THE KINGFISHER

Illustrated Children's Dictionary

THE KINGFISHER
Illustrated Children's Dictionary

Editor-in-Chief
John Grisewood
Consultant Editors
John Bollard Joanne Grumet

Kingfisher

NEW YORK

Editor-in-Chief
John Grisewood

Consultant Editors
John Bollard, Joanne Grumet

Senior Editor
Debra Miller

Text Editors
Nicola Barber, Richard Northcott

Text Database
Catherine Schwarz, George Davidson
Elaine Higgleton, Howard Sargeant, Anne Seaton

Text Input
Tracey McNerney, Ruth Barratt, Clive Barratt

Proofreaders
Eleanor Martlew, Sean Connolly, Coleen Degnan-Veness, Sarah Hewetson

Designers
Siân Williams, David Anstey, Earl Neish, Smiljka Surla (including cover/jacket design), Nigel Bradley

Additional Artwork Preparation
Julian Ewart, Janet Woronkowicz, Matthew Gore, Andy Archer, Narinder Sahotay

Artwork Research
Robert Perry, Bernard Nussbaum

Production Managers
Susan Latham, Oonagh Phelan

Production Assistant
Selby Sinton

KINGFISHER
Larousse Kingfisher Chambers Inc.
95 Madison Avenue
New York, New York 10016

First American edition 1994
4 6 8 10 9 7 5 3
Copyright © Larousse plc 1994

LIBRARY OF CONGRESS CATALOGING-IN-PUBLICATION DATA
The Kingfisher illustrated children's dictionary / editor in chief,
John Grisewood; consultant editors, John Bollard and Joanne Grumet.
—1st American ed.
p.   cm.
1. English language—Dictionaries, Juvenile. [1. English
language—Dictionaries]   I. Grisewood, John.   II. Bollard, John K.
III. Grumet, Joanne.
PE1628.5.K54   1994
423–dc20   93-45414   CIP   AC

ISBN 1-85697-841-9
Printed in China

WELCOME TO YOUR DICTIONARY

Any good dictionary must of course be useful. At the very least it should give the correct spelling of a word, the meaning (or different meanings) of a word, and the pronunciation. A dictionary can also give the part of speech to which a word belongs; it can give examples of how a word is used in context; it may explain how certain words originated. Some dictionaries warn readers of words that can be confused (*affect* and *effect* for example) and may even give its opinion on correct grammar and punctuation.

The Kingfisher Illustrated Children's Dictionary has all these features and more. It is a completely new and up-to-date dictionary; in some ways it is quite unlike any other children's dictionary. While we believe that this dictionary is enormously useful, we also think that it is thoroughly friendly and enjoyable to use, whether for browsing or specific consultation. The superb illustrations and diagrams and a wealth of encyclopedic information make *The Kingfisher Illustrated Children's Dictionary* strikingly different from other dictionaries.

We hope that this reliable, lively, and imaginative dictionary and reference book will show how much fun learning about words and the world around us can be.

John Grisewood

HOW TO MAKE THE MOST OF YOUR DICTIONARY

The Kingfisher Illustrated Children's Dictionary is an up-to-date dictionary combined with a basic encyclopedia. You can have fun finding out about the history and meaning of words, and enrich your vocabulary and word power. By following the "paragraphs of knowledge," marked with a ●, you can find out more about the world around you, its people, and its places. Become a better speller, a better reader, a better writer, a better speaker, and better informed.

The Kingfisher Illustrated Children's Dictionary is a completely new dictionary—not simply a revision of an old work. It is right up-to-date in its coverage of the language of today, especially the terms used in science, technology, and computing. The dictionary is full of useful features that make it an exciting adventure to explore words and track down information.

Full-color topic feature boxes provide a highly visual, in-depth look at selected subjects.

Guide words give the first and last entry on each double-page spread for speedy reference.

A pronunciation guide appears regularly throughout.

Discover the history of a word's origins and the difference between confusable words from the blue boxes.

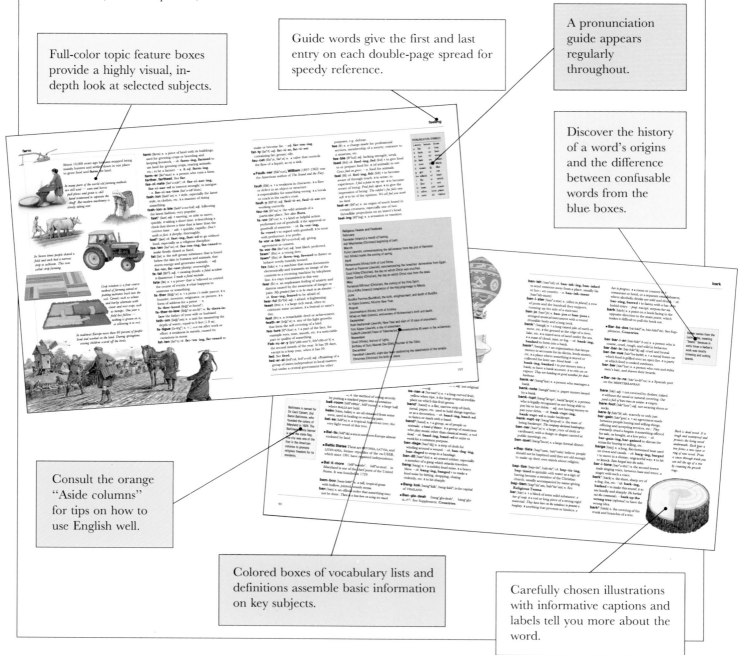

Consult the orange "Aside columns" for tips on how to use English well.

Colored boxes of vocabulary lists and definitions assemble basic information on key subjects.

Carefully chosen illustrations with informative captions and labels tell you more about the word.

The headword printed in **bold type** shows how the word is spelled. All headwords are in alphabetical order.

Follow the "paragraphs of knowledge" for:
- More encyclopedic information on the headword.
- Basic facts about people and places.

Cross references in SMALL CAPITAL LETTERS identify related words in the dictionary.

Irregular and alternative plural forms of nouns are shown in small bold type: **goose, geese; cactuses** or **cacti**. The plural of regular nouns is formed by adding *-s*.

End-of-line breaks are given in headwords and inflected forms.

Alternative spellings are given in **bold type**.

A repeated spelling with a little number above the headword means that there are two or more words spelled in the same way but with different meanings. They are *homographs*.

You are told how to pronounce the word. Where a word has more than one way of being pronounced, these are shown.

The headword's part of speech appears in abbreviated form and is printed in *italic: n., vb., adj., adv., pron., conj., prep.,* and *interj.* for noun, verb, adjective, adverb, pronoun, conjunction, preposition, and interjection.

be·cause (bi-kôz) *conj.* for the reason that: *I can't write the letter because I don't have any paper.*

● **Beck·et, Thomas** (1118-70) was Archbishop of CANTERBURY. He was murdered for opposing Henry II's attempts to control the clergy. He was made a saint in 1173.

bee (bē) *n.* a type of four-winged, stinging insect; some species live in large groups and make honey. − **a bee in your bonnet** an idea which has become an obsession.

bel·ly (bel'ē) *n.* **bel·lies** the part of the body containing the organs used for digesting food.

be·long (bi-lông') *vb.* **be·long·ing, be·longed** **1** to be the property or right of: *This book belongs to me.* **2** to be a member of a group, etc. **be·longings** *n.* (*plural*) personal possessions.

bi·as (bī'əs) *n.* a prejudice. **bi·ased** or **bi·assed** *adj.* favoring one side.

big (big) *adj.* **big·ger, big·gest** large or largest in size, weight, or number.

bill¹ (bil) *n.* **1** a piece of paper stating the amount of money owed for goods or services received. **2** a written plan for a proposed law.

bill² (bil) *n.* a bird's beak.

The definition is the part of the entry that tells you what the headword means.

An example sentence or phrase after a definition shows how the word is used. It is printed in *italic* type.

Idioms appear in **bold type** at the end of an entry. An idiom is a phrase with a different meaning from that of its individual words.

Other forms of verbs, inflections, are shown. They are the present participle: **belonging**; and the past tense and past participle: **belonged**.

Other forms of adjectives, the comparative and superlative, are shown using the addition *-er* and *-est* where the spelling of the main word changes. So *harder* and *hardest* are not given but *cagier, cagiest* are. Some longer adjectives take *more* and *most* instead of *-er* and *-est: more successful; most successful.*

Numbered definitions each give a different meaning or use of the word. Nouns, verbs, and adjectives are grouped and numbered.

FROM ENGLISC TO ENGLISH

In A.D. 408 the Roman army withdrew from Britain, leaving the country in the charge of the native British, a people of Celtic origin. Very soon Britain began to be invaded and settled by a new people from Scandinavia and northern Germany. We call them the Anglo-Saxons and they spoke Old English, a Germanic language and ancestor of the English we speak today. By the end of the 5th-century "coming of the Saxons," much of what is now England had submitted to the newcomers. The British were driven into Wales and Cornwall. Who among those early Anglo-Saxons could ever have imagined that 1,500 years later their speech would have become the international language of commerce, science, technology, and diplomacy? Or that it would be the main language of a vast new continent—North America—which was to remain unknown and undiscovered by Europeans for another 1,000 years and more?

So what kind of language was Old English? It was a mixture of the language of the Anglo-Saxon invaders and that of the later Viking invaders and settlers. In 890, King Alfred the Great wrote a preface to a translation of a book written by Pope Gregory. Here is what Alfred wrote in what was then called *Englisc*:

Ælfred kyning hateth gretan Waerferth biscep his
Alfred the king bids greet bishop Waerferth with his
wordum luflice ond freondlice.
words lovingly and friendly.

William the Conqueror's armies crushed any revolt by English rebels. For nearly three centuries French was the language of England's rulers; but English survived and evolved among the peasantry.

At a glance this looks very little like the English we know. But look closer and you will see likenesses between *kyning, gretan, biscep, wordum,* and *freondlice* with our modern *king, greet, bishop, word,* and *friendly*.

After Alfred had written this the peace of England was shattered by more Viking invasions of Danes and Norwegians, and in 1066 the country was conquered by the French-speaking Normans under William. William the Conqueror gave all the important jobs in government, law, and the church to Normans. For the next two hundred years two languages were spoken in England: the court spoke French, the ordinary people spoke English. Almost all writing was in Norman French or Latin.

Many thought the English of the ordinary people to be a "rough, uncouth language." Nevertheless poets continued to write in it. Here is an example from the 1200s:

> *Sumer is icumen in*
> *Lhude sing cuccu;*
> *Groweth sed and bloweth med*
> *And springth the wude nu.*
> *Sing cuccu . . .*

At the end of the 1300s the first really great English poet, Geoffrey Chaucer, was writing *The Canterbury Tales*. One hundred years later, William Caxton set up his printing press in London. One of the first books he published was Malory's *Morte d'Arthur*. Here is an extract with the spelling modernized:

Then the king got his spear in both his hands, and ran toward Sir Mordred, crying and saying, "Traitor, now is thy death-day come." And when Sir Mordred saw King Arthur, he ran until (unto) him with his sword drawn in his hand. And there King Arthur smote Sir Mordred under the shield, with a foin (thrust) of his spear, throughout the body, more than a fathom.

Geoffrey Chaucer (*c.* 1340-1400)—his works were among the first to be written and printed in the English language. He is regarded as one of England's greatest poets.

MIXED ENGLISH

English is very adaptable and keeps up with the times. In its long history it has been enriched by words from other languages—with *cotton*, *sofa*, and *syrup* from Arabic; *barbecue* and *hammock* from the Caribbean; *deck* and *yacht* from Dutch; plus words from Irish, German, Hebrew, Japanese, and Spanish; and thousands of words derived from Greek (*alphabet*, *geography*, *character*, *philosophy*) and many more thousands from Latin (*circus*, *exit*, *index*, *nil*). Despite all this enrichment, English is basically a mixture of two main languages, Old English and Latin-based Norman French. Old English provided the language with basic essential words: parts of the body, names of near relations, colors, names of wild animals, and geographical features. Norman French gave English new ways of expressing more abstract ideas and emotions: *charity*, *grace*, *passion*, *intellect* are examples. Some "foreign" words have duplicated Old English words—"folk" (Old English) and "people" (Norman French), "wed" and "marry," "freedom" and "liberty," and "forgive" and "pardon" are some examples. And the English pig turned into "pork," and sheep into "mutton" when it was served at the Norman rulers' tables.

It is not difficult to recognize this as the English we know today. The changes to the language that have since taken place are not so great as those that happened to English from the time of Alfred to Caxton's day.

Although in his printed books Caxton helped to provide a regular way of spelling, people still spelled very much as they liked. In 1639 Lady Harley wrote to her son at Oxford University:

My deare Ned, I beleeue (believe) *you are confident that you are more deare to me, thearefore thinke it not strange, if I am stuedious and carefull; that your peace should be kept with your God. whous favor is better than life. I longe to see you, and I hope I shall doo it shortly. I hope before this you haue reseued* (received) *your hate* (hat) *and stockens, but Burigh is sometime ngligent. Your father is thanke God well; he ride abroode. In hast I giue this ascurance that I am your affectionat mother.*

The erratic spelling of those like Lady Harley was one of the reasons that Samuel Johnson brought out his great English dictionary in 1755. Since then our spelling has, with a few minor changes (notably in American spelling), remained unchanged. But our pronunciations are very different. And like living human beings and the places they inhabit, our language is constantly changing and being enriched by its travels to foreign lands. English has a rich and fascinating past—the language of poets and orators (of Shakespeare and Whitman, of Lincoln and Churchill), of thinkers and scientists, of business people and teachers. It is a language that we should love and cherish. It is part of our heritage and our future. It is our duty to use it well and to look after it.

In 1474 William Caxton printed the first book in English.

SOME HELPFUL HINTS

Abbreviations used in the Dictionary

A.D. anno domini
adj. adjective
adv. adverb
B.C. before Christ
c. circa (Latin) about
cm centimeter
conj. conjunction
e.g. exempli gratia (Latin) for example
etc. et cetera (Latin) and so on
ft. feet
in. inches
i.e. id est (Latin) that is
interj. interjection
kg kilogram
km kilometer
m meter
mi. miles
n. noun
prep. preposition
pron. pronoun
sq. square
U.S.A. United States of America
vb. verb

Spelling Variants

Some words have more than one correct spelling. The most common alternative spellings are shown in **bold type** in this dictionary:

judg·ment or **judge·ment**

Variant inflected forms are also shown after the headword:

wharf . . . *n.* **wharves** . . . or **wharfs**

Parts of Speech

If a word is used as more than one part of speech, the definitions are grouped together after a part-of-speech abbreviation. These groups are separated by dashes:

waste (wāst) *vb.* **wast·ing, wast·ed** 1 . . . 2 . . . 3 . . . *–adj.* 1 . . . 2 . . . *–n.* 1 . . . 2 . . . 3

Run-on Entries

After the definitions for the main entry word, you will sometimes find derivatives of the headword, often formed by adding a common suffix such as *-ing, -ly, -ness*. If the meaning of this run-on entry is clear from the suffix, no definition is given:

yearn (yurn) *vb.* **yearn·ing, yearned** to feel a great desire; to long.–*n.* **yearn·ing**.

At the end of an entry, you may also find phrases and idioms that have meanings that cannot be guessed easily from the words themselves:

waste . . . *vb.*–**lay waste** to devastate.

Word Divisions

Most entry words of more than one syllable are printed with raised dots separating the syllables. These divisions indicate where to put a hyphen if there is not enough room for the whole word on a line. If it is necessary to break a word at the end of a line, try to divide it in a place that will not confuse the reader. For example, *re-appear* is a better choice than *reap-pear*, and *water-color* is preferable to both *wa-tercolor* and *watercol-or*.

Pronunciation

The pronunciation is shown for all main entry words, and for all inflected forms and run-on entries except those for which the pronunciation is obvious. Below is a list of the symbols we use and the sounds they represent.

ə	away, lemon, focus	i	fin	p	pen
		ī	fine	r	red
a	fat	j	jump	s	slice
ā	fade	k	cake	t	tip
ä	hot	kh	loch	th	think
âr	fair	l	lip	th	this
b	ball	m	map	u	cut
ch	each	n	net	ur	hurt
d	did	ng	sing	v	very
e	met	ô	often	y	yes
ē	mean	ō	note	yōō	music
f	fish	oi	boy	yoor	pure
g	get	oo	foot	z	zoo
h	home	ōō	moon	zh	vision
hw	which	ou	house		

The syllable that is most heavily stressed in a word is marked with an accent mark in bold type, a syllable with light stress is marked with a light accent mark: **abdicate** (ab′di-kāt′).

A pronunciation guide (right) to symbols that are different from the usual value of a letter is shown on pages throughout your dictionary.

PRONUNCIATION SYMBOLS			
ə away	lemon	focus	
a fat		oi	boy
ā fade		oo	foot
ä hot		ōō	moon
âr fair		ou	house
e met		th	think
ē mean		th	this
g get		u	cut
hw which		ur	hurt
i fin		w	witch
ī line		y	yes
îr near		yōō	music
ô often		yoor	pure
ō note		zh	vision

Aa

a (ə, ā) or **an** (ən, ān) the indefinite article, used before a noun: *a fossil; an elephant.*

aard·vark (ärd′värk′) *n.* an African animal with a long snout, that feeds on ants.

ab·a·cus (ab′ə-kəs) *n.* a frame holding a number of wires along which small balls can be moved, used for counting.

a·ban·don (ə-ban′dən) *vb.* **a·ban·don·ing, a·ban·doned 1** to give up completely: *Never abandon hope.* **2** to leave behind, usually intending not to return.

a·bate (ə-bāt′) *vb.* **a·bat·ing, a·bat·ed** to become or make less strong or severe.

ab·bey (ab′ē) *n.* **ab·beys 1** a group of monks or nuns living as a community. **2** the buildings occupied by such a community.

ab·bre·vi·ate (ə-brē′vē-āt′) *vb.* **ab·bre·vi·at·ing, ab·bre·vi·a·ted** to shorten; to represent a long word by a shortened form. — *n.* **ab·bre·vi·a·tion** (ə-brē′vē-ā′shən). See Supplement.

ab·di·cate (ab′di-kāt′) *vb.* **ab·di·cat·ing, ab·di·cat·ed 1** to give up the right to the throne. **2** to refuse to carry out. — *n.* **ab·di·ca·tion** (ab′di-kā′shən).

ab·do·men (ab′də-mən, ab-dō′mən) *n.* **1** the front part of the body containing the stomach and other digestive organs. **2** the rear part of the body of insects and crabs, etc.

ab·duct (əb-dukt′) *vb.* **ab·duct·ing, ab·duct·ed** to lead or carry away by force. — *n.* **ab·duc·tion** (əb-duk′shən).

Abbeys in the Middle Ages were like small self-supporting villages. As the plan shows, grouped around the church were cloisters (where the monks studied and exercised), a refectory (where they ate), a dormitory (where they slept), as well as kitchens, workshops, and gardens.

Church

Cloister

ab·hor (əb-hôr′) *vb.* **ab·hor·ring, ab·horred** to hate or dislike very much.

a·bil·i·ty (ə-bil′ət-ē) *n.* **a·bil·i·ties** the power, skill, or knowledge to do something.

ab·ject (ab′jekt′) *adj.* **1** miserable or poor. **2** showing lack of courage.

a·ble (ā′bəl) *adj.* **1** having the necessary knowledge, power, time, etc. to do something. **2** clever, skillful. – *adv.* **a·bly** (ā′blē, ā′bə-lē).

-able (-ə bl′) *suffix* forming adjectives meaning **1** that may or must be: *eatable; payable.* **2** that is suitable for: *fashionable.*

a·board (ə-bôrd′, ə-bōrd′) *adv. & prep.* on, onto, in, or into a ship, train, aircraft, etc.

a·bol·ish (ə-bäl′ish) *vb.* **a·bol·ish·ing, a·bol·ished** to stop or put an end to.

ab·o·li·tion·ist (ab′ə-lish′ə-nəst) *n.* a person who tries to abolish a custom or practice.

ab·o·rig·i·ne (ab′ə-rij′ə-nē) *n.* **1** (usually **Aborigine**) a member of the race of people who were the original inhabitants of AUSTRALIA. (The noun **Aboriginal** is now the preferred form.) **2** a member of any race of people who were the first people to live in a country or region. – *n. & adj.* **ab·o·rig·i·nal** or **Ab·o·rig·i·nal** (ab′ə-rij′ə-nəl).

a·bort (ə-bôrt′) *vb.* **a·bort·ing, a·bort·ed 1** to lose an offspring because it is born before it has developed enough to survive outside the womb. **2** to stop a plan or space flight, etc. because of technical problems.

a·bor·tion (ə-bôr′shən) *n.* an operation to remove a fetus from the womb.

a·bout (ə-bout′) *prep.* **1** concerning; relating to: *She was worried about her puppy.* **2** here and there: *There are daisies dotted about the lawn.* **3** all around; surrounding. – *adv.* **1** nearly; approximately: *The apples weighed about a pound.* **2** halfway or all around: *Turn yourself about.*

a·bove (ə-buv′) *prep.* **1** higher than; over. **2** more or greater than in quantity or degree: *The temperature was above boiling point.*

●**A·bra·ham** (ā′brə-ham′) is regarded as the founder of the Jewish people.

a·bra·sive (ə-brā′siv, ə-brā′ziv) *n.* a substance that can damage skin or rock, etc. by rubbing and scraping. – *adj.* rough; annoying.

a·breast (ə-brest′) *adv. & adj.* side by side and facing in the same direction.

a·brupt (ə-brupt′) *adj.* **1** sudden and unexpected. **2** rather sharp and rude.

ab·scess (ab′ses′) *n.* a painful swelling in a part of the body resulting from infection.

ab·sence (ab′səns) *n.* the state of being away from school or work, etc.

ab·sent (ab′sənt) *adj.* not in the expected place. **ab·sent·ing, ab·sent·ed** to keep away from.

ab·so·lute (ab′sə-lōōt′) *adj.* complete; total; perfect: *He swore her to absolute secrecy.*

ab·sorb (əb-sôrb′, əb-zôrb′) *vb.* **ab·sorb·ing, ab·sorbed 1** to take in or suck up: *Cotton clothes absorb sweat.* **2** to have all of the attention of. – *adj.* **ab·sor·bent** (əb-sôr′bənt, əb-zôr′bənt).

ab·stain (ab-stān′, ab-stān′) *vb.* **ab·stain·ing, ab·stained 1** to choose not to do or take something. **2** to choose not to vote.

ab·stract (ab-strakt′, ab′strakt′) *adj.* referring to something which exists only as an idea or quality.

ab·surd (əb-surd′, əb-zurd′) *adj.* ridiculous.

a·bun·dance (ə-bun′dəns) *n.* a large amount.

a·bun·dant (ə-bun′dənt) *adj.* existing in large amounts.

a·buse (ə-byōōz′) *vb.* **a·bus·ing, a·bused 1** to use wrongly: *to abuse political power.* **2** to treat cruelly or wrongly. – (ə-byōōs′) *n.*

a·bu·sive (ə-byōō′siv, ə-byōō′ziv) *adj.* violent or using insulting language.

a·bys·mal (ə-biz′məl) *adj.* **1** extremely bad. **2** very deep; very great: *abysmal ignorance.*

a·byss (ə-bis′) *n.* a very large and deep hole or seemingly bottomless space.

An Aboriginal shield and boomerang or wooden throwing stick. The spear and boomerang were the main weapons used by the Aboriginals as they wandered around the desert hunting or gathering food.

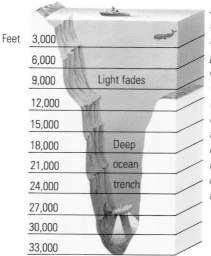

Feet

| 3,000 |
| 6,000 |
| 9,000 | Light fades |
| 12,000 |
| 15,000 |
18,000	Deep
21,000	ocean
24,000	trench
27,000
30,000
33,000

An abyss usually refers to the deepest parts of the oceans, below 6,500 feet (2,000 m). No light penetrates these waters and the pressure is many times heavier than at the surface.

ac·a·dem·ic (ak′ə-dem′ik) *adj.* having to do with study, education, or teaching.

a·cad·e·my (ə-kad′ə-mē) *n.* **a·cad·e·mies** **1** a school or college that gives training in a particular subject or skill. **2** a private school.

ac·cel·er·ate (ik-sel′ə-rāt′) *vb.* **ac·cel·er·at·ing, ac·cel·er·at·ed** to increase speed.

ac·cel·er·a·tion (ik-sel′ə-rā′shən) *n.* the rate of increase of speed.

ac·cel·er·a·tor (ik-sel′ə-rāt′ər) *n.* the lever that is pressed to make a vehicle move faster.

ac·cent (ak′sent′) *n.* **1** the way words are pronounced by certain people. **2** emphasis put on a syllable in speaking. **3** a mark put over or under a letter to show how it is pronounced.

ac·cept (ik-sept′) *vb.* **ac·cept·ing, ac·cept·ed 1** to receive with favor. **2** to agree to. **3** to believe to be true or correct.

ac·cep·tance (ik-sep′təns) *n.* the act of accepting something.

ac·cess (ak′ses′) *n.* a means of approaching or entering a place.

ac·ces·si·ble (ik-ses′ə-bəl) *adj.* able to be reached easily.

ac·ces·so·ry (ik-ses′ə-rē) *n.* **ac·ces·so·ries 1** something additional to, but less important than, something else. **2** an item of dress, such as a bag or tie that goes with a dress, etc.

ac·ci·dent (ak′sə-dənt, ak′sə-dent′) *n.* **1** an unexpected event which causes damage or harm. **2** something that happens by chance.

ac·ci·den·tal (ak′sə-dent′l) *adj.* not planned.

ac·claim (ə-klām′) *vb.* **ac·claim·ing, ac·claimed** to welcome with enthusiasm.

ac·com·mo·date (ə-käm′ə-dāt′) *vb.* **ac·com·mo·dat·ing, ac·com·mo·dat·ed 1** to provide with a place to stay. **2** to be large enough for.

ac·com·mo·da·tions (ə-käm′ə-dā′shənz) *n.* a room or rooms in a house or hotel.

ac·com·pa·ny (ə-kum′pə-nē) *vb.* **ac·com·pa·nies, ac·com·pa·ny·ing, ac·com·pa·nied 1** to come or go with. **2** to play a musical instrument as a support.

ac·com·plice (ə-käm′pləs) *n.* a person who helps another commit a crime.

ac·com·plish (ə-käm′plish) *vb.* **ac·com·plish·ing, ac·com·plished** to complete or carry out.

ac·com·plish·ment (ə-käm′plish-mənt) *n.* **1** a skill developed through practice. **2** the finishing or completing of something.

ac·cord (ə-kôrd) *vb.* **ac·cord·ing, a·ccord·ed 1** to agree or be in harmony.

ac·cord·ing (ə-kôr′ding) *adj.* **1** as said by. **2** in agreement with: *according to plan.*

ac·cord·ing·ly (ə-kôr′ding-lē) *adv.* **1** in an appropriate way: *act accordingly.* **2** therefore; for that reason.

ac·count (ə-kount′) *n.* **1** a description or report; an explanation. **2** a deposit of money in a bank. **3** (usually in *plural*) a record of money received and spent. – *vb.* **account for**; **ac·count·ing, ac·count·ed** to give a reason or explanation for.

ac·cu·mu·late (ə-kyōōm′yə-lāt′) *vb.* **ac·cu·mu·lat·ing, ac·cu·mu·lat·ed** to collect or gather in an increasing quantity. – *n.* **ac·cu·mu·la·tion** (ə-kyōōm′yə-lā′shən). – *adj.* **ac·cu·mu·la·tive** (ə-kyōōm′yə-lət-iv)

ac·cu·rate (ak′yə-rət) *adj.* exact; absolutely correct.

ac·cuse (ə-kyōōz′) *vb.* **ac·cus·ing, ac·cused** to charge with having done something wrong. – *n.* **ac·cu·sa·tion** (ak′yə-zā′shən).

ac·cus·tom (ə-kus′təm) *vb.* **ac·cus·tom·ing, ac·cus·tomed** to make used to something.

ace (ās) *n.* the playing card in each of the four suits with a single symbol on it.

ache (āk) *vb.* **ach·ing, ached** to feel a dull, continuous pain. – *n.* a dull, continuous pain.

●**A·che·be** (ä-chā′bā), **Chinua** (1930-) is a Nigerian novelist and poet.

a·chieve (ə-chēv′) *vb.* **a·chiev·ing, a·chieved** to reach or attain a goal, ambition, etc. especially through hard work.

a·chieve·ment (ə-chēv′mənt) *n.* something that has been done or gained by effort.

●**A·chil·les** (ə-kil′ēz) was a Greek hero in the siege of TROY in HOMER's poem the *Iliad*.

In the Trojan War Achilles kills Hector, the Trojan leader. The Iliad *is one of the great heroic epics of ancient Greece.*

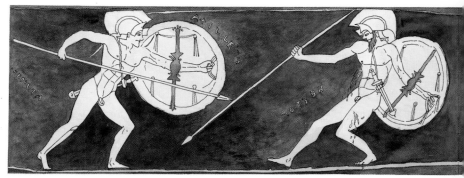

Gases react
with clouds

Acid rain

*Harmful gases may be carried
by the winds for hundreds of
miles before they are
washed to the
ground by
rain.*

Gases
carried by
wind

*Acid rain and the "greenhouse
effect" are the two main threats
to the earth's atmosphere. They
are both caused by gases sent
out by power stations, cars, and
factories. Acid rain causes
terrible damage to plant life.*

Forests and lakes
damaged by
acid rain

Waste
gases
produced by
industry

*The "greenhouse
effect" is caused by a
blanket of carbon dioxide
gas in the air. This traps
the sun's heat and stops it
from escaping into space.
As a result the earth could
become much warmer.*

The word acid comes
from a Latin word
meaning "sour," for
most acids taste sour.
Some acids are
dangerous; others, such
as citric acid in lemons,
are harmless. All acids
turn litmus, a special
kind of paper, red.
Some substances are
the opposite of acids.
They are alkalis and
turn litmus paper blue.

ac·id (as′əd) *n.* **1** any of a group of substances, usually in the form of liquids, that contain hydrogen, are usually sour, and are able to dissolve metals and form salts. **2** any sour substance. – *adj.* sour to taste.

a·cid·ic (ə-sid′ik) *adj.* like, or containing, acid.

acid rain *n.* rain that contains harmful acids formed from waste gases released into the atmosphere from factories, etc.

ac·knowl·edge (ik-näl′ij) *vb.* **ac·knowl·edg·ing, ac·knowl·edged** **1** to admit or accept the truth of. **2** to report receiving. **3** to express thanks for. **4** to recognize the authority of.

ac·me (ak′mē) *n.* the highest point of achievement, success, excellence, etc.

ac·ne (ak′nē) *n.* a skin condition in which pimples form on the face and upper body.

a·corn (ā′kôrn′, ā′kərn) *n.* the nutlike fruit of the oak tree.

a·cous·tic (ə-koo′stik) *adj.* having to do with sound or the sense of hearing.

a·cous·tics (ə-koo′stiks) *n.* (*plural*) the qualities of a room or theater that make it a good or bad place to listen to music or speech.

ac·quaint (ə-kwānt′) *vb.* **ac·quaint·ing, ac·quaint·ed** to make aware of or familiar with.

ac·quaint·ance (ə-kwānt′ns) *n.* **1** slight knowledge of something or someone. **2** a person you know slightly.

ac·quire (ə-kwīr′) *vb.* **ac·quir·ing, ac·quired** to achieve, gain, or develop, especially through skill or effort.

ac·qui·si·tion (ak′wə-zish′ən) *n.* a thing obtained.

ac·quis·i·tive (ə-kwiz′ət-iv) *adj.* very eager to obtain and possess things.

ac·quit (ə-kwit′) *vb.* **ac·quit·ting, ac·quit·ted** **1** to declare to be innocent of a crime. **2** to behave or conduct.

a·cre (ā′kər) *n.* a unit of measurement for land, equal to 43,560 square feet (4,047 sq. m).

ac·ro·bat (ak′rə-bat′) *n.* a person skilled in tumbling, balancing acts, tightrope walking, etc. – *adj.* **ac·ro·bat·ic** (ak′rə-bat′ik).

ac·ro·bat·ics *n.* (*plural*) acrobatic stunts.

ac·ro·nym (ak′rə-nim′) *n.* a word made from the first letters or syllables of other words.

ac·ro·pho·bi·a (ak′rə-fō′bē-ə) *n.* fear of heights.

a·cross (ə-krôs′) *prep.* **1** to, at, or on the other side of: *We saw the hotel across the lake.* **2** from one side of to the other: *She ran across the road.* **3** so as to cross: *He folded his arms across his chest.* – *adv.* from one side to the other.

act (akt) *n.* **1** a thing that is done; a deed. **2** the process of doing something. **3** a major division of a play or opera, etc. **4** a law passed by a law-making body such as Congress. – *vb.* **act·ing, act·ed** **1** to behave. **2** to do something. **3** to perform in a play or movie.

act·ing (ak′ting) *n.* the profession of performing in a play or movie. – *adj.* temporarily doing someone else's job: *She was the acting supervisor.*

ac·tion (ak′shən) *n.* **1** the process of doing something. **2** something that is done.

ac·ti·vate (ak′tə-vāt′) *vb.* **ac·tiv·at·ing, ac·tiv·at·ed** to make start working.

ac·tive (ak′tiv) *adj.* moving and doing things.

ac·tiv·ist (ak′tə-vəst) *n.* a person who is very

active, especially as a member of a group.

ac·tiv·i·ty (ak-tiv′ət-ē) *n.* **ac·tiv·i·ties 1** the state of being active or busy. **2** (often in *plural*) things that people do, especially for pleasure.

ac·tor (ak′tər) *n.* a man or woman whose job is performing in plays or movies.

ac·tress (ak′trəs) *n.* a woman whose job is performing in plays or movies.

ac·tu·al (ak′choo-əl, ak′shoo-əl) *adj.* real; not imagined.

actually (ak′choo-ə-lē, ak′shwə-lē) *adv.* really; in fact.

ac·u·punc·ture (ak′yə-pungk′chər) *n.* a method of treating illness and pain by sticking needles into the patient's skin at certain points.

a·cute (ə-kyoot′) *adj.* **1** very bad. **2** (describing the senses) keen or sharp. **3** (describing the mind) quick and intelligent. **4** (describing an illness) quickly becoming severe. **5** describing an angle that is less than 90°.

ad·age (ad′ij) *n.* a proverb or saying.

a·da·gio (ə-däj′ō, ə-dä′jē-ō). See **Musical Terms**.

●**Ad·am and Eve** (ad′əm, ēv) in the BIBLE, were the first people. They lived in the Garden of Eden.

ad·a·mant (ad′ə-mənt) *adj.* completely determined; stubborn.

a·dapt (ə-dapt′) *vb.* **a·dapt·ing, a·dapt·ed** to change so as to fit new circumstances.

a·dapt·a·ble (ə-dap′tə-bəl) *adj.* good at fitting into new circumstances or situations.

a·dap·ter (ə-dap′tər) *n.* a device that makes two mechanisms compatible.

add (ad) *vb.* **add·ing, add·ed 1** to put together or combine. **2** to put two or more numbers together to get their total. **3** to say or write something further: *Add your name to the list.*

add·er (ad′ər) *n.* **1** the common viper, a poisonous Old World snake. **2** any of various nonpoisonous snakes of North America.

The adder, or common viper, is the only snake found north of the Arctic Circle.

ad·di·tion (ə-dish′ən) *n.* **1** the act of adding. **2** a person or thing that is added to something else. – **in addition to** as well as; besides.

ad·di·tion·al (ə-dish′ən-l) *adj.* extra; more.

ad·dress (ə-dres′, ad′res′) *n.* **1** the number or name of the place where a person lives or works. **2** a speech. – *vb.* **ad·dress·ing, ad·dressed 1** to put the name and address on. **2** to make a speech to.

●**Ad·e·laide** (ad′l-ād′) is the capital of the state of South AUSTRALIA.

●**A·den** (ād′n) is the capital of YEMEN.

ad·e·noids (ad′n-oidz′) *n.* (*plural*) a mass of soft flesh situated behind the nose.

ad·e·quate (ad′ə-kwət) *adj.* enough; sufficient.

ad·here (ad-hîr′) *vb.* **ad·her·ing, ad·hered 1** to stick. **2** to remain loyal to: *to adhere to a belief.* **3** to follow exactly: *to adhere to a plan.*

ad·he·sive (ad-hē′siv, ad-hē′ziv) *adj.* sticky.

a·dieu (ə-doo′, ə-dyoo′) *n.* **a·dieus** or **a·dieux** (ə-dooz′, əd-yooz′) a good-bye.

ad·ja·cent (ə-jā′sənt) *adj.* lying beside or next to.

ad·jec·tive (aj′ik-tiv) *n.* a word that describes a noun or pronoun, as "dark" describes "hair" in *She has dark hair;* and "sad" describes "her" in *The book made her sad.* – *adj.* **ad·jec·ti·val** (aj′ik-tī′vəl).

ad·just (ə-just′) *vb.* **ad·just·ing, ad·just·ed** to change slightly. – *adj.* **ad·just·a·ble** (ə-jus′tə-bəl). – *n.* **ad·just·ment** (ə-just′mənt).

ad·min·is·ter (ad-min′ə-stər) *vb.* **ad·min·is·ter·ing, ad·min·ist·ered 1** to manage, govern, or direct. **2** to provide with or dispense: *to administer medicine.* – *n.* **ad·min·is·tra·tion** (ad-min′ə-strā′shən). – *adj.* **ad·min·is·tra·tive** (ad-min′ə-strāt′iv).

ad·mi·ral (ad′mə-rəl) *n.* **1** an officer commanding a navy or a fleet of ships. **2** a name applied to several species of butterfly.

ad·mire (əd-mīr′) *vb.* **ad·mir·ing, ad·mired** to regard with respect or approval. – *n.* **ad·mir·a·tion** (ad′mə-rā′shən). – *adj.* **ad·mi·ra·ble** (ad′mə-rə-bəl).

The Red Admiral is a common species of meadows, orchards, and gardens. It is found in North America, Europe, Asia, and North Africa.

INEVITABLE ADJECTIVES

Numerous nouns are always accompanied by an inevitable cliché of an adjective:

Shame is crying
Brides are blushing
Isolation is splendid
Efforts are concerted
Questions are burning
Beliefs are cherished
Negotiations are delicate
Conclusions are inevitable

Adobe is a Spanish word for sun-dried bricks and for a house built of such bricks. The ancient Egyptians and Babylonians used sun-dried mud and straw bricks. In North and South America, adobe was a common building material used by Pueblo Indians and Incas. Stone was mainly reserved for temples, but even important houses were built of adobe. Spanish settlers in Mexico, Texas, and California also used the material.

To make adobe, clay is mixed with water and straw. The mixture is placed in brick-shaped molds. When dry, the bricks are removed from the mold and allowed to bake in the sun.

ad·mit (əd-mit′) *vb.* **ad·mit·ting, ad·mit·ted 1** to agree to the truth of, especially unwillingly. **2** to allow to enter.

ad·mit·ted·ly (əd-mit′əd-lē) *adv.* as is known to be true.

a·do (ə-doo′) *n.* difficulty or trouble; fuss.

a·do·be (ə-dō′bē) *n.* **1** a brick made of clay and straw, which is dried in the sun. **2** a building made with these bricks. **3** the clay used in these bricks.

ad·o·les·cent (ad′l-es′ənt) *adj.* between childhood and adulthood, usually between the ages of 12 or 13 and 18. – *n.* a young person. – *n.* **ad·o·les·cence** (ad′l-es′əns).

a·dopt (ə-däpt′) *vb.* **a·dopt·ing, a·dopt·ed 1** to become the legal parent of. **2** to use as your own: *to adopt a new policy.* – *n.* **a·dop·tion** (ə-däp′shən).

a·dore (ə-dôr′, ə-dōr′) *vb.* **a·dor·ing, a·dored 1** to love deeply. **2** to worship as a god.

a·dorn (ə-dôrn′) *vb.* **a·dorn·ing, a·dorned** to decorate in order to make more beautiful.

●**A·dri·at·ic** (ā′drē-at′ik) an arm of the MEDITERRANEAN SEA east of ITALY.

> **ADORNMENT**
> An "adornment" is something that adorns, but it also describes words and expressions that have become overworked "fillers": Sort of; You know; Basically; Really; No problem; No way.

a·dult (ə-dult′, ad′ult′) *adj.* fully grown; mature. – *n.* a fully grown person, animal, bird, or plant. – *n.* **a·dult·hood** (ə-dult′hood′).

ad·vance (əd-vans′) *vb.* **ad·vanc·ing, ad·vanced 1** to move forward. **2** to make progress; to improve or promote. **3** to propose or suggest. **4** to move to an earlier time or date. – *n.* **1** progress; a move forward. **2** a payment made before it is due. – *adj.* done, made, or given, beforehand. – **in advance** ahead in time or place.

ad·vanced (əd-vanst′) *adj.* **1** having progressed or developed well. **2** modern; new.

ad·vant·age (əd-van′tij) *n.* **1** a favorable circumstance. **2** superiority over another. – **take advantage of** to make use of in such a way as to benefit yourself.

ad·van·ta·geous (ad′vən-tā′jəs) *adj.* giving help or benefit in some way.

ad·vent (ad′vent′) *n.* **1** coming or arrival; first appearance. **2 Advent** in the Christian calendar, the period before Christmas.

ad·ven·ture (əd-ven′chər) *n.* an exciting and often dangerous experience. – *n.* **ad·ven·tur·er**.

ad·ven·tur·ous (əd-ven′chə-rəs) *adj.* daring.

ad·verb (ad′vurb′) *n.* a word that describes or adds to the meaning of a verb, adjective, or another adverb, such as "very" and "quietly" in *They were talking very quietly.* – *adj.* **ad·ver·bi·al** (ad-vur′bē-əl).

ad·ver·sar·y (ad′vər-ser′ē) *n.* **ad·ver·sar·ies** an opponent.

ad·ver·tise (ad'vər-tīz') *vb.* **ad·ver·tis·ing,
ad·ver·tised** 1 to draw attention to or
describe goods for sale or services to encourage
people to buy or use them. 2 to make known
publicly. – *n.* **ad·ver·tis·er**.

ad·ver·tise·ment (ad'vər-tīz'mənt, ad-vurt'ə-
smənt) *n.* a public notice or a short television
film advertising something.

ad·vice (əd-vīs') *n.* suggestions or opinions
given to someone about what to do.

ad·vise (əd-vīz') *vb.* **ad·vis·ing, ad·vised** 1
to give advice to; to recommend. 2 to inform. –
n. **ad·vis·er** or **ad·vi·sor** (əd-vī'zər).

ad·vo·cate (ad'və-kət) *n.* a person who
supports an idea. – (ad'və-kāt') *vb.*
ad·vo·cat·ing, ad·vo·cat·ed to
recommend or support: *They advocated peace.*

●**Ae·ge·an** (i-jē'ən) the branch of the MEDITER-
RANEAN SEA between GREECE and TURKEY.

ae·ri·al (âr'ē-əl) *n.* a wire or rod on a radio or
television set, able to send or receive signals.

aero- 1 of air: *aerobic.* 2 of aircraft.

aer·o·bics (âr-ō'biks) *n.* (*singular*) physical
exercises which increase the supply of oxygen
in the blood and strengthen the heart and
lungs.

aer·o·nau·tics (âr'ə-nôt'iks, âr'ə-nät'iks) *n.*
(*singular*) the science of movement through the
air. – *adj.* **aeronautic** or **aer·o·nau·ti·cal**
(âr'ə-nôt'i-kəl, âr'ə-nät'i-kəl).

aer·o·sol (âr'ə-sôl, âr'ə-säl') *n.* a substance
packed under pressure, which is released from
a container in the form of a fine spray.

●**Ae·sop** (ē'säp') (500s B.C.) was the author of a
collection of Greek fables.

af·fa·ble (af'ə-bəl) *adj.* pleasant and friendly.

af·fair (ə-fâr') *n.* 1 a concern, matter, event, or
connected series of events: *The party was a noisy
affair.* 2 (in *plural*) matters of importance and
public interest. 3 (in *plural*) private business
matters.

af·fect (ə-fekt') *vb.* **af·fect·ing, af·fect·ed**
1 to influence. 2 to cause to feel strong
emotions. 3 to pretend: *He affected to walk with
a limp.*

●**affect** and **effect**. Affect means "to influence":
Nothing can affect our friendship. Effect as a verb
means "to cause to happen": *I want to effect a*
change. As a noun it means a "result": *The war
had a disastrous effect on the country.*

af·fec·tion (ə-fek'shən) *n.* love or strong liking.

af·fec·tion·ate (ə-fek'shə-nət) *adj.* showing
love.

af·firm (ə-furm') *vb.* **af·firm·ing, af·firmed**
to state firmly; to state as a fact.

af·flict (ə-flikt') *vb.* **af·flict·ing, af·flict·ed** to
cause physical or mental suffering.

af·flu·ent (af'lōō'ənt) *adj.* having plenty of
money; rich. – *n.* **af·flu·ence** (af'lōō'əns).

af·ford (ə-fôrd') *vb.* **af·ford·ing, af·ford·ed**
1 to have enough money or time to spend on:
*Only someone very rich could afford such a luxurious
car.* 2 to be able to do, without risk: *I can't
afford to lose my job.*

Af·ghan (af'gan') *adj.* belonging to
AFGHANISTAN. – *n.* 1 (also **Af·ghan·i** (af-gan')
a person born in or a citizen of AFGHANISTAN.
2 **afghan** a knitted blanket or shawl.

●**Af·ghan·i·stan** (af-gan'ə-stan'). See Supplement, **Countries**.

a·fraid (ə-frād') *adj.* 1 feeling fear or frightened;
worried: *The small child was afraid of the dark.*
2 politely sorry: *I'm afraid we're going to be late.*

PRONUNCIATION SYMBOLS		
ə away	lemon	focus
a fat	oi	boy
ā fade	oo	foot
ä hot	ōō	moon
âr fair	ou	house
e met	th	think
ē mean	th	this
g get	u	cut
hw which	ur	hurt
i fin	w	witch
ī line	y	yes
îr near	yōō	music
ô often	yoor	pure
ō note	zh	vision

Little is known about **Aesop** except that he
was born a slave and that he was ugly,
clownish, and witty. His fables were very
popular. They include "The Hare and the
Tortoise," in which a fast-running hare
and a slow, plodding tortoise run a
race. The hare is so sure he will win
that he stops for a rest along the way.
Meanwhile the tortoise goes on steadily. The
hare falls asleep, the tortoise plods past and
wins the race. The moral is that the slow but
sure are bound to succeed.

●**Af·ri·ca** (af′ri-kə) is the world's second largest continent. It stretches from the MEDITERRANEAN SEA in the north to the Cape of Good Hope in the south. The scorching SAHARA desert spreads over much of the northern part of the continent. Near the EQUATOR are thick rain forests. Over huge grasslands, called savannas, roam large herds of grazing animals such as ZEBRAS, GIRAFFES, and IMPALA. Other animals such as LIONS and CHEETAHS prey upon them. Africa is home to many groups of people with different languages, religions, and ways of life and is the site of one of the world's oldest civilizations, EGYPT. Many Africans are farmers. There

Most of Africa was colonized by Europeans in the 19th century; from the 1950s the colonies became independent countries. Today they are developing industries and natural resources.

are gold, copper, and tin mines, and industry is growing.

Af·ri·can (af′ri-kən) *adj.* belonging to or coming from the continent of AFRICA. – *n.* a person born or living in AFRICA, or whose ancestors came from AFRICA.

African-American (af′ri-kən-ə-mer′i-kən) or **Af·ro-A·mer·i·can** (af′rō-ə-mer′i-kən) *n.* an American whose ancestors came from AFRICA. – *adj.* of or relating to African-Americans.

aft (aft) *adv. & adj.* at or toward the stern.

af·ter (af′tər) *prep.* **1** coming later in time than. **2** following in position or importance; behind. **3** about: *She asked after the patient.* **4** in pursuit of: *He ran after her.* **5** given the same name as; in imitation of: *She was called Mary after her aunt.* – *adv.* **1** later in time. **2** behind in place. – *conj.* after the time when.

af·ter·life (af′tər-līf′) *n.* existence after death.

af·ter·math (af′tər-math′) *n.* circumstances that are a result of a great and terrible event.

af·ter·noon (af′tər-nōōn′) *n.* the period of the day between midday and the evening.

af·ter·thought (af′tər-thôt′) *n.* an idea or thought coming later.

af·ter·ward (af′tər-wərd) or **af·ter·wards** (af′tər-wərdz) *adv.* later.

a·gain (ə-gen′, ə-gin′, ə-gān′) *adv.* **1** once more; another time: *Play it again.* **2** back to a previous condition or situation: *I am well again.*

a·gainst (ə-genst′, ə-ginst′, ə-gānst′) *prep.* **1** close to or leaning on; in contact with: *She left the ladder against the wall.* **2** in opposition to: *Burglary is against the law.* **3** in contrast to: *His white suit stood out against the dark background.*

●**Ag·a·mem·non** (ag′ə-mem′nän′) was commander of the Greek army in the Trojan War. His quarrel with ACHILLES is the main theme of HOMER's *Iliad.*

This gold mask, once thought to be that of Agamemnon, was found in a grave at Mycenae by the German archaeologist, Heinrich Schliemann.

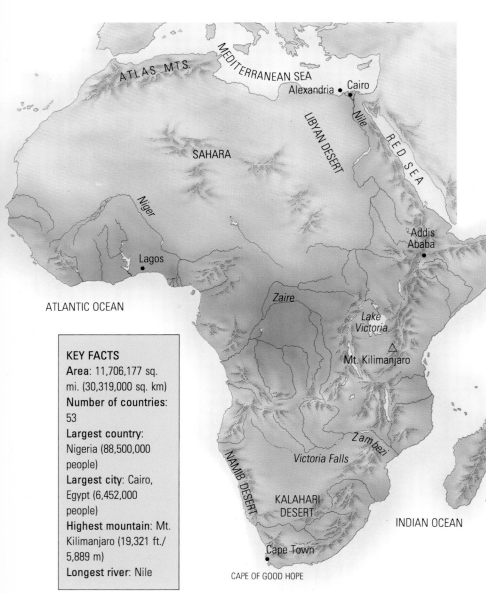

ATLAS MTS.
MEDITERRANEAN SEA
Alexandria • Cairo
LIBYAN DESERT
Nile
RED SEA
SAHARA
Niger
ATLANTIC OCEAN
Lagos
Addis Ababa
Zaire
Lake Victoria
Mt. Kilimanjaro
Zambezi
NAMIB DESERT
Victoria Falls
KALAHARI DESERT
INDIAN OCEAN
Cape Town
CAPE OF GOOD HOPE

KEY FACTS

Area: 11,706,177 sq. mi. (30,319,000 sq. km)

Number of countries: 53

Largest country: Nigeria (88,500,000 people)

Largest city: Cairo, Egypt (6,452,000 people)

Highest mountain: Mt. Kilimanjaro (19,321 ft./ 5,889 m)

Longest river: Nile

ag·ate (ag′ət) *n.* a type of semiprecious stone with layers of different colors.

age (āj) *n.* **1** the length of time a person or thing has existed. **2** a particular stage in life. **3** the fact of being old. **4** a period in the geological development or history marked by some particular feature: *We are studying the Bronze Age.* – *vb.* **ag·ing** or **age·ing, aged 1** to show signs of growing old. **2** to grow old; to mature. – **act** or **be your age** to behave sensibly.

aged *adj.* **1** having a particular age. **2** (ā′jəd) very old.

a·gen·cy (ā′jən-sē) *n.* **a·gen·cies** an office or business providing a particular service.

a·gen·da (ə-jen′də) *n.* a written list of subjects to be dealt with at a meeting.

a·gent (ā′jənt) *n.* **1** a person who represents an organization or who deals with someone else's business matters. **2** a person or thing that causes an effect: *an agent of change.*

ag·gra·vate (ag′rə-vāt′) *vb.* **ag·gra·vat·ing, ag·gra·vat·ed 1** to make worse. **2** to annoy. – *adj.* **ag·gra·vat·ing.** – *n.* **ag·gra·va·tion** (ag′rə-vā′shən).

ag·gres·sion (ə-gresh′ən) *n.* the act of attacking another person or country without being provoked; hostile behavior.

ag·gres·sive (ə-gres′iv) *adj.* **1** always ready to attack; hostile. **2** strong and determined.

ag·gres·sor (ə-gres′ər) *n.* in a fight or war, the person, group, or country that attacks first.

a·gile (aj′əl, aj′īl′) *adj.* able to move quickly and easily; nimble. – *n.* **a·gil·i·ty** (ə-jil′ət-ē).

ag·i·tate (aj′ə-tāt′) *vb.* **ag·i·tat·ing, ag·i·tat·ed 1** to excite or trouble: *She was agitated because she had lost her handbag.* **2** to try to stir up public interest: *The demonstrators were agitating for better working conditions.* – *n.* **ag·i·ta·tor.**

ag·i·ta·tion (aj′ə-tā′shən) *n.* **1** the act of stirring up public interest. **2** anxiety.

ag·nos·tic (ag-näs′tik) *n.* See **Religious Terms.**

ago (ə-gō′) *adv.* in the past; earlier.

ag·o·ny (ag′ə-nē) *n.* **ag·o·nies** severe bodily or mental pain.

a·gree (ə-grē′) *vb.* **a·gree·ing, a·greed 1** to be of the same opinion as someone else: *We agreed on a place to eat.* **2** to say yes to a suggestion or instruction: *He agreed to come with us.* **3** to be suitable or good for: *Milk doesn't agree with me.* – **agree to differ** to agree to accept each other's different opinions.

a·gree·able (ə-grē′ə-bəl) *adj.* **1** pleasant; friendly. **2** willing to accept a suggestion.

a·gree·ment (ə-grē′mənt) *n.* **1** a contract or promise. **2** the state of holding the same opinion.

ag·ri·cul·ture (ag′rə-kul′chər) *n.* the science of cultivating the land, especially for growing crops or rearing animals. – *adj.* **ag·ri·cul·tur·al** (ag′ri-kul′chə-rəl).

a·ground (ə-ground′) *adj. & adv.* describing ships that are stuck on the seabed or rocks.

a·head (ə-hed′) *adv.* **1** at or in the front; forward: *Full steam ahead!* **2** in advance: *We must plan ahead.*

aid (ād) *n.* **1** help. **2** help or support in the form of money, supplies, or services given to people who need it: *Many rich countries send aid to the poorer countries.* **3** a person or thing that helps do something: *She had to use a hearing aid in order to hear.* – *vb.* **aid·ing, aid·ed** to help or support.

aide (ād) *n.* an assistant or adviser.

AIDS (ādz) *abbreviation A*cquired *I*mmune *D*eficiency *S*yndrome, a condition transmitted by a virus which attacks the body's system of defense against disease.

ail·ment (āl′mənt) *n.* an illness.

aim (ām) *vb.* **aiming, aimed 1** to point or direct a weapon, attack, or remark. **2** to plan, intend, or try: *She was aiming to finish by 8 o'clock.* – *n.* **1** something a person intends to do. **2** the ability to hit what is aimed at.

aim·less (ām′ləs) *adj.* without any purpose.

air (âr) *n.* **1** the mixture of gases, consisting mainly of oxygen, nitrogen, and carbon dioxide, which people and animals breathe and which forms the earth's atmosphere. **2** the space above and around the earth, where birds and aircraft fly. **3** an appearance, look, or manner. **4** (in *plural*) behavior put on to impress others or to show off: *They put on airs to try to impress me.* **5** a tune. – *vb.* **air·ing, aired 1** to expose to the air. **2** to make known publicly: *She aired her opinions at the meeting.* – **by air** in an aircraft. – **clear the air** to remove or reduce disagreement by speaking openly.

air·borne (âr′bôrn′, âr′bōrn′) *adj.* describing aircraft that are flying in the air.

air con·di·tion·ing (âr′kən-dish′ə-ning) *n.* a system used to control the temperature, dryness, or dampness of the air in a building. – *adj.* **air-con·di·tioned** (âr′kən-dish′ənd).

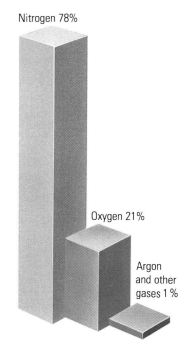

Nitrogen 78%

Oxygen 21%

Argon and other gases 1 %

Ninety-nine percent of air is composed of the colorless, tasteless, odorless gases nitrogen and oxygen. Without air, all living things, apart from a few micro-organisms, could not exist. The air cloaks the earth in a layer we call the atmosphere. The movement of air is responsible for weather.

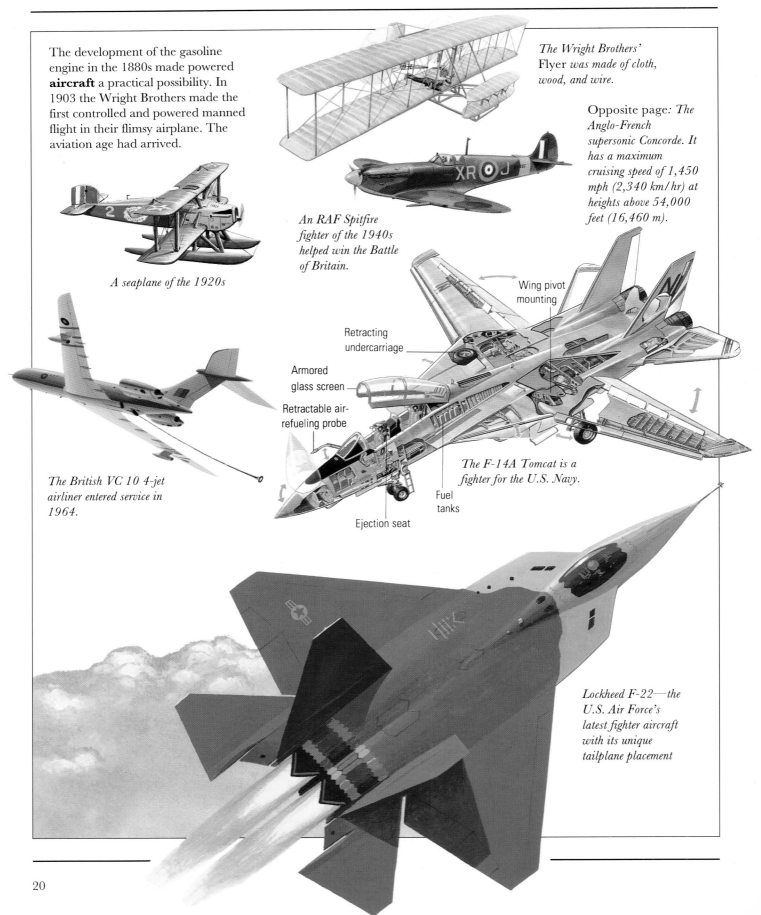

The development of the gasoline engine in the 1880s made powered **aircraft** a practical possibility. In 1903 the Wright Brothers made the first controlled and powered manned flight in their flimsy airplane. The aviation age had arrived.

The Wright Brothers' Flyer *was made of cloth, wood, and wire.*

Opposite page: The Anglo-French supersonic Concorde. It has a maximum cruising speed of 1,450 mph (2,340 km/hr) at heights above 54,000 feet (16,460 m).

A seaplane of the 1920s

An RAF Spitfire fighter of the 1940s helped win the Battle of Britain.

Wing pivot mounting

Retracting undercarriage

Armored glass screen

Retractable air-refueling probe

The British VC 10 4-jet airliner entered service in 1964.

The F-14A Tomcat is a fighter for the U.S. Navy.

Fuel tanks

Ejection seat

Lockheed F-22—the U.S. Air Force's latest fighter aircraft with its unique tailplane placement

air·craft (âr′kraft′) *n.* any of various types of machine that can fly in the air.

air force *n.* that part of a country's defense forces which uses aircraft for fighting.

air·line (âr′līn′) *n.* a company that provides a regular transportation service by aircraft.

air·lin·er (âr′lī′nər) *n.* a large passenger aircraft.

air·lock (âr′läk′) *n.* a small room with controllable air pressure, which allows a person to pass between places with different air pressures, as from outer space into a spaceship.

air·plane (âr′plān′) *n.* a vehicle with wings and engines, designed for flying.

air·port (âr′pōrt) *n.* a place where aircraft arrive and depart, with facilities for passengers and cargo.

air·ship (âr′ship′) *n.* a balloonlike aircraft.

air·strip (âr′strip′) *n.* a long narrow piece of ground where aircraft can land and take off.

air·tight (âr′tīt′) *adj.* describing a container which air cannot get into, out of, or through.

air·waves (âr′wāvz′) *n.* (*plural*) the radio waves used by radio and television stations.

air·y (âr′ē) *adj.* **air·i·er, air·i·est** **1** with plenty of fresh, cool air. **2** light or delicate.

aisle (īl) *n.* a passage between rows of seats in a church, theater, aircraft, etc.

●**Al·a·bam·a** (al′ə-bam′ə). See Supplement, **U.S.A.**

a·larm (ə-lärm′) *n.* **1** sudden fear produced by becoming aware of danger. **2** a bell or other noise which sounds to warn of danger, or on a clock to wake a person from sleep. – *vb.* **a·larm·ing, a·larmed** to frighten.

a·larm·ing (ə-lär′ming) *adj.* disturbing or frightening.

●**A·las·ka** (ə-las′kə). See Supplement, **U.S.A.**

●**Al·ba·ni·a** (al-bā′nē-ə). See Supplement, **Countries.**

Al·ba·ni·an (al-bā′nē-ən) *adj.* of Albania, its inhabitants, or language.

al·ba·tross (al′bə-tros′) *n.* a large, long-winged sea bird of the southern oceans.

al·che·my (al′kə-mē) *n.* medieval chemistry. One of the aims of alchemy was to discover how to make gold from other metals. – *n.* **al·che·mist** (al′kə-məst).

al·co·hol (al′kə-hôl′) *n.* **1** a colorless, flammable liquid made by the fermentation of sugar, used in making drinks, etc. **2** any drink containing this liquid, such as wine or beer.

al·co·hol·ic (al′kə-hô′lik, al′kə-häl′ik) *adj.* containing alcohol. – *n.* a person who is addicted to alcohol.

●**Al·cott** (ôl′kət, al′kät′), **Louisa May** (1832-1888) was an American novelist, the author of *Little Women.*

al·cove (al′kōv′) *n.* a recess in a wall.

ale (āl) *n.* a type of beer.

a·lert (ə-lurt′) *adj.* thinking and acting quickly; watchful and aware: *She was alert to all the dangers of her mission.* – *n.* a warning of danger: – *vb.* **a·lert·ing, a·lert·ed** to warn of danger; to make aware of a fact. – *n.* **a·lert·ness.** – **on the alert** watchful.

●**Al·ex·an·der the Great** (al′ig-zan′dər) (356 B.C.-323 B.C.), king of Macedonia (a former country in southern EUROPE). By 323 B.C. he ruled an empire that stretched from GREECE to INDIA.

al·ga (al′gə) *n.* **algae** (al′jē, al′gē) (usually in *plural*) a plant which grows in water or on moist ground, with no stem, leaves, or flowers, such as seaweed.

al·ge·bra (al′jə-brə) *n.* a branch of mathematics that uses letters and other symbols to represent numbers in calculations.

●**Al·ge·ri·a** (al-jir′ē-ə) is a large Arab republic on the MEDITERRANEAN coast in North AFRICA. The south of the country lies in the SAHARA. See also Supplement, **Countries.**

●**Al·gon·quin** (al-gäng′kwən) are a NATIVE AMERICAN people from southeast CANADA.

al·i·bi (al′ə-bī′) *n.* a plea of being somewhere else when a crime was committed.

a·li·en (ā′lē-ən) *n.* **1** a foreign-born resident of a country who has not adopted that country's nationality. **2** an inhabitant of another planet, especially in science fiction stories. – *adj.* foreign or strange.

alienate (ā′lē-ə-nāt′) *vb.* **a·li·en·a·ting, a·li·en·at·ed** to cause to feel unfriendly or hostile. – *n.* **a·li·en·a·tion** (ā′lē-ən-ā′shən).

A gold coin showing the head of Alexander the Great. Under him Greek culture spread throughout Asia. After his death his vast empire was divided among his generals.

PRONUNCIATION SYMBOLS		
ə away	lemon	focus
a fat	oi	boy
ā fade	oo	foot
ä hot	ōō	moon
âr fair	ou	house
e met	th	think
ē mean	th	this
g get	u	cut
hw which	ur	hurt
i fin	w	witch
ī line	y	yes
îr near	yōō	music
ô often	yoor	pure
ō note	zh	vision

Alligators (top and below) *are clumsy on land. They look like crocodiles* (center) *but have broader, flatter heads. When an alligator closes its mouth its teeth are hidden; a crocodile's fourth lower tooth is visible when its mouth is closed. The gharial* (bottom) *is related to the alligator.*

a·light (ə-līt′) *adj.* on fire.

a·lign (ə-līn′) *vb.* **a·lign·ing, a·ligned 1** to put in a straight line. **2** to bring into agreement with others: *The United States has aligned itself with Europe.* – *n.* **a·lign·ment** (ə-līn′mənt).

a·like (ə-līk′) *adj.* like one another; similar.

a·live (ə-līv′) *adj.* **1** living; having life; in existence. **2** lively; active.

al·kali (al′kə-lī′) *n.* a substance that reacts with an acid to form a salt.

all (ôl) *adj.* **1** the whole amount, number, or extent of: *They picked all the apples.* **2** any whatever: *beyond all doubt.* – *n.* someone's whole strength or resources: *She gave her all in the match.* – **after all** in spite of what has been said or done. – **all along** the whole time.

Al·lah (al′ə, äl′ə, ä-lä′) *n.* the MUSLIM name for GOD.

al·lege (ə-lej′) *vb.* **al·leg·ing, al·leged** to claim or declare to be the case without proof. – *adj.* **al·leged** (ə-lejd′, ə-lej′əd). – *adv.* **al·leg·ed·ly** (ə-lej′əd-lē).

al·le·giance (ə-lē′jəns) *n.* devotion or loyalty to your government, a cause, etc.

al·le·gro (ə-leg′rō, ə-lā′grō). See **Musical Terms**.

al·ler·gy (al′ər-jē) *n.* **al·ler·gies** sensitivity of the body to a substance such as dust which causes a reaction such as a rash or sneezing. – *adj.* **al·ler·gic** (ə-lur′jik).

al·ley (al′ē) *n.* **al·leys** (also **al·ley·way** (al′ē-wā)) a narrow passage between buildings.

alliance (ə-lī′əns) *n.* an agreement by which countries or people ally themselves.

allied (al′īd′, ə-līd′) *adj.* **1** joined by political agreement or treaty. **2** similar; related.

al·li·ga·tor (al′ə-gāt′ər) *n.* a kind of large reptile closely related to the CROCODILE.

al·lit·er·a·tion (ə-lit′ə-rā′shən) *n.* the repetition of a sound at the beginning of two or more words in a phrase, for example, "sing a song of sixpence."

al·lot (ə-lät′) *vb.* **al·lot·ting, al·lot·ted** to distribute; to give out a share of.

al·low (ə-lou′) *vb.* **al·low·ing, al·lowed 1** to permit. **2** to provide; to set aside.

al·low·ance (ə-lou′əns) *n.* a fixed amount of money or food, given regularly.

al·loy (al′oi) *n.* a mixture of two or more metals. – (ə-loi′, al′oi′) *vb.* **al·loy·ing, al·loyed** to mix so as to form an alloy.

all right 1 unhurt; safe. **2** adequate or satisfactory. **3** used to express agreement or approval: *"Oh, all right,"* she said.

al·lude (ə-lo͞od′) *vb.* **al·lud·ing, al·lud·ed** to speak of indirectly or mention in passing.

al·lure (ə-lo͞or′) *n.* attractiveness, appeal, or charm. – *adj.* **al·lur·ing.**

al·lu·vi·um (ə-lo͞o′vē-əm) *n.* **al·lu·vi·a** (ə-lo͞o′vē-ə) fertile soil and sand deposited by rivers or floods, especially in river valleys. – *adj.* **al·lu·vi·al** (ə-lo͞o′vē-əl).

al·ly (al′ī, ə-lī′) *n.* **allies** a country or person that has formally agreed to help and support another. – (ə-lī′, al′ī′) *vb.* **al·lies, al·ly·ing, al·lied** to join by political agreement, marriage, or friendship.

al·ma·nac (ôl′mə-nak′, al′mə-nak′) *n.* a book, published yearly, with a calendar, information about the moon and stars, public holidays, etc.

al·mond (äm′ənd, al′mənd) *n.* **1** a small tree related to the peach. **2** the oval nut of this tree.

al·most (ôl′mōst′, ôl-mōst′) *adv.* nearly but not quite.

alms (ämz) *n.* (*plural*) donations of money and food to the poor.

aloft (ə-lôft′) *adv.* in the air.

a·lone (ə-lōn′) *adj. & adv.* without anyone else; by yourself; apart from other people. – **go it alone** (*informal*) to act on your own and without help. – **leave alone** to stop bothering.

a·long (ə-lông′) *adv.* **1** in some direction: *I saw him walking along.* **2** in company with others: *Let's go along for the ride.* **3** into a more advanced state: *My essay is coming along nicely.* – *prep.* beside or part of the length of: *The bush lies along the wall.*

a·loof (ə-lo͞of′) *adj.* unfriendly and distant.

a·loud (ə-loud′) *adv.* not silently.

al·pac·a (al-pak′ə) *n.* a South American animal, related to the llama, with silky hair.

АБВГДЕЖЗИЙКЛМНО

The Cyrillic alphabet, based on the Greek, was invented by St. Cyril in the 800s when he was a missionary among the Slavic people.

ΑΒΓΔΕΖΗΘΙΚΛΜΝΞΠΟ

The Greeks took over many of the Phoenician signs, the first letter of which was aleph.

حخددز زسشصضطظغغغفقكلمنهو يلا

আমাদের পোস্টমাস্টার কলিকাতার মাছকে ডাঙ্গায় তজলিলে যেরষ

The Arabic (top) *and Bengali* (above) *systems developed from the Phoenician.*

al·pha·bet (al′fə-bet′) *n.* the set of letters, usually in a fixed order, used in writing.

al·pha·bet·i·cal (al′fə-bet′i-kəl) or **al·pha·bet·ic** (al′fə-bet′ik) *adj.* in the order of the letters of an alphabet. – *adv.* **al·pha·bet·i·cal·ly** (al′fə-bet′i-klē).

● **Alps** Europe's greatest mountain range. The Alps are centered in SWITZERLAND and stretch from FRANCE to SERBIA. Their highest point is Mont Blanc (15,771 feet or 4,807m).

al·read·y (ôl-red′ē) *adv.* before the present time or the expected time.

al·so (ôl′sō) *adv.* in addition; too; besides.

al·tar (ôl′tər) *n.* a special table where religious rites are performed.

al·ter (ôl′tər) *vb.* **al·ter·ing, al·tered** to make or become different. – *n.* **al·ter·a·tion** (ôl′tə-rā′shən).

al·ter·nate (ôl′tər-nət) *adj.* 1 arranged or coming one after the other by turns. 2 (with *plural* nouns) every other; one out of two. – (ôl′tər-nāt′) *vb.* **al·ter·nat·ing, al·ter·nat·ed** 1 to succeed or follow each other by turns. 2 to change from one thing to another by turns.

al·ter·na·tive (ôl-tur′nət-iv) *adj.* offering a choice. – *n.* the possibility of choice.

al·though or **al·tho** (ôl-thō′) *conj.* in spite of the fact that; except for the fact that; though.

al·ti·tude (al′tə-tōōd, al′tə-tyōōd′) *n.* height above sea level.

al·to (al′tō) *n.* **al·tos** 1 the lowest female singing voice. 2 the highest adult male singing voice. 3 a singer who has an alto voice.

al·to·geth·er (ôl′tə-geth′ər) *adv.* 1 completely. 2 on the whole; taking everything into consideration: *Altogether, I think we did very well.* 3 in total: *We made $300 altogether.*

a·lu·mi·num (ə-lōō′mə-nəm) *n.* a light, silvery metallic element (symbol **Al**) which is not corroded by the air.

al·ways (ôl′wēz, ôl′wāz) *adv.* 1 at all times; for all time. 2 in any case; if necessary: *You could always help him if he can't manage alone.*

A.M. or a.m. *abbreviation* for *ante meridien* (Latin) before midday; in the morning.

a·mal·gam (ə-mal′gəm) *n.* a mixture or blend.

am·a·teur (am′ə-tur′, am′ət-ər, am′ə-chər) *n.* 1 a person who takes part in a sport or pastime without being paid for it. 2 a person not very skilled in an activity. – *adj.* not professional.

am·a·teur·ish (am′ə-tur′ish, am′ə-toor′ish) *adj.* not very skillful.

a·maze (ə-māz′) *vb.* **a·maz·ing, a·mazed** to surprise greatly; to astonish. – *adj.* **a·mazed.** – *n.* **a·maze·ment** (ə-māz′mənt).

● **Am·a·zon** (am′ə-zän′) a great river in SOUTH AMERICA and the second longest river in the world (4,000 miles or 6,437 km) after the NILE.

Amateur comes from a Latin word for "love" and originally meant "a person who does something for the love of it rather than being paid for it." Sometimes the word is used to suggest a lack of talent, as in an *amateurish performance.*

The **Amazon** rain forest in Brazil is shrinking at an alarming rate as trees are cleared to provide timber. Much of the land is converted into farms and cattle ranches. Plant and animal species disappear and those found nowhere else become extinct.

1980s

1900

As the soil of cleared land becomes exhausted after a few harvests, farmers move on to new areas.

Soil is washed into rivers causing them to silt up.

In the dry season exposed soil may be baked hard and crack.

A piece of polished amber containing the body of an insect, preserved almost intact.

am·bas·sa·dor (am-bas′əd-ər) *n.* **1** a diplomat of the highest rank appointed by a government to represent it, usually abroad. **2** a representative or messenger.

am·ber (am′bər) *n.* a hard, clear, yellow or brownish fossil resin used in jewelry.

am·bi·dex·trous (am′bə-dek′strəs) *adj.* able to use both hands equally well.

am·bi·gu·ous (am-big′yōō-əs) *adj.* having more than one possible meaning; not clear.

am·bi·tion (am-bish′ən) *n.* **1** a strong desire for success, fame, or power. **2** a thing someone desires to do or achieve.

am·bi·tious (am-bish′əs) *adj.* **1** having a strong desire for success. **2** requiring hard work and skill: *an ambitious exercise program.*

am·ble (am′bəl) *vb.* **am·bling, am·bled** to walk without hurrying.

am·bu·lance (am′byə-ləns) *n.* a vehicle equipped for carrying sick or injured people.

am·bush (am′boosh′) *n.* the act of lying in wait to attack by surprise. – *vb.* **am·bush·ing, am·bushed** to attack in this way.

a·men (ä-men′, ā-men′) *interjection* (usually said at the end of a prayer) so be it.

a·mend (ə-mend′) *vb.* **a·mend·ing, a·mend·ed** to correct, improve, or make minor changes to. – *n.* **a·mend·ment** (ə-mend′mənt).

a·me·ni·ty (ə-men′ət-ē, ə-mē′nət-ē) *n.* **a·me·ni·ties 1** anything that makes life more comfortable and pleasant. **2** any agreeable way of manner; politeness: *social amenities.*

● **A·mer·i·ca** (ə-mer′ə-kə) is often used for the UNITED STATES. The original word, Americas, includes NORTH AMERICA, CENTRAL AMERICA, SOUTH AMERICA, and the CARIBBEAN. The Americas were named after the Italian explorer Amerigo VESPUCCI.

A·mer·i·can (ə-mer′ə-kən) *adj.* of the UNITED STATES of America or the continents of America, the people who live or were born there, and the languages they speak. – *n.* a person born in or a citizen of the United States of America, or the continents of America.

American Indian. See **Native American.**

Americanism (ə-mer′ə-kə-niz′əm) *n.* a word, phrase, or custom that is characteristic of Americans.

● **American Revolution** the war fought between the 13 American colonies and GREAT BRITAIN from 1775 to 1783. The colonies won their independence and became a new nation, the UNITED STATES of America. It is also called the **Revolutionary War**.

The American colonists declared that "taxation without representation is tyranny." The **American Revolution** began in 1775. At first the British were successful. Native Americans fought alongside the rebels. After six years' struggle the British surrendered at Yorktown, Virginia.

The map shows the main battles of the war.

Montreal
Great Lakes
Saratoga
Lexington (1775)
Bunker Hill
Princeton
Long Island
Trenton
Germantown
Chesapeake Bay
Jamestown
Indian territory
Yorktown
Camden
Atlantic Ocean

Battle of Bunker Hill (1775). The Americans defended the hill (Breed's Hill) from two British attacks but retreated at the third.

am·e·thyst (am′ə-thəst) *n.* a type of purple or violet quartz used as a gemstone.

a·mi·a·ble (ā′mē-ə-bəl) *adj.* likeable; friendly.

am·mo·ni·a (ə-mō′nē-ə) *n.* a strong-smelling gas used in making fertilizers, glue, etc.

am·mu·ni·tion (am′yə-nish′ən) *n.* bullets, shells, etc. made to be fired from a weapon.

am·ne·sia (am-nē′zhə) *n.* loss of memory.

am·nes·ty (am′nə-stē) *n.* **am·nes·ties** a general pardon, especially for people guilty of political crimes.

a·moe·ba (ə-mē′bə) *n.* **a·moe·bae** (ə-mē′bē), or **amoebas** a microscopic, single-celled organism which usually lives in water.

a·mong (ə-mung′) or **a·mongst** (ə-mungkst′) *prep.* **1** in the middle of a number of people or things: *She was among friends.* **2** between: *They divided the cake among them.*

a·mor·phous (ā-môr′fəs) *adj.* shapeless.

a·mount (ə-mount′) *n.* a quantity; a total or extent: *She earns a large amount of money.* – *vb.* **a·mount·ing, a·mount·ed** to be equal or add up to in size or number, etc.

am·phib·i·an (am-fib′ē-ən) *n.* a creature, such as a frog or toad, that spends part of its life on land and part in water.

●Amphibians were one of the earliest groups of animals on earth. Most amphibians lay their eggs in water in a protective layer of jelly.

am·phib·i·ous (am-fib′ē-əs) *adj.* living or operating both on land and in water.

am·phi·the·at·er (am′fi-thē′ət-ər) *n.* a round building without a roof, with tiers of seats around a central open area, used as a theater.

am·ple (am′pəl) *adj.* **1** more than enough; plenty. **2** extensive, abundant.

am·pli·fi·er (am′plə-fī′ər) *n.* a machine for increasing the strength of electrical signals, especially so as to produce sound.

am·pli·fy (am′plə-fī′) *vb.* **am·pli·fies, am·pli·fy·ing, am·pli·fied 1** to make stronger: *to amplify a sound.* **2** to add detail to a story: *Later, he amplified upon his explanation.*

am·pu·tate (am′pyə-tāt′) *vb.* **am·pu·tat·ing, am·pu·tat·ed** to cut off, especially part or all of a limb. – *n.* **am·pu·ta·tion** (am′pyə-tā′shən).

●**Am·ster·dam** (am′stər-dam′) is the biggest city in the NETHERLANDS, having many beautiful canals.

●**A·mund·sen** (ä′mən-sən), **Roald** (1872-1928) was a Norwegian explorer, and in 1911 the first to reach the SOUTH POLE.

a·muse (ə-myōoz′) *vb.* **a·mus·ing, a·mused** to make laugh; to keep entertained and interested. – *adv.* **a·mus·ed·ly** (ə-myōo′zəd-lē).

a·muse·ment (ə-myōoz′mənt) *n.* **1** the state of being amused. **2** something that amuses.

an See **a**.

an·ach·ro·nism (ə-nak′rə-niz′əm) *n.* the representation of something in a historical period in which it did not exist. – *adj.* **an·ach·ro·nis·tic** (ə-nak′rə-nis′tik).

an·a·con·da (an′ə-kän′də) *n.* a very large South American snake which squeezes its prey to death.

The anaconda lives on the banks of slow-moving rivers in South America. Like many snakes, anacondas can unhinge their jaws to swallow prey larger than themselves.

an·aes·thet·ic (an′əs-thet′ik) *n.* another spelling of ANESTHETIC.

an·a·gram (an′ə-gram′) *n.* a word or phrase formed from the letters of another. "Despair" is an anagram of "praised."

a·nal·o·gy (ə-nal′ə-jē) *n.* **a·nal·o·gies** a similarity in some aspects of two items.

a·nal·y·sis (ə-nal′ə-səs) *n.* **a·nal·y·ses** (ə-nal′ə-sēz′) a detailed examination of the structure and content of something.

analyst (an′l-əst) *n.* someone who is skilled in analysis, especially chemical, political, or economic.

an·a·lyze (an′l-īz′) *vb.* **an·a·lyz·ing, an·a·lyzed** to examine in detail.

an·ar·chy (an′ər-kē, an′är′kē) *n.* confusion and lack of order, especially political; lack of law and government. – *adj.* **an·ar·chic** (an-är′kik).

a·nat·o·my (ə-nat′ə-mē) *n.* **a·nat·o·mies 1** the science of the structure of animals or plants, especially studied through dissection. **2** the structure of an animal or plant. – *adj.* **an·a·tom·i·cal** (an′ə-täm′i-kəl).

Anchor comes from a Greek word meaning "hook." The earliest anchors were made of cast iron with a wooden crosspiece, or "stock." This type of anchor was replaced in the 19th century by one with a movable metal stock. This was known as the Admiralty anchor. Soon various stockless anchors came into use.

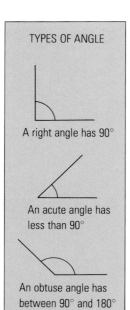

Stock

Shank

Arm

Crown

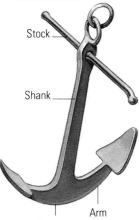

TYPES OF ANGLE

A right angle has 90°

An acute angle has less than 90°

An obtuse angle has between 90° and 180°

an·ces·tor (an'ses'tər) *n.* a person from whom you are descended.

an·ces·tral (an-ses'trəl) *adj.* of your ancestors.

an·chor (ang'kər) *n.* a heavy piece of metal with hooks which dig into the seabed, attached by a cable to a ship and used to restrict its movement.

an·cient (ān'shənt) *adj.* **1** dating from very long ago; very old. **2** dating from before the end of the ROMAN EMPIRE in A.D. 476.

and (ənd, and) *conj.* **1** used to show addition: *Two and two equals four.* **2** used to show a result or reason: *On ice it is easy to fall and bang your head.* **3** used to show repetition or duration: *It rained and rained.* **4** used to show progression: *The balloon got bigger and bigger.* **5** used to show variety or contrast: *good cars and bad cars.*

an·dan·te (än-dän'tā). See **Musical Terms**.

●**An·der·sen** (än'ər-sən, an'dər-sən), **Hans Christian** (1805-1875) was a Danish writer of fairy tales which include *The Little Mermaid*.

●**An·des** (an'dēz) the longest mountain range in the world, which runs the length (4,350 miles or 7,000 km) of western SOUTH AMERICA.

●**An·dor·ra** (an-dôr'ə). See Supplement, **Countries**.

an·ec·dote (an'ik-dōt') *n.* a short, interesting, and usually amusing account of an incident.

a·ne·mi·a (ə-nē'mē-ə) *n.* a condition in which there are not enough red cells or hemoglobin in the blood, causing tiredness and paleness. – *adj.* **a·ne·mic** (ə-nē'mik).

an·e·mom·e·ter (an'ə-mäm'ət-ər) *n.* an instrument for measuring the wind speed.

anesthetic (an'əs-thet'ik) *n.* a drug or gas that causes total unconsciousness or lack of feeling in part of the body , so that surgery may be performed without pain.

an·gel (ān'jəl) *n.* **1** a messenger of God, represented in human form with a halo and wings. **2** (*informal*) a very helpful person.

an·ger (ang'gər) *n.* a feeling of great or violent displeasure. – *vb.* **an·ger·ing, an·gered** to make angry; to displease.

an·gle[1] (ang'gəl) *n.* **1** the shape made by two straight lines or surfaces that meet. **2** a corner. – *vb.* **an·gling, an·gled** to place at an angle.

an·gle[2] (ang'gəl) *vb.* **an·gling, an·gled** to use a rod and line to try to catch fish.

Anglo- (ang'glō) *prefix* English; British; of English or British origin: *Anglo-American.*

An·glo-Sax·on (ang'glō-sak'sən) *n.* **1** a member of any of the Germanic tribes which settled in ENGLAND and parts of SCOTLAND in the 400s A.D. **2** Old English, the ENGLISH language before about 1150. – *adj.* relating to the Anglo-Saxons or the Old English language.

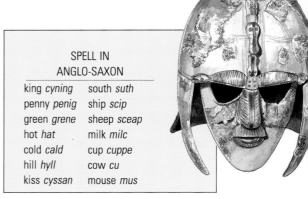

SPELL IN ANGLO-SAXON	
king *cyning*	south *suth*
penny *penig*	ship *scip*
green *grene*	sheep *sceap*
hot *hat*	milk *milc*
cold *cald*	cup *cuppe*
hill *hyll*	cow *cu*
kiss *cyssan*	mouse *mus*

A helmet showing skilled Anglo-Saxon metalwork.

●**An·go·la** (ang-gō'lə). See Supplement, **Countries**.

an·gry (ang'grē) *adj.* **an·gri·er, an·gri·est** feeling or showing anger. – *adv.* **an·gri·ly** (ang'grə-lē).

an·guish (ang'gwish) *n.* great pain or suffering, especially of the mind.

an·gu·lar (ang'gyə-lər) *adj.* **1** thin and bony. **2** having an angle or angles.

an·i·mal (an'ə-məl) *n.* a living being which can feel things and move by itself.

an·i·mos·i·ty (an'ə-mäs'ət-ē) *n.* **an·i·mos·i·ties** a strong dislike or hatred.

●**An·ka·ra** (ang'kə-rə) is the capital of TURKEY.

an·kle (ang'kəl) *n.* the joint connecting the leg and the foot.

an·nex (ə-neks', an'eks') *vb.* **annexing, annexed** to take possession of land or territory, especially by conquest or occupation. – (an'eks') *n.* a building added on to, or used as an addition to, another.

an·ni·hil·ate (ə-nī'ə-lāt') *vb.* **an·nih·il·at·ing, an·ni·hil·at·ed** to destroy completely. – *n.* **an·ni·hil·a·tion** (ə-nī'ə-lā'shən).

an·ni·ver·sa·ry (an'ə-vur'sə-rē) *n.*
an·ni·ver·sa·ries 1 the date on which an
event took place in a previous year. **2** the
celebration of this event each year.

an·nounce (ə-nouns') *vb.* **an·nounc·ing,**
an·nounced to make known publicly: *He*
announced his retirement. – *n.* **an·nounce·ment**
(ə-noun'smənt).

an·nounc·er (ə-noun'sər) *n.* a person who
introduces programs on radio or television.

an·noy (ə-noi') *vb.* **an·noy·ing, an·noyed** to
anger or distress: *His lack of concern annoys me.*

an·nu·al (an'yōō-əl) *adj.* happening every year.

annul (ə nul') *vb.* **an·nul·ling, an·nulled** to
declare publicly to be no longer valid: to annul
a marriage – *n.* **an·nul·ment** (ə nul' mənt).

a·noint (ə-noint') *vb.* **a·noint·ing,**
a·noint·ed to put oil or ointment on as part
of a religious ceremony. – *n.* **a·noint·ment**
(ə noint' mənt).

a·nom·a·ly (ə-näm'ə-lē) *n.* **a·nom·a·lies**
something which is different from the usual.

a·non·y·mous (ə-nän'ə-məs) *adj.* done or
written by a person whose name is not known.

an·o·rex·i·a (an'ə-rek'sē-ə) or **an·o·rex·i·a**
ner·vo·sa (an'ə-rek'sē-ə nər-vō'sə) *n.* an
illness in which the sufferer refuses to eat, and
loses a lot of weight. – *n.* & *adj.* **an·o·rex·ic**
(an'ə-rek'sik).

a·noth·er (ə-nuth'ər) *adj.* & *pron.* **1** one more.
2 one more of the same kind. **3** one of a
different kind: *another country.*

an·swer (an'sər) *n.* **1** something said or done in
response to a question or letter, etc. **2** the
solution to a problem. – *vb.* **an·swer·ing,**
an·swered 1 to make a reply or answer to. **2**
to respond to: *Please answer the door.* **3** to be the
same as: *His truck answers the police's description.*

an·swer·a·ble (an'sə-rə-bəl) *adj.* responsible
for.

ant (ant) *n.* a small, often wingless insect, which
lives in organized colonies.

an·tag·o·nist (an-tag'ə-nəst) *n.* an opponent
or enemy. – *adj.* **an·tag·o·nis·tic** (an-tag'ə-
nis'tik).

an·tag·o·nize (an-tag'ə-nīz') *vb.*
an·tag·o·niz·ing, an·tag·o·nized to
make angry or hostile.

Ant·arc·tic (ant-ärk'tik, ant-ärt'ik) *n.* the area
around the SOUTH POLE. – *adj.* of the area
around the SOUTH POLE.

● **Ant·arc·tic·a** (ant-ärk'ti-kə, ant-ärt'i-kə) is
the continent around the SOUTH POLE. Very
little can grow there as average temperatures
are below freezing.

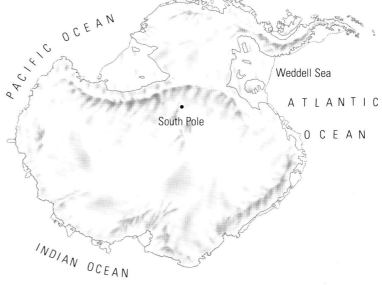

*In 1911 the Norwegian
Roald Amundsen became
the first person to reach
the South Pole. He was
closely followed by the
British explorer, Captain
Robert Falcon Scott.*

Amundsen Sea

PACIFIC OCEAN

South Pole

Weddell Sea

ATLANTIC OCEAN

INDIAN OCEAN

ant·eat·er (ant'ēt'ər) *n.* a South African
animal with a long snout, which eats mainly
termites.

an·te·lope (ant'l-ōp') *n.* **antelope** or
an·te·lopes any of several deerlike animals
with horns, related to the goat.

an·ten·na (an-ten'ə) *n.* **1 an·ten·nae** (an-
ten'ē) one of a pair of feelers on the head of
some insects or crustaceans, used for touching.
2 an·ten·nas an aerial.

an·them (an'thəm) *n.* a song of praise or
celebration, especially of a nation.

an·thol·o·gy (an-thäl'ə-jē) *n.* **anthologies** a
collection of poems or other writing.

● **An·tho·ny** (an'thə-nē), **Susan B**. (1820-1906)
campaigned for the ending of slavery in the UNI-
TED STATES and for the right of American
women to vote.

Worker ants with aphids

*Ants are "social" insects and live
together in colonies. In an ant
colony there are different chambers,
which the ants use to lay eggs and
bring up the young.*

Worker ants
with larvae

Wood ant

Adult
ants
emerging from pupae

Queen
ant lays
eggs

WHAT'S THE ANSWER
Answer is an Anglo-
Saxon word. The
second half has the
same root as "swear."
The first part "an"
means "facing," so the
whole word means "to
face and swear."

The main difference between horns and antlers is that horns are permanent, whereas antlers are shed each year. As a rule only male antelope have antlers, which may be used in combat as they compete for females during the mating season.

an·thro·pol·o·gy (an'thrǝ-päl'ǝ-jē) *n.* the study of the development of human beings, especially their society, physical characteristics, customs, and beliefs. – *n.*
 an·thro·pol·o·gist (an'thrǝ-päl'ǝ-jǝst).

anti- *prefix* **1** opposed to; against: *antifreeze.* **2** opposite to: *antimatter.*

an·ti·bi·ot·ic (ant'i-bī-ät'ik) *n.* any substance used to kill the bacteria that cause disease.

an·ti·bod·y (ant'i-bäd'ē) *n.* **an·ti·bod·ies** a substance produced by the blood to fight harmful bacteria.

an·tic·i·pate (an-tis'ǝ-pāt') *vb.*
 an·tic·i·pat·ing, an·tic·i·pat·ed 1 to foresee and plan for. **2** to expect. – *n.*
 an·tic·i·pa·tion (an-tis'ǝ-pā'shǝn).

an·ti·clock·wise (ant'i-kläk'wīz') *adv. & adj.* (*British*) counterclockwise.

an·ti·cy·clone (ant'i-sī'klōn') *n.* See **Weather Terms**.

an·ti·dote (ant'i-dōt') *n.* **1** a medicine given to stop the harmful effects of a poison. **2** anything that prevents something bad.

●**An·tig·ua and Bar·bu·da** (an-tē'gwǝ, bär-bōōd'ǝ). See Supplement, **Countries**.

 an·ti·quat·ed (ant'i-kwāt'ǝd) *adj.* out of date.

an·tique (an-tēk') *n.* an object which is very old and usually valuable. – *adj.* very old or old-fashioned: *an antique rug.*

an·ti·sep·tic (ant'ǝ-sep'tik) *n.* a substance that kills germs and so prevents infection or disease. – *adj.* **1** sterile; free from germs. **2** killing germs.

ant·ler (ant'lǝr) *n.* either of the two branched horns on the head of a stag.

an·to·nym (ant'ǝ-nim') *n.* a word opposite in meaning to another word.

a·nus (ā'nǝs) *n.* the opening at the lower end of the food canal.

an·vil (an'vǝl) *n.* a heavy iron block on which metal objects can be hammered into shape.

an·xious (angk'shǝs) *adj.* **1** worried or fearful. **2** very eager. – *n.* **an·xi·et·y** (ang-zī'ǝt-ē), **an·xi·et·ies**.

an·y (en'ē) *adj.* **1** one, no matter which: *I can't find any answer.* **2** some, no matter which: *Do you have any apples?* **3** a very small amount of: *I won't tolerate any nonsense.* **4** whichever or whatever: *Any child could tell you.* – *pron.* any one or any amount: *I don't have any at all.* – *adv.* in any way whatever: *Do you feel any better?*

an·y·bod·y (en'ē-bäd'ē, en'ē-bud'ē) *pron.* any person, no matter which: *Anybody could do it.*

an·y·how (en'ē-hou') *adv.* **1** in spite of what has been said or done. **2** carelessly; in an untidy state. **3** in any way or manner.

an·y·one (en'ē-wun') *pron.* same as **anybody**.

an·y·thing (en'ē-thing') *pron.* a thing of any kind; a thing, no matter which: *I can't think of anything to say.*

an·y·way (en'ē-wā') *adv.* **1** nevertheless; in spite of what has been said or done: *I don't agree, but I'll do it anyway.* **2** in any way.

an·y·where (en'ē-hwer') *adv.* in, at, or to any place. – *pron.* any place.

a·or·ta (ā-ôrt'ǝ) *n.* the main artery in the body, carrying blood from the heart.

●**A·pach·es** (ǝ-pach'ēz) a NATIVE AMERICAN tribe of the southwestern UNITED STATES.

a·part (ǝ-pärt') *adv.* **1** in or into pieces: *It fell apart in my hands.* **2** separated by a certain distance or time: *They've lived apart for two months.* **3** to or on one side: *The house was set apart from the rest of the town.*

a·part·ment (ǝ-pärt'mǝnt) *n.* a set of rooms or a single room for living in.

apartheid (ǝ-par'tāt', ǝ-par'tīt') *n.* in South Africa, the policy of keeping people of different races apart.

ap·a·thy (ap'ǝ-thē) *n.* lack of interest or enthusiasm. – *adj.* **ap·a·thet·ic** (ap'ǝ-thet'ik).

ape (āp) *n.* an animal related to monkeys, with little or no tail. – *vb.* **ap·ing, aped** to imitate.

There are four kinds of **ape**. The gorilla and chimpanzee are African; orangutans live in Borneo and Sumatra; gibbons live in southeast Asia. Apes have highly developed hands with "opposable" thumbs to help them swing from branches. Apes have large brains.

Gorilla

Chimpanzee

●**Ap·en·nines** (ap′ə-nīnz′) a mountain range in ITALY.

ap·er·ture (ap′ər-chər, ap′ə-chər) *n*. a small opening.

Aph·ro·di·te (af′rə-dīt′ē). See **Myths and Legends**.

A·pol·lo (ə-päl′ō). See **Myths and Legends**.

a·pol·o·get·ic (ə-päl′ə-jet′ik) *adj*. expressing regret for a fault, etc.

a·pol·o·gize (ə-päl′ə-jīz′) *vb*. **a·pol·o·giz·ing, a·pol·o·gized** to say you are sorry.

a·pol·o·gy (ə-päl′ə-jē) *n*. **a·pol·o·gies** an expression of regret for a mistake or failure.

a·pos·tle (ə-päs′əl) *n*. a person sent out to preach about Jesus Christ in the early Christian church, especially one of his 12 original disciples.

a·pos·tro·phe (ə-päs′trə-fē) *n*. a mark (') used to show the omission of a letter or letters, for example *I'm* for *I am*, and to show possession, for example *Anne's book*.

●**Ap·pa·la·chi·ans** (ap′ə-lā′chənz, ap′ə-lach′ənz) forested mountains forming the great eastern range that runs from Newfoundland, CANADA to Alabama in the UNITED STATES.

ap·pall or **appal** (ə-pôl′) *vb*. **ap·pall·ing, ap·palled** to shock or horrify.

ap·pa·ra·tus (ap′ə-rat′əs, ap′ə-rāt′əs) *n*. **ap·pa·ra·tus·es** or **apparatus** the equipment needed for a particular purpose.

ap·par·ent (ə-pâr′ənt) *adj*. **1** easy to see or understand. **2** seeming to be real but perhaps not actually so: *It was an apparent mistake.* – *adv*. **ap·par·ent·ly.**

ap·peal (ə-pēl′) *vb*. **ap·peal·ing, ap·pealed 1** to make an urgent or formal request. **2** to be pleasing, interesting, or attractive. **3** to request a higher authority or law court to change a decision given by a lower one. – *n*. **1** an urgent or formal request. **2** See **Law**. **3** the power to interest or attract.

ap·peal·ing *adj*. pleasing, attractive.

ap·pear (ə-pîr′) *vb*. **ap·pear·ing, ap·peared 1** to become visible or come into sight. **2** to seem: *They appear to be very happy.*

ap·pear·ance (ə-pîr′əns) *n*. **1** an act or instance of appearing. **2** how a person or thing looks.

ap·pen·di·ci·tis (ə-pen′də-sīt′əs) *n*. inflammation of the appendix.

ap·pen·dix (ə-pen′diks) *n*. **ap·pen·di·ces** (ə-pen′də-sēz′) **1** a small, tubelike sac attached to the lower end of the large intestine. **2** a section containing extra information at the end of a book or document.

ap·pe·tite (ap′ə-tīt′) *n*. **1** a natural physical desire, especially for food. **2** a liking or willingness for something.

ap·pe·tiz·ing (ap′ə-tī′zing) *adj*. increasing the appetite.

ap·plaud (ə-plôd′) *vb*. **ap·plaud·ing, ap·plaud·ed** to praise or show approval by clapping. – **ap·plause** (ə-plôz′).

ap·ple (ap′əl) *n*. **1** a firm, round, edible fruit with a green, red, or yellow skin and white flesh. **2** the tree bearing this fruit.

Four of the more than 1,800 named varieties of apple: 1. Granny Smith. 2. Cox's Orange Pippin. 3. McIntosh. 4. Golden Delicious.

ap·pli·ance (ə-plī′əns) *n*. a machine, instrument, or tool used for a particular job.

ap·pli·ca·tion (ap′lə-kā′shən) *n*. **1** a formal request. **2** the act of putting something on a surface. **3** something that is applied.

ap·ply (ə-plī′) *vb*. **ap·plies, ap·ply·ing, ap·plied 1** to make a formal request, as for a job. **2** to put or spread on a surface.

Gibbon

Orangutan

PRONUNCIATION SYMBOLS		
ə away	lemon	focus
a fat	oi	boy
ā fade	oo	foot
ä hot	ōō	moon
âr fair	ou	house
e met	th	think
ē mean	th	this
g get	u	cut
hw which	ur	hurt
i fin	w	witch
ī line	y	yes
îr near	yōō	music
ô often	yoor	pure
ō note	zh	vision

ap·point (ə-point′) *vb.* **ap·point·ing,
ap·point·ed 1** to designate or select. **2** to fix or agree on a date, time, or place.

ap·point·ment (ə-point′mənt) *n.* **1** an arrangement to meet someone. **2** the act of giving someone a job or position.

ap·pre·ci·ate (ə-prē′shē-āt′, ə-prish′ē-āt′) *vb.*
ap·pre·ci·at·ing, ap·pre·ci·at·ed 1 to be grateful or thankful for. **2** to be aware of the value or quality, etc. of. **3** to understand or be aware of.

ap·pre·ci·a·tion (ə-prē′shē-ā′shən, ə-prish′ē-ā′shən) *n.* **1** gratitude or thanks. **2** sensitive understanding and enjoyment.

ap·pre·cia·tive (ə-prē′shət-iv, ə-prish′ət-iv) *adj.* expressing appreciation.

ap·pre·hen·sion (ap′rē-hen′shən) *n.* fear or anxiety about the future.

ap·pre·hen·sive (ap′rē-hen′siv) *adj.* anxious.

ap·proach (ə-prōch′) *vb.* **ap·proach·ing,
ap·proached 1** to come near or nearer in space or time. **2** to suggest or propose something to. **3** to begin to deal with. – *n.* **1** the act of coming near. **2** a way to, or means of reaching, a place: *The approach to the castle was very steep.* **3** a method of handling something: *a new approach to the problem.*

ap·pro·pri·ate (ə-prō′prē-ət) *adj.* suitable.

ap·prov·al (ə-prōō′vəl) *n.* **1** a favorable opinion. **2** official permission.

ap·prove (ə-prōōv′) *vb.* **ap·prov·ing,
ap·proved 1** to agree to or permit. **2** to be pleased with or think well of.

ap·prox·i·mate (ə-präk′sə-mət) *adj.* almost exact or accurate.

a·pri·cot (ap′rə-kät′, ā′prə-kät′) *n.* a small, round, pale-orange fruit with a fuzzy skin.

A·pril (ā′prəl) *n.* the fourth month of the year. April has 30 days.

a·pron (ā′prən) *n.* a piece of cloth or plastic, etc. worn over the front of the clothes for protection from dirt.

apt (apt) *adj.* **1** suitable. **2** likely.

ap·ti·tude (ap′tə-tōōd′, ap′tə-tyōōd′) *n.* **1** a natural skill or talent. **2** ability or fitness.

a·quar·i·um (ə-kwâr′ē-əm) *n.* **a·quar·i·ums**
or **a·quar·i·a** (ə-kwâr′ē-ə) a glass tank, or a building containing several such tanks, for keeping fish and other water animals.

A·quar·i·us (ə-kwâr′ē-əs) *n.* See **zodiac**.

aq·ue·duct (ak′wə-dukt′) *n.* a bridgelike structure for carrying water across rivers or valleys.

Apricots grow on a small tree belonging to the plum family. They are sweet and peachlike to taste and can be eaten fresh, canned, or dried. People once thought that apricots came from the Americas; in fact they originate from China.

The most famous aqueducts were built by the Romans. Between 312 B.C. and A.D. 226 they built eleven aqueducts to supply Rome.

Ar·ab (ar′əb) *n.* **1** one of the Semitic people living in the MIDDLE EAST and North AFRICA. **2** a breed of horse famous for its grace and speed. – *adj.* of Arabs. – *adj.* **A·ra·bi·an** (ə-rā′bē-ən). – *adj.* **Ar·a·bic** (ar′ə-bik).

Ar·ab·ic (ar′ə-bik) *n.* the language of the Arabs.

Arabic numeral *n.* any of the numbers 0, 1, 2, 3, 4, 5, 6, 7, 8, or 9, brought to EUROPE from INDIA by the Arabs.

ar·a·ble (ar′ə-bəl) *adj.* describing land that is suitable or used for growing crops.

a·rach·nid (ə-rak′nəd) *n.* any of a class of eight-legged insectlike creatures, such as spiders.

ar·bi·trar·y (är′bə-trer′ē) *adj.* based on personal or random choice, not rules.

ar·bi·trate (är′bə-trāt′) *vb.* **ar·bi·trat·ing,
ar·bi·trat·ed** to act as a judge in a quarrel or disagreement. – *n.* **ar·bi·tra·tor** (är′bə-trāt′ər).

arc (ärk) *n.* a part of the line which forms a curve. – *vb.* **arc·ing, arced** to form an arc.

ar·cade (är-kād′) *n.* **1** a covered passage, usually lined with shops. **2** a row of arches supporting a roof or wall, etc.

arch (ärch) *n.* **1** a curved structure forming an opening, a support, or an ornament. **2** the raised part of the sole of the foot, between the heel and the toes. – *vb.* **arch·ing, arched** to form an arch.

arch- or **archi-** (ärch, ärk, är′kē) *prefix* chief; most important: *archangel*; *archduke*.

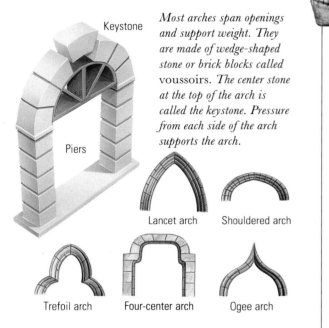

Keystone

Piers

Most arches span openings and support weight. They are made of wedge-shaped stone or brick blocks called voussoirs. *The center stone at the top of the arch is called the keystone. Pressure from each side of the arch supports the arch.*

Lancet arch

Shouldered arch

Trefoil arch

Four-center arch

Ogee arch

ar·chae·ol·o·gy (är′kē-äl′ə-jē) *n.* the study of the history and culture of ancient civilizations through studying remains such as tools or pots, etc. dug up from the ground. – *n.* **ar·chae·ol·o·gist** (är′kē-äl′ə-jəst).

ar·chae·op·ter·yx (är′kē-äp′tə-riks) *n.* an ancient fossil bird with sharp teeth.

ar·cha·ic (är-kā′ik) *adj.* **1** ancient; from a much earlier period. **2** out of date.

ar·cher (är′chər) *n.* a person who shoots with a bow and arrows.

ar·cher·y (är′chə-rē) *n.* the sport of shooting with a bow.

● **Ar·chi·me·des** (är′kə-mēd′ēz) (*c.*287 B.C.-212 B.C.) was a Greek mathematician and inventor who discovered the principle of the lever.

ar·chi·pel·a·go (är′kə-pel′ə-gō′, är′chə-pel′ə-gō′) *n.* **archipelagos 1** a group of islands. **2** an area of sea with many islands.

At first **archaeological** sites were ransacked for the treasures they contained, but by the early 1800s archaeologists had begun to uncover sites carefully, noting everything they found and where they found it. Today, carbon dating and dendrochronology (dating by tree rings) help tell archaeologists when objects were made.

Pottery

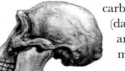

The skull of an early humanlike creature

WORDS USED IN ARCHAEOLOGY

artifact any object made by humans.

barrow an earth-covered dolmen.

Bronze Age from about 3000 B.C. to 1800 B.C.

cromlech a ring of standing stones.

dolmen a burial chamber consisting of several upright stones.

flint the most favored stone of prehistoric people.

henge a sacred circle of stones.

Iron Age began about 1400 B.C.

megaliths stone monuments.

menhir a single upright stone.

quern two circular stones used to grind corn.

sarcophagus a stone coffin.

shard a fragment of pottery.

Stone Age the name given to the time when people used only stone for toolmaking. It includes the Paleolithic (old Stone Age), the Mesolithic (middle Stone Age), and Neolithic (new Stone Age).

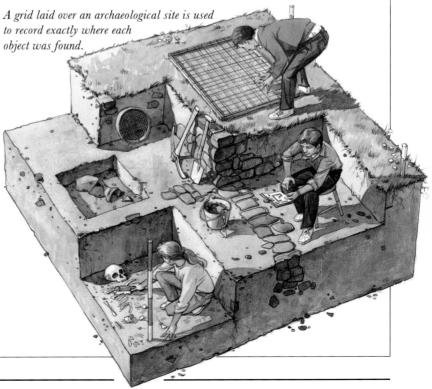

A grid laid over an archaeological site is used to record exactly where each object was found.

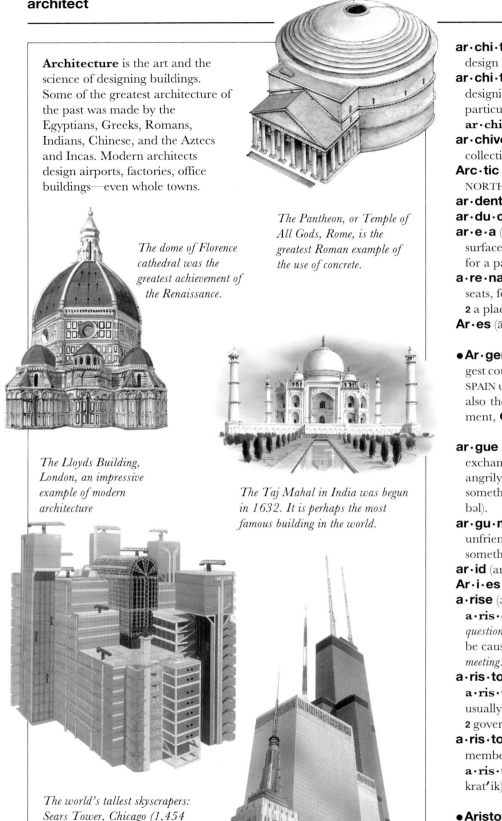

Architecture is the art and the science of designing buildings. Some of the greatest architecture of the past was made by the Egyptians, Greeks, Romans, Indians, Chinese, and the Aztecs and Incas. Modern architects design airports, factories, office buildings—even whole towns.

The Pantheon, or Temple of All Gods, Rome, is the greatest Roman example of the use of concrete.

The dome of Florence cathedral was the greatest achievement of the Renaissance.

The Lloyds Building, London, an impressive example of modern architecture

The Taj Mahal in India was begun in 1632. It is perhaps the most famous building in the world.

The world's tallest skyscrapers: Sears Tower, Chicago (1,454 ft./443 m) is the tallest.

ar·chi·tect (är′kə-tekt′) *n.* a person qualified to design buildings and other large structures.

ar·chi·tec·ture (är′kə-tek′chər) *n.* **1** the art of designing and constructing buildings. **2** a particular style of building: – *adj.* **ar·chi·tec·tur·al** (är′kə-tek′chə-rəl).

ar·chive (är′kīv′) *n.* (usually in *plural*) a collection of public documents or records, etc.

Arc·tic (ärk′tik, ärt′ik) *n.* the area around the NORTH POLE.

ar·dent (ärd′nt) *adj.* enthusiastic; passionate.

ar·du·ous (är′dū-əs) *adj.* difficult to do.

ar·e·a (âr′ē-ə) *n.* **1** the extent or size of a flat surface. **2** a region or part. **3** any space set aside for a particular purpose: *a dining area* .

a·re·na (ə-rē′nə) *n.* **1** an area surrounded by seats, for public shows or sports contests, etc. **2** a place of great activity, especially conflict.

Ar·es (âr′ēz). See **Myths and Legends**.

● **Ar·gen·ti·na** (är′jən-tē′nə) is the second largest country in SOUTH AMERICA. It was ruled by SPAIN until 1810. Buenos Aires is the capital and also the country's main port. See also Supplement, **Countries**.

ar·gue (är′gyōo′) *vb.* **ar·gu·ing, ar·gued 1** to exchange views with someone, especially angrily. **2** to suggest reasons for or against something. – *adj.* **ar·gu·a·ble** (är′gyōo-ə-bəl).

ar·gu·ment (är′gyə-mənt) *n.* **1** a quarrel or unfriendly discussion. **2** a reason for or against something.

ar·id (ar′əd) *adj.* dry; having very little water.

Ar·i·es (âr′ēz′, âr′ē-ēz′) *n.* See **zodiac.**

a·rise (ə-rīz′) *vb.* **a·ris·ing, a·rose** (ə-rōz′), **a·ris·en** (ə-riz′ən) **1** to come into being: *The question arose as we were speaking.* **2** to result or be caused: *His decision to go arose from our meeting.* **3** to get up or stand up.

a·ris·toc·ra·cy (ar′ə-stäk′rə-sē) *n.* **a·ris·toc·ra·cies 1** the highest social class, usually owning land and having titles. **2** government by this class.

a·ris·to·crat (ə-ris′tə-krat′, ar′əs-tə-krat′) *n.* a member of the aristocracy. – *adj.* **a·ris·to·crat·ic** (ə-ris′tə-krat′ik, ar′ə-stə-krat′ik).

● **Aristotle** (âr′ə-stät′l) (384 B.C.-322 B.C.) was a Greek philosopher who believed happiness comes from human reason.

a·rith·me·tic (ə-rith′mə-tik′) *n.* the science of adding, subtracting, multiplying, and dividing numbers.

●**Ar·i·zo·na** (ar′ə-zō′nə). See Supplement, **U.S.A.**

ark (ärk) *n.* **1** in the Bible, the vessel built by NOAH in which his family and animals survived the Flood. **2 Ark** a chest in a synagogue for keeping the Torah scrolls.

●**Ar·kan·sas** (är′kən-sô′). See Supplement, **U.S.A.**

arm¹ (ärm) *n.* **1** either of the two upper limbs of the body, from the shoulders to the hands. **2** anything shaped like this: *an arm of the sea.* **3** the sleeve of a garment. **4** the part of a chair, etc. that supports an arm. – **arm in arm** with arms linked together. – **with open arms** with a very friendly welcome.
arm² (ärm) *n.* **1** (usually in *plural*) a weapon. **2** (in *plural*) the symbol of a family, country, etc. – *vb.* **arm·ing, armed 1** to equip with arms. **2** to supply with whatever is needed.
ar·ma·da (är-mäd′ə) *n.* a fleet of fighting ships.

●In 1588 Spain sent a great fleet of armed ships, the Spanish Armada, to invade ENGLAND. The large, heavy Spanish ships were defeated by the smaller, faster English vessels.

The defeat of the Spanish Armada in 1588.

ar·ma·dil·lo (är′mə-dil′ō) *n.* **armadillos** a small burrowing animal covered with a hard bony shell, living in South America and as far north as Texas.

●**Ar·me·ni·a** (är-mē′nē-ə). See Supplement, **Countries**.

ar·mis·tice (är′mə-stəs) *n.* a stopping of hostilities.
ar·mor (är′mər) *n.* **1** a metal suit or covering formerly worn as a protection against injury in battle. **2** metal covering to protect ships or tanks, etc. against damage from weapons. **3** a protective covering on some animals and plants.
ar·mored (är′mərd) *adj.* protected by armor.

●**Arm·strong** (ärm′strông), **Neil** (1930-) was an American astronaut. On July 21, 1969 he became the first person to set foot on the moon.

ar·my (ar′mē) *n.* **ar·mies 1** a large number of people armed and organized for fighting on land. **2** a large number: *an army of children.*
a·ro·ma (ə-rō′mə) *n.* a distinctive, usually pleasant smell that a substance gives off.
a·ro·mat·ic (ar′ə-mat′ik) *adj.* having a strong, but sweet or pleasant smell.
a·round (ə-round′) *adv.* **1** on every side: *The children gathered around to listen to the story.* **2** here and there; in different directions or to different places: *They drove around for several hours.* – *prep.* **1** on all sides of: *She wore a bracelet around her wrist.* **2** at or to different points. **3** somewhere in or near: *Their house is around here.*
a·rouse (ə-rouz′) *vb.* **a·rous·ing, a·roused 1** to excite or stimulate. **2** to awake.
ar·range (ə-rānj′) *vb.* **ar·rang·ing, ar·ranged 1** to put into the proper order: *I arranged the words alphabetically.* **2** to plan in advance: *We arranged to meet at the station.* **3** to come to an agreement: *Arrange to get time off.*
ar·range·ment (ə-rānj′mənt) *n.* **1** (usually in *plural*) a plan or preparation for some future event. **2** the act of putting things into a proper order or pattern. **3** an agreement.
ar·rest (ə-rest′) *vb.* **ar·rest·ing, ar·rest·ed 1** to take into custody. **2** to stop or slow: – *n.* **1** See **Law**. **2** a stopping: *cardiac arrest.*

Armadillo is Spanish for "little armed one," an apt description for a creature whose body is encased in a kind of armor.

— Helmet

Visor —

— Breast plate

— Gauntlet

— Leg harness

— Sword

In the Middle Ages knights—and their horses—rode to battle encased in up to 60 pieces of plate armor. The invention of firearms made this type of armor obsolete.

Prehistoric people made arrowheads of stone or bone for hunting and for warfare. Together with spears, they have been used in all parts of the world throughout history. Illustrated are an arrow for a medieval longbow and a "bolt" used on the more powerful crossbow.

Artery is a Greek word meaning "air carrier." Because there is little blood in the arteries of dead bodies, ancient Greek doctors who dissected them thought arteries carried air around the body.

ar·riv·al (ə-rī′vəl) *n.* **1** the act of arriving. **2** a person or thing that has arrived, especially a newborn baby.

ar·rive (ə-rīv′) *vb.* **ar·riv·ing, ar·rived** to reach a place or destination: *She arrived at school earlier than expected.* – **arrive at** to come to: *He arrived at that conclusion after careful study.*

ar·ro·gant (ar′ə-gənt) *adj.* extremely proud; having or showing too high an opinion of your own importance. – *n.* **ar·ro·gance** (ar′ə-gəns).

ar·row (ar′ō) *n.* **1** a thin, straight stick with a point at one end and feathers at the other. It is fired from a bow. **2** an arrow-shaped symbol, used to indicate direction or position.

ar·se·nal (är′sə-nəl) *n.* **1** a factory or store for weapons or explosives. **2** a collection of weapons.

ar·se·nic (är′snik) *n.* a powerful poison.

ar·son (är′sən) *n.* the crime of deliberately setting fire to a building, etc. – *n.* **ar·son·ist** (är′sə-nəst).

art (ärt) *n.* **1** the creation of works of beauty. **2** (in *plural*) the different branches of creative activity, as music, painting, and literature. **3** a skill: *He has an art for dealing with people.*

Ar·te·mis (ärt′ə-məs). See **Myths and Legends**.

ar·ter·y (ärt′ə-rē) *n.* **ar·ter·ies** a tube that carries blood from the heart through the body.

art·ful (ärt′fəl) *adj.* **1** cunning. **2** skillful.

ar·thri·tis (är-thrīt′əs) *n.* inflammation of a joint or joints, causing pain and great difficulty in moving. – *n. & adj.* **ar·thrit·ic** (är-thrit′ik).

ar·thro·pod (är′thrə-päd′) *n.* a creature with a body in segments, limbs connected by joints, and its skeleton on the outside, such as a spider.

● **Ar·thur** (är′thər), **King** was a legendary British ruler of the A.D. 500s. In story he became leader of the Knights of the Round Table.

ar·ti·choke (ärt′ə-chōk′) *n.* a vegetable with large, thistlelike flower heads.

ar·ti·cle (ärt′i-kəl) *n.* **1** a thing or object: *an article of clothing.* **2** a usually short written composition in a newspaper or magazine. **3** in grammar, "the" (the **definite article**) or "a" or "an" (the **indefinite article**), or any equivalent word in other languages.

ar·tic·u·late (är-tik′yə-lāt′) *vb.* **ar·tic·u·lat·ing, ar·tic·u·lat·ed** to pronounce words or speak very distinctly.

ar·ti·fact (ärt′ə-fakt′) *n.* an object made by humans, for example a tool, especially with historical or archaeological interest.

ar·ti·fi·cial (ärt′ə-fish′əl) *adj.* made by humans; not occurring naturally.

artificial intelligence *n.* a branch of computer science which studies ways of making computers learn, understand, and make judgements as people do.

ar·til·ler·y (är-til′ə-rē) *n.* **ar·til·ler·ies** large guns or the part of an army using them.

Artillery include mounted guns and rocket launchers too heavy to be classed as small arms. Most artillery is mobile, such as antiaircraft artillery mounted on tanks.

art·ist (ärt′əst) *n.* a person who produces works of art, especially paintings.

ar·tis·tic (är-tis′tik) *adj.* **1** liking or skilled in painting or music, etc. **2** made or done with skill and good taste.

art·is·try *n.* artistic skill and imagination.

as (əz, az) *conj.* **1** when; while; during: *She played as I sang.* **2** because; since: *I couldn't carry it as it was so heavy.* **3** in the manner which: *Behave as you like.* **4** that which; what: *Do as you're told.* **5** although: *Try as he might, he still couldn't reach.* – *prep.* in the role of: *Speaking as her friend, I think you're mistaken.* – *adv.* to whatever extent or amount. – *pron.* **1** that, who, or which also: *She is a singer, as is her brother.* **2** for the reason that: *Come early so as to avoid the rush.* **3** a fact that: *He'll be late, as you know.* – **as for** or **to** with regard to; concerning. – **as it were** in a way; to some extent. – **as well** also.

as·bes·tos (as-bes′təs) *n.* a mineral made up of fibers that can be woven into fireproof cloth.

as·cend (ə-send′) *vb.* **as·cend·ing, as·cend·ed** to climb, go, or rise up.

as·cent (ə-sent′) *n.* **1** the act of climbing, going up, or rising. **2** an upward slope.

as·cer·tain (as′ər-tān′) *vb.* **as·cer·tain·ing, as·cer·tained** to find out; to discover.

AS·CII (as′kē) *abbreviation.* See **Computer Terms**.

As·gard (as′gärd′, az′gärd′). See **Myths and Legends**.

ash¹ (ash) *n.* the dust that remains after something is burned.

ash² (ash) *n.* a forest tree with silver-gray bark; the hard, pale wood from this tree.

a·shamed (ə-shāmd′) *adj.* **1** feeling shame or embarrassment. **2** hesitant or reluctant through shame or a fear of being wrong: *She was ashamed to show us her messy room.*

Ash Wednesday *n.* the first day of Lent.

●**A·sia** (ā′zhə, ā′shə) is the biggest continent. It stretches from the Arctic in the north to the equator in the south. It covers nearly a third of the earth's land surface. The world's highest mountains, the HIMALAYAS, are in Asia, and so is the lowest land surface, the shores of the Dead Sea. The river valleys of CHINA are among the most heavily populated places in the world. Most Asians are farmers and the chief crops are wheat and rice. JAPAN is the most industrialized Asian nation. There is a huge variety of animal life from elephants to pandas. Asia was the birthplace of civilization and many cultures have flourished there, including that of MESOPOTAMIA, CHINA, and the Indus Valley.

A·sian (ā′zhən, ā′shən) *n.* **1** a person born and living in ASIA. **2** a person of Asian descent. – *adj.* of ASIA, its people, languages, and culture.

A·si·at·ic (ā′zhē-at′ik, ā′zē-at′ik) *adj.* Asian.

a·side (ə-sīd′) *adv.* **1** on or to one side: *He pushed me aside as he ran along the corridor.* **2** apart: *Do you write anything else aside from poetry?*

ask (ask, äsk) *vb.* **asking, asked 1** to put a question to or call for an answer to a question: *He asked the girl what she thought about it.* **2** to inquire about: *Let's ask the way.* **3** to make a request; to seek: *The little boy asked for some ice cream.* **4** to invite: *Philip asked us to dinner.*

askew (ə-skyōō′) *adv.&adj.* not properly straight or level.

a·sleep (ə-slēp′) *adj. & adv.* in or into a sleeping state: *fall asleep.*

asp (asp) *n.* a small poisonous snake.

as·par·a·gus (ə-spar′ə-gəs) *n.* an edible plant related to the lily.

as·pect (as′pekt′) *n.* **1** a particular or distinct part of a problem or subject, etc.: *Which aspect of the matter shall we discuss first?* **2** look or appearance: *The old house has a spooky aspect.*

KEY FACTS
Area: 17,150,000 sq. mi. (44,418,500 sq. km)
Number of countries: 49
Largest country: China (1,169,619,000 people)
Highest mountain: Mt. Everest (29,028 ft./ 8,848 m)

Asia stretches from Turkey in the west to the Pacific Ocean in the east.

as·phalt (as′fôlt′) *n.* a black, tarlike substance used as a surface for roads or roofs, etc.

as·pire (ə-spīr′) *vb.* **as·pir·ing, as·pired** to have a strong desire to achieve or reach something: *She aspires to greatness.* – *n.* **as·pi·ra·tion** (as′pə rā′ shən).

as·pi·rin (as′prən, as′pə-rən) *n.* a drug widely used for relieving pain and fever.

The North African wild ass is probably the ancestor of the domestic donkey. The legs are often striped and the ears long. Wild asses live in semi-desert areas.

ass (as) *n.* **1** a donkey. **2** a fool.

as·sas·sin (ə-sas′ən) *n.* a person who murders someone, especially for political reasons.

as·sas·si·nate (ə-sas′ə-nāt′) *vb.* **as·sas·si·nat·ing, as·sas·si·nat·ed** to murder. — *n.* **as·sas·si·na·tion** (ə-sas′ə-nā′shən).

as·sault (ə-sôlt′) *n.* violent attack. — *vb.* **as·sault·ing, as·sault·ed** to make an assault on.

as·sem·ble (ə-sem′bəl) *vb.* **as·sem·bling, as·sem·bled** **1** to gather or collect together. **2** to put together.

as·sem·bly (ə-sem′blē) *n.* **as·sem·blies** a group of people gathered together, especially for a meeting.

assembly line *n.* a continuous series of machines and workers along which a product passes during its manufacture.

as·sert (ə-surt′) *vb.* **as·sert·ing, as·sert·ed** **1** to state firmly. **2** to insist on or defend your rights or opinions, etc.

as·sess (ə-ses′) *vb.* **as·sess·ing, as·sessed** **1** to judge the quality or importance of. **2** to estimate the cost or value of.

as·set (as′et′) *n.* **1** a valuable skill, quality, or person. **2** (in *plural*) the total value of the possessions of a person or company.

as·sign (ə-sīn′) *vb.* **as·sign·ing, as·signed** **1** to give out; to allot: *to assign a task to someone.* **2** to appoint to a position or task. **3** to fix or specify: *We assigned the date for our next outing.* — *n.* **as·sign·ment** (ə-sīn′mənt).

as·sist (ə-sist′) *vb.* **as·sist·ing, as·sist·ed** to help. — *n.* **as·sis·tance** (ə-sis′təns). — *n. & adj.* **as·sis·tant** (ə-sis′tənt).

as·so·ci·ate (ə-sō′sē-āt′, ə-sō′shē-āt′) *vb.* **as·so·ci·at·ing, as·so·ci·at·ed** **1** to connect in the mind. **2** to mix socially. — (ə-sō′sē-ət, ə-sō′shē-ət) *n.* **1** a business partner. **2** a colleague or friend.

as·so·ci·a·tion (ə-sō′sē-ā′shən, ə-sō′shē-ā′shən) *n.* **1** an organization or club. **2** a partnership. **3** a connection in the mind.

as·sort·ed (ə-sôrt′əd) *adj.* mixed; containing various different kinds: *assorted candies.*

as·sort·ment (ə-sôrt′mənt) *n.* a mixed collection.

as·sume (ə-sōōm′) *vb.* **as·sum·ing, as·sumed** **1** to accept, though without proof; to take for granted. **2** to take upon yourself: *He assumed the role of judge.* — *n.* **as·sump·tion** (ə-sump′shən).

as·sur·ance (ə-shoor′əns) *n.* **1** a promise, guarantee, or statement that a thing is true. **2** confidence.

as·sure (ə-shoor′) *vb.* **as·sur·ing, as·sured** **1** to state positively and confidently. **2** to convince: *I assured her of my innocence.*

as·ter·isk (as′tə-risk′) *n.* a star-shaped mark (*) used in printing and writing, to mark a reference to a note or an omission.

as·ter·oid (as′tə-roid′) *n.* any of the very small planets moving around the sun.

Ceres
Juno
Eunom
Psyche
Pallas
Vesta

Asteroids, or "minor planets," lie between Mars and Jupiter. The largest, Ceres, is less than 600 miles (1,000 km) wide.

asth·ma (az′mə) *n.* an illness, usually caused by an allergy, which makes breathing difficult.

as·ton·ish (ə-stän′ish) *vb.* **as·ton·ish·ing, as·ton·ished** to surprise greatly.

as·tound (ə-stound′) *vb.* **as·tound·ing, as·tound·ed** to amaze greatly or shock.

a·stray (ə-strā′) *adj. & adv.* out of the right or expected way. — **go astray** to get lost.

astro- of stars or space.

as·trol·o·gy (ə-sträl′ə-jē) *n.* the study of the movements of the stars and planets and their influence on people's lives. — *n.* **as·trol·o·ger** (ə-sträl′ə-jər).

as·tron·aut (as′trə-nôt′, as′trə-nät′) *n.* a person trained for space travel.

Astronomy is the oldest of all the sciences. Early astronomers divided the year into months, weeks, and days based on the movements of the Sun, Earth, and moon. Until the 1540s people believed that the Earth was the center of the universe.

Halley's Comet as depicted on the Bayeux Tapestry. Edmund Halley (1656 -1742) showed that the comet named after him appears at regular intervals.

The Hubble Space Telescope is above the Earth's atmosphere and so can send back pictures of distant objects.

A Mesopotamian "star map" of 2000 B.C.

The telescope that Galileo constructed in 1609. He challenged many accepted theories about the universe.

A terrestrial telescope at Mt. Palomar Observatory, California. Its reflecting mirror is 200 inches (508 cm) in diameter.

Hektor   Davida

---

as·tro·nom·i·cal (as′trə-näm′i-kəl) or **as·tro·nom·ic** (as′trə-näm′ik) *adj.* describing numbers or amounts, etc. that are very large.

as·tron·o·my (ə-strän′ə-mē) *n.* the scientific study of the stars and planets, etc. – *n.* **as·tron·o·mer** (ə-strän′ə-mər).

as·tute (ə-stoot′, ə-styoot′) *adj.* able to judge quickly; shrewd.

a·sy·lum (ə-sī′ləm) *n.* **1** a place of safety or protection. **2** a shelter for the mentally ill.

at (ət, at) *prep.* expressing **1** position or location: *We're staying at school.* **2** direction: *Look at the book.* **3** position in time: *We always eat at one o'clock.* **4** time during which: *He often works at night.* **5** cost: *She sold them at a high price.*

ate. See **eat**.

a·the·ism (ā′thē-iz′əm) *n.* See **Religious Terms**.

A·the·na (ə-thē′nə). See **Myths and Legends**.

●**Ath·ens** (ath′ənz) is the capital of GREECE and around 400 B.C. was a center of civilization.

ath·lete (ath′lēt′) *n.* a person who is good at sports.

ath·let·ic (ath-let′ik) *adj.* describing someone who is physically fit and strong.

ath·let·ics (ath-let′iks) *n.* (*plural*) sports and games that require physical strength and skill.

At·lan·tic (ət-lan′tik) *n.* the Atlantic Ocean, which separates EUROPE and AFRICA from the continents of AMERICA.

At·las (at′ləs). See **Myths and Legends**.

at·las (at′ləs) *n.* **at·las·es** a book of maps.

at·mos·phere (at′məs-fir′) *n.* **1** the gases surrounding a planet. **2** the air in a particular place. **3** the mood of a place.

a·toll (a′tôl′, a′täl′, ā′tôl′) *n.* a ring-shaped coral reef surrounding a lagoon.

at·om (at′əm) *n.* **1** the smallest particle of an element that can take part in a chemical reaction. **2** this particle as a source of nuclear energy. **3** a small amount.

atomic (ə-täm′ik) *adj.* **1** of or concerning an atom or atoms. **2** using nuclear energy.

a·tro·cious (ə-trō′shəs) *adj.*

Atoms are made up of a system of tiny particles. An atom has a nucleus, which contains protons (with a positive charge) and neutrons (no charge). Electrons (with a negative charge) spin around the nucleus.

Neutrons

Electron

Protons

1 very cruel or brutal. **2** very bad.

at·tach (ə-tach′) *vb.* **at·tach·ing, at·tached**
1 to fasten or join. **2** to attribute or assign.

at·tach·ment (ə-tach′mənt) *n.* **1** an act or
means of fastening. **2** liking or affection. **3** an
extra part that can be fitted to a machine.

at·tack (ə-tak′) *vb.* **at·tack·ing, at·tacked**
1 to make a sudden or violent attempt to hurt,
damage, or capture. **2** to criticize strongly in
speech or writing: *The article attacked his
decisions.* **3** to begin to do something with
enthusiasm or determination. – *n.* **1** an act of
attacking. **2** a sudden spell of illness.

at·tain (ə-tān′) *vb.* **at·tain·ing, at·tained 1** to
complete successfully or accomplish. **2** to
reach. – *adj.* **at·tain·able** (ə-tā′nə-bəl).

at·tempt (ə-tempt′) *vb.* **at·tempt·ing,
at·tempt·ed** to try. – *n.* **1** an endeavor to
achieve something. **2** an attack.

at·tend (ə-tend′) *vb.* **at·tend·ing,
at·tend·ed 1** to be present at: *Tom attended the
party.* **2** to go regularly: *She attends the local
school.* **3** to give attention to.

at·ten·dance (ə-ten′dəns) *n.* **1** the act of
attending. **2** the number of people present.

at·ten·tion (ə-ten′chən) *n.* **1** the act of
concentrating or directing the mind. **2** special
care and consideration.

at·ten·tive (ə-tent′iv) *adj.* **1** concentrating:
2 polite and courteous. – *adv.* **at·ten·tive·ly**.

at·tic (at′ik) *n.* a space or room at the top of a
house under the roof.

at·tire (ə-tīr′) *n.* clothing.

at·ti·tude (at′ə-tood′, at′ə-tyood′) *n.* a way of
thinking or behaving.

at·tor·ney (ə-tur′nē) *n.* **at·tor·neys 1** a
lawyer. **2** a person able to act for another in
legal or business matters.

at·tract (ə-trakt′) *vb.* **at·tract·ing,
at·tract·ed 1** to cause to come close or stay
close: *Light attracts moths.* **2** to be attractive to.

at·trac·tion (ə-trak′shən) *n.* **1** the act or power
of attracting. **2** a person or thing that attracts.

at·trac·tive (ə-trak′tiv) *adj.* **1** appealing: *This is
an attractive use of color.* **2** able to attract.

at·trib·ute (ə-trib′yət, ə-trib′yoot) *vb.*
at·trib·ut·ing, at·trib·ut·ed to think of as
being written, made, said, or caused by. –
at·tri·bute (a′trə-byoot′) *n.* a quality,
characteristic, or feature.

au·burn (ô′bərn) *adj.* of a reddish-brown color.

auc·tion (ôk′shən) *n.* a public sale in which
each item is sold to the person who offers the

most money. – *vb.* **auc·tion·ing,
auc·tioned** to sell in this way.

au·da·cious (ô-dā′shəs) *adj.* bold and daring.

au·di·ble (ôd′ə-bəl) *adj.* loud enough to be
heard.

au·di·ence (ôd′ē-əns) *n.* **1** a group of people
watching, listening, etc. a performance. **2** a
formal interview with an important person.

au·di·o (ôd′ē-ō) *adj.* of sound, hearing, or the
recording and broadcasting of sound in radio,
television, etc.

au·di·tion (ô-dish′ən) *n.* a short performance
to test the ability of an actor, singer, or
musician.

au·di·to·ri·um (ôd′ə-tôr′ē-əm, ôd′ə-tōr′ē-əm)
n. **auditoriums** or **au·di·tor·i·a** (ôd′ə-
tôr′ē-ə, ôd′ə-tōr′ē-ə) the part of a theater or
hall, etc. where the audience sits.

● **Au·du·bon** (ôd′ə-bən, ôd′ə-bän′) **John**
(1785-1857) was an American wildlife painter,
notably of birds.

Au·gust (ô′gəst) *n.* the eighth month of the
year. August has 31 days.

au·gust (ô-gust′) *adj.* noble; imposing.

auk (ôk) *n.* a sea bird with a heavy body, short
wings, and black and white feathers.

*Auks are found only in
the Northern Hemisphere.
Like penguins, they stand
erect and dive underwater
to catch fish. They spend
most of their lives at sea,
visiting land only to
breed.*

aunt (ant, änt) *n.* the sister of your father or
mother, or the wife of your uncle.

● **Aus·ten** (ô′stən), **Jane** (1775-1817) was one of
England's greatest novelists. *Emma* and *Pride and
Prejudice* are the best known of her six works.

aus·tere (ô-stîr′) *adj.* **1** severely simple and
plain. **2** serious; severe; stern. – *n.*
aus·ter·i·ty (ô-ster′ət-ē).

Aus·tral·a·sian (ô′strə-lā′zhən, ô′strə-lā′shən)
adj. of or relating to AUSTRALIA, NEW
ZEALAND, and the Pacific Islands.

Attorney is based on a
French word for "turn
over." It now applies to
someone to whom
people can turn for help
in legal matters.

●**Aus·tra·lia** (ô-strāl′yə, as-trāl′yə) is a huge island and the world's smallest continent, the last to be discovered by Europeans. Its first inhabitants were the ABORIGINES. Much of Australia is a dry flat desert and most of the population (17 million) live around the coasts. Cattle and sheep farming, and mining are all important. See also Supplement, **Countries**.

KEY FACTS
Capital: Canberra
Longest river: Darling
Largest reef: Great Barrier Reef

All marsupials— except opossums— live in Australia. The only food of koalas is eucalyptus leaves.

Aus·tra·lian (ô-strāl′yən) *adj.* of or relating to AUSTRALIA. − *n.* a person born or living in AUSTRALIA.

●**Aus·tri·a** (ô′strē-ə) is now a small central-European country. Under the HABSBURG rulers until 1918, it was one of the largest and most powerful nations. Its capital is VIENNA. See also Supplement, **Countries**.

au·then·tic (ô-then′tik) *adj.* **1** genuine. **2** reliable; trustworthy.

au·thor (ô′thər) *n.* **1** the writer of a book, play, article, etc. **2** the creator of something.

au·thor·i·ty (ə-thôr′ət-ē, ə-thär′at-ē) *n.* **au·thor·i·ties 1** the power or right to control or judge others. **2** (often in *plural*) the person or people who have power, especially political or administrative. **3** an expert.

au·tho·rize (ô′thə-rīz′) *vb.* **au·tho·riz·ing, au·tho·rized 1** to give authority to. **2** to approve.

auto- (ôt′ə) *prefix* of or by yourself or itself.

au·to·bi·og·ra·phy (ôt′ə-bī-äg′rə-fē) *n.* **au·to·bi·og·ra·phies** the story of a person's life written by that person. − *adj.* **au·to·bi·o·graph·i·cal** (ôt′ə-bī′ə-graf′i-kəl).

au·to·graph (ôt′ə-graf′) *n.* a person's signature, especially a famous person's.

au·to·mat·ic (ôt′ə-mat′ik) *adj.* **1** describing a machine that works by itself, with little or no control by people. **2** done without thinking; spontaneous.

au·to·ma·tion (ôt′ə-mā′shən) *n.* the use of automatic machines and equipment to control production in manufacturing.

au·to·mo·bile (ôt′ə-mō-bēl′, ôt′ə-mō-bēl′, ôt′ə-mō′bēl′) *n.* a car.

au·ton·o·my (ô-tän′ə-mē) *n.* **au·ton·o·mies 1** the power or right of a country, etc. to govern itself. **2** personal freedom.

au·tumn (ôt′əm) *n.* the season of the year coming between summer and winter; fall. − *adj.* **au·tum·nal** (ô-tum′nəl).

aux·il·ia·ry (ôg-zil′yə-rē, ôg-zil′ə-rē) *adj.* helping or supporting.

a·vail·a·ble (ə-vāl′ə-bəl) *adj.* able or ready to be obtained or used. − *n.* **a·vail·a·bil·i·ty** (ə-vāl′ə-bil′ət-ē).

av·a·lanche (av′ə-lanch′) *n.* a sudden, huge fall of snow and ice down a mountain.

●**Av·a·lon** (av′ə-län′) is the place where King ARTHUR was taken at his death.

av·a·rice (av′ə-rəs) *n.* a great desire for wealth.

a·venge (ə-venj′) *vb.* **a·veng·ing, a·venged** to take revenge for. − *n.* **a·veng·er.**

av·e·nue (av′ə-noo′, av′ə-nyoo′) *n.* a broad road or street, often with trees along the sides.

Much of Australia is dry flat desert. Most of its people live along the coasts in four main cities.

A AND AN
Use "a" before words beginning with a consonant or which are pronounced as if they begin with a consonant: a baseball, a caterpillar, a publication, a usual occurrence, a unit of currency.
Use "an" before words beginning with a vowel (a, e, i, o, u) or which are pronounced as if they begin with a vowel. Examples of these are: an average score, an heiress, an RBI, an SOS, an honest person.

av·e·rage (av′rij, av′ə-rij′) *n*. **1** the usual amount or number. **2** the result obtained by adding together a group of numbers and dividing the total by the number of numbers in the group; for example the average of 1 and 3 is (1+3) ÷ 2, or 2. − *adj*. **1** ordinary: *It's just an average day.* **2** estimated by taking an average: *What's the average number of visitors each year?*

a·verse (ə-vurs′) *adj*. reluctant or opposed.

a·ver·sion (ə-vur′zhən) *n*. a strong dislike.

a·vert (ə-vurt′) *vb*. **a·vert·ing, a·vert·ed** to turn away: *He averted his eyes from the sun.*

a·vi·a·tion (ā′vē-ā′shən) *n*. the science or practice of flying in aircraft.

av·id (av′əd) *adj*. enthusiastic: *I'm an avid reader.*

a·vo·ca·do (av′ə-käd′ō, äv′ə-käd′ō) *n*. **avocados** a pear-shaped fruit with a large pit, and creamy, light green flesh.

a·void (ə-void′) *vb*. **a·void·ing, a·void·ed 1** to keep away from: *Sam avoided her gaze by looking the other way.* **2** to stop or prevent: *It was impossible to avoid the catastrophe.* − *adj*. **a·void·a·ble** (ə-void′ə-bəl).

The **Aztec** empire was already a great civilization when Spanish soldiers discovered it. Within two years of the Spanish commander Hernando Cortés landing in Mexico in 1519, he had completely destroyed the empire. The invaders demolished the magnificent city of Tenochtitlán and built Mexico City on its site.

Quetzalcoatl, the plumed serpent, was one of the chief Aztec gods.

An Aztec pyramid with stairways leading to a temple at the top. Here the Aztecs sacrificed human beings to the gods.

a·wait (ə-wāt′) *vb*. **a·wait·ing, a·wait·ed** to wait for.

a·wake (ə-wāk′) *vb*. **a·wak·ing, a·woke** (ə-wōk′), **a·wok·en** (ə-wō′kən) to stop or to cause to stop sleeping. − *adj*. **1** not sleeping. **2** alert or aware.

a·wak·en (ə-wā′kən) *vb*. **a·wak·en·ing, a·wak·ened** to awake.

a·ward (ə-wôrd′) *vb*. **a·ward·ing, a·ward·ed** to give as a payment or prize. − *n*. a payment or prize.

a·ware (ə-wâr′) *adj*. knowing about or conscious of something: *I am aware of your contribution.* − *n*. **a·ware·ness** (ə-wâr′nəs).

a·way (ə-wā′) *adv*. **1** from a particular place; off: *We went away.* **2** in or to another or usual place: *We put the books away.* **3** gradually into nothing: *The music faded away.* − *adj*. distant: *They are miles away.*

awe (ô) *n*. admiration, fear, and wonder.

awe·some (ô′səm) *adj*. **1** causing or inspiring awe: *an awesome event.* **2** showing awe.

aw·ful (ô′fəl) *adj*. **1** very bad. **2** very great.

aw·ful·ly (ô′flē) *adv*. **1** very badly. **2** very.

a·while (ə-hwīl′, ə-wīl′) *adv*. for a short time.

awk·ward (ôk′wərd) *adj*. **1** clumsy and ungraceful. **2** embarrassed or embarrassing.

aw·ning (ô′ning, än′ing) *n*. a covering above the entrance to a store, hotel, etc. which can be pulled out to give shelter from the sun.

awoke, awoken. See **awake.**

ax or **axe** (aks) *n*. a tool with a long handle and a heavy metal blade, for cutting down trees or chopping wood, etc.

ax·i·om (ak′sē-əm) *n*. a fact or principle which is generally accepted as true.

axis (ak′səs) *n*. **axes** (ak′sēz′) **1** a real or imaginary line around which a body turns. **2** the line around which a figure is symmetrically distributed.

ax·le (ak′səl) *n*. a rod on which a wheel or pair of wheels turns.

ax·o·lotl (ak′sə-lät′l) *n*. a newtlike creature which lives in Mexican lakes.

●**Az·er·bai·jan** (az′ər-bī-zhän′). See Supplement, **Countries.**

Az·tec (az′tek′) *n*. a member of a Mexican Indian people whose great empire was overthrown by the Spanish in the 1500s. − *adj*. of the Aztecs, their language, and culture.

az·ure (azh′ər) *adj*. deep sky-blue.

B b

bab·ble (bab′əl) *vb.* **bab·bling, bab·bled** to talk quickly in a way that is hard to understand.

ba·boon (ba-boon′) *n.* a large African monkey.

● **Ba·bur** (bä′-boor′) (1483-1530) was the first Mogul emperor.

ba·by (bā′bē) *n.* **ba·bies** a newborn or very young child or animal.

ba·by-sit (bā′bē-sit′) *vb.* to take care of children while their parents are out. – *n.* **ba·by-sit·ter**.

● **Bab·y·lo·ni·a** (bab′ə-lō′nē-ə) in southern Mesopotamia, was a great ancient civilization. The Hanging Gardens of Babylon, the capital, were one of the SEVEN WONDERS OF THE WORLD.

Babylon: The Ishtar Gate.

● **Bach** (bäkh, bäk), **Johann Sebastian** (1685-1750) was the most famous member of a German family of composers.

bach·e·lor (bach′ə-lər) *n.* an unmarried man.

back (bak) *n.* **1** the rear part of the human body from the neck to the bottom of the backbone. **2** the upper part of an animal's body. **3** the part of an object that is opposite to or farthest from the front: *They sat at the back of the room.* – *adj.* **1** situated behind or at the back: *She went out the back door.* **2** away from or behind something more important: *We like to drive along the back roads.* – *adv.* **1** to or toward the rear; away from the front: *They moved back to let him pass.* **2** in or into an original position: *Please put the bowl back.*
– *vb.* **back·ing, backed**
1 to help or support, usually

The letter *B*, like all the letters, has a long history. The earliest alphabets were taken and adapted by the Greeks. The Greek *beta*, when combined with the first letter, *aleph*, gives us the word alphabet.

The Greeks passed on their letters to the Romans, who developed the alphabet we use today, although they used only capital letters. Small letters developed in the A.D. 700s.

An early form of the letter B, used in the Middle East more than 3,000 years ago.

This letter was taken by the Greeks and became beta.

Over the years different versions of the letter B have been developed.

BACK AT WORK
"Back" is an amazingly versatile little word — it can be used as a noun, verb, adjective, or adverb. It is also the root of many longer compound words—backache, backbone, backbreaking, backdraft, backfire, backlash, backhanded, backseat, backslide, backyard.

with money. **2** to move backward. **3** to bet on. – *vb.* **back up** (bak up′) **1** to assist. **2** to copy information kept on a computer onto a disk.

back·bone (bak′bōn′) *n.* **1** the spine. **2** the main support.

back·ground (bak′ground′) *n.* the space behind the main figures of a picture.

back·ward (bak′wərd) or **back·wards** (bak′wərdz) *adv.* **1** toward the back or rear. **2** with your back facing the direction you are going. **3** in reverse order.

ba·con (bā′kən) *n.* meat from the back and sides of a pig, usually salted or smoked.

bac·te·ri·a (bak-tîr′ē-ə) *n.* (*plural*) microscopic single-celled organisms.

● Bacteria are found everywhere. There are thousands of kinds. Most are harmless, although some can cause diseases. Antibiotic drugs, such as penicillin, can kill them.

bac·te·ri·um (bak-tîr′ē-əm) *n.* singular of **bacteria**.

bad (bad) *adj.* **worse** (wurs), **worst** (wurst) **1** not good. **2** naughty. **3** not skilled or clever: *I'm not athletic; I've always been bad at games.* **4** harmful: *Smoking is bad for you.* – *n.* unpleasant things.

badge (baj) *n.* a small emblem or button.

badg·er (baj′ər) *n.* an animal with a gray coat and black and white stripes on its head, which lives underground and is active at night. – *vb.* **badg·er·ing, badg·ered** to pester or worry.

European badgers live in woods in underground setts which they clean regularly by removing old bedding. American badgers live on the prairies.

bad·min·ton (bad′mint′n) *n.* a game for two or four people played with rackets and a shuttlecock which is hit across a high net.

baf·fle (baf′əl) *vb.* **baf·fling, baf·fled 1** to confuse or puzzle. **2** to hinder: *They baffled our attempts to find out the truth.* – *adj.* **baf·fling**.

bag (bag) *n.* a container made of cloth, plastic, paper, etc., for carrying things.

bag·gage (bag′ij) *n.* a traveler's luggage.

bag·gy (bag′ē) *adj.* **bag·gi·er, bag·gi·est** hanging loose.

● **Bagh·dad** (bag′dad′, bag-dad′) is the capital of IRAQ, on the river Tigris. It was founded in A.D. 762.

● **Ba·ha·mas** (bə-häm′əz). See Supplement, **Countries**.

● **Bah·rain** (bäkh-rān′, bä-rān′). See Supplement, **Countries**.

● **Bai·kal, Lake** (bī-kôl′, bī-käl′) in Siberia, is the world's deepest freshwater lake.

bail¹ (bāl) *n.* money given to a court of law to obtain a person's release, as a guarantee that he or she will return to court for trial. – *vb.* **bail out, bail·ing, bail** to provide bail for.

bail² (bāl) *vb.* **bail·ing, bailed** to remove water from a boat with a bucket.

bairn (bârn) *n.* a Scottish word for a child.

bait (bāt) *n.* **1** food put on a hook or in a trap to attract fish or animals. **2** anything intended to tempt. – *vb.* **bait·ing, bait·ed 1** to put food on a hook or in a trap. **2** to annoy or tease.

bake (bāk) *vb.* **bak·ing, baked 1** to cook cakes, bread, vegetables, etc. using dry heat in an oven. **2** to dry or harden using heat. – *n.* **bak·er**.

bak·ery (bā′kə-rē, bā′krē) *n.* **bak·er·ies** a place where bread and cakes are made or sold.

baking powder *n.* a powder containing sodium bicarbonate, starch, and an acid-forming substance, used to make cakes rise.

baking soda *n.* another name for sodium bicarbonate.

bal·ance (bal′əns) *n.* **1** an instrument for weighing, usually with two dishes hanging from a bar supported in the middle. **2** a state of stability in which the weight of a body is evenly distributed. **3** an amount left over. – *vb.* **bal·anc·ing, bal·anced** to be in or put into a

state of balance: *Can you balance a basketball on one finger?* – **in the balance** not decided.
balanced *adj.* **1** in a state of balance. **2** fair; considering all sides of an argument.

●**Bal·bo·a** (bal-bō′ə), **Vasco Nuñez de** (1475-1519) was a Spanish adventurer and explorer and the first European to discover the PACIFIC, in 1513. He named it *El Mar del Sur*, or "South Sea."

bal·co·ny (bal′kə-nē) *n.* **bal·co·nies 1** a platform surrounded by a wall or railing, projecting from the wall of a building. **2** a gallery in a theater or auditorium.

bald² (bôld) *adj.* **1** describing a person who has little or no hair on the head. **2** describing birds or animals with white on the face or head.

●**Bal·der** (bôl′dər). See **Myths and Legends**.

●**Bald·win** (bôl′dwən), **James** (1924-1987) was an American writer whose works include *Go Tell It on the Mountain.*

bale (bāl) *n.* a large bundle of cloth or hay, etc.

balk (bôk, bôlk) *vb.* **balk·ing, balked 1** to hesitate or refuse to go on. **2** (of a baseball pitcher) to make an illegal motion pretending to throw the ball when a runner is on base.

Bal·kan (bôl′kən) *adj.* **1** of the peninsula in southeastern EUROPE, bordered by the Adriatic, Aegean, and Black seas. **2** of its peoples or countries.

ball¹ (bôl) *n.* **1** a round or roundish object used in some sports. **2** anything round or nearly round in shape: *a snowball.*

ball² (bôl) *n.* a formal social meeting for dancing.

ball bear·ing (bôl bâr′ing) *n.* an arrangement of small steel balls between the moving parts of some machines, used to help reduce friction.

bal·lad (bal′əd) *n.* a slow, usually romantic, song.

bal·last (bal′əst) *n.* heavy material used to keep a ship without cargo steady.

bal·le·ri·na (bal′ə-rē′nə) *n.* a female ballet dancer.

bal·let (ba-lā′, bal′ā) *n.* a classical style of dancing and mime, using set steps and body movements. – *n.* **ballet dancer.**

ballistic missile (bə-lis′tik mis′əl) *n.* a self-propelled missile that is self-guided.

Classical **ballet** as we know it today began in France during the reign of Louis XIV (1638-1715). The king's dancing master, Pierre Beauchamp, worked out the five basic positions of the feet. These positions are the starting and finishing points of all steps. In ballet, dancers use their bodies to mime the story.

First position

Third position

Second position

In all five positions the shoulders are kept down; the elbows are rounded to create a flowing line through the arms to the fingertips.

Fourth position

Fifth position

Satin ballet shoes are delicate; they last at most a week!

BALLET TERMS

barre the exercise bar used in classwork.

choreography the art of dance composition.

corps de ballet the main body of dancers.

jeté a leap from one foot to another.

pas any dance step.

pirouette a spin on one foot.

pointes on the points of the toes.

positions five positions of the feet on which ballet is based.

The first successful airship flew in 1852. It was powered by a steam engine and could be steered.

The Montgolfier brothers' hot-air balloon rises over Paris, 1783. Balloons can only drift in the air.

In 1929 the German airship Graf Zeppelin *flew around the world.*

Hot-air balloons were used for reconnaissance in war during the 19th century.

Baltimore is named for Sir Cecil Calvert, 2nd Baron Baltimore, who founded the colony of Maryland in 1632. The Baltimore family banner is now the state flag. The city was one of the first in the American colonies to promote religious freedom for its residents.

bal·loon (bə-lōōn′) *n.* **1** a small rubber bag filled with air or other gas, often used as a toy. **2** a large bag, made of light material and filled with a light gas or hot air, designed to float in the air carrying people in a basket underneath. – *n.* **bal·loon·ing**.

bal·lot (bal′ət) *n.* the method of voting secretly by putting a marked paper into a container.

ball·room (bôl′rōōm′, bôl′room′) *n.* a large hall where BALLS are held.

balm (bäm, bälm) *n.* an oil obtained from some trees, used in healing or reducing pain.

bal·sa (bôl′sə) *n.* a tropical American tree; the very light wood of this tree.

● **Bal·tic** (bôl′tik) a sea in northern Europe almost enclosed by land.

● **Baltic States** These are ESTONIA, LATVIA, and LITHUANIA, former republics of the ex-USSR, which since 1991 have regained independence.

● **Bal·ti·more** (bôl′tə-môr′, bôl′tə-mər) in Maryland is one of the chief ports of the United States. It was founded in 1729.

bam·boo (bam-bōō′) *n.* a tall, tropical grass with hollow, jointed, woody stems.

ban (ban) *n.* an official order that something may not be done: *There is a ban here on using too much water in the summer.* – *vb.* **ban·ning, banned** to forbid or prevent.

ba·nal (bə-nal′, bə-näl′, bān′l) *adj.* not original or interesting.

ba·nan·a (bə-nan′ə) *n.* **1** a long curved fruit, yellow when ripe. **2** the large tropical treelike plant on which this fruit grows.

band[1] (band) *n.* a flat, narrow strip of cloth, metal, paper, etc. used to hold things together or as a decoration. – *vb.* **band·ing, band·ed** to fasten or mark with a band.

band[2] (band) *n.* **1** a group, as of people or animals: *a band of thieves.* **2** a group of musicians who play music other than classical music: *a rock band.* – *vb.* **band·ing, band·ed** to unite to work for a common purpose.

ban·dage (ban′dij) *n.* a strip of cloth for winding around a wound. – *vb.* **ban·dag·ing, ban·daged** to wrap in a bandage.

ban·dit (ban′dət) *n.* an armed robber, especially a member of a gang which attacks travelers.

bang (bang) *n.* **1** a sudden loud noise. **2** a heavy blow. – *vb.* **bang·ing, banged 1** to make a loud noise by hitting, dropping, closing violently, etc. **2** to hit sharply.

● **Bang·kok** (bang′käk′, bang-käk′) is the capital of THAILAND.

● **Ban·gla·desh** (bang′glə-desh′, bäng′glə-desh′). See Supplement, **Countries**.

ban·ish (ban′ish) *vb.* **ban·ish·ing, ban·ished** to send someone away from a place, usually his or her own country. – *n.* **ban·ish·ment** (ban′ish-mənt).

ban·i·ster (ban′ə-stər) *n.* (often in *plural*) a row of posts and the handrail they support, running up the side of a staircase.

ban·jo (ban′jō) *n.* **ban·jos** or **ban·joes** a stringed musical instrument with a round drumlike body and a long neck.

bank¹ (bangk) *n.* **1** a long raised pile of earth or snow, etc. **2** the ground at the edge of a river, lake, etc. **3** a raised area of sand under the sea. **4** a mass of cloud, mist, or fog. – *vb.* **bank·ing, banked** to form into a bank.

bank² (bangk) *n.* **1** an organization that keeps money in accounts for its clients, lends money, etc. **2** a place where something is stored or collected for later use: *blood bank.* – *vb.* **bank·ing, banked 1** to put money into a bank; to have a bank account. **2** to rely on or expect: *They are banking on good weather for their barbecue.*

bank·er (bang′kər) *n.* a person who manages a bank.

bank·note (bangk′note) *n.* paper money issued by a bank.

bank·rupt (bang′krupt′, bank′krəpt) *n.* a person who is legally recognized as not being able to pay his or her debts. – *adj.* not having money to pay your debts. – *vb.* **bank·rupt·ing, bank·rupt·ed** to make bankrupt.

bank·rupt·cy (bang′krəp-sē) *n.* the state of being bankrupt: *The company declared bankruptcy.*

ban·ner (ban′ər) *n.* a large piece of cloth or cardboard, with a design or slogan carried at public meetings, etc.

ban·quet (bang′kwət) *n.* a large formal dinner.

● **Bap·tists** (bap′təsts, bab′təsts) believe people should not be baptized until they are old enough to make up their own minds about religion.

bap·tize (bap-tīz′, bab-tīz′) *vb.* **bap·tiz·ing, bap·tized** to sprinkle with water as a sign of having become a member of the Christian church, usually accompanied by name-giving.

bap·tism (bap′tiz′əm, bab′tiz′əm) *n.* See **Religious Terms**.

bar (bär) *n.* **1** a block of some solid substance: *a bar of soap.* **2** a rod or long piece of a strong rigid material: *They have bars on the windows to prevent a burglary.* **3** anything that prevents or hinders: *a bar to progress.* **4** a room or counter in a restaurant or hotel, or a separate establishment, where alcoholic drinks are sold and drunk. – *vb.* **bar·ring, barred 1** to fasten with a bar. **2** to forbid entry. – *prep.* except: *everyone bar me.*

barb (bärb) *n.* a point on a hook facing in the opposite direction to the main point, which makes it difficult to pull the hook out.

● **Bar·ba·dos** (bä-bād′əs, bär-bād′ōz). See Supplement, **Countries**.

bar·bar·i·an (bär-bâr′ē-ən) *n.* a person who is coarse, cruel, rough, and wild in behavior.

bar·bar·ic (bär-bâr′ik) *adj.* cruel and brutal.

bar·be·cue (bär′bə-kyōō) *n.* **1** a metal frame on which food is grilled over an open fire. **2** a party at which food is cooked outdoors.

bar·ber (bär′bər) *n.* a person who cuts and styles men's hair, and shaves their beards.

● **Bar·ce·lo·na** (bär′sə-lō′nə) is a Spanish port on the MEDITERRANEAN.

bare (bâr) *adj.* **1** not covered by clothes; naked. **2** without the usual or natural covering: *Our yard is full of bare trees in winter.* **3** empty.

bare·foot (bâr′foot′) *adj.* not wearing shoes or socks.

bare·ly (bâr′lē) *adv.* scarcely or only just.

bar·gain (bär′gən) *n.* **1** an agreement made between people buying and selling things, offering and accepting services, etc.: *They eventually struck a bargain.* **2** something offered for sale, or bought, at a low price. – *vb.* **bar·gain·ing, bar·gained** to discuss the terms for buying or selling, etc.

barge (bärj) *n.* a long, flat-bottomed boat used on rivers and canals. – *vb.* **barg·ing, barged 1** to move in a clumsy, ungraceful way. **2** to hit or knock: *Sam barged into the table.*

bar·i·tone (bar′ə-tōn′) *n.* the second lowest male singing voice, between bass and tenor; a singer with such a voice.

bark¹ (bärk) *n.* the short, sharp cry of a dog, fox, etc. – *vb.* **bark·ing, barked 1** to make this sound. **2** to say loudly and sharply: *He barked out the commands.* – **bark up the wrong tree** (*informal*) to have the wrong idea.

bark² (bärk) *n.* the covering of the trunk and branches of a tree.

Barber comes from the Latin *barba*, meaning "beard," because in early times a barber's work was mostly trimming and cutting beards.

Bark is dead wood. It is tough and waterproof and protects the living wood underneath. Each year a tree forms a new layer or ring of new wood. From a sawn-through trunk you can tell the age of a tree by counting the growth rings.

Baseball is the American national game. It evolved from the 18th-century English game of rounders. It began in 1845 when Alexander Cartwright organized the Knickerbocker Club in New York and established the rules. He said the game would consist of nine innings and that each team would have nine players. It is played on a large field on which is marked a square known as the diamond. At the base of the square is the home plate, where the batter stands; in the center of the square is the pitcher's mound. Four bases are marked on the diamond, 90 feet apart. Each batter tries to advance around the bases safely to score runs.

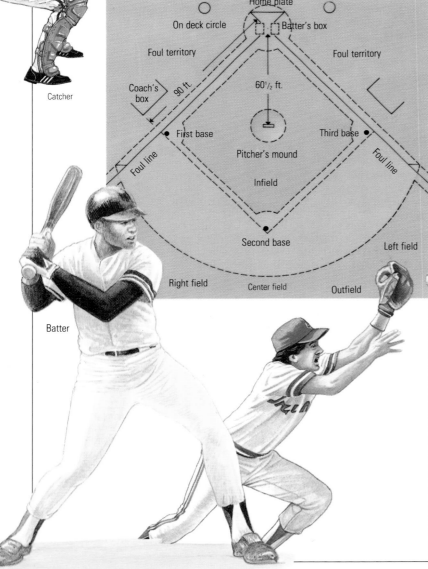

Pitcher

Catcher

Home plate

On deck circle

Batter's box

Foul territory

Foul territory

Coach's box

90 ft.

60½ ft.

First base

Third base

Pitcher's mound

Foul line

Foul line

Infield

Second base

Left field

Right field

Center field

Outfield

Batter

bar mitzvah (bär mits′və) *n.* See **Religious Terms**.

barn (bärn) *n.* a building in which grain or hay, etc. is stored, or for cattle, etc.

ba·rom·e·ter (bə-räm′ət-ər) *n.* an instrument which measures the pressure of the atmosphere, used to predict likely changes in the weather.

bar·rack (bar′ək) *n.* (usually in *plural*) a building or buildings for housing soldiers.

bar·ra·cu·da (bar′ə-kōō′də) *n.* any of a group of fish with sharp teeth found in warm waters throughout the world.

bar·rel (bar′əl) *n.* **1** a large round container, with a flat top and bottom and curving out in the middle, usually made of planks of wood held together with metal bands. **2** a U.S. standard quantity such a container may hold, as 31¹/₂ gallons (119.2 liters) of liquid. **3** the long, hollow, tube-shaped part of a gun.

bar·ren (bar′ən) *adj.* not able to produce crops or fruit, etc.: *Barren land surrounds the house.*

bar·ri·cade (bar′i-kād′) *n.* a barrier made of anything which can be piled up quickly. — *vb.* **bar·ri·cad·ing, bar·ri·cad·ed** to block with a barricade.

bar·ri·er (bar′ē-ər) *n.* **1** a fence, gate, or bar put up to defend, block, protect, or separate. **2** any thing that separates : *They can't communicate because of a language barrier.*

bar·row (bar′ō) *n.* **1** a small one-wheeled cart used to carry tools, earth, etc. **2** a prehistoric burial ground.

bar·ter (bär′tər) *vb.* **bar·ter·ing, bar·tered** to trade or exchange goods or services without using money.

base (bās) *n.* **1** the lowest part or bottom; the part which supports something or on which something stands. **2** the origin, root, or foundation of something. **3** the headquarters or center of activity or operations. **4** in baseball, one of several fixed points which players run between. — *vb.* **bas·ing, based 1** to make or use as the base: *This book is based on a true story.* **2** to give as a headquarters or center of operations: *The troops were based in France.*

base·ball (bās′bôl′) *n.* **1** a game played with a bat and ball by two teams of nine people each, in which the person batting may score a point, or run, by running around a path marked with four bases. **2** the ball used in this game.

base·ment (bā′smənt) *n.* the lowest floor of a building, usually below ground level.

bash·ful (bash′fəl) *adj.* lacking confidence; shy.

ba·sic (bā′sik) *adj.* **1** of, or forming, the base or basis. **2** of or at a very simple or low level: *I'm surprised you made such a basic mistake.* — *n.* **1** (usually in *plural*) the essential parts or simplest principles: *This is too confusing; let's get back to basics.* **2** BASIC. See **Computer Terms**.

ba·sic·al·ly (bā′sik-lē) *adv.* mostly, essentially; described in simple or general terms.

ba·sin (bā′sən) *n.* **1** a wide, open container, especially for holding water. **2** a bowl or sink for washing in. **3** a valley or an area of land drained by a river, or by streams running into a river.

ba·sis (bā′səs) *n.* **ba·ses** (bā′sēz) a principle on which an idea or theory is based.

bask (bask) *vb.* **bask·ing, basked 1** to lie in warmth or sunshine. **2** to enjoy and take great pleasure: *Beth is basking in our approval.*

bas·ket (bas′kət) *n.* a container made of strips of wood or cane, woven together.

bas·ket·ball (bas′kət-bôl′) *n.* **1** a game in which two teams of five players each score by throwing a ball into a net on a high post at each end of the court. **2** the ball used in this game.

● This game is played on a rectangular court. The ball can be advanced by bouncing it or by passing it to a teammate. A player cannot take more than one step while holding the ball.

Basque (bask) *n.* **1** a member of a people living in the western PYRENEES, in SPAIN and FRANCE. **2** the language spoken by these people.

bass¹ (bās) *n.* the lowest male singing voice; a singer with such a voice.

bass² (bas) *n.* **bass** a type of fish.

bass drum *n.* a large drum that produces a very low sound.

bas·soon (bə-sōōn′) *n.* a woodwind instrument with a deep sound and a double reed.

baste (bāst) *vb.* **bast·ing, bast·ed** to pour hot fat or juices over roasting meat, etc.

● **Bas·tille** (ba-stēl′) is the name of a fortress prison that was in Paris. The storming of the Bastille by a mob on July 14, 1789 marked the start of the FRENCH REVOLUTION.

bat¹ (bat) *n.* a shaped piece of wood for hitting the ball in baseball or other games. — *vb.* **bat·ting, bat·ted 1** to take a turn at hitting a ball with a bat, as in baseball. **2** to hit with a bat.

bat² (bat) *n.* a mouselike animal with wings that eats insects.

batch (bach) *n.* a number of things or people prepared, dealt with, etc. at the same time.

bath (bath, bäth) *n.* a washing of something, especially the body, in a bathtub.

bathe (bāth) *vb.* **bath·ing, bathed 1** to take a bath. **2** to wash part of the body with a liquid, etc. to clean it or to lessen pain: *She bathed her sore eyes in warm water.* — *n.* **bath·er** (bā′thər).

bath·tub (bath′tub, bäth′tub) *n.* a large, open container for water, in which to wash the whole body: *The bathtub is made out of enamel.*

bat mitz·vah (bät mits′və) or **bas mitz·vah** (bäs mits′və) *n.* See **Religious Terms**.

baton (bə-tän′) *n.* **1** a thin stick used by an orchestra conductor. **2** a short stick passed from one runner to another in a relay race. **3** a staff carried and twirled by a drum major.

bat·tal·ion (bə-tal′yən) *n.* an army unit made up of several smaller units (companies), and forming part of a larger unit (a brigade).

bat·ter¹ (bat′ər) *vb.* **bat·ter·ing, bat·tered** to strike or hit hard and often, or continuously: *We could hear the wind battering against the door.*

bat·ter² (bat′ər) *n.* eggs, flour, and usually either milk or water, beaten together.

bat·te·ry (bat′ə-rē) *n.* **bat·te·ries 1** a small container holding chemicals which produce or store electricity, or a container of two or more such cells. **2** any group or series of objects used for a common purpose: *a battery of tests.* **3** the illegal hitting or touching of someone: *assault and battery.*

bat·tle (bat′l) *n.* **1** a fight between opposing armies or people. **2** a competition between opposing groups or people: *It was a battle of wits.* **3** a long or difficult struggle: *a battle for equality.*

bat·tle·ment (bat′l-mənt) *n.* a low wall around the top of a castle, etc.

baux·ite (bôk′sīt′) *n.* a substance like clay, the main source of aluminum.

bay¹ (bā) *n.* a wide inward bend of a coastline.

bay² (bā) *vb.* to utter a long howl or moan.

Pipistrelle

Long eared bat

Greater horseshoe bat

Bats fly like birds but are mammals. Most bats are nocturnal. They produce high-pitched shrieks and use the echoes bouncing back from objects to tell where those objects are.

PRONUNCIATION SYMBOLS		
ə **away**	lemon	focus
a **fat**	oi	**boy**
ā **fade**	oo	**foot**
ä **hot**	o̅o̅	**moon**
âr **fair**	ou	**house**
e **met**	th	**think**
ē **mean**	th	**this**
g **get**	u	**cut**
hw **which**	ur	**hurt**
i **fin**	w	**witch**
ī **line**	y	**yes**
îr **near**	yo̅o̅	**music**
ô **often**	yoor	**pure**
ō **note**	zh	**vision**

Bears are carnivores (flesh-eating animals), but they also love honey! The largest bear is the brown bear of Alaska (standing); the smallest is the sun bear of southeast Asia (bottom left). The white fur of the polar bear (bottom center) makes it less noticeable against the ice and snow of the Arctic regions. The black bear, which can be brown (right), often approaches visitors to National Parks as it looks for handouts.

ba·zaar (bə-zär′) *n.* **1** a marketplace in Eastern countries. **2** a sale of goods.

be (bē) *vb.* **am** (am), **are** (är) , **is** (iz); **be·ing; was** (wuz, wəz), **were** (wur); **been** (bin) **1** to exist or live: *I think, therefore I am.* **2** to occur: *Lunch is in an hour.* **3** to occupy a position in space: *Sue is at home.* **4** used to link a subject and what is said about it: *She is a doctor.*

beach (bēch) *n.* the sandy or stony shore of a sea or ocean.

bea·con (bē′kən) *n.* a warning or guiding device for ships, etc., such as a lighthouse.

bead (bēd) *n.* a small ball of glass, stone, etc., often strung with others in a necklace.

bea·gle (bē′gəl) *n.* a type of small hunting dog with short legs and short hair.

beak (bēk) *n.* the hard part of a bird's mouth.

bea·ker (bēk′ər) *n.* a large drinking glass, or a large, often plastic, cup without a handle.

beam (bēm) *n.* **1** a long, straight, thick piece of wood, used in a building. **2** a ray of light. **3** a narrow wooden bar on which gymnasts perform balancing exercises. – *vb.* **beam·ing, beamed 1** to smile broadly with pleasure. **2** to send out rays as of light or radio waves.

bean (bēn) *n.* any of several kinds of climbing plant which produce edible seeds in long thin pods. – **full of beans** (*informal*) full of energy.

bear¹ (bâr) *vb.* **bear·ing, bore** (bôr), **borne** (bôrn) **1** to carry, bring, or take: *They came bearing gifts.* **2** to support a weight. **3** to produce: *This tree bears fruit every year.* **4** to put up with.

bear² (bâr) *n.* a large, heavily built, four-legged animal with thick fur.

bear·a·ble (bâr′ə-bəl) *adj.* able to be tolerated.

beard (bîrd) *n.* the hair that grows on a man's chin and neck. – *adj.* **beard·ed**.

bear·ing (bâr′ing) *n.* **1** the way a person stands, walks, etc. **2** a relation or effect: *Your remarks have no bearing on the situation.*

beast (bēst) *n.* **1** any large, especially four-footed, wild animal. **2** (*colloquial*) a difficult or unpleasant person or thing.

beat (bēt) *vb.* **beat·ing, beat, beat·en** (bēt′n) **1** to hit violently and repeatedly, especially to harm. **2** to strike repeatedly, e.g. to remove dust or make a sound. **3** to knock repeatedly: *The waves beat against the shore.* **4** to defeat; to do something better, sooner, or quicker than: *Joan beat me in the race.* **5** to mix or stir thoroughly: *Beat the eggs with a whisk.* **6** to move in a regular pattern of strokes, etc.: *Your heart beats quickly after exercise.* – *n.* **1** a regular stroke, or its sound: *the beat of a heart.* **2** the main accent in music.

● **the Beat·les** (bēt′lz) an English rock group of the 1960s and early 1970s.

Beau·fort scale (bō′fərt skāl) *n.* a scale of wind speeds, from 0 for calm to 12 for hurricane.

beau·ti·ful (byōōt′i-fəl) *adj.* with an appearance or qualities which please the senses; pleasing.

beau·ti·fy (byōōt′i-fī′) *vb.* **beau·ti·fies, beau·ti·fy·ing, beau·ti·fied** to make beautiful.

beau·ty (byōōt′ē) *n.* **beau·ties 1** a quality pleasing to the senses, especially the eye or ear. **2** a benefit: *The beauty of the plan is its simplicity.* **3** a person or thing that is beautiful.

bea·ver (bē′vər) *n.* a large, ratlike animal, with thick, soft fur, strong front teeth, and a large flat tail, which builds dams in rivers and streams.

became. See **become**.

be·cause (bi-kôz) *conj.* for the reason that.

Brown bear

Sun bear

Polar bear

Black bear

●**Beck·et** (bek'ət), **Thomas** (1118-1170) was Archbishop of CANTERBURY. He was murdered for opposing Henry II's attempts to control the clergy. He was made a saint in 1173.

be·come (bi-kum') *vb.* **be·com·ing, be·came** (bi-kām'), **be·come** 1 to come or grow to be: *He became an excellent juggler after years of practice.* 2 to happen to: *What became of him?*

bed (bed) *n.* 1 a piece of furniture for sleeping on. 2 the bottom of a river, lake, or sea. 3 an area of ground in a garden, for growing plants: *a bed of roses.*

bed·bug (bed'bug') *n.* a flat insect that sucks blood, often infesting beds.

bed·ding (bed'ing) *n.* 1 mattresses, blankets, etc. 2 straw, etc. for animals to sleep on.

bed·rock (bed'räk') *n.* 1 the solid rock forming the lowest layer under soil and rock fragments. 2 the basic principle or idea on which something rests: *The constitution is the bedrock of our law.*

Bed·ou·in (bed'ə-wən) *n.* **Bedouin** or **Bedouins** a member of a wandering Arab tribe that lives in the deserts of the MIDDLE EAST.

bee (bē) *n.* a type of four-winged, stinging insect, some species of which live in large groups and make honey. – **a bee in your bonnet** an idea that has become an obsession.

Bees use a "language" of tapping their legs to tell each other about the best places to find nectar.

Bumblebee

beech (bēch) *n.* a kind of forest tree with smooth silvery bark and small nuts.

beef (bēf) *n.* the meat of a bull, cow, or ox.

bee·line (bē'līn') *n.* a straight line for traveling.

been. See **be.**

beer (bîr) *n.* a type of alcoholic drink made from malt, barley, sugar, hops, and water.

beet (bēt) *n.* a leafy plant with a round, red root which is cooked as a vegetable.

●**Bee·tho·ven** (bā'tō'vən), **Ludwig van** (1770-1827) was a great German composer. He wrote nine symphonies and six concertos.

bee·tle (bē t'l) *n.* an insect with a pair of hard front wings that fold over its back.

be·fore (bi-fôr') *prep.* 1 earlier than: *Come before lunch.* 2 ahead of; in front of: *He was asked to stand before the table.* – *conj.* 1 earlier than the time when: *Do it before you forget.* 2 rather than; in preference to: *I'd die before I'd surrender to them.* – *adv.* previously; in the past: *Haven't we met somewhere before?*

beg (beg) *vb.* **beg·ging, begged** 1 to ask for money or food. 2 to ask earnestly or humbly.

be·gin (bi-gin') *vb.* **be·gin·ning, be·gan** (bi-gan'), **be·gun** (bi-gun') to start. – *n.* **beginning**.

be·have (bi-hāv') *vb.* **be·hav·ing, be·haved** 1 to act in a stated way: *She trained her puppy to behave well.* 2 to act in a suitable, polite, or orderly way: *Behave yourself at the party.*

be·hav·ior (bi-hā'vyər) *n.* way of behaving; manners: *good behavior.*

be·hind (bi-hīnd') *prep.* 1 at or toward the back of or the far side of. 2 later or slower than; after in time: *Our project is behind schedule.* 3 supporting: *We're all behind you.* 4 being the cause of: *The reasons behind his decision are not clear.* – *adv.* 1 in or to the back or far side of. 2 remaining: *Did you leave something behind?* 3 following: *The children ran behind the car.* – *adj.* not on time: *They are behind with their payments on the car.*

beige (bāzh) *adj.* a pale tan color.

Queen bee

Worker bees

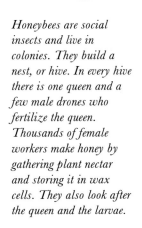

●**Bei·jing** (bā'jing'), (**Peking**) is the capital of CHINA.

●**Bei·rut** (bā-rōōt') is a port and capital of the LEBANON. In recent years it has been torn apart by civil war.

A ladybug in flight, showing the beetle's hard wing covers. Ladybugs are useful; they eat harmful insects. Many other beetles and their larvae do damage; Colorado beetles, for instance, attack potato crops.

Beehive

Honeybees are social insects and live in colonies. They build a nest, or hive. In every hive there is one queen and a few male drones who fertilize the queen. Thousands of female workers make honey by gathering plant nectar and storing it in wax cells. They also look after the queen and the larvae.

How a bell is cast
Bells are made by pouring molten metal between a solid core mold and an outer mold in the shape of the bell.

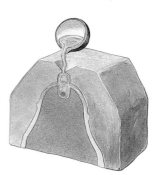

Below: *The Liberty Bell*

● **Belarus** (bel′ə-rus). See Supplement, **Countries**.

be·lat·ed (bi-lāt′əd) *adj.* happening late.

● **Bel·fast** (bel′fast′, bel-fast′) is the capital of NORTHERN IRELAND.

● **Bel·gium** (bel′jəm). See Supplement, **Countries**.

be·lief (bi-lēf′) *n.* **1** a principle or idea accepted as true, especially without proof: *belief in the afterlife.* **2** trust or confidence: *She has a strong belief in her ability.* **3** a person's religious faith.

be·lieve (bi-lēv′) *vb.* **be·liev·ing, be·lieved 1** to accept as true. **2** to think, assume, or suppose: *I believe this is the person you're looking for.* **3** to have religious faith.

● **Be·lize** (bə-lēz′). See Supplement, **Countries**.

bell (bel) *n.* **1** a deep, hollow, usually metal, object, rounded at one end and wide and open at the other, with a small hammer inside, which gives a ringing sound when struck. **2** any other device which makes a ringing sound.

● **Bell** (bel), **Alexander Graham** (1847-1922) was the Scottish-American inventor of the telephone.

bel·low (bel′ō) *vb.* **bel·low·ing, bel·lowed** to make a loud, deep cry like that of a bull.

● **Bel·low** (bel′ō), **Saul** (1915-) is a Canadian-born novelist living in the United States, whose works include *Herzog.*

bel·lows (bel′ōz) *n.* (*singular* or *plural*) a device consisting of or containing a baglike part which is squeezed to create a current of air.

bel·ly (bel′ē) *n.* **bel·lies** the part of the body containing the organs used for digesting food.

bel·ly·but·ton (bel′ē-but′n) *n.* (*informal*) the navel.

be·long (bi-lông′) *vb.* **be·long·ing, be·longed 1** to be the property or right of: *This book belongs to me.* **2** to be a member of a group, etc.: *He belongs to the chess club.* **3** to have a proper place: *The papers belong in this drawer.*

be·long·ings (bi-lông′ingz) *n.* (*plural*) personal possessions.

be·low (bi-lō′) *prep.* lower in position, rank, amount, etc.: *The water is below its usual level.* – *adv.* at, to, or in a lower place, point, or level.

belt (belt) *n.* **1** a long, narrow piece of leather or cloth worn around the waist to keep clothing in place or for decoration. **2** a strap passed across the body, to secure a person in a seat: *Fasten your seat belt!* **3** a band around the wheels of a machine: *a conveyor belt.*

bench (bench) *n.* **1** a long wooden or stone seat. **2** a worktable for a carpenter.

bend (bend) *vb.* **bend·ing, bent 1** to make or become angled or curved. **2** to move or stretch in a curve: *This road bends to the left.* **3** to move the body to form a curve: *He bent down to pick something up.* – *n.* a curve or bent part: *a bend in the road.*

be·neath (bi-nēth′) *prep.* **1** under; below. **2** not worthy of. – *adv.* below, underneath.

Ben·e·dic·tine *n.* (ben′ədik′tən, ben′ə-dik′tēn′) a member of the Christian community that follows the teachings of St. Benedict (480–543).

ben·e·fi·cial (ben′ə-fish′əl) *adj.* having good results.

ben·e·fit (ben′ə-fit) *n.* **1** something good gained. **2** advantage: *He ran the club for the children's benefit.* **3** (often in *plural*) a payment made by a government, company, or insurance plan, usually to someone who is ill or out of work. **4** an event held to raise money for a charitable cause: *a theatrical benefit for AIDS patients.* – *vb.* **ben·e·fit·ing, ben·e·fit·ed** to gain an advantage.

● **Be·nin** (bə-nin′, bə-nēn′). See Supplement, **Countries**.

bent (bent). *adj.* not straight. – *vb.* See **bend**.

be·queath (bi-wēth′, bi-kwēth′) *vb.* **be·queath·ing, be·queathed** to leave belongings in a will.

● **Be·ring Sea** (bâr′ing, ber′ing) the northern part of the PACIFIC Ocean between Alaska and Siberia, named after the Danish explorer, V. J. *Bering* (1681-1741).

● **Ber·lin** (bur-lin′) is the capital of Germany.

● **Ber·lin** (bur-lin′), **Irving** (1888-1989) was an American composer of musicals. His most famous song is *White Christmas.*

●**Ber·li·oz** (ber′lē-ōz′), **Hector** (1803-1869) was a French composer.

●**Ber·mu·da** (bər-myood′ə) is a British colony in the western ATLANTIC Ocean, 565 miles (922 km) from the UNITED STATES.

●**Bern·stein** (burn′stīn′, burn′stēn), **Leonard** (1918-1990) was an American composer.

Loganberry

Blueberry

Huckleberry

Strawberry

Gooseberry

Red currant

ber·ry (ber′ē) *n.* **ber·ries** a small, round, juicy fruit without a pit, various kinds of which are used as food, such as the strawberry.

berth (burth) *n.* a sleeping place in a ship or train.

be·side (bi-sīd′) *prep.* **1** next to, by the side of, or near. **2** compared with. **3** not relevant to: *Your remark is beside the point.*

be·sides (bi-sīdz′) *prep.* in addition to; as well as.

be·siege (bi-sēj′) *vb.* **besieging, besieged** to surround with an army: *The enemy besieged the town.*

●**Bes·se·mer** (bes′ə-mər), **Sir Henry** (1813-1898) was the inventor of a steel-making process.

best (best) *adj.* **1** most excellent, suitable, or desirable: *This is the best book I've ever read.* **2** most successful: *He is best at playing football.* – *adv.* **1** most successfully: *She wanted to do best in the exam.* **2** more than all others: *I like him best.* – *n.* the most excellent or suitable person or thing, most desirable quality, etc.: *She is the best of the bunch.*

bet (bet) *vb.* **bet·ting, bet** or **bet·ted 1** to risk money, etc. by guessing at the outcome or result of a future event, winning if the guess is right and losing if it is wrong. **2** (*informal*) to feel sure or confident that: *I bet she'll be late.* – *n.* a sum of money betted. – *n.* **bet·ting**.

●**Beth·le·hem** (beth′li-hem′, beth′lē-əm) is a small town in ISRAEL; birthplace of JESUS and home of King DAVID.

be·tray (bi-trā′) *vb.* **be·tray·ing, be·trayed 1** to be a traitor to: *They betrayed their country.* **2** to break a promise: *He betrayed my trust.* – *n.* **be·tray·al** (bi-trā′əl).

bet·ter (bet′ər) *adj.* **1** good to a greater extent; more suitable, or desirable: *Muriel is a better swimmer than I am.* **2** more successful at. **3** recovered from illness: *I had a headache yesterday, but I feel better today.* – *adv.* to a greater degree: *Carol likes cats better than dogs.* – **all the better for** very much better as a result of.

be·tween (bi-twēn′) *prep.* **1** in, to, through, or across the space dividing two people, places, times, etc.: *There is a park between the two roads.* **2** to and from: *There is a regular bus service between school and work.* **3** in combination; acting together: *They bought the car between them.* **4** shared out among.

be·ware (bi-wâr′) *vb.* to be careful; to be on your guard: *Beware of the dog!*

be·wil·der (bi-wil′dər) *vb.* **be·wil·der·ing, be·wil·dered** to confuse or puzzle: *Arithmetic bewilders some people.* – *adj.* **be·wil·der·ing**.

be·yond (bē-änd′) *prep.* **1** on the far side of: *We could see the sea beyond the hills.* **2** farther on than something in time or place: *I can't plan anything beyond July.* **3** out of the range, reach, power, understanding, or possibility of: *It's beyond me.* – *adv.* farther away; to or on the far side of.

●**Bhu·tan** (boo-tan′, boo-tän′). See Supplement, **Countries**.

bi- (bī-) *prefix* **1** having or involving two: *biceps.* **2** happening twice in every one, or once in every two: *biennial.* **3** on or from both sides.

bi·as (bī′əs) *n.* **1** a prejudice. **2** a tendency or principal quality of a person's character. – *vb.* **bi·as·ing, bi·ased** to influence or prejudice.

bi·ased *adj.* favoring one side.

PRONUNCIATION SYMBOLS		
ə **a**way	lemon	focus
a **fat**	oi	**boy**
ā **fade**	oo	**foot**
ä **hot**	oo	**moon**
âr **fair**	ou	**house**
e **met**	th	**think**
ē **mean**	<u>th</u>	**this**
g **get**	u	**cut**
hw **which**	ur	**hurt**
i **fin**	w	**witch**
ī **line**	y	**yes**
îr **near**	yoo	**music**
ô **often**	yoor	**pure**
ō **note**	zh	**vision**

Biscuit comes from Medieval Latin *bis coctus*, which means "twice cooked."

Bi·ble (bī′bəl) *n.* **1** the sacred writings of the Christian Church, consisting of the Old and New Testaments. **2** The sacred writings of the Jewish people, consisting of the Old Testament.

bib·li·cal or **Bib·li·cal** (bib′li-kəl) *adj.* of, like, or according to the Bible.

bi·ceps (bī′seps′) *n.* **biceps** a muscle with two heads or attachments, such as the muscle in the arm which bends the elbow.

bick·er (bik′ər) *vb.* **bick·er·ing, bick·ered** to argue or quarrel, usually about unimportant things. – *n.* **bick·er·ing.**

bi·cy·cle (bī′sik′əl) *n.* a vehicle consisting of a metal frame with two wheels and a seat, which is driven by turning pedals with the feet. – *vb.* **bi·cy·cling, bi·cy·cled** to ride a bicycle. – *n.* **bi·cy·clist** (bī′sik′ləst).

bid (bid) *vb.* **bid·ding, bid** to offer an amount of money when trying to buy something, especially at an auction. – *n.* **1** an offer of a price, especially at an auction. **2** an attempt to obtain: *They made a bid for freedom.* – *n.* **bid·der.**

bi·en·ni·al (bī-en′ē-əl) *adj.* **1** happening once in every two years. **2** lasting two years. – *n.* any event occurring every two years.

big (big) *adj.* **big·ger, big·gest 1** large or largest in size, weight, or number. **2** significant, important. **3** older or adult: *She is my big sister.*

big·ot (big′ət) *n.* a person who refuses to tolerate the opinions, religion, or race of other people. – *adj.* **big·ot·ed** (big′ət-əd).

bike (bīk) *n.* (*informal*) a bicycle or motorcycle.

bile (bīl) *n.* a yellowish or greenish thick bitter liquid produced by the liver to help digestion.

bill¹ (bil) *n.* **1** a piece of paper stating the amount of money owed for goods or services received. **2** a written plan for a proposed law.

● **Bill of Rights** the first ten amendments to the United States CONSTITUTION, dealing with human rights.

bill² (bil) *n.* a bird's beak.

bill·board (bil′bōrd′, bil′bôrd′) *n.* a large flat surface on which advertisements are displayed.

bil·liards (bil′yərdz) *n.* (*singular*) a game played on a cloth-covered table with pockets at the sides and corners, into which balls must be struck with long thin sticks called "cues."

bil·lion (bil′yən) *n.* **1** in the United States, and increasingly in Britain and Europe, a thousand million. **2** in Britain and Europe, a million million. – *n. & adj.* **bil·lionth** (bil′yənth).

bil·low (bil′ō) *n.* an upward-moving mass of water, smoke, mist, etc. – *vb.* **bil·low·ing, bil·lowed** to move in great waves or clouds.

bil·ly goat (bil′ē gōt′) *n.* a male goat.

bin (bin) *n.* a large container often used for storing grain or coal.

bi·na·ry (bī′nə-rē) *adj.* **1** consisting of two. **2** relating to the binary system.

binary system *n.* the system of calculating that uses only the numbers 0 and 1.

bind (bīnd) *vb.* **bind·ing, bound** (bound) **1** to tie or fasten tightly. **2** to be obliged or to promise to do something: *I am bound to secrecy.* **3** to fasten together the pages of a book.

bi·noc·u·lars (bi-näk′yə-lərz) *n.* (*plural*) an instrument with lenses for making distant objects look nearer.

bi·o·de·grad·a·ble (bī′ō-də-grād′ə-bəl) *adj.* able to be broken down by bacteria and other living things, and so decay naturally.

bi·og·ra·phy (bī-äg′rə-fē) *n.* **bi·og·ra·phies** a written account of another person's life.

bi·ol·o·gy (bī-äl′ə-jē) *n.* the science and study of living things. – *adj.* **bi·o·log·i·cal** (bī′ə-läj′i-kəl). – *n.* **bi·ol·o·gist** (bī-äl′ə-jəst). See **botany, zoology.**

bi·o·sphere (bī′ə-sfîr′) *n.* the parts of the Earth's atmosphere where living things exist.

bi·par·ti·san (bī-pärt′ə-zən) *adj.* including or concerning two political parties: *bipartisan support.*

birch (burch) *n.* a small tree with pointed leaves and smooth bark, valued for its wood.

bird (burd) *n.* a two-legged, egg-laying creature with feathers, a beak, and two wings. – **kill two birds with one stone** (*informal*) to achieve two things with a single action.

birth (burth) *n.* **1** the act or process of being born. **2** family history or origin: *He was of humble birth.* **3** beginning, origins.

birth control *n.* the prevention of pregnancy by the use of contraceptives.

birth·day (burth′dā′) *n.* the anniversary of the day on which a person was born.

bis·cuit (bis′kət) *n.* **1** a small bread raised with baking soda or powder.

bish·op (bish′əp) *n.* **1** a senior priest in the Christian Church. **2** a piece in the game of chess, which may only be moved diagonally.

● **Bis·marck** (biz′märk′), **Otto von** (1815-1898) was a German statesman.

Birds have hollow bones for lightness and strong breast muscles for working wings. While all birds lay eggs, some, such as the penguin, do not fly. Birds' beaks and claws have many different shapes for different purposes.

Broad wings help the vulture to soar high; the albatross on broad wings can glide for hours. The swallow's wings are built for speed enabling it to catch insects in flight.

Toucans, hummingbirds, and birds of paradise come from tropical rain forests.

Ostrich egg compared with that of a hummingbird.

American bull bison—"buffalo"—fighting during the mating season. Huge herds of bison once roamed the plains but hunters killed such great numbers that by 1889 there were only 500 left. Today bison are a protected species living in reserves.

bi·son (bī'sən, bī'zən) *n.* **bison** a shaggy wild relative of the ox with a large head, short horns, and a hump on its back.

bit[1] (bit) *n.* a small piece. — **a bit** (*colloquial*) **1** a short time or distance: *She shouted to him to wait a bit.* **2** a little; slightly; rather: *I feel a bit tired.* **3** a lot: *Lifting this weight takes a bit of doing.*

bit[2]. See **bite**.

bit[3] (bit) *n.* See **Horse Terms**.

bit[4] (bit) *n.* See **Computer Terms**.

bitch (bich) *n.* a female of the dog family.

bite (bīt) *vb.* **bit·ing, bit** (bit), **bit·ten** (bit'n) **1** to grasp, tear, or cut with the teeth. **2** (of insects and snakes) to make a hole in a person's skin and inject venom or suck blood. — *n.* a wound caused by biting.

bit·ter (bit'ər) *adj.* **1** having a sharp, acid, and often unpleasant taste. **2** feeling or causing sadness, pain, and resentment: *The divorce left them both with bitter memories.* **3** showing a lot of dislike, hatred, or opposition: *The war was a bitter struggle.* — *n.* **bit·ter·ness** (bit'ər-nəs).

bi·valve (bī'valv') *n.* any of several kinds of shellfish, such as an oyster, with a shell made up of two parts held together by a type of hinge.

Bivalves are mollusks whose shells consist of two parts hinged together. They include clams, mussels, scallops, and oysters. They all live in water, fresh or salt, and they all feed by sucking in water and filtering out the particles. Bivalves move on a foot poked out between both valves.

bizarre (bə-zär) *adj.* odd or very strange.

black (blak) *adj.* **1** of the color of coal, the night sky, etc. **2** without light. **3** (also **Black**) of dark-skinned people, especially of African origin. — *n.* **1** the color of coal, the night sky, etc. **2** (also **Black**) a dark-skinned person, especially of African origin. — *vb.* **blacking, blacked** to make black. — **in the black** with money on the credit side of an account.

black·ber·ry (blak'ber'ē) *n.* the edible black or purple fruit of certain prickly shrubs.

black·bird (blak'burd') *n.* **1** a small European bird, the male of which is black with a yellow beak. **2** any of several American birds with black feathers.

black hole *n.* an area in space which pulls matter into itself, thought to exist where a star has collapsed.

Black Muslim *n.* a member of an Islamic sect of mostly blacks.

● **Black Sea** an inland sea between RUSSIA, UKRAINE, TURKEY, BULGARIA, and ROMANIA.

black·smith (blak'smith') *n.* a person who makes and repairs by hand things made of iron.

black widow *n.* a black spider of warm regions of the United States and Central America, the female of which is poisonous.

blad·der (blad'ər) *n.* **1** the baglike organ in the body in which urine collects. **2** a small, air-filled pouch in certain plants, seaweed for example.

blade (blād) *n.* **1** the cutting part of a knife, sword, etc. **2** the wide flat part of an oar, etc.

blame (blām) *vb.* **blam·ing, blamed** to consider a person or thing as responsible for something wrong.

blame·less (blām'las) *adj.* innocent; free from blame.

bland (bland) *adj.* almost without taste; uninteresting: *The camp food was bland.*

blank (blangk) *adj.* **1** describing paper, magnetic tape, video tape, etc. with nothing printed or recorded on it. **2** not filled in; empty: *Fill in the blank form.* **3** showing no expression or interest: *She gave him a blank look.*

blan·ket (blang'kət) *n.* a thick, warm covering, often made of wool, used to cover beds.

blare (blâr) *vb.* **blar·ing, blared 1** to make a sound like a trumpet. **2** to sound or say loudly and harshly. – *n.* a loud, harsh sound: *The blare of her radio annoyed the neighbors.*

blast (blast) *n.* **1** an explosion. **2** a strong, sudden gust of air. **3** a sudden loud sound of a car horn. – *vb.* **blast·ing, blast·ed 1** to blow up with explosives. **2** to make a loud or explosive noise: *The radio was blasting out loud music.* – *vb.* **blast off** (of a spacecraft) to be launched.

blaze (blāz) *n.* **1** a bright, strong fire or flame. **2** a brilliant display: *The show opened in a blaze of publicity.* – *vb.* **blaz·ing, blazed** to burn or shine brightly.

bleach (blēch) *vb.* **bleach·ing, bleached** to make something become white or lose its color, through exposure to the sun or by chemicals. – *n.* a chemical used to bleach clothes or hair.

bleak (blēk) *adj.* **1** exposed and desolate; cold and not welcoming. **2** offering little or no hope: *The prospects for a recovery are bleak.*

bleat (blēt) *vb.* **bleat·ing, bleat·ed** to make a noise like a sheep, goat, or calf.

bleed (blēd) *vb.* **bleed·ing, bled** (bled) to lose or let out blood.

bleep (blēp) *n.* a short, high burst of sound, usually made by an electronic machine.

blem·ish (blem'ish) *n.* a stain, mark, or fault. – *vb.* **blem·ish·ing, blem·ished** to stain or spoil the beauty of.

blend (blend) *vb.* **blend·ing, blend·ed 1** to mix different things together. **2** to shade gradually into: *The sea blended into the sky.* – *n.* a mixture.

●**Blér·i·ot** (bler'ē-ō), **Louis** (1872-1936) was a French pilot who, on July 25, 1909, became the first person to cross the English Channel by air.

bless (bles) *vb.* **bless·ing, blessed** or **blest 1** to ask God to show favor to or protect. **2** to praise, to give honor or glory to.

bless·ing (bles'ing) *n.* **1** a wish or prayer for happiness or success. **2** a cause of happiness; a benefit or advantage. **3** approval or good wishes. **4** a prayer said before or after a meal.

●**Bligh** (blī), **William** (1754-1817) was a British naval officer whose crew mutinied during the voyage of the *Bounty*. Bligh survived an epic journey of 4,000 mi. (6,300 km) in a open boat.

blight (blīt) *n.* **1** a disease that causes plants to wither and die. **2** a person or thing that causes decay or destruction, or spoils things: *potato blight.*

blind (blīnd) *adj.* **1** not able to see. **2** unable or unwilling to understand or appreciate: *She was blind to his faults.* **3** unthinking, without reason or purpose: *He felt an overwhelming blind hatred.* – *n.* a screen to stop light coming through a window. – *vb.* **blind·ing, blind·ed 1** to make blind. **2** to make unreasonable or foolish: *She was blinded by anger.* – *n. & adj.* **blind·ing.** – *n.* **blind·ness** (blīnd'nəs). – **turn a blind eye to** to pretend not to notice.

blind·fold (blīnd'fōld') *n.* a piece of cloth used to cover the eyes to prevent a person from seeing.

blink (blingk) *vb.* **blink·ing, blinked 1** to open and shut the eyes very quickly: *I blinked and missed the shooting star.* **2** to flash a light on and off. – *n.* an act of blinking. – **on the blink** broken or in an unusable condition.

blip (blip) *n.* **1** a sudden, sharp sound produced by a machine. **2** a spot of light on a screen showing the position of an object, as on a radar screen.

bliss (blis) *n.* great happiness.

blis·ter (blis'tər) *n.* a thin bubble on the skin containing liquid, caused by something rubbing or burning the skin. – *vb.* **blistering, blistered** to come up in blisters.

bliz·zard (bliz'ərd) *n.* a storm with heavy snow and wind.

bloat (blōt) *vb.* **bloat·ing, bloat·ed** to swell or puff out: *I felt completely bloated after such an enormous meal.*

blob (bläb) *n.* **1** a small, soft, round mass of something: *He took a blob of jam.* **2** a small drop of liquid.

FINEST BLENDS
When parts of two words are put together to make a new word it is called blending. For example, the word "motel" is actually a blend of motor and hotel; "brunch" is a blend of breakfast and lunch; and "smog" is a blend of smoke and fog.

Blériot on his historic cross-Channel flight. He took off from Calais in northern France and 37 minutes later he touched down at the English port of Dover.

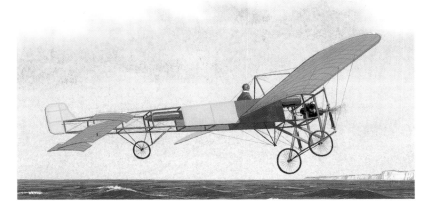

bloc (bläk) *n.* a group of countries that have a common interest, purpose, or policy.

block (bläk) *n.* **1** a mass of solid wood, stone, ice, etc., usually with flat sides. **2** a piece of wood or stone on which to chop and cut food. **3** a child's usually plastic or wooden, rectangular, cylindrical, etc. toy for building. **4** a rectangular area composed of four streets or one of these streets. **5** The buildings in such a rectangle. − *vb.* **block·ing, blocked** to make progress difficult or impossible; to obstruct.

block·ade (blä-kād′)*n.* the closing off of a port or region by surrounding it with soldiers or ships to stop people and goods from passing in and out. − *vb.* **block·ad·ing, block·ad·ed**.

blond (of a woman, usually **blonde**) (bländ) *adj.* having pale yellow hair and light skin.
blonde *n.* a woman with pale yellow hair.

blood (blud) *n.* the red liquid pumped through the body by the heart.

blood donor *n.* a person who gives blood for use by a person who is ill, in operations, etc.

blood group or **type** *n.* any one of the four types into which human blood is classified, A, B, AB, and O.

blood·hound (blud′hound′) *n.* a large dog with a very good sense of smell, used for tracking.

blood·stream (blud′strēm′) *n.* the blood flowing through the body.

bloom (bloom) *n.* a flower, especially on a plant valued for its flowers. − *vb.* **bloom·ing, bloomed 1** to be in flower. **2** to be healthy.

bloom·ing (bloo′ming) *adj.* **1** flowering. **2** bright; beautiful. **3** very healthy; flourishing.

blos·som (bläs′əm) *n.* **1** a flower or mass of flowers, especially on a fruit tree. **2** the state of flowering: *in blossom.* − *vb.* **blos·som·ing, blos·somed 1** to develop flowers. **2** to grow well or develop into.

Blossom of fruit trees. The aim of all plants is to produce seeds and so maintain the species. To do this they produce flowers, which are the plant's reproductive organs.

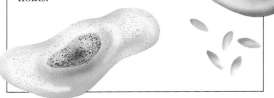

Blood is made up of four different substances: red cells, which carry oxygen around the body; white cells, which fight harmful bacteria; platelets, which help blood clot when we bleed; and plasma, the liquid in which blood floats.

blot (blät) *n.* **1** a spot or stain, especially of ink. **2** a stain on a person's good reputation.

blouse (blous, blouz) *n.* a lightweight woman's shirt.

blow¹ (blō) *vb.* **blow·ing, blew** (bloo), **blown** (blōn) **1** to be moving, especially rapidly: *The wind blew hard.* **2** to move or be moved, as by a current of air: *The wind blew the fence down.* **3** to send air from the mouth; to form or shape by blowing air from the mouth: *Let's blow bubbles!* − *vb.* **blow out** to put a flame out by blowing. − *vb.* **blow up 1** to explode. **2** to fill up or swell up with air or gas. **3** to make a photograph bigger.

blow² (blō) *n.* **1** a stroke or knock with the hand or a weapon. **2** a sudden shock or misfortune. − **come to blows** to end up fighting.

blow·hole (blō′hōl′) *n.* **1** a hole in ice through which animals such as seals can breathe. **2** a hole on top of a whale's head through which it blows air and water.

blub·ber (blub′ər) *n.* the fat of sea animals such as the whale. − *vb.* **blub·ber·ing, blub·bered** (*informal*) to weep noisily.

blue (bloo) *adj.* **1** describing the color of a bright sky. **2** sad or depressed. − *n.* **1** the color of a bright sky. **2** blue paint, dye, or material. −

once in a blue moon hardly ever.

blue·ber·ry (bloo′ber′ē) *n.* **blue·ber·ries** a dark blue berry from a bush common in North America.

blue·bird (bloo′burd′) *n.* a small blue-backed North American songbird.

blues (blooz) *n. (plural)* **1** feelings of sadness or depression. **2** slow, sad jazz music of black American origin.

blu·ish (bloo′ish) *adj.* somewhat blue; close to blue.

bluff¹ (bluf) *vb.* **bluff·ing, bluffed** to try to deceive someone by pretending to be stronger, cleverer, etc. than you really are.

bluff² (bluf) *n.* a steep cliff or bank of ground.

blun·der (blun′dər) *vb.* **blun·der·ing, blun·dered 1** to make a stupid, clumsy, and usually serious mistake. **2** to move about awkwardly and clumsily. – *n.* a stupid, clumsy, and usually serious mistake.

blunt (blunt) *adj.* **1** having no point or sharp edge. **2** honest and direct in a rough way.

blur (blur) *n.* **1** a thing not clearly seen or heard. **2** a smear or smudge. – *vb.* **blur·ring, blurred 1** to make or become less clear or distinct. **2** to rub over and smudge. – *adj.* **blurred**.

blush (blush) *n.* **1** a red or pink glow on the skin of the face, caused by shame or embarrassment. **2** a pink, rosy glow. – *vb.* **blush·ing, blushed 1** to become red or pink in the face because of shame or embarrassment. **2** to feel ashamed or embarrassed: *I blush when I think of my past mistakes.* – *adj.* **blush·ing**.

bo·a (bō′ə) *n.* any of several snakes that kill by winding around their prey and crushing it, especially a large snake of South America also called a **bo·a con·strict·or** (bō′ə kən-strik′tər).

boar (bōr, bôr) *n.* **1** (also **wild boar**) a wild pig. **2** a male pig kept for breeding.

board (bōrd, bôrd) *n.* **1** a long flat strip of wood or other material. **2** a flat piece of wood or card used for a specific purpose: *notice board; chessboard.* **3** an official group of people controlling or managing an organization: *She is head of the school board.*

boast (bōst) *vb.* **boast·ing, boast·ed** to talk with too much pride about your own abilities, achievements, etc.

boat (bōt) *n.* a small vessel for traveling over water.

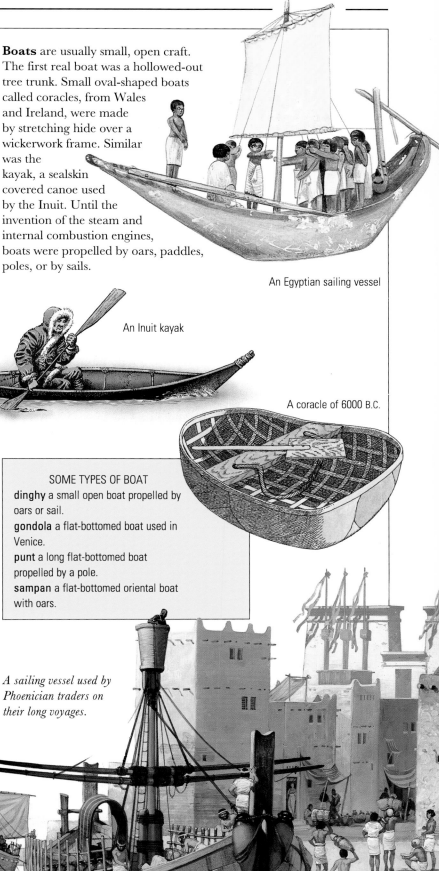

Boats are usually small, open craft. The first real boat was a hollowed-out tree trunk. Small oval-shaped boats called coracles, from Wales and Ireland, were made by stretching hide over a wickerwork frame. Similar was the kayak, a sealskin covered canoe used by the Inuit. Until the invention of the steam and internal combustion engines, boats were propelled by oars, paddles, poles, or by sails.

An Egyptian sailing vessel

An Inuit kayak

A coracle of 6000 B.C.

SOME TYPES OF BOAT
dinghy a small open boat propelled by oars or sail.
gondola a flat-bottomed boat used in Venice.
punt a long flat-bottomed boat propelled by a pole.
sampan a flat-bottomed oriental boat with oars.

A sailing vessel used by Phoenician traders on their long voyages.

The bobcat is active mainly at night. It uses its keen eyesight and hearing to track down the small animals it eats.

In the 15th century a bonfire was a *bone fire*, an open-air burning of bones, which was a common event in those days.

bob (bäb) *vb.* **bob·bing, bobbed** to move up and down quickly.

bob·bin (bäb′ən) *n.* a small cylindrical object on which thread is wound, used in sewing.

bob·cat (bäb′kat′) *n.* a wild cat of North America with brown fur marked with darker spots and lines. It eats rodents, snakes and sometimes livestock and poultry.

bob·sled (bäb′sled′) *n.* a racing sled with metal runners and a steering wheel.

bob·sleigh (bäb′slā′) *n.* (*British*) bobsled.

bod·i·ly (bäd′l-ē) *adj.* of the body: *the bodily functions.* – *adv.* concerning the whole body: *She picked the child up bodily.*

bod·y (bäd′ē) *n.* **bod·ies 1** the whole physical structure of a person or animal. **2** the physical structure of a person or animal excluding the head and limbs. **3** a corpse. **4** the main or central part of anything. **5** a group of people.

body building *n.* physical exercise which makes the muscles bigger and stronger.

bod·y·guard (bäd′ē-gärd′) *n.* a person or group of people who guard an important person.

bod·y·work *n.* the outer painted structure of an automobile etc.

Boer (bōr, bôr, boor) *n.* a descendant of the early Dutch settlers in SOUTH AFRICA. – *adj.* of or relating to the Boers.

bog (bôg, bäg) *n.* an area of very wet, spongy ground. – *vb.* **bog down, bog·ging, bogged** to prevent or be prevented from progressing: *She gets bogged down by details.*

bo·gey or **bo·gy** (boog′ē, bō′gē) *n.* an evil or mischievous spirit.

●**Bo·go·tá** (bō′gə-tä′) is the capital of Colombia.

bo·gus (bō′gəs) *adj.* false; not genuine.

●**Bohr** (bôr, bōr), **Niels** (1885-1962) was a Danish physicist.

boil[1] (boil) *vb.* **boil·ing, boiled 1** (of liquids) to start to bubble and turn to gas when heated. **2** to contain a liquid which is boiling: *The tea kettle is boiling.* **3** to cook by boiling.

boil[2] (boil) *n.* a red pus-filled swelling on the skin.

boil·er (boi′lər) *n.* an apparatus for heating a building's hot water supply.

boil·ing point (boi′ling point) *n.* the temperature at which a liquid boils.

boi·ster·ous (boi′stə-rəs) *adj.* very lively, noisy.

bold (bōld) *adj.* **1** daring or brave: *He made a bold attempt to rescue his friend.* **2** striking and clearly marked: *A zebra has bold markings.* **3** printed in thick, black letters, for example, **bold**.

bole (bōl) *n.* the trunk of a tree.

●**Bo·lí·var** (bō′lə-vär′, bō-lē′vär), **Simón** (1783-1830) was a South American hero who freed PERU, BOLIVIA, COLOMBIA, ECUADOR, and VENEZUELA from Spanish rule.

●**Bo·liv·ia** (bə-liv′ē-ə). See Supplement, **Countries**.

Bol·she·vik (bōl′shə-vik) *n.* a Russian communist or any communist. – *adj.* **1** of the Bolsheviks. **2** communist. – *n.* **Bol·she·vism** (bōl′shə-viz′əm).

bolt (bōlt) *n.* **1** a bar to fasten a door or gate. **2** a small, thick, round bar of metal, with a screw thread, used with a nut to fasten things

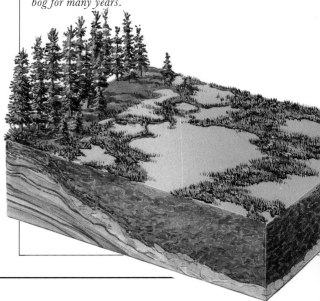

A bog contains peat (partially decayed plant life), which is acidic. The acid prevents things from decomposing, even if they have been buried in a bog for many years.

together. **3** a flash of lightning. **4** a sudden movement, especially to escape: *The thieving cat made a bolt for it.* – vb. **bolt·ing, bolt·ed 1** to fasten a door or window with a bolt. **2** to eat very quickly. **3** to run away suddenly and quickly: *The horse bolted, shedding its rider.*

bomb (bäm) *n.* **1** a hollow case or other device containing explosive substances. **2** the atomic bomb or any nuclear bomb. – vb. **bomb·ing, bombed** to attack with a bomb.

bom·bard (bäm-bärd′) *vb.* **bom·bard·ing, bom·bard·ed 1** to attack with large, heavy guns or bombs. **2** to direct attack at someone very quickly and without stopping.

●**Bom·bay** (bäm-bā′) is a city in western INDIA.

bomb·er (bäm′ər) *n.* an aircraft built for bombing.

bomb·shell (bäm′shel′) *n.* a piece of surprising news.

●**Bonaparte, Napoleon**. See **Napoleon**.

bond (bänd) *n.* **1** (usually in *plural*) something which restrains or imprisons a person. **2** something that joins people together. – vb. **bond·ing, bond·ed 1** to join or tie together. **2** to stick together.

bond·age (bän′dij) *n.* **1** slavery. **2** the state of being confined or imprisoned.

The face of a man who died more than 2,000 years ago. His body was found in the Tollund bog in Denmark in May 1950. The peat has preserved his hair and skin just as it was when he was put to death by hanging. (The noose is still visible around his neck.) He may have been sacrificed for ritual purposes or hanged for some crime.

Wooden figures found in a bog near Roos Carr, England. The acid in the peat has preserved them perfectly.

bone (bōn) *n.* **1** any of the pieces of hard tissue that form the skeleton. **2** the material from which this tissue is made.— vb. **bon·ing, boned 1** to take bones out of meat, etc. **2** to make a piece of clothing stiff by adding pieces of bone or some other hard substance.

bone-dry (bōn′drī′) *adj.* completely dry.

bon·fire (bän′fīr′) *n.* a large, outdoor fire, often burned to celebrate something.

●**Bonn** (bän, bôn) was the capital of West Germany until Germany reunited in 1990.

bon·net (bän′ət) *n.* **1** a hat with ribbons that are tied under the chin, worn by women and girls. **2** a Scottish cap worn by men and boys. **3** (*British*) the hinged cover, or hood, over a car's engine.

bo·nus (bō′nəs) *n.* an extra sum of money given on top of what is due.

bon·y (bō′nē) *adj.* **bon·i·er, bon·i·est 1** of or like bone. **2** thin.

book (book) *n.* **1** a number of printed pages bound together along one edge and protected by covers. **2** a number of blank pages bound together. – vb. **book·ing, booked** to reserve in advance: *We booked tickets to a show.* – n. **book·ing**.

● The first books were written on rolls of papyrus in ancient Egypt. The Romans also used parchment rolls, made from sheepskin. In the Middle Ages books were handwritten and beautifully decorated by monks. The first printed book was GUTENBERG's Bible in 1452.

boom[1] (boom) *n.* a loud, deep, resounding sound, like that made by a large drum or gun.

boom[2] (boom) *n.* a sudden increase or growth in business and prosperity. – vb. **boom·ing, boomed** to prosper rapidly.

boo·mer·ang (boo′mə-rang′) *n.* a piece of flat, curved wood used by Australian Aborigines for hunting, often so balanced that, when thrown to a distance, it returns to the thrower.

●**Boone** (boon), **Daniel** (1734-1820) was an American explorer and frontiersman.

boost (boost) *vb.* **boost·ing, boost·ed 1** to improve or encourage: *Her good exam results boosted her spirits.* **2** to increase. – n. **1** a piece of help or encouragement. **2** a rise or increase.

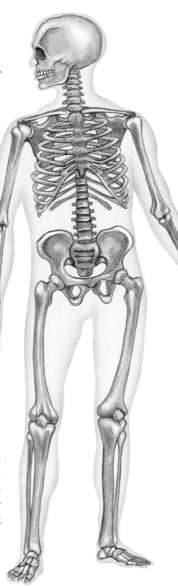

Adults have 206 bones in their bodies. Each arm has 32, each leg 31, the skull 29, the spine 26, and the chest 25. The smallest bone, the stapes, is in the ear. It is only $^1/_{12}$ inch (2 mm) long.

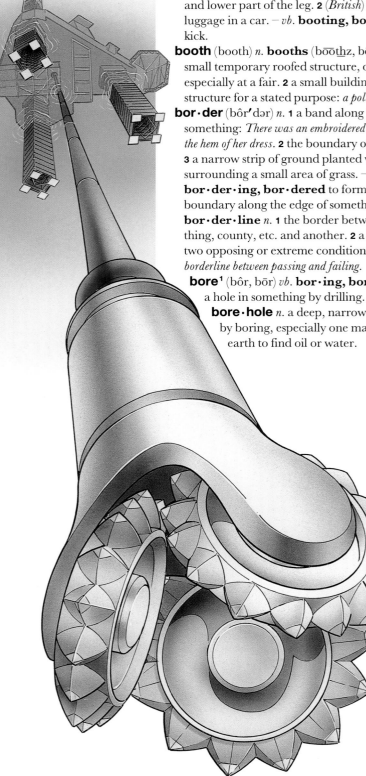

boot (boot) *n.* **1** a type of shoe that covers the foot and lower part of the leg. **2** (*British*) a place for luggage in a car. – *vb.* **booting, booted** to kick.

booth (booth) *n.* **booths** (bootͪz, booths) **1** a small temporary roofed structure, or a tent, especially at a fair. **2** a small building or structure for a stated purpose: *a polling booth.*

bor·der (bôr′dər) *n.* **1** a band along the edge of something: *There was an embroidered border along the hem of her dress.* **2** the boundary of a country. **3** a narrow strip of ground planted with flowers, surrounding a small area of grass. – *vb.* **bor·der·ing, bor·dered** to form a border or boundary along the edge of something.

bor·der·line *n.* **1** the border between one thing, county, etc. and another. **2** a line dividing two opposing or extreme conditions: *on the borderline between passing and failing.*

bore¹ (bôr, bōr) *vb.* **bor·ing, bored** to make a hole in something by drilling.

bore·hole *n.* a deep, narrow hole made by boring, especially one made in the earth to find oil or water.

bore² (bôr, bōr) *vb.* **bor·ing, bored** to make someone feel uninterested, by being dull and unimaginative. – *n.* a dull, tedious person or thing. – *adj.* **bored.** – *adj.* **bor·ing.**

bore³. See **bear¹**.

bore·dom (bôr′dəm) *n.* the state of being bored.

born (bôrn) *adj.* **1** brought into being by birth. **2** having a natural ability: *She is a born leader.* – **in all your born days** (*colloquial*) in all your lifetime or experience. – **not born yesterday** not a fool.

bor·ough (bur′ō, bur′ə) *n.* **1** a self-governing town or village chartered in certain states. **2** one of the five divisions of New York City.

bor·row (bär′ō, bôr′ō) *vb.* **bor·row·ing, bor·rowed** to take something temporarily, usually with permission and with the intention of returning it. – **live on borrowed time** to live longer than expected.

bor·zoi (bôr′zoi) *n.* a large dog originally used for hunting. It has a narrow head and a long, soft coat.

● **Bos·ni·a and Herz·e·go·vi·na** (bäz′nē-ə, hurt′sə-gō-vē′nə). See Supplement, **Countries**.

bos·om (booz′əm) *n.* **1** a woman's chest or breasts. **2** a loving or protective center. **bosom friend** *n.* a very close friend.

● **Bos·po·rus** (bäs′pə-rəs) a strip of water joining the Black Sea and the Sea of Marmara, dividing EUROPE from ASIA.

boss (bôs, bäs) *n.* (*informal*) a person who employs or who is in charge of others. **bos·sy** *adj.* **bossier, bossiest** (*informal*) liking to give orders and commands to others. – *adv.* **bossily.** – *n.* **bossiness.**

● **Bos·ton** (bôs′tən, bäs′tən) is the capital of Massachusetts. It is a major manufacturing center and seaport. Boston has many famous colleges and universities.

A seabed view of a rotary drill bit used to bore for oil. The drilling derrick is a tower that supports the drill pipes. The drill pipes are lengthened by adding extra sections. The drill pipes contain several channels. Mud pumped at high pressure down one channel cools and lubricates the boring bit and forces drilled rock up through the outer pipe channel.

● **Boston Tea Party** On December 16, 1773, a band of American colonists boarded a British ship in Boston harbor and dumped overboard its cargo of tea in protest at the high taxes collected by the British government. This was a crucial event leading to the AMERICAN REVOLUTION.

bot·a·ny (bät′n-ē) *n.* the scientific study of plants. − *adj.* **bo·tan·ic** (bə-tan′ik) or **bo·tan·i·cal** (bə-tan′i-kəl). − *n.* **bot·a·nist** (bät′n-ist).

● There are more than 300,000 different kinds of plants, from tiny algae to giant redwoods. In 1753 Carolus LINNAEUS, a Swedish botanist, invented the first real system for naming plants.

both (bōth) *adj. & pron.* the two: *Both girls owned bicycles.* − *adv.* as well: *She both works and raises a family.*

both·er (bä<u>th</u>′ər) *vb.* **both·er·ing, both·ered** **1** to annoy, worry, or trouble: *The flies bothered them.* **2** to take the time or trouble: *Don't bother about the dishes.* **3** to worry: *She was bothered about her exams.* − *n.* a minor trouble or worry.

● **Bot·swa·na** (bät-swän′ə). See Supplement, **Countries.**

● **Bot·ti·cel·li** (bät′ə-chel′ē), **Sandro** (1444-1510) was a famous painter of the Renaissance period in Italy.

bot·tle (bät′l) *n.* a hollow, usually glass or plastic container with a narrow neck, for holding liquids. − *vb.* **bot·tling, bot·tled** **1** to put into or store in bottles. **2** to restrain or hide feelings: *She had bottled up her sadness for many years.*

bot·tom (bät′əm) *n.* **1** the lowest position or part; the point farthest away from the top, most important, or most successful part: *He was bottom of the class.* **2** the part of the body on which a person sits. − *adj.* lowest or last.

bough (bow) *n.* a branch of a tree.

bought. See **buy.**

boul·der (bōl′dər) *n.* a large rock or stone, rounded and worn smooth by the weather.

boul·e·vard (bool′ə-värd′) *n.* a broad street, often lined with trees.

bounce (bowns) *vb.* **bounc·ing, bounced** **1** to spring or jump back from a surface. **2** to move or spring suddenly: *She bounced about the room.* −

American colonists disguised as Native Americans throwing a cargo of tea overboard into Boston harbor. They said that "taxation without representation is tyranny."

n. the act of springing back from a surface.

bound¹ (bownd) *adj.* **1** tied with a rope, etc. **2** restricted to or by: *housebound; snowbound.* **3** certain: *It was bound to happen.*

bound² (bownd) *adj.* going to or toward: *southbound.*

bound³ (bownd) *n.* a jump or leap upward. − *vb.* **bound·ing, bound·ed** to spring or leap.

bound·a·ry (bown′də-rē) *n.* **bound·a·ries** a line marking the farthest limit of an area, etc.

bou·quet (bō-kā′, boo-kā′) *n.* **1** a bunch of flowers arranged in an artistic way. **2** the delicate smell of wine.

bout (bowt) *n.* **1** a period of illness: *He has had a bout of the flu.* **2** a boxing or wrestling match.

bo·vine (bō′vīn′) *adj.* of or like cattle.

bow¹ (bow) *vb.* **bow·ing, bowed** **1** to bend the head or the upper part of the body forward and downward, usually as a sign of greeting or respect, or to acknowledge applause. **2** to accept or submit to, especially unwillingly: *I must bow to the inevitable.* − *n.* an act of bowing.

bow² (bō) *n.* **1** a knot with a double loop. **2** a weapon made of a piece of curved wood, bent by a string attached to each end, for shooting arrows. **3** a long thin piece of wood with horsehair stretched along its length, for playing the violin, cello, etc.

bow³ (bow) *n.* the front part of a ship or boat.

bow·el (bow′əl) *n.* (usually in *plural*) the organ for digesting food next after the stomach; the intestine.

● **Bow·ie** (boo′ē, bō′ē), **James** (1796-1836) was an American frontiersman and soldier. He died in the siege of the Alamo.

bowl¹ (bōl) *n.* **1** a round, deep dish for mixing or serving food, for holding liquids, etc. **2** the round, hollow part of an object, such as a spoon or pipe.

PRONUNCIATION SYMBOLS			
ə	away lemon		focus
a	fat	oi	boy
ā	fade	oo	foot
ä	hot	ōō	moon
âr	fair	ou	house
e	met	th	think
ē	mean	<u>th</u>	this
g	get	u	cut
hw	which	ur	hurt
i	fin	w	witch
ī	line	y	yes
îr	near	yōō	music
ô	often	yoor	pure
ō	note	zh	vision

bowl² (bōl) *vb.* **bowl·ing, bowled** to roll a ball in bowling. — *vb.* **bowl over** (*informal*) to impress greatly.

bowl·ing (bō′ling) *n.* a game played indoors in which a ball is rolled at a group of pins in order to knock them down.

box¹ (bäks) *n.* **1** a usually square or rectangular container made from wood, cardboard, plastic, etc. and with a lid, for holding things. **2** a separate compartment for a particular purpose, for example, for a group of people in a theater, or for a horse in a stable. — *vb.* **box·ing, boxed 1** to put into or provide with a box. **2** to stop from moving, confine or enclose.

box² (bäks) *vb.* **box·ing, boxed** to fight with hands protected by thick leather gloves, especially as a sport. — *n.* **box·ing**.

box·er (bäk′sər) *n.* **1** a person who boxes. **2** a medium-sized breed of dog with a short, smooth coat.

boy (boi) *n.* a male child. — *n.* **boy·hood** (boi′hood′).

boy·cott (boi′kät′) *vb.* **boy·cot·ting, boy·cot·ted** to refuse to have any business or social dealings with a company or a country because you disapprove of its actions.

● **Boyle** (boil), **Robert** (1627-1691) was an Irish chemist who formulated a law on the physical properties of gases.

brace (brās) *n.* **1** a device, usually made from metal, which supports or holds two things together. **2** a wire device worn on the teeth to straighten them. **3** (*British;* in *plural*) suspenders. — *vb.* **brac·ing, braced 1** to make tight or stronger, usually by supporting in some way. **2** to prepare yourself for a blow or a shock.

brace·let (brā′slət) *n.* a band or chain worn as a piece of jewelry around the arm or wrist.

brack·en (brak′ən) *n.* a type of fern.

brack·et (brak′ət) *n.* **1** either one of a pair of symbols, [ ], or < >, used to group together or enclose words, figures, etc. **2** a group or category falling within a certain range: *That bike is out of my price bracket.* **3** an L-shaped piece of metal or strong plastic, used for attaching shelves to walls. — *vb.* **brack·et·ing, brack·et·ed 1** to enclose words, etc. in brackets. **2** to put people or things into a group.

● **Brahms** (brämz), **Johannes** (1833-1897) was a German composer.

braid (brād) *n.* **1** a band or tape, often made from threads of gold and silver twisted together, used as a decoration on uniforms. **2** a length of hair consisting of several lengths which have been twisted together. — *vb.* **braid·ing, braid·ed** to twist several lengths of thread or hair together. — *adj.* **braid·ed**.

Braille (brāl) *n.* a system of printing using raised dots, which blind people can feel with their fingers and so read what is printed. It was invented by Louis *Braille* in the 1800s.

brain (brān) *n.* the soft gray organ inside the head which controls thought, sight, etc.

brain·teaser *n.* a difficult exercise or puzzle.

brake (brāk) *n.* **1** a device on a vehicle for making it slow down or stop. **2** anything which makes something stop or prevents progress: *There was a brake on public spending.* — *vb.* **brak·ing, braked** to use a brake.

bram·ble (bram′bəl) *n.* a wild prickly bush, as the one which produces blackberries.

bran (bran) *n.* the outer covering of grain often separated from flour.

branch (branch) *n.* **1** a shoot or stem growing out like an arm from the main body of a tree. **2** a main division of a railway line, river, road, or mountain range. **3** a division of a larger body: *a branch of the public library.* — *vb.* **branch·ing, branched** to divide from the main part.

Captain Charles Boycott worked for a British landlord in Ireland who, in the 1880s, charged his tenants high rents. Boycott evicted many tenants, so local people *boycotted* him.

Bracken is the world's commonest fern, but unlike most ferns has creeping underground stems, which can grow more than 3 feet in a year. In this way bracken spreads rapidly.

brand (brand) *n.* **1** a maker's name or trademark. **2** a variety or type: *Her brand of humor doesn't appeal to everybody.* **3** (also **brand·ing i·ron** [bran′ding ī′ərn]) an iron used for burning identifying marks on cattle, etc.

brass (bras) *n.* **1** a hard yellowish metal, a mixture of copper and zinc. **2** wind instruments made of brass, such as the trumpet; the brass instruments in an orchestra.

brave (brāv) *adj.* without fear of danger or pain. – *n.* **brav·er·y** (brā′və-rē, brāv′rē).

brawl (brôl) *n.* a noisy quarrel or fight.

bray (brā) *n.* the loud, harsh sound made by a donkey. – *vb.* **bray·ing, brayed** (of a donkey) to make such a noise.

● **Bra·zil** (brə-zil′). See Supplement, **Countries**.

bread (bred) *n.* a food made from flour, water, and yeast, baked in an oven.

breadth (bredth) *n.* the measurement from one side to the other.

break (brāk) *vb.* **break·ing, broke** (brōk), **brok·en** (brō′kən) **1** to become or cause to become divided into two or more parts by force: *The cup broke.* **2** to make or become damaged, so as to no longer work: *The lawnmower broke while she was cutting the grass.* **3** to do something not allowed: *David broke all the rules.* **4** to stop work, etc. for a short period of time: *At 10 o'clock we always break for coffee.* **5** to do better than: *Dan broke the school's high jump record.* **6** to become lower in tone, especially of the voice of a boy becoming an adult. – *n.* **1** an act of breaking. **2** a brief pause in work, lessons, etc. – *vb.* **break away** to escape from control. – *vb.* **break down 1** to use force to knock down: *We broke down the door.* **2** to stop working properly. – *vb.* **break in 1** to enter a building by force, especially to steal things inside. **2** to train or prepare for use. – *vb.* **break off 1** to remove or be removed by breaking. **2** to come to an end suddenly.

break·fast (brek′fəst) *n.* the first meal of the day.

breast (brest) *n.* **1** either of the two glands on the front of a woman's body which produce milk. **2** the front part of the body between the neck and stomach.

breath (breth) *n.* **1** the air drawn into and sent out from the lungs. **2** an act of breathing air in. **3** a slight breeze.

breathe (brēth) *vb.* **breath·ing, breathed** to draw air into, and force it out of, the lungs. – *n.* **breath·ing**.

breath·less (breth′ləs) *adj.* **1** having difficulty in breathing normally, either from illness or from hurrying, etc. **2** very eager or excited.

bred. See **breed**.

breed (brēd) *vb.* **breed·ing, bred** (bred) **1** to produce young, usually of animals. **2** to keep animals or plants for the purpose of producing more, or developing new types. – *n.* **1** a group of animals within a species which share characteristics. **2** a kind or type.

breeze (brēz) *n.* a gentle wind.

brew (broo) *vb.* **brew·ing, brewed 1** to make beer, etc. by mixing, boiling, and fermenting. **2** to make tea or coffee by mixing the leaves, grains, etc. with boiling water. **3** to get stronger and threaten: *There's a storm brewing.*

brew·er·y (broo′ə-rē) *n.* **brew·er·ies** a place where beer or ale is brewed.

bribe (brīb) *n.* a gift, usually money, offered to someone to persuade him or her to do something illegal or wrong. – *vb.* **brib·ing, bribed** to give or promise money, etc. to a person to persuade him or her to do something illegal or wrong. – *n.* **brib·er·y** (brī′bə-rē).

brick (brik) *n.* a rectangular block of baked clay used for building.

brick·lay·er (brik′lā′ər) *n.* a person who builds with bricks. – *n.* **bricklaying** (brik′lā′ing).

Bricks are generally laid in horizontal layers known as courses. *The patterns in which they are laid are called* bonds.

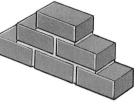

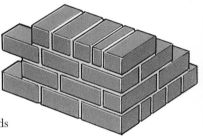

Bricks are made of clay. The clay is mined and crushed into small particles. Water is added, together with other chemicals, to make a stiff mud. Most bricks are shaped and cut by machine then oven-dried and "fired" at a very high temperature in kilns. Some specially shaped bricks are hand made in molds, air-dried, and then fired. In ancient Egypt bricks were made from the mud of the Nile, mixed with straw, and then dried in the sun.

brid·al (brīd′l) *adj.* of a wedding or a bride.

bride (brīd) *n.* a woman who has just been, or is about to be, married.

bride·groom (brīd′grōōm′, brīd′groom′) *n.* a man who has just been, or is about to be, married.

bridge¹ (brij) *n.* **1** a structure joining the two sides of a road, railroad, or river to allow people, vehicles, etc. to cross. **2** anything joining or connecting two separate things. **3** the narrow raised platform from which the captain of a ship directs its course. **4** a small piece of wood on a violin, guitar, etc. which keeps the strings stretched tight. **5** the hard, bony, upper part of the nose. – *vb.* **bridg·ing, bridged 1** to build a bridge over. **2** to make a connection.

bridge² (brij) *n.* a card game for four people.

There are three basic types of **bridge:** *beam,* in which a beam of steel is supported on each bank; *arch,* formed of one or several arches; *suspension* in which the main part is a beam supported by steel cables suspended from towers. The longest single-span bridge is the Humber Suspension bridge across the estuary of the River Humber, England.

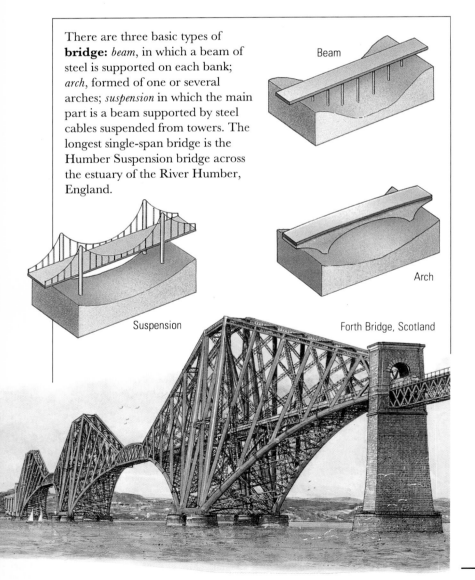

Beam

Arch

Suspension

Forth Bridge, Scotland

bri·dle (brīd′l) *n.* See **Horse Terms**.

brief (brēf) *adj.* lasting only a short time; short or small; concise. – *n.* **1** (in *plural*) a woman's or man's underpants without legs. **2** a summary of facts, legal points, etc., used by a lawyer in arguing a legal case. – *vb.* **brief·ing, briefed** to prepare a person by giving instructions in advance: *Rachel briefed him on the procedure.*

bri·gade (bri-gād′) *n.* an army unit made up of battalions and forming part of a division.

bright (brīt) *adj.* **1** giving out or shining with much light. **2** describing a color that is strong, light, and clear. **3** lively and cheerful. **4** clever and quick at learning. – *n.* **bright·ness**.

bright·en (brīt′n) *vb.* **bright·en·ing, bright·ened 1** to make or become bright or brighter. **2** to make or become happier.

bril·liant (bril′yənt) *adj.* **1** very bright and sparkling. **2** of outstanding intelligence or talent. **3** (*informal*) excellent. – *n.* **bril·liance** (bril′yəns).

brim (brim) *n.* **1** the top edge or lip of a cup, glass, bowl, etc. **2** the projecting edge of a hat.

bring (bring) *vb.* **bring·ing, brought** (brôt) **1** to carry or cause to come to a stated place or person: *to bring money home.* **2** to cause or result in: *War brings misery.* – *vb.* **bring a·bout** to cause to happen. – *vb.* **bring for·ward** to move to an earlier date or time. – *vb.* **bring out 1** to make clear, emphasize. **2** to publish. – *vb.* **bring up** to care for and educate from a young age.

brink (bringk) *n.* **1** the edge of a steep place or the edge of land before a body of water. **2** the point immediately before the start of something dangerous, unknown, exciting, etc.

brisk (brisk) *adj.* **1** lively, active, or quick: *We all went for a brisk walk.* **2** pleasantly cold and fresh: *It was a brisk day.* – *n.* **brisk·ness**.

bris·tle (bris′əl) *n.* a short, stiff hair on or from an animal's back, etc.

Brit·ish (brit′ish) *adj.* of GREAT BRITAIN or its people.

● **Brit·ish Co·lum·bi·a** (brit′ish kə-lum′bē-ə) the westernmost province of CANADA.

● **Brit·ish Isles** (brit′ish īlz′) made up of two large nations, the United Kingdom of GREAT BRITAIN and NORTHERN IRELAND (comprising ENGLAND, Northern Ireland, SCOTLAND, and WALES) and the Republic of IRELAND, and two small British dependencies, the Isle of Man and the Channel Islands.

brit·tle (brit′l) *adj.* hard but easily broken.

broad (brôd) *adj.* **1** large in extent from one side
to the other. **2** wide and open; spacious.
3 general, not detailed: *a broad inquiry.*

broad·cast (brôd′kast′) *vb.* **broad·cast·ing,**
broad·cast 1 to send out a program by radio
or television. **2** to make something widely
known. − *n.* a television or radio program.
− *n.* **broad·cast·er.** − *n.* **broad·cast·ing.**

broad·en (brôd′n) *vb.* **broad·en·ing,**
broad·ened to make or become broad or
broader.

broad·ly *adv.* widely; generally.

● **Broad·way** (brôd′wā′) is a street in New York
where most of the main theaters are found.

broc·co·li (bräk′ə-lē, bräk′lē) *n:* a variety of
cauliflower with green or purple flowerlike
heads.

broil (broil) *vb.* **broil·ing, broiled** to grill food.

broke[1] . See **break.**

broke[2] (brōk) *adj.* (*informal*) without money.

brok·en (brō′kən) *adj.* **1** smashed, fractured:
Robert has a broken leg. **2** interrupted: *They had a
broken sleep because of the noise.* **3** not working
properly: *The TV is broken.* **4** not kept or
followed: *broken promises.*

bron·chi·tis (bräng-kīt′əs) *n.* an infection of the
two large air tubes, the bronchi, in the lungs,
causing coughing, difficulty in breathing, etc.

bron·co (bräng′kō) *n.* **bron·cos** a wild or half-
tamed horse from the western United States.

● **Bron·të** (bränt′ē) All the Brontë sisters were
famous writers: Charlotte (1816-1855), author
of *Jane Eyre*, Emily (1818-1848) who wrote
Wuthering Heights, and Anne (1820-1849).

bronze (bränz) *n.* a mixture of copper and tin.
− *adj.* **1** made of bronze. **2** of the color of bronze.

Bronze Age *n.* the period in history when tools,
weapons, etc. were made out of bronze,
between about 3000 B.C. and 1000 B.C.

bronze medal *n.* a medal given to the person
who comes in third in a race or contest.

brooch (brōch, brōōch) *n.* **brooch·es** a
decoration or piece of jewelry, fastened to
clothes by a pin.

brood (brōōd) *n.* a number of young animals,
especially birds, born or hatched at the same
time. − *vb.* **brood·ing, brood·ed** (of birds) to
sit on eggs until the young are born.

In many parts of the world a
period called the Copper
Age was followed by the
Bronze Age, when people
learned how to strengthen
copper by adding tin, so
producing an *alloy.*

*A 7th-
century B.C.
bronze ax
head* (left)
and a bucket
(below left).

The Chinese bronze vessel
(above right) *was used for
preparing sacrificial
food for the dead.*

*Outside a copper mine near
Salzburg, Austria in about
1200 B.C. Mined copper ore
was carried out to be crushed
and washed out from the rock.
The concentrated ore was
smelted in furnaces. The molten
metal could then be cast in
molds. The oldest known molds
were open molds* (left).

brook (brook) *n.* a small stream.

● **Brook·lyn** (brook′lən) is the largest of the five boroughs (administrative divisions) of NEW YORK CITY. It is on Long Island. Brooklyn borders Queens, another borough. The Brooklyn Bridge connects Brooklyn with Manhattan.

● **Brooks** (brooks), **Gwendolyn** (1917-) is a famous poet. In 1950 she became the first black American to win the Pulitzer Prize. Her works include *Annie Allen* and *Bronzeville Boys and Girls*.

broom (brōōm, broom) *n.* a brush with a long handle for sweeping the floor.

broth (broth) *n.* a thin, clear soup made by boiling meat, fish, or vegetables.

broth·er (bru<u>th</u>′ər) *n.* **1** a boy or man with the same parents as another person or people. **2** (plural **breth·ren** [bre<u>th</u>′rən]) a man who is a member of a religious group, especially a monk.

broth·er-in-law (bru<u>th</u>′ər-ən-lô′) *n.* **broth·ers-in-law 1** the brother of someone's husband or wife. **2** the husband of someone's sister.

brought. See **bring**.

brow (brow) *n.* **1** (usually in *plural*) an eyebrow. **2** the forehead. **3** the top of a hill or road.

brown (brown) *adj.* having a color similar to that of bark, coffee, etc. – *n.* any of various dark colors similar to bark, coffee, etc. – *vb.* **brown·ing, browned** to make or become brown by cooking or burning in the sun, etc.

● **Brown** (brown), **John** (1800-1859) was a leader of the antislavery movement. He is remembered in the song *John Brown's Body*.

browse (browz) *vb.* **brows·ing, browsed** to look through a book, casually, reading only bits.

● **Brue·ghel** (broi′gəl) is the name of a family of Flemish painters of the 1500s and 1600s.

bruise (brōōz) *n.* an injury from a blow, turning the skin a darker color but not breaking it. – *vb.* **bruis·ing, bruised** to cause a bruise on.

● **Bru·nei** (brōō-nī′). See Supplement, **Countries**.

brush (brush) *n.* **brush·es** a tool with lengths of stiff bristles, etc., for tidying the hair, cleaning, painting, etc. – *vb.* **brush·ing, brushed** to rub with a brush to remove dirt, dust, etc.

● **Brus·sels** (brus′əlz) is the capital and largest city of BELGIUM.

Brus·sels sprout (brus′əlz sprowt) *n.* (usually in *plural*) a small, round, cabbagelike vegetable.

brutal (brōōt′l) *adj.* very cruel. – *n.* **bru·tal·i·ty** (brōō-tal′ət-ē), **bru·tal·i·ties**.

● **Bry·an** (brī′ən), **William Jennings** (1860-1925) was an American political leader.

bub·ble (bub′əl) *n.* **1** a thin film of liquid forming a ball around air or gas, especially one that floats in liquid: *soap bubbles*. **2** a ball of air or gas which has formed in a solid: *We found lots of air bubbles in the glass*. – *vb.* **bub·bling, bub·bled** to form or rise in bubbles.

buck (buk) *n.* the male of some animals, especially the rabbit, hare, or deer.

buck·et (buk′it) *n.* a round, open-topped container for holding liquids, etc.

buck·le (buk′əl) *n.* a flat piece of metal attached to one end of a strap or belt, with a pin in the middle which goes through a hole in the other end of the strap or belt to fasten it.

bud (bud) *n.* a small swelling on the stem of a tree or plant which will grow into leaves or a flower.

● **Bu·da·pest** (bōōd′ə-pest′) is the capital of HUNGARY.

A bud is an undeveloped shoot of a plant. If the covering of the bud is peeled back, the tightly packed leaves or flowers can be seen inside.

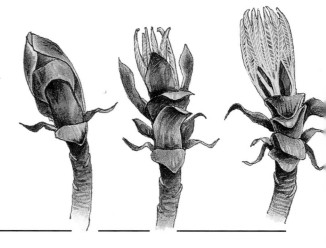

PRONUNCIATION SYMBOLS		
ə **away**	**lemon**	**focus**
a **fat**	oi	**boy**
ā **fade**	oo	**foot**
ä **hot**	ōō	**moon**
âr **fair**	ou	**house**
e **met**	th	**think**
ē **mean**	<u>th</u>	**this**
g **get**	u	**cut**
hw **which**	ur	**hurt**
i **fin**	w	**witch**
ī **line**	y	**yes**
îr **near**	yōō	**music**
ô **often**	yoor	**pure**
ō **note**	zh	**vision**

Buddhism The name Buddha means "enlightened one." He taught that a good cause will bring about a good consequence; bad cause, bad consequences. The ultimate goal is *nirvana*, a state of mind of complete peace. For Buddhists the wheel of life *(right)* is a symbol that life is an endless recurrence of cycles.

Left: *Buddha in a characteristic pose, with legs folded and with a restful expression.*

Saffron-robed Buddhist monks (above). They devote their time to prayer and meditation to achieve enlightenment.

Bud·dhism (bōōd′iz′əm, bood′iz′əm) *n.* the religion founded by the *Buddha*, Gautama, in the 500s B.C., which teaches spiritual purity and freedom from human concerns. – *n. & adj.* **Bud·dhist** (bōōd′əst, bood′əst).

budge (buj) *vb.* **budg·ing, budged** to move or cause to move: *I could not budge the heavy load.*

budg·et (buj′ət) *n.* a plan showing how money coming in will be spent. – *vb.* **budg·et·ing, budg·et·ed** to calculate so as not to spend more money than you earn.

●**Bue·nos Ai·res** (bwā′nəs âr′ēz′) is the capital of ARGENTINA.

buff (buf) *n.* **1** a dull yellow color. **2** a soft, undyed leather. **3** (*informal*) a person who knows a lot about, or takes great interest in, a certain subject: *Eleanor is an opera buff.*

buf·fa·lo (buf′ə-lō′) *n.* **buffalo** or **buf·fa·loes** **1** the American bison. **2** a wild or domesticated relative of the ox with long curved horns, several varieties of which are found in Asia and Africa.

●**Buf·fa·lo Bill** (buf′ə-lō′ bil) (1846-1917) was an American showman who traveled the United States and Europe with his Wild West Show. His real name was William Cody.

buf·fet¹ (bə-fā′, bōō-fā′) *n.* **1** a cold meal set out on tables from which people help themselves. **2** a sideboard for holding china, glasses, etc.

buf·fet² (buf′ət) *vb.* **buf·fet·ing, buf·fet·ed** to strike or knock about: *The ship was buffeted by the waves.*

bug (bug) *n.* **1** any insect with a flat body and a mouth which can suck blood; a bedbug. **2** any insect. **3** any germ or virus causing infection or illness: *She caught a stomach bug.* **4** a small, hidden microphone. **5** See **Computer Terms**.

bu·gle (byōō′gəl) *n.* a brass instrument like a small trumpet – *n.* **bu·gler** (byōō′glər).

build (bild) *vb.* **build·ing, built** (bilt) **1** to make or construct from parts: *Birds build nests from twigs and moss.* **2** to develop gradually: *The politician is building a good following.* – *n.* physical form, especially of the human body: *a slim build.*

build·er (bil′dər) *n.* a person who builds, or organizes the building of, houses, etc.

build·ing (bil′ding) *n.* a structure with walls and a roof.

bulb (bulb) *n.* **1** the onion-shaped part of the stem of certain plants from which the roots grow. **2** (also **light bulb**) a glass and metal device from which electric light is produced.

●**Bul·gar·i·a** (bul-gâr′ē-ə, bool-gâr′ē-ə). See Supplement, **Countries**.

bulge (bulj) *n.* a swelling, especially where you would expect to see something flat.

bulk (bulk) *n.* **1** large size; large body or shape. **2** the greater or main part of. **3** a large quantity: *We always buy in bulk.*

bull (bool) *n.* the uncastrated male of the cattle family; also the male elephant, whale, and other large animals. – **a bull in a china shop** a person who acts in a rough and careless way and is likely to break things.

bull·dog (bool′dôg′) *n.* a small, fierce, heavily built dog with a large head.

BUILDING TERMS
aqueduct a bridge that carries water across a river or valley.
barrage an artificial dam in a river.
cement a powdery substance that sets hard after being mixed with water.
foundation the underground structure supporting a building.
macadam a road surface made with small stones rolled in cement.
slate a rock that splits easily, used in roofing.

PRONUNCIATION SYMBOLS

ə **away**	lemon	focus
a	fat	oi	**boy**
ā	fade	oo	**foot**
ä	hot	ōō	**moon**
âr	**fair**	ou	**house**
e	met	th	**think**
ē	mean	th	**this**
g	get	u	**cut**
hw	**which**	ur	**hurt**
i	fin	w	**witch**
ī	line	y	**yes**
îr	near	yōō	**music**
ô	often	yoor	**pure**
ō	note	zh	**vision**

Bungalow comes from a Hindi word *bangla* meaning "belonging to Bengal," where thatched one-story houses are common.

bull·dozer (bool′dō′zər) *n.* a powerful tractor with a vertical blade at the front, for clearing the ground or making it level.

bul·let (bool′ət) *n.* a small metal cylinder with a pointed end, for firing from guns.

bul·let·in (bool′ət-n) *n.* **1** a short official statement of news issued as soon as the news is known. **2** a short leaflet produced regularly.

bull·frog (bool′frôg′, bool′fräg′) *n.* a large frog with a loud croak.

bull's-eye (bool′zī′) *n.* the small circular center of a target used in shooting, darts, etc.

bul·ly (bool′ē) *n.* **bul·lies** a person who hurts or frightens weaker or smaller people. – *vb.* **bul·lies, bul·ly·ing, bul·lied** to act like a bully.

bul·rush (bool′rush′) *n.* a tall strong grasslike water plant.

bum·ble·bee (bum′bəl-bē′) *n.* a large, hairy bee.

bump (bump) *vb.* **bump·ing, bumped** **1** to knock or hit something. **2** to hurt or damage by hitting. **3** to collide. – *n.* **1** a knock, jolt, or collision. **2** a dull sound caused by a knock or collision. **3** a lump or swelling on the body, especially one caused by a blow.

bump·y (bum′pē) *adj.* **bump·i·er, bump·i·est** having a lot of bumps: *a bumpy road.*

bun (bun) *n.* a round, often sweetened roll.

bunch (bunch) *n.* **1** a number of things fastened or growing together. **2** (*informal*) a group: *a bunch of friends.* – *vb.* **bunch·ing, bunched** to group together in a bunch.

bun·dle (bun′dəl) *n.* a number of things loosely tied together; a loose parcel.

bun·ga·low (bung′gə-lō′) *n.* a single-story house.

bunk (bungk) *n.* **1** a narrow bed attached to a wall. **2** one of two beds placed one above the other.

●**Bun·ker Hill** (bung′ker hil′), near Boston, was the first major battle of the AMERICAN REVOLUTION, fought in 1775.

buoy (bōō′ē, boi) *n.* a brightly colored floating object fastened to the bottom by an anchor, to mark a channel, to warn ships of rocks, etc.

●**Bur·bank** (bur′bangk′), **Lester** (1849-1926) was an American plant breeder who grew many new types of vegetables and flowers.

bur·den (burd′n) *n.* **1** something to be carried; a load. **2** a duty which is difficult, time consuming, costly, etc. – *vb.* **bur·den·ing, bur·dened** to load with a difficulty.

bu·reau (byoor′ō) *n.* **bu·reaus** or **bu·reaux** (byoor′ōz) **1** a chest of drawers. **2** an office or department: *Get the information from the appropriate bureau.*

bur·glar (bur′glər) *n.* a person who enters a building illegally to steal.

bur·i·al (ber′ē-əl) *n.* the burying of a dead body.

●**Bur·ki·na Fa·so** (bər-kē′nə fäs′ō). See Supplement, **Countries**.

●**Burma** (bur′ma). a former name of **Myanmar**.

burn (burn) *vb.* **burn·ing, burned** (burnd, burnt) or **burnt** (burnt) **1** to be or set on fire. **2** to damage or destroy by fire. – *n.* an injury or mark caused by fire, acid, etc.

burn·ing (bur′ning) *adj.* **1** on fire. **2** feeling extremely hot. **3** very strong or intense.

●**Burns** (burnz), **Robert** (1759-1796) was a Scottish lyric poet who wrote in the Scottish dialect.

burnt. See **burn**.

bur·row (bur′ō) *n.* a hole or tunnel dug by rabbits and other small animals for shelter. – *vb.* **bur·row·ing, bur·rowed** to make a hole or tunnel.

burst (burst) *vb.* **burst·ing, burst** **1** to break open or into pieces, usually suddenly and violently: *The balloon burst.* **2** to make your way suddenly or violently: *They burst into the room.* **3** to be full of a strong emotion: *Duncan is bursting with anger.* **4** to do something suddenly and noisily: *Jack burst out laughing.* – *n.* an instance of bursting or breaking open.

●**Bu·run·di** (boor-ōōn′dē). See Supplement, **Countries**.

bur·y (ber′ē) *vb.* **bur·ies, bur·y·ing, bur·ied** **1** to place a dead body in a grave, the sea, etc. **2** to hide in the ground: *The dog is burying a bone.*

bus (bus) *n.* a large road vehicle which carries passengers to and from stopping points.

bush (boosh) *n.* a thick, woody plant with many branches, smaller than a tree.

bushel (boosh′əl) *n.* a unit of dry measure

equaling 32 quarts (35.24 liters).

busi·ness (biz′nəs) *n.* **1** the buying and selling of goods and services. **2** a shop, firm, commercial company, etc. **3** your usual occupation, trade, or profession. **4** the things that are your proper or rightful concern: *Mind your own business.*

bust (bust) *n.* **1** the upper front part of a woman's body. **2** a sculpture of a person's head, shoulders, and chest.

bus·tle (bus′əl) *vb.* **bus·tling, bus·tled** to busy yourself noisily and energetically. *– n.* hurried, noisy activity.

bus·y (biz′ē) *adj.* **bus·i·er, bus·i·est 1** fully occupied, with a lot of work to do: *Terry was too busy to talk to me.* **2** full of activity: *a busy street.*

but (but, bət) *conj.* **1** opposite to what is expected: *She fell down but didn't hurt herself.* **2** in contrast: *You've been to Spain but I haven't.* **3** other than: *You can't do anything but wait. – prep.* except: *They are all here but him. – adv.* only: *I can but try.*

butch·er (booch′ər) *n.* a person or shop that sells meat. *– vb.* **butch·er·ing, butch·ered** to kill and prepare an animal for sale as food.

butt (but) *vb.* **butt·ing, butt·ed** to push or hit hard with the head like a goat. *– n.* a blow with the head or horns. *– vb.* **butt in** to interrupt.

but·ter (but′ər) *n.* a pale yellow solid fat made from cream or milk, which is spread on bread, etc. and used in cooking. *– vb.* **but·ter·ing, but·tered** to put butter on. *– adj.* **but·tered**. *– adj.* **but·ter·y**.

but·ter·cup (but′ər-kup′) *n.* a plant with a yellow flower shaped like a cup.

but·ter·fly (but′ər-flī′) *n.* **but·ter·flies** a type of insect with large, delicate, and usually brightly colored wings.

In the jungles of Southeast Asia and New Guinea there are vast numbers of butterflies including many varieties of birdwings (below and right). They come in all shapes and sizes, and an amazing range of beautiful patterns and dazzling colors. Males sometimes congregate in hundreds to drink from muddy river banks.

The Life Of A Butterfly
The female lays her eggs (1), the caterpillar hatches (2), eats and when fully grown spins a belt of silk and binds itself to a twig (3). It sheds its skin and becomes a pupa (4). Inside the caterpillar turns into a butterfly (5). This process is called "metamorphosis."

At rest, most butterflies fold their wings over their bodies (above), *while moths hold their wings spread out flat* (below).

The largest butterfly is the Queen Alexandra's birdwing; the smallest is the Western pygmy blue.

In A.D. 330 Constantine the Great transferred the capital of the Roman Empire from Rome to his new city (Constantinople), built on the Greek port of **Byzantium**. When the Roman empire finally collapsed in A.D. 476 Constantinople became the capital of what is called the Byzantine Empire. During the Emperor Justinian's reign (A.D. 527-A.D. 565) the empire became a center of learning and art and evolved its own form of Christianity in the Orthodox Church. It was eventually overthrown by the Turks in 1453, a date that marks the end of the Middle Ages.

Hagia Sophia— "Church of Holy Wisdom"— was built by Justinian as a Christian church, but was turned into a mosque.

The Byzantine navy had a secret weapon called "Greek Fire." It was a mixture of lime, petroleum, and sulfur, which burst into flames on contact with water.

Elaborate gold and enamel religious works of art were greatly prized.

but·tock (but′ək) *n.* **1** either of the two fleshy mounds at the hip. **2** (*in plural*) the rump.

but·ton (but′n) *n.* **1** a small usually round piece of metal, plastic, etc. sewn onto clothes, which fastens them. **2** a small round disk pressed to operate a door or bell, etc. – *vb.* **but·ton·ing, but·toned** to fasten using buttons.

but·tress (bu′trəs) *n.* a support built on to the outside of a wall.

buy (bī) *vb.* **buy·ing, bought** (bôt) to get something by paying for it. – *n.* a thing bought: *That bike was a good buy.*

buy·er (bī′ər) *n.* a person who buys; a customer.

buzz (buz) *vb.* **buzz·ing, buzzed 1** to make a continuous humming or rapidly vibrating sound like a bee. **2** to be filled with activity or excitement: *The factory is buzzing with activity.* – *n.* a buzzing sound.

buz·zard (buz′ərd) *n.* a kind of large hawk.

by (bī) *prep.* **1** next to, beside, near; past: *We drove by the house.* **2** through, along, or across: *The door was locked so we entered by the window.* **3** used to show the person or thing that does something: *John was bitten by a dog.* **4** used to show method or means: *Dan likes to travel by air.* **5** not later than: *You must be home by 10 P.M.* **6** used in stating rates of payment, etc.: *The workers are paid by the hour.* – *adv.* **1** near: *Louise lives close by.* **2** past: *Drive by without stopping.* – **by and by** after a short time.

by·pass (bī′pas′) *n.* **1** a road that avoids a busy area or town. **2** a tube inserted into a blood vessel to provide an alternative route for the blood flow, either temporarily during an operation or permanently to get around a blockage in the blood vessel.

by-prod·uct (bī′präd′əkt) *n.* **1** a substance or product obtained or formed during the making of something else. **2** an unexpected, extra result.

by·stand·er (bī′stan′dər) *n.* a person who watches but does not take part in what is happening.

●**Byrd** (burd), **Richard** (1888-1957) was an American pilot and polar explorer.

byte (bīt) *n.* a group of eight binary digits forming a unit of memory in a computer.

●**By·zan·ti·um** (bi-zant′ē-əm, bi-zan′shē-əm) was an ancient Greek city on the Bosporus. It was rebuilt in A.D. 330 by Constantine and named Constantinople. Today it is in TURKEY and is called Istanbul.

Cc

cab (kab) *n.* **1** a taxi. **2** the driver's compartment in a truck, train engine, etc.

cab·bage (kab′ij) *n.* a vegetable with green or red edible leaves forming a large round head.

cab·in (ka′bən) *n.* **1** a small house, especially one made of wood. **2** on a ship, a sleeping compartment. **3** the section of a plane for pilot and crew.

cab·i·net (kab′ə-nət) *n.* **1** a piece of furniture with shelves and doors, for storing or displaying things. **2** (often **Cabinet**) a group of official advisers to a head of state, in charge of the various departments of government.

ca·ble (kā′bəl) *n.* **1** a strong thick rope made of hemp or metal wire. **2** an enclosed set of wires carrying telephone signals or electricity.

ca·ble tel·e·vis·ion *n.* television transmitted by cable, rather than over radio waves.

cacao (kə-kou′) *n.* **cacaos** a tropical American evergreen tree that bears seeds used in making chocolate and cocoa.

cack·le (kak′l) *n.* **1** the sound that a hen or goose makes. **2** a laugh like this.

cac·tus (kak′təs) *n.* **cac·ti** (kak′tī′) or **cac·tus·es** any of many prickly desert plants whose thick stems store water.

ca·dav·er (kə-dav′ər) *n.* a dead body.

ca·det (kə-det′) *n.* a student at a military, naval, or police training school.

●**Cae·sar**(sē′zər)**, Julius** (100 B.C.-44 B.C.) was a Roman general, statesman, and author. He is most famous for his part in turning the ROMAN REPUBLIC into an empire ruled by one man. A group of enemies stabbed him to death in the forum at Rome.

cage (kāj) *n.* **1** a container with bars, etc., in which to keep captive birds or animals. **2** any structure or framework shaped like a cage. – *vb.* **cag·ing, caged** to put in a cage.

●**Cai·ro** (kī′rō), on the banks of the river NILE, is the capital of EGYPT and the biggest city in AFRICA. Nearby are the PYRAMIDS and the statue of the sphinx.

●**Ca·jun** (kā′jən) people are descended from French-speaking settlers in Louisiana. The name Cajun is a shortened form of "Acadian," because these settlers came from "Acadia" (the French name for Nova Scotia).

cake (kāk) *n.* **1** a food made by baking a mixture of flour, fat, eggs, sugar, etc. **2** a solid block of soap, etc. – *vb.* **cak·ing, caked** to dry as a hard crust; to cover in a thick crust: *His boots were caked with mud.*

●**Ca·lam·i·ty Jane** (kə-lam′ət-ē jān) (1852-1903) real name Martha Jane Canary, was an American pioneer and expert at shooting who toured in a Wild West show.

cal·ci·um (kal′sē-əm) *n.* an element (symbol **Ca**), a soft silvery metal, compounds of which are found in the ground and in such foods as milk and cheese.

The letter *C*, like all the letters, has a long history. The earliest alphabets were taken and adapted by the Greeks. The Greek *beta*, when combined with the first letter, *aleph*, gives us the word alphabet.

The Greeks passed on their letters to the Romans, who developed the alphabet we use today, although they used only capital letters. Small letters developed in the A.D. 700s.

7

An early form of the letter C, used in the Middle East more than 3,000 years ago.

Γ

This letter was taken by the Greeks and became gamma.

C

Over the years different versions of the letter C have been developed.

There are dozens of different cacti, but they all grow in hot desert climates. This is because they can store water in their fleshy stems. They are covered with prickly spines, which protect their store of water from desert animals.

Calculate comes from a Latin word meaning "pebble," because small stones were once used for counting.

cal·cu·late (kal′kyə-lāt) *vb.* **cal·cu·lat·ing, cal·cu·lat·ed 1** to work out or find out by mathematical means. **2** to make plans that depend on some possibility: *The ski shop had not calculated on a winter without snow.*

cal·cu·la·tion (kal′kyə-lā′shən) *n.* the act of calculating.

cal·cu·lat·or (kal′kyə-lāt′ər) *n.* a small electronic machine for doing mathematical calculations.

● **Cal·cut·ta** (kal-kut′ə) is the capital of the state of West Bengal in INDIA and is India's chief port.

cal·en·dar (kal′ən-dər) *n.* a table in the form of a booklet or chart that shows the months and days of the year.

calf[1] (kaf, käf) *n.* **calves** (kavz, kävz) the young of a cow, and of several other large animals.

calf[2] (kaf, käf) *n.* **calves** (kavz, kävz) the thick, fleshy, muscular back part of the leg below the knee.

● **Cal·ga·ry** (kal′gə-rē) is a city in Alberta, CANADA.

● **Cal·i·for·ni·a** (kal′ə-fôrn′yə). See Supplement, **U.S.A.**

ca·liph or **kha·lif** (kā′ləf) or (kal′əf) *n.* a title for a Muslim civil and religious leader.

call (kôl) *vb.* **call·ing, called 1** to shout or speak loudly in order to attract attention or in announcing something; to ask someone to come. **2** to telephone: *We called her from the airport.* **3** to waken: *Call me at eight.* **4** to make a visit: *We called at the neighbors'.* **5** to give a name to: *The Vikings called their new discovery Vinland.* **6** (of a bird, etc.) to make its typical or characteristic sound. − *n.* **1** a shout or cry. **2** the cry of a bird or animal: *I recognized the call of the loon.* **3** a brief visit. **4** the act of telephoning: *I'll give you a call tomorrow.* − *vb.* **call back** to telephone again; to visit again. − *vb.* **call for 1** to require: *Editing dictionaries calls for concentration.* **2** to collect; to fetch: *Kareem called for his laundry.*

cal·lig·ra·phy (kə-lig′rə-fē) *n.* handwriting as an art: *We admired the Chinese calligraphy.* − *n.* **cal·lig·ra·pher** (kə-lig′rə-fər).

cal·lus or **cal·lous** (kal′əs) *n.* an area of hard thick skin, often on the hand or foot, caused by constant pressure or rubbing: *I got a callus on my hand after sawing the logs.*

calm (käm) *adj.* **1** relaxed and in control; not anxious, upset, angry, etc.: *Dave's voice was calm despite the shock.* **2** (of weather, etc.) still, quiet, peaceful; not rough or stormy. − *vb.* **calm·ing, calmed** to make or become calmer. − *n.* **calm·ness** (käm′nəs).

cal·o·rie (kal′ə-rē) *n.* a unit of the energy-producing value of food.

Cal·vin·ism (kal′və-niz′əm) *n.* the teachings of the 16th-century Christian reformer John *Calvin* (1509-1564). − *n.* **Cal·vin·ist** (kal′və-nəst).

● **Cam·bo·di·a** (kam-bōd′ē-ə). See Supplement, **Countries.**

● **Cam·bridge** (kām′brij) **1** a city in Massachusetts, home of Harvard University. **2** a university town in eastern ENGLAND.

came. See **come.**

cam·el (kam′əl) *n.* an animal with a long neck and either one hump (the **dromedary**) or two (the **Bactrian camel**), that stores fat in its hump(s) as a source of energy, can survive long periods in the desert without food or water, and is used for carrying loads or for riding.

This stone shows the Aztec 20-day month. They had 18 months plus a final five, unlucky days.

Calligraphy is particularly beautiful handwriting, written very carefully. It is done using a pen or brush. Special documents such as scrolls or certificates are often written by a calligrapher.

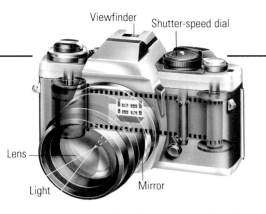

Viewfinder Shutter-speed dial

Lens

Light Mirror

cam·e·ra (kam′ə-rə, kam′rə) *n.* **1** an apparatus for taking still photographs or making moving films, with a lens through which light passes to form an image on film that is sensitive to light. **2** a similar apparatus used in television that receives the image of a scene and converts it into electrical signals.

●**Cam·e·roon** (kam′ə-roon′). See Supplement, **Countries**.

cam·ou·flage (kam′ə-fläzh′, kam′ə-fläj) *n.* **1** coloring used on military equipment, vehicles, or buildings, or for soldiers' uniforms, that imitates the colors of nature and so makes them difficult for an enemy to see. **2** coloring on an animal that blends with the animal's natural surroundings and makes it difficult to see. – *vb.* **cam·ou·flag·ing, cam·ou·flaged** to disguise or conceal with some kind of camouflage.

camp (kamp) *n.* **1** a piece of ground where people live in tents for a while. **2** a place, often in the country, where organized activities are held. **3** a permanent site where troops are housed or trained. – *vb.* **camp·ing, camped** to stay in a tent, cooking meals in the open, etc. – *n.* **camp·ing.**

cam·paign (kam-pān′) *n.* **1** an organized series of actions to gain a particular result. **2** the operations of an army while fighting in a particular area. – *vb.* **cam·paign·ing, cam·paigned** to take part in a campaign.

camp·er (kam′pər) *n.* a person who camps.

camp·site (kamp′sīt′) *n.* a piece of land for camping on.

To take a picture, the camera's shutter opens and light passes through a lens into a small aperture—the iris. There it is focused onto a light-sensitive film by a second set of lenses. The image formed is upside down.

cam·pus (kam′pəs) *n.* the grounds of a college, university, or school.

can¹ (kan, kən) *vb.* *(auxiliary)* **1** to be able to: *Can you lift that?* **2** to know how to: *Can he swim yet?* **3** to feel able to: *How can you believe that?* **4** used to express surprise: *Can it really be that late?* **5** to have permission to: *Can I take an apple?* **6** used when asking for help, etc.: *Can you give me more?*

can² (kan) *n.* a sealed metal container.

●**Can·a·da** (kan′əd-ə) is the second largest country in the world. The distance from the PACIFIC Ocean to the ATLANTIC is farther than from NORTH AMERICA to EUROPE. Most Canadians live in a narrow belt along the UNITED STATES border. The north of the country is covered by forests and lakes. The great central plains are given over to pasture and raising cattle. The west of the country is mountainous. Most Canadians speak English, but Quebec is French-speaking. The federal parliament is in Ottawa. See Supplement, **Countries**.

Ca·na·di·an (kə-nād′ē-ən) *n.* a person who comes from Canada. – *adj.* belonging to Canada.

PRONUNCIATION SYMBOLS		
ə **a**way	lemon	focus
a **fat**	oi	**boy**
ā **fade**	oo	**foot**
ä **hot**	ōō	**moon**
âr **fair**	ou	**house**
e **met**	th	**think**
ē **mean**	th	**this**
g **get**	u	**cut**
hw **which**	ur	**hurt**
i **fin**	w	**witch**
ī **line**	y	**yes**
îr **near**	yōō	**music**
ô **often**	yoor	**pure**
ō **note**	zh	**vision**

Canada is often called "the land of the future." The country's enormous mineral and oil reserves have hardly been touched.

PROVINCE OR TERRITORY	CAPITAL
1 Alberta	Edmonton
2 British Columbia	Victoria
3 Manitoba	Winnipeg
4 New Brunswick	Fredericton
5 Newfoundland	St. John's
6 Northwest Territories	Yellowknife
7 Nova Scotia	Halifax
8 Ontario	Toronto
9 Prince Edward Island	Charlottetown
10 Quebec	Quebec
11 Saskatchewan	Regina
12 Yukon Territory	Whitehorse

Until the 1500s **canals** could be built only across flat country. With the invention of the canal lock they could also be built across high ground. The Erie Canal *(below)* in New York State was completed in 1825. A total of 83 locks and a series of aqueducts allowed barges to travel through the Appalachian mountains and across gorges.

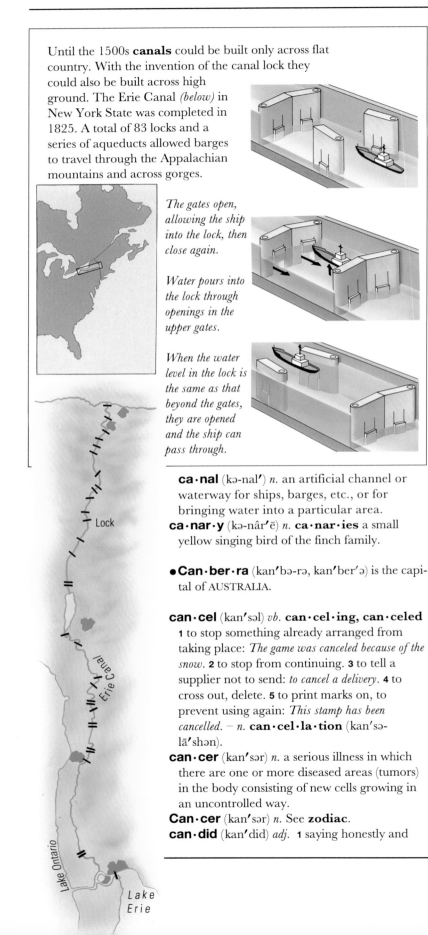

The gates open, allowing the ship into the lock, then close again.

Water pours into the lock through openings in the upper gates.

When the water level in the lock is the same as that beyond the gates, they are opened and the ship can pass through.

Lock

Erie Canal

Lake Ontario

Lake Erie

ca·nal (kə-nal′) *n.* an artificial channel or waterway for ships, barges, etc., or for bringing water into a particular area.

ca·nar·y (kə-nâr′ē) *n.* **ca·nar·ies** a small yellow singing bird of the finch family.

●**Can·ber·ra** (kan′bə-rə, kan′ber′ə) is the capital of AUSTRALIA.

can·cel (kan′səl) *vb.* **can·cel·ing, can·celed 1** to stop something already arranged from taking place: *The game was canceled because of the snow.* **2** to stop from continuing. **3** to tell a supplier not to send: *to cancel a delivery.* **4** to cross out, delete. **5** to print marks on, to prevent using again: *This stamp has been cancelled.* – *n.* **can·cel·la·tion** (kan′sə-lā′shən).

can·cer (kan′sər) *n.* a serious illness in which there are one or more diseased areas (tumors) in the body consisting of new cells growing in an uncontrolled way.

Can·cer (kan′sər) *n.* See **zodiac**.

can·did (kan′did) *adj.* **1** saying honestly and openly what you think; outspoken. **2** not posed; informal: *a candid photograph.*

can·di·date (kan′də-dāt′, kan′dəd-ət) *n.* **1** a person who is competing with others for a job, prize, political office, etc. **2** a person taking an examination.

can·dle (kan′dl) *n.* a stick of hard wax with a wick inside that is burned to provide light.

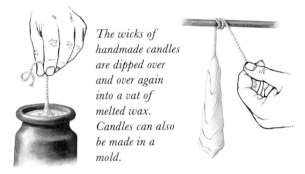

The wicks of handmade candles are dipped over and over again into a vat of melted wax. Candles can also be made in a mold.

can·dy (kan′dē) *n.* **can·dies** a sweet. – *vb.* **can·dies, can·dy·ing, can·died** to coat with sugar.

cane (kān) *n.* **1** walking stick. **2** the hollow stem of plants of the grass or reed families.

ca·nine (kā′nīn′) *adj.* of or relating to dogs or members of the dog family.

can·na·bis (kan′ə-bəs) *n.* **1** a drug obtained from the hemp plant. **2** the hemp plant itself.

can·non (kan′ən) *n.* **can·non** or **can·nons** a large gun on wheels.

can·not (kan′ät, kə-nät′, kan-ät′) *vb.* (*auxiliary*) can not.

can·ny (kan′ē) *adj.* **can·ni·er, can·ni·est** shrewd.

ca·noe (kə-nōō′) *n.* a light narrow boat moved by one or more paddles. – *vb.* **ca·noe·ing, canoed** to travel by canoe. – *n.* **ca·noe·ing.** – *n.* **ca·noe·ist** (kə-nōō′əst).

can·o·py (kan′ə-pē) *n.* **can·o·pies** a covering hung or held up over something or someone for shelter or ornament.

can·ter (kant′ər) *n.* a horse-riding pace between trotting and galloping.

●**Can·ter·bur·y** (kant′ər-ber′ē, kant′ər-brē) a cathedral and university city in Kent, England. The Archbishop of Canterbury is the senior bishop in the Church of England.

can·ti·le·ver (kan′l-ē′vər, kant′l-ev′ər) *n.* a beam or other support projecting from a wall to support a balcony or staircase, etc.

can·vas (kan′vəs) *n.* a thick cloth used for sails, tents, etc. and for painting pictures on.

can·vass (kan′vəs) *vb.* **can·vass·ing, can·vassed** to ask for votes or support for a person or proposal: *We all canvassed for Mrs. Hong in the election.*

can·yon (kan′yən) *n.* a deep river valley with steep sides; a gorge.

cap (kap) *n.* **1** a hat with a peak, of any of various types, some worn as part of a uniform or as an indication of occupation: *Nurses wear caps.* **2** a lid, cover, or top, for a bottle or pen. **3** a protective covering fitted over a damaged or decayed tooth. **4** a little metal or paper case containing a small amount of gunpowder, that explodes when struck. – *vb.* **cap·ping, capped** to put a cap on, or cover the top or end of, with a cap.

ca·pa·ble (kā′pə-bəl) *adj.* **1** having the ability or the personality for: *He was capable of much better work.* **2** clever; able; efficient.

ca·pac·i·ty (kə-pas′ət-ē) *n.* **ca·pac·i·ties** **1** the amount that something can hold. **2** ability; power: *She has a vast capacity for learning.* **3** function; role: *We are here in our capacity as referees.*

cape¹ (kāp) *n.* a short cloak.

cape² (kāp) *n.* a part of the coast that projects into the sea: *the Cape of Good Hope.*

●**Cape Horn** (kāp hôrn) is the southernmost tip of SOUTH AMERICA.

●**Cape Town** (kāp′ town) is SOUTH AFRICA's law-making capital.

●**Cape Verde** (kāp vurd′). See Supplement, **Countries**.

cap·i·tal (kap′ət-l) *n.* **1** the chief city of a country or state, usually where the government is based: *Springfield is the capital of Illinois.* **2** a capital letter used at the beginning of a sentence or a name, as in *My name is Jane.* **3** the amount of money or wealth possessed by a person or business, especially when used to produce more wealth. – *adj.* **1** chief. **2** (of a letter of the alphabet) in its large form, as used at the beginnings of names and sentences.

cap·i·tal·ism (kap′ət-l-iz′əm) *n.* an economic system based on private ownership of business and industry with free competition and profit making.

●**Cap·i·tol** (kap′ət-l) the building in Washington, D.C., where the United States CONGRESS meets. It stands on Capitol Hill.

ca·pit·u·late (kə-pich′ə-lāt′) *vb.* **ca·pit·u·lat·ing, ca·pit·u·lat·ed** to surrender and stop fighting.

Cap·ri·corn (kap′rə-kôrn′) *n.* See **zodiac**.

cap·size (kap′sīz, kap-sīz′) *vb.* **cap·siz·ing, cap·sized** (of a boat) to tip over completely.

cap·sule (kap′səl, kap′sool) *n.* **1** a small container holding a dose of medicine, that is swallowed whole and dissolves to release its contents. **2** (also **space capsule**) a part of a

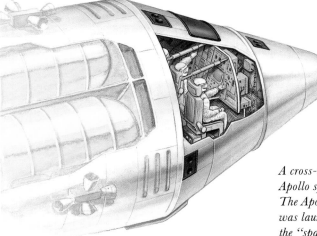

spacecraft designed to separate and travel independently.

cap·tain (kap′tən) *n.* **1** a leader, chief: *Linda was captain of the college ice hockey team.* **2** the commander of a ship or a company of troops.

cap·tion (kap′shən) *n.* the brief writing that accompanies a photograph or cartoon, etc.

cap·tive (kap′tiv) *n.* a person or animal that has been caught or taken prisoner. – *adj.* kept prisoner; unable to get away. – *n.* **cap·tiv·i·ty** (kap-tiv′ət-ē).

cap·ture (kap′chər) *vb.* **cap·tur·ing, cap·tured** **1** to catch. **2** to gain possession of.

The United States Capitol contains the chamber of the Senate in the north wing and that of the House of Representatives in the south wing. On top of the dome stands a 20-ft. (6-m) bronze statue of Freedom.

A cross-section of an Apollo space capsule. The Apollo spacecraft was launched as part of the "space race" between the United States and the former Soviet Union.

The first commercial three-wheeled, gasoline-driven **car** was produced by the German Karl Benz in 1885. Other makes soon followed, but it was Henry Ford in the United States who introduced the first successful way of producing cars quickly and inexpensively.

Karl Benz's Motorwagen—the world's first car to use an internal combustion engine.

An 1898 Renault, the world's first fully enclosed car.

An Italian racing car — the Ferrari 312T3

An aristocrat's automobile, the Bugatti Royale. Only six of these cars were built between 1927 and 1933. They had 12.8-liter, eight-cylinder engines.

Chrysler Imperial

"Much more car" for your money—American giants of the 1950s and 1960s. They were large, luxurious, and wasteful.

Cadillac

Ford Galaxie convertible

PARTS OF A CAR
accelerator a pedal that regulates engine speed by controlling fuel flow.
crankshaft is turned by the connecting rods from the pistons. The up-and-down motion of the pistons is converted into rotary motion.
disk brakes are operated by friction pads pressing against a metal disk, which turns with the wheel.
fanbelt drives the cooling fan from a pulley on the crankshaft.
spark plug a device that generates a spark to ignite the gasoline/ air mixture in the cylinder.
suspension a system of (usually) springs that supports a car's body.

Cars are quite complicated machines, made up of thousands of parts. They are driven by internal combustion engines, which burn a mixture of air and gasoline in cylinders.

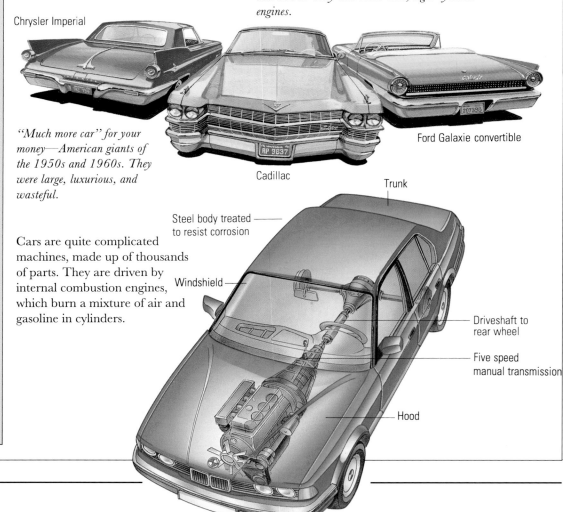

Trunk

Steel body treated to resist corrosion

Windshield

Driveshaft to rear wheel

Five speed manual transmission

Hood

car (kär) *n.* **1** a motor vehicle, usually with four wheels, for carrying a small number of people. **2** a railway carriage. **3** the enclosed part of an elevator for passengers or freight.

car·a·pace (kar′ə-pās′) *n.* the thick shell of certain creatures such as the turtle.

car·a·van (kar′ə-van′) *n.* **1** a group of travelers, usually with camels, crossing the desert on a journey. **2** any group of cars, trucks, etc. traveling together.

car·bo·hy·drate (kär′bō-hī′drāt′) *n.* a group of compounds of carbon with hydrogen and oxygen, especially the sugars and starches which form the main source of energy in food.

car·bon (kär′bən) *n.* an element (symbol **C**) found in diamonds, graphite, and charcoal, and present in all organic matter.

car·bon di·ox·ide (kär′bən dī-äk′sīd′) *n.* a gas (CO_2) present in the air, breathed out by humans and animals, and used by plants in PHOTOSYNTHESIS.

car·bu·ret·or (kär′bə-rāt′ər, kär′byə-rāt′ər) *n.* a device that mixes fuel with air and controls the amount of this mixture that is taken into an engine.

car·cass (kär′kəs) *n.* a dead body.

card (kärd) *n.* **1** a playing card. **2** a small paper or plastic rectangle, showing your identity, job, membership in an organization, etc. **3** a small plastic rectangle issued by a bank, for operating a cash machine. **4** a postcard.

card·board (kärd′bôrd′, kärd′bōrd′) *n.* a stiff material made from pulped waste paper, used for making boxes, etc.

car·di·ac (kär′dē-ak′) *adj.* relating to the heart.

●**Car·diff** (kärd′əf) is the capital of WALES.

car·di·nal (kärd′nəl, kärd′n-əl) *n.* **1** one of the leading clergymen in the ROMAN CATHOLIC CHURCH. **2** a North American songbird of which the male is bright red.

cardinal number *n.* a number expressing quantity, such as one, two, or three, as distinct from a number expressing order (an **ordinal number**), such as first, second, or third.

cardinal point *n.* any of the four main points of the compass – north, south, east, and west.

care (kâr) *n.* **1** attention: *Bill took great care with his work.* **2** caution; gentleness; regard for safety. **3** looking after someone or something, or the state of being looked after. **4** worry or anxiety: *She didn't have a care in the world.* – *vb.*

car·ing, cared 1 to mind or be upset by something: *I don't care if we have to leave the party early.* **2** to be interested in: *We all care about our welfare services.* **3** to have a wish for: *Would you care to join us?* – *vb.* **care for 1** to look after: *Nurses care for the ill.* **2** to be fond of.

ca·reer (kə-rir′) *n.* **1** your professional life; your progress in your job; **2** a job, occupation, or profession. – *vb.* **ca·reer·ing, ca·reered** to rush forward at high speed.

car·ing (kâr′ing) *adj.* showing concern for others.

ca·ress (kə-res′) *vb.* **ca·ress·ing, ca·ressed** to touch gently and lovingly. – *n.* a gentle touch.

car·go (kär′gō) *n.* **car·goes** the goods carried by a ship, aircraft, or other vehicle.

Ca·rib·be·an (kar′ə-bē′ən, kə-rib′ē-ən) *adj.* relating or belonging to the Caribbean Sea or its islands.

●**Caribbean Sea** the part of the ATLANTIC Ocean lying between the West Indies and South America.

car·i·bou (kar′ə-bōō) *n.* **caribous** or **caribou** a type of reindeer found in NORTH AMERICA.

car·i·ca·ture (kar′i-kə-choor′) *n.* a drawing of someone with their most distinctive features exaggerated for comic effect.

car·ies (kâr′ēz) *n.* (*plural*) the decay of a tooth.

●**Car·ne·gie** (kär′nə-gē, kär-neg′ē), **Andrew** (1835-1919) was a Scottish-American steel manufacturer and philanthropist.

car·ni·val (kär′nə-vəl) *n.* **1** a traveling amusement show, having games, rides, etc. **2** a period of festivity with street processions, costumes, and singing and dancing.

car·ni·vore (kär′nə-vôr′, kär′nə-vōr′) *n.* any of a group of animals with teeth specialized for eating flesh. – *adj.* **car·niv·o·rous** (kär-niv′ə-rəs).

●All carnivores have powerful jaws for chopping up their food, curved claws for tearing, and long sharp teeth for killing their victims. All have good eyesight, smell, and hearing, and are fast and intelligent.

car·ol (kar′əl) *n.* a religious song, especially one sung at CHRISTMAS.

PRONUNCIATION SYMBOLS		
ə **away**	lemon	focus
a **fat**	oi	**boy**
ā **fade**	oo	**foot**
ä **hot**	ōō	**moon**
âr **fair**	ou	**house**
e **met**	th	**think**
ē **mean**	th	**this**
g **get**	u	**cut**
hw **which**	ur	**hurt**
i **fin**	w	**witch**
ī **line**	y	**yes**
îr **near**	yōō	**music**
ô **often**	yoor	**pure**
ō **note**	zh	**vision**

A medieval carpenter at work. The design of many of the tools used then—and even in Roman times—have altered surprisingly little.

carp (kärp) *n.* a large edible fish of lakes and rivers.

car·pen·ter (kär′pən-tər) *n.* a person skilled in wood, as in building houses, or in making and repairing furniture. – *n.* **car·pen·try** (kär′pən-trē).

car·pet (kär′pət) *n.* a covering for floors, made of heavy, usually woven and tufted, fabric.

car·riage (kar′ij) *n.* **1** a four-wheeled horse-drawn passenger vehicle. **2** a light four-wheeled vehicle in which a baby is transported. **3** the way in which head and body are held; posture.

car·ri·on (kar′ē-ən) *n.* rotting flesh of dead animals.

● **Car·roll** (kar′əl), **Lewis** (1832-1898), real name Charles Dodgson, was a mathematician and writer of *Alice's Adventures in Wonderland*.

car·rot (kar′ət) *n.* a long and pointed orange-colored root vegetable.

car·ry (kar′ē) *vb.* **car·ries, car·ry·ing, car·ried 1** to hold something in your hands, have in a pocket, bag, etc., or support its weight on your body, while moving from one place to another: *We carried the groceries from the store to the car.* **2** to bring, take, or convey. **3** to have on your person: *Mark always carries a pen.* **4** to be able to be heard a distance away: *The sound of the traffic carried across the valley.* – **get carried away** (*informal*) to become over-enthusiastic.

● **Car·son** (kär′sən), **Kit** (1809-1868) was an American pioneer.

cart (kärt) *n.* **1** a two- or four-wheeled, horse-drawn vehicle. **2** a light vehicle pushed or pulled by hand.

● **Car·ti·er** (kär-tyā, kärt′ē-ā′), **Jacques** (1491-1557) was a French explorer of CANADA.

car·ti·lage (kärt′-l-ij) *n.* a tough flexible substance found in the body on the ends of the bones at joints and between the vertebrae.

car·ton (kärt′n) *n.* **1** a plastic or cardboard container in which food is packaged. **2** the amount such a container may hold.

car·toon (kär-to͞on′) *n.* **1** a humorous drawing in a newspaper, etc., often ridiculing someone or something. **2** (also **animated cartoon**) a film made by photographing a series of drawings, giving the impression of movement.

car·toon·ist (kär-to͞o′nəst) *n.* an artist who draws cartoons.

● Perhaps the most famous cartoonist was Walt Disney. His characters Mickey Mouse and Donald Duck are popular worldwide.

car·tridge (kär′trij) *n.* **1** a small case containing the explosive charge and bullet for a gun. **2** a plastic case containing film, for loading directly into a camera.

carve (kärv) *vb.* **carv·ing, carved 1** to cut wood, stone, etc. into a shape. **2** to cut meat into slices. – *n.* **carv·ing**.

cas·cade (kas-kād′) *n.* a waterfall or series of waterfalls.

case[1] (kās) *n.* **1** a box, container, or cover, for storage, protection, carrying, etc.: *My camera has a leather case.* **2** a suitcase.

— Moat

Castles were built to be safe from attack, with high, thick walls and a deep moat to prevent the enemy from getting in. Defending soldiers could fight off attacks and sit out long sieges by invading armies. Many castles were built on hills. After guns were invented in the 1300s castles were not much good as fortresses.

case² (kās) *n.* **1** a particular occasion, situation, or set of circumstances. **2** an example, instance, or occurrence. **3** a person receiving some sort of treatment or care. **4** a matter requiring investigation: *The police are looking into the case.* **5** a matter to be decided in a law court. **6** the argument for or against something with the relevant facts fully presented. – **as the case may be** according to how things turn out.

cash (kash) *n.* coins or paper money, as distinct from checks and credit cards. – *vb.* **cash·ing, cashed** to obtain or give cash in return for a check, etc.

cash flow *n.* the amount of money coming into, and going out of, a business, etc.

cash·ier (ka-shîr′) *n.* the person in a business, or store, etc. who deals with the cash.

cash·mere (kazh′mîr′, kash′mîr′) *n.* very fine soft wool from a long-haired Asian goat.

cask (kask) *n.* a barrel for holding liquids.

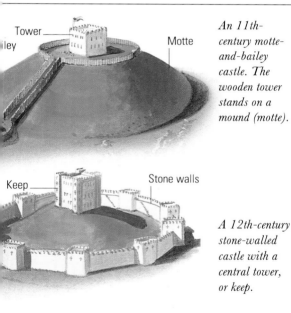

Tower
ley
Motte

An 11th-century motte-and-bailey castle. The wooden tower stands on a mound (motte).

Keep
Stone walls

A 12th-century stone-walled castle with a central tower, or keep.

A heavily fortified castle under siege. All kinds of siege machinery were needed. They included powerful catapults that hurled stones, giant siege towers, and scaling ladders.

cas·ket (kas′kət) *n.* **1** a coffin. **2** a small case for holding jewels, etc.

●**Cas·pi·an Sea** (kas′pē-ən sē) the world's largest inland body of water. It lies between the former USSR and Iran.

cas·se·role (kas′ə-rōl′) *n.* **1** a dish with a lid, in which food is cooked. **2** any food prepared in such a dish.

cas·sette (kə-set′) *n.* **1** a small sealed plastic case containing magnetic recording tape, for use in a tape recorder or video equipment. **2** a case containing a film, to load into a camera.

cast (kast) *vb.* **casting, cast 1** to throw: *Janet cast her fishing line into the stream.* **2** to turn, direct, shed, or cause to fall or rise: *cast doubt on*; *cast a shadow*; *cast a spell.* **3** to release from a secured state: *The boat was cast adrift.* **4** to shed or throw off: *Some insects cast their shells.* **5** to give an actor a part in a play or movie. **6** to shape in a mold: *They cast a bronze statue.* – *n.* **1** an act of throwing dice, a fishing line, etc. **2** an object shaped by pouring molten metal, plastic, plaster, etc. into a mold. **3** (also **plaster cast**) a covering of plaster around a broken limb to support it while it heals. **4** the set of actors or performers in a play, opera, or show.

cas·ta·nets (kas′tə-nets′) *n.* (*plural*) a Spanish musical instrument consisting of two shell-shaped pieces of wood or plastic attached to each other by string, held in the palm, and clicked together rhythmically with the fingers.

cast·a·way (kas′tə-wā′) *n.* a person who has been shipwrecked.

cas·tle (kas′əl) *n.* **1** a large fortified building with battlements and towers. **2** (also **rook** [rook]) a chess piece that can be moved any number of squares forward, backward, or sideways.

cas·trate (kas′trāt′) *vb.* **cas·trat·ing, cas·trat·ed** to remove the testicles of.

●**Cas·tro** (kas′trō), **Fidel** (1926-), the leader of CUBA's Communist regime since 1959.

ca·su·al (kazh′ə-wəl) *adj.* **1** happening by chance, without plan. **2** careless; without serious purpose: *He has a very casual attitude to work.* **3** (of clothes) informal.

cas·ual·ty (kazh′ə-wəl-tē) *n.* **cas·u·al·ties** a person who is killed or hurt in an accident or war.

Castanet comes from a Spanish word that originally meant "chestnut," because the shape of a castanet resembles a chestnut.

A feline family painting. In the back row are a lion and tiger. In the front row from left: a tabby cat, a wild cat, a lynx, a black panther, and a snow leopard.

The Charlotte Dundas, a catamaran built in 1801, had a boiler in one hull, an engine in the other, and a paddlewheel between.

cat (kat) *n.* any member of a family of four-legged furry carnivores with claws and whiskers. – **let the cat out of the bag** (*informal*) to give away a secret unintentionally.

cat·a·log or **cat·a·logue** (kat′l-ôg′, kat′l-äg′) *n.* **1** a list of items arranged in a systematic order, especially alphabetically. **2** a booklet, etc. containing a list of goods for sale.

cat·a·lyst (kat′l-əst) *n.* a substance that causes or speeds up a chemical reaction without going through a chemical change itself.

cat·a·ma·ran (kat′ə-mə-ran′, kat′ə-mə-ran′) *n.* a sailing boat with two hulls lying parallel to each other, joined across the top by the deck.

cat·a·ract (kat′ə-rakt′) *n.* **1** a condition of the eye in which the lens becomes clouded. **2** a huge, spectacular waterfall.

ca·tas·tro·phe (kə-tas′trə-fē) *n.* a great disaster, causing destruction and loss of life. – *adj.* **cat·a·stroph·ic** (kat′ə-sträf′ik).

catch (kach, kech) *vb.* **catch·ing, caught** (kôt) **1** to stop and hold: *Bill caught the falling apple.* **2** to manage to trap, especially after a hunt or chase: *Judy caught the foal.* **3** to be in time to get, reach, see, etc.: *I must catch the last train.* **4** to overtake or draw level with. **5** to discover so as to prevent the development of: *The disease can be cured if caught early.* **6** to surprise in some act; detect: *Dad caught me stealing some cookies.* **7** to become infected with: *Wrap up well so you don't catch cold.* **8** to get accidentally attached or held: *My dress caught on a nail.* – *n.* **1** an act of catching. **2** a small device for keeping a lid, door, etc. closed.

3 something caught. **4** the total amount of fish caught.

cat·e·go·ry (kat′ə-gôr′ē, kat′ə-gōr′ē) *n.* **cat·e·go·ries** a set of things classed together because of some quality or qualities they all have in common.

ca·ter (kāt′ər) *vb.* **ca·ter·ing, ca·tered** to supply food, accommodations, or entertainment for.

cat·er·pil·lar (kat′ər-pil′ər, kat′ə-pil′ər) *n.* the many-legged larva of a butterfly or moth.

ca·the·dral (kə-thē′drəl) *n.* the principal church of a diocese.

● **Cath·e·rine the Great** (kath′ə-rən, kath′rən) (1729-1796) deposed her husband, Czar Peter III, and became empress of RUSSIA in 1762.

Cath·o·lic (kath′ə-lik, kath′lik)) *adj.* **1** relating to the Roman Catholic Church. **2** relating to other churches that are descended from the original Christian church. – *n.* a member of the ROMAN CATHOLIC Church or other Catholic church.

cat·tle (kat′l) *n.* (*plural*) cows, bulls, and oxen.

caught. See **catch**.

cau·li·flow·er (kô′li-flow′ər, käl′i-flow′ər) *n.* a variety of cabbage with an edible white flower.

Cau·ca·sian (kô-kā′zhən) *n.* the division of mankind often called the white race.

cause (kôz) *n.* **1** something that produces an effect; the person or thing through which something happens: *The wind was the cause of the damage.* **2** a reason or justification. **3** an ideal, aim, etc., that people support and work for: *Training dogs for the blind is a good cause.* – *vb.* **caus·ing, caused** to bring about.

cau·tion (kô′shən) *n.* **1** care in avoiding danger. **2** a warning. **3** a scolding for an offense, with a warning not to repeat it. – *vb.* **cau·tion·ing, cau·tioned** to warn.

Cathedrals were built in many styles and with great splendor to the glory of God.

cau·tious (kô'shəs) *adj.* careful; wary.

cav·a·lier (kav'ə-lîr') *n.* **1** an armed horseman; a knight. **2** a dashing or courteous gentleman. – *adj.* thoughtless, offhand.

cave (kāv) *n.* a large natural hollow in a cliff or hillside, or underground. – *vb.* **cave in, cav·ing, caved** to collapse inwards.

cav·i·ty (kav'ət-ē) *n.* **cav·i·ties 1** a hollow or hole. **2** a hole in a tooth, caused by decay.

● **Cax·ton** (kak'stən), **William** (1421-1491) introduced the printing press to ENGLAND.

cease (sēs) *vb.* **ceas·ing, ceased** to end.

ce·dar (sēd'ər) *n.* a tall evergreen tree with spreading branches and needle-like leaves.

cede (sēd) *vb.* **ced·ing, ceded** to hand over or give up formally.

ceil·ing (sē'ling) *n.* the inner roof of a room.

cel·e·brate (sel'ə-brāt') *vb.* **cel·e·brat·ing, cel·e·brat·ed 1** to mark a success or other happy occasion, such as a birthday, with festivities. **2** to conduct a religious ceremony. – *n.* **cel·e·bra·tion** (sel'ə-brā'shən).

ce·leb·ri·ty (sə-leb'rət-ē) *n.* **ce·leb·ri·ties** a famous person.

cel·e·ry (sel'ə-rē, sel'rē) *n.* a vegetable with crisp stalks.

cell (sel) *n.* **1** a small room for an inmate in a prison or monastery. **2** the smallest unit of living matter. **3** a battery.

cel·lar (sel'ər) *n.* a room or series of rooms, usually underground, used for storage.

cel·lo (chel'ō) *n.* **cel·los** a stringed musical instrument similar to a violin but much larger.

cel·lu·lar (sel'yə-lər) *adj.* composed of cells.

cellular phone *n.* a movable telephone operating on radio signals that are passed on from one area to another.

cel·lu·lose (sel'yə-lōs') *n.* the substance of which the cell walls of plants chiefly consist.

Cel·si·us (sel'sē-əs, sel'shəs) *adj.* according to the scale on a centigrade thermometer.

● Invented by the Swedish scientist, Anders **Celsius** (1701-1744), this scale is divided into 100 degrees. Zero degrees is the temperature at which water freezes, 100 degrees is boiling point.

Celt (kelt, selt) *n.* a member of one of the ancient peoples that inhabited most parts of EUROPE in pre-Roman and Roman times, or of the peoples descended from them, now

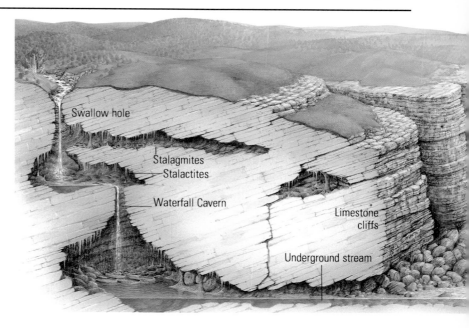

Swallow hole

Stalagmites
Stalactites

Waterfall Cavern

Limestone cliffs

Underground stream

mostly in SCOTLAND, WALES, and IRELAND.

Celt·ic (kel'tik, sel'tik) *adj.* relating to the Celts.

ce·ment (si-ment') *n.* a gray powder consisting of clay and lime, to which sand and water are added to produce mortar or concrete. – *vb.* **ce·ment·ing, ce·ment·ed** to stick together with cement; to cover with cement.

cem·e·te·ry (sem'ə-ter'ē) *n.* **ce·me·ter·ies** a burial ground for the dead.

cent (sent) *n.* a coin of the United States, Canada, and certain other countries worth a hundredth of the dollar.

cen·taur (sen'tôr') *n.* See **Myths and Legends**.

cen·ter (sent'ər) *n.* **1** a part at the middle of something. **2** a point inside a circle or sphere that is an equal distance from all points on the circumference or surface. **3** a central area. **4** a place where a particular activity is concentrated: *a sports center.* **5** a person or thing that acts as a focus of interest. – *adj.* at the center; central. – *vb.* **cen·ter·ing, cen·tered 1** to place in or at the center. **2** to focus your thoughts.

center of gravity *n.* the point on a body at which it balances.

cen·ti·grade (sent'ə-grād') *adj.* **1** (of a scale) divided into 100 degrees. **2** same as **Celsius**.

cen·ti·me·ter or (*British*) **cen·ti·me·tre** (sent'ə- mēt'ər) *n.* the 100th part of a meter.

cen·ti·pede (sent'ə-pēd') *n.* a small insectlike creature with a long body of many sections, each section having a pair of legs.

Most caves are formed in limestone and are the result of the rock being dissolved or worn away by water mixed with carbon dioxide over thousands of years. Scientists who study caves are known as speleologists.

PRONUNCIATION SYMBOLS			
ə	away lemon		focus
a	fat	oi	boy
ā	fade	oo	foot
ä	hot	o͞o	moon
âr	fair	ou	house
e	met	th	think
ē	mean	t͟h	this
g	get	u	cut
hw	which	ur	hurt
i	fin	w	witch
ī	line	y	yes
îr	near	yo͞o	music
ô	often	yoor	pure
ō	note	zh	vision

cen·tral (sen′trəl) *adj.* **1** at, or forming, the center of something; near the center: *The bus station is in a central part of the city.* **2** principal or chief: *Tom Sawyer is the central character in Mark Twain's famous novel.*

●**Cen·tral Af·ri·can Re·pub·lic** (sen′trəl af′ri-kən ri-pub′lik). See Supplement, **Countries.**

●**Cent·ral A·mer·i·ca** (sen′trəl ə-mer′i-kə) is the name for the neck of land between MEXICO and COLOMBIA that joins NORTH and SOUTH AMERICA. It consists of the independent republics of COSTA RICA, EL SALVADOR, GUATEMALA, HONDURAS, NICARAGUA, PANAMA, and BELIZE.

central bank *n.* a bank, such as the Federal Reserve in the United States, that issues currency and overseas lending and other banking practices in a country.

cen·trif·u·gal (sen-trif′yə-gəl, sen-trif′ə-gəl) *adj.* describing the force that appears to keep a circling body away from the center it is revolving around.

cen·tri·fuge (sen′trə-fyōōj) *n.* a device that rotates at high speeds in order to separate substances by means of centrifugal force: *the pharmacist separated the liquids in his centrifuge.*

cen·tu·ri·on (sen-toor′ē-ən, sen-tyoor′ē-ən) *n.* in the army of ancient Rome, the commander of a century.

cen·tu·ry (sen′chə-rē) *n.* **cen·tu·ries** **1** a period of 100 years: *From 1894 to 1994 is a century.* **2** in the army of ancient Rome, a company of (originally) one hundred foot soldiers.

ce·ram·ics (sə-ram′iks) *n.* (*singular*) the art of making pottery: *The pupils are learning about ceramics in their art class.*

ce·re·al (sir′ē-əl) *n.* **1** any plant that produces an edible grain: *Wheat, oats, and rice are cereals.* **2** a breakfast food prepared from grain. – *adj.* relating to edible grains.

cer·e·mo·ni·al (ser′ə-mō′nē-əl) *adj.* used for, or involving, a ceremony.

cer·e·mo·ny (ser′ə-mō′nē) *n.* **cer·e·mo·nies** a ritual or formal act performed to mark a particular occasion. – **stand on ceremony** to insist on behaving formally.

cer·tain (surt′n) *adj.* **1** definite or known beyond doubt; absolutely sure. **2** particular, and, though known, not named or specified: *I met a certain friend of yours.*

cer·tain·ly (surt′n-lē) *adv.* without any doubt; definitely.

cer·tain·ty (surt′n-tē) *n.* **cer·tain·ties** something that cannot be doubted or is bound to happen.

cer·tif·i·cate (sur-tif′i-kət) *n.* an official document that formally states particular facts (*a marriage certificate*), an achievement, or qualification (*a first aid certificate*).

cer·ti·fy (sur′tə-fī′) *vb.* **cer·ti·fies, cer·ti·fy·ing, cer·ti·fied** to declare or confirm officially.

●**Cer·van·tes** (sər-van′tēz′), **Miguel de** (1547-1616) was a Spanish writer best known for his novel, *Don Quixote de la Mancha.*

●**Cé·zanne** (sā-zan′, sā-zän′), **Paul** (1839-1906) was a French painter noted for his solid shapes and use of tones of color.

●**Chad** (chad). See Supplement, **Countries.**

●**Cha·gall** (shə-gäl′, shə-gal′), **Marc** (1887-1985) was a Russian-born painter, best known for his stage sets, tapestries, and stained glass.

chain (chān) *n.* **1** a series of connected links or rings, usually of metal. They are used to fasten, hold, support, or to transmit motion. **2** any series of things connected: *a chain of events.* **3** a number of stores, hotels, etc. under common ownership. **4** in chemistry, a number of atoms linked in a series to form a molecule. – *vb.* **chain·ing, chained** to fasten with a chain.

chain·saw (chān′sô′) *n.* a power-driven saw, the blade of which is a fast-revolving chain made of metal teeth.

chair (chār) *n.* **1** a seat for one person, with a back support and usually four legs. **2** a chairperson. – *vb.* **chair·ing, chaired** to control a meeting.

---

cereal and serial sound the same, but a cereal is a plant that produces grain, whereas a serial is a story told in episodes.

Cereals belong to the grass family. Rice is the main food crop for more than half the world's population.

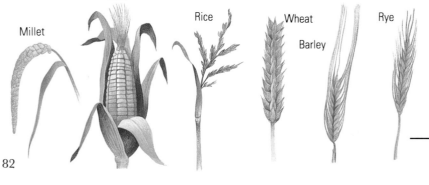

Millet
Corn
Rice
Wheat
Barley
Rye

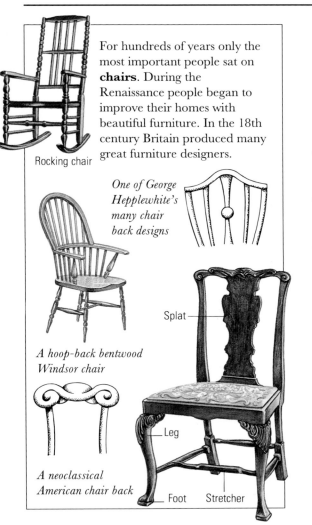

For hundreds of years only the most important people sat on **chairs**. During the Renaissance people began to improve their homes with beautiful furniture. In the 18th century Britain produced many great furniture designers.

Rocking chair

One of George Hepplewhite's many chair back designs

A hoop-back bentwood Windsor chair

Splat

A neoclassical American chair back

Leg

Foot   Stretcher

chair·per·son (châr′pur′sən) *n.* a person in charge of a meeting, a board, an institution, etc.: *She was chairperson of the English Department.*

chal·et (shal-ā′) *n.* a style of house typical of Alpine regions, with a sloping roof.

chalk (chôk) *n.* **1** a soft white rock composed of calcium carbonate from fossilized sea shells. **2** a stick of this substance used for writing.

chal·lenge (chal′ənj) *vb.* **chal·leng·ing, chal·lenged 1** to call on someone to take part in a fight or contest: *Matthew challenged him to a duel.* **2** to test, especially in a stimulating way: *This puzzle will challenge you.* – *n.* an invitation to a contest. – *n.* **chal·leng·er.**

cham·ber (chām′bər) *n.* **1** a bedroom or other private room. **2 chambers** (*plural*) the office of a judge. **3** hall for the meeting of an assembly, especially a legislative body. **4** a legislative or judicial branch of government.

cha·me·le·on (kə-mēl′yən, kə-mē′lē-ən) *n.* a type of lizard that changes color to match its surroundings.

cham·o·mile (kam′ə-mīl′, kam′ə-mēl′) *n.* a sweet-smelling herb with white or yellow flowers which are used for tea and medicine.

cham·pi·on (cham′pē-ən) *n.* **1** in games, competitions, etc., a competitor that has defeated all others. **2** the supporter or defender of a person or cause. – *vb.* **cham·pi·on·ing, cham·pi·oned** to strongly support or defend a person or cause.

chance (chans) *n.* **1** the way that things happen unplanned and unforeseen. **2** a possibility or probability: *There is a chance it may snow.* **3** a possible or probable success: *I don't stand a chance.* **4** an opportunity: *This is your big chance to meet the president.* **5** a risk: *It looks like rain, but I'll take a chance.* – *vb.* **chanc·ing, chanced 1** to risk. **2** to do or happen by chance.

chan·cel·lor (chan′sə-lər) *n.* the head of the government in certain European countries.

change (chānj) *vb.* **chang·ing, changed 1** to make or become different; to alter: *Jan changed her hairstyle.* **2** to give, leave, or substitute one thing for another: *Can I change this hat for another?* **3** to exchange, usually your position, with another person, etc.: *Do you mind if we change places?* **4** to remove clothes, etc. and replace them with clean or different ones. **5** to make into or become something different. **6** to obtain or supply another kind of money for: *Can you change these dollars into quarters?* **7** on a trip, to leave one vehicle and get into another: *You must change trains at Chicago.* – *n.* **1** the process of changing or an instance of it. **2** a variation from your regular habit: *Let's eat out for a change.* **3** money returned from the amount given in payment.

chan·nel (chan′l) *n.* **1** a natural or artificial water course, such as the bed of a stream or an irrigation ditch. **2** a narrow stretch of water joining two seas. **3** a set of frequencies on which television or radio programs are transmitted.

The chameleon is a remarkable lizard. It can change color to suit its surroundings or mood; it can move its eyes independently of each other; and it has a tongue that shoots out at lightning speed to a length greater than its body.

Of the 80 films that Chaplin made, probably the best known are The Kid *(1921),* City Lights *(1931), and* The Great Dictator *(1940), the "talkie" in which he satirized the German Nazi dictator, Adolf Hitler.*

The Egyptians, Assyrians (below), Greeks, and Romans (right) all built chariots.

chant (chant) *vb.* **chant·ing, chant·ed** to recite in a singing voice; to keep repeating, especially loudly and rhythmically: *The football crowd chanted "Touchdown.".* – *n.* a type of singing used in religious services.

Cha·nu·kah (hän′ə-kə, khän′ə-kə). Same as **Hanukkah.**

cha·os (kā′äs) *n.* complete confusion; utter disorder. – *adj.* **cha·ot·ic** (kā-ät′ik). – *adv.* **cha·ot·i·cal·ly** (kā-ät′i-klē).

chap·el (chap′əl) *n.* a small church.

chap·lain (chap′lən) *n.* a clergyman or -woman attached to a school, hospital, etc.

● **Chap·lin** (chap′lən), **Charles** (1889-1977) was an English-American movie star whose role as a baggy-trousered tramp endeared him to millions.

chap·ter (chap′tər) *n.* a main part of a book: *The book I'm reading has 17 chapters.*

char·ac·ter (kar′ik-tər) *n.* **1** the combination of qualities that makes up a person's nature or personality; the qualities that typify anything. **2** strong, admirable qualities such as determination, courage, and honesty. **3** interesting qualities: *We've bought a house with character.* **4** a person in a story or play.

char·ac·ter·is·tic (kar′ik-tə-ris′tik) *adj.* **1** typical. **2** distinctive. – *adv.* **char·ac·ter·is·ti·cal·ly.**

char·ac·ter·ize or **char·ac·ter·ise** (kar′ik-tə-rīz′) *vb.* **char·ac·ter·iz·ing, char·ac·ter·ized 1** to describe; give the chief qualities of. **2** to be a distinctive and typical feature of.

char·coal (chär′kōl′) *n.* a form of carbon, produced by partially burning wood, used for drawing and as a fuel.

charge (chärj) *vb.* **charg·ing, charged 1** to ask for as the price of something; to ask someone for an amount as payment. **2** to record as a debt against: *Charge the damages to me.* **3** to accuse officially. **4** to rush at in attack: *The bull charged at the dog.* **5** to give a task to: *He was charged with looking after the books.* **6** to fill up with electricity: *We charged the battery.* – *n.* **1** a price, cost, or fee. **2** control, care, responsibility: *The police arrived and took charge.* **3** something of which you are accused: *She was arrested on a charge of murder.* **4** a rushing attack: *The cavalry charge saved the day.*

char·i·ot (char′ē-ət) *n.* a two-wheeled vehicle pulled by two or more horses, used in ancient times in war or for racing. – *n.* **char·i·o·teer** (char′ē-ə-tir′).

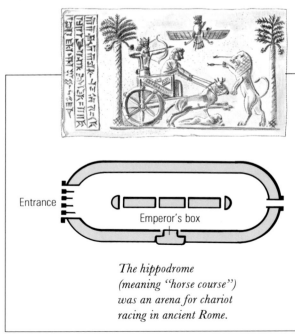

Entrance

Emperor's box

The hippodrome (meaning "horse course") was an arena for chariot racing in ancient Rome.

char·i·ta·ble (char′ət-ə-bəl) *adj.* **1** generous to those in need. **2** of or concerned with charity. **3** kind and understanding toward others.

char·i·ty (char′ət-ē) *n.* **char·i·ties 1** assistance given to those in need. **2** an organization established to provide such assistance.

●**Char·le·magne** (shär′lə-mān′) (747-814) was king of the Franks and extended his territory into GERMANY and ITALY. He tried hard to maintain the customs and traditions of the lands he conquered, and was a patron of learning.

●**Charles** (chärlz)**, Prince of Wales** (1948-) is the eldest son and heir of ELIZABETH II.

●**Charles I** (chärlz) (1600-1649) was king of ENGLAND and SCOTLAND. After the English Civil War he was beheaded.

charm (chärm) *n.* **1** the power of delighting, attracting, or fascinating. **2** (in *plural*) delightful qualities possessed by a person, place, or thing. **3** an object believed to have magical powers: *A rabbit's foot was his lucky charm.*

charm·ing (chär′ming) *adj.* delightful; pleasing; attractive.

chart (chärt) *n.* **1** a map, especially one designed to aid navigation by sea or air, or one on which weather developments are shown. **2** information presented as a diagram.

chart·er (chärt′ər) *n.* **1** a document guaranteeing certain rights and privileges issued by a ruler or government. **2** the hire of aircraft, buses, etc. for private use. — *vb.* **chart·er·ing, chart·ered 1** to hire by charter. **2** to give a charter to.

chase (chās) *vb.* **chas·ing, chased 1** to go after in an attempt to catch: *The dog chased after the rabbit.* **2** to force away, out, etc.: *Edna chased the pigeons away.* **3** to rush; to hurry.

chasm (kaz′əm) *n.* a deep crack in the ground, found for example close to a cliff edge: *The explorers had to stop at the chasm.*

chat (chat) *vb.* **chat·ting, chat·ted** to talk in a friendly, informal way. — *n.* informal, familiar talk; a friendly conversation.

chat·ter (chat′ər) *vb.* **chat·ter·ing, chat·tered 1** to talk rapidly and unceasingly, usually about trivial matters. **2** (of the teeth) to keep knocking together because of cold or fear.

chat·ter·box (chat′ər-bäks′) *n.* a person who talks continuously.

●**Chau·cer** (chô′sər), **Geoffrey** (1345-1400) was an early English writer. He wrote *The Canterbury Tales.*

Geoffrey Chaucer on horseback, from a manuscript of his works.

THE COOK (from *The Canterbury Tales*)

A Cook they hadde with hem for the nones
 They had a Cook with them who stood alone
To boille the chicknes with the marybones
 For boiling chicken with a marrow-bone
And poudre-marchant tart and galyngale
 Sharp flavoring-powder and a spice for savor
Wel koude he knowe a draughte of London ale,
 He could distinguish London ale by flavor,
He coude rooste, and sethe, and broille, and frye,
 And he could roast and seethe and broil and fry,
Maken mortreux, and wel bake a pye.
 Make good thick soup and bake a tasty pie
 Geoffrey Chaucer (*with a translation by Nevill Coghill, Penguin*)

---

cheap (chēp) *adj.* **1** low in price; less than the usual price; good value for money. **2** low in price but of poor quality. — *n.* **cheap·ness.**

cheat (chēt) *vb.* **cheat·ing, cheat·ed 1** to trick, deceive, swindle. **2** to act dishonestly so as to gain an advantage: *Martin cheats at cards.*

check (chek) *vb.* **check·ing, checked 1** to investigate or inspect. **2** to hold back, stop: *She nearly swore, but checked herself.* **3** to mark with a check. **4** to leave in someone's temporary care: *We checked our coats at the restaurant.* **5** to test the accuracy of: *Check your answers.* — *n.* **1** an inspection or investigation: *We were delayed by the unexpected Customs check at the airport.* **2** a printed form on which to fill in instructions to a bank to pay a person or organization a certain amount of money. **3** a bill for a meal in a restaurant. **4** a pattern of squares.

check·ers (chek′ərz) *n.* a game for two people in which 24 pieces are moved across a board with red and black squares.

check·mate (chek′māt′) *n.* in chess, a winning position, putting your opponent's king under an attack from which it cannot escape.

check·up (chek′up′) *n.* a thorough examination, especially a medical one.

cheek (chēk) *n.* **1** either side of the face below the eye. **2** rude speech or behavior.

PRONUNCIATION SYMBOLS			
ə	**away** lemon		focus
a	**fat**	oi	**boy**
ā	**fade**	oo	**foot**
ä	**hot**	o͞o	**moon**
âr	**fair**	ou	**house**
e	**met**	th	**think**
ē	**mean**	<u>th</u>	**this**
g	**get**	u	**cut**
hw	**which**	ur	**hurt**
i	**fin**	w	**witch**
ī	**line**	y	**yes**
îr	**near**	yo͞o	**music**
ô	**often**	yoor	**pure**
ō	**note**	zh	**vision**

Cheetahs have a top speed of nearly 60 mph (100 km/h). Unlike other cats that stalk their prey slowly and pounce, cheetahs chase their prey.

cheer (chir) *n.* a shout of approval or encouragement. – *vb.* **cheer·ing, cheered** to give approval or encouragement by shouting: *They came to cheer her on.* – *vb.* **cheer up** to make or become more cheerful.

cheer·ful (chir′fəl) *adj.* **1** happy; optimistic. **2** in a good mood; willing – *n.* **cheer·ful·ness.**

cheer·lead·er (chîr′lēd′ər) *n.* a person who directs the cheering section at a sports event.

cheese (chēz) *n.* a soft or hard food made from milk.

chee·tah (chēt′ə) *n.* a large long-legged spotted animal of the cat family found in AFRICA and ASIA, the fastest running of all mammals.

chef (shef) *n.* the chief cook in a restaurant, etc.

● **Che·khov** (chek′ôf, chek′ôv), **Anton** (1860-1904) was a Russian playwright. His works include *Uncle Vanya* and *The Cherry Orchard.*

chem·i·cal (kem′i-kəl) *adj.* relating to, or made using, chemistry or chemicals. – *n.* a substance produced by or used in chemistry.

chem·ist (kem′əst) *n.* **1** a scientist specializing in chemistry. **2** (*British*) a pharmacist.

chem·is·try (kem′ə-strē) *n.* the science of elements and compounds and how they work together.

● The true science of chemistry began in the 1600s when chemists discovered the elements, simple substances which make up all other substances.

cher·ish (cher′ish) *vb.* **cher·ish·ing, cher·ished** to care for lovingly.

● **Cher·no·byl** (chər-nō′bəl) is a city in UKRAINE where, in April 1986, explosions at a nuclear power station caused a serious escape of radio-activity.

● **Cher·o·kees** (cher′ə-kēz) are a NATIVE AMERICAN people who now live in Oklahoma.

cher·ry (cher′ē) *n.* **cher·ries** a small round red, yellow, or dark purple fruit with a pit.

chess (ches) *n.* a board game for two people each with 16 playing pieces, the most important pieces being the kings. The object of the game is to trap your opponent's king.

chest (chest) *n.* **1** the part of the body between the neck and the waist that contains the heart and lungs, or the front part of this. **2** a big, strong, box with a hinged lid used for storage or transport.

chest·nut (ches′nut′) *n.* a reddish-brown edible nut with a prickly covering.

● **Chev·ro·let** (shev′rə-lā′), **Louis** (1879-1941) an American racing driver and car manufacturer.

chew (choo) *vb.* **chew·ing, chewed** to use the teeth to crush food before swallowing.

● **Chey·enne** (shī-an′) are a tribe of NATIVE AMERICANS of Montana and Oklahoma.

chic (shēk) *adj.* elegant or fashionable.

● **Chi·ca·go** (shə-käg′ō, shə-kô′gō) is a city in Illinois on Lake Michigan. Its O'Hare Airport is the busiest in the world. The first skyscraper was built there in 1884.

chick (chik) *n.* a baby chicken or other bird.

chick·en (chik′ən) *n.* the farmyard fowl bred for its eggs and flesh; its flesh used as food.

chick·en·pox (chik′ən-päks′) *n.* a mild infectious disease, especially of childhood, with itchy spots.

chief (chēf) *n.* **1** a leader; the person in charge of any group, organization, etc. **2** the head of a tribe or clan.– *adj.* most important.

chief·tain (chēf′tən) *n.* the head of a tribe or clan; a leader or commander.

chil·blain (chil′blān′) *n.* a painful itchy red swelling usually on the fingers or toes.

child (chīld) *n.* **chil·dren** (chil′drən) **1** a boy or girl who is not an adult. **2** someone's son or daughter: *Mary is my friend's only child.*

child·hood (chīld′hood′) *n.* the state or time of being a child.

Male domestic chickens (cockerels or roosters) have a fleshy comb and wattles at the sides of the beak.

child·ish (chīl′dish) *adj.* silly; immature.

● **Chi·le** (chil′ē, chē′lā). See Supplement, **Countries**.

chil·i (chil′ē) *n.* **chil·ies 1** a hot red pepper. **2** (also **chili con carne**) a dish made of meat, hot pepper, and beans.

chill (chil) *n.* **1** a feeling of coldness: *There's a wintry chill in the air.* **2** a feverish cold. **3** a sudden feeling of fear. **4** a coldness of manner; hostility. – *vb.* **chill·ing, chilled** to make or become cold: *Mark chilled the wine.*

chill·ing (chil′ing) *adj.* frightening.

chill·y (chil′ē) *adj.* mildly cold. – *n.* **chill·i·ness** (chil′ē-nəs).

chime (chīm) *n.* a set of tuned bells; the sound made by them.

chim·ney (chim′nē) *n.* **chimneys** a narrow shaft through which smoke from a fire in a furnace, stove, or fireplace escapes.

chim·pan·zee (chim′pan′zē′, chim-pan′zē) *n.* an African ape.

● Chimpanzees can walk upright although they often use their hands to help push themselves along the ground. They live in family groups and are very fond of their young. They are playful and intelligent animals.

chin (chin) *n.* the part of your face below your mouth. – **keep your chin up** (*informal*) to stay cheerful in spite of misfortune.

● **Chi·na** (chī′nə) is the nation with the biggest population (one billion). The HIMALAYAS and deserts cut China off from its Asian neighbors. Most people live in the east along the great rivers, YANTZE and HUANG HO. China has an ancient civilization. For most of its history it was an empire. In 1949 it became a communist republic. Its capital is Beijing and its principal language is Mandarin Chinese. See also Supplement, **Countries**.

Chi·nese (chī-nēz′, chī-nēs′) *n.* **1** a native of CHINA. **2** a person of Chinese descent. **3** the language of the main ethnic group of CHINA. – *adj.* of CHINA, its people, etc.

The giant panda is found in the bamboo forests of western China. It is in danger of extinction.

The earliest ancient Chinese civilization grew up on the banks of **China**'s great rivers. The farmers relied on the rivers for water to grow crops and for transportation. The first dynasty (ruling family) we know of was called the Shang (ca 1500 B.C.). They grew crops, kept animals, and wove silk. The Chou dynasty (ca 1027 B.C.) used iron for weapons and tools. The Chi'n dynasty (ca 221 B.C.) united a vast empire, but was soon succeeded by the Han dynasty, which ruled until A.D. 220.

The bronze model of a horse and chariot was made in the A.D. 100s. Chinese art also included carving, painting, and fine porcelain.

我要马上找医生
我这里痛上
请别理得太短

The Chinese language is written in picture-signs, or characters. There are more than 40,000 characters, but a Chinese person can manage with 5,000. While Chinese is written the same through the country, the spoken language varies from area to area with hundreds of dialects. The most common is Mandarin.

The Chinese began building the Great Wall of China more than 2,000 years ago to keep out enemies from the north. Stretching 1,500 miles (2,400 km), it is the longest wall in the world.

chink (chingk) *n.* a small slit or crack: *Light shone through the chink in the door.*

chip (chip) *vb.* **chip·ping, chipped 1** to knock or strike small pieces off a hard object or material; to be broken off in small pieces. **2** to shape by chipping. — *n.* **1** a small piece chipped off: *a chip of marble.* **2** a place from which a piece has been chipped off. **3** a thin slice of food: *a potato chip.* **4** (*British*) a french-fried potato. **5** a plastic counter used as a money token in gambling. **6** (also **mi·cro·chip** [mī′krō-chip′] or **silicon chip**) a very small piece of silicon, on which a large amount of information can be stored electronically.

A microchip contains thousands of electronic components all mounted in a single block of plastic. Microchips can perform at almost the speed of light, more than a million operations per second.

chip·munk (chip′mungk′) *n.* a small striped relative of the squirrel.

chirp (chûrp) *vb.* **chirp·ing, chirped** a short high sound made by birds, grasshoppers, etc.

chis·el (chiz′əl) *n.* a tool with a strong metal blade, used for shaping wood or stone.

●**Chis·holm** (chiz′əm), **Shirley** (1924-) was the first black woman to be elected to the United States House of Representatives.

chlo·rine (klôr′ēn′, klōr′ēn′) *n.* an element (symbol **Cl**), a poisonous strong-smelling gas used in bleaches and disinfectants.

chlo·ro·phyll (klôr′ə-fil′, klōr′ə-fil′) *n.* the green coloring matter in plants that absorbs the energy from the sun.

choc·o·late (chäk′lət, chôk′lət) *n.* the roasted and ground seeds of the cacao, a tropical American tree, used in the form of a powder, paste, or solid block.

choice (chois) *n.* **1** the act or process of choosing: *I've made my choice in this matter.* **2** the right, power, or opportunity to choose: *I'd rather not go but I have no choice.* **3** something or someone chosen: *It was a good choice.* — *adj.* of specially good quality: *These are choice tomatoes.*

choir (kwīr) *n.* a group of singers.

choke (chōk) *vb.* **chok·ing, choked** to be prevented, wholly or partially, from breathing.

cho·les·te·rol (kə-les′tə-rôl′) *n.* a fatty substance found in body tissues and in animal fats. It is thought to cause fatty deposits in the blood vessels that narrow and harden them.

choose (chōōz) *vb.* **choosing, chose** (chōz), **cho·sen** (chō′zən) **1** to select one or more things or persons from a larger number. **2** to decide; to think fit: *She chose to travel alone.*

chop (chäp) *vb.* **chop·ping, chopped 1** to cut with a vigorous downward or sideways slicing action, with an ax, knife, etc. **2** to reduce or cut off: *to chop funds.* — *n.* **1** a slice of pork, lamb, or mutton containing a bone, especially a rib. **2** a chopping action or stroke.

chop·sticks (chäp′stiks′) *n.* (*plural*) slender sticks, used in pairs for eating by the Chinese, Japanese, and others.

●**Cho·pin** (shō-pan′), **Frédéric** (1810-1849) was a Polish-born composer of piano works.

chore (chôr, chōr) *n.* a boring task.

cho·re·og·ra·phy (kôr′ē-äg′rə-fē) *n.* the arrangement of the sequence and pattern of movements in dancing. — *n.* **cho·re·og·ra·pher** (kôr′ē-äg′rə-fər).

cho·rus (kôr′əs, kōr′əs) *n.* **1** a set of lines in a song, sung after each verse. **2** a large choir.

chose, chosen. See **choose.**

chris·ten (kris′ən) *vb.* **chris·ten·ing, chris·tened** to give a person a name, as part of the religious ceremony of receiving him or her into the Christian Church. — *n.* **chris·ten·ing** (kris′ə-ning, kris′ning).

Chris·tian (kris′chən) *n.* a person who believes in, and follows the teachings and example of, JESUS CHRIST.

●Christians believe that JESUS CHRIST is the son of God. They read of his teachings, life, and death by crucifixion in the New Testament of the BIBLE. Christianity teaches that salvation is achievable through Jesus.

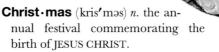

Christ·mas (kris′məs) *n.* the annual festival commemorating the birth of JESUS CHRIST.

chron·i·cle (krän′i-kəl) *n.* a record of events in the order in which they happened.

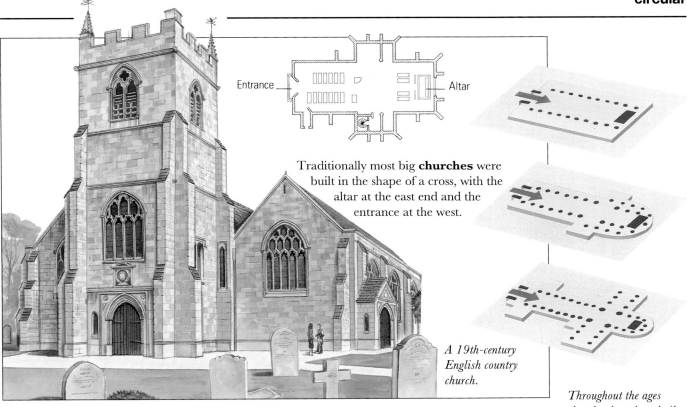

Entrance — Altar

Traditionally most big **churches** were built in the shape of a cross, with the altar at the east end and the entrance at the west.

A 19th-century English country church.

Throughout the ages churches have been built in many different styles; but all serve the same purpose, as places for prayer and the performing of religious services and as places that house all kinds of religious objects.

church (church) *n.* **1** a building for public Christian worship. **2** the profession of the clergy. **3** Christian services.

● **Churc·hill** (chur′chil′, church′hil′), **Winston** (1874-1965) was a British statesman and prime minister (1940-1945).

churn (churn) *n.* a container in which milk is shaken to make butter. – *vb.* **churn·ing, churned** to move or cause to move violently: *The storm churned the ocean waves.*

chut·ney (chut′nē) *n.* a spicy relish.

● **Cid, El** (el sid′) (1040-1099) was a Spanish hero in Spain's struggle against the Moors.

ci·der (sīd′ər) *n.* a juice or an alcoholic drink made from apples.

cin·der (sin′dər) *n.* a piece of burnt coal or wood.

● **Cin·de·rel·la** (sin′də-rel′ə) is a character in a fairy tale by Perrault, and a symbol of a person whose merits and charms go unnoticed.

cin·e·ma (sin′ə-mə) *n.* **1** a theater in which motion pictures are shown. **2** the art or

business of making movies.

● The art of making motion pictures came from an invention called the kinetoscope, built by an American, Thomas Edison, in 1891. At about the same time the French Lumière brothers invented a similar machine and, in 1896, gave the world's first public movie show, in Paris.

cin·na·mon (sin′ə-mən) *n.* a spice obtained from the bark of an Asian tree.

ci·pher (sī′fər) *n.* a secret code.

cir·cle (sur′kəl) *n.* **1** a line evenly and continuously curved so as to form a round figure, with every point on it an equal distance from the center. **2** anything in the form of a circle: *We sat around the reader in a circle.* **3** a group of people associated in some way: *I met his circle of friends.* – *vb.* **cir·cling, cir·cled** to move in a circle; to draw a circle around.

cir·cuit (sur′kət) *n.* **1** a complete course, journey, or route around something. **2** the regular trip from one place to another taken as part of one's job. **3** the area in which such a trip is made: *She was made judge of this circuit.* **4** the path of an electric current.

cir·cu·lar (sur′kyə-lər) *adj.* having the form of a circle.

cir·cu·late (sur′kyə-lāt′) *vb.* **cir·cu·lat·ing, cir·cu·lat·ed 1** to move around freely, especially in a fixed route. **2** to spread; to pass around: *Please circulate the report.*

cir·cu·la·tion (sur′kyə-lā′shən) *n.* **1** the act of circulating. **2** the flow of blood around the body. **3** the number of copies sold of a newspaper, etc.

cir·cum- round about.

cir·cum·cise (sur′kəm-sīz′) *vb.* **cir·cum·cis·ing, cir·cum·cised** to cut away the foreskin of the penis. – *n.* **cir·cum·ci·sion** (sur′kəm-sizh′ən).

circumference (sir **kum** fĕ rĕns) *n.* the outer line or edge of a circle.

cir·cum·stance (sur′kəm-stans′) *n.* a fact, occurrence, or condition, relating to an act or event: *He died in mysterious circumstances.*

cir·cus (sur′kəs) *n.* a traveling company of performers including acrobats, clowns, etc.

cis·tern (sis′tərn) *n.* a tank storing water.

cit·i·zen (sit′ə-zən) *n.* **1** a member of a country by birth or by naturalization. **2** an inhabitant of a city or town. – *n.* **cit·i·zen·ship** (sit′ə-zən-ship′).

cit·ric acid (si′ trik as′əd) *n.* a weak acid found in citrus fruits.

cit·rus (si′trəs) *n.* any tree of the group that includes the lemon and orange.

cit·y (sit′ē) *n.* **cit·ies** any large or major town.

civ·il (siv′əl) *adj.* **1** relating to the community and citizens of a country: *We heard about the civil disturbances.* **2** relating to ordinary citizens; not military, legal, or religious. **3** polite.

civil engineer *n.* someone who designs and builds roads, bridges, tunnels, etc.

ci·vil·ian (sə-vil′yən) *n.* anyone who is not in the armed forces or the police.

civ·i·li·za·tion (siv′ə-lə-z′shən) *n.* **1** the state of being civilized; the act of civilizing. **2** a stage of development in human society that is socially, politically, culturally, and technologically advanced.

civ·i·lize (siv′ə-līz′) *vb.* **civ·i·liz·ing, civ·i·lized** to educate and enlighten.

civil rights *n.* (*plural*) the personal rights of any citizen, especially to freedom and equality regardless of race, religion, sex, or sexuality.

civil war *n.* a war between citizens of the same country.

● **Civil War, American** (1861-1865) was fought between the government (Union) and the South-

The American Civil War
When Abraham Lincoln was elected president in 1860, the South feared that he would abolish slavery and the southern economy would suffer as a result. Eleven southern states seceded and formed the Confederate States of America. The war started on April 12, 1861. More than 600,000 Americans died. But the Union was preserved.

States of the Union
Confederate States

The rapid-fire gun, the Gatling gun, developed in 1861 by the American inventor Richard Gatling.

The major battles of the American Civil War were fought in the east and southeast of the United States.

Ulysses S. Grant (left) *(1822-1885) was the commander of the Union forces. He was tough and determined.*
Robert E. Lee (right) *(1807-1870) led the forces of the South.*

The English Civil War
King Charles I believed in "divine right," claiming his right to rule came directly from God. He quarreled with parliament over taxes and his right to imprison those who opposed him. In 1629 he dissolved parliament and for 11 years tried to rule alone. The first major battle of the war took place at Edgehill in 1642; the last at Worcester in 1651.

A musketeer of the New Model Army, which defeated the Royalists.

Oliver Cromwell, who led the Roundheads to victory over the King.

Charles was tried for treason and executed.

The Confederates won the first big battle of the war at Bull Run, Virginia in 1861.

ern states (Confederacy). The main quarrel was over slavery. After the Confederate army was defeated, slaves were freed.

● **Civil War, English** (1642-1649) was fought between the Royalists under CHARLES I and the Parliamentarians over the king's right to raise taxes. The Royalists lost the war and the king was executed.

claim (klām) *vb.* **claim·ing, claimed 1** to state something firmly, insisting on its truth: *John claimed he had seen a ghost.* **2** to demand as a right or as your own: *The settlers claimed the area.* – *n.* **1** a statement you insist is true. **2** a demand for something that you believe you have a right to.

clam·my (klam′ē) *adj.* **clam·mi·er, clam·mi·est** moist or damp: *Nick has clammy hands.*

clamp (klamp) *n.* a tool with adjustable jaws for gripping things firmly; a fastening device, used in woodwork, etc. – *vb.* **clamp·ing, clamped** to hold with a clamp.

clan (klan) *n.* a group of families, as in Scotland, generally with the same surname.

clap (klap) *vb.* **clap·ping, clapped** to strike the palms of your hands together with a loud noise; to applaud. – *n.* an act of clapping.

clar·i·fy (klar′ə-fī′) *vb.* **clar·i·fies, clar·i·fy·ing, clar·i·fied** to make easier to understand.

clar·i·net (klar′ə-net′) *n.* a woodwind instrument with keys and a single reed. **clar·i·net·ist** (klar′ə-net′əst).

clar·it·y (klar′ət-ē) *n.* the state or quality of being clear; clearness.

clash (klash) *n.* **1** a loud noise, like pieces of metal striking each other. **2** a serious disagreement; a quarrel or argument. – *vb.* **clash·ing, clashed 1** to strike against each other noisily. **2** to fight; to disagree violently. **3** to conflict: *Those colors clash.*

clasp (klasp) *n.* **1** a fastening on jewelry, a bag, etc. **2** a firm grip, or act of gripping. – *vb.* **clasp·ing, clasped 1** to take hold of firmly. **2** to fasten or secure with a clasp.

class (klas) *n.* **1** a lesson. **2** a number of pupils taught together. **3** a category or type. – *vb.* **class·ing, classed** to put into a category.

clas·sic (klas′ik) *adj.* of the highest quality; established as the best. – *n.* an established work of literature: *The Iliad is a Greek classic.*

Scottish clans carried on bitter feuds—the Macdonalds and Campbells, for example, were longstanding enemies. Each clan was distinguished by its tartan.

Nails and claws are made of hard skin, like animals' horns. When they are broad and flat they are called nails, but if they are sharp and pointed they are called claws. If you take a close look, an animal's claws will tell you about its way of life. Cats and birds of prey have very sharp claws. They are hooked for holding onto and tearing prey.

CLICHE CORNER...
Clichés are words or phrases that have been used too often and so have become tired and trite. Here are some clichés using "twinned" words:
by leaps and bounds
nook and cranny
to pick and choose
tooth and nail
trials and tribulations
slow but sure
fast and furious
give-and-take

---

clas·si·cal (klas′i-kəl) *adj.* **1** of ancient Greek and Roman literature, art, etc. **2** showing the influence of ancient Greece and Rome in architecture, etc. **3** having an established formal style: *He prefers classical music.*

clas·si·fy (klas′ə-fī′) *vb.* **clas·si·fies, clas·si·fy·ing, clas·si·fied** to put into a particular group.

clause (klôz) *n.* a simple sentence, or part of a sentence that has its own subject and verb.

claus·tro·pho·bia (klô′strə-fō′bē-ə) *n.* fear of being in confined spaces. – *adj.* **claus·tro·pho·bic** (klô′strə-fō′bik).

claw (klô) *n.* one of the sharply pointed hooked nails of an animal or bird; the foot of an animal or bird with claws: *Lions have sharp claws.*

clay (klā) *n.* soft sticky earth that can be formed into pottery, bricks, etc. and baked hard.

clean (klēn) *adj.* **1** free from dirt. **2** not containing anything harmful to health; pure: *clean water.* **3** unused; unmarked: *Write on a clean sheet of paper.* **4** neat and even: *It was a clean cut.* **5** clear of legal offenses: *She has a clean driving record.* **6** (of nuclear installations, etc.) not producing a harmful level of radioactivity. – *vb.* **clean·ing, cleaned 1** to make free from dirt. **2** to dust, polish floors and furniture, etc.

clean·ly (klēn′lē) (*adv., adj.*) **clean·li·er, clean·li·est.** *adv.* smoothly and easily. – (klen′lē) *adj.* clean by habit: *a cleanly person.* – *n.* **cleanliness** (klen′lē-nəs).

clear (klîr) *adj.* **1** easy to see through. **2** (of weather, etc.) not misty or cloudy. **3** easy to see, hear, or understand: *Your simple explanation makes it clear.* **4** bright; sharp: *What a clear photograph!* **5** free from flaws or blemishes: *Her skin is clear.* **6** well away from: *Stay well clear of the rocks.* **7** free from guilt, etc.: *My conscience is clear.* – *adv.* **1** in a clear manner. **2** completely: *They got clear away.* **3** out of the way of: *Keep or steer clear of trouble!* – *vb.* **clear·ing, cleared 1** to make or become clear, free of obstruction, etc. **2** to move out of the way. **3** to prove to be innocent. – *n.* **clearness** (klîr′nəs).

clear·ing (klîr′ing) *n.* an area in a forest, etc. that has been cleared of trees, etc.

clear·ly (klîr′lē) *adv.* obviously.

clench (klench) *vb.* **clench·ing, clenched** to close tightly: *John clenched his fist in anger.*

● **Cle·o·pat·ra** (klē′ə-pa′trə) (69 B.C.-30 B.C.) was Queen of Egypt.

cler·gy (klur′jē) *n.* **cler·gies** (*plural* or, sometimes, *singular*) ministers, priests, and rabbis.

cler·i·cal (kler′i-kəl) *adj.* **1** relating to clerks, office workers, or office work. **2** relating to the clergy.

clerk (klurk) *n.* a person in an office or bank who deals with letters, accounts, files, etc.

● **Cleve·land** (klēv′lənd), Ohio is a major port on Lake ERIE.

clev·er (klev′ər) *adj.* good or quick at learning and understanding: *Mary is clever at math.*

cli·ché (klē-shā′, kli-shā′, klē′shā) *n.* a phrase that has become stale through repetition.

click (klik) *n.* a short sharp sound like that of two parts of a mechanism locking into place.

cli·ent (klī′ənt) *n.* a person using the services of a lawyer, bank, etc.

North Pole

Rays hit Earth at an angle

Rays hit Earth directly

South Pole

Places near the equator get more of the sun's rays than those farther north or south.

cli·mate (klī′mət) *n.* the average weather conditions of a particular region or part of the world.

cli·max (klī′maks′) *n.* the high point of a series of events or of an experience.

climb (klīm) *vb.* **climb·ing, climbed** to go toward the top of a hill, ladder, etc.

cling (kling) *vb.* **cling·ing, clung** (klung) to hold tightly; to stick: *Mud clings to your boots.*

clin·ic (klin′ik) *n.* a department of a hospital where outpatients receive treatment or advice without staying overnight.

● **Clin·ton** (klint′n), **William Jefferson** (1946-) was elected president of the UNITED STATES in 1992. He was governor of Arkansas 1978-1980 and 1982-1992.

clip (klip) *vb.* **clip·ping, clipped** **1** to cut or trim, as with scissors or shears. **2** to cut out.

cloak (klōk) *n.* a loose outdoor garment, usually sleeveless. − *vb.* **cloak·ing, cloaked** to cover up or conceal: *The affair was cloaked in mystery.*

The first mechanical clocks, driven by weights, appeared around 1300 in Europe, and the pendulum clock in 1656. Today's electric clocks are remarkably accurate.

A ship's chronometer of the 1700s, with a slowly unwinding spring.

This clock's pendulum controls its speed.

clock (kläk) *n.* an instrument for measuring and showing time by means of pointers on a dial or displayed figures. − **against the clock** very fast, because of lack of time. − **around the clock** throughout the day and night.

clock·wise (kläk′wīz′) *adj. & adv.* in the same direction as the moving hands of a clock.

clock·work (kläk′wurk′) *n.* a mechanism like that of a clock, working by means of gears and a spring. − *adj.* operated by clockwork.

clod (kläd) *n.* a lump of earth or clay, etc.

clog (klôg, kläg) *n.* a shoe carved from wood. − *vb.* **clog·ging, clogged** to block.

clois·ter (kloi′stər) *n.* a covered walk built against the wall of a church, college, etc.

close¹ (klōs) *adj.* **1** near in space or time; at a short distance: *at close range.* **2** near in relationship, friendship **3** dense or compact; with little space between. **4** (of a contest) with little difference between entrants. **5** stuffy.

close² (klōz) *vb.* **clos·ing, closed** **1** to shut: *Please close the window.* **2** to finish; to come or bring to an end: *The meeting closed with the national anthem.* − *n.* an end or conclusion. − *vb.* **close in** to come nearer and surround: *The enemy closed in on them.* − *vb.* **close down 1** (of a business) to close permanently. **2** (of a television or radio station) to stop broadcasting

at the end of the day.

closed *adj.* shut; blocked.

clot (klät) *n.* a soft mass, especially of solidified liquid matter such as blood. − *vb.* **clot·ting, clot·ted** to form into clots.

cloth (klôth) *n.* **cloths** (klôthz, klôths) woven or knitted material.

clothe (klōth) *vb.* **cloth·ing, clothed** to cover or provide with clothes.

clothes (klōthz, klōz) *n.* (*plural*) things people wear to cover the body for warmth or decoration.

● Cloth fabric from as far back as 6000 B.C. has been found. Once the secret of weaving had been discovered, it spread around the world.

cloth·ing (klō′thing) *n.* clothes.

cloud (kloud) *n.* **1** a gray or white mass floating in the sky, made of particles of water or ice. **2** a mass of dust or smoke in the air. **3** a mass of things in motion: *A cloud of locusts.* − *vb.* **cloud·ing, cloud·ed** to become overcast with clouds. − *adj.* **cloud·less** (klowd′ləs). − **on cloud nine** (*informal*) extremely happy.

cloud·y (kloud′ē) *adj.* **cloud·i·er, cloud·i·est 1** full of clouds; overcast. **2** (of a liquid) not clear; milky.

Clouds form when water vapor condenses into droplets. Three main types of cloud are cirrus (streaky), cumulus (fluffy) and stratus (layer). Heights are indicated by: cirro (very high), alto (high), strato (low), and nimbo (rain cloud).

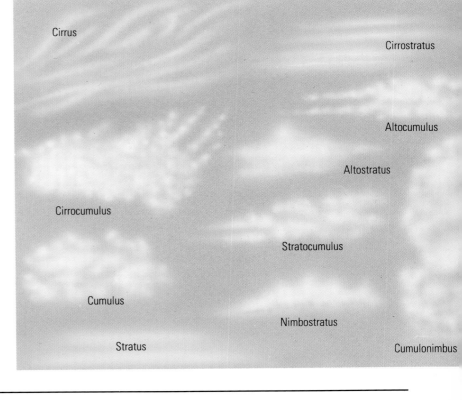

clove (klōv) *n.* the strong-smelling dried flower-bud of a tropical tree, used as a spice.

clo·ver (klō′vər) *n.* a plant grown as cattle fodder, with leaves divided into usually three parts and pink, purple, or white flowers.

clown (kloun) *n.* a comic performer in a circus or pantomime, usually wearing ridiculous clothes and makeup. – *vb.* **clown·ing, clowned** to behave ridiculously.

club (klub) *n.* **1** a stick, usually thicker at one end, used as a weapon. **2** a stick with a specially shaped head, for playing golf. **3** a society or association; the place where such a group meets. **4** a playing card of the suit **clubs,** bearing a black clover-shaped symbol. – *vb.* **club·bing, clubbed 1** to beat or strike with a club. **2** to contribute money for a special purpose: *The class clubbed together and bought the teacher a present.*

clue (kloo) *n.* a fact which helps to solve a problem, crime, or mystery.

clump (klump) *n.* **1** a group of like things placed or standing close together. **2** a dull heavy sound. **3** a mass or lump. – *vb.* **clump·ing, clumped 1** to walk with a heavy tread. **2** to form into clumps.

clum·sy (klum′zē) *adj.* **clum·si·er, clum·si·est** not skillful with the hands; awkward.

clung. See **cling.**

clus·ter (klus′tər) *n.* **1** a small group or gathering. **2** a number of flowers growing together on one stem.

clutch (kluch) *vb.* **clutch·ing, clutched** to grasp tightly: *Sheila clutched her little brother's hand.* – *n.* **1** (usually in *plural*) control or power: *He is in his boss's clutches.* **2** a pedal in a motor vehicle that you press when changing gear.

clut·ter (klut′ər) *n.* an untidy accumulation of things. – *vb.* **clut·ter·ing, clut·tered** to overcrowd or make untidy.

coach (kōch) *n.* **1** a railroad car for passengers. **2** (*British*) a bus. **3** a trainer or instructor in a sport, or a private tutor. **4** a large closed horse-drawn carriage. – *vb.* **coach·ing, coached** to train in a sport, or teach privately.

coal (kōl) *n.* a hard black mineral made of carbon formed by decayed and compressed plants, mined and used as a fuel.

coarse (kôrs, kōrs) *adj.* **1** rough or open in texture. **2** crude; not refined. – *n.* **coarse·ness.**

coast (kōst) *n.* the edge of the land, alongside the sea; the seaside or seashore. – *adj.* **coast·al** (kōs′təl).

Coast Guard *n.* a branch of the United States military that protects its coasts and waterways.

coast·line (kōst′līn′) *n.* the shape of the coast.

coat (kōt) *n.* **1** an outer garment with long sleeves usually worn outdoors. **2** the hair, fur, or wool of an animal. **3** a covering or application of paint, dust, sugar, etc. – *vb.* **coat·ing, coat·ed** to cover with a layer of something. – *n.* **coat·ing.**

coax (kōks) *vb.* **coax·ing, coaxed** to persuade using flattery, promises, kind words, etc.

cob (käb) *n.* **1** a strong horse with short legs. **2** a corncob. **3** a male swan.

cob·web (käb′web′) *n.* a web made by a spider.

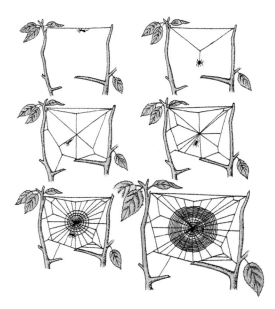

Nature at its most fascinating—a spider spins a beautifully constructed web. It lays out a line of silk as it moves around, anchoring it at intervals in much the same way as a mountaineer with a safety line.

co·caine (kō-kān′) *n.* a habit-forming drug derived from the leaves of a tropical plant and used in medicine to deaden pain.

cock (käk) *n.* **1** a male bird. **2** a valve or faucet.

cock·a·too (käk′ə-too′) *n.* a large, pale-colored crested parrot of Australia.

Cock·ney (Käk′nē) *n.* a dialect of English spoken in London, England.

cock·roach (käkr′ōch′) *n.* a large black or brown beetlelike insect.

Coal is found in seams or layers under the ground. It is called a fossil fuel because it was made from dead plants millions of years ago. The dead plants in swamps first became peat and under great pressure turned into coal. The hardest coal is known as anthracite.

Coal forests

Peat is buried and compressed

Anthracite

Lignite

co·coa (kō′kō) *n.* **1** a powder made from the roasted and ground seeds of the cacao tree. **2** a hot drink made with this powder.

co·co·nut (kō′kə-nut′) *n.* the large oval fruit of the **coconut palm**. It has a hard hairy brown shell filled with solid edible white flesh and a whitish sweet liquid (**coconut milk**).

co·coon (kə-kōōn′) *n.* the silky casing spun around itself by an insect larva, inside which it transforms into its adult form.

cod (käd) *n.* **cod** a large edible white fish.

code (kōd) *n.* **1** a system of words, letters, or symbols, used in place of those really intended, for secrecy or brevity. **2** a set of signals for sending messages, etc. **3** in computing, a set of programming instructions. **4** a set of principles of behavior. − *vb.* **cod·ing, cod·ed** to put into a code.

● **Codes** using the alphabet can usually be broken by experts because they know that some letters occur more often than others. In English *e*, *t*, *a*, and *o* are the most common letters.

● **Cod·y** (kōd′ē), **William**. See **Buffalo Bill**.

coe·la·canth (sē′lə-kanth′) *n.* a primitive fish believed extinct until one was found in 1938.

cof·fee (kô′fē) *n.* a tropical shrub whose roasted and ground seeds (beans) are used to make a drink.

cof·fer (kô′fər) *n.* a large chest.

cof·fin (kô′fən) *n.* a box in which to bury or cremate a corpse.

cog (käg) *n.* one of a series of teeth on the edge of a wheel which turns a similar wheel.

co·her·ent (kō-hir′ənt) *adj.* **1** logically and clearly developed; consistent: *Her argument was coherent.* **2** speaking intelligibly. − *n.* **co·her·ence** (kō-hir′əns).

coil (koil) *vb.* **coil·ing, coiled** to wind around and around in loops to forms rings or a spiral. − *n.* something looped into a spiral.

coin (koin) *n.* a small stamped piece of metal used as money.

coin·age (koi′nij) *n.* the currency of a country.

co·in·cide (kō′ən-sīd′) *vb.* **co·in·cid·ing, co·in·cid·ed** **1** to happen at the same time. **2** to agree: *Your ideas coincide with mine.*

co·in·ci·dence (kō-in′sə-dəns) *n.* a combination of events happening by chance: *It was a coincidence that we both have red hair.*

coke (kōk) *n.* the solid fuel left after gases have been extracted from coal.

cold (kōld) *adj.* **1** having a low temperature; not hot or warm. **2** unfriendly. − *n.* **1** lack of heat or warmth; cold weather. **2** an illness of the nose and throat, with running nose, sneezing, coughing, etc. − *n.* **cold·ness** (kōld′nəs).

cold-blood·ed (kōld′blud′əd) *adj.* (of fish, reptiles, etc.) having a body temperature that varies with that of the environment.

● **Co·le·ridge** (kō′lə-rij), **Samuel Taylor** (1772-1834) was an English poet. He wrote *The Rime of the Ancient Mariner.*

col·i·se·um (käl′ə-sē′əm) *n.* a large stadium or amphitheater for sports, entertainment, etc.

col·lab·o·rate (kə-lab′ə-rāt′) *vb.* **col·lab·o·rat·ing, col·lab·o·rat·ed** to work together with others on something.

col·lage (kə-läzh′) *n.* a design or picture made by pasting pieces of paper or cloth, or parts of photographs, etc. to a background surface.

col·lapse (kə-laps′) *vb.* **col·laps·ing, col·lapsed** **1** to fall, give way, or cave in. **2** to drop exhausted or helpless: *The hikers collapsed in the heat.* **3** to break down emotionally. **4** to fold up compactly for storage or space-saving.

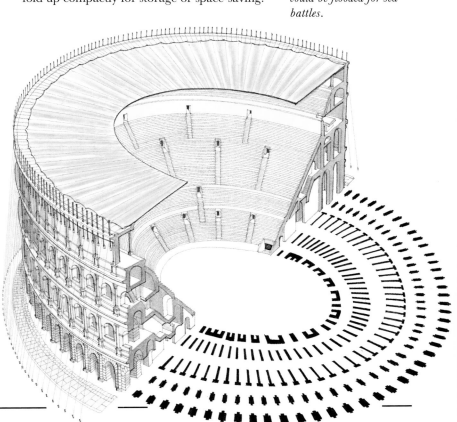

The Colosseum in Rome was a giant sports stadium holding more than 50,000 people. It was started in A.D. 72. A sheet, or awning, could be put over the spectators to protect them from the sun or bad weather. The arena (floor) was used for gladiatorial combats and could be flooded for sea battles.

Sunlight looks colorless, but it is really a mixture of **colors**. We can see the colors when the light from the sun is shone through a glass prism. The spectrum, or rainbow of colors, that comes out of the prism are red, orange, yellow, green, blue, indigo, and violet.

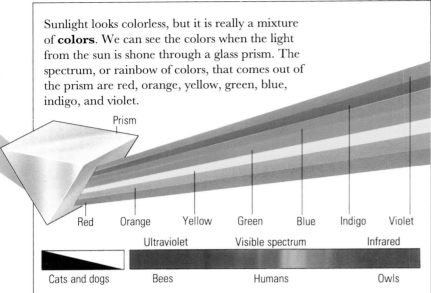

Prism

Red Orange Yellow Green Blue Indigo Violet

Ultraviolet | Visible spectrum | Infrared

Cats and dogs | Bees | Humans | Owls

Not all animals can see light from the same part of the spectrum.

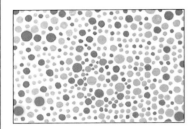

People who are color-blind cannot tell some colors apart. If your color vision is normal you should be able to see the number 6.

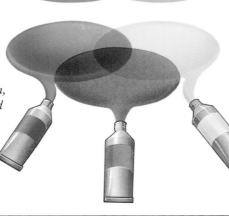

The three "primary colors" when mixing light are red, green, and blue. Added together, these primary colors make white light; but they can be mixed in such a way as to give virtually any other color.

The "primary colors" of paint, or the primary pigment colors, are red, yellow, and blue, or more accurately, magenta, yellow, and cyan. All three added together make brown, or they can be mixed in such a way as to make all other colors.

col·lar (käl′ər) *n.* **1** a band or flap around the neck of a garment; the neck of a garment: *There is a mark on your shirt collar.* **2** a band placed around the neck of a dog, etc.

col·lar·bone (käl′ər-bōn′) *n.* either of two bones linking the shoulder blades to the breastbone.

col·league (käl′ēg′) *n.* a fellow worker.

col·lect (kə-lekt′) *vb.* **col·lect·ing, col·lect·ed 1** to bring or come together; to gather; to accumulate. **2** to build up an assortment of things of a particular type: *collect stamps.* **3** to call for and pick up: *They collect the garbage on Mondays.*

col·lec·tion (kə-lek′shən) *n.* an accumulated assortment of things of a particular type.

col·lege (käl′ij) *n.* a school attended after high school that awards a bachelor's degree.

col·lide (kə-līd′) *vb.* **col·lid·ing, col·lid·ed** to crash into: *The motorbike collided into the wall.*

col·lie (käl′ē) *n.* a long-haired kind of sheepdog.

col·li·sion (kə-lizh′ən) *n.* a crash.

col·lo·qui·al (kə-lō′kwē-əl) *adj.* (of language) used in informal conversation.

●**Co·lom·bi·a** (kə-lum′bē-ə). See Supplement, **Countries**.

co·lon[1] (kō′lən) *n.* a punctuation mark (:), used to introduce a list or an example.

co·lon[2] (kō′lən) *n.* the main part of the large intestine, above the rectum.

colo·nel (kur′nəl) *n.* an army officer, in charge of a regiment, below a brigadier in rank.

col·o·nize (käl′ə-nīz′) *vb.* **col·o·niz·ing, col·o·nized** to establish a colony or settlement in.

col·o·ny (käl′ə-nē) *n.* **col·o·nies 1** a settlement abroad controlled by the founding country; the settlers living there. **2** a group of animals, birds, etc. of one type living together.

col·or (kul′ər) *n.* **1** red, blue, green, etc. **2** a property that surfaces have when light falls on them and is reflected or absorbed: *The lake is a clear blue color.* **3** a coloring substance, especially paint. − *vb.* **col·or·ing, col·ored 1** to put color on; to paint or dye. **2** to influence.

●**Col·o·ra·do** (käl′ə-räd′ō, käl′ə-rad′ō). See Supplement, **U.S.A.**

col·or-blind (kul′ər-blīnd′) *adj.* unable to

distinguish certain colors. – *n.* **col·or·blind·ness** (kul′ər-blīnd′nəs).

col·ored (kul′ərd) *adj.* **1** having colors in addition to black and white. **2** of or relating to nonwhite, especially Negro people. This term is considered offensive by many.

col·or·ful (kul′ər-fəl) *adj.* **1** full of bright color. **2** lively or interesting: *She is a colorful character.*

co·los·sal (kə-läs′əl) *adj.* huge; vast.

colt (kōlt) *n.* See **Horse Terms.**

● **Co·lum·bus** (kə-lum′bəs), **Christopher** (1451-1506) was a Genoese sailor and explorer who discovered AMERICA for SPAIN in 1492 while seeking a westward route to the Spice Islands of the East Indies.

col·umn (käl′əm) *n.* **1** in architecture, a usually cylindrical pillar with a base and capital. **2** something similarly shaped: *A column of smoke rose from the chimney.* **3** a vertical row of numbers: *He added up the column of figures.* **4** a vertical strip of print on a newspaper page; a regular section in a newspaper.

col·um·nist (käl′əm-nəst) *n.* a person writing a regular section of a newspaper.

● **Co·man·che** (kə-man′chē), a NATIVE AMERICAN tribe, now in Oklahoma.

comb (kōm) *n.* **1** a rigid toothed object for tidying and arranging hair. **2** the fleshy crest on the head of some cock birds.

com·bat (käm′bat′) *n.* fighting; a struggle. – *vb.* **com·bat** (kəm-bat′, käm′bat′) **com·bat·ing, com·bat·ed** to fight against.

com·bine (kəm-bīn′) *vb.* **com·bin·ing, com·bined** to join together; to unite.

com·bi·na·tion (käm′bə-nā′shən) *n.* a group of things, people, etc. combined; the resulting mixture or union.

com·bus·tion (kam-bus′chən) *n.* the process of catching fire and burning.

come (kum) *vb.* **com·ing, came** (kām), **come 1** to move in the direction of the speaker. **2** to reach a place; to arrive. **3** to form in the mind, etc.: *She came to the conclusion it was a good idea.* **4** to meet with: *I hope they don't come to any harm.* **5** to extend to or reach a level or standard. **6** to total: *That comes to $20.* **7** to have as a source or place of origin: *Where does he come from?* **8** to happen: *How did he come to hurt himself?* **9** to turn out: *Her wish came true.* – *vb.* **come**

On the first of his four voyages Columbus discovered the Bahamas and went on to explore Cuba.

The Niña, *the* Pinta, *and the* Santa Maria *set sail for the New World in August 1492.*

across to discover; to encounter. – *vb.* **come along 1** to progress; to improve. **2** to hurry up. – *vb.* **come back** to be recalled to mind: *It's all coming back to me now.* – *vb.* **come through** to survive.

co·me·di·an (kə-mēd′ē-ən) *n.* an entertainer who tells jokes, performs comic sketches, etc.

co·me·di·enne (kə-mēd′ē-en′) *n.* a woman who entertains by telling jokes, etc.

com·e·dy (käm′əd-ē) *n.* **com·e·dies** an amusing play or movie with a happy ending.

com·et (käm′ət) *n.* a heavenly body with a tail-like trail, traveling around the Sun.

● The tail of a comet always points away from the Sun. The head is a frozen ball of ice, dust, and chunks of rock. The most famous comet is Halley's Comet which returns to Earth every 76 or 77 years. It is due to return in 2062.

A comet tail is so fine that a rocket can pass through it unharmed. Comets are believed to be leftover particles from the beginning of the solar system.

COME, COME
A phrasal verb is a verb that is combined with an adverb or with a preposition. Examples using "come" are: come about; come across; come along; come back; come down; come from; come in; come into; come out; come over; come around; come through; come up; come under.

PRONUNCIATION SYMBOLS

ə	away	lemon	focus
a	fat	oi	boy
ā	fade	oo	foot
ä	hot	ōō	moon
âr	fair	ou	house
e	met	th	think
ē	mean	th	this
g	get	u	cut
hw	which	ur	hurt
i	fin	w	witch
ī	line	y	yes
îr	near	yōō	music
ô	often	yoor	pure
ō	note	zh	vision

The Commonwealth of Independent States (CIS) was formed in 1991 as an attempt to preserve a loosely unified association of independent ex-Soviet republics, following the breakup of the Soviet Union. At nearly 6.6 million sq. miles (17 million sq. km), Russia—the largest CIS member—is easily the world's biggest country by area.

com·fort (kum'fərt) *n.* **1** a pleasant feeling of physical and mental contentedness or well-being. **2** a person or thing that provides such relief or consolation. – *vb.* **com·fort·ing, com·fort·ed** to console.

com·for·ta·ble (kum'fərt-ə-bəl, kumf'tər-bəl) *adj.* **1** in a state of physical well-being; at ease. **2** providing comfort: *This is a comfortable bed.*

com·ic (käm'ik) *adj.* amusing; funny. – *n.* **1** a comedian. **2 comics** (*plural*) comic strips.

com·i·cal (käm'i-kəl) *adj.* funny; amusing.

comic book *n.* a magazine containing stories told through a series of pictures.

com·ma (käm'ə) *n.* a punctuation mark (,) indicating a break in a sentence.

com·mand (kə-mand') *vb.* **com·mand·ing, com·mand·ed 1** to order formally. **2** to have authority over, be in control of. – *n.* **1** an order. **2** control; charge: *He is second in command.* **3** knowledge of and ability to use: *Her command of the Italian language is second to none.* **4** an instruction to a computer.

com·mence (kə-mens) *vb.* **com·menc·ing, com·menced** to begin.

com·ment (käm'ent') *n.* **1** a remark or observation, especially a critical one. **2** talk or discussion. – *vb.* **com·ment·ing, com·ment·ed** to make observations.

com·merce (käm'urs) *n.* the buying and selling of goods and services; trade, banking etc.

com·mer·cial (kə-mur'shəl) *adj.* relating to commerce, business, or trade. – *n.* a radio or television advertisement.

com·mit (kə-mit') *vb.* **com·mit·ting, com·mit·ted 1** to carry out or perform: *to commit a crime.* **2** entrust into the care of: *He was committed to a hospital.*

com·mit·tee (kə-mit'ē) *n.* a group of people selected from a larger body to do certain work on its behalf.

com·mod·i·ty (kə-mäd'ət-ē) *n.* **com·mod·i·ties** something that is bought and sold, especially raw materials.

com·mon (käm'ən) *adj.* **1** happening often; frequent; familiar: *Storms are common in that area.* **2** shared by two or more people, things, etc.: *characteristics common to both animals.* **3** widespread: *His opinions are common knowledge.*

common sense *n.* practical good sense.

com·mon·place (käm'ən-plās') *adj.* ordinary.

com·mon·wealth (käm'ən-welth') *n.* **1** the people of a state or nation. **2** a republic or democracy. **3** an association of states or nations joined together for their common good.

● The **Commonwealth** is an association of countries and territories, such as AUSTRALIA, CANADA, INDIA, and NIGERIA, which were part of the British Empire. Queen ELIZABETH is head of the Commonwealth.

● **Commonwealth of Independent States** is formed of 12 independent countries that made up most of what was the Union of Soviet Socialist Republics. There were 15 republics, which are now separate countries.

COMMONWEALTH OF INDEPENDENT STATES

State:	Capital
ARMENIA	Yerevan
AZERBAIJAN	Baku
BELARUS	Minsk
GEORGIA	Tbilisi
KAZAKHSTAN	Alma-Ata
KYRGYZSTAN	Bishkek
MOLDOVA	Kishinev
RUSSIA	Moscow
TAJIKISTAN	Dushanbe
TURK-MENISTAN	Ashkhabad
UKRAINE	Kiev
UZBEKISTAN	Tashkent

com·mo·tion (kə-mō'shən) *n.* a disturbance; an upheaval: *The scuffle caused a commotion in the street.*

com·mu·ni·cate (kə-myōō'ni-kāt') *vb.* **com·mu·ni·cat·ing, com·mu·ni·cat·ed** **1** to make known; to exchange information about. **2** to get in touch.

com·mu·ni·ca·tion (kə-myōō'ni-kā'shən) *n.* **1** the exchanging or giving of ideas and information, etc. **2** (in *plural*) the systems involved in sending information, etc. especially by electronic means or radio waves.

com·mu·nism (käm'yə-niz'əm) *n.* a political doctrine which believes private property should be abolished, and land, factories, etc. owned and controlled by the people. – *n.* & *adj.* **com·mu·nist** (käm'yə-nəst).

com·mu·ni·ty (kə-myōō'nət-ē) *n.* **com·mu·ni·ties** the group of people living in a particular locality.

● **Com·o·ros** (käm'ə-rōz'). See Supplement, **Countries**.

com·pact (kəm-pakt', käm'pakt') *adj.* **1** firm and dense in form or texture. **2** small, but with all essentials neatly contained; taking up little space: *My computer is very compact.* – *vb.* **com·pact·ing, com·pact·ed** to compress.

com·pact disc (käm'pakt' disk') *n.* a plastic disk containing digitally stored information or music, played on a special machine (**compact disc player**) using a laser beam.

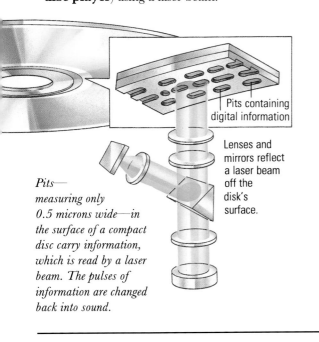

Pits—measuring only 0.5 microns wide—in the surface of a compact disc carry information, which is read by a laser beam. The pulses of information are changed back into sound.

Pits containing digital information

Lenses and mirrors reflect a laser beam off the disk's surface.

com·pan·ion (kəm-pan'yən) *n.* a person who spends a lot of time with another; a friend.

com·pa·ny (kum'pə-nē) *n.* **com·pa·nies** **1** the presence of another person or other people; guests or visitors. **2** a business organization. **3** a military unit forming part of a battalion.

com·par·a·tive (kəm-par'ət-iv) *adj.* **1** as compared with others: *This show is a comparative success.* **2** as observed by comparing one another: *We discussed their comparative strengths.* – *n.* a comparative adjective or adverb, as in *This book is **smaller** than that book* and *Peg runs **faster** than Rana.*

com·pare (kəm-pâr') *vb.* **com·par·ing, com·pared** to examine in order to see differences and likenesses: *Mary compared Mark's handwriting with Sam's.*

com·par·i·son (kəm-par'ə-sən) *n.* an act of, or a reasonable basis for, comparing: *There can be no comparison between them.*

com·part·ment (kəm-pärt'mənt) *n.* a separated section: *The drawer has a secret compartment.*

com·pass (kum'pəs) *n.* **1** an instrument for finding direction containing a dial marked with 32 points, with a magnetic needle that always points to magnetic north. **2** (often in *plural*) an instrument consisting of two hinged legs, for drawing circles, etc.

com·pat·i·ble (kəm-pat'ə-bəl) *adj.* See **Computer Terms**.

com·pel (kəm-pel') *vb.* **com·pel·ling, com·pelled** to force.

com·pel·ling *adj.* irresistibly fascinating: *I found that novel compelling.*

com·pete (kəm-pēt') *vb.* **com·pet·ing, com·pet·ed** **1** to take part in a contest. **2** to be a rival.

com·pe·tent (käm'pət-ənt) *adj.* having sufficient skill to do something.

com·pe·ti·tion (käm'pə-tish'ən) *n.* **1** an event in which people compete to find out who is best at something. **2** rivals, as in business.

com·pet·i·tive (kəm-pet'ət-iv) *adj.* **1** involving rivalry. **2** enjoying rivalry; aggressive; ambitious. – *n.* **com·pet·i·tive·ness**.

com·pet·i·tor (kəm-pet'ət-ər) *n.* a person, team, firm, or product that competes; a rival.

com·pla·cent (kəm-plā'sənt) *adj.* self-satisfied; smug: *They became complacent after building up a big lead.* – *n.* **com·pla·cen·cy** (kəm-plā'sən-sē).

Companion comes from Latin words meaning "with" and "bread," so producing a word meaning "one who eats bread with another."

In a magnetic compass the needle, fixed to a pivot and free to swing round, always points north and south when at rest. The earth acts like a big magnet.

com·plain (kəm-plān′) *vb.* **com·plain·ing, com·plained** 1 to express that you are not satisfied or pleased: *Dad complained when the plane was late.* 2 to say that you are suffering from: *Tina complained of having a toothache.*

com·ple·ment (käm′plə-mənt) *n.* something that completes, perfects, or goes well with: *The music is a complement to the mood of the movie.*

com·plete (kəm-plēt′) *adj.* 1 whole; finished; with nothing missing: *The jigsaw puzzle is complete.* 2 thorough; absolute; total. – *vb.* **com·plet·ing, com·plet·ed** to finish. – *n.* **com·ple·tion** (kəm-plē′shən).

com·plex (käm-pleks′, käm′pleks) *adj.* 1 composed of many interrelated parts: *An automobile is a complex machine.* 2 complicated: *a complex problem.*

com·plex·ion (kəm-plek′shən) *n.* the color of the skin, especially of the face.

com·pli·cate (käm′plə-kāt′) *vb.* **com·pli·cat·ing, com·pli·cat·ed** to make complex.

com·pli·ment (käm′plə-mənt) *n.* an expression of admiration or approval. – *vb.* **com·pli·ment·ing, com·pli·ment·ed** to congratulate; to pay a compliment to.

com·pli·men·ta·ry (käm′plə-ment′ə-rē) *adj.* 1 admiring or approving. 2 given free: *complimentary tickets.*

com·pose (kəm-pōz′) *vb.* **com·pos·ing** 1 to create music; to write a poem. 2 to make up or constitute.

com·posed *adj.* calm; controlled.

com·pos·er *n.* someone who composes music.

com·po·si·tion (käm′pə-zish′ən) *n.* 1 something composed, especially a musical or literary work. 2 what something consists of.

com·pound (käm′pownd′) *n.* 1 in chemistry, a substance made up of the atoms of two or more elements. 2 something made up of two or more parts: *Flies have compound eyes.*

com·pre·hend (käm′pri-hend′) *vb.* **com·pre·hend·ing, com·pre·hend·ed** to understand.

com·pre·hen·si·ble (käm′pri-hen′sə-bəl) *adj.* capable of being understood.

com·pre·hen·sive (käm′pri-hen′siv) *adj.* covering or including everything or a great deal.

com·press (kəm-pres′) *vb.* **com·press·ing, com·pressed** to press together or squeeze.

com·prise (kəm-prīz′) *vb.* **com·pris·ing, com·prised** to contain, include, or consist of: *The magazine comprises text and pictures.*

com·pro·mise (käm′prə-mīz′) *n.* something agreed on after each side has given up claims or demands.

com·pul·so·ry (kəm-pul′sə-rē) *adj.* required by the rules, law, etc.; obligatory.

com·put·er (kəm-pyoot′ər) *n.* an electronic machine that can quickly process, store, analyze, and retrieve data.

con·cave (kän-kāv′, kän′kāv′) *adj.* curving inward: *The inside of a cup is concave.*

con·ceal (kən-sēl′) *vb.* **con·ceal·ing, con·cealed** to hide.

con·cede (kən-sēd′) *vb.* **con·ced·ing, con·ced·ed** to admit to be true or correct.

con·cen·trate (kän′sən-trāt′) *vb.* **con·cen·trat·ing, con·cen·trat·ed** 1 to give all your attention and energy to something. 2 to bring or come together in one place: *Big cities are concentrated in the east of the country.* 3 to make stronger by removing water or other diluting substance.

con·cen·tra·tion (kän′sən-trā′shən) *n.* intensive mental effort.

con·cept (kän′sept) *n.* an abstract idea.

con·cep·tion (kən-sep′shən) *n.* 1 the idea you have of something. 2 the fertilization in the womb of a female egg by the male sperm.

con·cern (kən-surn′) *vb.* **con·cern·ing, con·cerned** 1 to have to do with; to be about: *It concerns your son.* 2 to worry, bother, or interest: *Matt's illness concerns his wife a lot.* – *n.* a cause of worry; a subject of interest.

con·cerned *adj.* worried.

con·cern·ing *prep.* about; regarding.

con·cert (kän′surt′, kän′sərt) *n.* a musical performance given before an audience by singers or players.

con·cer·to (kən-chert′ō) *n.* **con·cer·tos** a musical composition for one or more solo instruments and orchestra.

con·cise (kən-sīs′) *adj.* brief, but covering essential points. – *n.* **con·cise·ness.**

con·clude (kən-klood′) *vb.* **con·clud·ing, con·clud·ed** 1 to come or bring to an end. 2 to reach an opinion.

con·clu·sion (kən-kloo′zhən) *n.* 1 an end. 2 an opinion based on reasoning: *My advice helped him come to a conclusion.* 3 a result or outcome.

con·clu·sive (kən-kloo′siv) *adj.* decisive: *The evidence is conclusive, she is innocent.*

con·course (kän′kôrs′) *n.* a large open area for people, in a railroad station, airport, etc.

PRONUNCIATION SYMBOLS			
ə	away lemon	focus	
a	fat	oi	boy
ā	fade	oo	foot
ä	hot	ōō	moon
âr	fair	ou	house
e	met	th	think
ē	mean	th	this
g	get	u	cut
hw	which	ur	hurt
i	fin	w	witch
ī	line	y	yes
îr	near	yōō	music
ô	often	yoor	pure
ō	note	zh	vision

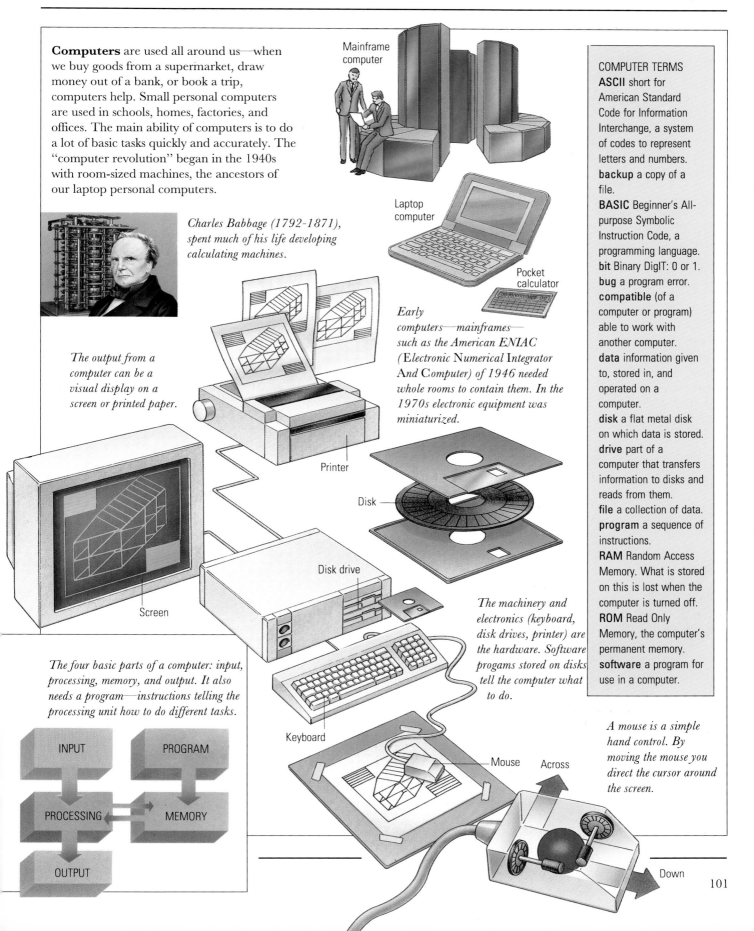

Computers are used all around us—when we buy goods from a supermarket, draw money out of a bank, or book a trip, computers help. Small personal computers are used in schools, homes, factories, and offices. The main ability of computers is to do a lot of basic tasks quickly and accurately. The "computer revolution" began in the 1940s with room-sized machines, the ancestors of our laptop personal computers.

Mainframe computer

Laptop computer

Pocket calculator

Charles Babbage (1792-1871), spent much of his life developing calculating machines.

Early computers—mainframes—such as the American ENIAC (Electronic Numerical Integrator And Computer) of 1946 needed whole rooms to contain them. In the 1970s electronic equipment was miniaturized.

The output from a computer can be a visual display on a screen or printed paper.

Printer

Disk

Disk drive

Screen

Keyboard

Mouse

Across

Down

The machinery and electronics (keyboard, disk drives, printer) are the hardware. Software progams stored on disks tell the computer what to do.

The four basic parts of a computer: input, processing, memory, and output. It also needs a program—instructions telling the processing unit how to do different tasks.

INPUT

PROGRAM

PROCESSING

MEMORY

OUTPUT

A mouse is a simple hand control. By moving the mouse you direct the cursor around the screen.

COMPUTER TERMS
ASCII short for American Standard Code for Information Interchange, a system of codes to represent letters and numbers.
backup a copy of a file.
BASIC Beginner's All-purpose Symbolic Instruction Code, a programming language.
bit Binary DigIT: 0 or 1.
bug a program error.
compatible (of a computer or program) able to work with another computer.
data information given to, stored in, and operated on a computer.
disk a flat metal disk on which data is stored.
drive part of a computer that transfers information to disks and reads from them.
file a collection of data.
program a sequence of instructions.
RAM Random Access Memory. What is stored on this is lost when the computer is turned off.
ROM Read Only Memory, the computer's permanent memory.
software a program for use in a computer.

The 20th century has seen widespread use of reinforced concrete in building. One example is the Habitat scheme (above), designed in 1967.

To make the sections of the Habitat scheme, concrete was poured around reinforcing mesh in molds, and left to dry and harden.

con·crete (kän′krēt′, kän-krēt′) *n.* a building material made by mixing cement, sand, gravel, and water. – *adj.* **1** made of concrete. **2** able to be felt, touched, seen, etc.: *concrete objects.*

con·demn (kən-dem′) *vb.* **con·demn·ing, con·demned 1** to consider wrong or evil. **2** to find guilty; to convict.

con·dense (kən-dens′) *vb.* **con·dens·ing, con·densed 1** to compress; to make denser: *This story has been condensed from a novel.* **2** to turn from gas or vapor to liquid or solid.

con·den·sa·tion (kän′den′sā′shən) *n.* condensed water vapor.

con·di·tion (kən-dish′ən) *n.* **1** a particular state: *The book is in good condition.* **2** a state of health: *He is overweight and out of condition.* **3** a disorder: *He has a heart condition.* **4** (in *plural*) circumstances: *They suffer poor working conditions.* **5** a qualification.

con·dom (kän′dem) *n.* a thin rubber sheath worn on the penis as a contraceptive, and to prevent the spread of disease.

con·dor (kän′dər, kän′dôr′) *n.* a large South American vulture.

The Andean condor is the world's largest flying bird. It can reach heights of more than 13,000 feet (4,000 m), gliding upward in rising air currents.

con·duct (kən-dukt′) *vb.* **con·duct·ing, con·duct·ed 1** to lead or guide. **2** to direct an orchestra or choir. **3** to transmit heat or electricity: *Metal conducts heat.* – (kän′dukt′) *n.* behavior. – *n.* **con·duc·tion** (kən-dək′shən).

con·duc·tor (kən-dukt′ər) *n.* **1** the director of a choir or orchestra. **2** a material, etc. that conducts heat or electricity, e.g. copper wires. **3** a person in charge of a train, subway, etc.

cone (kōn) *n.* **1** in geometry, a solid figure that has a round base and ends in a point. **2** the oval fruit of a coniferous tree, made up of overlapping woody scales.

con·fer (kən-fur′) *vb.* **con·fer·ring, con·ferred 1** to consult together. **2** to give as an honor.

con·fer·ence (kän′fə-rəns, kän′frəns) *n.* a formal meeting.

con·fess (kən-fes′) *vb.* **con·fess·ing, con·fessed 1** to own up to a fault, wrongdoing, etc. **2** to tell your sins to a priest.

con·fes·sion (kən-fesh′ən) *n.* the admission of a sin, fault, etc.

con·fide (kən-fīd′) *vb.* **con·fid·ing, con·fid·ed** to speak about personal matters to someone you trust.

con·fi·dence (kän′fəd-əns, kän′fə-dens′) *n.* **1** trust in a person or thing. **2** faith in your own ability. – *n.* **con·fi·dent** (kän′fəd-ənt, kän′fə-dent′).

con·fi·den·tial (kän′fə-den′chəl) *adj.* secret.

con·fine (kən-fīn′) *vb.* **con·fin·ing, con·fined 1** to restrict; to limit. **2** to keep prisoner. – *adj.* **con·fined** (kən-fīnd′).

con·firm (kən-furm′) *vb.* **con·firm·ing, con·firmed 1** to prove correct. **2** to support or prove. **3** to accept someone into full membership of a church or synagogue.

con·fis·cate (kän′fə-skāt′) *vb.* **con·fis·cat·ing, con·fis·cat·ed** to take away from someone, as a penalty. – *n.* **con·fis·ca·tion** (kän′fə-skā′shən).

con·flict (kän′flikt) *n.* **1** disagreement; fierce argument; a quarrel. **2** a fight, battle, or war. – (kən-flikt′) *vb.* **con·flict·ing, con·flict·ed** to be incompatible or in opposition.

con·form (kən-fôrm′) *vb.* **con·form·ing, con·formed** to act in agreement with rules or customs.

con·front (kən-frunt′) *vb.* **con·front·ing,**

con·front·ed 1 to face defiantly or accusingly. 2 to deal firmly with.

con·fuse (kən-fyōōz′) *vb.* **con·fus·ing, con·fused** 1 to put into a muddle or mess. 2 to fail to distinguish: *I confuse left and right.*

con·fu·sion (kən-fyōō′zhən) *n.* disorder.

con·gest·ed (kən-jes′təd) *adj.* 1 crowded. 2 (of the nose) blocked with mucus. — *n.* **con·ges·tion** (kən-jes′chən).

●**Con·go** (käng′gō). See Supplement, **Countries**.

con·grat·u·late (kən-grach′ə-lāt′) *vb.* **con·grat·u·lat·ing, con·grat·u·lat·ed** to express your pleasure at someone's success. — *n.* **con·grat·u·la·tion** (kən-grach′ə-lā′shən). — *adj.* **con·grat·u·la·to·ry** (kən-grach′ə-lə-tôr′ē).

con·gre·gate (käng′gri-gāt′) *vb.* **con·gre·gat·ing, con·gre·gat·ed** to come together in a crowd.

con·gre·ga·tion (käng′gri-gā′shən) *n.* a gathering or assembly of people, especially for religious worship.

con·gress (käng′grəs) 1 a large meeting gathered to discuss something. 2 **Congress**, the lawmaking body in some countries, especially of the UNITED STATES. — *adj.* **con·gres·sion·al** (kən-gresh′ən-l).

con·i·fer (kän′ə-fər, kō′nə-fər) *n.* a tree that bears cones, such as pines and larches.

con·jure (kän′jər) *vb.* **con·jur·ing, con·jured** to perform tricks that deceive the eye, by skillful use of the hands. — **conjure up.** to make appear or seem to appear by or as if by magic. — *n.* **con·jur·er** or **con·jur·or** (kän′jər-ər).

con·nect (kə-nekt′) *vb.* **con·nect·ing, con·nect·ed** 1 to join; to link. 2 to associate or involve: *They are connected with the advertising industry.*

con·nec·tion (kə-nek′shən) *n.* 1 a link: *There is a strong connection between smoking and heart disease.* 2 a relationship. 3 an influential contact.

●**Con·nec·ti·cut** (kə-net′i-kət). See Supplement, **U.S.A.**

con·quer (käng′kər) *vb.* **con·quer·ing, con·quered** 1 to gain possession over by force: *In 1066 the Normans conquered England.*

Conifers produce their pollen and seeds in cones, instead of in flowers. They also have narrow, needle-like leaves, and most types are evergreen. Among the best known conifers are spruce (Christmas tree), Scotch pine, cedar, and yew.

Fir

Monkey puzzle

Cedar of Lebanon

Cypress

Cypress

Larch

2 to defeat. — *n.* **con·quer·or**.

con·quest (käng′kwest) *n.* 1 the act of conquering. 2 a conquered territory.

●**Con·rad** (kän′rad′)**, Joseph** (1857-1924) was a Polish novelist who wrote in English after a career at sea. His works include *Lord Jim* and *Heart of Darkness.*

con·science (kän′shəns) *n.* a feeling about what is right and wrong that guides your behavior: *I have a clear conscience.*

con·sci·en·tious (kän′shē-en′shəs) *adj.* careful; thorough; painstaking.

con·scious (kän′shəs) *adj.* 1 awake and aware of your surroundings. 2 deliberate: *She made a conscious effort to be polite.*

con·sec·u·tive (kən-sek′yət-iv) *adj.* following one after the other.

con·sent (kən-sent′) *vb.* **con·sent·ing, con·sent·ed** to agree. — *n.* permission.

con·se·quence (kän′sə-kwens′) *n.* something that follows from an action.

con·se·quent·ly (kän′sə-kwent′lē) *adv.* as a result; therefore.

PRONUNCIATION SYMBOLS			
ə	**a**way lemon		focus
a	f**a**t	oi	b**oy**
ā	f**a**de	oo	f**oo**t
ä	h**o**t	ōō	m**oo**n
âr	f**air**	ou	h**ou**se
e	m**e**t	th	**th**ink
ē	m**ea**n	th	**th**is
g	**g**et	u	c**u**t
hw	**wh**ich	ur	h**ur**t
i	f**i**n	w	**w**itch
ī	l**i**ne	y	**y**es
îr	n**ear**	yōō	m**u**sic
ô	**o**ften	yoor	p**u**re
ō	n**o**te	zh	vi**s**ion

Over the last 30 years we have become aware of the damage we do to the environment. International agreements now exist to protect endangered species and to preserve their habitats. The map shows countries with agreements to protect United Nations World Heritage Sites and Wetlands of international importance.

- World Heritage Sites Protected
- Wetlands of International Importance Protected
- Wetlands and World Heritage Sites Protected

con·ser·va·tion (kän′sər-vā′shən) *n.* the preservation and protection of wildlife, etc.

con·ser·va·tive (kən-sur′vət-iv) *adj.* **1** favoring what is established or traditional; disliking change. **2** restrained; not flamboyant.

con·serve (kən-surv′) *vb.* **con·serv·ing, con·served** to keep safe from damage or loss.

con·sid·er (kən-sid′ər) *vb.* **con·sid·er·ing, con·sid·ered** to think about carefully.

con·sid·er·a·ble (kən-sid′ər-ə-bəl) *adj.* large; great: *There is still a considerable amount of work to do.* – *adv.* **con·sid·er·a·bly.**

con·sid·er·ate (kən-sid′ə-rət) *adj.* careful and thoughtful to others.

con·sist (kən-sist′) *vb.* **con·sist·ing, con·sist·ed** to be made up of.

con·sis·tent (kən-sis′tənt) *adj.* unchanging, reliable, regular, steady. – *n.* **con·sis·ten·cy** (kən-sis′tən-sē).

con·so·la·tion (kän′sə-lā′shən) *n.* a person or thing that brings you comfort.

con·sole[1] (kən-sōl′) *vb.* **con·sol·ing, con·soled** to comfort in distress or grief.

con·sole[2] (kän′sōl′) *n.* **1** a small cabinet that stands on the floor, holding a television, radio, etc. **2** a panel of dials, switches, etc. for operating an electronic machine.

con·so·nant (kän′sə-nənt) *n.* a letter representing a sound you make by obstructing the passage of the breath; not a vowel.

con·spic·u·ous (kən-spik′yōō-əs) *adj.* noticeable.

con·spir·a·cy (kən-spîr′ə-sē) **conspiracies** *n.* a secret plan for an illegal act; a plot.

con·spire (kən-spīr′) *vb.* **con·spir·ing, con·spired** to plot secretly together especially for an unlawful purpose.

con·sta·ble (kän′stə-bəl, kan′stə-bəl) *n.* (*British*) a policeman or policewoman.

●**Con·sta·ble** (kän′stə-bəl, kan′stə-bəl), **John** (1776-1837) was an English landscape painter.

con·stant (kän′stənt) *adj.* **1** never stopping or letting up. **2** unchanging: *Her temperature is now constant.*

●**Con·stan·ti·no·ple** (kän′stant′n-ō′pəl), a former name of Istanbul, TURKEY, was named after the emperor Constantine in A.D. 330.

con·stel·la·tion (kän′stə-lā′shən) *n.* a group of stars having a name.

Northern Hemisphere

Southern Hemisphere

The Babylonians named many **constellations** 4,000 years ago after heroes and animals whose shapes they saw in the patterns of the stars. The earliest named are the 12 forming the zodiac.

Northern Hemisphere

con·sti·tute (kän′stə-tōōt′) *vb.*
con·sti·tut·ing, con·sti·tut·ed to go
together to make.

con·sti·tu·tion (kän′stə-tōō′shən) *n.* **1** a set of
rules governing an organization. **2** the way in
which something is made up. **3** your physical
makeup, health, etc. − *adj.*
con·sti·tu·tion·al (kän′stə-tōō′shən-l).

● The United States Constitution was written in
1787 at a convention held in Philadelphia. It
states that the UNITED STATES will have an
elected president, a CONGRESS, and a SU-
PREME COURT.

con·strict (kənstrikt′) *vb.* **con·strict·ing,**
con·strict·ed to enclose tightly. − *n.*
con·stric·tion (kən-strik′shən).

con·struct (kən-strukt′) *vb.* **con·struct·ing,**
con·struct·ed 1 to build. **2** to form, compose.

con·struc·tion (kən-struk′shən) *n.* **1** the
process of building. **2** a building.

con·struc·tive (kən-struk′tiv) *adj.* useful in a
positive way: *The talks were most constructive.*

con·sult (kən-sult′) *vb.* **con·sult·ing,**
con·sult·ed 1 to ask the advice of: *She
consulted a lawyer.* **2** to refer to a map, book, etc.

con·sult·ant (kən-sult′nt) *n.* a person who
gives professional advice.

con·sume (kən-sōōm′) *vb.* **con·sum·ing,**
con·sumed 1 to eat or drink. **2** to use up. **3** to
destroy: *The fire consumed the office building.*

con·sump·tion (kən-sump′shən) *n.* the
amount consumed.

con·tact (kän′takt′) *n.* **1** a physical touching.
2 a means of communication. − (kän′takt′,
kən-takt′) *vb.* **con·tact·ing, con·tact·ed** to
get in touch with.

con·tain (kən-tān′) *vb.* **con·tain·ing,**
con·tained 1 to hold or have. **2** to control or
prevent the spread of.

con·tain·er (kən-tā′nər) *n.* a box, can, carton,
etc.

con·tam·i·nate (kən-tam′ə-nāt′) *vb.*
con·tam·i·nat·ing, con·tam·i·nat·ed to
make impure; to pollute or infect; to make
radioactive. − *n.* **con·tam·i·na·tion** (kən-
tam′ə-nā′shən).

con·tem·po·ra·ry (kən-tem′pə-rer′ē) *adj.*
1 belonging to the same period or time.
2 modern; present day: *contemporary art.*

con·tempt (kən-tempt′) *n.* scorn; a low
opinion.

con·tent¹ (kən-tent′) *adj.* satisfied; happy;
uncomplaining. − *n.* **con·tent·ment** (kən-
tent′mənt).

con·tent² (kän′tent′) *n.* **1** the subject matter of
a book, speech, etc. **2** (in *plural*) the things
contained in something.

con·tent·ed (kən-tent′əd) *adj.* peacefully
happy or satisfied.

con·test (kän′test′) *n.* a competition; a
struggle. (kən-test′)− *vb.* **con·test·ing,**
con·test·ed 1 to enter a competition. **2** to
dispute a decision.

con·test·ant (kən-tes′tənt) *n.* a competitor.

NOT DISCONTENTED
If you say that you are
"not discontented" you
really mean that you
are contented. In the
same way we say "not
bad" to mean "good"
or "not unlike" to mean
"like." This is a not
uncommon verbal
device known as litotes
(lī′tə′tēz), a means of
understating what we
wish to say. It is often
used to create an
amusing or
sophisticated effect in
everyday speech.

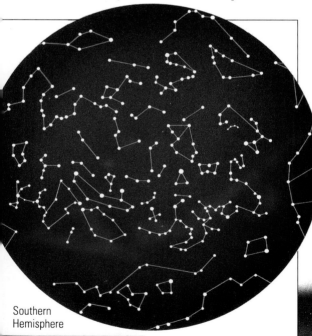

Southern
Hemisphere

*Lupus, the wolf, a
constellation in the
Southern Hemisphere.*

Southern Cross
Constellation

*The flag of Australia shows the Southern Cross
constellation and the Commonwealth Star. New
Zealand's flag displays four stars of
the Southern Cross.*

Australia

New Zealand

North America

Eurasia

Africa

South America

For a long time scientists have seen that the shapes of Europe, North and South America, and Africa looked as if they could fit together like pieces in a jigsaw puzzle. Then in 1912 the idea of continental drift was put forward. It was suggested that South America was once joined to Africa. The illustration shows how over millions of years the single continent we call Pangea broke up to produce the jigsaw puzzle of continents we know today.

con·ti·nent (känt′n-ənt, känt′nənt) *n.* any large land mass of the world – EUROPE, ASIA, AFRICA, NORTH and SOUTH AMERICA, AUSTRALIA, and ANTARCTICA.

con·tin·u·al (kən-tin′yōō-əl) *adj.* constantly happening or done; frequent.

con·tin·ue (kən-tin′yōō) *vb.* **con·tin·u·ing, con·tin·ued 1** to go on; not to stop. **2** to start again after a break.

con·tin·u·ous (kən-tin′yōō-əs) *adj.* never ceasing; unbroken; uninterrupted.

con·tour (kän′tōōr′) *n.* **1** (usually in *plural*) the distinctive outline of something **2** (also **contour line**) a line on a map joining points of the same height or depth.

con·tra·cep·tive (kän′trə-sep′tiv) *n.* a drug or device that prevents pregnancy.

con·tract (kän′trakt′) *n.* a legal agreement setting out terms. – (kən-trakt′) *vb.* **con·tract·ing, con·tract·ed 1** to make or become shorter: *His muscles contracted.* **2** to acquire or catch: *She contracted the flu.*

con·trac·tion (kən-trak′shən) *n.* a shortened form of a word or phrase: *"Aren't" is a contraction of "are not."*

con·tra·dict (kän′trə-dikt′) *vb.* **con·tra·dict·ing, con·tra·dict·ed 1** to say the opposite of: *Don't contradict me all the time.* **2** to disagree or be inconsistent with. – *n.* **con·tra·dic·tion** (kän′trə-dik′shən). – *adj.* **con·tra·dic·to·ry** (kän′trə-dik′tə-rē).

con·tral·to (kən-tral′tō) *n.* **con·tral·tos** the female singing voice that is lowest in pitch.

con·trar·y *adj.* (kän′trer′ē) opposite; quite different; opposed.

con·trast (kän′trast′) *n.* **1** difference between things or people that are being compared: *It snowed yesterday – today is warm by contrast.* **2** a person or thing that is strikingly different from another. – (kən-trast′, kän′trast′) *vb.* **con·trast·ing, con·trast·ed 1** to compare so as to reveal differences. **2** to show a contrast.

con·trib·ute (kən-trib′yət, kən-trib′yōōt) *vb.* **con·trib·u·ting, con·trib·ut·ed** to give for some joint purpose: *We contribute money to charity.* – *n.* **con·trib·u·tor** (kən-trib′yət-ər).

con·tri·bu·tion (kän′trə-byōō′shən) *n.* something contributed, as money, or an article for a magazine.

con·trol (kən-trōl′) *n.* **1** authority or charge; power to influence or guide: *in control; take control; under control; out of control.* **2** a method of limiting: *The government has imposed strict controls on spending.* **3** (in *plural*) the levers, switches, etc. by which a machine, etc. is operated. – *vb.* **con·trol·ling, con·trolled 1** to have control over: *Please control your dog.* **2** to regulate.

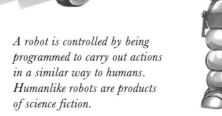

A robot is controlled by being programmed to carry out actions in a similar way to humans. Humanlike robots are products of science fiction.

con·tro·ver·sy (kän′trə-vur′sē) *n.*
con·tro·ver·sies a disagreement, often a
prolonged one. – *adj.* **con·tro·ver·sial**
(kän′trə-vur′shəl).

co·nun·drum (kə-nun′drəm) *n.* **1** a problem.
2 a riddle whose answer involves a pun.

con·va·les·cent (kän′və-les′ənt) *n.* a person
recovering from an illness. – *n.*
con·va·les·cence (kän′və-les′ənt).

con·ve·nient (kən-vēn′yənt) *adj.* fitting in with
plans, etc.; handy.

con·vent (kän′vent′, kän′vənt) *n.* a building
where a community of nuns live.

con·ven·tion (kən-ven′chən) *n.* **1** a large
conference. **2** a custom.

con·ven·tion·al (kən-ven′chən-l) *adj.*
1 traditional; customary. **2** (of weapons or war)
nonnuclear.

con·ver·sa·tion (kän′vər-sā′shən) *n.* informal
talk between people.

con·verse¹ (kən-vurs′) *vb.* **con·vers·ing,**
con·versed to talk informally.

converse² (kän′vurs′) *adj.* reverse; opposite. –
n. opposite.

con·vert (kən-vurt′) *vb.* **con·vert·ing,**
con·vert·ed 1 to change in form or function.
2 to win over to another religion, opinion, etc.
– (kän′vurt′) *n.* a person who has converted to
a religion.

con·vex (kän-veks′, kän′veks′) *adj.* outward
curving, like the surface of the eye.

con·vey (kən-vā′) *vb.* **con·vey·ing,**
con·veyed 1 to carry; to transport. **2** to
communicate: *It is hard to convey what I mean.*

con·vict (kən-vikt′) *vb.* **con·vict·ing,**
con·vict·ed to prove someone guilty of a
crime. – (kän′vikt′) *n.* a person serving a prison
sentence.

con·vince (kən-vins′) *vb.* **con·vinc·ing,**
con·vinced to persuade: *Peter convinced me that
he was telling the truth.* – *adj.* **con·vinc·ing.**

cook (kook) *vb.* **cook·ing, cooked** to prepare
food by heating.

● **Cook** (kook), **James** (1728-1779) was the
first European to cross the ANTARCTIC
Circle.

cool (kool) *adj.* **1** somewhat cold; not
warm. **2** lacking enthusiasm;
unfriendly: *She gave me a cool response.*
– *vb.* **cool·ing, cooled** to make or
become cool. – *n.* **cool·ness.**

coop·er·ate (kō-äp′ə-rāt′) *vb.*
coop·er·at·ing, coop·er·at·ed to work or
act together. – *n.* **coop·er·a·tion** (kō-äp′ə-
rā′shən).

cope (kōp) *vb.* **cop·ing, coped** to deal
successfully: *She coped with the problem.*

● **Co·pen·ha·gen** (kō′pən-hā′gən, kō′pən-
häg′ən) is a port and capital of DENMARK.

● **Co·per·ni·cus** (kə-pur′ni-kəs), **Nicolaus**
(1473-1543) was a Polish scientist. He showed
that the Earth is not the center of the universe
and that the Earth itself rotates.

co·pi·ous (kō′pē-əs) *adj.* plentiful.

● **Cop·land** (kōp′lənd), **Aaron** (1900-1990) was
an American composer who used folk music and
jazz in his compositions.

cop·per (käp′ər) *n.* an element (symbol **Cu**), a
brownish-red metal. – *adj.* of the brownish-red
color of copper.

● Copper was one of the first metals to be used.
Pure copper is soft, but if mixed with other
metals it makes harder alloys, such as brass
and bronze. It conducts electricity easily and
so is used to make electric wires.

copse (käps) *n.* a small wood.

Copper comes from the
Latin name for Cyprus,
Cyprium, where copper
was first found.

*When he reached New
Zealand, Captain Cook
met warlike Maoris with
tattooed faces who
paddled out to him in
their elaborately carved
canoes.*

cop·y (käp′ē) *n.* **cop·ies 1** an imitation or reproduction. **2** one of the many specimens of a book, or of a particular issue of a magazine, newspaper, etc. – *vb.* **cop·ies, cop·y·ing, cop·ied 1** to imitate. **2** to make a copy of.

cor·al (kôr′əl, kär′əl) *n.* a hard pink, red, or white material made up of the skeletons of tiny sea creatures.

cord (kôrd) *n.* **1** thin rope or thick string. **2** a cordlike structure in the body: *the spinal cord.* **3** electrical wire covered in plastic.

cor·du·roy (kôr′də-roi′) *n.* **1** a thick ribbed cotton fabric. **2** (in *plural*) pants made of corduroy.

core (kôr, kōr) *n.* **1** the center of an apple, etc., containing the seeds. **2** the essential part. **3** the inner part of the earth.

cork (kôrk) *n.* **1** the light outer bark of a Mediterranean tree, the cork oak. **2** a piece of this used as a stopper for a bottle, etc.

corn[1] (kôrn) *n.* **1** a tall cereal plant bearing large ears of kernels. **2** the edible kernels of this plant. **3** (*British*) any cereal plant or its seeds.

corn[2] *n.* (kôrn) a small patch of hardened skin, especially on a toe.

cor·ne·a (kôr′nē-ə) *n.* the transparent covering of the eyeball.

cor·ner (kôr′nər) *n.* a point or place where lines or surface-edges meet; the inside or outside of the angle so formed.

co·rol·la (kə-räl′ə, kə-rō′lə) *n.* the grouping of petals on a flower.

cor·o·na·tion (kôr′ə-nā′shən) *n.* the ceremony of crowning a king or queen.

corps (kôr) *n.* **corps** (kôr, kôrz) **1** a branch of the military: *the signal corps.* **2** people engaged in particular work: *the diplomatic corps.*

corpse (kôrps) *n.* a dead human being.

cor·pus·cle (kôr′pus′əl) *n.* a blood cell.

cor·rect (kə-rekt′) *vb.* **cor·rect·ing, cor·rect·ed 1** to set or put right; to remove errors from. **2** to mark the errors in. **3** to adjust or make better. – *adj.* **1** free from error; accurate. **2** right; proper; appropriate.

cor·rec·tion (kə-rek′shən) *n.* **1** the act of correcting. **2** a change that corrects something.

cor·res·pond (kôr′ə-spänd′, kär′ə-spänd′) *vb.* **cor·res·pond·ing, cor·res·pond·ed 1** to be similar or equivalent. **2** to exchange letters.

cor·res·pon·dent (kôr′ə-spän′dənt, kär′ə-spän′dent) *n.* **1** a person with whom you exchange letters. **2** a person employed by a newspaper to write reports.

cor·ri·dor (kôr′əd-ər, kär′əd-ər) *n.* a passageway, especially one off which rooms open.

cor·rode (kə-rōd′) *vb.* **cor·rod·ing, cor·rod·ed** to eat away little by little; to rust.

cor·ro·sion (kə-rō′zhən) *n.* the process of corroding or eating away. – *adj.* **cor·ro·sive** (kə-rō′siv).

cor·rupt (kə-rupt′) *vb.* **cor·rupt·ing, cor·rupt·ed 1** to change for the worse, especially morally. **2** to spoil, deform, or make impure. **3** to bribe. **4** to decay or deteriorate. – *adj.* morally evil.

●**Cor·tés** (kôr-tez′, kôr-tes′), **Hernando** (1485-1547) was a Spanish soldier who conquered the AZTEC Empire in MEXICO.

Hernando Cortés was the best known of the Spanish conquistadors. He was welcomed by Montezuma, the Aztec ruler, and showered with gifts. In return, Cortés plundered the Aztec empire and captured Montezuma.

cos·mic (käz′mik) *adj.* belonging or relating to the universe. – *adv.* **cos·mi·cal·ly** (käz′mi-klē).

cos·mo·naut (käz′mə-nôt′, käz′mə-nät′) *n.* a Russian astronaut.

cost (kôst) *vb.* **cost·ing, cost 1** to be obtainable at a certain price. **2** to involve the loss or sacrifice of. – *n.* **1** what something costs. **2** loss or sacrifice.

●**Cos·ta Ri·ca** (kô′stə rē′kə, käs′tə rē′kə). See Supplement, **Countries**.

cost·ly (kôst′lē) *adj.* **costl·i·er, costl·i·est 1** expensive. **2** involving big losses or sacrifices.

One kind of coral island is the atoll, a ringed reef that encloses a central lagoon. The original volcanic island sinks and more coral and sand build up on top of the reef.

Egyptian

Minoan

1640s
England

1920s

Roman

Viking

Costumes in the ancient world were based on the tunic. In Europe in the Middle Ages the rich alone could afford fine materials. In the Renaissance the rich liked exaggerated styles.

19th Century

1960s

cos·tume (käs′tōōm′, käs′tyōōm) *n.* clothing, especially of a particular period or country.
cot (kät) *n.* a narrow canvas bed.

● **Côte d'I·voire** (kōt′ dēv-wär′) (**Ivory Coast**). See Supplement, **Countries**.

cot·tage (kät′ij) *n.* a small house, especially one used for vacation.
cot·ton (kät′n) *n.* **1** the soft downy fibers that cover the seeds of the a low shrub. **2** the plant itself. **3** thread or cloth made from the fibers. − *vb.* (*informal*) **cot·ton on, cot·ton·ing, cot·toned** to understand.

● The Cotton Belt of the UNITED STATES produces over 15% of the world's cotton. The cotton gin, invented by Eli WHITNEY in 1793 increased production greatly.

couch (kouch) *n.* a sofa or settee.
cou·gar (kōō′gər) *n.* a mountain lion.

The cougar is a North American mountain lion.

cough (kôf) *vb.* **cough·ing, coughed** to force out air, mucus, etc. from the throat or lungs with a rough sharp noise.
could (kood) *vb.* (*auxiliary*) **1** *past tense* of **can**: *I found I could lift it.* **2** used to express a possibility or a possible course: *You could try telephoning her.* **3** used in making requests: *Could you help me?*
coun·cil (koun′səl) *n.* a group of people who advise, administer, discuss, or legislate.
coun·cil·lor (kown′sə-lər) *n.* a member of a council.
coun·sel (koun′səl) *n.* **1** advice. **2** a lawyer or group of lawyers that gives legal advice and fights cases in court. − *vb.* **coun·sel·ing, counsel·ed** to advise.
counselor (koun′sə-lər) *n.* **1** a person who gives professional advice. **2** a lawyer. **3** a person in charge of children at a camp.
count¹ (kount) *vb.* **count·ing, count·ed** **1** to say numbers in order. **2** to find the total amount of, by adding up item by item. **3** to include. − *n.* **1** an act of counting. **2** the number counted. − *adj.* **count·a·ble** (kount′ə-bəl). − **count me in** I'm willing to be included.
count² (kount) *n.* a European nobleman.
count·down (kount′doun′) *n.* a count backward, having zero as the moment for action, used especially in launching a rocket.
count·er¹ (kount′ər) *n.* **1** the long table in a store, bank, etc. over which goods are sold, food is served, or business done. **2** a small disk used in various board games.

Counter in the first sense was once used to describe a table on which money was counted; it then was used for any narrow table. A counter is also an object for counting in certain games. Counter in the second sense comes from a French word meaning "against."

PRONUNCIATION SYMBOLS

ə	**away**	lemon	focus
a	fat	oi	**boy**
ā	fade	oo	foot
ä	hot	ōō	moon
âr	**fair**	ou	house
e	met	th	think
ē	mean	<u>th</u>	this
g	**get**	u	cut
hw	**which**	ur	hurt
i	fin	w	witch
ī	line	y	yes
îr	**near**	yōō	music
ô	**often**	yoor	**pure**
ō	note	zh	vision

Squash courts are enclosed within four walls and have an entrance in the back. The game originates from Harrow School, England, where boys practiced knocking a ball around in a courtyard while waiting to get into a rackets court. The rackets ball is hard but the boys practiced with a soft, or "squash" ball.

count·er² (kount′ər) *adv.* in the opposite direction to: *Results ran counter to expectations.*

counter- *prefix* **1** against: *counteract.* **2** corresponding: *counterpart.*

coun·ter·clock·wise (kount′ər-kläk′wīz′) *adj. & adv.* in the opposite direction to that in which the hands of a clock move.

coun·ter·feit (kount′ər-fit′) *adj.* **1** made in imitation of a genuine article, especially with a dishonest purpose. **2** not genuine; insincere. – *vb.* **coun·ter·feit·ing, coun·ter·feit·ed** to copy for a dishonest purpose; to forge.

coun·tess (kount′əs) *n.* a European noblewoman.

coun·try (kun′trē) *n.* **countries** **1** the land of any of the nations of the world. **2** your native land. **3** open land. **4** an area or district: *mining country.* **5** the government of a land: *Our country is a democracy.* **6** the people of a nation.

country-and-western *n.* popular music of a style from the western and southern UNITED STATES.

coun·try·side (kun′trē-sīd′) *n.* land away from towns.

coun·ty (kount′ē) *n.* **coun·ties** any of the geographical divisions of local government within a state or country.

coup·le (kup′əl) *n.* **1** a man and wife, or other pair of people romantically attached. **2** two of a kind: *a couple of pears.*

cou·rage (kur′ij) *n.* **1** bravery; lack of fear. **2** cheerfulness in coping with setbacks.

cou·ra·geous (kə-rā′jəs) *adj.* having courage.

cou·ri·er (koor′ē-ər, kur′ē-ər) *n.* a messenger.

course (kôrs, kōrs) *n.* **1** the path that anything moves in. **2** a direction taken or planned: *The rocket went off course.* **3** the normal progress of something: *the course of history.* **4** a series of lessons or a program of study: *a science course.* **5** any of the successive parts of a meal: *Veal was the main course.* **6** the ground over which a game is played or a race run. – **of course 1** as expected. **2** without doubt. **3** admittedly.

court (kôrt, kōrt) *n.* **1** the judge, law officials, and members of the jury gathered to hear and decide on a legal case. **2** the place (**courtroom**) or building used for such a hearing. **3** an area marked out for a particular game: *a squash court.* – *vb.* **court·ing, court·ed 1** to try to win the favor of. **2** to risk or invite: *He courts danger with his rash behavior.* – **the ball is in your court** you must make the next move. – **go to court** to take legal action.

court·yard (kôrt′yärd′, kōrt′yärd′) *n.* an open space surrounded by buildings or walls.

cour·te·ous (kurt′ē-əs) *adj.* polite; considerate.

cour·te·sy (kurt′ə-sē) *n.* **cour·te·sies 1** polite and thoughtful behavior: *She treats everyone with the same courtesy.* **2** a courteous act.

cous·in (kuz′ən) *n.* **1** a son or daughter of your uncle or aunt. **2** a close relative.

cov·er (kuv′ər) *vb.* **cov·er·ing, co·vered 1** to form a layer over: *Ice covered the lake.* **2** to protect or conceal by putting something over: *Sheila covered her head with a blanket.* **3** to extend over: *Forests cover huge areas of Canada.* **4** to sprinkle, mark all over, etc. **5** to deal with a subject: *The book covers the French Revolution.* – *n.* **1** something that covers; a lid, top, protective casing, etc. **2** the covering of something: *She has filled her garden with plants that give good ground cover.* **3** the binding of a book, magazine, etc. **4** shelter, protection: *Take cover!* – *vb.* **cover for** to take over the duties of. – *n. & adj.* **cov·er·ing.** – *vb.* **cover up** to conceal a mistake, etc. – **under cover** in secret.

The markings on a tennis court are always the same regardless of its surface. Lines are painted on hard courts, but chalk lines mark grass courts. In doubles matches the playing area is enlarged by including the alleys. Serves in double games must still land in the service courts.

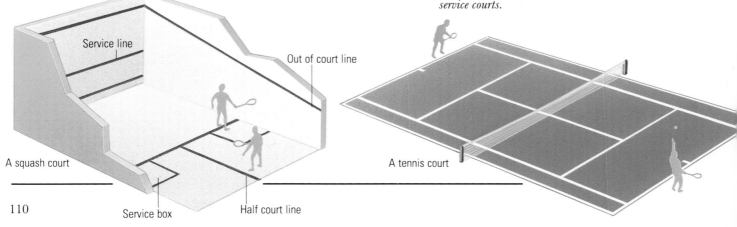

Service line

Out of court line

A squash court

A tennis court

Service box

Half court line

cov·er·age (kuv′ə-rij) *n.* **1** protection against risks in an insurance policy. **2** the reporting of news. **3** the manner or extent to which something is covered.

cow (kou) *n.* **1** the female of cattle. **2** the female of other large animals, as the elephant, whale, seal, and moose. – **till the cows come home** (*informal*) for a very long time.

cow·boy (kou′boi′) *n.* a man in charge of cattle on a ranch.

cow·girl (kou′gurl′) *n.* a woman in charge of cattle on a ranch.

cow·ard (kou′ərd) *n.* someone easily frightened, or lacking courage to face danger. – *n.* **cow·ard·ice** (kou′ərd-əs) – *adj.* **cow·ard·ly**.

coy (koi) *adj.* shy or pretending to be shy. – *n.* **coy·ness**.

coy·ot·e (kī′ōt′, kī-ōt′ē) *n.* **coyote** or **coy·ot·es** a small North American wolf.

crab (krab) *n.* an edible shellfish with a wide flat shell and five pairs of legs, the front pair taking the form of pincers. See CRUSTACEANS.

crack (krak) *vb.* **crack·ing, cracked 1** to fracture partially without falling to pieces: *Although the jug was cracked we still used it.* **2** to split, making a sudden sharp noise: *Ned cracked a nut with his teeth.* **3** to strike sharply. **4** to force open a safe. **5** to solve a code or problem. – *n.* **1** a sudden sharp sound. **2** a partial fracture. **3** a narrow opening. – *vb.* **crack down on** to take firm action against.

crack·er *n.* **1** a thin crisp biscuit. **2** a small noisy firework.

-cracy *suffix* rule or domination by a particular group, etc.: *democracy*.

cra·dle (krād′l) *n.* **1** a bed for a small baby that can be rocked. **2** a place of origin; the home of something: *The city of Ur is the cradle of civilization.*

craft (kraft) *n.* **1** a skill or occupation, especially one requiring the use of the hands: *They practiced crafts such as weaving and pottery.* **2** a boat or ship, or an air or space vehicle.

craft·y (kraf′tē) *adj.* **craft·i·er, craft·i·est** clever, shrewd.

cram (kram) *vb.* **cram·ming, crammed 1** to stuff full: *He crammed all he could get into the case.* **2** to study intensively for an examination.

cramp (kramp) *n.* a painful involuntary contraction of a muscle. – *vb.* **cramp·ing, cramped** to restrict or confine tightly.

cran·ber·ry (kran′ber′ē, kran′bə-rē) *n.*

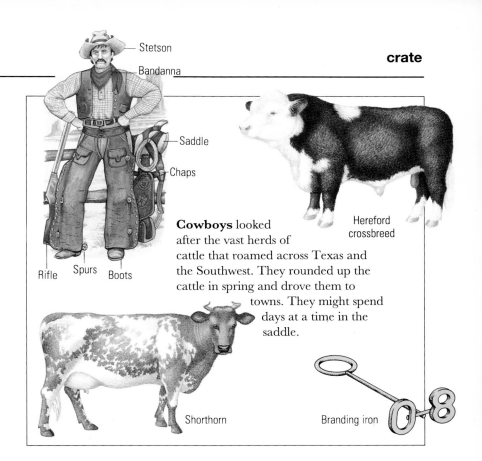

Stetson
Bandanna
Saddle
Chaps
Rifle Spurs Boots
Hereford crossbreed
Shorthorn
Branding iron

Cowboys looked after the vast herds of cattle that roamed across Texas and the Southwest. They rounded up the cattle in spring and drove them to towns. They might spend days at a time in the saddle.

cran·ber·ries 1 a sour red berry that grows on a shrub in bogs. **2** the plant itself.

crane (krān) *n.* **1** a machine for lifting heavy weights, having a long arm from which lifting gear is suspended. **2** any of various large, long-legged, long-necked birds.

● A crane's long arm is called a "jib." Modern cranes have a powerful motor, which winches the hook, raises and lowers the jib, and turns the cab around.

cra·ni·um (krā′nē-əm) *n.* **cra·ni·a** (krā′nē-ə) or **craniums** the dome of the skull, enclosing the brain.

crash (krash) *vb.* **crash·ing, crashed 1** to fall or strike with a banging or smashing noise. **2** to collide; to hit something destructively on landing: *The plane crashed into the mountain.* **3** (of a business or a stock exchange) to collapse. **4** (of a computer or program) to fail completely. – *n.* **1** a violent impact or breakage. **2** a deafening noise. **3** a traffic or aircraft accident. **4** the failure of a computer.

crash helmet *n.* a protective helmet worn by motorcyclists, pilots, etc.

crate (krāt) *n.* a strong box made of slats, for carrying goods: *a milk crate.*

Cranes can be fixed in one place, like the tower cranes erected on building sites.

Craters on the moon

Most of the craters on the moon were formed when smaller bodies crashed into its surface and blasted out a crater 10 times their own width.

In the blast rocky material was thrown out for hundreds of miles.

The violent impact produced shock waves, causing mountains to be formed in the center of the crater.

Over time dust settled in the crater.

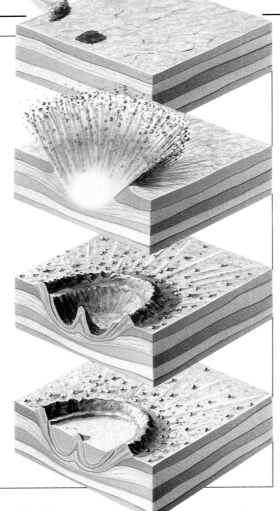

cra·ter (krāt′ər) *n.* **1** the bowl-shaped mouth of a volcano. **2** a hole made by an explosion.

crave (krāv) *vb.* **crav·ing, craved** to desire overwhelmingly: *An addict craves drugs.*

crawl (krôl) *vb.* **crawl·ing, crawled 1** (of insects, worms, etc.) to move along the ground. **2** to move along on hands and knees. **3** to progress very slowly: *Rush hour traffic crawls along.* **4** to be covered with crawling insects. – *n.* **1** a crawling motion. **2** a very slow pace. **3** a rapid overhand swimming stroke in which the feet kick continually.

craze (krāz) *n.* a fashion or something that is popular for a short time; a fad.

cra·zy (krā′zē) *adj.* **cra·zi·er, cra·zi·est 1** mad; insane. **2** very enthusiastic. – *adv.* **cra·zi·ly** (krā′zə-lē). – *n.* **cra·zi·ness**.

creak (krēk) *n.* a squeaking noise, as made by an unoiled hinge. – *vb.* **creak·ing, creaked** to make this noise.

cream (krēm) *n.* **1** the yellowish-white fatty substance on top of milk, from which butter and cheese are made. **2** any of many cosmetic preparations similar to cream in texture.

crease (krēs) *n.* a line made by folding, pressing, or crushing.

cre·ate (krē-āt′) *vb.* **cre·at·ing, cre·at·ed 1** to form from nothing. **2** to produce or cause: *His behavior created a riot.*

cre·a·tion (krē-ā′shən) *n.* **1** the act of creating. **2** something created.

cre·a·tive (krē-āt′iv) *adj.* having the ability to make something new; imaginative. – *n.* **cre·a·tiv·i·ty** (krē′ā-tiv′ət-ē).

cre·a·tor (krē-āt′ər) *n.* a person who creates.

crea·ture (krē′chər) *n.* any living thing.

cred·it (kred′ət) *n.* **1** faith placed in something. **2** a cause of honor: *To her credit, she didn't say anything.* **3** acknowledgment, recognition, or praise: *Give him credit for trying.* **4** trust given to someone promising to pay later for goods already supplied. **5** reputation for paying back: *Her credit is good.* **6** a balance in your favor, as in a bank. – *vb.* **cred·it·ing, cred·it·ed 1** to believe; to place faith in. **2** to attribute a quality or achievement to. **3** to note credit due.

creed (krēd) *n.* a statement of the main points of personal or religious beliefs.

creek (krēk, krik) *n.* a small stream.

creep (krēp) *vb.* **creep·ing, crept** (krept) **1** to move slowly and silently. **2** to move with the body close to the ground; to crawl. **3** (of plants) to grow along the ground, up a wall, etc.

creep·y (krēp′ē) *adj.* **creep·i·er, creep·i·est** (*informal*) frightening.

cre·mate (krē′māt′, kri-māt′) *vb.* **cre·mat·ing, cre·mat·ed** to burn a corpse to ashes. – *n.* **cre·ma·tion** (kri-mā′shən).

cres·cent (kres′ənt) *n.* **1** the moon in its first or last quarter. **2** a figure with that shape.

As the new moon moves through the first quarter of its orbit, a crescent moon is seen, followed by half and then full moon. The "phases" continue in reverse order until the moon is new again.

crest (krest) *n.* **1** a comb or vertical tuft of feathers on the head of certain birds. **2** the topmost ridge of a mountain. – *adj.* **crest·ed**.

●**Crete** (krēt') is a Greek island in the MEDITERRANEAN where the Minoan civilization flourished 5,000 years ago.

crew (krōō) *n.* a team of people operating a ship, aircraft, train, bus, etc.

crib (krib) *n.* **1** a baby's bed enclosed with rails. **2** a bin or structure for storing grain, fodder, etc. – *vb.* **crib·bing, cribbed** to copy or plagiarize.

crick·et[1] (krik'ət) *n.* a grasshopperlike insect, the male of which makes a chirping noise by rubbing its forewings together.

There are about 2,500 species of cricket, most of which live in tropical regions. Their long thin antennae distinguish them from grasshoppers.

crick·et[2] (krik'ət) *n.* an outdoor game played with a ball, bats, and wickets, between two sides of eleven players. – *n.* **crick·e·ter**.

crime (krīm) *n.* an illegal act; an act punishable by law; an act gravely wrong morally.

crim·i·nal (krim'ən-l) *n.* a person guilty of a crime. – *adj.* against the law: *The gang was involved in criminal activities.*

crim·son (krim'zən) *n. & adj.* dark red.

cri·sis (krī'səs) *n.* **cri·ses** (krī'sēz') **1** a crucial or decisive event. **2** a serious time.

crisp (krisp) *adj.* **1** dry and brittle: *Crisp crackers break into crumbs.* **2** (of vegetables or fruit) firm and fresh. **3** (of weather) fresh; bracing. – *adj.* **crisp·y, crisp·i·er, crisp·i·est**.

cri·te·ri·on (krī-tîr'ē-ən) *n.* **cri·te·ri·a** (krī-tîr'ē-ə) a standard on which to base a judgment.

crit·ic (krit'ik) *n.* **1** a person whose job it is to review literature, art, drama, or music. **2** a person who finds fault with something.

crit·i·cal (krit'i-kəl) *adj.* **1** always finding fault. **2** relating to a critic or criticism: *a critical review.* **3** relating to a crisis; decisive; crucial.

crit·i·cism (krit'ə-siz'əm) *n.* **1** fault-finding. **2** reasoned assessment, as of art, music, etc.

crit·i·cize or **crit·i·cise** (krit'ə-sīz') *vb.* **crit·i·ciz·ing, crit·i·cized** to find fault, express disapproval.

croak (krōk) *n.* the noise made by a frog.

●**Cro·a·tia** (krō-ā'shə). See Supplement, **Countries**.

cro·chet (krō-shā') *n.* decorative needlework made with a hooked needle. – *vb.* **cro·chet·ing, cro·cheted**.

crock·er·y (kräk'ə-rē) *n.* plates, cups, etc.

●**Crock·ett** (kräk'ət)**, Davy** (1786-1836) was an American politician and frontiersman.

croc·o·dile (kräk'ə-dīl') *n.* a large, thick-scaled, long-tailed reptile with huge jaws.

cro·cus (krō'kəs) *n.* **crocuses** a spring-flowering plant that grows from a bulb.

●**Crom·well** (kräm'wel', kräm'wəl)**, Oliver** (1599-1658) English ruler and general.

crook (krook) *n.* **1** a bend or curve: *He carried it in the crook of his arm.* **2** a thief or swindler.

crook·ed (krook'əd) *adj.* bent, curved.

crop (kräp) *n.* **1** a cereal or other plant grown as food; the season's yield from such a plant. **2** a batch: *This year's crop of graduates is one of the best ever.* **3** a horse rider's short whip. **4** a pouch projecting from the neck of certain birds, in which food is prepared for digestion. – *vb.* **crop·ping, cropped 1** to trim; to cut short. **2** to grow a plant for its produce.

Crop rotation is a system of planting different crops grown in rotation on the same land. On three fields, for example, the rotation might be corn, oats, and clover. This allows the soil to rest and be restored so that it can remain in use and give high yields.

Over the years the basic design of the cross has been elaborated and embellished in many ways. Here are a few different types of cross.

Greek

St. Andrew's

Celtic

St. Anthony's

Latin

Maltese

cro·quet (krō-kā′) *n.* a game played on a lawn, in which mallets are used to drive wooden balls through wire hoops.

cross (krôs) *n.* **1** a mark, structure, or symbol composed of two lines, one crossing the other in the form + or ×. **2** an upright post with a horizonal bar, used to crucify prisoners in ancient Rome. **3** (often **Cross**) the cross on which Jesus died. **4** intermingling between breeds or species; the resulting hybrid: *Our dog is a cross between a spaniel and a poodle.* – *vb.* **cross·ing, crossed 1** to move, pass, or get across. **2** to place one across the other: *He crossed his legs.* **3** to meet; to intersect. **4** to delete or cancel by drawing a line through: *Paul crossed out the message on the letter.* **5** to interbreed: *They tried to cross a sheep with a goat.* **cross out** to delete some words by drawing a line through them. – *adj.* angry; in a bad temper.

cross·ex·am·ine (krô′sig-zam′ən) *vb.* **cross·ex·am·in·ing, cross-ex·am·ined** to question, especially a witness, so as to develop or throw doubt on his or her statement. – *n.* **cross-ex·am·i·na·tion** (krô′sig-zam′ə-nā′shən).

crouch (krouch) *vb.* **crouch·ing, crouched** to bend low or squat with legs close to the chest and with hands on the ground.

crow (krō) *n.* **1** a large black bird or any of several related large birds including the raven, jackdaw, and magpie. **2** the shrill cry of a cock. – *vb.* **crow·ing, crowed** or **crew** (krōō) **1** to cry shrilly. **2** to triumph gleefully; to gloat: *The winning team crowed over the losers.* – **as the crow flies** in a straight line.

crow·bar (krō′bär′) *n.* a heavy iron bar with a bent, flattened end, used as a lever.

crowd (kroud) *n.* **1** a large number of people gathered together. **2** the spectators or audience at an event. – *vb.* **crowd·ing, crowd·ed** to move in a large, tightly-packed group.

crown (kroun) *n.* **1** the circular, usually jeweled, gold headdress of kings and queens. **2** the part of a tooth projecting from the gum. **3** the top part, as of the head; a hat, etc. – *vb.* **crown·ing, crowned 1** to place a crown ceremonially on the head of; to make king or queen. **2** to make perfect: *Her efforts were crowned with success.* **3** to put an artificial crown on a tooth.

crown·ing (krou′ning) *adj.* greatest: *her crowning moment.*

cru·cial (krōō′shəl) *adj.* decisive; critical.

cru·ci·fix (krōō′sə-fiks′) *n.* a representation of Christ on the cross.

crude (krōōd) *adj.* **1** in its natural, unrefined state: *crude oil.* **2** vulgar; tasteless.

cru·el (krōō′əl) *adj.* **1** deliberately causing pain or suffering. **2** harsh or severe: *a cruel wind.* – *adv.* **cru·el·ly** (krōō′əl-tē). – *n.* **cru·el·ty, cru·el·ties.**

cruise (krōōz) *vb.* **cruis·ing, cruised 1** to sail about for pleasure, calling at different places. **2** to go at a steady, comfortable speed.

crumb (krum) *n.* a tiny piece of cake, etc.

crum·ble (krum′bəl) *vb.* **crum·bling, crumbled** to break into crumbs or powdery fragments: *The fragile pots crumbled in her hands.*

crum·ple (krum′pəl) *vb.* **crum·pling, crum·pled 1** to make or become creased or crushed: *She crumpled the letter in her hand.* **2** to collapse.

crunch (krunch) *vb.* **crunch·ing, crunched** to crush or grind noisily between the teeth or under the foot: *She crunched a carrot.*

cru·sade (krōō-sād′) *n.* **1** a CHRISTIAN military expedition in medieval times to regain the Holy Land of Palestine from the MUSLIMS. **2** a campaign in aid of a cause: *Our school started a no-smoking crusade.* – *vb.* **cru·sad·ing, cru·sad·ed** to campaign. – *n.* **cru·sad·er.**

THE CRUSADES

Palestine, Holy Land of the Bible, was overrun by Muslims in 638. In 1095 the Pope called on Christian warriors to recover the Holy Land from the "infidels." The numerous expeditions—until the end of the 13th century—were known as crusades, from the Spanish word *cruzada*—"marked with the cross."

The crossed legs of this effigy of a Norman knight show that he had been on a crusade.

crush (krush) *vb.* **crush·ing, crushed 1** to break, damage, or distort by compressing violently. **2** to crumple or crease. **3** to defeat or subdue. − *n.* **1** violent compression. **2** a dense crowd. **3** a strong but not serious love for another person.

crust (krust) *n.* **1** the hard-baked outer surface of a loaf of bread; a piece of this. **2** the outer surface of the Earth.

crus·ta·cean (krus-tā′shən) *n.* a large group of mainly aquatic creatures with hard shells, as crabs, lobsters, crayfish, and shrimps.

● Crustaceans are a large group of about 10,000 creatures. They are invertebrates (animals without backbones). Many have pincers on their front legs.

crux (kruks) *n.* **cruxes** a crucial point.

cry (krī) *vb.* **cries, cry·ing, cried 1** to shed tears; to weep. **2** to shout or shriek, in pain or fear, or to get attention or help. **3** (of an animal or bird) to utter its characteristic noise. − *n.* **cries 1** a shout or shriek. **2** an excited utterance or exclamation. **3** an appeal or demand: *Her act was a cry for help.* **4** the characteristic sound of an animal or bird.

crypt (kript) *n.* an underground chamber beneath a church, used for burials.

Krak des Chevaliers, a crusader castle in Tripoli, defied 12 sieges.

Richard I "the Lion-Hearted" was an ardent crusader but failed to recapture Jerusalem.

cryp·tic (krip′tik) *adj.* puzzling.

crys·tal (krist′l) *n.* **1** a colorless transparent quartz. **2** a solid body having flat surfaces forming regular, characteristic patterns. − *adj.* like crystal in brilliance and clarity. − **crystal clear** as clear as can be.

● Snowflakes, salt grains, and diamonds are all crystals. In a crystal the molecules are arranged in a regular pattern: for example, all snowflakes are six-sided crystals.

crys·tal·lize (krist′l-iz′) *vb.* **crys·tal·liz·ing, crys·tal·lized 1** to form into crystals. **2** (of plans, ideas, etc.) to make or become clear.

cub (kub) *n.* the young of certain animals, as the fox, bear, lion, or wolf.

● **Cuba** (kyōō′bə). See Supplement, **Countries**.

cube (kyōōb) *n.* **1** a solid figure having six equal square faces. **2** in math, the product of a number multiplied by itself twice.

cu·bi·cle (kyōō′bə-kəl) *n.* a small compartment, room, or enclosed area.

cuck·oo (kook′ōō′, kōō′koo′) *n.* a bird known for its two-note call.

cu·cum·ber (kyoo′kum′bər) *n.* a long green vegetable with juicy white flesh, used in salads. − **cool as a cucumber** (*informal*) calm.

cud (kud) *n.* the half-digested food that a cow or other ruminant brings back into the mouth from the stomach to chew again.

cud·dle (kud′l) *vb.* **cud·dling, cud·dled** to hug or embrace affectionately. − *n.* a hug.

cue¹ (kyōō) *n.* the final words of an actor's speech that serve as a prompt for another to say or do something.

cue² (kyōō) *n.* a stick tapering to a point, used to strike the ball in billiards, and pool.

cuff (kuf) *n.* **1** the lower end of a sleeve. **2** the turned-up part of a pant leg.

cul·prit (kul′prət) *n.* a person guilty of a misdeed.

cul·ti·vate (kul′tə-vāt′) *vb.* **cul·ti·vat·ing, cul·ti·vat·ed 1** to prepare and use land or soil for crops. **2** to develop or improve.

cul·ture (kul′chər) *n.* **1** the customs, ideas, art, etc. of a particular civilization or social group. **2** appreciation of art, music, etc. **3** a crop of bacteria grown for study. − *adj.* **cul·tur·al** (kul′chə-rəl).

cul·tured (kul′chərd) *adj.* well-educated.

Snowflake crystal

Diamond

Graphite

The scientific study of crystals is called crystallography. Scientists measure the angles between crystal faces and analyze the surface arrangements.

PRONUNCIATION SYMBOLS			
ə	**away** lemon		focus
a	**fat**	oi	**boy**
ā	**fade**	oo	**foot**
ä	**hot**	ōō	**moon**
âr	**fair**	ou	**house**
e	**met**	th	**think**
ē	**mean**	<u>th</u>	**this**
g	**get**	u	**cut**
hw	**which**	ur	**hurt**
i	**fin**	w	**witch**
ī	**line**	y	**yes**
îr	**near**	yōō	**music**
ô	**often**	yoor	**pure**
ō	**note**	zh	**vision**

cum·ber·some (kum′bər-səm) *adj.* awkward.

cun·ning (kun′ing) *adj.* clever, sly, crafty, or artful. – *n.* skill used in a crafty manner.

cup (kup) *n.* **1** a small round container with a handle, from which to drink. **2** the amount a cup will hold; a measure of eight ounces. **3** an ornamental vessel awarded as a prize.

cup·board (kub′ərd) *n.* a piece of furniture, or a recess, fitted with doors, shelves, etc., for storing food, etc.

curb (kurb) *n.* **1** something that restrains or controls. **2** a raised border of stone or concrete along a street. – *vb.* **curbing, curbed** to restrain or control: *Curb your temper.*

One of the earliest coins, from Anatolia, and a spade-shaped early Chinese coin. Bottom: A 7th century Chinese banknote.

> **CURIOUS CURRENCY WORDS**
> Many strange words appear on coins and bank-notes. Here is the meaning of a few:
>
> **Latin words**
> | | |
> |---|---|
> | REGINA | Queen |
> | REX | King |
>
> **Countries**
> | | |
> |---|---|
> | DANSKE | Denmark |
> | DEUTSCHLAND | Germany |
> | EIRE | Ireland |
> | ESPAÑA | Spain |
> | HELVETIA | Switzerland |
> | ISLAND | Iceland |
> | MAGYAR | Hungary |
> | NORGE | Norway |
> | ÖSTERREICH | Austria |
> | SUOMI | Finland |
> | SVERIGES | Sweden |

cure (kyoor) *vb.* **cur·ing, cured 1** to restore to health; to heal; to get rid of an illness, harmful habit, etc. **2** to preserve meat, fish, etc. by salting, smoking, etc. – *n.* something that cures or remedies: *Many people rely on herbal cures.* – *adj.* **cur·a·ble** (kyoor′ə-bəl).

●**Cu·rie** (kyoor′ē, kyoor-ē′), **Marie** (1867-1934) was a Polish-born scientist who, with her husband, Pierre, was one of the earliest workers in the science of RADIOACTIVITY.

cu·ri·o (kyoor′ē-ō′) *n.* **cu·ri·os** an article valued for its rarity or unusualness.

cu·ri·os·i·ty (kyoor′ē-äs′ət-ē) *n.* eagerness to know.

cu·ri·ous (kyoor′ē-əs) *adj.* **1** strange; odd: *A curious thing happened last night.* **2** eager or interested: *I am curious to see what happens.* **3** inquisitive.

curl (kurl) *vb.* **curl·ing, curled 1** to twist or roll into coils or ringlets: *Norma curled her hair in the lastest fashion.* **2** to move in, or form into, a spiral, coil, or curve. – *n.* a ringlet of hair. – *vb.* **curl up** to sit or lie with the legs tucked up.

cur·lew (kur′lōō′, kurl′yōō′) *n.* a long-legged wading bird with a long curved beak and loud cry.

cur·rant (kur′ənt) *n.* **1** a small dried seedless grape. **2** any of several small soft berries.

cur·ren·cy (kur′ən-sē) *n.* **cur·ren·cies** the money, or the coins and notes, in use in a country.

cur·rent (kur′ənt) *adj.* **1** generally accepted: *Smoke is bad for you according to the current view.* **2** belonging to the present: *Who is your current boyfriend?* – *n.* **1** a continuous flow of water or air. **2** the flow of electricity through a circuit or wire.

cur·rent·ly *adv.* at the present time.

cur·ric·u·lum (kə-rik′yə-ləm) *n.* **cur·ric·u·la** (kə-rik′yə-lə) a course of study at school or college.

curriculum vi·tae (vē′tī′) *n.* **curricula vitae** a resumé.

cur·ry (kur′ē) *n.* **cur·ries 1** a powder made from ground spices. **2** a sauce made from this powder. **3** a dish of meat or vegetables cooked with this powder or sauce.

curse (kurs) *n.* **1** a word used in swearing; a proface expression of anger; an oath. **2** an evil; a cause of harm: *the curse of drugs.* **3** a wish for something bad to happen to someone. – *vb.* **curs·ing, cursed**.

cur·sor (kur′sər) *n.* a flashing marker on a computer screen indicating the current position of the operator.

curt (kurt) *adj.* rudely brief; abrupt.

cur·tail (kur-tāl′) *vb.* **cur·tail·ing, cur·tailed** to restrict: *The plans for a new town were curtailed.*

cur·tain (kurt′n) *n.* a hanging cloth over a window or open space for privacy or to exclude light. A curtain is also hung in front of a stage to screen it from the auditorium.

curve (kurv) *n.* **1** a line no part of which is straight, or a surface no part of which is flat: *There is a curve in the road.* **2** any smoothly arched line or shape, like part of a circle or sphere. – *vb.* **curv·ing, curved** to form a curve; to bend or move in a curve.

cush·ion (koosh′ən) *n.* a pillow or a stuffed fabric case used for making a seat comfortable, for kneeling on, etc. – *vb.* **cush·ion·ing, cush·ioned** to reduce the unpleasant or violent effect of: *The mattress cushioned her fall.*

● **Cus·ter** (kus′tər), **George** (1839-1876) was an American army general ordered to resettle CHEYENNE and SIOUX people in reservations. He was killed at a SIOUX village at Little Big-horn River in an attack led by Chief SITTING BULL.

cus·tod·y (kus′təd-ē) *n.* **1** protective care; the right to be guardian of a child, awarded to someone by a court of law. **2** imprisonment.

cus·tom (kus′təm) *n.* **1** a traditional activity or practice. **2** a personal habit.

cus·tom·ar·y (kus′tə-mer′ē) *adj.* usual. – *adv.* **cus·tom·ar·i·ly** (kus′tə-mer′ə-lē).

cus·tom·er (kus′tə-mər) *n.* a person who buys from a store or company.

cus·toms (kus′təmz) *n.* **1** taxes imposed on items brought into a country. **2** the government agency responsible for these taxes. **3** the place at a port, airport, etc. where baggage is inspected to determine these taxes.

cut (kut) *vb.* **cut·ting, cut 1** to slit, pierce, slice, or sever with a sharp-edged instrument; to be so slit, pierced, etc. **2** to divide by cutting. **3** trim: *Barbara cut his hair.* **4** to reap or harvest: *He cut some flowers.* **5** make or form by cutting. **6** to injure or wound with a sharp edge or instrument. **7** to reduce: *The working week was cut to 35 hours.* – *n.* **1** an act of cutting. **2** a slit, incision, or injury made by cutting. **3** a reduction. – *vb.* **cut back** to reduce spending, etc. – *vb.* **cut down 1** to fell: *They cut down a tree.* **2** to reduce: *He tried to cut down on spending.*

cut·ting (kut′ing) *n.* an extract, article, or picture cut from a newspaper, etc. – *adj.* hurtful; sarcastic.

cut·ler·y (kut′lə-rē) *n.* knives, forks, and spoons.

cy·cle (sī′kəl) *n.* **1** a constantly repeating series of events: *the cycle of the seasons.* **2** a bicycle or motorcycle. – *vb.* **cy·cling, cy·cled** to ride a bicycle or motorcycle.

cy·clone (sī′klōn′) *n.* **1** a system of winds blowing spirally inward toward a center of low pressure; a depression. **2** a violent wind storm.

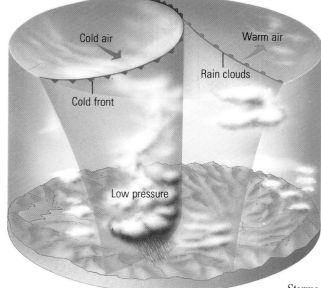

Storms usually occur with cyclones. The cold air along a cold front forces the warmer air to rise along a warm front. Clouds develop and as the air rises and cools, the water vapor it carries condenses, and rain begins to fall.

cyg·net (sig′nət) *n.* a young swan.

cyl·in·der (sil′ən-dər) *n.* **1** a solid or hollow object shaped like a tube. **2** a container of this shape. **3** in an internal combustion engine, the chamber inside which the piston moves.

cym·bal (sim′bəl) *n.* a platelike brass musical instrument, either beaten with a drumstick, or used as one of a pair that are struck together.

cyn·ic (sin′ik) *n.* a person who believes the worst about people. – *adj.* **cyn·i·cal**.

cy·press (sī′prəs) *n.* a slim coniferous tree.

Cyp·ri·ot (sip′rē-ət, sip′rē-ät′) *n.* a native of CYPRUS, a MEDITERRANEAN island.

● **Cy·prus** (sī′prəs). See Supplement, **Countries**.

cys·tic fi·bro·sis (sis′tik fī-brō′səs) *n.* an inherited disease of children causing the formation of cysts and excess mucus, which interfere with breathing and digestion.

czar (zär, tsär) *n.* the title given to the emperors of Russia until 1917.

cza·ri·na (zä-rē′nə, tsä-rē′nə) *n.* the title given to the empress of Russia or to the wife or widow of a czar.

Czech (chek) *n.* **1** a native of the CZECH REPUBLIC of Bohemia and Moldavia. **2** the official language of the CZECH REPUBLIC.

● **Czech Republic** (chek). See Supplement, **Countries**.

PRONUNCIATION SYMBOLS			
ə	away lemon		focus
a	fat	oi	boy
ā	fade	oo	foot
ä	hot	ōō	moon
âr	fair	ou	house
e	met	th	think
ē	mean	t̲h̲	this
g	get	u	cut
hw	which	ur	hurt
i	fin	w	witch
ī	line	y	yes
îr	near	yōō	music
ô	often	yoor	pure
ō	note	zh	vision

D d

dab (dab) *vb.* **dab·bing, dabbed** to touch lightly, etc.: *I dabbed at the stain with a damp cloth.* – *n.* a small amount of something.

dab·ble (dab′əl) *vb.* **dab·bling, dab·bled** to do or study something without serious effort: *He dabbles in Eastern religions.* – *n.* **dab·bler** (dab′lər).

dachs·hund (däks′hoont′, däk′sənd) *n.* a breed of dog with a long body and short legs.

dad·dy (dad′ē) *n.* **dad·dies** (*informal*) a father.

dad·dy-long·legs (dad′ē-lông′legz′) *n.* **dad·dy-long·legs** a relative of the spider having long, thin legs.

daf·fo·dil (daf′ə-dil′) *n.* a plant which grows from a bulb, with a yellow trumpet-shaped flower.

dag·ger (dag′ər) *n.* a knife or short sword with a pointed end, used for stabbing.

dai·ly (dā′lē) *adj.* happening, appearing, etc. every day, or every weekday. – *adv.* every day. – *n.* a newspaper published every day.

● **Daim·ler** (dām′lər), **Gottlieb** (1834-1900) was a German inventor who built the first motor-cycle.

dain·ty (dān′tē) *adj.* **dain·ti·er, dain·ti·est** small, pretty, and usually delicate. – *adv.* **dain·ti·ly** (dān′təl-ē). – *n.* **dain·ti·ness**.

dair·y (dâr′ē) *n.* **dair·ies 1** a place where milk, butter, cheese, etc. are sold. **2** the building on a farm where milk is kept, and butter and cheese are made.

da·is (dā′əs, dī′əs) *n.* a raised platform in a hall, used by speakers.

dai·sy (dā′zē) *n.* **dai·sies** a small flower with a yellow center and usually white petals.

dale (dāl) *n.* a valley.

Dal·ma·tian (dal-mā′shən) *n.* a large short-haired dog, white with dark spots.

dam (dam) *n.* a wall built across a river, etc. to hold back the water. – *vb.* **dam·ming, dammed** to hold back with a dam.

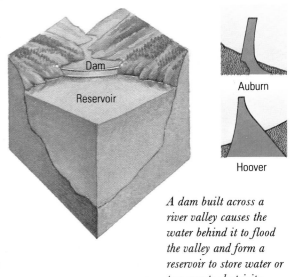

Dam
Reservoir
Auburn
Hoover

A dam built across a river valley causes the water behind it to flood the valley and form a reservoir to store water or to generate electricity.

dam·age (dam′ij) *n.* **1** harm or injury, or loss caused by injury. **2** (in *plural*) payment due for loss or injury caused by another person, organization, etc. – *vb.* **dam·ag·ing, dam·aged** to cause harm to.

● **Da·mas·cus** (də-mas′kəs) is the capital of SYRIA and the world's oldest continuously inhabited city.

damp (damp) *adj.* slightly wet. – *n.* slight wetness, as in walls or the air. – *n.* **damp·ness**.

damp·en (damp'ən) *vb.* **damp·en·ing, damp·ened 1** to make slightly wet. **2** (of emotions) to make less strong.

dance (dans) *vb.* **danc·ing, danced 1** to make a repeated series of rhythmic steps or movements, usually in time to music. **2** to perform by making such steps: *Can you dance the tango?* – *n.* **1** a series of fixed steps, usually made in time to music. **2** a social gathering at which people dance. – *n.* **danc·er**.

Tap dancing — popular in the 1930s

Dancers depicted on a wall of ancient Egypt.

Terpsichore, one of the nine Muses, presided over dancing.

Throughout history people the world over have **danced** — for pleasure, to act out stories, to prepare for battle, or as part of religious rituals.

dan·de·li·on (dan'dl-ī'ən) *n.* a common wild plant with indented leaves and yellow flowers.

dan·druff (dan'drəf) *n.* small pieces of dead skin on the head under the hair.

Dane (dān) *n.* a person born in DENMARK.

dan·ger (dān'jər) *n.* **1** a situation or state in which someone or something may suffer harm, an injury, or a loss: *Danger is all around us.* **2** something that may cause harm, injury, or loss: *You're a danger to other drivers.*

dan·ger·ous (dān'jə-rəs) *adj.* likely to cause harm or injury.

dan·gle (dang'gəl) *vb.* **dan·gling, dan·gled** to hang loosely.

Dan·ish (dā'nish) *adj.* of DENMARK or its inhabitants. – *n.* the language spoken in DENMARK.

dank (dangk) *adj.* unpleasantly wet and cold: *The unheated cellar was dank.*

● **Dan·te** (dän'tā), **Alighieri** (1265-1321) is ITALY's greatest poet, the author of the *Divine Comedy*.

● **Dan·ube** (dan'yo͞ob') a long river in EUROPE, flowing from Germany to the Black Sea.

dap·pled (dap'əld) *adj.* marked with patches of a different color.

dare (dâr) *vb.* **dar·ing, dared 1** to be brave enough to do something frightening, difficult, or dangerous. **2** to challenge someone to do something dangerous, etc. – *n.* a challenge to do something dangerous, etc.

dar·ing (dâr'ing) *adj.* bold or courageous.

dark (därk) *adj.* **1** without light. **2** (of a color) not light or pale; closer to black than white. **3** (of a person or the color of skin or hair) not light or fair. – *n.* **1** the absence of light: *Can you see in the dark?* **2** the time of day when night begins and there is no more light: *Don't go out after dark.* – *n.* **dark·ness** (därk'nəs).

Dark Ages *n.* (*plural*) in European history, the period of time from about the 5th to the 11th centuries when Goths, Vandals, and Huns swept down from the north and destroyed many fine buildings and works of art of the ROMAN EMPIRE.

dark·en (där'kən) *vb.* **dark·en·ing, dark·ened** to make or become dark or darker.

dar·ling (där'ling) *n.* **1** a much loved person. **2** a lovable person or thing: *He's a real darling.*

darn (därn) *vb.* **darn·ing, darned** to mend by sewing with rows of stitches.

dart (därt) *n.* **1** a narrow, pointed weapon that can be thrown or fired. **2** a small sharp-pointed missile used in the game of **darts**. **3** a sudden, quick movement. – *vb.* **dart·ing, dart·ed 1** to move suddenly and quickly. **2** to send or throw quickly: *He darted a quick look at the answer book.*

Dar·win·ism (där'wə-inz'əm) *n.* the theory of the development of the various species of plants and animals by evolution, proposed by Charles *Darwin* (1809-1882).

dash (dash) *vb.* **dash·ing, dashed 1** to run quickly; to rush: *Quick! Dash for cover.* **2** to destroy or put an end to: *Hopes of a quiet evening were quickly dashed.* – *n.* **1** a quick run or sudden rush. **2** a small amount of something added: *a dash of color.* **3** a short line (–) used in writing to show a break in a sentence, etc.

dash·ing *adj.* elegant, stylish.

King David, the first king of a united Israel, with his son, the future King Solomon. As a boy David had been a shepherd and the slayer of the Philistine warrior Goliath. He was also a musician and wrote many of the psalms in the Bible.

da·ta (dā′tə, da′tə, dä′tə) *n.* (originally *plural* but now also treated as *singular*. See also **datum**) **1** facts or information. **2** See **Computer Terms**.

da·ta·base (dāt′ə-bās′, dat′ə-bās′) *n.* a large amount of information stored in a computer.

date¹ (dāt) *n.* **1** the day of the month, and/or the year, in which something happened, is happening, or is going to happen. **2** a statement on a letter, document, etc. giving usually the day, the month, and the year when it was written, sent, etc. **3** a planned meeting or social outing. **4** a person whom you are meeting or going out with. – *vb.* **dat·ing, dat·ed 1** to put a date on: *This check hasn't been dated.* **2** to find, decide on, or guess the date of. **3** to meet socially on a regular basis.

date² (dāt) *n.* the fruit of a palm tree – brown, sticky, and sweet-tasting when dried.

dat·ed (dāt′əd) *adj.* old-fashioned.

da·tum (dā′təm, da′təm, dä′təm) *n.* **da·ta** a piece of information. See also **data**.

daugh·ter (dô′tər) *n.* a female child considered in relation to her parents.

daughter-in-law (dô′tər-ən-lô′) *n.* **daughters-in-law** a son's wife.

daunt (dônt) *vb.* **daunt·ing, daunt·ed** to frighten or discourage. – *adj.* **daunt·ing**.

● **Da·vid** (dā′vəd) (1018-993 B.C.) was the second king of ISRAEL. He united the people of ISRAEL and made Jerusalem their capital.

daw·dle (dô′dl) *vb.* **daw·dling, daw·dled** to waste time, especially by moving or doing something very slowly. – *n.* **daw·dler** (dô′dlər).

dawn (dôn) *n.* **1** the time of day when light first appears as the sun rises. **2** the beginning of a new period of time, etc. – *vb.* **dawn on, dawn·ing, dawned** to be realized by: *It suddenly dawned on me that she was right.*

day (dā) *n.* **1** the period of 24 hours from one midnight to the next. **2** the period of time from sunrise to sunset. **3** the period of time in any 24 hours normally spent doing something, especially working.

day·dream (dā′drēm′) *n.* pleasant thought which takes your attention away from what you are doing. – *vb.* to have daydreams.

daze (dāz) *vb.* **daz·ing, dazed** to make confused or unable to think clearly.

daz·zle (daz′əl) *vb.* **daz·zling, daz·zled 1** to cause to be unable to see properly, with or because of a strong light. **2** to impress greatly by beauty, charm, skill, etc. – *adj.* **daz·zling**.

dead (ded) *adj.* **1** no longer living. **2** with nothing living or growing in or on it: *Mars is almost certainly a dead planet.* **3** not, or no longer, functioning: *The radio's gone dead.* **4** no longer in use: *Latin is a dead language.* **5** having little or no excitement or activity; boring: *After Rio de*

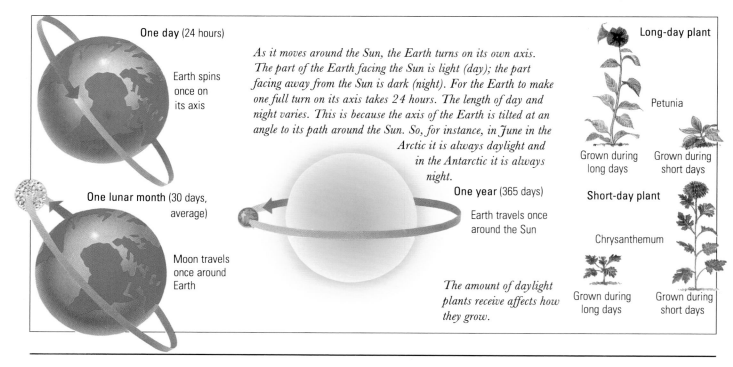

One day (24 hours)

Earth spins once on its axis

One lunar month (30 days, average)

Moon travels once around Earth

As it moves around the Sun, the Earth turns on its own axis. The part of the Earth facing the Sun is light (day); the part facing away from the Sun is dark (night). For the Earth to make one full turn on its axis takes 24 hours. The length of day and night varies. This is because the axis of the Earth is tilted at an angle to its path around the Sun. So, for instance, in June in the Arctic it is always daylight and in the Antarctic it is always night.

One year (365 days)

Earth travels once around the Sun

The amount of daylight plants receive affects how they grow.

Long-day plant

Petunia

Grown during long days

Grown during short days

Short-day plant

Chrysanthemum

Grown during long days

Grown during short days

Janeiro, home seems pretty dead. – *n.* **the dead**
dead people: *Don't speak ill of the dead.*

dead heat (ded hēt′)*n.* in a race, competition,
etc., the result when two or more competitors
produce equally good performances.

dead·line (ded′līn′) *n.* a time by which
something must be done.

dead·lock (ded′läk′) *n.* a situation in which no
further progress toward an agreement is
possible.

dead·ly (ded′lē) *adj.* **dead·li·er, dead·li·est**
1 causing or likely to cause death. **2** (*informal*)
very dull or uninteresting.

● **Dead Sea** (ded) a saltwater lake on the ISRAEL-
JORDAN border.

deaf (def) *adj.* **1** unable to hear at all or to hear
well. **2** not willing to listen to: *He was deaf to all
protests.* – *n.* **the deaf** deaf people. – **turn a
deaf ear to** to ignore.

deaf·en (def′ən) *vb.* **deaf·en·ing, deaf·ened**
to make deaf or temporarily unable to hear.

*Sign language is used by deaf people to communicate.
As well as finger spelling, based on the shapes of
letters, there are about 1,500 other signs.*

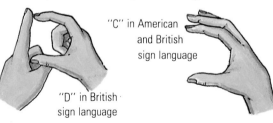

"C" in American
and British
sign language

"D" in British
sign language

deal (dēl) *n.* **1** a bargain, agreement, or
arrangement, especially in business or politics.
2 treatment: *Passengers in economy class got a raw
deal.* **3** the process of giving out cards in a card
game, or a turn to do so. – *vb.* **deal·ing,
dealt** (delt) **1** to buy and sell: *They deal in
oriental carpets.* **2** to divide among the players in
a card game. – *n.* **deal·er.**

deal·ings (dēl′ingz) *n.* (*plural*) business
contacts.

dealt. See **deal.**

dean (dēn) *n.* **1** a senior official in a college or
university: *dean of students.* **2** a senior clergyman
in a cathedral.

dear (dir) *adj.* **1** used in addressing someone at
the start of a letter. **2** loved: *They are dear
friends.* **3** high in price; expensive.

dearth (durth) *n.* a lack.

death (deth) *n.* **1** the time, act, or manner of
dying, or the state of being dead. **2** something
that causes you to die: *Smoking will be the death
of him.* – **at death's door** almost dead.

de·bat·a·ble (di-bāt′ə-bəl) *adj.* open to
debate; uncertain.

de·bate (di-bāt′) *n.* **1** a formal discussion, often
in front of an audience, in which two or more
people put forward opposing views on a
particular subject. **2** any general discussion on
a subject. – *vb.* **de·bat·ing, de·bat·ed** to
hold or take part in a debate about something.

de·bris or **dé·bris** (də-brē′, dā-brē′, dā′brē′)
n. what remains of something crushed,
smashed, destroyed, etc.

debt (det) *n.* **1** something that is owed. **2** the
state of owing something: *in debt.*

de·cade (dek′ād′, de-kād′) *n.* a period of ten
years.

dec·a·dence (dek′əd-əns) *n.* a falling to low
standards in morals, art, etc. – *adj.*
dec·a·dent (dek′əd-ənt).

de·cap·i·tate (di-kap′ə-tāt′) *vb.*
de·cap·i·tat·ing, de·cap·i·tat·ed to cut
off the head of.

de·cay (di-kā′) *vb.* **de·cay·ing, de·cayed** **1** to
make or become rotten. **2** weaker in health or
power, etc. **3** (of radioactive substances) to lose
radioactivity. – *n.* the state or process of
decaying.

de·ceased (di-sēst′) *adj.* dead.

de·ceit (di-sēt′) *n.* dishonesty.

de·ceit·ful (di-sēt′fəl) *adj.* deceiving.

de·ceive (di-sēv′) *vb.* **de·ceiv·ing, de·ceived**
to convince that something is true when it is
not.

De·cem·ber (di-sem′bər) *n.* the twelfth month
of the year. December has 31 days.

de·cen·cy (dē′sən-sē) *n.* **de·cen·cies** decent
behavior.

de·cent (dē′sənt) *adj.* **1** suitable; modest, not
vulgar or immoral. **2** kind, tolerant, or likeable.

*The Dead Sea is
1,296ft. (395m) below
sea level, the lowest place
on the earth's surface.
Nothing can live in the
Dead Sea, which is six
times more salty than
ordinary seawater. The
water is so dense that
even nonswimmers can
float on it.*

PRONUNCIATION SYMBOLS			
ə	away	lemon	focus
a	fat	oi	boy
ā	fade	oo	foot
ä	hot	ōō	moon
âr	fair	ou	house
e	met	th	think
ē	mean	th̲	this
g	get	u	cut
hw	which	ur	hurt
i	fin	w	witch
ī	line	y	yes
îr	near	yōō	music
ô	often	yoor	pure
ō	note	zh	vision

de·cep·tion (di-sep′shən) *n.* **1** an act of deceiving. **2** something that deceives or misleads.

dec·i·bel (des′ə-bel′) *n.* a unit used to measure the loudness of a sound.

de·cide (di-sīd′) *vb.* **de·cid·ing, de·cid·ed 1** to make up your mind; to reach a decision: *We've decided against a camping trip.* **2** to determine or solve: *You must decide the issue quickly.*

de·cid·u·ous (di-sij′oo-əs) *adj.* (of trees or shrubs) having leaves that drop off in fall.

dec·i·mal (des′ə-məl, des′məl) *adj.* based on ten.

de·ci·pher (di-sī′fər) *vb.* **de·ci·pher·ing, de·ci·phered 1** to translate using a key; to decode: *She learned to decipher Egyptian hieroglyphics.* **2** to work out the meaning of: *She deciphered his handwriting.*

de·ci·sion (di-sizh′ən) *n.* **1** the act of deciding. **2** something decided.

de·ci·sive (di-sī′siv) *adj.* **1** putting an end to doubt. **2** willing and able to make decisions with certainty and firmness. – *n.* **de·ci·sive·ness**.

deck (dek) *n.* **1** a platform forming a floor of a ship. **2** a platform attached to a building. **3** a pack of playing cards. **4** a component of an audio system that plays tapes or cassettes.

de·clare (di-klâr′) *vb.* **de·clar·ing, de·clared 1** to announce publicly: *War was declared in 1941.* **2** to say firmly. – *n.* **de·cla·ra·tion** (dek′lə-rā′shən).

● **Declaration of Independence** a historic document adopted on July 4, 1776, declaring the 13 American colonies independent of Britain. It ranks as one of the most important documents in history and the ideas it expresses have inspired people around the world.

de·cline (di-klīn′) *vb.* **de·clin·ing, de·clined 1** to refuse an invitation, etc., especially politely. **2** to become less in quality or quantity.

de·com·pose (dē′kəm-pōz′) *vb.* **de·com·pos·ing, de·com·posed** to decay or rot.

de·co·rate (dek′ə-rāt′) *vb.* **dec·o·rat·ing, dec·o·rat·ed 1** to beautify with ornaments, etc. **2** to design the inside of: *He decorated the apartment.* **3** to award a medal to: *awarded the Purple Heart.*

The Purple Heart is the oldest U.S. military decoration. George Washington issued the first three in 1782 and the medal still bears his profile. This award is for being killed or wounded in action.

dec·o·ra·tion (dek′ə-rā′shən) *n.* something used to decorate.

dec·o·ra·tive (dek′ə-rət-iv) *adj.* ornamental.

de·crease (di-krēs′, dē′krēs′) *vb.* **de·creas·ing, de·creased** to make or become less. – (dē′krēs′) *n.* a lessening or loss.

de·cree (di-krē′) *n.* a formal order or ruling made by someone in high authority. – *vb.* **de·cree·ing, de·creed** to order officially.

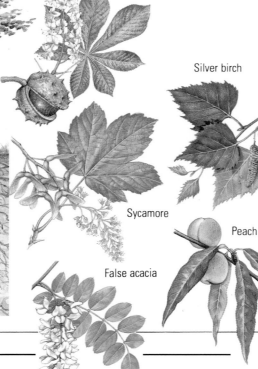

Conifers (softwoods) carry their needlelike leaves all the year round. Broad-leaved trees (hardwoods) in cooler climates are **deciduous** (they shed their leaves in autumn). The leaves of deciduous trees have many shapes: oval, with smooth or toothed edges, narrow (peach), compound (acacia) and forked (the European horse chestnut).

Horse chestnut

Silver birch

A typical broadleaf tree has spring flowers, which develop into fruits, and a spreading crown.

Sycamore

Peach

False acacia

ded·i·cate (ded′i-kāt′) *vb.* **ded·i·cat·ing,**
ded·i·cat·ed to devote wholly or chiefly to:
He dedicated all his time to tennis.

ded·i·cat·ed *adj.* **1** working very hard at or
spending a great deal of time and energy on
something. **2** (of computers, etc.) designed to
carry out one particular function.

de·duce (di-dōōs′, di-dyōōs′) *vb.* **de·duc·ing,**
de·duced to think out or judge on the basis of
what you know or assume to be fact.

de·duct (di-dukt′) *vb.* **de·duct·ing,**
de·duct·ed to take away a number or an
amount. – *n.* **de·duc·tion** (di-duk′shən).

deed (dēd) *n.* something someone has done; a
notable achievement.

deep (dēp) *adj.* **1** reaching far down from the
top or surface: *The water's not very deep here.*
2 going or being far in from the outside
surface or edge. **3** coming from or going
far down; long and full: *Take a deep
breath.* **4** (of a color) strong and relatively
dark. **5** low in pitch: *He has a deep voice.*
6 obscure; hard to understand: *Parts of this novel
are very deep.* – *adv.* **1** deeply. **2** far down or in.
3 late on in, or well into, a period of time: *deep
in the past.* – *n.* the ocean.

deep·en (dēp′ən) *vb.* **deep·en·ing,**
deep·ened to make or become deeper,
greater, more intense, etc.

deep·ly (dēp′lē) *adv.* very greatly.

deer (dîr) *n.* **deer** a large, four-footed,
hoofed animal, the male of which often
has antlers.

● Deer chew the cud and have cloven hooves
(divided in half). They eat leaves, fruit, grass,
and bark. The world's largest deer is the North
American moose.

de·feat (di-fēt′) *vb.* **de·feat·ing, de·feat·ed**
1 to beat or win a victory over, as in a war,
competition, game, or argument. **2** to cause to
fail: *Locking the door but leaving the key in defeats
the whole object.* – *n.* the act of defeating or state
of being defeated.

de·fect (dē′fekt′) *n.* a flaw, fault, or
imperfection. – (di-fekt′) *vb.* **de·fect·ing,**
de·fect·ed to leave your country, political
party, or group, especially to support or join
an opposing one.

de·fec·tive (di-fek′tiv) *adj.* imperfect; having
defects.

de·fend (di-fend′) *vb.* **de·fend·ing,**

de·fend·ed 1 to guard or protect against
attack. **2** to be the lawyer acting on behalf of
the accused person in a trial. – *n.* **de·fend·er**.

de·fense (di-fens′) *n.* **1** the act of defending
against attack. **2** the method, means,
equipment, or (often in *plural*) fortifications
used to protect against attack. **3** the armed
forces of a country. **4** in a court of law, the
person on trial and the lawyer acting for him
or her.

de·fen·sive (di-fen′siv) *adj.* **1** defending or
ready to defend. **2** attempting to justify your
actions when criticized or when expecting
criticism: *You'll never improve if you're always so
defensive.*

de·fer¹ (di-fur′) *vb.* **de·fer·ring,**
de·ferred to leave until a later
time. – *n.* **de·fer·ment** (di-
fur′mənt).

Moose

Red deer

Fallow deer

Muntjac

Reindeer

de·fer² (di-fur′) *vb.* **de·fer·ring, de·ferred** to
give in to the wishes, opinions, or orders of.

de·fi·ance (di-fī′əns) *n.* open disobedience;
boldness. – *adj.* **de·fi·ant** (di-fī′ənt).

de·fi·cient (di-fish′ənt) *adj.* not having all that
is needed: *Your diet is deficient in protein.*

de·fine (di-fīn′) *vb.* **de·fin·ing, de·fined 1** to
give the exact meaning of a word, etc. **2** to fix
or explain limits of: *Can you define the job?*

def·i·nite (def′ə-nət) *adj.* **1** not liable to change.
2 sure; certain. **3** clear and precise.

def·i·ni·tion (def′ə-nish′ən) *n.* a statement of
the meaning of a word or phrase.

de·fin·i·tive (də-fin′ət-iv) *adj.* providing a
definite solution. – *adv.* **de·fin·i·tive·ly.**

*Unlike their relatives,
cattle and antelope, deer
have antlers rather than
permanent horns. Female
deer, except reindeer or
caribou, do not grow
antlers. Deer are
naturally wild, but some
of them, such as reindeer
or caribou, have been
domesticated.*

de·flate (di-flāt′) *vb.* **de·flat·ing, de·flat·ed**
1 to make or grow smaller by the release of gas.
2 to take away the hopes, etc. of.

●**De·foe** (di-fō′), **Daniel** (1660-1731) was the English author of *Robinson Crusoe.*

deft (deft) *adj.* skillful, quick, and neat.
de·fy (di-fī′) *vb.* **de·fies, de·fy·ing, de·fied**
to resist or disobey boldly and openly.

●**de Gaulle** (də gôl′, də gōl′), **Charles** (1890-1970) was a French general, statesman, and president (1958-1969).

de·gree (di-grē′) *n.* **1** an amount or extent.
2 (*symbol* °) a unit of temperature. **3** (*symbol* °) a unit by which angles are measured, one 360th part of a complete revolution. **4** an award or title given by a university or college.
de·i·ty (dē′ət-ē, dā′ət-ē) *n.* **de·i·ties** a god or goddess.
de·ject·ed (di-jek′təd) *adj.* sad; miserable.

●**Del·a·ware** (del′ə-wâr′). See Supplement, **U.S.A.**

A delta may form where a river flowing slowly across a plain into the sea deposits sand and soil. Mudbanks build up and the river flows through them in channels. This blocked-up river mouth is called a delta because its shape is often like the Greek letter delta △.

de·lay (di-lā′) *vb.* **de·lay·ing, de·layed 1** to slow down or cause to be late: *The train was delayed when a tree fell onto the track.* **2** to put off to a later time. **3** to be slow in doing something; to linger. – *n.* **1** the act of delaying or state of being delayed. **2** the amount of time by which someone or something is delayed.
del·e·gate (del′i-gāt′) *vb.* **del·e·gat·ing, del·e·gat·ed 1** to give over to someone else: *to delegate power.* **2** to name someone as a representative, as the one to do a job, etc. – (del′i-gət, del′i-gāt′) *n.* someone chosen to be the representative at a conference or meeting.
de·lete (di-lēt′) *vb.* **de·let·ing, de·let·ed** to strike out or remove, especially from something written.

●**Del·hi** (del′ē) is the capital of INDIA.

de·lib·e·rate (di-lib′ə-rət) *adj.* **1** done on purpose. **2** slow and careful. – (di-lib′ə-rāt′) *vb.* **de·lib·e·rat·ing, de·lib·e·rat·ed** to think about carefully: *The jury deliberated on their verdict.*
del·i·ca·cy (del′i-kə-sē) *n.* **del·i·ca·cies 1** the state or quality of being delicate. **2** something considered particularly delicious to eat.
del·i·cate (del′i-kət) *adj.* **1** easily damaged or broken. **2** not strong or healthy. **3** small, neat, and careful: *She danced with delicate movements.* **4** requiring tact: *a delicate situation.*
de·li·cious (di-lish′əs) *adj.* very pleasant, especially to taste or smell.
de·light (di-līt′) *vb.* **de·light·ing, de·light·ed 1** to please greatly. **2** to take great pleasure: *He delights in teasing everybody.* – *n.* **1** great pleasure. **2** something or someone that gives great pleasure. – *adj.* **de·light·ed.**
de·liv·er (di-liv′ər) *vb.* **de·liv·er·ing, de·liv·ered 1** to carry to a person or place: *She delivered the mail..* **2** to set free. **3** to assist in the birth of. **4** to rescue or save. – *n.* **de·liv·er·y** (di-liv′ər-ē).
del·ta (del′tə) *n.* a roughly triangular area of land at the mouth of a river whose main stream has split into several channels.
de·luge (del′yo͞oj′, del′yo͞ozh′) *n.* **1** a flood. **2** a very heavy fall of rain.
de·mand (di-mand′) *vb.* **de·mand·ing, de·mand·ed 1** to ask for firmly, forcefully, or urgently. **2** to require or need: *This wound demands urgent medical attention.* – *n.* **1** a forceful request or order. **2** the desire or ability to buy

Democracy in ancient Greece was supposed to be government of the people, by the people, for the people — yet this did not apply to women or slaves. Voting took place in the open air and politicians took it in turn to address the people.

or obtain goods, etc.: *There is a constant demand for gloves and scarfs in winter.*

demi- (de'mē) *prefix* half or partly.

de·moc·ra·cy (di-mäk'rə-sē) *n.* **de·moc·ra·cies** a form of government in which the people govern themselves or elect representatives to govern them.

dem·o·crat (dem'ə-krat') *n.* **1** a person who believes in democracy. **2 Democrat** a supporter of the Democratic Party, a political party in the UNITED STATES. – *adj.* **dem·o·crat·ic** (dem'ə-krat'ik).

de·mol·ish (di-mäl'ish) *vb.* **de·mol·ish·ing, de·mol·ished** to pull or tear down; destroy. – *n.* **dem·o·li·tion** (dem'ə-lish'ən).

de·mon (dē'mən) *n.* an evil spirit.

dem·on·strate (dem'ən-strāt') *vb.* **dem·on·strat·ing, dem·on·strat·ed 1** to show or prove by reasoning or providing evidence. **2** to show how something is done, operates, etc. **3** to show one's views by protesting or marching in public. – *n.* **dem·on·stra·tion** (dem'ən-strā'shən). – *n.* **dem·on·stra·tor** (dem'ən-strāt'ər).

den (den) *n.* **1** a wild animal's home. **2** a room in a home for relaxing.

de·ni·al (di-nī'əl) *n.* **1** the act of denying. **2** a statement that something is not true.

den·im (den'əm) *n.* a tough cotton cloth used for making jeans, etc.

● **Den·mark** (den'märk'). See Supplement, **Countries**.

de·nom·i·na·tion (di-näm'ə-nā'shən) *n.* **1** a religious group with its own particular beliefs and practices. **2** a particular unit of value of a coin, or banknote, etc.

de·note (di-nōt') *vb.* **de·not·ing, de·not·ed 1** to mean; to be the name of or sign for. **2** to be a sign, mark, or indication of.

de·nounce (di-nowns') *vb.* **de·nounc·ing, de·nounced** to condemn.

dense (dens) *adj.* **1** closely packed or crowded together. **2** thick.

den·si·ty (den'sət-ē) *n.* **den·si·ties 1** the state of being dense. **2** the number or quantity of something in a given unit of area or volume.

dent (dent) *n.* a hollow in the surface of something, made by pressure or a blow. – *vb.* **dent·ing, dent·ed** to make a dent in.

den·tal (dent'l) *adj.* concerned with teeth.

den·tist (dent'əst) *n.* a person qualified to repair or remove decayed teeth, fit false teeth, etc.

den·tist·ry (dent'ə-strē) *n.* the work of a dentist.

de·ny (di-nī') *vb.* **de·nies, de·ny·ing, de·nied 1** to declare something not to be true. **2** to refuse to give or allow.

de·o·dor·ant (dē-ōd'ə-rənt) *n.* a substance that prevents or conceals odor.

de·part (di-pärt') *vb.* **de·part·ing, de·part·ed 1** to leave. **2** to vary or change. **3** to die. – *n.* **de·par·ture** (di-pär'chər).

de·part·ment (di-pärt'mənt) *n.* a section or division of any business or organization.

de·pend (di-pend') *vb.* **de·pend·ing, de·pend·ed 1** to be able to trust. **2** to be decided by or vary according to.

de·pend·a·ble (di-pen'də-bəl) *adj.* trustworthy or reliable.

de·pen·dant (di-pen'dənt) *n.* a person who is kept or supported financially by another.

de·pend·ent (di-pen'dənt) *adj.* **1** relying on for financial or other support. **2** decided or influenced by.

de·pict (di-pikt') *vb.* **de·pict·ing, de·pict·ed 1** to paint or draw. **2** to describe. – *n.* **de·pic·tion** (di-pik'shən).

DEPENDENT CLAUSE
A main clause is one that can stand alone as a sentence and make sense: *The cat was sitting on the mat.* A dependent clause is one that cannot stand alone and makes incomplete sense: *when I looked through the window.* The whole sentence should read: *When I looked through the window, the cat was sitting on the mat.*

Denim takes its name from Nîmes, France, where the cloth was first made in the 1600s.

An area of low air pressure is called a depression. As the air rises, its moisture condenses, clouds form, and it rains.

Depression

Derrick gets its name from gallows on which criminals were hanged in London. The name of the hangman was Derrick, after whom the gallows were named.

de·plore (di-plôr, di-plōr′) *vb.* **de·plor·ing, de·plored** to feel or express great disapproval of.

de·plor·a·ble (di-plôr′ə-bəl, di-plōr′ə-bəl) *adj.* very bad or regrettable.

de·port (di-pôrt′, di-pōrt′) *vb.* **de·port·ing, de·port·ed** to exile; to send out of the country.

de·pos·it (di-päz′ət) *vb.* **de·pos·it·ing, de·pos·it·ed 1** to put or leave. **2** to put in a bank: *They deposited money in their account.* – *n.* **1** a sum of money deposited in a bank, etc. **2** solid matter that has settled at the bottom of a liquid.

de·pot *n.* **1** (dē′pō) a railroad or bus station. **2** (dep′ō, dē′pō) a warehouse.

de·press (di-pres′) *vb.* **de·press·ing, de·pressed** to make sad and gloomy. – *adj.* **de·press·ing**.

de·pressed *adj.* **1** sad and gloomy. **2** suffering from high unemployment and poverty.

de·pres·sion (di-presh′ən) *n.* **1** a feeling of sadness. **2** a period of low business and industrial activity accompanied by a rise in unemployment. **3** a sunken place or hollow.

de·prive (di-prīv′) *vb.* **de·priv·ing, de·prived** to take or keep from; to prevent from using or enjoying.

de·prived *adj.* lacking in food, housing, etc.

depth (depth) *n.* **1** deepness; the distance from the top downward. **2** (of feelings) intensity or strength. **3** extensiveness: *I'm always amazed at the depth of his knowledge.* **4** somewhere far from the surface or edge of: *We hiked to the depths of the forest.* **5** (of sound) lowness of pitch.

dep·u·ty (dep′yət-ē) *n.* **dep·u·ties** a person appointed to act on behalf of or as an assistant to someone: *the sheriff's deputy.*

der·i·va·tion (der′ə-vā′shən) *n.* the act of deriving or the state of being derived.

de·rive (di-rīv′) *vb.* **de·riv·ing, de·rived 1** to obtain: *He derives a lot of pleasure from his work.* **2** to come from, or be traced back to, a source.

der·ma·tol·o·gy (dur′mə-täl′ə-jē) *n.* the branch of medicine concerned with the skin.

der·rick (der′ik) *n.* **1** a type of crane with a movable arm. **2** a framework built over an oil well, used for raising and lowering the drill.

● **Des·cartes** (dā-kärt′), **René** (1596-1650) was a French philosopher. The basis of his thinking was, "I think, therefore I am."

de·scend (di-send′) *vb.* **de·scend·ing, de·scend·ed 1** to go or move down from a higher to a lower place or position. **2** to lead or slope downward. **3** to come from a certain source: *We descend from a proud people.*

des·cen·dant (di-sen′dənt) *n.* a person or animal that is the child, grandchild, etc. of another.

de·scent (di-sent′) *n.* **1** the act or process of coming or going down. **2** a slope downward. **3** origin or ancestry.

de·scribe (di-skrīb′) *vb.* **de·scrib·ing, de·scribed** to tell about: *Can you describe how you felt?*

de·scrip·tion (di-skrip′shən) *n.* a statement of what someone or something is like.

de·scrip·tive (di-skrip′tiv) *adj.* describing, especially describing well or vividly.

de·sert[1] (di-zurt′) *vb.* **de·sert·ing, de·sert·ed** to abandon a place or person.

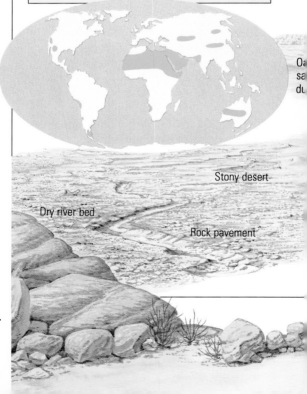

Some of the main deserts of the world. The driest is the Atacama in South America, the largest is the Sahara in Africa.

Sahara	3,560,000 sq. mi.
Great Australian	1,500,000 sq. mi.
Libyan	500,000 sq. mi.
Gobi	300,000 sq. mi.
Rub'al Khali	250,000 sq. mi.
Kalahari	120,000 sq. mi.
Kara Kum	110,000 sq. mi.
Atacama	25,000 sq. mi.

Stony desert

Dry river bed

Rock pavement

des·ert² (dez′ərt) *n.* an area of land where there is little water or rainfall.

de·sert·ed (di-zurt′əd)*adj.* empty or abandoned.

de·serve (di-zurv′) *vb.* **de·serv·ing, de·served** to have earned or be worthy.

des·ic·cate (des′i-kāt′) *vb.* **des·ic·cat·ing, des·ic·cat·ed** to dry out. − *adj.* **des·ic·cat·ed**.

de·sign (di-zīn′) *vb.* **de·sign·ing, de·signed** **1** to prepare a plan, drawing, or model of. **2** to plan, intend, or develop for a particular purpose: *This pen has been designed especially for left-handed people.* − *n.* **1** a plan, drawing, or model showing how something is to be made. **2** the art or job of making such drawings, plans, etc. **3** the way in which something has been made.

de·sign·er *n.* a person whose job it is to make designs, plans, patterns, drawings, etc.

de·sig·nate (dez′ig-nāt′) *vb.* **de·sig·nat·ing, des·ig·nat·ed** to appoint to a job or post.

de·sir·a·ble *adj.* pleasing; worth having.

de·sire (di-zīr′) *n.* a longing for something. − *vb.* **de·sir·ing, de·sired** to long for.

desk (desk) *n.* a table, often with drawers, used for writing, reading, etc.

des·o·late (des′ə-lət) *adj.* **1** (of a place) deserted, barren, and lonely. **2** very sad: *Life is pretty desolate now that my friends have moved.*

de·spair (di-spâr′) *vb.* **de·spair·ing, de·spaired** to be without or lose hope.

des·per·ate (des′pə-rət) *adj.* **1** willing to take large risks because of hopelessness and despair: *He's desperate and will try anything.* **2** very serious, difficult, dangerous, and almost hopeless: *With winter approaching the plight of the refugees is desperate.* **3** in great or urgent need: *They are desperate for money; please give what you can.* − *n.* **des·per·a·tion** (des′pə-rā′shən).

de·spise (di-spīz′) *vb.* **de·spis·ing, de·spised** to look down on with contempt. − *adj.* **despicable**.

de·spite (di-spīt′) *prep.* in spite of.

de·spon·dent (di-spän′dənt) *adj.* sad.

des·pot (des′pət, des′pät′) *n.* a person who has total power, especially one who uses such power in a cruel or oppressive way. − *adj.* **des·pot·ic** (des-pät′ik).

des·sert (di-zurt′) *n.* sweet food served after the main course of a meal.

des·ti·na·tion (des′tə-nā′shən) *n.* the place to which someone or something is going or sent.

des·tined (des′tənd) *adj.* intended for a particular purpose: *He was destined to be a politician.*

des·ti·ny (des′tə-nē) *n.* **des·ti·nies** a person's purpose or future as arranged by fate.

des·ti·tute (des′tə-tüt′, des′tə-tyüt′) *adj.* extremely poor.

de·stroy (di-stroi′) *vb.* **de·stroy·ing, de·stroyed** to damage something beyond repair: *The bomb destroyed a row of stores.*

de·stroy·er *n.* **1** a person or thing that destroys. **2** a type of small, fast warship.

de·struc·ti·ble (di-struk′tə-bəl) *adj.* able to be destroyed.

de·struc·tion (di-struk′shən) *n.* **1** the act of destroying. **2** something that destroys.

des·truc·tive (di-struk-tiv) *adj.* causing destruction or serious damage: *We remembered the destructive hurricane.*

Deserts are not necessarily hot. The polar regions are deserts. Most deserts are rocky, not sandy. Sand covers only 11 percent of the Sahara.

Salt pan

Oasis

Sandy desert

Camels are ideally suited for the job of making long journeys across deserts. They are powerful and swift and can go for days without eating or drinking, living off the fat stored in their humps.

PRONUNCIATION SYMBOLS			
ə	**a**way lem**o**n f**o**cus		
a	f**a**t	oi	b**oy**
ā	f**a**de	oo	f**oo**t
ä	h**o**t	o͞o	m**oo**n
âr	f**air**	ou	h**ou**se
e	m**e**t	th	**th**ink
ē	m**ea**n	t͟h	**th**is
g	**g**et	u	c**u**t
hw	**wh**ich	ur	h**ur**t
i	f**i**n	w	**w**itch
ī	l**i**ne	y	**y**es
îr	n**ear**	yo͞o	m**u**sic
ô	**o**ften	yoor	p**ure**
ō	n**o**te	zh	vi**s**ion

de·tach (di-tach′) *vb.* **de·tach·ing, de·tached** to unfasten or separate.

de·tail (di-tāl′, de′tāl′) *n.* **1** a small feature, fact, or item. **2** particular items in relation to the whole: *She has good eye for detail.*

de·tain (di-tān′) *vb.* **de·tain·ing, de·tained** **1** to stop, hold back, keep waiting, or delay. **2** to keep in a cell, prison, or elsewhere, especially before trial.

de·tect (di-tekt′) *vb.* **de·tect·ing, de·tect·ed** to discover or perceive. – *adj.* **de·tect·a·ble** (di-tek′tə-bəl).

de·tect·ive (di-tek′tiv) *n.* a person whose job is to solve crime by gathering evidence.

de·ter (di-tur′) *vb.* **de·ter·ring, de·terred** to discourage from doing something.

de·ter·gent (di-tur′jənt) *n.* a chemical substance used for cleaning.

de·te·ri·o·rate (di-tir′ē-ə-rāt′) *vb.* **de·te·ri·o·rat·ing, de·te·ri·o·rat·ed** to grow worse. – *n.* **de·te·ri·o·ra·tion** (di-tir′ē-ə-rā′shən).

de·ter·mi·na·tion (di-tur′mə-nā′shən) *n.* firmness or strength of will.

de·ter·mine (di-tur′mən) *vb.* **de·ter·min·ing, de·ter·mined** **1** to fix or find out exactly. **2** to decide or cause someone to decide: *I determined to finish on time.*

de·ter·mined (di-tur′mən) *adj.* **1** having firmly decided: *He was determined to win.* **2** having a strong will.

de·test (di-test′) *vb.* **de·test·ing, de·test·ed** to hate.

de·tour (dē′toor) *n.* a route away from or longer than a planned or more direct route.

de·tract (di-trakt′) *vb.* **de·tract·ing, de·tract·ed** to take away from or lessen.

●**De·troit** (di-troit′) is the largest city in Michigan.

Deutsch·mark (doich′märk′) *n.* (*symbol* **DM**) the standard unit of currency in GERMANY.

dev·as·tate (dev′ə-stāt′) *vb.* **dev·as·tat·ing, dev·as·tat·ed** to cause great destruction in or to. – *adj.* **dev·as·tat·ed.** – *n.* **dev·as·ta·tion** (dev′ə-stā′shən).

de·vel·op (di-vel′əp) *vb.* **de·vel·op·ing, de·vel·oped** **1** to make or become more mature, more advanced, etc. **2** to begin to have: *I'm developing an interest in politics.* **3** to make the picture visible by using a chemical process: *We developed the negative.*

de·vel·op·ment (də-vel′əp-mənt) *n.* **1** the act of developing or the process of being developed. **2** a new stage, event, or situation: *This is a worrisome development.*

de·vi·ate (dē′vē-āt′) *vb.* **de·vi·at·ing, de·vi·at·ed** to depart from what is considered correct.

de·vice (di-vīs′) *n.* something made for a special purpose, such as a tool or instrument.

dev·il (dev′əl) *n.* **1** any evil or wicked spirit. **2** also **Devil** the supreme evil spirit in some religions.

de·vi·ous (dē′vē-əs) *adj.* not honest; cunning.

de·vise (di-vīz′) *vb.* **de·vis·ing, de·vised** to invent, make up, or put together.

de·vote (di-vōt′) *vb.* **de·vot·ing, de·vot·ed** to give up wholly to or use entirely for.

de·vour (di-vour′) *vb.* **de·vour·ing, de·voured** to eat up greedily.

de·vout (di-vout′) *adj.* **1** sincerely religious. **2** deeply felt; earnest.

dew (do͞o, dyo͞o) *n.* moisture, in drops, coming from the air as it cools at night.

dex·ter (dek′stər) *n.* See **Flag Terms**.

di·a·be·tes (dī′ə-bēt′ēz, dī′ə-bēt′əs) *n.* a disease in which the body fails to absorb sugar and starch properly from the blood.

di·a·bet·ic (dī′ə-bet′ik) *n.* a person suffering from diabetes.

●**Di·a·ghi·lev** (dē-ä′gə-lef′), **Sergei** (1872-1929) was a Russian impresario and founder of *Ballets Russes*, a ballet company in Paris.

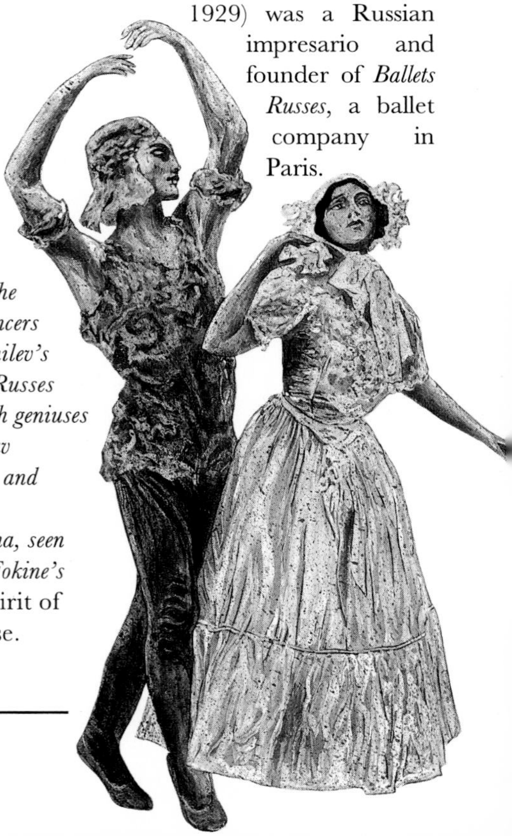

Among the great dancers in Diaghilev's Ballets Russes were such geniuses as Vaslav Nijinsky and Tamara Karsavina, seen here in Fokine's The Spirit of the Rose.

di·ag·no·sis (dī-əg-nō′səs) *n.* **di·ag·no·ses** (dī′əg-nō′sēz′) the identification of a disease from looking at symptoms, x-rays, etc.

di·ag·o·nal (dī-ag′ən-l) *adj.* sloping or slanting.

di·a·gram (dī′ə-gram′) *n.* a simple line drawing, showing how a machine, etc. works.

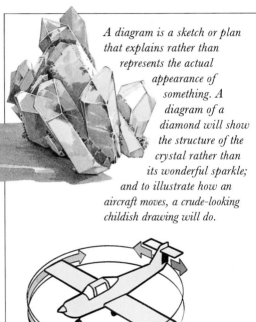

A diagram is a sketch or plan that explains rather than represents the actual appearance of something. A diagram of a diamond will show the structure of the crystal rather than its wonderful sparkle; and to illustrate how an aircraft moves, a crude-looking childish drawing will do.

di·al (dī′əl, dīl) *n.* a disk or plate on a clock, radio, meter, etc., with numbers or other measurements marked on it and a pointer, used to indicate speed, time, etc.

di·a·lect (dī′ə-lekt′) *n.* a form of a language spoken by a particular group.

di·a·logue (dī′ə-lôg′, dā′ə-läg′) *n.* **1** the words spoken by the characters in a play, book, etc. **2** a discussion of ideas.

di·al·y·sis (dī-al′ə-səs) *n.* **di·al·y·ses** (dī-al′ə-sēz) the removal of wastes from the blood of people suffering from kidney failure.

di·am·e·ter (dī-am′ət-ər) *n.* a straight line drawn from one side of a circle to the other side and passing through its center; the length of the line.

di·a·mond (dī′ə-mənd, dī′mənd) *n.* **1** a usually colorless transparent precious stone, a crystallized form of carbon, the hardest of all minerals. **2** a shape or figure with four equal straight sides and angles which are not right

angles. **3** (in *plural*) one of the four suits of playing cards with red symbols of this shape. **4** a baseball field.

di·a·per (dī′ə-pər, dī′pər) *n.* a baby's undergarment, consisting of absorbent cloth or paper and fastened at the waist.

di·a·phragm (dī′ə-fram′) *n.* the wall of muscle which separates the chest from the abdomen in the bodies of mammals.

di·a·ry (dī′ə-rē, dī′rē) *n.* **di·a·ries** a written record of daily events in a person's life.

● **Di·as** (dē′əs, dē′əsh), **Bartolomeu** (1450-1500) was a Portuguese explorer.

dice (dīs) *n. pl., sing.* **die** small cubes with a different number of spots, from 1 to 6, on each of their sides, used in games of chance. – *vb.* **dic·ing, diced** to cut into small cubes.

● **Dick·ens** (dik′ənz), **Charles** (1812-1870) was an English novelist.

● **Dick·in·son** (dik′ən-sən), **Emily** (1830-1886) was an American poet.

dic·tate (dik′tāt′, dik-tāt′) *vb.* **dic·tat·ing, dic·tat·ed 1** to say or read out for someone else to write down. **2** to give orders to or try to impose your wishes on someone.

dic·tio·nar·y (dik′shə-ner′ē) *n.* **dic·tio·nar·ies** a book containing words of a language arranged alphabetically with their meanings or translations into another language.

did. See **do**.

did·n't (did′nt) did not.

die (dī) *vb.* **dies, dy·ing, died 1** to stop living, cease to be alive: *Shakespeare died in 1616.* **2** to cease to exist, come to an end, or fade away: *The fight for equality will never die.* **3** to stop working suddenly and unexpectedly: *The motor*

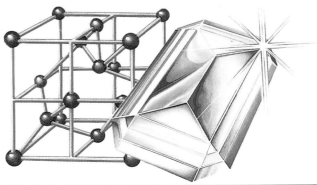

Diamonds are crystals. They are harder than anything else in the world. They are made of pure carbon. The atoms in a diamond are arranged in a dense latticework. This is why diamonds are so hard.

Lambeosaurus

Parasaurolophus

The Archaeopteryx ("ancient wing") was about the size of a crow. It had small, sharp teeth and bony fingers halfway down its wings.

The word **dinosaur** means "terrible lizard." Dinosaurs lived between 65 million and 225 million years ago. They included the largest and most ferocious animals ever to have lived. About 65 million years ago the dinosaurs mysteriously died out. Most of the knowledge we have about dinosaurs comes from bones and tracks that have been preserved as fossils in rocks. The first dinosaur discoveries were made in England. In 1822 Mary Mantell, a doctor's wife, noticed some fossil teeth in a pile of road-menders' stones. They belonged to what became named as *Iguanodon.*

Hadrosaurids ("big reptiles") had broad beaks like a duck's, so many people called them duckbilled dinosaurs.

The skull of a Camarasaurus, a member of the sauropod group.

Deinonychus had three strong, clasping fingers on its hands. Each finger was armed with a heavy claw (shown here).

The sauropod group of dinosaurs were the largest animals that have ever lived on land. Most of these huge creatures looked like enormous elephants with long necks and tails. These harmless plant-eating creatures could use their long necks to reach food.

Stegosaurus was a plant eater. It developed bony plates along its back to help protect itself from large flesh eaters such as Allosaurus. It had a tiny brain for its size.

just died. – **be dying for** (*informal*) to have a strong desire or need for. – *vb.* **die away** to become steadily weaker and finally stop: *The applause gradually died away.*

di·et (dī′ət) *n.* **1** the sort of food normally eaten by a person or animal. **2** a limited variety or quantity of food that a person is allowed to eat, especially in order to lose weight or because of illness. – *vb.* **di·et·ing, di·et·ed** to limit your food to what is allowed by a prescribed diet.

dif·fer (dif′ər) *vb.* **dif·fer·ing, dif·fered 1** to be different, unlike, or of more than one kind: *Earth differs from the other planets.* **2** to disagree: *We differ on several issues.*

dif·fer·ence (dif′ə-rəns, dif′rəns) *n.* **1** what makes one thing or person unlike another. **2** the amount by which one quantity or number is greater or less than another. **3** a quarrel.

dif·fer·ent (dif′ə-rənt, dif′rənt) *adj.* **1** not the same. **2** separate; distinct; various: *They all like different things.*

dif·fi·cult (dif′i-kult′, dif′i-kəlt) *adj.* **1** requiring great skill, intelligence, or effort. **2** not easy to please.

dif·fi·cul·ty (dif′i-kul′tē, dif′i-kəl-tē) *n.* **dif·fi·cul·ties 1** the state or quality of being difficult. **2** a difficult thing to do or understand. **3** (usually in *plural*) trouble or embarrassment, especially financial.

dif·fi·dent (dif′əd-ənt) *adj.* lacking in confidence; shy. – *n.* **dif·fi·dence** (dif′əd-əns).

dig (dig) *vb.* **dig·ging, dug** (dug) **1** to turn up or move earth, etc., especially with a spade. **2** to make a hole, etc. by digging. **3** to poke. – *n.* a place where archaeologists are digging to uncover ancient ruins, etc.

di·gest (dī-jest′, də-jest′) *vb.* **di·gest·ing, di·gest·ed** to break down by digestion.

di·ges·tion (dī-jes′chən, də-jes′chən) *n.* the process of breaking food down in the stomach, etc., into a form the body can use.

dig·it (dij′ət) *n.* any of the ten figures 0 to 9.

dig·i·tal (dij′ət-l) *adj.* **1** showing quantity, time, etc. by numbers rather than by a pointer on a scale, dial, etc. **2** processing information in the form of a series of digits, generally in binary form: *a digital computer.* – *adv.* **dig·i·tal·ly.**

dig·ni·ty (dig′nət-ē) *n.* **1** seriousness and formality. **2** goodness and nobility of character.

dike (dīk) *n.* a wall or bank built to prevent flooding or keep back the sea.

di·lap·i·dat·ed (di-lap′ə-dāt′əd) *adj.* falling to pieces because of neglect or age.

di·lem·ma (də-lem′ə) *n.* a situation in which one must choose between two courses of action, both equally undesirable.

dil·i·gent (dil′ə-jənt) *adj.* hard working; done with care and serious effort. – *n.* **dil·i·gence** (dil′ə-jəns).

di·lute (dī-lōōt′, də-lōōt′) *vb.* **di·lut·ing, di·lut·ed 1** to make thinner or weaker by mixing with water or another liquid. **2** to make weaker or less pure by adding something.

dim (dim) *adj.* **dim·mer, dim·mest 1** not bright or distinct. **2** lacking enough light to see clearly. **3** faint; not clearly remembered: *I have a dim memory of what happened.* – *vb.* **dim·ming, dimmed** to make or become dim. – *n.* **dim·ness.**

dime (dīm) *n.* a coin of the UNITED STATES and CANADA worth ten cents.

di·men·sion (də-men′chən) *n.* a measurement of length, breadth, height, etc.

di·min·ish (də-min′ish) *vb.* **di·min·ish·ing, di·min·ished** to become less or smaller.

di·min·u·tive (də-min′yət-iv) *adj.* very small.

dim·ple (dim′pəl) *n.* a small hollow, especially in the skin of the cheeks or chin.

din (din) *n.* a continuous and unpleasant noise.

dine (dīn) *vb.* **din·ing, dined 1** to eat dinner. **2** (on) to eat for dinner: *We dined on lobster.*

din·ghy (ding′ē, ding′gē) *n.* **din·ghies** a small open boat.

din·go (ding′ō) *n.* **din·goes** a species of wild dog found in AUSTRALIA.

din·ner (din′ər) *n.* the main meal of the day, usually eaten in the evening.

di·no·saur (dī′nə-sôr) *n.* any animal of the large number of species of extinct reptiles of the order *Dinosauria*.

di·o·cese (dī′ə-səs, dī′ə-sēz′) *n.* **di·o·ces·es** (dī′ə-sēz′, dī′ə-sē′zəz) the district over which a bishop has authority.

dip (dip) *vb.* **dip·ping, dipped 1** to put into a liquid for a short time. **2** to lower or go down briefly and then up again. **3** to slope downward. **4** to put your hand, etc. into a dish, container, etc. and take out some of the contents. – *n.* **1** an act of dipping. **2** a downward slope, especially in a road. **3** a short swim or bath. **4** a creamy food preparation scooped up with crackers, chips, etc.

Pteranodon (*"winged and toothless"*) had a turkey-sized body, but its wingspan measured up to 23ft. (7m).

diph·thong (dif′thông′, dip′thông′) *n.* two vowel sounds pronounced as one syllable, as the sound represented by *ou* in *sounds.*

di·plo·ma (də-plō′mə) *n.* a document certifying that you have completed a course of study.

dip·lo·ma·cy (də-plō′mə-sē) *n.* the art or profession of making agreements, treaties, etc. between countries.

dip·lo·mat (dip′lə-mat′) *n.* a government representative engaged in diplomacy.

di·rect (də-rekt′, dī-rekt′) *adj.* **1** straight; following the quickest and shortest path. **2** (of a person's manner, etc.) open, straightforward. − *vb.* **di·rect·ing, di·rect·ed 1** to point, aim, or turn in a particular direction. **2** to show the way. **3** to order or instruct.

di·rect·ly (də-rekt′lē, dī-rekt′lē) *adv.* **1** in a direct manner. **2** by a direct path. **3** at once; immediately.

di·rec·tion (də-rek′shən, dī-rek′shən) *n.* **1** the place or point towards which something moves or faces. **2** (usually in *plural*) instructions on how to operate a piece of equipment, etc.

di·rec·tor (də-rek′tər, dī-rek′tər) *n.* **1** any of the most senior managers of a business firm. **2** the person directing a play, movie, etc.

di·rec·to·ry (də-rek′tə-rē, dī-rek′tə-rē) *n.* **di·rec·to·ries** a book with a list of names and addresses, usually arranged alphabetically.

PRONUNCIATION SYMBOLS			
ə **away**	lemon	focus	
a	fat	oi	boy
ā	fade	oo	foot
ä	hot	ōō	moon
âr	**fair**	ou	house
e	met	th	think
ē	mean	th	this
g	get	u	cut
hw	**which**	ur	hurt
i	fin	w	witch
ī	line	y	yes
îr	near	yōō	music
ô	often	yoor	pure
ō	note	zh	vision

SOME RECENT DISASTERS OF THE 20TH CENTURY

1979 March. Water pump breaks down releasing radioactive steam at Three Mile Island, Pennsylvania.

1980s. Great areas of Africa, notably Ethiopia, suffer prolonged drought, crop failure, and famine.

1984 December. Toxic gas leaked from a pesticide plant at Bhopal, India. Possibly 10,000 deaths.

1986 January. Space shuttle *Challenger* explodes after takeoff, killing all seven astronauts on board.

1986 April. Nuclear reactor explodes at Chernobyl, Ukraine. 100,000 may die from radiation-induced cancer, a further 30,000 fatalities are possible worldwide in the years to come.

1988 December 21. American Pan Am Boeing 747 explodes in Lockerbie, Scotland. 270 deaths.

1991 February. Iraqi forces set alight 600 oil wells causing serious contamination of agricultural land and water supplies.

1991 July. *Kirki,* Greek tanker, breaks up off Western Australia spilling millions of gallons of crude oil, causing marine pollution of a conservation zone.

1993 Summer. Mississippi River Valley floods, causing millions of dollars' worth of damage throughout the U.S. Midwest.

dirt (durt) *n.* **1** any unclean substance, as mud or dust. **2** soil; earth.

dirt·y (durt′ē) *adj.* **dirt·i·er, dirt·i·est 1** marked with dirt. **2** which involves becoming marked with dirt: *a dirty job.* **3** indecent or obscene: *dirty language.* **4** mean or nasty: *a dirty lie.* − *vb.* **dirt·ies, dirt·y·ing, dirt·ied** to make dirty.

dis- *prefix* turns the main word into the opposite, usually negative, e.g. *disconnect, discontinue, dislike, disloyal, disobey.*

dis·ad·van·tage (dis′əd-van′tij) *n.* **1** a difficulty, drawback, or weakness. **2** an unfavorable situation.

dis·a·gree (dis′ə-grē′) *vb.* **dis·a·gree·ing, dis·a·greed 1** to have a different opinion. **2** to be opposed to. **3** to conflict with each other: *The two theories disagree.*

dis·a·gree·ment (dis′ə-grē′mənt) *n.* a quarrel.

dis·ap·pear (dis′ə-pîr′) *vb.* **1** to go out of sight; to vanish. **2** to cease to exist. − *n.* **dis·ap·pearance** (dis′ə-pir′əns).

dis·ap·point (dis′ə-point′) *vb.* to fail to fulfill the hopes or expectations of.

dis·ap·point·ment (dis′ə-point′mənt) *n.* **1** the state of being disappointed. **2** something that disappoints.

dis·ap·prove (dis′ə-prōōv′) *vb.* **dis·ap·prov·ing, dis·ap·proved** to have a low opinion of. − *n.* **dis·ap·proval** (dis′ə-prōō′vəl).

di·sas·ter (diz-as′tər) *n.* **1** an event causing great damage, injury, or loss of life. **2** a total failure: *The meal was a disaster.* − *adj.* **di·sas·trous** (diz-as′trəs).

disc (disk) *n.* also **disk 1** a phonograph record. **2** a compact disk. **3** in computing, a disk.

disc jockey *n.* **disc jockeys** a person who presents a program of recorded pop music.

dis·card (dis-kärd′) *vb.* **dis·card·ing, dis·card·ed** to get rid of as useless or unwanted.

dis·cern (dis-urn′) *vb.* **dis·cern·ing, dis·cerned** to notice; to judge.

dis·cern·ing (dis-ur′ning) *adj.* having good judgment.

dis·charge (dis-chärj′) *vb.* **dis·charg·ing, dis·charged 1** to allow to leave; to send away or dismiss, especially from employment. **2** to perform or carry out. **3** to flow out. − (dis′chärj′) *n.* **1** the act of discharging. **2** something discharged, as pus. **3** a release or dismissal. **4** a certificate of release.

dis·ci·ple (dis-ī′pəl) *n.* a person who follows the teachings of another.

dis·ci·pline (dis′ə-plən) *n.* **1** strict training intended to produce ordered and controlled behavior; the ordered behavior resulting from this. **2** punishment designed to create obedience. – *vb.* **dis·ci·plin·ing, dis·ci·plined** to train to behave in an ordered way.

dis·close (dis-klōz′) *vb.* **dis·clos·ing, dis·closed** to make known.

dis·co (dis′kō) *n.* **dis·cos** a discotheque.

dis·com·fit (dis-kum′fit) *vb.* **dis·com·fit·ing, dis·com·fit·ed** to confuse or embarrass.

dis·com·fort (dis-kum′fərt) *n.* slight pain.

dis·cord (dis′kôrd′) *n.* disagreement; conflict.

dis·co·theque (dis′kə-tek′, dis′kə-tek′) *n.* a nightclub with dancing to recorded pop music.

dis·count (dis′kount′) *n.* a deduction or the amount deducted from the normal price. – *vb.* (dis′kount′, dis-kount′) **dis·count·ing, dis·count·ed 1** to disregard as unlikely, untrue, or irrelevant. **2** to make a deduction from a price.

dis·cour·age (dis-kur′ij) *vb.* **dis·cour·ag·ing, dis·cour·aged 1** to deprive of confidence, hope, or the will to continue. **2** to try to prevent by persuasion: *Mom discouraged us from eating candy.* – *n.* **dis·cour·age·ment** (dis-kur′ij-mənt).

dis·cov·er (dis-kuv′ər) *vb.* **dis·cov·er·ing, dis·cov·ered 1** to be the first person to find. **2** to find by chance, especially for the first time.

dis·cov·er·y (dis-kuv′ə-rē, dis-kuv′rē) *n.* **dis·cov·er·ies 1** the act of discovering. **2** a person or thing discovered.

dis·crim·i·nate (dis-krim′ə-nāt′) *vb.* **dis·crim·i·nat·ing, dis·crim·i·nat·ed 1** to recognize a difference. **2** to give different treatment to different people or groups in identical circumstances, usually without justification.

dis·crim·i·na·tion (dis-krim′ə-nā′shən) *n.* unjustifiably different treatment given to different people or groups.

dis·cus (dis′kəs) *n.* a heavy disk thrown in athletic competitions.

dis·cuss (dis-kus′) *vb.* **dis·cuss·ing, dis·cussed** to talk about. – *n.* **dis·cus·sion** (dis-kush′ən).

dis·ease (diz-ēz′) *n.* illness or lack of health caused by infection rather than by an accident.

dis·fig·ure (dis-fig′yər) *vb.* **dis·fig·ured, dis·fig·ur·ing** to destroy the beauty or appearance of.

dis·grace (dis-grās′) *n.* shame or loss of favor or respect, or something likely to cause this. – *vb.* **dis·grac·ing, dis·graced** to bring shame upon. – *adj.* **dis·grace·ful** (dis-grās′fəl).

dis·guise (dis-gīz′) *vb.* **dis·guis·ing, dis·guised 1** to hide the identity of by a change of appearance. **2** to conceal the true nature of.

dis·gust (dis-gust′) *vb.* **dis·gust·ing, dis·gust·ed** to sicken; to provoke intense dislike. – *adj.* **dis·gust·ed**.

dish (dish) *n.* **1** any shallow, usually roundish container in which food is served. **2** a food prepared in a certain way.

di·shev·eled (di-shev′əld) *adj.* untidy; messy.

dis·hon·est (dis-än′əst) *adj.* likely to deceive or cheat. – *n.* **dis·hon·es·ty** (dis-än′ə-stē).

dis·hon·or (dis-än′ər) *n.* shame; loss of honor. – *vb.* **dis·hon·or·ing, dis·hon·ored** to bring dishonor on. – *adj.* **dis·hon·or·a·ble** (dis-än′ə-rə-bəl).

Most discuses are made of wood but have rounded metal rims. Women's discuses are lighter and smaller than men's.

Women's discus

Men's discus

An ancient Greek statue of a discus thrower. Discus throwing was a popular event in the Greek Olympic Games. Competitors get extra force by spinning several times before releasing the discus. The athlete who achieves the greatest distance after 6 throws is the winner.

dis·il·lu·sioned (dis'ə-loo'zhənd) *adj.* sad at having discovered the unpleasant truth.

dis·in·fect (dis'in-fekt') *vb.* **dis·in·fect·ing, dis·in·fect·ed** to clean with a substance that kills germs.

dis·in·te·grate (dis-int'ə-grāt') *vb.* **dis·in·te·grat·ing, dis·in·te·grat·ed** to shatter.

dis·in·ter·est·ed (dis-in'trə-stəd, dis-int'ə-res'təd) *adj.* unbiased; objective.

disk (disk) *n.* **1** any flat thin circular object. **2** in computing, a hard disk or a floppy disk. **3** a layer of cartilage between vertebrae. **4** a phonograph record.

dis·lo·cate (dis-lō'kāt') *vb.* **dis·lo·cat·ing, dis·lo·cat·ed** to put out of joint. − *n.* **dis·lo·ca·tion** (dis'lō-kā'shən).

dis·mal (diz'məl) *adj.* not cheerful.

dis·man·tle (dis-mant'l) *vb.* **dis·man·tling, dis·man·tled** to take to pieces.

dis·may (dis-mā', diz-mā') *n.* a mixture of sadness and deep disappointment or discouragement. − *vb.* **dis·may·ing, dis·mayed** to fill with dismay.

dis·miss (dis-mis') *vb.* **dis·miss·ing, dis·missed** **1** to refuse to consider or accept. **2** to put out of employment. − *n.* **dis·miss·al** (dis-mis'əl).

dis·o·be·di·ent (dis'ō-bēd'ē-ənt) *adj.* refusing or failing to obey. − *n.* **dis·o·be·di·ence** (dis'ō-bēd'ē-əns).

dis·o·bey (dis'ə-bā') *vb.* **dis·o·bey·ing, dis·o·beyed** to refuse to obey.

dis·or·der (dis-ôrd'ər, diz-ôrd'ər) *n.* **1** confusion or disturbance. **2** a disease or illness.

dis·patch (dis-pach') *vb.* **dis·patch·ing, dis·patched** to send to a place for a particular reason. − *n.* a report carried by a government official, or sent to a newspaper by a journalist.

dis·pel (dis-pel') *vb.* **dis·pel·ling, dis·pelled** to drive away or banish.

dis·pense (dis-pens') *vb.* **dis·pens·ing, dis·pensed** **1** to give out: *The courts dispense justice.* **2** to prepare and distribute: *A drugstore dispenses medicine.*

dis·perse (dis-purs') *vb.* **dis·pers·ing, dis·persed** **1** to spread out over a wide area. **2** to break up and leave. − *n.* **dis·pers·al** (dis-pur'səl) or **dis·per·sion** (dis-pur'zhən).

dis·play (dis-plā') *vb.* **dis·play·ing, dis·played** **1** to put on view. **2** to show or

The disposal of the millions of tons of waste from mines, factories, and homes is a growing problem. Most of the waste is buried in landfill sites, the base of which is lined to prevent harmful liquids leaking into nearby water. At the end of each day the trash is leveled and covered with topsoil.

Pollutants leach into water table

betray: *You displayed great courage.* − *n.* **1** the act of displaying: *There's going to be a fireworks display.* **2** something that is displayed.

dis·pose (dis-pōz') *vb.* **dis·pos·ing, dis·posed** to get rid of; to deal with or settle. − *n.* **dis·pos·al** (dispō'zəl).

dis·pute (dis-pyoot') *vb.* **dis·put·ing, dis·put·ed** **1** to question or deny the validity of. **2** to quarrel over. − *n.* an argument.

dis·re·gard (dis'ri-gärd') *vb.* **dis·re·gard·ing, dis·re·gard·ed** to pay no attention to; to dismiss as unworthy of consideration. − *n.* a lack of attention or concern.

dis·rupt (dis-rupt') *vb.* **dis·rupt·ing, dis·rupt·ed** to disturb the order or peaceful progress of. − *n.* **dis·rup·tion** (dis-rup'shən). − *adj.* **dis·rup·tive** (dis-rup'tiv).

dis·sect (dis-ekt', dī-sekt') *vb.* **dis·sect·ing, dis·sect·ed** to cut open for scientific or medical examination. − *n.* **dis·sec·tion** (dis-ek'shən, dī-sek'shən).

dis·sent (dis-ent') *n.* difference of opinion.

dis·si·dent (dis'əd-ənt) *n.* a person who disagrees publicly, especially with a government.

dis·solve (diz-älv', diz-ôlv') *vb.* **dis·solv·ing, dis·solved** **1** to break up and merge with a liquid. **2** to bring an assembly to a close.

dis·tance (dis'təns) *n.* **1** the separation between points in space or time; the extent of this separation. **2** any faraway point or place. − *vb.* **dis·tanc·ing, dis·tanced** to put at a distance.

dis·tant (dis'tənt) *adj.* **1** far apart in space or time. **2** not closely related. **3** unfriendly.

dis·till (dis-til') *vb.* **dis·till·ing, dis·tilled** **1** to purify by converting to a vapor, then cooling

Dismal comes from *dies mali*, Latin words meaning "evil days," referring to unlucky days in the medieval calendar.

the vapor to liquid form again. **2** to produce in this way: *Alcohol is distilled from grain.*

dis·tinct (dis-tingkt′) *adj.* **1** easily seen, heard, or recognized. **2** noticeably different.

dis·tinc·tive (dis-tingk′tiv) *adj.* easily recognized because very individual.

dis·tin·guish (dis-ting′gwish) *vb.* **dis·tin·guish·ing, dis·tin·guished 1** to mark or recognize as different: *Male birds are distinguished from females by their brighter plumage.* **2** to see the difference between. **3** to identify.

dis·tin·guished (dis-ting′gwisht) *adj.* **1** famous and well respected. **2** with a dignified appearance.

dis·tort (dis-tôrt′) *vb.* **dis·tort·ing, dis·tort·ed 1** to twist out of shape. **2** to change the meaning or tone of by inaccurate retelling. – *n.* **dis·tor·tion** (dis-tôr′shən).

dis·tract (dis-trakt′) *vb.* **dis·tract·ing, dis·tract·ed** to divert the attention of.

dis·tract·ed (dis-trak′təd) *adj.* anxious and confused.

dis·trac·tion (dis-trak′shən) *n.* **1** something that diverts the attention, especially an amusement. **2** anxiety; confusion.

dis·tress (dis-tres′) *n.* **1** mental or emotional pain. **2** financial difficulty. **3** great danger; peril. – *vb.* **dis·tress·ing, dis·tressed** to cause distress to; to upset.

dis·trib·ute (dis-trib′yət) *vb.* **dis·trib·ut·ing, dis·trib·ut·ed 1** to give out. **2** to supply or sell in an area: *They distribute milk.* **3** to scatter or spread out. – *n.* **dis·tri·bu·tion** (dis′trə-byo͞o′shən).

dis·trict (dis′trikt) *n.* an area or region.

dis·turb (dis-turb′) *vb.* **dis·turb·ing, dis·turbed 1** to interrupt. **2** to inconvenience. **3** to upset the order of. – *adj.* **dis·turb·ing.**

dis·tur·bance (dis-tur′bəns) *n.* **1** an outburst of noise or violence. **2** an act of disturbing.

dis·turbed (dis-turbd′) *adj.* emotionally upset.

ditch (dich) *n.* a narrow channel dug in the ground for drainage or irrigation.

dit·to (dit′ō) *n.* **dittos** the same thing; that which has just been said.

dive (dīv) *vb.* **div·ing, dived** or **dove** (dōv) **1** to leap head first into water. **2** to fall steeply through the air. **3** to throw oneself down: *He dived for the ball.* – *n.* an act of diving.

div·er (dī′vər) *n.* a person who dives into water or works underwater.

di·verse (dī-vurs′) *adj.* **1** various; assorted. **2** different; dissimilar. – *n.* **di·ver·si·ty** (də-vur′sət-ē, dī-vur′sət-ē).

di·ver·sion (də-vur′zhən, dī-vur′zhən) *n.* **1** a detour from a usual route. **2** something intended to draw attention away. **3** amusement or entertainment.

di·vert (də-vurt′, dī-vurt′) *vb.* **di·vert·ing, di·vert·ed 1** to cause to change direction. **2** to draw away, especially attention: *The news from abroad has diverted public attention from the troubles at home.*

di·vide (də-vīd′) *vb.* **di·vid·ing, di·vid·ed 1** to split up or separate into parts. **2** to share. **3** to determine how many times one number is contained in another.

di·vine (di-vīn′) *adj.* of, from, or relating to a god.

di·vis·i·ble (də-viz′ə-bəl) *adj.* able to be divided.

di·vi·sion (də-vizh′ən) *n.* **1** the act of dividing; the state of being divided. **2** something that divides or separates; a gap or barrier. **3** the process of determining how many times one number is contained in another.

di·vorce (də-vôrs′) *n.* **1** the legal ending of a marriage. **2** a complete separation.

Di·wa·li (də-wäl′ē) *n.* the HINDU or SIKH festival of light, held in October or November.

diz·zy (diz′ē) *adj.* **diz·zi·er, diz·zi·est** experiencing or causing a spinning sensation and loss of balance. – *adv.* **diz·zi·ly** (diz′ə-lē). – *n.* **diz·zi·ness** (diz′ē-nəs).

●**Dji·bou·ti** (jə-bo͞ot′ē). See Supplement, **Countries**.

The deep-sea pressure suit, like a spacesuit, has joints in the limbs and a porthole face mask. A mixture of gases for deep diving is contained in tanks. The diver can communicate with surface workers by microphones and headphones. Divers in such suits can descend to 2,000ft (600m).

Three stylish dives often used in competitions. Divers sometimes add fancy midair movements.

do (doo) *vb.* **does** (duz), **doing, did** (did), **done** (dun) **1** to carry out, perform, or commit. **2** to finish or complete. **3** to be enough or suitable: *That will do.* **4** to be in a particular state: *Business is doing well.* **5** to provide as a service: *Do they do lunches here?* – *vb.* (*auxiliary*) **1** used in questions and negative statements or commands: *Do you smoke? I don't like wine. Don't do that!* **2** used to avoid repetition of a verb: *She eats as much as I do.* **3** used for emphasis: *She does know you've arrived.* – *n.* **dos** or **do's** (*informal*) something done as a rule or custom: *dos and don'ts.* – *vb.* **do away with 1** to murder. **2** to abolish. – *vb.* **do out of** to deprive of, especially by trickery: *They had been done out of their rightful inheritance.* – *vb.* **do up** (*informal*) **1** to repair, clean, or improve the decoration of: *We did up the house just before selling it.* **2** to fasten; to tie or wrap up: *Leila did up the present with a long, pink ribbon.*

doc·ile (däs′əl, däs′īl′) *adj.* willing to obey.

dock (däk) *n.* a harbor where ships are loaded, unloaded, and repaired; (in *plural*) the area surrounding this. – *vb.* **dock·ing, docked 1** to bring or come into a dock. **2** to link up in space: *The two spaceships docked.*

doc·tor (däk′tər) *n.* a person trained and qualified to practice medicine.

doc·trine (däk′trən) *n.* a set of religious or political beliefs.

doc·u·ment (däk′yə-mənt) *n.* any piece of official writing, such as a certificate. – (däk′yə-mənt′) *vb.* **doc·u·ment·ing, doc·u·ment·ed** to provide written evidence to support or prove.

dodge (däj) *vb.* **dodg·ing, dodged 1** to avoid by moving quickly away, especially sideways: *He dodged through the traffic.* **2** to escape or avoid by cleverness or deceit.

do·do (dō′dō) *n.* **do·dos** or **do·does** a large gray flightless bird of Mauritius, now extinct.

doe (dō) *n.* **does** or **doe** an adult female deer, rabbit, hare, or other certain animals.

does·n't (duz′ənt) does not.

dog (dôg) *n.* **1** any of a family of four-legged mammals that includes the wolf and the fox; especially a domesticated species of this family. **2** the male of any such animal.

DOG TERMS

bitch a female dog.

dam the female parent.

dewclaw a rudimentary pad and claw on the inside of the leg.

litter a group of puppies born at one time to one female.

purebred a dog whose parents belong to the same breed.

sire the male parent.

whelp to give birth to puppies.

Dogs can be grouped according to the kind of work they do. There are sporting dogs, such as pointers, setters, and retrievers, which scent out game and retrieve it; hounds, which are trained for hunting; working and herding dogs, such as police dogs, rescue dogs, and sheepdogs; terriers, bred to drive game out of holes in the ground; and toy dogs, kept as pets or to keep guard.

American cocker spaniel

Boston terrier

Standard smooth-haired dachshund

Standard long-haired dachshund

Withers — Eye

Flank

Croup; rump — Loin — Cheek — Muzzle

Point of shoulder

Elbow

Boxer

Hock

Front pastern

Beagle

Bloodhound

Rhodesian ridgeback

● Prehistoric people tamed dogs to help them hunt wild animals. Today there are more than 100 breeds of dog. The Saint Bernard is the largest; the chihuahua is one of the smallest. Dogs live for about 12 years.

dog·fish (dôg′fish′) *n.* any of various kinds of small shark.

dog·ged (dô′gəd) *adj.* determined.

Dog Star *n.* Sirius, the brightest star in the sky.

dog·ge·rel (dô′gə-rəl) *n.* badly written poetry.

dog·ma (dôg′mə) *n.* a belief or principle laid down by an authority as unquestionably true.

dog·mat·ic (dôg-mat′ik) *adj.* (of a person) stating opinions very forcefully; intolerant.

doll (däl′, dôl′) *n.* a toy in the form of a model of a human being, especially a baby.

dollar (däl′ər) *n.* (*symbol* **$**) the standard unit of currency in the UNITED STATES, CANADA, and certain other countries, divided into 100 cents.

dol·phin (däl′fən, dôl′fin) *n.* **1** a highly intelligent marine mammal of the whale family. **2** a food fish living in warm waters.

dome (dōm) *n.* a roof in the shape of a hemisphere.

do·mes·tic (də-mes′tik) *adj.* **1** of or relating to the home, the family, or private life. **2** (of animals) not wild. − *n.* a household servant.

do·mes·ti·cate (də-mes′ti-kāt′) *vb.* **do·mes·ti·cat·ing, do·mes·ti·cat·ed** to train or cultivate for human use.

dom·i·nant (däm′ə-nənt′) *adj.* most important, evident, or active; foremost.

dom·i·nate (däm′ə-nāt′) *vb.* **dom·i·nat·ing, dom·i·nat·ed 1** to have command or influence over: *Don't let them dominate you.* **2** to be the most important or evident person or thing in: *The election dominates the news.*

● **Do·mi·ni·ca** (däm′ə-nē′kə, də-min′i-kə). See Supplement, **Countries**.

● **Do·min·i·can Republic** (də-min′i-kən). See Supplement, **Countries**.

do·min·ion (də-min′yən) *n.* **1** rule; power; influence. **2** a territory or country governed by a single ruler or government.

dom·i·no (däm′ə-nō′) *n.* **dom·i·noes** a small rectangular tile, marked with a varying number of dots (or left blank), used to play the game of **dominoes**.

do·nate (dō′nāt′, dō-nāt′) *vb.* **do·nat·ing, do·nat·ed** to give, especially to charity. − *n.* **do·na·tion** (dō-nā′shən).

● **Don·a·tel·lo** (dän′ə-tel′ō) (*c.*1386-1466) was a sculptor from Florence, ITALY, who lived during the RENAISSANCE.

done *adj.* **1** finished. **2** (of food) fully cooked. − *vb.* See **do.**

● **Don Juan** (dän hwän′, dän jōō′ən) in legend was a Spanish nobleman famous for seducing women.

don·key (däng′kē, dung′kē, dông′kē) *n.* **don·keys** an animal of the horse family, smaller than a horse and with longer ears. Also known as an ass.

● **Donne** (dun), **John** (?1572-1631) was an English churchman and poet.

● **Don Qui·xo·te** (dän′kē-hōt′ē) is a novel by the Spanish writer CERVANTES which describes the adventures of a crazy old knight. See **quixotic**.

Dollar is from a German word *taler*, the name of a silver coin made in 1518 from metal found at Joachims*thal*, Bohemia.

A cutaway showing the structure of a dome.

The inverted bowl shape of domes is found on many religious buildings such as mosques and churches. The Taj Mahal in India and the Mosque of Omar in Jerusalem carry one as does St. Peter's, Rome, and St. Paul's Cathedral, London, shown here.

don't (dōnt) do not.

doo·dle (dōod′l) *vb.* **doo·dling, doo·dled** to scribble aimlessly. – *n.* a meaningless scribble.

doom (dōom) *n.* unavoidable death, ruin, or other unpleasant fate. – *vb.* **doom·ing, doomed** to condemn to some horrible fate: *He was doomed to sail the seas forever.*

door (dôr, dōr) *n.* a movable barrier opening and closing an entrance, as to a room.

dor·mant (dôr′mənt) *adj.* inactive; hibernating.

dor·mi·to·ry (dôr′mə-tôr′ē, dôr′mə-tōr′ē) *n.* **dor·mi·tor·ies** a building providing accommodations at a school or college.

dor·mouse (dôr′mous′, dōr′mous′) *n.* **dor·mice** (dôr′mīs′, dōr′mīs′) an Old World animal, like a mouse with a squirrel's tail.

dose (dōs) *n.* a quantity of medicine taken at one time.

● **Dos·toy·ev·sky** (däs′toi-ef′skē), **Fyodor** (1821-1881) was the Russian author of *Crime and Punishment*, and other novels.

dot (dät) *n.* a small round mark; a spot; a point. – *vb.* **dot·ting, dot·ted** **1** to put a dot on. **2** to be scattered. – **on the dot** exactly.

dou·ble (dub′əl) *adj.* **1** made up of two similar parts; paired; in pairs. **2** of twice the usual weight, size, etc.: *A double portion of dessert, please.* **3** for two people: *We had a room with a double bed.* **4** with two different uses or aspects: *Everything he says has a double meaning.* – *adv.* **1** twice. **2** with one half over the other: *Towels should be folded double.* – *vb.* **dou·bling, dou·bled** **1** to make or become twice as large in size, number, etc. **2** to have a second use: *This wine bottle doubles as a vase.* **3** to act as a substitute. – **on the double** very quickly. – *vb.* **double back** to turn and go back.

dou·ble-cross (dub′əl-krôs′) *vb.* **dou·ble-cross·ing, dou·ble-crossed** to betray or deceive by breaking a promise.

double play *n.* a play in baseball in which two runners are put out.

doubt (dout) *vb.* **doubt·ing, doubt·ed** **1** to feel uncertain about; to be suspicious or show mistrust of. **2** to be inclined to disbelieve. – *n.* **1** uncertainty, suspicion, or mistrust. **2** an inclination to disbelieve; a reservation.

doubt·ful (dout′fəl) *adj.* **1** feeling doubt. **2** uncertain; able to be doubted. **3** likely not to be the case.

dough (dō) *n.* **1** a mixture of flour, water, and other ingredients, the basis of bread, etc. **2** (*informal*) money.

dour (dowr, dōor) *adj.* stern; sullen.

dove (duv) *n.* a bird of the pigeon family.

● **Dow-Jones** (dou′ jōnz′) an index of stocks and shares prices on the New York Stock Exchange.

down¹ (doun) *adv.* **1** toward or in a low or lower position, level, or state; on or to the ground. **2** from a greater to a lesser size, amount, or level: *We saw a scaled down model of the building.* **3** in writing; on paper: *Please take down notes.* **4** as a deposit: *Henry put down $50 for the bike.* **5** from earlier to later times: *This story has been handed down through generations.* – *prep.* **1** in a lower position on. **2** along; at a farther position on, by, or through: *Our good friends live down the road.* **3** from the top to, or toward, the bottom. – *adj.* **1** sad; in low spirits. **2** going toward or reaching a lower position: *a down pipe.* **3** made as a deposit: *a down payment.* **4** (of a computer, etc.) not working.

down² (doun) *n.* soft fine feathers or hair.

down·fall (doun′fôl′) *n.* the cause of failure or ruin.

down·heart·ed (doun-härt′əd) *adj.* dejected; discouraged.

down·stream (doun-strēm′) *adj. & adv.* farther along a river toward the sea.

down-to-earth (doun′tə-urth′) *adj.* sensible and practical.

down·ward (doun′wərd) or **down·wards** (doun′wərdz) *adv.* to or toward a lower position or level.

● **Doyle** (doil), **Arthur Conan** (1859-1930) was a Scottish novelist, creator of Sherlock HOLMES.

doze (dōz) *vb.* **doz·ing, dozed** to sleep lightly. – *n.* a brief period of light sleeping.

doz·en (duz′ən) *n.* **dozen** or **dozens** a set of twelve.

drab (drab) *adj.* **drab·ber, drab·best** **1** dull; dreary. **2** of a dull greenish-brown color.

● **Dra·cu·la** (dra′kyə-lə), **Count** was a Transylvanian vampire in a novel by Bram Stoker.

draft (draft) *n.* **1** a current of air, especially indoors. **2** a sketch or rough copy of something to be built or written. **3** the selection of personnel for compulsory military service.

PRONUNCIATION SYMBOLS			
ə	**away**	lemon	focus
a	**fat**	oi	**boy**
ā	**fade**	oo	**foot**
ä	**hot**	ōō	**moon**
âr	**fair**	ou	**house**
e	**met**	th	**think**
ē	**mean**	th	**this**
g	**get**	u	**cut**
hw	**which**	ur	**hurt**
i	**fin**	w	**witch**
ī	**line**	y	**yes**
îr	**near**	yōō	**music**
ô	**often**	yoor	**pure**
ō	**note**	zh	**vision**

Dragonflies are found near fresh water in all parts of the world. They are useful to people because they feed on harmful pests such as mosquitoes. They are swift, skillful fliers and superb hunters. Dragonflies have long, narrow, red, blue, green, or black bodies and two pairs of transparent, veined wings.

drag (drag) *vb.* **drag·ging, dragged 1** to pull along slowly and with force. **2** to move along scraping the ground. **3** to search a lake with a hook. – *n.* **1** an act of dragging; a dragging effect. **2** (*informal*) a tedious person or thing.

drag·on (drag'ən) *n.* a large mythical fire-breathing reptilelike creature with wings.

drag·on·fly (drag'ən-flī') *n.* **drag·on·flies** an insect with a long thin body and two sets of wings.

drain (drān) *vb.* **drain·ing, drained 1** to cause or allow liquid to escape; to empty a container in this way. **2** (of liquid, etc.) to escape; to flow away. – *n.* a pipe for carrying away liquid.

drain·age (drā'nij) *n.* the process or system of draining.

drake (drāk) *n.* a male duck.

●**Drake** (drāk), **Francis** (*c.*1543-1596) was an English sailor and adventurer who helped defeat the Spanish ARMADA in 1588.

dra·ma (dräm'ə, dram'ə) *n.* **1** a play; any work performed by actors. **2** plays in general. **3** a situation full of excitement and emotion.

dra·mat·ic (drə-mat'ik) *adj.* **1** of or relating to plays, the theater, or acting. **2** exciting; sudden and striking; drastic. – *adv.* **dra·mat·i·cal·ly** (drə-mat'i-klē).

dra·ma·tist (dräm'ət-əst, dram'ət-əst) *n.* a writer of plays.

drank. See **drink**.

drape (drāp) *vb.* **drap·ing, draped 1** to cover with cloth in loose folds. **2** to arrange in attractive folds. – *n.* (often in *plural*) cloth hung in folds, used as a window curtain.

dras·tic (dras'tik) *adj.* extreme; severe.

draw (drô) *vb.* **drawing, drew** (drōō), **drawn 1** to make a picture of something or someone with a pencil, pen, etc. **2** to pull out, take out, or extract: *They had to draw water from a well.* **3** to move: *Please draw nearer.* **4** to take from a fund or source: *During the game we needed to draw on extra reserves of energy.* **5** to attract: *Don't show off and draw attention to yourself.* **6** to end a game, etc. with neither side winning. **7** to suck air; (of

a chimney) to cause air to flow through a fire, allowing burning. – *n.* **1** a result in which neither side is the winner; a tie. **2** a person or thing with the potential to attract many people.

draw·back (drô'bak') *n.* a disadvantage.

draw·bridge (drô'brij') *n.* a bridge that can be lifted to prevent access across.

draw·ing (drô'ing) *n.* any picture drawn in pencil, pen, chalk, etc.

-drawn pulled by: *horse-drawn.*

draw·er (drôr, drô'ər) *n.* a sliding lidless storage box fitted as part of a piece of furniture.

dread (dred) *vb.* **dread·ing, dread·ed** & *n.* to look ahead to with great fear or apprehension: *I dread going to the dentist.*

Outlines with shading

Pen and ink drawing

You can use many media to **draw**—crayons, pencils, chalk, markers. Remember that straight lines seem to converge at one place, called a vanishing point; and circles, the top of a tower for instance, will look oval at various eye-levels.

Light source

Soft pencil shading

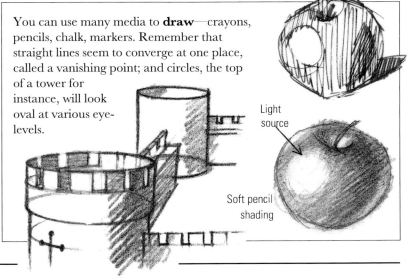

dream (drēm) *n.* **1** a series of thoughts and images occurring during sleep. **2** a goal or ambition. – *vb.* **dream·ing, dreamed** (drēmd, dremt) or **dreamt** (dremt) **1** to have thoughts and visions during sleep. **2** to have an ambition or hope. **3** to imagine: *I never dreamed I could win the high jump.* – *n.* **dream·er.**

drea·ry (drîr′ē) *adj.* **drea·ri·er, drea·ri·est** **1** dull and depressing. **2** uninteresting.

dredge (drej) *vb.* **dredg·ing, dredged** to clear the bottom of or deepen by bringing up mud and waste: *They had to dredge the harbor.* – *n.* a machine for dredging.

drench (drench) *vb.* **drenching, drenched** to make soaking wet.

dress (dres) *vb.* **dress·ing, dressed** **1** to put clothes on. **2** to treat and bandage: *The nurse cleaned and dressed the cut.* – *n.* a woman's garment with top and skirt in one piece.

dres·sage (dra-säzh′) *n.* See **Horse Terms.**

dress·ing *n.* **1** a sauce added to food, especially salad. **2** a covering for a wound. **3** a stuffing of breadcrumbs, herbs, etc.

drew. See **draw.**

drib·ble (drib′əl) *vb.* **drib·bling, drib·bled** **1** to fall or flow in drops. **2** to allow saliva to run slowly down from the mouth. **3** in basketball and soccer, to move by bouncing or short kicks: *He dribbled the basketball.*

drift (drift) *n.* **1** a pile or mass formed by the wind or a current: *a snow drift.* **2** a general movement or tendency to move. – *vb.* **drift·ing, drift·ed** **1** to float or be blown along. **2** to move about aimlessly.

drill (dril) *n.* **1** a tool for boring holes. **2** a training exercise, or a session of it. – *vb.* **drill·ing, drilled** **1** to make a hole with a drill. **2** to exercise or teach through repeated practice.

drink (dringk) *vb.* **drinking, drank** (drangk), **drunk** (drungk) **1** to swallow a liquid. **2** to drink alcohol: *The problem is, he drinks.* **3** to drink a toast. – *n.* **1** a liquid suitable for drinking. **2** a glass of alcohol of any kind.

drip (drip) *vb.* **drip·ping, dripped** **1** to fall in drops. **2** to release a liquid in drops: *That faucet is dripping.* – *n.* **1** the action or noise of dripping. **2** a liquid that falls in drops. **3** (*informal*) a stupid or dull person.

drive (drīv) *vb.* **driving, drove** (drōv), **driven** (driv′ən) **1** to control the movement of a vehicle. **2** to travel in a vehicle. **3** to produce motion in; to cause to function. – *n.* **1** a trip in a vehicle, especially for pleasure. **2** a path for

vehicles. **3** energy and enthusiasm.

driz·zle (driz′əl) *n.* fine light rain. – *vb.* **driz·zling, driz·zled** to rain lightly.

drom·e·dar·y (dräm′ə-der′ē) *n.* **drom·e·dar·ies** a camel with a single hump.

droop (drōōp) *vb.* **droop·ing, drooped** **1** to hang loosely. **2** to be weak with tiredness.

drop (dräp) *vb.* **drop·ping, dropped** **1** to fall or allow to fall: *Drop your weapons!* **2** to decline, lower, or weaken: *The temperature dropped.* **3** to stop discussing: *Let's drop the subject.* **4** to set down from a vehicle; to deliver or hand in: *Could you drop this parcel off at the post office?* – *n.* **1** a small mass of liquid, especially falling. **2** a descent; a fall. **3** a vertical distance.

drought (drout) *n.* lack of rainfall.

drove. See **drive.**

drown (droun) *vb.* **drown·ing, drowned** **1** to kill or die by suffocating in a liquid. **2** to soak or flood: *They drown everything in ketchup.*

drowse (drouz) *vb.* **drows·ing, drowsed** to sleep lightly for a short while.

drows·y (drou′zē) *adj.* sleepy.

drug (drug) *n.* **1** any substance used in the treatment of disease. **2** any substance taken for its effect on the mind, especially a habit-forming or illegal one. – *vb.* **drug·ging, drugged** **1** to make sleepy or unconscious with a drug. **2** to poison with a drug.

drug·gist (drug′əst) *n.* **1** a person who fills prescriptions. **2** the owner of a drugstore.

drug·store (drug′stôr′, drug′stōr′) *n.* a store where medicines, drugs, and a variety of other items are sold.

drum (drum) *n.* a percussion instrument consisting of a hollow frame with a skin or other membrane stretched tightly across its

Drums of various kinds are the oldest musical instruments. The kettledrum (timpani) is a large shell with a single drumhead. The pedal enables the player to tune the drum.

PRONUNCIATION SYMBOLS			
ə	away lemon	focus	
a	fat	oi	boy
ā	fade	oo	foot
ä	hot	ōō	moon
âr	fair	ou	house
e	met	th	think
ē	mean	th	this
g	get	u	cut
hw	which	ur	hurt
i	fin	w	witch
ī	line	y	yes
îr	near	yōō	music
ô	often	yoor	pure
ō	note	zh	vision

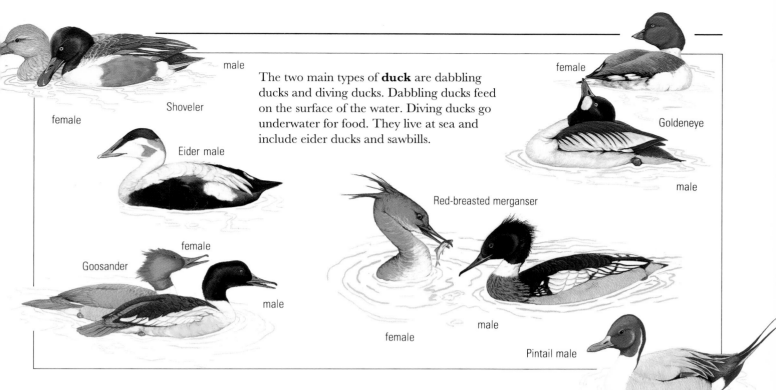

The two main types of **duck** are dabbling ducks and diving ducks. Dabbling ducks feed on the surface of the water. Diving ducks go underwater for food. They live at sea and include eider ducks and sawbills.

male

Shoveler

female

female

Goldeneye

Eider male

male

Red-breasted merganser

female

Goosander

male

male

female

Pintail male

opening. – *vb.* **drum·ming, drummed 1** to beat a drum. **2** to make continuous tapping or thumping sounds. – *n.* **drum·mer**.

drunk (drungk) *vb.* See **drink**. – *adj.* lacking control in movement, speech, etc. through having drunk too much alcohol.

dry (drī) *adj.* **dri·er, dri·est 1** free from moisture or wetness. **2** with little or no rainfall. **3** not in or under water: *dry land.* **4** thirsty. – *vb.* **dries, dry·ing, dried 1** to make or become dry. **2** to preserve by removing all moisture.

du·al (dōo′əl, dyōo′əl) *adj.* consisting of or representing two separate parts: *dual brakes.*

du·bi·ous (dōo′bē-əs) *adj.* feeling doubt; unsure: *I'm a bit dubious about taking the car.*

●**Dub·lin** (dub′lən) is the capital of the Republic of IRELAND. It lies on the River Liffey.

duch·ess (duch′əs) *n.* the wife of a duke.

duck¹ (duk) *n.* **1** any of a family of water birds with short legs, webbed feet, and a broad flat beak. **2** the female of such a bird, as opposed to the male drake.

duck² (duk) *vb.* **duck·ing, ducked 1** to lower the head or body suddenly, so as to avoid a blow. **2** to push briefly under water.

duck-billed plat·y·pus (duk′bild′ plat′ə-pəs, plat′ə-poos′) *n.* an Australian egg-laying amphibious mammal with a ducklike beak.

duck·ling (duk′ling) *n.* a young duck.

duct (dukt) *n.* **1** any tube in the body carrying liquids, such as tears. **2** a pipe or channel carrying liquids, protecting electric cables, etc.

due (dōo, dyōo) *adj.* **1** owed; payable. **2** expected according to schedule or prearrangement. – *adv.* directly: *due north.*

du·el (dōo′əl, dyōo′əl) *n.* a prearranged fight between two people.

du·et (dōo-et′, dyōo-et′) *n.* a piece of music for two singers or players; a pair of musicians.

dug (dug). See **dig**.

duke (dōok, dyōok) *n.* a nobleman of the highest rank outside the royal family. – *n.* **duke·dom** (dook′dəm, dyook′dəm).

dull (dul) *adj.* **1** (of color or light) lacking brightness or clearness. **2** (of sounds) deep and low; muffled. **3** slow to learn: *a dull student.* **4** not sharp. **5** uninteresting.

●**Du·mas** (dōo-mä′, dyōo-mä′), **Alexandre** (1802-1870) was the French author of *The Three Musketeers.*

dumb (dum) *adj.* **1** not able to speak. **2** (*informal*) stupid: *a dumb answer.*

dumb·found (dum′found′) *vb.* **dumb·found·ing, dumb-found·ed** to astonish into silence.

dum·my (dum′ē) *n.* **dum·mies** a life-size model of the human body, for displaying clothes, etc.

Desert sand **dunes** are shaped by the wind. A "barchan" has a crescent-shaped front and a long tail. "Linear" dunes are created in strong steady winds which cut troughs in the desert floor.

Barchan

Linear dune

dump (dump) *vb.* **dump·ing, dumped 1** to put down heavily or carelessly: *Don't just dump your bag in the hall.* **2** to dispose of trash, especially improperly. **3** to transfer from a computer's memory to a disk or printed page. – *n.* a place where rubbish may be dumped.

●**Dun·can** (dung′kən), **Isadora** (1878-1927) was an American dancer whose style was controversial.

dune (dōōn, dyōō) *n.* a low ridge of sand.

dun·geon (dun′jən) *n.* a prison cell, especially underground.

du·pli·cate (dōō′pli-kət, dyōō′pli-kət) *adj.* identical to another: *duplicate keys.* – *n.* an exact copy, as of a key or a document. – (dōō′pli-kāt′, dyōō′pli-kāt′) *vb.* **du·pli·cat·ing, du·pli·cat·ed 1** to make an exact copy of. **2** to repeat. – *n.* **du·pli·ca·tion** (dōō′pli-kā′shən, dyōō′pli-kā′shən). – *n.* **du·pli·ca·tor** (dōō′pli-kāt-ər, dyōō′pli-kāt′ər).

du·ra·ble (door′ə-bəl, dyoor′ə-bəl) *adj.* sturdy; long-lasting.

du·ra·tion (door-ā′shən, dyoor-ā′shən) *n.* the length of time that something lasts or continues.

●**Dü·rer** (door′ər, dyoor′ər), **Albrecht** (1471-1528) was a German artist and engraver.

du·ring (door′ing, dyoor′ing) *prep.* **1** throughout the time of: *The store is out of bounds during school hours.* **2** in the course of: *The phone rang during the night.*

dusk (dusk) *n.* twilight, the period of half darkness before night.

dust (dust) *n.* **1** earth, sand, or household dirt in the form of a fine powder. **2** any substance in powder form: *When the explorers tried to lift the mummy, it turned to dust.* – *vb.* **dust·ing, dust·ed 1** to remove dust from furniture, etc. **2** to sprinkle: *Dust the cake with sugar.*

dust·y (dus′tē) *adj.* **dust·i·er, dust·i·est** covered with, or containing, dust.

Dutch (duch) *n.* **1** the language of the NETHERLANDS. **2** the people of the NETHERLANDS. – *adj.* of the NETHERLANDS, its people, or their language.

du·ti·ful (dōōt′i-fəl, dyōōt′i-fəl) *adj.* showing a sense of duty.

du·ty (dōōt′ē, dyōōt′ē) *n.* **du·ties 1** something you are obliged to do; a moral or legal responsibility: *I feel it's my duty to warn you that he is a dangerous influence.* **2** a task to be performed, especially in connection with a job: *My duties include answering the phone.* **3** a tax on imported or exported goods.

dwell (dwel) *vb.* **dwell·ing, dwelt** or **dwelled** to reside. – *n.* **dwell·er.** – *vb.* **dwell on** or **upon** to think or speak about at length.

dwell·ing (dwel′ing) *n.* a place of residence; a house.

dwin·dle (dwin′dl) *vb.* **dwin·dling, dwin·dled** to shrink in size, number, or intensity.

dye (dī) *vb.* **dye·ing, dyed** to color or stain permanently. – *n.* any coloring substance.

dy·ing (dī′ing) *vb.* present participle of **die.** – *adj.* **1** occurring immediately before death: *It was his dying wish.* **2** at the point of death. **3** coming to an end.

dyke (dīk) *n.* another spelling of **dike.**

dy·nam·ic (dī-nam′ik) *adj.* full of energy, enthusiasm, and new ideas.

dy·na·mite (dī-nə-mīt′) *n.* an explosive. – *vb.* **dy·na·mit·ing, dy·na·mit·ed** to blow up using dynamite.

dy·na·mo (dī′nə-mō′) *n.* **dy·na·mos** a device that converts mechanical movement into electrical energy.

dy·nas·ty (dī′nə-stē) *n.* **dy·nas·ties** a succession of rulers from the same family.

dys·en·te·ry (dis′ən-ter′ē) *n.* an intestinal infection.

dys·lex·i·a (dis-lek′sē-ə) *n.* difficulty in reading and spelling, unrelated to intelligence. – *adj.* & *n.* **dys·lex·ic** (dis-lek′sik).

dys·pep·si·a (dis-pep′sē-ə) *n.* indigestion.

E e

each (ēch) *adj. & pron.* every one of two or more people, animals, or things considered separately: *Each girl took an apple.*

ea·ger (ē′gər) *adj.* showing enthusiasm; keen.

ea·gle (ē′gəl) *n.* any of various kinds of large birds of prey.

● Eagles soar into the sky on broad wings then swoop to seize their prey in powerful talons. They eat by tearing off flesh with their strong hooked beaks. The bald eagle is the national emblem of the UNITED STATES. It is not really bald, but has white feathers on its head.

ear (îr) *n.* one of the two parts of the body on either side of the head with which we hear.

ear·drum (îr′drum′) *n.* the thin membrane inside the ear that transmits vibrations made by sound waves to the inner ear.

earl (url) *n.* a male member of the British nobility.

ear·ring (îr′ring) *n.* a piece of jewelry that is attached to the earlobe.

ear·ly (ur′lē) *adv. & adj.* **ear·li·er, ear·li·est** **1** happening or existing near the beginning of a period of time: *He found traces of an early Roman settlement.* **2** happening or arriving sooner than usual, or sooner than expected or intended: *I was early, and the show had not yet begun.*

earn (urn) *vb.* **earn·ing, earned** **1** to gain money by working. **2** to deserve: *She felt that she had earned a rest.*

earn·ings (ur′ningz) *n.* (*plural*) money earned.

earn·est (ur′nəst) *adj.* serious.

● **Earp** (urp), **Wyatt** (1848-1929) was a UNITED STATES lawman in the days of the Wild West.

Imperial eagle

Golden eagle

Bald eagle

Eagles belong to the same family as hawks and vultures. They all have strong curved talons. Two species, the bald eagle and the golden eagle, breed in North America. The bald eagle is found nowhere else in the world.

The letter *E*, like all the letters, has a long history. The earliest alphabets were taken and adapted by the Greeks. The Greek *beta*, when combined with the first letter, *aleph*, gives us the word alphabet.

The Greeks passed on their letters to the Romans, who developed the alphabet we use today, although they used only capital letters. Small letters developed in the A.D. 700s.

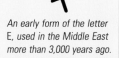

An early form of the letter E, used in the Middle East more than 3,000 years ago.

This letter was taken by the Greeks and became epsilon.

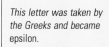

Over the years different versions of the letter E have been developed.

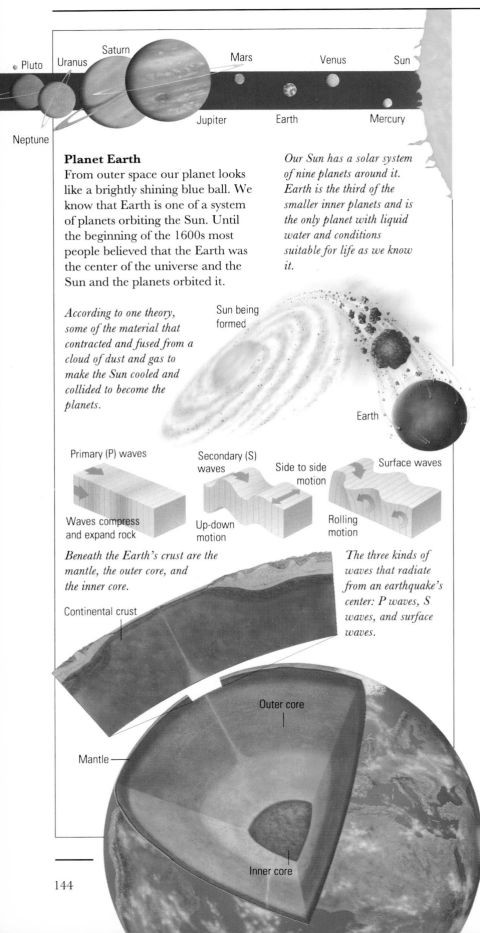

Pluto

Uranus

Saturn

Mars

Venus

Sun

Neptune

Jupiter

Earth

Mercury

Planet Earth

From outer space our planet looks like a brightly shining blue ball. We know that Earth is one of a system of planets orbiting the Sun. Until the beginning of the 1600s most people believed that the Earth was the center of the universe and the Sun and the planets orbited it.

Our Sun has a solar system of nine planets around it. Earth is the third of the smaller inner planets and is the only planet with liquid water and conditions suitable for life as we know it.

According to one theory, some of the material that contracted and fused from a cloud of dust and gas to make the Sun cooled and collided to become the planets.

Sun being formed

Earth

Primary (P) waves

Secondary (S) waves

Side to side motion

Surface waves

Waves compress and expand rock

Up-down motion

Rolling motion

Beneath the Earth's crust are the mantle, the outer core, and the inner core.

The three kinds of waves that radiate from an earthquake's center: P waves, S waves, and surface waves.

Continental crust

Outer core

Mantle

Inner core

earth (urth) *n.* **1** (also **Earth**) the planet on which we live, the third planet in order of distance from the sun. **2** dry land; the ground.

earth·quake (urth′kwāk′) *n.* a shaking of the earth's surface.

earth·worm (urth′wurm′) *n.* the common worm.

ear·wig (īr′wig′) *n.* an insect with pincers at the end of its body.

ease (ēz) *n.* **1** freedom from pain or anxiety. **2** absence of difficulty: *She completed the course with ease.* – *vb.* **eas·ing, eased 1** to free from pain, trouble, or anxiety: *The drugs eased the pain of his wound.* **2** to move or place gently or gradually: *We eased the piano through the door.*

ea·sel (ē′zəl) *n.* a stand for supporting an artist's canvas.

eas·i·ly (ē′zə-lē) *adv.* **1** without difficulty. **2** clearly; beyond doubt.

east (ēst) *n.* the direction from which the sun rises, or any part of the earth lying in that direction. – *adj.* **1** in the east; on the side which is on or nearest the east. **2** coming from the direction of the east: *An east wind was blowing.* – *adv.* toward the east. – **the East** the countries of ASIA, east of EUROPE.

east·ern (ē′stərn) *adj.* of the east.

east·ward (ēst′wərd) *adv.* (also **eastwards** [ēst′wərdz]) & *adj.* toward the east.

Eas·ter (ē′stər) *n.* See **Religious Terms**.

eas·y (ē′zē) *adj.* **eas·i·er, eas·i·est 1** not difficult: *The test was easy.* **2** not stiff or formal; leisurely. – *n.* **eas·i·ness** (ē′zē-nəs).

eat (ēt) *vb.* **eat·ing, ate** (āt), **eat·en** (ēt′n) **1** to bite, chew, and swallow food. **2** to destroy something by chemical action.

eat·a·ble (ēt′ə-bəl) *adj.* fit to be eaten.

eaves·drop (ēvz′dräp′) *vb.* **eaves·drop·ping, eaves·dropped** to listen secretly to a private conversation.

ebb (eb) *vb.* **eb·bing, ebbed** (of the tide) to move away from the land.

eb·o·ny (eb′ə-nē) *n.* a type of hard, almost black wood. – *adj.* **1** made from this wood. **2** black or almost black.

ec·cen·tric (ik-sen′trik) *adj.* odd; unusual. – *n.* an eccentric person.

ech·o (ek′ō) *n.* **ech·oes 1** the repeating of a sound caused by the sound waves striking a surface and coming back. **2** an imitation or repetition. – *vb.* **echo·es, echo·i·ng, echo·ed 1** to sound loudly with an echo; to send back an echo. **2** to repeat; to imitate.

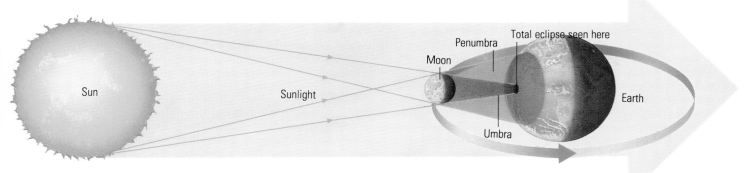

Labels on diagram: Sun; Sunlight; Moon; Penumbra; Total eclipse seen here; Umbra; Earth

e·clipse (i-klips′) *n.* a complete or partial darkening of a heavenly body. In a **solar eclipse** the sun is blocked when the moon comes between the sun and the earth and in a **lunar eclipse** the moon is blocked by the earth's shadow. – *vb.* **e·clips·ing, e·clipsed** **1** to cause an eclipse. **2** to surpass.

e·col·o·gy (i-käl′ə-jē) *n.* **1** the relationship between living things and their surroundings. **2** the scientific study of this relationship.

e·con·o·my (i-kän′ə-mē) *n.* **e·con·o·mies** **1** the system used by a country to organize its money and resources. **2** careful management of money or other resources to avoid waste and cut down on spending. – *adj.* of the cheapest kind: *They always fly economy class to save money.*

ec·sta·sy (ek′stə-sē) *n.* **ec·sta·sies** a feeling of immense joy.

●**Ec·ua·dor** (ek′wə-dôr′). See Supplement, **Countries**.

ec·ze·ma (ig-zē′mə, eg′zə-mə, ek′sə-mə) *n.* a skin disorder in which red blisters form on the skin.

-ed *suffix* **1** used to form past tenses: *walked*. **2** used to form adjectives from nouns: *bearded*; *bald-headed*.

ed·dy (ed′ē) *n.* **ed·dies** **1** a current of water running back against the main stream or current, forming a small whirlpool. **2** a movement of air, smoke, fog, etc. similar to this. – *vb.* **ed·dies, ed·dy·ing, ed·died** to move in this way; to whirl.

E·den (ēd′n) *n.* in the BIBLE, the garden where Adam and Eve originally lived.

edge (ej) *n.* **1** the part farthest from the middle of something; a border or boundary. **2** the area beside a cliff or steep drop. **3** the cutting side of something sharp such as a knife. – *vb.* **edg·ing, edged** **1** to form or make a border

to: *She edged the dress with lace.* **2** to move little by little: *She edged toward the cake.* – **have the edge on** or **over** to have an advantage over. – **on edge** uneasy; nervous.

edg·y (ej′ē) *adj.* **edg·i·er, edg·i·est** easily annoyed; nervous or tense.

ed·i·ble (ed′ə-bəl) *adj.* fit to be eaten; suitable to eat. – *n.* **ed·i·bil·i·ty** (ed′ə-bil′ət-ē).

ed·i·fice (ed′ə-fəs) *n.* a large building.

ed·i·fy (ed′ə-fī′) *vb.* **ed·i·fies, ed·i·fy·ing, ed·i·fied** to improve the mind or morals of. – *n.* **ed·i·fi·ca·tion** (ed′ə-fə-kā′shən). – *adj.* **ed·i·fy·ing**.

●**Ed·in·burgh** (ed′n-bur′ə) is the capital of SCOTLAND. It stands on a sea inlet, the Firth of Forth.

●**Ed·i·son** (ed′ə-sən), **Thomas Alva** (1847-1931) was an American inventor, notably of the phonograph and the electric light bulb.

In a solar eclipse (eclipse of the Sun) — the Moon passes between the Sun and Earth and casts its shadow across the Earth. An eclipse is total only if seen from within the Moon's central shadow or umbra.

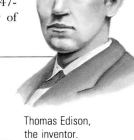

Thomas Edison, the inventor.

Edison was responsible for over 1,000 inventions – although many were modifications of already existing inventions (for example his improvement on Bell's telephone). But his phonograph was completely new and original.

Phonograph

Telephone

Radio receiver

Electricity comes from a Greek word for amber. This is because amber, when rubbed, can be given an electric charge and made to attract small pieces of paper or cloth.

ed·it (ed′ət) *vb.* **ed·it·ing, ed·it·ed** **1** to prepare a book, newspaper, etc. especially by making corrections or alterations. **2** to prepare a movie, or a television or radio program, by cutting and putting together material previously photographed or recorded.

e·di·tion (i-dish′ən) *n.* a number of copies of a book, etc. printed at one time.

ed·i·tor (ed′ət-ər) *n.* a person who edits.

●**Ed·mon·ton** (ed′mən-tən) is the capital of Alberta, CANADA.

ed·u·cate (ej′ə-kāt′) *vb.* **ed·u·cat·ing, ed·u·cat·ed** to train and teach; to provide school instruction for. – *adj.* **ed·u·ca·tive** (ej′ə-kāt′iv) – *n.* **ed·u·ca·tor** (ej′ə-kāt′ər).

ed·u·cat·ed (ej′ə-kāt′əd) *adj.* **1** having received an education, especially to a level higher than average. **2** based on experience or knowledge: *He made an educated guess.*

ed·u·ca·tion (ej′ə-kā′shən) *n.* **1** the process of teaching at school, college, and university. **2** the process of training and improving through learning and experience. – *adj.* **ed·u·ca·tion·al** (ej′ə-kā′shən-l).

●**Ed·ward** (ed′wərd) was the name of nine kings of ENGLAND.

eel (ēl) *n.* any of several kinds of fish with a long smooth snakelike body and very small fins.

ee·rie (îr′ē) *adj.* **eer·i·er, eer·i·est** strange and frightening. – *adv.* **eer·i·ly** (îr′ə-lē).

ef·face (i-fās′) *vb.* **ef·fac·ing, ef·faced** to rub or wipe out.

ef·fect (i-fekt′) *n.* **1** a result. **2** an impression given or produced: *She has had a good effect on him.* **3** operation; working state: *They put their plans into effect.* – *vb.* **ef·fect·ing, ef·fect·ed** to cause to happen.

ef·fec·tive (i-fek′tiv) *adj.* **1** having power to produce, or producing, a desired result. **2** in, or coming into, operation.

ef·fi·cient (i-fish′ənt) *adj.* capable of producing good results with an economy of effort and a minimum of waste.

ef·fi·gy (ef′ə-jē) *n.* **ef·fi·gies** a portrait, sculpture, or model of a person.

ef·flu·ent (ef′loo-ənt) *n.* industrial waste or sewage that is released into a river or the sea.

ef·fort (ef′ərt) *n.* **1** something that requires hard mental or physical work. **2** an attempt to do something: *She made an effort to win the race.*

effortless (ef′ərt-ləs) *adj.* done without apparent effort.

egg[1] (eg, āg) *n.* **1** the reproductive cell produced by a female animal from which a young one develops. **2** a reproductive cell produced in a hard shell by female birds, reptiles, and certain animals. **3** a hen's egg, used as food.

egg[2] (eg, āg) **egg on** *vb.* **eg·ging, egged** to urge or encourage.

egg·plant (eg′plant′, āg′plant′) *n.* **1** the edible purple fruit of a bushy plant. **2** this plant.

e·go (ē′gō) *n.* **e·gos** **1** personal pride. **2** the part of a person that is conscious and thinks.

e·go·tism (ē′gə-tiz′əm) *n.* the habit of having too high an opinion of oneself. – *n.* **e·go·tist** (ē′gə-təst, ē′gə-tist).

e·gret (ē′grət) *n.* any of various white, long-legged wading birds similar to herons.

●**E·gypt** (ē′jəpt). More than 5,000 years ago the people of ancient Egypt built a great civilization on the banks of the river NILE. The kings, or pharaohs, built huge temples and PYRAMIDS as tombs. See also Supplement, **Countries**.

E·gyp·tian (i-jip′shən) *adj.* of or belonging to Egypt. – *n.* a citizen of Egypt.

For most of their history, the ancient **Egyptians** were united under one ruler — the pharaoh (king), who was worshiped as a god. The Egyptians believed in an afterlife and developed the custom of embalming the dead. They built elaborate tombs in pyramids or in caves.

Top: *A shadoof is used to raise water for irrigation.* Right: *Important places in Egyptian history.*

Alexandria
Giza
Nile
Luxor
Abu Simbel

ei·der (īd′ər) or **eider duck** *n.* a large sea duck.

ei·der·down (īd′ər-doun′) *n.* a quilt usually filled with the down of the eider.

●**Eif·fel Tower** (ī′fəl) made of wrought iron, it soars 984 feet (300 meters) above Paris, France, and is a symbol of the city.

eight (āt) *n.* the number or figure 8. – *n., adj., & adv.* **eighth** (ātth, āth).

eigh·teen (āt-tēn′, ā-tēn′) *n.* the number or figure 18. – *n., adj., & adv.* **eigh·teen·th** (āt-tēnth′, ā-tēnth′).

eight·y (āt′ē) *n.* **eight·ies** the number or figure 80. – *n., adj., & adv.* **eight·i·eth** (āt′ē-əth).

●**Ein·stein** (īn′stīn′), **Albert** (1879-1955) was a German-American physicist whose theory of RELATIVITY revolutionized the way we look at the world.

either (ē′thər, ī′thər) *adj.* **1** any one of two: *Either chair is comfortable.* **2** each of two; both: *She had a garden with a fence on either side.* – *pron.* any one of two things, people, etc. – *adv.* also: *I found him rather unpleasant, and I didn't like his*

The pharaohs wielded immense power over their people and were looked upon as gods.

The mummified bodies of the pharaohs were buried on boats so that they could travel to the next world.

wife either. – **either ... or** introducing two choices or possibilities: *Either he goes or I do.*

e·ject (i-jekt′) *vb.* **e·ject·ing, e·ject·ed** to throw out with force. – *n.* **e·jec·tion** (i-jek′shən).

eke (ēk): **eke out** *vb.* **ek·ing, eked 1** to make but just barely: *to eke out a living.* **2** to make last longer by adding something or by careful use.

e·lab·o·rate (i-lab′ə-rət) *adj.* **1** complicated in design: *an elaborate sweater.* **2** carefully planned or worked out: *an elaborate plan.* – (i-lab′ə-rāt′) *vb.* **e·lab·o·rat·ing, e·lab·o·rat·ed** to add detail. – *n.* **e·lab·o·ra·tion** (i-lab′ə-rā′shən).

e·land (ē′lənd) *n.* **elands** or **eland** a large African antelope with spiral horns.

e·lapse (i-laps′) *vb.* **elaps·ing, elapsed** (of time) to pass.

e·las·tic (i-las′tik) *adj.* able to return to its original shape or size after being pulled or pressed out of shape. – *n.***1** a stretchable cord or fabric woven with strips of rubber. **2** a rubber band.

el·bow (el′bō′) *n.* the joint where the human arm bends.

el·der[1] (el′dər) *adj.* older. – *n.* an older person, especially regarded as having authority.

el·der[2] (el′dər) *n.* a kind of bush with white flowers and purple-black or red berries.

el·der·ly (el′dər-lē) *adj.* rather old.

el·dest (el′dəst) *adj.* oldest.

e·lect (i-lekt′) *vb.* **e·lect·ing, e·lect·ed 1** to choose by vote. **2** to choose to do something: *She elected to stay at home.* – *adj.* (following the noun) elected to a position, but not yet formally occupying it: *He is the president elect.*

e·lec·tion (i-lek′shən) *n.* the process of choosing people for an official position by taking a vote.

e·lec·tric (i-lek′trik) *adj.* produced by, worked by, or generating electricity.

e·lec·tri·cal (i-lek′tri-kəl) *adj.* related to or operated by electricity.

e·lec·tri·cian (i-lek-trish′ən) *n.* a person whose job is to install and repair electrical equipment.

e·lec·tric·i·ty (i-lek-tris′ət-ē) *n.* the energy that is used to make heat and light, etc.

e·lec·trode (i-lek′trōd′) *n.* either of the two conducting points by which electric current enters or leaves a battery or other electrical apparatus.

e·lec·tro·mag·net (i-lek′trō-mag′nət) *n.* a piece of soft metal, usually iron, made magnetic by the passage of an electric current

Democratic elections began to develop in Athens in the 400s B.C. All male citizens had a say in government. They used metal disks to vote.

through a coil of wire wrapped around the metal. – *adj.* **e·lec·tro·mag·net·ic** (i-lek′trō-mag-net′ik).

e·lec·tron (i-lek′trän′) *n.* a particle, present in all atoms, which has a negative electric charge.

e·lec·tron·ic (i-lek-trän′ik) *adj.* operated by means of very small electrical circuits which handle very low levels of electric current.

e·lec·tron·ics (i-lek-trän′iks) *n.* (*singular*) the study of the behavior of electronic circuits and how they are used in machines, etc.

el·e·gant (el′i-gənt) *adj.* having good taste in dress or style. – *n.* **el·e·gance** (el′i-gəns).

el·e·gy (el′ə-jē) *n.* **el·e·gies** a song or poem, especially one whose subject is death.

el·e·ment (el′ə-mənt) *n.* **1** a part of anything which combines with other features to make a whole. **2** any one of 105 known substances that cannot be split by chemical means into simpler substances.

el·e·men·tal (el′ə-ment′l) *adj.* basic or primitive.

el·e·men·ta·ry (el′ə-ment′ə-rē) *adj.* dealing with basic facts.

el·e·phant (el′ə-fənt) *n.* **elephants** or **elephant** the largest living land animal, with thick grayish skin, a nose in the form of a long hanging trunk, and two curved tusks.

el·e·vate (el′ə-vāt′) *vb.* **el·e·vat·ing, el·e·vat·ed** to raise or lift.

el·e·va·tion (el′ə-vā′shən) *n.* **1** the act of raising. **2** the height above sea level.

There are two species of elephant: the Indian elephant (above) and the much larger African elephant. Both the male and female African elephant have tusks; in the Indian elephant only the male has tusks. The Indian elephant can be trained to move heavy loads.

el·e·va·tor (el′ə-vāt′ər) *n.* a movable enclosed platform or cage for transporting people or freight from one floor to another.

e·lev·en (i-lev′ən) *n.* the number or figure 11. – *n., adj.,* & *adv.* **e·lev·enth** (i-lev′ənth).

elf (elf) *n.* **elves** (elvz) a tiny fairy with magical powers. – *adj.* **elf·ish** (el′fish).

el·i·gi·ble (el′ə-jə-bəl) *adj.* **1** suitable, or deserving to be chosen. **2** having a right. – *n.* **el·i·gi·bil·i·ty** (el′ə-jə-bil′ət-ē).

e·lim·i·nate (i-lim′ə-nāt′) *vb.* **e·lim·i·nat·ing, e·lim·i·nat·ed** to get rid of or exclude. – *n.* **e·lim·i·na·tion** (i-lim′ə-nā′shən).

● **El·i·ot** (el′ē-ət), **T. S.** (1888-1965) was an American-born British poet and playwright.

● **E·liz·a·beth I** (i-liz′ə-bəth) (1533-1603) became queen of ENGLAND in 1558.

● **E·liz·a·beth II** (i-liz′ə-bəth) (1926-) is queen of the UNITED KINGDOM and head of the British Commonwealth.

elk (elk) *n.* **elk** or **elks** **1** a large deer of NORTH AMERICA. **2** a large Old World deer.

el·lipse (i-lips′) *n.* a regular oval shape.

el·lip·ti·cal (i-lip′ti-kəl) or **el·lip·tic** (i-lip′tik) *adj.* having the shape of an ellipse.

elm (elm) *n.* any of various tall trees with broad leaves and clusters of small flowers; the hard heavy wood of these trees.

el·o·quence (el′ə-kwəns) *n.* the power of using words well. – *adj.* **el·o·quent** (el′ə-kwənt).

● **El Sal·va·dor** (el sal′və-dôr′, el′ säl′-və-dôr′). See Supplement, **Countries**.

else (els) *adj.* & *adv.* different from or in addition to something already mentioned: *Would you like something else?* – **or else** otherwise.

e·lude (ē-lo͞od′) *vb.* **e·lud·ing, e·lud·ed** **1** to escape or avoid. **2** to baffle.

e·lu·sive (ē-lo͞o′siv, ē-lo͞o′ziv) *adj.* **1** difficult to find or catch. **2** difficult to remember.

elves See **elf**.

e·man·ci·pate (i-man′sə-pāt′) *vb.* **e·man·ci·pat·ing, e·man·ci·pat·ed** to set free, especially from slavery. – *adj.* **e·man·ci·pat·ed**. – *n.* **e·man·ci·pa·tion** (i-man′sə-pā′shən).

em·balm (im-bäm′, im-bälm′) *vb.*

em·balm·ing, embalmed to preserve from decay by treatment with chemicals.

em·bank·ment (im-bangk′mənt) *n.* a wall of earth made to carry a road or to hold back water.

em·bar·go (im-bär′gō) *n.* **em·bar·goes** an official order forbidding trade with another country.

em·bark (im-bärk′) *vb.* **em·bark·ing, em·barked 1** to go, or put, on board ship. **2** to begin.

em·bar·rass (im-bar′əs) *vb.* **em·bar·rass·ing, em·bar·rassed** to cause to feel anxious, self-conscious, or ashamed. – *n.* **em·bar·rass·ment** (im-bar′ə-smənt).

em·bas·sy (em′bə-sē) *n.* **em·bas·sies** the official residence of an ambassador.

em·bel·lish (im-bel′ish) *vb.* **em·bel·lish·ing, em·bel·lished 1** to make more interesting by adding details. **2** to decorate.

em·ber (em′bər) *n.* (usually in *plural*) a piece of glowing or smoldering coal or wood in a fire.

em·bez·zle (im-bez′əl) *vb.* **em·bez·zling, em·bez·zled** to steal by fraud for one's own use: *They embezzled the company's money.*

em·blem (em′bləm) *n.* an object chosen to represent an idea or a country.

em·brace (im-brās′) *vb.* **em·brac·ing, embraced 1** to hold closely in the arms affectionately or as a greeting. **2** to accept sincerely and enthusiastically.

em·broi·der (im-broid′ər) *vb.* **em·broi·der·ing, em·broi·dered 1** to decorate cloth with sewn designs. **2** to make more interesting by adding details.

em·broi·der·y (im-broid′ə-rē) *n.* **1** the sewing of designs on to cloth. **2** embroidered cloth.

em·bry·o (em′brē-ō′) *n.* **embryos** a human or animal in the earliest stages of development before birth.

e·mend (ē-mend′) *vb.* **e·mend·ing, e·mend·ed** to correct.

em·er·ald (em′ə-rəld) *n.* **1** a bright-green precious stone. **2** a bright green color.

e·merge (i-murj′) *vb.* **e·merg·ing, e·merged 1** to come out from hiding or into view. **2** to become known or apparent.

e·mer·gen·cy (i-mur′jən-sē) *n.* **e·mer·gen·cies** an unexpected and serious happening which calls for immediate action.

●**Em·er·son** (em′ər-sən), **Ralph Waldo** (1803-1882) was an American philosopher and writer.

em·i·grant (em′ə-grənt) *n.* a person who leaves a native country and settles in another.

em·i·grate (em′ə-grāt′) *vb.* **em·i·grat·ing, em·i·grat·ed** to leave a native country and settle in another. – *n.* **em·i·gra·tion** (em′ə-grā′shən).

em·i·nent (em′ə-nənt) *adj.* widely admired.

em·i·nent·ly (em′ə-nənt-lē) *adv.* notably; very.

e·mis·sion (i-mish′ən) *n.* **1** the act of releasing a substance. **2** something released, especially heat, light, or gas.

e·mit (ē-mit′) *vb.* **e·mit·ting, e·mit·ted** to give out or send forth: *A lamp emits light.*

e·mo·tion (i-mō′shən) *n.* a strong feeling.

e·mo·tion·al (i-mō′shən-l) *adj.* **1** of the emotions. **2** tending to express emotions easily or excessively. **3** exciting the emotions.

em·per·or (em′pər-ər) *n.* the male ruler of an empire.

em·pha·sis (em′fə-səs) *n.* **em·pha·ses** (em′fə-sēz′) importance or extra stress to show that something has a special meaning.

em·pha·size (em′fə-sīz′) *vb.* **em·pha·siz·ing, em·pha·sized** to stress.

em·phat·ic (em-fat′ik) *adj.* expressed with or expressing emphasis.

em·pire (em′pīr′) *n.* a group of nations or states under the control of a single ruler or country.

em·ploy (im-ploi′) *vb.* **em·ploy·ing, em·ployed 1** to give paid work to. **2** to occupy the time or attention of.

Canada

Australia

New Zealand

South Africa

Many countries try to find some object that uniquely represents them as an emblem on their flags, crests, etc. Examples are the maple leaf in the national arms of Canada, sprays of wattle around the Australian arms, four stars of the Southern Cross for New Zealand, and a trekker's wagon on the arms of South Africa.

Endangered species
Throughout time animals and plants have died out naturally. Most of the animals and plants in danger of becoming extinct today are threatened by humans. Overhunting, overfishing, the destruction of habitats, and the pollution of the air and seas are taking their toll.

Bald eagle

Pampas deer

Bareheaded rock fowl

Tasmanian wolf

Giant panda

Monkey-eating eagle

em·ploy·ee (im-ploi′ē′, im-ploi′ē′) *n.* a person who works for another in return for payment.

em·ploy·er (im-ploi′ər) *n.* a person or company that employs workers.

em·ploy·ment (im-ploi′mənt) *n.* an occupation, especially regular paid work.

emp·ty (em′tē, emp′tē) *adj.* **emp·ti·er, emp·ti·est** having nothing inside; not occupied, inhabited, or furnished. – *vb.* **emp·ties, emp·ty·ing, emp·tied** to make or become empty.

e·mu (ē′myo͞o) *n.* a large Australian flightless bird with gray or brown plumage.

e·nam·el (in-am′əl) *n.* **1** a hardened colored glasslike substance applied to metal or glass. **2** the hard white covering of the teeth.

en·chant (in-chant′) *vb.* **en·chant·ing,**

en·chant·ed to charm or delight.

en·cir·cle (in-sur′kəl) *vb.* **en·cir·cling, en·cir·cled** to form a circle around.

en·close (in-klōz′) *vb.* **en·clos·ing, en·closed 1** to put inside a letter or its envelope. **2** to shut in or surround.

en·com·pass (in-kum′pəs) *vb.* **en·com·pass·ing, en·com·passed 1** to include. **2** to encircle or surround.

en·coun·ter (in-kount′ər) *vb.* **en·coun·ter·ing, en·coun·tered** to meet unexpectedly. – *n.* **1** a chance meeting. **2** a fight.

en·cour·age (in-kur′ij) *vb.* **en·cour·ag·ing, en·cour·aged 1** to give support, confidence, or hope to. **2** to urge or recommend. – *n.* **en·cour·age·ment** (in-kur′ij-mənt).

en·cy·clo·pe·di·a or **en·cy·clo·pae·di·a** (in-sī′klə-pēd′ē-ə) *n.* a reference work containing information on every branch of knowledge, or on one particular branch, usually arranged in alphabetical order.

end (end) *n.* **1** the point where something stops. **2** a finish or conclusion. **3** an object or purpose. – *vb.* **end·ing, end·ed** to finish or cease to exist.

en·dan·ger (in-dān′jər) *vb.* **en·dan·ger·ing, en·dan·gered** to put in danger.

endangered species *n.* a species of animal threatened with extinction.

en·deav·or (in-dev′ər) *vb.* **en·deav·or·ing, en·deav·ored** to try very hard. – *n.* a determined attempt or effort.

en·dorse (in-dôrs′) *vb.* **en·dors·ing, en·dorsed 1** to write your signature on. **2** to state your support for.

en·dur·ance (in-door′əns) *n.* the ability to withstand hardship.

en·dure (in-door′) *vb.* **en·dur·ing, en·dured 1** to bear patiently, put up with. **2** to last.

en·e·my (en′ə-mē) *n.* **en·e·mies** a hostile person, nation, or force. – *adj.* hostile.

en·er·get·ic (en′ər-jet′ik) *adj.* having or displaying energy; forceful; vigorous.

en·er·gy (en′ər-jē) *n.* **en·er·gies 1** vigorous activity; liveliness or vitality. **2** the capacity for doing work or yielding power.

●Energy can exist in different forms: as stored energy (potential energy), as energy of motion (kinetic energy), electrical energy (produced by generators), and nuclear energy, etc.

In the explosion of an atomic bomb vast quantities of energy are released. The splitting of an atom's nucleus is called nuclear fission.

en·gage (in-gāj′) *vb.* **en·gag·ing, en·gaged** **1** to take on as a worker. **2** to involve or occupy: *She engaged him in conversation.*

en·gaged (in-gājd′) *adj.* **1** bound by a promise to marry. **2** busy; occupied.

en·gage·ment (in-gāj′mənt) *n.* **1** a firm agreement between two people to marry: *They announced their engagement today.* **2** an appointment.

en·gine (en′jən) *n.* **1** a machine that turns energy into movement. **2** a locomotive.

en·gi·neer (en′jə-nîr′) *n.* **1** a person who designs or constructs roads, railroads, bridges, machines, equipment, etc. **2** a person who operates an engine, especially a train.

●**Eng·land** (ing′glənd, ing′lənd) is the largest country in the UNITED KINGDOM.

Steam locomotives are now rare. In the 1700s steam engines powered factory engines that made the Industrial Revolution possible.

Eng·lish (ing′glish, ing′lish) *adj.* **1** of England or its people. **2** of or using the English language. – *n.* the main language of GREAT BRITAIN, the UNITED STATES, CANADA, and many other countries.

en·grave (in-grāv′) *vb.* **en·grav·ing, en·graved** **1** to carve letters or designs on stone, wood, metal, etc. **2** to fix or impress deeply on the mind, etc. – *n.* **en·grav·er.**

en·gulf (in-gulf′) *vb.* **en·gulf·ing, en·gulfed** to swallow up completely; to overwhelm.

en·joy (in-joi′) *vb.* **en·joy·ing, en·joyed** **1** to find pleasure in. **2** to have the benefit of. – *n.* **en·joy·ment** (in-joi′mənt).

en·large (in-lärj′) *vb.* **en·larg·ing, en·larged** to make larger or more detailed.

en·list (in-list′) *vb.* **en·list·ing, en·list·ed** **1** to join one of the armed forces. **2** to obtain or secure for some cause: *We enlisted their help.*

e·nor·mous (i-nôr′məs) *adj.* extremely large.

e·nough (i-nuf′) *adj.* in the number or quantity needed: *Is there enough food to eat?* – *adv.* to the necessary degree or extent. – *pron.* the amount needed: *I've eaten enough, thank you.*

en·rage (in-rāj′) *vb.* **en·rag·ing, en·raged** to make very angry. – *adj.* **en·raged.**

en·rich (in-rich′) *vb.* **en·rich·ing, en·riched** to improve in quality, value, flavor, etc.

en·roll or **en·rol** (in-rōl′) *vb.* **en·roll·ing, en·rolled** to add the name of a person to a list, for example to join a course or a club. – *n.* **en·roll·ment** (in-rōl′mənt).

en·sign (en′sən) *n.* **1** a national flag flown by a ship. **2** the lowest ranking commissioned officer in the UNITED STATES Navy.

en·sure (in-shoor′) *vb.* **en·sur·ing, en·sured** to make certain; to guarantee.

en·tan·gle (in-tang′gəl) *vb.* **en·tan·gling, en·tan·gled** to catch in some obstacle.

en·ter (ent′ər) *vb.* **en·ter·ing, en·tered** **1** to come in or go in. **2** to register for a competition. **3** to record in a book or diary.

en·ter·prise (ent′ər-prīz′) *n.* **1** a project or undertaking. **2** boldness and initiative: *Their plan showed great enterprise.*

en·ter·tain (ent′ər-tān′) *vb.* **en·ter·tain·ing, en·ter·tained** **1** to provide amusement. **2** to give hospitality to a guest.

PRONUNCIATION SYMBOLS			
ə	away	lemon	focus
a	fat	oi	boy
ā	fade	oo	foot
ä	hot	ōō	moon
âr	fair	ou	house
e	met	th	think
ē	mean	th	this
g	get	u	cut
hw	which	ur	hurt
i	fin	w	witch
ī	line	y	yes
îr	near	yōō	music
ô	often	yoor	pure
ō	note	zh	vision

en·ter·tain·er (ent'ər-tā'nər) *n.* a person who provides amusement, especially professionally.

en·thu·si·asm (in-thoō'zē-az'əm, in-thyoō'zē-az'əm) *n.* lively or passionate interest or eagerness.

en·thu·si·ast (in-thoō'zē-ast', in-thyoō'zē-ast') *n.* a person filled with enthusiasm, a fan. — *adj.* **en·thu·si·as·tic** (in-thoō'zē-as'tik, in-thyoō'zē-as'tik).

en·tice (in-tīs') *vb.* **en·tic·ing, en·ticed** to tempt or persuade to do something.

en·tire (in-tīr') *adj.* whole, complete.

en·ti·tle (in-tīt'l) *vb.* **en·ti·tling, en·ti·tled** to give the right to; to qualify.

en·trance[1] (en'trəns) *n.* **1** a way in, for example a door. **2** the act of entering.

en·trance[2] (in-trans') *vb.* **entrancing, en·tranced 1** to grip the attention and imagination of. **2** to put in a trance.

en·try (en'trē) *n.* **1** the act of coming or going in. **2** a place of entering, such as a door. **3** an item written on a list.

e·nu·mer·ate (i-noō'mə-rāt', i-nyoō'mə-rāt') *vb.* **e·nu·mer·at·ing, e·nu·mer·at·ed** to list one by one.

en·vel·op (in-vel'əp) *vb.* **en·vel·o·ping, en·vel·oped** to cover, surround, or conceal.

en·ve·lope (en'və-lōp', än'və-lōp') *n.* a flat paper container, especially for a letter.

en·vi·ous (en'vē-əs) *adj.* feeling envy.

en·vi·ron·ment (in-vī'rən-mənt) *n.* the surroundings or conditions within which something or someone exists. — *adj.* **en·vi·ron·men·tal** (in-vī'rən-ment'l).

en·vis·age (in-viz'ij) *vb.* **en·vis·ag·ing, en·vis·aged** to picture in the mind.

en·voy (en'voi', än'voi') *n.* **1** a diplomat ranking below an ambassador. **2** a messenger.

en·vy (en'vē) *n.* bitterness combined with a desire for another person's better fortune, success, or possessions. — *vb.* **en·vies, en·vy·ing, en·vied** to feel envy toward.

e·phem·er·al (i-fem'ə-rəl) *adj.* lasting for only a very short time.

ep·ic (ep'ik) *n.* **1** a long poem that tells a story about heroic acts, the history of nations, etc. **2** a long adventure story or movie.

ep·i·dem·ic (ep'ə-dem'ik) *n.* a sudden and widespread outbreak of a disease.

ep·i·gram (ep'ə-gram') *n.* a witty or sarcastic saying, or a short poem with such an ending.

ep·i·graph (ep'ə-graf') *n.* a quotation or motto at the beginning of a book or chapter.

ep·i·sode (ep'ə-sōd') *n.* one of several events, sections, or distinct periods making up a longer sequence.

e·pis·tle (i-pis'əl) *n.* a letter, especially a long one dealing with important matters.

ep·i·taph (ep'ə-taf') *n.* an inscription on a gravestone.

e·pit·o·me (i-pit'ə-mē) *n.* a perfect or typical example of something.

ep·och (ep'ək, ep'äk') *n.* **1** a particular period of history. **2** a division of a geological period.

ep·o·nym (ep'ə-nim) *n.* a person after whom something is named.

e·qual (ē'kwəl) *adj.* **1** the same in size, amount, or value. **2** having or entitled to the same rights. — *n.* a person or thing of the same age, rank, ability, worth, etc. — *vb.* **e·qual·ing** or **e·qual·ling, e·qualed** or **e·qualled** to be the same in amount, value, or size; to match. — *n.* **e·qual·i·ty** (i-kwäl'ət-ē) **e·qual·i·ties**.

e·qual·ize (ē-kwə-līz') *vb.* **e·qual·iz·ing, e·qual·ized** to make or become equal.

e·qua·tion (i-kwā'zhən) *n.* **1** a mathematical formula which states that two quantities or groups are equal. **2** a scientific formula expressing the reaction of chemical compounds.

e·qua·tor (i-kwāt'ər) *n.* an imaginary line passing around the earth at an equal distance from the NORTH and SOUTH POLES.

e·qua·to·ri·al (e'kwə-tôr'ē-əl) *adj.* of or near the equator.

● **Equatorial Guin·ea** (gin'ē). See Supplement, **Countries**.

e·ques·trian (i-kwes'trē-ən) *adj.* of horses.

e·qui·lat·e·ral (ē'kwə-lat'ə-rəl, ek'wə-lat'ə-rəl) *adj.* having all sides of equal length.

e·qui·lib·ri·um (ē'kwə-lib'rē-əm, ek'wə-lib'rē-əm) *n.* a state in which weights, forces, etc. are equally balanced.

e·qui·nox (ē'kwə-näks', ek'wə-näks') *n.* either of the two occasions each year on which the sun crosses the equator and night and day are equal in length.

e·quip (i-kwip') *vb.* **e·quip·ping, e·quipped** to provide with tools, supplies, etc.

e·quip·ment (i-kwip'mənt) *n.* the clothes, machines, tools, instruments, etc. necessary for a particular kind of work or activity.

e·quiv·a·lent (i-kwiv'ə-lənt) *adj.* equal in value, power, meaning, etc.

e·ra (îr′ə, er′ə) *n.* **1** a distinct period in history marked by an important event. **2** in geology, a main division of time.

e·rase (i-rās′) *vb.* **e·ras·ing, e·rased** to rub out; to remove all trace of .

e·rect (i-rekt′) *adj.* upright; not bent or leaning. – *vb.* **e·rect·ing, e·rect·ed** to build.

e·rec·tion (i-rek′shən) *n.* the process of erecting something.

●**E·rie** (îr′ē), **Lake** is one of the GREAT LAKES between CANADA and the UNITED STATES.

●**Er·i·tre·a** (er′ə-trē′ə). See Supplement, **Countries**.

e·rode (i-rōd′) *vb.* **e·rod·ing, e·rod·ed** to wear away or be destroyed gradually.

E·ros (e′räs′, î′räs′). See **Myths and Legends**.

e·ro·sion (e-rō′zhən) *n.* the wearing away of rock or soil by the action of wind, water, or ice. – *adj.* **e·ro·sive** (i-rō′siv, i-rō′ziv).

err (er, ur) *vb.* **err·ing, erred** to make a mistake or do wrong.

er·rand (er′ənd) *n.* a short trip made to get or do something, especially for someone else.

er·rat·ic (i-rat′ik) *adj.* irregular; having no fixed pattern or course.

er·ror (er′ər) *n.* a mistake or inaccuracy.

e·rupt (i-rupt′) *vb.* **e·rupt·ing, e·rupt·ed** **1** (of a volcano) to throw out lava, ash, and gases. **2** to break out suddenly and violently. – *n.* **e·rup·tion** (i-rup′shən).

es·ca·late (es′kə-lāt′) *vb.* **es·ca·lat·ing, es·ca·lat·ed** to increase rapidly.

es·ca·lat·or (es′kə-lāt′ər) *n.* a continuous moving staircase.

es·cape (is-kāp′) *vb.* **es·cap·ing, es·caped** **1** to gain freedom. **2** to manage to avoid. – *n.* **1** an act of escaping. **2** the avoiding of danger or harm: *That was a narrow escape.*

es·cort (es′kôrt′) *n.* one or more persons or vehicles that accompany others for protection, guidance, or as a mark of honor. – (is-kôrt′) *vb.* **es·cort·ing, es·cort·ed** to accompany.

Es·ki·mo (es′kə-mō′) *n.* **Eskimos** or **Eskimo** a member of any of several peoples who inhabit northern CANADA, GREENLAND, Alaska, and eastern Siberia. (See **Inuit**.)

e·soph·a·gus (i-säf′ə-gəs) *n.* **e·soph·a·gi** (i-säf′ə-gī) a tube connecting the throat and stomach, through which food passes during digestion.

es·pi·o·nage (es′pē-ə-näzh′, es′pē-ə-näj′) *n.* the activity of spying.

-ess (es) *suffix* indicating a female.

es·say (es′ā′) *n.* a short formal piece of writing, usually dealing with a single subject.

es·sence (es′əns) *n.* **1** the basic quality of something that determines its nature or character. **2** a concentrated liquid obtained from a plant, and often used to flavor food: *vanilla essence.*

es·sen·tial (i-sen′chəl) *adj.* absolutely necessary. – *n.* a basic piece of equipment or information. – *adv.* **es·sen·tial·ly**.

LESS-ESS

-ess is a suffix that is often added to words to denote a feminine person or animal. Because they sound demeaning and pejorative, many are quite rightly rarely used, for example authoress, conductress, poetess, sculptress. A few -ess words, such as actress, hostess, waitress, lioness remain, and the feminine of titles such as baroness, duchess, goddess are still used.

Rain containing carbon dioxide from the air will dissolve limestone.

Scree formed by frost erosion

Erosion of river valley

A rock tower weathered by wind and rain

Rivers carry rock debris to the sea

Erosion and weathering both help to shape the earth. The action of wind, rain, ice, and snow physically break down rocks into smaller particles such as sand and grit. These bits are transported elsewhere by ice, wind, running water, or gravity. This is erosion.

In deserts sand-laden wind can sculpt rocks into weird shapes.

es·tab·lish (is-tab′lish) *vb.* **es·tab·lish·ing, es·tab·lished 1** to set up on a permanent basis: *to establish a university.* **2** to show or prove.

es·tab·lish·ment (is-tab′lish-mənt) *n.* **1** the act of establishing something. **2** a business organization, such as a store or a public institution.

es·tate (i-stāt′) *n.* **1** a large piece of land, usually with a large house. **2** possessions, especially money and property.

es·ti·mate (es′tə-māt′) *vb.* **es·ti·mat·ing, es·ti·mat·ed** to calculate size, amount, value, etc. roughly or without measuring. – (es′tə-mət) *n.* a rough assessment of size, cost, etc.

● **Es·to·ni·a** (es-tō′nē-ə) was a republic of the former USSR but since 1991 has been independent. See also Supplement, **Countries**.

es·tu·a·ry (es′chōō-er′ē) *n.* **es·tu·ar·ies** the wide lower part of a river where it flows into the sea.

etc. *abbreviation.* ET CETERA.

et cet·era (et set′ə-rə) and so forth; and so on.

etch (ech) *vb.* **etch·ing, etched** to make designs on metal or glass using an acid to eat out the lines.

etch·ing (ech′ing) *n.* a print made from an etched plate.

e·ter·nal (i-turn′l) *adj.* without beginning or end; everlasting and unchanging.

e·ter·ni·ty (i-tur′nət-ē) *n.* **e·ter·ni·ties** time regarded as having no end.

e·ther (ē′thər) *n.* a colorless sweet-smelling liquid, used as an anesthetic.

eth·i·cal (eth′i-kəl) *adj.* **1** of or concerning morals, justice, or duty. **2** morally right.

eth·ics (eth′iks) *n.* **1** (*singular*) the study or the science of beliefs about right and wrong. **2** (*plural*) rules or principles of behavior.

● **E·thi·o·pi·a** (ē′thē-ō′pē-ə). See Supplement, **Countries**.

eth·nic (eth′nik) *adj.* having a common race, language, or cultural tradition.

et·i·quette (et′i-kət) *n.* conventions of correct or polite social behavior.

et·y·mol·o·gy (et′ə-mäl′ə-jē) *n.* **et·y·mol·o·gies 1** the study of the origin and development of words and their usage. **2** the history of a word.

The flag of the EC has 12 gold stars.

More of **Europe**'s land can be farmed than of any other continent's, and it is rich in coal, iron, and other raw materials. The people of Europe are made up of many different nationalities. Each has its own language and customs. The largest European country is Russia; the smallest is Vatican City in Rome.

Key facts
Number of countries: 45
Area: 4,048,356 sq. mi.
Highest point: Mt. Elbrus (18,493 ft.)
Longest river: Volga (2,294 mi.)
Biggest lake: Caspian Sea
Biggest island: Great Britain

eu·ca·lyp·tus (yōō′kə-lip′təs) *n.* **eucalyptuses** or **eu·ca·lyp·ti** (yōō′kə-lip′tī) a tall evergreen tree, native to AUSTRALIA.

● **Eu·clid** (yōō′kləd) was a Greek mathematician who lived and worked around 300 B.C.

eu·phe·mism (yōō′fə-miz′əm) *n.* a mild term used in place of one considered offensive or unpleasantly direct, as *pass on* instead of *die.*

● **Eu·phra·tes** (yōō-frāt′ēz) is a river that flows through TURKEY into the Tigris River.

● **Eu·rip·i·des** (yoo-rip′əd-ēz′) was a Greek dramatist (5th century B.C.).

● **Eu·rope** (yoor′əp) is the sixth biggest continent but is second in population size. Most of Europe has a mild climate and fertile soil. There are some high mountains including the ALPS and URAL MOUNTAINS. Much of Europe's wealth comes from its factories, farms, and mines.

Eu·ro·pe·an (yoor′ə-pē′ən) *adj.* of, or relating to, Europe. – *n.* a native or inhabitant of the

continent of Europe.

e·vac·u·ate (i-vak′yə-wāt′) *vb.*
e·vac·u·at·ing, e·vac·u·at·ed to leave,
especially because of danger.

e·vade (i-vād′) *vb.* **e·vad·ing, e·vad·ed** to
escape or avoid by trickery or skill.

e·val·u·ate (i-val′yōō-āt′) *vb.*
e·val·u·at·ing, e·val·u·at·ed to form a
judgment about the worth or value of.

e·vap·o·rate (i-vap′ə-rāt′) *vb.*
e·vap·o·rat·ing, e·vap·o·rat·ed to
change from a solid or liquid into gas. – *n.*
e·vap·o·ra·tion (i-vap′ə-rā′shən).

eve (ēv) *n.* **1** the evening or day before some
notable event. **2** the period immediately
before: *She died on the eve of war.*

e·ven (ē′vən) *adj.* **1** smooth and flat; level.
2 constant or regular: *They were traveling at an
even 50 miles per hour.* **3** (of a number) divisible
by 2, with nothing left over: *8 is an even number.*
4 equal: *The score was even.* – *adv.* **1** used with a
comparative *adj.* or *adv.* to emphasize a
comparison with something else: *He's good, but
she's even better.* **2** used with an expression
stronger than a previous one: *He looked sad,
even depressed.* **3** used to introduce a surprising

piece of information: *Even John was there!*
4 used to emphasize that whether or not
something is true, the following or preceding
statement would remain the same: *He'd be
unhappy even if he did get the job.*

eve·ning (ēv′ning) *n.* the last part of the day,
from late afternoon until bedtime.

e·vent (i-vent′) *n.* **1** something that happens; an
incident, especially an important one. **2** an
item in a program of sports, etc.

e·ven·tu·al (i-ven′chōō-əl) *adj.* happening
gradually, or at the end of a period of time.

ev·er (ev′ər) *adv.* at any time: *Have you ever been
to New York?*

● **Ev·e·rest** (ev′ə-rəst, ev′rəst), in the
HIMALAYAS, is the world's highest peak at
29,028 feet (8,848 meters) above sea
level.

● **Ev·er·glades** (ev′ər-glādz′) a swamp that covers 3,860 sq. mi. (10,000 sq. km) of southern
Florida.

ev·er·green (ev′ər-grēn′) *adj.* having leaves all
the year round. – *n.* an evergreen tree or shrub.

ev·er·y (ev′rē) *adj.* **1** each single, omitting none.
2 the greatest or best possible: *We're making
every effort to avoid war.* – *adv.* at the end of each
stated period of time, distance, etc.: *every fourth
week*; *every six inches.* – **every now and then**
or **every so often** occasionally; from time to
time.

ev·er·y·bod·y (ev′rē-bäd′ē, ev′rē-bud′ē) *pron.*
every person.

ev·er·y·day (ev′rē-dā′) *adj.* **1** used on ordinary
days, rather than on special occasions.
2 common or usual.

ev·er·y·one (ev′rē-wun′, ev′rē-wən) *pron.*
every person.

ev·er·y·thing (ev′rē-thing′) *pron.* **1** all things;
all. **2** the most important thing: *Fitness is
everything in sports.*

ev·er·y·where (ev′rē-hwer′, ev′rē-wer′) *adv.*
in or to every place.

ev·i·dence (ev′ə-dəns) *n.* **1** information that
gives grounds for belief and which points to,
reveals, or suggests something. **2** See **Law**.

ev·i·dent (ev′ə-dənt) *adj.* clear to see or
understand; obvious.

e·vil (ē′vəl) *adj.* bad, wicked, or offensive;
harmful. – *n.* a source of wickedness or harm;
a harmful influence.

**CHANGES OF
MEANING**
Etymologists study word
origins and also how
words can change their
meaning, for instance:
acre once meant
simply "a field."
clown once meant
"a countryman."
cunning used to mean
"knowing or clever."
gallon once meant
"a bucket or container."
knave once meant
"a servant."
nice once meant "hard
to please" or "fussy."
silly once meant
"blessed or holy."
paradise once meant
"royal park."
villain once meant
"peasant."
yard was once
"a wand or stick."

Millions of years

Era	Period	Millions of years
CENOZOIC 65–0	**Pleistocene** The great Ice Ages First modern humans appear	0 2
	Pliocene First cattle and sheep	5
	Miocene Many new mammals appear First mice, rats, and apes	24
	Oligocene First deer, monkeys, pigs, and rhinoceroses	37
	Eocene First dogs, cats, rabbits, elephants, and horses	58
	Paleocene Mammals spread rapidly. First owls and shrews	65
MESOZOIC 245–65	**Cretaceous** Dinosaurs die out. First snakes, modern mammals	144
	Jurassic Dinosaurs rule the land. First birds appear.	208
	Triassic First dinosaurs, mammals, turtles, crocodiles, and frogs	245
PALEOZOIC 570–245	**Permian** First sail-back reptiles. Many sea and land animals die out.	286
	Carboniferous First reptiles. Great coal swamp forests	360
	Devonian First amphibians, insects, and spiders	408
	Silurian Giant sea scorpions First land plants	438
	Ordovician First nautiloids. Corals and trilobites common	505
	Cambrian First fishes, trilobites, corals, and shellfish	570
PRECAMBRIAN 4600–570	**Precambrian** 700—first jellyfish and worms 3500—life begins in the sea	4.6 billion years

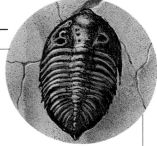

Fossils like this trilobite are the hardened remains of dead animals and plants. Fossils are found in rocks millions of years old. Dating rocks where fossils are found fills in the history of life.

Evolution

The story of life on Earth began millions of years before the appearance of the first humans. The age of the Earth has been estimated to be about 4.5 billion years. Evolution — scientists say — is the gradual process by which all living things have changed since life began some 3.5 billion years ago. The first creatures were very simple forms of life. They evolved into more complicated plants and animals. Fish evolved from simpler sea creatures. Some fish began breathing air and crawled on to dry land. They were the first amphibians. The chart shows how we mark Earth's prehistory by eras lasting millions of years: Precambrian, Paleozoic, Mesozoic, and Cenozoic. You can see how the evolution of species has shaped the "family tree" of life. Plants and animal species have died out and other species have developed.

The diagrams show how the lobe fins of the prehistoric fish, Eusthenopteron, evolved into the legs of the amphibian Icthyostega. The same bones can be seen in both.

The Irish elk, now extinct, had horns measuring up to 10ft. (3m) across from tip to tip.

e·vo·lu·tion (ev′ə-lōō′shən, ē′və-lōō′shən) *n.*
1 the process of gradual development. **2** the
gradual development of plants and animals,
including humans, from earlier forms of life. –
adj. **e·vo·lu·tion·ar·y** (ev′ə-lōō′shə-ner′ē,
ē′və-lōō′shə-ner′ē).

e·volve (i-välv′, i-vôlv′) *vb.* **e·volv·ing,**
e·volved 1 to develop or produce gradually.
2 to develop from a simpler into a more
complex form.

ewe (yōō) *n.* a female sheep.

ex- *prefix* **1** former: *ex-wife.* **2** out: *exhale.*

ex·act (ig-zakt′) *adj.* absolutely accurate or
correct: *She gave him the exact amount.*

ex·ag·ger·ate (ig-zaj′ə-rāt′) *vb.*
ex·ag·ger·at·ing, ex·ag·ger·at·ed to
describe as being greater in extent, etc. than is
really the case. – *n.* **ex·ag·ger·a·tion** (ig-
zaj′ə-rā′shən).

ex·am·i·na·tion (ig-zam′ə-nā′shən) *n.* **1** a set
of tasks to test knowledge or ability. **2** an
inspection or investigation.

ex·a·mine (ig-zam′ən) *vb.* **ex·am·in·ing,**
ex·am·ined 1 to inspect, consider, or look
into closely. **2** to check the health of. **3** to test
the knowledge or ability of.

ex·am·ple (ig-zam′pəl) *n.* **1** something or
someone that is a typical specimen.
2 something that illustrates a fact or rule.

ex·ceed (ik-sēd′) *vb.* **ex·ceed·ing,**
ex·ceed·ed to be greater than; to go beyond.

ex·cel (ik-sel′) *vb.* **ex·cel·ling, ex·celled** to
be exceptionally good; to be better than.

ex·cel·lence (ek′sə-ləns) *n.* great worth; very
high quality. – *adj.* **ex·cel·lent** (ek′sə-lənt).

ex·cept (ik-sept′) *prep.* not including.

ex·cep·tion (ik-sep′shən) *n.* a person or thing
not included; someone or something that does
not follow a general rule.

ex·cep·tion·al (ik-sep′shən-l) *adj.* remarkable
or outstanding.

ex·cess (ik-ses′, ek′ses′) *n.* **1** an amount greater
than is usual, necessary, or wise. **2** an amount
left over. – *adj.* greater than is usual, necessary,
or permitted.

ex·change (iks-chānj′) *vb.* **ex·chang·ing,**
ex·changed to give in return for something
else: *The two leaders exchanged gifts.* – *n.* **1** the
giving and taking of one thing for another. **2** a
conversation or argument. **3** a place where
shares are traded, or financial deals made.

ex·cite (ik-sīt′) *vb.* **ex·cit·ing, ex·cit·ed 1** to
arouse feelings. **2** to stir up. **3** to stimulate

action or motion in. – *adj.* **ex·cit·ed.**

ex·cite·ment (ik-sīt′mənt) *n.* the state of being
excited.

ex·claim (ik-sklām′) *vb.* **ex·claim·ing,**
ex·claimed to call or cry out suddenly. – *n.*
ex·cla·ma·tion (ek′sklə-mā′shən).

exclamation mark *n.* the punctuation mark (!)
used after an exclamation: *What an ugly tie!*

ex·clude (ik-sklōōd′) *vb.* **ex·clud·ing,**
ex·clud·ed to prevent from sharing or taking
part; to omit. – *n.* **ex·clu·sion** (ik-
sklōō′zhən).

ex·clu·sive (ik-sklōō′siv, ik-sklōō′ziv) *adj.* **1** not
including others: *an exclusive interest in tennis.*
2 excluding certain groups: *The lounge is for the
exclusive use of teachers.* **3** not including.

ex·cuse (ik-skyōōz′) *vb.* **ex·cus·ing,**
ex·cused 1 to pardon or forgive. **2** to serve as
an explanation for. **3** to free from an obligation
or a duty. – (ik-skyōōs′) *n.* an explanation for
something wrong.

ex·e·cute (ek′si-kyōōt′) *vb.* **ex·e·cut·ing,**
ex·e·cut·ed 1 to put to death by order of the
law. **2** to perform or carry out. – *n.*
ex·e·cu·tion (ek′si-kyōō′shən).

ex·ec·u·tive (ig-zek′yət-iv) *adj.* concerned
with management or administration.

ex·er·cise (ek′sər-sīz′) *n.* **1** physical training for
health or pleasure. **2** an activity intended to
develop a skill: *piano exercises.* **3** a task designed
to test ability: *a spelling exercise.* – *vb.*
ex·er·cis·ing, ex·er·cised 1 to keep fit and
healthy by training. **2** to use, bring into use.

ex·ert (ig-zurt′) *vb.* **ex·ert·ing, ex·ert·ed** to
bring into action forcefully: *She exerted her
authority.* – **exert one's self** to make a
strenuous effort. – *n.* **ex·er·tion** (ig-zur′shən).

ex·hale (eks-hāl′, ek-sāl′) *vb.* **ex·hal·ing,**
ex·haled to breathe out.

ex·haust (ig-zôst′) *vb.* **ex·haust·ing,**
ex·haust·ed 1 to make very tired. **2** to use up
completely. **3** to discuss or treat thoroughly. –
n. **1** the waste gases from an engine. **2** the parts
of an engine through which the gases escape. –
n. **ex·haus·tion** (ig-zôs′chən).

ex·hib·it (ig-zib′ət) *vb.* **ex·hib·it·ing,**
ex·hib·it·ed 1 to present or display for
public appreciation. **2** to show or reveal. – *n.*
an object displayed publicly, as in a museum.

ex·hi·bi·tion (ek′sə-bish′ən) *n.* a display, for
example of works of art, to the public.

ex·hil·a·rate (ig-zil′ə-rāt′) *vb.*
ex·hil·a·rat·ing, ex·hil·a·rat·ed to fill

Early explorers relied on three basic navigational aids: the astrolabe and backstaff were used to calculate a ship's latitude (how far north or south of the equator). The compass showed in which direction the ship was sailing.

Astrolabe

Backstaff

Compass

The Norwegian Roald Amundsen arrived at the South Pole using dogs to pull the sleds.

with a lively cheerfulness.

ex·ile (eg′sīl′, ek′sīl′) *n.* **1** enforced absence from someone's home country or town. **2** a person suffering such an absence. – *vb.* **ex·il·ing, ex·iled** to send into exile.

ex·ist (ig-zist′) *vb.* **ex·ist·ing, ex·ist·ed 1** to be, especially to be present in the real world. **2** to occur or be found.

ex·is·tence (ig-zis′təns) *n.* **1** the state of existing. **2** a way of living.

ex·it (eg′zət, ek′sət) *n.* **1** a way out of a building, off a highway, etc. **2** an act of going out or departing. – *vb.* **ex·it·ing, ex·it·ed** to go out, leave, or depart.

ex·ot·ic (ig-zät′ik) *adj.* **1** of or from a foreign place. **2** interestingly different or strange.

ex·pand (ik-spand′) *vb.* **ex·pand·ing, ex·pand·ed 1** to make or become greater in size, extent, or importance. **2** to give additional information to.

ex·panse (ik-spans′) *n.* a wide area or space.

ex·pan·sive (ik-span′siv) *adj.* **1** ready or eager to talk; open. **2** wide or extensive.

ex·pect (ik-spekt′) *vb.* **ex·pect·ing, ex·pect·ed 1** to think of as likely: *We expect them to come at noon.* **2** to require, or regard as

Exploring the World: Marco Polo traveled overland to China. Dias and da Gama pioneered the way around Africa. Columbus and Vespucci explored the New World. Magellan was the first to sail around the world.

Marco Polo 1271-1275
Vespucci 1499
Magellan 1519-1522
Columbus 1492

normal or reasonable. **3** (*informal*) to suppose.

ex·pec·ta·tion (ek′spek′tā′shən) *n.* **1** the state of expecting. **2** something expected.

ex·pe·di·tion (ek′spə-dish′ən) *n.* an organized trip: *a climbing expedition.*

ex·pel (ik-spel′) *vb.* **ex·pel·ling, ex·pelled** to force out: *She was expelled from school for fighting.*

ex·pense (ik-spens′) *n.* the act of spending money, or money spent; cost. – **at the expense of** with the loss of or damage to.

ex·pen·sive (ik-spen′siv) *adj.* costing a large amount.

ex·pe·ri·ence (ik-spîr′ē-əns) *n.* **1** practice in an activity. **2** knowledge or skill gained through practice. – *vb.* **ex·pe·ri·enc·ing, ex·pe·ri·enced** to feel or undergo.

ex·per·i·ment (ik-sper′ə-mənt) *n.* **1** a trial carried out in order to test a theory, a machine's performance, etc. or to discover something unknown. **2** an attempt at something original. – (ik-sper′ə-ment′) *vb.* **ex·per·i·ment·ing, ex·per·i·ment·ed** to make such a trial or attempt.

ex·pert (ek′spurt′) *n.* a person who knows a lot about a particular subject. – *adj.* highly skilled.

ex·per·tise (ek′spər-tēz′) *n.* special skill or knowledge.

ex·pire (ik-spīr′) *vb.* **ex·pir·ing, ex·pired 1** to come to an end, cease to be valid. **2** to breathe out. – *n.* **ex·pir·a·tion** (ek′spə-rā′shən).

ex·plain (ik-splān′) *vb.* **ex·plain·ing, ex·plained 1** to make clear or easy to understand. **2** to give, or be, a reason for.

ex·pla·na·tion (ek′splə-nā′shən) *n.* **1** the act of explaining. **2** a statement or fact that explains.

ex·plan·a·to·ry (ik-splan′ə-tôr′ē, ik-splan′ə-tōr′ē) *adj.* serving to explain.

ex·plic·it (ik-splis′ət) *adj.* stated clearly.

ex·plode (ik-splōd′) *vb.* **ex·plod·ing, ex·plod·ed 1** to burst or shatter violently; to blow up. **2** to suddenly show a strong emotion.

ex·ploit (ek′sploit′, ik-sploit′) *n.* (often in *plural*) an act or feat, especially a bold or daring one. – (ik-sploit′, ek′sploit′) *vb.* **ex·ploit·ing, ex·ploit·ed 1** to take unfair advantage of so as to achieve one's own aims. **2** to make good use of: *to exploit oil resources.*

ex·plore (ek′splôr′, ik-splōr′) *vb.* **ex·plor·ing, ex·plored 1** to search or travel through for the purpose of discovery. **2** to examine carefully: *We must explore every possibility.* – *n.* **ex·plor·a·tion** (ek′splə-rā′shən). – *n.* **ex·plor·er.**

ex·plo·sion (ik-splō′zhən) *n.* a blowing up, or the noise caused by this.

ex·plo·sive (ik-splō′siv, ik-splō′ziv) *adj.* likely to, or able to explode. – *n.* a substance capable of exploding.

ex·port (ek-spôrt′, ek-spōrt′) *vb.* **ex·port·ing, ex·port·ed** to send, take, or sell to another country, especially for sale. – (ek′spôrt′, ek′spōrt′) *n.* **1** the act or business of exporting. **2** something exported.

ex·pose (ik-spōz′) *vb.* **ex·pos·ing, ex·posed 1** to remove cover, protection, or shelter from. **2** to discover or make known a crime, etc.

When you look at something, the light rays reflected from the object are focused upside down on the retina, but the brain interprets this as the right way up.

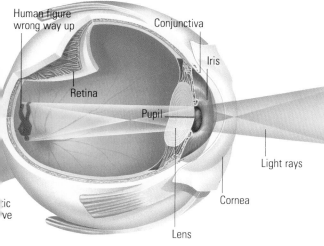

Human figure wrong way up

Conjunctiva

Iris

Retina

Pupil

Light rays

Cornea

Lens

ex·po·sure (ik-spō′zhər) *n.* the act of exposing or the state of being exposed.

ex·press (ik-spres′) *vb.* **ex·press·ing, ex·pressed 1** to put into words. **2** to show or reveal. – *adj.* making few stops: *an express bus.*

ex·pres·sion (ik-spresh′ən) *n.* **1** the act of expressing. **2** a look on the face that displays feelings. **3** a word or phrase.

ex·pres·sive (ik-spres′iv) *adj.* showing meaning or feeling in a clear or lively way.

ex·qui·site (ek-skwiz′ət, ek′skwiz-ət) *adj.* extremely delicate and beautiful.

ex·tend (ik-stend′) *vb.* **ex·tend·ing, ex·tend·ed 1** to make longer or larger. **2** to stick out. **3** to include, go as far as.

ex·ten·sion (ik-sten′chən) *n.* an added part.

ex·ten·sive (ik-sten′siv) *adj.* large in area or amount.

ex·tent (ik-stent′) *n.* **1** the area over which something extends. **2** amount; degree.

ex·te·ri·or (ek-stir′ē-ər) *adj.* on, from, or for use on the outside. – *n.* an outside part or surface.

ex·ter·mi·nate (ik-stur′mə-nāt′) *vb.* **ex·ter·mi·nat·ing, ex·ter·mi·nat·ed** to get rid of or destroy.

ex·ter·nal (ek-sturn′l) *adj.* from, on, or used on the outside.

ex·tinct (ik-stingkt′) *adj.* **1** no longer in existence. **2** (of a volcano) no longer active. – *n.* **ex·tinc·tion** (ik-stingk′shən).

ex·tin·guish (ik-sting′gwish) *vb.* **ex·tin·guish·ing, ex·tin·guished** to put out: *to extinguish a fire.*

ex·tra (ek′strə) *adj.* additional; more than is usual, necessary, or expected.

ex·tract (ik-strakt′) *vb.* **extracting, extracted 1** to pull out, especially by force. **2** to squeeze out. – (ek′strakt′) *n.* a passage selected from a book, etc.

ex·tra·or·di·nar·y (ik-strôrd′n-er′ē, ek′strə-ôrd′n-er′ē) *adj.* unusual; surprising.

ex·trav·a·gant (ik-strav′ə-gənt) *adj.* using, spending, or costing too much. – *n.* **ex·trav·a·gance** (ik-strav′ə-gəns).

ex·treme (ik-strēm′) *adj.* **1** very high in degree or intensity: *extreme cold.* **2** farthest, in any direction: *She stood on the extreme left.* **3** very violent or strong; not moderate; severe.

eye (ī) *n.* **1** the organ of sight in humans and animals. **2** (often in *plural*) sight; vision: *Surgeons need good eyes.* **3** attention, gaze, or observation: *Keep your eye on the ball.* **4** the ability to appreciate and judge: *He has an eye for beauty.* **5** any rounded thing, especially when hollow, for example the hole in a needle. – *vb.* **ey·ing** or **eye·ing, eyed** to look at carefully.

eye·brow (ī′brou′) *n.* the arch of hair above each eye.

eye·lash (ī′lash′) *n.* any of the short hairs that grow on the edge of the eyelid.

eye·let (ī′lət) *n.* a small hole through which a lace, etc. is passed.

eye·lid (ī′lid′) *n.* either of the two folds of skin that can be moved to cover or open the eye.

eye-o·pen·er (ī′ō′pə-nər, ī′ōp′-nər) *n.* something that suddenly surprises you or makes you suddenly understand.

eye·sight (ī′sīt′) *n.* the ability to see.

eye·wit·ness (ī′wit′nəs) *n.* a person who sees something happen, especially a crime.

PRONUNCIATION SYMBOLS		
ə **away**	le**m**on	**focus**
a **fat**	oi	**boy**
ā **fade**	oo	**foot**
ä **hot**	ōō	**moon**
âr **fair**	ou	**house**
e **met**	th	**think**
ē **mean**	t̲h̲	**this**
g **get**	u	**cut**
hw **which**	ur	**hurt**
i **fin**	w	**witch**
ī **line**	y	**yes**
îr **near**	yōō	**music**
ô **often**	yoor	**pure**
ō **note**	zh	**vision**

Ff

fa·ble (fā′bəl) *n.* **1** a story with a moral, usually with animals as characters. **2** a lie; a false story.

fab·ric (fab′rik) *n.* woven or knitted cloth.

fa·cade or **fa·çade** (fə-säd′) *n.* the front of a building.

face (fās) *n.* **1** the front part of the head, from forehead to chin. **2** facial expression: *The basset has such a sad face.* **3** a surface or side of a mountain, gem, geometrical figure, etc. − *vb.* **fac·ing, faced 1** to be opposite to; to look at or look in some direction. **2** to confront, brave, or accept: *She faced the sad news bravely.* − *vb.* **face up to** to accept an unpleasant fact, etc.

fa·cial (fā′shəl) *adj.* of the face.

fa·cil·i·ty (fə-sil′ət-ē) *n.* **fa·cil·i·ties 1** skill or ability with little effort. **2** a building, service, or piece of equipment for a particular activity.

fact (fakt) *n.* a thing known to be true or to exist.

fac·tor (fak′tər) *n.* **1** something that helps bring about a result. **2** one of two or more numbers that when multiplied together produce a given number.

fac·to·ry (fak′tə-rē, fak′trē) *n.* **fac·to·ries** a building where things are made.

fac·tu·al (fak′choo-əl, fak′shəl) *adj* **1** concerned with facts. **2** based on facts.

fac·ul·ty (fak′əl-tē) *n.* **fac·ul·ties 1** any of the mental or physical powers. **2** a particular talent or aptitude for something. **3** the staff of a college or university.

fad (fad) *n.* a short-lived fashion; a craze.

fade (fād) *vb.* **fad·ing, fad·ed** to lose strength, freshness, or color.

Fahr·en·heit (far′ən-hīt′) *n.* a scale of temperature on which water boils at 212° and freezes at 32°.

fail (fāl) *vb.* **fail·ing, failed 1** to be unsuccessful. **2** to judge not good enough to pass. **3** to neglect or not bother. **4** to let down; to disappoint. **5** to become weaker.

fail·ure (fāl′yər) *n.* **1** lack of success. **2** a person or thing that is unsuccessful. **3** a stoppage in functioning. **4** a failing to pass in school.

faint (fānt) *adj.* **1** pale; dim; indistinct. **2** weak and dizzy. **3** not enthusiastic. − *vb.* **faint·ing, faint·ed** to lose consciousness.

fair¹ (fâr) *adj.* **1** just; not using dishonest methods or discrimination. **2** having light-colored hair or skin. **3** average; moderately good. **4** fine: *fair weather.* − *adv.* in a fair way.

fair² (fâr) *n.* **1** an entertainment of sideshows, amusements, rides, etc. **2** an exhibition of goods from different countries, firms, etc.

fair ball *n.* a baseball that is hit within the foul lines.

fair·ly *adv.* **1** in a just way; honestly. **2** somewhat; pretty: *The party was fairly good.*

fair·y (fâr′ē) *n.* **fair·ies** an imaginary small creature with magical powers.

Winged fairies − illustrated in a children's book.

fairy tale *n.* a story about fairies, magic, etc.

faith (fāth) *n.* **1** trust or confidence. **2** strong belief, as in God.

faith·ful (fāth′fəl) *adj.* loyal and true; accurate.

fake (fāk) *n.* a person, thing, or act that is not genuine. – *adj.* not genuine; false. – *vb.* **fak·ing, faked** to make up; to pretend to feel an emotion or have an illness.

fal·con (fal′kən, fôl′kən) *n.* any of various hawks or hawklike birds of prey.

fall (fôl) *vb.* **fall·ing, fell** (fel), **fall·en 1** to descend or drop: *The book fell.* **2** to drop to the ground after losing balance. **3** (of rain, snow, etc.) to come down. **4** to become less: *The temperature fell suddenly.* **5** to pass into a certain state: *Luke fell asleep.* – *n.* **1** an act or way of falling: *a long fall.* **2** something, or an amount, that falls. **3** a drop in quality, quantity, value, temperature, etc. **4** a defeat or collapse.

false (fôls) *adj.* **1** untrue; mistaken. **2** artificial; not genuine. **3** insincere.

fal·ter (fôl′tər) *vb.* **fal·ter·ing, fal·tered 1** to move unsteadily. **2** to speak hesitantly.

fame (fām) *n.* the condition of being famous.

famed (fāmd) *adj.* famous.

fa·mil·iar (fə-mil′yər) *adj.* **1** well known or recognizable. **2** frequently met with: *Cycling in the park is a familiar sight.* **3** having knowledge of: *I am familiar with her work.* **4** friendly.

fam·i·ly (fam′lē, fam′ə-lē) *n.* **fam·i·lies 1** a group consisting of parents and their children. **2** a group of related people; relatives. **3** a related group of races, languages, plants, animals, etc.

fam·ine (fam′ən) *n.* a severe shortage of food.

fa·mous (fā′məs) *adj.* well known.

fan¹ (fan) *n.* **1** a hand-held object made of paper, silk, etc., for creating a current of air to cool the face. **2** an electric machine with revolving blades, for producing a current of air.

fan² (fan) *n.* an enthusiastic admirer.

fa·nat·ic (fə-nat′ik) *n.* someone with an excessive enthusiasm for something. – *adj.* excessively enthusiastic. – *adj.* **fa·nat·i·cal** (fə-nat′i-kəl).

fan·cy (fan′sē) *n.* **fan·cies 1** the imagination. **2** an idea or whim. **3** a sudden liking: *Pat took a fancy to the pony.* – *adj.* **fan·ci·er, fan·ci·est** elaborate. – *vb.* **fan·cies, fan·cy·ing, fan·cied 1** to think or believe. **2** to imagine.

fan·fare (fan′fâr′) *n.* **1** a short piece of music played on trumpets to announce an important event. **2** any noisy display.

Falcons, together with hawks, are day-flying birds of prey, and are found all over the world. Falcons are fast fliers and swoop down on their victims from above, hitting them with their claws. They use their large, hooked beaks for tearing flesh.

The peregrine falcon is one of the fastest fliers in the world. In a dive, it can reach 170 mph (280 km/h).

Peregrine falcon

male

Lesser kestrel

female

Hobby

Kestrel

The kestrel is a small falcon.

male

female

The merlin, sometimes known as the pigeon hawk, is the smallest of the falcons.

fang (fang) *n.* **1** a long pointed tooth. **2** the tooth of a poisonous snake.

fan·tas·tic (fan-tas′tik) *adj.* **1** splendid. **2** amazing. **3** strange or weird. – *adv.* **fan·tas·ti·cal·ly** (fan-tas′ti-klē).

fan·ta·sy (fant′ə-sē) *n.* **fan·ta·sies** a longed-for but unlikely happening.

far (fär) *adv.* **far·ther** (fär′thər), **far·thest** (fär′thəst) or **fur·ther** (fur′thər), **fur·thest** (fur′thəst) **1** at, to, or from, a great distance: *We flew far from the city.* **2** to or by a great extent: *Jim's far nicer than his brother.* **3** at or to a distant time. – *adj.* **1** distant; remote: *the far west of Canada.* **2** more distant: *the far side of the room.* – **far and wide** extensively.

farce (färs) *n.* a comedy with a series of ridiculously unlikely turns of events.

fare (fâr) *n.* the price paid by a passenger to travel on a bus, train, etc.

Far East (fär′ ēst′) *n.* the countries of East and Southeast ASIA.

far-fetched (fär′fecht′) *adj.* unlikely.

Fan (2nd def.) is simply an abbreviation of fanatic, someone who is devoted to an idea.

Plow

Winnowing rice

Plowing with oxen

Picking tea

Tractor

About 10,000 years ago humans stopped being mainly hunters and settled down in one place to grow food and **farm** the land.

In many parts of the world old farming methods are still used — oxen and horses pull plows and grain is still hand winnowed to separate the chaff. But modern machinery is slowly taking over.

In Saxon times people shared a field and each had a narrow strip to cultivate. This was called strip farming.

Crop rotation is a four-course method of farming aimed at putting nutrients back into the soil. Cereals such as wheat and barley alternate with clover and root crops such as turnips. One year a field lies fallow — nothing is grown on it, so allowing it to rest.

In medieval Europe more than 80 percent of people lived and worked on the land. During springtime sowing children scared off the birds.

farm (färm) *n.* a piece of land with its buildings, used for growing crops or breeding and keeping livestock. – *vb.* **farm·ing, farmed** to use land for growing crops, rearing animals, etc.; to be a farmer. – *n.* & *adj.* **farm·ing**.

farm·er (fär′mər) *n.* a person who runs a farm.

farther, farthest. See far.

fas·ci·nate (fas′ə-nāt′) *vb.* **fas·ci·nat·ing, fas·ci·nat·ed** to interest strongly; to intrigue. – *n.* **fas·ci·na·tion** (fas′ə-nā′shən).

fash·ion (fash′ən) *n.* **1** style, especially the latest style, in clothes, etc. **2** a manner of doing something.

fash·ion·a·ble (fash′ə-nə-bəl) *adj.* following the latest fashion; very popular.

fast[1] (fast) *adj.* **1** moving, or able to move, quickly. **2** taking a short time. **3** describing a clock that shows a time that is later than the correct time. – *adv.* **1** quickly; rapidly: *Don't walk so fast.* **2** deeply; thoroughly.

fast[2] (fast) *vb.* **fast·ing, fast·ed** to go without food, especially as a religious discipline.

fas·ten (fas′ən) *vb.* **fas·ten·ing, fas·tened** to make firmly closed or fixed.

fat (fat) *n.* the soft greasy substance that is found below the skin in humans and animals, that stores energy and generates warmth. – *adj.* **fat·ter, fat·test** plump; overweight.

fa·tal (fāt′l) *adj.* **1** causing death: *a fatal accident.* **2** disastrous: *I made a fatal mistake.*

fate (fāt) *n.* **1** a power that is believed to control the course of events. **2** what happens to someone or something.

fa·ther (fä<u>th</u>′ər) *n.* **1** a person's male parent. **2** a founder, inventor, originator, or pioneer. **3** a form of address for a priest. – *n.* **fa·ther·hood** (fä<u>th</u>′ər-hood′).

fa·ther-in-law (fä<u>th</u>′ər-ən-lô′) *n.* **fa·thers-in-law** the father of your wife or husband.

fath·om (fa<u>th</u>′əm) *n.* a unit for measuring the depth of water, equal to 6 feet (1.8 m).

fa·tigue (fə-tēg′) *n.* **1** tiredness after work or effort. **2** weakness in metals, caused by variations in stress.

fat·ten (fat′n) *vb.* **fat·ten·ing, fat·tened** to

make or become fat. − *adj.* **fat·ten·ing**.

fat·ty (fat′ē) *adj.* **fat·ti·er, fat·ti·est**
containing fat; greasy; oily.

fau·cet (fôs′ət, fäs′ət) *n.* a valve that controls
the flow of a liquid, as on a sink.

● **Faulk·ner** (fôk′nər), **William** (1897-1962) was
the American author of *The Sound and the Fury*.

fault (fôlt) *n.* **1** a weakness in character. **2** a flaw
or defect in an object or structure.
3 responsibility for something wrong. **4** a break
or crack in the earth's crust.

fault·y (fôl′tē) *adj.* **faul·ti·er, faul·ti·est** not
working correctly.

fau·na (fô′nə) *n.* the wild animals of a
particular place. See also **flora**.

fa·vor (fā′vər) *n.* **1** a kind or helpful action
performed out of goodwill. **2** the approval or
goodwill of someone. − *vb.* **fa·vor·ing,**
fa·vored 1 to regard with goodwill. **2** to treat
with preference. **3** to prefer.

fa·vor·a·ble (fā′və-rə-bəl) *adj.* giving
agreement or consent.

fa·vor·ite (fāv′rət) *adj.* best liked; preferred.

fawn¹ (fôn) *n.* a young deer.

fawn² (fôn) *vb.* **fawn·ing, fawned** to flatter or
behave overly humbly toward.

fax (faks) *n.* **1** a machine that scans documents
electronically and transmits an image of the
contents to a receiving machine by telephone
line. **2** a copy transmitted in this way.

fear (fîr) *n.* an unpleasant feeling of anxiety and
distress caused by the awareness of danger or
pain: *My greatest fear is to be stuck in an elevator.* −
vb. **fear·ing, feared** to be afraid of.

fear·ful (fîr′fəl) *adj.* **1** afraid. **2** frightening.

feast (fēst) *n.* **1** a large rich meal, often to
celebrate some occasion. **2** a festival or saint's
day.

feat (fēt) *n.* a remarkable deed or achievement.

feath·er (feth′ər) *n.* any of the light growths
that form the soft covering of a bird.

fea·ture (fē′chər) *n.* **1** a part of the face, for
example eyes, nose, mouth, etc. **2** a noticeable
part or quality of something.

Feb·ru·ar·y (feb′yōō-wer′ē, feb′rōō-er′ē) *n.*
the second month of the year. It has 28 days,
except in a leap year, when it has 29.

fed. See **feed**.

fed·er·al (fed′rəl, fed′ə-rəl) *adj.* consisting of a
group of states independent in local matters
but under a central government for other
purposes, e.g. defense.

fee (fē) *n.* a charge made for professional
services, membership of a society, entrance to
a museum, etc.

fee·ble (fē′bəl) *adj.* lacking strength; weak.

feed (fēd) *vb.* **feed·ing, fed** (fed) **1** to give food
to or prepare food for. **2** (of animals) to eat:
Cows feed on grass. − *n.* food for animals.

feel (fēl) *vb.* **feel·ing, felt** (felt) **1** to become
aware of through touch. **2** to sense; to
experience: *I feel a pain in my ear.* **3** to become
aware of being: *Fred feels upset.* **4** to give the
impression of being: *The rabbit's fur feels very
soft.* **5** to be of the opinion: *We all feel you work
too hard.*

feel·er (fēl′ər) *n.* an organ of touch found in
certain creatures, especially one of two
threadlike projections on an insect's head.

feel·ing (fēl′ing) *n.* a sensation or emotion.

PRONUNCIATION SYMBOLS		
ə **away**	lemon	focus
a **fat**	oi	**boy**
ā **fade**	oo	**foot**
ä **hot**	ōō	**moon**
âr **fair**	ou	**house**
e **met**	th	**think**
ē **mean**	th	**this**
g **get**	u	**cut**
hw **which**	ur	**hurt**
i **fin**	w	**witch**
ī **line**	y	**yes**
îr **near**	yōō	**music**
ô **often**	yoor	**pure**
ō **note**	zh	**vision**

Religious Feasts and Festivals
February
Ramadan (Islamic), a month of fasting.
Ash Wednesday (Christian), beginning of Lent.
March
Purim (Jewish), commemorating the deliverance from the plot of Hamman.
Holi (Hindu) marks the coming of spring.
April
Ramanavami (Hindu), birth of Lord Rama.
Pesach or Passover (Jewish), commemorating the Israelites' deliverance from Egypt.
Good Friday (Christian), the day on which Jesus was crucified.
Easter Sunday (Christian), the day on which Christ rose from the dead.
May
Pentecost/Whitsun (Christian), the coming of the Holy Spirit.
Id al-Adha (Islamic), major four-day festival.
June
Buddha Purnima (Buddhist), the birth, enlightenment, and death of Buddha.
Al Hijara (Islamic), Muslim New Year.
August
Janamashtami (Hindu), birth of Krishna.
Milad-un-Nabi (Islamic), anniversary of Muhammad's birth and death.
September
Rosh Hashannah (Jewish), New Year and start of 10 days of atonement.
Yom Kippur (Jewish), the Day of Atonement.
Sukkoth (Jewish) Feast of Tabernacles, commemorating 40 years in the wilderness.
November
Diwali (Hindu), festival of lights.
Birthday of Guru Nanak Dev (Sikh), founder of the Sikhs.
December
Hanukkah (Jewish), eight-day feast celebrating the rededication of the temple.
Christmas (Christian), the birth of Jesus.

Ferret comes from a Latin word *fur* meaning "thief," probably because the animal invades the burrows of other creatures.

Fencing was one of the original sports included in the modern Olympic Games. Fencers use one of three types of weapon — the foil, which has no cutting edge; the epeé, which has a stiff blade; and the saber, which has two cutting edges and a point.

Competitions begin with fencers on guard.

feet. See **foot**.

feign (fān) *vb.* **feign·ing, feigned** to pretend to have or be: *Suzie feigned illness.* — *adj.* **feigned**.

fe·line (fē′līn′) *adj.* **1** of or relating to cats. **2** like a cat.

fell¹. See **fall**.

fell² (fel) *vb.* **fell·ing, felled** to cut down.

fel·low (fel′ō) *n.* **1** a man or boy. **2** a companion or equal.

felt¹. See **feel**.

felt² (felt) *n.* a fabric formed by pressing together wool fibers, etc.

fe·male (fē′māl′) *adj.* **1** of the sex that gives birth to children, produces eggs, etc. **2** relating to, or belonging to, a woman. — *n.* a female person, animal, or plant.

fem·i·nine (fem′ə-nən) *adj.* womanly or belonging to a woman. — *n.* **fem·i·nin·i·ty** (fem′ə-nin′ət-ē).

fem·i·nism (fem′ə-niz′əm) *n.* a movement supporting the attitude that women's rights and opportunities should be equal to those of men. — *n.* **fem·i·nist** (fem′ə-nəst).

fe·mur (fē′mər) *n.* the thighbone.

fen (fen) *n.* low marshy land.

fence (fens) *n.* a barrier of wood, wire, etc. for enclosing or protecting land. — *vb.* **fenc·ing, fenced 1** to enclose or separate with a fence. **2** to practice the sport of fencing. — *n.* **fenc·er**.

fenc·ing *n.* the sport of fighting with swords.

fen·der (fen′dər) *n.* a protecting piece of metal over the wheel of a car, bicycle, etc.

●**Fer·mi** (fer′mē), **Enrico** (1901-1954) was an Italian-born scientist who built the first nuclear reactor in the UNITED STATES, in 1942.

fern (furn) *n.* a flowerless plant that reproduces by spores rather than seeds.

fe·ro·cious (fə-rō′shəs) *adj.* fierce; cruel; savage. — *n.* **fe·roc·i·ty** (fə-räs′ət-ē).

fer·ret (fer′ət) *n.* a small albino European polecat, used for driving rabbits and rats from their holes.

fer·ry (fer′ē) *n.* **fer·ries** a boat that carries passengers and often cars across a river or strip of water. — *vb.* **fer·ries, fer·ry·ing, fer·ried** to transport or go by ferry.

fer·tile (furt′l) *adj.* **1** capable of producing abundant crops: *fertile land.* **2** capable of producing babies, young, or fruit. — *n.* **fer·til·i·ty** (fur-til′ət-ē).

fer·til·ize (furt′l-īz′) *vb.* **fer·til·iz·ing, fer·til·ized 1** to make fertile: *Bees fertilize flowers.* **2** to add nutrients to soil. — *n.* **fer·til·i·za·tion** (furt′l-ə-zā′shən).

fer·til·iz·er (furt′l-ī′zər) *n.* a substance added to soil to make it more fertile.

fer·vent (fur′vənt) *adj.* enthusiastic; earnest. — *n.* **fer·vor** (fur′vər).

fes·ter (fes′tər) *vb.* **fes·ter·ing, fes·tered** to become infected.

fes·ti·val (fes′tə-vəl) *n.* **1** a day or time of celebration. **2** a saint's day.

fes·tive (fes′tiv) *adj.* of, or suitable for, a celebration; lively and cheerful.

fes·tiv·i·ty (fes-tiv′ət-ē) *n.* **fes·tiv·i·ties** celebration.

fetch (fech) *vb.* **fetch·ing, fetched 1** to go and get, and bring back. **2** to sell for.

fetch·ing *adj.* charming; attractive.

fete or **fête** (fāt, fet) *n.* a party or festival.

fet·lock (fet′läk) *n.* **1** the projection on a horse's leg just above the hoof. **2** the tuft of hair growing on this projection.

fe·tus (fēt′əs) *n.* the embryo of a human or other animal in its later stages of development in the womb.

feud (fyood) *n.* a long and bitter quarrel.

To attack, a fencer uses a lunge.

A fencer may block an attack with a parry; *but the action ends with a* touch.

Under the **feudal** system the king owned all the land but granted certain powerful lords land in return for their promising to help him fight his enemies. The lords in turn granted land to lesser lords called knights, who promised to fight for them in return. Below the knights came yeomen, or farmers, who were free men. At the lowest level were the peasants, known as villeins or serfs, who worked for the lord.

The feudal system created a society with the most powerful people at the top and the mass of the people at the bottom.

King John's great seal which was attached to the Magna Carta in 1215. The charter, which the English barons compelled the king to sign, made the king answerable to the law and promised a fair trial and justice to everyone.

---

feu·dal (fyōod′l) *adj.* of the social system of medieval EUROPE, in which tenants were obliged to serve under their lord in battle, and were in return protected by him. – *n.* **feu·dal·ism** (fyood′l-iz′əm).

fe·ver (fē′vər) *n.* **1** an illness with an abnormally high body temperature and racing pulse. **2** agitation or excitement.

few (fyōo) *adj.* not many; hardly any. – *pron.* hardly any things, people, etc. – **a few** a small number; some. – **as few as** no more than.

fi·an·cé (fē′än′sā′, fē-än′sā′) *n.* a man engaged to be married.

fi·an·cée (fē′än′sā′, fē-än′sā′) *n.* a woman engaged to be married.

fi·as·co (fē-as′kō, fē-äs′kō) *n.* **fi·as·coes** a complete failure.

fi·ber (fī′bər) *n.* **1** a fine thread of a natural or artificial substance. **2** the indigestible parts of edible plants that help to move food quickly through the body. **3** character; stamina.

fiberglass *n.* a material made of fine threadlike pieces of glass.

fiber optics *n.* (*singular*) the use of threads of glass to carry information in the form of light.

fib·u·la (fib′yə-lə) *n.* **fib·u·lae** (fib′yə-lē, fib′yə-lī′) or **fibulas** the outer and narrower of the two bones in the lower leg.

fic·tion (fik′shən) *n.* **1** literature concerning imaginary characters or events. **2** a pretense; a lie. – *adj.* **fic·ti·tious** (fik-tish′əs). – *adj.* **fic·tion·al** (fik′shən-l).

fid·dle (fid′l) *n.* (*informal*) a violin. – *vb.* **fid·dling, fid·dled** to play about aimlessly.

fidg·et (fij′ət) *vb.* **fidg·et·ing, fidg·et·ed** to move restlessly; to feel nervous.

field (fēld) *n.* **1** a piece of land enclosed for growing crops or for using as pasture for animals. **2** an area marked off as a ground for a sport, etc. **3** an area of knowledge or study. **4** See **Flag Terms**. – *vb.* **field·ing, field·ed** (in baseball) to catch or pick up and then make the next play with: *The player fielded the ball.*

field event *n.* in a tract meet, a contest involving jumping, throwing, etc., as distinct from an event on the running track.

field hockey *n.* a game for two teams of 11 players in which each team tries to score goals, played with long sticks which are bent at one end and a hard ball.

field mouse (fēld′mous′) *n.* a small long-tailed mouse inhabiting fields, woods, etc.

fierce (fîrs) *adj.* violent and aggressive.

fi·er·y (fī′ə-rē, fîr′ē) *adj.* **fi·er·i·er, fi·er·i·est 1** like fire. **2** passionate; spirited.

fif·teen (fif-tēn′) *n.* the number or figure 15. – *n., adj., & adv.* **fif·teenth** (fif-tēnth′).

fifth. See **five**.

fif·ty (fif′tē) *n.* **fif·ties** (fif′tēz) the number or figure 50. – *n., adj., & adv.* **fif·ti·eth** (fif′tē-əth).

fig (fig) *n.* a soft fruit full of tiny seeds; the tree bearing it.

Turkey and California are two of the world's main fig-producing areas. Because figs are too delicate to store easily, much of the crop is canned or dried.

fight (fīt) *vb.* **fight·ing, fought** (fôt) **1** to attack or engage in combat with fists or weapons, etc. **2** to struggle. **3** to campaign: *We must fight for equal rights.* **4** to quarrel. – *n.* **1** a battle; a violent struggle; a quarrel. **2** a contest.

fig·ure (fig′yər) *n.* **1** an indistinctly seen person: *There were three figures in the distance.* **2** the shape of the body. **3** a symbol representing a number; a numeral. **4** a well-known person: *a public figure.* **5** a diagram or illustration. **6** a geometrical shape. – *vb.* **fig·u·ring, fig·ured 1** to play a part in a story, incident, etc.: *The witches figure in Macbeth.* **2** to think; to reckon.

● **Fi·ji** (fē′jē). See Supplement, **Countries**.

fil·a·ment (fil′ə-mənt) *n.* a fine thread or fiber.

file[1] (fīl) *n.* a tool with a rough surface for smoothing or rubbing away wood, metal, etc.

file[2] (fīl) *n.* **1** a folder or box in which to keep loose papers. **2** a collection of papers kept in this way. **3** See **Computer Terms**. **4** a line of people or things moving one behind the other.

fill (fil) *vb.* **fill·ing, filled 1** to make full. **2** to take up the space in: *People filled the office.* **3** to become full. **4** to put material into so as to level the surface: *to fill a hole.*

film (film) *n.* **1** a strip of thin flexible plastic or other substance, coated so as to be sensitive to light and exposed inside a camera to produce still or moving pictures. **2** a motion picture. **3** a fine skin or coating: *A film of dirt covered the car.* – *vb.* **film·ing, filmed** to use a camera to take moving pictures.

fil·ter (fil′tər) *n.* a device that allows liquid, gas, smoke, etc. through but traps solid matter, impurities, etc. – *vb.* **fil·ter·ing, fil·tered** to pass through a filter.

filth (filth) *n.* **1** repulsive dirt. **2** obscenity. – *adj.* **filth·y** (fil′thē) **filth·i·er, filth·i·est**.

fin (fin) *n.* a thin winglike projection on a fish's body, with which it balances and steers itself.

fi·nal (fīn′l) *adj.* **1** occurring at the end; last. **2** definite; not to be altered: *That is my final decision.* – *n.* (often in *plural*) the last round, game, or match in a competition.

fi·nance (fī′nans′, fə-nans′) *n.* **1** money affairs; their study or management. **2** (in *plural*) one's financial state: *I must put my finances in order.* – *vb.* **fi·nanc·ing, fi·nanced** to provide funds for.

finch (finch) *n.* a small songbird with a short sturdy beak adapted for crushing seeds.

male

female

Finches are found throughout the world. They eat seeds, insects, and leaves and live in wooded areas. Most species have attractive songs. The sexes usually differ in color.

Bullfinch

find (fīnd) *vb.* **find·ing, found** (found) **1** to discover through search, inquiry, or chance. **2** to seek out and provide. **3** to realize or discover: *Jim found it difficult to ask for help.* **4** to experience as being: *She finds it hard to express herself.* **5** to get or experience: *I find pleasure in reading.* – *vb.* **find out** to discover.

fine[1] (fīn) *adj.* **1** of high quality; excellent. **2** (of weather) bright; not rainy. **3** well; healthy. **4** pure; refined. **5** thin; delicate. **6** intricately detailed: *fine embroidery.* – *adv.* satisfactorily: *It works fine.*

fine[2] (fīn) *n.* money to be paid as a penalty.

fin·ger (fing′gər) *n.* one of the five jointed parts of the hand; any of the four of these except the thumb. – *vb.* **fin·ger·ing, fin·gered** to touch or feel with the fingers: *Sue fingered the beads.*

fin·ger·nail (fing′gər-nāl′) *n.* the hard layer at the tip of one's finger.

fin·ger·print (fing′gər-print′) *n.* a mark, unique to each individual, left on a surface by the tip of a finger, useful as a means of identification.

PRONUNCIATION SYMBOLS		
ə **away**	lem**on**	**focus**
a fat	oi	boy
ā fade	oo	foot
ä hot	o͞o	moon
âr fair	ou	house
e met	th	think
ē mean	th̲	this
g get	u	cut
hw which	ur	hurt
i fin	w	witch
ī line	y	yes
îr near	yo͞o	music
ô often	yoor	pure
ō note	zh	vision

fin·ish (fin′ish) *vb.* **fin·ish·ing, fin·ished 1** to come to an end; to stop. **2** to complete or perfect. **3** to use, eat, drink, etc. the last of: *Bob finished off the cake.* **4** to give a particular treatment to the surface of cloth, wood, etc. – *n.* **1** the end. **2** the surface texture given to cloth, wood, etc.

●**Fin·land** (fin′lənd). See Supplement, **Countries**.

Finn (fin) *n.* a native or citizen of FINLAND.

Finn·ish (fin′ish) *adj.* of, belonging to, or relating to FINLAND. – *n.* the language of FINLAND.

fiord. See **fjord**.

fir (fur) *n.* an evergreen tree with cones and thin needlelike leaves.

fire (fīr) *n.* **1** flames coming from something that is burning. **2** a destructive burning. **3** a pile of burning fuel, used for warmth or cooking. **4** enthusiasm; passion: *Her speech was full of fire.* – *vb.* **fir·ing, fired 1** to send off a bullet or other missile from a gun, catapult, bow, etc. **2** to launch a rocket. **3** to dismiss from employment. **4** to bake or harden in a kiln.

fire alarm *n.* a bell or other device activated to warn people of fire.

fire·arm (fīr′ärm′) *n.* a gun, pistol, revolver, or rifle.

fire engine *n.* a vehicle carrying equipment for fighting fires.

fire·fight·er (fīr′fīt′ər) *n.* a person who puts out large fires. – *n.* **fire fight·ing** (fīr′fīt′ing).

fire·fly (fīr′flī′) *n.* **fireflies** a beetle that glows in the dark.

fire·place (fīr′plās′) *n.* a recess for a fire in a room, with a chimney above it.

fire·proof (fīr′proof′) *adj.* resistant to fire.

fire·works (fīr′wurk′) *n.* (*plural*) devices containing explosive chemicals that are ignited to produce bangs and spectacular flashes.

firm¹ (furm) *adj.* **1** strong; steady; solid; not soft.

firm² (furm) *n.* a business company.

first (furst) *adj.* **1** earliest in time or order. **2** foremost in importance. – *adv.* **1** before anything or anyone else. **2** foremost: *Kay jumped in feet first.* **3** before doing anything else: *First make sure of the facts.* – **at first** at the beginning.

first aid *n.* immediate emergency treatment given to an ill or injured person.

first-class (furst′klas′) *adj.* **1** of the highest grade or quality: *a first-class hotel.* **2** excellent.

first lady *n.* **first ladies** the wife of a president of the United States.

first·ly (first′lē) *adv.* first; to begin with.

fish (fish) *n.* **fish** or **fish·es** a cold-blooded creature with fins that lives in water and breathes through gills. – *vb.* **fish·ing, fished 1** to try to catch fish. **2** to search or grope. **3** to seek information, etc. by indirect means: *He's fishing for compliments.*

fish·y (fish′ē) *adj.* **fish·i·er, fish·i·est 1** of or like a fish. **2** (*informal*) odd; suspicious.

fis·sion (fish′ən) *n.* (usually **nuclear fission**) the splitting of the nucleus of an atom, with a release of energy.

fist (fist) *n.* a clenched hand.

fit¹ (fit) *vb.* **fit·ting, fit·ted 1** to be, or be made, the right shape or size for: *My shoes fit well.* **2** to be small or few enough to go into: *Will these books fit in the box?* **3** to be suitable or appropriate for: *This punishment fits the crime.* – *adj.* **fit·ter, fit·test 1** suitable; good enough. **2** healthy. – *n.* **fit·ness** (fit′nəs).

Fire was possibly human beings' earliest discovery — and probably made by accident. Fire meant that people could be warm in cold winter months. With fire meat and vegetables could be cooked so they became more tasty and tender. Fire could also scare off wild animals at night.

Using a bow drill was one way of making sparks.

When certain stones, such as flints, are rubbed together they send out sparks. If this is done near tinder-dry wood, a fire can be kindled.

fit² (fit) *n.* **1** a sudden loss of consciousness with uncontrolled movements. **2** a sudden burst: *Tim burst into a fit of giggles.*

● **Fitz·ger·ald** (fits-jer′əld), **F. Scott** (1896–1940) was an American writer. His novels include *Tender is the Night* and *The Great Gatsby.*

five (fīv) *n.* the number or figure 5. – *adj.* 5 in number. – *n., adj., & adv.* **fifth** (fifth, fif<u>th</u>).

fix (fiks) *vb.* **fix·ing, fixed 1** to attach firmly. **2** to mend or repair. **3** to direct; to concentrate: *Roland fixed his eyes on her.* **4** to arrange or set: *We fixed the time for lunch.* **5** to prepare.

fixed *adj.* **1** fastened; immovable. **2** not changing: *She has fixed ideas on this.*

fix·ture (fiks′chər) *n.* a permanently fixed piece of furniture or equipment.

fjord or **fiord** (fē-ôrd′) *n.* a long narrow inlet in a high rocky coast, especially in NORWAY.

flac·cid (flas′əd, flak′səd) *adj.* limp and soft.

flag (flag) *n.* a usually rectangular piece of cloth with a distinctive design, flown from a pole to represent a country, party, etc., or used for signaling. – *vb.* **flag·ging, flagged.**

flair (flâr) *n.* a natural talent for something.

flake (flāk) *n.* a small flat particle: *snowflakes.*

flam·boy·ant (flam-boi′ənt) *adj.* dashing and colorful. – *n.* **flam·boy·ance** (flam-boi′əns).

flame (flām) *n.* the flickering mass of burning gases coming from something that is on fire.

fla·min·go (flə-ming′gō) *n.* **flamingos** or **fla·min·goes** a large long-legged wading bird with a curved beak and pink plumage.

flam·ma·ble (flam′ə-bəl) *adj.* liable to catch fire; inflammable.

flank (flangk) *n.* the side of an animal or human body, between ribs and hip. – *vb.* **flank·ing, flanked** to be or move at the side of.

flan·nel (flan′l) *n.* a soft cotton or wool fabric with a nap, used in making clothes and sheets.

flap (flap) *vb.* **flap·ping, flapped** to wave up and down or backward and forward: *A bird flaps its wings.* – *n.* **1** a broad piece of something attached along one edge and hanging loosely: *pocket flaps.* **2** a hinged section on an aircraft wing adjusted to control speed.

flare (flâr) *vb.* **flar·ing, flared 1** to burn with sudden brightness. **2** to widen toward the edge

Canton

Quarterly

Border

Triangle

Flags are often divided into various geometrical patterns consisting of horizontal or vertical stripes, rectangles, triangles, etc.

Flags are symbols of many things. They represent nations, international organizations (UN, EU), U.S. states, business companies, labor unions, and individual people. They can also be used for signaling (semaphore) and act as warnings. The study of flags and their meanings is called *vexillology.*

During the French Revolution of 1789 the flag of the monarchy (left) was replaced by the Bastille flag and then by the French national colors.

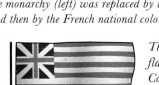

The first U.S. flag — the Continental Colors of 1776 had 13 red and white stripes.

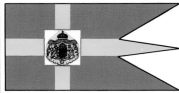

The Swedish royal flag is based on the national flag.

Japan's naval ensign adds rays to the Sun disk shown on the national flag.

The Red Cross was founded in Switzerland. Its flag is a reversed version of the Swiss national flag.

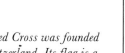

FLAG TERMS

canton upper rectangular corner of a flag, often used for a special design (e.g. the stars in the "Stars and Stripes").

dexter being on the right.

field the background color.

hoist to raise a flag.

pennant a triangular flag.

standard the personal flag of a ruler.

or bottom: *flared jeans.* – *n.* **1** a sudden blaze of bright light. **2** a device for producing a blaze of light.

flash (flash) *n.* **1** a sudden brief blaze of light. **2** an instant. **3** a brief but intense occurrence: *flash of inspiration.* – *vb.* **flash·ing, flashed** **1** to shine briefly. **2** to move or pass quickly: *The train flashed past.* – *adj.* sudden and severe: *flash floods.*

flash·light (flash′līt′) *n.* a battery-operated hand-held light.

flask (flask) *n.* **1** a narrow-necked bottle used in chemical experiments, etc. **2** a small flat bottle.

flat (flat) *adj.* **flat·ter, flat·test** **1** level; horizontal; even. **2** without depth: *a flat dish.* **3** not bent or crumpled. **4** toneless and expressionless. **5** (in music) below the intended pitch. – *adv.* **1** stretched out rather than curled up, etc. **2** into a flat compact shape: *This chair folds flat .* **3** exactly: *I'll be there in two minutes flat .* – *n.* (*British*) an apartment.

flat·fish (flat′fish′) *n.* a flat-bodied fish with both eyes on one side, that lies on the seabed.

flat·ten (flat′n) *vb.* **flat·ten·ing, flat·tened** to make or become flat or flatter.

flat·ter (flat′ər) *vb.* **flat·ter·ing, flat·tered** to compliment excessively or insincerely.

flat·ter·y (flat′ər-ē) *n.* **flat·ter·ies** excessive praise.

flaunt (flônt) *vb.* **flaunt·ing, flaunt·ed** to display or parade, in the hope of being admired.

flaut·ist (flôt′əst, flaut′əst) *n.* a flutist.

fla·vor (flā′vər) *n.* the taste of any particular food or drink: *strawberry flavor.*

flaw (flô) *n.* a crack, blemish, or weakness.

flax (flaks) *n.* a blue-flowered plant used for making linen and linseed oil.

flax·en (flak′sən) *adj.* describing very fair hair.

flea (flē) *n.* a tiny wingless jumping insect that sucks blood.

fleck (flek) *n.* a spot or speck. – *adj.* **flecked.**

fled. See **flee.**

fledg·ling (flej′ling) *n.* a young bird learning to fly.

flee (flē) *vb.* **flee·ing, fled** (fled) to run away.

fleece (flēs) *n.* a sheep's woolly coat.

fleet (flēt) *n.* **1** a number of ships under one command. **2** a number of buses, taxis, under the same management.

fleet·ing (flēt′ing) *adj.* brief.

Flem·ing (flem′ing) *n.* a native of the FLEMISH-speaking part of BELGIUM.

●**Flem·ing** (flem′ing), **Alexander** (1881-1955) was a Scottish doctor who discovered penicillin.

Flem·ish (flem′ish) *adj.* of, or relating to, the Flemings of BELGIUM or their language. – *n.* the language of the Flemings; Dutch.

flesh (flesh) *n.* **1** the body's soft tissues covering the bones under the skin. **2** the pulp of a fruit or vegetable.

flew. See **fly².**

flex (fleks) *vb.* **flex·ing, flexed** to bend.

flex·i·ble (flek′sə-bəl) *adj.* **1** bending easily. **2** readily adaptable to suit circumstances. – *n.* **flex·i·bil·i·ty** (flek′sə-bil′ət-ē).

flick·er (flik′ər) *vb.* **flick·er·ing, flickered** **1** to burn or shine unsteadily. **2** to move lightly to and fro: *Shadows flickered across the lawn.* – *n.* an unsteady light.

flight (flīt) *n.* **1** the action or power of flying. **2** a journey made by or in an aircraft. **3** a set of steps or stairs leading straight up or down.

In 1928 Fleming noticed that a spot of green mold stopped the growth of some bacteria he was cultivating. This led to the development of the life-saving antibiotic, penicillin.

Ostrich Emu Rhea Adélie penguin Kiwi

flight·less (flīt′ləs) *adj.* (of birds, etc.) unable to fly.

flim·sy (flim′zē) *adj.* **flim·si·er, flim·si·est** **1** light and thin. **2** without strength; frail. – *adv.* **flim·si·ly** (flim′zə-lē).

fling (fling) *vb.* **flinging, flung** (flung) to throw violently or vigorously. – *n.* a try; a go.

flint (flint) *n.* a hard quartz found in limestone or chalk. – *adj.* **flint·y, flin·t·ier, flint·i·est.**

flip (flip) *vb.* **flip·ping, flipped** to toss a coin, so as to turn over in midair. – *n.* **1** a flipping action. **2** a somersault performed in midair.

flip·per (flip′ər) *n.* a limb on a whale, seal, penguin, etc., used for swimming.

Five birds with something very unusual in common: they cannot fly. 1. Ostrich, the largest of all birds. 2. Adélie penguin stands erect and can swim. 3. Emu, from Australia. 4. Kiwi, nocturnal from New Zealand. 5. Rhea, from South America.

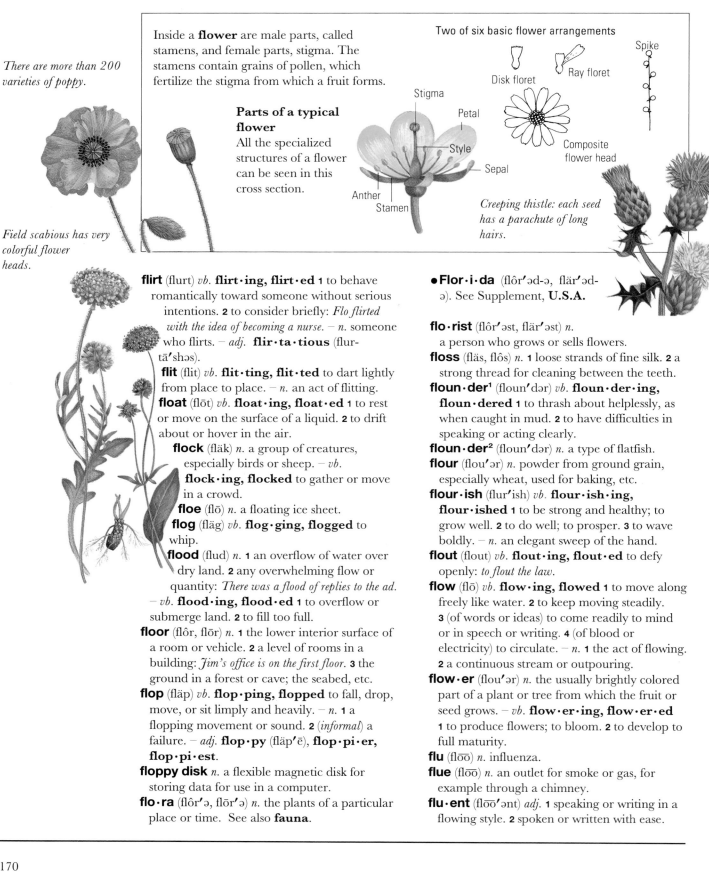

There are more than 200 varieties of poppy.

Field scabious has very colorful flower heads.

Inside a **flower** are male parts, called stamens, and female parts, stigma. The stamens contain grains of pollen, which fertilize the stigma from which a fruit forms.

Parts of a typical flower
All the specialized structures of a flower can be seen in this cross section.

Stigma
Petal
Style
Sepal
Anther
Stamen

Two of six basic flower arrangements

Spike
Disk floret
Ray floret
Composite flower head

Creeping thistle: each seed has a parachute of long hairs.

flirt (flurt) *vb.* **flirt·ing, flirt·ed 1** to behave romantically toward someone without serious intentions. **2** to consider briefly: *Flo flirted with the idea of becoming a nurse.* – *n.* someone who flirts. – *adj.* **flir·ta·tious** (flur-tā′shəs).

flit (flit) *vb.* **flit·ting, flit·ted** to dart lightly from place to place. – *n.* an act of flitting.

float (flōt) *vb.* **float·ing, float·ed 1** to rest or move on the surface of a liquid. **2** to drift about or hover in the air.

flock (fläk) *n.* a group of creatures, especially birds or sheep. – *vb.* **flock·ing, flocked** to gather or move in a crowd.

floe (flō) *n.* a floating ice sheet.

flog (fläg) *vb.* **flog·ging, flogged** to whip.

flood (flud) *n.* **1** an overflow of water over dry land. **2** any overwhelming flow or quantity: *There was a flood of replies to the ad.* – *vb.* **flood·ing, flood·ed 1** to overflow or submerge land. **2** to fill too full.

floor (flôr, flōr) *n.* **1** the lower interior surface of a room or vehicle. **2** a level of rooms in a building: *Jim's office is on the first floor.* **3** the ground in a forest or cave; the seabed, etc.

flop (fläp) *vb.* **flop·ping, flopped** to fall, drop, move, or sit limply and heavily. – *n.* **1** a flopping movement or sound. **2** (*informal*) a failure. – *adj.* **flop·py** (fläp′ē), **flop·pi·er, flop·pi·est**.

floppy disk *n.* a flexible magnetic disk for storing data for use in a computer.

flo·ra (flôr′ə, flōr′ə) *n.* the plants of a particular place or time. See also **fauna**.

● **Flor·i·da** (flôr′əd-ə, flär′əd-ə). See Supplement, **U.S.A.**

flo·rist (flôr′əst, flär′əst) *n.* a person who grows or sells flowers.

floss (fläs, flôs) *n.* **1** loose strands of fine silk. **2** a strong thread for cleaning between the teeth.

floun·der¹ (floun′dər) *vb.* **floun·der·ing, floun·dered 1** to thrash about helplessly, as when caught in mud. **2** to have difficulties in speaking or acting clearly.

floun·der² (floun′dər) *n.* a type of flatfish.

flour (flou′ər) *n.* powder from ground grain, especially wheat, used for baking, etc.

flour·ish (flur′ish) *vb.* **flour·ish·ing, flour·ished 1** to be strong and healthy; to grow well. **2** to do well; to prosper. **3** to wave boldly. – *n.* an elegant sweep of the hand.

flout (flout) *vb.* **flout·ing, flout·ed** to defy openly: *to flout the law.*

flow (flō) *vb.* **flow·ing, flowed 1** to move along freely like water. **2** to keep moving steadily. **3** (of words or ideas) to come readily to mind or in speech or writing. **4** (of blood or electricity) to circulate. – *n.* **1** the act of flowing. **2** a continuous stream or outpouring.

flow·er (flou′ər) *n.* the usually brightly colored part of a plant or tree from which the fruit or seed grows. – *vb.* **flow·er·ing, flow·er·ed 1** to produce flowers; to bloom. **2** to develop to full maturity.

flu (flo͞o) *n.* influenza.

flue (flo͞o) *n.* an outlet for smoke or gas, for example through a chimney.

flu·ent (flo͞o′ənt) *adj.* **1** speaking or writing in a flowing style. **2** spoken or written with ease.

fluff (fluf) *n.* small bits of soft woolly material. – *vb.* **fluff·ing, fluffed** to shake or arrange into a soft mass. – *adj.* **fluf·fy** (fluf′ē), **fluf·fi·er, fluf·fi·est**.

flu·id (floo′əd) *n.* a substance, such as liquid or gas, that can flow freely. – *adj.* able to flow.

flung. See **fling**.

flur·ry (flur′ē) *n.* **flur·ries** 1 a brief shower of rain, snow, etc. 2 a commotion.

flush¹ (flush) *vb.* **flush·ing, flushed** 1 to blush or go red. 2 to clean out with a rush of water.

flush² (flush) *adj.* 1 level with an adjacent surface. 2 (*informal*) having plenty of money.

flus·ter (flus′tər) *n.* a state of agitation. – *vb.* **flus·ter·ing, flus·tered** to agitate.

flute (floot) *n.* a woodwind instrument that is held horizontally out to the side of the head.

flut·ist (floot′əst) *n.* a flute player.

flut·ter (flut′ər) *vb.* **flut·ter·ing, flut·tered** 1 to fly with a rapid wing movement or drift with a twirling motion. 2 to move about in a restless, aimless way. – *n.* agitation; excitement.

fly¹ (flī) *n.* **flies** any of a large group of insects with two wings, as the housefly or gnat.

fly² (flī) *vb.* **flies, fly·ing, flew** (floo), **flown** (flōn) 1 to move through the air on wings; to travel through the air or through space. 2 to operate and control an aircraft, kite, etc. – *n.* 1 the flap covering a zipper or buttons on the front of trousers. 2 a baseball hit high above the field.

flying saucer *n.* any of a number of unidentified circular flying objects reported in the sky from time to time, believed by some to be from outer space.

foal (fōl) *n.* the young of a horse or of a related animal.

foam (fōm) *n.* a mass of tiny bubbles. – *adj.* **foam·y** (fō′mē), **foam·i·er, foam·i·est**.

fo·cus (fō′kəs) *n.* **focuses** or **fo·ci** (fō′sī′) 1 the point at which rays of light or sound waves meet or from which they seem to diverge. 2 the point where an object must stand to appear as a clear image in a lens or mirror. 3 the adjustment of the eye or the lens of an instrument, etc., to obtain a clear image. 4 a center of interest or attention. – *vb.* **fo·cus·ing, fo·cused** 1 to bring or be brought into focus; to meet at a focus. 2 to adjust the focus of your eye or an instrument. 3 to concentrate: *Tim focused his mind on the game.*

fod·der (fäd′ər) *n.* food, especially hay and straw, for cattle and other farm animals.

foe·tus (fēt′əs) *n.* See **fetus**.

fog (fôg, fäg) *n.* a thick cloud of condensed watery vapor suspended in the air reducing visibility; thick mist. – *vb.* **fog·ging, fogged** to obscure. – *adj.* **fog·gy** (fô′gē, fäg′ē), **fog·gi·er, fog·gi·est**.

foil¹ (foil) *vb.* **foil·ing, foiled** to prevent or frustrate: *We foiled their evil plan.*

foil² (foil) *n.* metal beaten or rolled out into thin sheets.

foil³ (foil) *n.* a blunt slender sword.

fold¹ (fōld) *vb.* **fold·ing, fold·ed** 1 to double over so that one part lies on top of another: *Fold the paper in two.* 2 to bring in close to the body: *The bird folded its wings.* 3 to stir an ingredient gently into a mixture. 4 (*informal*) (of a business, etc.) to fail. – *n.* a doubling of one layer over another.

fold² (fōld) *n.* an enclosure for sheep or cattle.

-fold *suffix* multiplied by a stated number: *The company's profits increased threefold.*

fold·er (fōl′dər) *n.* a cardboard or plastic cover in which to keep loose papers.

fo·li·age (fō′lē-ij) *n.* the leaves on a tree or plant.

folk (fōk) *n.* (*plural*) 1 people. 2 **folks** family or relatives. – *adj.* traditional.

folk·lore (fōk′lôr′) *n.* the customs, beliefs, stories, traditions, etc. of particular peoples.

fol·low (fäl′ō) *vb.* **fol·low·ing, fol·lowed** 1 to go or come after. 2 to result; to be a consequence. 3 to go along: *They followed the river.* 4 to watch or observe: *Her eyes followed him up the street.* 5 to obey: *You must follow my advice.* 6 to copy: *Follow her example.* 7 to understand: *Beth could not follow the explanation.*

fol·low·ing (fäl′ō-ing) *n.* a body of supporters. – *adj.* coming after; next: *We need to deal with the following points.* – *prep.* after.

fol·ly (fäl′ē) *n.* **fol·lies** foolishness.

fond (fänd) *adj.* having a liking for; loving. – *n.* **fond·ness** (fänd′nəs).

fon·dle (fän′dl) *vb.* **fon·dling, fon·dled** to stroke.

font (fänt) *n.* the basin in a church that holds water for baptisms.

food (food) *n.* 1 a substance taken in, or absorbed, by a living thing, that provides energy or helps growth. 2 something that provides stimulation: *food for thought.*

food chain *n.* a series of living organisms, each of which is fed on by the next in the series.

PRONUNCIATION SYMBOLS

ə away	lemon	focus
a fat	oi	boy
ā fade	oo	foot
ä hot	ōō	moon
âr fair	ou	house
e met	th	think
ē mean	<u>th</u>	this
g get	u	cut
hw which	ur	hurt
i fin	w	witch
ī line	y	yes
îr near	yōō	music
ô often	yoor	pure
ō note	zh	vision

fool (fōōl) *n.* a person lacking common sense or intelligence. – *vb.* **fool·ing, fooled 1** to mislead; to deceive. **2** to behave stupidly or playfully: *Stop fooling around.*

fool·ish (fōō′lish) *adj.* unwise; senseless.

foot (foot) *n.* **feet** (fēt) **1** the part of the leg on which a human being or animal stands or walks. **2** the bottom or lower part of something: *at the foot of the hill.* **3** a measure of length equal to 12 inches (30.48 cm).

foot·ball (foot′bôl′) *n.* **1** a game played with an oval ball by two teams of eleven players. **2** the ball used in the game. **3** (*British*) any of other similar team games, such as soccer or rugby.

foot·ing (foot′ing) *n.* **1** the stability of your feet on the ground. **2** basis or status.

foot·step (foot′step′) *n.* the sound of a step.

foot·wear (foot′wâr′) *n.* shoes, socks, etc.

for (fər, fôr) *prep.* **1** intended to be given or sent to: *This present is for Patrick.* **2** toward: *We are heading for home.* **3** throughout a time or distance: *I've known him for two years.* **4** in order to have, etc.: *Let's meet for a chat.* **5** at a cost of: *I bought a ticket for $5.* **6** to the benefit of: *What can I do for you?* **7** on account of: *This town is famous for its school.* **8** suitable to the needs of.

for·age (fôr′ij, fär′ij) *vb.* **for·ag·ing, for·aged** to search around, especially for food.

for·bid (fər-bid′) *vb.* **for·bid·ding, for·bade** (fər-bad′, fər-bād′) or **for·bad** (fər-bad′), **for·bid·den** (fər-bid′n)**1** to order not to do something: *I forbid you to go!* **2** to prohibit.

for·bid·ding (fər-bid′ing) *adj.* threatening; grim.

force (fôrs, fōrs) *n.* **1** strength; power; impact. **2** in physics, a power causing movement, alteration, etc.: *the force of gravity.* **3** any organized body: *the police force.* – *vb.* **forc·ing, forced 1** to make or compel: *Tim was forced to sell his car.* **2** to obtain by effort, strength, threats, violence, etc.

ford (fôrd, fōrd) *n.* a shallow place in a river for crossing. – *vb.* **ford·ing, ford·ed** to cross at a ford.

fore- *prefix* **1** before: *foresee.* **2** in front: *foreground.*

fore·arm (fôr′ärm′, fōr′ärm′) *n.* the part of the arm between wrist and elbow.

fore·cast (fôr′kast′, fōr′kast′) *vb.* **fore·cast·ing, fore·cast** or **fore·cast·ed** to predict. – *n.* a warning or prediction.

fore·fa·ther (fôr′fä<u>th</u>′ər, fōr′fä<u>th</u>′ər) *n.* an ancestor.

fore·fin·ger (fôr′fing′gər, fōr′fing′ər) *n.* the finger next to the thumb; the index finger.

fore·front (fôr′frunt′, fōr′frunt′) *n.* the very front; the most prominent or active position.

fore·ground (fôr′ground′, fōr′ground′) *n.* the part of a view or picture nearest to the viewer.

fore·head (fär′əd, fôr′əd, fôr′hed′, fōr′hed′) *n.* the part of the face between the eyebrows and hairline; the brow.

for·eign (fôr′ən, fär′ən) *adj.* **1** of, from, or relating to, another country. **2** concerned with relations with other countries: *foreign affairs.*

for·eign·er (fôr′ə-nər, fär′ə-nər) *n.* a person from another country.

fore·man (fôr′mən, fōr′mən), **fore·men** (fôr′mən, fōr′mən) or **fore·wom·an** (fôr′woom′ən, fōr′woom′ən), **fore·wom·en** (fôr′wim′ən, fōr′wim′ən) *n.* a man or woman in charge of a body of fellow workers.

fore·most (fôr′mōst′, fōr′mōst′) *adj.* leading; best. – *adv.* in the first place.

fore·see (fôr-sē′, fōr-sē′) *vb.* **fore·see·ing, fore·saw** (fôr′sô′, fōr′sô′), **fore·seen** to see or know in advance.

fore·sight (fôr′sīt′, fōr′sīt′) *n.* the ability to foresee.

for·est (fôr′əst, fär′əst) *n.* a dense growth of trees extending over a large area.

for·est·ry (fôr′ə-strē, fär′ə-strē) *n.* the

Below: *A mixed forest of aspens and larch in the Nevada Rockies.* Right: *A South American rain forest. The crowns of the trees merge to form a canopy of leafy vegetation, the home of many frogs, lizards, birds, mammals, and insects.*

management of forests.

for·ev·er (fə-rev′ər) *adv.* always; eternally.

fore·word (fôr′wərd, fōr′wərd) *n.* an introduction to a book.

for·feit (fôr′fət) *vb.* **for·feit·ing, for·feit·ed** to hand over as a penalty.

forgave. See **forgive**.

forge[1] (fôrj) *n.* a furnace for heating metals; a workshop where metal is shaped into horseshoes, tools, etc. – *vb.* **forg·ing, forged** **1** to shape by heating and hammering: *to forge metal.* **2** to make an imitation of for a dishonest purpose : *to forge a signature.*

forge[2] (fôrj) *vb.* **forg·ing, forged** – **forge ahead** to progress swiftly.

for·ger·y (fôr′jə-rē) *n.* **for·ger·ies** an illegal copy or copying of a signature, document, etc.

for·get (fər-get′, fər-gät′) *vb.* **for·get·ting, for·got, for·got·ten** (fər-gät′n) **1** to be unable to remember. **2** to stop being aware of: *Mike forgot his headache in the excitement.* **3** to leave behind accidentally: *I forgot my books.*

for·get·ful (fər-get′fəl) *adj.* tending to forget.

for·get-me-not (fər-get′mē-nät′) *n.* a small plant with blue flowers.

for·give (fər-giv′) *vb.* **for·giv·ing, for·gave** (fər-gāv′), **for·giv·en** (fər-giv′ən) to stop being angry with someone who has done something wrong. – *n.* **for·give·ness** (fər-giv′nəs).

forgot, forgotten. See **forget**.

fork (fôrk) *n.* **1** an eating or cooking implement with prongs, for spearing and lifting food. **2** a pronged digging or lifting tool. **3** the division of a road, etc. into branches: *Take the right fork.* – *vb.* **fork·ing, forked** to divide into two branches: *The road forks at that point.*

form (fôrm) *n.* **1** shape; figure or outward appearance. **2** kind, type, variety: *Karate is a form of martial art.* **3** a document with spaces for inserting information. – *vb.* **form·ing, formed** **1** to organize or set up. **2** to take shape. **3** to make a shape.

for·mal (fôr′məl) *adj.* **1** involving etiquette, ceremony, or conventional procedure generally: *formal dress.* **2** stiffly polite.

for·mal·i·ty (fôr-mal′ət-ē) *n.* a procedure gone through merely for the sake of correctness or legality.

for·mat (fôr′mat′) *n.* **1** the size and shape of something, especially a book or magazine. **2** an arrangement of data to suit the input system of a computer. – *vb.* **for·mat·ting, for·mat·ted** to organize in a particular way.

for·ma·tion (fôr-mā′shən) *n.* **1** the process of forming. **2** a particular pattern or order.

for·mer (fôr′mər) *adj.* **1** belonging to an earlier time. **2** previous; earlier. – *adv.* **for·mer·ly.**

for·mi·da·ble (fôr′məd-ə-bəl, fôr-mid′ə-bəl) *adj.* impressive.

for·mu·la (fôr′myə-lə) *n.* **formulas** or **for·mu·lae** (fôr′myə-lē′, fôr′myə-lī′) **1** the make-up of a chemical compound expressed in symbols: *H_2O is the formula for water.* **2** a mathematical rule expressed in figures and letters. **3** powdered milk for infants.

for·sake (fər-sāk′) *vb.* **for·sak·ing, for·sook** (fər-sook′), **for·sak·en** (fər-sāk′ən) to desert.

fort (fôrt) *n.* a fortified military building, enclosure, or position.

for·te (fôr′tā′, fôrt′ē). See **Musical Terms.**

forth (fôrth) *adv.* forward.

for·ti·fy (fôrt′ə-fī′) *vb.* **for·ti·fies, for·ti·fy·ing, for·ti·fied** **1** to strengthen in preparation for an attack, as by building walls.

for·tis·si·mo (fôr-tis′ə-mō′). See **Musical Terms.**

for·tress (fôr′trəs) *n.* a fortified town, or large fort or castle.

for·tu·nate (fôr′chə-nət) *adj.* lucky.

for·tune (fôr′chən) *n.* **1** luck. **2** your destiny. **3** a large sum of money.

for·ty (fôrt′ē) *n.* **for·ties** the number or figure 40. – *n., adj., & adv.* **for·ti·eth** (fôrt′ē-əth).

Format is the size and shape of a book. In a portrait *format (upper picture) the book is taller than it is wide; in a* landscape *(lower picture), it is wider than it is tall.*

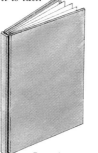
Portrait

Landscape

Forest is a shortening of the Latin *forestis silva*, which meant "an enclosed woodland" — as opposed to a park.

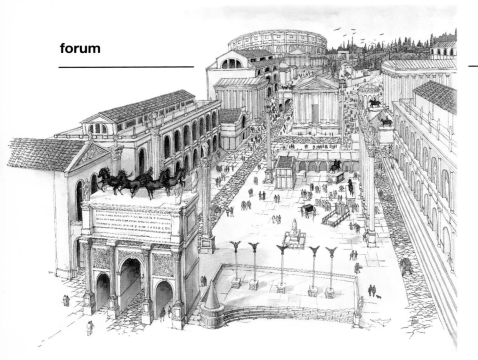

In the center of all Roman towns was the forum around which were grouped all the important buildings — government offices and temples, and a marketplace.

The word fossil comes from a Latin word meaning "dug up." Most fossils are found in sedimentary rocks — limestone and shale — which have been formed in the sea. So fossils of sea creatures are more common than those of land creatures.

fo·rum (fôr′əm, fōr′əm) *n.* **1** a public square in ancient Rome. **2** a place where opinions can be aired and discussed.

for·ward (fôr′wərd) *adv.* **1** (also **for·wards** (fôr′wərdz)) in the direction in front or ahead of one. **2** (also **forwards**) progressing from first to last. **3** on or onward; to a later time: *Don't forget to put the clocks forward.* **4** to an earlier time: *They decided to bring the wedding forward a month.* **5** into view or public attention: *Please put forward your suggestions.* — *adj.* **1** in the direction in front or ahead of you. **2** at the front. **3** advanced in development: *How far forward are the plans?* **4** concerning the future: *It's wise to do a little forward planning.* **5** bold or impolite. — *n.* a player in soccer, hockey, etc., whose task is to score rather than defend.

fos·sil (fäs′əl) *n.* the remains of, or the impression left by, an animal or plant in rock.

fossil fuel *n.* a fuel, as coal or petroleum, formed when prehistoric organic matter decomposed.

fos·sil·ize (fäs′ə-līz′) *vb.* **fos·sil·iz·ing, fos·sil·ized** to change into a fossil.

fos·ter (fôs′tər, fäs′tər) *vb.* **fos·ter·ing, fos·tered 1** to bring up or rear. **2** to encourage the development of. — *adj.* having a family relationship that is temporary rather than by birth or adoption: *foster care.*

fought. See **fight**.

foul (foul) *adj.* **1** disgusting: *What a foul smell.* **2** filthy. **3** contaminated: *The factory was surrounded by foul air.* — *n.* in sports, a breaking of the rules. — *vb.* **foul·ing, fouled.**

foul ball *n.* in baseball, a ball that is hit outside of the foul lines.

foul line *n.* a line in various games that must not be crossed by the ball or by a player.

found¹. See **find**.

found² (found) *vb.* **found·ing, found·ed 1** to start or establish. **2** to base: *They founded their argument on a lie.* — *n.* **found·er.**

foun·da·tion (foun-dā′shən) *n.* **1** See **Building Terms**. **2** the basis of a theory, etc.

foun·der (foun′dər) *vb.* **foun·der·ing, foun·dered 1** (of a ship) to sink. **2** (of a business, etc.) to fail.

found·ry (foun′drē) *n.* **found·ries** a place where metal or glass is melted and cast.

foun·tain (fount′n) *n.* **1** a structure producing a jet of water for drinking or for ornamental effect. **2** a spring of water.

four (fôr, fōr) *n.* the number or figure 4. — *n., adj., & adv.* **fourth** (fôrth, fōrth).

four·score (fôr′skôr′, fōr′skōr′) *n.* eighty.

fourth dimension *n.* time, as opposed to the dimensions of length, breadth, and height.

four·teen (fôrt-tēn′, fōrt-tēn′) *n.* the number or figure 14. — *n., adj., & adv.* **four·teenth** (fôrt-tēnth′, fōrt-tēnth′).

fowl (foul) *n.* **fowls** or **fowl** a farmyard bird.

fox (fäks) *n.* a wild member of the dog family

A sea animal such as an ammonite dies, sinks to the seabed and is covered in protective sediment.

The material around the shell hardens into rock and the shell itself may be replaced with lime. Over millions of years what was once seabed may be thrown up into a mountain range. The dug up fossil may not be the original animal preserved, but scientists can tell a great deal from it.

with a bushy tail, especially the reddish-brown variety of NORTH AMERICA and EUROPE.

fox·glove (fäks′gluv′) *n.* a tall plant with hanging purple or white flowers.

fox ter·ri·er (fäks ter′ē-ər) *n.* a breed of dog originally trained to hunt foxes.

foy·er (foi′ər, foi′ā′) *n.* the entrance hall of a theater, hotel, or home.

frac·tion (frak′shən) *n.* **1** a quantity that is not a whole number, as 0.25 or $^3/_7$. **2** a small part.

frac·ture (frak′chər) *n.* a break in anything hard, especially bone. – *vb.* **frac·tur·ing, frac·tured** to break.

fra·gile (fraj′əl, fraj′īl′) *adj.* easily broken or damaged. – *n.* **fra·gil·i·ty** (frə-jil′ət-ē).

frag·ment (frag′mənt) *n.* a small piece of something.

fra·grance (frā′grəns) *n.* a scent or odor.

fra·grant (frā′grənt) *adj.* having a pleasant smell.

frail (frāl) *adj.* **1** easily broken or destroyed; delicate; fragile. **2** in poor health.

frame (frām) *n.* **1** a structure around which something is built or to which other parts are added. **2** a structure that surrounds and supports: *Jill chose a red picture frame.* **3** a body, especially a human one, as a structure of a certain size and shape: *He eased his tall frame into the chair.* – *vb.* **fram·ing, framed 1** to put a frame around. **2** manufacture false evidence against, so as to make appear guilty of a crime.

frame·work (frām′wurk′) *n.* **1** a basic supporting structure. **2** a basic plan or system.

franc (frangk) *n.* the standard unit of currency in FRANCE, BELGIUM, SWITZERLAND, and several other French-speaking countries.

● **France** (frans) is the largest country in western EUROPE. The capital and biggest city is Paris. France is a republic and a member of the EUROPEAN UNION. See also Supplement, **Countries**.

fran·chise (fran′chīz′) *n.* **1** the right to vote. **2** right or privilege, granted by a government. **3** permission granted by a business to sell its products or services.

Frank (frangk) *n.* a member of a Germanic people that invaded Gaul in the late 400s A.D.

frank (frangk) *adj.* open and honest in speech or manner.

Fran·ken·stein (frang′kən-stīn′) *n.* a name for a creation or creature that destroys its creator.

● *Frankenstein* was the title of Mary Shelley's novel (written in 1818) and the name of the person in the book who created a human monster.

frank·furt·er (frangk′fərt-ər) *n.* a type of spicy smoked sausage often served on a bun.

● **Frank·lin** (frangk′lən), **Benjamin** (1706-1790) was an American statesman and inventor.

fran·tic (frant′ik) *adj.* **1** desperate, with fear or anxiety. **2** rushed: *We made a frantic dash for the train.* – *adv.* **fran·ti·cal·ly** (frant′i-klē).

fra·ter·nal (frə-turn′l) *adj.* of, or relating to, a brother; brotherly.

fraud (frôd) *n.* **1** an act of deliberate deception. **2** someone who pretends to be something that he or she is not.

fray¹ (frā) *vb.* **fray·ing, frayed** (of cloth or rope) to wear away so that the threads come loose.

fray² (frā) *n.* a fight, quarrel, or argument.

freak (frēk) *n.* a person, animal, or event that is abnormal: *A three-headed dog would be a freak.*

frec·kle (frek′əl) *n.* a small brown mark on the skin.

free (frē) *adj.* **fre·er, fre·est 1** allowed to move as one pleases; not shut in; not tied or fastened. **2** allowed to do as one pleases; not controlled: *Hungary is now a free nation.* **3** costing nothing. **4** not busy: *I'll be free after lunch.* – *adv.* **1** without payment: *We traveled free of charge.* **2** without restriction: *The horses were allowed to wander free.* – *vb.* **free·ing, freed** to make free; to release.

free·dom (frēd′əm) *n.* **1** the condition of being free to act, move, etc. without restriction. **2** liberty or independence. **3** the state of being without: *freedom from pain.*

free enterprise *n.* business done without government interference or control.

freeze (frēz) *vb.* **freez·ing, froze** (frōz), **froz·en** (frō′zən) **1** to turn into ice or solidify as a result of cold. **2** to cover or become covered with ice. **3** to become blocked up or stop operating because of frost or ice. **4** (of the weather, temperature, etc.) to be below the freezing point. **5** to be or make very cold: *My hands are freezing.* **6** to preserve by refrigeration at below freezing point. **7** to become motionless: *Fred froze with fear.*

In 1752 the American scientist Benjamin Franklin proved that lightning is electric by flying a kite in a thunderstorm. Attached to the kite was a metal key. When lightning struck the kite, a spark flashed as electricity passed down the string from the key.

freez·er *n.* a refrigerated cabinet or compartment in which to preserve food at below the freezing point.

freezing point *n.* the temperature at which water freezes. At sea level it is 32° Fahrenheit and 0° Celsius.

freight (frāt) *n.* **1** transportation of goods by rail, road, sea, or air. **2** the goods transported.

French (french) *adj.* **1** belonging to FRANCE or its inhabitants. **2** relating to the French language. – *n.* **1** the Romance language spoken in FRANCE, BELGIUM, SWITZERLAND, and elsewhere. **2** the people of FRANCE.

French Canadian *n.* a native of the French-speaking part of CANADA.

french fries (french'frīz') or **French fries** *n.* (*plural*) thin strips of deep-fried potatoes.

French windows *n.* (*plural*) a pair of glass

In 1789 a group of women marched to the palace of Versailles and seized the royal family.

The French Revolution was sparked off on July 14, 1789, when an angry Paris mob stormed the fortress prison of the Bastille. France had to live through years of upheaval until order was restored in 1795 and a republic established.

Anyone who was considered an enemy of the Revolution was beheaded on the guillotine.

doors that open onto a garden, balcony, etc.

● **The French Revolution** began in 1789 when the people of France demanded a fairer government and equality for all. The democratic ideas of the Revolution had a great influence all over the world.

fren·zy (fren'zē) *n.* **fren·zies** wild agitation or excitement; frantic activity. – *adj.* **fren·zied**.

fre·quen·cy (frē'kwən-sē) *n.* **fre·quen·cies** **1** the condition of happening often. **2** the rate at which something recurs: *He sneezes with great frequency.* **3** in radio, the particular rate of waves per second at which a signal is sent out.

fre·quent (frē'kwənt) *adj.* recurring at short intervals: *We are frequent visitors to the galleries.*

fres·co (fres'kō) *n.* **fres·cos** a picture painted on a wall, usually while the plaster is still damp.

fresh (fresh) *adj.* **1** newly made, gathered, etc. **2** another; different; clean: *Start on a fresh sheet of paper.* **3** new; additional: *We received fresh supplies.* **4** original: *This is a fresh approach to an old problem.* **5** bright and alert. **6** (of water) not salt. **7** rude or forward.

fresh·en (fresh'ən) *vb.* **fresh·en·ing, fresh·ened** to make fresh or fresher.

fresh·water (fresh' wôt'ər, fresh' wät'ər) *adj.* found in rivers and lakes, not in the sea.

fret¹ (fret) *vb.* **fret·ting, fret·ted** to worry; to show or express anxiety.

fret² (fret) *n.* a narrow metal ridge across the neck of a guitar or similar musical instrument.

fret·saw (fret'sô') *n.* a narrow-bladed saw for cutting designs in wood or metal.

Frey (frā). See **Myths and Legends**.

Frey·ja (frā'ə). See **Myths and Legends**.

fric·tion (frik'shən) *n.* **1** the rubbing of one thing against another. **2** the resistance met with by an object that is moving against another or through liquid or gas. **3** quarreling; conflict.

Fri·day (frīd'ē, frīd'ā) *n.* the sixth day of the week.

friend (frend) *n.* **1** someone known and liked. **2** someone who gives support or help: *Edward is a true friend of the poor.* **3** an ally.

friend·ly (fren'dlē) *adj.* **friend·li·er, friend·li·est** **1** kind; behaving as a friend. **2** on close or affectionate terms.

friend·ship (frend'ship') *n.* the relationship between friends.

Frig·ga (frig′ə). See **Myths and Legends**.

frig·id (frij′əd) *adj.* extremely cold.

fright (frīt) *n.* sudden fear; a shock.

fright·en (frīt′n) *vb.* **fright·en·ing, fright·ened 1** to make afraid. **2** to scare away.

fright·ful (frīt′fəl) *adj.* **1** ghastly; frightening. **2** (*informal*) bad; awful.

frill (fril) *n.* **1** a pleated strip of cloth attached along one edge to a garment, etc. as a decoration. **2** something extra serving no very useful purpose. – *adj.* **frill·y, frill·i·er, frill·i·est**.

fringe (frinj) *n.* **1** a border of loose threads on a carpet, tablecloth, garment, etc. **2** the edge; the part farthest from the main area or center.

frit·ter (frit′ər) *vb.* **frit·ter·ing, frit·tered** to waste a little at a time.

friv·o·lous (friv′ə-ləs) *adj.* silly; not sufficiently serious; not useful and sensible. – *n.* **fri·vol·i·ty** (fri-väl′ət-e), **fri·vol·i·ties**.

frock (fräk) *n.* a woman's or girl's dress.

frog (frôg, fräg) *n.* a small amphibious animal with webbed feet and long powerful hind legs.

frol·ic (fräl′ik) *vb.* **frol·ick·ing, frol·icked** to frisk or run about playfully.

from (frəm, frum, främ) *prep.* indicating **1** a starting point in place or time: *It was a long journey from London to New York.* **2** a lower limit: *You can get tickets from $12 upwards.* **3** movement out of: *She took a letter from the drawer.* **4** distance away: *The hotel is 16 miles from Boston.* **5** a viewpoint: *I can see the house from here.* **6** removal: *They took it away from her.* **7** point of attachment: *The hat was hanging from a nail.* **8** source or origin: *The covers are made from an old curtain.*

front (frunt) *n.* **1** the side or part of anything that is farthest forward or nearest to the viewer; the most important side or part, for example the side of a building where the main door is. **2** the part of a vehicle or vessel that faces the direction in which it moves: *Joe prefers to sit at the front of the bus.* **3** in war, the area where the soldiers are nearest to the enemy. **4** See **Weather Terms**. – *adj.* situated, formed, etc. at the front.

fron·tier (frun-tīr′, frun′tīr′) *n.* **1** a boundary between countries. **2** the edge of a settled community, near wilderness. **3** (in *plural*) limits: *the frontiers of knowledge.*

frost (frôst) *n.* a thin layer of frozen water vapor.

frost·bite (frôst′bīt′) *n.* the destruction of bodily tissues by freezing.

Frogs breathe through their skins as well as their lungs. It is important that frogs keep their skins wet to breathe, which is one reason why they live not far from water.

The main power for a frog's leap comes from the strong muscles in its hips and thighs. They pull on the leg bones.

frost·ing (frôst′ing) *n.* cake icing.

frost·y (frôst′ē) *adj.* **frost·i·er, frost·i·est** cold enough for frost to form.

● **Frost** (frôst), **Robert** (1874-1963) was an American poet, author of *A Boy's Will.*

Common gray tree frog. Tree frogs are less than 2 in. (5cm) long.

froth (frôth) *n.* a mass of tiny bubbles.

frown (froun) *vb.* **frown·ing, frowned 1** to wrinkle the forehead in an expression of worry, disapproval, thought, etc. **2** to disapprove of. – *n.* a disapproving expression.

froze, frozen. See **freeze**.

fru·gal (froo′gəl) *adj.* thrifty.

fruit (froot) *n.* **1** the seed-carrying product of a plant, especially if it has sweet, edible flesh. **2** whatever is gained as a result of hard work, etc. – *vb.* **fruit·ing, fruit·ed** to bear fruit.

fruit·less (froot′ləs) *adj.* useless; done in vain.

frus·trate (frus′trāt′) *vb.* **frus·trat·ing, frus·trat·ed 1** to prevent from doing or getting; to thwart: *We frustrated their plans.* **2** to make feel disappointed, useless, etc. – *n.* **frus·tra·tion** (frus-trā′shən).

frus·trat·ed *adj.* **1** disappointed. **2** unfulfilled in one's ambitions.

fry[1] (frī) *vb.* **fries, fry·ing, fried** to cook in hot oil or fat.

fry[2] (frī) *n.* (*plural*) young or newly spawned fish.

fry·ing pan (frī′ing-pan′) *n.* a shallow long-handled pan for frying food in.

PRONUNCIATION SYMBOLS		
ə **away**	lemon	focus
a **fat**	oi	**boy**
ā **fade**	oo	**foot**
ä **hot**	oo	**moon**
âr **fair**	ou	**house**
e **met**	th	**think**
ē **mean**	th	**this**
g **get**	u	**cut**
hw **which**	ur	**hurt**
i **fin**	w	**witch**
ī **line**	y	**yes**
îr **near**	yoo	**music**
ô **often**	yoor	**pure**
ō **note**	zh	**vision**

fudge (fuj) *n.* a soft candy made from butter, sugar, and usually chocolate.

fu·el (fyōō′əl) *n.* something that can be burned as a source of heat or power.

ful·crum (fool′krəm, ful′krəm) *n.* **fulcrums** the point on which a lever is supported.

ful·fill or **fulfil** (fool-fil′) *vb.* **ful·fil·ling, ful·filled 1** to carry out or perform: *Sarah fulfilled her promises.* **2** to satisfy or meet: *to fulfill a quota.* **3** to achieve: *Jack fulfilled his ambition by winning.* – *n.* **ful·fill·ment** (fool-fil′mənt).

full (fool) *adj.* **1** holding, containing, or having as much as possible. **2** complete: *We always do a full day's work.* **3** detailed: *I'd like a full report.* **4** occupied: *My hands are full.* **5** rich and varied: *Andrew has led a full life.* **6** (of the moon) at the stage when it is a complete disk. – *adv.* **1** completely; at maximum capacity: *Is the heater on full?* **2** exactly; directly: *The ball hit him full on the nose.*

full-time (fool′tīm′) *adj.* & *adv.* occupying your working time completely: *Fran has a full-time job.*

ful·ly (fool′ē, fool′lē) *adv.* **1** to the greatest possible extent. **2** completely.

●**Ful·ton** (foolt′n), **Robert** (1765-1815) was an American inventor who developed a steamboat.

fum·ble (fum′bəl) *vb.* **fum·bling, fum·bled 1** to handle things, or grope, clumsily. **2** to fail to manage because of clumsy handling: *The fielder fumbled the catch.* – *n.* an act of fumbling.

fume (fyōōm) *n.* smoke or vapor, especially if unpleasant or poisonous. – *vb.* **fum·ing, fumed 1** to be furious. **2** to give off fumes.

fun (fun) *n.* **1** enjoyment. **2** a source of amusement or entertainment. – **make fun of** to laugh at unkindly; to tease or ridicule.

func·tion (fungk′shən) *n.* **1** the special purpose or task of a machine, person, bodily part, etc. **2** an organized event such as a party, reception, meeting, etc. – *vb.* **func·tion·ing, func·tioned** to work; to operate.

func·tion·al (fungk′shən-l) *adj.* designed for efficiency rather than decoration.

fund (fund) *n.* **1** a sum of money for a special purpose. **2** a large store or supply: *Archie has a fund of jokes.* – *vb.* **fund·ing, fund·ed** to provide money for.

fun·da·men·tal (fun′də-mənt′l) *adj.* basic: *These are the fundamental rules of physics.*

fu·ne·ral (fyōō′nə-rəl, fyōōn′rəl) *n.* the

Fulcrum originally referred to the back-support of a couch. That use of the word, like the modern meaning, came from the original Latin word, which meant "to hold up or support." The word fulcrum can now also describe the parts of an animal that act as a hinge or support.

But the term fulcrum is most commonly used in physics.

Puffballs (below left) *are fungi which range in size from a golf ball to a volleyball. If a puffball is squeezed, spores (reproductive cells) escape in what looks like a smokelike puff.*

All species of chanterelles (above right) *have funnel-shaped fruit bodies growing on the ground. The group includes some of the most highly prized edible mushrooms.*

ceremonial burial or cremation of a dead person. – *adj.* of or relating to funerals.

fun·gus (fung′gəs) *n.* **fun·gus·es** or **fun·gi** (fun′jī′, fung′gī′) any of a group of plantlike growths, including mushrooms and toadstools, that reproduce by spores, and have no roots or leaves. – *adj.* **fun·gal** (fung′gəl).

fun·nel (fun′l) *n.* **1** a tube with a cone-shaped opening through which liquid, etc. can be poured into a narrow-necked container. **2** a chimney on a steamship or steam engine.

fun·ny (fun′ē) *adj.* **fun·ni·er, fun·ni·est**

Unlike higher plants, **fungi** lack chlorophyll and so cannot make their food (photosynthesize). Instead some live off dead matter such as rotting leaves and wood, while others are parasites and feed off living plants and animals.

Fly agaric

which heat is produced, for heating water or melting metal.

fur·nish (fur′nish) *vb.* **fur·nish·ing, fur·nished 1** to provide with furniture. **2** to supply or equip with whatever is required.

fur·ni·ture (fur′ni-chər) *n.* movable household equipment, such as tables, chairs, beds, etc.

fur·row (fur′ō) *n.* a groove or trench cut into the earth by a plow. – *vb.* **fur·row·ing, fur·rowed 1** to plow into furrows. **2** to make wrinkled: *Mandy furrowed her brow.*

fur·ther (fur′thər) *adj.* **1** more extended: *There will be a further delay.* **2** additional: *The police could find no further clues.* – *adv.* **1** at or to a greater distance or more distant point: *He could not walk any further.* **2** to or at a more advanced point: *His idea was further developed.* **3** to a greater extent or degree: *The plan can be modified even further.*

fur·ther·more (fur′thər-môr′, fur′thər-mōr′) *adv.* in addition; moreover.

fur·thest (fur′thəst) *adj.* most distant or remote. – *adv.* **1** at or to the greatest distance or most distant point. **2** at or to the most advanced point; to the greatest extent or degree.

fur·tive (furt′iv) *adj.* secretive; shy.

fu·ry (fyoor′ē) *n.* **fu·ries** violent anger.

fuse[1] (fyōoz) *n.* a safety device in an electrical circuit that breaks the circuit when the current becomes too strong.

fuse[2] (fyōoz) *vb.* **fused, fus·ing 1** to melt or unite by melting together. **2** to become united by or as if by melting together.

fu·se·lage (fyōo′sə-läzh′) *n.* the main body of an aircraft, carrying crew and passengers.

fu·sion (fyōo′zhən) *n.* **1** the process of melting together. **2** the combining of atomic nuclei with the resulting release of energy.

fuss (fus) *n.* agitation and excitement, especially over something trivial. – *vb.* **fuss·ing, fussed** to worry needlessly.

fuss·y (fus′ē) *adj.* **fuss·i·er, fuss·i·est 1** difficult to please: *a fussy eater.* **2** too concerned with details.

fu·tile (fyōot′l, fyōo′tīl′) *adj.* unproductive or pointless. – *n.* **fu·til·i·ty** (fyōo-til′ət-ē).

fu·ture (fyōo′chər) *n.* the time to come; events that are still to occur. – *adj.* **1** yet to come or happen: *I'm still planning my future career.* **2** about to become: *Have you met my future wife?*

fuzz (fuz) *n.* a mass of fine fibers or hair.

fuzz·y (fuz′ē) *adj.* **fuzz·i·er, fuzz·i·est 1** covered with fuzz. **2** blurred or not clear.

A chest of drawers with elements of ancient Greek and Roman design.

A plain, undecorated American rocking chair.

1 amusing; causing laughter. **2** strange; odd; mysterious. – *adv.* **fun·ni·ly** (fun′l-ē).

funny bone *n.* a place in the elbow joint where the nerve passes close to the skin.

fur (fur) *n.* **1** the thick fine soft coat of a hairy animal. **2** the skin of an animal with the hair attached. – *vb.* **fur·ring, furred** to coat or become coated with a furlike deposit.

fu·ri·ous (fyoor′ē-əs) *adj.* **1** violently angry. **2** raging; stormy. **3** frenzied: *There was furious activity just before the parade.*

fur·nace (fur′nəs) *n.* an enclosed chamber in

G g

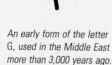
gab·ble (gab′əl) *vb.* **gab·bling, gab·bled** to talk quickly and unclearly.

ga·ble (gā′bəl) *n.* the triangular part of the side wall of a house between the sloping parts of the roof.

●**Ga·bon** (ga-bōn′). See Supplement, **Countries**.

gadg·et (gaj′ət) *n.* any small device or tool.

Gael·ic (gā′lik, gal′ik) *n.* any of the closely related Celtic languages spoken in IRELAND and the highlands of SCOTLAND. − *adj.* of or relating to these languages, the people who speak them, or their customs.

gag¹ (gag) *vb.* **gag·ging, gagged 1** to silence by putting a gag on. **2** to deprive of free speech. **3** to choke or retch.

gag² (gag) *n.* (*informal*) a joke or trick.

●**Ga·ga·rin** (gə-gär′in), **Yuri** (1934-1968) was a Russian cosmonaut. He made the first human space flight in 1961. He died in a plane crash.

gag·gle (gag′əl) *n.* a flock of geese.

gai·ly (gā′lē) *adv.* in a light-hearted, merry way.

gain (gān) *vb.* **gain·ing, gained 1** to get, obtain, or earn. **2** to benefit or profit: *She gained from the experience.* **3** to experience an increase in: *The car gained speed.* **4** (of a clock) to go too fast. **5** to advance or come nearer, as in a race. − *n.* an increase.

gait (gāt) *n.* a way of walking. See also **Horse Terms**.

gal·ax·y (gal′ək-sē) *n.* **gal·ax·ies** a group of stars and planets held together by the force of gravity.

gale (gāl) *n.* a very strong wind.

●**Gal·i·le·o** (gal′ə-lē′ō, gal′ə-lā′ō) (1564-1642) was an Italian astronomer and physicist who perfected the telescope and established Copernicus's theory of the universe in which the Sun is the center.

gal·lant *adj.* **1** (gal′ənt) brave. **2** (gə-lant′, gə-länt′) polite or courteous to women.

gal·leon (gal′yən) *n.* a large Spanish sailing ship used for war or trade from the 1400s to the 1700s.

Galleons had square sails on two front masts and three-cornered lateen sails on one or two rear masts. This meant that galleons could sail against the wind.

gal·ler·y (gal′ə-rē) *n.* **gal·ler·ies 1** a room or building used to display works of art. **2** a balcony along an inside upper wall.

gal·ley (gal′ē) *n.* **gal·leys 1** a long ship propelled by sails and oars. **2** the kitchen on a ship.

gal·lon (gal′ən) *n.* a measure of liquid equal to four quarts or 231 cubic in. (3.785 liters).

gal·lop (gal′əp) *n.* the fastest pace at which a horse moves, with all four legs leaving the ground together. − *vb.* **gal·lop·ing, gal·loped** to move at a gallop.

gal·lows (gal′ōz) *n.* (*singular*) a wooden frame on which criminals were hanged to death.

ga·lore (gə-lôr′, gə-lōr′) *adv.* in large amounts.

●**Gam·bi·a** (gam′bē-ə, gäm′bē-ə). See Supplement, **Countries**.

gam·ble (gam′bəl) *vb.* **gam·bling, gam·bled 1** to bet money on the result of a card game, horse race, etc. **2** to take a chance or risk. − *n.* **1** an act of gambling; a bet. **2** a risk, or a situation involving risk: *We were forced to take a gamble.* − *n.* **gam·bler** (gam′blər).

game (gām) *n.* **1** an amusement or pastime. **2** a competitive activity with rules, involving some form of skill; the equipment used for this.

gan·der (gan′dər) *n.* a male goose.

●**Gan·dhi** (gän′dē), **Indira** (1917-1984) was an Indian prime minister.

●**Gan·dhi** (gän′dē), **Mohandas** (1869-1948), known as Mahatma, was an Indian statesman who led nonviolent opposition to British rule.

gang (gang) *n.* a group of people, such as friends, who work or socialize together.

●**Gan·ges** (gan′jēz) a river in northern India.

gang·ster (gang′stər) *n.* a member of a gang of usually armed criminals.

gan·net (gan′ət) *n.* a large white seabird.

gan·try (gan′trē) *n.* **gan·tries** a large metal supporting framework.

gaol (jāl) *n.* (*British*) same as **jail**.

gap (gap) *n.* **1** a break or open space: *The dog escaped through a gap in the fence.* **2** a break in time; an interval: *a gap of three years.*

gape (gāp) *vb.* **gap·ing, gaped** to stare with the mouth open, especially in surprise or

Rose

In the ancient world the Egyptian Royal **Gardens** were famous, while the terraced gardens at Babylon became one of the Seven Wonders of the World as the "Hanging Gardens." Many Roman villas had sumptuous gardens. In the Middle Ages monasteries were noted for their herb and cloister gardens. In the 1700s English landscape gardeners placed natural-looking lawns around big houses.

Informal garden border

Formal herb garden

wonder. − *adj.* **gap·ing** wide open.

ga·rage (gə-räzh′, gə-räj′) *n.* **1** a building or area in a building in which cars, etc. are kept, repaired or serviced.

gar·bage (gar′bij) *n.* kitchen waste; refuse.

gar·den (gärd′n) *n.* **1** a piece of ground attached to a house, on which flowers, vegetables, trees, etc. are grown. **2** (usually in *plural*) a large area where plants are grown and displayed for public enjoyment: *They walked around the botanical gardens.* − *adj.* grown in a garden; not wild. − *vb.* **gar·den·ing, gar·dened** to work at the care of a garden and its plants, usually as a hobby. − *n.* **gar·den·er** (gärd′nər). − *n.* **gar·den·ing**.

gar·de·nia (gär-dēn′yə) *n.* a tropical shrub with large fragrant white or yellow flowers.

gar·gle (gär′gəl) *vb.* **gar·gling, gar·gled** to blow air from the lungs through a liquid held in the mouth without swallowing the liquid.

gar·goyle (gär′goil′) *n.* an ugly carved head or figure acting as a rainwater spout from a roof gutter or a decoration.

gar·ish (gār′ish) *adj.* unpleasantly bright.

gar·lic (gär′lik) *n.* a plant of the onion family, whose strong-tasting bulb is used as a flavoring

The gargoyles on Notre Dame cathedral in Paris are probably the best known of all those on Gothic cathedrals.

in cooking. – *adj.* **gar·lick·y** (gär′li-kē).

gar·ment (gär′mənt) *n.* an article of clothing.

gar·net (gär′nət) *n.* any of various hard minerals, especially a deep red variety used as a gemstone.

gar·nish (gär′nish) *n.* something, as parsley or lemon slices, used to decorate food.

gar·ret (gar′ət) *n.* an attic room.

gar·ri·son (gar′ə-sən) *n.* **1** a group of soldiers stationed in a town or fortress in order to defend it. **2** the building they occupy.

gar·ter (gärt′ər) *n.* a band of tight material, worn on the leg to hold up a stocking or sock.

● **Gar·vey** (gär′vē), **Marcus** (1887-1940) was a Jamaican who founded the Universal Negro Improvement Association in the UNITED STATES.

gas (gas) *n.* **1** any freely moving substance which is neither solid nor liquid. **2** gasoline.

gas·o·line (gas′ə-lēn′, gas′ə-lēn′) *n.* a fuel obtained from petroleum and natural gas, used in automobiles, etc.

gash (gash) *n.* a deep open cut or wound.

gasp (gasp) *vb.* **gasp·ing, gasped** to take a sharp breath in, through surprise, sudden pain, etc. – *n.* a sharp intake of breath.

gas·tric (gas′trik) *adj.* of the stomach.

gate (gāt) *n.* **1** a hinged barrier, moved to open or close an entrance in a wall, fence, etc. **2** a numbered exit at an airport through which passengers board or leave an aircraft.

gate·way (gāt′wā′) *n.* an entrance, especially to a city or park, with a gate across it.

gath·er (gat̶h′ər) *vb.* **gath·er·ing, gath·ered** **1** to come together in one place: *Huge crowds gathered in the marketplace.* **2** to collect, pick, or harvest. **3** to increase in speed or force: *The car gathered speed.* **4** to learn or understand from information received: *I gather that you won.*

gath·er·ing (gat̶h′ə-ring) *n.* a meeting or assembly.

gau·cho (gou′chō) *n.* **gauchos** a cowboy of the South American plains.

gau·dy (gôd′ē, gäd′ē) *adj.* **gau·di·er, gau·di·est** coarsely and brightly colored or decorated. – *adv.* **gau·di·ly** (gôd′l-ē, gäd′l-ē).

gauge (gāj) *vb.* **gaug·ing, gauged 1** to estimate or guess the measurement, size, etc. of. **2** to judge: *She gauged the seriousness of the situation immediately.* – *n.* a measuring instrument: *The fuel gauge read empty.*

● **Gau·guin** (gō-gan′), **Paul** (1848-1903) was a French painter whose works are classified as POSTIMPRESSIONISM.

gaunt (gônt) *adj.* thin or thin-faced through hunger or illness. – *n.* **gaunt·ness** (gônt′nəs).

gauze (gôz) *n.* thin transparent cloth, especially cotton used to dress wounds.

gay (gā) *adj.* **1** carefree. **2** bright and attractive. **3** homosexual. – *n.* a homosexual.

gaze (gāz) *vb.* **gaz·ing, gazed** to stare fixedly for a long time. – *n.* a fixed stare.

ga·zelle (gə-zel′) *n.* **gazelles** or **gazelle** a small graceful antelope of AFRICA and ASIA.

gear (gîr) *n.* **1** one of a set of small wheels with interlocking teeth, which combine to change the speed or direction of motion in a machine. **2** the equipment, clothes, or tools needed for a particular job, sport, etc. – *vb.* **gear·ing, geared** to adapt or design to suit a particular need: *The course is geared to nurses.*

Gei·ger count·er (gī′gər kount′ər) *n.* an instrument for measuring radioactivity.

gel. See **jell.**

gel·a·tine or **gelatin** (jel′ət-n) *n.* a clear jellylike substance made by boiling animal bones and hides, used in foods and glues.

geld (geld) *v.* See **Horse Terms.**

gem (jem) *n.* **1** (also **gem·stone** [jem′stōn′]) a precious stone cut and polished for use in jewelry. **2** a valued person or thing.

Gem·i·ni (jem′ə-nī, jem′ə-nē) *n.* See **zodiac.**

gen·der (jen′dər) *n.* the condition of being

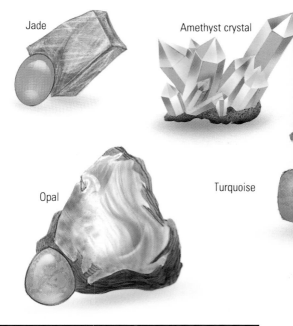

Jade

Amethyst crystal

Opal

Turquoise

male or female; sex.

gene (jēn) *n.* a basic component in cells responsible for passing characteristics from parents to children, such as the color of eyes, hair, etc.

gen·e·ral (jen′rəl, jen′ə-rəl) *adj.* **1** involving or applying to all or most parts, people, or things; widespread. **2** not detailed or definite; rough; vague. **3** not specialized: *His general knowledge is very wide.* – *n.* a senior army officer.

gen·er·al·ize (jen′rə-līz′, jen′ə-rə-līz′) *vb.* **gen·er·al·iz·ing, gen·er·al·ized** to speak in general terms or form general opinions, leaving out details.

gen·er·al·ly (jen′rə-lē) *adv.* usually.

gen·er·ate (je něrāt) *vb.* **gen·er·at·ing, gen·er·at·ed** to produce or create.

gen·er·a·tion (jen′ə-rā′shən) *n.* **1** the act of producing, for example electricity. **2** all people born and living at about the same time, considered as a group: *the younger generation.* **3** the average period between a person's birth and the birth of his or her children, considered to be about 30 years.

gen·er·a·tor (jen′ə-rāt′ər) *n.* a machine which produces one form of energy from another, such as electricity from wind power.

gen·er·os·i·ty (jen′ə-räs′ət-ē) *n.* a generous act.

gen·er·ous (jen′ə-rəs) *adj.* **1** willing to give money or gifts unselfishly; large and given unselfishly. **2** large; ample.

gen·e·sis (jen′ə-səs) *n.* **gen·e·ses** (jen′ə-sēz′) **1** a beginning or origin. **2 Genesis** the first

book in the Old Testament.

ge·net·ics (jə-net′iks) n. (*singular*) the study of the transmission of hereditary characteristics.

ge·nie (jē′nē) *n.* **genies** or **ge·ni·i** (jē′nē-ī′) in fairy stories, a spirit with the power to grant wishes.

gen·i·tals (jen′ət-lz) *n.* (*plural*; also **gen·i·ta·lia** [jen′ə-tāl′yə]) the external reproductive organs.

ge·ni·us (jēn′yəs, jē′nē-əs) *n.* **ge·ni·us·es 1** a person of outstanding creative or intellectual ability. **2** great intelligence and creativity.

gen·tile or **Gen·tile** (jen′tīl′) *n.* a person who is not Jewish.

gen·tle (jent′l) *adj.* **1** moderate and mild-mannered, not stern, coarse, or violent. **2** light and soft; not harsh, loud, or strong: *There was a gentle breeze.* – *adv.* **gent·ly** (jent′lē).

gen·u·ine (jen′yōō-ən) *adj.* **1** authentic, not artificial or fake. **2** honest; sincere.

ge·og·ra·phy (jē-äg′rə-fē) *n.* **1** the scientific study of the earth's physical features, climate, and population. **2** the layout of a place. – *n.* **ge·og·ra·pher** (jē-äg′rə-fər). – *adj.* **ge·o·graph·ic** (jē′ə-graf′ik).

ge·ol·o·gy (jē-äl′ə-jē) *n.* the scientific study of the earth's structure, especially its history and development as shown in the formation of rocks. – *adj.* **ge·o·log·ic** (jē′ə-läj′ik) or **ge·o·log·i·cal** (jē′nə-läj′i-kəl). – *n.* **ge·ol·o·gist** (jē-äl′ə-jəst).

ge·o·met·ric (jē′ə-me′trik) or **ge·o·met·ri·cal** (jē′ə-me′tri-kəl) *adj.* **1** measured using geometry. **2** using the kinds

Obsidian and granite are igneous rocks; marble and slate are metamorphic rocks; coal, limestone, and sandstone are sedimentary rocks.

In **geology** there are three kinds of rock: igneous, formed from molten rock; sedimentary, which is hardened layers of sediment; and metamorphic, which is either igneous or sedimentary rock changed by heat or pressure inside the earth.

Granite

Slate

Obsidian

Marble

Coal

Limestone

Sandstone

Areas of volcanic activity are rich in minerals that have crystallized after being forced to the surface under pressure.

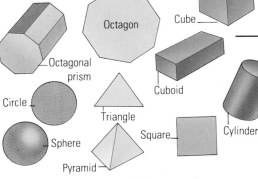

Octagon · Cube · Octagonal prism · Cuboid · Circle · Triangle · Square · Cylinder · Sphere · Pyramid

In geometry two-dimensional figures are plane figures; *three-dimensional shapes are* solids.

of basic forms dealt with in geometry, for example lines, circles, and triangles.

ge·om·e·try (jē-äm′ə-trē) *n.* the branch of mathematics dealing with lines, angles, shapes, and their relationships.

●**George** (jôrj) is the name of six British kings.

●**Geor·gia** (jôr′jə). See Supplement, **Countries**.

●**Geor·gia** (jôr′jə). See Supplement, **U.S.A.**

ge·ra·ni·um (jə-rā′nē-əm) *n.* a house or garden plant with fragrant leaves and bright red, pink, or white flowers.

ger·bil (jur′bəl) *n.* a mouselike desert animal with long hind legs, native to AFRICA and ASIA.

ger·i·at·ric (jer′ē-a′trik) *adj.* for or dealing with the very old and ill.

germ (jurm) *n.* any microscopic plant or creature, especially one causing disease.

Ger·man (jur′mən) *n.* **1** a native of GERMANY. **2** the official language of GERMANY, AUSTRIA, and parts of SWITZERLAND. – *adj.* of GERMANY, its people, or their language.

●**Ger·ma·ny** (jur′mə-nē) lies in the middle of EUROPE and has the largest population of any European nation. Its capital is Berlin. See Supplement, **Countries**.

ger·mi·nate (jur′mə-nāt′) *vb.* **ger·mi·nat·ing, ger·mi·nat·ed** to cause a seed or an idea, etc. to begin to grow. – *n.* **ger·mi·na·tion** (jur′mə-nā′shən).

●**Ge·ron·i·mo** (jə-rän′ə-mō) (1829-1909) was a warrior and leader of the APACHE tribe of Native Americans.

ges·ture (jes′chər) *n.* **1** a movement of a part of the body as an expression of feelings, especially when speaking. **2** something done simply as a formality. – *vb.* **ges·tur·ing, ges·tured** to move a part of the body to express feelings.

get (get) *vb.* **getting, got** (gät), **got** or **got·ten** (gät′n) **1** to receive or obtain: *I'm getting a new car.* **2** to have or possess: *I've got a new car.* **3** to go, move, travel, or arrive: *I got to Paris on Friday.* **4** to fetch, take, or bring: *I'll get it down from the shelf.* **5** to put into a particular state or condition: *She got him into trouble.* **6** to become: *He began to get angry.* **7** to understand: *I don't get the joke.*

●**Get·tys·burg** (get′əz-burg′), **Battle of** took place between July 1 and 3, 1863, during the American CIVIL WAR.

gey·ser (gī′zər) *n.* an underground spring that spouts out hot water and steam.

●**Gha·na** (gän′ə). See Supplement, **Countries**.

ghast·ly (gast′lē) *adj.* **ghast·li·er, ghast·li·est** extremely frightening; horrible.

gher·kin (gur′kən) *n.* a small variety of cucumber, usually pickled.

ghet·to (get′ō) *n.* **ghettos** or **ghet·toes** a section of a city where minority groups live.

ghost (gōst) *n.* **1** the spirit of a dead person. **2** a suggestion, hint, or trace. – *adj.* **ghost·ly**.

gi·ant (jī′ənt) *n.* **1** in fairy stories, a huge, strong, often cruel creature of human form. **2** a person who is usually large in size or importance: *a giant of industry.* – *adj.* unusually large; huge.

gib·bon (gib′ən) *n.* a small tailless tree-dwelling ape with very long arms, native to ASIA.

gib·lets (jib′ləts) *n.* (*plural*) the heart, liver, and other edible internal organs of fowl.

●**Gi·bral·tar** (jə-brôl′tər) is a tiny British colony, a rocky peninsula, on the south coast of SPAIN.

gid·dy (gid′ē) *adj.* **gid·di·er, gid·di·est 1** suffering a spinning sensation because of tiredness or illness. **2** light-hearted; frivolous.

gift (gift) *n.* **1** something given; a present. **2** a natural ability: *He has a gift for music.*

gift·ed (gif′təd) *adj.* having a great natural ability.

gi·gan·tic (jī-gant′ik) *adj.* huge; enormous.

gig·gle (gig′əl) *vb.* **gig·gling, gig·gled** to laugh quietly or in a nervous or silly way. – *n.*

1 such a laugh. **2** (in *plural*) a fit of giggling.

gild (gild) *vb.* **gild·ing, gild·ed** or **gilt** (gilt) to cover with a thin coating of gold.

gill (gil) *n.* the breathing organ of many sea animals, especially the slit on either side of a fish's head.

gin[1] (jin) *n.* an alcoholic spirit made from barley, rye, or corn, flavored with juniper berries.

gin[2] (jin) *n.* (also **cotton gin**) a machine that removes the seeds from cotton.

gin·ger (jin′jər) *n.* **1** a root used in medicine and as a spice in cooking; also the Asian plant from which it is taken. **2** a reddish-brown color.

gin·ger·bread (jin′jər-bred′) *n.* a cookie or cake flavored with ginger and molasses.

gin·ger·ly (jin′jər-lē) *adv. & adj.* with caution.

ging·ham (ging′əm) *n.* striped or checked cotton cloth.

gi·raffe (jə-raf′) *n.* a tall African mammal with a very long neck and long legs.

gird·er (gurd′ər) *n.* a large beam of wood, iron, or steel used to support a structure.

girl (gurl) *n.* **1** a female child. **2** a female sweetheart. **3** a woman.

girth (gurth) *n.* distance around something, as a tree or a person's waist.

gist (jist) *n.* general meaning; main point.

give (giv) *vb.* **giv·ing, gave** (gāv), **giv·en** (giv′ən) **1** to transfer ownership or possession to: *She gave him my watch.* **2** to provide or produce: *Cows give milk.* **3** to perform: *She gave a lecture on beetles.* **4** to pay: *I gave 20 cents for it.* **5** to break: *The chair gave under his weight.* – *n.* flexibility. – *vb.* **give in** to admit defeat; to yield. – *vb.* **give out 1** to distribute. **2** to emit. **3** to break down or come to an end: *Their resistance gave out.* – *vb.* **give over 1** to transfer. **2** to set aside or devote: *The morning was given over to games.* – *vb.* **give up 1** to admit defeat; to stop making an effort. **2** to renounce a habit: *He has given up smoking.* – **give way 1** to give priority. **2** to collapse under pressure.

giv·en (giv′ən) *adj.* **1** stated or specified. **2** likely or prone: *He is given to cheating.*

gla·cial (glā′shəl) *adj.* of or relating to glaciers or ice.

gla·cier (glā′shər) *n.* a slow-moving mass of ice, formed from an accumula-tion of snow.

glad (glad) *adj.* **glad·der, glad·dest** happy or pleased: *I'll be glad to go back to school.*

glad·den (glad′n) *vb.* **glad·den·ing, glad·dened** to make happy or pleased.

glad·i·a·tor (glad′ē-āt′ər) *n.* in ancient Rome, a man trained to fight against other men or animals in an arena.

glam·our or **glam·or** (glam′ər) *n.* great attractiveness, especially created on a person by makeup, clothes, etc.: *The models had a natural sense of glamour.* – *adj.* **glam·or·ous** (glam′ə-rəs).

glance (glans) *vb.* **glanc·ing, glanced 1** to look very quickly or indirectly. **2** to hit and bounce off: *The ball glanced off my arm.* – *n.* a brief look, often indirect.

gland (gland) *n.* an organ that produces chemical substances that are used by, or excreted from, the body, for example sweat and tears.

Glamour once meant "magic" or "spell," but by the 1800s had come to mean "magic beauty."

The results of the action of **glaciers** millions of years ago can be seen today. Valleys contained huge glaciers, creeping slowly downhill. The glacier's scouring action wore away the sides and floor of its valley.

Pyramidal peak

Cirque

Crevasses

Lakes may form in the armchair-shaped cirques made by glaciers.

Movement of glacier

Sometimes a glacier carries rocks a long distance away. These are known as erratics.

To make stained glass artists fitted pieces of colored glass together with lead to make designs or pictures.

In traditional **glass**-blowing a gob of molten glass at the end of a tube was blown to produce a bubble that could be shaped before it cooled.

Glass is made from melting sand, limestone, and soda ash. Lead replaces limestone to give crystal its sparkle.

GLASS-MAKING METHODS

blowing Today blowing is done by machines, to make bottles, light bulbs, etc.

pressing Glass is pushed into a mold and then cooled, e.g. to make ovenware.

casting Molten glass is poured into molds to make, for example, optical telescopes.

rolling Rollers squeeze molten glass into sheets.

floating A way of making sheet glass, done by floating molten glass across a bath of molten tin.

glare (glâr) *vb.* **glar·ing, glared** to stare angrily. − *n.* **1** an angry stare. **2** dazzling light.

glar·ing (glâr′ing) *adj.* **1** unpleasantly bright. **2** obvious.

glas·nost (gläs′nəst) *n.* openness about government policies (especially Soviet).

glass (glas) *n.* **1** a hard, brittle, usually transparent substance made by melting together and then rapidly cooling a mixture of compounds. **2** an article made from this substance, especially a drinking cup. **3** (in *plural*) spectacles. − *adj.* made of glass.

glass·blow·ing (glas′blō′ing) *n.* the process of shaping molten glass by blowing air into it through a tube.

glass·y (glas′ē) *adj.* **glass·i·er, glass·i·est 1** like glass. **2** without expression: *glassy eyes.*

glaze (glāz) *vb.* **glaz·ing, glazed 1** to fit with glass panes. **2** to give a hard shiny transparent coating to: *to glaze pottery.* **3** to become dull and expressionless: *His eyes glazed over with boredom.* − *n.* a hard glassy coating on pottery. − *adj.* **glazed**.

gleam (glēm) *n.* **1** a gentle glow. **2** a brief flash of light. **3** a brief appearance or sign: *There was a gleam of excitement in his eyes.* − *vb.* **gleam·ing, gleamed 1** to glow gently. **2** to shine with brief flashes of light. − *adj.* **gleam·ing**.

glee (glē) *n.* great delight; joy.

glee·ful (glē′fəl) *adj.* joyful; merry.

glen (glen) *n.* a long narrow valley.

● **Glenn** (glen)**, John** (1921-) was the first American to orbit the earth, on February 20, 1962.

glide (glīd) *vb.* **glid·ing, glid·ed 1** to move smoothly: *They glided along the ice.* **2** (of birds) to sail through the air without beating the wings. **3** (of an aircraft) to fly without engine power.

glid·er (glīd′ər) *n.* a small aircraft with no engine.

glim·mer (glim′ər) *vb.* **glim·mer·ing, glim·mered** to glow faintly. − *n.* **1** a faint glow. **2** a hint or trace: *a glimmer of hope.*

glimpse (glimps) *n.* a very brief look. − *vb.* **glimps·ing, glimpsed** to see for only a moment.

glis·ten (glis′ən) *vb.* **glis·ten·ing, glis·tened** to reflect faint flashes of light.

glit·ter (glit′ər) *vb.* **glit·ter·ing, glit·tered** to shine with bright flashes of light; to sparkle.

gloat (glōt) *vb.* **gloat·ing, gloat·ed** to feel or show smug satisfaction. − *n.* an act of gloating.

glo·bal (glō′bəl) *adj.* **1** affecting the whole world. **2** total; including everything.

globe (glōb) *n.* **1** the earth. **2** a sphere with a map of the world on it.

gloom (gloom) *n.* **1** darkness or dimness. **2** sadness or despair. − *adv.* **gloom·i·ly** (gloo′mə-lē). − *adj.* **gloom·y** (gloo′mē), **gloom·i·er, gloom·i·est**.

glo·ri·fy (glôr′ə-fī′, glōr′ə-fī′) *vb.* **glo·ri·fies, glo·ri·fy·ing, glo·ri·fied 1** to praise or honor. **2** to exaggerate the beauty, importance, etc. of.

glo·ri·ous (glôr′ē-əs, glōr′ē-əs) *adj.* having or bringing glory; splendidly beautiful.

glo·ry (glôr′ē, glōr′ē) *n.* **glo·ries 1** great honor and prestige. **2** great beauty or splendor.

gloss[1] (gläs, glôs) *n.* **1** shiny brightness on a surface. **2** a superficial pleasantness or attractiveness.

gloss[2] (gläs, glôs) *n.* a short explanation of a difficult word or phrase in a text.

glos·sa·ry (gläs′ə-rē, glôs′ə-rē) *n.* **glos·sa·ries** a list of glosses, often at the end of a book.

gloss·y (gläs′ē, glōs′ē) *adj.* **gloss·i·er, gloss·i·est** smooth and shiny.

glove (gluv) *n.* a covering for the hand, usually with separate fingers.

glow (glō) *vb.* **glow·ing, glowed 1** to give out a steady heat or light without flames. **2** to shine brightly, as if very hot. – *n.* **1** a steady heat or light. **2** a feeling of warmth or excitement.

glow·er (glau′ər) *vb.* **glow·er·ing, glow·ered** to stare angrily.

glu·cose (gloo′kōs′, gloo′kōz′) *n.* a sugar present in plant and animal tissue.

glue (gloo) *n.* any adhesive. – *vb.* **glu·ing** or **glue·ing, glued 1** to join with glue. **2** to stay very close to; to fix on: *She was glued to the TV.*

glum (glum) *adj.* **glum·mer, glum·mest** in low spirits; sullen.

glut (glut) *n.* an excessive supply of goods, etc.

glut·ton (glut′n) *n.* **1** a person who eats too much. **2** a person whose behavior suggests an eagerness for something unpleasant. – *adj.* **glut·ton·ous** (glut′n-əs).

glut·tony (glut′n-ē) *n.* the practice of eating too much.

gnarled (närld) *adj.* twisted; with knots and lumps, usually as a result of age: *a gnarled oak.*

gnat (nat) *n.* any of various small biting flies, some of which suck blood.

gnaw (nô) *vb.* **gnaw·ing, gnawed 1** to bite with a scraping action, causing a gradual wearing away. **2** to persistently cause physical or mental pain: *Jealousy gnawed at her for years.*

gnome (nōm) *n.* a small fairy-tale creature who lives underground, often guarding treasure.

gnu (noo, nyoo) *n.* **gnu** or **gnus** a type of large African antelope.

go (gō) *vb.* **goes** (gōz), **go·ing, went** (went), **gone** (gon) **1** to walk, move, or travel. **2** to lead or extend: *There is a path going across the field.* **3** to visit or attend, once or regularly: *I go to school.* **4** to be destroyed or taken away; to disappear: *The peaceful atmosphere has gone.* **5** to proceed: *The plan is going well.* **6** to be used up: *All his money goes on candy.* **7** to belong: *Where does this go?* **8** to apply: *The same goes for you.* **9** (of colors, etc.) to match or blend. – *n.* **go, goes 1** a turn: *It's my go.* **2** an attempt: *Have a go.* – *vb.* **go against** to be contrary to; to be decided unfavorably for. – *vb.* **go ahead** to proceed. – *vb.* **go off** to explode. – *vb.* **go out** to become extinguished. – *vb.* **go through with** to carry out to the end.

goal (gōl) *n.* **1** the set of posts through which the ball is struck to score points in various games. **2** an act of scoring in this way. **3** an aim.

goat (gōt) *n.* a horned and bearded animal of the sheep family, bred for its milk and wool.

gob·ble (gäb′əl) *vb.* **gob·bling, gob·bled 1** to eat hurriedly and noisily. **2** (of turkeys) to make a loud swallowing noise in the throat.

gob·lin (gäb′lən) *n.* in fairy tales, an evil or mischievous spirit in the form of a small man.

god (gäd) *n.* **1 God** in the CHRISTIAN, JEWISH, and MUSLIM religions, the creator and ruler of the universe. **2** in other religions, a super-human being with power over nature and humans, an object of worship.

god·child (gäd′chīld′) *n.* **god·child·ren** gäd′chil′drən) a child for whom a godparent is responsible.

god·dess (gâd′əs) *n.* a superhuman feminine being with power over nature and humans, an object of worship.

god·par·ent (gäd′pâr′ənt) *n.* a person with responsibility for a child, as at a baptism.

●**Goe·the** (gurt′ə), **Johann Wolfgang von** (1749-1832) was a German poet and play-wright as well as a scientist and statesman.

gog·gles (gäg′əlz) *n.* (*plural*) protective spectacles with edges fitting against the face.

Alpine ibex are amazingly nimble and sure footed.

The various breeds of domestic **goat** are descended from the Persian wild goat.

Cretan wild goat

Apennine mountain goat

Feral goat

The chamois is unusual in having horns that point backward.

Pure gold bars. A country's wealth is measured by the quantity of gold it has. The vast stock of U.S. gold is in Fort Knox, Kentucky.

gold (gōld) *n.* **1** an element (symbol **Au**), a soft yellow precious metal used for making jewelry, coins, etc. **2** articles made from it. **3** its deep yellow color. – *adj.* **1** made of gold. **2** gold-colored.

gold·en (gōl′dən) *adj.* **1** gold-colored. **2** made of or containing gold. **3** excellent; extremely valuable: *She was given a golden opportunity.* **4** (of an anniversary) 50th.

golden eagle *n.* a large northern mountain eagle with golden-brown plumage.

gold·finch (gōld′finch′) *n.* an American finch the male of which has bright yellow plumage.

gold·fish (gōld′fish′) *n.* **goldfish or gold·fish·es** a small yellow or orange freshwater fish, often kept in aquariums.

golf (gälf, gôlf, gäf, gôf) *n.* a game played on a large outdoor course, the object being to hit a small ball into each of a series of holes using a set of long-handled clubs, taking as few strokes as possible. – *n.* **golf·er**.

gon·do·la (gän′də-lə) *n.* a long narrow flat-bottomed boat with pointed upturned ends, used on the canals of Venice.

gone (gôn). See **go**. – *adj.* **1** moved away; departed. **2** lost. **3** dead. **4** used up.

gong (gäng, gông) *n.* a hanging metal plate which sounds when struck.

good (good) *adj.* **better** (bet′ər), **best** (best) **1** pleasant: *They had good weather.* **2** competent; talented: *She is good at sports.* **3** morally correct; virtuous. **4** beneficial: *The medicine is good for you.* **5** bringing happiness or pleasure: *He brought good news.* **6** well behaved. **7** thorough: *He had a good look.* – *n.* **1** moral correctness; virtue. **2** benefit; advantage: *It will do you good.* – **as good as** almost; virtually.

good-bye or **good-by** (good-bī′) *n.* a remark at leaving.

Good Friday See **Religious Feasts and Festivals**.

good·ness (good′nəs) *n.* **1** the state or quality of being good; kindness. **2** nourishing quality.

goose (goos) *n.* **geese** (gēs) **1** a long-necked, web-footed bird like a large duck. **2** the female, as opposed to the gander, the male.

go·pher (gō′fər) *n.* any of various burrowing ratlike animals found in NORTH and CENTRAL AMERICA, EUROPE, and ASIA.

gore[1] (gôr, gōr) *n.* blood from a wound.

gore[2] (gôr, gōr) *vb.* **gor·ing, gored** to pierce with a horn or tusk.

gorge (gôrj) *n.* a deep narrow valley, usually containing a river. – *vb.* **gorg·ing, gorged** to eat or swallow greedily.

GOLF TERMS
birdie 1 stroke under par
bogey 1 stroke over par
drive the first shot off the tee
driver a No 1 wood
eagle 2 shots under par
handicap a stroke or shot allowance given to a player so that he or she can play on equal terms with a superior player
par the number of shots it should take a player without a handicap to complete the hole or round

---

Some people think that the forerunner to the game of **golf** was played by the Chinese 2,000 years ago. Others claim that the Romans were the first to knock balls into holes. The game we know probably developed in Scotland where the first written rules for the game appeared in 1744.

Everything that a golfer needs can be put in a golf bag. Bags are often carried by hired caddies.

Modern golf balls comprise long strips of rubber wound around a core. The dimples on the casing help the ball to fly smoothly.

A golf course has 9 or 18 holes in well-mown areas called greens. The golfer hits his ball into each hole in turn. The object is to finish each hole in the fewest number of strokes.

gor·geous (gôr′jəs) *adj.* extremely beautiful or attractive; magnificent.

go·ril·la (gə-ril′ə) *n.* a powerfully built brown ape, the largest of all apes, native to AFRICA.

gos·ling (gäz′ling) *n.* a young goose.

gos·pel (gäs′pəl) *n.* **1** the life and teachings of Christ. **2 Gospel** any of the NEW TESTAMENT books attributed to Matthew, Mark, Luke, and John. **3** (*informal*) the absolute truth.

gos·sip (gäs′əp) *n.* **1** talk or writing about the private affairs of others, often spiteful and untrue. **2** a person who engages in or spreads such talk. **3** casual and friendly talk. – *vb.* **gos·sip·ing, gos·siped 1** to take part in, or pass on, malicious gossip. **2** to talk idly.

got. See **get**.

Goth (gäth) *n.* a member of a Germanic people who invaded parts of the ROMAN EMPIRE.

gouge (gouj) *n.* **1** a chisel with a rounded hollow blade. **2** a groove or hole made using this. – *vb.* **goug·ing, gouged** to cut or press out.

gou·lash (gŌŌ′läsh′) *n.* a thick meat stew originally from HUNGARY.

gourd (gôrd, gōrd, goord) *n.* **1** any of various plants related to the cucumber which bear a large hard-skinned fruit. **2** the hollowed-out dried skin of the fruit.

gov·ern (guv′ərn) *vb.* **gov·ern·ing, gov·erned** to control and direct the affairs of a country, state, or organization.

gov·ern·ment (guv′ər-mənt, guv′ərn-mənt) *n.* **1** a body of people, usually elected, with the power to control the affairs of a country or state. **2** the way in which a country is run.

gov·er·nor (guv′ə-nər, guv′nər) *n.* **1** the elected head of a state in the UNITED STATES. **2** the appointed ruler of a colony, territory, etc.

gown (goun) *n.* **1** a woman's long formal dress. **2** an official robe worn by clergy, judges, etc.

●**Goy·a** (goi′ə), **Francisco de** (1746-1828) was a Spanish painter whose works criticized society.

grab (grab) *vb.* **grab·bing, grabbed** to seize suddenly and often with violence. – *n.* an act of taking suddenly or greedily.

grace (grās) *n.* **1** elegance and beauty of form or movement. **2** decency: *He had the grace to offer.* **3** a short prayer of thanks to God said before or after a meal. – *vb.* **grac·ing, graced** to honor; to add beauty or charm to.

grace·ful (grās′fəl) *adj.* having or showing elegance and beauty of form or movement.

Graces *n.* (*plural*) See **Myths and Legends**.

gra·cious (grā′shəs) *adj.* **1** kind and polite. **2** having qualities of luxury and elegance.

grade (grād) *n.* **1** a stage or level on a scale of quality, rank, size, etc. **2** a mark given for an exam or an essay. **3** a particular class or year in school. – *vb.* **grad·ing, grad·ed 1** to arrange in different levels. **2** to award a mark indicating a grade to.

gra·di·ent (grād′ē-ənt) *n.* the steepness of a slope.

grad·u·al (graj′ŌŌ-əl) *adj.* changing or happening slowly, by degrees.

grad·u·ate (graj′ŌŌ-āt′) *vb.* **grad·u·at·ing, grad·u·at·ed 1** to receive an academic degree after completing studies. **2** to move up from a lower to a higher level, often in stages. – (graj′ŌŌ-ət) *n.* a person with an academic degree or diploma.

grad·u·a·tion (graj′ŌŌ-ā′shən) *n.* the ceremony to mark the receiving of an academic degree or diploma.

graf·fi·ti (grə-fēt′ē) *n.* (*plural*) words or drawings, scratched or painted on walls in public places.

graft (graft) *n.* **1** a living plant shoot inserted into another to form a new growth. **2** a healthy piece of skin or bone used to replace an unhealthy piece of the body. – *vb.* **graft·ing, graft·ed** to attach as a graft.

●**Gra·ham** (grā′əm, gram), **Martha** (1894-1991) was an American pioneer of modern dance.

grain (grān) *n.* **1** a single seed of a cereal plant. **2** cereal plants or their seeds as a whole. **3** a very small amount: *There was a grain of truth in his story.*

gram or **gramme** (gram) *n.* the basic unit of weight in the metric system, one thousandth of a kilogram, equal to 0.035 ounces.

gram·mar (gram′ər) *n.* the branch of language study dealing with the rules by which words are formed and combined into sentences.

gram·mat·i·cal (grə-mat′i-kəl) *adj.* **1** relating to grammar. **2** following the rules of grammar.

gra·na·ry (grā′nə-rē. gran′ə-rē) *n.* **gra·na·ries** a building where grain is stored.

grand (grand) *adj.* large or impressive in size, appearance, or style.

GOOD GRAMMAR
Grammar is the way a language is arranged and fits together to make a message that can be clearly and easily understood. "Words up jumbled and difficult to read to understand are." This is a nonsense sentence. We all understand "Jumbled up words are difficult to read and understand." Grammar can change through usage. In the 1700s it was perfectly correct to say "you was" when referring to one person. That seems perfectly logical. And we all say sentences such as "Aren't I lucky to be alive?" Would we say "I are lucky to be alive?" Strange, am it not?!

Many gourds have attractive names such as Aladdin's turban, Warted gourd, Nest-egg gourd, and Luffa.

The Grand Canyon in Arizona is the world's deepest gorge. It is about 210 mi. (350 km) long, up to 12 mi. (20 km) across and more than a mile (1.6 km) deep. The Colorado river runs through the canyon.

●**Grand Cany·on** (grand′ kan′yən), carved by the Colorado River in Arizona, is a wonder of nature.

grand·child (gran′chīld′), **grand·chil·dren** (gran′chil′drən), **grand·daugh·ter** (gran′dôt′ər), **grand·son** (gran′sun′) *n.* a child, daughter, or son, of one's child.

grand·fa·ther (gran′fä̱th′ər), **grand·moth·er** (gran′mu̱th′ər), **grand·par·ent** (gran′pâr′ənt) *n.* the father or mother of one's father or mother.

gran·deur (gran′jər) *n.* impressive beauty; magnificence.

gran·i·te (gran′ət) *n.* a hard gray or red rock, often used for building.

grant (grant) *vb.* **grant·ing, grant·ed** to give, allow, or fulfill. – *n.* something granted, especially an amount of money from a fund or property. – **grant·ed** admitting that is true. – **take for granted 1** to assume to be true. **2** to treat casually, without appreciation.

●**Grant** (grant)**, Ulysses** (1822-1885) was a Union general in the American CIVIL WAR and president of the UNITED STATES (1869-1877).

grape (grāp) *n.* a green or dark-purple berry growing on vines, eaten as a fruit, pressed to make wine, and dried to make raisins.

grape·fruit (grāp′fro̅o̅t′) *n.* **grapefruits** or **grapefruit** a large yellow citrus fruit.

grape·vine (grāp′vīn′) *n.* a vine on which grapes grow.

graph (graf) *n.* a diagram which shows changes or comparisons in value or quantity, by means of printed dots, lines, or blocks.

grap·ple (grap′əl) *vb.* **grap·pling, grap·pled** to grasp and struggle or fight.

grasp (grasp) *vb.* **grasp·ing, grasped 1** to take a firm hold of; to clutch. **2** to understand. – *n.* **1** a grip or hold. **2** ability to understand: *The lecture was beyond their grasp.*

grass (gras) *n.* any of numerous wild plants with green bladelike leaves, covering the ground in fields, lawns, etc., and eaten by various animals.

grass·hop·per (gras′häp′ər) *n.* an insect with long back legs suited for jumping.

grate[1] (grāt) *n.* **1** a framework of bars covering a window, door, or drain. **2** a framework of bars for holding coal, etc. in a fireplace.

grate[2] (grāt) *vb.* **grat·ing, grat·ed** to cut into shreds by rubbing against a rough surface.

grate·ful (grāt′fəl) *adj.* feeling thankful; showing or giving thanks.

Grape cultivation is one of the oldest human arts. Grapes are grown in vineyards, mostly in warm, temperate lands such as the Mediterranean zone, California, and Australia.

There are many varieties of grape such as the Cabernet, Sauvignon, Chardonnay, and Pinot Noir.

Different wines are put into bottles of different shapes: Bordeaux, Burgundy, and Chianti, for example.

grat·i·fy (grat′ə-fī′) *vb.* **grat·i·fies, grat·i·fy·ing, grat·i·fied** to please, satisfy, or indulge: *to gratify a whim.*

grat·i·tude (grat′ə-tōōd′, grat′ə-tyōōd′) *n.* the feeling of being grateful.

grave¹ (grāv) *n.* a hole dug in the ground for burying a dead body in.

grave² (grāv) *adj.* giving cause for great concern; very serious: *grave danger.*

grav·el (grav′əl) *n.* a mixture of small stones and coarse sand, used for the surface of paths.

grav·i·ty (grav′ət-ē) *n.* **1** the natural force which causes objects to be drawn toward each other, especially the force that attracts things toward the earth, causing them to fall toward or stay on the ground. **2** seriousness.

gra·vy (grā′vē) *n.* **gra·vies** a sauce made from the juices released by meat as it is cooking.

gray or **grey** (grā) *adj.* **1** of a color between black and white. **2** (of weather) dull and cloudy. **3** (of hair) turning white. — *n.* any shade of a color between black and white.

graze¹ (grāz) *vb.* **graz·ing, grazed** (of animals) to eat grass.

graze² (grāz) *vb.* **graz·ing, grazed** **1** to suffer a break in the skin of as a result of scraping. **2** to brush against lightly in passing.

grease (grēs) *n.* **1** animal fat softened by melting. **2** any thick oily substance, especially to lubricate the moving parts of machinery. — (grēs, grēz) *vb.* **greas·ing, greased** to lubricate with grease.

greas·y (grē′sē, grē′zē) *adj.* **greas·i·er,** **greas·i·est** containing, or covered in, grease.

great (grāt) *adj.* **1** very large in size, quantity, intensity, or extent. **2** very enjoyable. **3** most important. **4** enthusiastic: *She is a great reader.*

Great Bear *n.* a constellation of stars in the northern hemisphere.

●**Great Brit·ain** (grāt brit′n) *n.* the largest island in EUROPE, containing ENGLAND, WALES, and SCOTLAND, and forming, together with NORTHERN IRELAND, the UNITED KINGDOM.

●**Great Lakes** a chain of five lakes between CANADA and the UNITED STATES: Superior, Michigan, Huron, Erie, and Ontario.

●**Great Wall of China** the world's longest defensive wall stretching for 1,500 miles (2,400 km). It was built more than 2,000 years ago.

great- *in compounds* indicating a family relationship that is one generation more remote than that of the base word: *great-grandmother; great-granddaughter.*

●**Greece** (grēs). See Supplement, **Countries.**

●**Greece** (grēs), **ancient** was a great civilization which started about 2,500 years ago. In the city of Athens, the Greeks established a new form of government, democracy. They developed arts and sciences and built fine buildings.

Many fine examples of Greek "red figured" and "black figured" painted pottery have survived.

A silver four drachma ancient Greek coin, the "owl" piece, symbolizing the owl-eyed goddess, Athena.

The building of the Parthenon in Athens, completed in 432 B.C., it was one of the finest of all Greek temples.

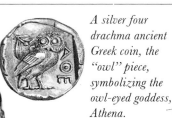

A bronze head of Aphrodite (left), the goddess of love, beauty, and fertility.

greed (grēd) *n.* an excessive and selfish desire for something.

greed·y (grēd′ē) *adj.* **greed·i·er, greed·i·est** filled with greed.

Greek (grēk) *n.* **1** the official language of GREECE. **2** a native or inhabitant of GREECE. – *adj.* of GREECE, its people, or their language.

green (grēn) *adj.* **1** of the color between yellow and blue in the visible spectrum, the color of the leaves of most plants. **2** covered with grass, bushes, etc.: *green fields.* **3** consisting mainly of leaves: *green salad.* **4** showing concern for, or designed to be harmless to, the environment. **5** extremely jealous or envious: *He was green with envy when he saw my new bike.* – *n.* **1** any shade of color between yellow and blue in the visible spectrum. **2** an area of grass, especially in a public place; an area of specially prepared turf. **3** (in *plural*) vegetables with edible green leaves and stems.

green bean *n.* Same as **string bean.**

green·house (grēn′hous′) *n.* a building with walls and a roof made of glass, used for growing plants.

greenhouse effect *n.* the effect of masses of man-made carbon dioxide and other gases in the atmosphere, preventing the escape of the sun's heat reflected by the earth's surface, causing warming of the earth's atmosphere.

● **Green·land** (grēn′land) is a large island in the north ATLANTIC belonging to Denmark.

● **Green·wich** (gren′ij, gren′ich) near London, is where the 0° line of longitude runs.

greet (grēt) *vb.* **greet·ing, greet·ed** to address or welcome, especially in a friendly way.

grem·lin (grem′lən) *n.* an imaginary mischievous creature blamed for faults in machinery or electronic equipment.

● **Gre·na·da** (grə-nād′ə). See Supplement, **Countries.**

grew. See **grow.**

grey (grā) Same as **gray.**

grey·hound (grā′hound′) *n.* a breed of dog capable of great speed.

grid (grid) *n.* **1** a pattern of lines that cross each other to form squares. **2** a network of cables and pipes for supplying power to a large area.

grid·dle (grid′l) *n.* a flat iron plate which is heated for baking or frying.

grid·i·ron (grid′ī′ərn) *n.* a football field.

grief (grēf) *n.* great sorrow and unhappiness.

grieve (grēv) *vb.* **griev·ing, grieved 1** to feel grief. **2** to upset or distress.

grill (gril) *n.* a framework on which food can be broiled over open heat. – *vb.* **grill·ing, grilled** to cook on a grill.

grim (grim) *adj.* **grim·mer, grim·mest 1** stern and unsmiling. **2** not changing: *She showed grim determination.* **3** depressing; gloomy.

gri·mace (grim′əs, grim-ās′) *n.* an ugly twisting of the face, expressing pain or disgust, or for amusement.

grime (grīm) *n.* dirt or soot. – *adj.* **grim·y** (grī′mē), **grimier, grimiest.**

grin (grin) *vb.* **grin·ning, grinned** to smile broadly, showing the teeth. – *n.* a broad smile. something unpleasant without complaining.

grind (grīnd) *vb.* **grind·ing, ground** (ground) to crush into small particles or powder between two hard surfaces.

grip (grip) *vb.* **grip·ping, gripped 1** to take or keep a firm hold of. **2** to capture the imagination or attention of. – *n.* **1** a firm hold. **2** a part that can be gripped.

grip·ping (grip′ing) *adj.* holding the attention.

gris·ly (griz′lē) *adj.* **gris·li·er, gris·li·est** horrible; ghastly; gruesome.

grit (grit) *n.* **1** small hard particles of stone, sand, etc. **2** (*informal*) courage and determination. – *vb.* **grit·ting, grit·ted** to clench the teeth to overcome pain. – *adj.* **grit·ty** (grit′ē), **grit·ti·er, grit·ti·est.**

grits (grits) *n.* (*plural*) coarsely ground hominy, used as a cereal or in baking.

griz·zly bear (griz′lē bâr′) *n.* a large fierce gray or brown North American bear.

groan (grōn) *vb.* **groan·ing, groaned** to make a long deep sound in the back of the throat,

Greenwich in London is at 0 degrees longitude. A place halfway round the world from Greenwich is 180 degrees longitude.

The racing greyhound is the fastest breed of dog and can achieve speeds of more than 35mph (60km/h). Greyhounds are depicted on ancient Egyptian wall paintings hunting gazelles. Today, many greyhounds compete on oval racetracks where they chase a mechanical hare.

expressing pain, distress, disapproval, etc. − *n.* the sound of groaning.

gro·cer (grō′sər) *n.* a person selling food and general goods.

gro·cer·y (grō′sə-rē, grōs′rē) *n.* **gro·cer·ies** **1** a grocer's store. **2** (in *plural*) merchandise, especially food, sold in a grocer's store.

groom (grōōm) *n.* **1** a person who looks after horses and cleans stables. **2** a bridegroom. − *vb.* **groom·ing, groomed 1** to clean and brush generally: *to groom horses*. **2** to train or prepare for a specific purpose or job.

groove (grōōv) *n.* a long narrow channel.

grope (grōp) *vb.* **grop·ing, groped** to search by feeling about with the hands, for example in the dark.

gross (grōs) *adj.* **1** total, with no deductions: *What is your gross income?* **2** very great; glaring: *gross negligence*. − *n.* gross twelve dozen, 144.

gro·tesque (grō-tesk′) *adj.* very unnatural or strange-looking, so as to cause fear or laughter.

grot·to (grät′ō) *n.* **grot·tos** or **grot·toes** a cave, especially small and picturesque.

ground[1] (ground) *n.* **1** the solid surface of the earth; soil; land. **2** (in *plural*) an area of land attached to or surrounding a building: *They strolled around the grounds.* **3** the range of subjects under discussion: *The book covers a lot of ground.* **4** (usually in *plural*) a reason or justification: *He had grounds for complaint.* − *vb.* **ground·ing, ground·ed 1** to base or establish: *They grounded their theory on the facts.* **2** to hit the seabed or shore and remain stuck.

ground control *n.* the people or equipment on the ground that direct and monitor the flight of an aircraft or spacecraft.

ground[2]. See **grind.**

group (grōōp) *n.* a number of people or things gathered or classed together. − *vb.* **group·ing, grouped** to form a group.

grouse (grous) *n.* **grouse** or **grous·es** a small plump game bird with feathered legs.

grow (grō) *vb.* **grow·ing, grew** (grōō), **grown** (grōn) **1** to develop into a larger, more mature form. **2** (of hair, nails, etc.) to increase in length or develop. **3** to cultivate plants. − *vb.* **grow up** to become, or be in the process of becoming, an adult.

growl (groul) *vb.* **growl·ing, growled** (of animals) to make a deep rough sound in the throat, showing hostility.

grown *adj.* fully developed and mature.

grown-up (grō′nup′) *n. & adj.* adult.

growth (grōth) *n.* **1** the process or rate of growing. **2** an increase in economic activity or profitability: *Tourism is a growth industry.*

grub (grub) *n.* the wormlike larva of an insect, especially a beetle.

Grub (larva)

The grub is an early stage in the development of the beetle. Drastic changes in appearance at various stages of growth can be seen in several animal groups — insects (as here) and in amphibians (for example frogs). This change of form is called metamorphosis.

grudge (gruj) *vb.* **grudg·ing, grudged** to feel a sense of unfairness or resentment at. − *n.* a long-standing feeling of resentment.

gruel·ing or **gruel·ling** (grōō′ling) *adj.* exhausting.

grue·some (grōō′səm) *adj.* inspiring horror.

gruff (gruf) *adj.* (of a voice) deep; unfriendly.

grum·ble (grum′bəl) *vb.* **grum·bling, grum·bled 1** to complain in a bad-tempered way. **2** to make a low rumbling sound. − *n.* **1** a complaint. **2** a rumbling sound.

grum·py (grum′pē) *adj.* **grum·pi·er, grum·pi·est** ill-tempered.

grunt (grunt) *vb.* **grunt·ing, grunt·ed** to make a low rough sound in the back of the throat. − *n.* the sound of grunting.

guar·an·tee (gar′ən-tē, gär′ən-tē) *n.* **1** a formal promise, especially by a manufacturer to repair or replace an article found to be faulty. − *vb.* **guar·an·tee·ing, guar·an·teed 1** to promise. **2** to ensure.

guard (gärd) *vb.* **guard·ing, guard·ed 1** to protect from danger or attack, or from escaping. **2** to take precautions to prevent: *He guarded against robbery.* − *n.* **1** a person or group whose job is to provide protection from danger or attack, or to prevent escape. **2** anything that gives protection.

guard·ed *adj.* **1** cautious. **2** protected.

guard·i·an (gärd′ē-ən) *n.* a person legally responsible for the care of another.

The **groom** in bridegroom has nothing to do with horses. The original word was *gome*, meaning "man." The word *grome* crept in by mistake.

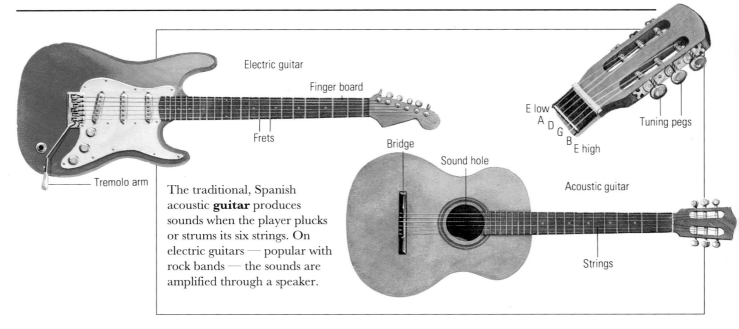

Electric guitar
Finger board
Frets
Tremolo arm
Bridge
Sound hole
E low
A
D
G
B
E high
Tuning pegs
Acoustic guitar
Strings

The traditional, Spanish acoustic **guitar** produces sounds when the player plucks or strums its six strings. On electric guitars — popular with rock bands — the sounds are amplified through a speaker.

A **guerrilla** (sometimes spelled guerilla) is a member of an irregular army whereas gorilla is the name of particular species of great ape.

●**Gua·te·ma·la** (gwät′ə-mäl′ə). See Supplement, **Countries**.

guer·ril·la or **gue·ril·la** (gə-ril′ə) *n.* a member of a small, unofficial army that makes surprise attacks, as against government troops.

guess (ges) *vb.* **guess·ing, guessed** to make an estimate or form an opinion, based on little or no information. – *n.* an estimate.

guest (gest) *n.* **1** a person who receives hospitality from another. **2** a person staying at a hotel, etc.

guide (gīd) *vb.* **guid·ing, guid·ed 1** to lead, direct, or show the way to. **2** to advise or influence. – *n.* **1** a person who leads the way, for example for tourists. **2** a book containing information on a particular subject.

guide dog *n.* a dog specially trained to guide a blind person safely.

guide·line (gīd′līn′) *n.* (often in *plural*) an indication of what future action is recommended.

guil·lo·tine (gil′ə-tēn′, gē′ə-tēn′) *n.* an instrument for beheading, consisting of a large heavy blade sliding rapidly down between two upright posts. – *vb.* **guil·lo·tin·ing, guil·lo·tined** to use a guillotine on.

guilt (gilt) *n.* **1** shame or regret for doing wrong. **2** the state of having done wrong or having broken a law.

guilt·y (gil′tē) *adj.* **guil·ti·er, guil·ti·est 1** judged to be responsible for a crime or wrongdoing. **2** feeling or showing guilt: *He gave her a guilty look.* – *adv.* **guilt·i·ly** (gil′tə-lē).

●**Gui·nea** (gin′ē). See Supplement, **Countries**.

●**Gui·nea-Bis·sau** (gin′ē-bə-sou′). See Supplement, **Countries**.

gui·tar (gə-tär′, gi′tär′) *n.* a musical instrument with a long neck and strings that are plucked or strummed. – *n.* **gui·tar·ist** (gə-tär′əst).

gulf (gulf) *n.* a stretch of sea with land on most sides; a huge bay.

gull (gul) *n.* any of various species of sea bird with white, gray, and black feathers.

gul·let (gul′ət) *n.* the tube by which food passes from the mouth to the stomach.

gul·li·ble (gul′ə-bəl) *adj.* easily tricked.

gul·ly (gul′ē) *n.* **gul·lies** a channel worn by running water.

gulp (gulp) *vb.* **gulp·ing, gulped 1** to swallow food or drink eagerly or in large mouthfuls. **2** to make a swallowing motion. – *n.* **1** a swallowing motion. **2** a mouthful.

gum¹ (gum) *n.* the firm flesh around the roots of the teeth.

gum² (gum) *n.* **1** a sticky substance from the trunks and stems of certain trees and plants. **2** a sticky preparation made for chewing.

gun (gun) *n.* **1** any weapon that fires bullets or shells from a metal tube. **2** any instrument which forces something out under pressure: *He used a spray gun to paint the car.*

gun·fire (gun′fīr′) *n.* the sound of firing.

gun·pow·der (gun'pou'dər) *n.* an explosive mixture of potassium nitrate, sulphur, and charcoal.

gur·gle (gur'gəl) *vb.* **gur·gling, gur·gled** to make a bubbling noise. – *n.* a bubbling noise.

gu·ru (gōō'rōō', goor'ōō) *n.* a HINDU or SIKH spiritual leader.

gush (gush) *vb.* **gush·ing, gushed** to flood out with sudden force. – *n.* a sudden flood.

gut (gut) *n.* the intestines; the insides of a person or animal. – *vb.* **gut·ting, gut·ted 1** to take the guts out of, especially fish. **2** to destroy the insides of: *Fire gutted the building.*

●**Gu·ten·berg** (gōōt'n-burg'), **Johann** (1400-1468) was the German inventor of printing with movable type.

gut·ter (gut'ər) *n.* a channel for carrying away rainwater, fixed to the edge of a roof or built between a sidewalk and a road.

guy[1] (gī) *n.* (*informal*) a man or boy.

guy[2] (gī) *n.* a rope or wire used to hold something, especially a tent, firm or steady.

●**Guy·a·na** (gī-an'ə, gī-än'ə). See Supplement, **Countries**.

gym·na·si·um (jim-nā'zē-əm) *n.* **gymnasiums** or **gym·na·si·a** (jim-nā'zē-ə) a building or room with equipment for physical exercise.

gym·nast (jim'nast', jim'nəst) *n.* a person skilled in gymnastics.

gym·nas·tics (jim-nas'tiks) *n.* **1** (*plural*) physical exercises designed to strengthen the body and improve agility. **2** (*singular*) the practice or sport of these exercises.

gy·ne·col·o·gy (gī'nə-käl'ə-jē) *n.* the branch of medicine dealing with disorders of the female body, especially the reproductive system. – *n.* **gy·ne·col·o·gist** (gī'nə-käl'ə-jəst).

Gyp·sy (jip'sē) *n.* **Gyp·sies** a member of a traveling people, originally from northwest INDIA, now scattered throughout EUROPE and NORTH AMERICA.

gy·rate (jī'rāt') *vb.* **gy·rat·ing, gy·rat·ed** to move with a circular or spiraling motion.

gy·ro·scope (jī'rə-skōp') *n.* an apparatus consisting of a circular frame containing a disk which spins rapidly around a freely moving axis. The axis keeps the same position regardless of any movement of the frame. Gyroscopes are used in ships' compasses, etc.

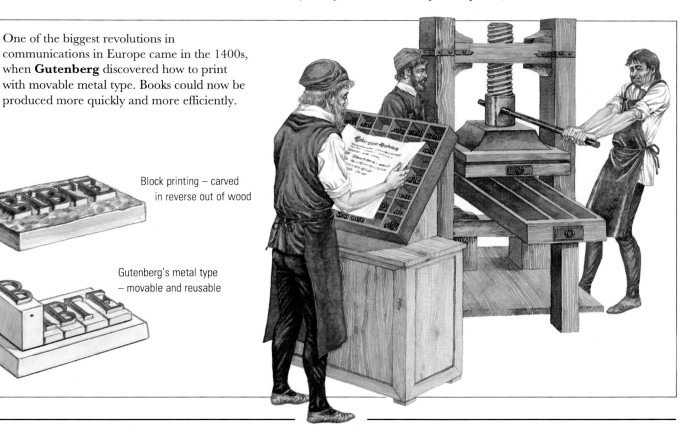

One of the biggest revolutions in communications in Europe came in the 1400s, when **Gutenberg** discovered how to print with movable metal type. Books could now be produced more quickly and more efficiently.

Block printing – carved in reverse out of wood

Gutenberg's metal type – movable and reusable

H h

hab·it (hab′ət) *n.* **1** a regular activity or tendency which is hard to give up. **2** a long loose garment worn by monks and nuns.

hab·i·tat (hab′ə-tat′) *n.* the natural home of an animal or plant.

ha·ci·en·da (hä′sē-en′də) *n.* in Spanish-speaking countries, a large estate.

hack·er (hak′ər). *n.* a person skilled at programming and solving problems with a computer.

had. See **have**.

had·dock (had′ək) *n.* **haddock** a small, North Atlantic saltwater fish used as food.

Ha·des (hād′ēz) *n.* See **Myths and Legends**.

hag·gard (hag′ərd) *adj.* looking very tired and ill, because of pain, worry, etc.

hag·gle (hag′əl) *vb.* **hag·gling, hag·gled** to bargain over or argue about a price.

hail[1] (hāl) *n.* frozen rain falling as ice from the clouds. − *vb.* **hail·ing, hailed** (of hail) to fall from the clouds.

hail[2] (hāl) *vb.* **hail·ing, hailed** **1** to call out to attract attention: *to hail a taxi*. **2** to greet.

hail·stone (hāl′stōn′) *n.* a single lump of hail.

hair (hâr) *n.* **1** a threadlike strand that grows from the skin of animals and humans. **2** a mass of these strands, especially on a person's head.

hair-rais·ing (hâr′rā′zing) *adj.* extremely frightening.

hair·y (hâr′ē) *adj.* **hair·i·er, hair·i·est** **1** covered in hair. **2** (*informal*) dangerous.

● **Hai·ti** (hāt′ē). See Supplement, **Countries**.

hale (hāl) *adj.* strong and healthy: *hale and hearty*.

half (haf, häf) *n.* **halves** (havz, hävz) **1** one of two equal parts which together form a whole. **2** the fraction equal to one divided by two. − *adj.* forming or equal to half. − *adv.* **1** to the extent or amount of one half. **2** almost.

half·back (haf′bak′) *n.* **1** in football, a player or position immediately behind the line of scrimmage. **2** in soccer, field hockey, etc. a position immediately behind the forwards.

half-broth·er (haf′bruth′ər) or **half-sist·er** (haf′sis′tər) *n.* a brother or sister through one parent.

Hail is formed when raindrops in a storm cloud are repeatedly lifted by air currents and frozen high in the cloud. When heavy enough, the hailstones fall out of the cloud.

half-heart·ed (haf'härt'əd) *adj.* not eager.

half-sister. See **half-brother.**

half·way (haf-wā') *adj.* & *adv.* at or to a point at an equal distance from two other points.

hal·i·but (hal'ə-bət) *n.* **halibut** a kind of large, flat, saltwater fish used for food.

hall (hôl) *n.* **1** a room or passage just inside the entrance to a house. **2** a building or large room, used for concerts, meetings, etc.

Hal·low·een or **Hal·low·e'en** (hal'ō-ēn') *n.* the evening of October 31.

ha·lo (hā'lō) *n.* **ha·los** or **ha·loes** a ring of light around the head of a saint or angel in paintings, etc.

halt (hôlt) *n.* a short or temporary stop. *– vb.* **halt·ing, halt·ed** to stop or cause to stop.

hal·ter (hôl'tər) *n.* a rope or strap for holding and leading a horse by its head.

halve (hav, häv) *vb.* **halv·ing, halved 1** to divide into two equal parts. **2** to reduce by half.

ham¹ (ham) *n.* the top part of the back leg of a pig, salted and smoked and used as food.

ham² (ham) *n.* (*informal*) **1** a bad actor. **2** an amateur radio operator.

ham·bur·ger (ham'bur'gər, ham'bər-gər) *n.* a flat, round patty of finely chopped beef.

ham·let (ham'lət) *n.* a small village.

ham·mer (ham'ər) *n.* **1** a tool with a heavy metal head on the end of a handle, used for driving nails into wood. **2** the part of a bell, piano, clock, etc. that hits against some other part, making a noise. *– vb.* **ham·mer·ing, ham·mered 1** to hit with a hammer. **2** to strike loudly and repeatedly.

ham·mock (ham'ək) *n.* a piece of canvas, netting, etc. hung at each end and used as a bed.

ham·per¹ (ham'pər) *vb.* **ham·per·ing, ham·pered** to hinder the progress or movement of.

ham·per² (ham'pər) *n.* a large basket with a lid.

ham·ster (ham'stər) *n.* a small rodent with a short tail and pouches in its mouth for storing food, often kept as a pet.

hand (hand) *n.* **1** the part of the body at the end of each arm, with a thumb, four fingers, and a palm. **2** help; assistance: *Let me give you a hand.* **3** a needle or pointer on a clock, watch, or gauge. **4** (*informal*) applause: *Give him a big hand.* **5** See **Horse Terms.** *– vb.* **hand·ing, hand·ed** to deliver or give using the hands. *– at hand* nearby; about to happen.

hand·bag (hand'bag') *n.* a small bag for carrying money and other small items.

hand·book (hand'bag') *n.* a short manual or guidebook.

hand·cuffs (han'kufs', hang'kufs') *n.* (*plural*) a pair of steel rings, joined by a short chain, for locking around the wrists of a prisoner.

● **Han·del** (han'dəl), **George Frederick** (1685-1759) was a German-born composer who wrote the *Messiah*.

han·di·cap (han'di-kap') *n.* a physical, mental, or social disability.

han·di·capped (han'di-kapt') *adj.* physically or mentally disabled. *– n.* (*plural*) handicapped people.

han·di·craft (han'dē-kraft') *n.* an activity which requires skillful use of the hands.

hand·ker·chief (hang'kər-chəf, hang'kər-chēf') *n.* **hand·ker·chiefs** a small piece of cloth used for blowing your nose.

han·dle (hand'l) *n.* the part of an object by which it is held so that it may be used or operated. *– vb.* **han·dling, han·dled 1** to touch, hold, move, or operate with the hands. **2** to deal with or manage, especially successfully or in the correct way.

han·dle·bars (hand'l-bärz') *n.* (*plural*) a curved metal bar with handles at each end, for steering a bicycle or motorcycle.

han·dler (hand'lər) *n.* **1** a person who trains and controls an animal, especially a dog. **2** a person who handles something.

hand·out (han'dout') *n.* money or food given to people in need.

hand·rail (hand'rāl') *n.* a railing used as a support on a staircase, balcony, etc.

hand·some (han'səm) *adj.* **1** good-looking, often in a masculine way; attractive. **2** generous: *He made a handsome donation.*

hand·y (han'dē) *adj.* **hand·i·er, hand·i·est 1** conveniently placed and easy to use. **2** skillful.

hang (hang) *vb.* **hang·ing, hung** (hung) (except for sense **2** which has **hanged** for its past tenses) **1** to fasten or be fastened from above. **2** to suspend by a rope around the neck until dead: *The prisoner hanged himself.* **3** to remain without moving, especially in the air or in a threatening way. **4** to droop: *She hung her head in shame.* *– n.* the way something falls or droops.

han·gar (hang'ər, hang'gər) *n.* a large shed in which aircraft are kept.

Parts of the body were once used as measuring units. A finger's breadth was a digit and two digits made an inch. From thumb to little finger (stretched) was a span. A yard was measured from the nose to the fingertip of an outstretched arm.

HANGING, DANGLING & MISPLACED
"Gazing out of the window, the boys were playing" or "Sleeping in my bed, the burglar startled me." These are examples of "hanging" participles not relating to the correct subject. The boys are not gazing out of the window; and the burglar is not sleeping in my bed. Correct sentences would be: "Gazing out of the window, I saw the boys were playing," and "Sleeping in my bed, I was startled by the burglar."

hang·er (hang′ər, hang′gər) *n.* a metal, wooden, or plastic frame on which clothes are hung to keep their shape.

hang glid·er (hang′glīd′ər) *n.* a large, light, metal frame with cloth stretched across it, which flies using air currents, with a harness hanging below it for the pilot. – *n.* **hang glid·ing** ((hang′glīd′ing).

hang-up (hang′up′) *n.* (*informal*) an emotional problem.

● **Han·ni·bal** (han′ə-bəl) (247-183 B.C.) was a general from Carthage who led his army over the Alps to invade ROME.

● **Ha·nuk·kah** (hän′ə-kə, k͟hän′ə-kə) is a Jewish festival, usually in December, that lasts eight days. It is celebrated by the lighting of candles.

hap·haz·ard (hap-haz′ərd) *adj.* done by chance; random. – *adv.* at random.

hap·pen (hap′ən) *vb.* **hap·pen·ing, hap·pened 1** to take place or occur. **2** to have the good or bad luck to: *I happened to meet him.*

hap·py (hap′ē) *adj.* **hap·pi·er, hap·pi·est 1** feeling or showing pleasure or contentment. **2** willing. – *n.* **hap·pi·ness** (hap′i-nəs).

hap·pi·ly (hap′ə-lē) *adv.* **1** in a happy way.

ha·rangue (hə-rang′) *n.* a loud, forceful speech to persuade people to do something. – *vb.* **ha·rangu·ing, ha·rangued** to give such a speech to.

ha·rass (hə-ras′, har′əs) *vb.* **ha·rass·ing, ha·rassed** to annoy or trouble constantly or often. – *adj.* **ha·rassed**. – *n.* **ha·rass·ment** (hə-ras′mənt, har′əs-mənt).

har·bor (här′bər) *n.* a place of shelter for ships. – *vb.* **har·bor·ing, har·bored** to give shelter or protection to; to hide: *to harbor a criminal.*

hard (härd) *adj.* **1** firm or solid: *The rock was hard beneath her feet.* **2** difficult to do, understand, solve, or explain: *He found his French homework hard to do.* **3** harsh; cruel: *She had a hard heart.* **4** causing or suffering hardship: *They were hard times.* **5** (of information) proven and reliable: *hard evidence.* – *adv.* **1** with great effort or energy: *I told him to work hard.* **2** with difficulty; as a result of great effort: *It was a hard-won victory.* – *n.* **hard·ness** (härd′nəs).

hard disk *n.* a metal disk with a magnetic coating, used for storing data in a computer.

hard·en (härd′n) *vb.* **hard·en·ing, hard·ened 1** to make or become hard or harder. **2** to become less sympathetic.

hard·ened (härd′nd) *adj.* toughened through experience and not likely to change.

hard·ly (härd′lē) *adv.* only with difficulty; scarcely: *She could hardly keep her eyes open.*

hard·ship (härd′ship′) *n.* suffering and pain.

hard·ware (härd′wâr′) *n.* **1** metal goods such as pots, cutlery, tools, etc. **2** the mechanical and electronic equipment used in computing.

hard·wood (härd′wood′) *n.* wood from a slow-growing deciduous tree, such as the oak or ash.

har·dy (här di) *adj.* **har·di·er, har·di·est** tough; strong; able to bear difficult conditions.

● **Har·dy** (härd′ē), **Thomas** (1840-1928) was an English novelist and poet whose works include *Tess of the d'Urbervilles.*

hare (hâr) *n.* an animal like a rabbit but slightly larger, with longer legs and ears.

harm (härm) *n.* physical or mental injury or damage. – *vb.* **harm·ing, harmed** to cause harm to.

har·mon·i·ca (här-män′i-kə) *n.* a small, rectangular, musical wind instrument with metal reeds along one side.

har·mo·nize (här-mə-nīz′) *vb.* **harmonizing, harmonized** to add notes to a simple tune to form harmonies.

har·mo·ny (här′mə-nē) *n.* **har·mo·nies 1** in music, a pleasing combination of two or more notes produced at the same time. **2** agreement in opinions and feelings: *The friends worked together in harmony.*

har·ness (här′nəs) *n.* **1** a set of leather straps used to attach a cart to a horse, and to control the horse's movements. **2** a similar set of straps for attaching to a person's body. *– vb.* **har·ness·ing, har·nessed 1** to put a harness on. **2** to control and make use of, especially to produce power.

harp (härp) *n.* a large, three-sided musical instrument with a series of strings stretched vertically across it, played by plucking the strings with the fingers. *– n.* **harp·ist** (här′pəst).

har·poon (här-pōōn′) *n.* a spear with barbs, fastened to a rope, used for catching whales.

harp·si·chord (härp′si-kôrd′) *n.* a keyboard instrument in which the strings are plucked mechanically when the player presses the keys.

harsh (härsh) *adj.* **1** grating; unpleasant to the senses. **2** strict, cruel, or severe.

har·vest (här′vəst) *n.* **1** the gathering in of ripened crops, usually in late summer or early autumn. **2** the crops gathered. *– vb.* **har·vest·ing, har·vest·ed** to gather crops.

has. See **have**.

has·sle (has′əl) (*informal*) *n.* trouble and inconvenience. *– vb.* **has·sling, has·sled** to annoy or bother.

haste (hāst) *n.* great urgency of movement.

has·ten (hās′ən) *vb.* **has·ten·ing, has·tened** to move or do something quickly.

hast·y (hā′stē) *adj.* **hast·i·er, hast·i·est** hurried; done without enough preparation.

● **Has·tings** (hā′stingz)**, Battle of** In 1066 near a town called Hastings on the southeast coast of England, the Normans under William the Conqueror defeated the English and became rulers of ENGLAND.

hat (hat) *n.* a covering for the head, usually worn outdoors.

hatch[1] (hach) *n.* **1** a door covering an opening in a ship's deck. **2** a door in an aircraft or spacecraft.

hatch[2] (hach) *vb.* **hatch·ing, hatched 1** to break out of an egg. **2** to plan or devise in secret: *They hatched up a scheme to rob the bank.*

hatch·et (hach′ət) *n.* a small ax.

hate (hāt) *vb.* **hat·ing, hat·ed** to dislike very much. *– n.* great dislike.

hate·ful (hāt′fəl) *adj.* causing or deserving great dislike.

ha·tred (hā′trəd) *n.* extreme dislike.

haugh·ty (hôt′ē) *adj.* **haugh·ti·er, haugh·ti·est** very proud; arrogant.

haul (hôl) *vb.* **haul·ing, hauled** to pull with great effort or difficulty. *– n.* **1** the distance to be traveled: *It's only a short haul.* **2** an amount gained at any one time, for example of fish caught in a single net.

haunt (hônt) *vb.* **haunt·ing, haunt·ed 1** (of a ghost) to live in a place or visit a person or place regularly. **2** (of unpleasant thoughts) to keep coming back to: *I was haunted by the memory of his leaving.* *– n.* (*informal*) a favorite place that is visited frequently.

● **Ha·van·a** (hə-van′ə) is the capital of CUBA.

At the Battle of Hastings in 1066 the English fought on foot with axes and spears — no match for the Normans, who fought on horseback.

PRONUNCIATION SYMBOLS			
ə	away	lemon	focus
a	fat	oi	boy
ā	fade	oo	foot
ä	hot	ōō	moon
âr	fair	ou	house
e	met	th	think
ē	mean	th	this
g	get	u	cut
hw	which	ur	hurt
i	fin	w	witch
ī	line	y	yes
îr	near	yōō	music
ô	often	yoor	pure
ō	note	zh	vision

have (hav) *vb.* **has** (haz), **hav·ing, had 1** to possess or own. **2** to receive, obtain, or take. **3** to think of or hold in the mind: *I've had an idea.* **4** to experience, enjoy, or suffer: *I have a headache.* **5** to be in a certain state: *The book has a page missing.* **6** to take part in or hold: *Let's have a party.* **7** to be required to: *I had to run fast.* **8** to show or feel: *She pleaded with him to have pity.* – *vb.* *(auxiliary)* used with past participles of verbs to show that an action has been completed: *I have seen the movie.*

ha·ven (hā′vən) *n.* a place of safety or rest.

hav·oc (hav′ək) *n.* great destruction or damage.

●**Ha·wai·i** (hə-wä′ē, hə-wī′ē, hə-wô′ē). See Supplement, **U.S.A.**

hawk (hôk) *n.* a bird of prey with short, rounded wings, and which is believed to have very good eyesight.

haw·thorn (hô′thôrn′) *n.* a thorny tree with pink or white flowers and red berries.

●**Haw·thorne** (hô′thôrn′), **Nathaniel** (1804-1864) was an American novelist.

hay (hā) *n.* grass that has been cut and dried, used as food for cattle.

hay fever *n.* an allergic reaction to pollen, which causes sneezing and sore eyes.

●**Haydn** (hīd′n), **Franz** (1732-1809) was an Austrian composer.

haz·ard (haz′ərd) *n.* something that is likely to cause harm or danger.

haz·ard·ous (haz′ərd-əs) *adj.* dangerous.

haze (hāz) *n.* a thin mist, cloud of dust, or smoke which makes it difficult to see.

haz·y (hā′zē) *adj.* **haz·i·er, haz·i·est 1** misty. **2** vague; not clear. – *adv.* **haz·i·ly** (hā′zə-lē).

ha·zel (hā′zəl) *n.* a small tree or shrub on which nuts grow; its wood. – *adj.* of a green-brown color: *hazel eyes.*

he (hē) *pron.* a male person or animal already referred to.

head (hed) *n.* **1** the top or front part of a body, containing the eyes, nose, mouth, brain, and ears. **2** the head, thought of as the center of intelligence, imagination, ability, etc.: *Use your head!* **3** the person with the most authority in an organization, country, etc.: *He is head of the civil service.* **4** the top or upper part of something, as a nail or pin. **5** the top part of a plant which produces leaves or flowers. **6** the side of a coin bearing the head of a person: *Heads or tails?* – *vb.* **head·ing, head·ed 1** to be at the front of or top of: *We headed the line.* **2** to be in charge of. **3** to move in a certain direction.

head·ache (hed′āk′) *n.* a pain in the head.

head·gear (hed′gir′) *n.* anything worn on the head.

head·light (hed′līt′) *n.* a powerful light on the front of a vehicle.

head·line (hed′līn′) *n.* a title of a newspaper article, written in large letters.

head·quar·ters (hed′kwôrt′ərz, hed′kwôrt′ərz) *n.* the center of an organization or group from which activities are controlled.

head·wind (hed′wind′) *n.* a wind that is blowing toward someone.

heal (hēl) *vb.* **heal·ing, healed** to make or become healthy or normal again. – *n.* **heal·er.**

health (helth) *n.* the state of being physically and mentally fit and free from illness.

health·y (hel′thē) *adj.* **health·i·er, health·i·est 1** having or showing good health. **2** in a good state: *a healthy economy.* **3** promoting good health: *healthy food.*

heap (hēp) *n.* a collection of things in an untidy pile or mass: *a heap of logs.* – *vb.* **heap·ing, heaped** to collect or be collected in a heap.

Scientists have listed nearly 300 different kinds of **hawk**. Falcons form one group. Hawking, or falconry, is an ancient sport dating back to ancient China and very popular in the Middle Ages. It is the art of training these birds of prey to hunt game. The trainer (falconer) hoods the bird to calm it and attaches leg straps (*jesses*).

A 16th-century falconer

hear (hîr) *vb.* **hear·ing, heard** (hurd) **1** to perceive sounds with the ear; to listen to. **2** to be told about or informed of: *I have heard about the problems.* **3** to be contacted by letter or telephone: *I heard from my Swedish friend last week.* – *n.* **hear·er**.

hear·ing (hîr′ing) *n.* **1** the sense by which sound is perceived. **2** the distance within which something can be heard. **3** an opportunity to state a case: *They gave him a fair hearing.*

hear·say (hîr′sā′) *n.* rumor; gossip.

hearse (hurs) *n.* a car used for carrying a coffin at a funeral.

heart (härt) *n.* **1** the hollow, muscular organ inside the chest, which pumps blood around the body. **2** this organ considered as the center of a person's thoughts, emotions, etc. **3** the central or most important part. **4** a usually red symbol representing the heart, with two curves at the top meeting in a point at the bottom. **5** a playing card with a red symbol of such a shape on it. – **by heart** by or from memory.

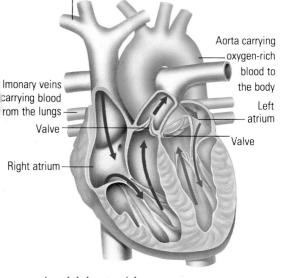

Superior vena cava carrying blood from the body

Aorta carrying oxygen-rich blood to the body

lmonary veins carrying blood from the lungs

Left atrium

Valve

Valve

Right atrium

An adult heart weighs about 11 ounces (300g) and beats over 100,000 times a day.

In an adult person the **heart** works at between 70 and 80 beats a minute. The blood carries OXYGEN from the LUNGS and energy from the food we eat. Arteries carry this rich red blood to feed the body. Veins carry away "tired blood" to the heart to be recharged with OXYGEN.

heart attack *n.* a sudden failure of the heart to work properly, causing severe pain and sometimes death.

heart·beat (härt′bēt′) *n.* one complete pulse of the heart pumping blood.

heart·less (härt′ləs) *adj.* cruel; very unkind.

hearth (härth) *n.* the floor of a fireplace, or the area surrounding it.

heat (hēt) *n.* **1** the state of being hot; the high temperature produced by something. **2** warmth of feeling, especially anger or excitement. **3** in sports, a preliminary race or contest which eliminates competitors. – *vb.* **heat·ing, heat·ed** to make or become hot.

● Heat is a form of energy. It travels in three ways: by conduction (a conductor such as a metal iron allows heat to pass through it); by convection (molecules in the air carrying heat from a radiator); by radiation (the sun's heat travels in the form of electromagnetic waves).

heat·ed (hēt′əd) *adj.* **1** having been made hot or warm. **2** angry or excited.

heat·er (hēt′ər) *n.* an apparatus for heating a room, building, water in a tank, etc.

heat·wave (hēt′wāv′)*n.* a period of unusually hot weather.

hea·then (hē′thən) *n.* a person who does not follow one of the established religions.

heave (hēv) *vb.* **heav·ing, heaved** to lift or pull with great effort.

heav·en (hev′ən) *n.* **1** the place believed to be the abode of God, angels, and the righteous after death. **2** (usually in *plural*) the sky.

heav·en·ly (hev′ən-lē) *adj.* **1** very pleasant; beautiful. **2** of or from heaven or the sky.

The heart is a pump which powers our blood or circulatory system, which is a network of blood vessels. Arteries take blood rich in food and oxygen from the heart to all parts of the body. Blood which has used up all its oxygen is carried back to the heart by veins.

heav·y (hev′ē) *adj.* **heav·i·er, heav·i·est**
1 having great weight. **2** great in size, amount, force, power, etc.: *There was heavy traffic in the city.* **3** severe, intense, or excessive: *heavy fighting.* – *n.* **heav·i·ness** (hev′ē-nəs). –
heavy going difficult or slow progress.

He·brew (hē′brōō′)*n.* **1** the ancient language of the Hebrews, revived and spoken in a modern form by Jews in ISRAEL. **2** a member of an ancient people, originally based in Palestine. – *adj.* of the Hebrew language or people.

● **He·brews** (hē′brōōz′) The Jewish people were once known as Hebrews or Israelites. There were 12 tribes descended from ABRAHAM.

hec·tare (hek′târ′, hek′tär′) *n.* a metric unit of land measurement, equivalent to 10,000 square meters, or about $2^1/_2$ acres.

● **Hec·tor** (hek′tər) in Greek mythology, was a prince of TROY, killed by ACHILLES.

hedge (hej) *n.* a fence or boundary formed by bushes and shrubs planted close together. – *vb.* **hedg·ing, hedged 1** to avoid making a decision or giving a clear answer. **2** to enclose an area of land with a hedge.

hedge·hog (hej′hôg′, hej′häg′) *n.* a small insect-eating animal with a thick spiny coat.

heel (hēl) *n.* **1** the rounded back part of the foot. **2** the part of a sock, shoe, etc. that covers the heel. – *vb.* **heel·ing, heeled** (of dogs) to walk at, or go to, a person's side.

He·gi·ra (hə-jī′rə, hej′ə-rə) *n.* See **Religious Terms**.

heif·er (hef′ər) *n.* a young cow, especially one that has not yet had a calf.

height (hīt) *n.* **1** the distance from the bottom of something to the top. **2** a distance above the ground from a recognized point, especially above sea level. **3** the most intense part.

height·en (hīt′n) *vb.* **height·en·ing, height·ened** to make or become higher, greater, or stronger.

heir (âr) *n.* a person who by law receives wealth, a title, etc. when the owner or holder dies.

held. See **hold**.

● **Hel·en** (hel′ən) of TROY, in Greek mythology, was the wife of a Greek king, but ran away with PARIS, prince of Troy, thus starting the Trojan War.

PRONUNCIATION SYMBOLS		
ə **a**way	**le**mon	**fo**cus
a f**a**t	oi	b**oy**
ā f**a**de	oo	f**oo**t
ä h**o**t	ōō	m**oo**n
âr f**air**	ou	h**ou**se
e m**e**t	th	**th**ink
ē m**ea**n	<u>th</u>	**th**is
g **g**et	u	c**u**t
hw **wh**ich	ur	h**ur**t
i f**i**n	w	**w**itch
ī l**i**ne	y	**y**es
îr n**ear**	yōō	m**u**sic
ô **o**ften	yoor	p**u**re
ō n**o**te	zh	vi**s**ion

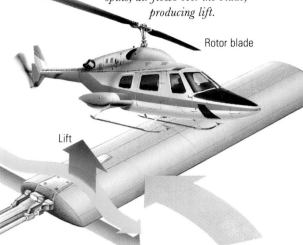

A helicopter has spinning rotor blades, which provide both "lift" and "thrust." The blade has the same airfoil shape as a plane's fixed wing. As it spins, air flows over the blade, producing lift.

Rotor blade

Lift

he·li·cop·ter (hel′ə-käp′tər, hē′lə-käp′tər) *n.* an aircraft, lifted and propelled by rotating blades, which takes off and lands vertically, and can hover above the ground.

he·li·um (hē′lē-əm) *n.* a light gas (symbol **He**) which does not burn, used in balloons and airships.

hell (hel) *n.* believed to be the place of punishment for the wicked after death.

he'll (hēl) he will.

helm (helm) *n.* the wheel or tiller by which a ship is steered. – **at the helm** in control.

hel·met (hel′mət) *n.* a hard, protective covering for the head.

help (help) *vb.* **help·ing, helped 1** to assist; to contribute toward making difficulties, pain, etc. less severe; to improve a situation. **2** to prevent or control. – *n.* **1** a person or thing that helps. **2** a remedy or relief. – *n.* **help·er.**

help·ful (help′fəl) *adj.* giving help; useful.

help·less (hel′pləs) *adj.* weak and defenseless.

hem (hem) *n.* a bottom edge of a piece of clothing, folded over and sewn down.

● **Hem·ing·way** (hem′ing-wā′), **Ernest** (1899-1961) was an American author and journalist.

hem·i·sphere (hem′ə-sfīr′) *n.* **1** one half of a sphere. **2** one half of the earth's sphere divided by the equator into the **Northern Hemisphere** and the **Southern Hemisphere**. A line through GREENWICH,

England, divides the earth into the **Eastern Hemisphere** and the **Western Hemisphere**.

hem·lock (hem′läk′) *n.* **1** a poisonous plant with small white flowers and a spotted stem. **2** a poison made from this plant.

hemp (hemp) *n.* **1** a plant producing coarse fiber and a drug. **2** the coarse fiber obtained from this plant, used to make rope and fabrics.

hen (hen) *n.* a female bird, especially a fowl.

hence (hens) *adv.* **1** for this reason. **2** from this time: *a few days hence.*

henge (henj) *n.* a circular prehistoric monument consisting of large upright stones.

●**Hen·ry** (hen′rē) is the name of eight English kings.

He·phaes·tus (hi-fes′təs, hi-fē′stəs). See **Myths and Legends**.

hep·ta·gon (hep′tə-gän′) *n.* a shape with seven sides. − *adj.* **hep·tag·o·nal** (hep-tag′ən-l).

her (hur) *pron. & adj.* (of or belonging to) a female person or animal, or a thing thought of as female, for example a ship. − *adj.* of or belonging to a female person or animal, or a thing thought of as female.

He·ra (hîr′ə, her′ə). See **Myths and Legends**.

Her·a·cles (her′ə-klēz′). See **Myths and Legends**.

her·ald (her′əld) *vb.* **her·ald·ing, her·ald·ed** to be a sign of the approach of; to proclaim.

herb (urb) *n.* a plant, especially one used to flavor food or to make medicines.

her·bi·vore (ur′bə-vôr′, ur′bə-vōr′) *n.* an animal that eats only plants.

Her·cu·les (hur′kyə-lēz′). See **Myths and Legends**.

herd (hurd) *n.* a large group of animals.

here (hîr) *adv.* at, in, or to this place: *Put the dish down here.* − *n.* this place.

he·red·i·tar·y (hə-red′ə-ter′ē) *adj.* able to be passed on from parents to children.

he·red·i·ty (hə-red′ət-ē) *n.* **he·red·i·ties** the passing on of physical and mental traits.

Her·mes (hur′mēz′). See **Myths and Legends**.

her·mit (hur′mət) *n.* a person who lives alone.

her·mit crab *n.* a small crab that lives in another creature's discarded shell.

he·ro (hîr′ō, hē′rō) *n.* **heroes 1** a person who is admired for bravery and courage. **2** the main male character in a story, play, etc.

●**Herod** (her′əd) **the Great** (74-4 B.C.) was a ruler in Judea who, according to the New Testament, ordered all the male infants in the town of BETHLEHEM to be slaughtered.

he·ro·ic (hi-rō′ik) *adj.* very brave.

The rear parts of a hermit crab are not protected by a shell, so for protection it backs into the disused shell of a sea snail.

Stonehenge — a prehistoric circle of standing stones on Salisbury Plain, England — is the most dramatic and most famous of such early monuments. It was probably built as a place of worship to the sun and moon sometime after 1800 B.C. The illustration shows how the massive stone blocks were dragged to the site on wooden rollers.

PRONUNCIATION SYMBOLS			
ə	away	lemon	focus
a	fat	oi	boy
ā	fade	oo	foot
ä	hot	ōō	moon
âr	fair	ou	house
e	met	th	think
ē	mean	th	this
g	get	u	cut
hw	which	ur	hurt
i	fin	w	witch
ī	line	y	yes
îr	near	yōō	music
ô	often	yoor	pure
ō	note	zh	vision

her·o·ine (her′ō-ən) *n*. **1** a woman admired for her bravery and courage. **2** the main female character in a play, story, etc.

he·ro·ism (her′ō-iz′əm) *n*. the qualities of a hero, especially great bravery.

her·on (her′ən) *n*. a large gray and white wading bird, with long legs, and a long neck.

her·ring (her′ing) *n*. **herring** or **herrings** a small, silvery saltwater fish valued as food.

hers (hurz) *pron*. someone or something belonging to her. − **of hers** of or belonging to her.

her·self (hur-self′) *pron*. **1** the reflexive form of **her** and **she**: *She made herself a dress.* **2** used for emphasis: *She did it herself.* **3** (also **by herself**) alone; without help.

hes·i·tate (hez′ə-tāt′) *vb*. **hes·i·tat·ing, hes·i·tat·ed** to be slow or unwilling in speaking or acting, especially because of uncertainty. − *n*. **hes·i·ta·tion** (hez′ə-tā′shən).

het·er·o·sex·u·al (het′ə-rō-sek′shōō-əl) *adj*. sexually attracted to the opposite sex.

hex·a·gon (hek′sə-gän′) *n*. a shape with six sides. − *adj*. **hex·ag·o·nal** (hek-sag′ən-l).

hi·ber·nate (hī′bə-nāt′) *vb*. **hi·ber·nat·ing, hi·ber·nat·ed** (of certain animals) to pass the winter in a sleeplike state with the temperature of the body and heartbeat lower than normal. − *n*. **hi·ber·na·tion** (hī′bər-nā′shən).

hic·cup or **hic·cough** (hik′up′, hik′əp) *n*. a gasp caused by a spasm in the diaphragm.

hid·den (hid′ən) *adj*. difficult to see.

hide¹ (hīd) *vb*. **hid·ing, hid** (hid), **hid·den** (hid′n) **1** to put in a place not easily found. **2** to keep secret. **3** to make difficult to see; to obscure: *There were trees hiding the house.* **4** to keep one's self out of sight.

hide² (hīd) *n*. the skin of an animal.

hid·e·ous (hid′ē-əs) *adj*. extremely ugly.

hi·ero·glyph (hīr′ə-glif′) *n*. a picture or symbol used to represent a word, syllable, or sound, especially in the ancient Egyptian language.

hi·ero·glyph·ic (hīr′ə-glif′ik) *adj*. of or relating to hieroglyphs.

Early Egyptian hieroglyphs represented different objects. Later ones stood for sounds, rather than things.

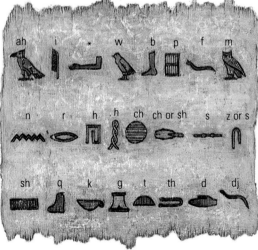

hi-fi (hī-fī′) *n*. equipment that reproduces sound accurately.

high (hī) *adj*. **1** reaching up to or situated at a great distance from the bottom. **2** of a particular height: *The tree is about 20 feet high.* **3** great; intense: *There was a high wind.* **4** very important in rank or position: *She ran for a high office.* − *adv*. at or to a height; in or into a raised position. − *n*. a high point.

high·brow (hī′brou′) *adj*. (of art, literature, etc.) suitable for intellectuals.

high fidelity *n*. the reproduction of sound with great accuracy.

high·land (hī′lənd) *n*. (often in *plural*) a high, mountainous area.

high·light (hī′līt′) *n*. **1** the best or most memorable part of something. **2** a bright spot or area in a painting. − *vb*. **high·light·ing, high·light·ed** to draw attention to or emphasize.

high·ly (hī′lē) *adv*. **1** very: *Snow is highly unlikely today.* **2** with approval: *She speaks highly of him.*

high-pow·ered (hī-pou′ərd) *adj*. **1** very powerful; very efficient. **2** hard-working.

high school *n*. a school attended after elementary or junior high school, often from grades nine to twelve.

high tide *n*. the time when the tide is farthest up the shore; the highest level reached by the water at this time.

high·way (hī′wā′) *n*. a public road, especially a large or main road.

high·way·man (hī′wā′mən) *n*. **high·way·men** (hī′wā′mən, hī′wā′men′) a robber, usually on horseback, who formerly attacked and robbed travelers.

hi·jack (hī′jak′) *vb*. **hi·jack·ing, hi·jacked** to take control of and force to go to a place chosen by the hijacker: *to hijack an airplane.* − *n*. **hi·jack·er.** − *n*. **hi·jack·ing.**

hike (hīk) *n*. a long walk, usually in the country, often carrying equipment in a knapsack on one's back. − *vb*. **hik·ing, hiked** to go on a hike. − *n*. **hik·er.**

hi·lar·i·ous (hil-âr′ē-əs) *adj*. very funny.

hill (hil) *n*. **1** an area of high land, smaller than a mountain. **2** a slope on a road.

hilt (hilt) *n*. the handle of a sword or dagger.

him (him) *pron*. a male person or animal.

him·self (him-self′) *pron*. **1** the reflexive form of **him** and **he**: *He taught himself to dance.* **2** used for emphasis: *He did it himself.* **3** (also **by himself**) alone; without help.

* vowel sound does not exist in English

●**Hi·ma·la·yas** (him′ə-lā′əz, hə-mäl′yəz) This mountain range is the highest in the world and separates INDIA from CHINA.

hind (hīnd) *adj.* at the back: *The dog sat up on its hind legs.*

hin·der (hin′dər) *vb.* **hin·der·ing, hin·dered** to delay or keep back; to prevent progress.

Hindi (hin′dē) *n.* one of the official languages of India, spoken in northern India.

Hin·du (hin′dōō) *n.* a person who practices Hinduism. – *adj.* of Hindus or Hinduism.

Hin·du·ism (hin′dōō-iz′əm) *n.* the main religion of INDIA, which includes worship of many gods and a belief in reincarnation.

hinge (hinj) *n.* the movable joint by which a door is fastened to its frame, and on which the door turns when it opens or closes. – *vb.* **hing·ing, hinged** **1** to hang or turn on. **2** to depend on: *Our success hinges on your help.*

hint (hint) *n.* **1** an indirect suggestion; a clue: *She gave him a hint to help him answer the question.* **2** a very small amount; a slight impression or suggestion of: *She wore a hint of perfume.* – *vb.* **hint·ing, hint·ed** to suggest, especially slightly or indirectly.

hip (hip) *n.* the upper, fleshy part of the thigh just below the waist.

Hip·po·crat·ic oath (hip′ə-krat′ik ōth′) *n.* an oath taken by doctors by which they agree to observe a code about rules of behavior.

hip·po·pot·a·mus (hip′ə-pät′ə-məs) *n.* **hip·po·pot·a·mus·es** or **hip·po·pot·a·mi** (hip′ə-pät′ə-mī′) a large African mammal with very thick, wrinkled skin and short legs, living near rivers and lakes.

hire (hīr) *vb.* **hir·ing, hired** **1** to employ to do some work. **2** to use temporarily in exchange for money. – *n.* an act of hiring.

●**Hi·ro·shi·ma** (hir′ə-shē′mə, hi-rō′shə-mə) is a Japanese city on which the first atomic bomb was dropped on August 6, 1945.

hir·sute (hur′sōōt′, hîr′sōōt′) *adj.* hairy; shaggy.

his (hiz) *adj.* of or belonging to a male person or animal. – *pron.* someone or something belonging to him.

His·pan·ic (his-pan′ik) *adj.* of SPAIN, the Spanish, or other Spanish-speaking countries and peoples, as Mexican. – *n.* a Spanish-speaking American of Latin-American descent.

hiss (his) *n.* a sharp sound like that of a long *s.*

– *vb.* **hiss·ing, hissed** to make a hiss.

his·tor·i·an (his-tôr′ē-ən, his-tōr′ē-ən, his-tär′ē-ən) *n.* a person who studies or writes about history.

his·tor·ic (his-tôr′ik, his-tär′ik) *adj.* famous or important in history; significant.

his·tor·i·cal (his-tôr′i-kəl, his-tär′i-kəl) *adj.* of or about history; of or about people or events from history: *She writes historical novels.*

his·to·ry (his′tə-rē) *n.* **his·to·ries** **1** the study of events that happened in the past. **2** a record or account of past events and developments.

hit (hit) *vb.* **hit·ting, hit** **1** to strike with a blow, missile, etc. **2** to knock against something, especially hard or violently: *She hit her head on the door.* **3** to drive with a stroke: *He hit the ball over the fence.* – *n.* **1** a blow, stroke, or shot. **2** something that is popular or successful.

HISTORY HIGHLIGHTS

B.C.

ca. 2600	Pyramids built in Egypt
400	Age of Pericles began in Athens
4	Probable birth of Jesus at Bethlehem

A.D.

476	End of Western Roman Empire
800	Charlemagne crowned Holy Roman Emperor
1066	Norman invasion of England
1096	Start of first Crusade
1260	Kublai Khan became ruler of China
1341-1351	Bubonic plague (Black Death) ravaged Europe
1453	Turks captured Constantinople: end of Eastern Roman Empire
1492	Christopher Columbus landed in the New World
1588	English fleet defeated the Spanish Armada
1620	*Mayflower* sailed to America with Pilgrim Fathers
1642-1646	English Civil War
1775-1783	American Revolutionary War
1789	French Revolution
1815	Napoleon finally defeated at Waterloo
1861-1865	American Civil War
1914-1918	World War I
1917	Russian Revolution
1939-1945	World War II
1945	Atomic bombs dropped on Hiroshima and Nagasaki
1947	India became independent
1949	Mao Zedong established Communist China
1969	First person landed on the moon
1980	AIDS virus first recognized
1990	Germany was reunited
1991	USSR was officially dissolved. Civil War in Yugoslavia

hitch (hich) *vb.* **hitch·ing, hitched 1** to fasten with a piece of rope. **2** (*informal*) to hitchhike: *They hitched a ride.* – *n.* a minor, temporary delay or difficulty: *The concert went without a hitch.*

hitch·hike (hich′hīk′) *vb.* **hitch·hik·ing, hitch·hiked** to travel by means of free rides in other people's vehicles. – *n.* **hitch·hik·er.**

● **Hit·ler** (hit′lər), **Adolf** (1889-1945) was the *Führer*, or leader, of Nazi Germany during WORLD WAR II. Millions of people died in Nazi death camps.

● **HIV** (āch′ī′vē′) *abbreviation* human immunodeficiency virus, any of several types of virus that cause AIDS.

hive (hīv) *n.* **1** a box for housing bees. **2** a colony of bees living in a hive. **3** place where people are working busily.

hoard (hôrd, hōrd) *n.* a store of money, food, treasure, usually hidden away for use in the future. – *vb.* **hoard·ing, hoard·ed** to store for use in the future. – *n.* **hoard·er.**

hoarse (hôrs, hōrs) *adj.* (of the voice) rough and croaking, especially because of a sore throat or too much shouting.

hoax (hōks) *n.* a trick played to deceive people. – *vb.* **hoax·ing, hoaxed** to trick or deceive with a hoax. – *n.* **hoax·er.**

hob·ble (häb′əl) *vb.* **hob·bling, hob·bled** to walk with difficulty, taking unsteady steps.

hob·by (häb′ē) *n.* **hob·bies** an activity or occupation done in spare time for relaxation and pleasure.

hock¹ (häk) *n.* a joint on the hind leg of a horse, sheep, etc. that corresponds to the human ankle.

hock² *vb.* (*informal*) to pawn.

hock·ey (häk′ē) *n.* **1** Same as **ice hockey. 2** (*British*) same as **field hockey.**

hoe (hō) *n.* a long-handled tool with a metal blade at one end, used for loosening soil, removing weeds, etc. – *vb.* **hoe·ing, hoed** to use a hoe.

hog (hôg, häg) *n.* **1** a grown male pig. **2** (*informal*) a greedy or selfish person. – *vb.* **hog·ging, hogged** (*informal*) to use or occupy selfishly.

hoist (hoist) *vb.* **hoist·ing, hoist·ed 1** to lift or heave up using ropes and pulleys. **2** See **Flag Terms.** – *n.* equipment for lifting heavy objects.

---

hoard and **horde**
The first word means a store or stockpile, whereas "horde" is a large group of people or insects.

● **Hol·bein** (hol′bīn′), **Hans** (1497-1543) was a German painter who worked in England.

hold¹ (hōld) *vb.* **hold·ing, held** (held) **1** to have or keep in your hand, or in something else stated. **2** to support, keep, or stay in a particular position or state: *Despite all his pulling, the knot held firm.* **3** to detain: *She was held in prison for three months.* **4** to contain or be able to contain: *The bottle holds three liters.* **5** to cause to take place; to conduct: *Let's hold a meeting.* **6** to have or possess: *She holds the world record.* – *n.* power; influence: *She has a hold over him.* – *n.* **hold·er.** – **get hold of 1** to manage to speak to: *He's impossible to get hold of on weekends.* **2** to get, buy, or obtain: *I can't get hold of that color of paint anywhere.* – *vb.* **hold down** to manage to keep: *He cannot hold down a job.* – *vb.* **hold off** to delay, not begin: *I hope the rain holds off.* – *vb.* **hold on 1** to keep: *I'm holding on to the receipt in case I want to get my money back.* **2** (especially when telephoning) to wait: *Can you hold on a minute?* – *vb.* **hold out** to continue to stand firm, resist difficulties: *We can hold out against the enemy until they surrender.* **2** to continue to demand or fight for something: *I held out for more money.* – *vb.* **hold with** to approve of.

hold² (hōld) *n.* the place where cargo is stored in ships and aircraft.

hole (hōl) *n.* **1** an opening or gap in or through something: *There was a hole in the wall.* **2** an animal's burrow. **3** (*informal*) an unpleasant or gloomy place. **4** in golf, the round can-shaped hollow in the middle of the green into which the ball is hit. – *adj.* **hol·ey** (hō′lē), **hol·i·er, hol·i·est.**

hol·i·day (häl′ə-dā′) *n.* (often in *plural*) **1** a day on which school and ordinary business are suspended in order to celebrate an event or to honor a person. **2** (*British*) a vacation.

● **Hol·i·day** (häl′ə-dā′), **Billie** (1915-1959) was an American JAZZ singer.

● **Hol·land** (häl′ənd). See **Netherlands.**

hol·low (häl′ō) *adj.* **1** containing an empty space; not solid. **2** sunken: *The old man had hollow cheeks.* **3** (of sounds) echoing as if made in a hollow place. **4** worthless; insincere. – *n.* a small valley or depression in the land. – *vb.* **hol·low·ing, hol·lowed** to make a hole or hollow in.

Otto I, who became King of Germany in 936, wanted to revive the old Roman Empire. In 962 he had the pope crown him Emperor Augustus, of the **Holy Roman Empire**. By 1100 the Holy Roman Empire stretched from the North Sea and the Baltic, nearly to the Mediterranean.

Otto I, also known as Otto the Great, the first Holy Roman Emperor

hol·ly (häl′ē) *n.* **hol·lies** a tree or shrub with dark, shiny evergreen leaves, usually with prickly edges and red berries.

hol·ly·hock (häl′ē-häk′) *n.* a tall garden plant with colorful flowers.

●**Hol·ly·wood** (häl′ē-wood′) is a district of Los Angeles, California, center of the motion picture industry.

●**Holmes** (hōmz), **Sherlock** is the detective who appears with his friend Dr. Watson in the stories of Arthur Conan DOYLE (1859-1930).

ho·lo·caust (hō′lə-kôst′, häl′ə-kôst′) *n.* **1** large-scale destruction and loss of life. **2 Holocaust** the mass murder of Jews by the Nazis during WORLD WAR II.

ho·lo·gram (häl′ə-gram′, hō′lə-gram′) *n.* a kind of photograph created by lasers, which shows objects in three dimensions.

hol·ster (hōl′stər) *n.* a leather case for a pistol, usually worn attached to a belt around a person's hips.

ho·ly (hō′lē) *adj.* **ho·li·er, ho·li·est** **1** belonging to or associated with God or gods; sacred. **2** pure and perfect; saintly. – *n.* **ho·li·ness** (hō′lē-nəs).

●**Holy Roman Empire** is the name of the German empire founded by Otto I in 962 and which continued in name until 1806.

home (hōm) *n.* **1** the place where someone lives. **2** the country or area someone originally comes from. **3** a place where a thing first occurred or was first invented: *America is the home of the hamburger.* **4** an institution where people who need care or rest live, for example orphans or old people. – *adj.* **1** of your home, country, or family. **2** (of a sports contest) played on your team's own ground rather than the opponent's. – *adv.* at or to a person's home. – *vb.* **hom·ing, homed 1** (of a bird) to return home safely. **2** to be directed accurately toward a target. – **at home** feeling at ease or familiar with a place – **bring home to** to make quite obvious to. – **home free** having achieved a goal. – **home away from home** a place where you feel as comfortable, relaxed, and happy as you feel at home.

home·less (hōm′ləs) *n.* (*plural*) people without a place to live. – *adj.* (of people) having nowhere to live.

ho·me·op·a·thy (hō′mē-äp′ə-thē) *n.* a way of healing a patient with medicines made from natural substances.

Around the fire, poets of ancient Greece, such as Homer, told stories of shipwrecks and the capture of cities, and warriors dying bravely.

SOME HOMOPHONES	
flour	flower
here	hear
lie	lye
mail	male
meet	meat
nose	knows
sum	some
there	their
wait	weight
ware	wear

PRONUNCIATION SYMBOLS		
ə away	lemon	focus
a fat	oi	boy
ā fade	oo	foot
ä hot	ōō	moon
âr fair	ou	house
e met	th	think
ē mean	<u>th</u>	this
g get	u	cut
hw which	ur	hurt
i fin	w	witch
ī line	y	yes
îr near	yōō	music
ô often	yoor	pure
ō note	zh	vision

● **Ho·mer** (hō′mər) was a Greek poet who lived around 800 B.C. He composed two great poems, the *Iliad* and the *Odyssey*.

home·sick (hōm′sik′) *adj.* missing one's home or country.

hom·o·nym (häm′ə-nim′) *n.* a word having the same sound and spelling as another word, but a different meaning, for example *kind* (helpful) and *kind* (sort).

hom·o·phone (häm′ə-fōn′) *n.* a word having the same sound as another, but a different spelling and meaning, as in *bear* and *bare*.

ho·mo·sex·u·al (hō′mə-sek′shōō-əl) *adj.* sexually attracted to the same sex.

● **Hon·du·ras** (hän-door′əs, hän-dyoor′əs). See Supplement, **Countries**.

hon·est (än′əst) *adj.* truthful; trustworthy; not likely to steal, cheat, or lie.

hon·est·ly (än′əst-lē) *adv.* **1** in an honest way. **2** truly.

hon·est·y (än′ə-stē) *n.* the state of being honest.

hon·ey (hun′ē) *n.* **hon·eys** the edible, thick, sweet substance made by bees.

hon·ey·comb (hun′ē-kōm′) *n.* the wax structure in which bees store honey.

hon·ey·moon (hun′ē-mōōn′) *n.* a vacation taken by a newly married couple.

hon·ey·suck·le (hun′ē-suk′əl) *n.* a climbing garden shrub with sweet-smelling flowers.

● **Hong Kong** (hông′ kông′, häng′ käng′) is a tiny British colony off the coast of CHINA. It will be returned to the Chinese government in 1997.

hon·or (än′ər) *n.* **1** great respect or public regard. **2** a pleasure or privilege: *It was an honour to accompany him.* – *vb.* **hon·or·ing, hon·ored 1** to respect greatly. **2** to give an award, title, or honor as a mark of respect.

hon·or·a·ble (än′ə-rə-bəl) *adj.* deserving or worthy of honor.

hon·our (än′ər) *n.* a British spelling of **honor**.

hood (hood) *n.* **1** a usually loose covering for the whole head, often attached to a coat at the collar. **2** the hinged cover over a car's engine.

hoof (hoof, hōōf) *n.* **hooves** or **hoofs** (hoovz, hōōvz) the horny part at the end of the feet of horses, cows, etc.

hook (hook) *n.* a small piece of plastic, wood, or metal shaped like a J, used for catching and holding things. – *vb.* **hook·ing, hooked** to catch with or fasten with a hook.

hoop (hoop, hōōp) *n.* a ring of metal around barrels, or a large wooden ring used as a toy.

hoot (hōōt) *n.* **1** the call of an owl. **2** the sound of a car horn, siren, steam whistle, etc.

hop (häp) *vb.* **hop·ping, hopped 1** (of people) to jump on one leg. **2** (of other animals) to jump on both or all legs. – *n.* a short jump.

hope (hōp) *n.* **1** a desire for something, with some confidence of obtaining it. **2** a person, thing, or event upon which someone is relying for help. – *vb.* **hop·ing, hoped** to wish or desire that something may happen.

hope·ful (hōp′fəl) *adj.* **1** feeling hope. **2** giving a reason for hope; likely to succeed.

hope·ful·ly (hōp′fə-lē) *adv.* **1** in a hopeful way. **2** it is to be hoped: *Hopefully, they won't be late.*

hope·less (hōp′ləs) *adj.* **1** not likely to be successful. **2** not likely to be cured: *a hopeless case.* **3** not good: *I'm hopeless at drawing.*

horde (hôrd, hōrd) *n.* a crowd or large group.

ho·ri·zon (hə-rī′zən) *n.* the line at which the earth and the sky seem to meet.

hor·i·zon·tal (hôr′ə-zänt′l, här′ə-zänt′l) *adj.* at right angles to vertical; parallel to the horizon.

hor·mone (hôr′mōn′) *n.* a chemical substance produced by some part of a plant or animal body, which has a specific effect on that body.

horn (hôrn) *n.* **1** either of a pair of hard, bony objects which grow on the heads of cows, sheep, etc.; a deer's antlers. **2** the bonelike substance of which horns are made. **3** any of other brass wind instruments, especially the French horn. **4** an apparatus for making a warning sound, especially on a vehicle.

hor·net (hôr′nət) *n.* a large wasp which can give a very bad sting.

hor·o·scope (hôr′ə-skōp′, här′ə-skōp′) *n.* a description of a person's future based on the position of the stars and planets at the time of birth.

hor·ri·ble (hôr′ə-bəl, här′ə-bəl) *adj.* **1** causing horror, dread, or fear. **2** unpleasant.

hor·rid (hôr′əd, här′əd) *adj.* **1** horrible or shocking. **2** unpleasant.

hor·ror (hôr′ər, här′ər) *n.* great fear, loathing, or disgust. – *adj.* (of a movie) violent and frightening.

horse (hôrs) *n.* a large, four-legged animal with a long mane and tail, ridden for pleasure and used to pull carts and do other work.

horse·pow·er (hôrs′pou′ər) *n.* a unit for measuring the power of an engine.

horse·rad·ish (hôrs′rad′ish) *n.* a plant with a long, white, sharp-tasting root.

horse·shoe (hôrs′shoo′) *n.* a piece of curved iron nailed to the bottom of a horse's hoof.

hor·ti·cul·ture (hôrt′i-kul′chər) *n.* the science and art of gardening.

hose (hōz) *n.* a flexible tube for directing water.

Percheron

The **horse** was one of the first animals to be tamed, valued for its speed and strength. The horse we know today developed over millions of years from a creature the size of a fox with short legs and four-toed feet. It was called Eohippus, or "dawn horse."

Thoroughbred   Arabian   Morgan

American Saddlebred

Camargue   Lusitano   Lipizzaner

EVOLUTION OF THE HORSE

Eohippus — Four toes

Mesohippus — Three toes

Merychippus — Large middle toe

Pliohippus — One toe

Equus caballus

HORSE TERMS

aids the signals given by a rider to guide a horse or pony.

bit the metal or rubber device attached to the bridle and placed in the horse's mouth.

bridle the part of the saddlery placed over the horse's head.

colt a young, male ungelded horse.

dressage a horse's performance of set maneuvers.

eventing a (usually) three-day competition: dressage, cross-country, and show jumping.

filly a female foal.

gait a pace of a horse: walk, trot, canter, gallop.

geld to remove a male horse's testicles.

hand a unit of measurement of a horse's height.

mare an adult female horse.

near side the left side of a horse

off side the right side of a horse.

stallion an adult male horse.

The different parts of a horse are called points. Together, the points of a horse make up its conformation — the way it looks. A horse of good conformation looks good because its parts are of the right size and shape.

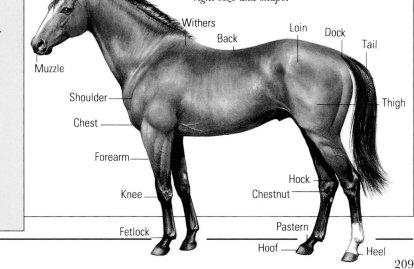

Forelock Ear Poll Mane

Muzzle

Shoulder

Chest

Forearm

Knee

Fetlock

Hoof Heel

Withers Back Loin Dock Tail

Thigh

Hock

Chestnut

Pastern

hos·pice (häs′pəs) *n.* **1** a home which cares for people suffering from incurable diseases. **2** a shelter for travelers.

hos·pit·a·ble (häs-pit′ə-bəl) *adj.* showing kindness to guests or strangers.

hos·pit·al (häs′pit′l) *n.* a place where people who are sick receive care and nursing.

hos·pit·al·i·ty (häs′pə-tal′ət-ē) *n.* a friendly welcome for guests or strangers.

host[1] (hōst) *n.* **1** a person who receives and entertains guests or strangers in their own home. **2** a person who introduces performers, etc. on a television or radio show. – *vb.* **host·ing, host·ed** to act as a host.

host[2] (hōst) *n.* a very large number.

hos·tage (häs′tij) *n.* a person who is held prisoner as a guarantee that the conditions of an agreement will be carried out.

hos·tel (häs′təl) *n.* **1** a building that provides overnight accommodations as a charity, especially for the homeless. **2** a youth hostel.

host·ess (hō′stəs) *n.* **1** a woman who entertains guests in her home. **2** a woman employed at a restaurant to seat customers. **3** a stewardess.

hos·tile (häs′təl, häs′tīl′) *adj.* **1** unfriendly; aggressive. **2** of or belonging to an enemy.

hos·til·i·ty (häs-til′ət-ē) *n.* **hos·til·i·ties 1** aggression. **2** (in *plural*) acts of war; battles.

hot (hät) *adj.* **hot·ter, hot·test 1** having or producing a great deal of heat. **2** having a higher temperature than is normal or desirable. **3** (of food) spicy; causing a burning sensation on the tongue. **4** very popular: *a hot new song.* **5** radioactive.

hot dog *n.* a hot frankfurter served in a long, split, soft roll.

ho·tel (hō-tel′) *n.* a large house or building where travelers or people on vacation receive food and lodging in return for payment.

hound (hound) *n.* any of various dogs that were originally bred for hunting. – *vb.* **hound·ing, hound·ed** to chase or bother relentlessly.

hour (our) *n.* **1** 60 minutes. There are 24 hours in a day. **2** a point in time: *They woke at an early hour.* **3** the time allowed or fixed for some activity: *I work strictly office hours.*

hour·ly (our′lē) *adj.* happening, done, or computed for every hour. – *adv.* every hour.

house (hous) *n.* **hou·ses** (hou′zəz, hou′səz) **1** a building in which people, especially a single family, live. **2** a building used for a particular purpose: *We visited the opera house.* **3** a business

firm: *She works as an editor for a publishing house.* **4** a family, especially an important or noble one: *Mary Queen of Scots was a member of the House of Stuart.* – (houz) *vb.* **hous·ing, housed 1** to provide with a house or similar shelter. **2** to store.

house·boat (hous′bōt′) *n.* a boat that is built to be lived in, and is usually moored in one place.

house·fly *n.* **house·flies** a fly that lives in or around houses and feeds on garbage.

house·hold (hous′hōld′, hou′sōld′) *n.* the people who live together in a house and make up a family.

House of Commons *n.* in Britain, the lower, elected assembly in Parliament.

House of Lords *n.* in Britain, the upper assembly in Parliament, made up of nobility and bishops.

House of Representatives *n.* the lower house or chamber of CONGRESS and of many state legislatures.

hous·ing (hou′zing) *n.* houses as a group.

Chinese thatch house of 2000 B.C.

People in prehistoric times lived in caves. The first **houses** were shelters made of mud and branches. Later people learned to make bricks from clay, to quarry stone, and to use timber. And so until quite recent times the style of houses has been influenced by building materials available locally, including straw and reeds (for thatch), flints, and clay (for adobe). Weather, too, has influenced house styles.

An Indonesian house built on stilts

●**Hous·ton** (hyŌŌ′stən, yŌŌ′stən) is the largest city in Texas and a major center for space research.

hov·el (huv′əl, häv′əl) *n.* a small, dirty, dismal dwelling.

hov·er (huv′ər, häv′ər) *vb.* **hov·er·ing, hov·ered** 1 to remain in the air without moving in any direction. 2 to move around while still remaining near a person or thing.

how (hou) *adv.* 1 in what way; by what means: *How did it happen?* 2 to what extent: *How old is he?* 3 in what condition, especially of health: *How is she feeling now?* 4 to what extent is something good or successful: *How was your trip?*

how·ev·er (hou-ev′ər) *adv.* in spite of that; nevertheless: *I tried my best; however, I failed.*

howl (houl) *n.* a long, loud cry, for example made by a wolf or dog. – *vb.* **howl·ing, howled** 1 to make a long, loud cry or similar wailing noise. 2 to cry or laugh loudly.

●**Huang Ho** (hwäng′hō′) or **Yellow River**, is

An American timber house

English Tudor house (1500s)

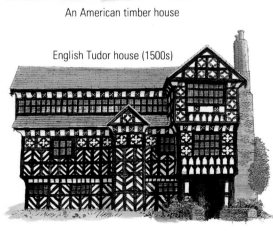

the second longest river in China (3,010 miles or 4,845 km).

hud·dle (hud′l) *vb.* **hud·dling, hud·dled** 1 to heap or crowd together closely. 2 to sit curled up. – *n.* 1 a confused mass or crowd. 2 a secret or private conference: *They went into a huddle.*

●**Hud·son** (hud′sən), **Henry** (*ca.*1550-1611) was an English explorer after whom the Hudson River in New York State is named.

hue (hyŌŌ) *n.* a color or shade.

hug (hug) *vb.* **hug·ging, hugged** 1 to hold tightly in your arms, especially to show affection. 2 to keep close to: *The ship hugged the shore.* – *n.* a tight grasp with the arms.

huge (hyŌŌj, yŌŌj) *adj.* very large.

●**Hughes** (hyŌŌz), **Langston** (1902-1967) was an African-American poet.

●**Hu·go** (hyŌŌ′gō), **Victor** (1802-1885) was a French writer, author of *Les Misérables*.

Hu·gue·not (hyŌŌ′gə-nät′) *n.* a French Protestant of the 1500s and 1600s.

hull[1] (hul) *n.* the frame or body of a ship or airship.

hull[2] (hul) *n.* the outer covering of certain fruit and vegetables, especially the pod of beans and peas. – *vb.* **hull·ing, hulled** to remove the hulls from.

hum (hum) *vb.* **hum·ming, hummed** to make a sound as though you are saying "m-m-m-m" without opening your mouth.

hu·man (hyŌŌ′mən, yŌŌ′mən) *adj.* 1 of or belonging to people. 2 having the better qualities of people, for example in being kind, thoughtful, etc. – *n.* a person.

hu·mane (hyŌŌ-mān′, yŌŌ-mān′) *adj.* kind.

hu·man·i·ty (hyŌŌ-man′ət-ē, yŌŌ-man′ət-ə) *n.* **humanity** 1 the human race. 2 the qualities of humans, especially in being kind or merciful: *We appealed to their humanity.*

hu·man·kind (hyŌŌ′mən-kind′, yŌŌ′mən-kind′) *n.* human beings as a race.

hum·ble (hum′bəl, um′bəl) *adj.* 1 modest, not vain. 2 low in status or condition.

●**Hum·boldt** (hum′bōlt′), **Baron Alexander von** (1767-1835) was a German explorer.

HUMBLE PIE
Humble comes from the Latin, meaning "lowly" or "mean." But the phrase "to eat humble pie" has quite a different origin. It comes from "umbles," the cheaply bought inner parts of an animal.

hum·bug (hum'bug') *n.* nonsense.

hum·drum (hum'drum') *adj.* dull; ordinary.

hu·mer·us (hyōō'mə-rəs) *n.* **hu·mer·i** (hyōō'mə-rī') the bone in the upper arm.

hu·mid (hyōō'məd, yōō'məd) *adj.* damp; moist.

hu·mil·i·ate (hyōō-mil'ē-āt') *vb.* **hu·mil·i·at·ing,** **hu·mil·i·at·ed** to make feel ashamed or look foolish in front of another person. – *adj.* **hu·mil·i·at·ing.** – *n.* **hu·mil·i·a·tion** (hyōō-mil'ē-ā'shən).

●**hum·ming bird** (hum'ing-burd') the smallest bird in the world, hardly larger than a bumblebee. It can beat its wings up to 70 times a second, which allows it to hover in midair. This also causes the distinctive humming sound.

hu·mor (hyōō'mər, yōō'mər) *n.* the ability to amuse or be amused. – *vb.* **hu·mor·ing, hu·mored** to please by doing what is wished.

hu·mor·ous (hyōō'mə-rəs, yōō'mə-rəs) *adj.* funny; amusing.

hump (hump) *n.* a small, rounded lump, as on the back of a camel.

Hun (hun) *n.* a member of a people who invaded EUROPE in the A.D. 300s and 400s.

hunch (hunch) *n.* an idea or belief based on feelings or suspicions rather than on clear evidence. – *vb.* **hunch·ing, hunched** to sit with your body curled up or bent.

hunch·back (hunch'bak') *n.* a person whose back has a large rounded lump, usually caused by a problem with the spine.

hun·dred (hun'drəd) *n.* **hun·dreds** or (after another number) **hundred 1** the number that is ten times ten; 100. **2** (usually in *plural*; *informal*) very many: *There were hundreds of people.* – *adj.* totaling one hundred. – *n. & adj.* **hun·dredth** (hun'drədth, hun'drətth).

hung (hung) *vb.* see **hang**.

●**Hun·ga·ry** (hung'gə-rē). See Supplement, **Countries**.

hun·ger (hung'gər) *n.* the desire or need, especially very great, for food. – *vb.* **hun·ger·ing, hun·gered** to have a strong desire or need: *We all hunger for affection.*

hun·gry (hung'grē) *adj.* **hun·gri·er, hun·gri·est** wanting or needing food. – *adv.* **hun·gri·ly** (hung'grə-lē).

hunk (hungk) *n.* a lump broken or cut off from a larger piece.

hunt (hunt) *vb.* **hunt·ing, hunt·ed 1** to chase and kill animals for food or for sport. **2** to search for: *They are hunting for a new house.*

hunt·er (hunt'ər) *n.* a person or animal that hunts.

hur·dle (hurd'l) *n.* **1** one of a series of light frames to be jumped in various races. **2** (in *plural*) a race in which hurdles must be jumped over. **3** a problem or difficulty. – *vb.* **hur·dling, hur·dled** to jump over.

hurl (hurl) *vb.* **hurl·ing, hurled 1** to throw violently. **2** to speak with force and spite: *to hurl insults.*

hur·ri·cane (hur'ə-kān', her'ə-kān') *n.* a violent storm, especially one with winds blowing at over 75 miles (120 km) per hour.

hur·ry (hur'ē) *vb.* **hur·ries, hur·ry·ing, hur·ried** to move or act quickly. – *n.* great haste or speed; eagerness. – *vb.* **hurry up** to move more quickly.

hur·ried (hur'ēd) *adj.* forced to act quickly, especially too quickly.

hurt (hurt) *vb.* **hurt·ing, hurt 1** to injure or cause physical pain to. **2** to upset or cause emotional pain to: *She hurt my feelings with her harsh words.* – *n.* **1** an injury or wound. **2** mental pain or suffering. – *adj.* **1** injured. **2** upset.

hurt·ful (hurt'fəl) *adj.* causing emotional pain.

hus·band (huz'bənd) *n.* a man to whom a woman is married.

hush (hush) *interjection* be quiet; be still. – *n.* silence, especially after noise. – *vb.* **hush·ing, hushed** to make or become quiet, calm, or still.

husk (husk) *n.* the thin, dry covering of certain fruits and seeds.

hus·ky[1] (hus'kē) *adj.* **hus·ki·er, hus·ki·est** (of a voice) rough and dry in sound.

At rest

At speed

Lift

Water flow

A hydrofoil can travel faster than ordinary craft because its design reduces water resistance. It has wings beneath its hull. At rest the hydrofoil floats low in the water. As it gains speed, the wings lift the craft so that it skims across the water.

hus·ky² (hus′kē) *n.*
hus·kies a large, strong dog used to pull sleds across snow.

hut (hut) *n.* a small house or shelter, often made of wood.

hutch (huch) *n.* **1** a box with a wire front in which small animals, as rabbits, are kept. **2** a cabinet with open shelves on top.

hy·a·cinth (hī′ə-sinth′, hī′ə-sənth) *n.* a plant which grows from a bulb and has sweet-smelling flowers.

hy·brid (hī′brəd) *n.* **1** an animal or plant produced by crossing different species or varieties. **2** anything produced by combining elements from different sources. – *adj.* produced by combining elements from different species, varieties, etc.

hy·drant (hī′drənt) *n.* a pipe connected to the main water supply with a nozzle for attaching a hose when fighting fires.

hy·drau·lic (hī-drô′lik) *adj.* worked by the pressure of liquid carried in pipes.

hy·dro·e·lec·tric·i·ty (hī′drō-i-lek-tris′ət-ē) *n.* electrical power produced from water. – *adj.* **hy·dro·e·lec·tric** (hī′drō-i-lek′trik).

hy·dro·foil (hī′drə-foil′) *n.* **1** a wing-shaped device on a boat which lifts it out of the water as its speed accelerates. **2** a boat fitted with such a device.

hy·dro·gen (hī′drə-jən) *n.* a gas (symbol **H**), the lightest element known, which produces water when combined with oxygen.

hy·e·na (hī-ē′nə) *n.* a doglike animal with a shrill cry that lives in AFRICA and ASIA.

hy·giene (hī′jēn′) *n.* the practice or study of staying healthy and preventing the spread of disease, especially by keeping yourself and your surroundings clean. – *adj.* **hy·gi·en·ic** (hī′jē-en′ik, hī-jē′nik, hī-jen′ik).

hymn (him) *n.* a song of praise.

hyper- *prefix* over, beyond, more than: *hyperactive.*

hy·per·bo·le (hī-pur′bə-lē) *n.* the use of an overstatement or exaggeration.

hy·phen (hī′fən) *n.* a punctuation mark (-) which is used to join up two words, for example bare-headed, or two parts of a word split over the end of one line and the beginning of the following one.

hy·phen·ate (hī′fə-nāt′) *vb.* **hy·phen·at·ing, hy·phen·at·ed** to join with a hyphen. – *n.* **hy·phen·a·tion** (hī′fə-nā′shən).

hyp·no·sis (hip-nō′səs) *n.* **hy·pno·ses** (hip-nō′sēz) a sleeplike state in which someone is totally relaxed and acts only on the suggestion of another person.

hyp·not·ic (hip-nät′ik) *adj.* **1** causing, or caused by, hypnosis. **2** causing sleepiness.

hyp·no·tism (hip′nə-tiz′əm) *n.* the practice of hypnosis. – *n.* **hyp·no·tist** (hip′nə-təst).

hyp·no·tize (hip′nə-tīz′) *vb.* **hyp·no·tiz·ing, hyp·no·tized** to put in a state of hypnosis.

hy·poc·ri·sy (hip-äk′rə-sē) *n.* **hy·poc·ri·sies** the act of pretending to have beliefs which you do not actually have.

hyp·o·crite (hip′ə-krit′) *n.* a person who pretends to have feelings or beliefs they do not actually hold. – *adj.* **hypocritical** (hip′ə-krit′i-kəl).

hy·po·der·mic sy·ringe (hī′pə-dur′mik sə-rinj′) *n.* a syringe with a fine hollow needle, used for injecting drugs under the skin.

hy·poth·e·sis (hī-päth′ə-səs) *n.* **hy·poth·e·ses** (hī-päth′ə-sēz′) a statement that is assumed to be true and on which an argument may be based.

hy·po·thet·i·cal (hī′pə-thet′i-kəl) *adj.* based on hypothesis; assumed.

hys·te·ri·a (his′ter′ē-ə, his-tir′ē-ə) *n.* a wild or uncontrolled emotional state.

hys·ter·i·cal (his-ter′i-kəl) *adj.* **1** suffering from hysteria. **2** (*informal*) very funny.

The spotted hyena is a powerful and aggressive animal. It hunts in packs at night.

Husband is from a Norse word meaning "someone who has a household."

I i

I (ī) *pron.* used by the speaker or writer to refer to himself or herself.

I·be·ri·an (ī-bîr′ē-ən) *adj.* of the Iberian Peninsula (now divided into SPAIN and PORTUGAL), its inhabitants and history.

i·bex (ī′beks′) *n.* **ibex** or **ibexes** a wild mountain goat with large, backward-curving horns, found in EUROPE, AFRICA, and ASIA.

I·bis (ī′bəs). See **Myths and Legends**.

i·bis (ī′bəs) *n.* **ibis** or **i·bis·es** a wading bird with a long, slender, downward-curving beak.

ice (īs) *n.* **1** frozen water. **2** a sheet of this. — *vb.* **ic·ing, iced 1** to become covered with ice. **2** to cover with icing. — *adj.* **iced.**

ice age *n.* a period during which large areas of the earth's surface are covered with ice.

ice·berg (īs′bûrg′) *n.* a huge mass of ice floating in the sea.

ice·cap (īs′kap′) *n.* a permanent covering of ice, for example at the North or South Poles.

ice cream (ī′skrēm′) *n.* a sweet, creamy frozen dessert, made usually from cream.

ice hock·ey (īs′häk′ē) *n.* a game played on ice in which two teams of six players try to shoot a hard rubber puck into the opposite goal.

● **Ice·land** (ī′slənd). See Supplement, **Countries**.

Ice·lan·dic (ī′slan′dik) *adj.* of ICELAND or its language. — *n.* the Icelandic language.

ice skate *n.* a skate with a metal blade for use on ice.

ic·i·cle (ī′sik′əl) *n.* a long hanging spike of ice.

ic·ing (ī′sing) *n.* a mixture of sugar, egg whites, water, and flavoring used to coat cakes.

ic·y (ī′sē) *adj.* **ic·i·er, ic·i·est 1** very cold. **2** covered with ice. **3** not friendly.

● **I·da·ho** (īd′ə-hō′). See Supplement, **U.S.A.**

Sea level

Water increases in volume and so decreases in density as it freezes to a solid. This is why **icebergs** float, with about seven-eighths of their volume below the surface. Some Antarctic icebergs are more than 60 miles (100km) long.

Under the Antarctic ice sheet (right) there is land. The Arctic is mostly a mass of pack ice covering an ocean.

i·de·a (ī-dē′ə) *n.* **1** a thought, image, or concept formed by the mind. **2** a plan or intention. **3** a main aim or feature. **4** an opinion or belief.

i·de·al (ī-dē′əl, ī-dēl′) *adj.* perfect; highest or best possible: *Flying is the ideal way of traveling.* – *n.* the highest standard of behavior, etc.

i·den·ti·cal (ī-dent′i-kəl) *adj.* being exactly alike in every respect: *They wore identical ties.*

i·den·ti·fi·ca·tion (ī-dent′ə-fə-kā′shən) *n.* something which identifies a person or thing.

i·den·ti·fy (ī-dent′ə-fī′) *vb.* **i·den·ti·fies, i·den·ti·fy·ing, i·den·ti·fied** **1** to recognize as being a particular person or thing; to establish the identity of. **2** to associate.

i·den·ti·ty (ī-dent′ət-ē) *n.* **i·den·ti·ties** who or what a person or thing is.

id·i·ot (id′ē-ət) *n.* (*informal*) a foolish or stupid person. – *adj.* **id·i·ot·ic** (id′ē-ät′ik).

i·dle (īd′l) *adj.* **1** not being used. **2** not wanting to work; lazy. – *adv.* **i·dly** (īd′lē).

i·dol (īd′l) *n.* an image, especially of a god, used as an object of worship.

if (if) *conj.* **1** in the event that; supposing that: *If what you say is true, we'll have to go.* **2** although; even though. **3** whenever: *I like to visit John if I can.* **4** whether: *I merely asked if I could help you.*

ig·loo (ig′lōō′) *n.* a dome-shaped INUIT house built with blocks of snow and ice.

ig·ne·ous (ig′nē-əs) *adj.* formed by molten rock from the earth's core becoming hard.

ig·nite (ig-nīt′) *vb.* **ig·nit·ing, ig·nit·ed** to set fire to; to catch fire: *You must ignite the gas first.*

ig·ni·tion (ig-nish′ən) *n.* the process of igniting the fuel in an engine.

ig·no·rant (ig′nə-rənt) *adj.* knowing very little; uneducated. – *n.* **ig·no·rance** (ig′nə-rəns).

ig·nore (ig-nôr′, ig-nōr′) *vb.* **ig·nor·ing, ig·nored** to take no notice of deliberately.

i·gua·na (ig-wän′ə) *n.* **i·gua·nas** a large gray-green, tree-dwelling lizard.

● **Il·i·ad** (il′ē-əd, il′ē-ad′) This epic poem by HOMER tells the story of the war between the Greeks and Trojans (the people of TROY).

ill (il) *adj.* **worse** (wurs), **worst** (wurst) **1** not in good health; sick. **2** bad or harmful: *She suffered ill effects from the oysters.* – *adv.* **worse** (wurs), **worst** (wurst) badly; poorly: *He thought ill of the neighbors.* – *n.* a sickness or disease.

ill- *prefix* meaning badly: *ill-informed; ill-treat.*

il·le·gal (il-ē′gəl) *adj.* against the law.

il·leg·i·ble (il-ēj′ə-bəl) *adj.* difficult to read.

● **Il·li·nois** (il′ə-noi′). See Supplement, **U.S.A.**.

il·lit·er·ate (il-it′ər-ət) *adj.* unable to read and write. – *n.* **il·lit·er·a·cy** (il-it′ər-ə-sē).

ill·ness (il′nəs) *n.* a disease.

il·log·i·cal (il-äj′i-kəl) *adj.* not based on reason.

il·lu·mi·nate (il-ōō′mə-nāt′) *vb.* **il·lu·mi·nat·ing, il·lu·mi·nat·ed** **1** to light up or make bright. **2** to make clearer. **3** to decorate with gold and colored designs.

il·lu·mi·na·tion (il-ōō′mə-nā′shən) *n.* **1** the amount of light present. **2** decoration, as with gold and colors in a manuscript.

il·lus·trate (il′ə-strāt′) *vb.* **il·lus·trat·ing, il·lus·trat·ed** to provide with pictures and diagrams. – *n.* **il·lus·tra·tor** (il′ə-strāt′ər).

il·lus·tra·tion (il′ə-strā′shən) *n.* **1** a picture or diagram in a book, etc. **2** an example.

I'm (īm) I am.

im·age (im′ij) *n.* **1** a likeness of a person or thing. **2** a person or thing that resembles another person or thing closely.

i·mag·i·nar·y (i-maj′ə-ner′ē) *adj.* not real.

i·mag·i·na·tion (i-maj′ə-nā′shən) *n.* the ability to form mental images of things, etc.

i·mag·i·na·tive (i-maj′ə-nət-iv) *adj.* having a lively imagination.

i·mag·ine (i-maj′ən) *vb.* **i·mag·in·ing, i·mag·ined** **1** to form a mental picture of. **2** to believe or suppose that one sees or hears. **3** to think, suppose, or guess.

im·i·tate (im′ə-tāt′) *vb.* **im·i·tat·ing, im·i·tat·ed** to copy the behavior, appearance, etc. of.

im·i·ta·tion (im′ə-tā′shən) *n.* **1** an act of imitating. **2** a copy.

im·ma·ture (im′ə-toor′, im′ə-tyoor′) *adj.* not fully grown or developed.

im·me·di·ate (i-mēd′ē-ət) *adj.* **1** happening or done at once and without delay. **2** nearest or next in space, time, or relationship. **3** urgent.

im·me·di·ate·ly (i-mēd′ē-ət-lē) *adv.* at once.

im·mense (i-mens′) *adj.* very large or great.

im·mi·grant (im′ə-grənt) *n.* a person who moves to a new country.

im·mi·grate (im′ə-grāt′) *vb.* **im·mi·grat·ing, im·mi·grat·ed** to move to a foreign country to settle there. – *n.* **im·mi·gra·tion** (im′ə-grā′shən).

A medieval illumination showing Bede, a monk at Jarrow, England. These decorations were usually painted in the hand-written Bibles and religious books.

im·mi·nent (im′ə-nənt) *adj.* likely to happen very soon.

im·mo·bile (im-ō′bəl) *adj.* motionless.

im·mod·er·ate (im-äd′ər-ət) *adj.* extreme.

im·mor·al (im-ôr′əl, im-är′əl) *adj.* morally wrong or bad; evil.

im·mor·tal (im-ôrt′l) *adj.* living forever and never dying; lasting forever. – *n.* **im·mor·tal·i·ty** (im′ôr-tal′ət-ē).

im·mune (im-yōōn′) *adj.* protected by inoculation from, or having a natural resistance to, a disease. – *n.* **im·mu·ni·ty** (im-yōō′nət-ē), **im·mu·ni·ties**.

im·mu·nize (im′yə-nīz′) *vb.* **im·mu·niz·ing**, **im·mu·nized** to make immune. – *n.* **im·mu·ni·za·tion** (im′yə-nə-zā′shən).

im·pact (im′pakt′) *n.* **1** a collision. **2** a strong effect or impression.

im·pa·la (im-pal′ə, im-päl′ə) *n.* **im·pa·las** a graceful African antelope with curving horns.

im·par·tial (im-pär′shəl) *adj.* not favoring one person, etc. more than another; fair.

im·pa·tient (im-pā′shənt) *adj.* **1** unwilling to wait; intolerant of delay. **2** restlessly eager. – *n.* **im·pa·tience** (im-pā′shəns).

im·peach (im-pēch′) *vb.* **im·peach·ing**, **im·peached** to accuse with misconduct while in public or governmental office.

im·pede (im-pēd′) *vb.* **im·ped·ing**, **im·ped·ed** to delay the progress of.

im·per·fect (im-pur′fikt) *adj.* having faults.

im·pe·ri·al (im-pîr′ē-əl) *adj.* of or suitable for an empire, emperor, or empress.

im·per·ti·nent (im-purt′n-ənt) *adj.* rude. – *n.* **im·per·ti·nence** (im-purt′n-əns).

im·ple·ment (im′plə-mənt) *n.* a tool or utensil; a piece of equipment. – (im′plə-ment′) *vb.* **im·ple·ment·ing, im·ple·ment·ed** to carry out or perform.

im·plore (im-plôr′, im-plōr′) *vb.* **im·plor·ing, im·plored** to beg. – *adj.* **im·plor·ing**.

im·ply (im-plī′) *vb.* **im·plies, im·ply·ing, im·plied** to suggest or express indirectly; to hint at. – *adj.* **im·plied**.

im·po·lite (im′pə-līt′) *adj.* not polite; rude.

im·port (im-pôrt′, im-pōrt′) *vb.* **im·port·ing, im·port·ed** to bring goods, etc. in from another country. – (im′pôrt′, im′pōrt′) *n.* something imported.

im·por·tant (im-pôrt′nt) *adj.* **1** having great value, influence, or effect. **2** of great value to. – *n.* **im·por·tance** (im-pôrt′ns).

im·pose (im-pōz′) *vb.* **im·pos·ing, im·posed** to force one's self or opinions on.

im·pos·ing (im-pō′zing) *adj.* impressive.

im·pos·si·ble (im-päs′ə-bəl) *adj.* **1** that cannot be done or cannot happen. **2** that cannot be true; difficult to believe.

im·prac·ti·ca·ble (im-prak′ti-kə-bəl) *adj.* not able to be done, put into practice, or used.

im·prac·ti·cal (im-prak′ti-kəl) *adj.* lacking common sense.

im·preg·na·ble (im-preg′nə-bəl) *adj.* not able to be seized, defeated, or taken by force.

im·press (im-pres′) *vb.* **im·press·ing, im·pressed** to produce a strong, lasting, and usually favorable impression on.

im·pres·sion (im-presh′ən) *n.* **1** an idea or effect produced in the mind or made on the senses. **2** a vague or uncertain idea or belief. **3** an imitation of a person, or a sound, done for entertainment.

Im·pres·sion·ism (im-presh′ə-niz′əm) *n.* **1** a movement in painting in the 1800s which aimed to represent nature, especially the play of light on objects, by the use of many small strokes of unmixed colors. **2** a style of music or writing which aims to give a general impression of feelings and events . – *n. & adj.* **Im·pres·sion·ist** (im-presh′ə-nəst).

im·pres·sive (im-pres′iv) *adj.* causing admiration; making a strong impression.

im·pris·on (im-priz′ən) *vb.* **im·pris·on·ing, im·pris·oned** to put in prison.

im·prob·a·ble (im-präb′ə-bəl) *adj.* **1** unlikely to happen or exist. **2** hard to believe.

When threatened a group of impala leap in the air in all directions in order to confuse the predator.

PRONUNCIATION SYMBOLS			
ə **a**way	l**e**mon	foc**u**s	
a	fat	oi	boy
ā	fade	oo	foot
ä	hot	ōō	moon
âr	fair	ou	house
e	met	th	think
ē	mean	t̲h̲	this
g	get	u	cut
hw	which	ur	hurt
i	fin	w	witch
ī	line	y	yes
îr	near	yōō	music
ô	often	yoor	pure
ō	note	zh	vision

The first **implements** or tools in the stone age were sharp flint stones. From these evolved hammers, chisels, and saws. Today we have power driven tools such as the steam rammer and all kinds of machine tools such as drills and lathes.

With the typewriter writing became mechanical.

A Viking ironing board with a smoothing stone.

From the open-fire spit to the microwave oven.

216

im·promp·tu (im-prämp′tōō, im-prämp′tyōō) *adj.* & *adv.* done without preparation.

im·prove (im-prōōv′) *vb.* **im·prov·ing, im·proved** to make or become better, of higher quality or value; to make progress.

im·pro·vise (im′prə-vīz′) *vb.* **im·pro·vis·ing, im·pro·vised** to compose, recite, or perform music, verse, etc. without preparing it in advance.

im·pulse (im-puls′) *n.* **1** a sudden push forward; a force producing sudden movement forward. **2** a sudden desire or urge to do something without thinking of the consequences. – *adj.* **im·pul·sive** (im-pul′siv).

in (in) *prep.* **1** used to express the position or inclusion of a person or thing: *He is in the room.* **2** into: *Get in the car.* **3** after: *Come back in an hour.* **4** during: *Birds nest in spring.* **5** used to express arrangement or shape: *List them in order.* **6** by means of; using: *She sang in Italian.* – *adv.* **1** to or toward the inside; indoors: *The cat came in.* **2** at home or work: *I won't be in tomorrow.* **3** so as to add: *Beat in the eggs.*

in- *prefix* (also **il-** before words beginning with **l**; **im-** before **b**, **m**, and **p**; and **ir-** before **r**) **1** not; non-; lack of: *inhospitable*; *irrelevant*. **2** toward; within: *imprison*.

in·an·i·mate (in-an′ə-mət) *adj.* without life.

in·au·gu·rate (in-ôg′yə-rāt′) *vb.* **in·au·gu·rat·ing, in·au·gu·rat·ed 1** to place in office with a formal ceremony. **2** to mark the beginning of with a ceremony. – *n.* **in·au·gu·ra·tion** (in-ôg′yə-rā′shən).

●**In·ca** (ing′kə) The Inca civilization was centered in modern PERU from about A.D. 1200 until its eventual destruction by Spanish conquistadors in the 1500s.

in·cense¹ (in′sens′) *n.* a spice or other substance that gives off a pleasant smell when burned.

in·cense² (in-sens′) *vb.* **in·cens·ing, in·censed** to make very angry.

in·cen·tive (in-sent′iv) *n.* something that encourages action, work, etc.

in·ces·sant (in-ses′ənt) *adj.* continual.

inch (inch) *n.* a measure of length equal to one twelfth of a foot (2.54 centimeters).

in·ci·dent (in′səd-ənt, in′sə-dent′) *n.* an event or occurrence.

in·ci·den·tal (in′sə-dent′l) *adj.* of minor importance: *incidental expenses.*

in·ci·den·tal·ly (in′sə-dent′lē) *adv.* by the way.

Inca headdress was often elaborate

Inca rule, at its height, extended from Ecuador to southern Chile. Inca society, headed by a godlike emperor, was ruthlessly efficient. The people were divided into groups of ten with an overseer; a local chief was appointed over 100 people. Higher officials were responsible for 1000 or 10,000 people. The Incas constructed elaborate irrigation systems and had an extensive road system.

The Incas of Peru built the mountain fortress-city of Machu Picchu, "lost" until rediscovered in 1911.

Inca soldiers used slings, spears, clubs, and bolas, *which were stones linked by lengths of string.*

The Incas used hand-held, stone hammers to shape their building stone.

in·cin·er·ate (in-sin′ə-rāt′) *vb.* **in·cin·er·at·ing, in·cin·er·at·ed** to burn.

in·cline (in-klīn′) *vb.* **in·clin·ing, in·clined** to slope from a horizontal or vertical line.

in·clude (in-klōōd′) *vb.* **in·clud·ing, in·clud·ed 1** to take in as part of a whole. **2** to contain or be made up of.

An Indian maharajah, or ruler.

The Indian emperor Asoka erected many stone pillars to remind people of his power.

The earliest **Indian** civilization was that of the Indus valley (*c.* 2500-1600 B.C.). From about 1500 B.C. Aryans (or Indo-Europeans) from Russia overran the north and settled down with the native Indians the Dravidians. The whole subcontinent was first unified under the Mauryan emperors (321-184 B.C.). Much later the Mogul Muslim empire was established in the north. It lasted until 1858.

Under the old caste system society was divided into four classes. The highest were the Brahman, the priests, scholars, and rulers. Such people as street traders were of the lowest caste.

A statue of the Buddha, the founder of Buddhism, which spread from India to China and the Far East.

The main station in Bombay opened in 1866 was a mixture of European styles with Indian style domes.

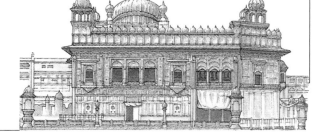

in·come (in′kum′) *n.* money received as payment for work, etc.

in·com·pe·tent (in-käm′pət-ənt) *adj.* lacking the necessary skill, ability, or qualifications.

in·con·ve·nience (in′kən-vēn′yəns) *n.* something which causes trouble or difficulty.

in·cor·po·rate (in-kôr′pə-rāt′) *vb.* **in·cor·po·rat·ing, in·cor·po·rat·ed 1** to contain as part of a whole. **2** to include or be included as part of a whole.

in·crease (in krēs) *vb.* **in·creas·ing, in·creased** to make or become greater in size, intensity, or number. – (in′krēs′) *n.* growth.

in·cred·i·ble (in-kred′ə-bəl) *adj.* difficult to believe; amazing.

in·cu·bate (ing′kə-bāt′) *vb.* **in·cu·bat·ing, in·cu·bat·ed** to hatch by keeping warm.

in·deed (in-dēd′) *adv.* **1** without any question. **2** used for emphasis: *It's very wet indeed.*

in·def·i·nite (in-def′ə-nət) *adj.* vague.

indefinite article *n.* either of the words **a** or **an**, which describe no particular person or thing.

In·de·pen·dence Day (in′di-pen′dəns) *n.* a United States public holiday celebrating the Declaration of Independence, on July 4.

in·de·pen·dent (in′di-pen′dənt) *adj.* **1** not under the control or authority of others, especially of a country or state. **2** not relying on others for money, care, or help. – *n.* **in·de·pen·dence** (in′di-pen′dəns).

in·dex (in′deks′) *n.* **in·dex·es** an alphabetical list of names, subjects, etc. dealt with in a book.

index finger *n.* the finger next to the thumb.

● **In·di·a** (in′dē-ə) is a part of ASIA and has more people than any other country except CHINA. To the north are the HIMALAYAS. Bombay and Calcutta are among the world's biggest cities and New Delhi is the capital. Modern India, the world's biggest democracy, became a republic in 1947. See also Supplement, **Countries**.

In·di·an (in′dē-ən) *n.* **1** a person born in INDIA. **2** a name of any of the various NATIVE AMERICAN peoples (excluding the INUIT). – *adj.* **1** relating to INDIA or the Indian subcontinent (INDIA, BANGLADESH, and PAKISTAN), its inhabitants, languages, and culture. **2** relating to the native peoples of America, their languages, and culture.

● **In·di·an·a** (in′dē-an′ə). See Supplement, **U.S.A.**

in·di·cate (in′di-kāt′) *vb.* **in·di·cat·ing, in·di·cat·ed** to point out or show.

in·di·ca·tion (in′di-kā′shən) *n.* a sign.

in·dif·fer·ent (in-dif′ə-rənt) *adj.* **1** showing no interest or concern. **2** average; mediocre.

in·dig·e·nous (in-dij′ə-nəs) *adj.* belonging naturally to an area; native: *indigenous plants*.

in·dig·nant (in-dig′nənt) *adj.* showing anger or a sense of ill-treatment.

in·di·vid·u·al (in′də-vij′ōo-əl) *adj.* **1** relating to a single person or thing. **2** particular to one person. − *n.* a particular person, animal, or thing.

● **In·do·ne·sia** (in′də-nē′zhə). See Supplement, **Countries**.

in·door (in′dôr′, in′dōr′) *adj.* used, done, happening, etc. inside a building.

in·doors (in-dôrz′, in-dōrz′) *adv.* in or into a building: *Stay indoors today*.

in·dus·tri·al (in-dus′trē-əl) *adj.* **1** of, relating to, or concerned with industry. **2** having highly developed industry: *an industrial country*.

in·dus·tri·al·ize (in-dus′trē-ə-līz′) *vb.* **in·dus·tri·al·iz·ing, in·dus·tri·al·ized** to make or become industrially developed.

● **Industrial Revolution** This is the name given to the expansion of the use of machinery and factories in EUROPE (especially ENGLAND) from 1750 to 1850. The main inventions were steam power and textile machinery.

in·dus·tri·ous (in-dus′trē-əs) *adj.* hard-working; diligent.

in·dus·try (in′dus′trē, in′də-strē) *n.* **in·dus·tries 1** the business of producing goods. **2** a branch of manufacturing and trade: *the coal industry*. **3** hard work or effort.

in·ed·i·ble (in-ed′ə-bəl) *adj.* not fit to eat.

in·ept (in-ept′) *adj.* **1** awkward. **2** silly; foolish.

in·e·qual·i·ty (in′i-kwäl′ət-ē) *n.* **in·e·qual·i·ties** a lack of equality or fairness.

in·ev·i·ta·ble (in-ev′ət-ə-bəl) *adj.* that cannot be avoided; certain to happen.

in·fant (in′fənt) *n.* a very young child.

in·fan·try (in′fən-trē) *n.* **in·fan·tries** soldiers who are trained and equipped to fight on foot.

in·fect (in-fekt′) *vb.* **in·fect·ing, in·fect·ed** to give germs, viruses, or a disease to.

in·fec·tion (in-fek′shən) *n.* a disease caused by germs.

in·fec·tious (in-fek′shəs) *adj.* describing a disease that can be passed from one person to another.

in·fer (in-fur′) *vb.* **in·fer·ring, in·ferred** to form an opinion from the facts given.

in·fe·ri·or (in-fîr′ē-ər) *adj.* poorer in quality; lower in value, rank, or status.

in·fest (in-fest′) *vb.* **in·fest·ing, in·fest·ed** (of something harmful, as vermin) to be present in large numbers.

in·fi·nite (in′fə-nət) *adj.* having no boundaries or limits in size, extent, time, or space.

in·fin·i·tive (in-fin′ət-iv) *n.* a verb form that expresses an action but which has no person or number, in English often used with *to*.

in·flam·ma·ble (in-flam′ə-bəl) *adj.* easily set on fire: *Gasoline is highly inflammable*.

in·flam·ma·tion (in′flə-mā′shən) *n.* a place in the body showing redness and swelling.

in·flate (in-flāt′) *vb.* **in·flat·ing, in·flat·ed 1** to expand with air or gas. **2** to increase prices.

in·fla·tion (in-flā′shən) *n.* a general increase in the level of prices.

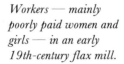

The Spinning Jenny, the first multireel spinning machine, was made by James Hargreaves in 1764.

The first steam engine — built by Thomas Newcomen in 1712 — was used to pump water out of mines. Steam power was to cause a revolution in industry.

Workers — mainly poorly paid women and girls — in an early 19th-century flax mill.

in·flu·ence (in'floo-əns) *n.* **1** the power that one person or thing has to affect another. **2** a person or thing that has such a power: *Try to be a good influence on him.* – *vb.* **in·flu·enc·ing, in·flu·enced** to have an effect on; sway.

in·flu·en·tial (in'floo-en'shəl) *adj.* having influence or power.

in·flu·en·za (in'floo-en'zə) *n.* an infectious illness caused by a virus.

in·form (in-fôrm') *vb.* **in·form·ing, in·formed** to give knowledge or information to.

in·for·mal (in-fôr'məl) *adj.* without ceremony; relaxed and friendly.

in·for·ma·tion (in'fər-mā'shən) *n.* knowledge gained or given; facts; news.

in·for·ma·tive (in-fôr'mət-iv) *adj.* giving useful or interesting information.

in·ge·ni·ous (in-jēn'yəs) *adj.* showing skill.

in·ge·nu·i·ty (in'jə-noo'ət-ē, in'jə-nyoo'ət-ē) *n.* inventive cleverness, skill, or originality.

in·gre·di·ent (in-grēd'ē-ənt) *n.* one of several things that goes into a mixture or a recipe.

in·hab·it (in-hab'ət) *vb.* **in·hab·it·ing, in·hab·it·ed** to live or dwell in a place.

in·hab·i·tant (in-hab'ət-ənt) *n.* a person or animal that lives permanently in a place.

in·hale (in-hāl') *vb.* **in·hal·ing, in·haled** to breathe in air, gas, etc.

in·her·it (in-her'ət) *vb.* **in·her·it·ing, in·her·it·ed 1** to receive from someone on his or her death. **2** to receive from your parents and ancestors as a characteristic.

in·her·i·tance (in-her'ət-əns) *n.* something inherited.

in·hu·man (in-hyoo'mən, in-yoo'mən) *adj.* cruel and unfeeling; brutal.

in·i·tial (i-nish'əl) *adj.* of or at the beginning. – *n.* the first letter of a word or name. – *adv.* **in·i·tial·ly** (i-nish'ə-lē).

in·i·tia·tive (i-nish'ət-iv) *n.* the ability or skill to make decisions.

in·ject (in-jekt') *vb.* **in·ject·ing, in·ject·ed** to introduce a liquid, such as medicine, into, using a syringe. – *n.* **in·jec·tion** (in-jek'shən).

in·jure (in'jər) *vb.* **in·jur·ing, in·jured 1** to harm or damage. **2** to do an injustice to.

in·jur·y (in'jə-rē) *n.* **in·jur·ies 1** physical harm or damage. **2** an injustice.

in·jus·tice (in-jus'təs) *n.* **1** unfairness or lack of justice. **2** an unjust act.

ink (ingk) *n.* a colored liquid used in writing, printing, and drawing.

in·land (in'lənd) *adj.* of or in that part of a country that is not beside the sea.

in·let (in'lət, in'let') *n.* a narrow length of water running inland from a sea coast.

inn (in) *n.* a small hotel or tavern.

in·ner (in'ər) *adj.* situated inside or close to the center.

in·ning (in'ing) *n.* a division of a baseball game in which each team has three outs.

in·no·cent (in'ə-sənt) *adj.* **1** pure. **2** not guilty. **3** trusting. – *n.* **in·no·cence** (in'ə-səns).

in·oc·u·late (in-äk'yə-lāt') *vb.* **in·oc·u·lat·ing, in·oc·u·lat·ed** to give a mild form of a disease so as to create immunity against that disease, usually by injection. – *n.* **in·oc·u·la·tion** (in-äk'yə-lā'shən).

in·or·gan·ic (in'ôr-gan'ik) *adj.* not made of or found in living animal or plant material.

in·put (in'poot') *n.* the information put into a computer.

in·quire (in-kwīr') *vb.* **in·quir·ing, in·quired** to ask for information about.

The eight-spotted forester moth of North America.

in·quir·y (in'kwə-rē, in'kwī'rē) *n.* **in·quir·ies 1** a request for information. **2** an investigation.

in·quis·i·tive (in-kwiz'ət-iv) *adj.* eager for information. – *n.* **in·quis·i·tive·ness**.

in·sane (in-sān') *adj.* not of sound mind.

in·san·i·ty (in-san'ət-ē) *n.* the state of being insane.

in·sect (in'sekt') *n.* any of many kinds of small invertebrates with a body consisting of a head, thorax, and abdomen, three pairs of legs, and usually one or two pairs of wings.

in·sec·ti·cide (in-sek'tə-sīd') *n.* a substance for killing insects.

in·sert (in-surt') *vb.* **in·sert·ing, in·sert·ed** to put, place, or fit: *Insert the coin into the slot.*

in·side (in'sīd', in'sīd') *n.* **1** the inner side, surface, or part of something. **2** (in *plural*; *informal*) the stomach and bowels. – *adj.* being

Of all forms of life, the most varied are the **insects**. More than 900,000 species are known but the number of individual insects is beyond count. They are highly adaptable and have conquered all environments.

The male goliath beetle of Africa, the world's heaviest insect, can weigh more than 4 ounces (100g). Silverfish are primitive wingless insects.

Compound eye • Two pairs of wings • Head • Thorax • Antenna • Abdomen • Six jointed legs

Most insects (like the bee) have four wings, but flies have only two. Insects breathe through tiny holes called "spiracles" along the sides of their body.

A lacewing — a member of a large and varied group of carnivorous insects.

A praying mantis — the female may eat the male while mating!

Male stag beetles wrestling with their antlers (enlarged jaws) when competing for a female.

Ants (bottom) are social insects, living in colonies.

on, near, toward, or from the inside. – *adv.* **1** to, in, or on the inside or interior. **2** indoors.

in·sig·nia (in-sig′nē-ə) *n.* **insignia** or **insignias** a badge or emblem of office.

in·sin·cere (in′sən-sîr′) *adj.* false; hypocritical. – *n.* **in·sin·cer·i·ty** (in′sin-ser′ət-ē).

in·sist (in-sist′) *vb.* **in·sist·ing, in·sist·ed** to demand firmly: *You must insist upon your rights.*

in·so·lent (in′sə-lənt) *adj.* rude or insulting. – *n.* **in·so·lence** (in′sə-ləns).

in·som·ni·a (in-säm′nē-ə) *n.* a continual inability to sleep.

in·spect (in-spekt′) *vb.* **in·spect·ing, in·spect·ed** to look at or examine closely. – *n.* **in·spec·tion** (in-spek′shən).

in·spi·ra·tion (in′spə-rā′shən) *n.* **1** a power which stimulates the mind, especially to artistic activity or creativity. **2** a brilliant or inspired idea. – *adj.* **in·spi·ra·tion·al** (in′spə-rā′shən-l).

in·spire (in-spīr′) *vb.* **in·spir·ing, in·spired 1** to stimulate to activity, especially artistic or creative activity. **2** to arouse feeling of confidence in. – *adj.* **in·spir·ing**.

in·stall (in-stôl′) *vb.* **in·stall·ing, in·stalled** to put equipment, machinery, etc. in place.

in·stall·ment or **in·stal·ment** (in-stôl′mənt) *n.* **1** one of a series of payments of a debt. **2** one of several parts published or broadcast at regular intervals.

in·stance (in′stəns) *n.* an example; a particular case. – **for instance** for example.

in·stant (in′stənt) *adj.* **1** immediate: *He was an instant success.* **2** (of food, etc.) very quickly prepared. – *n.* **1** a particular moment in time: *Come here this instant.* **2** a very brief period of time. – *adj.* **in·stan·ta·ne·ous** (in′stən-tā′nē-əs).

in·stant·ly (in′stənt-lē) *adv.* immediately.

in·stead (in-sted′) *adv.* as an alternative.

in·stinct (in′stingkt′) *n.* **1** a natural, involuntary, and usually unconscious reaction, response, or impulse: *Birds build nests by instinct.* **2** intuition.

in·sti·tute (in′stə-tōōt′, in′stə-tyōōt′) *n.* an organization which promotes research, education, or a particular cause.

in·struct (in-strukt′) *vb.* **in·struct·ing, in·struct·ed 1** to teach. **2** to direct or order.

in·struc·tion (in-struk′shən) *n.* **1** (often in *plural*) a direction, order, or command. **2** (in *plural*) clear, detailed guidelines, such as on how to operate a machine.

in·struc·tor (in-struk′tər) *n.* a teacher.

The Colorado beetle, originally from North America, is now a notorious potato pest on other continents.

United States Air Force

Royal Air Force

Insignia are emblems, badges, or signs identifying an organization, rank, or honor. In the U.S. army, for instance, a corporal wears two chevron stripes on both arms and a sergeant three stripes as insignia of rank.

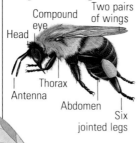

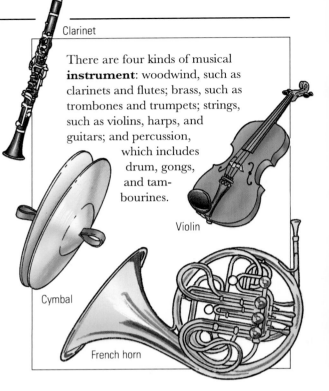

Clarinet

Violin

Cymbal

French horn

There are four kinds of musical **instrument**: woodwind, such as clarinets and flutes; brass, such as trombones and trumpets; strings, such as violins, harps, and guitars; and percussion, which includes drum, gongs, and tambourines.

in·stru·ment (in′strə-mənt) *n.* **1** a tool. **2** (also **musical instrument**) any of several devices which can be made to produce music.

in·su·late (in′sə-lāt′, in′syə-lāt′) *vb.* **in·su·lat·ing, in·su·lat·ed** to cover with a material which prevents the passing of heat, sound, electricity, etc.

in·sult (in-sult′) *vb.* **insulting, insulted** to behave or speak rudely or offensively to. − (in′sult′) *n.* a rude remark or action.

in·sur·ance (in-shoor′əns) *n.* protection against financial loss from loss or theft of property, illness, or injury by paying regular amounts to an **insurance company.**

in·sure (in-shoor′) *vb.* **in·sur·ing, in·sured** to arrange insurance for.

in·tact (in-takt′) *adj.* whole; not broken.

in·te·grate (int′ə-grāt′) *vb.* **in·te·grat·ing, in·te·grat·ed 1** to fit parts together to form a whole. **2** to mix freely with other groups. − *n.* **in·te·gra·tion** (int′ə-grā′shən).

in·tel·lect (int′l-ekt′) *n.* the ability to think.

in·tel·lec·tu·al (int′l-ek′shōō-əl) *adj.* devoted to study, thought, and reason. − *n.* a person with such interests.

in·tel·li·gence (in-tel′ə-jəns) *n.* **1** the ability to learn. **2** the gathering of secret information.

in·tel·li·gent (in-tel′ə-jənt) *adj.* clever or smart.

intend (in-tend′) *vb.* **in·tend·ing, in·tend·ed** to plan or have in mind as a purpose.

in·tense (in-tens′) *adj.* **1** very great or extreme. **2** very deeply felt: *a moment of intense happiness.*

in·ten·si·ty (in-ten′sət-ē) *n.* **in·ten·si·ties** the quality or state of being intense.

in·ten·sive (in-ten′siv) *adj.* **1** requiring considerable effort, time, etc. **2** thorough; concentrated.

in·tent (in-tent′) *n.* **1** intention or aim; a purpose. **2** meaning. − *adj.* firmly determined.

in·ten·tion (in-ten′chən) *n.* that which you plan or intend to do; an aim or purpose.

in·ten·tion·al (in-ten′chən-l) *adj.* said, done, etc. on purpose.

in·ter (in-tur′) *vb.* **in·ter·ring, in·terred** to bury.

in·ter- *prefix* between or among.

in·ter·cept (int′ər-sept′) *vb.* **in·ter·cept·ing, in·ter·cept·ed** to stop or catch on the way from one place to another.

in·ter·com (int′ər-käm′) *n.* a system of microphones and loudspeakers that allows communication within a building, aircraft, etc.

in·ter·est (in′trəst, int′ə-rəst) *n.* **1** concern or curiosity: *He showed interest in buying a house.* **2** the power to attract attention and curiosity: *The TV program lacked any interest.* **3** a hobby or pastime. **4** money paid as a charge for borrowing money. − (in′trəst, int′ə-rəst, int′ə-rest′) *vb.* **in·ter·est·ing, in·ter·est·ed 1** to attract the attention and curiosity of: *The new movie interests me.* **2** to cause to take a part in or be concerned about some activity: *Can I interest you in signing our petition?*

in·ter·fere (int′ər-fîr′) *vb.* **in·ter·fer·ing, in·ter·fered 1** to involve yourself in matters that do not concern you. **2** to get in the way or hinder the progress of.

in·te·ri·or (in-tîr′ē-ər) *adj.* of, or on the inside; inner: *interior design.* − *n.* **1** the inside. **2** the part of a country farthest from the coast.

in·ter·jec·tion (int′ər-jek′shən) *n.* a word, phrase, or sound used as an exclamation to express surprise, disappointment, pain, etc.

in·ter·me·di·ate (int′ər-mēd′ē-ət) *adj.* in the middle; placed between two points, stages, or extremes in place or time.

in·ter·nal (in-tur′nəl) *adj.* of, on, in, or suitable for the inside; inner. − *adv.* **in·ter·nal·ly** (in-tur′nə-lē).

in·ter·na·tion·al (int′ər-nash′ən-l) *adj.* of or involving two or more nations.

in·ter·plan·e·tar·y (int′ər-plan′ə-ter′ē) *adj.*

Insulate comes from the Latin word insula meaning "island," expressing the idea of "to isolate, to detach."

in·ter·pret (in-tur′prət) *vb.* **in·ter·pret·ing, in·ter·pret·ed 1** to explain the meaning of. **2** to bring out your understanding of. – *n.* **in·ter·pre·ta·tion** (in-tur′prə-tā′shən).

in·ter·pret·er (in-tur′prət-ər) *n.* a person who translates speech in a foreign language as the words are spoken.

in·ter·ro·gate (in-ter′ə-gāt′) *vb.* **in·ter·ro·gat·ing, in·ter·ro·gat·ed** to question or examine closely.

in·ter·rupt (int′ə-rupt′) *vb.* **in·ter·rupt·ing, in·ter·rupt·ed 1** to break in on by asking a question or making a comment. **2** to break the continuity of something.

in·ter·rup·tion (int′ə-rup′shən) *n.* **1** the act of interrupting. **2** something that interrupts.

in·ter·sect (int′ər-sekt′) *vb.* **in·ter·sect·ing, in·ter·sect·ed** to divide by passing or cutting through or across. – *n.* **in·ter·sec·tion** (int′ər-sek′shən, int′ər-sek′shən).

in·ter·val (int′ər-vəl) *n.* **1** a period of time between two events. **2** a space or distance between two things.

in·ter·view (int′ər-vyōō′) *n.* **1** a meeting, especially one at which an employer meets and judges a prospective employee. **2** a conversation in which a journalist asks questions and which is broadcast or published. – *vb.* **in·ter·view·ing, in·ter·viewed** to hold an interview with.

in·tes·tine (in-tes′tən) *n.* (often in *plural*) the tubelike part of the food canal leading from the stomach to the anus.

in·ti·mate (int′ə-mət) *adj.* **1** sharing a close and affectionate friendship. **2** very personal.

in·tim·i·date (in-tim′ə-dāt′) *vb.* **in·tim·i·dat·ing, in·tim·i·dat·ed** to frighten into doing what one wants. – *n.* **in·tim·i·da·tion** (in-tim′ə-dā′shən).

in·to (in′tə, in′tōō) *prep.* **1** toward the inside or middle of: *The customers went into the store.* **2** against; into contact or collision with: *The bull smashed into the fence.* **3** expressing a change of state or condition: *Tim changed into a suit for the wedding.* **4** used to express division: *Divide four into 20.*

in·tol·er·ant (in-täl′ə-rənt) *adj.* unwilling to accept ideas, behavior, etc. different from one's own. – *n.* **in·tol·er·ance** (in-täl′ə-rəns).

in·tri·cate (in′tri-kət) *adj.* full of complicated details or parts: *an intricate pattern.*

in·trigue (in′trēg′, in-trēg′) *n.* a secret plot or plan. – (in-trēg′) *vb.* **in·trigu·ing, in·trigued 1** to excite the curiosity or interest of: *This problem intrigues me.* **2** to plot secretly.

in·tro·duce (in′trə-dōōs′, in′trə-dyōōs′) *vb.* **in·tro·duc·ing, in·tro·duced 1** to make a person known by name to another. **2** to bring into a place, situation, etc. for the first time. – *adj.* **in·tro·duc·to·ry** (in′trə-duk′tə-rē).

in·tro·duc·tion (in′trə-duk′shən) *n.* **1** the act of introducing or process of being introduced. **2** a section at the beginning of a book which explains briefly what it is about.

in·trude (in-trōōd′) *vb.* **in·trud·ing, in·trud·ed** to force or impose one's self where one is unwanted and unwelcome. – *n.* **in·trud·er**.

in·tu·i·tion (in′tōō-ish′ən, in′tyōō-ish′ən) *n.* immediate, instinctive understanding or belief.

In·u·it (in′ōō-ət, in′yōō-ət) *n.* **Inuit** or **Inuits** a member of any of several native peoples living in GREENLAND, CANADA, and North Alaska. (**Eskimo** is the established English name for these peoples but many of them prefer **Inuit**.)

in·vade (in-vād′) *vb.* **in·vad·ing, in·vad·ed 1** to enter by force; to attack. **2** to interfere with or intrude on.

in·va·lid[1] (in′və-lid) *n.* a person who is constantly ill or who is disabled.

in·val·id[2] (in-val′əd) *adj.* having no legal force.

in·val·u·a·ble (in-val′yōō-ə-bəl, in-val′yə-bəl) *adj.* of a value too great to be measured.

in·va·sion (in-vā′zhən) *n.* an act of invading or process of being invaded.

in·vent (in-vent′) *vb.* **in·vent·ing, in·vent·ed 1** to make or use for the first time: *Samuel Morse invented the telegraph.* **2** to think or make up.

INTO AND IN TO
Two separate words are needed when in is an adverb belonging to the verb that comes before it, and *to* is part of an infinitive verb that comes after it: *The players went in to shelter from the rain.* Into as one word is a preposition: *He crashed the car into the wall.*

The biggest invasion in history — the Allied landings in Normandy, northern France, in June 1944. Some 350,000 troops were put ashore.

SOME GREAT INVENTIONS

B.C.
7000 Pottery
3000 Wheel (Asia)
3000 Plow (Mesopotamia)

A.D.
105 Paper from pulp (China)
1440 Printing press (Germany)
1590 Microscope (Netherlands)
1593 Thermometer (Italy)
1608 Telescope (Netherlands)
1650 Air Pump (Germany)
1712 Steam engine (England)
1793 Cotton gin (U.S.A.)
1800 Lathe (England)
1804 Steam locomotive (England)
1822 Camera (France)
1837 Telegraph (U.S.A.)
1858 Refrigerator (France)
1866 Dynamite (Sweden)
1876 Telephone (Scotland)
1885 Motor car engine (Germany)
1895 Radio (Italy)
1903 Airplane (U.S.A.)
1925 Television (USA/Scotland)
1940 Penicillin (England)
1946 Electronic computer (U.S.A.)
1948 Transistor (U.S.A.)
1955 Hovercraft (England)
1960 Laser (U.S.A.)
1970 Floppy disk (U.S.A.)
1979 Compact disc (Japan)

The wheel — driving force of many other inventions.

Powered flight — an ancient dream only recently realized.

Zippers — one of thousands of revolutionary ordinary inventions like safety pins and safety razors!

Human civilization is largely a story of discovery and **invention**. Many important inventions have come from the work of one person, others have been the result of many people working patiently together as a team.

A potter's wheel.

The computer, the modern successor to Charles Babbage's mechanical "Analytical Engine" of 1823.

Hans Lippershey's telescope of 1608.

in·ven·tion (in-ven′chən) *n.* **1** something invented, as a device or machine. **2** a lie.

in·ven·to·ry (in′vən-tôr′ē, in′vən-tōr′ē) *n.* **in·ven·to·ries** a list of the articles, goods, etc. found in a particular place.

in·ver·te·brate (in-vurt′ə-brət) *n.* an animal without a backbone.

in·vest (in-vest′) *vb.* **in·vest·ing, in·vest·ed** **1** to put money into a business in order to make a profit. **2** to give or devote to. – *n.* **in·ves·tor** (in-ves′tər).

in·ves·ti·gate (in-ves′tə-gāt′) *vb.* **in·ves·ti·gat·ing, in·ves·ti·gat·ed** to carry out a detailed inquiry into. – *n.* **in·ves·ti·ga·tion** (in-ves′tə-gā′shən).

in·vin·ci·ble (in-vin′sə-bəl) *adj.* that cannot be defeated.

in·vis·i·ble (in-viz′ə-bəl) *adj.* **1** not able to be seen. **2** unseen. – *n.* **in·vis·i·bil·i·ty** (in-viz′ə-bil′ət-ē).

in·vite (in-vīt′) *vb.* **in·vit·ing, in·vit·ed 1** to ask to come to a party, etc. **2** to ask for: *to invite comments.*

in·vi·ta·tion (in′və-tā′shən) *n.* a request to a person to come or go to a party, meal, etc.

in·voice (in′vois′) *n.* a list delivered with goods giving details of price and quantity.

in·vol·un·ta·ry (in-väl′ən-ter′ē) *adj.* describing an action, movement, muscle action, etc. that is done without being controlled by the will.

in·volve (in-välv′, in-vôlv′) *vb.* **in·volv·ing,**

in·volved 1 to require as a necessary part. **2** to cause to take part in. **3** to make emotionally concerned in.

in·ward (in′wərd) *adj.* & *adv.* **1** placed or being within. **2** moving toward the inside.

i·o·dine (ī′ə-dīn′, ī′ə-dən, ī′ə-dēn′) *n.* a nonmetallic element (symbol **I**), usually occurring as dark blue or black crystals.

i·on (ī′ən, ī′än′) *n.* an electrically charged atom.

●**I·o·wa** (ī′ə-wə). See Supplement, **U.S.A.**

●**I·ran** (i-ran′, ī-ran′, i-rän′). See Supplement, **Countries**.

●**I·raq** (i-rak′, i-räk′). See Supplement, **Countries**.

●**Ire·land** (īr′lənd) one of the British Isles. NORTHERN IRELAND is part of the UNITED KINGDOM. Its capital city is Belfast. The rest of Ireland forms the Republic of Ireland. Its capital is Dublin. See also Supplement, **Countries**.

ir·i·des·cent (îr′ə-des′ənt) *adj.* having many rainbowlike colors which seem to shimmer. – *n.* **ir·i·des·cence** (ir′ə-des′əns).

i·ris (ī′rəs) *n.* **1** the colored, central membrane in the eye. It controls the size of the pupil. **2** a tall flower with long, sword-shaped leaves.

I·rish (ī′rish) *adj.* of IRELAND, its inhabitants,

history, culture, or its Celtic language.

irk·some (urk′səm) *adj.* annoying, irritating.

i·ron (ī′ərn) *n.* **1** a heavy gray metallic element (symbol **Fe**), used for making tools and in engineering. **2** a flat-bottomed tool used for smoothing the creases out of clothes. – *adj.* **1** made of iron: *iron railings*. **2** like iron, especially in being very strong and inflexible: *an iron will.* – *vb.* **ironing, ironed** to smooth the creases out of with an iron.

Iron Age *n.* the period in history following the BRONZE AGE, when people made weapons and tools out of iron, from about 1000 B.C.

i·ro·ny (ī′rə-nē) *n.* **i·ro·nies** a form of humor, or a way of mocking by saying the opposite of what is clearly true.

i·ron·ic (ī-rän′ik) *adj.* (also **i·ron·i·cal** [ī-rän′i-kəl]) containing or expressing irony.

ir·ra·tio·nal (ir-ash′ən-l) *adj.* **1** not the result of logical thought. **2** not able to think logically.

ir·reg·u·lar (ir-eg′yə-lər) *adj.* **1** not happening at regular or equal intervals. **2** not smooth or balanced. **3** not conforming to accepted behavior or routine. **4** in grammar, having forms which do not fit the pattern: *"To be" is an irregular verb.*

ir·re·sis·ti·ble (ir′i-zis′tə-bəl) *adj.* too tempting or attractive to be resisted.

ir·re·spon·si·ble (ir′i-spän′sə-bəl) *adj.* **1** reckless; careless. **2** not reliable or trustworthy. – *n.* **ir·re·spon·si·bil·i·ty** (ir′i-spän′sə-bil′ət-ē).

ir·ri·gate (ir′ə-gāt′) *vb.* **ir·ri·gat·ing, ir·ri·gat·ed** to supply land with water through canals, ditches, etc. – *n.* **ir·ri·ga·tion** (ir′ə-gā′shən).

ir·ri·tate (ir′ə-tāt′) *vb.* **ir·ri·tat·ing, ir·ri·tat·ed** **1** to make angry or annoyed. **2** to make sore and red: *The dust irritated their eyes.* – *n.* **ir·ri·ta·tion** (ir′ə-tā′shən).

is. See **be**.

-ish *suffix* forming adjectives meaning **1** slightly; having a trace of: *bluish*. **2** like: *childish*. **3** having as a nationality: *Swedish*. **4** about; roughly: *fiftyish*.

I·sis (ī′səs). See **Myths and Legends**.

Is·lam (is-läm′, iz-läm′) *n.* the MUSLIM religion, based on the worship of one god (Allah) and the teachings of his prophet MUHAMMAD. – *adj.* **Is·lam·ic** (is-läm′ik, iz-läm′ik).

● Islam is the main religion in North AFRICA, much of the MIDDLE EAST, and central ASIA, and in parts of Southeast Asia. It was first preached by the prophet MUHAMMAD who was born in Mecca in A.D. 570. The followers of Islam are called MUSLIMS. Their holy book is the KORAN and their place of worship is a mosque.

is·land (ī′lənd) *n.* **1** a piece of land completely surrounded by water. **2** anything that is like an island or is detached. – *n.* **is·land·er**.

isle (īl) *n.* an island, often a small one.

-ism *suffix* forming nouns meaning **1** a formal set of ideas etc.: *feminism*. **2** a quality: *heroism*. **3** an activity or practice: *criticism*. **4** discrimination on the grounds of: *racism*.

iso- *prefix* same; equal.

i·so·bar (ī′sə-bär′) *n.* See **Weather Terms**.

i·so·late (ī′sə-lāt′) *vb.* **i·so·lat·ing, i·so·lat·ed** to separate from others. – *adj.* **i·so·lat·ed**. – *n.* **i·so·la·tion** (ī′sə-lā′shən).

i·sos·ce·les (ī-säs′ə-lēz′) *n.* a triangle having two sides of equal length.

● **Is·ra·el** (iz′rē-əl, iz′rā-əl). See Supplement, **Countries**.

Is·ra·e·li (iz-rā′lē) *adj.* of the modern state of Israel or its inhabitants. – *n.* a person born in Israel.

is·sue (ish′ōō) *n.* **1** the giving out, publishing, or making available of something: *I bought the first issue of the magazine.* **2** a subject for discussion: *Unemployment is the main issue of the debate.* **3** a result or consequence. – *vb.* **is·su·ing, is·sued** **1** to give or send out, distribute, publish, or make available. **2** to supply: *The troops were issued with weapons.*

-ist *suffix* **1** a believer in some formal system of ideas, principles, or beliefs: *feminist*. **2** a person who carries out some activity or practices some art: *novelist*.

● **Is·tan·bul** (is′tan-bool′, is′tan-bōōl′) is the largest city in TURKEY, on the BOSPHORUS.

it (ət, it) *pron.* **1** the thing, animal, baby, or group already mentioned: *We watched the movie and enjoyed it very much.* **2** the person in question: *Who is it?* **3** used as the subject with impersonal verbs and when describing the weather or distance or telling the time: *It's raining. What time is it?* **4** used to refer to a general situation or state of affairs: *How's it going?*

IRISH WORDS AND TERMS

The form of Gaelic spoken in parts of Ireland has given a number of words to the English language. They include:

blarney, brat, brogue, galore, leprechaun, shamrock and smithereens. Also *banshee* a female spirit that wails when a death is about to occur; *machree* a term of endearment meaning "my heart;" and *shillelagh* a club-like weapon; *whiskey* from the Gaelic for "water of life." The Prime Minister of the Republic of Ireland is the *Taoiseach*.

Sloping italic type is a streamlined version of the Small Roman hand developed by Italian scholars in the 1300s. It is based on lettering from books of the 700s.

I·tal·ian (ə-tal′yən) *adj.* of ITALY, its inhabitants, culture, history, or its language. – *n.* **1** a person born or living in ITALY or of Italian descent. **2** the Romance language spoken in ITALY and in parts of SWITZERLAND.

i·tal·ic (ə-tal′ik) *n.* (usually in *plural*) a typeface, first used in ITALY, with characters that slope upward to the right, as italic.

● **It·a·ly** (it′l-ē) is a peninsula in southern EUROPE and is noted for its impressive ruins of the ROMAN EMPIRE, for the VATICAN, and for its medieval cities such as Florence and VENICE. It was the birthplace of the RENAISSANCE. The northern cities are highly industrialized and there is much rich farmland. See also Supplement, **Countries**.

Throughout history, **Italy** has played an enormously powerful part in the culture and development of Europe. The Romans ruled and gave their civilization and administration to a vast area of the world. The Latin language is the ancestor of all Europe's Romance languages. The Renaissance flowered in Italy. For a long time the whole Christian Church was governed from there. In the arts, science, and industry Italy's contribution has been great.

Perhaps best known of Italian food are pizza and, in all its different guises, pasta.

A street scene in 15th-century Florence, one of the great centers of Renaissance learning and art. But it was trade that made Florence grow.

Pisa's cathedral and Leaning Tower.

itch (ich) *n.* an unpleasant irritation on the surface of the skin which makes you want to scratch. – *vb.* **itch·ing, itched 1** to have an itch and want to scratch. **2** to feel a strong or restless desire. – *n.* **itch·i·ness** (ich′ē-nəs). – *adj.* **itch·y** (ich′ē), **itch·i·er, itch·i·est**.

-ite *suffix* forming nouns denoting **1** a place or national group: *Israelite*. **2** a follower of: *laborite*. **3** a mineral: *bauxite*.

i·tem (īt′əm) *n.* **1** a separate unit, especially one on a list. **2** a separate piece of information or news.

i·tin·er·ar·y (ī-tin′ə-rer′ē) *n.* **i·tin·er·ar·ies** a plan of a route for a trip.

-itis *suffix* in the names of diseases, inflammation of: *appendicitis*.

its (its) *adj.* belonging to it: *The dog scratched its ear.* – *pron.* the one or ones belonging to it. – **of its** of or belonging to it.

● **its** and **it's**. The first word means "belonging to it": *The dog is eating its bone. It's* is an abbreviation of *it is*: *It's time to go.*

it's it is.

it·self (it-self′) *pron.* **1** the reflexive form of **it** meaning its own self: *The cat licked itself.* **2** used for emphasis: *It's the book itself that interests me, not the contents.* **3** (also **by itself**) alone; without help.

-ive *suffix* having a quality, performing an action, etc.: *creative; detective*.

i·vo·ry (īv′rē, ī′və-rē) *n.* the hard, bony, creamy-white substance which forms the tusks of elephants, hippopotamuses, and walruses. – *adj.* of or like ivory, especially in color.

Ivory Coast. See **Côte d'Ivoire**.

i·vy (ī′vē) *n.* **i·vies** an evergreen shrub with dark leaves with five points which climbs on walls and trees.

-ize *suffix* forming verbs meaning **1** to make or become: *equalize*. **2** to treat or react to: *criticize*. – *n. suffix* **-ization** .

J j

jab (jab) *vb.* **jab·bing, jabbed 1** to poke or prod. **2** to hit with quick, short blows. – *n.* **1** a poke or prod. **2** a quick, short punch.

jack (jak) *n.* **1** a device for raising heavy objects off the ground. **2** in cards, (also **knave**) the card bearing a picture of a young man. **3** the male of certain animals, as the donkey. – *vb.* **jack·ing, jacked** to raise with a jack: *Ed jacked the car to repair the flat tire.*

jack·al (jak′əl) *n.* a long-legged, yellowish, wild dog of AFRICA and ASIA, that feeds on the remains of creatures killed by other animals.

jack·daw (jak′dô′) *n.* a bird of the crow family and native to EUROPE.

jack·et (jak′ət) *n.* **1** a short coat, especially a long-sleeved hip-length one. **2** something worn over the top half of the body. **3** a loose paper cover for a book. **4** the skin of a potato.

jack·knife (jak′nīf′) *n.* **1** a pocket knife with a folding blade. **2** a dive in which the diver bends and straigthens before touching the water head first. – *vb.* **jack·knif·ing, jack·knifed** to fold like a jackknife.

jack·pot (jak′pät′) *n.* the maximum win to be made in a lottery, card game, etc.

jade (jād) *n.* either of two hard, usually green semiprecious stones.

jag·ged (jag′əd) *adj.* having a rough or sharp uneven edge.

jag·uar (jag′wär′, jag′wər) *n.* a large spotted South American animal of the cat family.

jail (jāl) *n.* prison. – *vb.* **jail·ing, jailed** to put in prison.

jam¹ (jam) *n.* a thick sticky food made from fruit boiled with sugar, used as a spread.

jam² (jam) *vb.* **jam·ming, jammed 1** to block up by crowding. **2** to push or shove; to cram, press, or pack. **3** to stick or wedge. **4** to stick and stop working. **5** to put on with sudden force: *Mom jammed on the brakes to avoid the dog.* – *n.* **1** a mass of vehicles, etc. so tightly crowded together that movement comes to a stop: *traffic jams*. **2** a stoppage of machinery, etc., caused by something jamming.

●**Ja·mai·ca** (jə-mā′kə). See Supplement, **Countries**.

jamb (jam) *n.* the vertical post at the side of a door.

jam·bo·ree (jam′bə-rē′) *n.* a large party.

●**James** (jāmz) is the name of six kings of SCOTLAND and two of GREAT BRITAIN.

●**James** (jāmz), **Henry** (1843-1916) was an American novelist whose works include *The Turn of the Screw*, and *The Portrait of a Lady*.

jan·gle (jang′gəl) *vb.* **jan·gling, jan·gled** to make an unpleasant ringing noise.

Jan·u·ar·y (jan′yoo-er′ē) *n.* the first month of the year. January has 31 days.

A finely carved Chinese jade pot of the 1700s. It was made to hold brushes used in Chinese writing, an art form that has been described as "dancing on paper."

Tokugawa Ieyasu, who in 1603 became the shogun, or military commander, of Japan.

Japan is the richest country in Asia. It is made up of four large and many small islands. Mountains cover most of Japan; the highest is a beautiful volcano called Fujiyama. Most Japanese live in cities and work in factories. Japan was defeated in World War II (1939-1945), but afterwards became the "workshop." The capital is Tokyo. See also Supplement, **Countries**.

The four main islands of Japan. There is evidence of people living there from around 30,000 B.C.

Hokkaido

Honshu

Shikoku

Kyushu

A bullet-shaped high-speed electric train — symbol of Japan's technical efficiency.

A beautifully carved netsuke, or toggle.

A Chinese-style Buddhist temple. But Shinto, "the way of the gods," is Japan's main religion.

Jap·a·nese (jap′ə-nēz′, jap′ə-nēs′) *adj.* of JAPAN, its people or language. – *n.* **1** a native of JAPAN. **2** the language of JAPAN.

jar¹ (jär) *n.* a wide-mouthed cylindrical container, usually of glass; the contents of this: *a jar of coffee.*

jar² (jär) *vb.* **jar·ring, jarred 1** to have a harsh effect. **2** to jolt or vibrate. **3** to clash or conflict. – *n.* a shock or jolt.

jar·gon (jär′gən) *n.* the specialized vocabulary of a particular trade or profession.

jaun·dice (jôn′dəs) *n.* a condition in which there is an excess of bile in the blood, a pigment of which turns the skin yellow.

jaun·diced (jôn′dəst) *adj.* **1** suffering from jaundice. **2** (of a person) bitter or resentful.

jav·e·lin (jav′ə-lən) *n.* a light spear for throwing as a weapon or in sport.

jaw (jô) *n.* either of the two hinged parts of the skull in which the teeth are set.

jay (jā) *n.* a noisy bird of the crow family, with feathers of various colors.

jazz (jaz) *n.* popular music of black American origin, with strong, catchy rhythms, performed with much improvization.

● Jazz was first played by blacks of New Orleans in the late 1800s. Famous jazz performers include Duke Ellington, Charlie Parker, and Billie HOLIDAY.

jeal·ous (je′ləs) *adj.* envious of someone else, his or her possessions, talents, etc.

jeal·ous·y (jel′ə-sē) *n.* **jeal·ous·ies** envy.

jeans (jēnz) *n.* (*plural*) denim trousers.

jeep (jēp) *n.* a light military vehicle capable of traveling over rough country.

jeer (jîr) *vb.* **jeer·ing, jeered** to mock; to laugh unkindly. – *n.* a taunt or insult.

● **Jef·fer·son** (jef′ər-sən), **Thomas** (1743-1826) was the chief author of the DECLARATION OF INDEPENDENCE and third president of the UNITED STATES.

jell or **gel** (jel) *vb.* **jell·ing, jelled** or **gell·ing, gelled** to become firm; to set.

jel·ly (jel′ē) *n.* **jellies** a thick preparation of fruit, sugar, water, and often pectin.

jelly bean *n.* a soft candy with a hard shell, shaped like a bean.

● **Jen·ner** (jen′ər), **Edward** (1749-1823) was an English doctor who discovered vaccination by showing that injections of a related virus produce immunity against SMALLPOX.

jeop·ar·dy (jep′ər-dē) *n.* danger of harm or loss.

jeop·ar·dize (jep′ər-dīz′) or (especially *British*) **jeop·ar·dise** *vb.* **jeop·ar·diz·ing, jeop·ar·dized** to put at risk of harm, loss, or destruction.

jer·bo·a (jur-bō′ə) *n.* a small ratlike animal of AFRICA and ASIA, with long hind legs.

●**Jer·i·cho** (jer′i-kō′) is a village in JORDAN on the site of a biblical city captured by the Israelites.

jerk (jurk) *n.* **1** a quick tug or pull. **2** a sudden movement. – *vb.* **jerk·ing, jerked 1** to pull sharply. **2** to move with sharp suddenness.

jer·sey (jur′zē) *n.* **jer·seys** a knitted garment worn on the upper part of the body; a pullover.

●**Je·ru·sa·lem** (jə-rōō′zə-ləm, jə-rōō′sə-ləm) is the capital of ISRAEL and a holy city of JEWS, CHRISTIANS, and MUSLIMS.

jest·er (jes′tər) *n.* a professional clown employed by a king or noble.

Je·su·it (jezh′ōō-ət) *n.* a member of the Society of Jesus, a Roman Catholic order.

●**Je·sus Christ** (jē′zəz krīst′, jē′zəs) (*ca.*6 B.C.-*ca.*A.D. 30) was the founder of CHRISTIANITY. He was born in BETHLEHEM and was brought up as a Jew. His life and teachings are contained in the New Testament of the BIBLE. CHRISTIANS believe he is the son of GOD and that he rose from the dead.

jet (jet) *n.* **1** a strong fast stream of liquid or gas, forced under pressure from a narrow opening. **2** (also **jet aircraft**) an aircraft powered by a jet engine. – *vb.* **jet·ting, jet·ted 1** to travel by jet aircraft. **2** to come out in a jet; to spurt.

jet·ti·son (jet′ə-sən) *vb.* **jet·ti·son·ing, jet·ti·soned 1** to throw overboard to lighten a ship, aircraft, etc. in an emergency: *to jettison cargo.* **2** to abandon, reject, or get rid of.

jet·ty (jet′ē) *n.* **jet·ties 1** a pier or wharf. **2** a stone barrier built out into the sea to protect a harbor from currents and high waves.

Jew (jōō) *n.* **1** a member of the HEBREW people. **2** someone whose religion is JUDAISM.

jew·el (jōō′əl) *n.* a precious stone.

jew·el·er or **jew·el·ler** (jōō′ə-lər, jōō′lər) *n.* a person who deals in, makes, or repairs jewelery.

jew·el·ry or (especially *British*) **jew·el·ler·y** (jōō′əl-rē, jōōl′rē) *n.* articles worn for personal decoration, such as bracelets, necklaces, etc.

Jew·ish (jōō′ish) *adj.* relating or belonging to the Jews or to JUDAISM.

jig (jig) *n.* a lively country dance or folk dance. – *vb.* **jig·ging, jigged** to dance a jig.

jig·saw (jig′sô′) *n.* a fine-bladed saw for cutting intricate patterns.

jig·saw puzzle (jig′sô′ puz′l) *n.* a picture mounted on wood or cardboard, and sawn into pieces. The pieces are put together again to rebuild the picture.

jin·gle (jing′gəl) *n.* **1** a short sharp ringing sound, as of coins or keys. **2** a simple rhyming verse or song. – *vb.* **jin·gling, jin·gled** to make a ringing sound.

●**Joan of Arc** (jōn′əv ärk′) (1412-1431) was a French heroine who led a force against the English in a war. She was burned for witchcraft.

job (jäb) *n.* **1** a person's regular paid employment. **2** a piece of work. **3** a completed task: *Mary made a good job of the pruning.* **4** a function or responsibility.

jock·ey (jäk′ē) *n.* **jock·eys** a rider, especially professional, in horse races.

jog (jäg, jôg) *vb.* **jog·ging, jogged 1** to nudge slightly. **2** to prompt the memory. **3** to run at a gentle, steady pace, for exercise. – *n.* **jog·ger.**

The jerboa, or desert rat, looks like a miniature kangaroo. It can hop up to 10ft. (3m) in each bound.

Joan of Arc was convinced that the "voices" she heard were from heaven telling her to rescue France from the English. She commanded the French army.

Jewelry has been made since prehistoric times, when the bones and teeth of animals were used. Today jewelry is mostly made of gems and precious metals.

An eagle-shaped brooch made by an Ostrogoth in Spain (A.D. 400s)

A jewel bearing the inscription "Alfred had me made." It was probably one of a set of book pointers that Alfred, King of Wessex, ordered to be made.

This gold ring is a fine example of Viking craftsmanship.

The crown used at the coronation of King Stephen of Hungary on Christmas Day, A.D. 1000.

● **Jo·han·nes·burg** (jō-han′əs-burg′) the largest city in SOUTH AFRICA.

● **John the Bap·tist** (jän′t͟hə bap′təst, bab′təst) was a preacher and cousin of JESUS whom he baptized. He was put to death by King HEROD.

● **John·son** (jän′sən), **Samuel** (1709-1784) was an English writer, wit, and dictionary editor.

join (join) *vb.* **join·ing, joined** **1** to connect, attach, link, or unite. **2** to become a member: *Darleen joined the glee club.* **3** to meet: *Roads join at a crossroad.* **4** to come together with: *We joined them for supper.* – *n.* a seam or joint. – *vb.* **join in** to take part.

joint (joint) *n.* **1** the place where two or more pieces join. **2** a part of the skeleton, such as the knee or elbow, where two bones meet. **3** a piece of meat, usually containing a bone. – *adj.* owned, done, etc. in common; shared: *We have a joint account at the bank.*

joist (joist) *n.* a horizontal beam supporting a floor or ceiling.

joke (jōk) *n.* a humorous story: *Steve is always telling jokes.* – *vb.* **jok·ing, joked** to make jokes; to speak in jest, not in earnest. – *adv.* **jok·ing·ly.**

jok·er *n.* **1** an extra card in a pack, usually bearing a picture of a jester, used in certain games. **2** a cheerful person, always full of jokes.

● **Jol·li·et** (jō′lē-et′, zhō′lē-ā′), **Louis** (1645-1700) was a French-Canadian explorer of NORTH AMERICA.

jol·ly (jäl′ē) *adj.* **jol·li·er, jol·li·est** **1** cheerful. **2** happy; enjoyable.

Jol·ly Rog·er (jäl′ē räj′ər) *n.* a pirate flag, depicting a skull and crossbones.

jolt (jōlt) *vb.* **jolt·ing, jolt·ed** **1** to move along jerkily. **2** to jog or jar: *The bus jolted to a halt.* – *n.* **1** a jarring shake. **2** an emotional shock.

jon·quil (jäng′kwəl) *n.* a plant with sweet-smelling white or yellow flowers.

● **Jor·dan** (jôrd′n). See Supplement, **Countries.**

jos·tle (jäs′əl) *vb.* **jos·tling, jos·tled** to push and shove: *The people jostled to get on the train.*

jot (jät) *n.* the least bit. – *vb.* **jot·ting, jot·ted** to write down hastily.

jour·nal (jurn′l) *n.* **1** a magazine. **2** a diary in which to recount daily activities.

jour·na·lism (jurn′l-iz′əm) *n.* the profession of writing news for newspapers and magazines, or for television and radio. – *n.* **jour·na·list** (jurn′l-əst).

jour·ney (jur′nē) *n.* **jour·neys** **1** a process of traveling from one place to another. **2** the distance covered by a journey. – *vb.* **jour·ney·ing, jour·neyed** to make a journey.

joust (joust) *n.* a contest between two knights on horseback, armed with lances. – *vb.* **joust·ing, joust·ed** to take part in a joust.

jo·vi·al (jō′vē-əl) *adj.* merry; cheerful.

jowl (joul) *n.* loose flesh under the chin.

joy (joi) *n.* **1** a feeling of happiness. **2** a cause of this: *The puppy was a great joy to Liz.*

joy·ful (joi′fəl) *adj.* happy; full of joy.

joy·ride (joi′rīd′) *n.* a reckless drive in a stolen vehicle.

● **Joyce** (jois), **James** (1882-1941) was an Irish novelist whose works include *Ulysses* and *Dubliners.*

ju·bi·lee (jōō′bə-lē′, jōō′bə-lē′) *n.* a special anniversary, especially the 25th, 50th, or 60th (respectively a **silver, golden,** and **diamond jubilee**) of an important event.

Ju·da·ism (jōōd′ə-iz′əm) *n.* the religion of the JEWS, having its basis in the Old Testament and the TALMUD. – *adj.* **Ju·da·ic** (jōō-dā′ik).

● Observances in Judaism include the Sabbath as a day of rest, and the holy days of YOM KIPPUR, PASSOVER, and Shabuoth.

judge (juj) *n.* **1** a public officer who hears and decides cases in a law court. **2** a person appointed to decide the winner of a contest. **3** a person qualified to give an expert opinion. – *vb.* **judg·ing, judged** **1** to try a case in a law court as judge. **2** to decide the winner of: *to judge a contest.* **3** to form an opinion about.

judg·ment or (especially *British*) **judge·ment** (juj′mənt) *n.* **1** the decision of a judge in a court of law. **2** the ability to make wise or sensible decisions.

ju·do (jōōd′ō) *n.* a Japanese form of wrestling.

jug (jug) *n.* a large container for liquids with a handle, a narrow mouth, and sometimes a cork or stopper.

PRONUNCIATION SYMBOLS

ə	away	lemon	focus
a	fat	oi	boy
ā	fade	oo	foot
ä	hot	ōō	moon
âr	fair	ou	house
e	met	th	think
ē	mean	t͟h	this
g	get	u	cut
hw	which	ur	hurt
i	fin	w	witch
ī	line	y	yes
îr	near	yōō	music
ô	often	yoor	pure
ō	note	zh	vision

Jubilee is of Hebrew origin and refers to a year of celebrations every 50 years. The word comes *jobel*, a ram's horn, for jubilee year was proclaimed by blowing a horn.

jug·gle (jug′əl) *vb.* **jug·gling, jug·gled** to keep several objects in the air by skillful throwing and catching. – *n.* **jug·gler** (jug′lər).

juice (jōōs) *n.* **1** liquid from fruit or vegetables: *carrot juice.* **2** the body's natural fluids.

juic·y (jōō′sē) *adj.* **juic·i·er, juic·i·est** full of juice; rich and succulent.

●**Ju·li·us Cae·sar** (jōōl′yəs sē′zər). See **Caesar**.

Ju·ly (joo-lī′) *n.* the seventh month of the year. July has 31 days.

jum·ble (jum′bəl) *vb.* **jum·bling, jum·bled** to mix; to throw together untidily. – *n.* a confused mass: *She left a jumble of clothes in the bedroom.*

jum·bo (jum′bō) (*informal*) *adj.* extra large.

jump (jump) *vb.* **jump·ing, jumped 1** to spring off the ground, pushing off with the feet; to leap. **2** to get over or across by jumping: *Kim jumped over the fence.* **3** to make a startled movement: *Jamal jumped when the alarm went off.* – *n.* an act of jumping.

junc·tion (jungk′shən) *n.* a place where roads or railroad lines meet; an intersection.

June (jōōn) *n.* the sixth month of the year. June has 30 days.

jun·gle (jung′gəl) *n.* dense tropical forest.

ju·nior (jōōn′yər) *adj.* **1** low, or lower, in rank, class, etc. **2** younger, as in the name of a son: *John Smith, Junior.* – *n.* **1** a person of low, or lower, rank in a profession, organization, etc. **2** a third-year college or high school student.

junior high school *n.* a school between elementary and high school, usually for grades seven through nine.

ju·ni·per (jōō′nə-pər) *n.* an evergreen shrub with prickly leaves and purple berries used as a medicine and for flavoring.

junk (jungk) *n.* worthless or rejected material; trash. – *adj.* cheap and worthless.

Ju·no (jōō′nō). See **Myths and Legends**.

●**Ju·pi·ter**¹ (jōō′pət-ər) is the largest planet in the solar system.

Ju·pi·ter² (jōō′pət-ər). See **Myths and Legends**.

ju·ry (jōōr′ē) *n.* **juries** a group of usually 12 people sworn to give an honest verdict on the evidence presented to a law court on a particular case.

just¹ (just) *adj.* fair; reasonable; based on justice: *The judge's decision was just.* – *n.* **just·ness** (just′nəs).

just² (just, jəst, jest) *adv.* **1** exactly; precisely. **2** a short time before: *He had just gone.* **3** at this or that very moment: *I was just leaving.* **4** and no more: *There was only just enough.* **5** barely; narrowly: *The knife just missed his ear.* **6** only; merely; simply: *Pam sent just a brief note.* – **just in case** as a precaution. – **just now** at this particular moment. – **not just yet** not immediately, but soon.

jus·tice (jus′təs) *n.* **1** the quality of being just; fairness. **2** the quality of being reasonable. **3** administration of the law: *a miscarriage of justice.* **4** a judge.

jus·ti·fy (jus′tə-fī′) *vb.* **jus·ti·fies, jus·ti·fy·ing, jus·ti·fied** to prove or show to be right, just, or reasonable. – *n.* **jus·ti·fi·ca·tion** (jus′tə-fə-kā′shən).

jut (jut) *vb.* **jut·ting, jut·ted** to stick out, to project.

ju·ve·nile (jōō′və-nīl′, jōō′vən-l) *adj.* young, of young people.

Unmanned space probes have collected information about Jupiter.

Jupiter is so huge that a thousand Earths could fit on it. It spins faster than any of the other planets; a day on Jupiter lasts 10 hours. Jupiter consists of 90 percent hydrogen and 10 percent helium. Jupiter's main features are its ring and its Great Red Spot, probably a swirling mass of gases in a never-ending storm.

Callisto

Ganymede

Io

Europa

Jupiter's core is hotter than the surface of the sun. Its clouds exposed to space are bitterly cold.

Io is a sulfur-covered world of constantly erupting volcanoes.

K k

The letter *K*, like all the letters, has a long history. The earliest alphabets were taken and adapted by the Greeks. The Greek *beta*, when combined with the first letter, *aleph*, gives us the word alphabet.

The Greeks passed on their letters to the Romans, who developed the alphabet we use today, although they used only capital letters. Small letters developed in the A.D. 700s.

Ψ

An early form of the letter K, used in the Middle East more than 3,000 years ago.

K

This letter was taken by the Greeks and became kappa.

ʞ

Over the years different versions of the letter K have been developed.

K. See **Computer Terms**.

ka·lei·do·scope (kə-līd′ə-skōp′) *n.* a tube inside which fragments of colored glass, etc. are reflected in mirrors, so as to form constantly changing symmetrical patterns.

kan·ga·roo (kang-gə-roo′) *n.* an Australian MARSUPIAL animal with powerful hind legs used for leaping long distances. The female carries her young in a pouch on her abdomen.

●**Kan·sas** (kan′zəs). See Supplement, **U.S.A.**

ka·ra·o·ke (kar′ē-ō′kē, kə-rō′kē) *n.* a form of entertainment in which amateur performers sing pop songs to the accompaniment of recorded music from a **karaoke machine**.

ka·ra·te (kə-rät′ē) *n.* Japanese system of unarmed self-defense, using blows and kicks.

kay·ak (kī′ak′) *n.* **1** a canoe covered with seal skin, used by the INUIT. **2** a similar fiberglass canoe.

●**Ka·zakh·stan** (käz′äk-stan′). See Supplement, **Countries**.

●**Keats** (kēts), **John** (1795-1821) was an English Romantic poet.

keel (kēl) *n.* the timber or metal bar extending along the base of a ship, from which the hull is built up. – *vb.* **keel over; keel·ing, keeled 1** (of a ship) to tip over sideways. **2** to fall over.

keen (kēn) *adj.* **1** (of the mind or senses) quick; acute. **2** (of competition, rivalry, etc.) fierce. **3** eager; willing. **4** enthusiastic about; fond of: *Kate is keen on hockey.*

keep¹ (kēp) *vb.* **keep·ing, kept** (kept) **1** to have; to possess. **2** to save. **3** to store: *I always keep stamps in my desk.* **4** to remain in a certain state, position, place, etc.: *Please keep quiet.* **5** to continue or be frequently doing something: *Keep smiling.* **6** to own an animal, etc. for use or pleasure: *Mark keeps hens in his yard.*

keep² (kēp) *n.* the central tower in a castle.

keep·er (kē′pər) *n.* a person who looks after animals in a zoo or people in an institution.

keg (keg) *n.* a small barrel.

●**Kel·ler** (kel′ər), **Helen** (1880-1968) was an

The keep, or donjon, *was a massive tower and the strongest point in a castle. It stood in a courtyard called a* bailey. *The keep contained garrison quarters, a wellhead, a Great Hall, and the lord's sleeping quarters.*

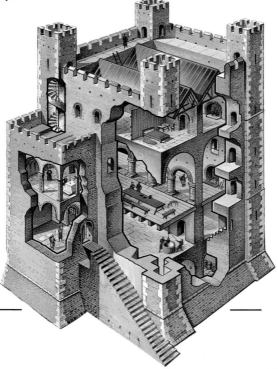

American author and social reformer who, despite being both blind and deaf, was taught to read BRAILLE and to talk.

● **Ken·ned·y** (ken′əd-ē), **John F.** (1917-1963) was the thirty-fifth president of the UNITED STATES.

ken·nel (ken′l) *n.* a small shelter for a dog.

● **Ken·tuck·y** (kən-tuk′ē). See Supplement, **U.S.A.**

● **Ken·ya** (ken′yə, kēn′yə). See Supplement, **Countries**.

kept. See **keep**.

ker·nel (kurn′l) *n.* a seed within a husk, the edible part of a nut, or the pit of a fruit.

ker·o·sene (ker′ə-sēn′, ker′ə-sēn′) *n.* an oil distilled from petroleum used for fuel.

ketch·up (kech′əp) *n.* a thick sauce made from tomatoes, vinegar, spices, etc.

ket·tle (ket′l) *n.* a kitchen vessel with a lid and handle, for boiling water in.

key (kē) *n.* **1** a piece of shaped metal designed to turn a lock, wind a clock, grip and turn a nut, etc. **2** one of a series of buttons or levers pressed to sound the notes on a musical instrument, or on a computer, calculator, etc. **3** a system of musical notes related to one another in a scale. **4** something that provides an answer or solution. **5** a table explaining signs and symbols used on a map, etc. – *adj.* centrally important. – *vb.* **key·ing, keyed** to type into a computer by operating keys.

key·board (kē′bôrd′, kē′bōrd′) *n.* the set of keys on a piano, typewriter, computer, etc.

kha·ki (kak′ē, käk′ē) *n.* a yellowish-brown color.

kib·butz (kib-oots′, kib-o͞ots′) *n.* **kib·but·zim** (kib-oot′sēm′, kib-o͞ot′sēm′) in ISRAEL, a farm owned and run by the people who work on it.

kick (kik) *vb.* **kick·ing, kicked** **1** to hit or propel with the foot: *The cow kicked my leg.* **2** to swing or jerk the leg vigorously. **3** to get rid of: *to kick a habit.* – *n.* **1** a blow with the foot. **2** a swing of the leg: *high kicks.* – *n.* **kick·er.** – *vb.* **kick off 1** to start a football game by kicking the ball. **2** to begin a discussion, etc.

kid¹ (kid) *n.* **1** (*informal*) a young person. **2** a young goat. – *adj.* (*informal*) younger: *Have you met my kid sister?*

kid² (kid) *vb.* **kid·ding, kid·ded** (*informal*) **1** to pretend. **2** to fool or deceive, especially for fun.

kid·nap (kid′nap′) *vb.* **kid·nap·ping, kid·napped** to seize illegally, usually demanding ransom.

kid·ney (kid′nē) *n.* **kid·neys** one of a pair of abdominal organs that filter waste from the blood and pass it out of the body as urine.

● **Kil·i·man·ja·ro** (kil′ə-mən-jär′ō) an extinct VOLCANO in TANZANIA is the highest mountain in AFRICA at 19,321 feet (5,889 m).

kill (kil) *vb.* **kill·ing, killed 1** to cause the death of. **2** (*informal*) to cause pain to: *My feet are killing me.* **3** (*informal*) to put an end to. – *n.* an act of killing. – *n.* **kill·er.**

killer whale *n.* a toothed WHALE closely related to dolphins.

kiln (kiln) *n.* an oven for baking pottery or bricks, or for drying grain.

ki·lo (kē′lō) *n.* **kilos** a kilogram or kilometer.

kilo- *prefix* one thousand.

kil·o·gram (kil′ə-gram′) *n.* a unit of weight equal to 1,000 grams (2.2 pounds).

kil·o·me·ter (kə-läm′ət-ər, kil′ə-mēt′ər) *n.* a unit of length equal to 1,000 meters (0.62 miles).

kil·o·watt (kil′ə-wät′) *n.* a unit of electrical power equal to 1,000 watts.

kilt (kilt) *n.* a pleated tartan knee-length skirt, worn by men of the Scottish Highlands.

ki·mo·no (kə-mō′nə) *n.* **ki·mo·nos** a long loose wide-sleeved Japanese garment.

kin (kin) *n.* relatives.

kind¹ (kīnd) *n.* **1** a group, class, sort, or type: *Foxes and wolves are kinds of dogs.* **2** nature or character: *They differ in kind.* – **kind of** (*informal*) slightly.

kind² (kīnd) *adj.* friendly, helpful, generous. – *n.* **kind·ness** (kīnd′nəs).

kin·der·gar·ten (kin′dər-gärt′n) *n.* a class or school for children aged between four and six.

An 18th-century kiln, or furnace (above), *and an African kiln of about 400 B.C.* (below). *The process of placing objects in a kiln is known as "firing."*

king (king) *n.* **1** a male ruler of a nation. **2** a person, creature, or thing considered supreme in strength, importance, etc. **3** in a pack of cards, the one bearing a picture of a king.

king·dom (king'dəm) *n.* **1** a country ruled by a king or queen. **2** any of the three divisions of the natural world: *the animal, plant, or mineral kingdoms.*

● **King** (king), **Martin Luther, Jr.** (1929-1968) was an American civil rights leader who worked for racial justice. He was awarded the NOBEL peace prize in 1964.

king·fish·er (king'fish'ər) *n.* a bird with brilliant plumage that dives for fish.

ki·osk (kē'äsk') *n.* a small structure with an open side, as a stand to sell newspapers.

● **Kip·ling** (kip'ling), **Rudyard** (1865-1936) was an English writer of adventure stories and poems including *The Jungle Books* and *Just So Stories.*

● **Ki·ri·bati** (kir'ə-bas'). See Supplement, **Countries.**

kiss (kis) *vb.* **kiss·ing, kissed** to touch with the lips, as a greeting or sign of affection. – *n.* **1** an act of kissing. **2** a gentle touch.

kit (kit) *n.* **1** a set of instruments, equipment, etc. needed for a purpose. **2** a set of clothing and personal equipment for a soldier. **3** a set of parts ready for assembling.

kitch·en (kich'ən) *n.* a room where food is prepared and cooked.

kite (kīt) *n.* **1** a long-tailed bird of prey of the hawk family. **2** a light frame covered in a light material, with a long holding string attached to it, for flying in the air for fun.

kit·ten (kit'n) *n.* a young cat.

ki·wi (kē'wē) *n.* a flightless, long-beaked bird from NEW ZEALAND.

knack (nak) *n.* the ability to do something with ease: *She has a knack for fixing machines.*

knap·sack (nap'sak') *n.* a bag for food, books, etc. carried on the back by means of straps over the shoulders.

knead (nēd) *vb.* **knead·ing, knead·ed** to press and squeeze with one's hands.

knee (nē) *n.* **1** the middle joint of the leg between ankle and hip; the same joint in an animal. **2** the lap: *The child sat on her knee.*

kneel (nēl) *vb.* **kneel·ing, knelt** (nelt) **or**

The kiwi gets its name from the shrill cries made by the male. Kiwis live in forests and at night hunt for worms and grubs. They have poor eyesight and smell out their food with the help of nostrils at the tip of their long beaks.

kneeled to go down on one or both knees: *He knelt and began to pray.*

knew. See **know**.

knife (nīf) *n.* **knives** (nīvz) a cutting instrument in the form of a blade fitted into a handle. – *vb.* **knif·ing, knifed** to stab with a knife.

knight (nīt) *n.* **1** in the MIDDLE AGES, a soldier, usually on a horse, serving a FEUDAL lord. **2** in chess, a piece shaped like a horse's head.

knit (nit) *vb.* **knit·ting, knit·ted** or **knit** to make a fabric or garment by looping wool or cotton around a pair of long needles.

knit·ting (nit'ing) *n.* knitted work.

knob (näb) *n.* **1** a handle, especially rounded, on a door or drawer. **2** a button pressed or turned to operate a piece of equipment.

knock (näk) *vb.* **knock·ing, knocked 1** to tap with the knuckles or some object. **2** to strike and so push, especially accidentally: *Kate knocked the cup off the table.* **3** to strike, bump, or bang against: *The gate knocked against the wall.* – *n.* **1** an act of knocking: *I jumped when I heard the knock on the door.* **2** a tap.

knoll (nōl) *n.* a small round hill.

● **Knos·sos** (näs'əs) is a ruined city in Crete with remains of the MINOAN civilization (1700-1450 B.C.).

In the Middle Ages in Europe both **knights** and their strong horses wore heavy plate armor. A knight's armor weighed up to 65 pounds (30kg), so heavy that he would have to be winched onto his horse.

knot (nät) *n.* **1** a join or tie in string, etc. made by looping the ends around each other and pulling tight. **2** a bond. **3** a tangle in hair, string, etc. **4** a hard mass in a tree trunk where a branch has grown out from it. – *vb.*
knot·ting, knot·ted 1 to tie in a knot. **2** to tangle.

know (nō) *vb.* **know·ing, knew** (nōō), **known** (nōn) **1** to be aware of; to be certain; to have an understanding of. **2** to be familiar with: *I know her well.* **3** to recognize or identify: *I know your face from somewhere.* **4** to consider.

know·ing (nō′ing) *adj.* **1** shrewd; clever. **2** (of a glance) showing secret awareness.

know·how (nō′hou′) *n.* (*informal*) skill; ability.

knowl·edge (näl′ij) *n.* **1** the fact of knowing; awareness. **2** information acquired through learning or experience: *a knowledge of science.*

knowl·edge·a·ble (näl′ij-ə-bəl) *adj.* well-informed.

●**Knox** (näks), **John** (1514-1572) was a Scottish religious reformer who established Presbyterianism.

knuck·le (nuk′əl) *n.* a joint of a finger.

Knights jousting in a tournament. They used blunt swords and lances but even so, many were killed or wounded.

A knight's shield carried his coat-of-arms so that he could be recognized in battle.

ko·al·a (kō-äl′ə) *n.* (also **koala bear**) an Australian tree-climbing MARSUPIAL animal that looks like a small bear.

●**Kohl** (kōl), **Helmut** (1930-) is Chancellor of GERMANY.

kook·a·bur·ra (kook′ə-bur′ə) *n.* a large Australian bird of the kingfisher family.

Ko·ran (kə-ran′, kə-rän′) *n.* the holy book of ISLAM, believed by MUSLIMS to be composed of the revelations of ALLAH to MUHAMMAD.

●**Ko·re·a** (kə-rē′ə), **North**. See Supplement, **Countries**.

●**Ko·re·a** (kə-rē′ə), **South**. See Supplement, **Countries**.

●**Ko·re·an War** (kə-rē′ən wôr′) (1950-1953) began when North Korea, a Communist country, attacked South Korea. Nearly 3 million people died, including 50,000 Americans.

ko·sher (kō′shər) *adj.* cooked, prepared, or otherwise in agreement with Jewish law.

●**Krak·a·to·a** (krak′ə-tō′ə) is an island VOLCANO in INDONESIA which erupted with great violence in 1883.

krem·lin (krem′lən) *n.* the citadel of a Russian town, especially that of Moscow.

●**Kub·lai Khan** (kōō′blə kän′, kōō′blī′ kän′) (1214-1294) was a Mongol ruler, grandson of Genghis Khan.

●**Ku Klux Klan** (kōō′ kluks′ klan′, kyōō′ kluks′ klan′) This secret organization was formed after the American CIVIL WAR (1861-1865) by white southerners, using violence against blacks, Jews, and Catholics.

●**Ku·wait** (kə-wāt′, kōō-āt′). See Supplement, **Countries**.

●**Kwan·za** or **Kwan·zaa** (kwän′zə) is an African-American festival held in late December.

●**Kyr·gyz·stan** (kur′gə-stan′) became independent of the USSR in 1991. See also Supplement, **Countries**.

Clove hitch

Reef knot

Bowline

Sheepshank

Two half hitches

Stone Age hunters used knots to tie arrowheads to shafts. Today everyone needs to tie a knot at some time or other.

A KNOCKOUT
Until about the end of the 1300s — the time of Chaucer — the *k* was still pronounced in words such as knee, knife, knight, and know. In the same way the *g* was pronounced in gnat and gnaw and the *gh* was pronounced in words such as light, sight, and ought. What we have is a ghost spelling of a former pronunciation.

L l

The letter *L*, like all the letters, has a long history. The earliest alphabets were taken and adapted by the Greeks. The Greek *beta*, when combined with the first letter, *aleph*, gives us the word alphabet.

The Greeks passed on their letters to the Romans, who developed the alphabet we use today, although they used only capital letters. Small letters developed in the A.D. 700s.

An early form of the letter L, used in the Middle East more than 3,000 years ago.

This letter was taken by the Greeks and became lambda.

Over the years different versions of the letter L have been developed.

la·bel (lā′bəl) *n.* a small written note attached to a parcel, object, etc. giving details of its contents, owner, manufacturer, etc.

lab·o·ra·to·ry (lab′rə-tôr′ē, lab′rə-tōr′ē) *n.* **lab·o·ra·to·ries** a room or building specially equipped for scientific experiments and research.

la·bor (lā′bər) *n.* **1** physical or mental work, especially when hard. **2** workers as a group: *They were hired as skilled labor.* **3** the process of giving birth to a baby: *She had an easy labor.* – *vb.* **la·bor·ing, la·bored 1** to work hard or with difficulty. **2** to progress or move slowly and with difficulty: *The car labored up the hill.*

Labor Day *n.* a legal holiday in the UNITED STATES honoring working people.

Lab·ra·dor (lab′rə-dôr′) *n.* a breed of large dog with a short black or golden coat.

● **Lab·ra·dor** (lab′rə-dôr′) is a region of northeastern CANADA.

lab·y·rinth (lab′ə-rinth) *n.* a complicated network of passages.

lace (lās) *n.* **1** a delicate material made from fine thread woven into netlike patterns. **2** a string drawn through holes, used for fastening shoes, etc. – *vb.* **lac·ing, laced** to fasten with a lace.

lack (lak) *n.* something missing or in short supply. – *vb.* **lack·ing, lacked** to be completely without or to have too little of.

lac·quer (lak′ər) *n.* a clear substance used to form a protective, shiny covering.

la·crosse (lə-krôs′) *n.* a game in which two teams use long sticks with triangular nets at one end (lacrosse sticks) to throw a small ball into their opponent's goal.

lac·y (lā′sē) *adj.* **lac·i·er, lac·i·est** of or like lace, especially in being fine and delicate.

lad (lad) *n.* a boy or a youth.

lad·der (lad′ər) *n.* a piece of equipment consisting of a set of horizontal rungs or steps between two long vertical supports, used for climbing up or down.

la·den (lād′n) *adj.* heavily loaded.

la·dle (lād′l) *n.* a large spoon with a long handle and deep bowl, for serving liquid. – *vb.* **la·dling, la·dled** to serve with a ladle.

la·dy (lād′ē) *n.* **ladies** a polite word for a woman.

la·dy·bug (lād′ē-bug′) or **la·dy·bird** (lād′ē-burd′) *n.* a small red beetle with black spots.

● **La·fay·ette** (lä′fē-et′, lä′fā-et′), **Marquis de** (1757-1834) was a French soldier

Lakes may contain fresh water or saltwater. The water in some of the largest saltwater lakes, such as the Caspian Sea and the Aral Sea, is mildly salty. Other saltwater lakes, such as the Great Salt Lake and the Dead Sea, are much saltier than seawater.

—Superior
—Huron
Michigan—
Erie Ontario

Four of the five Great Lakes lie on the border of Canada and the United States.

The Caspian Sea is up to 3,300ft. (1,000m) deep. It is rich in marine life.

who fought for the American colonists in the AMERICAN REVOLUTION and in the FRENCH REVOLUTION.

la·goon (lə-goon′) *n.* a shallow stretch of water separated from the sea by rocks, etc.

laid (lād) See **lay¹**.

lain. See **lie²**.

lair (lâr) *n.* a wild animal's den.

lake (lāk) *n.* an area of water surrounded by land.

● The world's largest lake is the salty Caspian Sea, 169,390 sq. miles (438,695 sq. km). The largest freshwater lake is Lake Superior, one of the GREAT LAKES.

lamb (lam) *n.* a young sheep.

lame (lām) *adj.* **1** not able to walk properly. **2** not convincing: *a lame excuse.*

la·ment (lə-ment′) *vb.* **la·ment·ing, la·ment·ed** to feel or express regret or sadness. – *n.* an expression of sadness, etc.

lamp (lamp) *n.* an appliance for producing a steady light, using electricity, oil, or gas.

lance (lans) *n.* a long spear with a hard, pointed head at one end, used by horse riders.

● **Lan·ce·lot** (lan′sə-lät′), in legend, was one of ARTHUR's knights and lover of Guinevere.

land (land) *n.* **1** the part of the earth's surface

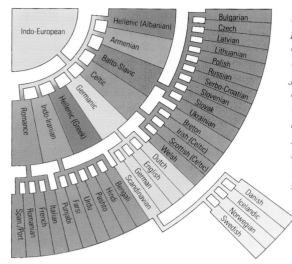

From the Indo-European parent have developed eight families or groups of languages, shown on this family tree. English, for example, belongs to the Germanic family, which also includes German, Dutch, and the Scandinavian languages. The Romance family includes Italian, French, Spanish, Portuguese, and Romanian.

not covered by water. **2** the ground or soil, especially in terms of its use or quality: *This is good land for farming.* – *vb.* **1** to come to rest on the ground or water after flight through the air. **2** to bring on to land from a ship.

land·ing (lan′ding) *n.* **1** the process of coming to land. **2** the level part of a staircase between flights of steps, or at the very top.

land·mark (land′märk′) *n.* **1** a conspicuous or well-known object on land. **2** an event of great importance.

land·scape (land′skāp′) *n.* the area and features of land seen from a single point.

land·slide (land′slīd′) *n.* a fall of land or rock down the side of a hill or cliff.

lane (lān) *n.* **1** a narrow road or street. **2** a division of a road for a single line of traffic.

lan·guage (lang′gwij, lang′wij) *n.* **1** human speech. **2** the speech of a particular nation or group of people. **3** any other way of communication: *She expressed herself using sign language.* **5** a system of signs and symbols, used to write computer programs.

lank (lank) *adj.* (of hair) long, straight, and limp.

lank·y (lang′kē) *adj.* **lank·i·er, lank·i·est** thin, tall, and awkward.

lan·tern (lan′tərn) *n.* a case for holding a light and shielding the flame from the wind.

● **La·os** (lā′äs′, lä′ōs′, lows). See Supplement, **Countries**.

lap¹ (lap) *vb.* **lap·ping, lapped 1** to drink in with the tongue. **2** (of water) to wash against with a light splashing sound: *The ocean lapped the shore.* – *n.* the sound of waves gently

PRONUNCIATION SYMBOLS			
ə	**away** lemon		focus
a	**fat**	oi	**boy**
ā	**fade**	oo	**foot**
ä	**hot**	o͞o	**moon**
âr	**fair**	ou	**house**
e	**met**	th	**think**
ē	**mean**	t͟h	**this**
g	**get**	u	**cut**
hw	**which**	ur	**hurt**
i	**fin**	w	**witch**
ī	**line**	y	**yes**
îr	**near**	yo͞o	**music**
ô	**often**	yoor	**pure**
ō	**note**	zh	**vision**

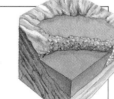

A barrier lake is where a river valley has become naturally blocked as a result of a landfall, for example, or debris left by a glacier.

A volcanic lake is where the crater of an extinct volcano fills up. Lakes may also form where hollow lava flows have collapsed.

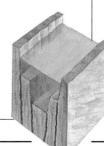

Rift valley lakes occur along major faults or fissure lines such as the long, narrow lochs in the Great Glen fault in Scotland.

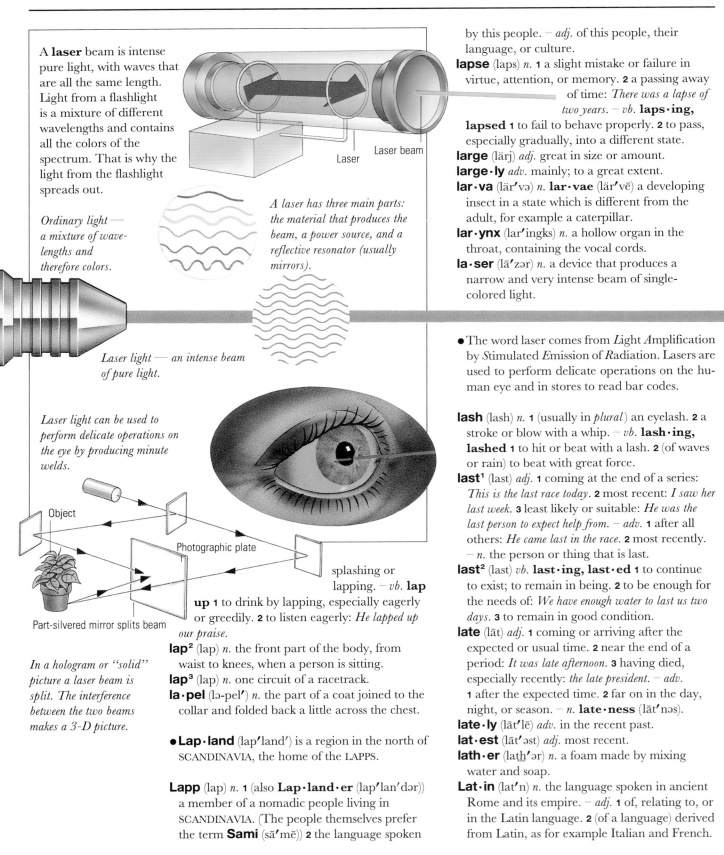

A **laser** beam is intense pure light, with waves that are all the same length. Light from a flashlight is a mixture of different wavelengths and contains all the colors of the spectrum. That is why the light from the flashlight spreads out.

Ordinary light — a mixture of wavelengths and therefore colors.

A laser has three main parts: the material that produces the beam, a power source, and a reflective resonator (usually mirrors).

Laser

Laser beam

Laser light — an intense beam of pure light.

Laser light can be used to perform delicate operations on the eye by producing minute welds.

Object

Photographic plate

Part-silvered mirror splits beam

In a hologram or "solid" picture a laser beam is split. The interference between the two beams makes a 3-D picture.

splashing or lapping. – *vb.* **lap up 1** to drink by lapping, especially eagerly or greedily. **2** to listen eagerly: *He lapped up our praise.*

lap² (lap) *n.* the front part of the body, from waist to knees, when a person is sitting.

lap³ (lap) *n.* one circuit of a racetrack.

la·pel (lə-pel') *n.* the part of a coat joined to the collar and folded back a little across the chest.

● **Lap·land** (lap'land') is a region in the north of SCANDINAVIA, the home of the LAPPS.

Lapp (lap) *n.* **1** (also **Lap·land·er** (lap'lan'dər)) a member of a nomadic people living in SCANDINAVIA. (The people themselves prefer the term **Sami** (sä'mē)) **2** the language spoken

by this people. – *adj.* of this people, their language, or culture.

lapse (laps) *n.* **1** a slight mistake or failure in virtue, attention, or memory. **2** a passing away of time: *There was a lapse of two years.* – *vb.* **laps·ing, lapsed 1** to fail to behave properly. **2** to pass, especially gradually, into a different state.

large (lärj) *adj.* great in size or amount.

large·ly *adv.* mainly; to a great extent.

lar·va (lär'və) *n.* **lar·vae** (lär'vē) a developing insect in a state which is different from the adult, for example a caterpillar.

lar·ynx (lar'ingks) *n.* a hollow organ in the throat, containing the vocal cords.

la·ser (lā'zər) *n.* a device that produces a narrow and very intense beam of single-colored light.

● The word laser comes from *L*ight *A*mplification by *S*timulated *E*mission of *R*adiation. Lasers are used to perform delicate operations on the human eye and in stores to read bar codes.

lash (lash) *n.* **1** (usually in *plural*) an eyelash. **2** a stroke or blow with a whip. – *vb.* **lash·ing, lashed 1** to hit or beat with a lash. **2** (of waves or rain) to beat with great force.

last¹ (last) *adj.* **1** coming at the end of a series: *This is the last race today.* **2** most recent: *I saw her last week.* **3** least likely or suitable: *He was the last person to expect help from.* – *adv.* **1** after all others: *He came last in the race.* **2** most recently. – *n.* the person or thing that is last.

last² (last) *vb.* **last·ing, last·ed 1** to continue to exist; to remain in being. **2** to be enough for the needs of: *We have enough water to last us two days.* **3** to remain in good condition.

late (lāt) *adj.* **1** coming or arriving after the expected or usual time. **2** near the end of a period: *It was late afternoon.* **3** having died, especially recently: *the late president.* – *adv.* **1** after the expected time. **2** far on in the day, night, or season. – *n.* **late·ness** (lāt'nəs).

late·ly (lāt'lē) *adv.* in the recent past.

lat·est (lāt'əst) *adj.* most recent.

lath·er (la<u>th</u>'ər) *n.* a foam made by mixing water and soap.

Lat·in (lat'n) *n.* the language spoken in ancient Rome and its empire. – *adj.* **1** of, relating to, or in the Latin language. **2** (of a language) derived from Latin, as for example Italian and French.

● With the fall of the ROMAN EMPIRE in A.D. 476, local variations of spoken Latin evolved into the Romance languages, including Italian, French, Catalan, Spanish, Portuguese, and Romanian. Latin words form a large part of the vocabulary of many European languages.

Latin America *n.* Mexico and the countries of Central and South America, where the official language is either Spanish or Portuguese. – *n.* & *adj.* **Latin American**.

Lines of latitude and longitude are marked on maps so that you can pinpoint specific places.

lat·i·tude (lat′ə-tōōd′, lat′ə-tyōōd′) *n.* **1** a distance north or south of the equator, measured in degrees. **2** scope for freedom of action or choice.

lat·ter (lat′ər) *adj.* **1** nearer to the end. **2** being the second of two people, things, etc. mentioned. **3** recent; modern. – *n.* the second of two people, things, etc. mentioned.

lat·ter-day (lat′ər dā′) *adj.* recent or modern.

lat·ter·ly (lat′ər-lē) *adv.* **1** recently. **2** lately.

● **Lat·vi·a** (lat′vē-ə). See Supplement, **Countries**.

laugh (laf) *vb.* **laugh·ing, laughed** to make sounds with the voice as a sign of happiness or amusement. – *n.* an act or sound of laughing. – *vb.* **laugh at** to make fun of or ridicule.

laugh·a·ble (laf′ə-bəl) *adj.* deserving to be laughed at; not very good.

laugh·ter (laf′tər) *n.* the act or sound of laughing.

launch¹ (lônch, länch) *vb.* **launch·ing, launched 1** to send into the water, especially for the first time: *to launch a ship.* **2** to send into the air: *to launch a missile.* **3** to introduce onto the market. – *n.* an act of launching, especially a ship or spacecraft.

launch² (lônch, länch) *n.* a large motorboat.

laun·dry (lôn′drē, län′drē) *n.* **laun·dries 1** a place where clothes and linen are washed, especially in return for payment. **2** clothes and linen which have been, or are to be, washed.

lau·rel (lôr′əl, lär′əl) *n.* a small evergreen tree with smooth, dark, shiny leaves. – **rest on your laurels** to be satisfied with your past successes and not try to achieve anything more.

la·va (läv′ə, lav′ə) *n.* the molten rock and liquid that flows from a volcano, becoming solid as it cools.

lav·a·to·ry (lav′ə-tôr′ē, lav′ə-tōr′ē) *n.* **lavatories 1** a room equipped with a sink for washing hands and face, and a toilet for eliminating waste. **2** a toilet.

lav·en·der (lav′ən-dər) *n.* **1** a plant or shrub with sweet-smelling pale bluish-purple flowers. **2** the pale bluish-purple color of the flowers.

● **La·voi·sier** (lav-wäz′ē-ā′), **Antoine** (1743-1794) was a French chemist who discovered the composition of air.

law (lô) *n.* **1** a collection of rules which govern what people can and cannot do, and by which people live or a country or state is governed. **2** a rule in science based on practice or observation, which says that under certain conditions certain things will always happen. – **lay down the law** to state your opinions and orders forcefully.

law·ful (lô′fəl) *adj.* allowed by or according to law; just or rightful.

law·less (lô′ləs) *adj.* ignoring or breaking the law.

law·man (lô′man′, lô′mən) *n.* a person who enforces the law, as a sheriff.

lawn (lôn, län) *n.* an area of smooth, mown grass.

lawn mow·er (lôn′mō′ər, län′mō′ər) *n.* a machine for cutting lawns.

lawsuit (lô′sōōt′) *n.* a legal proceeding in which a claim is made in a court.

law·yer (lô′yər, loi′ər) *n.* a person who gives legal advice and represents clients' lawsuits.

lax (laks) *adj.* slack; not careful or strict: *Discipline at the school is rather lax.*

lay¹ (lā) *vb.* **lay·ing, laid 1** to place or put on a surface. **2** to design or prepare: *He laid plans for his escape.* **3** to put plates and cutlery on for a meal: *to lay a table.* **4** to produce eggs. – *vb.* **lay off** to dismiss when there is no work available.

lay². See **lie².**

● **lay** and **lie.** The verb to lie means "to rest" or "to be horizontal." The verb to lay means "to put down or to place." A confusion arises because the past tense of lie is lay: *It is a warm day so*

The Supreme Court is the highest court in the United States. The president appoints judges, subject to Senate consent, to decide whether laws are constitutional.

TERMS USED IN LAW
advocate a lawyer employed in a law case to represent a party in court.

appeal a request to a higher court to change a decision given by a lower one.

arrest the taking into custody by the police of a person suspected of a crime.

bail money offered by an arrested person in order to be allowed free until the trial. If the person does not appear at the trial, the bail is forfeited.

evidence written or spoken information that helps the court to find out the facts of a case.

statute law made by a legislature (lawmaking body), such as Congress.

trial the hearing of a legal dispute in court.

verdict the decision of the judge (or the jury) after hearing the evidence in a trial in court.

Latitude 90°N
45°N
0°
35°S
90°S
0°

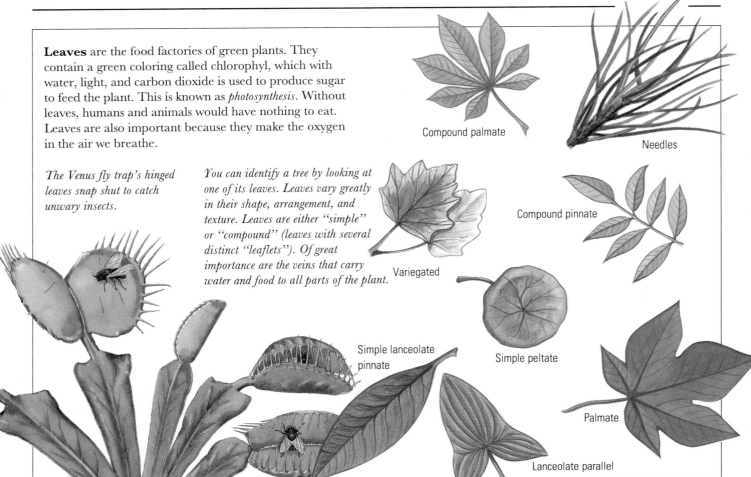

Leaves are the food factories of green plants. They contain a green coloring called chlorophyl, which with water, light, and carbon dioxide is used to produce sugar to feed the plant. This is known as *photosynthesis*. Without leaves, humans and animals would have nothing to eat. Leaves are also important because they make the oxygen in the air we breathe.

The Venus fly trap's hinged leaves snap shut to catch unwary insects.

You can identify a tree by looking at one of its leaves. Leaves vary greatly in their shape, arrangement, and texture. Leaves are either "simple" or "compound" (leaves with several distinct "leaflets"). Of great importance are the veins that carry water and food to all parts of the plant.

Compound palmate

Needles

Compound pinnate

Variegated

Simple lanceolate pinnate

Simple peltate

Palmate

Lanceolate parallel

PRONUNCIATION SYMBOLS		
ə away	lemon	focus
a fat	oi	boy
ā fade	oo	foot
ä hot	ōō	moon
âr fair	ou	house
e met	th	think
ē mean	<u>th</u>	this
g get	u	cut
hw which	ur	hurt
i fin	w	witch
ī line	y	yes
îr near	yōō	music
ô often	yoor	pure
ō note	zh	vision

I will lie in the sun. Yesterday, I lay in bed thinking. Now here are examples of the verb to lay: *After you finish reading, lay the book down. I'm sure I laid my pen on the desk yesterday.* Laid here is the past tense of lay. There is another verb to lie meaning "not to tell the truth." Its past tense is lied: *Tom has never lied to me; he is truthful.*

lay·er (lā'ər) *n.* a thickness or covering.
la·zy (lā'zē) *adj.* **la·zi·er, la·zi·est** not wanting to do exercise, work hard, etc.; idle. – *adv.* **la·zi·ly** (lā'zə-lē).
lead¹ (lēd) *vb.* **lead·ing, led** (led) **1** to guide by going in front. **2** to cause to feel or think in a certain way: *Her encouraging words led him to try harder.* **3** to experience: *He leads a miserable existence.* **4** to go: *All roads lead to Rome.* **5** to have as an end or consequence: *This decision will lead to problems.* **6** to be the most important in a particular field. – *n.* **1** the guidance given by leading; an example: *Follow the first singer's lead.* **2** the position of being ahead, as in a race or contest. **3** the extent by which a person is ahead in a race or contest. **4** a clue. **5** the main role in a play or movie.
lead² (led) *n.* **1** a soft, heavy, bluish-gray metallic element (symbol **Pb**) used in alloys. **2** a thin stick of graphite, used in pencils.
lead·er (lēd'ər) *n.* a person, animal, or thing that leads or guides others.
leaf (lēf) *n.* **leaves** (lēvz) **1** a thin, flat, usually green part most often growing from the stem of a plant. **2** a single sheet of paper forming two pages in a book. – *vb.* **leaf·ing, leafed** to turn the pages quickly.
league (lēg) *n.* an organization of people, nations, sports teams, etc.
leak (lēk) *n.* **1** an unwanted crack or hole that allows liquid or gas to pass through. **2** liquid or gas that has passed through such a crack or hole. – *vb.* **leak·ing, leaked** to allow liquid or gas to pass through: *Our roof leaks.*
lean¹ (lēn) *vb.* **lean·ing, leaned 1** to slope or be placed in a sloping position; to bend. **2** to

rest or be rested against something for support. **3** to rely on or be supported by.

lean² (lēn) *adj.* **1** (of a person or animal) thin. **2** (of meat) not containing much fat.

leap (lēp) *vb.* **leap·ing, leaped** or **leapt** (lēpt, lept) **1** to jump suddenly, high in the air or over a long distance. **2** to accept eagerly.

leap year *n.* a year of 366 days, February 29 being the extra day.

● Leap years are necessary because the calendar year is slightly shorter than the solar year.

learn (lurn) *vb.* **learn·ing, learned** (lurnd, lurnt) or **learnt** (lurnt) **1** to gain knowledge or a skill through experience, study, or by being taught. **2** to be informed.

learn·ed (lur′nəd) *adj.* having great learning.

learn·er (lur′nər) *n.* a person who is in the process of learning something.

learn·ing (lur′ning) *n.* knowledge gained through study.

lease (lēs) *n.* a contract for the use of property, a car, etc. for a specified period of time. − *vb.* **leas·ing, leased** to give or borrow on lease.

leash (lēsh) *n.* a strip of leather or a chain used for leading or holding a dog or other animal.

least (lēst) *adj. & adv.* smallest; slightest. − *pron.* the smallest amount. − **at least 1** at all events; anyway. **2** not less than.

leath·er (leth′ər) *n.* the skin of an animal made smooth by tanning.

leave¹ (lēv) *vb.* **leav·ing, left** (left) **1** to go away from; to move out of. **2** to go without taking: *I left all my luggage behind.* **3** to allow to remain in a particular state or condition: *Leave the window open.* **4** to have as a remainder: *Three minus one leaves two.*

leave² (lēv) *n.* permission to do something. − **on leave** officially absent from work.

●**Leb·a·non** (leb′ə-nən, leb′ə-nän′). See Supplement, **Countries**.

lec·ture (lek′chər) *n.* a formal talk on a particular subject given to an audience, for example at a university. − *vb.* **lec·tur·ing, lec·tured** to give a lecture.

led. See **lead¹**.

ledge (lej) *n.* a narrow horizontal shelf, as in the wall of a building or on the side of a mountain.

left¹ (left). See **leave¹**.

left² (left) *adj.* the opposite side to right. − *adv.* on or toward the left side. − *n.* **1** the left side, part, direction, etc. **2 Left** people or political parties that support liberal or radical policies.

left-hand·ed (left-han′dəd) *adj.* having the left hand more skillful than the right.

left·o·ver (left′ō′vər) *n.* (in *plural*) food that has not been eaten up at a meal.

left·wing (left′wing′) *adj.* of, relating to, or supporting the political Left.

leg (leg) *n.* **1** one of the limbs on which animals, birds, and people walk and stand. **2** a long narrow support of a table, chair, etc. **3** one stage in a journey, competition, or race.

le·gal (lē′gəl) *adj.* **1** lawful; allowed by the law. **2** of or relating to the law.

le·gal·ize (lē′gə-līz′) *vb.* **le·gal·i·zing, le·gal·ized** to make legal or lawful.

leg·end (lej′ənd) *n.* **1** a traditional story which may or may not be true. **2** a famous person.

leg·i·ble (lej′ə-bəl) *adj.* (of handwriting) clear enough to be read. − *adv.* **leg·i·bly** (lej′ə-blē).

le·gion (lē′jən) *n.* a unit in the ancient Roman army, containing between 3,000 and 6,000 soldiers. − *adj.* great in number.

leg·is·late (lej′ə-slāt′) *vb.* **leg·is·lat·ing, leg·is·lat·ed** to make laws. − *n.* **leg·is·lat·or** (lej′ə-slāt′ər).

leg·is·la·tion (lej′ə-slā′shən) *n.* **1** the act of legislating. **2** a group of laws.

leg·is·la·ture (lej′ə-slā′chər) *n.* the part of the government with power to make laws.

In every Roman legion a bearer carried a standard into battle. It was a great disgrace for a legion to lose its standard.

●**Leif Er·iks·son** (lēf er′ik-sən, lāf) (970-?) was a Viking who in about A.D. 1000 landed in an area he called Vinland, possibly Maine.

lei·sure (lē′zhər, lezh′ər) *n.* time when someone does not have to work.

lei·sure·ly *adj.* not hurried; relaxed. − *adv.* without hurrying and taking plenty of time.

An old Icelandic saga describes how Leif Eriksson sailed to where the land was green with trees and sweet "grapes." He named the place Vinland (wineland).

A concave lens is thinner in the middle than at the edges. It makes things look smaller.

A convex lens is thicker in the middle than at the edges. It makes things look bigger.

lem·on (lem′ən) *n.* a small citrus fruit with pale yellow skin and very sour flesh.

lem·o·nade (lem′ə-nād′) *n.* a drink flavored with or made from lemons.

lend (lend) *vb.* **lend·ing, lent** (lent) **1** to give the use of something on the understanding that it is to be returned: *Please lend me your pen.* **2** to allow someone the use of money. – *n.* **lend·er**.

length (length, lenth) *n.* **1** the distance from one end of an object to the other. **2** a period of time. **3** trouble or effort; action taken.

length·en (leng′thən, len′thən) *vb.* **length·en·ing, length·ened** to make or become longer.

length·y (leng′thē, len′thē) *adj.* **length·i·er, length·i·est** of great length.

le·ni·ent (lē′nē-ənt, lēn′yənt) *adj.* punishing only lightly; not severe.

● **Len·in** (len′ən), **Vladimir** (1870-1924) was the first leader of the Soviet Union.

● **Len·in·grad** former name of the city of St. Petersburg in Russia.

lens (lenz) *n.* **1** a piece of glass or clear plastic curved on one or both sides, used to focus light rays in cameras, glasses, etc. **2** a clear substance behind the iris in the eye which focuses light rays and images on the retina.

Lent (lent) *n.* in the Christian religion, the time from Ash Wednesday to EASTER Sunday.

Le·o (lē′ō) *n.* See **zodiac**.

● **Le·o·nar·do da Vin·ci** (lē′ə-när′dō də vin′chē) (1452-1519) was an Italian painter and versatile inventor.

leop·ard (lep′ərd) *n.* a large animal of the cat family, usually with a yellowish coat and black spots, found in AFRICA and ASIA.

le·o·tard (lē′ə-tärd′) *n.* a tight-fitting garment covering the body and not the limbs.

lep·re·chaun (lep′rə-kän′, lep′rə-kôn′) *n.* a small mischievous elf in Irish folklore.

les·bi·an (lez′bē-ən) *n.* a woman who is sexually attracted to other women.

● **Le·so·tho** (lə-sōō′tōō, lə-sōt′ō). See Supplement, **Countries**.

less (les) *adj.* smaller in size, quantity, duration, etc.: *There is less milk in these new bottles.* – *adv.*

Lenin was the leading figure in the Russian Revolution. When uprisings broke out in war-exhausted Russia in 1917, Lenin led the Bolshevik party, which overturned the government and took control.

In 1917 armed workers and Bolshevik-led soldiers attacked the Winter Palace.

not so much; to a smaller extent: *I am eating less than before.* – *prep.* without; minus.

● **less** and **fewer**. As a rough guide, use "less" for a quantity and "fewer" for a number of things: *The less ground we clear, the fewer flowers can be grown.*

les·sen (les′ən) *vb.* **les·sen·ing, les·sened** to make or become less.

les·ser (les′ər) *adj.* smaller than another in size, quantity, or importance.

les·son (les′ən) *n.* a period of teaching in a particular subject: *I enjoyed my art lesson today.*

let (let) *vb.* **let·ting, let 1** to allow or permit: *She let him in the house.* **2** to rent out in return for payment. **3** used to give orders, requests, warnings, permission, etc.: *Let him go!* – *vb.* **let down 1** to lower. **2** to disappoint.

le·thal (lē′thəl) *adj.* causing or enough to cause death.

let·ter (let′ər) *n.* **1** a written symbol, usually part of an alphabet, used to express a speech sound. **2** a written or printed message usually sent by mail in an envelope.

let·tuce (let′əs) *n.* a green plant with large edible leaves used as a salad vegetable.

lev·el (lev′əl) *n.* **1** a height, value, or extent: *She measured the level of the liquid in the jar.* **2** position, status, or importance: *The discussions were at government level.* – *adj.* **1** having a flat, smooth, even surface. **2** having the same height as something else: *The table is level with the bed.* — *vb.* **lev·el·ing** or **lev·el·ling, lev·eled** or **lev·elled** to make flat, smooth, or horizontal.

le·ver (lev′ər, lē′vər) *n.* **1** a simple device for lifting and moving loads, being a rigid bar resting on a fixed point, one end being raised by pushing down on the other. **2** a handle for operating a machine. — *vb.* **le·ver·ing, le·vered** to move or open using a lever.

le·ver·age (lev′rij, lēv′rij) *n.* the mechanical power gained by using a lever.

lex·i·con (lek′sə-kän′) *n.* a dictionary.

li·a·ble (lī′ə-bəl, lī′bəl) *adj.* **1** legally bound or responsible: *He is liable for the damage to my car.* **2** likely to do, have, or suffer: *She is liable to fail.*

li·ai·son (lē′ə-zän, lē-ā′zän′) *n.* communication or contact between groups.

li·ar (lī′ər) *n.* a person who tells lies.

lib·er·al (lib′ə-rəl, lib′rəl) *adj.* **1** given or giving generously, freely, or abundantly: *He gave her a liberal helping of ice cream.* **2** tolerant of different opinions. — *n.* an open-minded person.

lib·er·al·ize (lib′ə-rə-līz′) *vb.* **lib·er·al·iz·ing, lib·er·al·ized** to make or become more liberal.

lib·er·ate (lib′ə-rāt′) *vb.* **lib·er·at·ing, lib·er·at·ed** to set free.

●**Li·be·ri·a** (lī-bîr′ē-ə). See Supplement, **Countries**.

lib·er·ty (lib′ərt-ē) *n.* **lib·er·ties 1** freedom from captivity or from slavery. **2** freedom to do, think, and speak as one pleases.

Li·bra (lē′brə) *n.* See **zodiac**.

li·brar·i·an (lī-brer′ē-ən) *n.* a person who is employed in or is in charge of a library.

li·brar·y (lī′brer′ē) *n.* **li·brar·ies 1** a collection of books, either for public or private use. **2** the building or room which houses such a collection.

●**Library of Congress** in Washington, D.C., the world's largest library. It contains more than 80 million items in 470 languages.

●**Li·by·a** (lib′ē-ə). See Supplement, **Countries**.

li·cense (lī′səns) *n.* a document giving official permission to own a dog, gun, etc., or to do something such as sell alcohol. — *vb.* **li·cens·ing, li·censed** to give a license or permit for something.

Levers are the simplest of all machines. They are also among the most useful. By changing a small force into a big force, they make it easier to lift and move heavy objects. Levers involve three things: effort — the work put into the job, such as lifting or pulling; the fulcrum — the place where the lever pivots; and load — the thing you want to move. The three classes of lever *(bottom)* differ in the positions of the effort, fulcrum, and load.

A crowbar is a 1st class lever: A small effort on the crowbar handle is turned into a big upward force to raise the rock (load). The small rock acts as the fulcrum.

A hammer is a 3rd class lever: The shoulder is the fulcrum. The load is the hammer.

A wheel-barrow is a 2nd class lever: The handles (effort) lift loads behind the wheel (fulcrum).

1st class lever
Fulcrum is between effort and load.

2nd class lever
Load is between effort and fulcrum.

3rd class lever
Effort is between fulcrum and load.

li·chen (lī′kən) *n.* any of a large group of organisms formed from fungi and algae, which grow in patches on stones, trees, and soil.

lick (lik) *vb.* **lick·ing, licked 1** to pass the tongue over to moisten, taste, or clean. **2** to flicker over or around: *The flames licked around the coals in the fire.* — *n.* an act of licking with the tongue.

lic·o·rice (lik′ə-ris, lik′ə-rish) *n.* **1** a Mediterranean plant with sweet roots used in medicine and in candy. **2** a candy made from the juice of the root of this plant. — *adj.* flavored with or tasting of licorice.

lid (lēd′ō) *n.* a removable or hinged cover for a can, box, etc.

Library comes from a Latin word meaning a "bookseller's shop." The French still use the word *librairie* in the same way.

lie¹ (līʹ) *n.* a false statement made with the intention of deceiving. – *vb.* **lies, ly·ing, lied** to say something which is not true, intending to deceive.

lie² (līʹ) *vb.* **ly·ing, lay** (lā), **lain** (lān) **1** to be in or move into a flat position on a supporting surface. **2** to be or remain in a particular state: *Many animals lie dormant throughout the winter.* **3** to be situated; to stretch or be spread out to view: *The harbor lay before us.* – *n.* the way or direction in which something is lying.

● **Liech·ten·stein** (likʹtən-stīnʹ). See Supplement, **Countries**.

lieu·ten·ant (lōō-tenʹənt) *n.* **1** a deputy acting for a superior. **2** a junior officer in the army or navy.

life (līf) *n.* **lives** (līvz) **1** the state of being able to grow, develop, and change which distinguishes living animals and plants from dead ones and from matter such as rocks, etc. **2** the period between birth and death. **3** the length of time a thing exists or is able to function: *These batteries have a long life.* **4** living things as a group: *She studies marine life.* **5** liveliness; energy.

life·boat (līfʹbōtʹ) *n.* a boat for rescuing people in trouble at sea.

life cycle (līfʹsīʹkəl) *n.* the various stages through which a living thing passes.

life·time (līfʹtīmʹ) *n.* the length of time a person is alive.

lift (lift) *vb.* **lift·ing, lift·ed 1** to raise to a higher position. **2** (of cloud, fog, etc.) to clear. **3** to remove a barrier or restriction: *As soon as they reached an agreement the ban was lifted.* – *n.* **1** an act of lifting. **2** (*British*) an elevator. **3** a ride in a person's car or other vehicle: *My dad gives me a lift to school.* – *vb.* **lift off** (of a spacecraft) to rise from the ground.

lig·a·ment (ligʹə-mənt) *n.* a band of tough tissue that joins bones and cartilages together.

light¹ (līt) *n.* **1** the natural power from the sun, lamps, candles, etc. that makes sight possible and things visible. **2** any source of light, such as the sun, a lamp, a candle, etc. **3** daylight; dawn: *They got up at first light.* **4** a traffic light: *Turn left at the light.* – *adj.* **1** having light; not dark. **2** (of a color) pale; closer to white than black. – *vb.* **light·ing, lit** (lit) or **light·ed 1** to bring light to. **2** to cause to begin to burn: *She lit the fire.* – *n.* **light·ness** (lītʹnəs).

Without **light** from the sun, all life on earth would come to an end. Green plants need sunlight to make food, and humans and all the other animals on earth depend on plants for food. Light is a form of energy. It radiates freely though space and does not involve the movement of any material such as air. In empty space, light travels at about 186,000 miles (300,000km) per second. The light from the sun takes eight minutes to reach the earth.

Light on the electromagnetic spectrum. On either side are ultraviolet and infrared rays.

Short wavelengths
Cosmic rays
X-rays
Visible light
Gamma rays
Ultraviolet rays
Microwaves
Television waves
Infrared rays
Radar waves
Long wavelengths
Radio waves

When light rays pass from one substance to another (for example from air to water), they are bent. This bending distorts the image (in the example below, the straws) seen by the eye. This is called refraction.

Polarized light

Light waves vibrate in all directions. In polarized light the direction of the waves is limited.

Unpolarized light

Refraction

Clear glass is transparent — you can see objects through it. Frosted glass is translucent — you can see light through it. Cardboard is opaque — no light passes through it.

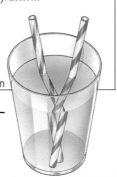

light·en (līt′n) *vb.* **light·en·ing, light·ened**
to make or become brighter, less dark.

light·house (līt′hows′) *n.* a building on a coast
with a flashing light to guide ships.

light² (līt) *adj.* **1** of little weight; easy to lift or
carry. **2** low in amount: *It is only light rain.*
3 easy to do: *She is only capable of light work.*
4 not serious or profound, but for amusement
only: *She took some light reading for the trip.* – *adv.*
1 in a light manner. **2** with little luggage: *We
like to travel light.* – *adv.* **light·ly**.

light·en (līt′n) *vb.* **light·en·ing, light·ened**
1 to make less heavy. **2** to make or become
happier or more cheerful.

light·heart·ed (līt′härt′əd) *adj.* **1** (of a person)
happy and free from worry. **2** not serious.

light·ning (līt′ning) *n.* a flash of light caused by
electricity between clouds or between a cloud
and the earth, especially during a storm.

light-year *n.* the distance light travels in a year,
5.88 trillion miles (9.46 trillion km).

like¹ (līk) *adj.* **1** similar; resembling: *She is very like
her mother.* **2** typical of: *It's just like him to forget.*
3 in the correct state or mood for: *I feel like a
drink.* – *prep.* in the same manner as; to the
same extent as: *He can run like a deer.* – *conj.*
(*informal*) as if: *You look like you haven't slept.*

like² (līk) *vb.* **lik·ing, liked 1** to find pleasant or
agreeable. **2** to be fond of.

like·ly (līʹklē) *adj.* probable: *It's likely that he will
be late.* – *adv.* probably. – *n.* **like·li·ness.**

lik·en (līʹkən) *vb.* **lik·en·ing, lik·ened** to
think or speak of as being similar to.

like·ness (līkʹnəs) *n.* **1** a similarity. **2** an image.

like·wise (līkʹwīz′) *adv.* in the same
or a similar manner; also.

li·lac (līʹlək, līʹlak′, līʹläk′) *n.*
a small tree or shrub which
has bunches of white or
pale purple, sweet-smelling
flowers.

*The lily family is large: as well as
true lilies, it includes the hyacinth,
bluebell, tulip, onion, and
asparagus!*

Wood lily

lil·y (lilʹē) *n.* **lil·ies** a plant
grown from a bulb, with white or
colored trumpet-shaped flowers.

limb (lim) *n.* **1** an arm, leg, or wing. **2** a main
branch on a tree. – *adj.* **limbed** (limd). – **out
on a limb** isolated, in a dangerous position.

lime¹ (līm) *n.* a white substance, a compound of
calcium and oxygen, made from limestone and
used for making cement and fertilizer.

lime² (līm) *n.* **1** a small, sour, green citrus fruit.
2 a tree bearing this fruit.

lim·e·rick (limʹə-rik) *n.* a humorous poem of
five lines with the first, second, and fifth lines,
and the third and fourth lines, rhyming.

lime·stone (līmʹstōn′) *n.* a rock made mainly
of calcium.

lim·it (limʹət) *n.* **1** a point or amount beyond
which something does not or may not pass.
2 (often in *plural*) the boundary or edge of an
area. – *vb.* **lim·it·ing, lim·it·ed** to be a
limit or boundary to; to restrict.

lim·it·ed *adj.* **1** having a limit or limits. **2** not
great: *He has a limited understanding of math.*

limp¹ (limp) *vb.* **limp·ing, limped** to walk with
an awkward or uneven step, because one leg is
weak or injured. – *n.* a limping walk.

limp² (limp) *adj.* not stiff or firm; hanging
loosely. – *n.* **limp·ness**
(limpʹnəs).

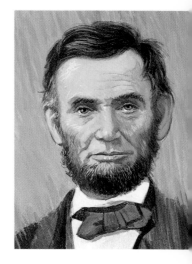

*The Civil War, which
Lincoln hoped would be
over in a few months,
dragged on for four years
and cost the lives of half
a million men.*

●**Lin·coln** (lingʹkən), **Abraham**
(1809-1865) was the 16th president of the United States who
led the Union during the CIVIL WAR.

●**Lind·bergh** (linʹburg′), **Charles** (1902-1974)
was an American pilot who made the first solo
flight across the ATLANTIC, in 1927.

line¹ (līn) *n.* **1** a long narrow mark, streak, or
stripe. **2** a length of thread, rope, wire, etc.,
especially for a particular purpose: *fishing
line.* **3** (often in *plural*) an outline or
shape, especially as part of the design:
They admired the clean lines of the car. **4** a row
of words. **5** (in *plural*) the words of an
actor's part. **6** a boundary: *the county
line.* **7** a number of persons or
objects in a row.

line² (līn) *vb.* **lin·ing, lined**
to cover the inside of a
garment, box, etc. with some
other material: *She lined the skirt
with silk.* – *n.* **lin·ing**

lin·e·ar (linʹē-ər) *adj.*
consisting of or like a line.

lin·en (linʹən) *n.* cloth made from
flax. – *adj.* made of or like linen.

lin·er (līʹnər) *n.* a large passenger ship.

*Lindbergh took off from
Roosevelt Field in New
York in a plane called
Spirit of St. Louis.
Thirty-three hours and
3,600 miles later he
landed in Paris to a
hero's welcome.*

Evergreen oak
Quercus ilex

Pedunculate oak
Quercus robur

Red oak
Quercus borealis

Linnaeus used his two-word (binomial) naming system to name many common plants and trees. The first name is the plant's genus; the second the species. The three trees shown are of the genus Quercus *(oak).*

lin·ger (ling′gər) *vb.* **lin·ger·ing, lin·gered** to be slow to do something; to delay.

lin·guist (ling′gwəst) *n.* **1** a person who studies languages. **2** a person who speaks various languages.

link (lingk) *n.* **1** a ring of a chain. **2** a connection between two people, places, or things. – *vb.* **link·ing, linked** to connect or join.

links (lingks) *n.* (*plural*) a golf course.

●**Lin·nae·us** (lə-nē′əs, lə-nā′əs)**, Carolus** (1707-1778) was a Swedish botanist who established a method of classifying living things.

li·no·le·um (lə-nō′lē-əm) *n.* a smooth hard-wearing covering for floors.

Lions of the African plains live in groups (prides) of up to 30 animals. The females do most of the hunting.

lin·seed (lin′sēd′) *n.* the seed of flax.

lin·tel (lint′l) *n.* a horizontal wooden or stone beam placed over a doorway or window.

li·on (lī′ən) *n.* a large flesh-eating animal of the cat family, with a tawny yellow coat.

lip (lip) *n.* **1** either of the folds of flesh which form the edge of the mouth. **2** an edge or rim.

liq·ue·fy (lik′wə-fī′) *vb.* **liq·ue·fies, liq·ue·fy·ing, liq·ue·fied** to make or become liquid.

liq·uid (lik′wəd) *n.* a fluid or watery substance. – *adj.* (of a substance) able to flow and change shape; in a state between solid and gas.

●**Lis·bon** (liz′bən) is the capital of PORTUGAL.

lisp (lisp) *vb.* **lisp·ing, lisped** to pronounce the sounds (s) and (z) as (th) and (th) respectively.

list (list) *n.* a series of names, numbers, prices, etc. written down or said one after the other.

lis·ten (lis′ən) *vb.* **lis·ten·ing, lis·tened** to give attention so as to hear something.

●**Lis·ter** (lis′tər)**, Joseph** (1827-1912) was an English surgeon who first used antiseptics.

lit. See **light¹**.

li·ter (lēt′ər) *n.* a metric unit of capacity equal to one cubic decimeter, or .908 quart dry measure and 1.057 quarts liquid measure.

lit·er·a·cy (lit′ə-rə-sē) *n.* the ability to read and write.

lit·er·al (lit′ə-rəl) *adj.* following the exact meaning of words or a text: *a literal translation.*

lit·er·ate (lit′ə-rət) *adj.* **1** able to read and write. **2** experienced in: *She is computer literate.*

lit·er·a·ture (lit′ə-rə-chər) *n.* written material of high quality, such as novels, poems, and plays.

●**Lith·u·a·ni·a** (lith′ōō-ā′nē-ə). See Supplement, **Countries**.

lit·mus (lit′məs) *n.* **1** a substance obtained from certain lichens, which is turned red by acids and blue by alkalis.

lit·ter (lit′ər) *n.* **1** a mess of paper and trash in a public place. **2** straw and hay used as bedding for animals. **3** a number of animals born to the same mother at the same time. — *vb.* **lit·ter·ing, lit·tered** **1** (of objects) to lie untidily around a place. **2** to scatter litter or mess up with litter: *Don't litter.*

lit·tle (lit′l) *adj.* small in size, extent, or amount: *She was little for her age.* — *n.* anything small in size, amount, or extent: *I can do a little to help out.* — *adv.* **1** to a small degree or extent: *Run around a little to keep warm.* **2** not much or at all.

live¹ (liv) *vb.* **liv·ing, lived** **1** to have life; to be alive. **2** to continue or last: *The memory of the accident lives on.* **3** to have as your home: *She lives next door.*

live² (līv) *adj.* **1** having life; not dead. **2** (of a radio or television broadcast) heard or seen as the event takes place and not from a recording. **3** (of a wire) connected to a source of electrical power.

live·stock (līv′stäk′) *n.* domestic animals, especially horses, cattle, sheep, and pigs.

live·li·hood (līv′lē-hood′) *n.* a job that provides income to live on.

live·ly (līv′lē) *adj.* **live·li·er, live·li·est** **1** active and full of energy and high spirits. **2** brisk. — *n.* **live·li·ness.**

liv·er (liv′ər) *n.* a large organ in the body which carries out several functions, including cleaning the blood.

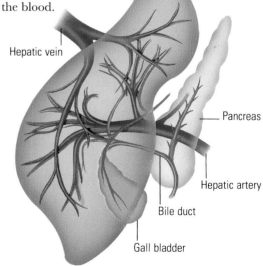

Hepatic vein

Pancreas

Hepatic artery

Bile duct

Gall bladder

The liver is a large gland that produces the digestive juices that burn up the fat you eat. It also makes proteins used in the blood. It stores vitamins and minerals until needed.

● The liver is often called the body's laboratory. It manufactures bile, a digestive fluid; urea, a waste product; and various blood proteins. It stores essential proteins, vitamins, and minerals.

● **Liv·er·pool** (liv′ər-pool′) is a big seaport in northwest ENGLAND.

liv·id (liv′əd) *adj.* (*informal*) extremely angry.

liv·ing (liv′ing) *adj.* having life; alive. — *n.* livelihood or means of earning money.

liv·ing room (liv′ing-room′, liv′ing-room′) *n.* a room in a house for sitting and relaxing in.

● **Liv·ing·stone** (liv′ing-stən), **David** (1813-1873) was a Scottish doctor who explored AFRICA.

liz·ard (liz′ərd) *n.* a reptile with a long body and tail, four legs, and a scaly skin.

lla·ma (lä′mə) *n.* a domesticated South American mammal of the camel family.

load (lōd) *n.* **1** something that is carried; a burden. **2** (in *plural*; *informal*) a large amount. — *vb.* **load·ing, load·ed** **1** to put a load of something on or in. **2** to put film, videotape, etc. into. **3** to put a disk into: *to load the computer.*

loaf (lōf) *n.* **loaves** (lōvz) **1** a mass of bread when baked. **2** a mass of some other food.

loan (lōn) *n.* anything lent, but especially a sum of money. — *vb.* **loan·ing, loaned** to lend.

loathe (lōth) *vb.* **loath·ing, loathed** to feel dislike or disgust for.

lob·by (läb′ē) *n.* **lob·bies** **1** an entrance hall or public lounge. **2** a group of people who try to influence the government, politicians, etc. in favor of a particular cause.

lobe (lōb) *n.* the soft, lower part of the ear.

lob·ster (läb′stər) *n.* a large edible shellfish with large claws, which turns red when boiled.

lo·cal (lō′kəl) *adj.* **1** of or belonging to one's home area or neighborhood. **2** (of a train or bus) stopping at all the stations or stops in a small area. **3** affecting a small area or part only: *He was given a local anesthetic.*

lo·cate (lō′kāt′) *vb.* **lo·cat·ing, lo·cat·ed** to find the exact position of.

lo·ca·tion (lō-kā′shən) *n.* a position or situation.

Lizards vary greatly. The Komodo dragon of Indonesia (above) *is the largest living lizard. It can grow up to 10ft. (3m) long. It hunts for food such as deer, pigs, and monkeys. The thorny devil of Australia* (top) *has grooved skin that channels rain or dew toward its mouth.*

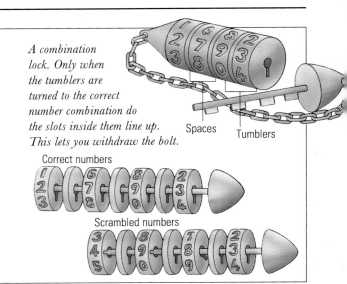

Simple wooden **locks** were developed in ancient Egypt. The Yale lock was invented in 1861. It contains a series of pins and drivers, which are all raised only when the correct key is inserted. Combination locks have no key. They are worked by a dial.

Locking cylinder

When the door is locked, springs push a row of pins into the metal cylinder so it cannot be turned.

The notches on the key push the pins free of the cylinder so the key can turn the cylinder.

Correct key

Wrong key

A combination lock. Only when the tumblers are turned to the correct number combination do the slots inside them line up. This lets you withdraw the bolt.

Spaces   Tumblers

Correct numbers

Scrambled numbers

Locusts have huge appetites and in swarms they do immense damage to crops. For much of the time, locusts lead solitary lives but from time to time they swarm in hundreds of millions.

lock¹ (läk) *n.* **1** a small device for fastening doors, lids, etc., with a bolt that usually needs a key to move it. **2** a closed part of a canal or river where the water level may be controlled, allowing boats to pass between higher and lower sections of the canal or river.

lock² (läk) *n.* curl of hair.

lock·er (läk′ər) *n.* a small, lockable compartment.

lo·co·mo·tive (lō′kə-mōt′iv) *n.* a railroad engine for pulling trains.

lo·cust (lō′kəst) *n.* any of several kinds of large insects related to the grasshopper, which travel around in swarms and eat and destroy crops.

lodge (läj) *n.* **1** a small house often used to vacation in. **2** a hotel or house for guests. **3** the home of a beaver or otter. – *vb.* **lodg·ing, lodged 1** to live in rented accommodations. **2** to bring officially to the authorities: *to lodge a complaint.* **3** to become firmly fixed: *A piece of bone lodged in his throat.*

lodg·er (läj′ər) *n.* a person who rents accommodations in someone else's home.

lodg·ing (läj′ing) *n.* (usually in *plural*) a room or rooms rented in someone else's home.

loft (lôft) *n.* a room or space under a roof.

loft·y *adj.* **loft·i·er, loft·i·est 1** of great or imposing height: *a lofty ceiling.* **2** of high or noble character: *She has lofty ideals.*

log (lôg, läg) *n.* **1** part of a tree trunk or thick bare branch, especially when used as firewood. **2** a detailed record of events occurring during a ship's voyage.

log·ic (läj′ik) *n.* **1** the science of reasoning correctly. **2** sound or proper reasoning.

log·i·cal (läj′i-kəl) *adj.* **1** relating to or based on logic. **2** using logic or capable of using logic: *a logical mind.* – *adv.* **log·i·cal·ly** (läj′i-klē).

lo·go (lō′gō, läg′ō) *n.* **logos** a small design used as the symbol of an organization.

loi·ter (loit′ər) *vb.* **loi·ter·ing, loi·tered** to stand around or pass time doing nothing in particular. – *n.* **loi·ter·er.**

lol·li·pop (läl′ē-päp′) *n.* a hard candy on a stick.

● **Lon·don** (lən′dən) is the capital of the UNITED KINGDOM and stands on the Thames River.

● **Lon·don** (lən′dən), **Jack** (1876-1916) was an American novelist who wrote more than 50 books.

lone (lōn) *adj.* alone; isolated.

lone·ly (lōn′lē) *adj.* **lone·li·er, lone·li·est 1** (of a person) sad because without companions or friends; solitary: *He leads a lonely existence.* **2** (of a place) isolated and rarely visited. – *n.* **lone·li·ness** (lōn′lē-nəs).

long¹ (lông) *adj.* **1** measuring a great distance from one end to the other. **2** measuring a stated amount in space or time: *My ruler is 12 inches long.* **3** having a large number of items: *a long list.* **4** lasting for an extended period of time – *adv.* **1** for or during a long period of time: *He died long ago.* **2** throughout the whole time: *She cried all night long.* – **as long as 1** provided that. **2** while; during the time that.

long² (lông) *vb.* **long·ing, longed** to want very much. – *adv.* **long·ing·ly.**

●**Long·fel·low** (lông′fel′ō), **Henry Wads-worth** (1807-1882) was an American poet who wrote *The Song of Hiawatha.*

long·ing (lông′ing) *n.* a great desire.

long·i·tude (län′jə-tood′, län′jə-tyood′) *n.* a distance measured in degrees east or west of 0°, the imaginary line passing from north to south through Greenwich, England.

look (look) *vb.* **look·ing, looked 1** to turn the eyes in a certain direction so as to see. **2** to consider, examine, or give your attention. **3** to seem to be or appear: *She looked unhappy.* **4** to search: *I'm looking for my friend.* **5** to rely on or refer to: *I look to you for support.* **6** to investigate: *She looked into the matter for him.* − *n.* **1** an act of looking; a glance or view: *Let's have a good look.* **2** the general appearance of a thing or person: *I don't like the look of those dark clouds.* − *vb.* **look after** to take care of. − *vb.* **look ahead** to consider what will happen in the future. − *vb.* **look forward to** to wait for with pleasure. − *vb.* **look out** to keep watch. − *vb.* **look up to** to respect the opinions of.

look·out (look′out′) *n.* **1** a careful watch. **2** a person assigned to watch.

loom¹ (loom) *n.* a machine for weaving thread into fabric.

loom² (loom) *vb.* **loom·ing, loomed 1** to appear indistinctly and usually in some enlarged or threatening form: *A large ship loomed up in the mist.* **2** (of an event) to be imminent, especially in some threatening way.

loon (loon) *n.* a diving bird with a sharp beak.

loop (loop) *n.* **1** the oval-shaped coil formed in a piece of rope, chain, etc. as it crosses over itself. **2** any object resembling this. − *vb.* **loop·ing, looped** to form into a loop.

loose (loos) *adj.* **1** no longer tied or held in confinement; free. **2** not tight or close-fitting. **3** not held together; not fastened or firmly fixed in place; not packaged. − *vb.* **loos·ing, loosed 1** to release or set free. **2** to make less tight, compact, or dense.

loos·en (loo′sən) *vb.* **loos·en·ing, loos·ened 1** to make or become loose or looser. **2** to make or become less tense or stiff.

loot (loot) *n.* stolen goods. − *vb.* **loot·ing, loot·ed** to steal money or goods from.

lop (läp) *vb.* **lop·ping, lopped** to cut.

lop·sid·ed (läp′sīd′əd) *adj.* with one side smaller, lower, or lighter than the other.

lord (lôrd) *n.* **1** a person with authority over others, a ruler. **2** a male member of the nobility. **3** **Lord** God or Jesus.

lore (lôr, lōr) *n.* the whole body of knowledge, especially traditional knowledge, on a subject.

●**Los An·ge·les** (lôs an′jə-ləs, lôs an′jə-lēz′) in California, is the second largest city in the UNITED STATES.

In 1801 the French inventor Joseph-Marie Jacquard designed the first automatic loom. It used punched cards which enabled it to weave patterned fabrics.

lor·ry (lôr′ē, lär′ē) *n.* **lor·ries** (*British*) a truck.

lose (looz) *vb.* **los·ing, lost** (lôst) **1** to stop having; to fail to keep, especially through carelessness. **2** to suffer the loss of through death. **3** to leave accidentally or be unable to find: *I lost my way in the fog.* **4** to fail to win. − *vb.* **lose out 1** to suffer loss or be at a disadvantage. **2** to fail to get something you desire.

los·er (loo′zər) *n.* **1** a person who loses. **2** (*informal*) a person who seems likely always to fail.

los·ing *adj.* failing; never likely to be successful.

loss (lôs) *n.* **1** the act of losing something. **2** the thing, amount, etc. that is lost.

lost (lôst) *past participle* of **lose**. − *adj.* **1** missing; no longer to be found. **2** unable to find the way. **3** confused, puzzled.

lot (lät) *n.* **1** (*informal*; often in *plural*) a great

Path of sound waves

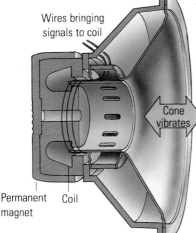

Wires bringing signals to coil

Cone vibrates

Permanent magnet

Coil

Most loudspeakers consist of a cone attached to an electromagnet. The cone is made of a special paper. The electric signals are fed to the coil of the electromagnet, and the coil vibrates as the electrical signals change. The vibrations move the cone, which vibrates the air and so creates sound waves.

Lunch is not a shortening of "luncheon." In fact the second word is a lengthening of the first. The word was based on the English dialect word *nuncheon*, meaning "drink taken at noon."

---

number or amount: *He ate a lot at the picnic.* **2** a slip of paper, drawn from among a group, used to reach a decision by chance: *They drew lots to decide who should go first.* **3** an item or set of items for sale by auction. **4** an area of land: *a parking lot.*

lo·tion (lō'shən) *n.* a liquid that is put on the skin to protect or clean it.

lot·tery (lät'ə-rē) *n.* **lot·ter·ies** a way of raising money by selling tickets and giving prizes or cash for those tickets drawn at random.

loud (loud) *adj.* **1** making a great sound; noisy. **2** capable of making a great sound: *His car has a loud horn.* – *adv.* **loud·ly.** – **out loud** aloud; loudly.

loud·speak·er (loud-spē'kər) *n.* a device which converts electrical signals into sound in televisions, radios, etc.

Low-frequency reflex cabinet — Midrange horn

High-frequency bullet radiators

● **Louis** (lōō'ē) was the name of eighteen kings of FRANCE. Louis XIV (1638-1715) ruled for 72 years and built the palace of VERSAILLES. Louis XVI (1754-1793) was put to death in the FRENCH REVOLUTION.

● **Lou·i·si·an·a** (lōō-ē'zē-an'ə, lōō'ə-zē-an'ə). See Supplement, **U.S.A**.

lounge (lounj) *vb.* **loung·ing, lounged 1** to lie or recline comfortably. **2** to be idle or lazy. – *n.* a large room for sitting or waiting in.

louse (lous) *n.* **lice** (līs) a wingless, blood-sucking insect with a flat body and short legs.

lout (lout) *n.* a bad-mannered, rough, and aggressive person. – *adj.* **lout·ish** (lout'ish).

● **Louvre** (lōōv, lōōv'rə) a museum and art gallery in Paris.

lov·a·ble or **love·a·ble** (luv'ə-bəl) *adj.* worthy of or inspiring love or affection.

love (luv) *n.* **1** a feeling of great affection for, and devotion to, another person. **2** a strong liking

for something: *a love for music.* **3** in tennis, no score. – *vb.* **lov·ing, loved 1** to feel great affection for. **2** to enjoy very much; to like.

love·ly (luv'lē) *adj.* **love·li·er, love·li·est** very beautiful; attractive; delightful. – *n.* **love·li·ness** (luv'lē'nəs).

lov·ing (luv' ing) *adj.* feeling and showing affection or love.

low¹ (lō) *adj.* **1** not reaching up to a high level; not tall: *They sat on a low wall.* **2** situated close to the ground, sea level, or the horizon: *The sun was low in the sky.* **3** of less than average amount: *This cheese is low in fat.* **4** making little sound; soft: *She spoke in a low voice.* **5** (of notes) produced by slow vibrations and having a deep pitch. – *adv.* **1** in or to a low position, state, or manner. **2** in a small quantity. **3** with a low voice; quietly. – *n.* **low·ness** (lō'nəs).

low² (lō) *vb.* **low·ing, lowed** (of cattle) to make a low, gentle, mooing sound.

Low Countries *n.* (*plural*) the NETHERLANDS, BELGIUM, and LUXEMBOURG.

low·er (lō'ər) *adj.* not as high as something else in position, status, height, value, etc. – *adv.* in or to a lower position. – *vb.* **low·er·ing, low·ered 1** to make or become lower in amount, sound, etc.

low tide *n.* the time the tide is at its lowest level.

loy·al (loi'əl) *adj.* faithful and true to someone.

loy·al·ist (loi'əl-əst) *n.* a loyal supporter.

loy·al·ty (loi'əl-tē) *n.* **loy·al·ties** the state or quality of being loyal.

loz·enge (läz'ənj) *n.* a small candy or tablet.

lu·bri·cate (lōō'brə-kāt') *vb.* **lubricating, lubricated** to cover with oil, grease, etc., to make smooth or slippery. – *n.* **lu·bri·ca·tion** (lōō'brə-kā'shən).

lu·cid (lōō'səd) *adj.* **1** easily understood; expressed clearly: *He gave a lucid account of the battle.* **2** having a clear mind, sane. – *n.* **lu·cid·i·ty** (lōō-sid'ət-ē).

luck (luk) *n.* **1** chance, especially when thought of as bringing good fortune. **2** events in life which cannot be controlled and seem to happen by chance: *He's had his share of bad luck.*

luck·y (luk'ē) *adj.* **luck·i·er, luck·i·est 1** having good luck. **2** bringing good luck: *a lucky charm.* **3** fortunate: *a lucky coincidence.* – *adv.* **luck·i·ly** (luk'ə-lē).

lu·di·crous (lōōd'ə-krəs) *adj.* ridiculous.

lug (lug) *vb.* **lug·ging, lugged** to pull or drag.

lug·gage (lug'ij) *n.* the suitcases and bags of a traveler: *Linda had lost her luggage.*

●**Luke** (look), **Saint** is the author of the third gospel and the Acts of the Apostles in the New Testament.

luke·warm (look-wôrm′) *adj.* **1** moderately warm. **2** not enthusiastic; indifferent.

lull (lul) *vb.* **lull·ing, lulled** to make or become calm or quiet. – *n.* a period of calm.

lul·la·by (lul′ə-bī′) *n.* **lul·la·bies** a soothing song to lull children to sleep.

lum·ber[1] (lum′bər) *n.* timber, especially cut up and ready for use.

lum·ber[2] (lum′bər) *vb.* **lum·ber·ing, lum·bered** to move around heavily.

lum·ber·jack (lum′bər-jak′) *n.* a person employed to fell, saw up, and move trees.

lump (lump) *n.* **1** a small, solid, shapeless mass. **2** a swelling on the surface of something. – *vb.* **lump·ing, lumped** to form into a lump.

lu·na·cy (loo′nə-sē) *n.* **lu·na·cies** great foolishness or stupidity.

lu·nar (loo′nər) *adj.* like or caused by the moon.

lu·na·tic (loo′nə-tik′) *adj.* **1** mad or insane. **2** foolish, stupid, or eccentric. – *n.* an insane, foolish, stupid, eccentric, or dangerous person.

lunch (lunch) *n.* a meal eaten in the middle of the day between breakfast and dinner.

lung (lung) *n.* an organ for breathing.

lunge (lunj) *n.* a sudden plunge forward. – *vb.* **lung·ing, lunged** to make a sudden strong or thrusting movement forward.

lure (loor) *vb.* **lur·ing, lured** to attract or entice by offering some reward. – *n.* a person or thing that tempts or attracts.

lurk (lurk) *vb.* **lurk·ing, lurked** to lie in wait, especially in ambush.

lush (lush) *adj.* green and growing abundantly; luxurious. – *n.* **lush·ness**.

lus·ter (lus′tər) *n.* the shiny appearance of a surface in reflected light.

lute (loot) *n.* an ancient guitarlike instrument with a pear-shaped body and a fretted neck.

●**Lu·ther** (loo′thər), **Martin** (1483-1546) was a German priest who quarreled with the ROMAN CATHOLIC Church and started the REFORMATION.

●**Lux·em·bourg** (luk′səm-burg′). See Supplement, **Countries**.

lux·u·ri·ous (lug-zhoor′ē-əs, luk-shoor′ē-əs) *adj.* enjoying or providing luxury.

lux·u·ry (luk′shə-rē, lug′zhə-rē) *n.* **lux·u·ries** **1** expensive, rich, extremely comfortable surroundings and possessions. **2** something pleasant, often expensive, but not necessary. – *adj.* relating to or providing luxury.

-ly *suffix* used to form adverbs: *cleverly*.

lymph (limf) *n.* a clear liquid containing white blood cells, found in the tissues in animal bodies.

lynx (lingks) *n.* an animal of the cat family, with long legs, a short tail, and tufted ears.

●**Lyons** (lē-ôn′, lī′ənz) is a large city in FRANCE.

lyre (līr) *n.* a U-shaped, harplike instrument.

lyr·ic (lir′ik) *adj.* having the form of a song. – *n.* (usually in *plural*) the words of a song.

Saint Luke's Gospel contains the parable of the Good Samaritan in which a person from Samaria, a country despised by the Jews, comes to the aid of a traveler who had been beaten up by robbers.

Martin Luther pinning up the list of 95 arguments, setting out what he thought was wrong with the Church.

Mm

ma·ca·bre (mə-käb′rə, mə-käb′) *adj.* strange and ghastly.

ma·cad·am (mə-kad′əm) *n.* a road surface made of layers of broken stones and tar.

mac·a·ro·ni (mak′ə-rō′nē) *n.* pasta usually in the form of short tubes.

●**Mac·Ar·thur** (mə-kär′thər), **Douglas** (1880-1964) was an American general.

ma·caw (mə-kô′) *n.* a large, long-tailed, brightly colored tropical American parrot.

●**Mac·beth** (mək-beth′) (*died* 1057) was a king of SCOTLAND and the main character in SHAKESPEARE's play of that name.

●**Mac·don·ald** (mək-dän′ld), **Sir John** (1815-1891) was the first prime minister of CANADA.

ma·chine (mə-shēn′) *n.* any device with moving parts, designed to perform a particular task. *– vb.* **ma·chin·ing, ma·chined** to make or cut with a machine.

●There are six kinds of simple machine: the wheel and axle, lever, pulley, screw, wedge, and inclined plane.

machine language *n.* a code used for writing instructions that a computer can understand.

machine gun (mə-shēn′ gun′) *n.* any of various portable guns that fire a continuous stream of bullets.

ma·chin·er·y (mə-shē′nə-rē) *n.* **1** machines in general. **2** the moving parts of a machine.

ma·chin·ist (mə-shē′nəst) *n.* a person who operates, designs, or fixes machines.

Machines change energy from one form into another more useful form; they make jobs easier. Until the Industrial Revolution in the 1700s, there were very few machines. Steam engines became common in the 1700s. In the 1800s came other forms of energy such as the internal combustion engine and the electric motor making possible motor cars, aircraft, and many types of electrical machines.

The small electric motor in a drill is powerful. Its turning force is increased as it is slowed down by the gearing mechanism.

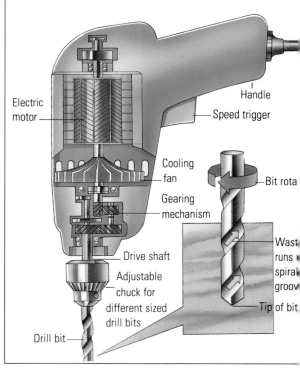

Electric motor
Cooling fan
Gearing mechanism
Drive shaft
Adjustable chuck for different sized drill bits
Drill bit
Handle
Speed trigger
Bit rota
Wast runs spira groov
Tip of bit

mack·er·el (mak′ə-rəl, mak′rəl) *n.* **mackerel** or **mackerels** a North Atlantic saltwater fish.

mad (mad) *adj.* **mad·der, mad·dest 1** very angry. **2** insane. **3** foolish or senseless: *It was a mad idea to dive from the bridge.* – *n.* **mad·ness** (mad′nəs).

●**Mad·a·gas·car** (mad′ə-gas′kər). See Supplement, **Countries**.

mad·am (mad′əm) *n.* a polite form of address to any woman.

●**Ma·drid** (mə-drid′) is the capital of SPAIN.

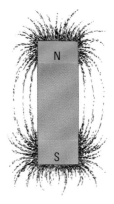

Pulleys change the direction of a force. A lifting tackle has several pulleys and makes lifting easier. Pulling the rope a long distance lifts the load a shorter distance.

Effort

Distance moved by load = 1

Load

A forklift truck is a hydraulic machine. It uses liquid pressure to transmit power because liquid cannot be compressed. Inside a hydraulic jack, a large movement of the smaller piston causes a small change of the large piston.

Large piston

Small piston

Oil Force

mag·a·zine (mag′ə-zēn′, mag′ə-zēn′) *n.* a weekly or monthly paperback publication.

●**Ma·gel·lan** (mə-jel′ən), **Ferdinand** (1480-1521) was a Portuguese mariner and explorer.

mag·got (mag′ət) *n.* the larva of various flies.

mag·ic (maj′ik) *n.* **1** in stories, the power of supernatural forces to affect people, objects, and events. **2** the art of performing entertaining illusions and conjuring tricks. **3** the quality of being wonderful, charming, or delightful: *The magic of the music crept over him.* – *adj.* of or used in sorcery or conjuring.

mag·i·cal (maj′i-kəl) *adj.* **1** relating to the art or practice of magic. **2** fascinating; wonderful.

ma·gi·cian (mə-jish′ən) *n.* **1** a performer of illusions. **2** in stories, a person with supernatural powers.

mag·istrate (maj′ə-strāt′) *n.* a judge in a lower court of law dealing with minor offenses.

mag·ma (mag′mə) *n.* molten rock beneath the earth's crust.

●**Mag·na Carta** (mag′nə kärt′ə) an agreement signed in 1215 by King John of ENGLAND. It gave rights to the nobles and made the king answerable to the law.

mag·ne·si·um (mag-nē′zē-əm) *n.* an element (symbol **Mg**), a light silvery-white metal.

mag·net (mag′nət) *n.* a piece of metal, especially iron, with the power to attract and repel iron, and the tendency to point in a north-south direction when freely suspended.

mag·net·ic (mag-net′ik) *adj.* having the powers of or operating by means of a magnet or magnetism.

magnetic tape *n.* any of various kinds of thin plastic tape coated with magnetic material, on which data can be recorded.

mag·ne·tism (mag′nə-tiz′əm) *n.* the properties of attraction possessed by magnets.

mag·nif·i·cent (mag-nif′ə-sənt) *adj.* impressive. – *n.* **mag·nif·i·cence** (mag′nif′ə-səns). – *adv.* **mag·nif·i·cent·ly**.

mag·ni·fy (mag′nə-fī′) *vb.* **mag·ni·fies, mag·ni·fy·ing, mag·ni·fied** to cause to appear larger.

magnifying glass *n.* a hand-held lens through which objects appear larger.

mag·no·li·a (mag-nō′lē-ə) *n.* a tree or shrub with large sweet-smelling flowers.

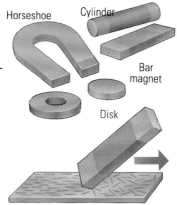

Horseshoe   Cylinder

Bar magnet

Disk

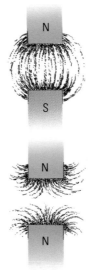

N

S

N

N

N

S

The pushing and pulling forces around a magnet are invisible. But if you scatter iron filings on a piece of paper and place a magnet under the paper some of the lines of force become clear.

The Magyars are a race of people who came originally from the steppes (plains) of Russia. Under their leader, Prince Arpad, they occupied what we now call Hungary in the A.D. 800s. This illustration is from a manuscript showing their arrival in Hungary.

Malaria was once believed to have been caused by "bad air" given off in marshy places. It was therefore named *mal'aria* in Italy, meaning "bad air."

Mag·yar (mag'yär') *n.* **1** a member of the predominant ethnic group in HUNGARY. **2** the Hungarian language. – *adj.* of the Magyars or their language.

ma·hog·a·ny (mə-häg'ə-nē) *n.* **ma·hog·a·nies** a tropical American tree; any of various related African and Asian trees.

maid (mād) *n.* **1** a female servant. **2** a maiden.

maid·en (mād'n) *n.* an unmarried woman or girl. – *adj.* **1** unmarried. **2** first ever.

mail (māl) *n.* **1** the postal system. **2** letters, parcels, etc. sent by mail. – *vb.* **mail·ing, mailed** to send by mail.

mail·man (māl'man', māl'mən) *n.* **mail·men** (also **mail carrier**) a person who delivers the mail.

main (mān) *adj.* most important; chief. – *n.* a main pipe or cable for water, power, etc.

●**Maine** (mān). See Supplement, **U.S.A**.

main·ly (mān'lē) *adv.* for the most part; largely.

main·tain (mān-tān') *vb.* **main·tain·ing, main·tained 1** to continue; to keep in existence. **2** to keep in good condition. **3** to pay the expenses of: *She is maintained by her parents.* **4** to continue to argue; to assert.

main·te·nance (mānt'n-əns) *n.* **1** the process of keeping something in good condition. **2** money or support.

maize (māz) *n.* (*British*) the corn plant or its grain.

maj·es·ty (maj'ə-stē) *n.* **ma·jes·ties** great and impressive dignity; splendor. – *adj.* **majestic** (mə-jes'tik).

ma·jor (mā'jər) *adj.* great in number, size, importance, etc. – *n.* an army officer below a colonel in rank.

major general *n.* a middle-ranking army general.

ma·jor·i·ty (mə-jôr'ət-ē, mə-jär'ət-ē) *n.* **ma·jor·i·ties** the greater number; the largest group.

make (māk) *vb.* **mak·ing, made 1** to create, manufacture, or produce by mixing, combining, or shaping materials. **2** to cause to be or become; to bring about: *He made me angry.* **3** to force: *She made him jump off the wall.* **4** to cause to appear: *Long hair makes her look younger.* **5** to gain, earn, or acquire: *They have made a fortune.* **6** to add up to or amount to: *4 and 4 makes 8.* **7** to carry out or produce: *He made a good speech.* **8** to tidy after use: *to make a bed.* – *n.* a manufacturer's brand: *What make of car did you buy?* – **make believe** to pretend. – *vb.* **make for** to move quickly toward. – *vb.* **make out** to see, hear, or understand. – *vb.* **make up 1** to fabricate or invent. **2** to compose: *He made up a poem about me.* **3** to compensate: *To make up for the argument, he cooked dinner.*

ma·lar·i·a (mə-lâr'ē-ə) *n.* an infectious disease producing bouts of fever.

●**Ma·la·wi** (mə-lä'wē). See Supplement, **Countries**.

Ma·lay (mə-lā', ma'lā') *n.* **1** a member of a race of people that inhabit MALAYSIA, SINGAPORE, and INDONESIA. **2** their language. – *adj.* of the Malays or their language.

●**Ma·lay·sia** (mə-lā'zhə). See Supplement, **Countries**.

●**Mal·dives** (môl'dēvz', môl'dīvz'). See Supplement, **Countries**.

male (māl) *adj.* **1** of the sex that has a sperm-producing or similar organ, not of the sex that gives birth to young. **2** having flowers with stamens which can fertilize female flowers. **3** of or characteristic of men. – *n.* a male person, animal, or plant.

ma·lice (mal'əs) *n.* the desire or intention to harm or hurt others.

ma·lig·nant (mə-lig'nənt) *adj.* **1** feeling or showing hatred. **2** a medical term describing cancerous tumors.

mall (môl) *n.* **1** a wide street or promenade. **2** a shopping area.

mal·le·a·ble (mal′ē-ə-bəl) *adj.* **1** able to be shaped easily. **2** easily influenced.

mal·let (mal′ət) *n.* a hammer with a wooden head.

malt (môlt) *n.* barley or other grain prepared for making beer or whiskey.

●**Mal·ta** (môl′tə). See Supplement, **Countries**.

Mal·tese (môl-tēz′) *n.* **1** a native or inhabitant of Malta. **2** one of the official languages of Malta. − *adj.* of Malta, its people, or their language.

mam·mal (mam′əl) *n.* any warm-blooded animal, the female of which gives birth to live young and produces milk to feed them.

mam·moth (mam′əth) *n.* a large hairy prehistoric elephantlike animal. − *adj.* huge.

man¹ (man) *n.* **men** (men) **1** an adult male human being. **2** the human race.

Man² *n.* **Isle of** is an island in the Irish Sea and is part of the UNITED KINGDOM.

man·a·cle (man′ə-kəl) *n.* a handcuff.

man·age (man′ij) *vb.* **man·ag·ing, man·aged 1** to be in control or charge of. **2** to succeed in doing or producing something.

man·age·ment (man′ij-mənt) *n.* **1** the skill or practice of controlling something. **2** the managers of a company as a group.

man·a·ger (man′ə-jər) *n.* a person in charge.

mane (mān) *n.* the long hair growing from the neck of horses, lions, and other animals.

●**Ma·net** (mə-nā′), **Edouard** (1832-1883) was a French painter, whose works are classified as IMPRESSIONISM.

ma·neu·ver (mə-nōō′vər) *n.* **1** a movement performed with considerable skill. **2** (in *plural*) military exercises. − *vb.* **ma·neu·ver·ing, ma·neu·vered** to move or handle accurately and with skill.

man·gan·ese (mang′gə-nēz′) *n.* an element (symbol **Mn**), a brittle gray-white metal.

●**Man·hat·tan** (man-hat′n) is an island at the mouth of the Hudson River and a borough of NEW YORK CITY.

ma·ni·a (mā′nē-ə) *n.* **1** a form of mental illness characterized by overly active, overly excited behavior. **2** a great enthusiasm; a craze.

man·i·fest (man′ə-fest′) *vb.* **man·i·fest·ing, man·i·fest·ed** to show or display clearly.

man·i·fes·to (man′ə-fes′tō) *n.* **manifestos** or **man·i·fes·toes** a declaration of policy.

ma·nip·u·late (mə-nip′yə-lāt′) *vb.* **ma·nip·u·lat·ing, ma·nip·u·lat·ed 1** to handle, especially skillfully. **2** to control or influence especially to your own advantage.

●**Man·i·to·ba** (man′ə-tō′bə) is a province of CANADA.

A kid suckling a goat. Mammals are the most highly developed of the many different forms of animal. All mammals give birth to live young (not hatched from an egg) and the young feed on milk from the mother's body. Mammals usually have four limbs.

man·kind (man-kīnd′) *n.* the human race.

man·ner (man′ər) *n.* **1** way; fashion: *She dresses in a sloppy manner.* **2** behavior toward others: *She has a good manner with children.* **3** (in *plural*) polite social behavior: *Mind your manners!*

man·ner·ism (man′ə-riz′əm) *n.* an individual characteristic, for example a gesture or facial expression.

man·or (man′ər) *n.* **1** in medieval Europe, an area of land under the control of a lord. **2** a large house on a country estate.

●**Mans·field** (manz′fēld′) , **Katherine** (1888-1923) was a New Zealand short-story writer.

man·sion (man′shən) *n.* a large house.

man·slaugh·ter (man′slôt′ər) *n.* the crime of killing someone without intending to do so.

man·tel·piece (mant′l-pēs′) *n.* the ornamental frame around a fireplace.

man·tis (mant′əs) *n.* **man·tis·es** or **man·tes** (man′tēz′) (also **praying mantis**) an insect-eating insect with a long body, large eyes,

PRONUNCIATION SYMBOLS			
ə	away lemon		focus
a	fat	oi	boy
ā	fade	oo	foot
ä	hot	o͞o	moon
âr	fair	ou	house
e	met	th	think
ē	mean	th	this
g	get	u	cut
hw	which	ur	hurt
i	fin	w	witch
ī	line	y	yes
îr	near	yo͞o	music
ô	often	yoor	pure
ō	note	zh	vision

which often carries its two front legs raised.

man·u·al (man′yoo-əl) *adj.* **1** of the hand or hands. **2** using the body, rather than the mind; physical: *manual labor*. **3** operated by hand; not automatic. – *n.* a book of instructions.

man·u·fac·ture (man′yə-fak′chər) *vb.* **man·u·fac·tur·ing, man·u·fac·tured** to make from raw materials, especially in large quantities using machinery. – *n.* the practice or process of manufacturing.

ma·nure (mə-noor′, mən-yoor′) *n.* a substance, especially animal dung, used on soil as a fertilizer.

man·u·script (man′yə-skript′) *n.* a handwritten or typed version of a book before it has been printed.

man·y (men′ē) *adj.* **more**, **most** great in number; numerous. – *pron.* a great number of people or things.

● **Mao Ze·dong** (moud′zu′doong′) (1893-1976) was a Chinese communist statesman and president of the People's Republic of CHINA until 1959.

Mao·ri (mou′rē) *n.* **Maori** or **Maoris 1** a member of the aboriginal Polynesian people of NEW ZEALAND. **2** the language of this people. – *adj.* of this people or its language.

map (map) *n.* a diagram of the earth's surface, showing geographical and other features, for example the position of towns and roads.

A conical projection

Mercator projection

Polar zenithal projection

A projection is the way in which mapmakers show the curved surface of the earth on a flat map.

Different types of **map**. A relief map shows the surface of the land, the hills, rivers, forests, etc. Maps of the seabed are important for plotting a ship's course, and in the search for minerals. Star maps help navigation. Perhaps the most commonly used are road maps.

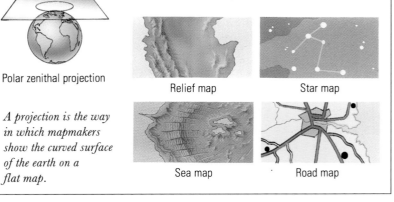

Relief map   Star map

Sea map   Road map

mar·a·thon (mar′ə-thän′) *n.* **1** a long-distance running race, usually 26 miles (42 km). **2** any lengthy and difficult task.

● The marathon is named after a Greek soldier's run from Marathon to Athens in 490 B.C. to bring news of a victory over the Persians.

mar·ble (mär′bəl) *n.* **1** hard streaky-looking limestone rock that can be highly polished, used in building and sculpture. **2** a small hard ball of glass, used in children's games.

March (märch) *n.* the third month of the year, following February. March has 31 days.

march (märch) *vb.* **march·ing, marched 1** (of soldiers, etc.) to walk in a formal manner, usually at a brisk pace and in step with others. **2** to walk in a purposeful and determined way. – *n.* **1** an act of marching; a distance traveled by marching. **2** a brisk walking pace.

An early Marconi radio, with a speaker and headphones. Modern radios use tiny transistors instead of glass tubes.

● **Mar·co·ni** (mär-kō′nē), **Guglielmo** (1874-1937) was the Italian inventor of the radio.

● **Mar·co Po·lo** (mär′kō pō′lō) (1254-1324) was a Venetian merchant who traveled to CHINA.

mar·ga·rine (mär′jə-rən, mär′jə-rēn′) *n.* a butterlike substance made from vegetable oils.

mar·gin (mär′jən) *n.* **1** the blank space around a page. **2** any edge or border.

mar·gin·al (mär′jə-nəl) *adj.* **1** small and unimportant. **2** appearing in the margin.

mar·i·gold (mâr′ə-gōld)′ *n.* any of various garden plants with bright orange or yellow flowers and strongly scented leaves.

ma·rine (mə-rēn′) *adj.* **1** concerned with the sea. **2** of ships, shipping trade, or the navy. – *n.* a soldier trained to serve on land or at sea.

Marine Corps *n.* a branch of the United States NAVY trained to launch attacks on land from the sea.

mar·i·o·nette (mar′ē-ə-net′) *n.* a puppet with jointed limbs moved by strings.

mar·i·time (mar′ə-tīm′) *adj.* **1** of the sea or ships. **2** living or growing near the sea.

mark (märk) *n.* **1** a visible blemish, for example a scratch or stain. **2** a number or letter used to grade a student's or competitor's performance. **3** a sign or symbol: *a question mark.* **4** an indication or representation: *We keep a minute's silence as a mark of respect.* – *vb.* **mark·ing, marked 1** to spoil with a blemish or mark. **2** to award a grade to. **3** to show; to be a sign of.

marked *adj.* obvious or noticeable.

marks·man (märk′smən) *n.* **marks·men** a person able to shoot a gun accurately.

●**Mark** (märk), **Saint** was the writer of one of the gospels in the New Testament.

mar·ket (mär′kət) *n.* **1** a gathering of people to buy and sell various goods. **2** the building or other public location in which this takes place. **3** a particular section of the population considered as a potential customer. – *vb.* **mar·ket·ing, mar·ket·ed** to offer for sale.

mar·ma·lade (mär′mə-lād′) *n.* a jam made from any citrus fruit, especially oranges.

mar·mo·set (mär′mə-set′, mär′mə-zet′) *n.* any of various small South American monkeys.

ma·roon¹ (mə-rōōn′) *n.* a dark brown-red color.

ma·roon² (mə-rōōn′) *vb.* **ma·roon·ing, ma·rooned** to leave in isolation in a deserted place: *Robinson Crusoe was marooned on an island.*

mar·riage (mar′ij) *n.* **1** the relationship of being husband and wife. **2** a wedding.

mar·ried *adj.* having a husband or wife.

mar·row (mar′ō) *n.* (also **bone marrow**) the soft tissue in the hollow center of bones.

mar·ry (mar′ē) *vb.* **mar·ries, mar·ry·ing, mar·ried 1** to take as a husband or wife. **2** to perform a wedding between two people.

Mars¹ (märz). See **Myths and Legends**.

●**Mars²** (märz) is also called the "Red Planet." It is about half the size of Earth and has two moons.

●**Mar·seil·les** (mär-sā′, mär-sālz′) is an important French port on the MEDITERRANEAN.

marsh (märsh) *n.* an area of low-lying wetlands.

mar·shal (mär′shəl) *n.* an officer of a federal court who has certain law enforcement duties.

mar·su·pi·al (mär-sōō′pē-əl) *n.* any member of a class of mammals, including kangaroos and koalas, whose young are carried in an external pouch on the mother's body.

mar·tial (mär′shəl) *adj.* of or relating to war or the military.

martial art *n.* any of various fighting sports or self-defense techniques of Far Eastern origin.

mar·tin (märt′n) *n.* a small bird of the swallow family, with a square or slightly forked tail.

mar·tyr (märt′ər) *n.* a person who chooses to die rather than give up his or her beliefs.

mar·vel (mär′vəl) *n.* an astonishing or wonderful person or thing.

mar·ve·lous (mär′və-ləs) *adj.* so wonderful or astonishing as to be almost beyond belief.

Marx·ism (märk′siz′əm) *n.* the theories of Karl Marx (1818-1883), German political philosopher, stating that the struggle between different social classes is the main influence on political and economic change. – *n.* & *adj.* **Marx·ist** (märk′səst).

●**Ma·ry·land** (mâr′ə-lənd). See Supplement, **U.S.A.**

●**Ma·ry** (mâr′ē, mā′rē), **Queen of Scots** (1542-1587) was heir to ELIZABETH I of England who had her executed for treason.

Two Viking probes visited Mars in 1976. The probe in the picture is viewing the enormous volcanic mountain of Olympus Mons. The planet's atmosphere is only about a hundredth part as thick as Earth's. On the left of the picture is Phobos, one of the two tiny moons of Mars.

MATH TERMS

bisect divide into two equal parts.

factor 2 multiplied by 6 are factors of 12.

fraction part of a whole.

greatest common divisor the largest integer that is a factor of two numbers. 3 is the GCD of 12 and 15.

integer a whole number, e.g. 2.

prime number 7, 11, etc. — numbers that can only be divided evenly by themselves or one.

square a number multiplied by itself: 7 × 7 = 49.

square root a number multiplied by itself to produce a given number: 4 is the square root of 16.

mas·cot (mas′kät′) *n.* a person, animal, etc. thought to bring good luck, as to a sports team.

mas·cu·line (mas′kyə-lən) *adj.* typical of or suitable for men.

mash (mash) *vb.* **mash·ing, mashed** to beat or crush into a pulpy mass: *Mash the potatoes!*

mask (mask) *n.* any covering for the face, worn for amusement, for protection, or as a disguise. – *vb.* **mask·ing, masked** to disguise.

In ancient Greece plays were acted in huge open-air theaters. Men wearing stylized masks (depicting comedy or tragedy, etc.) played all the parts.

ma·son (mā′sən) *n.* a person trained in the craft of working with stone.

mass¹ (mas) *n.* **1** a body of material; a lump. **2** a large quantity or number. **3** a measure of the quantity of matter in a body. **4 the masses** ordinary people. – *adj.* involving a large number of people.

mass² or **Mass** (mas) *n.* in some Christian churches, the ceremony of Holy Communion.

●**Mas·sa·chu·setts** (mas′ə-chōō′səts). See Supplement, **U.S.A.**

mas·sa·cre (mas′ə-kər) *n.* a cruel killing of large numbers of people or animals. – *vb.* **mas·sa·cring, mas·sa·cred.**

mas·sage (mə-säzh′, mə-säj′) *n.* a technique of easing pain or stiffness in the body, especially the muscles, by rubbing with the hands. – *vb.* **mas·sag·ing, mas·saged** to perform a massage on.

mas·sive (mas′iv) *adj.* **1** very big, solid, and heavy. **2** very large.

mast (mast) *n.* any upright supporting pole, especially one carrying the sails of a ship.

mas·ter (mas′tər) *n.* a person who commands or has authority over someone or something. – *adj.* fully qualified; highly skilled; expert. – *vb.* **mas·ter·ing, mas·tered 1** to overcome or defeat: *She mastered her disappointment.* **2** to become skilled in.

mas·to·don (mas′tə-dän′) *n.* a prehistoric elephant-like mammal.

mat (mat) *n.* **1** a flat piece of carpet, used to decorate or protect floors, or for wiping shoes on to remove dirt. **2** a tangled mass, as of hair. – *vb.* **mat·ting, mat·ted** to become tangled into an untidy mass.

mat·a·dor (mat′ə-dôr′) *n.* the principal toreador in a bullfight, who kills the bull.

match¹ (mach) *n.* a short thin piece of wood coated on the tip with a substance that produces a flame when struck.

match² (mach) *n.* **1** a contest or game. **2** a person or thing that has similar qualities to, or combines well with, another. – *vb.* **match·ing, matched 1** to combine well. **2** to be equal to; to make an equivalent to: *I can't match that offer.*

mate (māt) *n.* **1** an animal's breeding partner. **2** a person's spouse. **3** one of a pair: *I lost the mate to this glove.*

ma·te·ri·al (mə-tîr′ē-əl) *n.* **1** any substance out of which something is made. **2** cloth; fabric.

ma·ter·nal (mə-turn′l) *adj.* **1** of or like a mother. **2** related on the mother's side.

math·e·ma·ti·cian (math′ə-mə-tish′ən) *n.* an expert in mathematics.

math·e·mat·ics (math′ə-mat′iks) *n.* (*singular*) the science dealing with measurements, numbers, quantities, and shapes.

●**Ma·tisse** (mə-tēs′), **Henri** (1869-1954) was a French painter and sculptor.

mat·ri·mo·ny (ma′trə-mō′nē) *n.* the state of being married.

mat·ter (mat′ər) *n.* **1** the substance from which all physical things are made; material. **2** material of a particular kind: *She took plenty of reading matter with her.* **3** (often in *plural*) a subject or topic; a concern, affair, or question: *I leave financial matters to my accountant.* – *vb.* **mat·ter·ing, mat·tered** to be important or significant: *Does the extra cost matter to you?*

●**Mat·thew** (math′yōō), **Saint** was one of Jesus' apostles and author of the first gospel in the NEW TESTAMENT.

mat·tress (ma′trəs) *n.* a large flat fabric-covered pad, used on a bed for sleeping on.

ma·ture (mə-toor′, mə-choor′) *adj.* **1** fully grown or developed. **2** behaving with adult good sense. – *vb.* **ma·tur·ing, ma·tured** to make or become fully developed. – *n.* **ma·tur·i·ty** (mə-toor′ət-ē, mə-choor′ət-ē).

●**Mau·na Lo·a** (mou′nə lō′ə), on the island of Hawaii, is the world's largest active volcano.

●**Mau·ri·ta·ni·a** (môr′ə-tā′nē-ə). See Supplement, **Countries**.

●**Mau·ri·tius** (môr-ish′əs). See Supplement, **Countries**.

max·i·mum (mak′sə-məm) *adj.* greatest possible. – *n.* the greatest possible amount.

May (mā) *n.* the fifth month of the year, following April. May has 31 days.

may (mā) *vb.* **might** (mīt) expressing: **1** permission: *You may go now.* **2** possibility: *I may well leave.* **3** request: *May I help you?* **4** used to introduce the first of a pair of statements, with the sense of "although": *You may be rich, but you're not happy.*

may·be (mā′bē) *adv.* it is possible; perhaps.

●**May·flow·er** (mā′flou′ər) This was the ship which, in 1620, carried the PILGRIMS from Plymouth in ENGLAND to AMERICA.

The Mayflower *was a small sailing ship about 88 feet long. Its Puritan Pilgrim passengers were looking for religious freedom in the New World.*

may·on·naise (mā′ə-nāz′, mā′ə-nāz′) *n.* an uncooked creamy sauce made of egg yolk, oil, vinegar or lemon juice, and seasoning.

may·or (mā′ər, mâr) *n.* the head of a town or city. – *adj.* **may·or·al** (mā′ə-rəl, mâr′əl).

maze (māz) *n.* a confusing network of paths or passages; any confusingly complicated system.

me (mē) *pron.* used by a speaker or writer to refer to himself or herself.

●**Mead** (mēd), **Margaret** (1901-1978) was an American anthropologist.

mead·ow (med′ō) *n.* a field of grass.

mea·ger (mēg′ər) *adj.* inadequate; scanty.

meal[1] (mēl) *n.* **1** a time in which food is eaten. **2** an amount of food eaten on one occasion.

meal[2] (mēl) *n.* coarsely ground grain.

mean[1] (mēn) *vb.* **mean·ing, meant** (ment) **1** to intend: *He didn't mean any harm.* **2** to be sincere about: *She means what she says.* **3** to result in; to involve.

mean[2] (mēn) *adj.* **1** unkind. **2** not generous.

mean[3] (mēn) *n.* **1** a midway position between two extremes. **2** a mathematical average.

mean·ing (mē′ning) *n.* the sense in which a statement, action, or word is intended to be understood.

means (mēnz) *n.* **1** (*singular* or *plural*) the instrument or method used to achieve some object. **2** (*plural*) wealth; resources.

mean·while (mēn′hwīl′) *adv.* at the same time.

mea·sles (mē′zəlz) *n.* (*singular*) an infectious disease, common in children.

mea·sure (mezh′ər, mā′zhər) *n.* **1** size, volume, etc. determined by comparison with an instrument graded in standard units. **2** a standard unit of size; a system of such units; a standard amount: *We use a metric measure.* **3** an action: *drastic measures.* – *vb.* **mea·sur·ing, mea·sured** to determine the size, volume, etc. of.

meat (mēt) *n.* the flesh of animals used as food.

●**Mec·ca** (mek′ə) in Saudi Arabia, is the holy city of the MUSLIMS and MUHAMMAD's birthplace.

me·chan·ic (mə-kan′ik) *n.* a skilled worker who repairs or maintains machinery.

The pyramid builders of Egypt more than 5,000 years ago used parts of the body to measure. The cubit was the length from fingers to elbow.

USEFUL MEASURES
American
3 teaspoons = 1 tablespoon.
1 tablespoon = $\frac{1}{2}$ fluid oz.
1 cup = 8 fluid oz.
2 cups = 1 pint.
1 pint = 16 fluid oz.
1 quart = 2 pints.
1 gallon = 4 quarts.
Imperial
1 pint = 20 fluid oz.
1 gallon = 1.25 U.S. gall.
Metric equivalents
1 teaspoon = 5 ml.
1 pint = 0.5 liters app.
1 lb = 0.5 kg app.

me·chan·i·cal (mə-kan′i-kəl) *adj.* of or concerning machines.

mech·a·nism (mek′ə-niz′əm) *n.* a working part of a machine, or its system of working parts.

med·al (med′l) *n.* a flat piece of metal decorated with a design or inscription and offered as an award for merit or bravery.

med·al·list (med′l-əst) *n.* a person awarded a medal, especially for excellence in sports.

med·dle (med′l) *vb.* **med·dling, med·dled** to interfere: *Stop meddling in my personal affairs!*

media. See **medium.**

med·i·cal (med′i-kəl) *adj.* of doctors or the science or practice of medicine.

Florence, city of the powerful Medici family, and one of the great centers of the Italian Renaissance.

● **Med·i·ci** (med′ə-chē, mə-dē′chē) was the name of the ruling family of Florence, ITALY, from the 1400s to the 1700s.

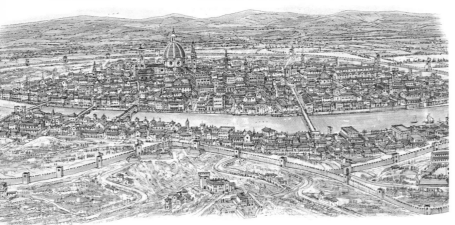

med·i·cine (med′ə-sən) *n.* **1** a substance used to treat or prevent disease or illness. **2** the practice of treating or preventing illness.

me·di·e·val or **me·di·ae·val** (mēd′ē-ē′vəl, med′ē-ē′vəl, mid-ē′vəl) *adj.* of or relating to the MIDDLE AGES.

med·i·tate (med′ə-tāt′) *vb.* **med·i·tat·ing, med·i·tat·ed** to spend time in deep thought.

Med·i·ter·ra·ne·an (med′i tə rā′ nē ən) *n.* a large sea between southern Europe, western Asia, and northern Africa.

me·di·um (mēd′ē-əm) *n.* **me·di·a** (med′ē-ə) or **mediums 1** something by or through which an effect is produced. **2** (usually in *plural*; also **mass medium**) a means by which news, etc. is communicated to the public.

meet (mēt) *vb.* **meet·ing, met** (met) **1** to come together by chance or arrangement. **2** to be present at the arrival of: *She met his train.* **3** to join; to come into contact with.

meet·ing (mēt′ing) *n.* an assembly or gathering.

meg·a·byte (meg′ə-bīt′) *n.* in computing, a unit of storage capacity of 1,048,576 bytes.

mel·an·chol·y (mel′ən-käl′ē) *adj.* sad.

● **Mel·bourne** (mel′bərn) is AUSTRALIA's second largest city.

mel·low (mel′ō) *adj.* **1** (of character) calm and relaxed with age or experience. **2** (of sound, color, light, etc.) soft, rich, and pure.

mel·o·dy (mel′əd-ē) *n.* **mel·o·dies** the sequence of single notes that form a tune.

mel·on (mel′ən) *n.* a large edible fruit with a thick skin, sweet juicy flesh, and many seeds.

melt (melt) *vb.* **melt·ing, melt·ed** to become soft through the action of heat; to dissolve.

● **Mel·ville** (mel′vil′, mel′vəl), **Herman** (1819-1891) was the American author of *Moby Dick.*

mem·ber (mem′bər) *n.* a person belonging to a group or organization.

mem·brane (mem′brān′) *n.* a thin film of skin covering, connecting, or lining organs or cells in plants or animals.

mem·o·ra·ble (mem′ə-rə-bəl) *adj.* worth remembering; easily remembered.

me·mo·ri·al (mə-môr′ē-əl, mə-mōr′ē-əl) *n.* a thing that honors or commemorates a person or an event, for example a statue.

mem·o·rize (mem′ə-rīz′) *vb.* **mem·o·riz·ing, mem·o·rized** to learn thoroughly, so as to reproduce from memory.

mem·o·ry (mem′ə-rē) *n.* **mem·o·ries 1** the power of the mind to remember. **2** everything one remembers. **3** the part of a computer in which information is stored.

men·ace (men′əs) *n.* **1** a source of danger. **2** a threat; a show of hostility: *a look full of menace.* −*vb.* **men·a·cing, men·aced** to threaten.

mend (mend) *vb.* **mend·ing, mend·ed 1** to repair. **2** to improve or correct.

● **Men·del** (men′dəl), **Gregor** (1822-1884) was an Austrian monk, founder of the science of GENETICS.

men·o·pause (men′ə-pôz′) *n.* the time in a woman's life when she stops menstruating, usually between the ages of 45 and 50.

A menorah stood in the first Temple at Jerusalem and is still used today. Its branches symbolize the seven days of creation recorded in the Bible.

me·no·rah (mə-nôr′ə, mə-nōr′ə) *n.* a holder for candles with seven or nine branches, used in Jewish worship.

men·stru·ate (men′strōō-āt′) *vb.* **men·stru·at·ing, men·stru·at·ed** to discharge blood monthly from the womb. – *n.* **men·stru·a·tion** (men′strōō-ā′shən).

men·tal (ment′l) *adj.* relating to or done in the mind or intelligence: *mental images.*

men·tion (men′chən) *vb.* **men·tion·ing, men·tioned** to speak of or make reference to. – *n.* a remark, usually a brief reference to.

men·u (men′yōō) *n.* **1** a list of the range of dishes available in a restaurant. **2** a list of computer functions displayed on a screen.

mer·chan·dise (mur′chən dīs′, mur′chən dīz) *n.* goods that are bought or sold.

mer·chant (mur′chənt) *n.* a person who buys and sells goods, especially a storekeeper.

mer·ci·ful (mur′sə-fəl) *adj.* showing mercy.

mer·ci·less (mur′sē-ləs) *adj.* without mercy; cruel; pitiless.

●**Mer·cu·ry** (mur′kyə-rē) is the smallest planet in the solar system and the closest to the sun.

mer·cu·ry (mur′kyə-rē) *n.* an element (symbol **Hg**), a heavy poisonous silvery-white metal that is liquid at ordinary temperatures, used in thermometers and barometers.

mer·cy (mur′sē) *n.* **mer·cies 1** kindness or forgiveness shown when punishment is possible or justified. **2** a piece of good luck; a welcome happening: *Let's be grateful for small mercies.*

merge (murj) *vb.* **merg·ing, merged** to blend, combine, or join with something else.

me·rid·i·an (mə-rid′ē-ən) *n.* an imaginary line on the earth's surface passing through the poles at right angles to the equator.

mer·it (mer′ət) *n.* **1** worth or excellence. **2** a good point or quality. – *vb.* **mer·it·ing, mer·it·ed** to deserve; to be worthy of.

mer·maid (mur′mād′) *n.* a mythical sea creature with a woman's head and upper body, and a fish's tail.

mer·ry (mer′ē) *adj.* **mer·ri·er, mer·ri·est** cheerful and lively.

mesh (mesh) *n.* **1** netting made of fine wire or thread. **2** the openings between the threads of a net. – *vb.* **mesh·ing, meshed** to fit together.

mes·mer·ize (mez′mə-rīz′) *vb.* **mes·mer·ing, mes·mer·ized** to grip the attention of.

Mesmerize, meaning ''to fascinate,'' is named after one of the earliest people to practice hypnotism, the Austrian physicist Friedrich *Mesmer* (1733-1815).

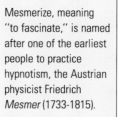

Mesopotamia, now mostly in Iraq, was a region between the Tigris and Euphrates rivers which was the center of many early civilizations, including the earliest, the Sumerian.

The Chaldean king, Nebuchadnezzar (604-561 B.C.), rebuilt the Mesopotamian city of Babylon in such fabulous splendor that it came to be regarded as one of the wonders of the world.

A Sumerian princess wearing an elaborate headdress, earrings, and necklaces, made of gold and silver, decorated with lapis-lazuli and carnelians.

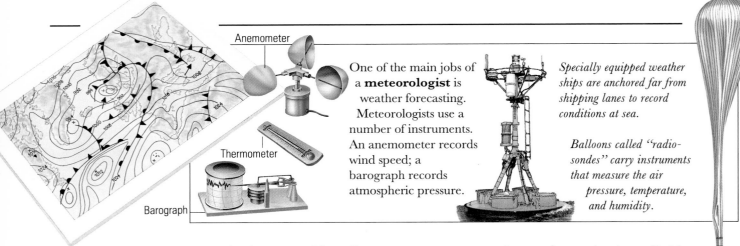

Anemometer

Thermometer

Barograph

One of the main jobs of a **meteorologist** is weather forecasting. Meteorologists use a number of instruments. An anemometer records wind speed; a barograph records atmospheric pressure.

Specially equipped weather ships are anchored far from shipping lanes to record conditions at sea.

Balloons called "radio-sondes" carry instruments that measure the air pressure, temperature, and humidity.

Weather maps record conditions using standard symbols. Isobars are lines connecting places where air pressure is the same. The closer the isobars, the stronger the winds. The chart also show warm (rounded symbols) and cold (triangular symbols) fronts.

The Old Woman meteorite weighs more than 3 tons. It was discovered in California in 1976. It is composed of iron and nickel and may have formed part of a planet that disintegrated 4 billion years ago!

mess (mes) *n.* **1** an untidy or dirty state; a state of disorder or confusion. **2** a communal dining room, especially in the armed forces. – *vb.* **mess·ing, messed 1** to interfere or meddle. **2** to put into an untidy, dirty, or damaged state. – *adv.* **mess·i·ly** (mes′ə-lē). – *adj.* **mess·y, mess·i·er, mess·i·est**.

mes·sage (mes′ij) *n.* a spoken or written communication from one person to another.

mes·sen·ger (mes′ən-jər) *n.* a person who carries communications between people.

Mes·si·ah (mə-sī′ə) *n.* **1** in Christianity, Jesus Christ. **2** in Judaism, the king of the Jews still to be sent by God to free them.

me·tab·o·lism (mə-tab′ə-liz′əm) *n.* the system of chemical processes in a living body, from which energy, growth, and waste matter are produced.

met·al (met′l) *n.* any of a group of elements that can conduct heat and electricity, can be worked into different shapes, and typically have a shiny appearance, for example iron.

met·al·lur·gy (met′l-ur′jē) *n.* the scientific study of the nature and properties of metals and their extraction from the ground.

met·a·mor·pho·sis (met′ə-môr′fə-səs) *n.* **met·a·mor·pho·ses** (met′ə-môr′fə-sēz′) a complete change of form, appearance, or character.

met·a·phor (met′ə-fôr′) *n.* an expression in which the person, action, or thing referred to is described as if it really were what it resembles, for example as when a rejection is referred to as "a slap in the face."

me·te·or (mēt′ē-ər, mēt′ē-ôr′) *n.* any of countless small bodies traveling through space, which become visible as streaks of light if they enter the earth's atmosphere.

me·te·or·ite (mēt′ē-ə-rīt′) *n.* a meteor fallen to earth as a lump of rock or metal.

me·te·o·rol·o·gy (mēt′ē-ə-räl′ə-jē) *n.* the study of the atmosphere and weather patterns. – *n.* **me·te·o·rol·o·gist** (mēt′ē-ə-räl′ə-jəst).

me·ter¹ (mēt′ər) *n.* an instrument for measuring and recording quantities of electricity, gas, water, etc. used.

me·ter² (mēt′ər) *n.* the principal unit of length in the metric system, equal to 39.37 inches.

me·ter³ (mēt′ər) *n.* **1** in poetry, the rhythmic pattern of words and syllables.

meth·od (meth′əd) *n.* a way of doing something, especially a set of procedures.

me·thod·i·cal (mə-thäd′i-kəl) *adj.* efficient and orderly; done in an orderly way.

met·ric (me′trik) *adj.* based on the metric system. – *adv.* **met·ri·cal·ly** (me′tri-klē).

metric system *n.* a decimal system of weights and measures with the meter, kilogram, and liter as its principal units.

me·trop·o·lis (mə-träp′ə-ləs) *n.* **metropolises** a large city. – *adj.* **met·ro·pol·i·tan** (me′trə-päl′ət-n).

● **Mex·i·co** (mek′si-kō′) is the southern neighbor of the UNITED STATES. Its capital is Mexico City. From 1519 the Spanish conquered the powerful AZTEC empire and ruled until 1821. See also Supplement, **Countries**.

● **Mi·am·i** (mī-am′ē, mī-am′ə) is Florida's second largest city and a popular tourist spot.

● **Mi·chel·an·ge·lo** (mī′kə-lanj′ə-lō′) (1475-1564) was a great Italian sculptor and painter.

● **Mich·i·gan** (mish′ə-gən). See Supplement, **U.S.A.**

mi·crobe (mī′krōb′) *n.* any tiny organism

invisible to the naked eye.

mi·cro·chip (mī′krō-chip′) *n.* (also **chip**) a tiny piece of silicon carrying several electrical circuits, used in computers and appliances.

● **Mic·ro·ne·sia** (mī′krə-nē′zhə). See Supplement, **Countries**.

mi·cro·phone (mī′krə-fōn′) *n.* an instrument that picks up sounds to be recorded or broadcast.

mi·cro·scope (mī′krə-skōp′) *n.* an instrument with a system of lenses for viewing objects too small to be seen with the naked eye.

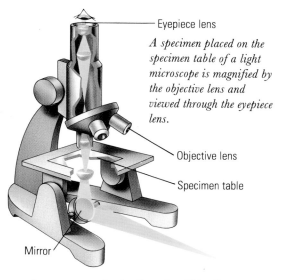

— Eyepiece lens

A specimen placed on the specimen table of a light microscope is magnified by the objective lens and viewed through the eyepiece lens.

— Objective lens

— Specimen table

Mirror

mi·cro·scop·ic (mī′krə-skäp′ik) *adj.* **1** too small to be seen without the aid of a microscope. **2** extremely small.

mi·cro·wave (mī′krə-wāv′) *n.* an electromagnetic wave of very short wavelength, used in cooking and radar.

microwave oven *n.* an oven that cooks food quickly by passing microwaves through it.

mid- (mid) *adj.* being the part at or in the middle: *She stopped me in mid sentence.*

mid·day (mid-dā′) *n.* twelve o'clock noon.

mid·dle (mid′l) *adj.* **1** at a point between two ends or extremes, and especially the same distance from each. **2** moderate, not extreme: *He steered a middle course.* – *n.* the middle point, part, or position. – **in the middle of** during.

middle age *n.* the years between youth and old age, approximately between ages 40 and 60.

Middle Ages *n.* (*plural*) the period of European history between the A.D. 1100s and 1400s.

During the **Middle Ages** in Europe people lived under the feudal system. Religion was a powerful force because the church had great authority. Monasteries were islands of learning in a sea of ignorance and superstition. Gradually universities were founded and trade expanded.

In 1085, William the Conqueror's officials toured England and recorded in the "Domesday Book" the names of all landowners.

William quickly crushed any revolt by English rebels, thus consolidating his rule over the land.

In the Middle Ages merchants bought spices and silks from the East in exchange for wool and cloth.

A European medieval town on market day was a bustling, noisy place. A dancing bear entertains the crowds.

Few people could read or write. In monasteries monks preserved ancient learning, copying books by hand.

PRONUNCIATION SYMBOLS			
ə	**away** lemon		focus
a	fat	oi	boy
ā	fade	oo	foot
ä	hot	ōō	moon
âr	**fair**	ou	house
e	met	th	think
ē	mean	<u>th</u>	this
g	get	u	cut
hw	**which**	ur	hurt
i	fin	w	witch
ī	line	y	yes
îr	near	yōō	music
ô	often	yoor	pure
ō	note	zh	vision

middle ear *n.* the system of tiny bones which transmits sounds from the eardrum to the inner ear.

Middle East *n.* all the countries between, but not including, Tunisia and Pakistan.

midge (mij) *n.* any of various kinds of small insects that gather near water.

mid·night (mid'nīt) *n.* twelve o'clock at night.

mid·sum·mer (mid-sum'ər) *n.* the period of time in summer around June 21.

Mid·west (mid-west') *n.* the central northern states of the UNITED STATES.

mid·wife (mid'wīf') *n.* **mid·wives** (mid'wīvz') a nurse trained to supervise childbirth.

might¹ (mīt) *vb.* **1** past tense of **may**: *He asked if he might be of assistance.* **2** used to express possibility: *She might win if she tries hard.* **3** used to request permission: *Might I speak to you?*

might² (mīt) *n.* power or strength.

might·y (mīt'ē) *adj.* **might·i·er, might·i·est 1** having great strength or power. **2** very large.

mi·grant (mī'grənt') *n.* a person or animal that migrates.

mi·grate (mī'grāt') *vb.* **mi·grat·ing, mi·grat·ed 1** (of animals, especially birds) to travel from one region to another at certain times. **2** to leave one country and settle in another. – *n.* **mi·gra·tion** (mī-grā'shən).

mild (mīld) *adj.* **1** gentle in temperament or behavior. **2** not sharp or strong in flavor or effect. **3** not great or severe. **4** (of climate) rather warm.

mil·dew (mil'dōō', mil'dyōō') *n.* a whitish growth of fungus on plants or other substances.

mile (mīl) *n.* a unit of distance equal to 1,760 yards (1.6km).

mile·age (mī'lij) *n.* the number of miles traveled.

mile·stone (mīl'stōn') *n.* an important event.

mil·i·tant (mil'ə-tənt) *adj.* ready to take strong or violent action; aggressively active.

mil·i·tar·y (mil'ə-ter'ē) *adj.* by or for the armed forces. – *n.* the armed forces.

milk (milk) *n.* **1** a whitish liquid produced by female mammals as food for their young; this liquid produced by a cow or goat and used by humans as food. **2** any similar liquid. – *vb.* **milk·ing, milked** to take milk from.

Milky Way *n.* the band of faint white light in the sky at night, formed by millions of stars.

mill (mil) *n.* **1** a building containing a large machine that grinds grain into flour. **2** any of various smaller machines or devices for grinding: *a pepper mill* . – *n.* **mil·ler** (mil'ər).

mil·len·ni·um (mə-len'ē-əm) *n.* **mil·len·ni·a** (mə-len'ē-ə) a period of a thousand years.

milli- *prefix* a thousandth part: *millisecond.*

mil·li·gram (mil'ə-gram') *n.* a metric unit of weight, equal to one thousandth of a gram.

mil·li·meter (mil'ə-mēt'ər) *n.* a metric unit of length, equal to one thousandth of a meter.

mil·lion (mil'yən) *n.* **mil·lions** the number 1,000,000.

mil·lion·aire (mil'yə-nâr', mil'yə-nâr') *n.* a person who has a million dollars or more.

mil·li·pede (mil'ə-pēd') *n.* a small wormlike creature with numerous pairs of legs.

● **Mil·ton** (milt'n), **John** (1608-1674) was an English poet, author of the epic *Paradise Lost.*

mime (mīm) *vb.* **mim·ing, mimed** to act using only movements and gestures.

mim·ic (mim'ik) *vb.* **mim·ick·ing, mim·icked** to imitate.

The 11th-century minaret at the Jami Mosque in Simnan, Iran.

min·a·ret (min'ə-ret') *n.* a tower on a mosque, from which MUSLIMS are called to prayer.

mind (mīnd) *n.* **1** the power of thinking and understanding; the place where thoughts, memory, and feelings exist; the intelligence. **2** attention: *His mind wanders easily.* **3** wish; inclination: *She has changed her mind.* – *vb.* **mind·ing, mind·ed 1** to take notice of: *Mind your own business.* **2** to object: *Do you mind if I don't come?* **3** to be careful of: *Mind the traffic.*

mine¹ (mīn) *pron.* something or someone belonging to, or connected with, me; those belonging to me: *That book is mine.*

mine² (mīn) *n.* **1** a place from which coal, minerals, metal ores, or precious stones are dug up. **2** an exploding device, designed to destroy enemy ships, troops, etc. – *vb.* **min·ing, mined** to dig for minerals, etc. – *n.* **min·ing**.

min·er (mī'nər) *n.* a person who works in a mine.

min·e·ral (min′ə-rəl, min′rəl) *n.* any solid substance such as iron ore, salt, etc. that forms naturally in the rocks in the earth. – *adj.* of the nature of a mineral; containing minerals.

min·gle (ming′gəl) *vb.* **min·gling, min·gled** **1** to become mixed. **2** to associate with.

mini *n.* a small or short one of its kind. – *adj.* small or short of its kind.

min·i·a·ture (min′ē-ə-choor′) *n.* a small copy or model of anything. – *adj.* small in scale.

min·i·mum (min′ə-məm) *n.* the lowest possible number, quantity, or degree, or the lowest reached or allowed. – *adj.* of the nature of a minimum; lowest possible; lowest reached or allowed: *Five dollars is the minimum investment.*

min·is·ter (min′ə-stər) *n.* **1** a member of the clergy in Protestant Churches. **2** in many countries, a senior politician who heads a government department.

min·is·try (min′ə-strē) *n.* **min·is·tries** the profession, duties, or period of service of a religious minister.

mink (mingk) *n.* **mink** a weasellike mammal of NORTH AMERICA, EUROPE, and ASIA.

● **Min·ne·so·ta** (min′ə-sōt′ə). See Supplement, **U.S.A.**

min·now (min′ō) *n.* a small freshwater fish.

Mi·no·an (mə-nō′ən) *adj.* relating to the Bronze Age civilization of CRETE and other Aegean islands, approximately 3000-1100 B.C.

mi·nor (mīn′ər) *adj.* **1** not as great in importance or size; fairly small or insignificant: *She has only minor injuries.* **2** below the age of legal adulthood. – *n.* a person below the age of legal adulthood.

mint¹ (mint) *n.* **1** any of various herbs of northern regions with leaves widely used as a flavoring. **2** a candy flavored with peppermint.

mint² (mint) *n.* a place where coins are produced under government authority.

mi·nus (mīn′əs) *prep.* without. – *n.* (also **minus sign**) a sign (-) indicating that a following quantity is to be subtracted. – *adj.* less than zero: *The temperature was minus ten degrees.*

min·ute¹ (min′ət) *n.* **1** a sixtieth part of an hour; sixty seconds. **2** (usually in *plural*) the official written record of a formal meeting.

min·ute² (mī-nōōt′, mī-nyōōt′) *adj.* very small.

mir·a·cle (mîr′i-kəl) *n.* **1** an act or event breaking the laws of nature, and therefore thought to be caused by a supernatural force. **2** a fortunate happening; an amazing event.

mi·rac·u·lous (mə-rak′yə-ləs) *adj.* **1** of the nature of a miracle. **2** amazing.

mi·rage (mə-räzh′) *n.* an optical illusion, especially of a distant mass of water.

mir·ror (mîr′ər) *n.* a glass surface coated with an alloy of mercury and other metals so as to reflect light and produce reflections. – *vb.* **mir·ror·ing, mir·rored** to reflect.

mis- *prefix* **1** wrong or wrongly: *misbehave; misclassify.* **2** negative; lack: *mistrust.*

The apple mint (above) is one of several mint plants used as a flavoring in cooking, or in making mint tea.

The first European civilization we know about started on the island of Crete about 4,500 years ago. It is called **Minoan** after the legendary king, Minos. The Minoans built several cities linked by paved roads.

A state room at the royal palace at Knossos being decorated (left). *Wall paintings show the dangerous but popular sport of bull-leaping* (shown above).

The royal palace at Knossos as it may have looked in Minoan times. The royal apartments lay around a central courtyard, with public rooms upstairs.

*Throughout the ages
people have attributed
magical properties to
mistletoe. It is
particularly familiar
through the Christmas
tradition of kissing under
a sprig of the plant.*

mis·chief (mis′chəf) *n.* behavior that annoys or irritates but causes no serious harm. – *adj.* **mis·chie·vous** (mis′chə-vəs).

mis·er·a·ble (miz′ə-rə-bəl) *adj.* marked by misery. – *adv.* **mis·er·a·bly** (miz′ə-rə-blē).

mis·er·y (miz′ə-rē) *n.* **mis·er·ies 1** great unhappiness. **2** poverty or squalor.

mis·lay (mis-lā′) *vb.* **mis·lay·ing, mis·laid** to put in a place but forget where.

mis·lead (mis-lēd′) *vb.* **mis·lead·ing, mis·led** (mis-led′) **1** to cause to take an undesirable course of action. **2** to cause to have a false impression or belief.

mis·place (mis-plās′) *vb.* **mis·plac·ing, mis·placed 1** to mislay. **2** to put in the wrong place.

miss (mis) *vb.* **miss·ing, missed 1** to fail to hit or catch. **2** to fail to arrive in time for: *I missed my plane.* **3** to fail to take advantage of: *You have missed your chance.* **4** to regret the absence of: *I miss my parents.* **5** to refrain from going to: *I'll have to miss the next class.* – *n.* a failure to hit, catch, or reach.

Miss (mis) *n.* a term used to address an unmarried woman.

mis·sile (mis′əl) *n.* **1** a self-propelled flying bomb. **2** any object that is thrown or fired.

mis·sing (mis′ing) *adj.* absent; lost.

mis·sion (mish′ən) *n.* **1** a purpose for which a person or group of people is sent. **2** the group of people sent on a mission.

●**Mis·sis·sip·pi** (mis′ə-sip′ē). See Supplement, **U.S.A.**

●**Mis·sou·ri** (mə-zoor′ē, mə-zoor′ə). See Supplement, **U.S.A.**

mis·spell (mis-spel′) *vb.* **mis·spell·ing, mis·spelt** or **mis·spelled** to spell incorrectly.

mist (mist) *n.* a cloud of condensed water vapor in the air near the ground; thin fog or low cloud. – *vb.* **mist·ing, mist·ed** to cover or become covered with mist.

mis·take (mə-stāk′) *vb.* **mis·tak·ing, mis·took** (mə-stook′), **mis·tak·en** (mə-stā′kən) to identify incorrectly. – *n.* **1** an error. **2** a misunderstanding.

mis·ter (mis′tər) *n.* (abbreviation **Mr.**) a term used to address an adult male.

mis·tle·toe (mis′əl-tō) *n.* an evergreen shrub that grows as a parasite on trees.

mis·treat (mis-trēt′) *vb.* **mis·treat·ing, mis·treat·ed** to treat cruelly or without care.

mist·y (mis′tē) *adj.* **mist·i·er, mist·i·est** covered with mist.

mis·un·der·stand (mis′un′dər-stand′) *vb.* **mis·un·der·stand·ing, mis·un·der·stood** (mis′un′dər-stood′) to fail to understand properly.

mis·un·der·stand·ing *n.* **1** a failure to understand properly. **2** a disagreement: *He was sorry about the misunderstanding.*

mite (mīt) *n.* any of various small spiderlike creatures, some of which are parasites.

mi·ter (mīt′ər) *n.* the ceremonial headdress of a pope, bishop, or abbot, a tall pointed hat with the front and back sections divided.

mix (miks) *vb.* **mix·ing, mixed 1** to put together or combine to form one mass. **2** to do at the same time; to combine: *Let's not mix business with pleasure.* – *vb.* **mix up** to confuse.

mixed (mikst) *adj.* consisting of different kinds.

mix·ture (miks′chər) *n.* **1** a blend of ingredients prepared for a purpose. **2** a combination.

moan (mōn) *n.* a low prolonged sound expressing sadness, grief, or pain. – *vb.* **moan·ing, moaned 1** to utter or produce a moan. **2** to complain. – *n.* **moan·er.**

moat (mōt) *n.* a deep trench around a castle.

mob (mäb) *n.* a large disorderly crowd.

mo·bile (mō′bəl, mō′bēl′, mō′bīl′) *adj.* able to move or be moved easily: *a mobile home.* – *n.* **mo·bil·i·ty** (mō-bil′ət-ē).

moc·ca·sin (mäk′ə-sən) *n.* **1** a shoe with a soft sole and no heel. **2** (also **water moccasin**) a poisonous aquatic snake of the southern UNITED STATES.

mock (mäk) *vb.* **mock·ing, mocked** to speak or behave with contempt toward. – *adj.* false.

mock·ing·bird (mäk′ing-burd′) *n.* a gray North American bird that imitates other birds.

mode (mōd) *n.* a way of doing something.

mod·el (mäd′l) *n.* **1** a small-scale representation or replica. **2** one of several types or designs of manufactured article: *He bought the latest model stereo.* **3** a person who displays clothes to potential buyers by wearing them. **4** a thing from which something else is to be derived; a basis. **5** an excellent example; an example to be copied: *She's a model of loyalty.* – *vb.* **mod·el·ing** or **mod·el·ling, mod·eled** or **mod·elled 1** to display clothes by wearing them. **2** to work as a model for an artist or photographer. **3** to shape into a particular form. – *adj.* built as a replica: *a model ship.*

mod·er·ate (mäd′ə-rət) *adj.* **1** not extreme; not strong or violent. **2** average: *moderate intelligence.*

mod·ern (mäd′ərn) *adj.* **1** belonging to the present or to recent times; not old or ancient. **2** involving the very latest available techniques, styles, etc.

mod·ern·ize (mäd′ər-nīz′) *vb.* **mod·ern·iz·ing, mod·ern·ized** to bring up to modern standards; to switch to more modern methods or techniques.

mod·est (mäd′əst) *adj.* not having or showing pride; humble. – *n.* **mod·es·ty** (mäd′ə-stē).

mod·i·fy (mäd′ə-fī′) *vb.* **mod·i·fies, mod·i·fy·ing, mod·i·fied** to change the form of slightly.

mod·ule (mäj′ool′) *n.* **1** a separate unit that combines with others to form a larger unit, structure, or system. **2** a separate self-contained part of a space vehicle used for a particular purpose. – *adj.* **mod·u·lar** (mäj′ə-lər).

●**Mo·gul** (mō′gəl) a member of the ruling dynasty in INDIA from the 1500s to 1900s.

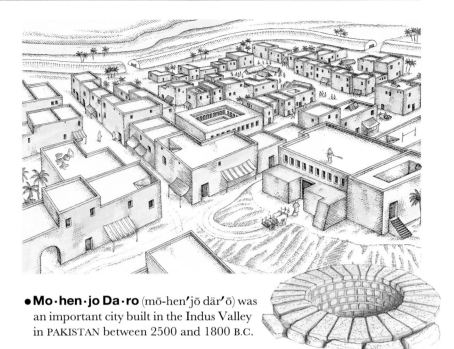

The magnificent tomb of the Akbar (1542-1605), the Mogul emperor of India. He supported writers and artists and allowed freedom of worship in his conquered empire.

●**Mo·ham·med** (mō-ham′əd). See **Muhammad**.

●**Mo·hawks** are a tribe of Iroquois who formerly lived in New York State.

●**Mo·hen·jo Da·ro** (mō-hen′jō där′ō) was an important city built in the Indus Valley in PAKISTAN between 2500 and 1800 B.C.

moist (moist) *adj.* damp; slightly wet.

mois·ten (moi′sən) *vb.* **mois·ten·ing, mois·tened** to make or become damp.

mois·ture (mois′chər) *n.* liquid in tiny drops in the air.

mo·lar (mō′lər) *n.* any of the large back teeth in humans and other mammals, used for chewing and grinding.

mold¹ (mōld) *n.* a growth of fungus on substances in damp warm conditions.

mold² (mōld) *n.* a hollow container into which a liquid substance is poured to take on the container's shape when it cools and sets.

●**Mol·do·va** (mäl-dō′və). See Supplement, **Countries**.

mole¹ (mōl) *n.* a raised dark spot on the skin.

mole² (mōl) *n.* a small burrowing insect-eating mammal with tiny eyes and soft dark fur.

mol·e·cule (mäl′ə-kyool′) *n.* the smallest unit into which a chemical compound can be divided without losing its basic nature.

mol·lusk or **mol·lusc** (mäl′əsk) *n.* any of numerous limbless invertebrate creatures with a soft body and usually a hard shell.

mol·ten (mōlt′n) *adj.* in a melted state.

mo·ment (mō′mənt) *n.* **1** a short while. **2** a particular point in time.

mo·men·tum (mō-ment′əm) *n.* the amount or force of motion in a moving object.

An artist's impression of the ancient city (top) of Mohenjo Daro as it may have looked at the height of power and prosperity. Like modern American cities, it was built on a grid pattern! Some of the houses had brick-lined shafts (above) in their courtyards. The shafts may have been used as wells or for storage.

●**Mo·na Li·sa** (mō'nə lē'sə) This is perhaps the world's most famous painting. It was painted by LEONARDO DA VINCI.

mon·arch (män'ərk) *n.* a king or queen.

mon·arch·y (män'ər-kē) *n.* **mon·arch·ies** a country ruled by a monarch.

Mon·day (mun'dē, mun'dā) *n.* the second day of the week, between Sunday and Tuesday.

●**Mo·net** (mō-nā'), **Claude** (1840-1926) was a French painter of the IMPRESSIONISM movement.

mon·ey (mun'ē) *n.* **1** coins or bills used as a means of buying things. **2** wealth in general.

●**Mon·go·li·a** (mäng-gō'lē-ə). See Supplement, **Countries**.

mon·goose (mäng'gōōs') *n.* **mon·goos·es** a long-tailed weasel-sized mammal of AFRICA and ASIA that preys on snakes and rats.

A mongoose can pounce so quickly that a cobra has no time to strike with its fangs.

mon·grel (mung'grəl, mäng'grəl) *n.* a dog of mixed breeding.

mon·i·tor (män'ət-ər) *n.* **1** any instrument or person that checks, records, or controls. **2** a small television screen.

monk (mungk) *n.* a member of a religious community of men.

mon·key (mung'kē) *n.* **monkeys** any of various kinds of apes, especially the smaller long-tailed varieties.

mon·o·logue (män'l-ôg') *n.* a long speech by one person, as in a movie or play.

mo·nop·o·ly (mə-näp'ə-lē) *n.* **mo·nop·o·lies** the exclusive control of a particular commodity or service.

mon·o·tone (män'ə-tōn') *n.* a single unvarying tone in speech or sound that does not vary.

mo·not·o·nous (mə-nät'n-əs) *adj.* lacking in variety; tediously unchanging.

mon·soon (män- sōōn') *n.* in southern ASIA, a wind that blows from the southwest in summer, bringing rain, and from the northeast in winter.

mon·ster (män'stər) *n.* **1** any large and frightening imaginary creature. **2** a cruel or evil person.

mon·strous (män'strəs) *adj.* **1** hideous or outrageous. **2** huge. **3** like a monster, horrible.

●**Mon·tan·a** (män-tan'ə). See Supplement, **U.S.A.**

●**Mon·te·zu·ma** (mänt'ə-zōō'mə) (1466-1520) was the last AZTEC emperor of MEXICO. He surrendered to the Spanish conquistador, Cortes.

month (munth) *n.* any of the twelve named divisions of the year, varying in length between 28 and 31 days.

month·ly (munth'lē) *adj.* happening, published, etc. once a month; lasting one month. – *adv.* once a month.

●**Mon·tre·al** (män'trē-ôl') is an island and the largest city in Quebec, CANADA. It is the largest French-speaking city outside of FRANCE.

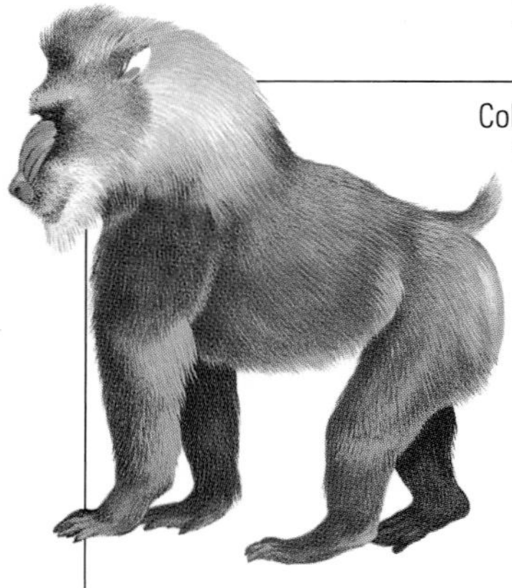

Colobus monkey from Africa

Monkeys are mammals that look rather like people. Monkeys and apes are called primates. American monkeys use their tail as an extra hand, to grasp tree branches. African and Asian monkeys cannot do this.

Spider monkey – from South America

Mandrill – from Africa

Woolly monkey from South America

mon·u·ment (män′yə-mənt) *n*. **1** something, for example a statue, built to preserve the memory of a person or event. **2** any ancient

This monument, called the Tempietto, was built in Rome at the time of the Renaissance to mark the probable spot where Jesus' apostle Peter was crucified. It is built in the classical Greek style.

structure preserved for its historical value.

mon·u·ment·al (män′yə-ment′l) *adj*. like a monument, especially huge and impressive.

mood (mo͞od) *n*. **1** a state of mind at a particular time. **2** an atmosphere.

mood·y (mo͞od′ē) *adj*. **mood·i·er, mood·i·est** tending to change mood often.

moon (mo͞on) *n*. **1** (often **Moon**) the heavenly body that moves once around the earth each month, often visible as a circle or crescent in the sky at night. **2** any similar smaller body circling another planet.

● On July 21, 1969 *Apollo 11* astronauts Neil Armstrong and Edwin Aldrin became the first humans to walk on the surface of the moon.

moon·light (mo͞on′līt′) *n*. sunlight reflected by the moon.

Moor (moor) *n*. a member of an ARAB people of northwest AFRICA.

moor (moor) *vb*. **moor·ing, moored** to fasten by a rope, cable, or anchor.

moose (mo͞os) *n*. **moose** a large North American deer with flat rounded antlers.

mop (mäp) *n*. a large sponge or a set of thick threads on a long handle for cleaning floors.

mor·al (môr′əl, mär′əl) *adj*. **1** of or relating to the principles of good and evil, or right and wrong. **2** conforming to what is considered by society to be good, right, or proper.

mo·rale (mə-ral′) *n*. level of confidence or optimism; spirits: *Our team's morale was high.*

more (môr, mōr) *adj*. a greater, or additional, number or quantity of: *I need more milk.* − *adv*. **1** used to form the comparative of many adjectives and adverbs, especially those of two or more syllables: *She is more graceful than I.* **2** to a greater degree; with a greater frequency: *I visit my aunt more than my uncle.* − *pron*. a greater, or additional, quantity: *May I have some more?*

Mor·mon (môr′mən) *n*. a member of the Church of Jesus Christ of Latter-day Saints.

morn·ing (môr′ning) *n*. the period from sunrise to midday, or from midnight to midday.

● **Mo·roc·co** (mə-räk′ō). See Supplement, **Countries**.

● **Mor·ri·son** (môr′ə-sən, mär′ə-sən), **Toni** (1931-) is an American novelist and the winner of the 1993 NOBEL PRIZE for literature.

Moon rocks brought back by the Apollo project can be dated back to 4.5 billion years — soon after the Moon was created.

The side of the Moon that faces Earth has huge plains called "maria." The far side is covered with craters and mountain ranges. Because the Moon has no air or atmosphere, there is nothing to protect it from the heat of the Sun in the day and the cold at night.

A mosaic from Pompeii in southern Italy depicting Alexander the Great leading a charge.

Morse code (môrs kōd′) *n.* a code used for sending messages, each letter being represented as a series of short or long signals.

mor·sel (môr′səl) *n.* a small piece of food.

mor·tal (môrt′l) *adj.* **1** certain to die at some future time: *All humans are mortal.* **2** of or causing death: *He received a mortal blow.*

mor·tar (môrt′ər) *n.* a mixture of sand, water, and cement or lime, used in building to bond bricks or stones.

mort·gage (môr′gij) *n.* a pledge or claim on property, securing a loan.

mo·sa·ic (mō-zā′ik) *n.* a design formed in small pieces of colored stone or glass.

●**Mos·cow** (mäs′kou′, mäs′kō′) is the capital of RUSSIA.

●**Mo·ses** (mō′zəz, mō′zəs) in the BIBLE, was a Jewish leader, lawgiver, and prophet.

●**Mo·ses** (mō′zəz, mō′zəs), **Grandma** (1860-1961) was an American artist.

Mos·lem (mäz′ləm). See **Muslim**.

mosque (mäsk) *n.* a Muslim place of worship.

mos·qui·to (mə-skēt′ō) *n.* **mos·qui·toes** or **mosquitos** a small insect with long legs. The females suck blood from animals and people and may pass on diseases, such as malaria.

moss (môs) *n.* any variety of small plant growing as a thick mass on rocks or tree trunks in damp conditions. – *adj.* **moss·y** (mô′sē) **moss·i·er, moss·i·est.**

most (mōst) *adj.* the greatest part, amount, or number of: *Let's see who can eat the most corn.* – *adv.* **1** used to form the superlative of many adjectives and adverbs, especially those of more than two syllables: *This is the most beautiful garden in town.* **2** to the greatest degree; with the greatest frequency: *I like chocolate the most.* – *pron.* the greatest number or quantity, or the majority of people or things: *Most of us were late.*

most·ly (mōst′lē) *adv.* mainly or principally.

mo·tel (mō-tel′) *n.* a hotel mainly for motorists.

moth (môth) *n.* a butterfly-like insect with a wide body and dull coloring, that usually flies at night.

moth·er (muth′ər) *n.* a female parent. – *vb.* **moth·er·ing, moth·ered** to treat with care and protection. – *n.* **moth·er·hood** (muth′ər-hood′).

moth·er-in-law (muth′ər-ən-lô′) *n.* **mothers-in-law** the mother of someone's husband or wife.

mo·tion (mō′shən) *n.* **1** the act of moving and changing position. **2** a gesture. **3** a proposal for formal discussion at a meeting. – *vb.* **mo·tion·ing, mo·tioned** to give a signal or direction: *She motioned to him to approach.*

motion picture *n.* **1** a series of pictures projected onto a screen that give the illusion of motion. **2** a story told in such pictures.

mo·tive (mōt′iv) *n.* a reason for action.

mo·tor (mōt′ər) *n.* any device for converting energy into movement. – *adj.* of, relating to, or having a motor.

mo·tor·bike (mōt′ər-bīk′) *n.* a small motorcycle.

mo·tor·cy·cle (mōt′ər-sī′kəl) *n.* any two-wheeled road vehicle powered by a gas engine. – *n.* **mo·tor·cy·clist** (mōt′ər-sī′kləst).

mo·tor·ist (mōt′ə-rəst) *n.* the driver of an automobile.

mot·to (mät′ō) *n.* **mot·toes** or **mottos** a phrase adopted as a principle of behavior: *"Never give up" was his motto.*

mount[1] (mount) *vb.* **mount·ing, mount·ed** **1** to go up: *We mounted the stairs.* **2** to get up onto: *to mount a horse.* **3** to increase in level or intensity: *The tension mounted as the match progressed.* **4** to put in a frame or on a background for display: *The picture was mounted on white paper.*

mount[2] (mount) *n.* mountain, used in a name: *Mount Rushmore.*

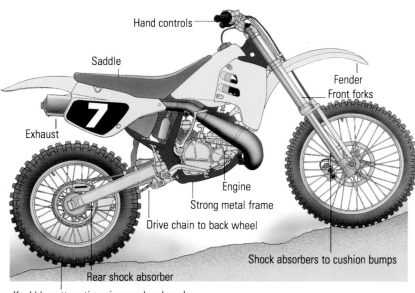

Hand controls

Saddle

Fender

Front forks

Exhaust

Engine

Strong metal frame

Drive chain to back wheel

Shock absorbers to cushion bumps

Rear shock absorber

Knobbly-pattern tire grips sand and mud

moun·tain (mount′n) *n.* a very high steep hill.

● The greatest mountain ranges are the Himalayas of ASIA, the Andes of SOUTH AMERICA, the Rockies of NORTH AMERICA and CENTRAL AMERICA, and the Alps of EUROPE.

moun·tain·ous (mount′n-əs) *adj.* **1** containing many mountains. **2** huge.

● **Mount Rush·more** (mount rush′môr′, rush′mōr′) in South Dakota, has carved into it the faces of four United States presidents.

mourn (môrn, mōrn) *vb.* **mourn·ing, mourned** to feel or show deep sorrow at the death or loss of a person or thing.

mourn·ing (môr′ning, mōr′ning) *n.* a period of grief felt or shown over a death.

mouse (mous) *n.* **mice** (mīs) **1** a small furry rodent with a slender tail. **2** a manual device connected by wire to a computer, used to control certain functions.

mous·tache (mə-stash′, mus′tash′) *n.* another spelling of **mustache**.

mouth (mouth) *n.* **mouths** (mou<u>th</u>z) **1** an opening in the head through which food is taken in and speech or sounds emitted. **2** an opening, for example of a cave or a bottle. **3** the part of a river that widens to meet the sea. – (mou<u>th</u>) *vb.* **mouth·ing, mouthed** to form with the mouth: *to mouth words.*

mov·a·ble or **mov·e·able** (mōō′və-bəl) *adj.* not fixed in one place; portable.

move (mōōv) *vb.* **mov·ing, moved 1** to change position or go from one place to another. **2** to make progress of any kind: *They are moving toward a solution.* **3** to change your place of living or working: *We are moving to New York.* **4** to affect the feelings or emotions of: *He was deeply moved by their singing.* – *n.* **1** an act of moving the body: *They watched his every move.* **2** an act of moving a piece in a board game.

move·ment (mōōv′mənt) *n.* **1** changing position or going from one point to another. **2** an organization of people who share the same beliefs: *She belongs to the women's movement.*

mov·ie (mōō′vē) *n.* a motion picture.

mov·ing *adj.* **1** having an effect on the emotions; touching; stirring: *The music at her wedding was very moving.* **2** in motion; not still.

mow (mō) *vb.* **mow·ing, mowed** or **mown** (mōn) to cut by hand or with a machine.

Young mountains, such as the Himalayas (top) are high and rugged. Old mountains are smoother and lower.

When two slow-moving plates of the earth's crust and mantle collide, a **mountain** belt is thrust upward. The sediments of the ocean floor are squeezed into folds.

● **Mo·zam·bique** (mō′zam-bēk′). See Supplement, **Countries**.

● **Mo·zart** (mōt′särt′), **Wolfgang Amadeus** (1756-1791) was a great Austrian composer of operas and symphonies.

much (much) *adj.* **more** (môr, mōr), **most** (mōst) of a great amount or quantity of something: *I haven't much time.* – *pron.* a great amount or quanity: *Much has been said of his abilities.* – *adv.* **1** by a great deal: *She is much prettier.* **2** to a great degree: *I don't like her much.*

mu·cus (myōō′kəs) *n.* thick sticky liquid secreted by glands in the nose.

mud (mud) *n.* soft wet earth.

mud·dle (mud′l) *vb.* **mud·dling, mud·dled 1** to put into a disordered, mixed-up state. **2** to confuse or be confused.

mudd·y (mud′ē) *adj.* **mudd·i·er, mudd·i·est 1** covered with or containing mud. **2** (of a color, liquid, etc.) dull or cloudy.

mu·ez·zin (mōō-ez′ən) *n.* the Muslim official who calls worshippers to prayer.

muf·fin (muf′ən) *n.* a small bread often made

Two hundred years after his death, Mozart's music is played and listened to by people all over the world. He died in poverty in his 36th year.

Biceps, the muscle in the upper arm, contracts when you bend your arm. The other muscle, the triceps, relaxes.

Biceps contracted

Triceps relaxed

Biceps relaxed

Triceps contracted

with blueberries, bran, etc.

muf·fle (muf'əl) *vb.* **muf·fling, muf·fled 1** to make quieter. **2** to wrap up in a coat or scarf.

mug[1] (mug) *n.* a large cup with a handle.

mug[2] (mug) *vb.* **mug·ging, mugged** to attack and rob violently. – *n.* **mug·ger.**

●**Mu·ham·mad** (mə-häm'əd, moo-ham'əd) (A.D. 570-632) was an Arab prophet and the founder of ISLAM.

mul·ber·ry (mul'ber'ē) *n.* **mul·ber·ries** a deciduous tree with purple edible berries.

mule (myool) *n.* the offspring of a donkey and a horse, used as a working animal.

multi- *prefix* many: *multicolored.*

mul·ti·ple (mul'tə-pəl) *adj.* involving or affecting many parts: *multiple injuries.*

mul·ti·ply (mul'tə-plī') *vb.* **mul·ti·plies, mul·ti·ply·ing, mul·ti·plied 1** to add a number to itself a given number of times. **2** to increase in number, especially by breeding.

mul·ti·tude (mul'tə-tood', mul'tə-tyood') *n.* **1** a great number. **2** a huge crowd of people.

mum·ble (mum'bəl) *vb.* **mum·bling, mum·bled** to speak unclearly.

mum·my (mum'ē) *n.* **mum·mies** a human or animal corpse preserved with spices.

mumps (mumps) *n.* a disease causing painful swelling of the salivary glands near the ears.

munch (munch) *vb.* **munching, munched** to chew, especially noisily.

mu·ral (myoor'əl) *n.* a wall painting.

mur·der (murd'ər) *n.* the act of unlawfully and intentionally killing a person. – *vb.* **mur·der·ing, mur·dered** to kill unlawfully and intentionally. – *n.* **mur·der·er.**

murk·y (mur'kē) *adj.* **murk·i·er, murk·i·est** gloomy; (of water) dark and dirty.

mur·mur (mur'mər) *n.* **1** a quiet continuous sound, for example of running water or low voices. **2** anything said in a low indistinct voice.

mus·cle (mus'əl) *n.* tissue in the body responsible for movement.

mus·cu·lar (mus'kyə-lər) *adj.* **1** relating to or consisting of muscle. **2** having strong muscles.

mu·se·um (myoo-zē'əm) *n.* a place where objects are displayed to the public.

mush·room (mush'room', mush'room') *n.* any of several types of fungus with an umbrella-shaped cap, many of which are edible.

mu·sic (myoo'zik) *n.* the art of making sound in a rhythmically organized harmonious form.

mu·si·cal (myoo'zi-kəl) *adj.* **1** of or producing music. **2** pleasant to hear; melodious.

mu·si·cian (myoo-zish'ən) *n.* a person skilled in performing or composing music.

Mus·lim (muz'ləm, moos'ləm, mooz'ləm) or **Mos·lem** (mäz'ləm) *n.* a follower of ISLAM.

mus·sel (mus'əl) *n.* a small edible shellfish.

must (must) *vb.* expressing **1** need: *I must earn some extra money.* **2** duty or obligation: *You must help him.* **3** certainty: *You must be Charles.* **4** determination: *I must remember.* **5** probability: *She must be there by now.* **6** inevitability: *We must all die some time.*

mus·tache (mə-stash', mus'tash') *n.* a line of hair on the upper lip.

mus·tard (mus'tərd) *n.* **1** any of several plants of the cabbage family with strong-smelling seeds. **2** a thick strong-tasting yellow or brown paste made from crushed mustard seeds.

mute (myoot) *adj.* not able to speak; dumb.

mu·ti·ny (myoot'n-ē) *n.* **mu·ti·nies** an act of rebellion against established authority.

mut·ton (mut'n) *n.* the flesh of an adult sheep.

mu·tu·al (myoo'choo-əl) *adj.* done or felt by each of two or more for the other or others.

muz·zle (muz'əl) *n.* **1** the jaws and nose of an animal, for example a dog. **2** an arrangement of straps fitted around an animal's jaws to prevent it biting.

my (mī) *adj.* of or belonging to me.

my·self (mī-self') *pron.* **1** the reflexive form of *me: I shaved myself.* **2** used to emphasize *I* or *me.* **3** (also **by myself**) alone.

●**Myan·mar** (myän-mä', mē-än'mär'). See Supplement, **Countries.**

mys·te·ri·ous (mə-stî'rē-əs) *adj.* difficult or impossible to understand or explain.

mys·ter·y (mis'tə-rē, mis'trē) *n.* **mys·ter·ies** an unexplained event.

mys·ti·fy (mis'tə-fī') *vb.* **mys·ti·fies, mys·ti·fy·ing, mys·ti·fied** to puzzle.

myth (mith) *n.* **1** an ancient story dealing with gods and heroes. **2** a false notion.

myth·i·cal (mith'i-kəl) *adj.* **1** relating to myth. **2** imaginary.

my·thol·o·gy (mi-thäl'ə-jē) *n.* **my·thol·o·gies** a collection of myths.

MYTHS & LEGENDS

GREEK & ROMAN MYTHOLOGY
(Roman names shown in parentheses)

Aphrodite (Venus) goddess of love and beauty.

Apollo son of Zeus and twin of Artemis. God of poetry, music, and archery.

Ares (Mars) god of war, son of Zeus.

Artemis (Diana) Moon goddess, twin of Apollo.

Athena (Minerva) goddess of wisdom, arts and crafts, and war.

Atlas one of the Titans who made war on Zeus and as a punishment was made to carry the world on his shoulders.

Centaur a creature with a man's head, arms, and trunk joined to the four-legged body of a horse.

Cronus one of the Titans.

Demeter (Ceres) the goddess of agriculture.

Dionysus (Bacchus) god of wine.

Eros (Cupid) god of love and son of Aphrodite.

Graces these three daughters of Zeus bestowed beauty, charm, and happiness: Aglaia (brilliance), Thalia (charm), and Euphrosyne (joy).

Hades (Pluto) ruler of the Underworld, which is also known as Hades, the world beneath the earth's surface where the souls of the dead live.

Hephaestus (Vulcan) the heavenly blacksmith.

Hera (Juno) queen of heaven.

Heracles (Hercules) son of Zeus, famous for his great strength.

Hermes (Mercury) the messenger of the gods.

Muses nine daughters of Zeus, they presided over the arts and sciences.

Orpheus a skilled musician who could even move inanimate things with his lyre.

Pan (Faunus) god of forests and flocks.

Perseus son of Zeus.

Pluto ruler of Hades.

Poseidon (Neptune) god of the sea.

Satyrs forest gods or demons attendant upon Bacchus.

Titans children of Uranus and Gaia, of immense size and strength, they overthrew Uranus and set up Cronos as king. He was overthrown by Zeus.

Uranus oldest of the Greek gods.

Zeus (Jupiter) lord of the Heavens and bringer of thunder and lightning.

The Greek supreme god, Zeus, asks Demeter, the corn goddess, why the crops have failed. "My daughter, Persephone, has disappeared. I cannot rest until I find her," she replies.

NORSE MYTHOLOGY

Asgard the home of the gods.

Balder god of summer sun, and son of Odin and Frigga.

Frey god of fertility and crops.

Freyja goddess of love, marriage, and the dead. Her chariot was drawn by two cats.

Frigga wife of Odin.

Odin the supreme god.

Thor the god of thunder.

Valhalla the hall in Asgard where the souls of heroes killed in battle were welcomed by Odin.

Valkyries Odin's nine handmaidens.

Odin, the king of the Norse gods *(far right)*.

Freyja, Odin's first wife.

EGYPTIAN MYTHOLOGY

Horus son of Osiris and Isis, represented as a winged sun-disk.

Isis the principal goddess of Egypt and wife of Osiris.

Osiris chief god of the underworld.

Ra the sun god, ancestor of the pharaohs. Represented with a falcon's head.

Set jealous brother of Osiris. He came to be regarded as the embodiment of evil.

Isis

Anubis

Ra

Osiris

Horus

Nn

na·dir (nād′îr or nād′ər) *n.* the very lowest point.

nag (nag) *vb.* **nag·ging, nagged 1** to keep urging to do something. **2** to cause anxiety to: *Fear kept nagging at me.* – *n.* a person who nags.

nail (nāl) *n.* **1** the small horny covering at the tip of a finger or toe. **2** a metal spike hammered into something, for example to join two objects together. – *vb.* **nail·ing, nailed** to fasten with a nail.

na·ked (nāk′əd) *adj.* **1** wearing no clothes. **2** without fur, feathers, or foliage. **3** blank; empty. **4** (of the eye) unaided by a telescope or microscope: *I could see the star with a naked eye.*

name (nām) *n.* **1** a word or words by which an individual person, place, or thing is called and referred to. **2** reputation. **3** a famous person, firm, etc.: *What are the big names in fashion this season?* – *vb.* **nam·ing, named 1** to give a name to. **2** to identify by name: *Name three Belgian poets.* **3** to choose or appoint: *Nick was named as leader.*

●**Na·mib·i·a** (nə-mib′ē-ə). See Supplement, **Countries**.

nanny goat (nan′nē gōt′) *n.* a female goat.

nap (nap) *n.* a short sleep. – *vb.* **nap·ping, napped** to take a nap.

nap·kin (nap′kən) *n.* (also **table napkin**) a piece of cloth or paper for wiping your mouth and fingers at meals.

●**Na·ples** (nā′pəlz) is a port in southern ITALY. It is dominated by Vesuvius, an active volcano.

●**Na·po·le·on** (nə-pō′lē-ən) (1769-1821) was a Corsican soldier who became emperor of FRANCE in 1804 and conquered ITALY, SPAIN, EGYPT, the NETHERLANDS, and most of central EUROPE. He was eventually defeated by the Prussians and British in 1815 at Waterloo.

nar·rate (nar′āt′) *vb.* **nar·rat·ing, nar·rated** to tell or relate. – *n.* **nar·ra·tion** (nar-ā′shən). – *n.* **nar·ra·tor** (nar′āt′ər).

nar·ra·tive (nar′ət-iv) *n.* an account of events. – *adj.* telling a story; recounting events: *Sir Walter Scott wrote narrative poetry.*

nar·row (nar′ō) *adj.* **1** of little breadth; not wide. **2** (of interests or experience) restricted; limited. **3** close; only just achieved, etc.: *a narrow victory.* – *n.* (usually in *plural*) a narrow part of a straight, bay, etc. – *vb.* **nar·row·ing, nar·rowed** to make or become narrow. – *adv.* **nar·row·ly** (nar′ō-lē).

nar·row-mind·ed (nar′ō-mīn′dəd) *adj.* intolerant; prejudiced.

nar·whal (när′hwäl′, när′wəl) *n.* an arctic whale, the male of which has a long spiral tusk.

na·sal (nā′zəl) *adj.* relating to the nose.

nas·ty (nas′tē) *adj.* **nas·ti·er, nas·ti·est 1** unpleasant; disgusting. **2** malicious; ill-natured. **3** worrying; serious: *a nasty wound.* **4** (of weather) wet or stormy.

na·tion (nā′shən) *n.* **1** the people living in, and together forming, a single state. **2** a group of people with a common history, language, etc.

As well as being a brilliant general Napoleon was a skillful statesman who restored order to France.

na·tion·al (nash′ən-l, nash′nəl) *adj.* **1** belonging to a particular nation: *The sari is a national dress of India.* **2** concerning the whole nation.

na·tion·al·ism (nash′nəl-iz′əm) *n.* pride in the history, culture, etc. of your own nation. – *n.* **na·tion·al·ist** (nash′nəl-əst).

na·tion·al·i·ty (nash′ə-nal′ət-ē) *n.* **na·tion·al·i·ties** the national group to which a person belongs.

national park *n.* an area of countryside, usually important for its natural beauty, wildlife, etc., under the ownership and care of the nation.

na·tive (nāt′iv) *adj.* **1** being or belonging to the place of one's birth. **2** born a citizen of a particular place: *Anna is a native Italian.* **3** originating in a particular place: *Elephants are native to Africa and India.*

●**Native Americans** were the first people to live in the Americas. They are sometimes called Indians because Christopher COLUMBUS thought he had arrived in India in 1492.

nat·u·ral (nach′ə-rəl) *adj.* **1** normal; not surprising. **2** instinctive; not learned; innate: *Kindness was natural to her.* **3** (of manner, etc.) simple, easy and direct; not artificial. **4** relating to nature. **5** (of materials) derived from plants and animals as opposed to artificial: *natural fibers.* – *n.* (*informal*) a person with an inborn feel for something.

nat·u·ral·ist (nach′ə-rəl-əst) *n.* a person who studies animal and plant life.

nat·u·ral·ly (nach′rə-lē) *adv.* **1** of course; not surprisingly. **2** by nature; as a natural characteristic: *Sympathy came naturally to her.*

na·ture (nā′chər) *n.* **1** the physical world not made by people; the forces that have formed it and control it. **2** what something is, or consists of. **3** an essential character; attitude, or outlook: *Philip is quiet and retiring by nature.* **4** a kind, type, etc.: *What nature of fish is this?*

naught (nôt) *n.* the figure 0; zero.

naugh·ty (nôt′ē) *adj.* **naugh·ti·er, naugh·ti·est** mischievous; disobedient.

nau·sea (nô′zē-ə, nô′sē-ə, nô′zhə) *n.* a feeling of wanting to vomit.

nau·ti·cal (nôt′i-kəl) *adj.* relating to ships.

●**Na·va·jos** (näv′ə-hōz′, nav′ə-hōz′) make up the largest NATIVE AMERICAN tribe. Originally from what is now Canada, many now live on reservations in Arizona, New Mexico, and Utah.

na·val (nā′vəl) *adj.* relating to ships.

nave (nāv) *n.* the main central part of a church.

na·vel (nā′vəl) *n.* the small hollow in the belly where the umbilical cord was attached.

nav·i·gate (nav′ə-gāt′) *vb.* **nav·i·gat·ing, nav·i·gat·ed** to direct and steer the course of a ship, aircraft, or other vehicle. – *n.* **nav·i·ga·tor** (nav′ə-gāt′ər).

nav·i·ga·tion (nav′ə-gā′shən) *n.* the act or skill of navigating.

na·vy (nā′vē) *n.* **na·vies 1** the warships of a state. **2** the organization to which they belong.

●**Naz·a·reth** (naz′ə-rəth) is a town in ISRAEL where JESUS spent much of his life.

Ne·an·der·thal (nē-an′dər-thôl′, nē-an′dər-tôl′) *adj.* denoting a primitive type of person of the early STONE AGE in Europe.

near (nîr) *prep.* **1** at a short distance from. **2** close to in amount, etc.: *She was near tears at the end of the sad movie.* – *adv.* close: *The ball came near to hitting her.* – *adj.* **1** being a short distance away; close: *The passengers had a near escape.* **2** closer of two. – *vb.* **nearing, neared** to approach. – *n.* **near·ness** (nîr′nəs).

near·by (nîr-bī′) *adj. & adv.* not far away.

Among Plains Indians tribal lore was passed from one generation to the next in long evening sessions around the fire.

Native Americans came to North and South America from Asia more than 20,000 years ago and developed many different lifestyles. The Spanish conquerors of the 1500s were amazed at the civilizations of the Incas and Aztecs. To the north most people lived as hunters and farmers in small villages.

Hiawatha was a Mohawk leader. The Indian in the poem The Song of Hiawatha *by Henry Wadsworth Longfellow was not based on the real Hiawatha.*

The Anasazi of what is now the southwestern United States lived in villages called pueblos. The houses were joined together to form a single large building.

PRONUNCIATION SYMBOLS		
ə away	lemon	focus
a fat	oi	boy
ā fade	oo	foot
ä hot	ōō	moon
âr fair	ou	house
e met	th	think
ē mean	th	this
g get	u	cut
hw which	ur	hurt
i fin	w	witch
ī line	y	yes
îr near	yōō	music
ô often	yoor	pure
ō note	zh	vision

The "empty" space between stars contains hydrogen atoms and tiny grains of solid material. In some regions of a galaxy the grains are found close together, forming dark clouds of dust and gas. Such regions are called nebulae.

near·ly (nîr′lē) *adv.* almost but not quite.

near·sight·ed (nîr′sīt′əd) *adj.* unable to see distant objects well.

neat (nēt) *adj.* **1** tidy; clean; orderly. **2** elegantly or cleverly simple: *a neat theory.* **3** (*informal*) excellent: *That's a neat new motorbike.*

●**Ne·bras·ka** (nə-bras′kə). See Supplement, **U.S.A**.

neb·u·la (neb′yə-lə) *n.* **neb·u·lae** (neb′yə-lē′, neb′yə-lī′) or **nebulas** a bright mass of remote stars, dust, and gases.

nec·es·sar·y (nes′ə-ser′ē) *adj.* **1** needed; essential; indispensable. **2** unavoidable.

ne·ces·si·ty (nə-ses′ət-ē) *n.* **necessity** **1** something necessary or essential. **2** circumstances that make something necessary or unavoidable: *She went from necessity not choice.*

neck (nek) *n.* **1** the part of the body between the head and the shoulders. **2** the part of a garment at or covering the neck.

neck·lace (nek′ləs) *n.* a string of beads or other ornaments worn around the neck.

need (nēd) *vb.* **need·ing, need·ed** **1** to require. **2** to be required or obliged: *Do you need to shout?* – *n.* **1** something required. **2** poverty: *The collection is for children in need.*

nee·dle (nēd′l) *n.* **1** a thin pointed steel sewing instrument with an eye for the thread. **2** a slender rod of metal, wood, plastic, etc. for knitting, crocheting, etc. **3** the pointed end of a hypodermic syringe. **4** the pointer on a compass or other instrument. **5** the needle-shaped leaf of a tree such as the pine.

nee·dle·work (nēd′l-wurk′) *n.* sewing and embroidery.

need·y (nēd′ē) *adj.* **need·i·er, need·i·est** poverty-stricken; destitute.

neg·a·tive (neg′ət-iv) *adj.* **1** meaning or saying "no"; expressing denial, refusal, or prohibition. **2** unenthusiastic or pessimistic: *His feelings for the scheme are entirely negative.* **3** in mathematics, less than zero. **4** in medicine, showing that something has not happened or is not present: *The result of the cancer test was negative.* **5** (of film) having the light and shade of the actual image reversed, or complementary colors in place of actual ones. – *n.* denial.

ne·glect (ni-glekt′) *vb.* **ne·glect·ing, ne·glect·ed** **1** not to give proper care and attention to. **2** to leave undone. **3** to fail to do. – *n.* lack of proper care.

neg·li·gent (neg′lə-jənt) *adj.* **1** showing neglect. **2** careless or indifferent. – *n.* **neg·li·gence**.

ne·go·ti·ate (ni-gō′shē-āt′) *vb.* **ne·go·ti·at·ing, ne·go·ti·at·ed** to discuss together so as to reach a satisfactory arrangement. – *n.* **ne·go·ti·a·tion** (ni-gō′shē-ā′shən). – *n.* **ne·go·ti·a·tor** (ni-gō′shē-āt′ər).

Ne·gro (nē′grō) *n.* **Ne·groes** (sometimes *offensive*) a person belonging to the black-skinned race originally from AFRICA. – *adj.* of, belonging to, or relating to this race.

●**Neh·ru** (ner′ōō′, nā′rōō′), **Jawaharlal** (1889-1964) was India's first prime minister.

neigh (nā) *vb.* **neigh·ing, neighed** to make the loud sound of a horse.

neigh·bor (nā′bər) *n.* **1** a person living near or next door to another. **2** an adjacent territory, person, etc.

neigh·bor·hood (nā′bər-hood′) *n.* a district or locality; the area near something or someone.

neigh·bor·ly (nā′bər-lē) *adj.* friendly.

nei·ther (nē′thər, nī′thər) *adj. & pron.* not the one nor the other: *Neither proposal is acceptable.* – *conj.* (introducing the first of two or more alternatives; usually paired with **nor**) not: *I neither know nor care.* – *adv.* nor; also not: *If you won't, neither will I.*

neo- *prefix* new, or a new form of; modern.

ne·on (nē′än) *n.* an element (symbol **Ne**), a clear gas that glows red when electrified.

●**Ne·pal** (nə-pôl′, nə-päl′, nə-pal′). See Supplement, **Countries**.

neph·ew (nef′yōō) *n.* the son of a brother or sister, or of a brother- or sister-in-law.

Nep·tune[1] (nep′tōōn′, nep′tyōōn′). See **Myths and Legends**.

Neptune[2] (nep′tōōn′, nep′tyōōn′) is a large planet, far out in the solar system.

●**Ne·ro** (nē′rō, nîr′ō) (A.D. 37-68) was a Roman emperor, famous for his cruelty to CHRISTIANS. A great fire destroyed much of Rome during his reign.

nerve (nurv) *n.* **1** one of the cords, consisting of a bundle of fibers, that carry instructions for movement and information on sensation between the brain or spinal cord and other parts of the body. **2** courage.

ner·vous (nur′vəs) *adj.* **1** timid; easily agitated. **2** apprehensive; uneasy.

nervous system *n.* the network of communication including the brain, nerves, and spinal cord.

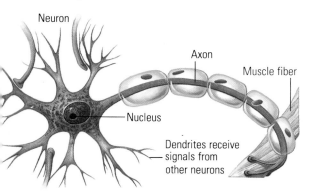

A muscle nerve cell or neuron, the nerve's control center. The axon is a tubelike extension that carries messages.

-ness *suffix* used to form nouns indicating a state, condition, or degree: *slowness*; *darkness*.

nest (nest) *n.* a structure built by creatures in which to lay eggs or give birth to and look after young.

net¹ (net) *n.* **1** a material made of thread, cord, etc. knotted or woven so as to form regularly shaped meshes. **2** a piece of this in any of various shapes or sizes appropriate to different uses.

net² (net) *adj.* of profit, remaining after all expenses, etc. have been paid.

● **Neth·er·lands** (neth′ər-ləndz). See Supplement, **Countries**.

net·tle (net′l) *n.* a plant covered with hairs that sting if touched.

net·work (net′wurk′) *n.* **1** any system resembling a mass of crossing lines: *a network of streets*. **2** any coordinated system involving large numbers of people, branches, etc.: *a telecommunications network*. **3** in computers, a system of linked terminals. — *vb.*

net·work·ing, net·worked 1 to broadcast on a network. **2** (of computer users) to pass information to one another's machines.

neu·ter (no͞ot′ər, nyo͞ot′ər) *adj.* neither masculine nor feminine.

neu·tral (no͞o′trəl, nyo͞o′trəl) *adj.* **1** not taking sides in a quarrel or war. **2** not belonging or relating to either side: *neutral ground*.

neu·tron (no͞o′trän′, nyo͞o′trän′) *n.* one of the electrically uncharged particles in an atom.

● **Ne·vad·a** (nə-vad′ə, nə-väd′ə). See Supplement, **U.S.A.**

nev·er (nev′ər) *adv.* not ever; at no time.

nev·er·the·less (nev′ər-thə-less′) *adv.* in spite of that.

new (no͞o, nyo͞o) *adj.* **1** recently made, bought, built, opened, etc. **2** recently discovered: *They appear to have found a new planet.* **3** just invented, etc.: *The surgeon is using new techniques.* — *adv.* only just, or freshly: *a newborn baby.*

● **New Bruns·wick** (no͞o brunz′wik, nyo͞o) is a province of CANADA.

● **New En·gland** (no͞o ing′glənd, nyo͞o ing′lənd) is a region in the United States made up of six states: MAINE, NEW HAMPSHIRE, VERMONT, MASSACHUSETTS, RHODE ISLAND, and CONNECTICUT.

● **New·found·land** (no͞o′fənd-land′, no͞o′fənd-lənd, no͞o′fənd-land′) is a province of CANADA.

● **New Hamp·shire** (no͞o hamp′shər, nyo͞o). See Supplement, **U.S.A.**

● **New Jer·sey** (no͞o jur′zē, nyo͞o). See Supplement, **U.S.A.**

● **New Mex·i·co** (no͞o mek′si-kō, nyo͞o). See Supplement, **U.S.A.**

● **New Or·leans** (no͞o ôr′lē-ənz, nyo͞o ôr′lənz) is a city on the Mississippi River in Louisiana.

news (no͞oz, nyo͞oz) *n.* (*singular*) information about recent events.

news·cast (no͞oz′kast′, nyo͞oz′kast′) *n.* a broadcast of news on radio or television.

news·pa·per (no͞oz′pā′pər, no͞os′pā′pər) *n.* a daily or weekly publication containing news and often advertisements.

newt (no͞ot, nyo͞ot) *n.* a small amphibious animal with a long body and tail.

The tiny hairs on a nettle leaf are like hollow needles. If they pierce the skin and break off, poison enters the wound from a small reservoir at the base of the hair.

In a darkened room Isaac Newton put a prism in a beam of sunlight shining through a tiny hole in the wall. He noticed that the white light was split into the colors of the rainbow: red, orange, yellow, green, blue, indigo, violet.

Niagara Falls is made up of two waterfalls: the American Falls in the United States, and Horseshoe Falls in Canada.

●**New·ton** (nōōt′n, nyōōt′n), **Sir Isaac** (1642-1727) was an English scientist and mathematician. He was the first to explain the force of gravity and his experiments showed that white light is a mixture of all the colors of the rainbow.

●**New York Cit·y** (nōō′ yôrk′ sit′ē, nyōō) at the mouth of the Hudson River, is the largest city in the UNITED STATES. The city is made up of five sections, or boroughs: Manhattan, Queens, Brooklyn, the Bronx, and Staten Island.

●**New York State**. See Supplement, **U.S.A.**

●**New Zea·land** (nōō zē′lənd, nyōō) is a country east of Australia in the south Pacific, consisting of two main islands. About 8 percent of the population are MAORIS, the original inhabitants. The capital is Wellington.

next (nekst) *adj.* **1** following in time or order: *The next day was bright and sunny.* **2** following this one: *Let's visit the museum next week.* **3** adjoining; neighboring: *They sat in the next compartment.* – *adv.* **1** immediately after that or this: *What happened next?* **2** on the next occasion: *When I next saw her she was ill.* **3** following, in order of degree: *the next longest river after the Amazon.* – **next door** in the neighboring house.
next of kin *n.* someone's closest relative.

●**Ni·ag·ara Falls** (nī-ag′rə-fôlz′). A waterfall standing on the border between CANADA and the UNITED STATES. It is one of the most spectacular sights in North America.

nib·ble (nib′əl) *vb.* **nib·bling, nib·bled 1** to take very small bites of.

●**Ni·ca·rag·ua** (nik′ə-räg′wə). See Supplement, **Countries**.

nice (nīs) *adj.* **1** pleasant. **2** good; satisfactory.
nic·e·ty (nī′sət ē) *n.* **niceties** a small point of detail.
niche (nich) *n.* a recess in a wall, suitable for a lamp or ornament, etc.
nick (nik) *n.* a small cut. – *vb.* **nick·ing, nicked** to make a small cut in.
nick·el (nik′əl) *n.* **1** an element (symbol **Ni**), a silvery metal used especially in alloys. **2** in the UNITED STATES and CANADA, a coin worth five cents.

nick·name (nik′nām′) *n.* a name, additional to the real one, given to a person or place in fun, affection, or contempt.
niece (nēs) *n.* the daughter of a sister or brother, or of a sister- or brother-in-law.

●**Ni·ger** (nī′jər, nē-zher′). See Supplement, **Countries**.

●**Ni·ge·ri·a** (nī-jîr′ē-ə). See Supplement, **Countries**.

night (nīt) *n.* **1** the time of darkness between sunset and sunrise.
night·fall (nīt′fôl′) *n.* the beginning of night; dusk.
night·in·gale (nīt′n-gāl′) *n.* a small bird with a melodious song, heard especially at night.

●**Night·in·gale** (nīt′n-gāl′), **Florence** (1820-1910) was the founder of modern nursing. Against much opposition she organized hospitals in the Crimean War (1854–1856), so saving thousands of lives.

night·ly (nīt′lē) *adj. & adv.* happening every night.
night·mare (nīt′mâr′) *n.* **1** a frightening dream. **2** an unpleasant or frightening experience.
night·time (nīt′tīm′) *n.* the time between sunset and sunrise.
nil (nil) *n. & adj.* amounting to zero.

●**Nile** (nīl) the world's longest river. It flows 4,150 miles (6,671 km) from near the equator in AFRICA to the MEDITERRANEAN SEA.

nim·ble (nim′bəl) *adj.* quick and light in movement; agile. – *adv.* **nim·bly** (nim′blē).
nine (nīn) *n.* the number or figure 9. – *n., adj., & adv.* **ninth** (nīnth).
nine·teen (nīn-tēn′) *n.* the number or figure 19. – *n., adj., & adv.* **nine·teenth** (nīn-tēnth′).
nine·ties (nīnt′ēz) *n.* (*plural*) **1** the period of time between a person's 90th and 100th birthdays. **2** the period of time between the 90th and 100th years of a century, 1990s.
nine·ty (nīnt′ē) *n.* **nine·ties** the number or figure 90. – *n., adj., & adv.* **nine·ti·eth** (nīnt′ē-əth).
nip (nip) *vb.* **nip·ping, nipped 1** to pinch or squeeze sharply. **2** to give a sharp little bite to: *The parrot nipped my ear.* – *n.* **1** a pinch or squeeze. **2** a sharp little bite. **3** a sharp biting

coldness, or stinging quality.

nip·ple (nip′əl) *n.* **1** the pointed projection on a breast; in the female the outlet of the ducts from which the young suck milk. **2** the rubber tip on a baby's bottle.

ni·tro·gen (nī′trə-jən) *n.* an element (symbol **N**), a gas making up four-fifths of the air.

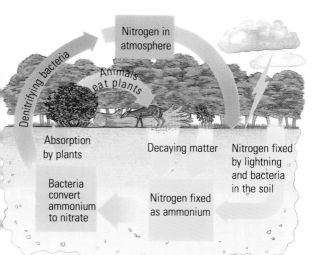

The nitrogen cycle: nitrogen passes from air to soil, to plants, to animals which eat plants, and eventually back into the air.

no¹ (nō) *interjection* used as a negative reply, expressing denial, refusal, or disagreement.

no² (nō) *adj.* **1** not any. **2** certainly not a; far from a: *He's no fool.* **3** hardly any. **4** not allowed.

No·bel prize (nō-bel′ prīz′) *n.* any of the prizes awarded annually for work in physics, chemistry, medicine, literature, and the promotion of peace.

no·bil·i·ty (nō-bil′ət-ē) *n.* the quality of being noble, in character, conduct, or rank.

no·ble (nō′bəl) *adj.* **1** honorable. **2** generous. **3** of high birth or rank. — *n.* a person of noble rank. — *adv.* **no·bly** (nō′blē).

no·bod·y (nō′bəd-ē, nō′bäd′ē) *pron.* no person; no one.

noc·tur·nal (näk-turn′l) *adj.* **1** (of animals) active at night. **2** of or belonging to the night.

nod (näd) *vb.* **nod·ding, nod·ded 1** to make a brief bow with the head, in agreement, greeting, etc. **2** to let the head droop with sleepiness; to become drowsy.

noise (noiz) *n.* **1** a sound: *I can hear no noise in the church.* **2** a harsh, disagreeable sound; a din.

nois·y (noi′zē) *adj.* **nois·i·er, nois·i·est 1** making a lot of noise: *noisy children.* **2** full of noise: *noisy streets.* — *adv.* **nois·i·ly** (noi′zə-lē).

no·mad (nō′mad) *n.* a member of a people without a permanent home, who travel from place to place seeking food or pasture.

no-man's-land (nō′manz′ land′) *n.* **1** unclaimed land. **2** neutral territory between opposing armies or between two countries with a common border.

nom·i·nate (näm′ə-nāt′) *vb.* **nom·i·nat·ing, no·mi·na·ted** to suggest formally as a candidate for election, for a job, etc. — *n.* **nom·i·na·tion** (näm′ə-nā′shən).

nom·i·nee (näm′ə-nē′) *n.* a person who is nominated as a candidate, or for a job, etc.

non- *prefix* **1** not; the opposite of: *nonexistent.* **2** not belonging to the category of: *nonfiction.* **3** not having the skill or desire to be: *nonswimmers, nonsmokers.*

non·cha·lant (nän′shə-länt′) *adj.* coolly unconcerned.

none (nun) *pron.* (with *singular* or *plural* verb) **1** not any. **2** no one: *None were as kind as she.* — **none but** only: *Robert uses none but the finest ingredients.*

non·sense (nän′sens′, nän′səns) *n.* **1** words or ideas that do not make sense. **2** silly behavior.

noo·dle (nōōd′l) *n.* a thin strip of pasta, usually made with eggs.

noon (nōōn) *n.* midday; twelve o'clock.

no one (nō′wən, nō′wun′) *n.* nobody; no person.

noose (nōōs) *n.* a loop made in the end of a rope with a sliding knot.

nor (nər, nôr) *conj.* (used to introduce alternatives after **neither**) *She neither knows nor cares.*

Nor·dic (nôr′dik) *adj.* of or belonging to SCANDINAVIA or its inhabitants.

norm (nôrm) *n.* an accepted way of behaving, etc.: *Adam followed all the social norms.*

nor·mal (nôr′məl) *adj.* usual; typical; not extraordinary. — *n.* what is average or usual. — *n.* **nor·mal·i·ty** (nôr-mal′ət-ē).

nor·mal·ly (nôr′mə-lē) *adv.* usually.

Nor·man (nôr′mən) *n.* a person from Normandy, a region in northwest FRANCE; one of the Scandinavian settlers of France who conquered England in 1066. — *adj.* of or belonging to the Normans, their language, etc.

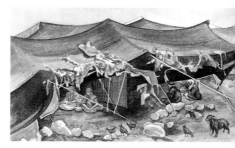

Nomads are found mainly in Africa and Asia, the Arab Bedouin being the best known.

PRONUNCIATION SYMBOLS		
ə away	lemon	focus
a fat	oi	boy
ā fade	oo	foot
ä hot	ōō	moon
âr fair	ou	house
e met	th	think
ē mean	th	this
g get	u	cut
hw which	ur	hurt
i fin	w	witch
ī line	y	yes
îr near	yōō	music
ô often	yoor	pure
ō note	zh	vision

Odin, the chief of the Norse gods. He owned two ravens, Thought and Memory. He sent them out daily to report on what was going on in the world.

Norse (nôrs) *adj.* of or belonging to ancient or medieval SCANDINAVIA. – *n.* (*plural*) the Scandinavians, especially the Norwegians.

north (nôrth) *n.* the direction to your left when you face the rising sun, or any part of the earth, a country, town, etc. lying in that direction. – *adj.* **1** in the north; on the side that is on or nearest the north. **2** coming from the direction of the north: *a north wind.*

●**North A·mer·i·ca** (nôrth′ ə-mer′i-kə) includes CANADA, the UNITED STATES, MEXICO, Central America and the West Indian islands of the Caribbean Sea. It covers cold Arctic lands, hot deserts, and subtropical swamps. High mountains include the Rocky Mountains. The Great Lakes are the world's largest group of freshwater lakes. Most people in North America speak English, Spanish, or French.

●**North Car·o·li·na** (nôrth′ kar′ə-lī′nə). See Supplement, **U.S.A.**

●**North Da·ko·ta** (nôrth′ də-kōt′ə). See Supplement, **U.S.A.**

north·east (nôr-thēst′) *n.* the direction midway between north and east or any part of the earth, a country, etc. lying in that direction. – *adj.* **1** in the northeast. **2** from the direction of the northeast: *a northeast wind.* – *adj.* **north·east·ern** (nôr-thē′stərn).

north·er·ly (nôr′thər-lē) *adj.* **1** (of a wind, etc.) coming from the north. **2** looking, lying, etc. toward the north.

north·ern (nôr′thərn) *adj.* of the north.

●**Northern Ireland** (nôr′thərn īr′lənd) a country in the northeastern part of Ireland that is part of the UNITED KINGDOM.

●**North Ko·re·a** (nôrth′ kə-rē′ə). See Supplement, **Countries**.

●**North Pole** *n.* the point on the earth's surface representing the northern end of its axis.

north·ward (nôrth-wərd) *adv.* & *adj.* toward the north.

north·west (nôrth-west′) *n.* the direction midway between north and west or any part of the earth, a country, etc. lying in that direction. – *adj.* **1** in the northwest. **2** from the direction of the northwest: *a northwest wind.* – *adj.* **north·west·ern** (nôrth-wes′tərn).

●**Nor·way** (nôr′wā′) is a country with many mountains. The coast is pierced with inlets called fjords. The capital is Oslo. See Supplement, **Countries**.

Nor·we·gian (nôr-wē′jən) *adj.* of or belonging to NORWAY, its inhabitants, or their language. – *n.* **1** a native of Norway. **2** the language of Norway.

nose (nōz) *n.* **1** the projecting organ above the mouth, with which you smell and breathe; an animal's snout or muzzle. **2** the sense of smell. – *vb.* **nos·ing, nosed** to edge forward.

nos·tal·gia (nə-stal′jə) *n.* a yearning for the past. – *adj.* **nos·tal·gic** (nə-stal′jik).

nos·tril (näs′trəl) *n.* either of the two openings

The continent of North America stretches north from tropical Panama to the icy Arctic Ocean, and east from the Pacific Ocean to the Atlantic Ocean.

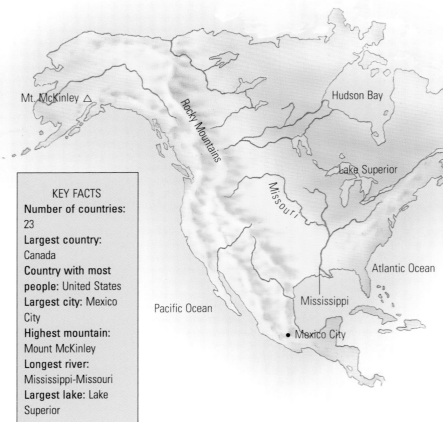

Mt. McKinley △
Rocky Mountains
Hudson Bay
Missouri
Lake Superior
Atlantic Ocean
Pacific Ocean
Mississippi
Mexico City

KEY FACTS
Number of countries: 23
Largest country: Canada
Country with most people: United States
Largest city: Mexico City
Highest mountain: Mount McKinley
Longest river: Mississippi-Missouri
Largest lake: Lake Superior

in the nose, through which one breathes, etc.

not (nät) *adv.* (often shortened to **-n't** (nt, ənt))
1 used to make a sentence negative: *It's not fair* or *It isn't fair.* **2** used with verbs of opinion, intention, etc. to make the clause or infinitive following the verb negative: *I don't think he's right.* **3** used in place of a negative clause or predicate: *I might be late, but I hope not.* **4** absolutely no.

no·ta·ble (nōt′ə-bəl) *adj.* **1** worth noting; significant. – *adv.* **no·ta·bly** (nōt′ə-blē).

notch (näch) *n.* a small V-shaped cut.

note (nōt) *n.* **1** a brief record made for later reference. **2** a short informal letter. **3** a piece of paper issued as money. **4** attention; notice: *Take note of the warning.* **5** a musical sound. **6** an agreement in writing promising to pay a sum of money. – *vb.* **not·ing, not·ed** **1** to write down. **2** to notice; to be aware of: *Note this.*

not·ed (nōt′əd) *adj.* well known.

noth·ing (nuth′ing) *n.* **1** no thing; not anything. **2** very little; something of no importance or not very impressive. **3** the number 0. – **have nothing to do with** **1** to avoid. **2** to be unconnected with. **3** to be no concern of.

no·tice (nōt′əs) *n.* **1** an announcement displayed or delivered publicly. **2** attention: *Your success was brought to my notice.* **3** a warning given before leaving, or dismissing someone from, a job: *Natasha has given her boss notice.* – *vb.* **no·tic·ing, no·ticed** **1** to observe. **2** to remark on. – **at short notice** with little warning.

no·tice·a·ble (nōt′ə-sə-bəl) *adj.* easily seen.

no·ti·fy (nōt′ə-fī′) *vb.* **no·ti·fies, no·ti·fy·ing, no·ti·fied** to inform or warn.

no·tion (nō′shən) *n.* **1** an impression, idea, or understanding. **2** a belief. **3** an inclination: *He had a notion to go swimming.*

no·to·ri·ous (nə-tôr′ē-əs, nə-tōr′ē-əs) *adj.* well known for a bad reason. – *n.* **no·to·ri·e·ty** (nōt′ə-rī′ət-ē).

nought (nôt) *n.* (*British*) naught.

noun (noun) *n.* a word used as the name of a person, animal, thing, place, or quality.

nou·rish (nur′ish) *vb.* **nou·rish·ing, nou·rished** to supply with food needed for survival and growth. – *adj.* **nou·rish·ing**.

nou·rish·ment (nur′ish-mənt) *n.* something that nourishes; food.

●**No·va Sco·tia** (nō′və skō′shə) is a province of CANADA.

nov·el¹ (näv′əl) *n.* a long fictional story.

The novels of Charles Dickens were often illustrated and first appeared as serials in magazines. This scene is from David Copperfield.

nov·el² (näv′əl) *adj.* new; original: *a novel idea.*

nov·el·ist (näv′əl-əst) *n.* the writer of a novel.

nov·el·ty (näv′əl-tē) *n.* **nov·el·ties** something new and strange.

No·vem·ber (nō-vem′bər) *n.* the eleventh month of the year. November has 30 days.

nov·ice (näv′əs) *n.* **1** a beginner. **2** a person who has recently joined a religious community.

now (nou) *adv.* **1** at the present time or moment. **2** immediately: *You'd better go now.* **3** in these circumstances; as things are: *I planned to, but now I can't.* **4** up to the present: *She has now been teaching for 13 years.*

now·a·days (nou′ə-dāz′) *adv.* these days.

no·where (nō′hwer′) *adv.* not anywhere.

noz·zle (näz′əl) *n.* an attachment with an opening for the end of a hose or pipe.

nu·cle·ar (nōō′klē-ər, nyōō′klē-ər) *adj.* **1** of or relating to atoms or their nuclei. **2** relating to or produced by the fission or fusion of atomic nuclei.

nuclear reactor *n.* an apparatus for producing nuclear energy.

nu·cle·us (nōō′klē-əs, nyōō′klē-əs) *n.* **nu·cle·i** (nōō′klē-ī′, nyōō′klē-ī′) **1** the positively charged central part of an atom, consisting of neutrons and protons. **2** the central part of a plant or animal cell.

nude (nōōd, nyōōd) *adj.* wearing no clothes.

nudge (nuj) *vb.* **nudg·ing, nudged** **1** to poke gently with the elbow, to get attention, etc. **2** to push slightly. – *n.* a gentle prod.

Nostalgia comes from the Greek *nostos* "return home" and *algos* "pain." Together they produce the meaning "homesickness."

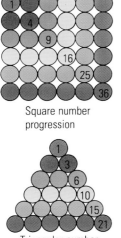

Square number progression

Triangular number progression

Some sequences of numbers can be shown as patterns. A number multiplied by itself is called a square (top). *A triangular arrangement gives the progression 1, 3, 6, 10, 15, 21, and so on.*

The **numbers** 1, 2, 3, 4, etc. we use so often in everyday life are called natural numbers because they were thought to be natural, in existence, and correspond to something in reality such as two eyes, four legs, etc.

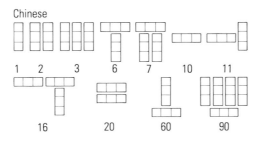

Chinese

| 1 | 2 | 3 | 6 | 7 | 10 | 11 |
| 16 | 20 | 60 | 90 |

Roman

I II III IV V VI VII VIII IX X

1 2 3 4 5 6 7 8 9 10

XI XV XX L XC C CX CL D M

11 15 20 50 90 100 110 150 500 1000

Over the centuries different peoples have devised various ways of writing numbers. Our modern Arabic numbers were originally developed in India.

١	٢	٣	٤	٥	٦	٧	٨	٩		·	Arabic
											Spanish 976
										٥	W. Europe 1360
										٥	Italy 1400
1	2	3	4	5	6	7	8	9	10	0	Modern
											Computer

This diagram shows how our modern numerals were derived from ancient Arabic.

nug·get (nug′ət) *n.* a lump, especially of gold.

nui·sance (no͞o′səns, nyo͞o′səns) *n.* an annoying or troublesome person, thing, or circumstance.

numb (num) *adj.* **1** deprived completely, or partly, of the ability to feel: *My fingers are numb with cold.* **2** too stunned to feel emotion: *I am numb with shock.*

num·ber (num′bər) *n.* **1** the means or system by which groups of individual things are counted. **2** a numeral or set of numerals. **3** a numeral or set of numerals identifying something or someone: *What is your telephone number?* **4** quantity of individuals. **5** a single issue of a magazine, etc. – *vb.* **num·ber·ing, num·bered 1** to give a number to; to mark with a number. **2** to include. **3** to amount to.

nu·mer·al (no͞o′mə-rəl, nyo͞o′mə-rəl) *n.* an arithmetical symbol used to express a number; a figure: *5 and V are numerals for five.*

nu·mer·i·cal (no͞o-mer′i-kəl, nyo͞o-mer′i-kəl) *adj.* relating to, or consisting of, numbers.

nu·mer·ous (no͞o′mə-rəs, nyo͞o′mə-rəs) *adj.* many; a large number.

nu·mis·mat·ics (no͞o′miz-mat′iks, nyo͞o′miz-mat′iks) *n.* (*singular*) the study, or collecting, of coins and medals.

nun (nun) *n.* a woman who lives in a convent in obedience to certain vows.

nurse (nurs) *n.* a person who is trained to look after sick or injured people, especially in a hospital. – *vb.* **nurs·ing, nursed 1** to look after sick or injured people. **2** to feed a baby at the breast. – *n.* **nurs·ing.**

nurs·ing home (nur′sing hōm′) *n.* a small hospital or home, for example for old people.

nur·ser·y (nur′sə-rē, nus′rē) *n.* **nur·ser·ies 1** a room or area in a house for small children. **2** a place where plants are grown for sale.

nut (nut) *n.* **1** a fruit consisting of a kernel contained in a hard shell; the kernel itself. **2** a small piece of metal with a hole through it, for screwing on the end of a bolt.

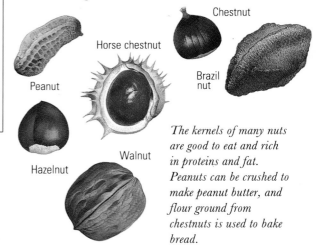

Chestnut

Horse chestnut

Peanut

Brazil nut

Walnut

Hazelnut

The kernels of many nuts are good to eat and rich in proteins and fat. Peanuts can be crushed to make peanut butter, and flour ground from chestnuts is used to bake bread.

nut·meg (nut′meg′) *n.* the hard aromatic seed of the fruit of an Indian tree, used as a spice.

nu·tri·tion (no͞o-trish′ən, nyo͞o-trish′ən) *n.* **1** the process of nourishment. **2** food. – *adj.* **nu·tri·tious** (no͞o-trish′əs, nyo͞o-trish′əs).

nuz·zle (nuz′əl) *vb.* **nuz·zling, nuz·zled** to rub with the nose.

ny·lon (nī′län) *n.* a synthetic material from which a wide variety of products are made, including clothing, ropes, and brushes.

O o

oak (ōk) *n*. **1** a large tree of the beech family, with lobed leaves. **2** its hard wood, used especially for building furniture.

oar (ôr, ōr) *n*. a long pole with a broad, flat blade used for rowing a boat.

o·a·sis (ō-ā′səs) *n*. **o·a·ses** (ō-ā′sēz′) a fertile area in a desert where water is found and plants grow.

● An oasis may be just a clump of trees or much bigger. Egypt's NILE Valley is a huge oasis. Oases can be made by drilling wells and digging irrigation ditches.

Saturated sand

Fault — Impermeable rock

Impermeable rock (rock through which water cannot penetrate)

Aquifer

Where water fills an aquifer (a rock that holds water), and where the aquifer breaks the surface, an oasis will form. If the water is trapped between two layers of rock wells can be drilled.

oat (ōt) *n*. **1** a cereal plant grown for its seeds. **2** (in *plural*) the seeds of this plant.

oath (ōth) *n*. **1** a solemn promise to tell the truth, be loyal, etc. **2** a swearword.

o·be·di·ence (ō-bēd′ē-əns) *n*. the act or practice of obeying.

o·bey (ō-bā′) *vb*. **o·bey·ing, o·beyed** to follow the commands of.

o·bit·u·ar·y (ō-bich′o͞o-er′ē) *n*.

o·bit·u·ar·ies a written announcement of a person's death.

ob·ject¹ (äb′jikt, äb′jekt) *n*. **1** a thing that can be seen or touched. **2** an aim or purpose. **3** in grammar, the noun, etc. affected by the action of the verb or a preposition.

ob·ject² (əb-jekt′) *vb*. **ob·ject·ing, ob·ject·ed** **1** to express dislike or disapproval. **2** to give as a reason for opposing.

ob·jec·tion (əb-jek′shən) *n*. **1** an expression of disapproval. **2** a reason for disapproving.

ob·jec·tive (əb-jek′tiv) *n*. a thing aimed at or wished for; a goal.

o·blige (ə-blīj′) *vb*. **o·blig·ing, o·bliged** to bind morally, legally, or by physical force.

o·blig·ing (ə-blī′jing) *adj*. willing to help.

o·blique (ə-blēk′, ə-blīk′) *adj*. **1** sloping; not vertical or horizontal. **2** not straight or direct.

o·blit·er·ate (ə-blit′ə-rāt′) *vb*. **o·blit·er·at·ing, o·blit·er·at·ed** to destroy completely.

o·blong (äb′lông′) *adj*. forming or being a rectangle which is longer than it is broad.

o·boe (ō′bō′) *n*. a treble wind instrument.

ob·scure (əb-skyoor′) *adj*. **1** dark; dim. **2** not clear; hidden; difficult to see or understand.

ob·ser·va·tion (äb′zər-vā′shən) *n*. **1** the act of noticing or watching; the state of being observed or watched. **2** perception: *Test her powers of observation*. **3** a remark or comment.

ob·ser·va·to·ry (əb-zur′və-tôr′ē, əb-zur′və-tōr′ē) *n*. **ob·ser·va·to·ries** a place specially equipped for observing the stars and weather.

ob·serve (əb-zurv′) *vb*. **ob·serv·ing, ob·served** **1** to notice or become conscious of. **2** to watch carefully.

ob·serv·er (əb-zur′vər) *n*. a person who observes.

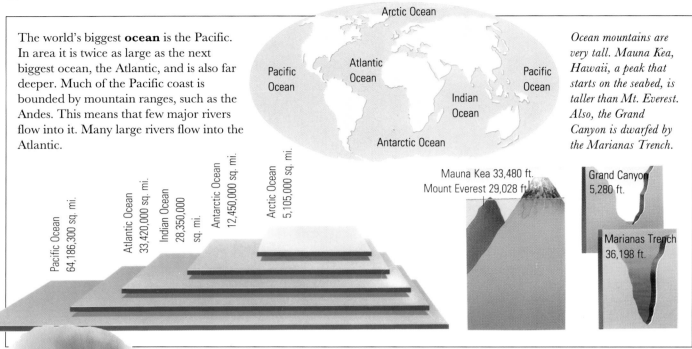

The world's biggest **ocean** is the Pacific. In area it is twice as large as the next biggest ocean, the Atlantic, and is also far deeper. Much of the Pacific coast is bounded by mountain ranges, such as the Andes. This means that few major rivers flow into it. Many large rivers flow into the Atlantic.

Ocean mountains are very tall. Mauna Kea, Hawaii, a peak that starts on the seabed, is taller than Mt. Everest. Also, the Grand Canyon is dwarfed by the Marianas Trench.

Arctic Ocean
Atlantic Ocean
Pacific Ocean
Pacific Ocean
Indian Ocean
Antarctic Ocean

Pacific Ocean 64,186,300 sq. mi.
Atlantic Ocean 33,420,000 sq. mi.
Indian Ocean 28,350,000 sq. mi.
Antarctic Ocean 12,450,000 sq. mi.
Arctic Ocean 5,105,000 sq. mi.

Mauna Kea 33,480 ft.
Mount Everest 29,028 ft.
Grand Canyon 5,280 ft.
Marianas Trench 36,198 ft.

In parts of the oceans there are holes — "smokers" — in the sea floor where hot liquids and gases leak into the water from the hot rocks beneath.

ob·so·lete (äb′sə-lēt′) *adj.* out-of-date.

ob·sta·cle (äb′stə-kəl) *n.* a person or thing that stands in a person's way or prevents progress.

ob·sti·nate (äb′stə-nət) *adj.* refusing to change one's opinion; stubborn.

ob·struct (əb-strukt′) *vb.* **ob·struct·ing, ob·struct·ed 1** to block or close. **2** to prevent or hinder the movement of.

ob·struc·tion (əb-strək′shən) *n.* **1** a thing that obstructs or blocks. **2** the act of obstructing.

ob·tain (əb-tān′) *vb.* **ob·tain·ing, ob·tained** to get or to come into possession of.

ob·tuse (äb-tōōs′, äb-tyōōs′) *adj.* (of an angle) between 90° and 180°.

ob·verse (äb′vurs′, äb-vurs′) *n.* the side of a coin with the head or main design on it.

ob·vi·ous (äb′vē-əs) *adj.* easily seen or understood; evident. – *adv.* **ob·vious·ly**.

oc·ca·sion (ə-kā′zhən) *n.* **1** a particular event or happening. **2** a special event. – *vb.* **oc·ca·sion·ing, oc·ca·sioned** to cause.

oc·ca·sion·al (ə-kā′zhən-l) *adj.* happening irregularly and infrequently.

Oc·ci·dent (äk′səd-ənt, äk′sə-dent′) *n.* the countries in the West, especially NORTH AMERICA, SOUTH AMERICA, and EUROPE, as opposed to the **Orient**.

oc·cu·pant (äk′yə-pənt) *n.* a person who occupies a place.

oc·cu·pa·tion (äk′yə-pā′shən) *n.* **1** a person's job or profession. **2** an activity that occupies a person's attention, free time, etc.

oc·cu·py (äk′yə-pī′) *vb.* **oc·cu·pies, oc·cu·py·ing, oc·cu·pied 1** to have possession of or live. **2** to fill: *I occupy my time drawing.* **3** to take possession of by force: *The Iraqis occupied Kuwait in 1991.*

oc·cur (ə-kur′) *vb.* **oc·cur·ring, oc·curred 1** to happen or take place. **2** to come into the mind, especially by chance.

oc·cur·rence (ə-kur′əns) *n.* an event.

o·cean (ō′shən) *n.* **1** the salt water that covers most of the earth's surface. **2** any one of its five main divisions: the ATLANTIC, Indian, PACIFIC, Arctic, and Antarctic oceans. – *adj.* **o·ce·an·ic** (ō′shē-an′ik).

o·ce·lot (äs′ə-lät′, ō′sə-lät′) *n.* a wild cat of the forests of South and Central America, which has dark yellow fur with spots and stripes.

o'·clock (ə-kläk′) *adv.* a phrase used in specifying the time: *It's nine o'clock.*

●**O'·Con·nor** (ō-kän′ər), **Flannery** (1925-1964) was an American novelist and short-story writer.

oc·ta·gon (äk′tə-gän′) *n.* a flat figure with eight straight sides and eight angles. – *adj.* **oc·tag·o·nal** (äk-tag′ən-l).

oc·tave (äk′tiv) *n.* the series of notes between

the first note and the eighth note on a major or minor scale.

Oc·to·ber (äk-tō′bər) *n.* the tenth month of the year. October has 31 days.

oc·to·pus (äk′tə-pəs, äk′tə-poos′) *n.* **octopuses** a sea creature with a soft oval body and eight tentacles.

odd (äd) *adj.* **1** left over when others are put into groups or pairs. **2** not matching. **3** not exactly divisible by two. **4** unusual; strange.

od·di·ty (äd′ət-ē) *n.* **od·di·ties** a strange person or thing.

odds (ädz) *n.* (*plural*) the chance or probability, expressed as a ratio, that something will or will not happen: *The odds are 10 to 1 in favor of our winning the game.*

odor (ōd′ər) *n.* a usually distinctive smell; scent.

●**Od·ys·sey** (äd′ə-sē) an epic poem by the Greek poet HOMER. It tells of the journeys of Ulysses (Odysseus) after the Trojan Wars.

of (əv, uv, äv) *prep.* **1** used to show origin, cause, or authorship: *people of Paris; die of hunger; poems of Whitman.* **2** belonging to; connected with. **3** used to define a component, ingredient, characteristic, etc.: *built of bricks; an area of marsh.* **4** about; concerning: *tales of Rome.*

off (ôf) *adv.* **1** away; at or to a distance: *The new school is a couple of miles off.* **2** in or into a position which is not attached; loose; separate: *The handle came off.* **3** ahead in time: *Easter is a week off.* **4** no longer operating: *Turn the radio off.* **5** stopped or canceled: *The game was called off.* **6** in or into a state of sleep: *He dozed off.* **7** away from work or duties: *Take an hour off.* **8** away from a course: *Turn off into a side street.* — *adj.* **1** not good; not up to standard: *He's having an off day.* **2** most distant; farthest away. — *prep.* **1** from; away from: *Please take your feet off the table!* **2** removed from; no longer attached to. **3** opening out of; leading from: *Olga lives on a side street off the main road.* **4** denying oneself: *He's off candy.*

of·fend (ə-fend′) *vb.* **of·fend·ing, of·fend·ed** to cause to feel hurt or angry; to insult.

of·fense (ə-fens′) *n.* **1** the breaking of a rule; a crime. **2** any cause of anger, annoyance, or displeasure. **3** the team playing offensive positions.

of·fen·sive (ə-fen′siv) *adj.* **1** giving or likely to give offense; insulting. **2** unpleasant, disgusting, repulsive, especially to the senses. — *n.* **1** an aggressive action or attitude: *Go on the offensive.* **2** an attack. **3** of or relating to a team in possession of the ball or puck.

of·fer (ô′fər) *vb.* **of·fer·ing, of·fered 1** to put forward a gift, payment, suggestion, etc. to be accepted, refused, or considered. **2** to provide: *This hill offers the best view.* **3** to state willingness to do something: *Jane offered to wash the car.* — *n.* **1** an act of offering. **2** that which is offered, especially an amount of money offered to buy something.

of·fer·ing (ô′fə-ring, ôf′ring) *n.* anything offered, especially a gift.

off·hand (ôf′hand′) or **off·hand·ed** (ôf′han′dəd) *adj.* casual or careless.

of·fice (äf′əs, ô′fəs) *n.* the room, set of rooms, or building in which business is done.

of·fic·er (äf′ə-sər, ô′fə-sər) *n.* **1** a person in a position of authority and responsibility in the armed forces or in an organization. **2** a policeman or policewoman.

of·fi·cial (ə-fish′əl) *adj.* **1** of or relating to an office or position of authority. **2** given or authorized by a person in authority: *an official report.* — *n.* a person in a position of authority.

off·spring (ôf′spring′) *n.* **1** a person's child. **2** the young of an animal.

of·ten (ôf′ən, ôf′tən) *adv.* **1** many times; frequently. **2** in many cases.

o·gre (ō′gər) *n.* in fairy stories, a cruel, ugly giant.

●**O·hi·o** (ō-hī′ō, ə-hī′ə). See Supplement, **U.S.A.**

oil (oil) *n.* **1** a usually thick liquid which will not mix with water, obtained from plants, animals, and minerals. **2** petroleum. — *vb.* **oil·ing, oiled** to apply oil to, or treat with oil.

oil rig *n.* a structure and the equipment used for drilling oil.

oil slick *n.* a patch of oil, especially one forming a film on water.

Each of the octopus's arms has two rows of suckers, which help it to seize its prey.

The derrick on an oil platform is a tall metal tower that houses the drilling equipment. The drill bit at the end of the drill pipe cuts through rock with metal teeth.

SOME -OLOGIES

Term	Study of
anthropology	*mankind*
astrology	*heavens*
cardiology	*heart*
chronology	*dates*
cosmology	*universe*
dendrology	*trees*
entomology	*insects*
etymology	*word origins*
genealogy	*ancestry*
hydrology	*water*
meteorology	*weather*
odontology	*teeth*
ornithology	*birds*
pathology	*diseases*
rhinology	*noses*
speleology	*caves*
topology	*shapes*
vexillology	*flags*

A Greek athlete competes in the long jump. Notice that he carries a weight in each hand.

oil tanker *n.* a large ship for carrying oil.

oil well *n.* a well bored in the ground or seabed to obtain petroleum.

oil·y (oi′lē) *adj.* **oil·i·er, oil·i·est** of, containing, or like oil; covered with oil.

oint·ment (oint′mənt) *n.* any greasy substance rubbed on the skin to heal injuries to protect it.

O.K. or **OK** (ō′kā′) *adj. adv. interj.* all right; fine.

okay. Same as O.K..

● **O·kla·ho·ma** (ō′klə-hō′mə). See Supplement, **U.S.A**.

old (ōld) *adj.* **1** having existed or lived for a long time. **2** having a stated age: *He is five years old.* **3** relating to the end period of a long life: *old age.* **4** worn out or shabby through long use: *old shoes.* **5** no longer in use; out-of-date. **6** belonging to the past. **7** former or earlier. – *n.* **1** an earlier time: *men of old.* **2** (*plural*) old people.

old-fa·shioned (ōld′fash′ənd) *adj.* **1** out-of-date. **2** in favor of acting according to the moral views of the past.

old wives' tale *n.* an ancient belief or theory considered foolish and unscientific.

Old World *n.* the Eastern Hemisphere, comprising EUROPE, ASIA, and AFRICA.

ol·ive (äl′əv) *n.* **1** an evergreen Mediterranean tree. **2** the small, oval fruit of this tree, eaten as a food or pressed to extract its oil.

-ol·o·gy (äl′ə jē′) *suffix* used to form words indicating the science or study of a subject.

O·lym·pi·an (ō-lim′pē-ən) *n.* in mythology, any of the 12 ancient Greek gods thought to live on Mount Olympus in Greece.

O·lym·pic (ō-lim′pik) *adj.* **1** of the Olympic Games. **2** of Olympia, a plain in ancient Greece.

Olympic Games *n.* (*plural*) **1** the games

celebrated every four years in Olympia in ancient Greece, including athletic, musical, and literary competitions. **2** a modern international sports competition held every four years.

● This is the world's oldest athletics competition. The first Olympic Games were held at Olympia in GREECE in 776 B.C. The modern Games have been held every four years since 1896, each time in a different country.

● **O·man** (ō-män′, ō-man′). See Supplement, **Countries**.

om·buds·man (äm′boodz′mən) *n.* **om·buds·men** an official appointed to investigate complaints against authorities.

om·elette or **om·elet** (äm′lət) *n.* a dish of beaten eggs fried in a pan.

Most olives come from countries around the Mediterranean. The oil we get from pressing olives is good for our health and is used for cooking.

o·men (ō′mən) *n.* a sign of a future event, either good or evil: *Some say owls are a bad omen.*

o·mis·sion (ō-mish′ən) *n.* something that has been left out or neglected.

o·mit (ō-mit′) *vb.* **o·mit·ting, o·mit·ted** to leave out, either by mistake or on purpose.

on (on, än) *prep.* **1** touching, supported by, attached to: *There's a sheet on the bed.* **2** carried with: *I have no money on me.* **3** very near to or along the side of: *I live in a house on the shore.* **4** at or during a certain time: *We'll see you on Sunday.* **5** within the limits of: *a picture on page nine.* **6** about: *Ruth is reading a book on Jane Austen.* **7** through contact with; as a result of: *Jill cut herself on the broken bottle.* **8** in the state or process of: *The house is on fire!* – *adv.* **1** (especially of clothes) covering: *When we are born we have no clothes on.* **2** ahead, forward: *Go on home. I'll see you later on.* **3** continuously;

without interruption: *He keeps on about his toothache.* **4** in or into operation: *Put the radio on.* – *adj.* **1** working, broadcasting, or performing: *You're on in two minutes.* **2** taking place.

once (wuns) *adv.* **1** a single time; on one occasion. **2** at some time in the past: *Once upon a time...* – *conj.* as soon as: *Once she's arrived we can watch the movie.* – *n.* one time or occasion.

one (wun) *adj.* **1** being a single unit, number, or thing. **2** being a particular person or thing, especially as distinct from others of the same kind: *Lift one leg and then the other.* **3** being a particular but unspecified instance or example: *We'll visit him one day soon.* **4** being the only such: *Olive is the one woman who can beat her.* – *n.* the number or figure 1, the lowest cardinal number. – *pron.* **1** (often referring to a noun already mentioned) an individual person, thing, or example: *Buy the blue one.* **2** anybody: *One can't do better than that.*

one-sid·ed (wun′sīd′əd) *adj.* with one person or side having a great advantage over the other.

one-way (wun′wā′) *adj.* of a road or street in which traffic can move in one direction only.

on·go·ing (ôn′gō′ing, än′gō′ing) *adj.* continuing; in progress.

on·ion (un′yən) *n.* a vegetable with an edible bulb which has a strong taste and smell.

on·look·er (ôn′look′ər, än′look′ər) *n.* a person who watches and does not take part; an observer.

on·ly (ōn′lē) *adj.* **1** without any others of the same type: *This is the only horse in this class.* **2** having no brothers or sisters: *He's an only child.* – *adv.* **1** not more than; just. **2** alone; solely. **3** not longer ago than; not until: *I spoke to her only a minute ago.* – *conj.* but; however: *Come if you want to, only don't complain.*

on·o·mat·o·poe·ia (än′ə-mät′ə-pē′ə) *n.* the use of a word which imitates the sound represented, such as *hiss* and *moo.*

on·set (ôn′set′, än′set′) *n.* **1** a beginning. **2** an attack.

on·slaught (än′slôt′, ôn′slôt′) *n.* a fierce attack.

● **On·tar·i·o** (än-ter′ē-ō′) is a province of CA-NADA.

on·to (ôn′tōō, än′tōō) *prep.* **1** to a position on; upon. **2** (*informal*) aware of: *We're onto your lies.*

o·nus (ō′nəs) *n.* **onuses** a burden.

on·ward (ôn′wərd, än′wərd) *adj.* moving forward in place or time.

ooze (ōōz) *vb.* **ooz·ing, oozed** to flow or leak out gently or slowly: *Mud oozed from the pipes.*

o·pal (ō′pəl) *n.* a blue-white precious stone, which has iridescent reflections in it.

o·paque (ō-pāk′) *adj.* not able to be seen through; not transparent.

o·pen (ō′pən) *adj.* **1** allowing things or people to go in or out. **2** (of a container) with the inside visible. **3** not enclosed or restricted: *They sailed on the open sea.* **4** (of a store, etc.) ready for business. **5** unprejudiced: *He's very fair, he has an open mind.* – *vb.* **o·pen·ing, o·pened 1** to make or become open or more open. **2** to unfasten or to allow access. **3** to start or begin working: *The store opens at nine.* – *n.* **1** an area of open country. **2** public notice or attention: *Let's bring the issue out into the open.*

o·pen-air (ō′pən âr′) *adj.* in the open air; outside.

o·pen·er (ō′pə-nər) *n.* **1** a device for opening something. **2** the first item on a program.

o·pen·ing (ō′pə-ning, ōp′ning) *n.* **1** a hole, gap. **2** the act of making or becoming open. **3** a beginning. **4** an opportunity or chance. – *adj.* of or forming an opening; first: *opening night.*

o·pen·ly (ō′pən-lē) *adv.* without trying to hide anything.

op·er·a (äp′ə-rə, äp′rə) *n.* a dramatic work set to music, in which the singers are usually accompanied by an orchestra.

The bulb of an onion is made up of tightly packed layers of leaves containing a special kind of oil. Vapor from the oil makes your eyes water.

● Opera started in ITALY in the late 1500s, and rapidly became a popular form of entertainment. Some of the greatest opera composers have come from Austria (Mozart), Germany (Wagner), and Italy itself Rossini).

op·er·ate (äp′ə-rāt′) *vb.* **op·er·at·ing, op·er·at·ed 1** to function or work. **2** to manage or direct: *Jenny operates a computer business.* **3** to perform surgery.

op·er·a·tion (äp′ə-rā′shən) *n.* **1** an act or

process of working or operating: *The operation of the machine is complicated.* **2** the state of working or being active: *The factory is not yet in operation.* **3** an activity; something done. **4** an act of surgery to treat a part of the body.

op·er·a·tion·al (äp′ə-rā′shən-l) *adj.* able or ready to work.

op·er·a·tor (äp′ə-rāt′ər) *n.* a person who operates a machine or apparatus.

o·pin·ion (ə-pin′yən) *n.* **1** a belief or judgment that seems likely to be true, but which is not based on proof. **2** a professional judgment given by an expert.

o·pos·sum (ə-päs′əm, päs′əm) *n.* a small North American or Australian MARSUPIAL with a strong tail for gripping branches.

● **Op·pen·hei·mer** (äp′ən-hī′mər), **J. Robert** (1904-1967) was an American physicist who helped develop the atomic bomb and later opposed development of the hydrogen bomb.

op·po·nent (ə-pō′nənt) *n.* a person on the opposing side in an argument, contest, etc.

op·por·tu·ni·ty (äp′ər-tōō′nət-ē, äp′ər-tyōō′nət-ē) *n.* **op·por·tu·ni·ties** an occasion offering a possibility; a chance.

op·pose (ə-pōz′) *vb.* **op·pos·ing, op·posed** **1** to resist or fight against by force or argument. **2** to object; to disagree: *I oppose capital punishment.* – *adj.* **op·pos·ing**.

op·po·site (äp′ə-zət) *adj.* **1** being on the other side of, or at the other end of, a real or imaginary line or space. **2** facing in a directly different direction: *opposite sides of the coin.* **3** completely or diametrically different: *We have opposite ideas about how to bring up dogs.* – *adv.* in or into an opposite position: *I live opposite.* – *prep.* **1** across from and facing: *There is a house opposite the station.* **2** (of an actor) starring with.

op·po·si·tion (äp′ə-zish′ən) *n.* the act of resisting or fighting something by force or argument.

op·press (ə-pres′) *vb.* **op·press·ing, op·pressed** **1** to govern with cruelty and injustice. **2** to trouble or make anxious; to weigh heavily upon: *Margaret was oppressed by her worries.* – *n.* **op·pres·sor** (ə-pres′ər).

op·pres·sion (ə-presh′ən) *n.* the state of suffering cruelty and injustice.

op·pres·sive (ə-pres′iv) *adj.* **1** cruel, tyrannical, and unjust. **2** causing worry or distress. **3** (of the weather) hot and sultry.

opt (äpt) *vb.* **opt·ing, opt·ed** to decide between or choose. – *vb.* **opt out** to choose or decide not to take part in something.

op·tic (äp′tik) *adj.* of or relating to sight or the eye: *optic nerve.*

op·ti·cal (äp′ti-kəl) *adj.* **1** of or relating to the sense of sight: *an optical illusion.* **2** made to improve sight: *an optical instrument.*

op·ti·cian (äp-tish′ən) *n.* a person who makes and sells glasses and contact lenses.

op·ti·mism (äp′tə-miz′əm) *n.* a tendency to take a bright, hopeful view of things. – *n.* **op·ti·mist** (äp′tə-məst). – *adj.* **op·ti·mis·tic** (äp′tə-mis′tik).

op·tion (äp′shən) *n.* **1** an act of choosing. **2** something which may be chosen.

op·tion·al (äp′shən-l) *adj.* not compulsory.

or (ər, ôr) *conj.* used to introduce: **1** alternatives: *red or pink or blue.* **2** a synonym or explanation: *a puppy or young dog.* **3** an afterthought: *She's laughing – or is she crying?* **4** the second part of an indirect question: *Ask her whether she thinks he'll come or not.* **5** because if not: *Run or you'll be late.* **6** and not: *He never joins in or helps.* – **or else** **1** otherwise. **2** (*informal*) expressing a threat or warning: *Give it to me or else!*

-or *suffix* used to form words meaning the person or thing performing the action: *actor.*

or·a·cle (ôr′ə-kəl) *n.* a holy place in ancient GREECE or ROME where a god was asked to give prophecy through a priest or priestess.

o·ral (ôr′əl, ōr′əl, är′əl) *adj.* **1** spoken or verbal; not written. **2** of or used in the mouth: *oral hygiene.*

or·ange (är′ənj, ôr′ənj) *n.* **1** a round, juicy citrus fruit with a thick reddish-yellow skin and sharp, sweet taste. Orange trees are evergreens and grow in warm climates. **2** the reddish-yellow color of its skin.

o·rang·u·tan (ə-rang′ə-tang′, ə-rang′ə-tan′) *n.* a large ape with shaggy reddish-brown hair and long strong arms, that lives in the forests of Borneo and Sumatra.

Ripe fruit

Unripe fruit

Oranges grow on a tree with dark leaves. The fruit develops from the ovaries of white, fragrant flowers. The delicious juice of the orange is rich in vitamin C.

● The name orangutan comes from the Malay words meaning "man of the woods." Human beings are orangutans' main enemies. Orangutans are already scarce; they could become extinct.

or·a·tor (ôr′ət-ər, är′ət-ər) *n.* a person who is skilled in persuading people through public speech.

or·a·to·ry (ôr′ə-tôr′ē, ōr′ə-tōr′ē, är′ə-tôr′ē) *n.* **or·a·to·ries** the art of speaking well in public.

orb (ôrb) *n.* anything in the shape of a globe.

or·bit (ôr′bət) *n.* **1** the curved path in which a moon or spacecraft moves around a planet or star. **2** one complete passage around this path. − *vb.* **or·bit·ing, or·bit·ed** to move in an orbit.

or·chard (ôr′chərd) *n.* a garden or piece of land where fruit trees are grown.

or·ches·tra (ôr′kə-strə, ôr′kes′trə) *n.* a group of musicians who play a variety of different instruments together, led by a conductor.

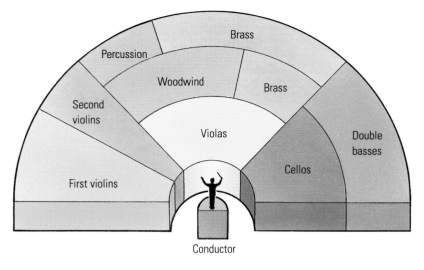

There are some 15,000 kinds of orchid. Most grow in warm, rainy forests.

— Early-purple orchid

The lower petal of the bee orchid resembles a bee, so it attracts a male insect to mate with it.

or·chid (ôr′kəd) *n.* any of several types of plant that usually have brightly colored flowers.

or·dain (ôr-dān′) *vb.* **or·dain·ing, or·dained** to make into a priest, vicar, etc. officially.

or·deal (ôr-dēl′, ôr′dēl′) *n.* a difficult, painful, or testing experience.

or·der (ôrd′ər) *n.* **1** a state in which everything is in its proper place; tidiness. **2** an arrangement of objects according to importance, value, position, etc.: *alphabetical order.* **3** a command, instruction, or direction. **4** a state of peace and harmony in society. **5** an instruction to a supplier, waiter, etc. to provide something. **6** a category in the classification of animals and plants which is below a class and above a family. − *vb.* **or·der·ing, or·dered** **1** to give a command to. **2** to instruct a waiter, etc. to supply. − **in order 1** in accordance with the rules. **2** properly prepared: *my travel documents are in order.* **3** in the correct sequence. − **in order to** so as to be able to.

or·der·ly (ôr′dər-lē) *adj.* **1** in good order; well arranged. **2** well behaved; quiet. − *n.* **or·der·li·ness** (ôr′dər-lē-nəs).

or·di·nar·y (ôrd′n-er′ē) *adj.* usual; normal; unexceptional; familiar.

ore (ôr) *n.* a rock or mineral from which a metal or other valuable substance can be removed.

● **Or·e·gon** (ôr′ə-gən, är′ə-gən). See Supplement, **U.S.A**.

or·gan (ôr′gən) *n.* **1** a part of a body or plant which has a special function, for example a kidney or leaf. **2** a usually large musical instrument with a keyboard and

The musicians in an orchestra are arranged like this in a semicircle in front of the conductor. This arrangement produces the best blend of sound.

The word orchestra once meant "dancing place," because in ancient Greek theaters dancers and musicians performed on a space between the audience and stage. When the Italians invented opera their theaters were arranged with the musicians in the same way. The word orchestra came to describe the group of musicians.

pedals, in which sound is produced by air being forced through pipes of different lengths.

or·gan·ic (ôr-gan′ik) *adj.* **1** of, relating to, or produced by a bodily organ or organs. **2** (of food, crops, etc.) produced without being treated with chemicals. − *adv.* **or·gan·i·cal·ly** (ôr-gan′i-klē).

or·gan·ist (ôr′gə-nəst) *n.* an organ player.

or·gan·ism (ôr′gə-niz′əm) *n.* a living animal or plant.

or·ga·ni·za·tion (ôr′gə-nə-zā′shən) *n.* **1** a group of people formed into a society, union, or especially a business. **2** the act of organizing.

or·ga·nize (ôr′gə-nīz′) *vb.* **or·ga·niz·ing, or·ga·nized 1** to give an orderly structure to. **2** to arrange, provide, or prepare.

o·ri·ent (ôr′ē-ənt, ōr′ē-ənt) *n.* **the Orient** the countries in eastern ASIA, as opposed to the **Occident**.

O·ri·en·tal or **oriental** (ôr′ē-ent′l, ōr′ē-ent′l) *adj.* of, from, or relating to the Orient.

o·ri·ga·mi (ôr′ə-gäm′ē) *n.* the art of folding paper into shapes and figures.

or·i·gin (ôr′ə-jən, är′ə-jən) *n.* a beginning or a source.

o·rig·i·nal (ə-rij′ən-l)*adj.* **1** existing from the beginning; earliest; first: *Who was the car's original owner?* **2** (of an idea) never thought of before; fresh or new: *He brought an original approach to the job.* **3** (of a person) creative or inventive. − *n.* **1** the first example of something which is copied to produce others. **2** a model from which a painting, etc. is made. − *n.* **o·rig·i·nal·i·ty** (ə-rij′ə-nal′ət-ē).

o·rig·i·nate (ə-rij′ə-nāt′) *vb.* **o·rig·i·nat·ing, o·rig·i·nat·ed** to bring or come into being.

or·na·ment (ôr′nə-mənt) *n.* a small, usually decorative object.

or·nate (ôr-nāt′) *adj.* highly or excessively decorated. − *n.* **or·nate·ness** (ôr-nāt′nəs).

or·ni·thol·o·gy (ôr′nə-thäl′ə-jē) *n.* the study of birds and their behavior.

or·phan (ôr′fən) *n.* a child who has lost both parents. − *vb.* **or·phan·ing, or·phaned** to cause to be an orphan.

or·phan·age (ôr′fə-nij) *n.* a home for orphans.

or·tho·dox (ôr′thə-däks′) *adj.* believing in or conforming with generally accepted opinions.

Orthodox Church *n.* the eastern Christian Church, especially in the Balkans and Russia.

or·tho·pe·dics (ôr′thə-pēd′iks) *n.* (*singular*) the branch of medicine concerned with curing diseases and injuries of the bones.

Goldsmiths and silversmiths are renowned for producing marvelously detailed ornaments.

●**Or·well** (ôr′wəl, ôr′wel), **George** (1903-1950) was an English writer whose novels include *1984.*

-ory *suffix* forming nouns meaning a place for: *dormitory; laboratory.*

●**O·sa·ka** (ō-säk′ə) is JAPAN's second largest city.

os·cil·late (äs′ə-lāt′) *vb.* **os·cil·lat·ing, os·cil·lat·ed** to swing or cause to swing backward and forward like a pendulum.

O·si·ris (ō-sī′rəs). See **Myths and Legends**.

●**Os·lo** (äz′lō, äs′lō) is the capital of NORWAY.

Frightened ostriches do not hide their heads in the sand, as people used to think! Ostriches can live for 50 years or more.

os·trich (äs′trich) *n.* the largest living bird, able to run quickly but not fly.

oth·er (u<u>t</u>h′ər) *adj.* **1** remaining from a group when one or some have been specified already: *Close the other eye.* **2** different from the ones already mentioned: *He knows many other people.* **3** far or opposite: *He's on the other side of the garden.* − *pron.* another person or thing.

oth·er·wise (u<u>t</u>h′ər-wīz′) *conj.* or else; if not: *I already have the book, otherwise I'd have to borrow yours.* − *adv.* **1** in other respects: *He is good at languages but otherwise not very bright.* **2** in a different way: *Muriel couldn't act otherwise.*

●**Ot·ta·wa** (ät′ə-wə, ät′ə-wô′, ät′ə-wä′) is the capital of CANADA in the province of Ontario.

ot·ter (ät′ər) *n.* a small fish-eating river animal with smooth dark fur, a slim body, and webbed feet with claws.

Ot·to·man (ät′ə-mən) *adj.* of the Ottomans or the Ottoman Empire, which lasted from the 1200s until the end of the WORLD WAR I, centered in what is now TURKEY.

ought (ôt) *vb.* (*auxiliary*) used to express **1** duty or obligation: *You ought to help.* **2** advisability: *You ought to see a doctor.* **3** expectation: *She ought to be here soon.* **4** shortcoming or failure: *He ought to have won.*

ounce (ouns) *n.* **1** a unit of weight equal to one sixteenth of a pound. **2** a unit of liquid measure equal to one sixteenth of a pint.

our (our, är) *adj.* of, belonging to, or done by us.

ours (ourz, ärz) *pron.* the one or ones belonging to us: *Those parcels are ours, not yours.*

our·selves (our-selvz′, är-selvz′) *pron.* **1** the reflexive form of **us** and **we**: *We helped ourselves to cakes.* **2** used for emphasis: *we ourselves.*

-ous *suffix* forming adjectives meaning having the character, quality, or nature of: *marvelous; venomous.*

out (out) *adv. & adj.* **1** away from the inside; not in or at a place: *Go out into the yard.* **2** not at home or at work: *I came by but you were out.* **3** to or at an end; to or into a state of being completely finished: *The milk has run out.* **4** aloud: *She cried out.* **5** in all directions from a central point: *Give out the cake.* **6** in baseball, not succeeding (as a batter) in getting on base, or

(as a base runner) prevented from advancing a base or bases: *He was tagged out at second base.* **7** removed; dislocated: *He has to have a tooth out.* **8** (of a flower) in bloom. **9** (of a tide) at the lowest level of water. — *n.* **1** a way out, a way of escape; an excuse. **2** in baseball, the failure of a batter or a runner to get to a base safely.

out- *prefix* **1** external; separate; from outside: *outpatient; outhouse.* **2** away from the inside, especially as a result: *output.* **3** going away or out of; outward: *outdoor.* **4** so as to excel or surpass: *outwit.*

out·back (out′bak′) *n.* isolated, remote areas of a country, especially AUSTRALIA.

out·board (out′bôrd′, out′bōrd′) *adj.* (of a motor or engine) portable and designed to be attached to the outside of a boat's stern.

out·break (out′brāk′) *n.* a sudden occurrence, usually of something unpleasant.

out·burst (out′burst′) *n.* **1** a sudden, violent expression of strong emotion, especially anger. **2** a sudden period of great activity.

out·come (out′kum′) *n.* a result or consequence.

out·cry (out′krī′) *n.* **out·cries** a noisy protest: *The new tax caused a public outcry.*

out·door (out-dôr′, out-dōr′) *adj.* done or taking place in the open air.

out·doors (out-dôrz′, out-dōrz′) *adv.* in or into the open air; outside a building. — *n.* (*singular*) the open air: *the great outdoors.*

The first **Ottomans** were nomadic Turkish tribes that migrated to the Middle East from Asia. The name comes from *Osman,* or *Othman,* who was the first sultan or ruler of the empire.

An Ottoman sipahi *or* cavalryman *(above). In return for military service he received a land grant from the government.*

A janissary *(right), an elite soldier.*

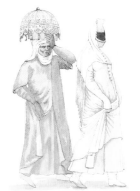

Women (below) *led a secluded life. When they went outside the house they had to be fully veiled and accompanied by a servant.*

The empire reached its greatest extent under Suleiman the Magnificent. Only his failure to capture Vienna in 1529 prevented an invasion of western Europe.

Ned Kelly, the outlaw, and his gang of bushrangers (bandits) roamed Australia, staging holdups and raiding banks. He often wore homemade armor.

out·er (out′ər) *adj.* **1** external; belonging to or for the outside. **2** farther from the center or middle: *The castle has an outer wall.*

outer space *n.* space beyond the earth's atmosphere.

out·fit (out′fit′) *n.* **1** a set of clothes worn for a particular occasion. **2** (*informal*) a group of people working as a team. – *vb.* **out·fit·ting, out·fit·ted** to provide with an outfit, especially clothes.

out·go·ing (out-gō′ing, out′gō′ing) *adj.* **1** friendly. **2** leaving: *The outgoing flight is full.*

out·grow (out-grō′) *vb.* **out·grow·ing, out·grew** (out-grōō′), **out·grown 1** to grow too large for. **2** to become too old for.

out·ing (out′ing) *n.* a short pleasure trip.

out·land·ish (out-lan′dish) *adj.* (of appearance, manner, habit, etc.) very strange; odd.

out·law (out′lô′) *n.* a criminal who is a fugitive from, or deprived of the protection of, the law. – *vb.* **out·law·ing, out·lawed 1** to declare an outlaw. **2** to forbid officially.

out·lay (out′lā) *n.* money spent on something.

out·let (out′lət, out′let′) *n.* **1** a way or passage out, especially for water or steam. **2** a way of releasing or using energy, talents, etc. **3** a place for plugging into an electric circuit.

out·line (out′līn′) *n.* **1** a line forming or marking the outer edge of an object. **2** a drawing with only the outer lines and no shading. **3** the main points without the details. – *vb.* **out·lin·ing, out·lined 1** to draw the outline of. **2** to give a brief description of the main features of.

out·look (out′look′) *n.* **1** a view from a particular place. **2** a person's mental attitude or point of view. **3** a prospect for the future.

out·ly·ing (out′lī′ing) *adj.* distant.

out-of-date (out′əv-dāt′) *adj.* no longer in style or in use; behind the times.

out·post (out′pōst′) *n.* a distant or remote settlement.

out·put (out′poot′) *n.* **1** the amount produced. **2** information after it has been processed by a computer. – *vb.* **out·put·ting, out·put·ted** to produce as output.

out·rage (out′rāj′) *n.* an act of great cruelty or violence.

out·ra·geous (out-rā′jəs) *adj.* **1** extravagant. **2** greatly offensive to accepted standards of decency, etc.

out·right (out-rīt′) *adv.* **1** completely: *She paid for it outright.* **2** immediately; at once: *The rabbit was killed outright.* **3** openly; honestly: *Ask outright.* – (out′rīt′) *adj.* **1** complete: *I felt an outright fool.* **2** clear: *the outright winner.* **3** open; honest.

out·set (out′set′) *n.* a beginning or start.

out·side (out-sīd′, out′-sīd′) *n.* **1** the outer surface; the external parts. **2** everything that is not within the bounds or scope of something: *We must view the problem from the outside.* **3** the farthest limit. – (owt sīd) *adj.* **1** of, on, or near the outside. **2** not forming part of your regular job, etc.: *Skating is my outside interest.* **3** unlikely; remote: *an outside chance of winning.* – (out-sid′) *adv.* on or to the outside; outdoors. – *prep.* **1** on or to the outside of. **2** beyond the limits of: *outside the city.* **3** except; apart from.

out·skirts (out′skurts′) *n.* (*plural*) the outer parts or area, especially of a town or city.

out·stand·ing (out-stand′ing) *adj.* **1** excellent; superior; remarkable: *an outstanding student.* **2** not yet paid, done, etc.: *outstanding debts.*

out·ward (out′wərd) *adj.* **1** on or toward the outside. **2** (of a trip) away from a place. – *adv.* (also **outwards**) toward the outside; in an outward direction.

o·val (ō′vəl) *adj.* shaped like an egg.

o·va·ry (ō′və-rē) *n.* **o·va·ries** either of the two female reproductive organs which produce eggs and hormones.

o·va·tion (ō-vā′shən) *n.* cheering or applause.

ov·en (uv′ən) *n.* an enclosed compartment for baking or roasting food, or drying clay, etc.

over- *prefix* **1** excessively: *overjoyed.* **2** above; in a higher position or authority: *overlord.* **3** across the surface; covering: *overcoat.* **4** down; away from an upright position: *overturn; overhang.*

o·ver (ō′vər) *adv.* **1** above and across. **2** outward and downward: *Try to knock it over.* **3** across a space; to or on the other side: *We came over from Australia.* **4** from one person, side, or condition to another: *We'll win them over.* **5** through, from beginning to end: *Think it over thoroughly.* **6** again; in repetition: *Do it twice over.* **7** remaining: *There were two left over.* – *prep.* **1** in or to a position which is above or higher in place, importance, authority, value, number, etc. **2** above and from one side to another: *They flew over the sea.* **3** so as to cover: *His hair was flopping over his eyes.* **4** out and down from: *It fell over the edge.* **5** throughout the extent of: *Read over that page again.* **6** during: *over the weekend.* **7** more than: *over a year ago.* **8** concerning; about.

o·ver·alls (ō′vər-ôlz′) *n.* (*plural*) a one-piece garment with pants and a biblike top.

o·ver·board (ō′vər-bôrd′, ō′vər-bōrd′) *adv.* over the side of a ship or boat into the water.

o·ver·cast (ō′vər-kast′) *adj.* cloudy.

o·ver·come (ō′vər-kum′) *vb.* **o·ver·com·ing, o·ver·came** (ō′vər-kām′), **o·ver·come 1** to defeat; to succeed in a struggle against. **2** to affect strongly; to overwhelm: *The children were overcome with sleep.*

o·ver·due (ō′vər-dōō′) *adj.* (of bills, work, etc.) not yet paid, delivered, etc. although the date for doing this has passed: *My rent is overdue.*

o·ver·flow (ō′vər-flō′) *vb.* **o·ver·flow·ing, o·ver·flowed** to flow over a brim or go beyond the limits or edge of.

o·ver·grown (ō′vər-grōn′) *adj.* **1** (of a garden, etc.) dense with plants. **2** grown too large.

o·ver·haul (ō′vər-hôl′) *vb.* **o·ver·haul·ing, o·ver·hauled** to examine and repair.

o·ver·head (ō′vər-hed′) *adv.* & *adj.* directly above; – (ō′vər-hed′) *n.* the regular costs of a business, such as rent, wages, etc.

o·ver·lap (ō′vər-lap′) *vb.* **o·ver·lap·ping, o·ver·lapped 1** to have one part partly covering another. **2** to coincide partially.

o·ver·look (ō′vər-look′) *vb.* **o·ver·look·ing, o·ver·looked 1** to give a view of from a higher position. **2** to fail to see or notice. **3** to allow to go unpunished: *to overlook an offense.*

o·ver·power (ō′vər-pou′ər) *vb.* **o·ver·power·ing, o·ver·powered** to defeat by greater strength.

o·ver·seas (ō′vər-sēz′) *adv.* abroad.

o·ver·see (ō′vər-sē′) *vb.* **o·ver·see·ing, o·ver·saw** (ō′vər-sô′), **o·ver·seen** (ō′vər-sēn′) to supervise. – *n.* **o·ver·seer** (ō′vər-sîr′).

o·ver·sight (ō′vər-sīt′) *n.* a mistake made through a failure to notice something.

o·ver·take (ō′vər-tāk′) *vb.* **o·ver·tak·ing, o·ver·took** (ō′vər-took′), **o·ver·tak·en** (ō′vər-tā′kən) **1** to catch up with. **2** to draw level with and begin to do better than.

o·ver·time (ō′vər-tīm′) *n.* time spent working at a job beyond regular hours.

o·ver·whelm (ō′vər-hwelm′) *vb.* **o·ver·whelm·ing, o·ver·whelmed 1** to overpower; to defeat by superior force or numbers. **2** to supply or offer something in great amounts to: *We were overwhelmed with offers of help.* – *adj.* **o·ver·whelm·ing**.

o·vum (ō′vəm) *n.* **ova** (ō′və) an egg cell which, when fertilized, can develop into a new individual.

owe (ō) *vb.* **ow·ing, owed 1** to have to pay money to someone: *Rick owes Olive $5.* **2** to be obliged to give: *You owe me an explanation.*

ow·ing (ō′ing) *adj.* still to be paid; due. – **owing to** because of; on account of.

owl (oul) *n.* a bird of prey with a large broad head, flat face, large eyes, a short hooked beak, and a hooting cry, active at night.

owl·et (ou′lət) *n.* a young owl.

own (ōn) *adj.* belonging to or for oneself or itself: *my own sister.* – *pron.* one or something belonging to oneself or itself: *to have a room of one's own.* – *vb.* **own·ing, owned 1** to have as a possession: *I own the house.* **2** to admit or confess: *He owned up to the robbery.* – **on one's own 1** alone. **2** without help.

own·er *n.* a person who owns something.

ox (äks) *n.* **ox·en** (äk′sən) **1** a bull or cow, used for pulling loads. **2** a castrated bull.

●**Ox·ford** (äks′fərd) is a famous industrial and university city in central southern ENGLAND.

ox·ide (äk′sīd′) *n.* a compound of oxygen and another element.

ox·y·gen (äk′sə-jən) *n.* a clear gas (symbol **O**) which forms part of the air and water and which is essential to life.

ox·y·mo·ron (äk′si-môr′än′, äk′si-mōr′än′) *n.* a figure of speech in which contradictory terms are used together: *a wise fool.*

oys·ter (oi′stər) *n.* an edible shellfish which sometimes produces a pearl.

o·zone (ō′zōn′) *n.* a type of oxygen with a powerful smell, used in bleaching, sterilizing water, and purifying air.

ozone layer *n.* the layer of ozone, high above the earth's surface, that protects the earth from harmful radiation from the sun.

PRONUNCIATION SYMBOLS			
ə **away**	lemon	focus	
a	**fat**	oi	**boy**
ā	**fade**	oo	**foot**
ä	**hot**	ōō	**moon**
âr	**fair**	ou	**house**
e	**met**	th	**think**
ē	**mean**	th̲	**th̲is**
g	**get**	u	**cut**
hw	**which**	ur	**hurt**
i	**fin**	w	**witch**
ī	**line**	y	**yes**
îr	**near**	yōō	**music**
ô	**often**	yoor	**pure**
ō	**note**	zh	**vision**

A plant (above) damaged by radiation. Harmful radiation from the sun is normally filtered before it reaches Earth by a layer of ozone in the stratosphere. Near the South Pole a "hole" has appeared caused by pollution.

Radiation from Sun

Hole in ozone layer

Radiation blocked off

Ozone layer

Some radiation gets through

P p

pace (pās) *n.* **1** a single step. **2** the distance covered by one step. **3** rate of movement or progress: *He can't stand the pace.* – *vb.* **pac·ing, paced** to keep walking about impatiently.

pace·maker (pās'mā'kər) *n.* an electronic device fitted next to the heart to regularize its beat.

Pa·cif·ic (pə-sif'ik) *adj.* relating to the **Pacific Ocean** between Asia and North and South America, the largest and deepest ocean.

pac·i·fist (pas'ə-fəst) *n.* someone who opposes violence. – *n.* **pac·i·fism** (pas'ə-fiz'əm).

pac·i·fy (pas'ə-fī') *vb.* **pac·i·fies, pac·i·fying, pac·i·fied 1** to calm or make quiet. **2** to make peaceful.

pack (pak) *n.* **1** things tied into a bundle for carrying; a rucksack. **2** a complete set of playing cards. **3** a troop of animals hunting together, for example dogs or wolves. – *vb.* **pack·ing, packed 1** to put goods, clothes, etc. in boxes, suitcases, etc. for transport or travel. **2** to cram: *a room packed with people.*

pack·age (pak'ij) *n.* something wrapped and secured with string, tape, etc.; a parcel.

pack·et (pak'ət) *n.* a bag or container, sometimes with its contents.

pact (pakt) *n.* an agreement reached between two or more opposing parties, states, etc.

pad (pad) *n.* **1** a thick soft piece of material used to cushion, protect, shape, or clean. **2** a quantity of sheets of paper fixed together into a block. **3** a water lily's large floating leaf. **4** the fleshy underside of an animal's paw. – *vb.* **pad·ding, pad·ded** to cover or fill with layers of soft material.

pad·dle[1] (pad'l) *n.* a short light oar with a blade at one or both ends. – *vb.* **pad·dling, pad·dled** to move a canoe, etc. with paddles.

pad·dle[2] (pad'l) *vb.* **pad·dling, pad·dled** to walk around barefoot in shallow water.

paddle wheel *n.* a large engine-driven wheel at the side or back of a ship which moves the ship through the water as it turns.

pad·dock (pad'ək) *n.* a small field for a horse.

pad·dy (pad'ē) *n.* **pad·dies** a field in which rice is grown.

pad·lock (pad'läk') *n.* a detachable lock with a U-shaped bar that can be passed through a ring or chain and locked in position.

pa·gan (pā'gən) *adj.* of or following a religion in which a number of gods are worshiped.

page[1] (pāj) *n.* one side of one of the sheets of paper in a book, magazine, etc.

page[2] (pāj) *n.* **1** a boy attendant serving a knight, and training for knighthood. **2** a boy attending the bride at a wedding.

pag·eant (paj'ənt) *n.* a series of dramatic scenes, usually depicting historical events; any colorful and varied spectacle. – *n.* **pag·eant·ry** (paj'ən-trē).

The roof of each story of a pagoda curves upward. In China pagodas usually have an odd number of storys and are octagonal; in Japan they usually have only five stories and are square.

pa·go·da (pə-gōd'ə) *n.* an Oriental temple, in the form of a tall tower, each story having its own projecting roof.

paid. See **pay**.

pail (pāl) *n.* a bucket.

pain (pān) *n.* **1** physical or emotional suffering. **2** (in *plural*) trouble taken or efforts made in doing something. – *vb.* **pain·ing, pained** to cause distress to.

pain·ful (pān′fəl) *adj.* causing pain.

pains·tak·ing (pān′stā′king) *adj.* thorough; showing great care and effort.

● **Paine** (pān)**, Thomas** (1737-1809) was an American writer (*The Rights of Man*) who fought in the AMERICAN REVOLUTION.

paint (pānt) *n.* colored liquid used to decorate buildings or create pictures. – *vb.* **paint·ing, paint·ed 1** to apply a coat of paint to. **2** to make using paint: *to paint pictures.*

paint·er *n.* **1** a person who decorates houses. **2** an artist who paints pictures.

Prehistoric art: early artists painted animals, like this bison, deep inside their caves.

paint·ing *n.* **1** the process of applying paint to walls, etc. **2** the art of creating pictures in paint. **3** a painted picture.

● STONE AGE hunters may have used painting as magic. They drew wounded beasts on their cave walls, perhaps with the idea that such pictures would help them kill real animals on their next hunt. In the MIDDLE AGES most artists worked for the Church. Later in Europe, princes and rich merchants paid artists to paint pictures to decorate their homes. Modern painters such as PICASSO, have produced pictures that concentrate on basic shapes and patterns and therefore appear more abstract.

● **Paint·ed Des·ert** (pānt′əd dez′ərt) is a 7,720 sq. mile (20,000 sq. km) area of plateau in Arizona, noted for its brilliant-colored rocks.

pair (pâr) *n.* **1** a set of two identical or corresponding things, as shoes or gloves, intended for use together. **2** something consisting of two joined, corresponding parts: *a pair of scissors.* – **in pairs** in twos.

pajamas (pə-jäm′əz, pə-jam′əz) *n.* (*plural*) an outfit for sleeping consisting of a loose jacket or top, and pants or shorts.

● **Pak·i·stan** (pak′i-stan′, päk′i-stän′). See Supplement, **Countries**.

pal (pal) *n.* (*informal*) a friend.

pal·ace (pal′əs) *n.* the official residence of a sovereign, bishop, archbishop, etc.

pal·ate (pal′ət) *n.* the roof of the mouth.

pale (pāl) *adj.* **1** (of a person, face, etc.) having less color than normal, for example from illness or fear. **2** (of a color) closer to white than black; light: *I like the color pale green.* **3** lacking brightness or vividness; subdued: *pale sunlight.* – *vb.* **pal·ing, paled** to become pale.

pal·ette (pal′ət) *n.* a small board with a thumb hole, on which an artist mixes colors.

pal·in·drome (pal′ən-drōm′) *n.* a word or phrase that reads the same backward and forward, as *eye*, or *Able was I ere I saw Elba.*

palm[1] (päm, pälm) *n.* the inner surface of the hand between the wrist and the fingers.

palm[2] (päm, pälm) *n.* a tree usually with a single trunk and a cluster of long bladelike leaves.

pal·o·mi·no (pal′ə-mē′nō) *n.* **palominos** a golden horse with a white tail and mane.

pam·per (pam′pər) *vb.* **pam·per·ing, pam·pered** to treat too indulgently; to spoil.

pan (pan) *n.* a metal pot, usually shallow, used for cooking.

● **Pan·a·ma** (pan′ə-mä′, pan′ə-mô′). See Supplement, **Countries**.

The coconut palm (right) *can grow as high as 100ft.* (30m). *Dates are the fruit of the date palm. Most palms grow in warm climates.*

Coconut

Dates

Before **paper** was invented, people wrote on clay tablets or animal skins. The Egyptians wrote on a kind of paper made from papyrus reed (from which we get the name paper).

Paper making was invented during the Chinese Han dynasty (202 B.C.- A.D. 220). Frames of hemp pulp were allowed to dry in the sun.

Modern paper making: A barking drum debarks specially treated logs to make pulp, which is made into a thin slurry with water. The slurry passes onto an endless web of wire mesh; the water is sucked out and the web of paper is squeezed between rollers.

Refiners

Washing unit

Paper reel

Press rollers

Steam heated cylinders (dry the paper)

Feeder

Wire suction services

Chipper

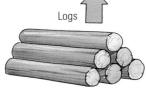

Barking drum

Debarked log

Logs

PRONUNCIATION SYMBOLS

ə away	lemon	focus
a fat	oi	boy
ā fade	oo	foot
ä hot	ōō	moon
âr fair	ou	house
e met	th	think
ē mean	th	this
g get	u	cut
hw which	ur	hurt
i fin	w	witch
ī line	y	yes
îr near	yōō	music
ô often	yoor	pure
ō note	zh	vision

● **Panama Canal** This canal crosses Panama and is used by ships as a short cut from the PACIFIC to the ATLANTIC OCEAN. Completed in 1914, it is 51 miles (81.6 km) long.

pan·cake (pan′kāk′) *n.* a round cake of thin batter cooked on both sides in a pan.

pan·cre·as (pang′krē-əs) *n.* a gland lying behind the stomach, that helps with digestion.

pan·da (pan′də) *n.* (also **giant panda**) a large black and white bearlike animal of CHINA.

pan·de·mo·ni·um (pan′də-mō′nē-əm) *n.* noise, chaos, and confusion.

pan·der (pan′dər) *n.* a person who caters to the base desires or vices of others. – *vb.* **pan·der·ing, pan·dered** to act as a pander; to indulge or gratify someone.

pane (pān) *n.* a sheet of glass, especially one fitted into a window or door.

pan·el (pan′l) *n.* **1** a rectangular wooden board forming a section of a wall or door. **2** any of the metal sections forming the body of a vehicle. **3** a board bearing the instruments and dials for controlling an aircraft, etc. **4** a team of people selected to judge a contest, or participate in a discussion before an audience.

pang (pang) *n.* a painfully acute feeling of hunger, remorse, etc.: *She felt a pang of regret.*

pan·ic (pan′ik) *n.* a sudden overpowering fear. – *vb.* **pan·ick·ing, pan·icked** to feel panic.

pan·o·ra·ma (pan′ə-ram′ə) *n.* an open and all around view. – *adj.* **panoramic** (pan′ə-ram′ik).

pan·sy (pan′zē) *n.* **pan·sies** a small garden plant with flowers of many colors.

pant (pant) *vb.* **pant·ing, pant·ed** to breathe in gasps as a result of exertion.

pan·ther (pan′thər) *n.* **1** the name usually given to a black leopard. **2** a puma. **3** a jaguar.

panties (pant′ēz) *n.* (*plural*) short underpants for girls and women.

pan·to·mime (pant′ə-mīm′) *n.* the use of gesture and movement to tell a story.

pan·try (pan′trē) *n.* **pan·tries** a room or cupboard for storing food in.

pants (pants) *n.* (*plural*) trousers.

pa·pal (pā′pəl) *adj.* of, or relating to, the pope.

pa·per (pā′pər) *n.* **1** a material manufactured in thin sheets from wood, rags, etc., used for writing and printing on, wrapping things, etc. **2** a newspaper. **3** (in *plural*) personal documents, for example a passport. **4** an essay or other written report. – *vb.* **pa·per·ing, pa·pered** to decorate with wallpaper.

pa·per·back (pā′pər-bak′) *n.* a book with a paper cover.

paper clip *n.* a metal clip formed from bent wire, for holding papers together.

pa·pier-mâ·ché (pā′pər-mə-shā′) *n.* a light material consisting of shredded paper mixed with glue and sometimes other substances, and molded into shape while wet.

pa·poose (pa-poōs′, pə-poōs′) *n.* a NATIVE AMERICAN baby or young child.

● **Pa·pu·a-New Gui·nea** (päp′ə-wə-noōgin′ē). See Supplement, **Countries**.

pa·py·rus (pə-pī′rəs) *n.* **pa·py·ri** (pə-pī′rē′, pə-pī′rī) or **papyruses** a tall water plant native to northern Africa used in ancient times to make a paperlike material.

par·a·ble (par′ə-bəl) *n.* a story whose purpose is to make a moral or religious lesson.

par·a·chute (par′ə-shoōt′) *n.* a fabric apparatus that slows the fall of a person dropped from an aircraft. – *n.* **par·a·chut·ist** (par′ə-shoō′əst).

pa·rade (pə-rād′) *n.* a ceremonial procession of people, vehicles, etc.

par·a·dox (par′ə-däks′) *n.* a statement that seems to contradict itself, for example *"More haste, less speed."* – *adj.* **par·a·dox·i·cal** (par′ə-däk′si-kəl).

par·a·graph (par′ə-graf′) *n.* a section of a piece of writing, starting on a fresh line, and dealing with a distinct point or idea.

● **Par·a·guay** (par′ə-gwī′, par′ə-gwā′). See Supplement, **Countries**.

par·a·keet (par′ə-kēt′) *n.* any of various small parrots with long tails.

par·al·lel (par′ə-lel′) *adj.* **1** (of lines) being at every point the same distance apart. **2** similar; exactly equivalent; corresponding. – *adv.* alongside and at an unvarying distance from. – *vb.* **par·al·lel·ing, par·al·leled** to equal; to correspond to or be equivalent to.

par·al·lel·o·gram (par′ə-lel′ə-gram′) *n.* a shape with four sides in which opposite sides are parallel to each other.

par·al·y·sis (pə-ral′ə-səs) *n.* **1** loss of the power of motion or of sensation in any part of the body. **2** a state of immobility; a standstill.

par·a·lyze (par′ə-līz′) *vb.* **par·a·lyz·ing, par·a·lyzed 1** to cause paralysis in. **2** to disrupt or bring to a standstill.

par·a·med·ic (par′ə-med′ik) *n.* a person who is trained to assist a doctor or do emergency first aid work.

par·a·mount (par′ə-mount) *adj.* foremost.

par·a·pet (par′ə-pət) *n.* a low wall along the edge of a bridge, balcony, etc.

par·a·phrase (par′ə-frāz′) *n.* a restatement of

something. – *vb.* **par·a·phras·ing, par·a·phrased** to express in other words.

par·a·site (par′ə-sīt′) *n.* an animal or plant that lives on, and obtains its nourishment from, another.

par·a·sol (par′ə-sôl′) *n.* a sunshade.

par·a·troops (par′ə-troōps′) *n.* (*plural*) troops trained to parachute into enemy territory.

par·a·troop·er (par′ə-troō′pər) *n.* a member of the paratroops.

par·cel (pär′səl) *n.* something wrapped in paper, etc. and secured with string or tape. – *vb.* **par·cel·ing** or **par·cel·ling, par·celed** or **par·celled 1** to wrap up in a parcel. **2** to divide into portions and share.

parch (pärch) *vb.* **parch·ing, parched 1** to dry up; to deprive of water. **2** to make thirsty.

parch·ment (pärch′mənt) *n.* a material formerly used for binding books and for writing on, made from animal skin.

par·don (pärd′n) *vb.* **par·don·ing, par·doned 1** to forgive or excuse for a fault or offense. **2** to cancel the punishment of. – *n.* **1** forgiveness. **2** the cancellation of a punishment. – *adj.* **par·don·a·ble** (pärd′n-ə-bəl).

par·ent (pâr′ənt) *n.* a father or mother. – *adj.* **pa·rent·al** (pə-rent′l). – *n.* **par·ent·hood** (pâr′ənt-hood′).

pa·ren·the·sis (pə-ren′thə-səs) *n.* **pa·ren·the·ses** (pə-ren′thə-sēz′) **1** a word or phrase inserted into a sentence, usually marked off by brackets. **2** (in *plural*) a pair of round brackets used to enclose such a comment.

● **Par·is¹** (par′əs, pa-rē) is the capital of FRANCE. It contains many famous landmarks: the Eiffel Tower, the Cathedral of Notre Dame, the Arc de Triomphe, and the Louvre museum.

● **Par·is²** (par′əs) was a Trojan prince whose abduction of HELEN caused the Trojan War.

Paris's most famous landmark: the 1,000ft. (300m) tall Eiffel Tower, built by Gustave Eiffel in 1889 for the Paris Exposition.

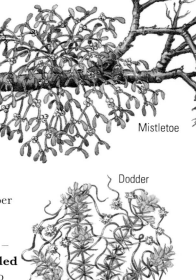

Mistletoe

Dodder

Mistletoe is really a semi-parasite; it takes some food from its host but also makes its own by photosynthesis. The dodder is a true parasite, depending solely on its host.

The much endangered parrot family includes these colorful macaws from South America. Their hooked beaks can open a brazil nut with ease — and cut off a finger just as easily!

par·ish (par′ish) *n.* a district or area served by its own church and priest or minister.

park (pärk) *n.* **1** an area in a town with grass and trees, reserved for public recreation. **2** an area of land kept as a nature reserve. – *vb.* **park·ing, parked** to maneuver into position and leave a vehicle temporarily.

par·ka (pär′kə) *n.* a hooded jacket.

● **Par·ker** (pär′kər), **Dorothy** (1893-1967) was an American poet and satirical writer.

Dorothy Parker is remembered as much for her quick wit in conversation as for her writing. When she was told that President Calvin Coolidge (who was a man of few words) had died, she replied: "How could they tell?" She was one of the most popular contributors to the *New Yorker* magazine.

parking lot *n.* a lot used for parking cars.

park·ing-me·ter (pär′king-mēt′ər) *n.* a coin-operated meter in the street beside which a car may be parked for a limited period.

par·lia·ment (pär′lə-mənt) *n.* the highest law-making assembly of some nations; **Parliament** in Britain, the House of Commons and House of Lords.

par·lia·men·tar·y (pär′lə-ment′ə-rē) *adj.* of, relating to, or issued by, a parliament.

par·o·dy (par′-əd-ē) *n.* **par·o·dies** a comic or satirical imitation of the work, or the style, of a writer, composer, etc.

pa·role (pə-rōl′) *n.* the release of a prisoner before the end of his or her sentence, on promise of good behavior.

par·rot (par′ət) *n.* a tropical, especially South American, bird with a hooked beak and colorful plumage.

par·sley (pär′slē) *n.* a plant with curled or flat feathery leaves used as a flavoring in cooking.

par·snip (pär′snəp) *n.* a root vegetable that looks like a thick white carrot.

part (pärt) *n.* **1** a portion, piece, or bit; some but not all of something. **2** a section of a book; any of the episodes of a story broadcast as a serial. **3** a performer's role in a play, opera, etc.: *He played the part of the villain.* – *vb.* **part·ing, part·ed 1** to separate. **2** to divide into parts.

● **Par·the·non** (pär′thə-nän′) a temple on the Acropolis in ATHENS, built in the 400s B.C.

par·tial (pär′shəl) *adj.* **1** incomplete; in part only. **2** having a liking for: *I'm rather partial to pizza.* **3** favoring one side or person unfairly.

par·tic·i·pate (pär-tis′ə-pāt′) *vb.* **par·tic·i·pat·ing, par·tic·i·pat·ed** to take part or be involved. – *n.* **par·tic·i·pant** (pär-tis′ə-pənt). – *n.* **par·tic·i·pa·tion** (pär-tis′ə-pā′shən).

par·ti·ci·ple (pärt′ə-sip′əl) *n.* a word formed from a verb and used as an adjective or to form different tenses of a verb. The **present participle** in English is formed with **-ing** (*We heard encouraging news; I was going*). The **past participle** is formed with **-ed, -t,** or **-en** (*The cookies were broken; The cakes will be burnt*).

par·ti·cle (pärt′i-kəl) *n.* **1** a tiny unit of matter such as a molecule, atom, or electron. **2** a tiny piece.

par·tic·u·lar (pär-tik′yə-lər) *adj.* **1** specific; single; individually known or referred to: *She was looking for a particular color.* **2** special: *He took particular care.* **3** difficult to satisfy; fastidious: *My mother is very particular about hygiene.* – *n.* (in plural) personal details: *He took down her particulars.* – **in particular** especially.

par·tic·u·lar·ly (pär-tik′yə-lər-lē) *adv.* **1** more than usually. **2** specifically; especially.

par·ti·tion (pär-tish′ən) *n.* a screen or thin wall dividing a room. – *vb.* **par·ti·tion·ing, par·ti·tioned** to separate with a partition.

part·ly (pärt′lē) *adv.* to a certain extent; not completely; in some parts.

part·ner (pärt′nər) *n.* one of two or more people who take part in an activity: *a business partner, a dancing partner, a tennis partner.*

part·ner·ship (pärt′nər-ship′) *n.* a business

jointly owned or run by two or more people.

par·tridge (pär′trij) *n.* a plump, game bird.

part-time (pärt-tīm′, pärt′tīm′) *adj. & adv.* during only part of the full working day.

par·ty (pärt′ē) *n.* **par·ties 1** a social event often with invited guests, for enjoyment or celebration. **2** a group of people involved in a certain activity together: *They came across a party of tourists.* **3** a national organization of people united by a common political aim.

pass (pas) *vb.* **pass·ing, passed 1** to come alongside and move beyond: *I passed her on the stairs.* **2** to run, flow, move: *Blood passes through our veins.* **3** to achieve the required standard in a test: *I passed my driving test first time.* **4** (of time) to go by; to use up in some activity: *We passed the time singing.* **5** to hand around or transfer; to circulate: *Pass the sugar around, please.* **6** in sports, to throw or kick the ball to another player on your team. **7** to vote into effect: *pass a law.* **8** to go away after a while: *Her nausea passed.* – *n.* **1** a route through a gap in a mountain range. **2** an official card or document permitting someone to enter somewhere, be absent from duty, etc. **3** in sports, a throw, kick, or hit to another player on your team. – *vb.* **pass away** to die.

pass·a·ble (pas′ə-bəl) *adj.* **1** barely adequate: *He gave a passable imitation of a chimpanzee.* **2** (of a road, etc.) able to be traveled along. – *adv.* **pass·a·bly** (pas′ə-blē).

pass·a·ge (pas′ij) *n.* **1** (also **pas·sage·way** (pas′ij-wā′)) a route through; a corridor, narrow street, or channel. **2** a section of a book or piece of music. **3** the process of passing.

pas·sen·ger (pas′ən-jər) *n.* a traveler in a vehicle driven by someone else.

pass·ing (pas′ing) *adj.* lasting only briefly.

pas·sion (pash′ən) *n.* **1** a strong emotion, for example hate, anger, or love. **2** great enthusiasm: *He has a passion for jogging.*

pas·sion·ate (pash′ə-nət) *adj.* strongly emotional; ardent.

Pass·o·ver (pas′ō′vər) *n.* an eight-day Jewish festival held in the spring, celebrating the sparing of the first-born Israelite children, and the freeing of the Israelites from Egypt.

pass·port (pas′pôrt′, pas′pōrt′) *n.* an official document issued by the government, giving proof of the holder's identity and nationality.

past (past) *adj.* **1** of a time before the present; of an earlier time. **2** over; finished: *The days when I could run that fast are past.* – *prep.* **1** up to and beyond: *She went past me.* **2** after in time or age: *It's ten past three.* – *adv.* so as to pass by: *Go past.* – *n.* the time before the present.

paste (pāst) *n.* a stiff moist mixture usually of powder and water, for example a mixture of flour and water used as a glue.

pas·tel (pas-tel′) *n.* a chalklike crayon. – *adj.* (of colors) delicately pale.

●**Pas·teur** (pas-tur′), **Louis** (1822-1895) was a French scientist who founded the science of microbiology.

pas·teur·ize (pas′chə-rīz′) *vb.* **pas·teur·iz·ing, pas·teur·ized** to kill bacteria by a heating process. – *n.* **pas·teur·i·za·tion** (pas′chə-rə-zā′shən).

pas·time (pas′tīm′) *n.* a hobby.

pas·tor (pas′tər) *n.* a member of the clergy.

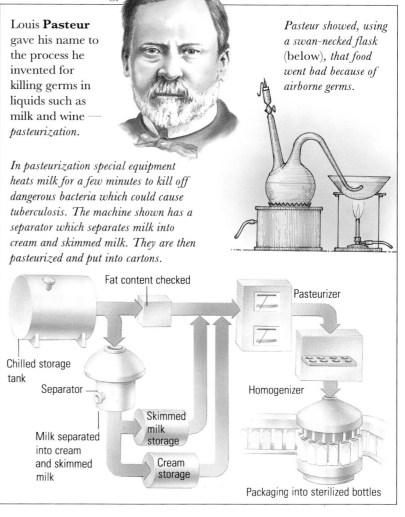

Louis **Pasteur** gave his name to the process he invented for killing germs in liquids such as milk and wine — *pasteurization.*

Pasteur showed, using a swan-necked flask (below), that food went bad because of airborne germs.

In pasteurization special equipment heats milk for a few minutes to kill off dangerous bacteria which could cause tuberculosis. The machine shown has a separator which separates milk into cream and skimmed milk. They are then pasteurized and put into cartons.

Fat content checked

Pasteurizer

Chilled storage tank

Separator

Homogenizer

Skimmed milk storage

Milk separated into cream and skimmed milk

Cream storage

Packaging into sterilized bottles

Saint Patrick, the patron saint of Ireland, was born in Britain but died in Ireland in 461 at the age of 76.

past·ry (pās′trē) *n.* **past·ries** dough made with flour, fat, and water, used for piecrusts.

pas·ture (pas′chər) *n.* an area of land suitable for the grazing of cattle, etc.

pat (pat) *vb.* **pat·ting, pat·ted** to strike lightly or affectionately with the palm of the hand.

patch (pach) *n.* **1** a piece of material sewn or glued on to cover a hole or reinforce a worn part. **2** a plot of earth: *a vegetable patch.* – *vb.* **patch·ing, patched 1** to mend by sewing patches on. **2** (*informal*) to settle a quarrel.

patch·work *n.* needlework done by sewing together pieces of contrasting fabric.

patch·y (pach′ē) *adj.* **patch·i·er, patch·i·est** forming patches; uneven or variable in quality.

pa·tel·la (pə-tel′ə) *n.* **pa·tel·lae** (pə-tel′ē) or **patellas** the triangular plate of bone covering the front of the knee joint; the kneecap.

pat·ent (pat′nt) *n.* an official license from the government granting a company the right to be the only manufacturer allowed to make and sell a particular article. – *vb.* **pat·ent·ing, pat·ent·ed** to obtain a patent for.

pa·ter·nal (pə-tur′nəl) *adj.* of, or appropriate to, a father.

path (path) *n.* (also **path·way** (path′wā′)) a track for walking.

pa·thet·ic (pə-thet′ik) *adj.* moving to pity; touching or pitiful.

pa·tience (pā′shəns) *n.* the ability to endure delay, trouble, pain, or hardship calmly: *Patience is a virtue.*

pa·tient (pā′shənt) *adj.* having or showing patience. – *n.* a person who is being treated by a doctor, dentist, etc. – *adv.* **pa·tient·ly.**

pa·tri·arch (pā′trē-ärk′) *n.* **1** the male head of a family or tribe. **2** in the Eastern Orthodox Church, a high-ranking bishop.

PATRON SAINTS

St. Andrew	Scotland	Nov. 30
St. Anthony	Lost articles	June 13
St. Cecilia	Music	Nov. 22
St. David	Wales	March 1
St. Denis	France	Oct. 9
St. George	England	April 23
St. Luke	Doctors	Oct. 18
St. Nicholas	Children	Dec. 6
St. Peter	Fishermen	June 29
St. Valentine	Sweethearts	Feb. 14

●**Pat·rick** (pa′trik)**, Saint** (A.D. 400s) is the patron saint of IRELAND.

pa·tri·ot (pā′trē-ət) *n.* someone who loves and serves his or her country devotedly.

pa·trol (pə-trōl′) *vb.* **pa·trol·ling, pa·trolled** to make a regular systematic tour of to see that there is no trouble. – *n.* a group of people performing this duty.

pa·tron (pā′trən) *n.* **1** a person who gives financial support, for example to an artist or charity. **2** a regular customer of a store, etc.

patron saint *n.* the guardian saint of a country, profession, craft, etc. See also **saints**.

pat·ter (pat′ər) *vb.* **pat·ter·ing, pat·tered** (of rain, footsteps, etc.) to make a light rapid tapping noise.

pat·tern (pat′ərn) *n.* **1** a model, guide, or set of instructions for making something. **2** a design.

pat·terned (pat′ərnd) *adj.* having a decorative design.

●**Pau·ling** (pôl′ing)**, Linus** (1901-) is an American chemist opposed to nuclear tests.

paunch (pônch, pänch) *n.* a protruding belly.

pau·per (pô′pər) *n.* a poor person.

pause (pôz) *n.* a short break in some activity, etc. – *vb.* **paus·ing, paused 1** to have a break; to stop briefly. **2** to hesitate.

pave (pāv) *vb.* **pav·ing, paved** to surface with stone slabs, cobbles, etc.: *to pave a road.*

pave·ment (pāv′mənt) *n.* a paved surface.

pa·vil·ion (pə-vil′yən) *n.* a building, often with open sides, used for amusement, shelter, or display exhibits at a trade fair, etc.

paw (pô) *n.* the foot of a mammal having four legs.

pawn¹ (pôn) *vb.* **pawn·ing, pawned** to deposit with a pawnbroker as a pledge for a sum of money borrowed.

pawn² (pôn) *n.* a chess piece of lowest value.

pawn·bro·ker (pôn′brō′kər) *n.* a person who lends money in exchange for pawned articles.

pay (pā) *vb.* **pay·ing, paid 1** to give money to in exchange for goods, services, etc. **2** to settle: *to pay a debt.* **3** to give wages or salary to. **4** to make a profit, or make as profit: *This business doesn't pay.* **5** to benefit; to be worthwhile: *It pays to be polite.* – *n.* money given or received for work, etc.; wages. – *vb.* **pay up** to pay what is due, especially reluctantly.

pay·a·ble (pā′ə-bəl) *adj.* that can or must be

paid: *Make the check payable to me.*

pay·ment (pā′mənt) *n.* **1** a sum of money paid.
2 the act of paying or process of being paid.

pay·off (pā′ôf) *n.* (*informal*) **1** the outcome of an
event. **2** a bribe.

pea (pē) *n.* the green seed of a climbing plant,
growing in pods and eaten as a vegetable.

peace (pēs) *n.* **1** freedom from war; a treaty or
agreement ending a war. **2** quietness or calm;
serenity: *At last she had found peace of mind.*

peace·ful (pēs′fəl) *adj.* **1** calm and quiet;
serene. **2** free from war, violence, or disorder.

peach (pēch) *n.* a round fruit with velvety
yellowish-pink skin, juicy yellow flesh, and a
large pit.

pea·cock (pē käk′) *n.* a bird of the pheasant
family, the male of which has magnificent tail
feathers that it can spread out like a fan.

pea·hen (pē′hen′) *n.* a female peacock.

*A peacock attracts its mates by spreading out its
spectacular tail. It looks very proud of itself — "as
proud as a peacock!"*

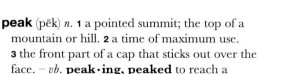

peak (pēk) *n.* **1** a pointed summit; the top of a
mountain or hill. **2** a time of maximum use.
3 the front part of a cap that sticks out over the
face. – *vb.* **peak·ing, peaked** to reach a
maximum.

peal (pēl) *n.* **1** the ringing of a bell or set of bells.
2 a burst of noise: *They heard peals of laughter.*

*Peanuts, sometimes
known as groundnuts,
grow underground. They
are covered by red, papery
skin and contained in
wrinkled yellowish pods.*

pea·nut (pē′nut′, pē′nət) *n.* an edible nutlike
seed that ripens underground in a shell.

pear (pâr) *n.* a fruit with white juicy flesh.

pearl (purl) *n.* **1** a bead of hard bluish-white
material formed by an oyster inside its shell,
prized as a gem; an imitation of this.
2 something valued or precious: *They listened
carefully to his pearls of wisdom.* – *adj.* like a pearl
in color or shape.

● **Pearl Harbor** (purl′ härbər) was a United
States naval base in Hawaii which was attacked
by the Japanese on December 7, 1941, thus
bringing the United States into WORLD WAR II.

● **Pea·ry** (pîr′ē), **Robert** (1856-1920) was an
American explorer who reached the NORTH
POLE in 1909.

peas·ant (pez′ənt) *n.* in poor agricultural
societies, a farm worker or small farmer.

peat (pēt) *n.* a material consisting of partly
rotted vegetable matter found in bogs and hilly
areas, and used dried as a fuel.

peb·ble (peb′əl) *n.* a small stone worn round
and smooth by water.

peck[1] (pek) *vb.* **peck·ing, pecked** **1** to strike,
nip, or pick up with the beak. **2** to kiss quickly.

peck[2] (pek) *n.* a unit of dry measure equalling 8
quarts or $1/4$ bushel (8.81 liters).

PRONUNCIATION SYMBOLS		
ə **a**way	lemon	focus
a	f**a**t	oi	b**oy**
ā	f**a**de	oo	f**oo**t
ä	h**o**t	o͞o	m**oo**n
âr	f**ai**r	ou	h**ou**se
e	m**e**t	th	**th**ink
ē	m**ea**n	th̲	**th**is
g	**g**et	u	c**u**t
hw	**wh**ich	ur	h**ur**t
i	f**i**n	w	**w**itch
ī	l**i**ne	y	**y**es
îr	n**ea**r	yo͞o	m**u**sic
ô	**o**ften	yoor	p**u**re
ō	n**o**te	zh	vi**s**ion

pe·cu·liar (pi-kyōōl′yər) *adj.* **1** strange; odd. **2** belonging exclusively or typically to: *This habit is peculiar to snails.*

pe·cu·li·ar·i·ty (pi-kyōō′lē-ar′ət-ē) *n.* **pe·cu·li·ar·i·ties 1** the quality of being strange or odd. **2** a distinctive feature.

ped·al (ped′l) *n.* a lever operated by the foot, for example on a machine or vehicle. – *vb.* **ped·al·ing** or **ped·al·ling, ped·aled, ped·alled** to operate by means of a pedal.

Bicycle pedals are linked to the back wheel with a chain. Pushing the pedals turns the back wheel, which moves the bicycle forward.

ped·dle (ped′l) *vb.* **ped·dling, ped·dled** to go from place to place selling goods.

ped·es·tal (ped′ə-stəl) *n.* the base on which a statue or column is mounted.

pe·des·tri·an (pə-des′trē-ən) *n.* a person traveling on foot, especially on a street.

pe·di·a·tri·cian (pēd′ē-ə-trish′ən) *n.* a doctor specializing in children's illnesses.

ped·i·gree (ped′ə-grē′) *n.* a person or animal's line of descent; a family tree.

peek (pēk) *vb.* **peek·ing, peeked** to glance briefly and secretly; to peep. – *n.* a brief glance.

peel (pēl) *vb.* **peel·ing, peeled 1** to strip the skin or rind off: *to peel an orange.* **2** (of skin, paint, etc.) to flake off in patches. – *n.* the skin or rind of vegetables or fruit.

peep¹ (pēp) *vb.* **peep·ing, peeped 1** to look quickly; to peek. **2** to emerge briefly or partially: *The sun peeped from behind the clouds.*

peep² (pēp) *n.* the faint high cry of a baby bird.

peer¹ (pîr) *n.* **1** someone who is equal in age, rank, etc.; a contemporary or companion. **2** a member of the nobility.

peer² (pîr) *vb.* **peer·ing, peered** to look hard, so as to see clearly.

peer·age (pîr′ij) *n.* the title or rank of a peer.

peg (peg) *n.* **1** a hook for a coat fixed to a wall, etc. **2** a clothespin. **3** any of several pins on a stringed instrument, turned to tune it.

pe·jor·a·tive (pə-jôr′ət-iv, pə-jär′ət-iv) *adj.* (of an expression) critical and disapproving.

Pe·kin·gese or **Pe·kin·ese** (pē′kə-nēz′, pē′kə-nēs′) *n.* a small dog with a silky coat.

● **Pe·king** (pē′king′, pā′king′). See **Beijing**.

pel·i·can (pel′ə-kən) *n.* **pelican** or **pelicans** a large water bird with a pouch in its beak.

pel·let (pel′ət) *n.* a small ball of material, for example paper, lead, etc.

pell-mell (pel-mel′) *adv.* in confused haste.

pelt¹ (pelt) *vb.* **pelt·ing, pelt·ed 1** to throw violently: *He was pelted with stones.* **2** (of rain, hail, etc.) to fall fast and heavily.

pelt² (pelt) *n.* the skin of a dead animal.

pel·vis (pel′vəs) *n.* the bony structure into which the base of the spine fits, enclosing the bowels, organs of reproduction, etc. – *adj.* **pel·vic** (pel′vik).

pen¹ (pen) *n.* a small enclosure for animals. – *vb.* **pen·ning, penned** to enclose in a pen.

pen² (pen) *n.* a writing instrument that uses ink.

pe·nal (pēn′l) *adj.* relating to punishment, especially by law.

pen·al·ty (pen′l-tē) *n.* **pen·al·ties** a punishment or disadvantage for doing wrong, breaking a contract or rule, etc.

pen·cil (pen′səl) *n.* an instrument used for writing and drawing, consisting of a wooden part containing a stick of graphite or other material.

pen·dant (pen′dənt) *n.* an ornament suspended from a neck chain, necklace, bracelet, etc.

pen·du·lum (pen′jə-ləm) *n.* any weight hung from a fixed point so as to swing freely, for example the swinging weight that regulates the movement of a clock.

● Each swing of a pendulum takes the same amount of time, no matter whether the swing is big or small. This makes pendulums useful for keeping time in clocks.

A pendulum at the top of its swing has potential energy stored in it. Gravity makes it swing, work is done, and potential energy becomes kinetic energy.

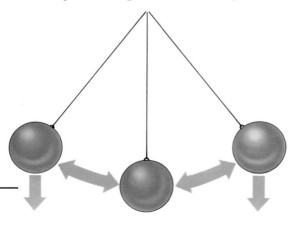

pen·e·trate (pen′ə-trāt′) *vb.* **pen·e·trat·ing, pen·e·trat·ed** to find a way in; to enter, especially with difficulty. – *n.* **pen·e·tra·bil·i·ty** (pen′ə-trə-bil′ət-ē).

pen·e·trat·ing *adj.* **1** (of a voice) loud and clear; strident. **2** (of a mind) acute; discerning. **3** (of a look) piercing; probing.

pen·guin (pen′gwən, peng′gwən) *n.* a black and white sea bird of the Antarctic and Southern Hemisphere, with webbed feet and wings adapted as flippers for swimming.

Rockhopper

Adélie

King

Emperor penguin

Penguins are swimming birds. They cannot fly. There are 18 different types of penguin.

pen·i·cil·lin (pen′ə-sil′ən) *n.* an antibiotic taken from molds, used to treat infection.

pen·in·su·la (pə-nin′sə-lə, pə-nin′chə-lə) *n.* a piece of land almost surrounded by water or projecting into water from a larger land mass.

pe·nis (pē′nəs) *n.* the male organ used for sexual intercourse and, in mammals, for urination.

pen·knife (pen′nīf′) *n.* a small pocket knife.

● **Penn** (pen), **William** (1644-1718) was an English QUAKER leader, founder of Pennsylvania.

pen·nant (pen′ənt) *n.* a small triangular flag, used on ships for identification or for signaling.

● **Penn·syl·va·nia** (pen′səl-vān′yə). See Supplement, **U.S.A.**

pen·ny (pen′ē) *n.* **pen·nies 1** in the UNITED STATES and CANADA, a coin equal to a hundredth part of one dollar. **2** in GREAT BRITAIN, a coin equal to a hundredth part of one pound.

pen·sion (pen′chən) *n.* a regular payment to a retired worker. – *vb.* **pen·sion·ing, pen·sioned** to grant a pension to.

pen·sion·er (pen′chə-nər) *n.* a person who receives a pension.

pen·ta·gon (pent′ə-gän′) *n.* **1** a shape with five sides and five angles. **2 Pentagon** the five-sided building in Washington, D. C., that is the headquarters of the United States Department of Defense.

Pen·te·cost (pent′ə-kôst′, pent′ə-käst′) *n.* **1** in the Christian Church, a festival on the seventh Sunday after EASTER. **2** the Jewish feast of Shabouth.

pent·house (pent′hous′) *n.* a luxurious apartment on the roof of a tall building.

pen·ul·ti·mate (pi-nul′tə-mət) *adj.* next to last.

pe·o·ny (pē′ə-nē) *n.* **pe·o·nies** a small shrub with large globular red, pink, or white flowers.

peo·ple (pē′pəl) *n.* **1** (*plural*) men, women, and children in general. **2** a nation, ethnic group, or race. – *vb.* **peo·pling, peo·pled** to fill a region with people; to populate.

pep·per (pep′ər) *n.* **1** a pungent seasoning prepared from the dried and crushed berries of a tropical climbing plant. **2** the red, yellow, or green fruit of several garden plants eaten as a vegetable.

pep·per·mint (pep′ər-mint′) *n.* a mint plant with a strong-tasting oil used as a flavoring.

per (pər, pur) *prep.* for each: *60 miles per hour.*

per·ceive (pər-sēv′) *vb.* **per·ceiv·ing, per·ceived 1** to observe or notice. **2** to understand, interpret, or view. – *adj.* **per·ceiv·a·ble** (pər-sē′və-bəl).

percent (pər sent′) *adv.* (symbol **%**) in every 100: *Only 40 percent of people voted.*

per·cent·age (per-sent′ij) *n.* an amount, number, or rate stated as a proportion of 100.

perch[1] (purch) *n.* a branch or other narrow support above ground for a bird to rest on. – *vb.* **perch·ing, perched** (of birds) to rest on a perch.

perch[2] (purch) *n.* **perch** or **perches** any of several edible fish with spiny fins.

per·co·late (pur′kə-lāt′) *vb.* **per·co·lat·ing, per·co·lated** to ooze, trickle, or filter.

per·cus·sion (pər-kussh′ən) *n.* musical instruments played by striking, for example drums, cymbals, xylophone, etc.

pe·ren·ni·al (pə-ren′ē-əl) *adj.* **1** (of a plant) living for at least two years. **2** constant; continual. – *n.* a perennial plant.

per·fect (pur′fikt) *adj.* **1** faultless; flawless;

PRONUNCIATION SYMBOLS			
ə	**a**way **l**emon		**fo**cus
a	**fa**t	oi	**bo**y
ā	**fa**de	oo	**fo**ot
ä	**ho**t	ōō	**moo**n
âr	**fair**	ou	**hou**se
e	**me**t	th	**think**
ē	**mea**n	<u>th</u>	<u>th</u>**is**
g	**g**et	u	**cu**t
hw	**wh**ich	ur	**hur**t
i	**fi**n	w	**w**itch
ī	**li**ne	y	**y**es
îr	**nea**r	yōō	**mu**sic
ô	**o**ften	yoor	**pure**
ō	**no**te	zh	vi**si**on

Perch are common freshwater fish. They generally swim in shoals.

303

PRONUNCIATION SYMBOLS			
ə	away lemon		focus
a	fat	oi	boy
ā	fade	oo	foot
ä	hot	ōō	moon
âr	fair	ou	house
e	met	th	think
ē	mean	t͟h	this
g	get	u	cut
hw	which	ur	hurt
i	fin	w	witch
ī	line	y	yes
îr	near	yōō	music
ô	often	yoor	pure
ō	note	zh	vision

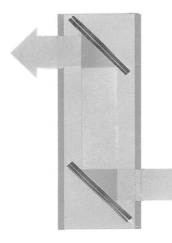

In its simplest form, a periscope is two mirrors at 45° angles near the top and bottom of a tube.

excellent; absolutely satisfactory. **2** (*informal*) absolute; utter: *She is talking perfect nonsense.* – (pər-fekt′) *vb.* **per·fect·ing, per·fect·ed** to improve to a high standard.

per·fec·tion (pər-fek′shən) *n.* **1** the state of being perfect. **2** the process of making something complete, etc.

per·form (pər-fôrm′) *vb.* **per·form·ing, per·formed 1** to carry out a task, job, action, etc. **2** to act, sing, play, dance, etc.

per·for·mance (pər-fôr′məns) *n.* **1** the performing of a play, dance, piece of music, etc. before an audience. **2** the act or process of performing a task, etc.

per·fume (pur′fyōōm′) *n.* **1** a sweet smell; a scent or fragrance. **2** a fragrant liquid.

per·haps (pər-haps′) *adv.* possibly; maybe.

per·il (per′əl) *n.* grave danger. – *adj.* **per·i·lous** (per′ə-ləs).

pe·rim·e·ter (pə-rim′ət-ər) *n.* the edge or boundary of an enclosed area or shape.

pe·ri·od (pîr′ē-əd) *n.* **1** a length of time. **2** a certain phase or stage in history, etc. **3** a woman's time of menstruation. **4** a punctuation mark (.) used at the end of a sentence or in an abbreviation.

pe·ri·od·ic (pîr′ē-äd′ik) *adj.* happening at regular intervals; occasional.

pe·ri·od·i·cal (pîr′ē-äd′i-kəl) *n.* a magazine published weekly, monthly, quarterly, etc.

per·i·scope (per′ə-skōp′) *n.* an optical instrument consisting of a tube containing mirrors so angled as to allow one to see things around corners, used especially in submerged submarines for looking above the surface.

per·ish (per′ish) *vb.* **per·ish·ing, per·ished 1** to die; to be destroyed or ruined. **2** (of materials) to decay or rot.

per·ish·a·ble (per′ish-ə-bəl) *adj.* (of food) liable to rot or go bad quickly.

perk (purk) *vb.* **perk·ing, perked** to become or make more lively: *I perked up after my bath.*

per·ma·frost (pur′mə-frôst′) *n.* land that is permanently frozen, in polar areas.

per·ma·nent (pur′mə-nənt) *adj.* lasting for ever; unlikely to alter.

per·mis·sion (per-mish′ən) *n.* consent, agreement, leave, or authorization.

per·mit (pər-mit′) *vb.* **per·mit·ting, per·mit·ted** to consent to or give permission for. – (pur′mit′, pər-mit′) *n.* a document authorizing something.

per·pen·dic·u·lar (pur′pən-dik′yə-lər) *adj.* **1** vertical; upright. **2** at right angles to.

per·pe·trate (pur′pə-trāt′) *vb.* **per·pe·trat·ing, per·pe·trat·ed** to commit or be guilty of: *to perpetrate a robbery.*

per·pe·tu·al (pər-pech′ōō-əl) *adj.* everlasting.

per·pe·tu·ate (pər-pech′ōō-āt′) *vb.* **per·pe·tu·at·ing, per·pe·tu·at·ed** to cause to last or continue.

per·se·cute (pur′si-kyōōt′) *vb.* **per·se·cut·ing, per·se·cut·ed** to oppress or torment. – *n.* **per·se·cu·tion** (pur′si-kyōō′shən).

per·se·vere (pur′sə-vîr′) *vb.* **per·se·ver·ing, per·se·vered** to keep on trying. – *n.* **per·se·ver·ance** (pur′sə-vîr′əns).

Per·sian (pur′zhən, pur′shən) *adj.* of Persia (modern IRAN), its people, or language. – *n.* **1** a native or citizen of Persia. **2** the language of Persia or IRAN.

per·sist (pər-sist′, pər-zist′) *vb.* **per·sist·ing, per·sist·ed 1** to continue in spite of resistance, discouragement, etc. **2** (of rain, etc.) to continue steadily.

per·sis·tent (pər-sis′tənt, per-zis′tənt) *adj.* **1** continuing with determination in spite of discouragement. **2** constant; endless. – *n.* **per·sis·tence** (pər-sis′təns, pər-zis′təns).

per·son (pur′sən) *n.* **1** an individual human being. **2** someone's body: *The police found drugs concealed on his person.* **3** in grammar, one of the three classes into which pronouns and verb forms fall. The **first person** describes the speaker (*I, we*), the **second person** the person addressed (*you*) and the **third person** the person(s) or thing(s) spoken of (*she, he, it, they*).

In the Arctic winter all moisture in the soil freezes. In summer the top layer may thaw. The subsoil remains permanently frozen.

The Trans-Alaska oil pipeline (below) was built on supports to prevent its thawing the permafrost.

Persia (now known as Iran, from the word "Aryan") ruled over a vast and flourishing empire from the 500s to 300s B.C. Under Darius I (reigned 521-486) Susa was its administrative center and Persepolis its magnificent center of state. Darius built roads to link all parts of his empire and encouraged trade by introducing a standard currency.

Darius I organized the empire into 20 provinces called satrapies.

The palace steps at Persepolis show people bringing gifts for the king.

A Persian foot soldier

The Parthians were a nomadic people who moved into Persia about 1000 B.C. They were famous for their way of fighting on horse-back. They would gallop away from the enemy, as if fleeing, then turn in the saddle and shoot arrows.

per·son·al (pur′snəl, purs′n-əl) *adj.* **1** coming from someone as an individual, not from a group or organization: *This is my personal opinion.* **2** done or attended to by the individual person in question, not by a substitute: *I will give it my personal attention.* **3** relating to someone's private concerns: *personal effects.*

personal computer *n.* a microcomputer.

personal pronoun *n.* in grammar, any of the pronouns representing a person or thing, for example *I, you, he, him, she, it, they, us.*

per·son·al·i·ty (pur′sə-nal′ət-ē) *n.* **per·son·al·i·ties 1** a person's nature; the qualities that give someone's character individuality. **2** a well-known person; a celebrity: *She is a television personality.*

per·son·nel (pur′sə-nel′) *n.* (*plural*) the people employed in a business, or other organization.

per·spec·tive (pər-spek′tiv) *n.* **1** the representation of objects in drawing and painting which gives a sense of depth by making them smaller the more distant they are. **2** a balanced view of a situation: *It is important to get things into perspective.*

per·spi·ra·tion (pər′spə-rā′shən) *n.* the salty moisture produced by the sweat glands of the skin.

per·spire (pər-spīr′) *vb.* **per·spir·ing, per·spired** to sweat.

per·suade (pər-swād′) *vb.* **per·suad·ing, per·suaded 1** to urge successfully: *We persuaded her to come for a walk.* **2** to convince.

per·sua·sion (pər-swā′zhən) *n.* the act of urging, coaxing, or persuading.

per·sua·sive (pər-swā′siv, pər-swā′ziv) *adj.* having the power to persuade; convincing.

per·tain (pər-tān′) *vb.* **per·tain·ing, per·tained** to concern or relate to.

per·ti·nent (purt′n-ənt) *adj.* relating to.

per·turb (pər-turb′) *vb.* **per·turb·ing, per·turbed** to make anxious or agitated.

●**Peru** (pə-roō′). See Supplement, **Countries**.

pes·si·mism (pes′ə-miz′əm) *n.* the tendency to emphasize the gloomiest aspects of anything, and to expect the worst to happen. – *n.* **pes·si·mist** (pes′ə-məst). – *adj.* **pes·si·mis·tic** (pes′ə-mis′tik).

pest (pest) *n.* **1** an insect or animal harmful to plants, food, or livestock. **2** a person or thing that is a constant nuisance.

pes·ter (pes′tər) *vb.* **pes·ter·ing, pes·tered** to annoy constantly: *Stop pestering me.*

pes·ti·cide (pes′tə-sīd) *n.* a chemical for killing insects or other pests.

pet (pet) *n.* **1** a tame animal or bird kept as a companion. **2** someone's favorite. – *adj.* **1** kept as a pet. **2** of or for pets. **3** favorite; own special. – *vb.* **pet·ting, pet·ted** to pat or stroke.

pet·al (pet′l *n.* any of the group of colored parts forming the head of a flower.

pe·ter (pēt′ər): **peter out** *vb.* **pe·ter·ing, pe·tered** to dwindle away to nothing.

Insect pests (for example locusts or Colorado beetles) are devastating. Chemicals can destroy such pests, but biological control — finding a natural predator, for instance — does less harm to other living things.

Peter's ambition was to make Russia a great European power. He had enormous energy and was constantly at work making laws, drilling troops, planning towns, and building ships.

Pharaoh comes from the word *peraa* which means "great house." This was the palace in which the pharaoh lived. Egyptians believed that each pharaoh was the same god in the shape of a different man.

●**Pe·ter** (pēt′ər), **Saint** (*died* A.D. 67) was the leader of JESUS' apostles in the New Testament and is regarded by ROMAN CATHOLICS as the first pope.

●**Pe·ter** (pēt′ər)**the Great** (1672-1725) was the czar of RUSSIA who built St. Petersburg.

pe·ti·tion (pə-tish′ən) *n.* a formal written request to an authority to take some action, signed by a large number of people.

pet·rel (pe′trəl) *n.* any of several sea birds that live far from land, especially the storm petrel.

pet·ri·fy (pe′trə-fī′) *vb.* **pet·ri·fies, pet·ri·fy·ing, pet·ri·fied 1** to terrify; to paralyze with fright: *Snakes petrify Sam.* **2** to change into stone; to become fossilized.

pet·rol (pe′trəl) *n.* (*British*) gasoline.

pe·trol·e·um (pə-trō′lē-əm) *n.* a dark oil, a mixture of hydrocarbons, found in the earth and refined into gasoline and other products.

pet·ti·coat (pet′ē-kōt′) *n.* a woman's underskirt.

pet·ty (pet′ē) *adj.* **pet·ti·er, pet·ti·est 1** of minor importance; trivial. **2** childishly spiteful.

pet·u·lant (pe′chə-lənt) *adj.* ill-tempered.

pe·tu·nia (pə-tōōn′yə, pə-tyōōn′yə) *n.* a plant native to tropical America, with white, pink, or purple funnel-shaped flowers.

pew (pyōō) *n.* one of the long benches with backs used as seating in a church.

pew·ter (pyōōt′ər) *n.* an alloy of tin and copper, and formerly tin and lead.

phan·tom (fant′əm) *n.* a ghost. – *adj.* not real.

pha·raoh (fâr′ō, fā′rō) *n.* a king of ancient EGYPT.

phar·ma·cist (fär′mə-səst) *n.* a person trained to prepare and dispense drugs and medicines.

phase (fāz) *n.* a stage or period in growth or development. – *vb.* **phas·ing, phased** to organize or carry out in stages.

pheas·ant (fez′ənt) *n.* **pheasant** or **pheasants** any of various species of long-tailed game birds.

phe·nom·e·non (fi-näm′ə-nän′) *n.* **phe·nom·e·na** (fi-näm′ə-nə) **1** something that happens or exists, especially something scientifically explainable. **2** something unusual.

phi·al (fī′əl) *n.* a little medicine bottle.

●**Phil·a·del·phi·a** (fil′ə-del′fē-ə) in Pennsylvania, is known as the "birthplace of the nation." The DECLARATION OF INDEPENDENCE was

signed there in 1776.

phi·lan·thro·py (fə-lan′thrə-pē) *n.* love for fellow human beings, especially in the form of generosity to those in need. – *adj.*
phi·lan·throp·ic (fil′ən-thräp′ik). – *n.*
phi·lan·thro·pist (fə-lan′thrə-pəst).

phi·lat·e·ly (fə-lat′l-ē) *n.* the study and collecting of postage stamps. – *n.*
phi·lat·e·list (fə-lat′l-əst).

●**Phil·ip·pines** (fil′ə-pēnz′). See Supplement, **Countries**.

phi·los·o·phy (fə-läs′ə-fē) *n.*
phi·los·o·phies 1 the search for truth and knowledge. **2** any particular system or set of beliefs.

phi·los·o·pher (fə-läs′ə-fər) *n.* a person who studies philosophy.

pho·bi·a (fō′bē-ə) *n.* a fear or hatred: *She has a phobia about spiders.* – *adj.* **pho·bic** (fō′bik).

SOME COMMON PHOBIAS	
Phobia	*A fear of*
acrophobia	*heights*
agoraphobia	*open spaces*
arachnophobia	*spiders*
aerophobia	*flying*
bibliophobia	*books*
claustrophobia	*confined spaces*
hippophobia	*horses*
hydrophobia	*water*
ornithophobia	*birds*
pyrophobia	*fire*
xenophobia	*strangers*
zoophobia	*animals*

Phoe·ni·cian (fə-nish′ən, fə-nē′shən) *adj.* of ancient Phoenicia on the coast of SYRIA, its people, colonies, language, and arts. – *n.* **1** one of the Phoenician people. **2** their language.

phoe·nix (fē′niks) *n.* in Arabian legend, a bird that every 500 years sets itself on fire and is reborn from its ashes.

phone (fōn) *n.* a telephone. – *vb.* **phon·ing, phoned** to telephone.

pho·net·ics (fə-net′iks) *n.* (*singular*) the study of speech sounds.

phos·pho·rus (fäs′fə-rəs) *n.* a poisonous, non-metallic element (symbol **P**).

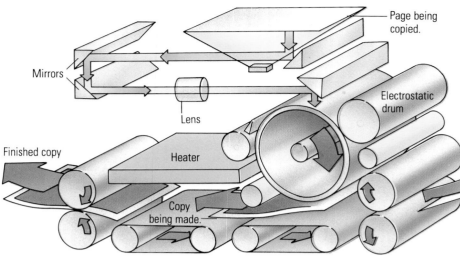

Page being copied.

Mirrors

Lens

Electrostatic drum

Finished copy

Heater

Plain copying paper

Copy being made.

Photocopying is based on the principle that static electricity attracts objects. (Rub a balloon on a wool sweater!) The electrostatic drum in a photocopier is charged with static electricity. The image to be copied is beamed onto the drum by mirrors and lenses, and it alters the pattern of the charges. The charged parts attract the toner (granules of ink). This is transferred to a blank sheet of paper and fixed in place by heat.

Charged image area

Toner dust attracted to charged image area

In a photocopier, powdered pigment called toner sticks to paper in a pattern that corresponds to electrical charges on a rotating drum.

pho·to·cop·i·er (fōt′ə-käp′ē-ər) *n.* a machine that quickly makes copies of documents, etc.

pho·to·cop·y (fōt′ə-käp′ē) *n.*
pho·to·cop·ies a copy of a document, drawing, etc. made on a photocopier. – *vb.*
pho·to·cop·ies, pho·to·copy·ing, pho·to·cop·ied to make a photocopy of.

pho·to·graph (fōt′ə-graf′) *n.* an image recorded by camera using the action of light on special film. – *vb.* **pho·to·graph·ing, pho·to·graphed** to take a photograph of.

pho·tog·ra·pher (fə-täg′rə-fər) *n.* a person who takes photographs.

pho·tog·ra·phy (fə-täg′rə-fē) *n.* the art or process of taking photographs.

pho·to·syn·the·sis (fōt′ō-sin′thə-səs) *n.* the manufacture by plants of substances essential for life from carbon dioxide and water, using the energy from sunlight.

phrase (frāz) *n.* a set of words expressing a single idea, forming part of a sentence.

phys·i·cal (fiz′i-kəl) *adj.* **1** of the body rather than the mind; bodily: *physical strength.* **2** relating to objects that can be seen or felt: *the physical world.*

phy·si·cian (fə-zish′ən) *n.* a doctor.

phys·ics (fiz′iks) *n.* (*singular*) the science that includes the study of heat, light, sound, electricity, mechanics, and magnetism. – *n.* **phys·i·cist** (fiz′ə-səst).

phy·sique (fə-zēk′) *n.* the structure of the body with regard to size, shape, and muscular development: *Gymnasts have powerful physiques.*

pi (pī) *n.* the Greek letter (π) used in mathematics as a symbol representing the ratio of the circumference of a circle to its diameter, in numerical terms it equals 3.142.

pi·an·o (pē-an′ō) *n.* **pianos** a large musical instrument with a keyboard and pedals. When the keys are pressed down they operate a set of hammers that strike tuned wires to produce sounds. – *n.* **pi·an·ist** (pē-an′əst, pē′ə-nəst).

●**Pi·cas·so** (pi-käs′ō, pi-kas′ō), **Pablo** (1881-1973) was a Spanish painter whose abstract style has greatly influenced artists of the 20th century.

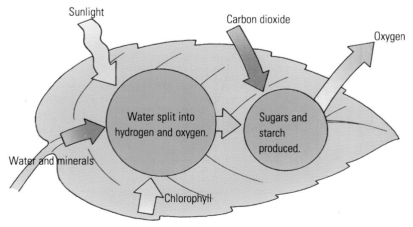

Sunlight

Carbon dioxide

Oxygen

Water split into hydrogen and oxygen.

Sugars and starch produced.

Water and minerals

Chlorophyll

Photosynthesis means "building with light." It is a remarkable and complex process in which plants combine water from the soil with carbon dioxide from the air to make food in the form of glucose sugar. The process takes place only in light and with the help of chlorophyll (the green coloring matter in plants).

Piccard's bathyscaphe, Trieste *in which he dived 40,000ft. (12,000m) in the Mariana Trench in the Pacific Ocean. It needed powerful lights to probe the inky blackness. Cameras filmed creatures that live at such depths and which had never before been seen alive.*

●**Pic·card** (pē-kär′), **Auguste** (1884-1962) was the Swiss inventor of the bathyscaphe, a submersible ship used for deep-sea exploration.

pic·co·lo (pik′ə-lō′) *n.* **piccolos** a musical wind instrument similar to, but smaller than, the flute.

pick¹ (pik) *vb.* **pick·ing, picked 1** to choose or select. **2** to gather from a plant, from a tree, etc.: *to pick fruit.* **3** to open with a device other than a key: *to pick a lock.* **4** to steal money or valuables from: *to pick someone's pocket.* – *n.* **1** (*singular* or *plural*) the best of a group: *He is the pick of the bunch.* **2** your own preferred selection: *Take your pick.* – *n.* **pick·er.** – *vb.* **pick at** to eat only small quantities of . – *vb.* **pick up 1** to lift or raise. **2** to learn or acquire: *to pick up a language.* **3** to give a lift to. **4** to fetch. **5** to increase; to improve: *The car picked up speed.*

pick² (pik) *n.* a tool with a long metal head for breaking ground, rock, ice, etc.

pick·ax or **pick·axe** (pik′aks′) *n.* Same as **pick².**

pick·et (pik′ət) *n.* **1** a person stationed outside a place of business as a striker. **2** a stake fixed in the ground, for example as part of a fence. – *vb.* **pick·et·ing, pick·et·ed** to station pickets or act as a picket.

pick·le (pik′əl) *n.* **1** a vegetable, especially a cucumber, preserved in vinegar and salt water or a tart sauce. **2** (*informal*) a mess; a quandary.

pick·pock·et (pik′päk′ət) *n.* a thief who steals from people's pockets.

pic·nic (pik′nik) *n.* a meal eaten out in the open air. – *vb.* **pic·nick·ing, pic·nicked** to have a picnic. – *n.* **pic·nick·er.**

pic·ture (pik′chər) *n.* **1** a representation of someone or something on a flat surface; a drawing, painting, or photograph. **2** a view; a mental image. – *vb.* **pic·tur·ing, pic·tured 1** to imagine or visualize; to describe vividly; to depict. **2** to represent or show in a picture or photograph.

pic·tur·esque (pik′chə-resk′) *adj.* (of places or buildings) charming to look at.

pie (pī) *n.* a sweet or savory dish, usually baked in a container, consisting of a filling with a covering of pastry: *apple pie; chicken pie.*

pie·bald (pī′bôld′) *adj.* having contrasting patches of color, especially black and white. – *n.* a piebald horse.

pie chart *n.* a diagram in which quantities are represented as parts of a circle.

piece (pēs) *n.* **1** a portion of some material or something; a bit or a section: *a piece of cake.* **2** a musical, artistic, literary, or dramatic work: *pieces of music.* **3** a coin: *a 50 cent piece.*

pier (pîr) *n.* a structure built of stone, wood, or iron, projecting into water for use as a landing-place or breakwater.

pierce (pîrs) *vb.* **pierc·ing, pierced 1** to puncture; to make a hole in with something sharp. **2** to penetrate or force a way through or into: *The wind pierced her thin clothing.*

Gloucester Old Spot • China • Poland • Tamworth

A pig's feet are called trotters. Its nose is called a snout. Above are four breeds of pig.

pig (pig) *n.* a plump short-legged farm animal raised for its meat (pork, ham, or bacon).

pi·geon (pij′ən) *n.* a bird of the dove family.

pig·let (pig′lət) *n.* a baby pig.

pig·ment (pig′mənt) *n.* any substance that gives something its color.

pig·sty (pig′stī′) *n.* **pig·sties 1** a pen on a farm for pigs. **2** any very dirty place.

pile¹ (pīl) *n.* a number of things lying on top of each other; a quantity of something in a heap. – *vb.* **pil·ing, piled** to form a pile.

pile² (pīl) *n.* the raised cropped threads that give a soft thick surface to carpet, velvet, etc.

pil·fer (pil′fər) *vb.* **pil·fer·ing, pil·fered** to steal in small quantities. – *n.* **pil·fer·er**.

pil·grim (pil′grəm) *n.* a person who journeys to a holy place as an act of religious faith.

pil·grim·age (pil′grə-mij) *n.* a journey to a shrine or other holy place, or to a place celebrated or made special by its associations.

The Pilgrim Fathers left England to escape persecution for their Protestant faith. Their disciplined lives and modest ways deeply influenced American life.

● **Pilgrims** members of a sect of PURITANS who on September 6, 1620 sailed from Plymouth, England in the *Mayflower* on a nine-week journey. They landed at what is now Plymouth Rock in Massachusetts.

pill (pil) *n.* a small tablet of medicine.

pil·lar (pil′ər) *n.* a vertical post serving as a support; a column.

pil·lion (pil′yən) *n.* a seat for a passenger on a motorcycle or horse, behind the rider.

pil·low (pil′ō) *n.* a cushion for the head, especially a large rectangular one on a bed.

pil·low·case (pil′ō-kās′) *n.* [also **pil·low·slip** (pil′ō-slip′)] a washable cover for a pillow.

pi·lot (pī′lət) *n.* **1** a person who flies an aircraft. **2** a person employed to conduct or steer ships into and out of harbor. – *adj.* serving as a first test; experimental. – *vb.* **pi·lot·ing, pi·lot·ed** to act as pilot to.

pim·ple (pim′pəl) *n.* a small swelling on the skin; a spot.

pin (pin) *n.* **1** a short stainless steel implement with a sharp point and small round head, for fastening, attaching, etc., used especially in clothing. **2** a piece of jewelry or an emblem fastened with a pin. **3** in bowling, a club-shaped object set upright for toppling with a ball. – *vb.* **pin·ning, pinned 1** to secure with a pin. **2** to hold fast or trap.

pin·a·fore (pin′ə-fôr′, pin′ə-fōr′) *n.* an apronlike dress worn over another dress.

pin·cers (pin′sərz, pin′chərz) *n.* (*plural*) **1** a hinged tool with clawlike jaws for gripping things. **2** the hinged end of a crab's or lobster's claw, adapted for gripping.

pinch (pinch) *vb.* **pinch·ing, pinched 1** to squeeze or nip flesh between thumb and finger; to squeeze painfully. **2** (*informal*) to steal. – *n.* **1** an act of pinching; a nip or squeeze. **2** a quantity, as of salt, that can be held between thumb and finger; a small amount.

pine¹ (pīn) *n.* a cone-bearing evergreen tree with dark green needlelike leaves.

pine² (pīn) *vb.* **pin·ing, pined** to long or yearn.

pine·ap·ple (pī′nap′əl) *n.* a large tropical fruit with juicy yellow flesh.

pink (pingk) *n.* **1** a color between red and white. **2** a type of plant with fragrant red, pink, or multiple-colored flowers. – *adj.* of the color pink.

pink·ie or **pink·y** (ping′kē) *n.* **pink·ies** the little finger.

pint (pīnt) *n.* a unit of liquid measure equal to one-eighth of a gallon or about 0.473 of a liter.

pi·o·neer (pī′ə-nîr′) *n.* an explorer of unknown lands; someone who does something that no one has done before in a particular field or discipline: *The Wright Brothers were pioneers in the history of flight.* – *vb.* **pi·o·neer·ing, pi·o·neered** to explore and open up a route, etc.; to try out or develop a new technique, etc.

pi·ous (pī′əs) *adj.* religiously devout.

pip (pip) *n.* the small seed of a fruit such as an apple, pear, orange, or grape.

pipe (pīp) *n.* **1** a hollow tube for water, gas, oil, etc. to flow along. **2** a little bowl with a hollow stem for smoking tobacco, etc. **3** a wind instrument consisting of a simple wooden or metal tube. – *vb.* **pip·ing, piped 1** to move through pipes: *Gas was piped to the house.* **2** to play on a pipe or on the bagpipes. – *vb.* **pipe down** (*informal*) to stop talking; to be quiet.

pipe·line (pī′plīn′) *n.* a series of connected pipes laid to convey gas, water, oil, etc.

Pineapples are so named because they look like pine cones. The plants grow to a height of just over 3ft. (1m), bearing long, rough-edged, and sharp-pointed leaves, from the center of which grow the flower stem. This develops into the fruit.

pip·er *n.* a player of a pipe or the bagpipes.

pi·ran·ha (pə-rän′ə) *n.* a carnivorous freshwater fish of SOUTH AMERICA.

pi·rate (pī′rət) *n.* someone who attacks and robs ships at sea. − *vb.* **pi·rat·ing, pi·rat·ed** to publish or reproduce without legal permission.− *n.* **pi·ra·cy** (pī′rə-sē).

●**Pi·sa** (pē′zə) is a city in ITALY, famous for its leaning tower.

Pis·ces (pī′sēz′) *n.* See **zodiac**.

pis·til (pis′təl) *n.* the female, seed-producing part of a flower.

pis·tol (pis′təl) *n.* a small gun held in one hand.

pis·ton (pis′tən) *n.* in engines, a disk or solid cylinder that slides within a hollow cylinder.

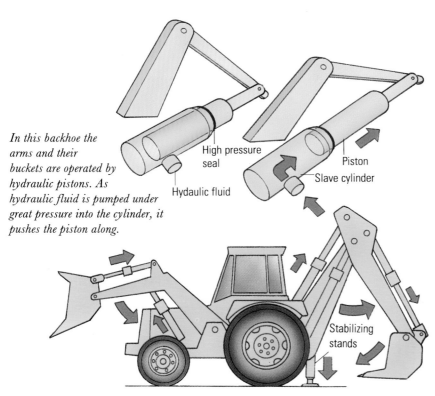

In this backhoe the arms and their buckets are operated by hydraulic pistons. As hydraulic fluid is pumped under great pressure into the cylinder, it pushes the piston along.

High pressure seal

Hydaulic fluid

Piston

Slave cylinder

Stabilizing stands

pit¹ (pit) *n.* **1** a big deep hole in the ground. **2** a coal mine. − *vb.* **pit·ting, pit·ted 1** to set or match in competition or opposition: *He was pitted against a tough opponent.* **2** mark with scars or holes: *The moon is pitted with craters.*

pit² (pit) *n.* the stone in a peach, plum, etc. − *vb.* **pit·ting, pit·ted** to remove the pit from.

pitch¹ (pich) *vb.* **pitch·ing, pitched 1** to set up: *to pitch a tent.* **2** to throw or fling. **3** (in baseball) to throw a ball to the batter. **4** to fall heavily forward. **5** (of a ship) to move around violently. − *n.* **1** the toss of a baseball to a batter. **2** a degree of intensity; a level: *The noise reached a deafening pitch.* **3** the angle of steepness of a slope: *The roof had a steep pitch.* **4** in music, the highness or lowness of a note.

pitch² (pich) *n.* a thick black substance obtained from tar, used for waterproofing ships, etc.

pitch·er¹ (pich′ər) *n.* a container for pouring liquids with a handle and a spout.

pitch·er² (pich′ər) *n.* a player in baseball who throws the ball to the batter.

pitch·fork (pich′fôrk′) *n.* a long-handled fork with sharp prongs, for tossing hay.

pit·fall (pit′fôl′) *n.* a hidden danger.

pit·i·ful (pit′ə-fəl) *adj.* **1** arousing pity; wretched or pathetic. **2** sadly inadequate or ineffective.

pit·i·less (pit′i-ləs) *adj.* showing no pity; cruel.

●**Pitts·burgh** (pits′burg′) in Pennsylvania, is the "steel capital" of the UNITED STATES.

pit·y (pit′ē) *n.* a feeling of sorrow for the troubles and sufferings of others; compassion. − *vb.* **pit·ies, pit·y·ing, pit·i·ed** to feel or show pity for. − *adj.* **pit·y·ing**.

piv·ot (piv′ət) *n.* the central point around which something turns, swivels, or revolves. − *vb.* **piv·ot·ing, piv·ot·ed** to turn or revolve.

piz·za (pēt′sə) *n.* a circle of dough spread with cheese, tomatoes, etc. and baked in an oven.

place (plās) *n.* **1** an area, region, district, etc.; a country, city, town, village, building, room, etc. **2** a seat or space at a table. **3** something or someone's usual position: *Put it back in its place!* **4** a point reached, for example in a conversation or a book: *The end of the chapter is a good place to stop.* **5** a position within an order, for example of competitors in a contest: *Pete finished in third place.*

plac·id (plas′əd) *adj.* calm; tranquil.

pla·gia·rize (plā′jə-rīz′) *vb.* **pla·gia·riz·ing, pla·gia·rized** to steal ideas from someone else's work, and use them as if they were one's own. − *n.* **pla·gia·rism** (plā′jə-riz′əm).

plague (plāg) *n.* **1** any of several highly infectious diseases which tend to occur on a large scale. **2** an overwhelming invasion by something unwelcome: *The crops were destroyed by a plague of locusts.* − *vb.* **plagu·ing, plagued** to afflict: *She is plagued by headaches.*

In the 1300s, a form of **plague** called the Black Death killed a quarter of the people of Europe. Plague is given to people by fleas from infected rats.

At night carts were loaded with corpses to be taken away for burial.

Artists depicted death in such forms as a skeleton on horseback.

plain (plān) *adj.* **1** all of one color; having no pattern or decoration. **2** simple; unsophisticated; without improvement: *We eat very plain food.* **3** obvious; clear; straightforward; direct: *Let me speak in plain language.* – *n.* (also in *plural*) a large level expanse of land.

plain sailing *n.* easy, unproblematic progress.

● **Plains Indians**, who traditionally lived on the grassy plains of NORTH AMERICA, were until the 1600s mainly nomadic hunters and gatherers. They hunted buffalo on foot. When the Spanish introduced horses, the Plains Indians could follow buffalo with ease. Later Plains Indians fought many battles with the United States Army, which was protecting settlers heading west across traditional NATIVE AMERICAN hunting grounds.

plait (plāt, plat) *vb.* **plait·ing, plait·ed** to arrange hair by interweaving three or more lengths. – *n.* a length of interwoven hair or other material.

plan (plan) *n.* **1** a thought-out arrangement or method for doing something. **2** a drawing or diagram of a floor of a house, the streets of a town, etc. done as though from above. – *vb.* **plan·ning, planned 1** to devise a scheme for; to prepare; to make plans: *It is important to plan ahead.* **2** to intend: *We planned on spending two weeks away.*

plane[1] (plān) *n.* an airplane.

plane[2] (plān) *n.* **1** a level surface. **2** a level or standard: *He is on a higher intellectual plane.*

plane[3] (plān) *n.* a carpenter's tool for smoothing wood. – *vb.* **plan·ing, planed** to make smooth with a plane.

plan·et (plan′ət) *n.* **1** any of the nine heavenly bodies – Mercury, Venus, Earth, Mars, Jupiter, Saturn, Uranus, Neptune and Pluto – that revolve around the sun. **2** any similar body revolving round any star. – *adj.* **plan·e·tar·y** (plan′ə-ter′ē).

plan·e·tar·i·um (plan′ə-ter′ē-əm) *n.* **planetariums** or **plan·e·tar·i·a** (plan′ə-ter′ē-ə) a building housing an apparatus that shows the motion of the planets by means of images projected on to a domed ceiling.

plank (plangk) *n.* a long flat piece of timber.

plank·ton (plangk′tən) *n.* tiny plants and animals that drift about near the water surface, in oceans or lakes: *Many sea creatures depend on plankton for food.*

PLANET FACTS
Mercury is the planet nearest the Sun.
Venus is the hottest planet, but hidden by clouds.
Earth is the only planet with air, water, and life.
Mars is known as the "red planet."
Jupiter is twice the size of all the other planets.
Saturn is famous for its rings.
Uranus was the first planet discovered by telescope.
Neptune's year lasts 165 Earth years.
Pluto is 40 times as far from the Sun as Earth.

The Native Americans depended on huge herds of buffalo (bison) for food, clothing, shelter, and fuel. When the bison were reduced to near extinction by the white settlers, the Native Americans succumbed. The remains of the Plains nations were forced on to reservations, often on poor land.

plant (plant) *n.* **1** any member of the vegetable kingdom; any living thing that grows from the ground, having a stem, root, and leaves. **2** a factory, its buildings and equipment. – *vb.* **plant·ing, plant·ed** to put seeds or plants into the ground to grow.

●**Plan·tag·e·net** (plan-taj′ə-nət) is the name applied to English kings from 1154 to 1483.

plas·ma (plaz′mə) *n.* the liquid content of blood, in which the blood cells are suspended.

plas·ter (plas′tər) *n.* a material consisting of lime, sand, and water, that is applied to walls when soft, and dries to form a hard smooth surface. – *vb.* **plas·ter·ing, plas·tered 1** to apply plaster to. **2** to coat or spread thickly.

plas·tic (plas′tik) *n.* any of many synthetic materials that can be molded to any shape when soft. – *adj.* made of plastic.

plastic surgery *n.* surgery to repair or replace damaged flesh, or to improve the appearance, especially of the face. – *n.* **plastic surgeon.**

Four varieties of tulip (below). The red flower is a common tulip; the other three are new cross-bred varieties.

plate (plāt) *n.* **1** a shallow dish for serving food on or eating food off. **2** a sheet of metal, glass, or other rigid material. **3** armor made from metal plate. **4** an illustration in a book.

pla·teau (pla-tō′, pla′tō′) *n.* **plateaus** (pla-tōz′, pla′tōz′) or **pla·teaux** an area of high land, more or less uniformly level.

plat·form (plat′fôrm′) *n.* **1** a raised floor for speakers, performers, etc. **2** the raised walkway alongside the track at a railroad station. **3** a floating structure moored to the seabed, for drilling oil, marine research, etc.

plat·i·num (plat′n-əm) *n.* an element (symbol **Pt**), a heavy silvery-white precious metal.

plat·i·tude (plat′ə-tōōd′, plat′ə-tyōōd′) *n.* an empty and unoriginal comment.

●**Pla·to** (plāt′ō) (429-347 B.C.) was a Greek philosopher. He believed the things we see around us are only poor copies of perfect things in an ideal world.

plat·y·pus (plat′i-pəs, plat′i-poos′) *n.* **platypuses** (also **duck-billed platypus**) a furry Australian egg-laying water mammal, with a ducklike beak and webbed feet.

play (plā) *vb.* **play·ing, played 1** to amuse oneself with games and toys; to have fun. **2** to fiddle or meddle: *He was playing with my emotions.* **3** to take part in: *to play tennis.* **4** to do for fun: *My sister played a trick on me.* **5** to act in a play, etc.; to perform: *He played the role of Hamlet.* **6** to perform music on: *to play the violin.* **7** to turn on so as to watch or listen: *We played the radio.* – *n.* **1** recreation; playing games. **2** a dramatic piece for the stage, or a performance of it. **3** a turn to move in a game.

play·er (plā′ər) *n.* **1** a participant in a game or sport. **2** a performer on a musical instrument.

play·ful (plā′fəl) *adj.* **1** full of fun. **2** humorous.

play·ground (plā′ground′) *n.* an area for children's play.

play·wright (plā′rīt′) *n.* an author of a play.

plea (plē) *n.* **1** an earnest appeal: *Listen to her pleas for help.* **2** a statement of guilty or not guilty made in a court of law by the defendant.

plead (plēd) *vb.* **plead·ing, plead·ed** or **pled** (pled) **1** to appeal earnestly: *The captives pleaded for their freedom.* **2** (of an accused person) to state in a court of law

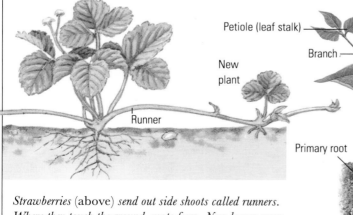

All our food ultimately comes from **plants** (meat comes from plant-eating animals). There are more than 335,000 different kinds of plant. They are placed in different groups such as algae, mosses, and flowering plants. Plants include the biggest living things, the giant redwood trees of California.

Terminal bud

Stem

Petiole (leaf stalk)

Branch

New plant

Runner

Primary root

Strawberries (above) *send out side shoots called runners. Where they touch the ground, roots form. New leaves grow and the runner dies away.*

that you are guilty or not guilty. **3** to argue in defense of.

plea·sant (plez′ənt) *adj.* **1** giving pleasure; enjoyable; agreeable. **2** (of a person) friendly.

please (plēz) *vb.* **pleas·ing, pleased** to give satisfaction, pleasure, or enjoyment; to be agreeable to. – *adv.* used politely to accompany a request, order, etc.: *Pass the salt, please.*

pleased (plēzd) *adj.* happy; satisfied; glad.

plea·sur·a·ble (plezh′ə-rə-bəl) *adj.* enjoyable; pleasant.

plea·sure (plezh′ər, plā′zhər) *n.* **1** a feeling of enjoyment or satisfaction: *I take pleasure in my surroundings.* **2** an enjoyable activity. – *adj.* used for or done for pleasure: *a pleasure trip.*

pleat (plēt) *n.* a fold sewn or pressed into cloth, etc. – *vb.* **pleat·ing, pleat·ed** to make pleats in. – *adj.* **pleat·ed.**

pledge (plej) *n.* **1** a solemn promise. **2** symbol. – *vb.* **pledg·ing, pledged** to promise.

plen·ti·ful (plent′i-fəl) *adj.* in good supply.

plen·ty (plent′ē) *pron.* **1** enough, or more than enough. **2** a lot: *Plenty of folks would agree.* – *n.* wealth or sufficiency: *We live in times of plenty.*

pleu·ri·sy (ploor′ə-sē) *n.* an illness in which the lungs become inflamed.

The platypus and the spiny anteater are the only members of the most primitive order of living mammals the monotremata *(egg-laying mammals). They are found only in Australia.*

pli·ers (plī′ərz) *n.* (*plural*) a hinged tool with jaws for gripping, bending, or cutting wire, etc.

plod (pläd) *vb.* **plod·ding, plod·ded** **1** to walk slowly with a heavy tread. **2** to work slowly, methodically, and thoroughly. – *n.* **plod·der.**

plot¹ (plät) *n.* **1** a secret plan; a conspiracy. **2** the story of a play, movie, novel, etc. – *vb.* **plot·ting, plot·ted** **1** to plan secretly. **2** to chart or make a diagram of.

plot² (plät) *n.* a piece of ground for various uses.

plo·ver (pluv′ər, plō′vər) *n.* any of various seashore birds, most with long wings and a short straight beak.

plow or **plough** (plou) *n.* a farm tool with blades used for turning up the soil in ridges and furrows. – *vb.* **plow·ing, plowed** to turn over soil with a plow.

pluck (pluk) *vb.* **pluck·ing, plucked** **1** to pull the feathers off. **2** to pick from a plant or tree. **3** to remove by pulling: *She plucked out her gray hairs.* **4** to play the strings using the fingers or a pick. – *n.* courage.

plug (plug) *n.* **1** a piece of rubber, plastic, etc. shaped to fit a hole as a stopper, for example in a bath or sink. **2** the device with metal prongs that is fitted to the end of the cord of an electrical appliance and is pushed into a socket to connect with the power supply. – *vb.* **plug·ging, plugged** **1** to stop or block with something. **2** (*informal*) to give favorable publicity to.

plum (plum) *n.* an oval red, purple, green, or yellow fruit with soft juicy flesh and a pit.

plum·age (ploo′mij) *n.* a bird's feathers.

plum·ber (plum′ər) *n.* a person who fits and repairs water pipes, heating systems, baths, etc.

plume (ploom) *n.* **1** a large feather. **2** a curling column of smoke, etc.

plump (plump) *adj.* rounded and somewhat fat.

plun·der (plun′dər) *vb.* **plun·der·ing, plun·dered** to steal valuable goods, or loot a place, especially during a war; to rob or ransack. – *n.* the goods plundered; loot; booty.

plunge (plunj) *vb.* **plung·ing, plunged** **1** to dive, throw oneself or fall: *He plunged into the pool.* **2** to involve oneself rapidly and enthusiastically. – *n.* an act of plunging; a dive.

plung·er (plun′jər) *n.* a rubber cup at the end of a long handle, used to clear blocked drains.

plu·ral (ploor′əl) *n.* the form of a noun, pronoun, or verb, etc. used for two or more people or things. For example, the plural of *house* is *houses* and the plural of *mouse* is *mice.*

plus (plus) *prep.* **1** with the addition of: *2 plus 5 equals 7.* **2** in combination with: *Bad luck, plus his own obstinacy, brought about his downfall.* – *n.* **pluses** (also **plus sign**) the symbol (+) meaning addition or positive value.

● **Plu·to**¹ (ploot′ō). See **Myths and Legends**.

● **Pluto**² (ploot′ō) is a planet. It is farther away from the sun than any of the other planets.

PLURALS

The plural in English is usually formed by adding an *s* to a noun, as in book, *books*; hand, *hands*. Words ending in *ch, s, sh, x,* and *z* add *es* for the plural, as in watch, *watches*; bus, *buses*; box, *boxes.*

When a noun ends in *y* with a consonant before it, the *y* is changed into an *i*, as in baby, *babies*; lady, *ladies*. If a vowel comes before the *y*, the plural usually remains *s*, as in boy, *boys*; tray, *trays*. Most nouns ending in *f* or *fe* change the *f* or *fe* into *v* and add *es*, as in leaf, *leaves*; wolf, *wolves*. There are exceptions: the following words keep the *f* and add *s*: belief, chief, reef, roof. Common words ending in *o* take *es* as a plural, as in cargo, *cargoes*; potato, *potatoes*. But there are many that simply add *s*: commando, *commandos.*

There are some irregular plurals. Certain words such as *deer, cod, sheep, aircraft* remain the same, whether singular or plural. A few words form their plural by adding *en*, as in ox, *oxen*. And some other words form the plural by changing the vowels in the middle of the word, as in foot, *feet*; tooth, *teeth.*

plu·to·ni·um (ploo-tō′nē-əm) *n.* a radioactive metallic element (symbol **Pu**).

ply (plī) *n.* **plies** thickness of yarn, rope, or wood, measured by the number of strands or layers that compose it.

ply·wood (plī′wood′) *n.* wood made up of thin layers glued together.

P.M. *abbreviation* for *post meridiem* (Latin), after midday; in the afternoon.

pneu·mat·ic (noo-mat′ik, nyoo-mat′ik) *adj.* containing or inflated with air: *pneumatic tires.*

pneu·mo·nia (noo-mōn′yə, nyoo-mōn′yə) *n.* a serious illness that affects the lungs.

poach¹ (pōch) *vb.* **poach·ing, poached 1** to cook in boiling water: *to poach an egg.* **2** to simmer in milk or other liquid: *to poach fish.*

poach² (pōch) *vb.* **poach·ing, poached** to catch fish, etc. illegally. – *n.* **poach·er.**

pock·et (pak′ət) *n.* an extra piece sewn into or onto a garment to form an enclosed section for carrying things in. – *adj.* small enough to be carried in a pocket; smaller than standard.

pod (pad) *n.* the long seedcase of a pea, etc.

● **Poe** (pō), **Edgar Allan** (1809-1849) was an American poet and story writer.

po·em (pō′əm, pō′im) *n.* a piece of writing in verse, sometimes with rhymes.

po·et (pō′ət, pō′it) *n.* a writer of poems.

po·et·ic (pō-et′ik) *adj.* **1** of, or relating to, poets or poetry. **2** having grace or beauty.

po·et·ry (pō′ə-trē, pō′i-trē) *n.* **1** the art of composing poems. **2** poems collectively.

● Almost all poetry uses meter (rhythm), and much of it uses rhyme. Other techniques are alliteration (words beginning with the same sound) and assonance (words with the same vowel sounds). The main kinds of poetry are lyric (dealing with personal emotion), dramatic (as in plays), and narrative (as in ballads and epics).

point (point) *n.* **1** a sharp end or tip: *She sharpened the point of her pencil.* **2** a dot, for example inserted before a decimal fraction, as in *2.1* or a period. **3** a position, place, or location: *He was posted at the lookout point.* **4** a stage, temperature, etc.: *The water reached boiling point.* **5** aim or intention: *That is the point of this procedure.* **6** a unit or mark in scoring: *You have scored 11 points.* **7** any of the 32 directions marked on a compass. – *vb.*

point·ing, point·ed 1 to aim: *He pointed the camera at them.* **2** to extend a finger toward someone or something, so as to direct attention there; (of a sign, etc.) to indicate a certain direction. **3** to face in a certain direction: *She lay with toes pointing upward.* **4** to indicate or suggest. – **beside the point** not relevant or important.

point·er (point′ər) *n.* **1** a rod, finger, or needle used to point at or indicate something. **2** a breed of dog used for hunting.

point of view *n.* **points of view** someone's own way of seeing something.

poise (poiz) *n.* self-confidence, calm.

poi·son (poi′zən) *n.* a substance that causes illness or death when swallowed or absorbed into the body. – *vb.* **poi·son·ing, poi·soned** to harm or kill with poison; to pollute.

poi·son·ous (poi′zə-nəs) *adj.* **1** liable to cause injury or death if swallowed or absorbed. **2** producing, or able to inject, a poison.

The little golden poison-arrow frog is the deadliest of animals.

Spiders are killers. They have sharp curved fangs for stabbing their prey. Poison is squirted through a tube in the fang into the prey's body.

Poison tube | Poison gland | Small teeth | Curved fang

The blue-ringed octopus lives in the seas around Australia. Its colored rings warn that its bite is deadly.

POET'S CORNER
Some of the terms used in poetry:
ballad a poem describing a historical or legendary event.
epic a long narrative poem about heroic or legendary people.
foot a unit of two or more syllables forming part of a poem's meter.
limerick a kind of nonsense verse in five lines.
meter the pattern and rhythm of poetry.
ode a medium-length poem, usually in praise of something.
sonnet a 14-lined poem.

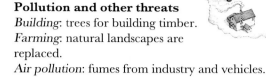

Pollution and other threats
Building: trees for building timber.
Farming: natural landscapes are replaced.
Air pollution: fumes from industry and vehicles.

Water pollution: outfalls from factories and sewage works spread dangerous chemicals in rivers and seas.
Land "reclamation": habitat loss through changing marsh, mudflats, or desert into farmland.

poke (pōk) *vb.* **pok·ing, poked 1** to thrust, prod, or jab. **2** to project. – *n.* a prod.

po·ker (pō′kər) *n.* a metal rod for stirring a fire.

●**Po·land** (pō′lənd). See Supplement, **Countries**.

po·lar (pō′lər) *adj.* relating to the earth's NORTH or SOUTH POLE or the regions around them.

polar bear *n.* a white bear found in the ARCTIC.

pole¹ (pōl) *n.* **1** (also **Pole**) either end of the earth's axis: *We flew over the North Pole.* **2** either end of a magnet.

pole² (pōl) *n.* a rod, especially fixed in the ground as a support.

pole·cat (pōl′kat′) *n.* **1** a dark-brown animal of the weasel family. **2** a skunk.

po·lice (pə-lēs′) *n.* (*plural*) the body of men and women employed by the government of a locality to keep order, enforce the law, prevent crime, etc. – *vb.* **po·lic·ing, po·liced** to keep law and order using the police, army, etc.

po·lice·man (pə-lēs′mən), **po·lice·men** (pə-lēs′mən) *n.* a member of a police force.

po·lice·wom·an (pə-lēs′woom′ən), **po·lice·wom·en** (pə-lēs′wim′ən) *n.* a member of a police force.

pol·i·cy (päl′ə-sē) *n.* **pol·i·cies** a plan of action, decided on by a body or individual.

po·li·o (pō′lē-ō′) *n.* a viral disease of the brain and spinal cord. Polio is a shortened form of **po·li·o·my·e·li·tis** (pō′lē-ō′mī′ə-līt′əs).

Po·lish (pō′lish) *adj.* of, or relating to, POLAND, its language, culture, or people. – *n.* the language of POLAND.

pol·ish (päl′ish) *vb.* **pol·ish·ing, pol·ished**
1 to make or become smooth and glossy by rubbing. **2** to improve or perfect: *She polished up her French for her interview.* – *n.* a substance used for polishing surfaces.

po·lite (pä-līt′) *adj.* having good manners.

po·lit·i·cal (pə-lit′i-kəl) *adj.* of or relating to government, public affairs, or politics.

pol·i·ti·cian (päl′ə-tish′ən) *n.* someone engaged in politics.

pol·i·tics (päl′ə-tiks′) *n.* (*singular*) the science or business of government.

poll (pōl) *n.* **1** (in *plural*) a political election. **2** the votes cast at an election. **3** (also **opinion poll**) a survey of public opinion.

pol·len (päl′ən) *n.* the fine powder produced by flowers in order to fertilize other flowers.

pol·li·nate (päl′ə-nāt′) *vb.* **pol·li·nat·ing, pol·li·nat·ed** to carry pollen out of or to.

pol·lute (pə-loot′) *vb.* **pol·lut·ing, pol·lut·ed** to make dirty or dangerous with harmful substances; to make impure. – *n.* & *adj.* **pol·lut·ant** (pə-loot′nə). – *n.* **pol·lu·tion** (pə-loo′shən).

po·lo (pō′lō) *n.* a ball game played on horseback using long-handled hammers to propel the ball along the ground.

poly- *prefix* many or much: *polytechnic.*

●**Pol·y·ne·sia** (päl′ə-nē′zhə), meaning "many islands," is one of the three divisions of the islands in the PACIFIC. The other two are Melanesia and Micronesia.

pol·y·syl·la·ble (päl′i-sil′ə-bəl) *n.* a word of three or more syllables.

pol·y·un·sa·tu·rat·ed (päl′ē-un′sach′ə-rāt′əd) *adj.* (of oils and fats) free of cholesterol.

PRONUNCIATION SYMBOLS		
ə **a**way	l**e**mon	f**o**cus
a f**a**t	oi	b**oy**
ā f**a**de	oo	f**oo**t
ä h**o**t	ōō	m**oo**n
âr f**air**	ou	h**ou**se
e m**e**t	th	**th**ink
ē m**ea**n	<u>th</u>	**th**is
g **g**et	u	c**u**t
hw **wh**ich	ur	h**ur**t
i f**i**n	w	**w**itch
ī l**i**ne	y	**y**es
îr n**ear**	yōō	m**u**sic
ô **o**ften	yoor	p**u**re
ō n**o**te	zh	vi**si**on

pom·e·gran·ate (päm′ə-gran′ət) *n.* a hard, round seedy fruit with red juicy flesh.

pomp (pämp) *n.* ceremonial grandeur.

● **Pom·pei·i** (päm-pā′) was a Roman town near Naples, ITALY, that was buried in volcanic ash from Vesuvius in A.D. 79.

pom·pous (päm′pəs) *adj.* self-important.

pon·cho (pän′chō) *n.* **ponchos** a garment like a blanket with a hole for the head.

pond (pänd) *n.* a small area of water.

pon·der (pän′dər) *vb.* **pon·der·ing, pon·dered** to consider or contemplate.

pon·der·ous (pän′də-rəs) *adj.* laborious; slow.

pon·tiff (pänt′əf) *n.* a title for the POPE.

po·ny (pō′nē) *n.* **po·nies** a small horse of any of several small breeds.

● **Po·ny Ex·press** a system of delivering mail by horseback in the United States during the 1860s that used a relay of riders and horses.

poo·dle (pōōd′l) *n.* a breed of dog with a curly coat, often clipped in an elaborate style.

On August 24, A.D. 79, a cloud appeared over the Roman town of Pompeii. Moments later a massive explosion blew the top off the nearby volcano, Mt. Vesuvius. The town was buried under 220ft. (67m) of ash and 2,000 people died of suffocation from the fumes. Pompeii was forgotten until it was rediscovered in the 1700s.

pool¹ (pōōl) *n.* **1** a small area of still water: *We played in the rock pools.* **2** a swimming pool.

pool² (pōōl) *n.* **1** a collection of money, vehicles, etc. shared by several people: *She is one of the secretaries in the typing pool.* **2** a game like billiards played with a white ball and numbered colored balls.

poor (poor, pōr) *adj.* **1** not having enough money to live comfortably. **2** not well supplied with: *a country poor in minerals.* **3** not good; weak; unsatisfactory: *a poor response.*

poor·ly (poor′lē, pōr′lē) *adv.* not well; badly. – *adj.* (*informal*) ill.

pop¹ (päp) *n.* **1** a sharp, explosive noise, like that of a cork coming out of a bottle. **2** same as **soda³**. – *vb.* **pop·ping, popped 1** to make a popping noise. **2** to spring out; to protrude: *His eyes popped with surprise.* **3** to go quickly: *I′ll just pop next door.*

pop² (päp) *n.* (also **pop music**) modern music, usually with a strong beat.

pop·corn (päp′kôrn′) *n.* a variety of corn with kernels that pop open when heated.

pope or **Pope** (pōp) *n.* the bishop of Rome, the head of the ROMAN CATHOLIC Church.

pop·lar (päp′lər) *n.* a tall slender tree.

pop·py (päp′ē) *n.* **pop·pies** a plant with large scarlet flowers and a hairy wiry stem.

pop·u·lace (päp′yə-ləs) *n.* (*plural*) the mass of ordinary citizens; the common people.

pop·u·lar (päp′yə-lər) *adj.* **1** liked or enjoyed by most people. **2** catering to the tastes and abilities of ordinary people: *He has written a popular history of science.*
　– *n.* **pop·u·lar·i·ty** (päp′yə-ler′ət-ē).

pop·u·lar·ize (päp′yə-lə-rīz′) *vb.* **pop·u·lar·iz·ing, pop·u·lar·ized** to make popular.

pop·u·late (päp′yə-lāt′) *vb.* **pop·u·lat·ing, pop·u·lat·ed** to inhabit or live in.

pop·u·la·tion (päp′yə-lā′shən) *n.* **1** all the people living in a particular country, area, etc. **2** the number of people living in a particular area, etc.: *The city has a population of two million.*

por·ce·lain (pôr′sə-lən) *n.* a fine earthenware, used to make crockery and ornaments.

porch (pôrch, pōrch) *n.* a structure forming a covered entrance to the doorway of a building.

por·cu·pine (pôr′kyə-pīn′) *n.* a large rodent covered with long spines.

A North African crested porcupine. The porcupine can rattle its quills to warn off enemies.

pore¹ (pôr, pōr) *n.* a tiny opening in skin or in a plant surface, through which fluids can pass.

pore² (pôr, pōr) *vb.* **por·ing, pored** to study with intense concentration.

pork (pôrk, pōrk) *n.* the flesh of a pig used as food.

por·poise (pôr′pəs) *n.* a sea mammal of the whale family, with a blunt snout.

por·ridge (pôr′ij, pär′ij) *n.* a dish of oatmeal or other cereal boiled in water or milk.

Ships use **ports** to take on and off-load passengers, cargo, and fuel. They also call at ports to be repaired and cleaned. The world's biggest and busiest ports cover vast areas. Rotterdam-Europoort in The Netherlands is the busiest port in the world and has 62 miles of docks, where many different types of ship can moor.

Oil Terminal

Oil is carried around the world by sea. At an oil terminal, tankers can load or unload into storage tanks.

Tankers can load or unload into storage tanks.

Container ships dock alongside docks.

Water is pumped out of a dry dock (left) after a ship has floated in so the ship's hull can be repaired.

Container ships moor alongside docks where special cranes load or unload their cargo containers.

Dry docks

Containers

port¹ (pôrt, pōrt) *n.* a town with a harbor.

port² (pôrt, pōrt) *n.* the left side of a ship or aircraft.

port·a·ble (pôrt′ə-bəl, pōrt′ə-bəl) *adj.* designed to be easily carried or moved. – *n.* a portable radio, television, typewriter, etc.

por·ter¹ (pôrt′ər, pōrt′ər) *n.* a doorkeeper.

porter² (pôrt′ər, pōrt′ər) *n.* a person employed to carry luggage or parcels.

port·hole (pôrt′hōl′, pōrt′hōl′) *n.* a round opening in a ship's side.

por·ti·co (pôrt′i-kō′, pōrt′i-kō′) *n.* **por·ti·coes** or **porticos** a porch or covered way alongside a building, supported by pillars.

por·tion (pôr′shən, pōr′shən) *n.* a piece or part of a whole; a share.

por·trait (pôr′trət, pōr′trət) *n.* a drawing, photograph, etc. of a person.

por·tray (pôr-trā′, pōr-trā′) *vb.* **por·tray·ing, por·trayed** to describe or depict; to act the part of in a play, movie, etc. – *n.* **por·tray·al** (pôr-trā′əl, pōr-trā′əl).

●**Por·tu·gal** (pôr′chə-gəl). See Supplement, **Countries**.

Por·tu·guese (pôr′chə-gēz′, pôr′chə-gēz′) *adj.* **1** of, or belonging to, PORTUGAL or its inhabitants. **2** of, or belonging to, the Portuguese language. – *n.* **1** a native or citizen of PORTUGAL. **2** the language of PORTUGAL, BRAZIL, ANGOLA, and MOZAMBIQUE.

pose (pōz) *n.* **1** a position or attitude of the body: *She adopted a relaxed pose.* **2** an artificial way of behaving, often purely for effect: *His punk style is just a pose.* – *vb.* **pos·ing, posed** **1** to take up a position for a photograph, portrait, etc. **2** to pretend to be. **3** to ask or put forward: *to pose a question.* **4** to cause or present: *to pose a problem.*

Po·sei·don (pə-sīd′n). See **Myths and Legends**.

po·si·tion (pə-zish′ən) *n.* **1** a place where something or someone is. **2** a way of sitting, standing, lying, or facing: *an upright position.* **3** someone's opinion or viewpoint. **4** a job or post: *She holds a senior position.* **5** the place of a competitor in a contest: *He is in fourth position.* – *vb.* **po·si·tion·ing, po·si·tioned** to place.

pos·i·tive (päz′ət-iv) *adj.* **1** sure; definite: *I have positive proof of her guilt.* **2** expressing agreement or approval: *We received a positive response.* **3** optimistic.

pos·sess (pə-zes′) *vb.* **pos·sess·ing, pos·sessed** to own; to have as a feature or quality: *He possesses a quick mind.*

pos·ses·sion (pə-zesh'ən) *n.* **1** the condition of possessing something; ownership. **2** something owned. **3** (*in plural*) someone's property or belongings.

pos·ses·sive (pə-zes'iv) *adj.* **1** not willing to share things: *He is very possessive about his car.* **2** in grammar, describing the form of a noun, pronoun, or adjective that shows possession, for example *Jack's, its,* or *her.*

pos·si·bil·i·ty (päs'ə-bil'ət-ē) *n.* **pos·si·bil·i·ties 1** something that is possible. **2** (*in plural*) promise or potential: *This idea has possibilities.*

pos·si·ble (päs'ə-bəl) *adj.* **1** able to be done. **2** imaginable: *It's possible that he's still there.*

pos·si·bly (päs'ə-blē) *adv.* **1** perhaps. **2** within the limits of possibility: *We're doing all we possibly can.*

post¹ (pōst) *n.* a strong pole fixed upright in the ground, as a support or a marker.

post² (pōst) *n.* a position or job.

post³ (pōst) *n.* **1** the official system for the delivery of mail. **2** letters and parcels delivered by this system; mail. – *vb.* **post·ing, post·ed** to mail.

A pottery head made by the Nok people of Nigeria between 400 B.C. and A.D. 200.

Muslim artists of the A.D. 700s concentrated on intricate designs, as can be seen in this Persian bowl.

Pottery was a key invention which followed when humans adapted to a settled way of life. The earliest known pottery, shaped by hand, dates from about 8000 B.C.

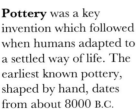

A Roman amphora (right), used to hold wine or olive oil.

A potter shaping a vessel on a wheel. For thousands of years potters have made pots by hand.

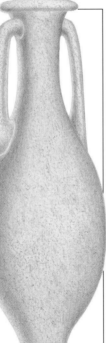

post- *prefix* after: *postwar.*

post·age (pō'stij) *n.* the charge for sending a letter, etc. through the mail.

postage stamp *n.* (also **stamp**) a small printed label stuck on a letter, etc. showing that the postage has been paid.

pos·tal (pō'stəl) *adj.* of or relating to the post office or delivery of mail.

post·card (pōst'kärd') *n.* a card for writing messages on, often with a picture on one side.

post·er (pō'stər) *n.* **1** a large advertisement for public display. **2** a large printed picture.

● **Post·im·pres·sion·ism** (pōst'-im-presh'ə-niz'əm) was the style of painting that arose between 1885 and 1905. It followed the IMPRESSIONISM movement. Artists experimented freely with expression, form, and design instead of representing nature realistically. The movement included such artists as CEZANNE, GAUGIN, and VAN GOGH.

post·man (pōst'mən) *n.* **post·men** (pōst'mən) Same as **mailman**.

post·mark (pōst'märk') *n.* a mark stamped on mail by the post office, canceling the stamp and showing the date and place of mailing.

post me·rid·i·em (pōst' mə-rid'ē-əm) after noon. Usually abbreviated to P.M.

post·mor·tem (pōst-môrt'əm) *n.* a medical examination of a dead person to establish the reason for death.

post office *n.* **1** the local office where one can buy stamps and mail letters. **2** the government department in charge of postal services.

post·pone (pōst-pōn') *vb.* **post·pon·ing, post·poned** to put off till later.

pos·ture (päs'chər) *n.* the position of the body in standing, sitting, or walking.

pot (pät) *n.* any of various deep round containers used for cooking or serving food, or for storage.

po·tas·si·um (pə-tas'ē-əm) *n.* an element (symbol **K**), a soft silvery-white metal.

po·ta·to (pə-tāt'ō) *n.* **po·ta·toes** a white root vegetable with a dark skin.

po·ten·tial (pə-ten'chəl) *adj.* possible or likely, though as yet not tested or actual: *He is a potential world champion.* – *n.* the ability to achieve something not yet developed.

pot·hole (pät'hōl') *n.* **1** a hole carved in a riverbed by the grinding action of stones. **2** a hole worn in a road surface.

pot·ter *n.* a person who makes pottery.

pot·ter·y (pät'ə-rē) *n.* **pot·ter·ies 1** pots, dishes, etc. made from baked clay. **2** a factory where such objects are produced. **3** the art or craft of the potter.

● There are two main kinds of pottery: porcelain, made with white clay that lets the light through; and stoneware, made from various colors of clay. Stoneware is usually thicker and does not let light through. Firing pots in kilns makes the pots rock hard and hardens the glaze.

pouch (pouch) *n.* **1** a purse or small bag. **2** in marsupials such as the kangaroo, a pocket of skin on the belly in which the young are carried. **3** any baglike part, as in the cheeks of a hamster for storing food.

poul·try (pōl'trē) *n. (plural)* farmyard birds such as hens, ducks, or geese.

pounce (pouns) *vb.* **pounc·ing, pounced** to leap; to grab eagerly. – *n.* an act of pouncing.

pound¹ (pound) *n.* **1** *(abbreviation* **lb**) a measure of weight equal to 16 ounces or 0.454 kilograms. **2** *(also* **pound sterling**) the currency of the UNITED KINGDOM, divided into 100 pennies. **3** the standard unit of currency in several other countries.

pound² (pound) *n.* an enclosure where stray animals or illegally parked cars that have been removed by the police are kept for collection.

pound³ (pound) *vb.* **pounding, pounded** to beat or bang vigorously.

pour (pôr, pōr) *vb.* **pour·ing, poured 1** to flow in a downward stream. **2** to empty liquid out of a pitcher, teapot, etc. **3** to rain heavily.

pov·er·ty (päv'ərt-ē) *n.* the state of being poor.

pow·der (poud'ər) *n.* any substance in the form of fine dustlike particles. – *vb.* **pow·der·ing, pow·dered** to sprinkle or cover with powder.

pow·er (pou'ər) *n.* **1** control and influence exercised over others. **2** strength, vigor, force, or effectiveness. **3** an ability or skill: *Animals do not have the power of speech.* **4** any of the forms of energy, for example *nuclear power, electrical power;* any of these as the driving force of a machine, etc. – *adj.* using mechanical or electrical power; motor-driven: *The store has a full range of power tools.* – *vb.* **pow·er·ing, pow·ered** to supply with power.

pow·er·ful (pou'ər-fəl) *adj.* having great power, strength, authority, or influence.

power station *n.* an electricity generating station.

The potato was introduced to Europe from South America in the 1500s. A potato plant has pink or white flowers. Tubers (the parts of the plant we eat) form underground on the stems.

prac·ti·cal (prak'ti-kəl) *adj.* **1** concerned with action instead of theory: *He can put his knowledge to practical use.* **2** (of a person) sensible and efficient in deciding and acting.

practical joke *n.* a trick played on someone.

prac·ti·cal·ly (prak'ti-klē) *adv.* **1** almost. **2** in a practical manner.

prac·tice (prak'təs) *n.* **1** the process of carrying something out: *She put her ideas into practice.* **2** repeated exercise to improve an ability in an art, sport, etc. **3** a doctor's or lawyer's business. – *vb.* **prac·tic·ing, prac·ticed** to do exercises repeatedly in an art, sport, etc. so as to improve performance.

prag·mat·ic (prag-mat'ik) *adj.* concerned with what is practicable and convenient.

● **Prague** (präg) is the capital of the CZECH REPUBLIC.

prai·rie (prer'ē) *n.* in NORTH AMERICA, a treeless grass-covered plain.

prairie dog *n.* a North American rodent that lives in burrows in large colonies and barks.

praise (prāz) *vb.* **prais·ing, praised 1** to express admiration or approval of. **2** to worship or glorify with hymns, etc.

prank (prangk'stər) *n.* a trick; a practical joke.

prawn (prôn, prän) *n.* an edible shellfish like a large shrimp.

pray (prā) *vb.* **pray·ing, prayed** to address God, making earnest requests or giving thanks.

prayer (prâr) *n.* **1** an address to God, making a request or giving thanks: *She says her prayers every day.* **2** an earnest hope or desire.

pre- prefix before in **1** time, for example *prearrange.* **2** position, for example *prefix.*

preach (prēch) *vb.* **preach·ing, preached** to deliver a sermon as part of a religious service.

pre·car·i·ous (pri-kâr'ē-əs) *adj.* not safe.

pre·cau·tion (pri-kô'shən) *n.* a measure taken to avoid a risk or danger. – *adj.* **pre·cau·tion·ar·y** (pri-kô'shə-ner'ē).

Prairie dogs sometimes place sentries on guard at the entrances to their burrows.

pre·cede (pri-sēd′) *vb.* **pre·ced·ing, pre·ced·ed** to go before, in time, order, position, rank, or importance.

pre·ce·dence (pres′ə-dəns) *n.* the greatest importance; priority: *Safety takes precedence.*

pre·ce·dent (pres′əd-ənt) *n.* a previous incident, legal case, etc. that serves as a basis for a decision in a present one.

pre·cinct (prē′singkt) *n.* any of the districts into which a city is divided for administrative or policing purposes.

pre·cious (presh′əs) *adj.* **1** valuable. **2** dear; beloved; treasured: *precious memories.*

precious stone *n.* a mineral valued for its beauty and rarity; a gem.

prec·i·pice (pres′ə-pəs) *n.* a sheer cliff.

pre·cise (pri-sīs′) *adj.* exact: *this precise moment.*

pre·cise·ly (pri-sīs′lē) *adv.* exactly.

pre·ci·sion (pri-sish′ən) *n.* accuracy. − *adj.* (of tools, etc.) designed to operate with extreme accuracy.

pred·a·tor (pred′ət-ər) *n.* a bird or animal that kills and feeds on others.

pred·a·to·ry (pred′ə-tôr′ē, pred′ə-tōr′ē) *adj.* (of creatures) killing and feeding on others.

pred·e·ces·sor (pred′ə-ses′ər, prēd′ə-ses′ər) *n.* **1** person who comes or came before another. **2** an ancestor.

pre·dict (pri-dikt′) *vb.* **pre·dict·ing, pre·dict·ed** to foretell or forecast.

pre·dic·tion (pri-dik′shən) *n.* something foretold.

preen (prēn) *vb.* **preen·ing, preened** (of a bird) to clean and smooth its feathers with its beak.

pref·ace (pref′əs) *n.* an explanatory statement at the beginning of a book. − *vb.* **pref·ac·ing, pref·aced** to introduce with some preliminary matter.

pre·fer (pri-fur′) *vb.* **pre·fer·ring, pre·ferred** to like better: *I prefer tea to coffee.*

pref·er·a·ble (pref′ə-rə-bəl) *adj.* more desirable, suitable, or advisable; better.

pref·er·ence (pref′ə-rəns) *n.* **1** the preferring of one thing, etc. to another: *She chose pink in preference to purple.* **2** favorable consideration.

pre·fix (prē′fiks′) *n.* a group of letters such as *un-, re-, non-, de-* added to the beginning of a word to create a new word.

preg·nant (preg′nənt) *adj.* carrying an unborn child or young in the womb. − *n.* **preg·nan·cy** (preg′nən-sē), **preg·nan·cies.**

pre·his·tor·ic (prē′is-tôr′ik, pre′is-tär′ik) *adj.* belonging or relating to the time before there were written historical records. − *n.* **pre·his·to·ry** (prē′his′tə-rē).

prej·u·dice (prej′əd-əs) *n.* a biased opinion or unreasonable dislike of something or someone. − *vb.* **prej·u·dic·ing, prej·u·diced**

The tiger is a skilled predator. It stalks its prey by creeping slowly toward it until it is near enough to pounce. The tiger makes sure that the wind is blowing its own scent away from the other animal.

to cause to feel unreasonable dislike; to bias.

pre·lim·i·nar·y (pri-lim′ə-ner′ē) *adj.* occurring at the beginning; introductory or preparatory.

pre·mier (pri-mîr′, prē′mē-ər) *adj.* first in rank; most important; leading. – *n.* a prime minister.

pre·miere or **pre·mière** (pri-myer′, pri-mîr′) *n.* the first public performance of a play or showing of a movie.

pre·mi·um (prē′mē-əm) *n.* **1** something offered free or at a reduced price to persuade someone to buy something. **2** an amount paid regularly to an insurance company. **3** an extra sum added to wages or to interest.

prep·a·ra·tion (prep′ə-rā′shən) *n.* the process of preparing or being prepared.

pre·pare (pri-pâr′) *vb.* **pre·par·ing, pre·pared** to make or get ready.

pre·pared (pri-pârd′) *adj.* willing or able.

pre·po·si·tion (prep′ə-zish′ən) *n.* a word such as *to, from, into, against,* that describes the position, movement, etc. of things or people in relation to one another.

pre·scribe (pri-skrīb′) *vb.* **pre·scrib·ing, pre·scribed** to advise as a remedy.

pre·scrip·tion (pri-skrip′shən) *n.* a set of instructions from a doctor for preparing and taking a medicine, etc.

pres·ence (prez′əns) *n.* **1** the state, or circumstance, of being in a place. **2** someone's physical bearing: *The actress has great presence.*

pres·ent[1] (prez′ənt) *adj.* **1** being here; being at the place or occasion in question. **2** existing now. – *n.* **1** the present time. **2** a verb in the present tense.

pre·sent[2] (pri-zent′) *vb.* **pre·sent·ing, pre·sent·ed** **1** to give formally or ceremonially. **2** to introduce.

pres·ent[3] (prez′ənt) *n.* something given; a gift.

pre·sent·ly *adv.* **1** soon; shortly. **2** now.

pre·ser·va·tive (pri-zur′vət-iv) *n.* a substance used to treat food to prevent it from decaying.

pre·serve (pri-zurv′) *vb.* **pre·serv·ing, pre·served** **1** to save from loss, damage, decay, or deterioration. **2** to treat to last, for example by freezing, pickling, or boiling in sugar. – *n.* **pres·er·va·tion** (prez′ər-vā′shən).

pre·side (pri-zīd′) *vb.* **pre·sid·ing, pre·sided** to take the chair at a meeting, etc.; to be in charge.

pres·i·den·cy (prez′əd-ən-sē) *n.* **pres·i·den·cies** the rank or period of office of a president.

pres·i·dent (prez′əd-ənt, prez′ə-dent′) *n.* **1** (also **President**) the elected head of state in a republic, as the UNITED STATES. **2** the head of an organization. – *adj.* **pres·i·den·tial** (prez′ə-den′chəl) in a manner typical of or fitting for a president.

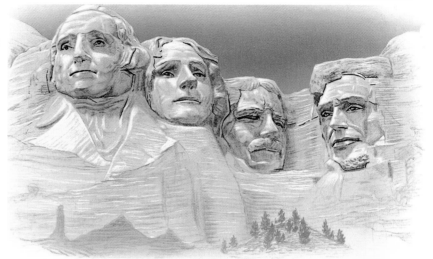

The faces of four U.S. presidents are carved into Mt. Rushmore. They are George Washington, Thomas Jefferson, Theodore Roosevelt, and Abraham Lincoln.

●**Pres·ley** (prez′lē, pres′lē), **Elvis** (1935-1977) was an American singer called "King of Rock 'n' Roll."

press (pres) *vb.* **press·ing, pressed** **1** to push steadily; to hold firmly against something. **2** to iron: *to press clothes.* **3** to ask insistently: *He is pressing for a raise.* – *n.* **1** any apparatus for pressing, flattening, squeezing, etc.: *clothes press.* **2** a printing press. **3** newspapers or journalists in general.

pressed (prest) *adj.* under pressure; in a hurry.

press·ing (pres′ing) *adj.* urgent.

pres·sure (presh′ər) *n.* **1** the force produced by pushing on something. **2** forceful persuasion: *They put pressure on her to resign.* **3** tension, strain, or stress: *He found the pressures of family life too much.*

pres·tige (pre-stēzh′, pre-stēj′) *n.* fame or reputation due to rank or success. – *adj.* **prestigious** (pre-stij′əs).

pre·sume (pri-zōōm′) *vb.* **pre·sum·ing, pre·sumed** to suppose to be the case; to take for granted: *We presumed he was right.*

Water pressure increases the deeper you go. At 12,326ft. (3,758m), where the wreck of the Titanic *lies, water pressure is 350 times that at the surface.*

Scuba diver 425 ft.

Nuclear sub 2,300 ft.

Wreck of *Titanic* 12,300 ft.

Trieste bathy-scaphe dived to 36,100 ft.

pre·tend (pri-tend′) *vb.* **pre·tend·ing,**
pre·tend·ed to make believe; to give the
impression that something is the case when it is
not: *He pretended to be asleep.*

pre·tense or **pre·tence** (prē′tens′, pri-tens′)
n. make-believe; an act put on deliberately to
mislead: *His anger was mere pretense.*

pre·ten·tious (pri-ten′chəs) *adj.* pompous and
self-important; showy.

pre·text (prē′tekst′) *n.* an excuse.

pret·ty (prit′ē) *adj.* **pret·ti·er, pret·ti·est**
charming to look at. – *adv.* fairly; rather: *I am
pretty tired.*

pret·zel (pret′səl) *n.* a salted stick or knot of
baked dough.

pre·vail (pri-vāl′) *vb.* **pre·vail·ing,**
pre·vailed 1 to win through. **2** to be
widespread or acceptable.

pre·vent (pri-vent′) *vb.* **pre·vent·ing,**
pre·vent·ed to stop someone from doing, or
from happening; to hinder: *The roadblock
prevented us from passing.* – *adj.* **pre·vent·a·ble**
or **pre·vent·i·ble** (pri-vent′ə-bəl). – *n.*
pre·ven·tion (pri-ven′chən).

pre·view (prē′vyōō′) *n.* an advance showing of
a movie, play, exhibition, etc., before
presentation to the general public.

pre·vi·ous (prē′vē-əs) *adj.* **1** earlier. **2** former.

prey (prā) *n.* a creature that is hunted and killed
for food: *The owl was in search of prey.* – *vb.*
prey on or **prey upon: preying, preyed**
1 to hunt for food. **2** to take advantage of.

*This anaconda is killing
its prey by squeezing it to
death. Like pythons and
boas, anacondas are
constrictors.*

prick (prik) *vb.* **prick·ing, pricked** to pierce
slightly with a fine point.

prick·le (prik′əl) *n.* a sharp point or thorn on a
plant or creature.

prick·ly (prik′lē) *adj.* **prick·li·er,**
prick·li·est 1 having prickles. **2** (*informal*)
irritable; too sensitive.

pride (prīd) *n.* **1** a feeling of pleasure and
satisfaction at one's own or someone else's
accomplishments, etc. **2** self-respect; personal
dignity. **3** a group of lions. – *vb.* **prid·ing,**
prid·ed to congratulate on: *He prided himself
on his youthful figure.*

priest (prēst) *n.* **1** in some Christian churches,
an ordained minister. **2** in many religions, an
official who performs religious rites.

priest·hood (prēst′hood′) *n.* **1** the period of
office of a priest. **2** priests collectively.

prim (prim) *adj.* **prim·mer, prim·mest**
formal and prudish; easily shocked by anything
rude.

pri·ma·ry (prī′mer′ē, prī′mə-rē) *adj.* **1** first or
most important; principal: *Money is our primary
concern.* **2** earliest in order or development.

pri·mar·i·ly (prī-mer′ə-lē) *adv.* chiefly; mainly.

primary color *n.* one of the colors from which
all others can be produced by mixing. The
primary colors of light are red, green, and
blue; those of paint are red, yellow, and blue.

pri·mate (prī′māt′) *n.* **1** member of the highest
order of mammals, including monkeys, lemurs,
apes, and humans. **2** (also prī′māt′) an
archbishop.

prime (prīm) *adj.* chief; fundamental.

●**Pri·am** (prī′əm) in Greek mythology, was king
of TROY.

price (prīs) *n.* **1** the amount, usually in money,
for which a thing is sold or offered. **2** what
must be given up in order to gain something:
Loss of privacy is the price of fame. – *vb.* **pric·ing,**
priced to fix a price for.

price·less (prī′sləs) *adj.* too valuable to have a
price: *The art collection was priceless.*

prime minister *n.* the chief minister of a
government.

prime number *n.* a number that is exactly
divisible only by itself and one, as 3, 5, 7.

primeval (prī-mē′vəl) *adj.* **1** belonging to the
early period of the history of the earth.
2 primitive.

prim·i·tive (prim′ət-iv) *adj.* **1** belonging to
earliest times, or the earliest stages of
development: *primitive man.* **2** simple, rough, or

crude: *They were living in primitive conditions*.

prim·rose (prim′rōz′) *n*. a small plant with pale yellow flowers that appear in spring.

prince (prins) *n*. a male member of a royal family, especially the son of a king and queen.

Edward, Prince of Wales, was known as the Black Prince from the color of his armor. A brilliant general, he died before his father, King Edward II.

prin·cess (prin′səs, prin′ses′)*n*. the wife or daughter of a prince; the daughter of a sovereign, or of a royal family.

●**Prince Ed·ward Is·land** (prins ed′wərd ī′lənd) **(P.E.I.)** is a province in CANADA.

prin·ci·pal (prin′sə-pəl) *adj*. first in rank or importance; chief; main. – *n*. the head of an elementary, junior high, or high school.

prin·ci·ple (prin′sə-pəl) *n*. **1** a general truth or scientific law, especially one that explains a natural phenomenon or the way a machine works. **2** a general rule that guides someone's behavior: *She is a woman of high principles*. – **in principle** in general, as opposed to in detail.

print (print) *vb*. **print·ing, print·ed 1** to reproduce on paper in large quantities, using a printing press or other mechanical means. **2** to write in separate letters instead of joined writing. – *n*. **1** a mark made on a surface by the pressure of something in contact with it. **2** a photograph made from a negative.

print·er *n*. a person or business engaged in printing books, newspapers, etc.

print·ing *n*. the art or business of producing books, etc. in print.

print·out (print′out′) *n*. information from a computer printed out on paper.

pri·or (prī′ər) *adj*. already arranged for the time in question; previous.

prism (priz′əm) *n*. a transparent solid with triangular ends that separates a beam of white light into the colors of the spectrum.

pris·on (priz′ən) *n*. a building where criminals are confined.

pris·on·er (priz′ə-nər, priz′nər) *n*. a person who is under arrest or held in captivity.

pri·vate (prī′vət) *adj*. **1** not open to the general public: *You may not enter the private rooms*. **2** kept secret from others; confidential: *This is a private matter*. **3** relating to your personal life: *His private affairs were widely reported in the papers*. **4** not coming under the state system of education, health care, social welfare, etc.; paid for individually: *My brother went to a private school*. **5** (of industries, etc.) owned and run by private individuals, not by the state. – **in private** not in public; in secret; confidentially. – *n*. **pri·va·cy** (prī′və-sē).

pri·va·tize (prī′və-tīz′) *vb*. **pri·va·tiz·ing, pri·va·tized** to transfer a state-owned business to private ownership.

priv·i·lege (priv′ə-lij, priv′lij) *n*. a special right or advantage granted to an individual or a select few.

priv·i·leged (priv′ə-lijd, priv′lijd) *adj*. enjoying the advantages of wealth and class.

prize (prīz) *n*. **1** something won in a

To print in color four different inks on four cylindrical printing plates are used. The four inks are yellow, magenta (red), cyan (blue), and black. Each color is printed in turn one after the other. Mixed together, these four colors can give the effect of all other colors.

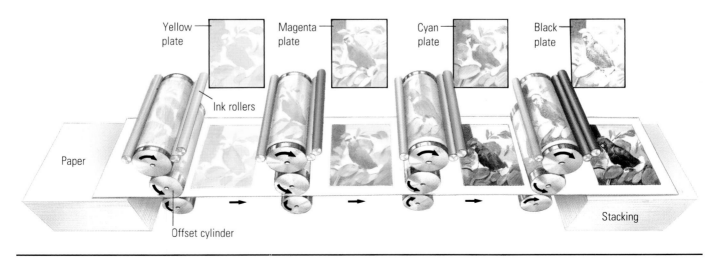

Yellow plate · Magenta plate · Cyan plate · Black plate

Ink rollers

Paper

Offset cylinder

Stacking

Pioneer-Venus 2 *acted as a carrier to four smaller probes on the way to Venus in 1978. As it approached Venus, Pioneer launched its four probes toward different parts of the planet.*

competition, game, etc. **2** a reward given in recognition of excellence. − *adj.* valued highly by a person. − *vb.* **priz·ing, prized** to value highly.

pro- *prefix* in favor of; admiring or supporting: *He is very pro-French.*

prob·a·ble (präb′ə-bəl) *adj.* **1** likely to happen: *A draw seems the probable outcome.* **2** likely to be the case: *It's probable that she's left.*

prob·a·bil·i·ty (präb′ə-bil′ət-ē) *n.* **prob·a·bil·i·ties** a likelihood.

prob·a·bly (präb′ə-blē) *adv.* almost certainly.

pro·ba·tion (prō-bā′shən) *n.* **1** the system under which someone convicted of a crime is allowed to go free under supervision: *He was put on probation for six months.* **2** a period during which a new employee is observed on the job, before he or she is given the job permanently.

probe (prōb) *n.* **1** a long slender usually metal instrument used by doctors to examine a wound. **2** a thorough investigation. **3** (also **space probe**) an unmanned spacecraft that records and transmits data back to earth. − *vb.* **prob·ing, probed 1** to examine with a probe. **2** to investigate closely.

prob·lem (präb′ləm) *n.* **1** a person, situation, or matter that is difficult to understand or deal with. **2** a puzzle or mathematical question.

pro·ce·dure (prə-sē′jər) *n.* the method and order followed in doing something.

pro·ceed (prō-sēd′) *vb.* **pro·ceed·ing, pro·ceed·ed 1** to make your way; to move. **2** to go on; to continue.

pro·ceeds (prō′sēdz) *n.* (*plural*) money made by an event, sale, etc.

pro·cess (präs′es′, prō′ses′) *n.* a series of operations or stages resulting in development or transformation. − *vb.* **pro·cess·ing, pro·cessed** to put through the required stages; to deal with appropriately.

pro·ces·sion (prä-sesh′ən) *n.* a line of people or vehicles proceeding in orderly formation.

pro·claim (prō-klām′) *vb.* **pro·claim·ing, pro·claimed** to announce publicly.

pro·cras·ti·nate (prə-kras′tə-nāt′) *vb.* **pro·cras·ti·nat·ing, pro·cras·ti·nat·ed** to keep putting off doing something.

prod (präd) *vb.* **prod·ding, prod·ded** to poke, jab, or nudge. − *n.* a poke, jab, or nudge.

prod·i·gal (präd′i-gəl) *adj.* extravagant or wasteful.

prod·i·gy (präd′ə-jē) *n.* **prod·i·gies** a person, especially a child, of extraordinary talent.

pro·duce (prə-dōōs′, prə-dyōōs′) *vb.* **pro·duc·ing, pro·duced 1** to bring out or present to view. **2** to make or manufacture. **3** to be responsible for the presentation of: *to produce a play.* − (prō′dōōs′, prō′dyōōs′) *n.* what is produced, especially from land or livestock. − *n.* **pro·duc·er** (prə-dōō′sər).

prod·uct (präd′ukt, präd′əkt) *n.* **1** something made to be sold for example through manufacture or agriculture. **2** a result. **3** in mathematics, the number gotten by multiplying.

pro·duc·tion (prə-duk′shən) *n.* **1** the process of manufacturing or growing something. **2** a particular presentation of a play, etc.

pro·duc·tive (prə-duk′tiv) *adj.* yielding a lot.

pro·fes·sion (prə-fesh′ən) *n.* **1** an occupation, especially one that requires extensive training, for example medicine, law, engineering. **2** the body of people engaged in a particular occupation: *the medical profession.*

pro·fes·sion·al (prə-fesh′ən-l) *adj.* **1** earning a living in the performance, practice, or teaching of something that is a pastime for others: *She is a professional tennis player.* **2** belonging to a trained profession. − *n.* someone who is trained in a certain field.

pro·fes·sor (prə-fes′ər) *n.* a teacher in a university.

pro·file (prō′fīl′) *n.* a side view of something, especially a face or head.

prof·it (präf′ət) *n.* money gained from selling something for more than was paid for it, or for more than it cost to make. − *vb.* **prof·it·ing, prof·it·ed** to benefit.

prof·it·a·ble (präf′ət-ə-bəl) *adj.* **1** (of a business, etc.) making a profit. **2** useful; fruitful. − *n.* **prof·it·a·bil·i·ty** (präf′ət-ə-bil′ət-ē).

A production line assembly using computer-controlled robots to do the routine jobs.

pro·found (prə-found′) *adj.* **1** deep; intense. **2** showing deep understanding.

pro·gram (prō′gram′, prō′grəm) *n.* **1** a leaflet giving information about a performance, ceremony, etc. **2** a plan or schedule. **3** a scheduled radio or television presentation. **4** a set of coded instructions to a computer. — *vb.* **pro·gram·ing** or **pro·gram·ming**, **pro·gramed** or **pro·grammed** to set a computer to perform a set of tasks.

prog·ress (präg′rəs, präg′res′) *n.* **1** movement while traveling in any direction; course. **2** movement toward a destination, goal, or state of completion. **3** advances or development. — **pro·gress** (prə-gres′) *vb.* **pro·gres·sing, pro·gressed** to advance or develop; to improve.

pro·gres·sive (prə-gres′iv) *adj.* advanced in outlook; using or favoring, new methods.

pro·hib·it (prō-hib′ət) *vb.* **pro·hib·it·ing, pro·hib·it·ed** to forbid, especially by law.

pro·hi·bi·tion (prō-ə-bish′ən) *n.* a law or decree prohibiting something.

proj·ect (präj′ekt′, präj′ikt) *n.* **1** a plan, scheme, or proposal. **2** a research or study assignment. — **pro·ject** (prə-jekt′) *vb.* **pro·ject·ing, pro·ject·ed** **1** to jut out; to protrude: *The headland projects into the bay.* **2** to throw a shadow or image on to a surface.

pro·jec·tile (prə-jek′təl) *n.* an object that is thrown with force.

pro·jec·tion (prə-jek′shən) *n.* **1** something that protrudes from a surface. **2** the showing of a movie or transparencies on a screen. **3** a forecast based on present trends and other known data.

pro·jec·tor (prə-jek′tər) *n.* a machine for projecting images onto a screen.

pro·lif·ic (prō-lif′ik) *adj.* abundant and plentiful; productive: *She is a prolific writer.*

pro·long (prō-lông′) *vb.* **pro·long·ing, pro·longed** to make longer; to extend.

prom·i·nent (präm′ə-nənt) *adj.* **1** jutting out; protruding; bulging: *He has a prominent chin.* **2** leading; notable: *She is a prominent politician.* — *n.* **prom·i·nence** (präm′ə-nəns).

prom·ise (präm′əs) *vb.* **prom·is·ing, prom·ised** **1** to give an assurance to do or not do something. **2** to look likely to do something. — *n.* **1** an undertaking to give, do, or not do, something. **2** signs of future excellence.

prom·on·to·ry (präm′ən-tôr′ē, präm′ən-tôr′ē) *n.* **prom·on·to·ries** a part of a coastline that projects into the sea.

pro·mote (prə-mōt′) *vb.* **pro·mot·ing, pro·mot·ed** **1** to raise to a more senior position. **2** to contribute to; to work for the cause of: *Exercise promotes health.* **3** to publicize; to try to boost the sales of by advertising. — *n.* **pro·mo·tion** (prə-mō′shən).

prompt (prämpt) *adj.* immediate; quick; punctual. — *adv.* punctually. — *vb.* **prompt·ing, prompt·ed** **1** to cause or remind to do something. **2** to produce in reaction or response: *What prompted that remark?*

prone (prōn) *adj.* **1** lying flat, especially face downward. **2** liable to suffer from.

prong (prông, präng) *n.* a point or spike.

pro·noun (prō′noun′) *n.* a word such as *she, him, they, it* used in place of a noun.

pro·nounce (prə-nouns′) *vb.* **pro·nounc·ing, pro·nounced** **1** to say: *to pronounce a word.* **2** to declare officially or formally.

pro·nounced *adj.* noticeable, distinct: *He runs with a pronounced limp.*

pro·nun·ci·a·tion (prə-nun′sē-ā′shən) *n.* the usual way of pronouncing words, sounds, etc.

proof (prōōf) *n.* **1** evidence that something is true or a fact. **2** a testing or trial of anything.

prop[1] (präp) *n.* **1** a stick or other object used to support things. **2** a person or thing that you depend on for help or emotional support. — *vb.* **propping, propped** **1** to support or hold upright with a prop. **2** to lean.

prop[2] (präp) *n.* an object used on stage in a theater.

prop·a·gan·da (präp′ə-gan′də) *n.* information presented so as to influence public feeling.

pro·pel (prə-pel′) *vb.* **pro·pel·ling, pro·pelled** to drive or push forward.

Political propaganda in China. Large posters of Party leaders formed the backdrop to speeches at a meeting of the Communist party in Shanghai in 1948. Propaganda posters are used to great effect for such things as road safety campaigns and health warnings.

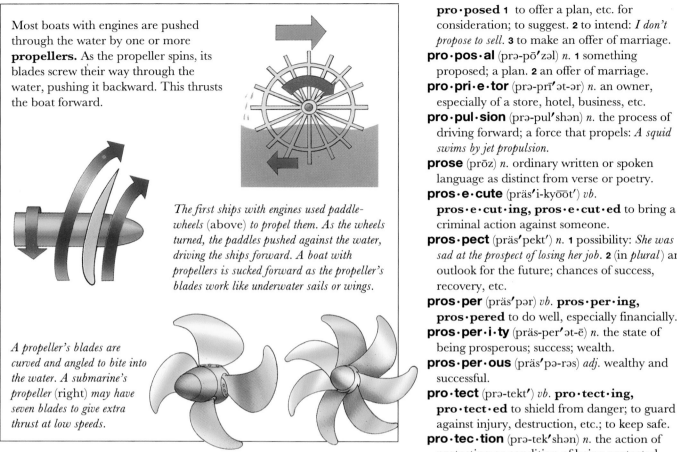

Most boats with engines are pushed through the water by one or more **propellers.** As the propeller spins, its blades screw their way through the water, pushing it backward. This thrusts the boat forward.

The first ships with engines used paddle-wheels (above) to propel them. As the wheels turned, the paddles pushed against the water, driving the ships forward. A boat with propellers is sucked forward as the propeller's blades work like underwater sails or wings.

A propeller's blades are curved and angled to bite into the water. A submarine's propeller (right) may have seven blades to give extra thrust at low speeds.

pro·pel·ler (prə-pel'ər) *n.* a device consisting of a shaft with blades that is turned by the engine to propel a ship or an aircraft.

prop·er (präp'ər) *adj.* **1** real; genuine: *We need a proper vacation.* **2** right; correct: *You must learn the proper grip.*

prop·er·ly (präp'ər-lē) *adv.* **1** suitably; appropriately; correctly. **2** with strict accuracy.

proper noun *n.* the name of a particular person, place, or thing.

prop·er·ty (präp'ər-tē) *n.* **prop·er·ties** **1** something that someone owns. **2** a piece of land. **3** a quality or feature.

proph·e·cy (präf'ə-sē) *n.* **prophecies** the foretelling of what will happen in the future.

proph·et (präf'ət) *n.* a person who predicts what may happen in the future.

pro·por·tion (prə-pôr'shən) *n.* **1** a part of a total. **2** the size of one element or group in relation to the whole or total. **3** the correct balance between parts or elements: *The hands are out of proportion with the head.*

pro·pose (prə-pōz') *vb.* **pro·pos·ing,**

pro·posed **1** to offer a plan, etc. for consideration; to suggest. **2** to intend: *I don't propose to sell.* **3** to make an offer of marriage.

pro·pos·al (prə-pō'zəl) *n.* **1** something proposed; a plan. **2** an offer of marriage.

pro·pri·e·tor (prə-prī'ət-ər) *n.* an owner, especially of a store, hotel, business, etc.

pro·pul·sion (prə-pul'shən) *n.* the process of driving forward; a force that propels: *A squid swims by jet propulsion.*

prose (prōz) *n.* ordinary written or spoken language as distinct from verse or poetry.

pros·e·cute (präs'i-kyŏŏt') *vb.* **pros·e·cut·ing, pros·e·cut·ed** to bring a criminal action against someone.

pros·pect (präs'pekt') *n.* **1** possibility: *She was sad at the prospect of losing her job.* **2** (in *plural*) an outlook for the future; chances of success, recovery, etc.

pros·per (präs'pər) *vb.* **pros·per·ing, pros·pered** to do well, especially financially.

pros·per·i·ty (präs-per'ət-ē) *n.* the state of being prosperous; success; wealth.

pros·per·ous (präs'pə-rəs) *adj.* wealthy and successful.

pro·tect (prə-tekt') *vb.* **pro·tect·ing, pro·tect·ed** to shield from danger; to guard against injury, destruction, etc.; to keep safe.

pro·tec·tion (prə-tek'shən) *n.* the action of protecting or condition of being protected.

pro·tec·tive (prə-tek'tiv) *adj.* giving protection; tending to protect.

pro·tein (prō'tēn') *n.* any of a group of organic compounds essential to the composition of all living cells.

pro·test (prə-test', prō'test') *vb.* **pro·test·ing, pro·test·ed** **1** to express an objection, opposition, or disagreement. **2** to declare in response to an accusation: *He protested his innocence.* – (prō'test') *n.* **1** a declaration of disapproval; an objection. **2** an organized public demonstration of disapproval.

Prot·es·tant (prär'ə-stənt) *n.* a member of any of the Christian churches that rejected the authority of the pope and separated from the Roman Catholic Church in the 1500s.

proto- *prefix* first or earliest: *prototype.*

pro·ton (prō'tän') *n.* a particle with a positive electrical charge forming part of the nucleus of an atom.

pro·to·type (prōt'ə-tīp') *n.* a first working version, for example of a vehicle or aircraft.

pro·trude (prə-trŏŏd') *vb.* **pro·trud·ing,**

pro·trud·ed to project; to stick out. – *n.* **pro·tru·sion** (prō-trōō′zhən).

proud (proud) *adj.* **1** feeling pride at one's own or another's accomplishments, one's possessions, etc. **2** arrogant; having too high an opinion of oneself.

prove (prōōv) *vb.* **prov·ing, proved 1** to show to be true, correct, or a fact. **2** to be found to be, when tried; to turn out to be.

prov·erb (präv′urb′) *n.* a saying that gives advice or expresses a supposed truth about life.

pro·vide (prə-vīd′) *vb.* **pro·vid·ing, pro·vid·ed 1** to supply. **2** to prepare for an emergency, etc.: *I have put money aside to provide for the future.* – *n.* **pro·vid·er.**

prov·ince (präv′əns) *n.* an administrative division of a country.

pro·vin·cial (prə-vin′chəl) *adj.* **1** belonging to or relating to a province. **2** relating to the parts of a country away from the capital. – *n.* **pro·vin·cial·ism** (prə-vin′chə-liz′əm).

pro·vi·sion (prə-vizh′ən) *n.* **1** something provided or made available; facilities: *There is provision for disabled pupils.* **2** preparations; measures taken in advance: *We must make provision for the future.* **3** (in *plural*) supplies of food.

pro·vi·sion·al (prə-vizh′ən-l) *adj.* temporary.

pro·voke (prə-vōk′) *vb.* **pro·vok·ing, pro·voked 1** to annoy or infuriate, especially deliberately. **2** to cause or stir up.

prow (prou) *n.* the front part of a ship.

prowl (proul) *vb.* **prowl·ing, prowled** to move about stealthily. – *n.* **prowl·er.**

prox·im·i·ty (präk-sim′ət-ē) *n.* nearness.

prude (prōōd) *n.* a person who is easily shocked or prim. – *adj.* **prud·ish** (prōōd′ish).

pru·dent (prōōd′nt) *adj.* wise or careful; frugal. – *n.* **pru·dence** (prōōd′ns).

prune¹ (prōōn) *vb.* **prun·ing, pruned** to cut off branches from to improve growth.

prune² (prōōn) *n.* a dried plum.

pry (prī) *vb.* **pries, pry·ing, pried** to investigate the personal affairs of others.

psalm (säm) *n.* a sacred song from the Book of Psalms in the OLD TESTAMENT of the Bible.

pseudo- or **pseud-** *prefix* false: *pseudoclassic.*

pseud·o·nym (sōōd′n-im′) *n.* a false name used by an author.

psy·chi·a·try (sə-kī′ə-trē) *n.* the medical study of the treatment of mental illness. – *adj.* **psy·chi·a·tric** (sī′kē-a′trik). – *n.* **psy·chi·a·trist** (sī-kī′ə-trəst).

psy·cho·log·i·cal (sī′kə-läj′i-kəl) *adj.* relating to the human mind.

psychology (sī-käl′ə-jē) *n.* the study of the human mind and the reasons for human behavior. – *n.* **psy·chol·o·gist** (sī-käl′ə-jəst).

psy·cho·path (sī′kō-path′) *n.* a person with a personality disorder who is liable to behave violently without feeling any guilt. – *adj.* **psy·cho·path·ic** (sī′kō-path′ik): *a psychopathic desire for revenge.*

pter·o·dac·tyl (ter′ə-dakt′l) *n.* an extinct flying reptile with a birdlike skull and leathery wings.

● **Ptol·e·my** (täl′ə-mē) (A.D. 100-168) was a Greek astronomer who proposed that the earth was the center of the universe.

pu·ber·ty (pyōō′bərt-ē) *n.* the stage in life during which the reproductive organs develop.

pub·lic (pub′lik) *adj.* **1** of, or concerning, all the people of a country or community. **2** provided for the use of the community: *The town has two public parks.* **3** made, done, held, etc. openly, for all to see and hear: *He made a public announcement.* – *n.* (*singular* or *plural*) the people or community.

pub·li·ca·tion (pub′li-kā′shən) *n.* **1** the process of publishing a printed work. **2** a book, magazine, newspaper, or other printed and published work.

pub·li·ci·ty (pə-blis′ət-ē) *n.* advertising or other activity designed to rouse public interest in something.

pub·li·cize (pub′lə-sīz′) *vb.* **pub·li·ciz·ing, pub·li·cized** to make generally or widely known; to advertise.

pub·lish (pub′lish) *vb.* **pub·lish·ing, pub·lished** to prepare, print or produce, and distribute for sale to the public.

Pterodactyls (meaning "winged fingers") belonged to the group pterosaurs or "winged lizards." Most pterodactyls had long wings, little or no tail, and a toothless beak. Some were as small as a sparrow; others bigger than an eagle.

FAMOUS PSEUDONYMS	
Pseudonym	*Real Name*
Mark Twain	*Samuel Langhorne Clemens*
George Eliot	*Mary Ann Evans*
O. Henry	*William S. Porter*
Lewis Carroll	*Charles Lutwidge Dodgson*
Voltaire	*François-Marie Arouet*

●**Puc·ci·ni** (pōō-chē′nē), **Giacomo** (1858-1924) was the Italian composer whose operas include *La Bohème* and *Tosca*.

puck (puk) *n.* a thick disk of hard rubber used in ice hockey in place of a ball.

pud·ding (pood′ing) *n.* a usually soft creamy cooked dessert: *rice pudding*.

pud·dle (pud′l) *n.* a small pool, especially of rainwater.

●**Puer·to Ri·co** (pôrt′ə rē′kō, pōrt′ə, pwert′ə), an island in the Caribbean, is a self-governing part of the UNITED STATES.

puff (puf) *n.* a small cloud of smoke, dust, or steam emitted from something. – *vb.* **puff·ing, puffed 1** to breathe with difficulty. **2** (of smoke, steam, etc.) to emerge in small gusts.

puf·fin (puf′ən) *n.* a black and white sea bird.

pug (pug) *n.* a small dog with a flattened snout.

●**Pu·lit·zer Prizes** (pool′ət-sər, pyōō′lət-sər) are awarded each year for outstanding achievements in American journalism, literature, and music. They are named after the newspaper magnate Joseph Pulitzer (1847-1911).

pull (pool) *vb.* **pull·ing, pulled** to draw or force toward the person or object exerting the force; to tug or drag: *The car was pulling a trailer.* – *n.* **1** an act of pulling. **2** attraction; attracting force: *He feels the pull of his homeland.* – *vb.* **pull in** (of a train) to halt at a station.

pul·ley (pool′ē) *n.* **pul·leys** a device for lifting and lowering weights, consisting of a wheel over which a rope or belt runs.

pull·o·ver (pool′ō′vər) *n.* a knitted garment pulled on over the head, as a shirt or sweater.

pulp (pulp) *n.* **1** the soft part of a fruit or vegetable. **2** a soft wet mass of mashed food or other material: *Paper is made from wood pulp.*

pul·pit (pool′pət) *n.* a small enclosed platform in a church, from which the preacher delivers the sermon.

pulse[1] (puls) *n.* **1** the rhythmical beat of blood being pumped through the body, noticeable where an artery nears the skin surface, for example at the wrist. **2** a regular throbbing beat in music. – *vb.* **puls·ing, pulsed** to throb.

pulse[2] (puls) *n.* the edible seeds of plants such as beans, peas, and lentils.

pu·ma (pyōō′mə) *n.* same as **cougar**.

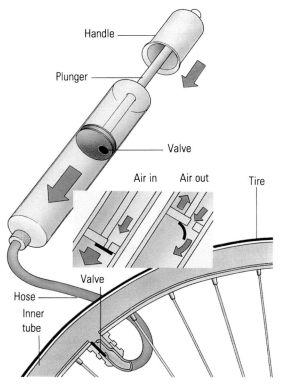

How a bicycle pump works. A valve allows the air to flow only one way.

pump (pump) *n.* any of various devices for forcing liquids or gases into or out of something, etc. – *vb.* **pump·ing, pumped**.

pum·per·nick·el (pum′pər-nik′əl) *n.* a dark heavy coarse rye bread.

pump·kin (pump′kən) *n.* a large round thick-skinned yellow-orange fruit often used in pies.

pun (pun) *n.* a play on words, especially one where an association is created between words of similar sound but different meaning, for

Most pumpkins are orange and they grow at ground level on a trailing plant. Pumpkin pie is a traditional dish on Thanksgiving Day. For Halloween children carve jack-o'-lanterns (hollowed out pumpkins).

example *A pun is a punishable offense.* – *vb.*
pun·ning, punned to make a pun.

punch¹ (punch) *vb.* **punch·ing, punched** to hit with the fist. – *n.* a blow with the fist.

punch² (punch) *n.* a tool for cutting holes or notches, or stamping designs, in leather, paper, metal, etc. – *vb.* **punch·ing, punched** to pierce, notch, or stamp with a punch.

punc·tu·al (pungk′chōō-əl) *adj.* arriving or happening at the arranged time; not late. – *n.* **punc·tu·al·i·ty** (pungk′chōō-al′ət-ē).

punc·tu·ate (pungk′chōō-āt′) *vb.* **punc·tu·at·ing, punc·tu·at·ed 1** to put punctuation marks into a piece of writing. **2** to interrupt repeatedly.

punc·tu·a·tion (pungk′chōō-ā′shən) *n.* the marks used in a text to make it easier for the reader to understand.

punctuation mark *n.* any of the set of marks such as the period, comma, question mark, colon, etc. used in written matter.

punc·ture (pungk′chər) *n.* a small hole pierced in something with a sharp point. – *vb.* **punc·tur·ing, punc·tured** to make a hole.

pun·ish (pun′ish) *vb.* **pun·ish·ing, pun·ished** to cause to suffer for an offense: *They punished the thief harshly.*

pun·ish·a·ble (pun′ish-ə-bəl) *adj.* (of offenses) liable to be punished, especially by law.

pun·ish·ment (pun′ish-mənt) *n.* the act of punishing or process of being punished.

punk (pungk) *n.* (*informal*) **1** a follower of punk rock, and styles such as brightly colored hair and torn black clothes. **2** a tough or worthless young person.

punk rock *n.* loud aggressive rock music popular in the 1970s and 1980s.

pu·pa (pyōō′pə) *n.* **pu·pae** (pyōō′pē, pyōō′pī) or **pupas** the form an insect takes during the stage when it is changing from larva to adult.

pu·pil¹ (pyōō′pəl) *n.* someone who is being taught; a child in school or a student.

pu·pil² (pyōō′pəl) *n.* the circular opening in the middle of the eye through which the light passes to the retina.

pup·pet (pup′ət) *n.* a doll that can be made to move in a lifelike way by strings or sticks attached to its limbs, or by fitting over the hand.

pup·py (pup′ē) *n.* **pup·pies** a young dog.

pur·chase (pur′chəs) *vb.* **pur·chas·ing, pur·chased** to obtain in return for payment; to buy. – *n.* something that has been bought. –

n. **pur·chas·er**.

pure (pyoor) *adj.* **1** consisting of itself only; unmixed with anything else: *My ring is pure gold.* **2** unpolluted; wholesome: *She tasted the pure water.* **3** virtuous; free from sin or guilt. – *n.* **pure·ness** (pyoor′nəs). – **pure and simple** and nothing else: *It's jealousy pure and simple.*

pure·bred (pyoor′bred′) *adj.* (of animals) of unmixed breed.

pure·ly (pyoor′lē) *adv.* **1** in a pure way. **2** completely; entirely: *She won purely on her merits.*

pu·rée (pyoor-ā′) *n.* fruit or vegetables reduced to a pulp by putting in a food processor, etc.

purge (purj) *vb.* **purg·ing, purged** to get rid of impure or unwanted elements.

pu·ri·fy (pyoor′ə-fī′) *vb.* **pu·ri·fies, pu·ri·fy·ing, purified** to make pure; to

Water from reservoirs goes to the water works to be purified. The water is filtered through beds of sand to remove dirt and bacteria particles. Chlorine may be added to kill germs. Fluoride is sometimes added to water to help strengthen teeth.

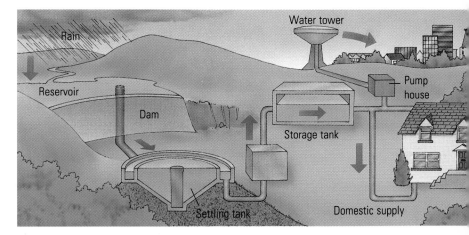

remove all harmful substances from. – *n.* **pu·ri·fi·ca·tion** (pyoor′ə-fə-kā′shən). – *n.* **pu·ri·fi·er** (pyoor′ə-fī-ər).

pu·ri·tan (pyoor′ət-n) *n.* **1 Puritan** a supporter of the Protestant movement in England and America in the 1500s and 1600s that tried to rid church worship of ritual. **2** a person of strict moral principles. – *adj.* **pu·ri·tan·i·cal** (pyoor′ə-tan′i-kəl).

pu·ri·ty (pyoor′ət-ē) *n.* the state of being pure.

pur·ple (pur′pəl) *n.* a color that is a mixture of blue and red. – *adj.* of this color.

pur·pose (pur′pəs) *n.* **1** the function for which something is intended. **2** an intention, aim, or goal. **3** determination. – **on purpose** intentionally; deliberately.

purr (pur) *vb.* **purr·ing, purred** (of a cat) to make a soft, low, vibrating sound when happy.

purse (purs) *n.* **1** a woman's handbag. **2** a small

PRONUNCIATION SYMBOLS		
ə **away**	lemon	focus
a **fat**	oi	**boy**
ā **fade**	oo	**foot**
ä **hot**	ōō	**moon**
âr **fair**	ou	**house**
e **met**	th	**think**
ē **mean**	th̲	**this**
g **get**	u	**cut**
hw **which**	ur	**hurt**
i **fin**	w	**witch**
ī **line**	y	**yes**
îr **near**	yōō	**music**
ô **often**	yoor	**pure**
ō **note**	zh	**vision**

Building a pyramid in the Egyptian desert. In the background, laborers drag blocks on wooden runners up the huge ramp built alongside the unfinished pyramid. In the foreground, skilled masons are smoothing and squaring the blocks as engineers look on.

Pythagoras is perhaps most famous for formulating his theory the Pythagorean Theorem, *which states that in a right-angled triangle the square on the hypotenuse equals the sum of the squares on the other two sides.*

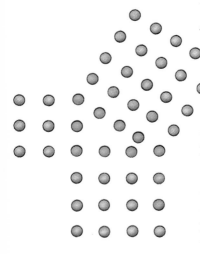

container carried in the pocket or handbag, for keeping cash, etc. in.

pur·sue (pər-soo′) *vb.* **pur·su·ing, pur·sued** to follow so as to overtake, capture, attack, etc.

pur·suit (pər-soot′) *n.* **1** the act of pursuing or chasing. **2** an occupation or hobby.

pus (pus) *n.* the thick yellowish liquid that forms in infected wounds.

push (poosh) *vb.* **push·ing, pushed** to force away from oneself; to press, thrust, or shove. – *n.* **1** an act of pushing; a thrust or shove. **2** determination, aggression, or drive.

push·o·ver (poosh′ō′vər) *n.* (*informal*) **1** someone easily gotten the better of. **2** a task easily accomplished.

puss (poos) *n.* (*informal*) a cat.

put (poot) *vb.* **put·ting, put 1** to place in, or move to, a position or situation. **2** to cause to be: *My joke put him in a good mood.* **3** to apply: *I put pressure on them to go.* **4** to estimate: *I would put the costs at $10,000.* – *vb.* **put aside** to save for future use. – *vb.* **put back 1** to replace. **2** to postpone: *We put the meeting back a month.* **3** to adjust to an earlier time: *We put back the clock one hour in the fall.* – *vb.* **put forward 1** to offer or suggest: *to put forward an idea.* **2** to propose for a post, etc.; to nominate. **3** to advance the time or date of: *We put the wedding forward a month.* – *vb.* **put off 1** to postpone; to cancel. **2** to cause to lose enthusiasm for: *Her accident put me off climbing.* – *vb.* **put on 1** to switch on. **2** to present: *to put on a play.* – *vb.* **put out 1** to extinguish. **2** to inconvenience.

put·ty (put′ē) *n.* a paste used to fasten glass to window frames, fill holes in wood, etc.

puz·zle (puz′əl) *vb.* **puz·zling, puz·zled 1** to perplex, bewilder, or baffle. **2** to wonder or worry: *We puzzled over his motives.* – *n.* **1** a baffling problem. **2** a game or toy designed to test knowledge, memory, powers of observation, etc. – *adj.* **puz·zling** (puz′ling).

py·lon (pī′län′) *n.* a tall steel structure for supporting electric power cables.

pyr·a·mid (pir′ə-mid′) *n.* **1** any of the huge ancient Egyptian royal tombs built on a square base, with four sloping triangular sides meeting at the top. **2** a solid of this shape, with a square or triangular base.

● The three most famous pyramids built by the Egyptians are near the city of Giza. Central and South American Indians also built pyramids as temples from the A.D. 100s to 500s.

● **Pyr·e·nees** (pîr′ə-nēz′) a mountain range forming the border between FRANCE and SPAIN.

Pyr·rhic vic·to·ry (pir′ik vik′tə-rē) *n.* a victory won at so great a cost in lives, etc. that it can hardly be regarded as a triumph at all.

● **Py·thag·o·ras** (pə-thag′ə-rəs) was a Greek mathematician of the 500s B.C. who laid the foundations of geometry.

py·thon (pī′thän′, pī′thən) *n.* any of several large non-poisonous snakes, including the boa constrictor, that kill their prey by crushing.

Q q

quack (kwak) *n.* the cry of a duck. – *vb.* **quack·ing, quacked** to make this cry.

quadr- or **quadri-** *prefix* four.

quad·ran·gle (kwä′drang′gəl) *n.* a square, rectangle, or other four-sided figure.

quad·rant (kwä′drənt) *n.* **1** a quarter of the circumference of a circle. **2** an instrument used for measuring altitude.

quad·ri·lat·er·al (kwä′drə-lat′ər-əl) *n.* a four-sided two-dimensional figure.

quad·ru·ped (kwä′drə-ped′) *n.* a four-footed animal, especially a mammal, as a horse.

quad·ru·ple (kwä-droo′pəl, kwä-drup′əl) *vb.* **quad·ru·pling, quad·ru·pled** to multiply by four or increase four times.

quag·mire (kwag′mīr′) *n.* an area of soft marshy ground; a bog.

quail (kwāl) *n.* a bird of the partridge family.

quaint (kwānt) *adj.* charmingly or pleasingly odd or old-fashioned.

quake (kwāk) *vb.* **quak·ing, quaked** (of people) to shake or tremble.

Quak·er (kwā′kər) *n.* a member of a Christian sect, the Society of Friends, founded by George Fox in the 1600s.

qual·i·fi·ca·tion (kwäl′ə-fə-kā′shən) *n.* a skill or ability that fits someone for some job.

qual·i·fy (kwäl′ə-fī′) *vb.* **qual·i·fies, qual·i·fy·ing, qual·i·fied 1** to complete a training, pass an examination, etc., that gives professional status: *Julia qualified as a doctor.* **2** to make suitable for a task, job, etc.: *George is hardly qualified to judge.*

qual·i·ty (kwäl′ət-ē) *n.* **qual·i·ties 1** standard of goodness. **2** high standard: *She writes novels of quality.* – *adj.* of high quality.

quan·ti·ty (kwänt′ət-ē) *n.* **quan·ti·ties 1** the property things have that makes them measurable or countable; size or amount. **2** an amount that can be counted or measured; a specified amount. **3** largeness of amount; bulk.

quan·tum (kwänt′əm) *n.* **quanta** (kwänt′ə) **1** an amount or quantity. **2** in physics, an indivisible unit of any form of physical energy.

quar·an·tine (kwôr′ən-tēn′, kwär′ən-tēn′) *n.* the isolation of people or animals to prevent the spread of any infectious disease.

quar·rel (kwôr′əl, kwär′əl) *n.* **1** an angry disagreement or argument. **2** a cause of such disagreement. – *vb.* **quar·rel·ing, quar·reled 1** to argue or dispute angrily. **2** to disagree and fall out. **3** to find fault.

quar·rel·some (kwôr′əl-səm, kwär′əl-səm) *adj.* inclined to quarrel.

quar·ry[1] (kwôr′ē, kwär′ē) *n.* **quar·ries** an open excavation for the purpose of extracting stone or slate for building.

quar·ry[2] (kwôr′ē, kwär′ē) *n.* **quar·ries** a hunted animal or bird; a prey.

quart (kwôrt) *n.* a liquid measure equivalent to quarter of a gallon or two pints (0.946 liter).

The common quail of Europe, Asia, and North Africa is 7 in. (18 cm) long, and is mottled brown in color. American quail such as the bobwhite and the crested quail are more colorful and slightly larger.

The letter *Q*, like all the letters, has a long history. The earliest alphabets were taken and adapted by the Greeks. The Greek *beta*, when combined with the first letter, *aleph*, gives us the word alphabet.

The Greeks passed on their letters to the Romans, who developed the alphabet we use today, although they used only capital letters. Small letters developed in the A.D. 700s.

An early form of the letter Q, used in the Middle East more than 3,000 years ago.

This letter was taken by the Greeks and became koppa.

Over the years different versions of the letter Q have been developed.

Quartz is found nearly everywhere. Sand is mostly made of quartz. In its pure form it has no color and is as clear as glass. Quartz forms six-sided crystals.

KEY QUESTION
What does *qwerty* stand for? It is simply an ACRONYM for the first six letters on a normal computer or typewriter keyboard and it is used to describe such keyboards.

Mary, queen of Scots, on her way to her execution at Fotheringhay Castle in 1587. She was said to have plotted against Elizabeth I, queen of England.

quar·ter (kwôrt′ər) *n.* **1** one of four equal parts into which something may be divided. **2** in the UNITED STATES and CANADA, a coin worth 25 cents. – *vb.* **quar·ter·ing, quar·tered** to divide into quarters. – *adj.* being one of four equal parts.

quar·tet or **quar·tette** (kwôr-tet′) *n.* **1** a group of four singers or instrumental players. **2** a piece of music for four performers.

quartz (kwôrts) *n.* a common rock-forming mineral, a form of silica.

qua·sar (kwā′zär′) *n.* a distant, highly luminous source of radio waves, outside our galaxy.

qua·ver (kwā′vər) *vb.* **qua·ver·ing, qua·vered** (of someone's voice) to be unsteady; to shake or tremble. – *n.* **1** a musical trill. **2** a tremble in the voice.

quay (kē) *n.* a wharf for the loading and unloading of ships.

● **Que·bec** (kwi-bek′, kā-bek′) is the largest province in CANADA. The largest city is Montreal, the second biggest French-speaking city in the world. The city of Quebec is the capital.

queen (kwēn) *n.* **1** a woman who rules a country, having inherited her position by birth. **2** the wife of a king. **3** a large female ant, bee, or wasp that lays eggs. **4** the most powerful chess piece.

● **Queens·land** (kwēnz′lənd). See **Australia**.

queer (kwîr) *adj.* odd, strange, or unusual.

quench (kwench) *vb.* **quench·ing, quenched** to satisfy by drinking: *to quench a thirst.*

que·ry (kwîr′ē) *n.* **que·ries** a question, often one that raises a doubt.

quest (kwest) *n.* a search or hunt.

ques·tion (kwes′chən) *n.* **1** an utterance that requests information or an answer; the form of words in which this is expressed: *Can you put your question in writing, please?* **2** a doubt or query: *Their behavior raises questions about their loyalty.* **3** an uncertainty: *There is no question about the cause of the fire.* – *vb.* **ques·tion·ing, ques·tioned 1** to ask questions to; to interrogate. **2** to raise doubts about: *I'd question whether it's possible.*

question mark *n.* a punctuation mark (?) placed after a question.

queue (kyo͞o) *n.* a line or file of people or vehicles waiting for something.

quick (kwik) *adj.* **1** taking little time; speedy: *The train trip to Baltimore is very quick.* **2** lasting briefly: *a quick glance.* **3** not delayed; immediate: *a quick response.* **4** intelligent; alert; sharp: *a quick wit.* – *adv.* rapidly.

qui·et (kwī′ət) *adj.* **1** making little or no noise; soft. **2** (of a place, etc.) peaceful; tranquil; without noise or bustle. **3** silent; saying nothing: *Katie kept quiet about it.* – *n.* absence of, or freedom from, noise. – *adv.* **qui·et·ly.**

quill (kwil) *n.* **1** a large stiff feather from a bird's wing or tail. **2** a pen made from a feather.

quilt (kwilt) *n.* a cover for a bed containing padding or a filling of feathers, etc. stitched in patterns.

quince (kwins) *n.* the acid fruit of an Asian tree.

qui·nine (kwī′nīn′) *n.* a bitter-tasting drug, used to treat malaria.

quin·tu·plet (kwin-tup′lət, kwin-to͞o′plət) *n.* one of five children born at one birth.

quip (kwip) *n.* a witty remark.

quirk (kwurk) *n.* an odd habit or mannerism that someone has.

quit (kwit) *vb.* **quit·ting, quit** or **quit·ted** to leave, give up, or resign: *to quit a job.*

quite (kwīt) *adv.* **1** completely; entirely: *I don't quite understand; it's not quite clear.* **2** really; to a high degree. **3** to a great extent.

quiv·er (kwiv′ər) *vb.* **quiv·er·ing, quiv·ered** to shake or tremble slightly; to shiver.

quiz (kwiz) *n.* **quiz·zes** any series of questions as a test of knowledge. – *vb.* **quiz·zing, quizzed** to question; to interrogate.

quo·ta (kwōt′ə) *n.* someone's allocated share: *I've done my quota of work for today.*

quo·ta·tion (kwō-tā′shən) *n.* **1** something quoted. **2** a price for a bond, stock, etc.

quotation marks *n.* (*plural*) punctuation marks (" " or ' ') used to show the beginning and end of a quotation, or on either side of a word or phrase on which attention is focused.

quote (kwōt) *vb.* **quot·ing, quot·ed** to repeat the exact words of.

R r

rab·bi (rab′ī′) *n.* **1** a Jewish religious official and community leader. **2** a Jewish scholar.

rab·bit (rab′ət) *n.* a small, long-eared, burrowing animal with a fluffy white tail.

ra·bies (rā′bēz′) *n.* a disease of the nervous system which is caught by being bitten by an infected animal.

The raccoon belongs to the same family as the panda. Most of the seven species are about the size of a cat.

rac·coon or **ra·coon** (ra-kōōn′) *n.* a small furry North American animal, with a black striped tail and black rings around the eyes.

race¹ (rās) *n.* **1** a contest of speed between runners, horses, cars, etc. **2** (in *plural*) a series of such contests over a fixed course, especially for horses or dogs. **3** any contest or rivalry, especially to be the first to do or get something: *the arms race.* – *vb.* **rac·ing, raced** **1** to take part in a race. **2** to have a race with. **3** to run or move quickly.

Reflected waves

Transmitted waves

Radar screen

race² (rās) *n.* **1** a major division of human beings having particular physical characteristics, such as size, hair type, or skin color. **2** a tribe, nation, or other group of people.

●**Rach·ma·ni·nov** (räk-män′ə-nôf′), **Sergei** (1873-1943) was a Russian composer.

ra·cial (rā′shəl) *adj.* **1** of, or relating to, a particular race. **2** based on race. – *adv.* **ra·cial·ly**.

ra·cism (rā′siz′əm) *n.* **1** a belief that a particular race is superior to others. **2** discrimination and prejudice caused by such a belief. – *n.* & *adj.* **ra·cist** (rā′səst).

rack·et or **rac·quet** (rak′ət) *n.* a wooden or metal oval frame with gut or nylon strings stretched across it, used for playing tennis, badminton, squash, etc.

ra·dar (rā′där′) *n.* a device for detecting the direction, speed, and distance away of an aircraft, ship, etc. by bouncing radio waves off it.

ra·di·ate (rā′dē-āt′) *vb.* **ra·di·at·ing, ra·di·at·ed** **1** to send out rays of light, heat, electromagnetic radiation, etc. **2** to be emitted in rays: *Light radiates from the stars.* **3** to spread out from a central point as radii.

ra·di·a·tion (rā′dē-ā′shən) *n.* the sending out of energy in the form of electromagnetic waves or particles, such as x-rays.

Radar sends out high-frequency radio waves and picks up the signals reflected by an object. The reflected signals displayed as "blips" on a screen show the distance and direction of an object.

The letter *R*, like all the letters, has a long history. The earliest alphabets were taken and adapted by the Greeks. The Greek *beta*, when combined with the first letter, *aleph*, gives us the word alphabet.

The Greeks passed on their letters to the Romans, who developed the alphabet we use today, although they used only capital letters. Small letters developed in the A.D. 700s.

An early form of the letter R, used in the Middle East more than 3,000 years ago.

P

This letter was taken by the Greeks and became rho.

Over the years different versions of the letter R have been developed.

PRONUNCIATION SYMBOLS		
ə **away**	lemon	focus
a	fat	oi	boy
ā	fade	oo	foot
ä	hot	ōō	moon
âr	fair	ou	house
e	met	th	think
ē	mean	th	this
g	get	u	cut
hw	which	ur	hurt
i	fin	w	witch
ī	line	y	yes
îr	near	yōō	music
ô	often	yoor	pure
ō	note	zh	vision

ra·di·a·tor (rād′ē-āt′ər) *n.* an apparatus for heating a room, consisting of a series of pipes through which hot water or steam is circulated.

rad·i·cal (rad′i-kəl) *adj.* **1** of or relating to the basic nature of something; fundamental: *radical changes.* **2** in favor of extreme political and social reforms. – *n.* a person who holds radical political views. – *adv.* **rad·i·cal·ly** (rad′i-klē).

radii. See **radius**.

ra·di·o (rād′ē-ō′) *n.* **radios** **1** the sending and receiving of messages, etc. without connecting wires, using electromagnetic waves. **2** an electrical apparatus that receives, transmits, or broadcasts signals using electromagnetic waves. – *adj.* **1** of, for, transmitting, or transmitted by radio. **2** controlled by radio. – *vb.* **ra·di·os, ra·di·o·ing, ra·di·oed** to send by radio: *to radio a message.*

ra·di·o·ac·tiv·i·ty (rād′ē-ō-ak-tiv′ət-ē) *n.* the spontaneous disintegrating of the atomic nuclei of some elements, for example uranium, resulting in the giving off of radiation. – *adj.* **ra·di·o·ac·tive** (rād′ē-ō-ak′tiv).

radio telescope *n.* a telescope that can pick up radio waves generated by stars, planets, etc.

rad·ish (rad′ish) *n.* a plant of the mustard family, with pungent-tasting roots.

ra·di·um (rād′ē-əm) *n.* a radioactive metallic element (symbol **Ra**).

ra·di·us (rād′ē-əs) *n.* **ra·di·i** (rād′ē-ī′) or **radiuses** a straight line running from the center of a circle to a point on its circumference.

raft (raft) *n.* a flat structure of logs, timber, etc. that floats on water, used for transportation.

raf·ter (raf′tər) *n.* any of the sloping beams supporting a roof.

rag (rag) *n.* a scrap of cloth, especially a piece which has been worn or torn off old clothes.

rag·ged (rag′əd) *adj.* **1** (of clothes) old, worn, and tattered. **2** with a rough and irregular edge; jagged. **3** untidy; straggly.

rage (rāj) *n.* **1** violent anger. **2** violent force. **3** a fashion or craze. – *vb.* **rag·ing, raged** **1** to be violently angry. **2** to move or progress with great force: *The hurricane raged all night.*

raid (rād) *n.* a sudden unexpected attack.

rail (rāl) *n.* **1** a usually horizontal bar supported by vertical posts, forming a fence or barrier. **2** either of a pair of lengths of steel forming a track for the wheels of a train.

rail·ing (rāl′ing) *n.* a fence or barrier.

rail·road (rāl′rōd′) *n.* **1** a track or set of tracks formed by two parallel steel rails fixed to ties, for trains to run on. **2** a system of such tracks, plus all the trains, buildings, and people required for it to function.

rail·way (rāl′wā′) *n.* **1** a rail line with lighter equipment than that used on normal railroad. **2** (*British*) a railroad.

rain (rān) *n.* water falling from the clouds in drops. – *vb.* **rain·ing, rained** **1** (of rain) to fall. **2** to fall like rain: *The bullets rained down.*

When it **rains**, the sky returns water to the earth that once evaporated through the heat of the sun from the land and sea. This is known as the "water cycle." Water falling from clouds is known as "precipitation" and may fall as rain, drizzle, hail, or snow.

Most rain is formed by snowflakes melting as they fall. Rising water vapor cools and condenses into water droplets which form into clouds. At "freezing level" the droplets become ice crystals and grow into snowflakes.

A rainbow forms when sunlight plays on tiny raindrops. When a beam of sunlight shines on a raindrop, the raindrop acts as a prism and splits the beam into different colors.

Temperature

Wet snow

Dry snow

Sleet

Rain

Drizzle

rain·bow (rān'bō') *n.* an arch of colors in the sky (red, orange, yellow, green, blue, indigo, and violet), caused by light from the sun's rays being reflected and refracted through rain.

rain for·est (rān'fôr'əst, rān'fär'əst) *n.* a dense tropical forest, with broad-leaved, evergreen trees and heavy rainfall.

rain·y (rā'nē) *adj.* **rain·i·er, rain·i·est** having a lot of heavy showers of rain.

raise (rāz) *vb.* **rais·ing, raised** 1 to move or lift to a high position or level: *All who agree, raise your hand.* 2 to put in an upright or standing position. 3 to build. 4 to increase the value, amount, or strength of: *Please don't raise your voice.* 5 to put forward for consideration or discussion: *to raise an objection.* 6 to collect or gather together: *We raised $200 for charity.* 7 to bring up or rear: *to raise a family.* – *n.* 1 an act of raising or lifting. 2 an increase in salary. – *adj.* **raised.** – *n.* **rais·ing.**

rai·sin (rā'zən) *n.* a dried grape.

rake (rāk) *n.* a long-handled tool with a comb-like part at one end, used for smoothing or breaking up earth, gathering leaves together, etc. – *vb.* **rak·ing, raked** to collect, gather, or remove with, or as if with, a rake: *Tomorrow you must rake the leaves.*

●**Ra·leigh** (rô'lē, rä'lē), **Sir Walter** (1552-1618) was an English soldier, explorer, and poet.

ral·ly (ral'ē) *vb.* **ral·lies, ral·ly·ing, ral·lied** 1 to come or bring together again after being dispersed: *The colonel rallied his troops after the battle.* 2 to come or bring together for some common cause or action: *We rallied behind our team when they were in trouble.* – *n.* **ral·lies** 1 a reassembling of forces to make a new effort. 2 a mass meeting of people with a common cause. 3 in tennis, a long series of strokes between players before one of them finally wins the point.

ram (ram) *n.* 1 a male sheep. 2 **the Ram** the constellation and sign of the zodiac Aries. 3 (also **battering ram**) a device consisting of a pole and heavy head used to knock down walls, doors, etc. – *vb.* **ram·ming, rammed** 1 to force down or into position by pushing hard. 2 to strike or crash against violently.

Ra·ma·dan (ram'ə-dän', ram'ə-dan') *n.* the ninth month of the Muslim year, during which Muslims fast between sunrise and sunset.

ram·ble (ram'bəl) *vb.* **ram·bling, ram·bled** 1 to go for a long walk or walks, especially in the countryside, for pleasure. 2 to speak or write in an aimless or confused way. – *n.* a walk for pleasure. – *n.* & *adj.* **ram·bling.**

ram·bler (ram'blər) *n.* 1 a climbing plant, especially a rose. 2 a person who rambles.

●**Ram·ses** (ram'sēz') or **Ram·e·ses** (ram'ə-sēz') is the name of any of 12 pharaohs of ancient EGYPT to about 1090 B.C.

ramp (ramp) *n.* a sloping surface between two different levels, especially one that can be used instead of steps.

ram·shack·le (ram'shak'əl) *adj.* badly made and likely to fall down: *a ramshackle old shed.*

ran. See **run.**

ranch (ranch) *n.* a large farm for rearing cattle or horses.

ran·dom (ran'dəm) *adj.* lacking a plan, system, or order; irregular; haphazard. – *n.* **ran·dom·ness** (ran'dəm-nəs).

rang. See **ring².**

range (rānj) *n.* 1 an area between limits within which things may move, function, etc.; the limits forming this area: *The range of local radio stations is 50 miles.* 2 the distance to which a gun may be fired or an object thrown. 3 a group of mountains forming a distinct series or row. 4 a large area of open land for grazing livestock. 5 a large cooking stove. – *vb.* **rang·ing, ranged** 1 to put in a row or rows. 2 to put into a specified group: *He ranged himself among her enemies.* 3 to vary or change between specified limits. 4 to roam freely.

rang·er (rān'jər) *n.* (also **forest ranger**) a person who looks after a forest or park.

rank (rangk) *n.* 1 a line or row of people or things. 2 a line of soldiers standing side by side. 3 a position of seniority within an organization, society, the armed forces, etc.

ran·sack (ran'sak') *vb.* **ran·sack·ing, ran·sacked** to search thoroughly and often roughly: *Rioters ransacked the church.*

ran·som (ran'səm) *n.* money paid in return for the release of a kidnapped person.

The temple of Rameses II was carved out of solid rock on the banks of the Nile. It was moved to a higher position in 1964 when the Aswan High Dam was built.

rap (rap) *n.* **1** the sound made by a quick sharp tap or blow. **2** (*slang*) blame or punishment: *She had to take the rap.* **3** a fast, rhythmic monologue recited over a musical backing with a pronounced beat. – *vb.* **rap·ping, rapped** to strike sharply: *Robert rapped on the window.*

rape (rāp) *n.* the crime of forcing someone to have sex. – *n.* **rap·ist** (rā′pəst).

●**Ra·pha·el** (raf′ē-əl, rā′fē-əl, räf′ē-əl) (1483-1520) was an artist of the RENAISSANCE in Italy. His real name was Raffaello Sanzio.

rap·id (rap′əd) *adj.* moving or happening quickly; fast. – *n.* **ra·pid·i·ty** (rə-pid′ət-ē).

ra·pi·er (rā′pē-ər) *n.* a thin two-edged sword.

rare (râr) *adj.* **1** not done, found, or occurring very often: *Rhinos are becoming rare.* **2** (of the atmosphere at high altitudes) thin; not dense.

rare·ly (râr′lē) *adv.* not often.

rash[1] (rash) *adj.* hasty: *a rash decision.*

rash[2] (rash) *n.* a redness or outbreak of red spots on the skin.

rasp (rasp) *n.* **1** a coarse, rough file. **2** a harsh, rough, grating sound.

rasp·ber·ry (raz′ber′ē) *n.* **rasp·ber·ries** an edible red berry that grows on a shrub.

rat (rat) *n.* a rodent like a large, long-tailed mouse.

rate (rāt) *n.* **1** the number of times something happens, etc. within a given period of time: *at the rate of 20 miles an hour.* **2** a price or charge, often measured per unit: *What is the rate of pay for the job?* **3** a price or charge fixed according to a standard scale: *rate of exchange.* **4** class or rank: *second-rate.* – *vb.* **rat·ing, rat·ed 1** to give a value to: *Roy is rated an excellent teacher.* **2** to be worthy of; to deserve.

rath·er (ra<u>th</u>′ər, rä<u>th</u>′ər) *adv.* **1** more readily; from preference: *I'd rather stay at home than go out.* **2** more truly or properly: *He is my father, or rather my stepfather.* **3** to a certain extent; somewhat: *They married rather late in life.*

ra·ti·o (rā′shē-ō′) *n.* **ratios** the number or degree of one class of things in relation to another class: *The ratio of dogs to cats is 5 to 3.*

ra·tion (rā′shən, rash′ən) *n.* a fixed allowance of food, clothing, gas, etc., especially during a time of shortage. – *vb.* **ra·tion·ing, ra·tioned** to share out especially something which is in short supply.

ra·tion·al (rash′ən-l) *adj.* **1** of or based on reason or logic. **2** able to think, form opinions, make judgments, etc. – *adv.* **ra·tion·al·ly**.

rat·tle (rat′l) *vb.* **rat·tling, rat·tled 1** to make a series of short sharp hard sounds in quick succession: *The snake rattled its tail.* **2** to move along rapidly, often with a rattling noise. **3** to chatter thoughtlessly or idly. **4** to say or recite rapidly, fluently, or glibly: *Sarah rattled off all the names of the team.* – *n.* **1** a series of short sharp hard sounds in quick succession. **2** a baby's toy filled with small pellets which rattle when shaken.

rat·tle·snake (rat′l-snāk′) *n.* a poisonous American snake with loose rings on the tail which rattle.

rave (rāv) *vb.* **rav·ing, raved 1** to talk wildly as if crazy or delirious. **2** to talk enthusiastically about: *Rose raved about her new kitten.*

ra·ven (rā′vən) *n.* a large black bird of the crow family. – *adj.* glossy black.

ra·vine (rə-vēn′) *n.* a deep steep-sided gorge.

raw (rô) *adj.* **1** not cooked: *Lions eat raw meat.* **2** not processed, purified, or refined. **3** not trained or experienced: *raw recruits.*

raw deal *n.* (*informal*) harsh unfair treatment.

raw·hide (rô′hīd′) *n.* untanned leather.

raw material *n.* any material, usually in its natural state, out of which something is made.

ray[1] (rā) *n.* **1** a narrow beam of light or radioactive particles. **2** a small amount of or the beginnings of: *a ray of hope.*

ray[2] (rā) *n.* a fish with a broad flat body, eyes on the top of its head, and a long narrow tail.

A 17th-century rapier. Rapiers were long and narrow, two-edged and pointed. Swords of various shapes and sizes were for centuries important battlefield weapons. Later men fought duels with swords.

A thornback ray. Like their relations the sharks, rays have skeletons made of cartilage rather than bone.

A rattlesnake rattles its tail as a warning that it is about to strike. Twenty-nine species of rattlesnake live in the Americas.

ra·zor (rā′zər) *n.* a sharp-edged instrument used for shaving.

reach (rēch) *vb.* **reach·ing, reached 1** to arrive at; to get as far as: *We reached the hotel by noon.* **2** to be able to touch or get hold of: *I can almost reach the ceiling.* **3** to project or extend: *The curtains reach the floor.* **4** to make contact or communicate with. – *n.* the distance you can stretch your arm, hand, etc.

One of the important "little inventions" — the safety razor invented in 1880 by King C. Gillette.

re·act (rē-akt′) *vb.* **re·act·ing, re·act·ed 1** to respond to something that has been done or said, has happened, etc. **2** to undergo a chemical reaction.

re·ac·tion *n.* **1** a reacting or response to something. **2** a complete change of opinions, feelings, etc. to the opposite of what they were. **3** a process of change occuring in the atoms and molecules of substances when different substances are put together.

re·ac·tion·ar·y *adj.* opposed to change or progress: *reactionary views.*

read (rēd) *vb.* **read·ing, read** (red) **1** to look at and understand printed or written words. **2** to speak aloud words which are printed or written. **3** to interpret or understand the meaning of: *Can you read a map?* **4** (of writing) to be, or not be, coherent, fluent, and logical: *This essay reads well but that one reads badly.* – (red) *adj.* educated through reading: *John is very well read.*

read·a·ble (rēd′ə-bəl) *adj.* **1** legible; able to be read. **2** pleasant or quite interesting to read.

read·ing (rēd′ing) *n.* **1** the action of a person who looks at and understands what is written or printed. **2** the ability to read: *His reading is poor.* **3** an event at which a play, poetry, etc. is read to an audience. **4** information, figures, etc. shown by an instrument or meter.

read·out (rēd′out′) *n.* information received from a computer or instrument.

read·y (red′ē) *adj.* **read·i·er, read·i·est 1** prepared and available for action or use. **2** willing and able: *Rob is always ready to help.* **3** prompt; quick: *Don't be too ready to find fault.* **4** likely or about to: *The plant is just ready to flower.* – *adv.* **read·i·ly** (red′l-ē).

real (rē′əl, rēl, ril) *adj.* **1** which actually exists; not imaginary. **2** not imitation; genuine: *real leather.* **3** actual; true: *What was the real reason?* **4** great, important, or serious: *a real problem.*

real estate *n.* property in the form of houses or land.

re·al·ism (rē′ə-liz′əm, rēl′iz′əm) *n.* **1** in art and literature, a style that presents things as they really are. **2** an acceptance of things as they really are. – *n.* **re·al·ist** (rē′ə-ləst, rēl′əst). – *adj.* **re·al·is·tic** (rē′ə-lis′tik).

re·al·i·ty (rē-al′ət-ē) *n.* **re·al·i·ties 1** the state or fact of being real. **2** the real nature of something; the truth. – **in reality** in fact.

re·al·ize (rē′ə-līz′) *vb.* **re·al·iz·ing, re·al·ized 1** to come to know or understand: *I now realize how lucky I am.* **2** to make real; to make come true: *Anna realized her ambition.*

real·ly (rē′ə-lē, rē′lē, ri′ə-lē, ril′ē) *adv.* **1** actually; in fact. **2** very; genuinely.

realm (relm) *n.* **1** a kingdom. **2** a field of interest, study, or activity: *the realm of music.*

rear[1] (rîr) *n.* the back part; the area at the back. – *adj.* at the back: *Look out the rear window.*

rear[2] (rîr) *vb.* **rear·ing, reared** to feed, care for, and educate: *They reared three children.*

rea·son (rē′zən) *n.* **1** a justification or motive for an action, belief, etc. **2** an underlying explanation or cause: *What is the reason for her rude behavior?* **3** the power of the mind to think, form opinions, reach conclusions, etc. – *vb.* **rea·son·ing, rea·soned 1** to use the mind to form opinions, reach conclusions, etc. **2** to argue using careful logic: *She reasoned with him.*

rea·son·a·ble (rē′zə-nə-bəl, rēz′nə-bəl) *adj.* **1** sensible; showing reason or good judgment. **2** fair; not excessive: *a reasonable price.*

PRONUNCIATION SYMBOLS		
ə **a**way	l**e**mon	f**o**cus
a	f**a**t	oi	b**o**y
ā	f**a**de	oo	f**oo**t
ä	h**o**t	o͞o	m**oo**n
âr	f**ai**r	ou	h**ou**se
e	m**e**t	th	**th**ink
ē	m**ea**n	t͟h	**th**is
g	**g**et	u	c**u**t
hw	**wh**ich	ur	h**ur**t
i	f**i**n	w	**w**itch
ī	l**i**ne	y	**y**es
îr	n**ea**r	yo͞o	m**u**sic
ô	**o**ften	yoor	p**u**re
ō	n**o**te	zh	vi**s**ion

reb·el (reb′əl) *n.* **1** a person who opposes or fights against people in authority or oppressive conditions. **2** a person who does not accept the rules of normal behavior, dress, etc. – **re·bel** (ri-bel′) *vb.* **re·bel·ling, re·belled 1** to resist authority or oppressive conditions openly and with force. **2** to reject the accepted rules of behavior, dress, etc.

re·bel·lion (ri-bel′yən) *n.* an act of rebelling.

re·bel·lious (ri-bel′yəs) *adj.* rebelling or likely to rebel.

re·ceipt (ri-sēt′) *n.* a written note saying that money or goods have been received.

re·ceive (ri-sēv′) *vb.* **re·ceiv·ing, re·ceived 1** to get, be given, or accept. **2** to experience or suffer: *to receive injuries.*

re·cent (rē′sənt) *adj.* happening, done, having appeared, etc. not long ago: *recent history.*

re·cess (rē′ses′, ri-ses′) *n.* **1** an open space or alcove set in a wall. **2** a temporary break from work.

rec·i·pe (res′ə-pē) *n.* a list of ingredients for, and set of instructions on how to prepare and cook, a particular kind of dish, cake, etc.

re·cite (ri-sīt′) *vb.* **re·cit·ing, re·cit·ed** to repeat aloud from memory.

reck·less (rek′ləs) *adj.* very careless; acting or done without any thought of the consequences.

reck·on (rek′ən) *vb.* **reck·on·ing, reck·oned 1** to calculate or compute: *The store clerk reckoned the bill.* **2** to think of as part of or belonging to.

rec·og·ni·tion (rek′əg-nish′ən) *n.* the act or state of recognizing.

rec·og·nize (rek′ig-nīz′) *vb.* **rec·og·niz·ing, re·cog·nized 1** to identify or know again: *I'd recognize Ellen anywhere.* **2** to admit or be aware of: *I recognize my mistakes.* **3** to show approval of and gratitude for. – *adj.* **re·cog·niz·a·ble** (rek′əg-nī′zə-bəl).

re·com·mend (rek′ə-mend′) *vb.* **re·com·mend·ing, re·com·mend·ed 1** to advise. **2** to suggest as being suitable to be accepted, chosen, etc. – *n.* **re·com·mend·ation** (rek′ə-mən-dā′shən).

rec·on·cile (rek′ən-sīl′) *vb.* **rec·on·cil·ing, rec·on·ciled 1** to make friendly again, for example after a quarrel. **2** to bring into agreement: *to reconcile differences.* **3** to make adjusted to; to resign. – *n.* **rec·on·cil·i·a·tion** (rek′ən-sil′ē-ā′shən).

rec·ord (rek′ərd) *n.* **1** a formal written report of facts, events, or information. **2** a round flat piece of usually black grooved plastic on which sound is recorded. **3** a performance that has never yet been beaten. – **re·cord** (ri-kôrd′) *vb.* **re·cord·ing, re·cord·ed 1** to set down in writing or some other permanent form. **2** to

A videorecorder stores signals for both sounds and pictures on magnetic tape. This tape is stored in a plastic cassette.

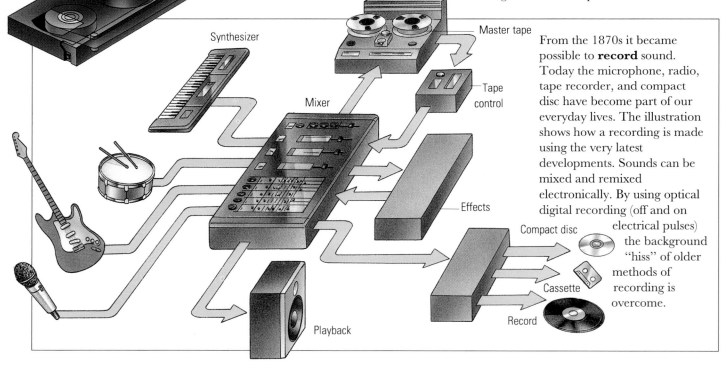

Synthesizer

Master tape

Mixer

Tape control

Effects

Compact disc

Cassette

Record

Playback

From the 1870s it became possible to **record** sound. Today the microphone, radio, tape recorder, and compact disc have become part of our everyday lives. The illustration shows how a recording is made using the very latest developments. Sounds can be mixed and remixed electronically. By using optical digital recording (off and on electrical pulses) the background "hiss" of older methods of recording is overcome.

register on a record or tape to be listened to in the future: *to record a song.*

re·count (ri-kount′) *vb.* **re·count·ing, re·count·ed** to tell in detail: *to recount a story.*

re·cov·er (ri-kuv′ər) *vb.* **re·cov·er·ing, re·cov·ered 1** to get or find again: *They recovered the lost kitten.* **2** to get well again. – *adj.* **re·cov·er·a·ble** (ri-kuv′ər-ə-bəl).

re·cov·er·y (ri-kuv′ə-rē) *n.* **re·cov·er·ies** an act of recovering or state of having recovered: *Bill made a quick recovery from the flu.*

rec·re·a·tion (rek′rē-ā′shən) *n.* a pleasant and often refreshing activity done in spare time. – *adj.* **rec·re·a·tion·al** (rek′rē-ā′shən′l).

re·cruit (ri-krōōt′) *n.* a newly enlisted member of the army, air force, navy, etc.

rec·tan·gle (rek′tang′gəl) *n.* a four-sided figure with opposite sides which are equal and four right angles. – *adj.* **rec·tan·gu·lar** (rek-tang′gyə-lər).

re·cur (ri-kur′) *vb.* **re·cur·ring, re·curred** to happen or come around again or at intervals. – *n.* **re·cur·rence** (ri-kur′əns).

red (red) *adj.* **red·der, red·dest 1** of the color of blood. **2** (of hair or fur) a color between a golden brown and a deep brown.

Red Cross *n.* an international organization which brings medical relief to the victims of wars and natural disasters.

●**Red Sea** (red sē′). This sea divides Arabia from northeast AFRICA. It is linked to the MEDITERRANEAN by the SUEZ CANAL.

re·duce (ri-dōōs′, ri-dyōōs′) *vb.* **re·duc·ing, re·duced 1** to make or become less, smaller, etc. **2** to lower the price of.

re·duc·tion (ri-duk′shən) *n.* **1** an act of reducing; the state of being reduced. **2** the amount by which something is reduced.

re·dun·dant (ri-dun′dənt) *adj.* **1** using or having more words than are needed. **2** not needed; superfluous.

red·wood (red′wood′) *n.* a large Californian conifer with reddish wood.

reed (rēd) *n.* a tall stiff grass growing in wet places.

reef (rēf) *n.* a ridge of rocks, sand, etc. just above or below the surface of the sea.

reel (rēl) *n.* **1** a cylindrical object on which thread, film, fishing line, etc. can be wound. **2** a lively traditional Scottish, Irish, or American dance. – *vb.*

reel·ing, reeled 1 to wind on a reel. **2** to pull in or up using a reel: *to reel in a fish.* **3** to stagger or sway; to move unsteadily. **4** to appear to whirl: *The room began to reel and then she fainted.*

re·fer (ri-fur′) *vb.* **re·fer·ring, re·ferred 1** to talk or write about; to mention. **2** to relate, concern, or apply to: *Does this refer to me?* **3** to look for information: *Please refer to your notes.*

ref·e·ree (ref′ə-rē′) *n.* an umpire or judge, for example of a game or in a dispute.

ref·er·ence (ref′rəns, ref′ə-rəns) *n.* **1** a mention of something; an illusion. **2** a direction in a book to another passage or book. **3** a book in which information can be found.

re·fine (ri-fīn′) *vb.* **re·fin·ing, re·fined** to make pure by removing dirt, waste substances, etc.

re·flect (ri-flekt′) *vb.* **re·flect·ing, re·flect·ed 1** to send back light, heat, sound, etc.: *White clothes reflect the sun's rays.* **2** (of a mirror, etc.) to give an image of. **3** to consider carefully: *Candice reflected on the poem.*

re·flec·tion (ri-flek′shən) *n.* **1** the act of reflecting. **2** the sound, heat, light, etc. reflected. **3** a reflected image: *Rose saw her reflection in the mirror.* **4** careful consideration.

re·form (ri-fôrm′) *vb.* **re·form·ing, re·formed 1** to improve or remove faults from: *to reform a criminal.* **2** to give up bad habits, improve behavior, etc. – *n.* a correction or improvement, as in a social or political system: *Freeing the slaves was a major reform.*

re·for·ma·tion (ref′ər-mā′shən) *n.* **1** the act of reforming or state of being reformed. **2 Reformation** the 16th-century religious movement which began by trying to reform abuses in the ROMAN CATHOLIC Church and which led to the development of the various PROTESTANT churches in Europe.

PRONUNCIATION SYMBOLS			
ə	**away**	lemon	focus
a	**fat**	oi	**boy**
ā	**fade**	oo	**foot**
ä	**hot**	ōō	**moon**
âr	**fair**	ou	**house**
e	**met**	th	**think**
ē	**mean**	t͟h	**this**
g	**get**	u	**cut**
hw	**which**	ur	**hurt**
i	**fin**	w	**witch**
ī	**line**	y	**yes**
îr	**near**	yōō	**music**
ô	**often**	yoor	**pure**
ō	**note**	zh	**vision**

The Reformation: In England between 1536 and 1540 the monasteries were dissolved (closed) by Henry VIII, who had broken all ties with the pope. He decided that the great wealth of the monasteries should go to the Crown. The money helped to pay for wars with France.

A refrigerator from about 1930 with a compartment for ice and shelves for food.

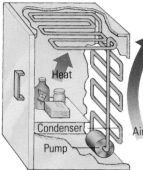

An electric refrigerator: a fluid called a refrigerant evaporates into a gas inside the coils in the freezing compartment, absorbing heat and lowering the temperature. A pump compresses the gas and turns it back into a liquid. It releases the heat absorbed from the freezer compartment to the room outside the refrigerator.

re·fract (ri-frakt′) *vb.* **re·fract·ing, re·fract·ed** to cause refraction in.

re·frac·tion (ri-frak′shən) *n.* the bending of a ray of light, sound, etc. to a different angle when that ray enters a different medium.

re·frain (ri-frān′) *vb.* **re·frain·ing, re·frained** to restrain or keep yourself back: *Please refrain from smoking.*

re·fresh (ri-fresh′) *vb.* **re·fresh·ing, re·freshed** to give renewed strength, energy, and enthusiasm to.

re·fresh·ment (ri-fresh′mənt) *n.* anything that refreshes, such as food and drink.

re·frig·er·ate (ri-frij′ə-rāt′) *vb.* **re·frig·er·at·ing, re·frig·er·at·ed** to make or keep cold to prevent spoilage.

re·frig·er·a·tor (ri-frij′ə-rāt′ər) *n.* a machine that keeps food cold to prevent spoilage.

ref·uge (ref′yōōj′, ref′yōōzh′) *n.* shelter or protection from danger or trouble.

ref·u·gee (ref′yoo-jē′, ref′yoo-jē′) *n.* a person who seeks shelter, especially from persecution.

re·fund (ri-fund′, rē′fund′) *vb.* **re·fund·ing, re·fund·ed** to pay back to someone: *to refund a deposit.* – (rē′fund′) *n.* **1** the paying back of money, etc. **2** the money, etc. paid back.

re·fus·al (ri-fyōō′zəl) *n.* an act of refusing.

re·fuse¹ (ri-fyōōz′) *vb.* **re·fus·ing, re·fused 1** to express unwillingness to do something. **2** to not accept: *I refused the offer of help.*

re·fuse² (ref′yōōs′) *n.* rubbish.

re·gal (rē′gəl) *adj.* of, or like, a king or queen.

re·gard (ri-gärd′) *vb.* **re·gard·ing, re·gard·ed 1** to consider. **2** to pay attention to; to take notice of. **3** to look at attentively or steadily. – *n.* **1** thought or attention. **2** care or consideration. **3** respect and affection.

re·gard·ing (ri-gärd′ing) *prep.* concerning.

re·gime (ri-zhēm′, rā-zhēm′) *n.* (also **régime**) a system of government: *a new regime.*

re·gion (rē′jən) *n.* **1** an area with particular geographical, social, etc. characteristics; a district: *the Arctic regions.* **2** any area, place, zone, etc.: *the region of the brain behind the eyes.*

reg·is·ter (rej′ə-stər) *n.* **1** a book containing a written list or record of names, events, etc. **2** a machine or device that records and lists information, especially one in a store (**cash register**) which lists sales and in which money is kept. – *vb.* **reg·is·ter·ing, reg·is·tered 1** to enter in an official register. **2** to enroll. – *n.* **reg·is·tra·tion** (rej′ə-strā′shən).

re·gret (ri-gret′) *vb.* **re·gret·ting, re·gret·ted** to feel sorry, distressed, disappointed about: *I regret missing your visit.* – *n.* a feeling of sorrow, disappointment, etc.

re·gret·ta·ble (ri-gret′ə-bəl) *adj.* that should be regretted; unwelcome; unfortunate. – *adv.* **re·gret·ta·bly** (ri-gret′ə-blē).

reg·u·lar (reg′yə-lər) *adj.* usual; normal; customary: *It's past Tom's regular bedtime.*

reg·u·late (reg′yə-lāt′) *vb.* **reg·u·lat·ing, re·gu·lat·ed 1** to control or adjust as required. **2** to control or direct according to rules: *to regulate trade.*

reg·u·la·tion (reg′yə-lā′shən) *n.* **1** a rule or instruction. **2** the act of regulating or state of being regulated.

re·hearse (ri-hurs′) *vb.* **re·hears·ing, re·hearsed** to practice a play, piece of music, etc. before performing it for an audience. – *n.* **re·hears·al** (ri-hur′səl).

reign (rān) *n.* the time during which a king or queen rules – *vb.* **reign·ing, reigned 1** to be a monarch. **2** to dominate: *Silence reigns.*

rein (rān) *n.* (usually in *plural*) one of two straps attached to a bridle for guiding a horse.

rein·deer (rān′dîr′) *n.* **reindeer** or **reindeers** a large deer found in ARCTIC regions.

The reindeer is the only deer in which the female carries antlers. Reindeer are related to caribou, but unlike the caribou, reindeer of Arctic Europe and Asia are domesticated.

re·in·force (rē′in-fôrs′, rē-in-fôrs′) *vb.*
re·in·forc·ing, re·in·forced to make
stronger or give additional support to.

re·ject (ri-jekt′) *vb.* **re·ject·ing, re·ject·ed**
1 to refuse to accept, agree to, admit, believe,
etc.: *Robin rejected my friendship.* **2** to throw away
or discard. – (rē′jekt′) *n.* a person or thing that
is rejected. – *n.* **re·jec·tion** (ri-jek′shən).

re·lapse (ri-laps′) *vb.* **re·laps·ing, re·lapsed**
to return to a former bad state or condition. –
(rē′laps′) *n.* the act or process of relapsing.

re·late (ri-lāt′) *vb.* **re·lat·ing, re·lat·ed 1** to
tell. **2** to connect or bring into relation.

re·lat·ed (ri-lāt′əd) *adj.* **1** belonging to the same
family. **2** connected.

re·la·tion (ri-lā′shən) *n.* **1** a connection
between one person or thing and another. **2** a
relative. **3** reference; respect: *in relation to.* **4** (in
plural) the social, political, or personal contact
between people, countries, etc.

rel·a·tive (rel′ət-tiv) *n.* a person who is related
to someone else by birth or marriage. – *adj.*
1 compared with something else; comparative:
the relative speeds of a car and train. **2** existing only
in relation to something else.

rel·a·tiv·i·ty (rel′ə-tiv′ət-ē) *n.* **1** the state of
being relative. **2** (also **special theory of
relativity**) Einstein's theory (published in
1905) that the mass of a body varies with its
speed, based on the premises that all motion is
relative and that the speed of light relative to
an observer is constant.

re·lax (ri-laks′) *vb.* **re·lax·ing, re·laxed 1** to
make or become less tense or worried. **2** to give
or take rest completely from work or effort.

re·lax·a·tion (rē′lak-sā′shən) *n.* **1** the act of
relaxing. **2** a relaxing activity.

re·lay (rē′lā′) *n.* a set of people that relieves
others doing some task, etc. – (rē′lā′) *vb.*
re·lay·ing, re·layed to receive and pass.

re·lease (ri-lēs′) *vb.* **re·leas·ing, re·leased**
1 to free from captivity. **2** to relieve from
something unpleasant, a duty, etc. **3** to loosen a
grip on and stop holding.

re·lent·less (ri-lent′ləs) *adj.* **1** never stopping:
relentless noise. **2** determined not to give up.

rel·e·vant (rel′ə-vənt) *adj.* connected with the
matter being discussed, etc.

re·li·a·ble (ri-lī′ə-bəl) *adj.* able to be trusted.

re·lief (ri-lēf′) *n.* **1** the lessening or removal of
pain, worry, oppression, or distress. **2** help,
often in the form of money, food, clothing, and
medicine, given to people in need.

re·lieve (ri-lēv′) *vb.* **re·liev·ing, re·lieved**
1 to lessen or stop. **2** to take a burden from.

re·li·gion (ri-lij′ən) *n.* **1** a belief in, or the
worship of, a god or gods. **2** a particular system
of belief or worship, such as CHRISTIANITY or
JUDAISM.

re·li·gious (ri-lij′əs) *adj.* **1** of, or relating to, religion. **2** pious; devout.

rel·ish (rel′ish) *vb.* **rel·ish·ing, rel·ished** to
enjoy greatly; to look forward to with great
pleasure. – *n.* **1** pleasure; enjoyment. **2** a spicy,
appetizing sauce often made of pickles.

re·luc·tant (ri-luk′tənt) *adj.* unwilling.

re·ly (ri-lī′) *vb.* **re·lies, re·ly·ing, re·lied** to
trust; to depend on or need: *The colonists relied
on help from France.*

re·main (ri-mān′) *vb.* **re·main·ing,
re·mained 1** to be left. **2** to stay in the same
place; not to leave. **3** to continue.

re·main·der (ri-mān′dər) *n.* the number or
part that is left after the rest has gone, been
taken away, etc.

RELIGIOUS TERMS

agnostic someone who belives that nothing can be known about the existence of God.

atheism the belief that there is no god.

baptism a Christian rite of immersion, or being sprinkled with water to signify purification.

bar mitzvah a Jewish ceremony in which usually a 13-year-old boy formally accepts full religious responsibilities. A similar ceremony for a girl is a **bas mitzvah**.

circumcision the cutting away of the foreskin, a practice especially important to the Jews.

Easter an annual Christian festival commemorating the resurrection of Jesus.

hegira Muhammad's escape from Mecca to Medina in A.D. 622. It was taken as the beginning of the history of Muslim people.

Koran the Holy Book of Islam.

kosher the term signifying that food is fit to be eaten according to Jewish ritual.

Rosh Hashanah the Jewish New Year.

Sabbath a day of the week set aside for rest and religious observance: for Jews it is Saturday.

Trinity a Christian term for God as existing in the form of three divine persons: the Father, Son, and Holy Spirit.

yoga a Hindu philosophy involving union with the Absolute Being.

Yom Kippur a Jewish fast day.

---

*All the major religions
have special symbols or
signs. The yin and yang
of Taoism (5th down),
for instance, are
two opposing
forces of
nature
which need
to be balanced
for harmony.*

Christian cross

Islam's crescent
moon and star

Hindu god Siva

Statue of
the Buddha

Taoist
symbol
of yin
and yang

Judaism's
Star of
David

Symbol of Sikhism

re·mains (ri-mānz′) *n.* (*plural*) **1** what is left after part has been taken away, eaten, destroyed, etc. **2** a dead body.

re·mark (ri-märk′) *vb.* **re·mark·ing, re·marked** to make a comment. – *n.* a comment; an observation.

re·mark·a·ble (ri-mär′kə-bəl) *adj.* worth mentioning or commenting on; unusual.

●**Rem·brandt** (rem′brant′) (1606-1669) was perhaps the greatest of the Dutch painters.

rem·e·dy (rem′əd-ē) *n.* **rem·e·dies 1** any drug or treatment that cures or controls a disease. **2** anything that solves a problem.

re·mem·ber (ri-mem′bər) *vb.* **re·mem·ber·ing, re·mem·bered 1** to recall to mind something from memory. **2** to keep a fact, idea, etc. in your mind.

re·mind (ri-mīnd′) *vb.* **re·mind·ing, re·mind·ed 1** to help to remember. **2** to make think about someone or something else, especially because of a similarity.

re·mote (ri-mōt′) *adj.* **1** far away or distant in time or place. **2** very small or slight.

re·move (ri-mo͞ov′) *vb.* **re·mov·ing, re·moved 1** to move out: *They removed the furniture.* **2** to take off: *Jack removed his coat.* **3** to get rid of: *Dave removed the stains with vinegar.*

re·nais·sance (ren′ə-sänts′) *n.* **1** a rebirth or revival. **2 Renaissance** the revival of arts, literature, and classical scholarship, and the beginnings of modern science, in Europe in the 1300s to the 1500s.

ren·der (ren′dər) *vb.* **ren·der·ing, ren·dered 1** to cause to become: *The drug rendered him helpless.* **2** to give or provide: *to render a service.* **3** to perform: *to render a song.* **4** to translate or put into other words. **5** to melt: *to render fat.*

ren·dez·vous (rän′di-vo͞o′) *n.* **rendezvous** (rän′di-vo͞oz′) an appointment to meet, or the meeting itself, at a specified time and in a specific place.

ren·di·tion (ren-dī′shən) *n.* **1** a performance of a musical or theatrical work: *a rendition of "Yankee Doodle."* **2** a translation.

re·new (ri-no͞o′, ri-nyo͞o′) *vb.* **re·new·ing, re·newed 1** to make fresh or like new again. **2** to begin again; to repeat. **3** to make valid for a further period of time.

●**Re·noir** (ren-wär′), **Pierre** (1841-1919) was a French painter whose works are classified as IMPRESSIONISM.

rent (rent) *n.* money paid to the owner of a property by a tenant in return for the use or occupation of that property. – *vb.* **rent·ing, rent·ed** to pay rent for a building, etc.

re·pair (ri-pâr′) *vb.* **re·pair·ing, re·paired** to restore to good working condition; to fix. – *n.* an act of repairing.

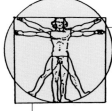

From the 1300s Europeans began to rediscover the learning of ancient Greece and Rome. This **Renaissance** ("rebirth") was an exciting time of thought and discovery. Artists such as Leonardo Da Vinci and Michelangelo produced great paintings and sculpture. Scientists such as Galileo and Copernicus had new ideas about the universe. Explorers such as Columbus discovered new lands.

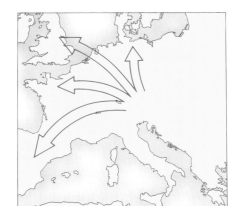

Italy in the late 1300s was the birthplace of the Renaissance. The invention of printing in the 1450s helped the spread of the Renaissance all over Europe.

A future idea anticipated: This sketch of a flying machine is by Leonardo da Vinci, who was both an artist and a scientist.

A merchant and his wife in Renaissance Italy. In the background is a French chateau built in the Italian style.

re·peal (ri-pēl′) *vb.* **re·peal·ing, re·pealed** to make no longer valid. − *n.* the act of repealing a law, etc.

re·peat (ri-pēt′) *vb.* **re·peat·ing, re·peat·ed** to say, do, etc. again: *He repeated his accusation in front of the teacher.* − *n.* an act of repeating.

re·pel (ri-pel′) *vb.* **re·pel·ling, re·pelled 1** to force or drive back or away. **2** to cause a feeling of disgust or loathing.

re·pent (ri-pent′) *vb.* **re·pent·ing, re·pent·ed** to feel great sorrow or regret.

rep·e·ti·tion (rep′ə-tish′ən) *n.* **1** the act of repeating. **2** a thing that is repeated.

rep·e·ti·tious (rep′ə-tish′əs) or **re·pet·i·tive** (ri-pet′ət-iv) *adj.* having too much repetition.

re·place (ri-plās′) *vb.* **re·plac·ing, re·placed 1** to put back in a previous or proper position. **2** to take the place of or be a substitute for. **3** to substitute or fill the place of.

re·place·ment (ri-plā′smənt) *n.* **1** the act of replacing something. **2** a person or thing that replaces another.

rep·li·ca (rep′li-kə) *n.* an exact copy.

re·ply (ri-plī′) *vb.* **re·plies, re·ply·ing, re·plied 1** to respond in words, writing, or action. **2** to say or do something in answer. − *n.* **re·plies** something said, written, or done in answer or response.

re·port (ri-pôrt′, ri-pōrt′) *n.* **1** a detailed statement, description, or account, especially after investigation. **2** a detailed account of the discussions and decisions of a committee. − *vb.* **re·port·ing, re·port·ed** to give an account or description of.

report card *n.* a statement of a pupil's work and behavior at school given to the parents.

re·pose (ri-pōz′) *n.* a state of rest.

rep·re·sent (rep′ri-zent′) *vb.* **rep·re·sent·ing, rep·re·sent·ed 1** to serve as a symbol or sign for; to stand for or correspond to: *Letters represent sounds.* **2** to speak or act on behalf of. **3** to be a good example of.

rep·re·sen·ta·tive (rep′ri-zent′ət-iv) *adj.* **1** representing. **2** being a good example of something; typical. − *n.* a person who represents someone or something else.

re·pro·duce (rē′prə-dōōs′, rē′prə-dyōōs′) *vb.* **re·pro·duc·ing, re·pro·duced 1** to make or produce a copy or imitation of; to duplicate. **2** to produce offspring.

re·pro·duc·tion (rē′prə-duk′shən) *n.* a copy or imitation, especially of a work of art.

rep·tile (rep′tīl′, rep′təl) *n.* any of the group of cold- blooded vertebrates which have a body covered with scales or bony plates, for example snakes, lizards, alligators, and turtles.

re·pub·lic (ri-pub′lik) *n.* a form of government in which there is no monarch, and in which power is held by the people or their elected representatives.

re·pub·li·can (ri-pub′li-kən) *adj.* **1** of, like, or for a republic. **2 Republican** of the Republican party, one of the two major political parties in the UNITED STATES.

rep·u·ta·ble (rep′yət-ə-bəl) *adj.* well thought of; trustworthy.

rep·u·ta·tion (rep′yə-tā′shən) *n.* the generally held opinion about a person with regard to abilities, character, etc.

re·quest (ri-kwest′) *n.* **1** the act of asking for something. **2** something asked for: *Our request is for money for the refugees.* − *vb.* **re·quest·ing, re·quest·ed** to ask for, especially politely.

re·quire (ri-kwīr′) *vb.* **re·quir·ing, re·quired 1** to need; to wish to have: *All living things require oxygen.* **2** to have as a necessary condition for success, etc.: *You require a brain to think.*

re·quire·ment (ri-kwīr′mənt) *n.* something that is needed, asked for, essential, etc.

res·cue (res′kyōō′) *vb.* **res·cu·ing, res·cued** to free from danger, trouble, captivity, etc.

re·search (ri-surch′, rē′surch) *n.* a detailed and careful investigation into some area of study. − *vb.* **re·search·ing, re·searched** to carry out such an investigation.

re·sem·ble (ri-zem′bəl) *vb.* **re·sem·bling, re·sem·bled** to look like or be similar to.

re·sent (ri-zent′) *vb.* **re·sent·ing, re·sent·ed** to feel anger or bitterness toward.

res·er·va·tion (rez′ər-vā′shən) *n.* **1** something that has been reserved, as at a hotel or restaurant. **2** (usually in *plural*) a doubt or objection. **3** an area of land set aside for a particular purpose, especially in the UNITED STATES and CANADA for the original native inhabitants.

Republic comes from two Latin words, *res* meaning "affair or thing," and *publica*, meaning "public." The word was originally *respublica*, but the *s* was dropped in French, which is the source of the English word.

A simple, single-celled organism such as an amoeba reproduces by splitting into two by the process of cell division or mitosis.

Parent amoeba

Cell divides

Two daughter amoebas

Georg Simon Ohm (1789-1854) was a German physicist who found that the electrical resistance of a conductor (the material through which an electric current flows) depends on its thickness, its length, and the material it is made from. The unit of resistance, the ohm, is named after him.

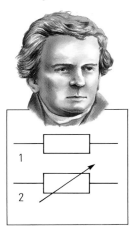

Symbols used to show fixed resistance (1) and variable resistance (2). In electronics a resistor is a circuit component that has resistance. The resistance in a variable resistor can be altered. It is used as a volume control in radios, for instance.

re·serve (ri-zurv´) *vb.* **re·serv·ing, re·served** **1** to order in advance. **2** to keep back or set aside for the use of a particular person or for a particular purpose. – *n.* **1** something set aside for later use. **2** land set aside for a particular purpose: *a nature reserve.*

res·er·voir (rez´ərv-wär´) *n.* a place, usually an artificial lake, where water is stored.

re·side (ri-zīd´) *vb.* **re·sid·ing, re·sid·ed** to live or have a home in, especially permanently.

res·i·dence (rez´əd-əns) *n.* **1** a house or dwelling. **2** the act of living in a place.

re·sign (ri-zīn´) *vb.* **re·sign·ing, re·signed** **1** to give up a job, etc. **2** to accept with patience and without resistance; to yield.

re·sig·na·tion (rez´ig-nā´shən) *n.* **1** the act of resigning. **2** the state of showing acceptance.

res·in (rez´ən) *n.* a sticky substance produced by certain trees, for example firs and pines.

re·sist (ri-zist´) *vb.* **re·sist·ing, re·sist·ed** **1** to oppose; to fight against someone or something; to refuse to give in to or comply with. **2** to remain undamaged by.

re·sis·tance (ri-zis´təns) *n.* **1** the act of resisting. **2** the ability to be unaffected by something, especially disease. **3** the force that one object exerts on the movement of another, causing it to slow down or stop. **4** the opposition to the passage of heat, electricity, etc. through a substance.

res·o·lu·tion (rez´ə-loo´shən) *n.* **1** the act of making a firm decision. **2** a formal expression of opinion, will, etc. by a group of people.

re·solve (ri-zälv´, ri-zôlv´) *vb.* **re·solv·ing, re·solved** **1** to make a firm decision to. **2** to pass a resolution, especially formally. **3** to find an answer to. – *n.* determination.

re·sort (ri-zôrt´) *vb.* **re·sort·ing, re·sort·ed** to turn to as a way of solving a problem, etc. when other methods have failed. – *n.* a place visited by many people on vacation.

re·sound (ri-zound´) *vb.* **re·sound·ing, re·sound·ed** (of sounds) to ring or echo.

re·sound·ing (ri-zoun´ding) *adj.* **1** echoing and ringing. **2** clear and decisive: *a resounding victory.*

re·source (rē´-sôrs´, rē´zôrs´, ri-zôrs´) *n.* **1** a person or thing that gives help, support, etc. when needed. **2** (usually in *plural*) a means of support, for example money and property. **3** (usually in *plural*) a country's or business's source of wealth: *natural resources.*

re·spect (ri-spekt´) *n.* **1** admiration; good opinion. **2** consideration of or attention to. **3** (in *plural*) a greeting or expression of admiration, esteem, and honor. – *vb.* **re·spect·ing, res·pect·ed** **1** to show or feel admiration or high regard for. **2** to show consideration, attention, or thoughtfulness to.

re·spec·tive (ri-spek´tiv) *adj.* belonging to or relating to each person or thing mentioned; separate: *We went to our respective homes.*

res·pi·ra·tion (res´pə-rā´shən) *n.* breathing.

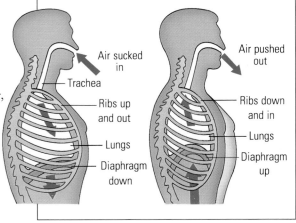

Land vertebrates have lungs for breathing or **respiration**. Breathe in and your diaphragm contracts, increasing the space inside your chest. Air flows in to fill the space. Breathe out and your diaphragm relaxes, reducing the space inside your chest. The air rushes out.

Air sucked in
Trachea
Ribs up and out
Lungs
Diaphragm down

Air pushed out
Ribs down and in
Lungs
Diaphragm up

re·spond (ri-spänd´) *vb.* **re·spond·ing, re·spond·ed** **1** to answer or reply. **2** to act or behave in reply or response: *I smiled at her, but she didn't respond.* **3** to react favorably or well.

re·sponse (ri-späns´) *n.* a reply or answer.

re·spon·si·bil·i·ty (ri-spän´sə-bil´ət-ē) *n.* **re·spon·si·bil·i·ties** something or someone for which one is responsible.

re·spon·si·ble (ri-spän´sə-bəl) *adj.* **1** having control over and being accountable for; having as a job. **2** having to answer or account for something: *You are responsible to the dean.* **3** having many important duties, especially the making of important decisions.

rest¹ (rest) *n.* **1** a short period of relaxation or freedom from work, activity, worry, etc. **2** sleep; repose. **3** calm; tranquillity. **4** a state of

not moving or working. – *vb.* **rest·ing,
rest·ed 1** to stop working or moving. **2** to relax, especially by sleeping. **3** to set, place, or lie on or against something for support.

rest² (rest) *n.*: **the rest** the remainder.

res·tau·rant (res′tə-rənt, res′tə-ränt′) *n.* a place where meals may be bought and eaten.

re·store (ri-stôr′, ri-stōr′) *vb.* **re·stor·ing,
re·stored 1** to return to an original condition by repairing, cleaning, etc. **2** to bring back, or bring back to, a normal, healthy state. **3** to return to the rightful owner.

re·strain (ri-strān′) *vb.* **re·strain·ing,
re·strained 1** to prevent someone from doing something. **2** to keep under control.

re·strict (ri-strikt′) *vb.* **re·strict·ing,
re·strict·ed 1** to keep within certain limits. **2** to limit or regulate the use of.

re·sult (ri-zult′) *n.* **1** an outcome or consequence of something. **2** a number or quantity obtained by calculation, etc. – *vb.*
re·sult·ing, re·sult·ed to be a consequence or outcome of some action, event, etc.

re·sume (ri-zoom′) *vb.* **re·sum·ing,
re·sumed** to return to or begin again after an interruption.

ré·su·mé (rez′ə-mā, rā′zə-mā′) *n.* **1** a summary of a person's education and work experience, used in applying for jobs. **2** a summary of a story.

re·tail (rē′tāl′) *n.* the sale of goods to customers who will not resell them. – *adj.* of, relating to, or concerned with such sale of goods. – *vb.*
re·tail·ing, re·tailed to sell goods in small quantities to customers. – *n.* **re·tail·er.**

re·tain (ri-tān′) *vb.* **re·tain·ing, re·tained
1** to continue to have, contain, use, etc. **2** to be able to remember. **3** to hold back or keep in place.

ret·i·na (ret′n-ə) *n.* **retinas** or **ret·i·nae**
(ret′n-ē′, ret′n-ī′) the light-sensitive lining at the back of the eye which receives the image from the lens.

re·tire (ri-tīr′) *vb.* **re·tir·ing, re·tired 1** to stop working permanently, usually on reaching an age at which a pension can be received. **2** to go away to rest, especially to go to bed.

re·tire·ment (ri-tīr′mənt) *n.* the state of being retired from work.

re·tir·ing (ri-tīr′ing) *adj.* shy and reserved.

re·treat (ri-trēt′) *vb.* **re·treat·ing,
re·treat·ed** to withdraw; to move back or away from a position or battle. – *n.* the act of retreating, especially from battle, danger, etc.

re·trieve (ri-trēv′) *vb.* **re·triev·ing,
re·trieved 1** to get or bring back again; to recover. **2** to rescue or save: *John retrieved the situation.*

re·turn (ri-turn′) *vb.* **re·turn·ing, re·turned
1** to come or go back again to a former place, state, or owner. **2** to give, send, put back, etc. in a former position. **3** to come back to in thought or speech. **4** to answer or reply: *I'm returning your telephone call.* **5** (of a jury) to announce officially: *to return a verdict.*– *n.* **1** an act of coming back from a place, state, etc. **2** an act of returning something to a former place, state, ownership, etc. **3** profit from work, a business, or investment.

re·u·nion (rē-yoo′yən) *n.* a meeting of people who have not met for some time.

re·veal (ri-vēl′) *vb.* **re·veal·ing, re·vealed
1** to make known: *to reveal a secret.* **2** to show.

rev·el·ry (rev′əl-rē) *n.* **rev·el·ries** (usually in *plural*) noisy festivities.

re·venge (ri-venj′) *n.* injury, harm, or wrong done in return for injury, harm, or wrong received. – *vb.* **re·veng·ing, re·venged** to do injury, harm, etc. in return for injury, harm, etc. received.

rev·e·nue (rev′ə-noo′, rev′ə-nyoo′) *n.* money from property or shares, especially the money raised by the government from taxes, etc.

●**Re·vere** (ri-vîr′), **Paul** (1735-1818) was a patriot and hero of the AMERICAN REVOLUTION. He is most famous for his night ride on April 18, 1775 to warn the Minutemen of Lexington and Concord, Massachusetts, that British troops were coming.

re·vere (ri-vîr′) *vb.* **re·ver·ing, re·vered** to feel or show great affection and respect for.

rev·er·ence (rev′ə-rəns) *n.* great respect; especially that shown to something sacred.

rev·er·end (rev′rənd, rev′ə-rənd) *adj.* **1** worthy of being respected. **2 Reverend** used as a title for members of the clergy.

rev·er·ent (rev′ə-rənt) *adj.* showing or feeling great respect.

re·verse (ri-vurs′) *vb.* **re·vers·ing, re·versed
1** to put into an opposite or contrary position, state, order, etc. **2** to change a policy, decision, etc. to the exact opposite or contrary. **3** to move in an opposite or backward direction. –
n. **1** the opposite or contrary of something. **2** an

Paul Revere in fact made two famous "rides." The first ride was to warn the revolutionaries to hide their arms.

Rhinoceros comes from the Greek *rhin-*, meaning "nose," and *keras*, meaning "horn," forming the word meaning "nose-horn."

act of changing to an opposite or contrary position, direction, state, etc. **3** the side of a coin, medal, note, etc. with a secondary design on.

re·view (ri-vyōō′) *n.* **1** an act of examining or revising, or the state of being examined or revised. **2** a general survey. **3** a survey of past events: *the newspaper's annual review of the year.* **4** a critical report on a book, play, movie, etc. – *vb.* **re·view·ing, re·viewed 1** to examine. **2** to look back on and examine: *to review the past.* **3** to inspect officially: *to review troops.* **4** to write a critical report on.

re·view·er (ri-vyōō′ər) *n.* a person who writes critical reviews of books, plays, etc.

re·vise (ri-vīz′) *vb.* **re·vis·ing, re·vised 1** to change in order to correct faults, improve, or bring up to date. **2** to change or alter.

re·vi·sion (ri-vizh′ən) *n.* **1** the act of revising. **2** a revised book, edition, article, etc.

re·viv·al (ri-vī′vəl) *n.* **1** the act of reviving. **2** a renewed interest.

re·vive (ri-vīv′) *vb.* **re·viv·ing, re·vived 1** to come or bring back to consciousness, strength, health, etc.: *Ron quickly revived from his fall.* **2** to come or bring back to use, to notice, etc.: *The theater group revived an old play.*

re·voke (ri-vōk′) *vb.* **re·vok·ing, re·voked** to cancel or make no longer valid: *to revoke a will.*

re·volt (ri-vōlt′) *vb.* **re·volt·ing, re·volt·ed 1** to rebel against a government, authority, etc. **2** to make feel disgust, loathing, horror, or revulsion. – *n.* a rebellion against authority.

re·volt·ing *adj.* causing a feeling of disgust.

re·vo·lu·tion (rev′ə-lōō′shən) *n.* **1** the usually violent overthrow of a government by the governed. **2** a complete and usually far-reaching change in ideas, ways of doing things, etc.: *the computer revolution.* **3** a complete circle or turn around an axis. **4** a planet's orbit.

re·vo·lu·tion·ar·y (rev′ə-lōō′shə-ner′ē) *adj.* **1** of or like a revolution. **2** completely new or different.

rev·o·lu·tion·ize (rev′ə-lōō′shə-nīz′) *vb.* **rev·o·lu·tion·iz·ing, re·vo·lu·tion·ized** to cause radical or fundamental changes in.

re·volve (ri-välv′, ri-vôlv′) *vb.* **re·volv·ing, re·volved 1** to move or turn in a circle around a central point; to rotate. **2** to have as a center, focus, or main point.

re·volv·er (ri-väl′vər, ri-vôl′vər) *n.* a pistol with a revolving cylinder that holds bullets.

re·ward (ri-wôrd′) *n.* something given or received in return for work done, good behavior, etc. – *vb.* **re·ward·ing, re·ward·ed** to give a reward to.

re·ward·ing (ri-wôrd′ing) *adj.* giving personal satisfaction.

rhe·a (rē′ə) *n.* a South American flightless bird resembling a small ostrich.

rheu·ma·tism (rōō′mə-tiz′əm) *n.* a disease marked by painful swelling of the joints and which causes stiffness and pain.

● **Rhine** (rīn) the main waterway of EUROPE, rising in the Swiss Alps and emptying into the sea near Rotterdam, Holland.

rhi·noc·er·os (rī-näs′ə-rəs) *n.* **rhinoceroses** or **rhinoceros** a large plant-

The rhinoceros is one of the heaviest of all land animals and may weigh over 3 tons. Africa has two species — black and white, but both are really gray! Egrets often follow rhinos to eat insects stirred up by their huge feet. They sometimes perch on the rhino's back.

eating animal with a thick skin and one or two horns on its nose, found in AFRICA and ASIA.

● **Rhode Island** (rōd ī′lənd). See Supplement, **U.S.A.**

rhu·barb (roo′bärb′) *n.* a garden plant with reddish stalks that can be cooked and eaten.

rhyme (rīm) *n.* **1** a word which has the same final sound as another: *"Beef" rhymes with "leaf."* **2** a short poem, verse, or jingle written in rhyme. – *vb.* **rhym·ing, rhymed** to have the same final sounds and so form rhymes.

rhythm (rith′əm) *n.* a regular repeated pattern, movement, beat, or sequence of events, for example, in a piece of music or in poetry; meter.

rhyth·mic (rith′mik) or **rhyth·mi·cal** (rith′mi-kəl) *adj.* of or with rhythm.

rib (rib) *n.* any of the slightly flexible bones that curve around from the spine, forming the chest wall and protecting the heart and lungs.

rib·bon (rib′ən) *n.* **1** a long narrow strip of material used for decorating clothes, tying hair and packages, etc. **2** any ribbonlike strip.

Young shoots of rice are planted in flooded fields called paddies. Young rice has long narrow leaves and fine clusters of flowers that turn into the grain that we eat.

rice (rīs) *n.* **1** a grass that grows in marshy ground. **2** its seed, highly valued as food.

rich (rich) *adj.* **1** having a lot of money, property, or possessions. **2** costly and elaborate: *rich clothes.* **3** high in value or quality: *a rich harvest.* **4** (of a soil, a region, etc.) productive, fertile. **5** (of colors) vivid and deep.

● **Rich·e·lieu** (rish′ə-loo′), **Cardinal** (1585-1642) was an influential French statesman.

People do not usually notice an earthquake until its strength reaches 4 on the **Richter scale**: (1) Felt only by seismographs. (2) Feeble: just noticeable. (3) Slight: similar to a heavy truck passing. (4) Moderate: loose objects rock. (5) Quite strong: noticed even when you are asleep. (6) Strong: trees rock. (7) Very strong: walls crack. (8) Destructive: weak buildings collapse. (9) Houses collapse. (10) Disastrous: ground cracks. (11) Very disastrous: few buildings remain. (12) Catastrophic: ground rises and falls in waves.

Earthquakes can be terribly destructive, and be the cause of huge casualties from collapsing buildings. In an earthquake in 1906 much of San Francisco burned down as the gas mains broke and caught fire (above).

Rich·ter scale (rik′tər skāl′) *n.* a scale used for measuring the strength of an earthquake.

ric·o·chet (rik′ə-shā′) *vb.* **ric·o·chet·ing, ric·o·cheted** to hit a flat surface and bounce off again at an angle.

rid (rid) *vb.* **rid·ding, rid** to free or clear from something unwanted.

rid·dle (rid′əl) *n.* a short humorous puzzle, often in the form of a question, which describes an object, person, etc. in a mysterious or misleading way.

ride (rīd) *vb.* **rid·ing, rode** (rōd), **rid·den** (rid′n) **1** to sit on and control a bicycle, horse, etc. **2** to travel or be carried in a car, train, etc. – *n.* a trip on horseback or by vehicle.

rid·er (rīd′ər) *n.* a person who rides, especially a horse.

ridge (rij) *n.* **1** any long, narrow, raised area on an otherwise flat surface: *a fabric with ridges.* **2** the top edge of something where two upward sloping surfaces meet, for example on a roof.

rid·i·cule (rid′i-kyool′) *n.* language, laughter, behavior, etc. which makes someone or something appear foolish; mockery. – *vb.* **rid·i·cul·ing, rid·i·culed** to laugh at, make fun of, or mock.

ri·dic·u·lous (ri-dik′yə-ləs) *adj.* silly or absurd.

ri·fle (rī′fəl) *n.* a gun fired from the shoulder.

rig (rig) *vb.* **rig·ging, rigged 1** to fit with ropes,

RHYMING PAIRS
Have you noticed what a lot of rhyming expressions we use? Here are some examples: chip and dip, brain-drain, double trouble, hi-fi, hoity-toity, namby-pamby, nitwit, nitty gritty, bigwig, no-go, pow-wow, hanky panky, high and dry, wear and tear, hodgepodge, silly billy, wheeler-dealer, fair and square.

sails, and rigging: *to rig a ship.* **2** to control or manipulate for dishonest purposes, for personal profit, or advantage. – *n.* **1** the arrangement of sails, ropes, and masts on a ship. **2** an oil rig. **3** gear or equipment, especially that used for a specific task.

rig·ging (rig′ing) *n.* the system of ropes, wires, etc. which control a ship's masts and sails.

right (rīt) *adj.* **1** of or on the side of someone or something which is toward the east when the front is facing north. **2** correct; true. **3** suitable; appropriate: *They are right for one another.* **4** in a correct, proper, satisfactory, or healthy condition: *Can you put things right?* – *adv.* **1** exactly or precisely. **2** immediately; without delay: *He'll be right over.* **3** completely; all the way: *Run right around the field.* **4** straight; directly: *They went right to the top.* **5** to or on the right side. – *n.* **1** (often in *plural*) a power, privilege, etc. that a person may claim legally or morally. **2** (often in *plural*) a just or legal claim to something: *mineral rights.* **3** fairness, truth, and justice. **4** the right side, part, or direction. **5** (in *plural*) the legal permission to print, publish, film, etc. a book, usually sold to a company by the author or by another company. – **right away** at once.

right angle *n.* an angle of 90°, formed by two lines that are perpendicular to each other.

rig·id (rij′əd) *adj.* **1** completely stiff and inflexible. **2** not able to be moved. **3** (of a person) strictly sticking to ideas, opinions, and rules: *She's a rigid disciplinarian.* – *n.* **ri·gid·i·ty** (ri-jid′ət-ē).

rim (rim) *n.* **1** a raised and often curved edge or border: *the rim of a cup.* **2** the outer circular edge of a wheel to which the tire is attached.

Rip Van Winkle returns to his village to learn that 20 years have passed since he fell asleep. During those years his wife has died, his children grown up, and the colonists won the Revolutionary War against the British.

rind (rīnd) *n.* a hard outer layer or covering as on cheese or bacon, or the peel of a fruit.

ring[1] (ring) *n.* **1** a small circle of gold, silver, or some other metal, worn on the finger. **2** any object, mark, or figure that is circular in shape. **3** a group of people or things arranged in a circle. **4** an enclosed and usually circular area for competitions or exhibitions.

ring[2] (ring) *vb.* **ring·ing, rang** (rang), **rung** (rung) **1** to make a sound, especially a bell-like sound. **2** to ring as a summons: *We rang the doorbell.* **3** (*British*) to telephone. – *n.* **1** the act or sound of ringing. **2** the act of ringing a bell. **3** the clear resonant sound of a bell, or a similar sound. **4** (*informal*) telephone call.

ring·leader (ring′lēd·ər) *n.* the leader of a group of people who are causing trouble.

rink (ringk) *n.* **1** an area of ice prepared for skating or ice hockey. **2** an area of smooth floor for roller skating.

rinse (rins) *vb.* **rins·ing, rinsed** to wash soap, detergent, etc. out of clothes, hair, dishes, etc. with clean water.

●**Ri·o de Ja·nei·ro** (rē′ō dā zhə-ner′ō) is BRAZIL's main seaport.

●**Ri·o Grande** (rē′ō grand′) a river that forms the boundary between Texas and MEXICO.

ri·ot (rī′ət) *n.* **1** an often violent disturbance by a large group of people. **2** (*informal*) a person or thing considered very funny. – *vb.* **ri·ot·ing, ri·ot·ed** to take part in a riot. – *n.* **ri·ot·er.**

ri·ot·ous (rī′ət-əs) *adj.* **1** likely to start, or like, a riot. **2** very active, noisy, and wild.

rip (rip) *vb.* **rip·ping, ripped** **1** to tear or come apart violently or roughly. **2** to remove quickly and violently: *Rita ripped pages out of the book.* – *n.* a violent or rough tear or split. – *vb.* **rip off** (rip′ôf′) (*informal*) to cheat or steal from.

ripe (rīp) *adj.* fully matured and ready to be picked and eaten: *ripe fruit.*

rip·en (rī′pen) *vb.* **rip·en·ing, rip·ened** to make or become ripe or riper.

rip·ple (rip′əl) *n.* a slight wave or series of slight waves on the surface of water. – *vb.* **rip·pling, rip·pled** to form ripples.

●**Rip van Win·kle** (rip van wing′kəl) is a character, in a story by the American writer Washington Irving (1783-1859), who sleeps for 20 years.

rise (rīz) *vb.* **ris·ing, rose** (rōz), **ris·en** (riz′ən) **1** to get or stand up, especially from a sitting, kneeling, or lying position. **2** to get up from bed, especially after a night's sleep. **3** to move upward; to ascend. **4** to increase in size, amount, volume, strength, degree, intensity, etc.: *The cheers rose to a loud pitch.* **5** (of the sun, moon, planets, etc.) to appear above the horizon. **6** to rebel: *The mob rose against the dictator.* − *n.* **1** an act of rising. **2** an increase in size, amount, volume, strength, status, rank, etc. **3** a slope or hill.

risk (risk) *n.* the chance or possibility of suffering loss, injury, damage, or failure. − *vb.* **risk·ing, risked 1** to expose to danger or risk. **2** to take the chance of. − *adv.* **risk·i·ly** (ris′kə-lē). − *adj.* **risk·y** (ris′kē), **risk·i·er, risk·i·est**.

rite (rīt) *n.* a religious ceremony or observance.

rit·u·al (rich′oo-əl) *n.* the set order or words used in a religious or other ceremony.

ri·val (rī′vəl) *n.* a person or group of people that tries to compete with another for the same goal or in the same field. − *adj.* being a rival: *A rival company developed our idea.* − *vb.* **ri·val·ing** or **ri·val·ling, ri·valed** or **ri·valled** to compete with.

riv·er (riv′ər) *n.* a large natural stream that usually flows along a definite course.

riv·et (riv′ət) *n.* a metal bolt for fastening plates of metal together.

ri·vet·ing (riv′ət-ing) *adj.* fascinating.

road (rōd) *n.* an open, usually specially surfaced or paved way, for people to travel on.

roam (rōm) *vb.* **roam·ing, roamed** to wander about without purpose.

roar (rôr, rōr) *vb.* **roar·ing, roared 1** to give a loud growling cry: *Lions roar.* **2** to laugh loudly. − *n.* **1** a loud deep cry. **2** a loud deep sound.

roast (rōst) *vb.* **roast·ing, roast·ed 1** to cook by exposure to dry heat, especially in an oven.

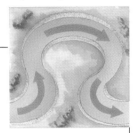

On the inner curve of a meander the river deposits sand and silt.

The neck of the loop may greatly narrow as the loop develops.

Rivers have helped to shape the landscape. They have provided means of transportation from the sea to inland areas. And rivers have supplied food, and water for drinking and irrigation. Some rivers start life as springs, others are fed by melting glaciers. Most rivers come from rain and snow that falls on uplands.

A river flowing quickly down a steep slope of hard rocks cuts a deep gorge.

When a river flows slowly over soft rock, the valley is worn back and widened into a V shape.

The old channel may be cut off to form an oxbow lake.

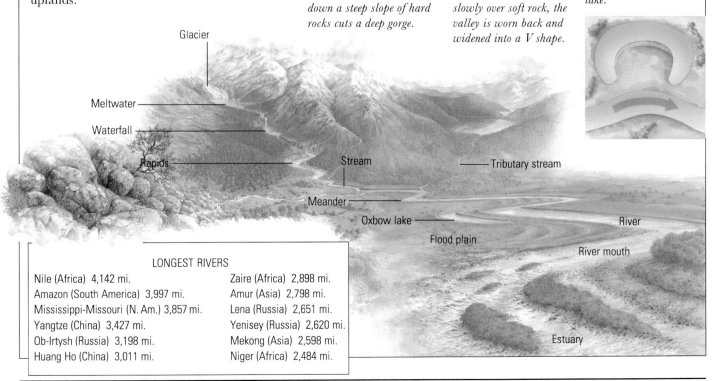

Glacier

Meltwater

Waterfall

Rapids

Stream

Tributary stream

Meander

Oxbow lake

Flood plain

River

River mouth

Estuary

LONGEST RIVERS

Nile (Africa) 4,142 mi.	Zaire (Africa) 2,898 mi.
Amazon (South America) 3,997 mi.	Amur (Asia) 2,798 mi.
Mississippi-Missouri (N. Am.) 3,857 mi.	Lena (Russia) 2,651 mi.
Yangtze (China) 3,427 mi.	Yenisey (Russia) 2,620 mi.
Ob-Irtysh (Russia) 3,198 mi.	Mekong (Asia) 2,598 mi.
Huang Ho (China) 3,011 mi.	Niger (Africa) 2,484 mi.

An 18th-century stagecoach being held up by highwaymen at gunpoint and its passengers robbed of their money and possessions.

rob (räb) *vb.* **rob·bing, robbed** to steal something from. – *n.* **rob·ber.**
rob·ber·y (räb′ə-rē) *n.*
rob·ber·ies the act of robbing.
robe (rōb) *n.* **1** (often in *plural*) a long loose garment, especially one worn for special ceremonies as a mark of office: *a judge's robes*. **2** a long loose garment worn at home, especially over a nightgown or pajamas.

● **Robe·son** (rōb′sən) **, Paul** (1898-1976) was an American singer and actor who fought for civil rights for blacks.

● **Robes·pierre** (rōb′spē-âr′), **Maximilien de** (1758-1794) was a French revolutionary leader who started the "Reign of Terror," the most violent period of the FRENCH REVOLUTION.

rob·in (räb′ən) *n.* a North American thrush with an orange-red breast.

● **Robin Hood** (räb′ən hood′) was a legendary English outlaw of the 1100s who robbed the rich to give to the poor.

ro·bot (rō′bät′, rō′bət) *n.* an automatic machine that performs specific tasks.
ro·bust (rō-bust′, rō′bust) *adj.* **1** strong and healthy; with a strong constitution. **2** strongly built or constructed.
rock¹ (räk) *n.* **1** the hard mineral matter which forms part of the earth's crust. **2** a mass of this mineral matter forming a cliff, peak, reef, etc. **3** a large stone or boulder. **4** a stone of any size.
rock² (räk) *vb.* **rock·ing, rocked 1** to sway gently backward and forward or from side to side. **2** to move or shake violently.
rock and roll or **rock 'n' roll** (räk′ən rōl′) *n.* a form of popular music with a lively beat and simple melodies. – *vb.* **rock·ing and roll·ing, rocked and rolled** or **rock'n'roll·ing, rock'n'rolled** to dance to or play rock and roll music.
rock crystal *n.* a transparent variety of quartz without color.

● **Rock·e·fel·ler** (räk′ə-fel′ər) is the name of a family noted for its activities in business, politics, and philanthropy.

Since far back in history, people have been obsessed with making machines with human brains or more daringly creating a mechanical being gifted with life – a **robot**. Philon of Byzantium (200s BC) is said to have created performing statues, powered entirely by water.

A Japanese computer-controlled automated "arm."

Lunakhods, *unmanned Soviet Moon cars, were controlled from Earth by radio and traveled the Moon's surface collecting information.*

In the Czech play R.U.R. mechanical men do all the work of the world. Few robots in fact look like such machines.

rock·et (räk′it) *n.* **1** a self-propelling, cylindrical projectile which is driven forward and upward by the gas it expels from burning fuel, for example one forming the basis of a jet engine. **2** such a device used as fireworks or a distress signal. **3** anything that is propelled by such a device, for example a missile or spacecraft.

● **Rock·well** (räk′wel′), **Norman** (1894-1978) was an American painter of realistic detail, famed for the covers he painted for the magazine, the *Saturday Evening Post.*

rock·y (räk′ē) *adj.* **rock·i·er, rock·i·est** **1** full of rocks. **2** full of problems.

● **Rocky Mountains** This mountain system stretches along the west side of NORTH AMERICA. The highest peak is Mount Elbert in the United States at 14,431 feet (4,399 meters) above sea level.

rod (räd) *n.* **1** a long slender stick or bar of wood, metal, etc.: *a curtain rod.* **2** (also **fishing rod**) a pole with a line and hook, often with a reel, used to catch fish.

ro·dent (rōd′nt) *n.* any of the group of small mammals with strong sharp teeth for gnawing, including mice, rats, and squirrels.

ro·de·o (rōd′-ē-ō, rə-dā′ō) *n.* **rodeos** a show or contest of cowboy skills.

● **Rodg·ers** (räj′ərz), **Richard** (1902-1979) was an American composer of musicals.

● **Ro·din** (rō-dan′), **Auguste** (1840-1917) was the French sculptor of *The Kiss* and *The Thinker.*

roe¹ (rō) *n.* the eggs of a fish.

roe² (rō) *n.* (also **roe deer**) a small deer found in EUROPE and ASIA.

role or **rôle** (rōl) *n.* **1** an actor's part in a play, movie, etc. **2** a part played in life, business, etc.

roll (rōl) *n.* **1** anything flat, such as paper, fabric, etc., which is rolled up to form a cylinder or tube: *a roll of wax paper.* **2** a small bread for one serving. **3** an official list of names, for example of school pupils, members of a club, etc. **4** an act of rolling. **5** a swaying or rolling movement: *the roll of a boat.* **6** a long low prolonged sound:

a roll of thunder. – *vb.* **roll·ing, rolled** **1** to move by turning over and over, as if on an axis. **2** to move on wheels, rollers, etc., or in a vehicle with wheels: *Roy rolled his bike into the shed.* **3** (of a person or animal, etc. lying down) to turn with a rolling movement to face in another direction. **4** to spread out or make flat or flatter: *to roll dough.* **5** to pronounce with a trill: *to roll "r's."* **6** to throw: *to roll the dice.*

roll·er (rō′lər) *n.* **1** any of a number of cylindrical objects or machines used for flattening, crushing, spreading, printing, applying paint, etc. **2** a small cylinder on which hair is rolled for curling. **3** a long sea wave: *The surfers waited for a good roller.*

roll·er·coast·er (rō′lər-kō′stər) *n.* a raised railroad with sharp curves and steep inclines, ridden on for excitement, usually at fairs.

Rodin's bronze statue, The Thinker.

roll·er skate (rō′lər-skāt′) *n.* a skate with wheels. – *vb.* **roll·er-skate, roll·er-skat·ing, roll·er-skat·ed** to move on roller skates. – *n.* **roller-skater.**

roll·ing pin (rō′ling-pin′) *n.* a cylinder for flattening out pastry, usually made of wood.

ROM (räm) *abbreviation* in computers, read-only memory, a memory that holds data and allows it to be used but not changed.

Ro·man (rō′mən) *adj.* **1** of, or related to, modern or ancient Rome. **2 roman** (of printing type) written in ordinary upright letters (as opposed to italic). – *n.* an inhabitant of modern or ancient Rome.

Ro·man Cath·o·lic (rō′mən kath′ə-lik) *adj.* of the Christian church that recognizes the Pope as its head. – *n.* a member of this church.

ro·mance (rō-mans′) *n.* **1** a love affair. **2** a sentimental story of a love affair. **3** a fictitious story that deals with imaginary, adventurous, and mysterious events, characters, places, etc. – *adj.* **Romance** of, or relating to, the languages that have developed from Latin.

A roller skate consists of either a series of wheels attached to a frame which can be fitted over a shoe, or a shoe with wheels attached to the sole. Inside the wheels of a roller skate are ball bearings. These help the wheels move round smoothly, reducing friction and wear.

The **Roman Empire** was founded by emperor Augustus in 27 B.C. and lasted for nearly 500 years. Until about A.D. 200 the empire was prosperous and peaceful. A network of roads linked all parts of the empire helping trade and defense. Towns had fine public buildings and in the countryside farming was efficient.

The empire had a common coinage.

According to tradition Rome was founded by Romulus and Remus in 753 B.C. The twins were abandoned as babies but were found by a she-wolf who raised them.

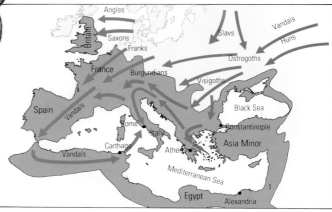

From about A.D. 200 the empire was under constant attack from invading tribes. Rome was finally overrun by Alaric, leader of the Visigoths, in A.D. 410.

The arch of Constantine, built in A.D. 312.

Everyday objects such as oil lamps were hand crafted.

The Roman army conquered a vast area. An ordinary Roman soldier carried a sword, a dagger, and a rectangular shield.

The Romans built long straight roads which enabled their armies to travel quickly.

Rome's chariot-racing stadium, the Circus Maximus, could hold up to 250,000 spectators.

● **Roman Empire** Legend says that Rome was founded in 753 B.C. by the twins ROMULUS and Remus. From a cluster of villages along the river Tiber, Rome grew to be the center of a mighty empire, covering most of Europe and the lands around the Mediterranean. The Romans set up a republic, but were later ruled by emperors. The Romans were practical people — splendid builders, engineers, and lawmakers. They took much of their learning and culture from the Greeks. By A.D. 476 the empire had collapsed.

● **Ro·ma·ni·a** (rō-mō′nē-ə). See Supplement, **Countries**.

Ro·ma·ni·an (rō-mā′nē-ən) *n.* **1** the official language of ROMANIA. **2** an inhabitant of or person from ROMANIA. – *adj.* of, or relating to, ROMANIA.

Roman numeral *n.* any of the figures used to represent numbers in the system developed by the ancient Romans, for example I (= 1), V (= 5), X (= 10), etc.

● **Ro·ma·nov** (rō-män′əf, rō′mə-nôf′) is the name of the dynasty that ruled RUSSIA from 1613 to 1917.

ro·man·tic (rō-mant′ik) *adj.* **1** of, like, or feeling sentimental and idealized love. **2** dealing with or suggesting adventure, mystery, and sentimentalized love.

● **Rome** (rōm) is today the capital of ITALY. It was once the center of the ROMAN EMPIRE.

● **Rom·u·lus** (räm′yə-ləs) according to legend, was the founder of ROME. He and his twin brother, Remus, were suckled by a wolf after they had been abandoned as babies.

roof (rōof, roof) *n.* **roofs 1** the covering of a building or vehicle. **2** the top inner surface of an oven, a cave, the mouth, etc. – *vb.* **roof·ing, roofed** to cover with a roof.

rook (rook) *n.* a chess piece; See **castle**.

room (rōom, room) *n.* **1** a part of a building that is separated from the rest of the building by having a ceiling, floor, and walls. **2** a space or area that is occupied by or is available to someone or something. **3** opportunity; scope.

room·mate (rōom′māt′, room′māt′) *n.* a person who shares a room with another.

room·y (rōo′mē, room′ē) *adj.* **room·i·er, room·i·est** spacious.

● **Roo·se·velt** (rō′zə-velt, rō′zə-velt′), **Franklin Delano** (1882-1945) was president of the UNITED STATES from 1933 to 1945.

roost (rōost) *n.* a branch, perch, etc. on which birds rest at night. – *vb.* **roost·ing, roost·ed** (of birds) to settle on a roost.

roost·er (rōo′stər) *n.* a male fowl; a cock.

root[1] (rōot, root) *n.* **1** the underground part of a plant that absorbs water and nourishment from the soil. **2** the part of a tooth, hair, nail, etc. which attaches it to the body. **3** the basic cause, source, or origin of something. **4** (in *plural*) ancestry or family origins. **5** the basic element in a word which may form the basis of a number of related words: *"Love"* is the root of *"lovable"* and *"loveliness."* – *vb.* **root·ing, root·ed** to grow roots; to become firmly established.

root[2] (rōot, root) *vb.* **root·ing, root·ed** (especially of pigs) to dig up the ground with the snout in search of food.

Franklin D. Roosevelt became president in 1933. He steered the United States out of the deepest economic Depression and led the country through most of World War II.

Roots anchor a plant firmly in the soil and supply it with water and mineral salts. Plants such as grasses have a mass of fibrous roots. Roots can store food for such plants as carrots and beets. Potato tubers and corms are really underground stems, not roots. A tree's roots grow deep into the soil and can find water even in a drought.

rope (rōp) *n.* **1** strong thick cord made by twisting fibers together. **2** a number of objects, as pearls strung together. – *vb.* **rop·ing, roped** to tie, fasten, or bind with a rope.

rose[1] (rōz) *n.* **1** any of a family of shrubs with prickly stems and often sweet-smelling flowers. **2** a darkish pink color. – *adj.* of or like roses, especially in color or scent.

rose[2]. See **rise**.

Rosh Ha·sha·nah (rōsh′ hə-shô′nə, räsh′hə-shän′ə) *n.* the Jewish festival of New Year, celebrated in September or October.

PRONUNCIATION SYMBOLS			
ə	away	lemon	focus
a	fat	oi	boy
ā	fade	oo	foot
ä	hot	ōō	moon
âr	fair	ou	house
e	met	th	think
ē	mean	th	this
g	get	u	cut
hw	which	ur	hurt
i	fin	w	witch
ī	line	y	yes
îr	near	yōō	music
ô	often	yoor	pure
ō	note	zh	vision

ros·in (räz′ən, rô′zən) *n.* a clear hard resin produced by distilling turpentine prepared from dead pine wood, rubbed on the bows of stringed musical instruments.

rot (rät) *vb.* **rot·ting, rot·ted** to decay. – *n.* decay; something that has rotted.

ro·ta·ry (rōt′ə-rē) *adj.* turning on an axis like a wheel. – *n.* **ro·ta·ries** a traffic circle.

ro·tate (rō′tāt′) *vb.* **ro·tat·ing, ro·tat·ed 1** to turn on an axis like a wheel. **2** to arrange in an ordered sequence.

ro·ta·tion (rō-tā′shən) *n.* **1** an act of rotating. **2** one complete turn around an axis. **3** (also **crop rotation**) the growing of different crops on a field, usually in an ordered sequence, to help keep the land fertile.

● **Roth·ko** (räth′kō), **Mark** (1903-1970) was a Latvian-born American abstract painter.

ro·tor (rōt′ər) *n.* a system of blades which rotate at high speed to provide the force to lift and propel a helicopter.

rot·ten (rä′n) *adj.* **1** having gone bad, decayed. **2** (*informal*) miserably unwell: *I have a cold and I'm feeling rotten.* **3** (*informal*) unsatisfactory: *That's a rotten plan.* **4** (*informal*) unpleasant: *What rotten weather!*

● **Rot·ter·dam** (rät′ər-dam′) is Europe's busiest port and a major manufacturing city in the NETHERLANDS.

Rott·wei·ler (rät′wī′lər, rôt′vī′lər) *n.* a large powerfully built black and tan dog, originally from Germany.

rough (ruf) *adj.* **1** (of a surface) not smooth, even, or regular. **2** (of ground) covered with stones, tall grass, bushes, etc. **3** harsh or grating: *a rough voice.* **4** (of a person's character, behavior, etc.) noisy, coarse, or violent. **5** stormy: *rough winds.* **6** requiring hard work or considerable physical effort, or involving great difficulty, tension, etc.: *Mom had a rough day at work.* **7** unpleasant and hard to bear: *The decision was rough on the employees.* **8** (of an estimate, etc.) approximate. – *n.* **rough·ness** (ruf′nəs). – *vb.* **rough·ing, roughed: rough it** (*informal*) to live without the usual comforts of life.

rough·age (ruf′ij) *n.* coarse bulky material in food, which helps digestion.

rough·en (ruf′ən) *vb.* **rough·en·ing, rough·ened** to make or become rough.

round (round) *adj.* **1** shaped like a circle or a ball. **2** not angular; curved and plump. **3** moving in or forming a circle. **4** (of numbers) complete and exact: *That makes a round dozen.* **5** (of a number) without a fraction. **6** (of a number) approximate. – *adv.* **1** throughout a period of time: *all year round.* **2** around: *the wheels turned round.* – *n.* **1** something round, and often flat, in shape. **2** a complete revolution around a circuit or path. **3** the playing of all 18 holes on a golf course in a single session. **4** one of a recurring series of events, actions, etc.: *a round of talks.* **5** (usually in *plural*) a doctor's visits to his or her patients, either in a hospital or in their own homes. **6** a stage in a competition. **7** a single bullet or charge of ammunition. – *vb.* **round·ing, round·ed 1** to make or become round. **2** to go round: *The car rounded the corner.* – *n.* **round·ness**. – *vb.* **round off 1** to make corners, angles, etc. smooth. **2** to complete successfully and pleasantly.

round·a·bout (roun′də-bout′) *adj.* not direct or short: *a roundabout route.* – *n.* (*British*) a traffic circle.

round·ed (roun′dəd) *adj.* curved.

Round·head (round′hed′) *n.* a supporter of the parliamentary party against Charles I in the English CIVIL WAR (1642-1649).

Round Table *n.* the legendary table at which King Arthur and his Knights met, made circular so that none could claim to sit near the head.

Arthur and the Knights of the Round Table. There are many romantic stories told about the British king, Arthur, his court at Camelot, and his Knights of the Round Table.

route (rōōt, rout) *n.* a particular group of roads followed to get to a place.

rou·tine (rōō-tēn′) *n.* a regular or fixed way of doing things. – *adj.* not varying; ordinary.

row[1] (rō) *n.* a number of people or things, such as seats, numbers, etc. arranged in a line.

row[2] (rō) *vb.* **row·ing, rowed** to move a boat through the water using oars.

row[3] (rou) *n.* a noisy quarrel; a disturbance.

rowd·y (roud′ē) *adj.* **rowd·i·er, rowd·i·est** noisy and rough. – *adv.* **rowd·i·ly** (roud′l-ē). – *n.* **rowd·i·ness** (roud′ē-nəs).

roy·al (roi′əl) *adj.* **1** of, or suitable for, a king or queen. **2** under the patronage or in the service of the king or queen: *Royal Geographical Society.* **3** being a member of the king's or queen's family.

The badge of the Royal Canadian Mounted Police.

● **Royal Canadian Mounted Police** (RCMP) the federal police force of CANADA, known as Mounties.

rub (rub) *vb.* **rub·bing, rubbed 1** to move your hand, an object, etc. backward and forward over a surface with pressure. **2** to move backward and forward over a surface with pressure and friction: *The dog rubbed its back against the tree.* **3** to apply by rubbing: *to rub lotion on the skin.* **4** to clean, polish, dry, smooth, etc. – *n.* an act of rubbing. – *vb.* – **rub off on** to have an effect on or be passed to: *Some of his bad habits have rubbed off on you.* – **rub the wrong way** to annoy or irritate.

rub·ber (rub′ər) *n.* **1** a strong elastic substance obtained from the latex of various trees or plants or produced synthetically. **2** waterproof rubber shoe, usually worn over other shoes. **3** a condom.– *adj.* of or producing rubber.

rubber band *n.* a loop of rubber used to hold things together.

rub·bish (rub′ish) *n.* **1** waste material; things that have been thrown away. **2** nonsense.

rub·ble (rub′əl) *n.* bricks, plaster, etc. from ruined or demolished buildings.

ru·by (rōō′bē) *n.* **rubies** a precious stone varying in color from deep red to pink.

ruck·sack (ruk′sak′) *n.* See **knapsack**.

rud·der (rud′ər) *n.* **1** a flat piece of wood, metal, etc. fixed vertically to a ship's stern for steering. **2** a similar device on an aircraft which helps control its movement.

rud·dy (rud′ē) *adj.* **rud·di·er, rud·di·est 1** having a healthy reddish complexion: *His face was ruddy after the run.* **2** reddish.

rude (rōōd) *adj.* **1** impolite; showing bad manners. **2** roughly made. **3** vulgar; indecent. – *n.* **rude·ness** (rōōd′nəs).

ruf·fi·an (ruf′ē-ən) *n.* a violent lawless person.

ruf·fle (ruf′əl) *vb.* **ruf·fling, ruf·fled 1** to make wrinkled or uneven; to spoil the smoothness of. **2** to make or become irritated. **3** (of a bird) to raise in display or anger: *to ruffle feathers.* – *n.* a frill worn either around the neck or wrists.

rug (rug) *n.* a thick heavy fabric, covering all or part of the floor.

Rug·by or **rug·by** (rug′bē) *n.* a form of football played with an oval ball which players may pick up and run with and may pass from hand to hand.

Ruffian has nothing to do with the word "rough," but comes from the Italian word *ruffiano,* taken from an older word *roffia* which means "beastly thing."

Rubber production. (1) & (2) A rubber tree is tapped and a white liquid called latex oozes out. (3) Formic acid is added to the latex to make it stick together. (4) & (5) The rubber is rolled into sheets and hung out to dry. (6) Crude rubber sheets ready for use.

From a ruin (of say, a castle) you can work out what it once looked like. For instance, fireplaces and holes for beams will show you where each floor was. The shape of some rooms will be shown by the remains of foundations.

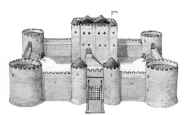

rug·ged (rug′əd) *adj.* **1** having a rough uneven surface; steep and rocky: *The Alps are a rugged range of mountains.* **2** (of the face) having features that are strongly marked and furrowed and which suggest physical strength. **3** involving physical hardships: *a rugged life.* **4** (of equipment, a machine, etc.) strongly or sturdily built: *a rugged mountain bike.* – *n.* **rug·ged·ness** (rug′əd-nəs).

ru·in (rōō′ən, rōō′in) *n.* **1** a broken, destroyed, decayed state: *The castle is a ruin.* **2** a complete loss of wealth, social position, power, etc.: *financial ruin.* **3** a cause of a complete loss of wealth, social position, etc., or of physical destruction, decay, etc.: *Smoking was his ruin.* – *vb.* **ru·in·ing, ru·ined** to cause ruin to; to destroy. – *adj.* **ru·ined**.

rule (rōōl) *n.* **1** a principle, order, or direction that controls some action, function, form, use, etc. **2** the period during which government or control is exercised. **3** a general principle or custom: *Make it a rule always to be punctual.* – *vb.* **rul·ing, ruled** **1** to govern; to exercise authority. **2** to keep control of or restrain. – *vb.* **rule out** to leave out or not consider.

rul·er (rōō′lər) *n.* **1** a person, for example a sovereign or president, who rules or governs. **2** a strip of wood, metal, or plastic with straight edges marked off in units and used for drawing straight lines and measuring.

rul·ing (rōō′ling) *n.* an official decision.

rum (rum) *n.* a spirit distilled from sugarcane.

ru·mi·nant (rōō′mə-nənt) *n.* any mammal that chews the cud, such as cattle and sheep.

rum·mage (rum′ij) *vb.* **rum·mag·ing, rum·maged** to search thoroughly or turn things over untidily in. – *n.* a thorough search.

ru·mor (rōō′mər) *n.* **1** information which is passed from person to person and which may or may not be true. **2** general talk or gossip.

rump (rump) *n.* the rear part of an animal.

rum·ple (rum′pəl) *vb.* **rum·pling, rum·pled** to make untidy or wrinkled. – *n.* a wrinkle.

run (run) *vb.* **run·ning, ran** (ran), **run** (run) **1** (of a person or animal) to move on foot so quickly that both or all feet are off the ground together for an instant during each step. **2** to cover, accomplish, or perform by, or as if by, running: *Sarah often runs errands for me.* **3** to move quickly and easily on, or as if on, wheels. **4** (of water, etc.) to flow; to allow to flow: *The river runs to the sea; Run cold water into the bathtub.* **5** to operate or work. **6** to organize or manage. **7** to travel on a regular route: *Is there a train running between Boston and Hartford?* **8** to stand as a candidate. – *n.* **1** an act of running; the distance covered by running. **2** a rapid running movement: *The walkers broke into a run.* **3** a continuous and unbroken period or series of something: *a run of bad luck.* **4** freedom to move about or come and go as you please: *You can have the run of the house.* **5** a route that is regularly traveled: *a train on the New York to Philadelphia run.* **6** a row of unraveled stitches, especially in hosiery. **7** an inclined course covered with snow and used for skiing. **8** a unit of scoring in baseball made after a runner touches all four bases. – *vb.* **run after** to

---

RUN RUNS RIOT

There are an almost innumerable number of ways that we can use the little verb "run." Like "get" and "pop" it is very useful.

to tend toward: *run to fat.*

to be an inherent or recurring part of: *Blue eyes run in the family.*

to be affected by or subjected to: *run a high temperature* or *run risks.*

to spread quickly: *The color in his shirt ran* or *The rumor ran through the office.*

to move or pass quickly: *Run your eyes over the report* or *Excitement ran through the audience.*

to continue or extend in a specified direction, time, or distance: *The play ran for ten years* or *This road runs south.*

to continue to have legal force: *Their lease still has a year to run.*

to accumulate: *He's run up debts at the bank.*

to get past or through: *run a blockade.*

Runs to a lot of examples!

chase. – *vb.* **run away 1** to escape or flee. **2** (of a horse) to gallop off uncontrollably. **3** to win an easy victory: *Ruby ran away with the competition.* – *vb.* **run down 1** (of a clock, battery, etc.) to stop working because of a gradual loss of power. **2** to knock to the ground: *The boys were run down in the street.* **3** to speak badly of, usually without good reason. – *vb.* **run into 1** (*informal*) to meet unexpectedly. **2** to crash into or collide with. **3** to reach as far as: *His debts run into hundreds.* – *vb.* **run out 1** to come to an end; to be used up: *The soap ran out.* **2** to use up: *The project has run out of money.* **3** to leak out. – *vb.* **run over 1** (of a vehicle or driver) to knock down and drive over. **2** to overflow. **3** to repeat or glance over quickly, especially for practice.

run·ner (run′ər) *n.* **1** a person or thing that runs. **2** a groove or strip along which a drawer, sliding door, etc. slides. **3** either of the strips of metal or wood running the length of a sled, on which it moves; a blade on an ice skate.

run·ner-up (run′ər-up′) *n.* **run·ners-up** (run′ər-zup′) a competitor who finishes in second place.

run·way (run′wā′) *n.* a wide hard surface from which aircraft take off and on which they land.

rung¹ (rung) *n.* a step on a ladder.

rung². See **ring².**

ru·ral (roor′əl) *adj.* of the countryside.

rush¹ (rush) *vb.* **rush·ing, rushed** to hurry or go quickly. – *n.* **1** a sudden quick movement, usually toward a single goal: *a gold rush.* **2** a sudden general movement. **3** haste; hurry.

rush² (rush) *n.* a tall grasslike plant that grows in or near water.

rush hour *n.* a period at the beginning or end of the day when traffic is at its busiest.

●**Rus·sia** (rush′ə) is a republic which until 1991 formed three-fourths of the former Union of Soviet Socialist Republics. Even without the other 14 republics, Russia is still by far the largest country in the world. Russia stretches from St. Petersburg (formerly Leningrad) on the Baltic Sea to Vladivostok on the Sea of Japan. Russia has a great variety of scenery and climate — Arctic wastes, vast forests, grassy plains, and high mountains. Until 1917 the country was ruled by Czars. Then communists under LENIN seized power and the U.S.S.R. was ruled as a strict communist state. In 1985 Mikhail Gorbachev became president and intro-

duced reforms, allowing greater freedom. Boris Yeltsin has been president of Russia since 1991. See Supplement, **Countries**.

Rus·sian (rush′ən) *n.* **1** a person born in or living in RUSSIA or (*loosely*) the other former Soviet republics. **2** the language spoken in Russia. – *adj.* of Russia or (*loosely*) the former Soviet republics.

Rusted metal

Rust is the visible evidence of a chemical reaction known as oxidation. Oxygen in the air takes electrons from the atoms in the metal. This produces the signs of rust. Salt water speeds rusting.

rust
(rust) *n.*
1 a reddish-brown brittle coating that forms on iron caused by the action of oxygen and moisture. **2** the color of rust, usually a reddish-brown. **3** a fungus causing a plant disease in which leaves take on a rusty appearance. – *vb.* **rust·ing, rust·ed** to become coated with rust.

rus·tic (rust′ik) *adj.* of or living in the country.

rus·tle (rus′əl) *vb.* **rus·tling, rus·tled 1** to make a soft whispering sound as of dry leaves. **2** to steal cattle or horses. – *n.* a quick succession of soft dry crisp whisperlike sounds. – *vb.* **rustle up** to arrange or prepare quickly.

rus·tler (rus′lər) *n.* a cattle or horse thief.

rust·y (rust′ē) *adj.* **rust·i·er, rust·i·est 1** covered with or affected by rust. **2** (of a skill, knowledge of a subject, etc.) not as good as it used to be. **3** rust-colored.

rut (rut) *n.* **1** a deep track or furrow in soft ground made by wheels. **2** an established and usually dreary routine. – *adj.* **rut·ted.**

●**Ruth** (rōōth)**, George Herman "Babe"** (1895-1948) was a baseball player who had many long-standing batting records.

ruth·less (rōōth′ləs) *adj.* without pity.

●**Rwan·da** (roo-än′də). See Supplement, **Countries**.

rye (rī) *n.* a cereal whose grain is used for making bread and whiskey, and as food for animals.

S s

The letter *S*, like all the letters, has a long history. The earliest alphabets were taken and adapted by the Greeks. The Greek *beta*, when combined with the first letter, *aleph*, gives us the word alphabet.

The Greeks passed on their letters to the Romans, who developed the alphabet we use today, although they used only capital letters. Small letters developed in the A.D. 700s.

An early form of the letter S, used in the Middle East more than 3,000 years ago.

Σ

This letter was taken by the Greeks and became sigma.

S

Over the years different versions of the letter S have been developed.

●**Saar·i·nen** (sär′ə-nən), **Eero** (1910-1961) was a Finnish-born American architect.

Sab·bath (sab′əth) *n.* a day of the week set aside for religious worship and rest, Saturday among the JEWS and Sunday among most CHRISTIANS.

sa·bot (sa-bō′) *n.* a wooden clog.

sab·o·tage (sab′ə-täzh′) *n.* deliberate damage or destruction, especially carried out for military or political reasons.

sa·bre (sā′bər) *n.* a curved single-edged sword.

●**Sac·a·ga·we·a** (sak′ə-jə-wē′ə) (1787-1812) was a NATIVE AMERICAN guide and interpreter who guided the explorers Lewis and Clark on their expedition to the PACIFIC.

sack¹ (sak) *n.* **1** a large bag, especially of coarse cloth or paper. **2** (*informal*) dismissal from employment: *Bob was given the sack.* – *vb.* **sack·ing, sacked 1** (in football) to tackle a quarterback behind the line of scrimmage. **2** (*informal*) to dismiss from employment.

sack² (sak) *vb.* **sack·ing, sacked** to plunder and destroy: *to sack a village.*

sa·cred (sā′krəd) *adj.* **1** devoted to God or a god and therefore regarded with solemn respect. **2** connected with religion or worship.

sac·ri·fice (sak′rə-fīs′) *n.* **1** an offering made to God or a god. **2** anything, especially something valuable, given up for the sake of another thing or person. – *vb.* **sac·ri·fic·ing, sac·ri·ficed** to offer as a sacrifice.

sad (sad) *adj.* **sad·der, sad·dest 1** feeling unhappy. **2** causing unhappiness: *sad news.* – *n.* **sad·ness** (sad′nəs).

sad·den (sad′n) *vb.* **sad·den·ing, sad·dened** to make or become sad.

sad·dle (sad′l) *n.* **1** a seat on a horse, usually made of leather, fitting on the horse's back. **2** a fixed seat on a bicycle or motorcycle. – *vb.*

When she was a little girl Sacagawea was captured by the Hidatsa tribe of Native Americans and sold to a French Canadian fur trader. She later proved invaluable as a guide on the Lewis and Clark expedition across North America.

sad·dling, sad·dled 1 to put a saddle on: *to saddle a horse.* **2** to burden: *Sam saddled Sally with his problems.*

safe (sāf) *adj.* **1** free from danger or harm. **2** giving protection from harm; secure: *a safe place.* **3** not dangerous: *It's safe to go out.* – *n.* a sturdily constructed metal cabinet in which valuables can be locked away.

safe·ty (sāf′tē) *n.* the condition of being safe.

sag (sag) *vb.* **sag·ging, sagged 1** to sink or bend, especially in the middle. **2** to hang loosely: *Tom's shoulders sagged.*

sa·ga (säg′ə) *n.* **1** a medieval Scandinavian tale of legendary heroes and events. **2** any long piece of fiction resembling this.

sage (sāj) *n.* a plant with aromatic leaves.

Sag·it·tar·i·us (saj′ə-ter′ē-əs). See **zodiac**.

● **Sa·ha·ra** (sə-hâr′ə, sə-här′ə) the world's largest hot desert, in northern AFRICA.

said. See **say**.

sail (sāl) *n.* **1** a sheet of canvas spread to catch the wind and make a ship move. **2** a trip in a boat or ship. **3** any of a windmill's revolving arms. – *vb.* **sail·ing, sailed 1** to travel by boat or ship: *to sail the Pacific.* **2** to control a boat or ship. **3** to depart by boat or ship.

Sailing into the wind, sails act as slotted wings and a strong suction force, similar to an airfoil's lift, is produced.

Mainsail

Lift

Foresail

Keel

Wind direction   Water flow

sail·or (sā′lər) *n.* any member of a ship's crew.

saint (sānt) *n.* a person whose holiness is formally recognized after death by a Christian church. – *n.* **saint·hood** (sānt′hood′).

● **St. Kitts-Ne·vis** (sānt kits′ nē′vəs). See Supplement, **Countries**.

● The **St. Law·rence Sea·way** (sānt lôr′əns sē′wā′) connects the GREAT LAKES with the ATLANTIC Ocean.

● **St. Lu·cia** (sānt loo′shə). See Supplement, **Countries**.

● **St. Vin·cent and the Gren·a·dines** (sānt vin′sənt, gren′ə-dēnz′). See Supplement, **Countries**.

sake (sāk) *n.* benefit; behalf: *Do it for my sake.*

sa·laam (sə-läm′) *n.* a word used as a greeting in Eastern countries, especially by Muslims.

sal·ad (sal′əd) *n.* a cold dish of usually raw vegetables, usually served with a dressing.

● **Sal·a·din** (sal′əd-n, sal′ə-din′) (1138-1193) was an Arab soldier who repelled the Third Crusade led by Richard I of England.

sal·a·man·der (sal′ə-man′dər) *n.* a lizardlike amphibious creature.

sal·a·ry (sal′ə-rē) *n.* **sal·a·ries** a fixed regular payment for work.

sale (sāl) *n.* **1** the act or practice of selling; the selling of an item: *the sale of a bicycle.* **2** an item sold. **3** a period during which goods are offered at reduced prices: *a Labor Day sale.*

● **Sal·in·ger** (sal′ən-jər), **Jerome David** (1919-) is an American novelist whose best-known work is *The Catcher in the Rye.*

sa·li·va (sə-lī′və) *n.* the watery liquid produced by glands in the mouth to aid digestion.

● **Salk** (sôk, sôlk), **Jonas** (1914-) is an American scientist who developed a vaccine that prevents poliomyelitis.

sal·mon (sam′ən) *n.* **salmon** or **salmons 1** a large silvery marine fish that lays its eggs in fresh water. **2** any of various related fishes.

salt (sôlt) *n.* **1** (also **common salt**) sodium chloride, a white crystalline substance found as a mineral (**rock salt**) or in solution in sea water (**sea salt**), used to season and preserve food. **2** a chemical compound in which one or more hydrogen atoms have been replaced by a metal atom or atoms. – *vb.* **salt·ing, salt·ed** to season or preserve with salt. – *adj.* **1** preserved with salt: *salt pork.* **2** containing salt: *salt water* – *adj.* **salt·ed**.

● **Salt Lake City** is the capital of UTAH.

salt·y (sôl′tē) *adj.* **salt·i·er, salt·i·est** containing salt or tasting of salt.

A fire salamander. There are some 300 species of these amphibians. They are sometimes mistaken for lizards. Unlike lizards they have rounded heads, moist skins without scales, and no claws on their toes.

Salary is from the Latin *salarium*, in turn from the word *sal*, meaning "salt." This is because a salary was originally money given to Roman soldiers to buy salt.

sa·lute (sə-lo͞ot′) *vb.* **sa·lut·ing, sa·lut·ed**
1 to pay formal respect to with a set gesture, especially with the right arm or a weapon. **2** to greet with a show of friendship.

sal·vage (sal′vij) *vb.* **sal·vag·ing, sal·vaged** to rescue from damage or loss.

sal·va·tion (sal-vā′shən) *n.* **1** the act of saving a person or thing from harm. **2** a person or thing that saves another from harm. **3** liberation from the influence of sin.

Salvation Army *n.* a Christian organization aiming to help the poor and spread Christianity.

salve (sav, säv, salv) *n.* ointment to heal or soothe. *– vb.* **salv·ing, salved** to ease or comfort: *to salve your conscience.*

same (sām) *adj.* **1** exactly alike or similar: *All the puppies look the same.* **2** not different.
3 unchanged or unchanging: *Sam is wearing the same shirt as yesterday.* **4** previously mentioned; the actual one in question: *Do you mean this same man? – pron.* the same person or thing, or the one previously mentioned: *She drank lemonade, and I drank the same.*

sam·o·var (sam′ə-vär′) *n.* a Russian tea urn.

sam·ple (sam′pəl) *n.* a part that shows what the whole is like: *This piece of cloth is a sample of my dress material. – vb.* **sam·pling, sam·pled** to take or try as a sample: *Sample the soup.*

sam·u·rai (sam′ə-rī′, sam′yə-rī′) *n.* **sam·u·rai** a member of a class of Japanese warriors between the 1000s and 1800s.

sanc·tion (sangk′shən) *vb.* **sanc·tion·ing, sanc·tioned** to authorize or confirm formally: *to sanction the use of force.*

sanc·tu·ar·y (sangk′cho͞o-er′ē) *n.* **sanc·tu·ar·ies 1** a holy place, for example a church or temple. **2** any place of safety and refuge. **3** safety as found in a sanctuary. **4** a nature reserve in which the animals or plants are protected by law: *a bird sanctuary.*

sand (sand) *n.* a grainy substance forming beaches and deserts, consisting of rock powdered by the action of the sea or wind. *– vb.* **sand·ing, sand·ed** to smooth or polish with sandpaper.

san·dal (san′dəl) *n.* an open shoe with straps for holding the sole on the foot.

sand·pa·per (sand′pā′pər) *n.* rough paper with a coating of sand, crushed glass, etc. for smoothing and polishing wood. *– vb.* **sand·pa·per·ing, sand·pa·pered**.

sand·stone (sand′stōn′) *n.* a type of rock formed from compressed sand, used in building.

sand·wich (san′wich′, san′dwich′) *n.* a food consisting of two or more slices of bread or a roll with a filling of cheese, meat, etc. *– vb.* **sand·wich·ing, sand·wiched** to squeeze in between two other things: *I just managed to sandwich a driving lesson into my busy schedule.*

sand·y (san′dē) *adj.* **sand·i·er, sand·i·est**
1 containing sand. **2** pale yellowish-brown.

sane (sān) *adj.* **1** not crazy. **2** sensible.

Samurai in battle, equipped with the newly introduced firearm. Meaning "one who serves," the samurai warrior of Japan gloried in warfare, in self-discipline, and toughness. To avoid capture in battle he would disembowel himself.

●**San Fran·cis·co** (san′fran-sis′kō) is one of the most colorful cities in the UNITED STATES and is its chief PACIFIC port. It is well known for its Golden Gate Bridge and cable cars.

san·i·ta·tion (san′ə-tā′shən) *n.* measures taken to preserve public health, especially waste and sewage disposal.

San·skrit (san′skrit′) *n.* a language of ancient INDIA.

●**São To·mé and Prín·ci·pe** (soun′tə-mā′ ā prin′sə-pə). See Supplement, **Countries**.

sap¹ (sap) *n.* a liquid circulating in plants, carrying food and water.

sap² (sap) *vb.* **sap·ping, sapped** to tire, weaken: *The long run has sapped her energy.*

sap·phire (saf′īr′) *n.* a precious stone of a transparent dark blue color.

sar·casm (sär′kaz′əm) *n.* bitter, usually ironical remarks expressing scorn or contempt.

sar·cas·tic (sär-kas′tik) *adj.* containing or using sarcasm. – *adv.* **sar·cas·ti·cal·ly**.

sar·dine (sär-dēn′) *n.* a small fish that is often sold in flat cans.

●**Sar·gent** (sär′jənt), **John Singer** (1856-1925) was an American portrait painter.

sa·ri (sär′ē) *n.* **saris** a traditional garment of women in INDIA, a single long piece of fabric wound around the body.

●**Sar·tre** (särt, sär′trə), **Jean-Paul** (1905-1980) was a French philosopher and writer.

sash¹ (sash) *n.* a broad band of cloth worn around the waist or over one shoulder.

sash² (sash) *n.* a frame for a window that holds panes of glass.

●**Sas·katch·e·wan** (sə-skach′ə-wən, sas-kash′ə-wän′) is one of CANADA's three "Prairie Provinces," which produce wheat and oil.

Sa·tan (sāt′n) *n.* the devil.

sat·el·lite (sat′l-īt′) *n.* **1** a heavenly body that orbits a larger planet or star, as the earth does the sun. **2** an artificial device set in orbit

around the earth, for example as an aid to communication.

satellite dish *n.* a dish-shaped aerial for receiving television programs via satellite.

sat·in (sat′n) *n.* a fabric with a shiny finish.

sat·ire (sa′tīr′) *n.* a variety of humor aiming at mockery or ridicule, often using sarcasm.

sat·is·fac·tion (sat′əs-fak′shən) *n.* the state or feeling of being satisfied.

sat·is·fac·to·ry (sat′əs-fak′tə-rē) *adj.* adequate; acceptable. – *adv.*
sat·is·fac·to·ri·ly (sat′əs-fak′tə-rə-lē).

sat·is·fy (sat′əs-fī′) *vb.* **sat·is·fies, sat·is·fy·ing, sat·is·fied 1** to fulfill the needs or desires of; to meet the requirements of: *The sandwich satisfied my hunger.*
2 to remove the doubts of; to convince: *Stephen satisfied us with his explanation.* – *adj.*
sat·is·fy·ing.

Sat·ur·day (sat′ər-dē, sat′ər-dā′) *n.* the seventh day of the week.

Sat·urn¹ (sat′ərn) the Roman god of farming.

●**Sat·urn**² (sat′ərn) is the second largest planet and famous for the rings that circle it.

Most Hindu women wear a sari. They place the loose end over the head or shoulder.

sauce (sôs) *n.* any seasoned liquid that food is cooked or served in.

sau·cer (sô′sər) *n.* a small dish under a cup.

●**Sau·di A·ra·bi·a** (sôd′ē ə-rā′bē-ə, soud′ē). See Supplement, **Countries**.

sau·na (sô′nə, sou′nə) *n.* a Finnish-style steam bath, created by pouring water on hot coals.

saun·ter (sônt′ər, sänt′ər) *vb.* **saun·ter·ing, saun·tered** to walk at a leisurely pace.

sau·sage (sô′sij) *n.* minced and seasoned meat enclosed in a tube-shaped casing.

Fresh sausages may be fried or boiled. There are also smoked sausages and dry sausages such as salami. The frankfurter, or hot dog, named after Frankfurt, Germany, is a cooked sausage and probably the most famous of all sausages.

PRONUNCIATION SYMBOLS

ə away	lemon	focus
a fat	oi	boy
ā fade	oo	foot
ä hot	ōō	moon
âr fair	ou	house
e met	th	think
ē mean	th	this
g get	u	cut
hw which	ur	hurt
i fin	w	witch
ī line	y	yes
îr near	yōō	music
ô often	yoor	pure
ō note	zh	vision

sav·age (sav′ij) *adj.* **1** not tamed; uncivilized: *a savage animal.* **2** ferocious.

sa·van·na or **sa·van·nah** (sə-van′ə) *n.* a grassy plain of tropical or subtropical areas.

The savanna is home to many species of grazing animals. Each species feeds differently so they do not compete with each other.

save (sāv) *vb.* **sav·ing, saved 1** to rescue from danger, harm, loss, or failure: *The firefighters saved the children from burning to death.* **2** to set aside money, etc. for future use: *Sol is saving up to buy a computer.* **3** to use economically so as to avoid waste: *You must save water in a drought.* **4** to cause to escape possible inconvenience; to spare: *That will save you the trouble of making the trip.* **5** to store computer data on a disk or tape: *Save the files in case there is a power cut.* **6** (in sports) to prevent a goal by blocking a ball or shot. *– n.* **1** (in sports) an act of saving a ball or shot, or preventing a goal. **2** an instruction for a computer to store data on a disk or tape.

sav·ing (sā′ving) *n.* **1** an economy made: *Renting the smaller car was a saving of about $20.* **2** (in *plural*) money saved up: *Do you have any savings?*

saw¹. See **see**¹.

saw² (sô) *n.* a tool with a toothed metal blade

The chainsaw has a never-ending blade in the shape of a chain loop bearing teeth. A small engine (electric or gasoline-driven) turns the drive cog and makes the chain move.

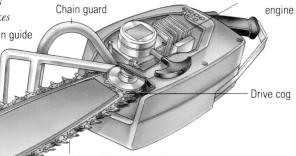

Chain guard

Small internal combustion engine

Chain guide

Drive cog

Chain with cutting teeth

for cutting, hand-operated or power-driven. *– vb.* **saw·ing, sawed, sawn** to cut with a saw.

saw·mill (sô′mil′) *n.* a factory in which timber is cut.

Sax·on (sak′sən) *n.* a member of a Germanic people that conquered much of Britain in the A.D. 400s and 500s.

sax·o·phone (sak′sə-fōn′) *n.* a wind instrument with a long metal body and keys. *– n.* **saxophonist**.

say (sā) *vb.* **say·ing, said** (sed) **1** to utter or pronounce. **2** to express in words: *Say what you mean.* **3** to state as an opinion: *I say we should refuse.* **4** to suppose: *Say he doesn't come, what do we do then?* **5** to judge or decide: *It's difficult to say which is best.* **6** to argue in favor of or against: *There's a lot to be said for it.* **7** to communicate: *She talked for ages but didn't actually say much.* **8** to indicate: *The clock says ten o'clock.* *– n.* a chance to express an opinion: *You've had your say.* *–* **go without saying** to be obvious.

say·ing (sā′ing) *n.* a proverb or expression.

scab (skab) *n.* a crust of dried blood formed over a healing wound.

scaf·fold (skaf′əld) *n.* a framework of metal poles and planks used as a platform for building repair or construction.

scald (skôld) *vb.* **scald·ing, scald·ed** to injure with hot liquid or steam.

scale¹ (skāl) *n.* **1** a series of markings or divisions at regular known intervals, for use in measuring; a system of such markings or divisions. **2** the relationship between actual size and size as represented on a model or drawing. **3** a complete sequence of notes in music. *– vb.* **scal·ing, scaled 1** to climb: *to scale a mountain.* **2** to change the size of something, making it larger (**scale up**) or smaller (**scale down**).

scale² (skāl) *n.* any of the small thin plates that cover the skin of fish and reptiles. *– vb.* **scal·ing, scaled** to remove the scales from.

scale³ (skāl) *n.* (*often in plural*) an instrument for weighing. *–* **tip the scales 1** to be the decisive factor. **2** to have your weight measured at: *He tips the scales at 250 pounds.*

sca·lene (skā′lēn′) *adj.* (of a triangle) having each side a different length.

scal·lop (skäl′əp, skal′əp) *n.* an edible shellfish that has a pair of hinged fan-shaped shells.

scalp (skalp) *n.* the skin on the head from which hair grows.

scal·pel (skal′pəl) *n.* a small surgical knife.

scam·per (skam′pər) *vb.* **scam·per·ing, scam·pered** to run quickly taking short steps: *Ted scampered back to the house.*

A patient having a body scan. The X-ray pictures are computerized into "slice" images.

scan (skan) *vb.* **scan·ning, scanned 1** to read through or examine carefully. **2** to look over quickly. **3** to produce an image of using any of various electronic devices. **4** (of a poem) to conform to a pattern of rhythm. – *n.* an image produced by scanning. – *n.* **scan·ner**.

scan·dal (skan′dəl) *n.* widespread public outrage; an event or fact causing this.

scan·dal·ous (skan′də-ləs) *adj.* disgraceful; outrageous.

Scan·di·na·vi·an (skan′də-nā′vē-ən) *adj.* of, or relating to, **Scandinavia**, SWEDEN, NORWAY, and DENMARK collectively, sometimes also including FINLAND and ICELAND. – *n.* a native or inhabitant of Scandinavia.

scar (skär) *n.* a mark left on the skin after a wound has healed. **2** a blemish. – *vb.* **scar·ring, scarred** to be marked with a scar.

scarce (skârs) *adj.* **1** not often found; rare. **2** in short supply: *Food was scarce during the war.*

scarce·ly (skâr′slē) *adv.* **1** only just. **2** hardly ever. **3** not at all.

scare (skâr) *vb.* **scar·ing, scared 1** to frighten or become afraid. **2** to startle. **3** to drive away

by frightening. – *n.* **1** a fright. **2** a sudden and widespread feeling of alarm: *a bomb scare.*

scarf (skärf) *n.* **scarfs** or **scarves** (skärvz) a strip or square of fabric worn around the neck.

scar·let (skär′lət) *n.* a bright red color.

scar·y *adj.* **scar·i·er, scar·i·est 1** frightening. **2** afraid or timid.

scat·ter (skat′ər) *vb.* **scat·ter·ing, scat·tered 1** to throw haphazardly: *Sam scattered grass seed on the lawn.* **2** to rush off in different directions: *The children scattered when the teacher arrived.*

scav·enge (skav′ənj) *vb.* **scav·eng·ing, scav·enged** to search among waste for usable things. – *n.* **scav·eng·er**.

scene (sēn) *n.* **1** the setting in which a real or imaginary event takes place. **2** a unit of action in a play or movie. **3** a landscape, etc. as seen by someone; a sight: *A delightful scene met their eyes.*

scen·e·ry (sē′nə-rē, sēn′rē) *n.* **1** landscape. **2** the items making up a stage or film set.

scent (sent) *n.* **1** the distinctive smell of a person, animal, or plant. **2** a trail of this left behind: *dogs on the scent.* **3** perfume. **4** the sense of smell.

scep·ter (sep′tər) *n.* a ceremonial rod carried by a

Ultrasound scanners are used in the treatment of heart or kidney disease.

monarch as a symbol of authority.

sched·ule (skej′ool, skej′əl) *n.* **1** a list of activities or events planned to take place at specific times. **2** any list or inventory. **3** a timetable. – *vb.* **sched·ul·ing, sched·uled** to plan to happen at a specific time.

scheme (skēm) *n.* **1** a plan of action, especially a crafty one. **2** a system or program. **3** a careful arrangement of different parts: *a color scheme.* – *vb.* **schem·ing, schemed** to plan secretly.

schol·ar (skäl′ər) *n.* **1** a learned person. **2** a person who studies; a pupil or student.

schol·ar·ship (skäl′ər-ship′) *n.* money awarded for the purposes of further study.

school[1] (skool) *n.* **1** a place where a formal general education is given. **2** a place offering formal instruction in a subject: *art school.*

PRONUNCIATION SYMBOLS		
ə **away**	lemon	focus
a **fat**	oi	**boy**
ā **fade**	oo	**foot**
ä **hot**	oo	**moon**
âr **fair**	ou	**house**
e **met**	th	**think**
ē **mean**	th	**this**
g **get**	u	**cut**
hw **which**	ur	**hurt**
i **fin**	w	**witch**
ī **line**	y	**yes**
îr **near**	yoo	**music**
ô **often**	yoor	**pure**
ō **note**	zh	**vision**

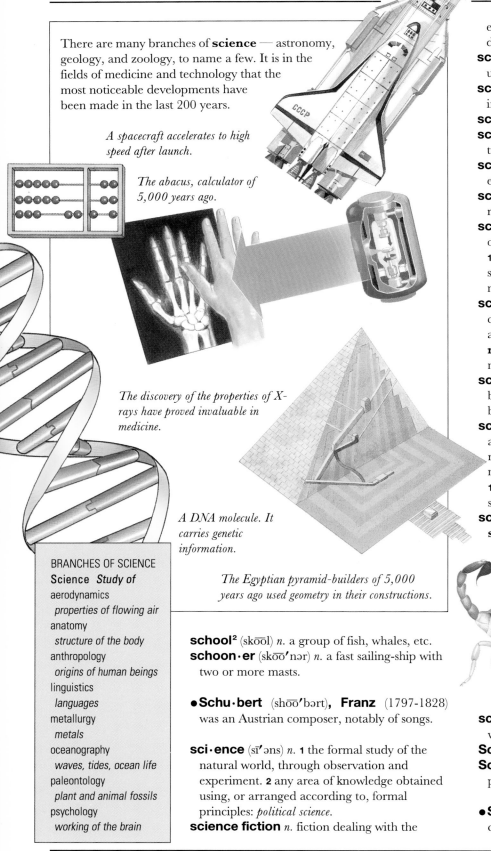

There are many branches of **science** — astronomy, geology, and zoology, to name a few. It is in the fields of medicine and technology that the most noticeable developments have been made in the last 200 years.

A spacecraft accelerates to high speed after launch.

The abacus, calculator of 5,000 years ago.

The discovery of the properties of X-rays have proved invaluable in medicine.

A DNA molecule. It carries genetic information.

BRANCHES OF SCIENCE
Science *Study of*
aerodynamics
  properties of flowing air
anatomy
  structure of the body
anthropology
  origins of human beings
linguistics
  languages
metallurgy
  metals
oceanography
  waves, tides, ocean life
paleontology
  plant and animal fossils
psychology
  working of the brain

The Egyptian pyramid-builders of 5,000 years ago used geometry in their constructions.

school² (skōōl) *n.* a group of fish, whales, etc.
schoon·er (skōō′nər) *n.* a fast sailing-ship with two or more masts.

●**Schu·bert** (shōō′bərt), **Franz** (1797-1828) was an Austrian composer, notably of songs.

sci·ence (sī′əns) *n.* **1** the formal study of the natural world, through observation and experiment. **2** any area of knowledge obtained using, or arranged according to, formal principles: *political science.*
science fiction *n.* fiction dealing with the

effects of science on human life, often describing space travel.
sci·en·tif·ic (sī′ən-tif′ik) *adj.* of, relating to, or used in science. – *adv.* **sci·en·tif·i·cal·ly**.
sci·en·tist (sī′ən-təst) *n.* a student of or expert in science.
sci-fi (sī′fī′) *n.* science fiction.
scis·sors (siz′ərz) *n.* (*plural*) a cutting tool with two long blades joined in the middle.
scoff (skäf, skôf) *vb.* **scoff·ing, scoffed** to express scorn or contempt; to jeer.
scold (skōld) *vb.* **scold·ing, scolded** to reprimand.
scoop (skōōp) *vb.* **scoop·ing, scooped** to lift or dig with a sweeping circular movement. – *n.* **1** a spoonlike implement for handling or serving food. **2** a shovellike part of a mechanical digger.
scoot·er (skōōt′ər) *n.* **1** a child's toy vehicle consisting of a board on two wheels, pushed along the ground with one foot. **2** (also **mo·tor-scoot·er** [mōt′ər-skōōt′ər]) a motorcycle with a small engine.
scorch (skôrch) *vb.* **scorch·ing, scorched** to burn slightly on the surface. – *n.* a mark made by scorching. – *adj.* **scorch·ing**.
score (skôr, skōr) *vb.* **scor·ing, scored 1** to achieve a point, etc. in games. **2** to keep a record of points gained during a game. **3** to make cuts or scratches in the surface of. – *n.* **1** a number of points, etc. scored. **2** a scratch or shallow cut. **3** a set of twenty.
scorn (skôrn) *n.* mocking contempt. – *vb.* **scorn·ing, scorned**.
  Scor·pi·o (skôr′pē-ō′) *n.* See **zodiac**.

Scorpions will not sting humans unless provoked. The main danger is their coming into houses and getting into clothing.

scor·pi·on (skôr′pē-ən) *n.* a spiderlike creature with a poisonous sting.
Scot (skät) *n.* a native of SCOTLAND.
Scotch (skäch) *adj.* (of things; not now of people) Scottish. – *n.* Scotch whiskey.

●**Scot·land** (skät′lənd) is one of the countries comprising the UNITED KINGDOM (the crowns of SCOTLAND and ENGLAND were united when James VI of Scotland became James I of Great Britain). Glasgow is the largest city; EDINBURGH is the capital.

●**Scotland Yard** is the headquarters for the police and criminal investigation in London.

Scots (skäts) *adj.* Scottish. – *n.* any of the dialects related to English used in SCOTLAND.

●**Scott** (skät), **Walter** (1771-1832) was a Scottish poet and novelist, author of *Ivanhoe*.

Scot·tish (skät′ish) *adj.* of SCOTLAND, or its language or people.

scoun·drel (skoun′drəl) *n.* a rogue or villain.

scour[1] (skour) *vb.* **scour·ing, scoured** to clean by hard rubbing.

scour[2] (skour) *vb.* **scour·ing, scoured** to make an exhaustive search of.

scout (skout) *n.* **1** a person or group sent out to observe the enemy and bring back information. **2 Scout** a member of the Boy Scouts of America (a **Boy Scout**) or the Girl Scouts of America (a **Girl Scout**). – *vb.* **scout·ing, scout·ed** to make a search.

scowl (skoul) *vb.* **scowl·ing, scowled** to wrinkle the brow in displeasure or anger.

scram·ble (skram′bəl) *vb.* **scram·bling, scram·bled 1** to mix together or jumble. **2** to crawl or climb using hands and feet, especially frantically: *We scrambled to safety behind the boulders.* **3** to cook eggs by whisking the whites and yolks.

scrap[1] (skrap) *n.* **1** a small piece; a fragment. **2** waste material; waste metal for recycling. **3** (in *plural*) leftover pieces of food. – *vb.* **scrap·ping, scrapped** to discard as useless.

scrap[2] (skrap) *n.* (*informal*) a fight or quarrel.

scrape (skrāp) *vb.* **scrap·ing, scraped 1** to push or drag along a hard or rough surface. **2** to damage by such contact: *Max scraped his elbow.* **3** to remove something from a surface with a grazing action: *Please can you scrape the mud off your boots?* – *n.* **1** an instance, or the action, of dragging or grazing. **2** a part damaged or cleaned by scraping.

scratch (skrach) *vb.* **scratch·ing, scratched 1** to rub or drag a sharp or pointed object across causing damage or making marks. **2** to rub lightly with the fingernails, for example to relieve itching. – *n.* **1** a mark made by

scratching. **2** an act of scratching. **3** a superficial wound or minor injury.

scrawl (skrôl) *vb.* **scrawl·ing, scrawled** to write or draw untidily or hurriedly.

scream (skrēm) *vb.* **scream·ing, screamed** to cry out in a loud high voice.

screech (skrēch) *n.* a harsh shrill cry, voice, or noise. – *vb.* **screech·ing, screeched**.

screen (skrēn) *n.* **1** a netting of mesh used to cover windows and doors. **2** movable hinged panel or panels, used to partition part of a room off. **3** the part of a television set on which the images are formed. **4** a white surface onto which movies or slides are projected. – *vb.* **screen·ing, screened 1** to separate with a screen. **2** to show at the cinema or on television. **3** to subject to an examination, for example to test trustworthiness or check for the presence of disease.

screw (skroō) *n.* **1** a type of nail with a spiral ridge down its length and a slot in its head, driven into place using a twisting action with a screwdriver. **2** the propeller of a ship or boat. – *vb.* **screw·ing, screwed** to twist into place.

screw·driv·er (skroō′drī′vər) *n.* a tool used to twist a screw.

scrib·ble (skrib′əl) *vb.* **scrib·bling, scrib·bled** to write quickly or carelessly.

scrim·mage (skrim′əj) *n.* a play in football after the ball has been snapped back. The **line of scrimmage** is an imaginary line across the football field parallel to the goals determined by the referee when the ball is no longer in play.

script (skript) *n.* **1** the printed text, or the spoken dialogue, of a play, movie, or broadcast. **2** a system of characters used for writing: *Chinese script.* **3** handwriting in which the letters are joined. – *vb.* **script·ing, script·ed** to write the script of. – *n.* **script·writ·er**.

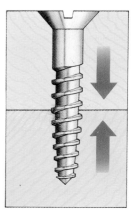

The screw is one of the six simple machines, acting like a long thin wedge that has been wrapped around a cylinder. When you turn the screw, the action of the wedge forces the two pieces of wood together.

Scrap metals, glass, paper, and organic waste can be recycled, thus enabling us to use smaller amounts of limited resources.

scrip·ture (skrip′chər) *n.* the sacred writings of a religion. – *adj.* **scrip·tur·al** (skrip′chə-rəl).

scroll (skrōl) *n.* **1** a roll of paper or parchment written on. **2** a decorative spiral shape, for example in stonework or handwriting. – *vb.* **scroll·ing, scrolled** to move the displayed text on a computer screen up or down.

scrub¹ (skrub) *vb.* **scrub·bing, scrubbed** to rub hard, especially with a brush, to remove dirt. – *n.* an act of scrubbing.

scrub² (skrub) *n.* land covered with low-growing bushes and shrubs.

scruff·y (skruf′ē) *adj.* **scruff·i·er, scruff·i·est** shabbily dressed and messy-looking.

The aqualung or scuba (self-contained underwater breathing apparatus) has a "demand" valve that regulates the exact amount of air needed by a diver to breathe.

scu·ba (skōōb′ə) *n.* a breathing device for underwater divers consisting of cylinders of compressed air connected to a mouthpiece.

scuf·fle (skuf′əl) *n.* a confused fight. – *vb.* **scuf·fling, scuf·fled** to take part in a scuffle.

sculpt (skulpt) *vb.* **sculpt·ing, sculpt·ed** to create a solid model in clay, etc.

sculp·tor (skəlp′tər) *n.* a person who creates sculpture.

sculp·ture (skalp′chər) *n.* **1** the art of carving or modeling with clay, wood, stone, etc. **2** a work or works of art produced in this way.

scum (skum) *n.* dirt or waste matter floating on the surface of a liquid.

scythe (sīth) *n.* a tool with a handle and a long curved blade, for cutting crops or grass.

Like many hand tools, the scythe dates back to prehistoric times. This Roman scythe was used for cutting grain.

sea (sē) *n.* **1** the great mass of salt water that covers most of the earth's surface; the ocean. **2** any named part of this, usually smaller than an ocean. **3** an area of this with reference to its calmness or turbulence: *choppy seas*. **4** a large inland saltwater lake: *the Dead Sea*. **5** a vast expanse or crowd: *a sea of*

worshipers. – **all at sea** completely at a loss.

sea·bed (sē′bed) *n.* the floor of an ocean or sea.

sea·board (sē-bôrd′, sē′bōrd′) *n.* a coast.

sea·far·ing (sē′fer′ing) *adj.* traveling by or working at sea.

sea·gull (sē′gul′). See **gull¹**.

sea horse *n.* a small fish with a curling tail and a horselike head.

seal¹ (sēl) *n.* **1** a device, for example a strip of plastic or metal, that keeps something closed. **2** a piece of rubber or other material serving to keep a joint airtight or watertight. **3** a piece of wax or other material attached to a document and stamped with an official mark to show authenticity: *the royal seal*. – *vb.* **seal·ing, sealed 1** to make securely closed, airtight, or watertight with a seal: *The plumber sealed up the pipes*. **2** to stamp with a seal. – *vb.* **seal off** to isolate, preventing entry: *to seal off an area*.

seal² (sēl) *n.* any of several types of fish-eating sea mammal, with flippers and webbed feet.

sea level *n.* the average level of the sea's surface, the point from which land height is measured.

sea li·on (sē′lī′ən) *n.* a PACIFIC seal with large ears.

seam (sēm) *n.* **1** a join between edges, especially one sewn or welded. **2** a layer of coal or ore in the earth. – *vb.* **seam·ing, seamed** to join by sewing: *Jim seamed the new curtains*.

search (surch) *vb.* **search·ing, searched** to carry out a thorough exploration to try to find something. – *n.* an act of searching.

search·light (surch′līt′) *n.* a pivoting exterior light with a powerful beam.

sea·shore (sē′shôr′, sē′shōr) *n.* land next to the sea.

sea·son (sē′zən) *n.* **1** any of the four major periods – spring, summer, autumn, and winter – into which the year is divided according to differences in weather patterns, etc. **2** a period of the year during which a particular sport or activity is carried out or which has a particular characteristic: *fishing season; rainy season*. – *vb.* **sea·son·ing, sea·soned** to flavor by adding salt, pepper, or other herbs and spices. – *adj.* **sea·soned**.

● As the earth travels around the sun, first one pole and then the other leans toward the sun. When the NORTH POLE tips toward the sun, it is summer in the northern half and winter in the southern half. Six months later it is the SOUTH POLE's turn to lean toward the sun.

sea·son·al (sē′zə-nəl) *adj.* available, happening, or taking place only at certain times of the year.

seat (sēt) *n.* **1** a thing designed for sitting on, for example a chair or bench. **2** a place for sitting, for example a chair. **3** an established center: *Universities are seats of learning.*

●**Se·at·tle** (sē-at′l) is an important port and the largest city in the state of WASHINGTON.

sec·ond¹ (sek′ənd) *adj.* **1** next after the first, in order of sequence or importance. **2** alternate: *They come every second week.* **3** additional; supplementary: *Have a second go.* **4** subordinate; inferior: *His designs are second to none.* − *n.* a person or thing next in sequence after the first. − *adv.* in second place: *George came second in the race.*

sec·ond² (sek′ənd) *n.* a 60th part of a minute.

sec·on·dar·y (sek′ən-der′ē) *adj.* of lesser importance than the primary concern.

second cousin *n.* the child of a parent's cousin.

sec·ond-rate (sek′ənd-rāt′) *adj.* inferior.

se·cre·cy (sē′krə-sē) *n.* the ability or tendency to keep information secret.

se·cret (sē′krət) *adj.* **1** hidden from or undisclosed to others, or to all but a few. **2** whose activities are unknown to or unobserved by others: *a secret army.* − *n.* a piece of information not to be revealed to others.

sec·re·tar·y (sek′rə-ter′ē) *n.* **sec·re·tar·ies** **1** a person employed to perform administrative or clerical tasks; the member of a club or society responsible for its correspondence and business records. **2** a person heading a government department: *Secretary of State.* − *adj.* **sec·re·tar·i·al** (sek′rə-ter′ē-əl).

se·cre·tive (sē′krət-iv) *adj.* fond of secrecy.

sec·tion (sek′shən) *n.* any of the parts into which a thing can be divided, or from which it is constructed.

sec·u·lar (sek′yə-lər) *adj.* not religious.

se·cure (si-kyōōr′) *adj.* **1** free from danger. **2** free from trouble or worry. **3** firmly fixed or attached. − *vb.* **se·cur·ing, se·cured** **1** to fasten or attach firmly. **2** to get or get possession of.

se·cur·i·ty (si-kyoor′ət-ē) *n.* **se·cur·i·ties** **1** the state of being secure. **2** freedom from the possibility of future financial difficulty. **3** something given as a guarantee, as for repayment of a loan.

sed·i·ment (sed′ə-mənt) *n.* solid matter that settles at the bottom of a liquid.

see¹ (sē) *vb.* **see·ing, saw** (sô), **seen** **1** to look at with the eyes: *I saw three ships sailing by.* **2** to have the power of vision: *I can see well with these lenses.* **3** to watch: *Shall we go and see a play?* **4** to understand: *I don't see what you mean.* **5** to find out: *Wait and see.* **6** to meet up with; to be in the company of: *I haven't seen her for ages.* **7** to speak to or consult: *The angry customer asked to see the manager.* − *vb.* **see about** to attend to. − *vb.* **see through something** to recognize an essential truth underlying a lie, trick, etc.

see² (sē) *n.* the post of bishop.

seed (sēd) *n.* **seeds** or **seed** **1** the fruit of a plant from which a new plant grows. **2** source or origin − *vb.* **seed·ing, seed·ed** **1** to plant seeds. **2** to remove seeds from.

The coconut is the hard-shelled seed or fruit of the coconut palm. It is a seed that is spread by being carried along on water.

At the center of a **seed** is a tiny embryo of a new plant. Around this there is a stock of food for the embryo, enclosed by a hard, protective outside. Seeds spread in many ways.

The maple's winged seeds fly through the air.

The seeds of the thistle and the dandelion are scattered by the wind.

The burdock seed (above) has tiny hooks that cling to animals.

Acorns and blackberries (above) are dispersed by being stored or eaten by animals.

Absorbing water, a seed swells and splits (1). An embryo root pushes into the soil (2). The shoot pushes up to the sunlight and leaves appear (3).

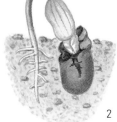

1   2   3

During an earthquake seismic waves travel through the earth. These waves are recorded on a seismograph. The word seismic comes from Greek and means "shaking."

●**See·ger** (sē′gər), **Pete** (1919-) is an American songwriter and folksinger.

seek (sēk) *vb.* **seek·ing, sought** (sôt) **1** to look for. **2** to try to get or achieve. **3** to try or endeavor: *Martha is always seeking to please.* **4** to ask for: *Wendy sought our advice.*

seem (sēm) *vb.* **seem·ing, seemed 1** to appear; to give the impression of being. **2** to be apparent: *There seems no good reason for refusing.*

seen. See **see¹**.

seep (sēp) *vb.* **seep·ing, seeped** (of a liquid) to escape slowly through a narrow opening.

see·saw (sē′sô′) *n.* a plank balanced in the middle, allowing people, especially children, seated on its ends to propel each other up and down by pushing off the ground with the feet.

seg·ment (seg′mənt) *n.* **1** a part, section, or portion. **2** a part of a circle or sphere separated off by an intersecting line. – (seg′ment′, seg-ment′) *vb.* **seg·ment·ing, seg·ment·ed** to divide into segments.

seg·re·gate (seg′rə-gāt′) *vb.* **seg·re·gat·ing, seg·re·gat·ed 1** to separate from others or from each other. **2** to impose segregation on: *to segregate a school.*

seg·re·ga·tion (seg′rə-gā′shən) *n.* **1** the act or process of segregating. **2** the practice of keeping racial, religious, or ethnic groups separate in schools, housing, etc.

seis·mic (sīz′mic) *adj.* to do with earthquakes.

seis·mo·graph (sīz′mə-graf′) *n.* an instrument that measures the force of earthquakes. – *n.*

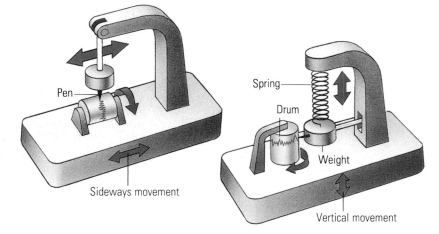

Pen

Sideways movement

Spring

Drum

Weight

Vertical movement

seis·mog·ra·phy (sīz-mäg′rə-fē).

seize (sēz) *vb.* **seiz·ing, seized 1** to take or grab suddenly. **2** to overcome.

sel·dom (sel′dəm) *adv.* rarely.

se·lect (sə-lekt′) *vb.* **se·lect·ing, se·lect·ed** to choose from among several: *Steve selected two apples.* – *adj.* picked out in preference to others.

se·lec·tion (sə-lek′shən) *n.* **1** the act or process of selecting or being selected. **2** a thing or set of things selected. **3** a range from which to choose.

self (self) *n.* **selves** (selvz) **1** personality, or a particular aspect of it. **2** a person as a whole, a combination of characteristics of appearance and behavior: *He isn't his usual happy self.*

self- *in compounds* **1** of, by, for, in, to, or in relation to yourself: *self-doubt; self-inflicted.* **2** acting automatically: *This door is self-closing.*

self-con·fi·dence (self-kän′fə-dəns) *n.* faith in one's own abilities.

self-con·scious (self-kän′shəs) *adj.* ill at ease in company as a result of feeling observed.

self·ish (sel′fish) *adj.* tending to be concerned only with personal welfare.

self-pit·y (self-pit′ē) *n.* excessive grumbling or moaning about one's own misfortunes.

self-re·spect (self′ri-spekt′) *n.* respect for oneself and concern for dignity and reputation.

self-sat·is·fied (self-sat′əs-fīd′) *adj.* smug.

self-sup·port·ing (self′sə-pôrt′ing) *adj.* earning enough money to meet expenses.

sell (sel) *vb.* **sell·ing, sold** (sōld) **1** to give in exchange for money: *Sam sold his bike for $50.* **2** to have available for buying: *This store sells video equipment.* **3** to be in demand: *Compact discs sell well.* – *n.* **sell·er.**

sem·a·phore (sem′ə-fôr′, sem′ə-fōr′) *n.* a system of signaling with flags.

se·men (sē′mən) *n.* a thick whitish liquid containing sperm, ejaculated by the penis.

semi- *prefix* **1** half: *semicircle.* **2** partly: *semiconscious.*

sem·i·cir·cle (sem′i-sur′kəl) *n.* one half of a circle.

sem·i·co·lon (sem′i-kō′lən) *n.* a punctuation mark (;) indicating a pause stronger than that marked by a comma.

sem·i·nar·y (sem′ə-ner′ē) *n.* **sem·i·nar·ies** a college for the training of the clergy.

sen·ate (sen′ət) *n.* **1** a government body that governs or makes laws. **2 Senate** the upper house of the United States CONGRESS or certain state legislatures.

sen·a·tor (sen′ət-ər) *n.* (also **Senator**) a member of a senate or the **Senate**.

send (send) *vb.* **send·ing, sent 1** to cause or order to go or be conveyed or transmitted. **2** to

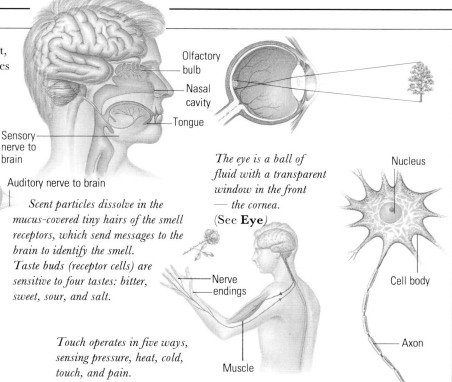

Through the five **senses** — hearing, sight, smell, taste, and touch — the brain receives information about the world outside. A sense contains receptor cells to collect information. This is passed to the sensory nerve cells which take it to the brain.

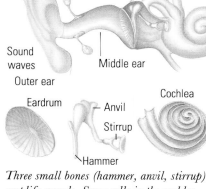

Sound waves
Outer ear
Middle ear
Eardrum
Anvil
Stirrup
Hammer
Cochlea

Three small bones (hammer, anvil, stirrup) amplify sounds. Sense cells in the cochlea send the vibrations as impulses to the brain.

Sensory nerve to brain

Olfactory bulb
Nasal cavity
Tongue

Auditory nerve to brain

Scent particles dissolve in the mucus-covered tiny hairs of the smell receptors, which send messages to the brain to identify the smell.
Taste buds (receptor cells) are sensitive to four tastes: bitter, sweet, sour, and salt.

Touch operates in five ways, sensing pressure, heat, cold, touch, and pain.

Nerve endings
Muscle

The eye is a ball of fluid with a transparent window in the front — the cornea. (See **Eye**)

Nucleus
Cell body
Axon
Muscle

A typical nerve cell (often called a neuron) has a cell body with short fibers called dendrites branching from it. These dendrites send electrical impulses (messages) to the cell body. A long fiber, or axon, carries messages away from the cell body.

cause to become in a state of: *My joke sent him into fits of laughter.* – *n.* **send·er.** – *vb.* **send away for** to order by mail. – *vb.* **send for 1** to ask or order to come; to summon. **2** to order to be brought or delivered. – *vb.* **send off** to dispatch by mail.

●**Sen·e·gal** (sen′i-gôl′). See Supplement, **Countries**.

se·nior (sēn′yər) *adj.* **1** higher in rank or authority than. **2** of or concerning the last year in high school or college. – *n.* **1** a person who is senior in age, rank, or authority. **2** a student in the senior year of high school or college. – *n.* **se·nior·i·ty** (sēn-yôr′ət-ē).

sen·sa·tion (sen-sā′shən) *n.* **1** awareness, by means of the nervous system, of the physical existence or characteristics of things; being able to hear, touch, smell, and taste. **2** a physical feeling: *a burning sensation.* **3** an emotion or general feeling.

sen·sa·tion·al (sen-sā′shən′l) *adj.* **1** causing widespread excitement, intense interest, or shock. **2** excellent: *What a sensational hat!*

sense (sens) *n.* **1** any of the five powers — hearing, taste, sight, smell, and touch — used to perceive the physical world or the condition of the body. **2** an awareness or appreciation of some specified thing: *He has a poor business sense.* **3** (often in *plural*) soundness of mind: *Gus has lost his senses.* **4** wisdom; practical worth: *There's no sense in doing it now.* – *vb.* **sens·ing, sensed 1** to perceive using any of the five senses. **2** to be aware of by means other than the five senses.

sen·si·ble (sen′sə-bəl) *adj.* wise; showing good judgment. – *adv.* **sen·si·bly** (sen′sə-blē).

sen·si·tive (sen′sət-iv) *adj.* **1** responding readily, strongly, or painfully. **2** able to feel or respond to. **3** easily upset or offended. **4** about which there is much strong feeling or difference of opinion: *Some people prefer to avoid discussing sensitive issues.* – *n.* **sen·si·tiv·i·ty** (sen′sə-tiv′ət-ē).

sent. See **send**.

sen·tence (sent′ns) *n.* **1** a sequence of words forming a complete grammatical structure, when written beginning with a capital letter and ending with a period. **2** a punishment determined by a court or judge. – *vb.* **sen·tenc·ing, sen·tenced** to announce the punishment to be given to; to condemn as punishment.

sen·ti·ment (sent′ə-mənt) *n.* an emotion, especially when expressed.

sen·ti·men·tal (sent′ə-ment′l) *adj.* **1** easily feeling or expressing tender emotions, especially love, friendship, and pity. **2** closely associated with fond memories of the past: *My mother cherishes these objects of sentimental value.* – *n.* **sen·ti·men·tal·i·ty** (sent′ə-men-tal′ət-ē).

sen·try (sen′trē) *n.* **sen·tries** a soldier or other person on guard to control entry or passage.

se·pal (sē′pəl) *n.* a group of leaflike parts protecting an unopened flower bud.

sep·a·rate (sep′ə-rāt′) *vb.* **sep·a·rat·ing, separated 1** to set, take, keep, or force apart: *A river separates the two countries.* **2** to move apart; to become detached; to cease to be or live together. – (sep′ə-rət) *adj.* distinctly different; unrelated: *That's a separate issue.*

sep·a·ra·tion (sep′ə-rā′shən) *n.* the act of separating or the state or process of being separated.

Sep·tem·ber (sep-tem′bər) *n.* the ninth month of the year. September has 30 days.

se·quel (sē′kwəl) *n.* **1** a book, movie, or play that continues an earlier story. **2** a result.

se·quence (sē′kwəns) *n.* a series of things following each other in a particular order.

se·quoi·a (si-kwoi′ə) *n.* either of two types of giant Californian coniferous trees.

●**Ser·bi·a** (sur′bē-ə) is a republic that formed part of the former YUGOSLAVIA.

se·rene (sə-rēn′) *adj.* calm; peaceful: *a serene night.* – *n.* **se·ren·i·ty** (sə-ren′ət-ē).

serf *n.* (surf) a medieval peasant who was bound to the land he worked on.

ser·geant (sär′jənt) *n.* an officer above the rank of corporal in the armed forces.

se·ri·al (sîr′ē-əl) *n.* a story published or broadcast in regular installments.

serial killer *n.* a person committing a succession of murders.

se·ries (sîr′ēz′) *n.* **series** a number of similar, related, or identical things arranged or produced one after the other.

ser·if (ser′əf) *n.* a short decorative line on the end of a printed letter, as in E as opposed to the sans serif (=without serifs) E.

se·ri·ous (sîr′ē-əs) *adj.* **1** solemn; not light-hearted or flippant. **2** dealing with important issues: *My father likes to read serious books.* **3** severe: *There's been a serious accident.* – *n.* **se·ri·ous·ness** (sîr′ē-əs-nəs).

ser·mon (sur′mən) *n.* **1** a public speech about morals, religious duties, etc., forming part of a church service. **2** any long talk about behavior, morals, etc.

ser·pent (sur′pənt) *n.* a snake.

ser·vant (sur′vənt) *n.* a person employed by another to do household work.

serve (surv) *vb.* **serv·ing, served 1** to work for the benefit of: *He served the community well.* **2** to carry out duties as a member: *They serve on a committee.* **3** to act as a member of the armed forces: *Simon served in the Marines.* **4** to give assistance to: *to serve a customer.* **5** to respond to the needs or demands of someone: *These shoes have served me well.* **6** to bring or present food or drink. **7** to provide specified facilities to.

ser·vice (sur′vəs) *n.* **1** (often in *plural*) work performed for or on behalf of others; use or usefulness; a favor, or any act with beneficial results: *Your services are no longer required.* **2** an organization working to serve or benefit others in some way: *the civil service.* **3** assistance given to customers. **4** a facility provided. **5** a religious ceremony: *the marriage service.* **6** a complete set of dishes: *a dinner service.* **7** repair or maintenance of a vehicle or equipment. **8** an act of putting the ball into play in sports; a serve. **9** any of the armed forces. – *vb.* **ser·vic·ing, ser·viced** to keep in repair or give service to.

The abbot is shown here entering the choir to celebrate solemn sung High Mass, one of the most important services in an abbey's day. Leading the procession is the thurifer, carrying a censer, followed by a cross-bearer and two acolytes with candles.

S S

Serifs were developed by Roman stonecutters who carved letters in stone. They found it difficult to end wide strokes without ugly, blunt lines. So they added a graceful decoration to the tops and bottoms of many letters.

ses·sion (sesh′ən) *n.* a meeting of a court, council, or legislature; a period during which such meetings are regularly held.

set¹ (set) *vb.* **set·ting, set 1** to put into a certain position or condition: *to set free; to set fire to.* **2** to become solid or motionless: *The cement hasn't set.* **3** to fix, establish, or settle: *Sasha set a new record in the high jump.* **4** to put into a state of readiness: *Set the table.* **5** to adjust to the correct reading: *Can you set the clock?* **6** to place in position for healing: *to set a broken bone.* **7** to place on or against a background, or in surroundings: *The story is set in France.* **8** to stir, provoke, or force into activity: *I set her to work.* **9** (of the sun or moon) to disappear below the horizon. *– n.* **1** form; shape: *the set of his jaw.* **2** the scenery and props used to create a particular location in filming. *– adj.* fixed; allowing no variations: *The restaurant had a set menu.* *– vb.* **set back 1** to delay or hinder the progress of. **2** to cause to return to an earlier and less advanced stage: *These delays will set us back. – vb.* **set in** to become firmly established: *Winter has set in. – vb.* **set off 1** to start out on a trip. **2** to provoke; to start or cause: *The sad movie set her off crying.* **3** to detonate.

set² (set) *n.* **1** a group of related or similar things regarded as a complete unit: *a set of books.* **2** a complete collection of pieces needed for a particular activity: *a chess set; a train set.* **3** one of the major divisions of a match in some sports, for example tennis. **4** an instrument for receiving broadcasts.

set·back (set′bak′) *n.* a defeat or hindrance.

set·tle (set′l) *vb.* **set·tling, set·tled 1** to make or become firmly or satisfactorily positioned or established. **2** to come to an agreement: *Let's settle on a date.* **3** to come lightly to rest: *The butterfly settled on the flower.* **4** to become calm or disciplined after a period of noisy excitement or upheaval: *Please settle down.* **5** to establish a permanent home or colony in: *The Pilgrims settled on the coast of Massachusetts.* **6** to pay off: *Settle up with her.* **7** to sink to the bottom of something; to sink lower: *The leaves settled at the bottom of the pond.*

set·tle·ment (set′l-mənt) *n.* **1** the act of settling. **2** a community of recently settled people. **3** an agreement ending a dispute.

set·tler (set′lər) *n.* a person who settles in a country that is being newly populated.

Pyramids of Egypt

Tomb of Mausolus at Halicarnassus, Turkey

Pharos (lighthouse), Alexandria, Egypt

Temple of Artemis at Ephesus

Colossus at Rhodes

Statue of Zeus at Olympia

sev·en (sev′ən) *n.* the number or figure 7. *– n., adj., & adv.* **seventh** (sev′ənth).

sev·en·teen (sev′ən-tēn′) *n.* the number or figure 17. *– n., adj., & adv.* **sev·en·teenth** (sev′ən-tēnth′).

seventh heaven *n.* a state of great joy: *She was in seventh heaven on her birthday.*

sev·en·ty (sev′ən-tē, sev′ən-dē) *n.* **sev·en·ties** the number or figure 70. *– n., adj., & adv.* **sev·en·ti·eth** (sev′ən-tē-əth, sev′ən-dē-əth).

sev·en·ties (sev′ən-tēz, sev′ən-dēz) *n.* (*plural*) the period of time between the seventieth and eightieth years of a century or a person's seventieth and eightieth birthdays.

● **Seven Wonders of the World** were seven outstanding objects which were built in ancient times. Only one Wonder, the PYRAMIDS, exists today. The others were: The Hanging Gardens of Babylon; the Temple of Artemis at Ephesus, in Turkey; the Statue of Zeus at Olympia, Greece; the Tomb of Mausolus at Halicarnassus, in Turkey; the Colossus at Rhodes; and the Pharos (lighthouse) at Alexandria, Egypt.

sev·er (sev′ər) *vb.* **sev·er·ing, sev·ered 1** to cut off physically: *to sever limbs.* **2** to discontinue.

Hanging Gardens of Babylon

sev·er·al (sev′ə-rəl) *adj.* more than a few, but not a great number.

se·vere (si-vîr′) *adj.* **1** extreme and difficult to endure; marked by extreme conditions: *severe weather.* **2** very strict toward others. **3** austere. **4** grave. − *n.* **se·ver·i·ty** (si-ver′ət-ē).

sew (sō) *vb.* **sew·ing, sewn** or **sewed** to stitch, attach, or repair fabric with thread.

sew·age (sōō′ij) *n.* waste matter carried away in drains.

sew·er (sōō′ər) *n.* an underground pipe for carrying away sewage from drains and water from road surfaces; a main drain.

sex (seks) *n.* **1** either of the two groups − male and female − into which animals and plants are divided. **2** sexuality.

sex·ism (sek′siz′əm) *n.* contempt shown for a particular sex based on prejudice or stereotype. − *n. & adj.* **sex·ist** (sek′səst).

sex·u·al (sek′shōō-əl) *adj.* concerned with or suggestive of sex or the sexes.

sex·u·al·i·ty (sek′shōō-al′ət-ē) *n.* the character of being masculine or feminine.

sex·tant (sek′stənt) *n.* an instrument like a small telescope, used for measuring distance.

sex·tet (sek-stet′) *n.* **1** a group of six singers or musicians. **2** any set of six.

●**Sey·chelles** (sā-shel′, sā-shelz′). See Supplement, **Countries**.

shab·by (shab′ē) *adj.* **shab·bi·er, shab·bi·est** old and worn.

shack (shak) *n.* a roughly built hut.

shade (shād) *n.* **1** an area from which sunlight has been partially blocked. **2** the state of appearing comparatively unimpressive: *His painting puts mine in the shade.* **3** any device used as a shield from direct light; a lampshade. **4** any of a number of varieties of a color: *different shades of brown.* − *vb.* **shad·ing, shad·ed 1** to block out sunlight from. **2** to draw or paint so as to indicate shade.

shad·ow (shad′ō) *n.* **1** a dark shape on a surface, produced when an object stands between the surface and a source of light. **2** an area darkened by the blocking out of light. **3** a slight amount. − *adj.* **shad·ow·y** (shad′ō-ē).

shaft (shaft) *n.* **1** the long straight handle of a tool or weapon. **2** any long straight part, as a rod that transmits motion in an engine. **3** a vertical passageway. **4** a ray or beam.

shake (shāk) *vb.* **shak·ing, shook** (shook), **shak·en** (shā′kən) **1** to move with quick side-to-side or up-and-down movements. **2** to mix in this way. **3** to wave violently and threateningly. **4** to tremble, totter, or shiver. **5** to cause intense shock: *His revelations shook the nation.* **6** to cause to waver; to weaken: *That incident shook my confidence.* **7** to shake hands. − *n.* an act or the action of shaking.

●**Shake·speare** (shāk′spîr′)**, William** (1564-1616) is the greatest English dramatist. He wrote comedies (e.g. *As You Like It*), tragedies (e.g. *Macbeth* and *Hamlet*), English histories (e.g. *Richard III*), and classical histories (e.g. *Antony and Cleopatra*).

A sextant, by means of mirrors and a telescope, measures the angle between a star and the horizon. From this the position of a ship or aircraft can be determined.

Shake·spear·e·an or **Shake·spear·i·an** (shāk-spîr′ē-ən) *adj.* of, or relating to, William **Shakespeare**.

shak·y (shā′kē) *adj.* **shak·i·er, shak·i·est 1** trembling, as with weakness or illness. **2** not solid or secure. − *adv.* **shak·i·ly** (shā′kə-lē).

shall (shal, shəl) *vb.* (*auxiliary*) **1** a question implying future action, often with the sense of an offer or suggestion, especially when the subject is *I* or *we*: *What shall we do? Shall I give you a hand?* **2** determination, intention, certainty, and obligation, especially when the subject is *you, he, she, it,* or *they*: *They shall succeed; You shall have what you want; He shall become king; You shall not kill.* **3** expressing the future tense of other verbs, especially when the subject is *I* or *we*: *We shall see you tomorrow.*

shal·low (shal′ō) *adj.* having little depth.

shame (shām) *n.* **1** an embarrassing or degrading sense of guilt, foolishness, or failure as a result of having done something wrong. **2** disgrace or loss of reputation. **3** a regrettable or disappointing event or situation: *It's a shame you can't come.* − *vb.* **sham·ing, shamed** to provoke by inspiring feelings of shame.

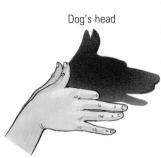

Dog's head

Chicken's head

Flying bird

Rabbit's head

Shadow play. You can use your hands to make different animal shapes.

shame·ful (shām′fəl) *adj.* bringing or deserving shame.

shame·less (shām′ləs) *adj.* showing no shame.

sham·poo (sham′poo′) *n.* **shampoos** a soapy liquid for washing the hair and scalp. – *vb.* **sham·poos, sham·poo·ing, sham·pooed**.

sham·rock (sham′räk′) *n.* a plant whose leaves have three rounded leaflets, as clover.

shan't (shant) (chiefly *British*) shall not.

shan·ty (shant′ē) *n.* **shan·ties** a roughly built hut.

shape (shāp) *n.* **1** the outline or form of anything. **2** a person's body or figure. **3** condition generally: *Her car is in bad shape.* – *vb.* **shap·ing, shaped 1** to give a particular form to; to fashion: *She shaped the clay into a pot.* **2** to influence: *These events shaped history.*

shape·less (shāp′ləs) *adj.* **1** having no definite shape. **2** having an ungraceful form.

shard (shärd) or **sherd** (shurd) *n.* a fragment of pottery, especially on an archaeological site.

share (shār) *n.* **1** a portion given to or contributed by each of two or more people or groups. **2** any of the units into which the total wealth of a business company is divided. – *vb.* **shar·ing, shared 1** to have joint use of, with another or others: *We share an office.* **2** to divide into portions.

shark (shärk) *n.* a large, sometimes fierce, flesh-eating fish.

● Sharks are sometimes called the "tigers of the sea." Some sharks, such as the dogfish, are small. The huge whale shark, the biggest of all fishes, is harmless, eating only tiny plankton. The most feared shark, the great white shark, sometimes attacks swimmers.

sharp (shärp) *adj.* **1** having a thin edge that can cut or a point that can pierce. **2** having a bitter taste. **3** severely felt: *sharp pain.* **4** sudden and acute: *Watch out for the sharp bend.* – *adv.* **1** punctually; on the dot. **2** suddenly: *The bus pulled up sharp.* – *n.* (in music) a note or tone one half note above a note of the same name.

sharp·en (shär′pən) *vb.* **sharp·en·ing, sharp·ened** to make or grow sharp.

shat·ter (shat′ər) *vb.* **shat·ter·ing, shat·tered** to break into tiny pieces, usually suddenly or forcefully: *The baseball shattered the window.* – *adj.* **shat·tered**. – *adj.* **shat·ter·ing**.

shave (shāv) *vb.* **shav·ing, shaved 1** to cut off hair from the face or other part of the body with a razor or shaver. **2** to remove thin slivers from the surface with a blade: *to shave wood.* – *n.* the act or process of shaving. – **a close shave** a near miss or lucky escape.

shawl (shôl) *n.* a large piece of fabric used as a loose covering for the head or shoulders.

she (shē) *pron.* the female person or animal named before or understood from the context.

shear (shîr) *vb.* **shear·ing, sheared, shorn** (shôrn) **1** to clip or cut off with a large pair of clippers. **2** to cut the fleece off: *to shear a sheep.* **3** (of metal) to twist or break under strain. – *n.* (in *plural*) a large scissorslike cutting tool.

shed¹ (shed) *n.* an outbuilding of any size, for working in or for storage or shelter.

shed² (shed) *vb.* **shed·ding, shed 1** to release or cause to flow: *to shed tears.* **2** to get rid of: *The tree shed its leaves.*

sheep (shēp) *n.* **sheep** an animal of the goat family, reared for its meat and its wool.

sheep·ish (shē′pish) *adj.* embarrassed because of having done something wrong or foolish.

sheer (shîr) *adj.* **1** complete; absolute; nothing but: *Your plan is sheer madness.* **2** (of a cliff, etc.) very steep.

sheet¹ (shēt) *n.* **1** a large broad piece of fabric, especially for covering a bed. **2** any large broad expanse: *a sheet of glass.* **3** a piece of paper.

sheet² (shēt) *n.* a controlling rope attached to the lower corner of a sail.

sheikh or **sheik** (shēk, shāk) *n.* a Muslim leader. – *n.* **sheikh·dom** or **sheik·dom** (shek′dəm, shāk′dəm).

shek·el (shek′əl) *n.* the standard unit of currency in ISRAEL.

shelf (shelf) *n.* **shelves** (shelvz) a flat board for laying things on, fixed to a wall or as part of a cupboard, etc.

PRONUNCIATION SYMBOLS			
ə **a**way	lemon	focus	
a	f**a**t	oi	b**oy**
ā	f**a**de	oo	f**oo**t
ä	h**o**t	o͞o	m**oo**n
âr	f**air**	ou	h**ouse**
e	m**e**t	th	**think**
ē	m**ea**n	th	**this**
g	**g**et	u	c**u**t
hw	**wh**ich	ur	h**ur**t
i	f**i**n	w	**w**itch
ī	l**i**ne	y	**y**es
îr	n**ear**	yo͞o	m**u**sic
ô	**o**ften	yoor	p**u**re
ō	n**o**te	zh	vi**s**ion

Sharks mostly hunt alone, but the smell and taste of blood is enough to bring them together as a pack, in a "feeding frenzy," when they will attack anything, including each other.

shell (shel) *n.* **1** the hard protective outer covering of numerous organisms, for example an egg, a nut, or a mollusk. **2** the empty covering of a mollusk. **3** any hard outer case: *the shell of a ship.* **4** a round of ammunition for artillery; a shotgun cartridge. – *vb.* **shell·ing, shelled 1** to remove the shell from. **2** to bombard with artillery shells: *The cannons shelled the fortress both day and night.* – *n.* **shell·ing**.

she'll (shēl, shil) she will; she shall.

shell·fish (shel′fish) *n.* any of numerous sea creatures with an outer shell, for example lobsters.

shel·ter (shel′tər) *n.* **1** protection against weather or danger. **2** a place or structure giving this. – *vb.* **shel·ter·ing, shel·tered 1** to protect from danger or the effects of weather. **2** to take cover.

● **Shep·ard** (shep′ərd), **Alan** (1923-) was the first United States astronaut to be launched into space, on May 5, 1961.

shep·herd (shep′ərd) *n.* a person who looks after sheep.

sher·iff (sher′əf) *n.* the chief police officer in a county.

● **Sher·man** (shur′mən), **William** (1820-1891) was a Union Army general in the AMERICAN CIVIL WAR.

Sher·pa (shur′pə) *n.* a member of an eastern Tibetan people living high in the HIMALAYAS.

shield (shēld) *n.* **1** a piece of armor carried to block an attack with a weapon. **2** a protective plate or screen. – *vb.* **shield·ing, shield·ed** to protect from harm or danger.

shift (shift) *vb.* **shift·ing, shift·ed 1** to change the position or direction of: *The wind shifted to the south.* **2** to transfer, switch, or direct somewhere else: *Why does he always shift the blame onto me?* **3** to remove or dislodge. – *n.* **1** a change or change of position. **2** the group of workers taking turns with other workers on duty. **3** a straight, often loose dress.

shift·y (shif′tē) *adj.* **shift·i·er, shift·i·est** sly.

shil·ling (shil′ing) *n.* **1** a former British coin worth one-twentieth of a pound.

shim·mer (shim′ər) *vb.* **shim·mer·ing, shim·mered** to shine and quiver with reflected light.

shin (shin) *n.* the bony front part of the leg below the knee.

shin·dig (shin′dig′) *n.* (*informal*) a lively party.

shine (shīn) *vb.* **shin·ing, shone** (shōn, shôn) or (sense **3**) **shined 1** to reflect light. **2** to direct the light from: *He shone the flashlight in my face.* **3** to make bright and gleaming by polishing. – *n.* shining quality.

Sea**shells** are the skeletons of animals we call mollusks. Unlike humans and other mammals, mollusks and a number of other animals such as insects and crabs have outer skeletons, which protect their soft bodies from other animals. There are five major groups of mollusk.

Philippine Nerite, a shell of estuary waters.

A pearl is made when a piece of grit irritates the soft tissue of a mollusk's mantle. The animal covers it with shell lining to protect itself, and this forms into a pearl.

Tusk shells burrow in sand.

Textile cone — one of some 500 species. All cone shells inject poison into their victims. The sting of some large species can kill a human.

Triton's trumpet is a snail-like gastropod. There are about 80,000 types of gastropod. Many are found on rocks or stones.

Scallops are two-part (bivalve) shells which live on the seabed.

Queen conch. The conch is a family of sea snails whose shells have been used as trumpets. They live in shallow tropical waters and feed on seaweed.

The largest seashell in the world — the Giant Clam, the biggest being 42 in. wide and weighing 580 lb.

shin·gle (shing′gəl) *n.* a piece of wood, slate, etc. laid in rows to cover a roof or wall.

Shin·to (shin′tō) *n.* the principal religion of JAPAN.

shin·y (shī′nē) *adj.* **shin·i·er, shin·i·est** reflecting light; polished to brightness.

ship (ship) *n.* **1** any large boat intended for sea travel. **2** a spaceship or airship. – *vb.* **ship·ping, shipped** to send or transport by ship. – **when your ship comes in** when you become rich.

Supertankers are not only the biggest ships, but the biggest vehicles of any kind. This oil supertanker is 1240 ft. long and 202 ft. wide.

●Today most ships are cargo vessels, such as tankers which carry liquids such as oil or wine, or container ships, refrigerator ships, and bulk carriers which transport wheat, coal, etc. Planes have replaced most passenger ships but there are still many ferries and cruise ships.

-ship *suffix* **1** rank, position, or status: *lordship.* **2** a period of office: *during his chairmanship.* **3** a state or condition: *friendship.* **4** a type of skill: *craftsmanship.* **5** a group of individuals: *membership.*

ship·ment (ship′mənt) *n.* a cargo.

ship·ping (ship′ing) *n.* ships as traffic: *The new port is open to shipping.*

ship·shape (ship′shāp′) *adj.* in good order.

ship·wreck (ship′rek′) *n.* **1** the accidental sinking or destruction of a ship. **2** the remains of a sunken or destroyed ship. – *vb.* **ship·wreck·ing, ship·wrecked.**

ship·yard (ship′yärd′) *n.* a place where ships are built.

shire (shīr) *n.* a county in GREAT BRITAIN.

shirk (shurk) *vb.* **shirk·ing, shirked** to avoid doing work. – *n.* **shirk·er.**

shirt (shurt) *n.* a garment with sleeves for the upper body, usually with a collar, especially worn by men.

shiv·er (shiv′ər) *vb.* **shiv·er·ing, shiv·ered** to quiver or tremble with cold or fear. – *n.* an act of shivering. – *adj.* **shiv·er·y.**

shoal[1] (shōl) *n.* a large number of fish.

shoal[2] (shōl) *n.* an area of shallow water.

shock (shok) *n.* **1** a strong emotional disturbance. **2** a convulsion caused by the passage of electricity through the body. **3** a heavy jarring blow or impact. – *vb.* **shock·ing, shocked** to cause to feel extreme surprise, outrage, etc.

shoe (shō͞o) *n.* a shaped outer covering for the foot, usually ending below the ankle.

shone. See **shine.**

shook. See **shake.**

shoot (shō͞ot) *vb.* **shoot·ing, shot** (shät) **1** to fire a gun or other weapon, or bullet, arrow, or other missile. **2** to hit, wound, or kill with a weapon or missile. **3** in sports, to strike the ball, etc. at the goal, basketball hoop, etc. **4** to film or take photographs. – *n.* **1** an act of shooting. **2** a new or young plant growth.

shooting star *n.* a meteor.

shop (shäp) *n.* **1** a small store where goods or services are sold: *a sandwich shop.* **2** a place in which work of a particular kind is carried out: *a machine shop.* – *vb.* **shop·ping, shopped** to visit a store in order to buy or look for goods.

shop·lift·er (shäp′lif′tər) *n.* someone who steals goods from stores.

shopping center *n.* an area, as in the suburbs, containing a large number of stores.

shore[1] (shôr, shōr) *n.* land bordering on the sea or any area of water.

shore[2] (shôr, shōr) *n.* a prop. – *vb.* **shor·ing, shored** to support with props.

short (shôrt) *adj.* **1** not long: *Simone's hair is short.* **2** of little height. **3** brief; concise: *a short trip; a short meeting.* **4** (of a temper) easily lost. **5** rudely abrupt; curt. **6** not having enough of; deficient: *We're short of glasses for the party.* – *adv.* abruptly: *She stopped short.*

short·age (shôrt′ij) *n.* a lack or deficiency.

short circuit *n.* a cut in an electrical circuit caused by a fault, which produces heat with a danger of fire.

short·com·ing (shôrt′kum′ing) *n.* a fault.

SHORT OR LITTLE?
A synonym is not always an exact equivalent of another word. Little can mean small — for example "a small boy" or "a little boy." But "Little Larry fights for his life" or "The little old lady who chased off a burglar" cannot be replaced by "small Larry" or "small old lady" The "little" here is suggesting defenselessness or weakness rather than actual height.

short·en (shôrt′n) *vb.* **short·en·ing, short·ened** to make or become shorter: *She shortened her skirt.*

short·hand (shôrt′hand′) *n.* a method of abbreviated writing.

short·list (shôrt′list′) *n.* a selection of the best candidates from the total number submitted.

short-lived (shôrt′livd′, shôrt′līvd′) *adj.* lasting or existing for a short time.

short·ly (shôrt′lē) *adv.* soon.

short-sight·ed (shôrt-sīt′əd) *adj.* **1** showing a lack of foresight. **2** near-sighted. — *n.* **short-sight·ed·ness** (shôrt-sīd′əd-nəs).

shot¹ (shät) *n.* **1** an act of firing a gun; the sound of a gun being fired. **2** small metal pellets fired from a shotgun. **3** an act of shooting or playing a stroke in a sport. **4** a single scene in a movie; a photograph. **5** (*informal*) an attempt: *Have a shot at driving.* — **like a shot** without hesitating.

shot². See **shoot**.

shot·gun (shät′gun′) *n.* a gun held at the shoulder that fires shot.

should (shood) *vb.* (*auxiliary*) expressing **1** obligation; ought to: *Students should be on time.* **2** likelihood or probability: *He should have left by now.* **3** condition: *if I should die before you.* **4** advice: *You should brush your teeth regularly.* **5** (with *1st person pronouns*) a past tense of *shall* in reported speech: *I told them I should be back soon.* **6** statements in clauses with *that*, following expressions of feeling or mood: *It seems odd that we should both have had the same idea.* **7** doubt or polite indirectness in statements: *I should imagine he's left.*

shoul·der (shōl′dər) *n.* **1** the part of the body between the neck and upper arm. **2** the part of a garment covering this. **3** (in *plural*) capacity to bear burdens: *He has a lot of responsibility on his shoulders.* — *vb.* **shoul·der·ing, shoul·dered** to bear or assume: *to shoulder a responsibility.* — **rub shoulders with** (*informal*) to meet or associate with.

shoulder blade *n.* the broad flat triangular bone behind either shoulder.

shout (shout) *n.* a loud cry or call. — *vb.* **shout·ing, shout·ed** to utter a loud cry or call.

shove (shuv) *vb.* **shov·ing, shoved** to push or thrust with force.

shov·el (shuv′əl) *n.* a tool with a deep spadelike blade and a handle, for lifting and carrying loose material. — *vb.* **shov·el·ing** or **shov·el·ling, shov·eled** or **shov·elled** to lift or carry with a shovel.

show (shō) *vb.* **show·ing, showed, shown** (shōn) or **showed** **1** to be or become visible or noticeable: *Her elbow showed through the hole in her shirt.* **2** to present or give to be viewed: *We showed our tickets.* **3** to display or exhibit. **4** to prove, indicate, or reveal: *Show me how it's done.* **5** to teach by demonstrating: *The art teacher showed me how to draw.* **6** to lead, guide, or escort: *The hotel porter showed them to their room.* **7** to give: *Show him some respect.* **8** to be part of a current program: *That play is now showing on Broadway.* — *n.* **1** an entertainment or spectacle of any kind. **2** an exhibition. **3** a pretence: *It was merely a show of friendship between sworn enemies.* **4** a display of true feeling: *no show of emotion.* — *vb.* **show off** **1** to display proudly, inviting admiration. **2** to display to good effect: *The cream sofa shows off the red carpet nicely.*

show business *n.* the entertainment industry.

show·er (shou′ər) *n.* **1** a sudden but brief fall of rain, snow, or hail. **2** a cubicle fitted with a device producing a stream of water for bathing under. — *vb.* **show·er·ing, show·ered** **1** to bathe under a shower. **2** to rain in showers.

show·ing (shō′ing) *n.* **1** an act of exhibiting or displaying. **2** a screening of a motion picture. **3** a performance.

shown. See **show**.

show·y (shō′ē) *adj.* **show·i·er, show·i·est** **1** attractive. **2** gaudy or tasteless.

shrank. See **shrink**.

shred (shred) *n.* **1** a thin strip cut or ripped off. **2** the smallest piece or amount: *There was not a shred of evidence.* — *vb.* **shred·ding, shred·ded** or **shred** to reduce to shreds by ripping.

shrew (shrōō) *n.* a small, mouselike animal, related to the mole, with a long pointed snout.

Shrews are related to moles. They spend most of their time above ground. They are intensely active, and must eat three times their own weight every day.

Pygmy shrew

Common shrew

PRONUNCIATION SYMBOLS

ə	**a**way	lemon	**fo**cus	
a	**fat**	oi	**boy**	
ā	**fade**	oo	**foot**	
ä	**hot**	ōō	**moon**	
âr	**fair**	ou	**house**	
e	**met**	th	**think**	
ē	**mean**	th	**this**	
g	**get**	u	**cut**	
hw	**which**	ur	**hurt**	
i	**fin**	w	**witch**	
ī	**line**	y	**yes**	
îr	**near**	yōō	**music**	
ô	**often**	yoor	**pure**	
ō	**note**	zh	**vision**	

shrewd (shrōōd) *adj.* having good judgment.

shriek (shrēk) *vb.* **shriek·ing, shrieked** to utter a piercing scream. – *n.* such a scream.

shrill (shril) *adj.* high in pitch and piercing: *a shrill voice.*

shrimp (shrimp) *n.* an edible shellfish with a long tail.

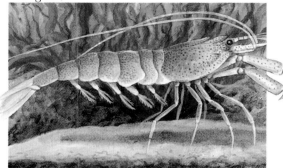

The common shrimp is abundant in coastal waters. By day it buries itself in sand or mud, coming out after dark to walk and feed on the sea bottom.

shrine (shrīn) *n.* a sacred place of worship.

shrink (shringk) *vb.* **shrink·ing, shrank** (shrangk), **shrunk** (shrungk) or (especially as *adj.*) **shrunk·en** (shrung′kən) **1** to make or become smaller. **2** to move away in horror.

shrub (shrub) *n.* a bushy plant with a woody stem.

shrug (shrug) *vb.* **shrug·ging, shrugged** to raise the shoulders briefly to show doubt or indifference. – *n.* an act of shrugging.

shud·der (shud′ər) *vb.* **shud·der·ing, shud·dered** to tremble, with fear or disgust.

shuf·fle (shuf′əl) *vb.* **shuf·fling, shuf·fled** **1** to move with short quick sliding movements: *to shuffle your feet.* **2** to rearrange carelessly. **3** to jumble up playing cards.

shun (shun) *vb.* **shun·ning, shunned** to avoid.

shut (shut) *vb.* **shut·ting, shut 1** to place or move so as to close an opening: *The door shut.* **2** to allow no access: *The office shuts on weekends.*

shut·ter (shut′ər) *n.* **1** a movable cover for a window. **2** a device in a camera that opens and closes to expose the film.

shut·tle (shut′l) *n.* **1** in weaving, the device carrying the horizontal thread (the **weft**) back and forth between the vertical threads (the **warp**). **2** an aircraft, train, or bus running a frequent service between two places.

shut·tle·cock (shut′l-käk′) *n.* a cone of feathers or plastic, used in badminton.

shy (shī) *adj.* **shy·er, shy·est** or **shi·er, shi·est 1** embarrassed or unnerved by the company or attention of others. **2** easily scared; timid.

Si·am·ese (sī′ə-mēz′) *n.* & *adj.* Same as **Thai.**

sib·ling (sib′ling) *n.* a brother or sister.

sick (sik) *adj.* **1** ill; unwell. **2** nauseous; feeling the desire to vomit. **3** relating to ill health: *sick pay.* **4** (also **sick and tired**) thoroughly weary or fed up: *We are sick of hearing your excuses.*

sick·en (sik′ənd) *vb.* **sick·en·ing, sick·ened 1** to cause to feel ill or like vomiting. **2** to annoy greatly or disgust. – *adj.* **sick·en·ing.**

sick·ness (sik′nəs) *n.* **1** an illness. **2** vomiting.

sick·le (sik′əl) *n.* a tool with a short handle and a curved blade for cutting grain.

sick·ly (sik′lē) *adj.* **sick·li·er, sick·li·est** often ill.

side (sīd) *n.* **1** any of the flat or flattish surfaces that form the shape of something; any of these surfaces other than the top and bottom; any of these surfaces other than the front, back, top, or bottom: *A cube has six sides. A barn has four sides.* **2** an edge or border: *the side of the road.* **3** either of the parts or areas produced when the whole is divided up the middle: *the right side of your body.* **4** either of the broad surfaces of a flat object: *the two sides of a coin.* **5** any of the lines forming a geometric figure: *A triangle has three sides.* **6** any of the groups or teams in a conflict or competition. – *adj.* **1** located at the side: *a side entrance.* **2** subsidiary: *a side road.* – *adj.* **sid·ed.**

side effect *n.* an additional, unexpected, and usually undesirable effect, especially of a drug.

The traditional shuttlecock comprises a hemispherical cork base to which 16 goose feathers are fastened.

For thousands of years farmers harvested grain by hand with a sickle or scythe. This illustration is of a medieval harvest scene.

side·track (sīd′trak′) *vb.* **side·track·ing, side·tracked** to turn aside or divert: *The new problem sidetracked us from our project.*

side·walk (sīd′wôk′) *n.* a paved walkway.

side·ways (sīd′wāz′) or **side·way** *adv. & adj.* **1** from, to, or toward one side. **2** with one side foremost: *The car slid sideways into the wall.*

siege (sēj) *n.* an attempt to capture a fort or town by surrounding it with troops and forcing surrender. – **lay siege to** to subject to a siege.

●**Si·er·ra Le·one** (sē-er′ə lē-ōn′). See Supplement, **Countries**.

●**Si·er·ra Ne·va·da** (sē-er′ə nə-väd′ə, nə-vad′ə) **1** a mountain range in eastern California. **2** a mountain range in southern Spain.

si·es·ta (sē-es′tə) *n.* an afternoon sleep.

sieve (siv) *n.* a utensil with a meshed or perforated bottom, used to separate solids from liquids or large particles from smaller ones. – *vb.* **siev·ing, sieved** to sift.

sift (sift) *vb.* **sift·ing, sift·ed 1** to pass through a sieve. **2** to separate out as if by passing through a sieve.

sigh (sī) *vb.* **sigh·ing, sighed** to release a long deep breath, especially indicating sadness, longing, or relief. – *n.* an act of sighing.

Silk is made from the cocoon of one kind of moth. Silkworms (caterpillars) are fed on mulberry leaves for about four weeks. They then spin their cocoons and start to turn into moths. The cocoons are unwound as a long thread of more than 2,000 ft.

(Above) *Silkworms feeding on mulberry leaves.*

Under the Manchus in China the silk industry employed thousands of workers to weave silk on looms.

sight (sīt) *n.* **1** the power of seeing; vision. **2** a thing seen. **3** one's field of vision: *It flew out of sight.* **4** (usually in *plural*) a thing that is particularly interesting to see: *We're seeing the sights of the town.* **5** an aiming device. – *vb.* **sight·ing, sight·ed 1** to get a look at or glimpse of. **2** to adjust the sight of a firearm.

sign (sīn) *n.* **1** a printed mark with a meaning; a symbol: *a multiplication sign.* **2** an indication: *There are signs of improvement.* **3** a board or panel displaying information for public view. **4** a signal. **5** a division of the zodiac. – *vb.* **sign·ing, signed 1** to write a signature on. **2** to express in sign language.

sig·nal (sig′nəl) *n.* a message in the form of a gesture, light, sound, radio waves, etc., conveying information. – *vb.* **sig·nal·ing** or **sig·nal·ling, sig·naled** or **sig·nalled** to transmit a message using signals.

sig·na·ture (sig′nə-chər) *n.* a person's name written by that person.

sig·nif·i·cance (sig′nif′i-kəns) *n.* meaning or importance.

sig·nif·i·cant (sig-nif′i-kənt) *adj.* **1** important; worth noting. **2** having some meaning.

sign language *n.* a language that uses gestures instead of speech.

Sikh (sēk) *n.* a follower of a religion founded in INDIA in the 1500s, worshiping one god.

si·lence (sī′ləns) *n.* absence of sound or speech. – *vb.* **si·lenc·ing, si·lenced** to cause someone to stop speaking, stop making a noise, or stop giving away information.

si·lent (sī′lənt) *adj.* **1** free from noise. **2** not speaking.

sil·hou·ette (sil′ə-wet′) *n.* **1** a dark shape seen against a light background. **2** an outline drawing of a person, especially a portrait in profile, usually filled in with black.

sil·i·con (sil′ə-kən, sil′i-kän′) *n.* a nonmetallic element (symbol **Si**), found in quartz and opal.

silicon chip *n.* a minute piece of silicon on which electronic circuits are formed.

silk (silk) *n.* a fine soft fiber produced by the silkworm; fabric made from such fibers.

silk·worm (silk′wurm′) *n.* the larva of a moth that spins silk to form its cocoon.

sill (sil) *n.* a ledge of wood, stone, or metal forming the bottom of a window or door.

sil·ly (sil′ē) *adj.* **sil·li·er, sil·li·est** not sensible; foolish; frivolous.

silt (silt) *n.* fine soil deposited by rivers, etc.

An ancient Greek silver coin — the owl, which symbolized the owl-eyed goddess of Athens, Athena.

Silver can be found as lumps of metal in the ground, but most silver is extracted from ores.

sil·ver (sil′vər) *n.* **1** an element (symbol **Ag**), a precious shiny gray metal. **2** coins made of this metal. **3** cutlery made of or coated with this metal. − *adj.* **1** of a whitish-gray color. **2** (of a wedding or other anniversary) 25th.

sil·ver·ware (sil′vər wâr′) *n.* forks, spoons, knives, etc. used for eating and as serving utensils.

sim·i·lar (sim′ə-lər) *adj.* alike; of the same kind, but not identical: *The two makes of car look very similar.* − *n.* **sim·i·lar·i·ty** (sim′ə-lar′ət-ē).

sim·i·le (sim′ə-lē) *n.* any phrase in which a thing is described by being likened to something, usually using "as" or "like," as in "eyes sparkling like diamonds."

sim·mer (sim′ər) *vb.* **sim·mer·ing, sim·mered** to cook gently at just below the boiling point.

sim·ple (sim′pəl) *adj.* **1** easy; not difficult; straightforward; not complex or complicated. **2** plain or basic; not elaborate or luxurious. **3** down-to-earth; unpretentious. **4** plain; mere.

sim·pli·fy (sim′plə-fī′) *vb.* **sim·pli·fies, sim·pli·fy·ing, sim·pli·fied** to make less complicated or easier to understand. − *n.* **sim·pli·fi·ca·tion** (sim′plə-fə-kā′shən).

sim·plis·tic (sim-plis′tik) *adj.* too simple.

sim·ply (sim′plē) *adv.* **1** in a straightforward, uncomplicated way. **2** just: *Your accusation is simply not true.* **3** absolutely: *The party was simply marvelous.* **4** merely: *I simply wanted to help.*

si·mul·ta·ne·ous (sī′məl-tā′nē-əs) *adj.* happening, or done, at exactly the same time.

sin (sin) *n.* an act that breaks religious law or teaching. − *vb.* **sin·ning, sinned** to commit a sin. − *adj.* **sin·ful** (sin′fəl). − *n.* **sin·ner**.

since (sins) *conj.* **1** during or throughout the period between now and some earlier stated time. **2** as; because. − *prep.* during or throughout the period between now and some earlier stated time: *I've been here since midday.*

sin·cere (sin-sīr′) *adj.* genuine; not pretended or affected. − *n.* **sin·cer·i·ty** (sin-ser′ət-ē).

sin·ew (sin′yōō′) *n.* a strong fiberlike tissue joining a muscle to a bone; a tendon.

sing (sing) *vb.* **sing·ing, sang** (sang), **sung** (sung) **1** to make sounds in a musical, rhythmic fashion. **2** to make a sound like a musical voice; to hum, ring, or whistle: *Can you hear the tea kettle singing on the stove?* − *n.* **sing·er**. − *n.* **sing·ing**. − *vb.* **sing out** to shout or call out.

● **Sing·a·pore** (sing′ə-pôr′, sing′ə-pōr′). See Supplement, **Countries**.

singe (sinj) *vb.* **singe·ing, singed** to scorch.

sin·gle (sing′gəl) *adj.* **1** of which there is only one; solitary. **2** unmarried. **3** for use by one person only: *a single room.* − *vb.* **single out; sin·gling, sin·gled** to pick from among others.

sin·gle-hand·ed (sing′gəl-han′dəd) *adj. & adv.* without help from others.

sin·gle-mind·ed (sing′gəl-mīn′dəd) *adj.* determinedly pursuing a single aim. − *n.* **sin·gle-mind·ed·ness**.

sin·gly (sing′glē) *adv.* one at a time.

sin·gu·lar (sing′gyə-lər) *adj.* **1** single; unique. **2** extraordinary; exceptional: *It's a singular sound to hear crickets in winter.* **3** strange; odd. **4** in grammar, referring to one person, thing, etc.

sin·i·ster (sin′ə-stər) *adj.* suggesting or threatening evil or danger.

sink (singk) *vb.* **sink·ing, sank** (sangk), **sunk** (sungk) or (especially as *adj.*) **sunk·en** (sung′kən) **1** to fall below the surface of water: *The boat sank in the storm.* **2** to collapse downwardly or inwardly; to fall because of a collapsing base or foundation. **3** to produce the sensation of a downward collapse within the body: *My heart sank at the news.* **4** to embed: *Sally sank the pole into the ground.* **5** (of the sun) to disappear below the horizon. − *n.* a basin with faucets and drainage. − *vb.* **sink in** to be fully understood.

si·nus (sī′nəs) *n.* any of the hollows in the bones of the skull connected with the nose.

● **Sioux** (sōō) a tribe of PLAINS INDIANS who lived mainly in what are now Minnesota, South Dakota, and Nebraska.

sip (sip) *vb.* **sip·ping, sipped** to drink in very small mouthfuls. − *n.* a small mouthful.

PRONUNCIATION SYMBOLS		
ə **away**	lemon	focus
a **fat**	oi	**boy**
ā **fade**	oo	**foot**
ä **hot**	ōō	**moon**
âr **fair**	ou	**house**
e **met**	th	**think**
ē **mean**	<u>th</u>	**this**
g **get**	u	**cut**
hw **which**	ur	**hurt**
i **fin**	w	**witch**
ī **line**	y	**yes**
îr **near**	yōō	**music**
ô **often**	yoor	**pure**
ō **note**	zh	**vision**

A straw in a carton of juice acting as a siphon. If the end of the straw dips below the level of the juice in the carton, the juice will flow.

si·phon or **sy·phon** (sī′fən) *n.* a bent pipe through which, by atmospheric pressure, a liquid is drawn from one container into a second container placed at a lower level.

sir (sur) *n.* a term of politeness used in addressing a man.

si·ren (sī′rən) *n.* **1** a device that gives out a loud wailing noise, usually as a warning signal. **2** in Greek mythology, a sea nymph, part woman, part bird, whose songs lured sailors to their death on the rocks.

sis·ter (sis′tər) *n.* **1** a female child of the same parents as another. **2** a nun.

sis·ter-in-law (sis′tər-ən-lô′) *n.* **sis·ters-in-law** **1** the sister of a person's husband or wife. **2** the wife of a person's brother.

sit (sit) *vb.* **sit·ting, sat** (sat) **1** to rest the body on the buttocks; (of a bird) to perch or lie. **2** to lie or rest: *The cup sitting on the shelf is an antique.* **3** to be a member, taking regular part in meetings: *Our dean sits on several committees.* **4** to assign a seat to: *Gail sat me next to her brother.* – *vb.* **sit in** **1** to be present, especially without taking part. **2** to act as a substitute.

site (sīt) *n.* **1** the place where something was, is, or is to be situated. **2** an area set aside for a specific activity: *a camping site.*

● **Sitting Bull** (*died* 1890) was a NATIVE AMERICAN chief who led the SIOUX in a war against the UNITED STATES army in which George CUSTER was killed at the Battle of Little Bighorn in 1876.

Sitting Bull fought fiercely against the wagon trains that crossed his people's lands.

sit·u·ate (sich′ōō-āt′) *vb.* **sit·u·at·ing, sit·u·at·ed** to put in a certain position or place: *We situated the summer house by the lake.*

sit·u·a·tion (sich′ōō-ā′shən) *n.* **1** a set of circumstances; a state of affairs. **2** a position.

six (siks) *n.* the number or figure 6. – *adj., n., & adv.* **sixth** (siksth).

six·teen (sik-stēn′) *n.* the number or figure 16. – *adj., n., & adv.* **six·teenth** (sik-stēnth′).

six·ty (sik′stē) *n.* **six·ties** the number or figure 60. – *adj., n., & adv.* **six·ti·eth** (sik′stē-əth).

six·ties (sik′stēz) *n.* (*plural*) **1** the period of time between a person's sixtieth and seventieth birthdays. **2** the period of time between the sixtieth and seventieth years of a century; 1960s.

size (sīz) *n.* **1** length, breadth, height, or volume, or a combination of all or any of these. **2** largeness: *I was astonished by its size.*

siz·zle (siz′əl) *vb.* **siz·zling, siz·zled** to make a hissing sound when, or as if when, frying in hot fat: *The bacon is sizzling in the pan.*

skate[1] (skāt) *n.* a boot with a device fitted to the sole for gliding smoothly over surfaces, either a steel blade for use on ice (**ice skate**) or a set of small wheels for use on wooden and other surfaces (**roller skate**). – *vb.* **skat·ing, skat·ed** to move around on skates.

skate[2] (skāt) *n.* **skate** or **skates** a large flat fish of the ray family.

skate·board (skāt′bôrd′, skāt′bōrd′) *n.* a narrow-shaped board mounted on sets of small wheels, for riding on.

skel·e·ton (skel′ət-n) *n.* the framework of bones supporting a human or animal body. – *adj.* **skel·e·tal** (skel′ət-l).

● There are more than 200 bones in the human skeleton. These include the bones of the spine, skull, ribs, pelvis, breastbone, and limbs. Joints are places where bones meet. Some joints, like those in the skull, do not move. Others, like those in the shoulders and hips, help us to move about.

skep·tic (skep′tik) *n.* a person who doubts the beliefs of others. – *adj.* **skep·ti·cal** (skep′ti-kəl). – *n.* **skep·ti·cism** (skep′tə-siz′əm).

sketch (skech) *n.* **1** a rough drawing quickly done. **2** any of several short pieces of comedy presented as a program. – *vb.* **sketch·ing, sketched** to do a rough drawing.

sketch·y (skech′ē) *adj.* **sketch·i·er, sketch·i·est** lacking detail; not complete.

ski (skē) *n.* **skis** **1** a long narrow strip of wood, metal, or plastic, turned up at the front, for gliding over snow, attached to each of a pair of boots or to a vehicle. **2** (also **water ski**) a similar object worn on each foot for gliding over water. – *vb.* **skis, ski·ing, skied** to move on skis. – *n.* **ski·er**. – *n.* **ski·ing**.

skid (skid) *vb.* **skid·ding, skid·ded** to slide at an angle, especially out of control.

skill (skil) *n.* **1** expertness; dexterity. **2** a talent or accomplishment. – *adj.* **skilled**.

skill·ful (skil′fəl) *adj.* having or showing skill.

skim (skim) *vb.* **skim·ming, skimmed 1** to remove floating matter from the surface of. **2** to read superficially: *I skim through the headlines before reading the newspaper.*

skim or **skimmed milk** *n.* milk from which all the fat has been removed.

skin (skin) *n.* **1** the tissue forming the outer covering on the bodies of humans and animals. **2** the outer covering of some fruits and vegetables. **3** an animal hide, with or without fur or hair attached. − *vb.* **skin·ning, skinned 1** to strip the skin from. **2** to injure by

skip (skip) *vb.* **skip·ping, skipped 1** to go along with light springing or hopping steps on alternate feet. **2** to omit, leave out, or pass over. − *n.* a skipping movement.

skip·per (skip′ər) *n.* the captain of a ship.

skirt (skurt) *n.* a woman's garment that hangs from the waist. − *vb.* **skirt·ing, skirt·ed 1** to border. **2** to pass along or around the edge of.

skit (skit) *n.* a short, often humorous sketch performed as entertainment.

skit·tle (skit′l) *n.* **1** *(plural)* an English game similar to bowling played with a wooden ball. **2** any of several bottle-shaped targets used in

FIND THE SKIPPER
Skipper is from the Dutch *schipper*, from the word *schip* ("ship"). The English "equip" is from the same source. In early France the word for "boarding ship" was taken from the Dutch, becoming eskip or esquip. The "s" was dropped, forming the word "equip" which has, over the years, changed its meaning.

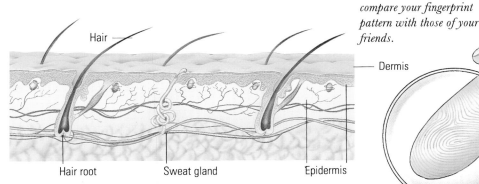

Skin helps to keep out harmful germs and stops us from getting too hot or too cold. The outer layer, called the epidermis, is constantly being rubbed away and replaced from beneath. The dermis beneath is thicker and contains nerves, blood vessels, hair roots, and sweat glands.

Fingerprints are unique. No two people have the same pattern of loops and whorls on their skin. Use a magnifying glass to compare your fingerprint pattern with those of your friends.

Hair

Dermis

Hair root   Sweat gland   Epidermis

The skin contains sweat glands, which carry moisture and waste material to the surface. Hair roots and little muscles cause "goose flesh" and make our hair "stand on end."

---

scraping the skin from. − **by the skin of one's teeth** very narrowly; only just. − **get under someone's skin** *(informal)* to greatly annoy or irritate someone. − **have a thick skin** *(informal)* to be insensitive to criticism or insult.

skin-deep (skin′dēp′) *adj.* superficial: *The wound was only skin-deep.*

skin div·ing (skin′dī′ving) *n.* underwater swimming with no wet suit and only simple breathing and other equipment. − *n.* **skin div·er** (skin′dī′vər).

skin·flint (skin′flint′) *n.* a person who is very mean and niggardly.

skin·ny (skin′ē) *adj.* **skin·ni·er, skin·ni·est** very thin.

the game of skittles.

skull (skul) *n.* **1** the head's framework of bone. **2** *(informal)* the head, considered as the center of learning or understanding: *You must get algebra into your skull.*

The human skull (far right) *has 22 bones. Eight of these bones form the cranium, which encloses the brain. The other 14 bones form the face and jaw. Only the jaw bone moves.* (Right) *A hyena's skull showing its stabbing canine teeth.*

Like all members of the weasel family the skunk has a musk gland at the base of its tail. It can squirt a foul-smelling liquid a distance of 12 feet (3.7 m) to drive off even the most intrepid attacker.

skunk (skungk) *n.* a North American animal with black and white fur, which defends itself by squirting bad-smelling liquid.

sky (skī) *n.* **skies** (often in *plural*) the vast area of space visible above the earth, in which the sun, moon and stars can be seen; the heavens.

sky blue *n.* a pale light blue color.

sky·div·ing (skī′dī′ving) *n.* the sport of diving from an aircraft with a long delay before the parachute is opened. – *n.* **sky·div·er** (skī′dī′vər).

sky·light (skī′līt′) *n.* a small window in a roof.

sky·line (skī′līn′) *n.* the outline of buildings, hills, and trees seen against the sky.

sky·scrap·er (skī′skrā′pər) *n.* an extremely tall building.

● The first skyscraper was built in 1884 in Chicago, Illinois. For many years the world's tallest building was the Empire State Building, in New York City, which is 102 stories high. Now there are two taller ones — the Sears Tower in Chicago and the World Trade Center in New York City, both 110 stories.

slab (slab) *n.* a thick flat rectangular piece, slice, or object.

slack (slak) *adj.* **1** loose; not pulled or stretched tight. **2** not careful or diligent: *Your work is full of errors; you've become slack.* **3** not busy: *Business is slack.* – *vb.* **slack·ing, slacked** (also **slack·en** (slak′ən), **slack·en·ing, slack·ened**) **1** to become slower; to slow your working pace through tiredness or laziness. **2** to make or become looser: *Slacken your belt.* **3** to become less busy.

slam (slam) *vb.* **slam·ming, slammed** to shut loudly and with violence: *Don't slam the door.*

slan·der (slan′dər) *n.* a false spoken (not written) statement about a person, intended to damage his or her reputation.

slang (slang) *n.* language used informally, not usually in writing or formal speech.

slant (slant) *vb.* **slant·ing, slant·ed** **1** to be at an angle, not horizontal or vertical; to slope.

2 to present in a biased way. – *n.* a sloping position, surface, or line.

slap (slap) *n.* **1** a blow with the palm of the hand or anything flat. **2** the sound made by such a blow. – *vb.* **slap·ping, slapped** to strike with the open hand or anything flat. – **a slap in the face** (*informal*) an insult or rebuff.

slap·dash (slap′dash′) *adj.* careless and hurried: *Your writing is messy and slapdash.*

slash (slash) *vb.* **slash·ing, slashed** **1** to make sweeping cuts or cutting strokes in or at, especially repeatedly: *Saul slashed the weeds with a knife.* **2** (*informal*) to reduce suddenly and drastically: *Prices have been slashed.*

slat (slat) *n.* a thin strip of wood or metal.

slate (slāt) *n.* **1** a usually dull gray rock splitting easily into thin layers, used to make roofing tiles, etc. **2** a small tablet for writing on.

slaugh·ter (slôt′ər) *n.* **1** the killing of animals for food. **2** cruel and violent murder. – *vb.* **slaugh·ter·ing, slaugh·tered** **1** to kill for food; to butcher. **2** to massacre.

Slav (släv) *n.* a member of any of various European peoples speaking Slavonic languages such as Russian and Polish.

slave (slāv) *n.* **1** a person owned by and acting as servant to another, with no personal freedom. **2** a person who works extremely hard for another. – *vb.* **slav·ing, slaved** to work hard.

slav·er·y (slā′və-rē, slāv′rē) *n.* **1** the state of being a slave. **2** the practice of owning slaves.

A slave market in Yemen in 1237. Slaves were mostly brought from Africa and from central Asia. The Koran forbade people from making other Muslims slaves.

PRONUNCIATION SYMBOLS			
ə	**away** lemon		focus
a	**fat**	oi	**boy**
ā	**fade**	oo	**foot**
ä	**hot**	ōō	**moon**
âr	**fair**	ou	**house**
e	**met**	th	**think**
ē	**mean**	th	**this**
g	**get**	u	**cut**
hw	**which**	ur	**hurt**
i	**fin**	w	**witch**
ī	**line**	y	**yes**
îr	**near**	yōō	**music**
ô	**often**	yoor	**pure**
ō	**note**	zh	**vision**

slay (slā) *vb.* **slay·ing, slew** (sloō), **slain** (slān) to kill: *St. George slew the dragon.*

sled (sled) *n.* **1** a vehicle with ski-like runners for traveling over snow, drawn by horses or dogs. **2** a small vehicle on runners for sliding down hills.

sledge·ham·mer (slej'ham'ər) *n.* a large heavy hammer swung with both arms.

sleek (slēk) *adj.* smooth, soft, and glossy.

Light sleep   Deep sleep   Light sleep

Hours 1   2   3   4   5   6   7   8

Periods of light and deep sleep can be measured from the electrical waves given off by the brain during sleep. Dreams occur during light sleep.

sleep (slēp) *n.* **1** rest in a state of near unconsciousness, with the eyes closed. **2** a period of such rest. – *vb.* **sleep·ing, slept** (slept) to rest in a state of sleep. – **go to sleep** **1** to pass into a state of sleep. **2** (*informal*) (of a limb) to be temporarily numb through lack of circulation of blood.

sleep·ing bag (slē'ping-bag') *n.* a large quilted sack for sleeping in when camping, etc.

sleep·y (slē'pē) *adj.* **sleep·i·er, sleep·i·est** **1** feeling the desire to sleep; drowsy. **2** suggesting sleep or drowsiness: *sleepy music.* – *adv.* **sleep·i·ly** (slē'pə-lē).

sleet (slēt) *n.* rain mixed with snow or hail.

sleeve (slēv) *n.* the part of a garment that covers the arm. – **up your sleeve** held secretly in reserve, for possible later use.

sleigh (slā) *n.* a large horse-drawn sled.

slen·der (slen'dər) *adj.* **1** attractively slim. **2** narrow; slight: *They won by a slender margin.*

slept. See **sleep**.

slew. See **slay**.

slice (slīs) *n.* a thin broad piece, or a wedge, cut off: *a slice of cake.* – *vb.* **slic·ing, sliced** **1** to cut up into slices. **2** to cut as, or as if as, a slice.

slick (slik) *adj.* **1** dishonestly or slyly clever: *Her sales talk was just too slick.* **2** superficially smart or efficient: *a slick organization.* **3** smooth and glossy; sleek. – *n.* (also **oil slick**) a wide layer of spilled oil floating on the surface of water.

slide (slīd) *vb.* **slid·ing, slid** (slid) **1** to move or run smoothly along a surface. **2** to move or place softly and gently: *I slid the letter into his pocket.* **3** to slip. – *n.* **1** an act or instance of sliding. **2** a structure for children to play on with a narrow sloping part to slide down. **3** a

transparent photograph for projecting onto a screen.

slight (slīt) *adj.* **1** small in extent, importance, or seriousness: *We have a slight difference of opinion.* **2** slender. **3** lacking solidity; flimsy. – *vb.* **slight·ing, slight·ed** to insult by ignoring or dismissing abruptly; to snub. – *adv.* **slight·ly**.

slim (slim) *adj.* **slim·mer, slim·mest** attractively thin; slender. – *vb.* **slim·ming, slimmed** to make or become slim.

slime (slīm) *n.* a thin unpleasantly slippery or mudlike substance.

sling (sling) *n.* **1** a cloth hoop supporting an injured arm that is suspended from the neck. **2** a weapon for launching stones. **3** a strap or loop for hoisting or carrying a weight.

slip[1] (slip) *vb.* **slip·ping, slipped** **1** to lose one's footing and slide accidentally. **2** to slide, move, or drop accidentally: *The soap slipped through my hands.* **3** to place quietly or secretively: *Lucy slipped the envelope into her pocket.* **4** to move quietly and unnoticed: *Sarah slipped out of the room as soon as the baby fell asleep.* **5** to pull free from smoothly and swiftly; to escape suddenly from: *The dog slipped its leash. The name has slipped my mind.* **6** to make a slight mistake. – *n.* **1** an instance of losing one's footing and sliding accidentally. **2** (also **slip-up**) a slight mistake: *a slip of the tongue.*

slip[2] (slip) *n.* a small strip or piece of paper.

slip·per (slip'ər) *n.* a soft loose indoor shoe.

slip·per·y (slip'ə-rē) *adj.* so smooth as to cause slipping.

slip·shod (slip'shäd') *adj.* carelessly done.

slip·stream (slip'strēm') *n.* a stream of air driven back by a moving vehicle.

slit (slit) *n.* a long narrow cut or opening. – *vb.* **slit·ting, slit·ted** to cut a slit in.

sliv·er (sliv'ər) *n.* a splinter.

slo·gan (slō'gən) *n.* a phrase used to identify a group, or to advertise a product; a motto.

slope (slōp) *n.* **1** a position or direction that is neither level nor upright; an upward or downward slant. **2** a slanting surface; an incline; the side of a hill or mountain. – *vb.* **slop·ing, sloped** to rise or fall at an angle.

slot (slät) *n.* a narrow opening into which something is fitted or inserted.

sloth (slôth, slōth) *n.* **1** a slow-moving tree-dwelling mammal of SOUTH AMERICA. **2** laziness. – *adj.* **sloth·ful** (slôth'fəl, slōth'fəl).

slouch (slouch) *vb.* **slouch·ing, slouched** to sit, stand, or walk with a drooping posture.

The sloth spends most of its life hanging upside down from branches, using its long curved claws as hooks. There are two main types of sloth: the two-toed and the three-toed.

Smart was once used only in the sense of a sharp stinging pain. In the 1100s it also came to mean "brisk" and later still "clever." The meaning of "well-dressed" dates from the 1700s.

Slo·vak *n.* (slō′vak′, slō′väk′) a person from or the language of SLOVAKIA.

●**Slo·va·ki·a** (slō-väk′ē-ə, slō-vak′ē-ə). See Supplement, **Countries**.

●**Slo·ve·ni·a** (slō-vē′nē-ə). See Supplement, **Countries**.

slow (slō) *adj.* **1** having little speed or pace; not moving fast or quickly. **2** taking a long time, or longer than usual. **3** (of a watch or clock) showing a time earlier than the correct time. **4** not quickly or easily learning: *a slow pupil.* − *adv.* in a slow manner. − *vb.* **slow·ing, slowed** to reduce speed, pace, or rate of progress. − *n.* **slow·ness** (slō′nəs).

slug (slug) *n.* **1** a land mollusk like a snail but with no shell. **2** (*informal*) someone who is lazy or idle.

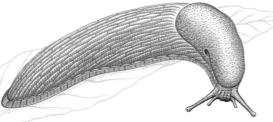

Slugs have two pairs of tentacles with eyes at the tips of the longer ones. A coating of thick, sticky slime helps to prevent desiccation (drying up). Slugs are most active at night or after a daytime rainshower.

slug·gish (slug′ish) *adj.* unenergetic; lazy; slow in movement.

sluice (sloōs) *n.* **1** a channel or drain for water. **2** an act of washing down or rinsing. − *vb.* **sluic·ing, sluiced** to wash down or rinse.

slum (slum) *n.* a poor, dirty, usually crowded urban neighborhood.

slump (slump) *vb.* **slump·ing, slumped 1** to drop or sink suddenly and heavily, for example with tiredness. **2** (of trade, etc.) to decline suddenly and sharply.

slush (slush) *n.* half-melted snow.

sly (slī) *adj.* **sli·er, sli·est** or **sly·er, sly·est 1** clever; cunning. **2** secretively deceitful.

smack (smak) *vb.* **smack·ing, smacked 1** to slap, especially with the hand. **2** to hit loudly and heavily. − *n.* **1** the sound of smacking. **2** a loud enthusiastic kiss.

small (smôl) *adj.* **1** little in size or quantity. **2** little in extent, importance, or worth; not great. **3** humble: *small beginnings.* **4** young.

small·pox (smôl′päks′) *n.* a highly contagious disease characterized by fever and a severe rash that usually leaves permanent scars.

●There have been no outbreaks of smallpox in the world for several years. It may have been wiped out.

Lady Mary Wortley Montagu, who pioneered an early form of vaccination against the killer disease smallpox. The next step was taken by Edward Jenner in 1796.

small print *n.* the details of a contract, etc. often printed very small.

small talk *n.* polite trivial conversation.

smart (smärt) *adj.* **1** clever; astute; shrewd. **2** expensive and sophisticated: *We're staying in a smart hotel.* **3** neat and well dressed. **4** brisk: *He always walks at a smart pace.* − *vb.* **smart·ing, smart·ed** to feel or be the cause of a sharp stinging pain: *My hand smarts from the smack.* − *n.* a sharp stinging pain. − *n.* **smart·ness** (smärt′nəs).

smash (smash) *vb.* **smash·ing, smashed 1** to break violently into pieces; to destroy or be destroyed in this way. **2** to strike with violence, often causing damage; to burst with great force: *The angry farmer smashed his fist down on the table.* − *n.* **1** an act, or the sound, of smashing. **2** a powerful overhead stroke in racket sports.

smear (smîr) *vb.* **smear·ing, smeared 1** to spread something sticky or oily thickly over a surface. **2** to smudge. − *n.* **1** a greasy mark or patch. **2** a damaging accusation; slander.

smell (smel) *n.* **1** the sense by which you become aware of the odor of things, located in the nose. **2** the quality perceived by this sense; odor or scent: *I love the smell of freshly cut hay.* − *vb.* **smell·ing, smelled** or **smelt** (smelt) **1** to be aware of, or take in, the odor of. **2** to give off an odor: *Susan smells of onions.*

●Some animals use smell to find food and to avoid enemies, and to recognize their own home territory. The human sense of smell is very weak but it can still identify more than 10,000 different odors.

smell·y (smel′ē) *adj.* **smell·i·er, smell·i·est** (*informal*) having a bad smell.

smile (smīl) *vb.* **smil·ing, smiled** to turn up the corners of the mouth, as an expression of pleasure or amusement. – *adj.* **smil·ing**.

smith (smith) *n.* (especially *in compounds*) **1** a person who makes articles in a particular metal: *silversmith*. **2** a blacksmith.

smog (smäg) *n.* fog mixed with smoke and fumes.

smoke (smōk) *n.* **1** the gases and fine particles given off by something burning. **2** visible fumes or vapors. – *vb.* **smok·ing, smoked 1** to give off smoke or visible fumes or vapors. **2** to draw in and puff out the smoke from the burning tobacco. **3** to preserve or flavor food by the action of smoke. – *adj.* **smoked**.

Photochemical smog is the result of chemical reactions caused by the action of sunlight on nitrogen oxides and unburnt fuel from car exhausts.

smoke·stack (smōk′stak′) *n.* a tall chimney.

smok·y (smō′kē) *adj.* **smok·i·er, smok·i·est 1** giving out too much smoke. **2** filled with smoke. **3** having a smoked flavor. – *n.* **smok·i·ness** (smō′kē-nəs).

smolder (smōl′dər) *vb.* **smoldering, smoldered** to burn slowly or without a flame.

smooth (smooth) *adj.* **1** having an even regular surface; not rough, coarse, bumpy, or wavy: *The sheets are smooth.* **2** free from problems or difficulties: *We had a smooth trip.* – *vb.* **smooth·ing, smoothed** to make smooth: *She smoothed the wrinkles in her blouse.*

smoth·er (smuth′ər) *vb.* **smoth·er·ing, smoth·ered 1** to suffocate. **2** to extinguish by cutting off the air supply: *They smothered the fire with a blanket.*

smudge (smuj) *n.* a mark or blot spread by rubbing. – *vb.* **smudg·ing, smudged** to make dirty.

smug (smug) *adj.* **smug·ger, smug·gest** overly satisfied with oneself. – *adv.* **smug·ly**. – *n.* **smug·ness**.

smug·gle (smug′əl) *vb.* **smug·gling, smug·gled** to take into or out of a country secretly and illegally. – *n.* **smug·gler**.

snack (snak) *n.* a light meal eaten quickly.

snail (snail) *n.* a slow-crawling mollusk with a spiral shell into which its whole body can fit.

snake (snāk) *n.* a crawling reptile with a long narrow body and no legs. Some species have a poisonous bite. – *vb.* **snak·ing, snaked 1** to follow a winding course. **2** to move like a snake.

● A snake's body is covered with a scaly skin which it sheds several times a year. Snakes move by wriggling along the ground or swinging their body in loops. They swallow their food whole.

snap (snap) *vb.* **snap·ping, snapped 1** to break cleanly with a sharp cracking noise. **2** to move quickly with a sharp sound: *The lid snapped shut.* **3** to make a biting or grasping movement. **4** to speak abruptly with anger or impatience. – *n.* **1** the act or sound of snapping. **2** a snapshot. **3** a fastening that closes with a snapping sound. – *adj.* briefly considered; sudden: *a snap decision.*

snap·py (snap′ē) *adj.* **snap·pi·er, snap·pi·est 1** irritable. **2** fashionable: *a snappy dresser.* **3** lively: *at a snappy tempo.*

snap·shot (snap′shät′) *n.* a photograph, especially one taken with simple equipment.

snare (snâr) *n.* an animal trap, especially one with a noose to catch the animal's foot. – *vb.* **snar·ing, snared** to trap.

snarl[1] (snärl) *vb.* **snarl·ing, snarled 1** (of an animal) to growl angrily. **2** to speak or say aggressively. – *n.* an act of snarling.

snarl[2] (snärl) *n.* **1** a knotted or tangled mass. **2** a confused or congested situation or state.

snatch (snach) *vb.* **snatch·ing, snatched 1** to seize or grab suddenly. **2** to make a sudden grabbing movement. **3** to pull suddenly and forcefully. – *n.* **1** an act of snatching. **2** a fragment overheard or remembered.

sneak (snēk) *vb.* **sneak·ing, sneaked** to move or go quietly and avoiding notice.

sneak·er (snē′kər) *n.* a sports shoe having a rubber sole.

sneak·y (snē′kē) *adj.* **sneak·i·er, sneak·i·est** done with secrecy or dishonesty.

sneer (snîr) *vb.* **sneer·ing, sneered** to show scorn or contempt for, especially by drawing the top lip up at one side.

sneeze (snēz) *vb.* **sneez·ing, sneezed** to blow air out through the nose suddenly, violently, and involuntarily. – *n.* an act of sneezing.

snick·er (sni′kər) *vb.* **snick·er·ing, snick·ered** to laugh quietly in a mocking way.

In Europe, the 1700s were the heyday of smuggling. Goods such as wine and liquor were secretly and illegally imported to avoid paying taxes or to get around trade bans between countries at war.

sniff (snif) *vb.* **sniff·ing, sniffed 1** to draw in air through the nose in short sharp bursts, for example when crying. **2** to smell at in this way. – *n.* an act or the sound of sniffing.

snip (snip) *vb.* **snip·ping, snipped** to cut, especially with a single quick action with scissors. – *n.* **1** an act or the action of snipping. **2** a small piece snipped off.

snipe (snīp) *n.* a wading bird of marshes with a long straight bill.

snip·pet (snip′ət) *n.* a scrap, as of information.

snob (snäb) *n.* someone who places too high a value on wealth or social status, admiring those higher up the social ladder and despising those lower down. – *n.* **snob·ber·y** (snäb′ə-rē). – *adj.* **snob·bish** (snäb′ish).

snooze (snōōz) *vb.* **snooz·ing, snoozed** to sleep lightly; to doze. – *n.* a nap.

snore (snôr, snōr) *vb.* **snor·ing, snored** to breathe with a snorting sound while sleeping.

snor·kel (snôr′kəl) *n.* a tube through which air from above the surface of water can be drawn into the mouth while a person is swimming just below the surface. – *vb.* **snor·kel·ing, snor·keled** to swim with a snorkel.

snort (snôrt) *vb.* **snort·ing, snort·ed** (especially of animals) to force air noisily out through the nostrils. – *n.* the sound of snorting.

snout (snout) *n.* the projecting nose and mouth parts of certain animals, as the pig.

snow (snō) *n.* **1** frozen water vapor falling to the ground in soft white flakes. **2** a fall of this: *heavy snows.* – *vb.* **snow·ing, snowed** to fall to earth as snow. – **snow in** to block with snow:

We were snowed in last winter. – *adj.* **snow·y** (snō′ē), **snow·i·er, snow·i·est**.

snow·ball (snō′bôl′) *n.* a small mass of snow pressed hard together. – *vb.* **snow·ball·ing, snow·balled 1** to throw snowballs at. **2** to develop or increase rapidly.

snow·flake (snō′flāk′) *n.* a single feathery crystal of snow.

snow line (snō′līn′) *n.* the level or height on a mountain above which there is a permanent layer of snow.

snow·mo·bile (snō′mō′bēl, snō′mə-bēl′) *n.* a vehicle, on skis or tracks, for traveling on snow.

snow·plow (snō′plou′) *n.* a vehicle fitted with a large shovellike device for clearing snow from roads.

snow·shoe (snō′shōō) *n.* a webbed, racket-shaped device strapped to a shoe to enable the wearer to walk on snow.

snub (snub) *vb.* **snub·bing, snubbed** to insult by openly ignoring. – *adj.* short and turned up at the end: *a snub nose.*

snug (snug) *adj.* **snug·ger, snug·gest 1** enjoying or providing warmth, comfort, and shelter: *snug as a bug in a rug.* **2** comfortably close-fitting: *a snug sweater.* – *adv.* **snug·ly**.

snug·gle (snug′əl) *vb.* **snug·gling, snug·gled** to settle into a position of warmth and comfort.

so (sō) *adv.* **1** to such an extent: *This chocolate is so expensive that nobody buys it.* **2** to this, that, or the

In very cold air water vapour can condense directly into ice crystals. These crystals may cling together to form **snow**flakes. Seen under a microscope, snow crystals are all six-sided. They all have wonderfully different shapes such as stars, needles, pyramids, and prisms.

Each crystal has six points or sides — but each crystal has a unique pattern.

Polar bears and seals live in the snow-covered Arctic. Northern forests with snow-clad mountains are home to such animals as beavers and moose.

Snowshoes were first used by the Native Americans. They distribute the wearer's weight over a broad area.

A snowmobile is a motorized sled that is designed to move easily and swiftly across snow or ice.

same extent; as: *This one is lovely, but that one is not so nice.* **3** very: *She is so talented!* **4** also; likewise: *She's my friend and so are you.* **5** used to avoid repeating a previous statement: *You have to take your medicine because I said so.* – *conj.* **1** therefore: *He insulted me, so I hit him.* **2** (often **so that**) in order that: *Lend me the book, so I can read it.* – *adj.* true: *You think I'm mad, but it's not so.* – *interjection* used to express discovery: *So, that's what you've been doing!* – **just so** neatly, precisely, or perfectly: *Her hair is always arranged just so.*

soak (sōk) *vb.* **soak·ing, soaked 1** to let stand in a liquid for some time: *You must soak the dried apricots overnight.* **2** to make thoroughly wet; to drench. **3** to absorb: *Sponges soak up water.* – *adj.* **soaked.** – *n. & adj.* **soak·ing.**

so-and-so (sō′ən-sō′) *n.* (*informal*) **1** a person whose name you cannot remember. **2** used in place of a vulgar word: *You little so-and-so!*

soap (sōp) *n.* a mixture of oils or fats, in the form of a liquid, powder, or solid block, used with water to remove dirt. – *vb.* **soap·ing, soaped** to wash with or apply soap to. – *adj.* **soap·y.**

soap·box (sōp′bäks′) *n.* **1** a box in which soap is sold. **2** an improvised platform for making public speeches.

soap opera *n.* a radio or television series dealing with the daily life and troubles of a regular group of characters.

soar (sôr, sōr) *vb.* **soar·ing, soared 1** to fly or glide high into the air. **2** to rise sharply.

sob (säb) *vb.* **sob·bing, sobbed** to cry uncontrollably with gulps for breath.

so·ber (sō′bər) *adj.* **1** not at all drunk. **2** serious or solemn; not frivolous: *The official dinner was a sober event.*

soc·cer (säk′ər) *n.* a form of football played between teams of eleven players with a round ball, in which the players attempt to kick or head the ball into the opposing team's goal.

so·cia·ble (sō′shə-bəl) *adj.* fond of the company of others; friendly.

so·cial (sō′shəl) *adj.* **1** of or for the welfare of people or society as a whole: *social policies.* **2** living with others: *Ants are social creatures.*

so·cial·ism (sō′shə-liz′əm) *n.* the economic system in which a nation's wealth, for example its industries, and transportation systems are owned by the public or government. – *n. & adj.* **so·cial·ist** (sō′shə-ləst).

so·ci·e·ty (sə-sī′ət-ē) *n.* **soc·i·e·ties 1** all human beings as a whole, or a group of them such as one nation, considered as a single community. **2** an organized group or association. **3** wealthy or fashionable people.

sock (säk) *n.* a fabric covering for the foot and ankle worn inside a shoe or boot.

sock·et (säk′ət) *n.* a hole or set of holes into which something is fitted: *an electrical socket.*

●**Soc·ra·tes** (säk′rə-tēz′) (470-399 B.C.) was a Greek philosopher who laid the bases of Western thinking.

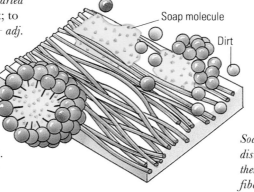

Soap molecule

Dirt

Soap and detergent molecules dislodge dirt particles by sticking to them, and squeezing them out of the fibers.

so·da (sōd′ə) *n.* **1** a common name given to various compounds of sodium in everyday use, as baking soda or washing soda. **2** soda water. **3** a fizzy soft drink of any kind.

soda water *n.* water made fizzy by the addition of carbon dioxide.

so·di·um (sōd′ē-əm) *n.* an element (symbol **Na**), a bluish-white metal of which many compounds exist as everyday substances, including common salt (sodium chloride).

so·fa (sō′fə) *n.* an upholstered seat with a back and usually arms, for two or more people.

soft (sôft) *adj.* **1** easily yielding or changing shape when pressed; pliable: *Clay is soft.* **2** (of fabric, etc.) having a smooth surface producing little or no friction. **3** quiet: *a soft voice.* **4** of little brightness: *soft colors.* **5** kind or sympathetic, especially excessively so. **6** lacking strength of character; easily influenced. **7** tender; loving: *soft words.*

soft·ball (sôft′bôl′) *n.* a game similar to baseball, played with a larger, softer ball.

soft drink *n.* a nonalcoholic drink.

soft·en (sô′fən) *vb.* **soft·en·ing, soft·ened** to make or become soft or softer.

soft spot *n.* a fondness: *to have a soft spot for.*

soft·ware (sôft′wâr′) *n.* computer programs, and the floppy disks, tapes, etc. on which information is recorded.

soft·wood (sôft′wood′) *n.* wood from conifers, as the pine.

sog·gy (säg′ē, sō′gē) *adj.* **sog·gi·er, sog·gi·est** thoroughly wet; saturated.

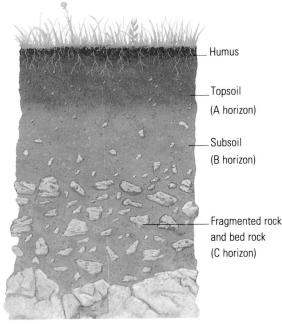

Soil forms in layers called "horizons." Horizon A is rich in decomposed plants and animal matter. The B horizon is mainly mineral particles.

soil¹ (soil) *n.* the upper layer of the earth's land surface, in which plants grow.

soil² (soil) *vb.* **soil·ing, soiled** to dirty or stain.

so·lar (sō′lər) *adj.* **1** of, or relating to, the sun. **2** using energy from the sun's rays: *solar heat.*

solar system *n.* the system of planets, asteroids, and comets that orbit our sun.

sold. See **sell.**

sol·der (säd′ər) *n.* an alloy melted over the join between two metals, hardening to form a seal.

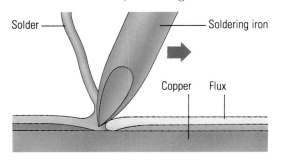

– *vb.* **sol·der·ing, sol·dered** to apply solder to; to join with solder.

sol·dier (sōl′jər) *n.* a member of a fighting force, especially a national army.

sole¹ (sōl) *n.* the underside of the foot or of a shoe or boot.

sole² (sōl) *n.* **sole** or **soles** a small edible fish.

sole³ (sōl) *adj.* **1** only. **2** exclusive: *This magazine has sole rights to the story.*

sole·ly (sōl′lē, sō′lē) *adv.* **1** alone: *He is solely to blame.* **2** excluding all else: *solely for profit.*

sol·emn (säl′əm) *adj.* earnest and serious. – *n.* **so·lem·ni·ty** (sə-lem′nət-ē).

sol·id (säl′əd) *adj.* **1** in a form other than a liquid or a gas, and resisting changes in shape. **2** of the same nature or material throughout; pure: *a solid oak table.* **3** firmly constructed or attached. **4** difficult to undermine or destroy; sound: *We found solid support for the plan.* – *n.* **1** a substance that is neither liquid nor gas. **2** a three-dimensional geometric figure. – *n.* **so·lid·i·ty** (sə-lid′ət-ē).

so·lid·i·fy (sə-lid′ə-fī′) *vb.* **so·lid·i·fies, so·lid·i·fy·ing, so·lid·i·fied** to make or become solid.

sol·i·tar·y (säl′ə-ter′ē) *adj.* **1** single; lone. **2** preferring to be alone; not social.

so·lo (sō′lō) *n.* **solos** a piece of music for a single voice or instrument. – *adj.* performed without assistance or accompaniment. – *adv.* alone: *to fly solo.* – *n.* **so·lo·ist** (sō′lō-əst).

●**Solomon Islands** (säl′ə-mən). See Supplement, **Countries.**

sol·u·ble (säl′yə-bəl) *adj.* **1** capable of being dissolved. **2** capable of being solved.

sol·u·tion (sə-lōō′shən) *n.* **1** an answer to a problem or puzzle. **2** a liquid which has a solid or gas dissolved in it.

solve (sälv, sôlv) *vb.* **solv·ing, solved** to discover a solution to a puzzle or a problem.

●**So·ma·li·a** (sə-mäl′-ē-ə). See Supplement, **Countries**.

som·ber (säm′bər) *adj.* **1** sad and serious; grave: *a somber occasion.* **2** dark and gloomy.

Solder is an alloy of tin and lead and is used in joining metals in plumbing and electrical circuits. The solder melts more easily than the metals to be joined. Flux is used to remove any oxide from the metals.

some (sum) *adj.* **1** denoting an unknown or unspecified amount or number of. **2** of unknown or unspecified nature or identity: *He's had some problem with the engine.* **3** quite a lot of: *I've been waiting for some time.* **4** at least a little: *Try to feel some excitement.* – *pron.* **1** certain unspecified things or people: *Some say he should resign.* **2** an unspecified amount or number: *Give him some, too.* – *adv.* to an unspecified extent: *Play some more.*

some·bod·y (sum′bud′ē, sum′bäd′ē, sum′bəd-ē) *pron.* an unknown or unnamed person; someone.

some·day (sum′dā′) *adv.* at an unknown time in the future.

some·how (sum′hou′) *adv.* **1** in a way not yet known: *We'll find the answer somehow.* **2** for a reason not easy to explain: *It just happened somehow.*

some·one (sum′wun′, sum′wən) *pron.* somebody: *Someone is shooting in the street.*

some·thing (sum′thing) *pron.* **1** a thing not known or not stated: *Take something to eat.* **2** an amount or number not known or not stated: *Something short of a thousand people were there.*

some·time (sum′tīm′) *adv.* at an unknown time in the future or the past: *I'll see you sometime.*

some·times (sum′tīmz′) *adv.* occasionally.

some·what (sum′hwät′, sum′hwut′) *adv.* rather; a little.

some·where *adv.* in or to some place or degree, or at some point, not known or not specified.

-some *suffix* **1** causing or producing: *troublesome.* **2** inviting: *cuddlesome.* **3** tending to: *quarrelsome.*

som·er·sault (sum′ər-sôlt′) *n.* a leap or roll in which the whole body turns a complete circle forward or backward, leading with the head. – *vb.* **som·er·sault·ing**, **som·er·sault·ed**.

son (sun) *n.* a male child.

so·nar (sō′när′) *n.* **1** a system of underwater navigation and missile targeting in which the echoes from projected sound waves indicate the presence of objects. **2** an echo-sounding navigation technique used by bats, etc.

so·na·ta (sə-nät′ə) *n.* a piece of music, in three or more movements, for a solo instrument.

song (sông) *n.* a set of words to be sung.

son·ic (sän′ik) *adj.* using sound or sound waves.

sonic boom *n.* a loud explosive noise heard when the shock wave produced by an aircraft traveling faster than the speed of sound reaches the ground.

son-in-law (sun′in-lô′) *n.* **sons-in-law** the husband of a person's daughter.

son·net (sän′ət) *n.* a poem with fourteen lines and a regular rhyming pattern.

soon (sōōn) *adv.* **1** in a short time from now or from a stated time: *Soon it will be summer.* **2** quickly; with little delay. **3** willingly: *I would as soon pay the fine as not.* – **as soon as** at or not before the moment when.

soot (soot, sut) *n.* a black powder produced when coal or wood is burned.

soothe (sōōth) *vb.* **sooth·ing, soothed 1** to bring relief from: *to soothe a pain.* **2** to comfort.

● **Soph·o·cles** (säf′ə-klēz′) (400s B.C.) was one of the greatest of the ancient Greek playwrights.

so·pra·no (sə-pran′ō, sə-prän′ō) *n.* **sopranos** a singing voice of the highest pitch.

sore (sôr, sōr) *adj.* **1** painful when touched; tender. **2** angry or resentful. – *n.* a diseased or broken area on the skin.

sor·row (sär′ō, sôr′ō) *n.* grief or deep sadness because of loss or disappointment. – *vb.* **sor·row·ing, sor·rowed** to have or express such feelings.

Sonar is a system that uses sound and echoes to detect objects in deep water. The word sonar is made from SOund Navigation And Ranging. (Ranging means measuring distance.) In nature, sonar is used by some animals, such as whales, to detect the animals they eat. Passive sonar means listening for sounds — submarines pick up the noise of a ship's engines. Active sonar works by sending bursts of sound and picking up the echoes that bounce back.

Active sonar

Passive sonar

Sonar in nature

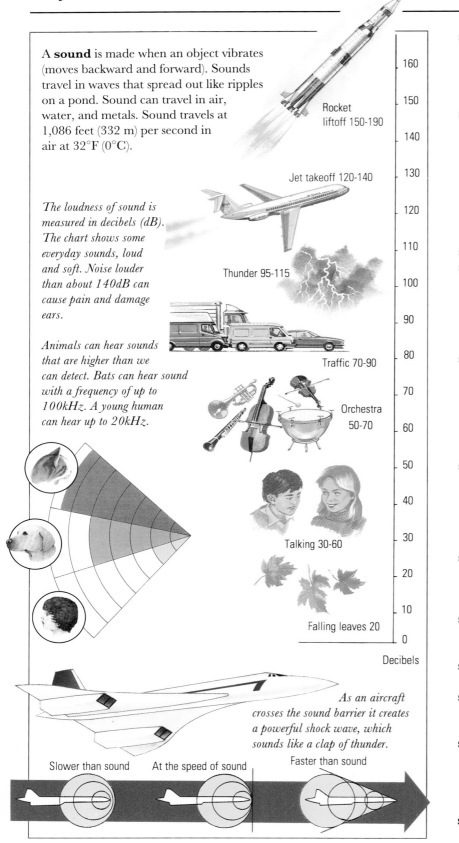

A **sound** is made when an object vibrates (moves backward and forward). Sounds travel in waves that spread out like ripples on a pond. Sound can travel in air, water, and metals. Sound travels at 1,086 feet (332 m) per second in air at 32°F (0°C).

The loudness of sound is measured in decibels (dB). The chart shows some everyday sounds, loud and soft. Noise louder than about 140dB can cause pain and damage ears.

Animals can hear sounds that are higher than we can detect. Bats can hear sound with a frequency of up to 100kHz. A young human can hear up to 20kHz.

Rocket
liftoff 150-190

Jet takeoff 120-140

Thunder 95-115

Traffic 70-90

Orchestra
50-70

Talking 30-60

Falling leaves 20

160
150
140
130
120
110
100
90
80
70
60
50
40
30
20
10
0

Decibels

As an aircraft crosses the sound barrier it creates a powerful shock wave, which sounds like a clap of thunder.

Slower than sound   At the speed of sound   Faster than sound

sor·ry (sär′ē, sôr′ē) *adj.* **sor·ri·er, sor·ri·est 1** feeling regret or shame. **2** feeling pity or sympathy: *We feel sorry for you.* **3** pitifully bad: *The house is in a sorry state.* – *interjection* used as an apology.

sort (sôrt) *n.* a kind, type, or class: *Carrots and turnips are different sorts of root vegetable.* – *vb.* **sort·ing, sort·ed** to arrange into different groups according to type or kind. – **a sort of** something like a: *It's a sort of bottle with a tube attached.* – **sort of** (*informal*) rather; in a way; to a certain extent: *Ed was feeling sort of embarrassed.* – *vb.* **sort out 1** to put into order; to arrange. **2** to put right.

sought. See **seek**.

soul (sōl) *n.* **1** the nonphysical part of a person, with personality, emotions, and intellect, widely believed to survive in some form after the death of the body. **2** ordinary human feelings of sympathy: *He has no soul.* **3** a person: *Not a soul was home.*

sound¹ (sound) *n.* **1** vibrations in the air carrying information to the brain by the sense of hearing. **2** a thing heard; a noise. **3** quality of sound: *The guitar has a nice sound.* – *vb.* **sound·ing, sound·ed 1** to cause or make a sound: *The whistle sounded.* **2** to pronounce: *Elaine doesn't sound her r's correctly.*

sound² (sound) *adj.* **1** not damaged or injured; in good condition; healthy: *The horse is sound after its fall.* **2** sensible; well-founded: *Ann always gives sound advice.* **3** thorough: *Tom gave the rug a sound beating.* **4** (of sleep) deep and undisturbed. – *adv.* deeply: *sound asleep.*

sound bar·ri·er *n.* increased air resistance met by an aircraft at around the speed of sound, requiring a huge increase in power for a small increase in speed.

soundtrack (sound′trak′) *n.* a band of magnetic tape along the edge of a movie film, on which the sound is recorded.

soup (sōōp) *n.* a liquid food made by stewing meat, vegetables, or grains.

sour (sour) *adj.* **1** having an acid taste or smell, similar to that of lemon juice or vinegar. **2** sullen; miserable: *a sour-faced old man.*

source (sôrs, sōrs) *n.* **1** the place, thing, person, or circumstance from which anything begins; origin. **2** a person or thing that supplies information: *This is a good source of information.* **3** the place where a river or stream begins.

south (south) *n.* **1** the direction to the right of a person facing the rising sun in the northern hemisphere, directly opposite north, or any part of the earth in that direction. **2 the South** the southeastern states of the UNITED STATES. – *adv.* toward the south. – *adj.* **1** of, facing, or lying in the south; on the side or in the part nearest the south. **2** (of wind) blowing from the south.

●**South Af·ri·ca** (south af′ri-kə) is a country in southern AFRICA. It is rich in minerals, is industrialized, and produces many crops. Almost three-fourths of the people are black Africans to whom in recent years democratic rights have slowly been extended. Pretoria is the government capital and Cape Town the legislative capital. See Supplement, **Countries**.

●**South A·mer·i·ca** (south ə-mer′i-kə) is the fourth largest continent. Some people there are American Indians, but many are descendants of people from EUROPE, especially SPAIN, AFRICA, ASIA, and in Brazil, from PORTUGAL. The land is rich in natural resources such as silver in Peru, tin in Bolivia, copper in Chile, and oil in Venezuela.

south·bound (south′bound′) *adj.* traveling or heading south: *the southbound lane of traffic.*

●**South Car·o·li·na** (south′ kar′ə-lī′nə). See Supplement, **U.S.A.**

●**South Da·ko·ta** (south′ də-kōt′ə). See Supplement, **U.S.A.**

south·east (sou-thēst′) and **south·west** (south-west′) *n.* the direction midway between south and east or south and west. – *adv.* in this direction. – *adj.* of, facing, or lying in the southeast or southwest.

south·er·ly (suth′ər-lē) *adj.* & *adv.* south.

south·ern (suth′ərn) *adj.* south; of the south.

south·ern·er (suth′ər-nər) *n.* a native or inhabitant of a southern region or country.

South Pole *n.* the southernmost point of the earth's axis of rotation, in ANTARCTICA.

south·ward (south′wərd) *adj.* traveling toward the south. – *adv.* (also **south·wards** (south′wərdz)) toward the south.

sou·ve·nir (sōō′və-nîr′) *n.* a thing bought, kept, or given as a reminder of a place, person, or occasion; a memento: *I brought souvenirs back from Florida for my family.*

sov·er·eign (säv′ə-rən, säv′rən, suv′rən) *n.* a supreme ruler or head, especially a monarch. – *adj.* having supreme power or authority.

So·vi·et (sō′vē-et′, sō′vē-ət, säv′ē-et′, säv′ē-ət) *n.* a native or inhabitant of the Soviet Union. – *adj.* of or concerning the Soviet Union.

●**Soviet Union** the common name of the former U.S.S.R. (Union of Soviet Socialist Republics). See **Russia**.

sow[1] (sō) *vb.* **sow·ing, sowed, sown** (sōn) or **sowed** to plant seeds; to plant with crops of a particular kind: *The farmer sowed barley.*

sow[2] (sou) *n.* an adult female pig.

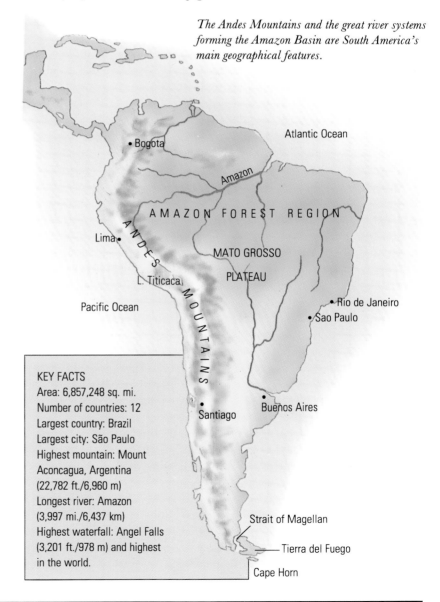

The Andes Mountains and the great river systems forming the Amazon Basin are South America's main geographical features.

Atlantic Ocean

Bogota

Amazon

AMAZON FOREST REGION

Lima

MATO GROSSO

L. Titicaca

PLATEAU

Pacific Ocean

Rio de Janeiro

Sao Paulo

ANDES MOUNTAINS

Santiago

Buenos Aires

KEY FACTS
Area: 6,857,248 sq. mi.
Number of countries: 12
Largest country: Brazil
Largest city: São Paulo
Highest mountain: Mount Aconcagua, Argentina (22,782 ft./6,960 m)
Longest river: Amazon (3,997 mi./6,437 km)
Highest waterfall: Angel Falls (3,201 ft./978 m) and highest in the world.

Strait of Magellan

Tierra del Fuego

Cape Horn

Eccentric orbit — Polar orbit
— Circular orbit

Geostationary orbit

Types of orbit. In an eccentric orbit the satellite's distance from the Earth keeps changing. In a geostationary, the satellite always faces the same part of the Earth.

The first **spacecraft** were launched in the 1950s. There were two types: satellites and probes. Satellites go into orbit around the Earth; probes zoom away from Earth to explore other planets. Most probes and satellites are unmanned. All spacecraft are thrust into space by powerful rockets. Satellites and probes are full of scientific equipment. Information collected is radioed back to Earth.

Vostok rocket

Titan 3

V2 rocket

A space shuttle is launched like an ordinary rocket into orbit but comes back to Earth landing like a glider. New fuel tanks are then fitted for the next launch.

Laika (left), the dog who spent a week in orbit in the Russian Sputnik 2 in 1957.

The V2 rocket was built by the Germans to attack London during the World War II (1939-1945). It had a range of 200 mi. and carried 5 tons of explosives. Titan 3 launches satellites into space.

Unless launched in the space shuttle, all satellites are carried in the upper stage of a launch rocket.

Rosat

IUE

IRAS

soy·bean (soi′bēn′) **soy·a bean** (soi′ə-bēn′) *n.* a bean from an Asian plant, eaten as a vegetable and used as a source of oil and flour.

space (spās) *n.* **1** the limitless area in which all physical things exist. **2** a portion of this; room: *Is there space in the yard for a pool?* **3** an interval of distance; a gap: *the space between the houses.* **4** an empty place: *a space at our table.* **5** (also **outer space**) the region beyond Earth, in which other planets and stars are located; the universe. – in *compounds*, for use or travel in the region beyond the earth: *spaceship.* – *vb.* **spac·ing, spaced** to arrange with intervals of distance or time between each.

space·craft (spās′kraft′) *n.* **space·craft** any vehicle, with or without a crew, that orbits a planet or travels through outer space.

space·ship (spās′ship′) *n.* a vehicle used for traveling in space.

space shuttle *n.* a spaceship designed to make repeated journeys into space.

space·walk (spās′wôk′) *n.* the act of going outside a spacecraft while in space.

spa·cious (spā′shəs) *adj.* extending over a large area. – *n.* **spa·cious·ness** (spā′shəs-nəs).

spade¹ (spād) *n.* a digging tool with a long handle and a broad metal blade for digging the earth. – **call a spade a spade** to speak plainly.

spade² (spād) *n.* a playing card that carries an emblem like a black blade.

spade·work (spād′wurk′) *n.* hard or boring preparatory work.

spa·ghet·ti (spə-get′ē) *n.* pasta in the form of long thin stringlike strands.

● **Spain** (spān) in southwestern Europe, beyond the Pyrenees, is covered mostly by high plains and mountains. Many Spaniards work as farm-ers or by fishing. Barcelona is a major industrial area. Spain was once occupied by Moors. Spain also had a huge empire which it lost in the 1800s. Spain is a monarchy. Madrid is the capital. See also Supplement, **Countries**.

span (span) *n.* **1** the length between the supports of a bridge or arch. **2** (often in *compounds*) length from end to end: *wingspan; timespan.* – *vb.* **span·ning, spanned** to extend across or over: *The bridge spans the river.*

Span·iard (span′yərd) *n.* a native or inhabitant of SPAIN.

span·iel (span′yəl) *n.* a breed of dog with long drooping ears and a silky coat.

Span·ish (span′ish) *n.* **1** (*plural*) the people of Spain. **2** their language, also spoken in the UNITED STATES and CENTRAL and SOUTH AMERICA. – *adj.* of the people or their language.

span·ner (span′ər) *n.* (*British*) a wrench. – **throw a spanner in the works** to upset a plan or system.

spare (spâr) *adj.* **1** held in reserve as a replacement: *a spare tire.* **2** available for use; unoccupied: *There's a spare seat next to me.* **3** lean; thin. – *vb.* **spar·ing, spared 1** to afford to give or give away: *Can you spare a minute?* **2** to be merciful, to refrain from harming: *Spare his life.*

spar·ing (spâr′ing) *adj.* economical or frugal.

spark (spärk) *n.* **1** a tiny red-hot glowing particle thrown off by burning material: *A spark flew from the match.* **2** an electric flash as produced by a spark plug in a car engine to explode a mixture of air and gasoline. – *vb.* **spark·ing, sparked** to throw off sparks.

spark plug *n.* an electrical device in a vehicle engine that produces a spark to ignite the air and gasoline mixture.

spar·kle (spär′kəl) *vb.* **spar·kling, spar·kled 1** to give off sparks. **2** to shine with tiny points of bright light. **3** to be lively or witty. – *adj.* **spar·kling**.

spar·row (spar′ō) *n.* any of a family of small brown or gray birds similar to finches.

sparse (spärs) *adj.* thinly distributed; not dense.

PRONUNCIATION SYMBOLS		
ə **a**way	l**e**mon	foc**u**s
a f**a**t	oi b**o**y	
ā f**a**de	oo f**oo**t	
ä h**o**t	ōō m**oo**n	
âr f**air**	ou h**ou**se	
e m**e**t	th **th**ink	
ē m**ea**n	th **th**is	
g **g**et	u c**u**t	
hw **wh**ich	ur h**ur**t	
i f**i**n	w **w**itch	
ī l**i**ne	y **y**es	
îr n**ear**	yōō m**u**sic	
ô **o**ften	yoor p**u**re	
ō n**o**te	zh vi**s**ion	

Many orbiting satellites send us valuable information. Rosat is recording X-ray sources from dim stars. The International Ultraviolet Explorer studies stellar ultraviolet light. IRAS stands for Infra-Red Astronomy Satellite. AXAS is the Advanced X-ray Astrophysics Facility.

AXAF

Spar·tan (spärt′n) *adj.* austere; frugal; basic: *She has little money and so leads a Spartan life.*

spasm (spaz′əm) *n.* a sudden uncontrollable jerk caused by a contraction of the muscles.

spat·u·la (spach′ə-lə) *n.* a tool with a broad flat flexible blade used for spreading, mixing, or in cooking to turn food over.

spawn (spôn, spän) *n.* the eggs of frogs, fish, and mollusks, laid in water in a soft transparent jellylike mass. – *vb.* **spawn·ing, spawned** (of frogs, fish, etc.) to lay eggs.

speak (spēk) *vb.* **speak·ing, spoke** (spōk), **spoken** (spō′kən) **1** to utter; to talk. **2** to talk to someone or each other: *They haven't spoken for years.* **3** to be able to communicate in: *He speaks French.*

spear (spîr) *n.* a weapon consisting of a long pole with a sharp point, for throwing.

spe·cial (spesh′əl) *adj.* **1** distinct from, especially better than, others of the same kind; exceptional: *Birthdays are special days.* **2** designed for a particular purpose: *There is a special tool for cutting tiles.*

spe·cial·ize (spesh′ə-līz′) *vb.* **spe·cial·iz·ing, spe·cial·ized** to devote all efforts to one particular activity, field of study, etc. – *n.* **spe·cial·i·za·tion** (spesh′ə-lə-zā′shən). – *n.* **spe·cial·ist** (spesh′ə-ləst).

spe·cial·ty (spesh′əl-tē) *n.* **spe·cial·ties** a thing specialized in: *Seafood is my specialty.*

spe·cies (spē′shēz, spē′sēz) *n.* **species 1** a group of closely related plants or animals able to breed together; a subdivision of a genus. **2** a kind or type.

spe·cif·ic (spi-sif′ik) *adj.* **1** precisely identified. **2** precise in meaning; not vague.

spec·i·fy (spes′ə-fī′) *vb.* **spec·i·fies, spec·i·fy·ing, spec·i·fied** to refer to or identify precisely: *Please specify what you want.*

spec·i·men (spes′ə-mən) *n.* a sample or example of something, especially an object studied or put in a collection.

spec·ta·cle (spek′ti-kəl) *n.* **1** a thing seen; a sight, especially impressive, wonderful, or ridiculous: *The parade is a wonderful spectacle.* **2** (in *plural*) eyeglasses.

spec·tac·u·lar (spek-tak′yə-lər) *adj.* impressively striking to see or watch.

spec·ta·tor (spek′tāt′ər, spek-tāt′ər) *n.* a person who watches an event or incident.

spec·trum (spek′trəm) *n.* **spec·tra** (spek′trə) or **spec·trums** the range of colors — red, orange, yellow, green, blue, indigo, and violet — that make up white light, separately visible when the light is passed through a prism.

spec·u·late (spek′yə-lāt′) *vb.* **spec·u·lat·ing,**

Fastest car: the British Thrust 2 *set the world land speed record in 1983. Using an aircraft jet engine, it reached 633.6 mph (1,020 km/h).*

Thrust 2

Fastest plane: The world record was set in 1976 when the USA's SR-71A, *nicknamed* Blackbird, *reached 2,192 mph (3,530 km/h).*

SR-71A Blackbird

spec·u·lat·ed 1 to make guesses; to consider possibilities: *We speculated about the future.* **2** to make purchases, as of stocks and shares, in the hope of making profitable sales. – *n.* **spec·u·la·tion** (spek′yə-lā-shən).

sped. See **speed.**

speech (spēch) *n.* **1** the ability to speak. **2** a talk addressed to other people.

speed (spēd) *n.* **1** rate of movement or action. **2** quickness; rapidity: *with speed.* **3** a gear setting

Fastest boat: in 1977 Ken Warby roared to 345 mph in his jet-powered hydroplane, Spirit of Australia.

Spirit of Australia

The black widow spider is one of the few spiders that is poisonous to humans.

on a vehicle: *a five-speed transmission.* – *vb.* **speed·ing, sped** (sped) **1** to move quickly: *The train was speeding down the line.* **2** to drive at a speed higher than the legal limit.

speed·om·e·ter (spi-däm′ət-ər) *n.* an instrument in a vehicle that indicates speed.

spell[1] (spel) *vb.* **spell·ing, spelled** or **spelt** (spelt) **1** to write or name the letters of words in their correct order: *Can you spell "accommodate?"* **2** to form a word when written in sequence: *B, A, D spells "bad."*

spell[2] (spel) *n.* a set of words believed to have magical power: *The fairy cast a spell over the boy.*

spell·ing (spel′ing) *n.* a way a word is spelled.

spend (spend) *vb.* **spend·ing, spent** (spent) **1** to use up or pay out. **2** to devote or pass: *We spend a lot of time in the garden.*

sperm (spurm) *n.* **1** fertilizing cells contained in semen. **2** semen.

sphere (sfir) *n.* **1** a round solid figure with a surface on which all points are an equal distance from the center; a globe or ball. **2** a field of activity: *the sphere of sport.*

spher·i·cal (sfir′i-kəl) *adj.* sphere-shaped.

Sphinx (sfingks) *n.* **1** in Greek mythology, a monster with the head of a woman and the body of a lioness, that killed travelers who could not solve the riddles it set. **2** a huge monument near the Egyptian pyramids with the head of a man and the body of a lion.

spice (spīs) *n.* any of various fragrant vegetable substances used to flavor food. – *adj.* **spic·y** (spī′sē), **spic·i·er, spic·i·est.**

Spice Islands *n.* former name for a group of islands in INDONESIA.

spi·der (spīd′ər) *n.* an eight-legged creature, many varieties of which spin silky webs to catch insects for food.

● When a spider catches something, it stuns or kills it with a poisonous bite. In most cases spiders do not harm humans. There are about 30,000 different kinds of spiders.

spike (spīk) *n.* **1** a pointed piece of metal, for example one of several on railings or the soles of shoes for running. **2** a large metal nail.

spill (spil) *vb.* **spill·ing, spilled** (spilt) or **spilt** to run or cause to run or flow out from a container, especially accidentally. – *n.* an act of spilling. – **spill the beans** (*informal*) to give away information, especially a secret.

spin (spin) *vb.* **spin·ning, spun** (spun) **1** to rotate repeatedly, especially quickly: *The wheels of a bike spin.* **2** to draw out and twist fibers, etc. into thread. **3** to make from thread: *Spiders spin webs.* – *n.* **1** an act of spinning or a spinning motion. **2** rotation in a ball thrown or struck.

spin·ach (spin′ich) *n.* a plant with dark green leaves eaten as a vegetable.

spi·nal (spī′nəl) *adj.* of, or relating to, the spine.

spinal column *n.* the spine.

● The spinal column is made up of a number of small bones called vertebrae. A child has 33 vertebrae, but some of these vertebrae grow together, so that an adult has only 26.

spinal cord *n.* a cordlike mass of nerve tissue running along the spine and connecting the brain to nerves in all other parts of the body.

spine (spīn) *n.* **1** the backbone; a series of linking bones forming a flexible column along the backs of many animals. **2** a projecting thornlike growth on a plant or animal.

Before refrigeration or canning, spices were often used to disguise food that was not quite fresh. Cloves (1) are the dried flower buds of a plant native to southeast Asia. Nutmeg (2) is the dried kernel of a fruit that looks like an apricot. Mace (3) comes from the outer covering of the nutmeg. Pepper (4) is a common spice widely used as a seasoning.

Most spires are tall and pointed and made of stone or of timber covered with slates.

Sport is an English word which has been adopted by many other languages. It comes from the verb disport, meaning "to divert, play, or frolic," and originally meant any kind of pleasant pastime.

spine·less (spīn′ləs) *adj.* **1** having no backbone. **2** lacking courage.

spin-off (spin′ôf′) *n.* a thing developed from an earlier product or idea, for example a television series derived from a movie.

spin·ster (spin′stər) *n.* a woman who never married, especially an older one.

spin·y (spīn′ē) *adj.* **spin·i·er, spin·i·est 1** like a spine or thorn; sharp. **2** having spines or thorns.

spi·ral (spī′rəl) *n.* the pattern made by a line winding downward from a point in near circles of the same or increasing size, as if around a cylinder or cone: *A corkscrew is a spiral.* – *adj.* of the shape or nature of a spiral: *a spiral staircase.*

spire (spīr) *n.* a tall structure tapering upwards to a point, especially on a church.

spir·it (spîr′ət) *n.* **1** the force within a person that is or provides the will to live: *Sad news broke his spirit.* **2** (usually in *plural*) emotional state; mood: *The children were in high spirits.* **3** a distilled alcoholic liquid for drinking, as whiskey, brandy, or gin.

spir·it·ed (spîr′ət-əd) *adj.* **1** full of courage or liveliness. **2** (in *compounds*) a mood or attitude: *public-spirited.*

spir·i·tu·al (spîr′ich-o͞o-əl, spîr′ich-wəl) *adj.* **1** of, or relating to, the spirit or soul, rather than to the body. **2** religious: *a spiritual leader.* – *n.* a religious folk song developed from the traditions of AFRICAN AMERICANS.

spit (spit) *vb.* **spit·ting, spit** or **spat** (spat) **1** to throw out saliva from the mouth, often as a gesture of contempt. **2** to force out of the mouth: *to spit out food.* – *n.* saliva spit out from the mouth.

spite (spīt) *n.* the desire to hurt or offend; ill-will. – *adj.* **spite·ful** (spīt′fəl). – *n.* **spite·ful·ness** (spīt′fəl-nəs).

splash (splash) *vb.* **splash·ing, splashed** to cause large drops of a liquid to be thrown about: *She splashed cold water over her face.* – *n.* **1** a sound of splashing. **2** an irregular spot or patch: *splashes of color.*

splash·down (splash′doun′) *n.* a landing at sea of a spacecraft. – *vb.* **splash down.**

splen·did (splen′dəd) *adj.* **1** magnificent; very grand: *a splendid palace.* **2** very good; excellent.

splin·ter (splint′ər) *n.* a thin sharp piece broken off a hard substance, for example wood or glass. – *vb.* **splin·ter·ing, splin·tered** to break into splinters: *The cup broke and splintered.*

split (split) *vb.* **split·ting, split 1** to break apart or into pieces. **2** to divide up into separate smaller amounts or groups: *Split up into pairs.*

split infinitive *n.* an infinitive with an adverb between "to" and the verb, as in *to boldly go,* considered grammatically incorrect by some.

spoil (spoil) *vb.* **spoil·ing, spoiled** or **spoilt** (spoilt) **1** to ruin, or make useless or valueless: *The rain has spoiled our game.* **2** to make selfish and unable to accept hardship by consistently giving in to all demands or wishes: *to spoil a child.* **3** (of food) to rot.

spoke[1]. See **speak.**

spoke[2] (spōk) *n.* a rod or bar attaching the rim of a wheel to its center.

spo·ken (spō′kən). See **speak.** – *adj.* expressed in speech: *Tapes can record the spoken word.*

Sponges are some of the earliest and simplest forms of living things. There are about 5,000 species.

sponge (spunj) *n.* **1** a simple sea creature with a body that has many holes. **2** a piece of the springy skeleton of such a creature, or a synthetic substitute, used in cleaning.

spong·y (spun′jē) *adj.* **spong·i·er, spong·i·est** soft and springy like a sponge.

spon·sor (spän′sər) *n.* **1** a person who assumes responsibility for another. **2** a person or organization that finances an event or broadcast in return for advertising. – *vb.* **spon·sor·ing, spon·sored** to act as a sponsor for.

spon·ta·ne·ous (spän-tā′nē-əs) *adj.* unplanned; occurring naturally or by itself: *Her welcome was spontaneous.* – *n.* **spon·ta·ne·i·ty** (spän′tə-nā′ət-ē, spän′tə-nē′ət-ē).

spool (spo͞ol) *n.* a small cylinder on which thread, film, tape, etc. is wound; a reel.

spoon (spo͞on) *n.* a utensil with a handle and a shallow bowllike part, for eating, serving, or stirring food.

spore (spôr, spōr) *n.* a cell produced by many plants that can grow into a new plant by itself.

sport (spôrt) *n.* **1** any activity or competition designed to test physical skills. **2** good-humored fun: *They did it in sport.*

sport·ing (spôrt′ing) *adj.* of, or relating to, sports: *sporting achievements.*

sports car *n.* a small fast car.

spot (spät) *n.* **1** a small mark or stain: *There's a red spot on your nose.* **2** a drop or small amount of liquid: *ink spots.* **3** a place: *What a great spot for a picnic!* – *vb.* **spot·ting, spot·ted 1** to mark with spots. **2** to see; to catch sight of.

spot·less (spät′ləs) *adj.* absolutely clean.

spot·light (spät′līt′) *n.* a lamp casting a concentrated circle of light on a small area, especially of a theater stage.

spot·ty (spät′ē) *adj.* **spot·ti·er, spot·ti·est 1** marked with spots. **2** not uniform.

spout (spout) *n.* **1** a tube or lip through which liquid is poured. **2** a jet or stream of liquid. – *vb.* **spout·ing, spout·ed 1** to flow out in a jet or stream: *Water spouted from the pipe.* **2** to speak or say, especially at length.

sprain (sprān) *vb.* **sprain·ing, sprained** to injure the muscles of by a sudden twisting or wrenching: *Sam sprained his ankle jumping from the wall.* – *n.* such an injury, causing swelling.

sprang. See **spring**.

sprawl (sprôl) *vb.* **sprawl·ing, sprawled** to sit or lie lazily with the arms and legs spread out.

spray (sprā) *n.* **1** a fine mist of small flying drops of liquid. **2** a device for dispensing a liquid as a mist; an atomizer. – *vb.* **spray·ing, sprayed** to apply spray to.

spread (spred) *vb.* **spread·ing, spread 1** to apply in a smooth coating over a surface: *She spread butter on the bread.* **2** to extend or scatter: *Spread the cards on the table.* **3** to open or unfold.

sprig (sprig) *n.* a twig: *a sprig of heather.*

spring (spring) *vb.* **spring·ing, sprang** (sprang), **sprung** (sprung) **1** to leap with a sudden quick launching action. **2** to move suddenly and swiftly by elastic force. **3** to appear or come into being suddenly: *Three new buildings have sprung up recently.* **4** to present suddenly and unexpectedly: *to spring a surprise on someone.* – *n.* **1** a device that expands and contracts freely, returning to its original shape when released. **2** a natural outflow of water from the ground. **3** the season between winter and summer, when most plants begin to grow. **4** a leap.

spring·bok (spring′bäk′) *n.* a South African antelope renowned for its high springing leaps.

spring·y (spring′ē) *adj.* **spring·i·er, spring·i·est** readily springing back into its original shape when released; elastic.

sprin·kle (spring′kəl) *vb.* **sprin·kling, sprin·kled** to scatter in tiny drops or particles: *Sprinkle salt on the popcorn.*

sprin·kler (springk′lər) *n.* a device that sprinkles water over plants or on a fire to extinguish it.

sprint (sprint) *n.* a race at high speed over a short distance. – *vb.* **sprint·ing, sprint·ed** to run at full speed. – *n.* **sprint·er**.

sprout (sprout) *vb.* **sprout·ing, sprout·ed** to develop a new growth, for example of leaves or hair. – *n.* a shoot or bud.

spruce (sprōōs) *n.* an evergreen tree with needlelike leaves.

spud (spud) *n.* (*informal*) a potato.

spun. See **spin**.

spur (spur) *n.* **1** a metal device fitted to the heel of a rider's boot used to make a horse go faster. **2** a ridge sticking out from a range of hills or mountains.

spurt (spurt) *vb.* **spurt·ing, spurt·ed** to flow out in a sudden sharp jet.

spy (spī) *n.* **spies 1** a person employed by a government to secretly gather information about political enemies. **2** a person observing others in secret. – *vb.* **spies, spy·ing, spied 1** to work as a spy. **2** to catch sight of; to spot.

squad (skwäd) *n.* a small group of soldiers or police; a group of people working together.

squa·lor (skwäl′ər) *n.* filth; dirt.

squan·der (skwän′dər) *vb.* **squan·der·ing, squan·dered** to use up or spend wastefully.

Dampers keep springs from bouncing back too quickly after the spring has been compressed by the vehicle going over a bump. The oil in the cylinder slows down the spring's "bounce back."

In most road vehicles the suspension system and its shock absorbers of springs and dampers is hidden inside. This off-road buggy reveals all. Without shock absorbers to swallow up bumps and jolts road travel would be very uncomfortable.

PRONUNCIATION SYMBOLS			
ə **away**	**lemon**	**focus**	
a	**fat**	oi	**boy**
ā	**fade**	oo	**foot**
ä	**hot**	ōō	**moon**
âr	**fair**	ou	**house**
e	**met**	th	**think**
ē	**mean**	<u>th</u>	**this**
g	**get**	u	**cut**
hw	**which**	ur	**hurt**
i	**fin**	w	**witch**
ī	**line**	y	**yes**
îr	**near**	yōō	**music**
ô	**often**	yoor	**pure**
ō	**note**	zh	**vision**

The squid sucks water into its body and then squirts it out through a narrow tube. The force of the jet can propel the squid through the water at enormous speeds. The squid's tentacles are covered with suckers, which hold the prey firmly while the squid bites it.

square (skwâr) *n.* **1** a two-dimensional figure with four sides of equal length and four right angles. **2** an open space in a town, shaped vaguely like this. – *adj.* **1** square-shaped. **2** measured in length and breadth; of an area equal to a square whose sides are the stated length: *One room is 12 feet square.*

square dance *n.* a folk dance performed by couples in a square formation.

square root *n.* the number which, when multiplied by itself, gives the number in question: *The square root of sixteen is four.*

squash¹ (skwäsh, skwôsh) *vb.* **squash·ing, squashed 1** to crush or flatten by pressing or squeezing. **2** to force into a confined space. – *n.* **1** a crushed or crowded state. **2** a tennislike game for two players on a walled indoor court.

squash² (skwäsh, skwôsh) *n.* any of a group of round or long vegetables related to the gourd.

squat (skwät) *vb.* **squat·ting, squat·ted 1** to sit in a low position with the knees fully bent and the weight on the soles of the feet. **2** to occupy land or an empty building without legal right. – *adj.* short and broad or fat.

squaw (skwô) *n.* a NATIVE AMERICAN woman or wife.

squawk (skwôk) *n.* a loud croak like that of a parrot. – *vb.* **squawk·ing, squawked** to utter such a cry.

squeak (skwēk) *n.* a short high cry or noise like that of a mouse or a rusty gate. – *vb.* **squeak·ing, squeaked** to make a squeak.

squeal (skwēl) *n.* a long high-pitched cry or yelp, like that of a pig or a child in pain. – *vb.* **squeal·ing, squealed 1** to utter a squeal. **2** (*informal*) to inform or tell tales.

squeeze (skwēz) *vb.* **squeez·ing, squeezed 1** to grasp or embrace tightly. **2** to press forcefully, especially from at least two sides: *We squeezed the box to see if it was empty.* **3** to press or crush so as to extract juice, etc.; to extract by pressing or crushing. – *n.* **1** an act of squeezing. **2** a crowded or crushed state. – *n.* **squeez·er.**

squid (skwid) *n.* **squid** or **squids** a sea creature with a long body and ten trailing tentacles.

squint (skwint) *n.* **1** the act or habit of looking with half closed eyes. **2** (*informal*) a quick look; a peep. – *vb.* **squint·ing, squint·ed** to look with a squint.

squirm (skwurm) *vb.* **squirm·ing, squirmed 1** to wriggle. **2** to show embarrassment, often with slight wriggling movements of the body.

squir·rel (skwur′əl) *n.* a tree-dwelling rodent with a large bushy tail and gray or reddish-brown fur.

●**Sri Lan·ka** (srē läng′kə). See Supplement, **Countries.**

stab (stab) *vb.* **stab·bing, stabbed 1** to wound or pierce with a pointed instrument or weapon. **2** to make a thrusting movement with something sharp. – *n.* **1** an act of stabbing. **2** (*informal*) a try: *Have a stab at doing this.*

sta·ble¹ (stā′bəl) *adj.* **1** firmly balanced or fixed; not likely to fall: *The shelves are stable.* **2** firmly established; not likely to be abolished: *a stable government.* – *n.* **sta·bil·i·ty** (stə-bil′ət-ē).

sta·ble² (stā′bəl) *n.* a building for horses.

stack (stak) *n.* **1** a large neat pile: *a hay stack.* **2** (in *plural*) the area in a library where books are kept. **3** (in *plural*) (*informal*) a large amount: *stacks of supplies.* – *vb.* **stack·ing, stacked 1** to arrange in stacks. **2** to arrange beforehand in a certain order: *to stack a deck of cards.*

sta·di·um (stād′ē-əm) *n.* **stadiums** or **sta·di·a** (stād′ē-ə) a large sports arena.

staff (staf) *n.* **1** the employees working in an organization. **2** (**staffs** or **staves** (stāvz)) a stick or rod carried in the hand.

stag (stag) *n.* an adult male deer.

stage (stāj) *n.* **1** a platform in the theater on which a performance takes place. **2** any of several distinct and successive periods. **3** theater as a profession: *She has devoted her life to the stage.* **4** a part of a journey or route. – *vb.* **stag·ing, staged 1** to present a performance of a play. **2** to organize or hold: *to stage an event.*

stag·ger (stag′ər) *vb.* **stag·ger·ing, stag·gered 1** to walk or move unsteadily. **2** to cause extreme shock or surprise to: *The bad* *news staggered her.* **3** to schedule or arrange so as to take place or begin at different times: *The traffic lights are staggered. n.* an act of staggering. – *adj.* **stag·ger·ing.**

stag·nant (stag′nənt) *adj.* (of water) dirty and foul-smelling because of its not flowing.

stain (stān) *vb.* **stain·ing, stained 1** to make or become marked or spotted: *She stained the carpet when she spilled the coffee.* **2** to change the color of by applying a dye or pigment: *to stain wood.* – *n.* **1** a mark or spot. **2** a pigment or coloring for changing the color of wood.

stair (stâr) *n.* one of a series of steps connecting the floors of a building.

stair·case (stâr′kās′) or **stair·way** (stâr′wā′) *n.* a set of stairs.

stake¹ (stāk) *n.* a stick or post, usually with one end pointed, driven into the ground as a support, for example for a young tree or as part of a fence. – *vb.* **stak·ing, staked.**

stake² (stāk) *n.* **1** a sum of money risked in betting. **2** an interest, especially financial: *They have a stake in the project's success.* – *vb.* **stak·ing, staked** to risk as a bet; to gamble.

sta·lac·tite (stə-lak′tīt′) *n.* an icicle-like mass of limestone attached to the roof of a cave, etc., formed by the dripping of water.

sta·lag·mite (stə-lag′mīt′) *n.* a spiky mass of limestone sticking up from the floor of a cave, formed by the dripping of water from above.

stale (stāl) *adj.* (of food) not fresh; dry and tasteless: *This cake tastes stale.*

stalk¹ (stôk) *n.* the principal stem of a plant.

stalk² (stôk) *vb.* **stalk·ing, stalked** to hunt, follow, or approach softly and quietly. – *n.* **stalk·er.**

stall¹ (stôl) *n.* **1** a space for a single animal in a shed, stable, etc. **2** a platform or stand on which goods for sale are displayed. – *vb.* **stall·ing, stalled** to stop or cause to stop: *My car's engine always stalls in the rain.*

stall² (stôl) *vb.* **stall·ing, stalled** to delay; to cause delay by being evasive: *to stall for time.*

stam·i·na (stam′ə-nə) *n.* energy needed to endure prolonged physical or mental exertion.

stam·mer (stam′ər) *n.* an uncontrolled repetition of a sound or syllable. – *vb.* **stam·mer·ing, stam·mered** to speak with a stammer.

stamp (stamp) *vb.* **stamp·ing, stamped 1** to bring down with force: *The horse stamped its hoof on the road.* **2** to walk with a heavy tread. **3** to imprint with a mark or design: *You must stamp the date on the incoming mail.* **4** to stick a postage stamp on. – *n.* **1** (also **postage stamp**) a small piece of gummed paper with the official mark of a nation's postal system, stuck to mail to show that postage has been paid. **2** an instrument for stamping a mark; the mark stamped. – *vb.* **stamp out 1** to put out by stamping: *to stamp out a fire.* **2** to put an end to; *to stamp out an uprising.*

The British "penny black" of 1840, the first stamp on which postage was prepaid, and a U.S. "local" stamp.

stam·pede (stam-pēd′) *n.* a sudden rush of frightened animals or of a frightened crowd of people. – *vb.* **stam·ped·ing, stam·ped·ed** to rush in a herd.

stand (stand) *vb.* **stand·ing, stood** (stood) **1** to be in, or move into, an upright position on the feet or a base. **2** to place or be placed: *Our*

As water drips into a limestone cave, lime deposits may come out of solution to form a rocky "icicle." These icicles are called stalactites if they hang from the ceiling or stalagmites if they build up from the ground.

STAMP TERMS
commemorative a stamp issued to celebrate an event.
mint an unused stamp in perfect condition.
perforation the row of holes punched in a sheet of stamps.
philately the study and collection of stamps.
postmark a mark stamped on mail to cancel the stamp.

Red Giant

Blue Giant

Main sequence star
(such as the Sun)

White dwarf

Red dwarf

Black hole

Neutron
star

*Our Sun shines with a
yellow light. The hottest
stars shine with a white-
blue light. They are
known as blue giants.
The cool stars are known
as red dwarfs. There are
also relatively cool red
giants and dim white
dwarfs. In a white dwarf
the atoms are crushed
together. A neutron star
is a dead star made from
solid nuclei of atoms, the
densest material in the
universe. A black hole is
a massive neutron star.*

house stands in a valley. **3** to be a particular
height: *The tower stands 90 feet tall.* **4** to tolerate
or put up with: *I can't stand him.* **5** to be a
symbol or representation of: *If Y equals 12,
what does X stand for?* – *n.* **1** a base on which
something is supported: *a cakestand.* **2** a stall
displaying goods or services for sale. **3** a
structure with sitting or standing facilities for
spectators. **4** a rack on which coats, hats,
umbrellas, etc. may be hung. **5** a firm attitude
or opinion. – *vb.* **stand by** (stand′bī′) **1** to be
in a state of readiness to act. **2** to give support
in time of difficulty: *Steve stood by Sarah when she
had her breakdown.* **3** to look on without taking
the expected action. – *vb.* **stand in** to act as a
substitute. – *vb.* **stand out** to be noticeable or
prominent.

stan·dard (stan′dərd) *n.* **1** an
accepted model against which
others are compared,
measured,
or judged. **2** a level of excellence,
value, or quality. **3** (often in *plural*)
a principle of behavior. **4** a flag
or other emblem. – *adj.* **1** of the
normal or accepted kind. **2** typical;
average; unexceptional.

stan·za (stan′zə) *n.* a verse in poetry.

star (stär) *n.* **1** any of the
innumerable bodies in the night sky
that appear as points of light. **2** a
figure with five or more radiating
points. **3** a celebrity, especially from the
sporting or entertainment world: *The
success of his first movie made him a star.*
– *vb.* **star·ring, starred** to feature
or appear as a principal performer.

star·board (stär′bərd) *n.* the right side of a ship
or aircraft, as viewed when facing forward.

starch (stärch) *n.* a carbohydrate stored in
plants in the form of tiny white granules.

stare (stâr) *vb.* **star·ing, stared** to look with a
fixed gaze. – *n.* an act of staring; a fixed gaze.

Star of David *n.* the symbol of JUDAISM, a six-
pointed star.

Stars and Stripes *n.* the national flag of the
UNITED STATES.

start (stärt) *vb.* **start·ing, start·ed 1** to begin;
to bring or come into being. **2** to set or be set
in motion, or put or be put into a working
state: *Can you start the engine?* **3** to be at first: *She
started as a truck driver.* **4** to initiate or get going;
to cause or set off. **5** to begin a trip. – *n.* **1** the
first or early part. **2** an origin or cause. **3** the
time or place at which something starts.

star·tle (stärt′l) *vb.* **star·tling, star·tled** to
give a sudden fright to; to surprise.

starve (stärv) *vb.* **starv·ing, starved** to suffer,
cause to suffer or die, through lack of food.

state (stāt) *n.* **1** the condition, as of health, etc.
of a person or thing at a particular time. **2** a
nation. **3** (also **State**) one of the constituents of
a federal government: *the state of Maine.* – *adj.*
of, or controlled by the state or a state. – *vb.*
stat·ing, stat·ed to express clearly.

state·ment (stāt′mənt) *n.* a thing stated.

sta·tion (stā′shən) *n.* **1** a stopping place for
subways, trains, or buses, with facilities for
purchasing tickets, etc. **2** a local headquarters.
3 a building equipped for some particular
purpose. **4** a radio or television channel.

sta·tion·ar·y (stā′shə-ner′ē) *adj.*
not moving.

sta·tion·er·y (stā′shə-ner′ē) *n.* writing
materials.

stat·ue (stach′ōō) *n.* a sculpted figure.

● **Statue of Liberty** This statue welcomes
immigrants to the United States.

*The Statue of Liberty, which was
given to the United States by
France in 1886, stands on Liberty
Island in New York Harbor. Two
spiral staircases wind up inside it.*

sta·tus (stāt′əs, stat′əs) *n.* **1** rank or position in relation to others. **2** legal state.

stay (stā) *vb.* **stay·ing, stayed 1** to remain in the same place or condition, without moving or changing: *The dog stayed in her basket all day.* **2** to reside temporarily, for example as a guest. – *n.* a period of temporary residence; a visit.

stead·y (sted′ē) *adj.* **stead·i·er, stead·i·est 1** firmly fixed or balanced; not tottering or wobbling. **2** regular; constant; not varying. – *vb.* **stead·ies, stead·y·ing, stead·ied** to make or become steady. – *adv.* **stead·i·ly** (sted′l-ē). – *n.* **stead·i·ness** (sted′ē-nəs).

steak (stāk) *n.* a thick slice of meat or fish, especially of beef.

steal (stēl) *vb.* **steal·ing, stole** (stōl), **stol·en** (stō′lən) **1** to take away another person's property without permission, especially secretly. **2** to go about quietly so as not to be noticed: *She stole out of the room.*

steam (stēm) *n.* **1** the gas into which water is converted by boiling, invisible but generally becoming visible as a white mist of fine water vapor. **2** this gas as a source of mechanical power. – *vb.* **steam·ing, steamed 1** to give off steam. **2** to cook with steam. **3** to move under the power of steam. – *adj.* powered by steam. – **let off steam** to release anger or energy.

● Steam will fill 1,700 times more space than the water it comes from. So if you squash steam into a small container it presses hard against the sides. If one side is free to move, the steam pressure will push it outward. This fact was used to build engines powered by steam. Steam engines powered factory machines that made the INDUSTRIAL REVOLUION possible.

steam·roll·er (stēm′rō′lər) *n.* a large vehicle, originally driven by steam, with huge solid metal cylinder wheels, used to flatten road surfaces.

steel (stēl) *n.* a tough metal alloy of iron and carbon, with numerous industrial uses.

steep¹ (stēp) *adj.* rising or sloping sharply: *a steep hill.* – *n.* **steep·ness** (stēp′nəs).

steep² (stēp) *vb.* **steep·ing, steeped** to soak thoroughly in liquid.

stee·ple (stē′pəl) *n.* a tower with a spire.

steer¹ (stîr) *vb.* **steer·ing, steered** to guide or control the direction of a vehicle or vessel.

steer² (stîr) *n.* a young bull reared for beef.

● **Stein·beck** (stīn′bek′)**, John** (1902-1968) was an American author noted for his portrayal of the poor. *Of Mice and Men, The Grapes of Wrath,* and *East of Eden* are his best-known works.

stel·lar (stel′ər) *adj.* of or like stars.

stem¹ (stem) *n.* **1** the central part of a plant, growing upward from the root. **2** any long slender part. – *vb.* **stem·ming, stemmed** to originate or spring.

stem² (stem) *vb.* **stem·ming, stemmed** to stop or hold back; to restrain: *to stem the flow of time.*

stench (stench) *n.* a very unpleasant smell.

The iron used in steel making is mined as iron ore. The ore is smelted in a furnace. It is then made into cast iron and poured into molds to make engine blocks, etc.; or the ore is mixed with small amounts of carbon to form steel.

step (step) *n.* **1** a single movement of the foot in walking or running. **2** one of a pattern in dancing. **3** (often in *plural*) a place to put the foot to climb up or down. **4** a single action proceeding toward an end: *steps to control noise.* – *vb.* **step·ping, stepped 1** to move by taking steps. **2** to lay your foot, often heavily: *You've stepped on the cat's tail!*

step- *prefix* indicating a relationship not by blood but through a second or later marriage or partnership: *stepfather; stepson.*

steppe (step) *n.* a vast dry grassy plain.

ster·ile (ster′əl) *adj.* **1** incapable of reproducing. **2** made free of germs.

ster·i·lize (ster′ə-līz′) *vb.* **ster·i·liz·ing, ster·i·lized** to make sterile.

ster·ling (stur′ling) *n.* **1** British money. **2** an alloy that is 92.5 percent silver. − *adj.* **1** excellent. **2** made of sterling.

stern[1] (sturn) *adj.* strict; authoritarian; harsh.

stern[2] (sturn) *n.* the rear of a ship or boat.

steth·o·scope (steth′ə-skōp′) *n.* an instrument for listening to sounds made inside the body.

●**Ste·ven·son** (stē′vən-sən), **Robert Louis** (1850-1894) was the Scottish author of adventure stories such as *Treasure Island* and *Kidnapped*.

stew (stoō, styoō) *vb.* **stew·ing, stewed** to cook by long simmering. − *n.* a dish, usually of meat and vegetables, prepared by stewing.

stick[1] (stik) *n.* **1** a twig or thin branch. **2** any long thin piece of wood shaped for a particular purpose: *a hockey stick.*

stick[2] (stik) *vb.* **stick·ing, stuck** (stuk) **1** to push or thrust. **2** to fasten by piercing with a pin or other sharp object: *Stick it to the wall.* **3** to fix, or be or stay fixed, with an adhesive. **4** to remain: *It's an episode that sticks in my mind.* **5** to be unable to move: *We're stuck in a traffic jam.* **6** to remain faithful to; to not stray from: *Stick to the point!*

stick·er (stik′ər) *n.* an adhesive label.

stick insect *n.* any of the many insect species whose bodies resemble sticks or twigs.

stick·y (stik′ē) *adj.* **stick·i·er, stick·i·est** **1** able or likely to stick: *sticky candy.* **2** (of weather) warm and humid; muggy.

stiff (stif) *adj.* **1** not easily bent or folded; rigid: *Cardboard is stiff.* **2** lacking suppleness; not moving or bending easily: *Sam's arm is stiff from playing too much tennis.* **3** (of punishment, etc.) harsh; severe. **4** (of a task, etc.) difficult. **5** (of a manner) not relaxed.

stiff·en (stif′ən) *vb.* **stiff·en·ing, stiff·ened** to make or become stiff or stiffer.

sti·fle (stī′fəl) *vb.* **sti·fling, sti·fled** **1** to hold back; to repress. **2** to have difficulty in breathing, because of heat and lack of air.

stig·ma (stig′mə) *n.* **stigmas** or **stig·mat·a** (stig-mät′ə) **1** a mark of disgrace or shame. **2** the part of a flower that receives pollen.

stile (stīl) *n.* a step for climbing over a fence.

still (stil) *adj.* **1** motionless; inactive: *The air is still.* **2** quiet and calm; tranquil: *The sea is still tonight.* − *adv.* **1** continuing as before, now, or at some future time: *Phil is still my best friend.* **2** up to the present time, or the time in question; yet: *I still haven't finished my homework.* **3** even

then; nevertheless: *Although it was raining, they still went out.* **4** quietly and without movement: *Please try to sit still.* **5** to a greater degree; even: *Sean is older still.* − *n.* **1** stillness; tranquillity. **2** a photograph used for publicity purposes.

stilt (stilt) *n.* either of a pair of long poles with foot supports, on which a person can walk around supported high above the ground.

stim·u·late (stim′yə-lāt′) *vb.* **stim·u·lat·ing, stim·u·lat·ed** **1** to excite or arouse the senses of. **2** to create interest and enthusiasm in. − *n.* **stim·u·la·tion** (stim′yə-lā′shən).

stim·u·lus (stim′yə-ləs) *n.* **stim·u·li** (stim′yə-lī′, stim′yə-lē′) a thing that stimulates.

sting (sting) *n.* **1** a sharp part of some plants or animals that can pierce skin and inject poison: *a bee sting.* **2** the poison injected or wound inflicted. − *vb.* **sting·ing, stung** (stung) **1** to pierce, poison, or wound with a sting. **2** to produce a sharp tingling pain.

stin·gy (stin′jē) *adj.* **stin·gi·er, stin·gi·est** mean; miserly. − *n.* **stin·gi·ness** (stin′jē-nəs).

stink (stingk) *n.* a strong and unpleasant smell. − *vb.* **stink·ing, stank** (stangk) or **stunk** (stungk) **1** to give off a stink. **2** to be bad or unpleasant: *I think the whole idea stinks.*

stir (stur) *vb.* **stir·ring, stirred** **1** to mix with circular strokes: *Stir the sauce until it is smooth.* **2** to arouse the emotions of; to move: *The rebels stirred up the crowd.* **3** to make a slight movement: *Not a leaf stirred.* − *n.* **1** an act of stirring a liquid, etc.: *Give it a good stir.* **2** a commotion: *His remarks caused quite a stir.*

stir·rup (stur′əp, stûr′əp) *n.* either of a pair of metal loops hanging on straps from a horse's saddle to support the rider's foot.

stitch (stich) *n.* **1** a single link of thread or yarn in sewing, knitting, etc. **2** a sharp ache in the side. **3** (*informal*) the least scrap of clothing: *without a stitch on.* − *vb.* **stitch·ing, stitched** to join, close up, or decorate with stitches.

stock (stäk) *n.* **1** the total goods stored in a warehouse, etc. **2** a supply kept in reserve. **3** ownership of a company divided into shares; such a share or shares. **4** family; lineage. **5** liquid in which meat or vegetables have been cooked, used as a base for a soup. **6** farm animals; livestock. − *adj.* of a standard type, size, etc., constantly in demand and always kept in stock. − *vb.* **stock·ing, stocked** to keep a stock of for sale.

stock·ade (stäk-ād′) *n.* a fence or enclosure made from tall heavy posts, built for defense.

The bodies of some stick insects are so twiglike that they are almost impossible to see as they sit on trees or bushes. There are about 2,000 species of the insect.

stock·ing (stäk′ing) *n.* a close-fitting covering for the legs.

stole. See **steal**.

stolen. See **steal**.

stom·ach (stum′ik) *n.* **1** the baglike organ of the body into which food passes when swallowed. **2** (*loosely*) the area around the abdomen. – *vb.* **stom·ach·ing, stom·ached** (*informal*) to put up with.

stone (stōn) *n.* **1** the hard solid mineral substance of which rocks are made. **2** a piece of rock. **3** a gem. **4** the hard seed in various fruits. – *vb.* **ston·ing, stoned 1** to pelt with stones. **2** to remove the stone from: *to stone a fruit.*

Stone Age *n.* the earliest period in human history, during which primitive tools and weapons were made of stone.

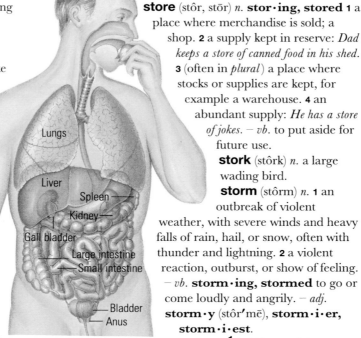

In your stomach, juices moisten and start digesting food. Stomach muscles churn the mixture, then force it into the small intestine.

● **Stone·henge** (stōn′henj′) is a prehistoric temple in southern ENGLAND. The main part is a great circle of huge standing stones.

A Stone Age fish spear and flint arrowhead.

stood. See **stand**.

stool (stōōl) *n.* a seat without a back.

stoop¹ (stōōp) *vb.* **stoop·ing, stooped** to bend from the waist: *She stooped to avoid the low beams.*

stoop² (stōōp) *n.* a set of stairs at an entrance.

stop (stäp) *vb.* **stop·ping, stopped 1** to bring or come to rest, a standstill, or an end; to cease moving, operating, or progressing. **2** to prevent. **3** to withhold or keep back. **4** to block, plug, or close. – *n.* **1** an act of stopping. **2** a place stopped at, for example on a bus route.

stop·page (stäp′ij) *n.* an act of stopping or the state of being stopped.

stop·watch (stäp′wäch′) *n.* a watch that can be stopped instantly, used for timing races, etc.

store (stôr, stōr) *n.* **stor·ing, stored 1** a place where merchandise is sold; a shop. **2** a supply kept in reserve: *Dad keeps a store of canned food in his shed.* **3** (often in *plural*) a place where stocks or supplies are kept, for example a warehouse. **4** an abundant supply: *He has a store of jokes.* – *vb.* to put aside for future use.

stork (stôrk) *n.* a large wading bird.

storm (stôrm) *n.* **1** an outbreak of violent weather, with severe winds and heavy falls of rain, hail, or snow, often with thunder and lightning. **2** a violent reaction, outburst, or show of feeling. – *vb.* **storm·ing, stormed** to go or come loudly and angrily. – *adj.* **storm·y** (stôr′mē), **storm·i·er, storm·i·est**.

sto·ry¹ (stôr′ē, stōr′ē) *n.* **stories 1** a written or spoken description of an event or series of events, real or imaginary. **2** a news article.

sto·ry² (stôr′ē, stōr′ē) *n.* **stories** a level or floor in a building.

stout (stout) *adj.* **1** rather fat: *a stout man.* **2** hard-wearing; robust: *stout boots.* **3** (also **stout-heart·ed** (stout-härt′əd)) courageous; brave.

stove (stōv) *n.* **1** an appliance for cooking food, often including an oven. **2** a heating device that burns coal, wood, oil, etc.

stow·a·way (stō′ə-wā′) *n.* someone who hides on a ship, etc. to avoid paying the fare.

strag·gle (strag′əl) *vb.* **strag·gling, strag·gled 1** to grow or spread untidily. **2** to lag behind or stray from the main group.

straight (strāt) *adj.* **1** not curved, bent, curly, or wavy. **2** without deviations or detours; direct: *Follow the straight path.* **3** level; not sloping, leaning, or twisted. **4** frank; open; direct.

straight·en (strāt′n) *vb.* **straight·en·ing, straight·ened** to make or become straight.

straight·for·ward (strāt-fôr′wərd) *adj.* **1** without complications. **2** honest and frank.

strain¹ (strān) *vb.* **strain·ing, strained 1** to injure or weaken. **2** to make violent efforts. **3** to pass through or pour into a sieve or strainer. **4** to tug violently. – *n.* **1** a wrenching of the muscles. **2** an extreme effort made by, or

PRONUNCIATION SYMBOLS		
ə **away**	lemon	focus
a **fat**	oi	**boy**
ā **fade**	oo	**foot**
ä **hot**	ōō	**moon**
âr **fair**	ou	**house**
e **met**	th	**think**
ē **mean**	<u>th</u>	<u>th</u>**is**
g **get**	u	**cut**
hw **which**	ur	**hurt**
i **fin**	w	**witch**
ī **line**	y	**yes**
îr **near**	yōō	**music**
ô **often**	yoor	**pure**
ō **note**	zh	**vi**sion

demand made on, the mind or the body.

strain² (strān) *n.* a breed of animals or plants.

strain·er (strā′nər) *n.* a kitchen utensil used to separate liquids from solid material.

strait (strāt) *n.* **1** (often in *plural*) a narrow strip of sea between two land masses. **2** (in *plural*) difficulty; hardship: *The company is in dire straits.*

strand¹ (strand) *vb.* **strand·ing, strand·ed** to leave in a helpless position.

strand² (strand) *n.* a single thread or fiber.

strange (strānj) *adj.* **1** not known or experienced before; unfamiliar or alien. **2** not usual; odd. **3** uncomfortable; vaguely ill or ill at ease.

strang·er (strān′jər) *n.* a person whom one does not know.

stran·gle (strang′gəl) *vb.* **stran·gling, stran·gled** to kill by squeezing the throat with the hands, a cord, etc. – *n.* **stran·gler.**

strap (strap) *n.* a narrow strip of material by which a thing is hung, carried, or fastened.

strat·e·gy (strat′ə-jē) *n.* **strat·e·gies** a long-term plan for future success or development.

straw (strô) *n.* **1** the dried cut stalks of grain after threshing. **2** a thin tube for sucking.

straw·ber·ry (strô′ber′ē) *n.* **straw·ber·ries** a small juicy red fruit of a low-growing plant.

stray (strā) *vb.* **stray·ing, strayed** to wander away: *Some of us strayed from the group.* – *n.* a lost or homeless pet or person. – *adj.* random.

streak (strēk) *n.* **1** a long irregular stripe or band. **2** a flash of lightning. **3** an element or characteristic: *a cowardly streak.* **4** a short period; a spell: *a lucky streak.* – *vb.* **streak·ing, streaked** to move at great speed; to dash.

stream (strēm) *n.* **1** a very narrow river. **2** a constant flow: *a stream of cars.* **3** an uninterrupted burst: *a stream of insults.* – *vb.* **stream·ing, streamed 1** to flow or move continuously and in large quantities. **2** to trail: *Her long hair streamed in the wind.*

stream·lined (strēm′līnd′) *adj.* shaped so as to move with minimum resistance to air or water.

street (strēt) *n.* a public road, especially one in a town with sidewalks and buildings at the sides.

strength (strength, strenth) *n.* **1** the quality or degree of being physically or mentally strong. **2** the ability to withstand pressure or force.

strength·en (streng′thən, stren′thən) *vb.* **strength·en·ing, strength·ened** to make or become stronger.

stren·u·ous (stren′yo͞o-əs) *adj.* requiring, or performed with, great effort or energy.

stress (stres) *n.* **1** mental or emotional pressure;

PRONUNCIATION SYMBOLS		
ə **away**	lemon	focus
a **fat**	oi	**boy**
ā **fade**	oo	**foot**
ä **hot**	o͞o	**moon**
âr **fair**	ou	**house**
e **met**	th	**think**
ē **mean**	<u>th</u>	**this**
g **get**	u	**cut**
hw **which**	ur	**hurt**
i **fin**	w	**witch**
ī **line**	y	**yes**
îr **near**	yo͞o	**music**
ô **often**	yoor	**pure**
ō **note**	zh	**vision**

---

acute anxiety. **2** physical pressure or tension. **3** importance or weight attached to something. **4** emphasis on a particular syllable or word.

stretch (strech) *vb.* **stretch·ing, stretched 1** to make or become longer or wider by pulling or drawing out. **2** to extend in space or time: *The ocean stretches from North America to Europe.* **3** to straighten and extend the body fully, for example when waking or reaching. – *n.* **1** an act of stretching, especially the body. **2** a period of time; a spell. **3** an expanse, for example of land or water.

stretch·er (strech′ər) *n.* a length of canvas or other sheeting with poles attached, for carrying a sick or wounded person.

stricken (strik′ən) *n.* See **strike.**

strict (strikt) *adj.* **1** demanding obedience or close observance of rules; severe. **2** that must be obeyed: *The rules are strict but fair.* **3** complete: *I told you in the strictest confidence.* – *adv.* **strict·ly** (strik′lē, strik′tlē).

stride (strīd) *n.* **1** a single long step in walking. **2** (usually in *plural*) a measure of progress or development: *We have made great strides.* – *vb.* **strid·ing, strode** (strōd), **strid·den** (strid′n) **1** to walk with long steps. **2** to step over.

strike (strīk) *vb.* **strik·ing, struck** (struk) or **strick·en** (strik′ən) **1** to hit; to give a blow to; to come or bring into heavy contact with. **2** to make a particular impression on: *It strikes me as a great idea.* **3** to come into the mind of; to occur to. **4** to ignite through friction: *to strike a match.* **5** (of a clock) to announce the time with a chime. **6** to happen suddenly: *Disaster struck.* **7** to find a source of: *We've struck oil.* **8** to stop working as part of a collective protest against an employer. – *n.* **strik·er.** – *n.* **1** an act of hitting or dealing a blow. **2** a refusal to work, as a protest against an employer. **3** in baseball, a ball judged to be pitched in the correct area but missed by the batter, or a ball swung at but missed. – *vb.* **strike out 1** to cross out. **2** in baseball, to lose or cause to lose one's turn at batting after three strikes.

strik·ing (strī′king) *adj.* **1** impressive. **2** on strike.

string (string) *n.* **1** thin cord. **2** any of a set of pieces of stretched wire, gut, etc., vibrated to produce sound in musical instruments.

strip (strip) *n.* a long narrow piece of anything: *a strip of paper.* – *vb.* **strip·ping, stripped 1** to remove by peeling or pulling off: *We stripped the wallpaper in the bedroom.* **2** to take one's clothes off.

stripe (strīp) *n.* a band of color. – *adj.* **strip·ed** (strīpt, strī′pəd).

strive (strīv) *vb.* **striv·ing, strove** (strōv), **striv·en** (striv′ən) to try hard; to struggle.

strode. See **stride**.

stroke (strōk) *n.* **1** an act of striking: *a stroke of the bat.* **2** a single movement with a pen, paintbrush, etc. **3** a single complete movement in a repeated series, as in the action of pistons in an engine. **4** the striking of a clock, or its sound. **5** a gentle caress. **6** a sudden loss of consciousness caused by the bursting or blocking of a blood vessel in the brain. – *vb.* **strok·ing, stroked** to caress.

stroll (strōl) *vb.* **stroll·ing, strolled** to walk in a slow leisurely way. – *n.* a leisurely walk.

strong (strông) *adj.* **1** exerting great force or power: *Elephants are very strong.* **2** able to withstand rough treatment; robust. **3** firmly held or boldly expressed: *Sam has strong views on politics.* **4** sharply felt or experienced; intense.

strove. See **strive**.

struck. See **strike**.

struc·ture (struk′chər) *n.* **1** the way in which the parts of a thing are arranged or organized. **2** a thing built from many smaller parts.

strug·gle (strug′əl) *vb.* **strug·gling, strug·gled 1** to move the body around violently in an attempt to get free. **2** to make a strenuous effort under difficult conditions. – *n.* **1** an act of struggling. **2** a contest.

strum (strum) *vb.* **strum·ming, strummed** to play a stringed musical instrument with sweeps of the fingers or a pick.

strut (strut) *vb.* **strut·ting, strut·ted** to walk in a proud or arrogant way.

● **Stu·arts** (stōō′ərts) The Stuarts were a royal family that ruled SCOTLAND from 1371 to 1603 and ENGLAND and Scotland from 1603 to 1715.

stub (stub) *n.* a short piece of a cigarette or a pencil, etc. – *vb.* **stub·bing, stubbed** to bump against a hard surface: *I stubbed my toe.*

stub·ble (stub′əl) *n.* **1** the mass of short stalks left in the ground after a crop has been harvested. **2** a short growth of beard.

stub·born (stub′ərn) *adj.* unwilling to change plans or opinions; obstinate.

stuck. See **stick²**.

stu·dent (stōōd′nt, styōōd′nt) *n.* **1** person following a course of study. **2** a person devoted to the study of some subject: *a student of foreign policy.*

stu·di·o (stōōd′ē-ō′, styōōd′ē-ō′) *n.* **studios 1** the workroom of an artist or photographer. **2** a room or large area used for recording or broadcasting.

The Stuart King James VI of Scotland became James I of England when the two crowns united in 1603. The first Union flag (above) was created in 1606 by combining the crosses of St. George and St. Andrew, the national flags of England and Scotland. With the union with Ireland in 1800 the saltire of St. Patrick was added.

The **structure** of something is the way it is put together. We see evidence of structure all around us. Things that are well constructed are efficient and last.

Scientists study the molecular structure of, for example, the crystals of an element.

The structure of a building such as a skyscraper — involving many people such as architects, builders, and civil engineers — is complex.

The sophisticated structure of an artifical limb requires careful and painstaking design.

Stupid is from the Latin word *stupidus,* taken from the verb *stupere* meaning "to be amazed." At one time the word meant "stunned with surprise," but took on its present meaning in the 1500s.

stud·y (stud′ē) *vb.* **stud·ies, stud·y·ing, stud·ied 1** to learn about a subject by giving time and attention to it. **2** to look at or examine closely, or think about carefully. – *n.* **stud·ies** a private room where quiet work or study is carried out.

stuff (stuf) *n.* **1** any material, substance, or equipment. **2** belongings. **3** matter; essence: *the very stuff of life.* – *vb.* **stuff·ing, stuffed 1** to fill the hollow or hollowed-out part of, for example a cushion. **2** to fill to capacity or over. **3** to cram or thrust in.

stuff·ing (stuf′ing) *n.* **1** padding. **2** a seasoned mixture used to stuff poultry, etc.

stuff·y (stuf′ē) *adj.* **stuff·i·er, stuff·i·est 1** lacking fresh, cool air; badly ventilated. **2** (*informal*) overly formal.

stum·ble (stum′bəl) *vb.* **stum·bling, stum·bled 1** to lose one's balance; to trip. **2** to walk unsteadily.

stum·bling block (stum′bling-bläk) *n.* an obstacle or difficulty.

stump (stump) *n.* the part of a tree left in the ground after the top has been removed. – *vb.* **stump·ing, stumped** to baffle or perplex.

stun (stun) *vb.* **stun·ning, stunned 1** to make unconscious. **2** to shock: *They were stunned when they saw the damage.*

stung. See **sting**.

stunt[1] (stunt) *vb.* **stunt·ing, stunt·ed** to prevent the full growth of.

stunt[2] (stunt) *n.* a daring act or spectacular event: *an acrobatic stunt.*

stu·pid (sto͞o′pəd, styo͞o′pəd) *adj.* having a lack of common sense. – *n.* **stu·pid·i·ty** (sto͞o-pid′ət-ē, styo͞o-pid′ət-ē).

stur·dy (sturd′ē) *adj.* **stur·di·er, stur·di·est** strongly built; robust: *a sturdy tree.*

stut·ter (stut′ər) *n.* a stammer. – *vb.* **stut·ter·ing, stut·tered** to stammer.

● **Stuy·ve·sant** (stī′və-sənt), **Peter** (1592-1672) was governor of the Dutch colony of New Netherland from 1646 to 1664 when he surrendered it to the British, who renamed it New York.

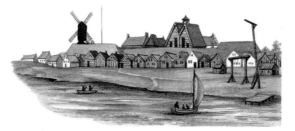

Peter Stuyvesant was an unpopular governor of the colony of New Netherland. When the British captured it in 1664, the colonists readily surrendered.

sty[1] (stī) *n.* **sties** a pen in which pigs are kept.

sty[2] or **stye** (stī) *n.* **sties** or **styes** a tiny swelling on the eyelid, at the base of the lash.

style (stīl) *n.* **1** a manner or way of doing something, as writing, speaking, painting, or designing buildings. **2** a striking elegance: *She dresses with style.* **3** a small stalklike part on the inside of a flower, bearing the stigma.

styl·ish (stī′lish) *adj.* elegant; fashionable.

● **Styx** (stiks) in Greek mythology, was a river in the Underworld (Hades) across which the souls of the dead were ferried.

sub- *prefix* **1** under or below: *submarine.* **2** secondary; lower in rank or importance: *subdivision.* **3** imperfectly; less than: *subhuman.* **4** a part or division of: *subcommittee.*

sub·ject (sub′jikt) *n.* **1** a matter or topic under discussion or consideration. **2** an area of learning that forms a course of study. **3** a person or thing represented by an artist or writer. **4** a person under the ultimate rule of a monarch or government: *a British subject.* **5** in grammar, a word or phrase referring to the person or thing that usually performs or receives the action of a verb, as in "*He* dropped it" and "*It* was dropped by him." – *adj.* **1** showing a tendency; prone: *She's subject to backaches.* **2** exposed; open. **3** governed; dependent: *We're all subject to the law.* – (səb-jekt′) *vb.* **sub·ject·ing, sub·ject·ed 1** to cause to undergo or experience. **2** to bring under the control.

sub·ma·rine (sub′mə-rēn′, sub′mə-rēn′) *n.* **1** a vessel, especially military, able to travel underwater. **2** a large sandwich on a long roll with a variety of fillings, such as meat, cheese, lettuce, tomato, etc., also called *grinder, hero, hoagie.* – *adj.* under the surface of the sea.

sub·merge (səb-murj′) *vb.* **sub·merg·ing, sub·merged** to plunge or sink under the surface of water or other liquid. – *n.* **sub·mer·sion** (səb-mur′zhən).

sub·mit (səb-mit′) *vb.* **sub·mit·ting, sub·mit·ted 1** to give in, especially to the wishes or control of another person. **2** to offer or present for consideration by others.

sub·mis·sive (səb-mis′iv) *adj.* meek; obedient.

sub·scribe (səb-skrīb′) *vb.* **sub·scrib·ing, sub·scribed** to agree to buy a certain number of issues, opera tickets, etc.: *to subscribe to a magazine.* – *n.* **sub·scrib·er.**

sub·scrip·tion (səb-skrip′shən) *n.* an agreement to buy issues of a magazine, etc.

sub·side (səb-sīd′) *vb.* **sub·sid·ing, sub·sid·ed 1** (of land, buildings, etc.) to sink to a lower level; to settle. **2** to die down.

sub·stance (sub′stəns) *n.* **1** the matter or material that a thing is made of; anything that can be seen or touched. **2** a particular kind of matter: *a sticky substance.* **3** the essence or basic meaning of something.

sub·stan·tial (səb-stan′chəl) *adj.* **1** large in amount, extent, or importance. **2** solidly built.

sub·sti·tute (sub′stə-tōōt′, sub′stə-tyōōt′) *n.* a person or thing that takes the place of, or is used instead of, another. – *vb.* **sub·sti·tut·ing, sub·sti·tut·ed.**

sub·tle (sut′l) *adj.* **1** not straightforward or obvious. **2** (of flavors, etc.) faint or delicate.

sub·tract (səb-trakt′) *vb.* **sub·tract·ing, sub·tract·ed** to take one number or quantity from another; to deduct. – *n.* **sub·trac·tion.**

sub·urb (sub′urb′) *n.* (often in *plural*) a district, especially residential, on the edge of a town.

sub·ur·ban (sə-bur′bən) *adj.* of or in a suburb.

sub·way (sub′wā′) *n.* an underground railroad, usually in a city.

suc·ceed (sək-sēd′) *vb.* **suc·ceed·ing, suc·ceed·ed 1** to achieve an aim or purpose. **2** to develop or turn out as planned. **3** to come next after; to follow.

suc·cess (sək-ses′) *n.* **1** the state of having succeeded; a favorable development or outcome. **2** the attainment of fame, power, or wealth. – *adj.* **suc·cess·ful.**

suc·ces·sion (sək-sesh′ən) *n.* a series of people or things coming one after the other.

such (such) *adj.* **1** of that kind, or the same or a similar kind: *You can't reason with such a person.* **2** so great: *I'm not such a fool as to believe that.* – *adv.* extremely: *It was such great weather.*

suck (suk) *vb.* **suck·ing, sucked 1** to draw liquid into the mouth. **2** to hold in the mouth and draw the flavor from: *to suck a candy.*

suck·le (suk′əl) *vb.* **suck·ling, suck·led** to give or suck milk from a breast or udder.

●**Su·dan** (sōō-dan′). See Supplement, **Countries**.

sud·den (sud′n) *adj.* happening quickly or unexpectedly. – *n.* **sud·den·ness.**

suds (sudz) *n.* (*plural*) lather of soapy water.

sue (sōō) *vb.* **su·ing, sued** to take legal proceedings against a person or company.

●**Su·ez Canal** (sōō′ez′, sōō-ez′) This is the world's longest canal, 99 miles (160km), and links the MEDITER-RANEAN and RED seas.

Submarines like this Deepstar IV can sink to depths of 3,900 ft. and are used in underwater exploration, surveying wrecks, laying pipelines, etc.

Submarines are specially designed so that they can sink and spend long periods underwater. Most submarines are military vessels; a few others are used for scientific research. Nuclear submarines can remain submerged for months. Diesel submarines have to surface to recharge their batteries.

George Washington class submarine, used by the U.S. Navy, first launched in 1959.

The sub sinks when air rushes out of the ballast tanks and water rushes in. When the water is forced out by pumping in air, the sub rises again.

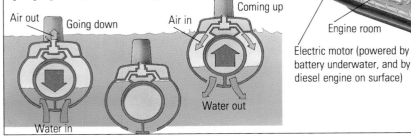

Air out
Going down
Air in
Coming up
Water in
Water out

Propeller
Engine exhaust
Conning tower
Lock-out chamber, used by divers entering and leaving underwater
Stern hydroplane
Engine room
Electric motor (powered by battery underwater, and by diesel engine on surface)
Torpedoes
Crew quarters
Bow hydroplane
Sonar

suf·fer (suf′ər) *vb.* **suf·fer·ing, suf·fered 1** to undergo or endure physical or mental pain or other unpleasantness. **2** to be afflicted with an illness. **3** to deteriorate as a result of something.

suf·fi·cient (sə-fish′ənt) *adj.* enough; adequate.

suf·fix (suf′iks) *n.* a word ending to mark a grammatical inflection or derivation, for example the *-s* in *monkeys*.

suf·fo·cate (suf′ə-kāt′) *vb.* **suf·fo·cat·ing, suf·fo·cat·ed** to kill with or die from lack of air. – *n.* **suf·fo·ca·tion** (suf′ə-kā′shən).

sug·ar (shoog′ər) *n.* a sweet-tasting substance found in sugarcane and other plants, refined into white or brown crystals, used to sweeten food and drinks. – *vb.* **sug·ar·ing, sug·ared.**

sug·gest (səg-jest′, sə-jest′) *vb.* **sug·gest·ing, sug·gest·ed 1** to put forward as a possibility. **2** to make someone think of.

sug·ges·tion (səg-jes′chən, sə-jes′chən) *n.* **1** a thing suggested. **2** a hint or trace.

su·i·cide (soo′ə-sīd′) *n.* the act of killing oneself. – *adj.* **su·i·cid·al** (soo′ə-sīd′l).

suit (soot) *n.* **1** a jacket with pants or a skirt, usually made from the same material. **2** any of the four groups into which a pack of playing cards is divided. **3** a legal action taken against someone. – *vb.* **suit·ing, suit·ed 1** to be acceptable to or required by. **2** to be in harmony with or attractive to.

suit·a·ble (soot′ə-bəl) *adj.* that suits; appropriate or agreeable; convenient.

suite *n.* **1** (swēt) a set of rooms. **2** (swēt, soot) a matching set of furniture.

sulk (sulk) *vb.* **sulk·ing, sulked** to be silent out of bad temper.

sul·len (sul′ən) *adj.* silently angry: *Jan was sullen after the criticism.*

sul·phur (sul′fər) *n.* an element (symbol **S**), a yellow brittle nonmetallic mineral.

sul·tan (sult′n) *n.* the ruler of a Muslim country.

sul·try (sul′trē) *adj.* **sul·tri·er, sul·tri·est** (of weather) hot and humid.

sum (sum) *n.* **1** the amount produced when numbers or quantities are added together. **2** an amount of money.

sum·ma·ry (sum′ə-rē) *n.* **sum·ma·ries** a short account outlining the main points.

sum·mer (sum′ər) *n.* the warmest season of the year, between spring and autumn.

sum·mit (sum′ət) *n.* the highest point; peak.

sum·mon (sum′ən) *vb.* **sum·mon·ing, sum·moned** to order to come or appear.

sum·mons (sum′ənz) *n.* **sum·mons·es** a written order to attend a court of law.

sun (sun) *n.* (often Sun) the star that is the source of light, heat, and gravitational pull for all the planets in the earth's planetary system.

Sun·day (sun′dē, sun′dā) *n.* the first day of the week, and for most Christians a day of worship.

sun·flow·er (sun′flou′ər) *n.* a large flower on a tall stem with yellow petals and edible seeds.

sung. See **sing.**

sunk. See **sink.**

sunk·en (sung′kən). See **sink.** – *adj.* at a lower level than the surrounding area: *a sunken pond.*

sun·light (sun′līt′) *n.* light from the sun.

sun·ny (sun′ē) *adj.* **sun·ni·er, sun·ni·est 1** filled with sunshine. **2** cheerful.

sun·rise (sun′rīz′) *n.* the sun's appearance above the horizon in the east in the morning.

sun·set (sun′set′) *n.* the sun's disappearance below the horizon in the west in the evening.

su·per (soo′pər) (*informal*) *adj.* excellent.

super- *prefix* **1** great or extreme in size or degree: *supertanker.* **2** above or beyond: *supernatural.* **3** outstanding: *superhero.*

su·perb (soo-purb′) *adj.* **1** outstandingly excellent. **2** magnificent; majestic.

su·per·fi·cial (soo′pər-fish′əl) *adj.* **1** of, on, or near the surface: *a superficial cut.* **2** not thorough or indepth. **3** only apparent; not real or genuine. **4** lacking the capacity for sincere emotion or serious thought; shallow.

su·pe·ri·or (soo-pîr′ē-ər) *adj.* **1** higher in rank or position. **2** better in a particular way; of high quality. **3** arrogant; self-satisfied. – *n.* a person of higher rank or position. – *n.* **su·pe·ri·or·i·ty** (soo-pîr′ē-ôr′ət-ē).

su·per·la·tive (soo-pur′lət-iv) *adj.* **1** superior to all others; supreme. **2** (of an adjective or adverb) expressing the highest degree of a particular quality, for example *nicest.*

su·per·son·ic (soo′pər-sän′ik) *adj.* capable of traveling faster than the speed of sound.

su·per·sti·tion (soo′pər-stish′ən) *n.* belief in a mysterious influence that certain objects, actions, or occurrences have on events, people's lives, etc. – *adj.* **su·per·sti·tious** (soo′pər-stish′əs).

su·per·vise (soo′pər-vīz′) *vb.* **su·per·vis·ing, su·per·vised** to be in overall charge of; to oversee. – *n.* **su·per·vi·sion** (soo′pər-vizh′ən).

Cane

Crusher

Lime to help purify

Filters

Carbon dioxide to help purify

Evaporating pan

Making sugar from sugarcane: the stems of the canes are crushed and the juice filtered and purified. The sugar solution is evaporated to produce sugar crystals. Sugar beet is treated in a similar way.

The **Sun** is a star. It is a fiercely hot globe of burning gas, mostly hydrogen, measuring about 870,000 miles across. It is the center of our solar system and has existed for over 4.5 billion years.

The hydrogen atoms at the Sun's center have so much energy that they break apart, coming together again as helium gas. This energy produces "sunshine."

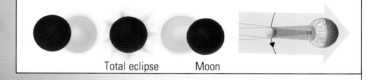

Total eclipse   Moon

During a total eclipse the Moon totally covers the Sun. This is visible from a narrow strip crossing the Earth's surface, usually about 90 miles (150 km) wide.

sup·per (sup′ər) *n.* the evening meal.

sup·ple (sup′əl) *adj.* bending easily; flexible.

sup·ple·ment (sup′lə-mənt) *n.* a thing added to make something complete or to make up a deficiency. – (sup′lə-ment′) *vb.* **sup·ple·ment·ing, sup·ple·ment·ed** to add to.

sup·ply (sə-plī′) *vb.* **sup·plies, sup·ply·ing, sup·plied** to provide or make available. – *n.* **sup·plies** (sə-plīz′) **1** an amount supplied regularly. **2** an amount that can be drawn from and used; a stock. – *n.* **sup·pli·er** (sə-plī′ər).

sup·port (sə-pôrt′, sə-pōrt′) *vb.* **sup·port·ing, sup·port·ed 1** to keep upright or in place; to bear the weight of: *The pillars support the roof.* **2** to give active encouragement to. **3** to provide with the means necessary for living or existing: *He supports his parents.* – *n.* **1** the act of supporting or the state of being supported. **2** a person, group, or thing that supports.

sup·pose (sə-pōz′) *vb.* **sup·pos·ing, sup·posed 1** to consider likely or probable. **2** to treat as a fact for the sake of argument.

su·preme (sə-prēm′, soo-prēm′) *adj.* **1** of highest rank, power, or importance. **2** most excellent; best.

sure (shoor, shōr) *adj.* **1** confident beyond doubt; convinced: *Eleanor was sure that she could drive the new car.* **2** guaranteed or certain: *It will be a sure winner.* – *n.* **sure·ness** (shoor′nəs, shōr′nəs).

sure·ly (shoor′lē, shōr′lē) *adv.* **1** without doubt; certainly. **2** (in questions and exclamations) it must be that: *Surely you're not leaving already!*

surf (surf) *n.* **1** the foam produced by breaking waves. **2** waves.

sur·face (sur′fəs) *n.* **1** the outer side of anything. **2** external appearance, rather than underlying reality. – *adj.* **1** at, on, or relating to a surface. **2** superficial. – *vb.* **sur·fac·ing, sur·faced**.

surge (surj) *n.* **1** a sudden sharp increase. **2** a rising and falling of a large area of sea.

sur·geon (sur′jən) *n.* a doctor specializing in surgery.

sur·ge·ry (sur′jə-rē) *n.* **sur·ge·ries 1** the treatment of disease or injury by cutting into the patient's body to operate directly on, or remove, the affected part: *The doctor recommended surgery.* **2** the branch of medicine dealing with such operations.

●**Sur·i·name** (soor′ə-nam′). See Supplement, **Countries**.

sur·name (sur′nām′) *n.* a family name or last name.

sur·pass (sər-pas′) *vb.* **sur·pass·ing, sur·passed** to exceed; to be better than.

sur·plus (sur′plus′, sur′pləs) *n.* an amount more than is required or used: *This year there is a surplus of apples; we can't sell them.* – *adj.* extra.

PRONUNCIATION SYMBOLS

ə away	lemon	focus
a fat	oi	boy
ā fade	oo	foot
ä hot	ōō	moon
âr fair	ou	house
e met	th	think
ē mean	th	this
g get	u	cut
hw which	ur	hurt
i fin	w	witch
ī line	y	yes
îr near	yōō	music
ô often	yoor	pure
ō note	zh	vision

sur·prise (sər-prīz′, sə-prīz′) *n.* something sudden or unexpected. – *vb.* **sur·pris·ing, sur·prised** to cause surprise to.

sur·ren·der (sə-ren′dər) *vb.* **sur·ren·der·ing, sur·ren·dered** to admit defeat by giving yourself up to an enemy; to give in. – *n.* the act of surrendering.

sur·round (sə-round′) *vb.* **sur·round·ing, sur·round·ed** to be on all sides; to encircle: *The sea surrounds the island.* – *adj.* **sur·round·ing**.

sur·round·ings *n.* (*plural*) environment.

sur·vey (sər-vā′, sur′vā′) *vb.* **sur·veys, sur·vey·ing, sur·veyed** 1 to look at or examine at length or in detail. 2 to measure land heights and distances for the purposes of drawing a detailed map. – (sur′vā′) *n.* **sur·veys** a detailed examination, for example public opinion.

sur·vive (sər-vīv′) *vb.* **sur·viv·ing, sur·vived** 1 to remain alive or undamaged in spite of; to come through. 2 to live on after the death of: *The grandparents survived their grandchildren.* – *n.* **sur·viv·al** (sər-vī′vəl). – *n.* **sur·vi·vor**.

sus·pect (sə-spekt′) *vb.* **sus·pect·ing, sus·pect·ed** 1 to consider likely: *We suspect you are wrong.* 2 to think a person possibly guilty of a crime or other wrongdoing. – (sus′pekt′) *n.* a person suspected of committing a crime, etc.

sus·pend (sə-spend′) *vb.* **sus·pend·ing, sus·pend·ed** 1 to hang or hang up. 2 to delay or postpone. 3 to remove from a job, a team, etc. temporarily, as punishment.

sus·pense (sə-spens′) *n.* a state of anxiety or excited uncertainty.

sus·pen·sion (sə-spen′chən) *n.* 1 the act of suspending or the state of being suspended. 2 a mixture of solid particles in a liquid or gas.

sus·pi·cion (sə-spish′ən) *n.* 1 the feeling of suspecting. 2 an act of suspecting; a belief or opinion based on slender evidence. – *adj.* **sus·pi·cious** (sə-spish′əs).

swal·low¹ (swäl′ō) *vb.* **swal·low·ing, swal·lowed** 1 to allow to pass down the throat to the stomach. 2 to stifle or repress. – *n.* an act of swallowing.

swal·low² (swäl′ō) *n.* an insect-eating bird with long pointed wings and a forked tail.

swam. See **swim**.

Leaves fall into the water of shallow lakes; a layer of peat accumulates to form a swamp.

swamp (swämp, swômp) *n.* permanently wet, spongy ground.

swan (swän) *n.* a large bird with a long curving neck and webbed feet.

swap (swäp) *vb.* **swap·ping, swapped** to exchange or trade.

swarm (swôrm) *n.* 1 a large group of bees flying in search of a new home. 2 a crowd of people, insects, etc. on the move.

swat (swät) *vb.* **swat·ting, swat·ted** to crush, especially a fly, with a heavy slapping blow.

sway (swā) *vb.* **sway·ing, swayed** 1 to move from side to side. 2 to waver. 3 to influence.

●**Swa·zi·land** (swäz′ē-land′). See Supplement, **Countries**.

swear (swâr) *vb.* **swear·ing, swore** (swôr), **sworn** (swôrn) 1 to use vulgar language. 2 to promise solemnly, as if by taking an oath.

sweat (swet) *n.* the salty moisture that the body gives off through the skin's pores; perspiration. – *vb.* **sweat·ing, sweat·ed** or **sweat** to give off sweat through the pores.

sweat·er (swet′ər) *n.* a knitted garment for the upper body, often of wool.

Swede (swēd) *n.* a native or citizen of SWEDEN.

Swallows return from South Africa to the same nesting site in Europe each year. Their nests are built against buildings.

●**Swe·den** (swēd′n) is a mountainous country in northwest EUROPE. Manufacturing, mining, and forestry are the main sources of the country's prosperity. The capital is Stockholm. See also Supplement, **Countries**.

Swed·ish (swēd′ish) *n.* the language of SWEDEN. – *adj.* of, or relating to, SWEDEN, its people, or their language.

sweep (swēp) *vb.* **sweep·ing, swept** (swept) **1** to clean or remove dirt, dust, etc. with a brush or broom: *He swept the room.* **2** to take, carry, or push suddenly and with irresistible force: *The crowd was swept against the railings.* – *n.* **1** an act of sweeping. **2** a sweeping movement, etc.

sweep·ing *adj.* wide-ranging and thorough: *The government brought in sweeping changes.*

sweet (swēt) *adj.* **1** tasting like sugar; not sour, salty, or bitter: *Honey is sweet.* **2** pleasing to any of the senses, especially smell and hearing: *It smells sweet.* **3** likable; charming: *Aren't the kittens sweet?* – *n.* (in *plural*) sweet food, as candies or pastry. – *n.* **sweet·ness** (swēt′nəs).

sweet corn *n.* a variety of corn grown especially for human consumption.

sweet·en (swēt′n) *vb.* **sweet·en·ing, sweet·ened** to make sweet or sweeter.

sweet tooth *n.* a fondness for sweet foods.

swell (swel) *vb.* **swell·ing, swelled, swoll·en** (swō′lən) or **swelled 1** to make or become bigger through injury, infection, or filling with liquid or air. **2** to increase in number, size, or intensity: *Membership has swelled in recent months.*

swept. See **sweep**.

swerve (swurv) *vb.* **swerv·ing, swerved** to turn or move aside suddenly and sharply.

swift (swift) *adj.* **1** fast-moving; able to move fast. **2** done quickly. – *n.* a small fast-flying bird similar to the swallow. – *adv.* **swift·ly**. – *n.* **swift·ness** (swift′nəs).

●**Swift** (swift), **Jonathan** (1667-1745) was an Irish writer whose most famous book is *Gulliver's Travels*.

swim (swim) *vb.* **swim·ming, swam** (swam), **swum** (swum) **1** to move through water by moving the arms and legs or in animals other parts of the body. **2** to cross a stretch of water in this way. **3** to be flooded or awash: *The cellar is swimming with water after the flood.* – *n.* a spell of swimming. – *n.* **swim·mer**.

swin·dle (swin′dəl) *vb.* **swin·dling, swin·dled** to cheat or trick: *She swindled me out of $50.* – *n.* an act of swindling.

swing (swing) *vb.* **swing·ing, swung** (swung) **1** to open and close; to move back and forth: *The door is swinging on its hinges.* **2** to undergo a sudden sharp change or changes. – *n.* **1** an act, manner, or spell of swinging: *a swing of the ax.* **2** a seat suspended from a frame or branch, for a person to swing on. **3** a sudden sharp change, for example in mood or pattern of voting.

Swiss (swis) *adj.* of, or relating to, SWITZERLAND or its people. – *n.* a native or citizen of SWITZERLAND.

switch (swich) *n.* a button, knob, or lever that makes or breaks an electrical circuit, turning an appliance on or off. – *vb.* **switch·ing, switched 1** to turn an appliance on or off by means of a switch. **2** to exchange, especially quickly and without notice.

●**Swit·zer·land** (swit′sər-lənd). See Supplement, **Countries**.

swoop (swōōp) *vb.* **swoop·ing, swooped** to fly down with a fast sweeping movement: *An eagle swoops on its prey.* – *n.* an act of swooping.

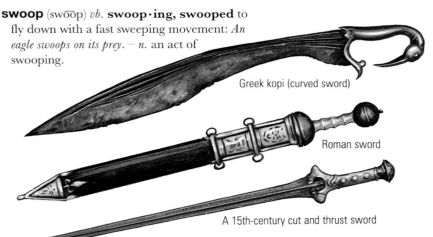

Greek kopi (curved sword)

Roman sword

A 15th-century cut and thrust sword

sword (sôrd) *n.* a hand weapon with a long blade.

sword·fish (sôrd′fish′) *n.* a large saltwater fish with a long and pointed upper jaw used as a weapon.

swore. See **swear**.

sworn (swôrn). See **swear**. – *adj.* bound by or as if by an oath: *sworn enemies.*

swum. See **swim**.

swung. See **swing**.

syc·a·more (sik′ə-môr′) *n.* a deciduous tree with large leaves and bark that flakes off.

The handle of a sword is called a hilt. Sword blades may have one or two cutting edges and some are curved. Very narrow swords are called rapiers. Today swords are used mainly in the sport of fencing or on military ceremonial occasions.

●**Syd·ney** (sid′nē) is the largest and oldest city in AUSTRALIA and the capital of the state of New South Wales.

Australia's most famous building — the Sydney Opera House — under construction. The saillike roofs were particularly difficult to erect. The building was completed in 1973.

syl·la·ble (sil′ə-bəl) *n.* any of the parts, consisting of one or more sounds and usually including a vowel, that a word can be divided into: *The word "telephone" has three syllables, "tel," "e," and "phone."*

sym·bol (sim′bəl) *n.* **1** a thing that represents or stands for another: *The dove is a symbol of peace.* **2** a letter or sign used to represent a quantity, idea, object, etc.

sym·bol·ic (sim-bäl′ik) *adj.* **1** relating to symbols. **2** serving as a symbol.

sym·bol·ize (sim′bə-līz′) *vb.*
sym·bol·iz·ing, sym·bol·ized to be a symbol of; to stand for.

sym·me·try (sim′ə-trē) *n.* **sym·me·tries** exact similarity between two parts or halves. – *adj.* **sym·met·ri·cal** (sə-me′tri-kəl).

sym·pa·thet·ic (sim′pə-thet′ik) *adj.* **1** acting or done out of sympathy. **2** in keeping with your mood or feelings. – *adv.*
sym·pa·thet·i·cal·ly (sim′pə-thet′i-klē).

sym·pa·thy (sim′pə-thē) *n.* **sym·pa·thies 1** a deep and genuine understanding of the sadness or suffering of others. **2** loyal or approving support or agreement: *The hospital orderlies are on strike in sympathy with the nurses.*

sym·pa·thize (sim′pə-thīz′) *vb.*
sym·pa·thiz·ing, sym·pa·thized to feel or express sympathy.

sym·pho·ny (sim′fə-nē) *n.* **sym·pho·nies** a long musical work in several parts, or movements, played by a full orchestra.

symp·tom (sim′təm, simp′təm) *n.* an indication of the presence of illness: *A fever and rash are symptoms of chickenpox.*

syn·a·gogue (sin′ə-gäg′) *n.* a Jewish place of worship.

syn·od (sin′əd) *n.* a council of church officials.

syn·o·nym (sin′ə-nim′) *n.* a word having the same, or very nearly the same, meaning as another: *"Anger" and "fury" are synonyms.* – *adj.* **sy·non·y·mous** (sə-nän′ə-məs).

sy·nop·sis (sə-näp′səs) *n.* **sy·nop·ses** (sə-näp′sēz′) a brief outline or summary, as of the plot of a book.

syn·tax (sin′taks′) *n.* the positioning of words in a sentence and their relationship to each other.

syn·thet·ic (sin-thet′ik) *adj.* created artificially by combining chemical substances; not natural: *Nylon is a synthetic fiber.*

syphon. Same as **siphon.**

●**Sy·ri·a** (sîr′ē-ə). See Supplement, **Countries.**

sy·ringe (sə-rinj′) *n.* a medical instrument for injecting or drawing off liquid, consisting of a hollow cylinder with a plunger inside and a thin hollow needle attached. – *vb.*
sy·ring·ing, sy·ringed to inject using a syringe.

sy·rup (sîr′əp, sur′əp) *n.* the thick sweet liquid made by boiling sugar and fruit, or from the sap of the sugar maple tree.

sys·tem (sis′təm) *n.* **1** a set of connected or related parts forming a complex whole: *the human digestive system.* **2** an arrangement of mechanical or electrical parts functioning as a unit. **3** a way of working; a method. **4** society, or the institutions that control it.

sys·te·mat·ic (sis′tə-mat′ik) *adj.* **1** making use of a method. **2** methodical. – *adv.*
sys·te·mat·i·cal·ly (sis′tə-mat′i-klē) methodically and regularly.

Tt

tab (tab) *n.* a small flap or strip of material attached to an article for holding it, etc.

tab·by (tab'ē) *n.* tabbies (also tabby cat) a gray or brown cat with darker stripes.

tab·er·na·cle (tab'ər-nak'əl) *n.* a place of worship for various religious groups.

ta·ble (tā'bəl) *n.* 1 a piece of furniture consisting of a flat surface supported by legs. 2 a group of figures, etc. arranged in columns and rows. 3 a short list: *a table of contents.*

An elaborately carved and gilded French 16th-century table with an onyx top.

A nest of red and gold lacquered French tables of 1860. The set of tables of different sizes are designed to fit one over the other.

tablespoon *n.* 1 a large spoon used to serve food. 2 a spoon equal to half a fluid ounce.

tab·let (tab'lət) *n.* 1 a small solid measured amount of a medicine; a pill. 2 a pad of paper.

table tennis *n.* a game based on tennis, played on a table with small paddles and a light ball.

tab·loid (tab'loid') *n.* a newspaper with small pages and many photographs.

tack (tak) *n.* 1 a short nail with a sharp point and a broad flat head. 2 a long loose stitch used to hold material together while it is being sewn properly. 3 riding harness for a horse.

tack·le (tak'əl) *n.* 1 the equipment needed for a particular sport or occupation, as fishing. 2 the act of knocking someone to the ground. — *vb.* tack·ling, tack·led 1 to try to solve. 2 to knock to the ground, as in football.

tact (takt) *n.* the ability to deal with difficult situations without offending others.

tac·tics (tak'tiks) *n.* (*singular*) the method used to achieve an end or aim.

tad·pole (tad'pōl') *n.* the larva of the frog or toad, with a rounded body and long tail.

tag (tag) *n.* a piece of material, etc. that carries information about the object to which it is attached: *a price tag.*

tail (tāl) *n.* 1 the part of an animal's, bird's, or fish's body that sticks out from the lower end of the back. 2 the last or rear part: *the tail of the storm.* 3 (in *plural*) the reverse side of a coin.

tai·lor (tā'lər) *n.* a person who makes clothes to measure, especially for men.

● Tai·wan (tī'-wän') See Supplement, Countries.

● Ta·jik·i·stan (taj-ik'ə-stan'). See Supplement, Countries.

The letter *T*, like all the letters, has a long history. The earliest alphabets were taken and adapted by the Greeks. The Greek *beta*, when combined with the first letter, *aleph*, gives us the word alphabet.

The Greeks passed on their letters to the Romans, who developed the alphabet we use today, although they used only capital letters. Small letters developed in the A.D. 700s.

$+$

An early form of the letter T, used in the Middle East more than 3,000 years ago.

T

This letter was taken by the Greeks and became tau.

t

Over the years different versions of the letter T have been developed.

Tadpole comes from two Old English words, the first meaning "toad" and the second meaning "head."

PRONUNCIATION SYMBOLS

ə away	lemon	focus
a fat	oi	boy
ā fade	oo	foot
ä hot	ōō	moon
âr fair	ou	house
e met	th	think
ē mean	th	this
g get	u	cut
hw which	ur	hurt
i fin	w	witch
ī line	y	yes
îr near	yōō	music
ô often	yoor	pure
ō note	zh	vision

take (tāk) *vb.* **tak·ing, took** (took), **tak·en** (tā′kən) **1** to reach out for and grasp, lift, pull, etc.: *She took the book down from the shelf.* **2** to move, carry, or lead to another place: *They took him some grapes.* **3** to accept as true or valid: *I'll have to take her word for it.* **4** to commit yourself to: *He took her side in the argument.* **5** to need or require: *This job will take all day to finish.* **6** to use as a means of transportation: *He took the bus.* **7** to remove or borrow without permission: *He took her coat by mistake.* **8** to eat or drink: *Do you take sugar in coffee?* **9** to measure: *My mother took my temperature.* — *vb.* **take after** to be like a parent or relation in appearance or character. — *vb.* **take down** to make a written note or record of. — *vb.* **take off 1** to remove. **2** (of an aircraft) to leave the ground. **3** (*informal*) (of a scheme, product, etc.) to become popular and successful. — *vb.* **take on 1** to agree to do; to undertake. **2** to give employment to. **3** to challenge or compete against. **4** to acquire: *to take on a new meaning.* — *vb.* **take over** to assume control of something.

take·o·ver (tā′kō′vər) *n.* the act of taking control of something, especially a company.

Tanks were first used in World War I (from 1916), but their full potential was not realized until the success of the German tank-borne invasion of France in World War II.

The French NC2 (1931) had a special suspension. The British Vickers Medium Mark II (below) was one of the most successful tanks built between the two World Wars. It carried a crew of five.

The Americans developed the M-60 tank in the 1950s when they were faced with the Russian-built tanks of the North Korean army.

talc (talk) or **tal·cum** (tal′kəm) *n.* a soft gray or silver-white mineral used to make talcum powder, pottery, etc. **2** talcum powder.

tale (tāl) *n.* a story.

tal·ent (tal′ənt) *n.* a natural skill or ability, especially for art, music, etc.

talk (tôk) *vb.* **talk·ing, talked** to express ideas, feelings, and thoughts to someone in words; to have a conversation or discussion about something. — *n.* **1** a conversation or discussion. **2** (often in *plural*) a formal discussion or series of negotiations. **3** an informal lecture. — *n.* **talk·er.**

talk·a·tive (tô′kə-tiv) *adj.* talking a lot.

tall (tôl) *adj.* **1** of above average height. **2** having a stated height. **3** difficult to believe; unlikely.

Tal·mud (tal′mood′) *n.* the books containing the ancient JEWISH law. — *adj.* **Tal·mud·ic** (tal-mood′ik).

tal·on (tal′ən) *n.* a hooked claw.

tame (tām) *adj.* (of animals) used to living or working with people; not wild or dangerous. — *vb.* **tam·ing, tamed 1** to make used to living or working with people. **2** to subdue.

tam·per (tam′pər) *vb.* **tam·per·ing, tam·pered** to interfere or meddle.

tan (tan) *n.* **1** the brown color of the skin after exposure to the sun's ultraviolet rays. **2** a tawny brown color. — *vb.* **tan·ning, tanned 1** to become brown in the sun. **2** to convert into leather by soaking in a chemical solution.

tan·dem (tan′dəm) *n.* a type of bicycle for two people. — **in tandem 1** together. **2** together or in partnership with.

tan·ge·rine (tan′jə-rēn′) *n.* a variety of orange with a loose reddish-orange skin.

tan·gi·ble (tan′jə-bəl) *adj.* **1** able to be felt by touch. **2** real or definite.

tan·gle (tang′gəl) *n.* **1** an untidy, confused, or knotted state, for example of hair. **2** a confused or complicated state or situation. — *vb.* **tan·gling, tan·gled.**

tank (tangk) *n.* **1** a large container for holding, storing, or transporting liquids or gas. **2** a heavy military vehicle armed with guns.

tank·er (tank′kər) *n.* a ship, large truck, or aircraft that transports liquid, often fuel.

tan·trum (tan′trəm) *n.* a fit of childish bad temper.

● **Tan·za·ni·a** (tan′zə-nē′ə). See Supplement, **Countries**.

Tao·ism (dou′əst) *n.* a Chinese philosophical and religious system based on the teachings of Lao-Tzu (*c.* 500s B.C.) and others. − *n.* & *adj.* **Tao·ist**.

A statue of a Taoist founder, Lao-Tzu, riding an ox.

tap¹ (tap) *n.* **1** the sound made by a quick or light touch, knock, or blow. **2** a piece of metal attached to the bottom of a shoe. − *vb.* **tap·ping, tapped** to strike or knock lightly.

tap² (tap) *n.* a device attached to a pipe that can be turned to control the flow of liquid or gas; a faucet. − *vb.* **tap·ping, tapped 1** to let out liquid from by opening a tap. **2** to start using.

tap dance (tap′dans′) *n.* a rhythmical dance performed wearing shoes with taps.

tape (tāp) *n.* **1** a narrow strip of woven cloth used for tying, fastening, etc. **2** a magnetic tape. **3** a ribbon of thin paper or plastic with a sticky surface, used for fastening, sticking, etc. − *vb.* **tap·ing, taped 1** to fasten, tie, or seal with tape. **2** to record.

tape deck *n.* the part of a tape recorder that includes the motor and the playing heads for the tape.

tape mea·sure (tāp′mezh′ər) *n.* a length of plastic, cloth, or metal tape marked with inches or centimeters for measuring.

ta·per (tā′pər) *n.* a long thin candle. − *vb.* **ta·per·ing, ta·pered** to make or become gradually narrower toward one end. − *adj.* **ta·pered** and **ta·pe·ring**.

tape-re·cord (tāp′ri-kôrd′) *vb.* **tape-re·cord·ing, tape-re·cord·ed** to record on magnetic tape. − *n.* **tape re·cord·ing**.

tape re·cord·er (tāp′ri-kôr′dər) *n.* a machine that records sounds on magnetic tape and reproduces them when required.

tap·es·try (tap′ə-strē) *n.* **tap·es·tries** a thick cloth with an ornamental design or picture woven into it.

ta·pir (tā′pər) *n.* **tapir** or **tapirs** a large hoofed mammal with hooves and a snout, found in SOUTH AMERICA and MALAYSIA.

tar (tär) *n.* a thick dark sticky liquid obtained by distilling matter such as wood, peat, or coal. − *vb.* **tar·ring, tarred** to cover with tar.

ta·ran·tu·la (tə-ran′chə-lə) *n.* any of several large, hairy spiders, some of which are poisonous.

tar·get (tär′gət) *n.* **1** an object aimed at in shooting practice or competitions, especially a flat round board marked with circles. **2** a goal.

tar·iff (tar′əf) *n.* the tax to be paid on a particular type of goods imported or exported.

tar·nish (tär′nish) *vb.* **tar·nish·ing, tar·nished 1** (of metal) to become dull and stained. **2** to spoil or damage.

tart (tärt) *adj.* sharp or sour in taste.

tar·tar (tärt′ər) *n.* a hard deposit that forms on the teeth.

task (task) *n.* a piece of work to be done, especially one which is unpleasant or difficult.

tas·sel (tas′əl) *n.* a decoration consisting of a hanging bunch of threads.

taste (tāst) *vb.* **tast·ing, tast·ed 1** to discover the flavor of by taking a small amount into your mouth. **2** to be aware of or recognize the flavor of. − *n.* **1** the sense by which flavors are distinguished by the tongue and nose. **2** a first, usually brief experience of something.

tast·y (tās′tē) *adj.* **tast·i·er, tast·i·est** having a good flavor. − *adv.* **tast·i·ly** (tās′tə-lē).

tat·ter (tat′ər) *n.* (usually in *plural*) a torn, ragged shred of cloth, especially of clothing.

tat·tered (tat′ərd) *adj.* ragged or torn.

tat·too¹ (ta-tōō′) *vb.* **tat·too·ing, tat·tooed** to mark designs or pictures on by pricking the skin and putting in colored dyes.

tat·too² (ta-tōō′) *n.* **tattoos 1** a steady rhythmic drumming sound. **2** a signal given to soldiers

Tarantula is the name given to the large spiders variously called bird spiders or monkey spiders. The original tarantula was the wolf spider, found near the town of Taranto, in southern Italy.

and sailors to return to quarters at night.

taunt (tônt) *vb.* **taunt·ing, taunt·ed** to say unpleasant things to in a cruel and hurtful way; to tease. – *n.* a cruel or provoking remark.

Tau·rus (tôr′əs) *n.* See **zodiac**.

taut (tôt) *adj.* pulled or stretched tight.

tav·ern (tav′ərn) *n.* a bar or inn.

taw·dry (tô′drē) *adj.* **taw·dri·er, taw·dri·est** cheap and showy.

taw·ny (tô′nē) *n. & adj.* **taw·ni·er, taw·ni·est** yellowish-brown.

tax (taks) *n.* a contribution toward the expenses of a country, state, etc. paid from people's salaries, property, and from the sale of goods and services. – *vb.* **tax·ing, taxed** to impose a tax on. – *adj.* **tax·a·ble.**

tax·i (tak′sē) *n.* **taxis** (also **tax·i·cab** (tak′sē-kab′)) a car that may be hired with its driver to take passengers on usually short trips.

● **Tchai·kov·sky** (chī-kôf′skē), **Peter Ilyich** (1840-1893) was a Russian composer, perhaps most famous for his ballet music: *Swan Lake* and *The Nutcracker.*

tea (tē) *n.* **1** an evergreen shrub or tree originally grown in ASIA. **2** the dried leaves of this plant used to make a hot drink by pouring on boiling water. **3** a similar drink made from other plants: *mint tea.*

teach (tēch) *vb.* **teach·ing, taught** (tôt) **1** to give knowledge to; to instruct in a skill or help to learn. **2** to give lessons in a subject.

  teach·er (tē′chər) *n.* a person who teaches, especially professionally in a school.

  teach·ing (tē′ching) *n.* **1** the work of a teacher. **2** (often in *plural*) that which is taught.

teak (tēk) *n.* **1** a large tree which grows in ASIA. **2** its hard yellowish-brown wood.

team (tēm) *n.* **1** a group of people forming one side in a game. **2** a group of people working together. – *vb.* **team·ing, teamed** to form or make into a team for some common action.

tear¹ (tîr) *n.* a drop of clear salty liquid that moistens and washes the eye and eyelid and is often shed as a result of emotion.

tear² (târ) *vb.* **tear·ing, tore** (tôr, tōr), **torn** (tôrn, tōrn) **1** to pull or rip apart by force; to make a hole, etc. by ripping. **2** to remove or take by force; to force or persuade to leave. – *n.* a hole or damage caused by tearing.

Most tea today is grown in China, northern India, Sri Lanka, and east Africa. The tea plant is pruned to keep it small and bushy so that all its energy goes into making new leaves. Unpruned it could grow 30 ft. high.

tease (tēz) *vb.* **teas·ing, teased** to laugh at or make fun of unkindly.

tech·ni·cal (tek′ni-kəl) *adj.* **1** of or related to a particular science, art, or practical skill. **2** having or showing technique: *She plays with technical brilliance.*

tech·nique (tek-nēk′) *n.* **1** skill in the practical aspects of an art, etc. **2** the method of doing something.

tech·nol·o·gy (tek-näl′ə-jē) *n.* **tech·nol·o·gies 1** the branch of science that has a practical value, especially in industry. **2** the technical skills and achievements of a particular time in history, civilization, or group of people. – *adj.* **tech·no·log·i·cal** (tek′nə-läj′i-kəl).

te·di·ous (tēd′ē-əs) *adj.* monotonous.

tee-shirt (tē′shurt′) *n.* Same as **T-shirt.**

teem¹ (tēm) *vb.* **teem·ing, teemed** to be full of; to be present in large numbers.

teem² (tēm) *vb.* **teem·ing, teemed** (of water, especially rain) to pour in torrents.

teen (tēn) *n.* **1** (in *plural*) the years of a person's life between the ages of 13 and 19. **2** (in *plural*) the numbers from 13 to 19.

teen·ag·er (tē′nā′jər) *n.* a person aged between 13 and 19.

teethe (tēth) *vb.* **teeth·ing, teethed** (of a baby) to grow the first teeth. – *n.* **teeth·ing.**

tel·e·com·mu·ni·ca·tions (tel′ə-kə-myōō′ni-kā′shənz) *n.* (*singular*) the technology of sending information or messages over a distance by telephone, television cable, etc.

tel·e·graph (tel′ə-graf′) *n.* a system of sending messages or information through electrical impulses along a wire.

tel·e·phone (tel′ə-fōn′) *n.* an instrument that allows a person to speak to someone in a different place by transmitting sound in the form of electrical signals. – *vb.* **tel·e·phon·ing, tel·e·phoned** to speak to someone by telephone.

tel·e·scope (tel′ə-skōp′) *n.* a tube-shaped instrument with a combination of lenses and mirrors inside that make distant objects seem closer and larger.

tel·e·vi·sion (tel′ə-vizh′ən) *n.* **1** the sending of pictures and sound in the form of radio waves to be reproduced on a screen in a person's home, etc. **2** (also **television set**) an apparatus with a screen and speakers which is able to receive radio waves and reproduce them in the form of pictures and sounds.

Some of the major technological changes of the last 150 years have been in **telecommunications** — the long distance communication by telephone, telegraph, radio, television, and telex. The electric telegraph was developed in the 1850s; the first electric telephone was made by Alexander Bell in 1876; and in 1926, John Logie Baird demonstrated his television set. Today most telephone systems and cable TV use optical fibers to carry signals in the form of light rays fired along each fiber by a laser.

Telecommunications 18th-century style. After 1794, coded messages could be sent by the semaphore telegraph invented by the French engineer, Claude Chappe. Movable metal arms on top of towers sent coded messages great distances.

(Above) *An early telephone; it carried a weak electrical wave over long distances.*

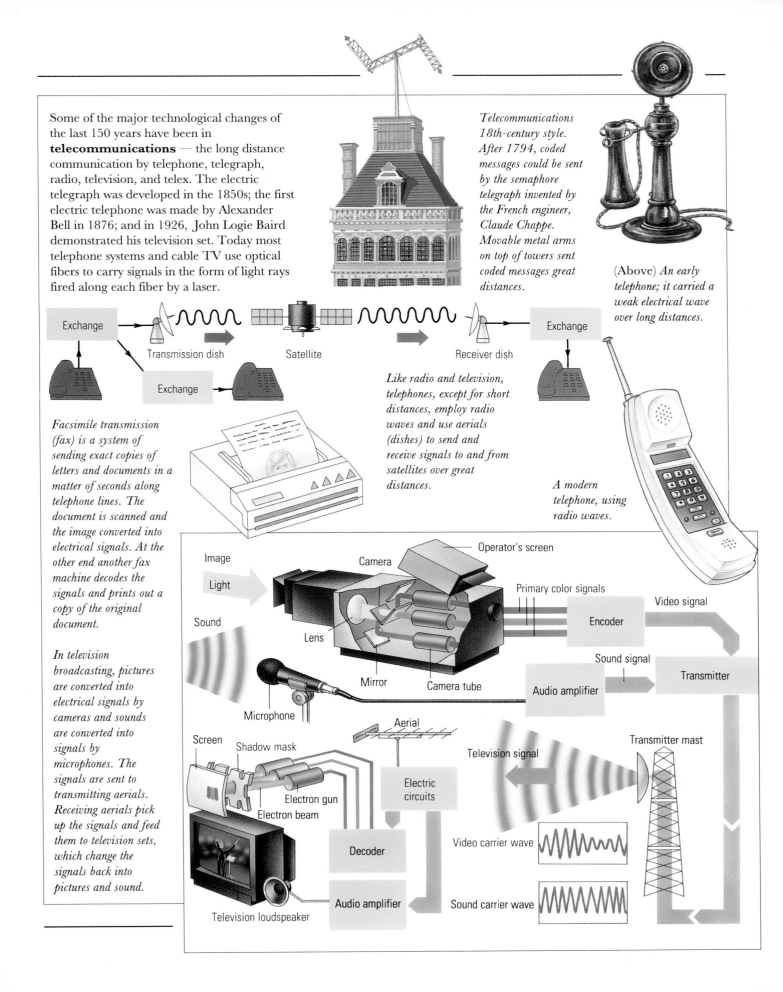

Exchange — Transmission dish — Satellite — Receiver dish — Exchange

Exchange

Like radio and television, telephones, except for short distances, employ radio waves and use aerials (dishes) to send and receive signals to and from satellites over great distances.

A modern telephone, using radio waves.

Facsimile transmission (fax) is a system of sending exact copies of letters and documents in a matter of seconds along telephone lines. The document is scanned and the image converted into electrical signals. At the other end another fax machine decodes the signals and prints out a copy of the original document.

In television broadcasting, pictures are converted into electrical signals by cameras and sounds are converted into signals by microphones. The signals are sent to transmitting aerials. Receiving aerials pick up the signals and feed them to television sets, which change the signals back into pictures and sound.

Image / Light — Camera — Operator's screen — Primary color signals — Video signal

Sound — Lens — Mirror — Camera tube — Encoder

Microphone — Audio amplifier — Sound signal — Transmitter

Screen — Shadow mask — Aerial — Television signal — Transmitter mast

Electron gun — Electron beam — Electric circuits

Decoder — Video carrier wave

Audio amplifier — Sound carrier wave

Television loudspeaker

PRONUNCIATION SYMBOLS

ə	*away*	lemon	focus
a	fat	oi	boy
ā	fade	oo	foot
ä	hot	ōō	moon
âr	fair	ou	house
e	met	th	think
ē	mean	th	this
g	get	u	cut
hw	which	ur	hurt
i	fin	w	witch
ī	line	y	yes
îr	near	yōō	music
ô	often	yoor	pure
ō	note	zh	vision

tell (tel) *vb.* **tell·ing, told** (tōld) **1** to give information to in speech or writing. **2** to order, command, or instruct. **3** to distinguish: *I can't tell copper from bronze.*

tell·ing (tel'ing) *adj.* having a marked effect.

tem·per (tem'pər) *n.* **1** a characteristic state of mind; mood or humor: *She has an even temper.* **2** a state of uncontrolled anger.

tem·per·a·ment (tem'prə-mənt) *n.* a person's natural character which governs the way he or she behaves and thinks.

tem·per·a·men·tal (tem'prə-men'təl) *adj.* given to extreme changes of mood.

tem·per·ate (tem'pə-rət) *adj.* **1** moderate and restrained in behavior. **2** (of a climate or region) having temperatures which are mild, and neither extremely hot nor extremely cold.

tem·per·a·ture (tem'pər-choor', tem'prə-chər) *n.* **1** the degree of hotness, for example of air or water as measured by a thermometer. **2** the level of body heat in a person: *The doctor took his temperature.* **3** a level of body heat that is higher than normal: *She has a temperature.*

tem·pest (tem'pəst) *n.* a violent storm with very strong winds.

tem·ple¹ (tem'pəl) *n.* a building used for worship by people in various religions.

The Temple of Heaven, Beijing, China, was built in 1751 to a traditional Chinese design.

temple² (tem'pəl) *n.* either of the flat parts of the head at the side of the forehead.

tem·po (tem'pō) *n.* **tempos** or **tem·pi** (tem'pē) **1** the speed at which a piece of music is played. **2** rate or speed.

tem·po·rar·y (tem'pə-rer'ē) *adj.* lasting, used, etc. for a limited period of time only.

tempt (tempt) *vb.* **tempt·ing, tempt·ed 1** to try to persuade to do something, especially something wrong. **2** to attract or entice.

temp·ta·tion (temp-tā'shən) *n.* **1** the state of being tempted. **2** something that tempts.

tempt·ing (temp'ting) *adj.* attractive; enticing.

ten (ten) *n.* the number or figure 10.

ten·ant (ten'ənt) *n.* a person who pays rent to another for the use of property or land.

tend¹ (tend) *vb.* **tend·ing, tend·ed** to take care of; to look after: *She tended her horse at the stables.*

tend² (tend) *vb.* **tend·ing, tend·ed** to be likely or inclined to: *I tend to fall asleep after lunch.*

ten·den·cy (ten'dən-sē) *n.* **ten·den·cies** a likelihood of acting or thinking a certain way.

ten·der (ten'dər) *adj.* **1** (of meat) easily chewed or cut. **2** easily damaged; sensitive: *She has a tender heart.*

ten·don (ten'dən) *n.* a cord of strong tissue that joins a muscle to a bone.

ten·e·ment (ten'ə-mənt) *n.* an apartment building that is poorly taken care of.

ten·et (ten'ət) *n.* a belief or opinion.

●**Ten·nes·see** (ten'ə-sē'). See Supplement, **U.S.A.**

ten·nis (ten'əs) *n.* a game in which two players or two pairs of players use rackets to hit a light ball across a net on a rectangular court.

ten·or (ten'ər) *n.* a singing voice of the highest normal range for an adult man.

tense¹ (tens) *n.* the form of a verb that shows whether the time of its action is in the past, present, or future.

tense² (tens) *adj.* feeling worried or nervous, showing mental strain. — *vb.* **tens·ing, tensed** to make or become taut and stiff: *He tensed his muscles, ready to throw the ball.*

tent (tent) *n.* a shelter made of material supported by poles or a frame and fastened to the ground with ropes and pegs, that can be taken down and carried from place to place.

ten·ta·cle (tent'ə-kəl) *n.* a long thin flexible organ used by an animal to feel, grasp, and feed: *An octopus has eight tentacles.*

tenth (tenth, tentth) *n.* **1** one of ten equal parts. **2** the last of ten; the next after the ninth.

te·pee or **tee·pee** (tē'pē') *n.* a NATIVE AMERICAN tent formed of skins stretched over a cone-shaped frame of poles.

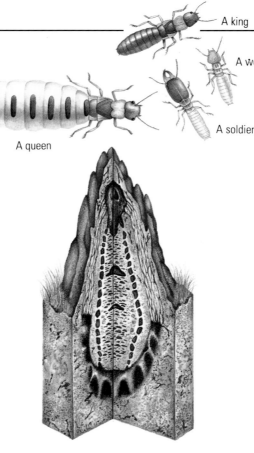

A king

A worker

A soldier

A queen

term (turm) *n.* **1** a word or expression, especially one used with a precise meaning in a specialized field: *That is a scientific term.* **2** (in *plural*) a particular way of speaking or describing something. **3** (in *plural*) a relationship between people or countries: *They are on good terms.* **4** one of the divisions into which the school year is divided.

ter·mi·nal (tur′mən-l) *adj.* **1** (of an illness) causing death; fatal. **2** forming or occurring at the end or boundary of something. – *n.* **1** an arrival and departure building at an airport. **2** a train or bus station. **3** a device consisting usually of a keyboard and screen, which allows a user to use a distant computer.

ter·mite (tur′mīt′) *n.* a pale-colored antlike insect which feeds on wood.

ter·race (ter′əs) *n.* **1** a series of raised level banks of earth, like large steps on the side of a hill, used for growing crops. **2** a paved area by the side of a house.

ter·ra cot·ta (ter′ə-kät′ə) *n.* an unglazed brownish-orange pottery. – *adj.* made of, or the color of, terra cotta.

ter·ra·pin (ter′ə-pən) *n.* any of several North American fresh or partly saltwater turtles.

ter·ri·ble (ter′ə-bəl) *adj.* **1** (*informal*) very bad: *He is a terrible singer.* **2** (*informal*) very great; extreme: *She is a terrible gossip.* **3** causing fear.

ter·rif·ic (tə-rif′ik) *adj.* (*informal*) **1** marvelous; excellent. **2** very great or powerful.

ter·ri·fy (ter′ə-fī′) *vb.* **ter·ri·fies, ter·ri·fy·ing, ter·ri·fied** to make very frightened; to fill with terror. – *adj.* **terrified**.

ter·ri·to·ry (ter′ə-tôr′ē, ter′ə-tōr′ē) *n.* **ter·ri·to·ries** **1** an area of land under the control of a ruler, government, or state. **2** an area that a bird or animal treats as its own.

ter·ror (ter′ər) *n.* very great fear or dread.

ter·ror·ism (ter′ə-riz′əm) *n.* the organized use of violence for political purposes.

test (test) *n.* an examination or trial of a person's or thing's qualities, abilities, etc.

tes·ta·ment (tes′tə-mənt) *n.* **1** a will. **2 Testament** either of the two main divisions of the BIBLE, the **Old Testament** or the **New Testament**.

tes·ti·cle (tes′ti-kəl) *n.* either of the two glands in the male body that produce sperm.

tes·ti·fy (tes′tə-fī′) *vb.* **tes·ti·fies, tes·ti·fy·ing, tes·ti·fied** **1** to give evidence in court. **2** to declare solemnly.

tes·ti·mo·ny (tes′tə-mō′nē) *n.*

These towers of mud are termites' nests. Inside are many tunnels where the termites live. Each colony has a king and queen. Thousands of small white workers dig the tunnels and find food and water. There are also soldier termites. They have huge heads and jaws to defend the nest from enemies. New males and females periodically swarm from the nests to mate and form new nests.

tes·ti·mo·nies **1** a statement made under oath, especially in a law court. **2** evidence.

teth·er (teth′ər) *n.* a rope or chain for tying an animal to a post.

●**Tex·as** (tek′səs). See Supplement, **U.S.A**.

text (tekst) *n.* the main body of printed words in a book rather than the pictures, etc.

text·book (tekst′book′) *n.* a book containing information on a certain subject.

tex·tile (tek′stəl, tek′stīl′) *n.* any cloth or fabric.

tex·ture (teks′chər) *n.* the way the surface of a material or substance feels when touched.

Thai (tī) *n.* **1** an inhabitant of THAILAND. **2** the main language of THAILAND. – *adj.* of, or relating to, THAILAND.

●**Thai·land** (tī′lənd). See Supplement, **Countries**.

●**Thames** (temz) a river in southern ENGLAND, flowing through London to the North Sea.

than (than, thən) *conj.* **1** used to introduce the second part of a comparison: *She is older than he*

Terra cotta is Italian, and literally means "cooked earth." The English use of the word to describe brownish-orange unglazed pottery dates from the 1700s.

is. **2** used to introduce the second of two alternatives: *I would rather swim than play ball.*

thank (thangk) *vb.* **thank·ing, thanked 1** to express gratitude to: *She thanked him for his help.* **2** to hold responsible for: *You have only yourself to thank for your failure.* — *n.* (in *plural*) an expression of gratitude.

thanks·giv·ing (thangks-giv′ing) *n.* **1** a formal act of giving thanks, especially to God. **2** (**Thanksgiving**, also **Thanksgiving Day**) a public holiday occurring on the fourth Thursday in November in the UNITED STATES and the second Monday in October in CANADA.

Wampanoag Native Americans joined the Pilgrims for the first Thanksgiving in 1621. Without their advice on farming and fishing, the Plymouth settlement may well not have survived.

● The first Thanksgiving Day was celebrated in North America by the PILGRIMS in 1621, the year after they had settled there. The Pilgrims and the Native Americans who gave them help in the New World gathered together for a feast of celebration.

that (that) *adj.* **those** (thōz) indicating the thing, person, or idea already mentioned or understood: *I would like that cake, please.* — (usually (that)) *relative pron.* used instead of **which, who,** or **whom** to introduce a relative clause. — *conj.* used to introduce a clause showing reason, purpose, consequence, a result, or expressing a wish or desire: *She spoke so quickly that no one could understand.*

thatch (thach) *n.* a roof covering of straw and reeds.

thaw (thô) *vb.* **thaw·ing, thawed 1** (of snow or ice) to melt. **2** (of anything frozen) to defrost.

the (thə, thē) the definite article, used to refer to a particular person or thing, or group of people or things.

the·a·ter or **the·a·tre** (thē′ət-ər, thē′āt′ər) *n.* **1** a building specially designed for the presenting of plays, movies, etc. **2** an area or place where something happens.

theft (theft) *n.* stealing.

their (thâr) *adj.* of, or belonging to, them.

theirs (thârz) *pron.* a person or thing that belongs to them: *That car is theirs.*

them (thəm, them) *pron.* people or things already mentioned or spoken about.

them·selves (thəm-selvz′, them-selvz′) *pron.* **1** the reflexive form of **them** and **they. 2** used for emphasis: *They did it themselves.*

theme (thēm) *n.* **1** the subject of a discussion, speech, or piece of writing. **2** a short melody that forms the basis of a piece of music.

then (then) *adv.* **1** at that time. **2** soon or immediately after that: *She looked at him, then turned away.* **3** in that case; that being so.

the·ol·o·gy (thē-äl′ə-jē) *n.* **the·ol·o·gies** the study of God and religion.

the·o·ry (thē′ə-rē, thir′ē) *n.* **the·o·ries 1** a series of ideas and general principles which explain some aspect: *the theory of relativity.* **2** an idea that has not yet been proved.

ther·a·py (ther′ə-pē) *n.* **ther·a·pies** the treatment of illness without using drugs or surgery. — *n.* **ther·a·pist** (ther′ə-pəst).

there (thâr) *adv.* **1** at, in, or to a place or position. **2** used to begin a sentence: *There are no mistakes in this.* — *n.* that place or point.

there·fore (thâr′fôr′) *adv.* for that reason.

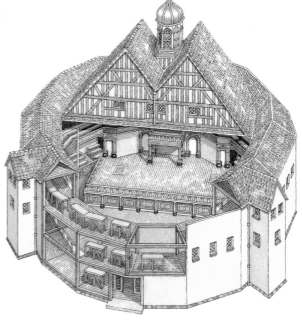

The Globe, one of London's first public theaters. Many of Shakespeare's plays were performed here.

ther·mal (thur′məl) *adj.* of, related to, or causing heat: *a thermal blanket.*

ther·mom·e·ter (ther-mäm′ət-ər) *n.* an instrument for measuring temperature.

A maximum thermometer contains mercury. As the temperature rises, the mercury expands and pushes a metal index up the tube, which remains there. An index in the minimum thermometer (containing alcohol) records the lowest temperature.

Minimum thermometer — Metal index — Maximum thermometer — Mercury — Alcohol

Many thermostats contain a coiled bimetallic strip made of two different metals welded together which expand and contract at different rates causing the strip to bend. Here a tube of mercury is used to complete the circuit between the contacts. The circuit is broken when the tube tips the mercury away.

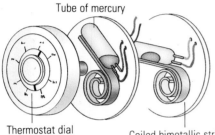

Tube of mercury — Thermostat dial — Coiled bimetallic strip

ther·mo·stat (thur′mə-stat′) *n.* an apparatus that automatically controls temperature.

the·sau·rus (thi-sôr′əs) *n.* **the·sau·ri** (thi-sôr′ī′) or **the·sau·rus·es** a book that lists words in groups according to their meaning.

they (thā) *pron.* the people, animals, or things already spoken about or being indicated.

they'd (thād) **1** they had. **2** they would.

they'll (thāl) **1** they will. **2** they shall.

they're (thâr) they are.

they've (thāv) they have.

thick (thik) *adj.* **1** having a large distance between opposite sides. **2** having a certain distance between opposite sides: *The rope is three inches thick.* **3** (of liquids) containing a lot of solid matter: *thick soup.* **4** grouped close together; dense: *He has nice thick hair.*

thick·ness (thik′nəs) *n.* **1** the state or degree of being thick. **2** a layer.

thick·et (thik′ət) *n.* a dense mass of bushes.

thief (thēf) *n.* **thieves** (thēvz) a person who steals things.

thieve *vb.* **thiev·ing, thieved** to steal.

thigh (thī) *n.* the fleshy part of the leg between the knee and hip.

thim·ble (thim′bəl) *n.* a small metal or plastic cap worn on the finger to protect it and push the needle when sewing.

thin (thin) *adj.* **thin·ner, thin·nest** **1** having a short distance between opposite sides. **2** having a small thickness; narrow or fine. **3** (of people or animals) not fat; lean. **4** (of liquids) containing very little solid matter. **5** set far apart; not dense or crowded: *thin hair.*

thing (thing) *n.* **1** any object, rather than an animal or a human being, especially one that cannot move. **2** an event, affair, or circumstance: *Things are getting out of hand.* **3** an obsession or interest: *She has a thing about horses.*

think (thingk) *vb.* **think·ing, thought** (thôt) **1** to have ideas in the mind about a subject, person, etc. **2** to consider, judge, or believe: *People once thought the world was flat.* **3** to consider: *We must think of the children first.* **4** to remember: *I couldn't think of his name.*

third (thurd) *adj.* **1** coming next after second in time, place, or order; last of three. **2** being one of three equal parts. — *n.* one of three equal parts. — *adv.* in the third position.

Third World *n.* a term sometimes used to describe the poorer countries of AFRICA, ASIA, and LATIN AMERICA.

thirst (thurst) *n.* the need to drink something. — *vb.* **thirst·ing, thirst·ed** to have a great desire or longing for.

thirst·y (thur′stē) *adj.* **thirst·i·er, thirst·i·est** **1** needing or wanting to drink. **2** causing thirst.

thir·teen (thurt-tēn′, thur-tēn′) *n.* the number or figure 13. — *n., adj., & adv.* **thir·teenth** (thurt-tēnth′, thur-tēnth′).

thir·ty (thurt′ē) *n.* **thirt·ies** the number or figure 30. — *n., adj., & adv.* **thirt·i·eth.**

this (this) *pron.* **these** (thēz) **1** a person, animal, thing, or idea already mentioned or about to be mentioned: *This is my house.* **2** the present time or place. — *adj.* the person, animal, thing, or idea which is nearby, especially closer than something else: *Do you want this book or that one?*

this·tle (this′əl) *n.* any of several plants with prickly purple flowers.

●**Thom·as** (täm′əs), **Dylan** (1914-1953) was a

Thesaurus is from a Greek word meaning "treasury," and was used in the early 1800s to describe a treasury of knowledge or words.

The spear thistle — one of several varieties of this vigorous plant. To gardeners the thistle is a troublesome weed. To the Scots it is their national emblem.

Welsh writer, perhaps best known for *A Child's Christmas in Wales.*

● **Thom·as** (täm′əs), **Saint**, also called "doubting Thomas," was one of the apostles of Jesus.

thong (thông) *n.* a narrow strip of leather, often used to fasten something.

tho·rax (thôr′aks′, thōr′aks′) *n.* **tho·rax·es** or **tho·ra·ces** (thôr′ə-sēz′, thōr′ə-sēz′) the part of the body between the head and abdomen, in humans the chest, and in insects the middle section that bears the wings and legs.

A threshing machine of 1860. It would have been powered by a steam engine standing on the edge of the field.

● **Tho·reau** (thə-rō′, thôr′ō), **Henry David** (1817-1862) was an American philosopher, best known for *Walden.*

thorn (thôrn) *n.* a hard, sharp point sticking out from the stem or branch of certain plants.

thorn·y (thôr′nē) *adj.* **thorn·i·er, thorn·i·est** 1 full of or covered with thorns. 2 difficult.

thor·ough (thur′ō) *adj.* 1 (of a person) extremely careful and attending to every detail. 2 carried out with great care and great attention to detail: *a thorough cleaning.*

thor·ough·bred (thur′ə-bred′) *n.* an animal, as a horse or dog, bred from the best specimens carefully chosen.

thor·ough·fare (thur′ə-fâr′) *n.* a public road.

though (thō) *conj.* 1 despite the fact that: *She ate her dessert even though she was full.* 2 if: *He looked as though he would cry.* 3 and yet; but: *I like the new car, though not as much as the old one.* – *adv.* however; nevertheless.

thought (thôt). See **think.** – *n.* 1 an idea or opinion. 2 the act of thinking. 3 serious and careful consideration.

thought·ful (thôt′fəl) *adj.* 1 appearing to be

thinking deeply; reflective. 2 showing careful or serious thought: *a thoughtful review of the book.* 3 thinking of other people; considerate.

thought·less (thôt′ləs) *adj.* inconsiderate.

thous·and (thou′zənd) *n.* **thousands** or (after another number) **thousand** the number or figure 1,000. – *n. & adj.* **thou·sandth** (thou′zəntth).

thrash (thrash) *vb.* **thrash·ing, thrashed** 1 to beat soundly. 2 to defeat thoroughly. 3 to move around violently or wildly.

thread (thred) *n.* 1 a fine strand of silk, cotton, or wool. 2 the spiral ridge around a screw or on the lid of a container. 3 a connecting element or theme in a story, argument, etc. – *vb.* **thread·ing, thread·ed** to pass a thread through the eye of: *to thread a needle.*

threat (thret) *n.* 1 a warning that someone is going to hurt or punish someone. 2 a sign that something unpleasant is about to happen.

threat·en (thret′n) *vb.* **threat·en·ing, threat·ened** 1 to make a threat to. 2 to seem likely to happen: *A storm was threatening.*

three (thrē) *n.* the number or figure 3.

three-di·men·sion·al (thrē′də-men′shə-nəl) *adj.* having or appearing to have three dimensions: height, width, depth.

thresh (thresh) *vb.* **thresh·ing, threshed** to beat stalks of cereal to extract the grain.

thres·hold (thresh′hōld′) *n.* 1 any doorway or entrance. 2 a starting-point.

thrift·y (thrif′tē) *adj.* **thrift·i·er, thrift·i·est** showing thrift; economical.

thrill (thril) *vb.* **thrill·ing, thrilled** to feel a sudden strong sensation of excitement, emotion, or pleasure.

thrive (thrīv) *vb.* **thriv·ing, throve** (thrōv) or **thrived** 1 to grow strong and healthy. 2 to prosper and be successful. – *adj.* **thriv·ing.**

throat (thrōt) *n.* 1 the top part of the passage that leads from the mouth and nose to the stomach. 2 the front part of the neck.

throb (thräb) *vb.* **throb·bing, throbbed** to beat or vibrate with a strong, regular rhythm.

throm·bo·sis (thräm-bō′səs) *n.* **throm·bo·ses** (thräm-bō′sēz) the forming of a clot in a blood vessel which prevents the flow of blood around the body.

throne (thrōn) *n.* the ceremonial chair of a king, queen, or bishop, used on official occasions.

throng (thrông) *n.* a large crowd of people. – *vb.* **throng·ing, thronged** to crowd or fill.

through (thrōō) *prep.* 1 going from one side of

something to the other: *A road ran through the village.* **2** from the beginning to the end of; during: *We stayed in Florida through the summer.* **3** up to and including: *He worked Tuesday through Thursday.* **4** because of: *He lost his job through stupidity.* **5** by way of; by: *They are related through marriage.* – *adv.* **1** into and out of; from one side to the other. **2** from the beginning to the end. **3** completely: *I was soaked through.*

throw (thrō) *vb.* **throw·ing, threw** (thrōō), **thrown** (thrōn) **1** to hurl through the air with force, especially with a rapid forward movement of the hand and arm. **2** to put into a certain condition, especially suddenly: *My words threw them into confusion.* **3** to put on quickly and carelessly: *to throw on clothes.* – *n.* **1** an act of throwing. **2** the distance something is thrown.

thrust (thrust) *vb.* **thrust·ing, thrust** to push suddenly and violently.

thumb (thum) *n.* the short thick finger on the side of the hand.

thun·der (thun′dər) *n.* **1** a deep rumbling or loud cracking sound heard after a flash of lightning. **2** any loud deep rumbling noise.

Thurs·day (thurz′dē, thurz′dā) *n.* the day between Wednesday and Friday.

thus (thus) *adv.* **1** in the way or manner shown: *You must tie the knot thus.* **2** to this degree, amount, or distance: *You have come thus far.* **3** therefore; accordingly.

thyme (tīm) *n.* any of several herbs and shrubs.

●**Ti·bet** (tə-bet′) is a country in central ASIA which was taken over by CHINA in 1959.

Ti·bet·an (tə-bet′n) *n.* **1** an inhabitant of TIBET. **2** the main language of TIBET. – *adj.* of, or relating to, TIBET.

tick¹ (tik) *n.* **1** a regular tapping or clicking sound, such as that made by a watch or clock. **2** a small spiderlike creature that feeds on the blood of animals. – *vb.* **tick·ing, ticked** to make a regular clicking sound.

tick² (tik) *n.* any of several bloodsucking insects living on the skin of some animals.

tick·et (tik′ət) *n.* a printed piece of paper or card which shows that the holder has paid money for a fare or for admission.

tick·le (tik′əl) *vb.* **tick·ling, tick·led** to touch a part of the body lightly in order to produce a tingling sensation and laughter.

tid·al (tīd′l) *adj.* caused or affected by tides.

tidal wave *n.* an enormous wave caused by movement of the sea floor.

tide (tīd′ē) *n.* **1** the regular rise and fall in the level of the sea. **2** a sudden or marked trend.

The Bay of Fundy, Canada boasts the world's greatest spring tidal range — 48 ft. between high and low tides.

The highest **tides**, spring tides, occur when the Earth, Moon, and Sun are in a straight line. The lowest tides, neap tides, occur when the Moon, Earth, and Sun form a right angle.

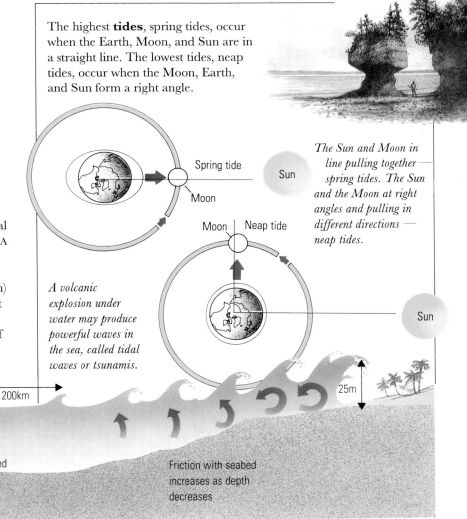

The Sun and Moon in line pulling together — spring tides. The Sun and the Moon at right angles and pulling in different directions — neap tides.

Spring tide

Sun

Moon

Moon   Neap tide

Sun

A volcanic explosion under water may produce powerful waves in the sea, called tidal waves or tsunamis.

200km

25m

Volcanic eruption

Seabed

Friction with seabed increases as depth decreases

ti·dy (tīd′ē) *adj.* **ti·di·er, ti·di·est 1** neat and in good order. **2** methodical. – *vb.* **ti·dies, ti·dy·ing, ti·died** to make neat.

tie (tī) *vb.* **ty·ing, tied 1** to fasten with a string, ribbon, rope, etc. using a bow or knot. **2** to have the same score or final position as another competitor in a contest. – *n.* **1** a narrow strip of material worn around the neck under a shirt collar and tied in a knot or bow at the front. **2** a link or bond: *strong ties of friendship*. **3** a competition in which the result is an equal final score or position for each competitor. **4** one of the horizontal wooden beams onto which railroad tracks are laid.

tier (tîr) *n.* any series of levels placed one above the other, for example of seats in a theater.

ti·ger (tī′gər) *n.* a very large wild cat with a striped tawny coat, found in ASIA.

The tiger is the largest member of the cat family. Males have been found up to 10 ft. in length.

tiger lily *n.* **tiger lilies** a tall lily with orange flowers spotted with black.

tight (tīt) *adj.* **1** fitting very closely: *These shoes are too tight*. **2** stretched so as not to be loose; tense; taut. **3** fixed or held firmly in place: *a tight knot*. **4** strictly and carefully controlled: *She keeps a tight rein on her emotions*. **5** (of a contest or game) closely or evenly fought. **6** (of a schedule, timetable, etc.) not allowing much time.

tight·en (tīt′n) *vb.* **tight·en·ing, tight·ened** to make or become tighter.

tight-fist·ed (tīt′fis′təd) *adj.* mean and ungenerous with money.

tight-knit (tīt′nit′) *adj.* closely organized or united.

tight·rope (tīt′rōp′) *n.* a tightly stretched rope or wire on which acrobats balance.

tights (tīts) *n.* (*plural*) a close-fitting garment covering the legs and body to the waist.

ti·gress (tī′grəs) *n.* a female tiger.

tile (tīl) *n.* a flat thin slab of clay, cork, or linoleum, used to cover roofs, floors, walls, etc. – *vb.* **til·ing, tiled** to cover with tiles.

till[1] (til) *prep.* up to the time of: *Wait till tomorrow*. – *conj.* up to the time when: *Go on till you reach the station*.

till[2] (til) *n.* a container or drawer in a store in which money taken from customers is put.

till[3] (til) *vb.* **till·ing, tilled** to prepare for growing crops: *to till land*.

till·er (til′ər) *n.* the lever used to turn the rudder of a boat.

tilt (tilt) *vb.* **tilt·ing, tilt·ed** to slope; to put in a slanting position. – *n.* a slant; a sloping position or angle.

tim·ber (tim′bər) *n.* **1** wood, especially prepared for building or making furniture. **2** a wooden beam in the framework of a ship or house.

tim·bered (tim′bərd) *adj.* **1** built completely or partly of wood. **2** having many trees.

tim·bre (tam′bər, tim′bər) *n.* the particular quality and characteristics of a sound produced by a musical instrument or voice.

time (tīm) *n.* **1** the continuous passing of minutes, days, years, etc. **2** a particular point in time expressed in hours and minutes, or days, months, and years: *The time is ten o'clock*. **3** a point or period which is marked by some event or some particular characteristic: *She was very thin at the time of her marriage*. **4** the period required or available for some particular activity: *How much time do we need to rehearse?* **5** one of a number or series of occasions: *I have been to Spain three times*. – *vb.* **tim·ing, timed 1** to measure the time taken by: *to time a race*. **2** to arrange or choose a time for. – **at times** occasionally; sometimes. – **behind the times** out-of-date; old-fashioned. – **for the time being** meanwhile; for the moment. – **from time to time** occasionally; sometimes. – **have no time for** to have no interest in or patience with. – **in no time** very quickly. – **take one's time** to not hurry.

time bomb *n.* a bomb that has been set to explode at a particular time.

time-hon·ored (tīm′än′ərd) *adj.* respected and upheld because of being a custom or tradition.

time·less (tīm′ləs) *adj.* not belonging to or typical of any particular time or date; ageless.

time·ly (tīm′lē) *adj.* coming at a suitable moment. – *n.* **time·li·ness**.

time-out (tīm′out′) *n.* a brief period of time for

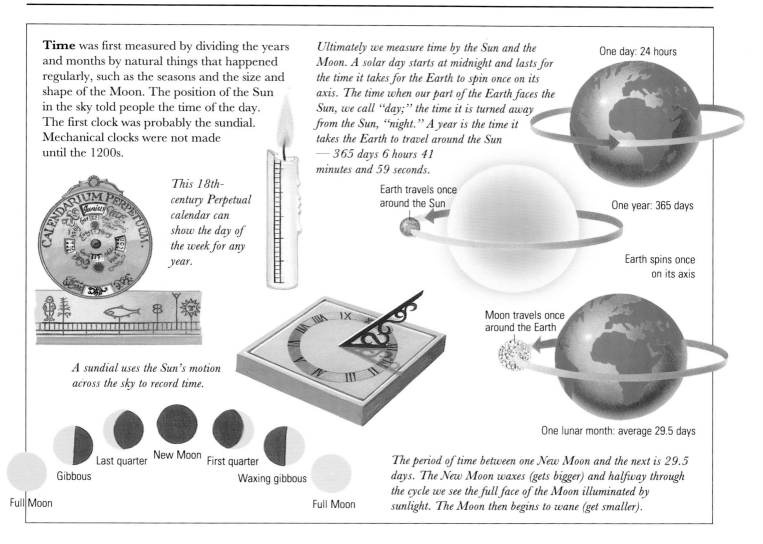

Time was first measured by dividing the years and months by natural things that happened regularly, such as the seasons and the size and shape of the Moon. The position of the Sun in the sky told people the time of the day. The first clock was probably the sundial. Mechanical clocks were not made until the 1200s.

This 18th-century Perpetual calendar can show the day of the week for any year.

A sundial uses the Sun's motion across the sky to record time.

Ultimately we measure time by the Sun and the Moon. A solar day starts at midnight and lasts for the time it takes for the Earth to spin once on its axis. The time when our part of the Earth faces the Sun, we call "day;" the time it is turned away from the Sun, "night." A year is the time it takes the Earth to travel around the Sun — 365 days 6 hours 41 minutes and 59 seconds.

One day: 24 hours

One year: 365 days

Earth spins once on its axis

Earth travels once around the Sun

Moon travels once around the Earth

One lunar month: average 29.5 days

Gibbous Last quarter New Moon First quarter Waxing gibbous

Full Moon Full Moon

The period of time between one New Moon and the next is 29.5 days. The New Moon waxes (gets bigger) and halfway through the cycle we see the full face of the Moon illuminated by sunlight. The Moon then begins to wane (get smaller).

rest in a sport or other occupation.

time·piece (tīm′pēs′) *n.* a watch or clock.

tim·er (tī′mər) *n.* a device like a clock which switches an appliance on or off at preset times.

times (tīmz) *prep.* multiplied by: *Three times two is six.*

time·ta·ble (tīm′tā′bəl) *n.* **1** a list of the departure and arrival times of trains, buses, etc. **2** a plan showing the order of events.

tim·ing (tī′ming) *n.* the skill of coordinating actions and events to achieve the best effect.

tim·id (tim′əd) *adj.* easily frightened or alarmed; nervous; shy.

tin (tin) *n.* a soft silvery-white metallic element (symbol **Sn**), which is used in alloys.

tinge (tinj) *n.* a trace or hint of a color.

tin·gle (ting′gəl) *vb.* **tin·gling, tin·gled** to feel a prickling or slightly stinging sensation. – *adj.* **tin·gling** or **tin·gly** (ting′glē), **tin·gli·er,** **tin·gli·est.**

tin·ker (ting′kər) *vb.* **tin·ker·ing, tin·kered** to fiddle with machinery, etc., especially to try to improve it.

tin·kle (ting′kəl) *vb.* **tin·kling, tin·kled** to make a sound like the ringing of small bells.

tin·sel (tin′səl) *n.* a long strip of glittering colored metal threads used as a decoration.

tint (tint) *n.* a variety of a color, especially one made softer by adding white. – *vb.* **tint·ing,** **tint·ed** to color slightly.

ti·ny (tī′nē) *adj.* **ti·ni·er, ti·ni·est** very small. – *n.* **ti·ni·ness.**

tip¹ (tip) *n.* the end of something long and usually thin: *She pointed with the tip of her finger.*

tip² (tip) *vb.* **tip·ping, tipped 1** to lean or slant. **2** to remove or empty from a container by overturning or upsetting it: *She tipped out the contents of her purse.* **3** to topple.

tip[3] (tip) *n.* **1** a gift of money given to a waiter, taxi driver, etc. in return for service. **2** a piece of useful information; a helpful hint. − *vb.* **tip·ping, tipped** to give a tip to.

tip·toe (tip′tō′) *vb.* **tip·to·ing, tip·toed** to walk quietly on the tips of the toes. − *n.* the tips of the toes. − *adv.* on the tips of the toes.

tire[1] (tīr) *vb.* **tir·ing, tired** (tīrd) **1** to make or become weary and in need of rest: *The walk tired him out.* **2** to lose patience with; to become bored with.

tire[2] (tīr) *n.* a thick rubber air-filled or hollow ring placed over a wheel.

tired (tīrd) *adj.* **1** wearied; exhausted. − **tired of** wearied or bored by: *I'm tired of stew.*

tire·less (tīr′ləs) *adj.* never becoming weary.

tis·sue (tish′ōō) *n.* **1** a group of cells with a similar structure and particular function in an animal or plant: *muscle tissue.* **2** a piece of thin soft paper used as a handkerchief.

tit (tit) *n.* any of several small songbirds.

● **Ti·tan·ic** (tī-tan′ik) the British ocean liner which struck an iceberg and sank in 1912.

ti·ta·ni·um (tī-tā′nē-əm) *n.* a white metallic element (symbol **Ti**), used to make alloys.

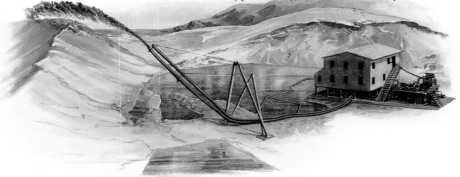

Titanium being extracted from the rich sands on the Australian coast.

● **Ti·tans** (tīt′nz) in Greek mythology, were the sons and daughters of the very first gods, Uranus (Sky) and Gaea (Earth).

ti·tle (tīt′l) *n.* **1** the name of a book, play, work of art, piece of music, etc. **2** a word of address used before a person's name to show rank or occupation. **3** in sports, a championship.

tit·ter (tit′ər) (*informal*) *vb.* **tit·ter·ing, tit·tered** to giggle or snicker. − *n.* a giggle.

to (tōō, tə) *prep.* **1** toward; in the direction of; with the destination of: *I am going to Mexico.* **2** used to express an aim or purpose: *You must boil the fruit to a pulp.* **3** used to express addition: *He added one to ten.* **4** before the hour of: *The time is ten minutes to three.* − *adv.* **1** into a nearly closed position: *He pulled the window to.* **2** back into consciousness: *He came to later.*

toad (tōd) *n.* a tailless amphibian related to the frog that spends much of its life on land.

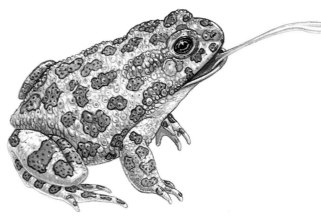

A toad darts out its long sticky tongue to capture a meal. Most toads and frogs eat insects and other small creatures.

toast (tōst) *vb.* **toast·ing, toast·ed** to make brown by putting near direct heat. − *n.* bread that has been browned, as in a toaster.

to·bac·co (tə-bak′ō) *n.* **tobaccos** **1** any of several American plants with large leaves. **2** the dried leaves of these plants which are smoked in a pipe, cigarette, etc.

to·bog·gan (tə-bäg′ən) *n.* a long, light sled which curves up at the front.

to·day (tə-dā′) *n.* **1** this day. **2** the present time. − *adv.* **1** on or during this day. **2** nowadays.

toe (tō) *n.* **1** any of the five fingerlike parts at the end of the foot. **2** the front part of a shoe or sock, covering the toes.

tof·fee (tô′fē, täf′ē) *n.* a sticky candy made by boiling sugar and butter.

to·fu (tō′fōō) *n.* a type of food made from soybeans, with bland flavor.

to·ga (tō′gə) *n.* a loose piece of clothing worn draped around the body in ancient ROME.

to·geth·er (tə-get͟h′ər) *adv.* **1** with someone or something else; in company. **2** at the same time. **3** in contact, joined, or united: *She pushed the tables together.*

● **To·go** (tō′gō). See Supplement, **Countries.**

toil (toil) *vb.* **toil·ing, toiled** to work long and hard; to labor. – *n.* long hard work.

toi·let (toi′lət) *n.* a bowl-like receptacle for the body's waste matter, with a water supply for washing this into a drain.

to·ken (tō′kən) *n.* **1** anything serving as a sign, reminder, or souvenir. **2** a small coinlike piece of metal or plastic which is used instead of money. – *adj.* having mostly symbolic value.

●**To·ky·o** (tō′kē-ō′) is the capital of JAPAN. It is one of the biggest cities in the world. It contains the Imperial Palace, and many ancient temples.

told. See **tell**.

tol·er·ance (täl′ə-rəns) *n.* **1** the ability to be fair toward other people's religious or political beliefs or opinions. **2** the ability to resist or endure pain or hardship. – *adj.* **tol·er·ant** (täl′ə-rənt). – *n.* **tol·er·a·tion** (täl′ə-rā′shən).

tol·er·ate (täl′ə-rāt′) *vb.* **tol·er·a·ting, tol·er·a·ted 1** to endure or put up with. **2** to treat fairly and accept: *to tolerate other beliefs.*

toll¹ (tōl) *vb.* **toll·ing, tolled 1** (of a bell) to sound with slow measured strokes. **2** to ring in this way. – *n.* the act or sound of tolling.

toll² (tōl) *n.* **1** a tax paid for the use of a bridge or road. **2** the cost in damage, injury, or lives of some disaster: *The hurricane took a terrible toll.*

●**Tol·stoy** (tôl′stoi′, tōl′stoi′), **Count Leo** (1828-1910) was a Russian writer. His finest works are *War and Peace* and *Anna Karenina.*

tom·a·hawk (täm′ə-hôk′) *n.* a small ax used as a weapon by NATIVE AMERICANS.

to·ma·to (tə-māt′ō, tə-mät′ō) *n.* **to·ma·toes** a round red juicy fruit eaten as a vegetable.

tomb (tōōm) *n.* a chamber for a dead body, either below or above ground; a grave.

to·mor·row (tə-mär′ō, tə-môr′ō) *n.* **1** the day after today. **2** the future.

ton (tun) *n.* **1** a unit of weight equal to 2,000 pounds (approximately 907.2 kg). **2** (British) a unit of weight equal to 2,240 pounds (approximately 1,016.05 kg).

tone (tōn) *n.* **1** the quality of a musical or vocal sound. **2** the character of the voice expressing a particular feeling, mood, etc.

●**Tonga** (tän′gə). See Supplement, **Countries**.

tongue (tung) *n.* **1** the fleshy muscular organ attached to the floor of the mouth, used for eating, licking, tasting and, in people, speaking. **2** a particular language.

to·night (tə-nīt′) *n.* the night of this present day.

ton·sil (tän′səl) *n.* either of two oval lumps of tissue at the back of the throat.

too (tōō) *adv.* **1** more than is required, desirable, or suitable: *I have too many things to do.* **2** in addition; also. **3** what is more; indeed.

took (took). See **take**.

tool (tōōl) *n.* any instrument held in the hand and used for cutting, digging, etc.

tooth (tōōth) *n.* **teeth** (tēth) **1** any of the hard enamel-coated objects set in the mouth and used for biting and chewing. **2** anything like a tooth in shape, such as the points on a comb.

●An animal's teeth are adapted to its diet. Gnawing creatures such as rats have sharp, pointed teeth, whereas grazing creatures such as horses have flat grinding teeth. Beavers use their teeth to fell trees.

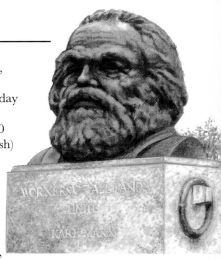

The tomb of Karl Marx is in London. Marx was probably the most influential of all modern political thinkers. His Das Kapital *formed the basis of modern Communism.*

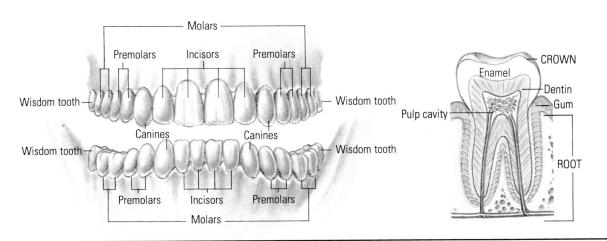

Children have 20 baby (first) teeth. These gradually fall out to be replaced by 32 adult teeth (far left).

A tooth has three main layers (left). The outside is made of hard enamel, to resist wear; underneath lies a hard dentine, over an inner pulpy cavity, which contains nerves and blood vessels.

Molars — Premolars — Incisors — Premolars — Wisdom tooth — Canines — Premolars — Incisors — Premolars — Molars

CROWN — Enamel — Dentin — Gum — Pulp cavity — ROOT

top[1] (täp) *n.* **1** the highest part, point, or level of anything. **2** the person or thing having the most important rank or position: *He is the top in his field.* **3** a lid for covering the top of something: *Put the top back on the jam, please.* – *adj.* being the highest or most important: *She stopped on the top step.* – *vb.* **top·ping, topped 1** to cover or form the top of: *She topped the cake with cream.* **2** to rise above or be better than; to reach the top of: *The song topped the charts.*

top[2] (täp) *n.* a toy that spins on a pointed base.

top·ic (täp′ik) *n.* a subject or theme.

to·pog·ra·phy (tə-päg′rə-fē) *n.* **to·pog·ra·phies** the natural and artifical features on the surface of land, such as rivers, mountains, valleys, bridges, and train lines.

top·ple (täp′əl) *vb.* **top·pling, top·pled 1** to fall over. **2** to overthrow.

To·rah (tôr′ə, tōr′ə, toi′ə) *n.* **1** the first five books of the Old Testament. **2** the scroll on which this is written, used in a synagogue.

torch (tôrch) *n.* a burning piece of wood or bundle of cloth, etc. used to give light.

to·re·a·dor (tôr′ē-ə-dôr′) *n.* a bullfighter, especially one on horseback.

tor·ment (tôr′ment′) *n.* very great pain, suffering, or anxiety. – (tôr-ment′) *vb.* **tor·ment·ing, tor·ment·ed** to cause great suffering or anxiety to.

torn (tôrn). See **tear**[2].

tor·na·do (tôr-nād′ō) *n.* **tor·na·does** a violent destructive storm accompanied by whirlwinds.

●**To·ron·to** (tə-ränt′ō) is the capital of Ontario province in CANADA.

●**Tor·que·ma·da** (tôr-kə-mä′də) **Tomás de** (1420-1498) was a ROMAN CATHOLIC monk in Spain who held the position of Inquisitor-General. He tortured people he believed were enemies of the Catholic Church.

tor·rent (tôr′ənt, tär′ənt) *n.* **1** a great rushing stream or downpour of water, lava, etc. **2** a nonstop flow of speech: *a torrent of abuse.* – *adj.* **tor·ren·tial** (tə-ren′chəl): *Torrential rain followed the hurricane.*

tor·rid (tôr′əd, tär′əd) *adj.* **1** (of land) scorched and parched by extremely hot dry weather: *torrid desert sands.* **2** passionate.

tor·so (tôr′sō) *n.* **torsos** the main part of the human body, without the arms, legs, and head: *The ancient statue depicted a torso.*

tor·til·la (tôr-tē′ə) *n.* a thin corn cake usually eaten hot with a filling of meat or cheese.

tor·toise (tôrt′əs) *n.* a turtle that lives on land.

The now rare desert tortoise lives in the American deserts. It feeds mainly on cacti, storing water from the plant in its body.

tor·ture (tôr′chər) *n.* severe pain or mental suffering deliberately caused in order to punish someone or to persuade them to give information. – *vb.* **tor·tur·ing, tor·tured** to cause great suffering to.

To·ry (tôr′ē, tōr′ē) *n.* **To·ries** a member or supporter of a British Conservative party.

toss (tôs) *vb.* **toss·ing, tossed 1** to throw up into the air. **2** to move restlessly or from side to side: *She tossed sleeplessly all night.* **3** to jerk or lift suddenly: *The pony tossed its head.* **4** to throw a coin into the air and guess which side will land facing up. – *n.* an act or an instance of tossing.

to·tal (tōt′l) *adj.* whole; complete. – *n.* the whole or complete amount, for example of various things added together. – *vb.* **to·tal·ing** or **to·tal·ling, to·taled** or **to·talled** to amount to; to add up. – *adv.* **totally.**

In 1493 Torquemada became Inquisitor-General and organized a campaign of imprisonment and torture against Arabs, Jews, and people with Protestant beliefs. Heretics were burned at the stake.

An early and intricate woodcarving by Maoris of New Zealand for a type of totem pole.

to·tem (tōt′əm) *n.* an animal, plant, etc. used as the symbol of a tribe or an individual person, especially among NATIVE AMERICANS.

to·tem pole *n.* a pole carved or painted with images called totems.

tou·can (tōō′kan′, tōō′kän′) *n.* a tropical American bird with a huge bright beak.

touch (tuch) *vb.* **touch·ing, touched** 1 to bring something into contact with so as to feel: *He touched her cheek gently.* 2 to come into contact with: *The branch touched the window.* 3 to be in contact with without overlapping. – *n.* 1 an act of touching or the sensation of being touched. 2 the sense by which a person feels objects through contact with the hands, feet, skin, lips, etc. 3 the particular qualities of an object as felt through contact with the skin. – *vb.* **touch down** (of aircraft or spacecraft) to land.

touch·down (tuch′doun′) *n.* a play in football worth six points, in which a team is in possession of the ball past the opponents' goal.

touch·ing (tuch′ing) *adj.* causing pity or sympathy; moving. – *prep.* concerning.

tough (tuf) *adj.* 1 strong and long-lasting; not easily cut, broken, torn, or worn out. 2 (of food) difficult to chew. 3 (of people and animals) strong and fit and able to endure hardship. 4 difficult to deal with or overcome.

tough·en (tuf′ən) *vb.* **tough·en·ing, tough·ened** to make or become tough.

tour (toor) *n.* 1 a long journey stopping at various places along the route. 2 a visit around a particular place. – *vb.* **tour·ing, toured** to make a tour of.

tour·ism (toor′iz′əm) *n.* the practice of traveling to places for pleasure and relaxation.

tour·ist (toor′əst) *n.* a person who travels for pleasure and relaxation.

tour·na·ment (toor′nə-mənt) *n.* a competition, for example in tennis or chess, between many players for a championship.

tour·ni·quet (toor′ni-kət) *n.* a bandage that is tied very tightly to stop the flow of blood.

tow (tō) *vb.* **tow·ing, towed** to pull behind.

to·ward (tôrd, tōrd, tə-wôrd′) or **to·wards** (tôrdz, tōrdz, tə-wôrdz′) *prep.* 1 in the direction of. 2 in relation to; about: *She has a strange attitude toward the new manager.* 3 as a contribution to: *I donated $500 toward the cost of a new hospital.* 4 near: *We sat toward the rear.*

tow·el (tou′əl, toul) *n.* a piece of thick soft cloth or paper for drying the body, dishes, etc.

tow·er (tou′ər) *n.* a tall narrow structure often forming part of a larger lower building such as a church. – *vb.* **tow·er·ing, tow·ered** to reach a great height or rise high above.

tow·er·ing (tou′ər-ing) *adj.* reaching a great height; very tall or elevated; intense; violent.

town (toun) *n.* a place with buildings and streets, smaller than a city.

tox·ic (täk′sik) *adj.* poisonous.

toy (toi) *n.* an object made for a child to play with. – *adj.* made to be played with: *a toy oven.*

trace (trās) *n.* 1 a mark or sign that some person, animal, or thing has been in that place. 2 a very small amount of something that can only just be detected. – *vb.* **trac·ing, traced** 1 to track and discover by following clues or a trail. 2 to follow step by step: *In his book he traces the development of medicine.* 3 to make a copy of by covering with a sheet of transparent paper and drawing over the visible lines.

tra·che·a (trā′kē-ə) *n.* **tra·che·ae** (trā′kē-ē′, trā′kē-ī) or **tracheas** the tube in the body that carries air from the throat to the lungs.

track (trak) *n.* 1 a mark or trail left by the passing of a person, animal, or thing, especially a footprint. 2 a rough path, especially one made by feet. 3 a specially prepared course for racing. 4 the rails along which a train runs.

tract (trakt) *n.* 1 a large area of land. 2 a system in the body with a particular function: *the digestive tract.* 3 a short essay or book.

track and field *n.* an outdoor or indoor sport consisting of track events as well as field events such as high-jumping and discus-throwing.

trac·tion (trak′shən) *n.* 1 the action of pulling or the force used in pulling. 2 a medical treatment using a series of pulleys and weights to pull on a muscle or limb. 3 the grip of a wheel, tire, etc. on a surface.

trac·tor (trak′tər) *n.* a vehicle with two large rear wheels, for pulling farm machinery, etc.

The Canadian National Tower in Toronto is taller than any skyscraper at 1,821 ft.

trade (trād) *n.* **1** the buying and selling of goods or services between people or countries. **2** an occupation or job. – *vb.* **trad·ing, trad·ed** to buy and sell.

trade·mark (trād′märk′) *n.* a name, word, or symbol shown on the goods made or sold by a company or individual.

trade name *n.* the name used by a manufacturer to identify a product or service.

trade union *n.* (also **labor union**) an organization of workers or employees formed to protect their interests and generally try to improve working conditions and pay.

tra·di·tion (trə-dish′ən) *n.* a belief, custom, or story that is passed on through generations. – *adj.* **tra·di·tion·al** (trə-dish′ə-nəl).

traf·fic (traf′ik) *n.* the vehicles, ships, aircraft, etc. that move along a particular route.

trag·e·dy (traj′əd-ē) *n.* **trag·e·dies 1** a serious drama, movie, opera, etc. with a sad ending. **2** a serious disaster or catastrophe.

trag·ic (traj′ik) *adj.* sad; very distressing.

trail (trāl) *vb.* **trail·ing, trailed 1** to drag loosely: *They trailed the fishing line behind the boat.* **2** to move along slowly and wearily. **3** to fall behind a competitor in a race or contest. – *n.* **1** a series of marks, footprints, etc. left by a passing person, animal, or thing. **2** a rough path through a wild or mountainous area.

trail·er (trāl′ər) *n.* **1** a vehicle for towing behind a car, truck, etc. equipped to transport something. **2** a similar vehicle used as living accommodations.

train (trān) *n.* **1** a string of cars pulled by a railroad engine. **2** the back part of a long dress or robe that trails behind the wearer. **3** a connected series of events, actions, ideas, or thought. – *vb.* **train·ing, trained 1** to teach to do something. **2** to prepare for performance in a sport by instruction, practice, diet, etc.

Today trains are particulary useful for carrying heavy freight long distances and for taking commuters to and from their jobs in city centers. The illustration shows a Union Pacific freight train.

trait (trāt) *n.* a distinguishing feature or quality, especially of a person's character.

trai·tor (trāt′ər) *n.* a person who betrays his or her country, or a friend's trust.

tramp (tramp) *vb.* **tramp·ing, tramped 1** to walk with firm heavy footsteps. **2** to make a trip on foot: *We tramped over the hills.* – *n.* a person who walks from place to place, and who lives by begging and doing odd jobs.

tram·ple (tram′pəl) *vb.* **tram·pling, tram·pled** to tread heavily or roughly; to tread on: *Cigarette ash was trampled into the rug.*

tram·po·line (tram′pə-lēn′, tram′pə-lēn′) *n.* a piece of tough canvas attached to a framework by cords or rope and stretched tight, for acrobats, gymnasts, etc. to jump on.

tran·quil (trang′kwəl, tran′kwəl) *adj.* quiet; peaceful; undisturbed.

trans- *prefix* **1** across; beyond: *transatlantic.* **2** into another state or place: *transform.*

tran·scribe (tran-skrīb′) *vb.* **tran·scrib·ing, tran·scribed** to make a copy of in writing or typing: *to transcribe notes.*

tran·script (trans′skript′) *n.* a typed or written copy: *a transcript of school grades.*

trans·fer (trans-fur′, trans′fur′) *vb.* **trans·fer·ring, trans·ferred** to move from one place, person, or group to another.

trans·form (trans-fôrm′) *vb.* **trans·form·ing, trans·formed** to change completely and often dramatically. – *n.* **trans·for·ma·tion** (trans′fər-mā′shən).

tran·sis·tor (tran-zis′tər) *n.* **1** a small electrical device in radios and televisions which performs serveral functions including amplification. **2** (in full **transistor radio**) a small portable radio.

trans·late (trans-lāt′) *vb.* **trans·lat·ing, trans·lat·ed** to put speech or written text into another language. – *n.* **trans·la·tor** (trans′lāt′ər).

trans·la·tion (trans-lā′shən) *n.* **1** speech or written text that has been put into one language from another. **2** the act of translating.

trans·lu·cent (trans-loo′sənt) *adj.* allowing some light to pass through.

trans·mis·sion (trans-mish′ən) *n.* something broadcast, especially a radio or television program.

trans·mit (trans-mit′) *vb.* **trans·mit·ting, trans·mit·ted 1** to pass or hand on: *The disease is transmitted through dirty water.* **2** to broadcast: *to transmit a radio program.*

trans·mit·ter (trans′mit′ər) *n.* an apparatus for transmitting radio signals.

trans·par·ent (trans-pâr′ənt) *adj.* **1** able to be seen through; clear. **2** obvious; evident.

trans·plant (trans-plant′) *vb.* **trans·plant·ing, trans·plant·ed 1** to move a growing plant from one place to another. **2** to transfer from one person or part of the body to another: *to transplant an organ.* – (trans′plant′) *n.* anything that has been transplanted.

trans·port (trans-pôrt′, trans-pōrt′) *vb.* **trans·port·ing, trans·port·ed** to carry from one place to another. – (trans′pôrt′, trans′pōrt′) *n.* **1** the act of transporting. **2** a ship or aircraft for transporting.

trans·por·ta·tion (trans′pər-tā′shən) *n.* **1** the act of transporting or process of being transported. **2** a means of transporting.

trap (trap) *n.* **1** a device or hole, usually with bait attached, for catching animals. **2** a plan or trick for surprising or catching someone. – *vb.* **trap·ping, trapped 1** to catch an animal in a trap. **2** to catch out, especially with a trick.

trap·door (trap-dôr′, trap-dōr′) *n.* a small door or opening in a floor or ceiling.

tra·peze (trap-ēz′) *n.* a swinglike apparatus on which acrobats perform tricks.

trash (trash) *n.* **1** rubbish. **2** nonsense.

trav·el (trav′əl) *vb.* **trav·el·ing** or **trav·el·ling, trav·eled** or **trav·elled 1** to go from place to place; to journey, especially abroad or far from home. **2** to move.

trawl (trôl) *n.* a large bag-shaped net used to catch fish in the sea. – *vb.* **trawl·ing, trawled** to search the sea for fish with a trawl.

trawl·er (trô′lər) *n.* a boat used in trawling.

tray (trā) *n.* a flat piece of wood, metal, plastic, etc. with a low edge, for carrying dishes, etc.

treach·er·ous (trech′ə-rəs) *adj.* **1** not able to be trusted. **2** having hidden dangers.

tread (tred) *vb.* **tread·ing, trod** (träd), **trod·den** (träd′n) or **trod 1** to walk or step on. **2** to crush or press into the ground; to trample: *Don't tread dirt into the carpet.* – *n.* **1** a manner or the sound of walking. **2** an act of treading. **3** the thick, grooved, and patterned surface of a tire. **4** the horizontal part of a step.

trea·son (trē′zən) *n.* disloyalty to one's country.

trea·sure (trezh′ər, trā′zhər) *n.* **1** a collection of gold, silver, jewels, etc., which have often been hidden for a period of time. **2** anything of great value. – *vb.* **trea·sur·ing, trea·sured** to value greatly or think of as very precious.

trea·sur·er (trezh′ər-ər, trā′zhər-ər) *n.* the person who is in charge of the money and accounts in an organization.

trea·sur·y (trezh′ə-rē, trā′zhə-rē) *n.* **trea·sur·ies 1** a place where funds or treasure is stored. **2 Treasury** the government department in charge of a country's finances.

treat (trēt) *vb.* **treat·ing, treat·ed 1** to behave toward in a certain manner: *She treated him badly.* **2** to give medical care to. – *n.* an outing, meal, present, etc. given as a gift.

treat·ment (trēt′mənt) *n.* **1** the medical care given to a patient. **2** the manner of dealing with someone or something.

trea·ty (trēt′ē) *n.* **trea·ties** an agreement between states or governments.

treb·le (treb′əl) *n.* **1** anything that is three times as much or as many. **2** in music, the highest part or voice; soprano. – *adj.* three times as much or as many; threefold; triple. – *vb.* **trebl·ing, trebled** to make or become three times as much.

Trees are the largest and oldest living things. The biggest is the giant redwood of the sequoia family. These trees come from North America and can grow up to 300 feet tall.

Bonsai is the ancient Japanese art of growing miniature trees. Grown in pots, the trees are constantly pruned and shaped.

tree (trē) *n.* a tall woody plant with a trunk and branches on its upper part.

trel·lis (trel′əs) *n.* a frame of narrow wooden strips used to support climbing plants.

trem·ble (trem′bəl) *vb.* **trem·bling, trem·bled** to shake with cold, fear, etc.

tre·men·dous (trə-men′dəs) *adj.* enormous.

trem·or (trem′ər) *n.* a shaking or quivering.

trench (trench) *n.* a long narrow ditch dug in the ground.

PRONUNCIATION SYMBOLS

ə away	lemon	focus
a fat	oi	boy
ā fade	oo	foot
ä hot	ōō	moon
âr fair	ou	house
e met	th	think
ē mean	th	this
g get	u	cut
hw which	ur	hurt
i fin	w	witch
ī line	y	yes
îr near	yōō	music
ô often	yoor	pure
ō note	zh	vision

trend (trend) *n.* **1** a general direction or tendency. **2** the current movement in style.

trend·set·ter (trend'set'ər) *n.* a person who sets a fashion.

trend·y (tren'dē) *adj.* **trend·i·er, trend·i·est** (*informal*) following the latest fashions.

tres·pass (tres'pas', tres'pəs) *vb.* **tres·pass·ing, tres·passed** to enter someone's property without permission. – *n.* the act of entering someone's property without permission. – *n.* **tres·pass·er.**

tri- *prefix* three or three times: *triweekly.*

tri·al (trī'əl) *n.* **1** a legal process by which a person accused of a crime is judged by a judge or jury in a court of law. **2** an experiment.

tri·an·gle (trī'ang'gəl) *n.* **1** a shape with three sides and three angles. **2** a musical percussion instrument consisting of a metal triangle that is struck with a small hammer.

tri·an·gu·lar (trī-ang'gyə-lər) *adj.* in the shape of a triangle.

tribe (trīb) *n.* a group of families or communities with the same customs, language, leader, etc.

trib·u·tar·y (trib'yə-ter'ē) *n.* **trib·u·tar·ies** a stream that flows into a larger river or lake.

trib·ute (trib'yōōt') *n.* something given or said as an expression of praise, thanks, admiration, or affection.

trick (trik) *n.* **1** a mischievous act or plan; a prank or joke. **2** a clever or skillful act or feat which astonishes, puzzles, or amuses. – *adj.* intended to deceive or give a certain illusion: *trick photography.* – *vb.* **trick·ing, tricked** to cheat or deceive.

trick·le (trik'əl) *vb.* **trick·ling, trick·led** to flow in a thin slow stream or drops. – *n.* a thin slow stream, flow, or movement.

trick·y (trik'ē) *adj.* **trick·i·er, trick·i·est** needing skill and care.

tri·cy·cle (trī'sik'əl) *n.* a vehicle with three wheels driven by pedals.

tri·dent (trīd'nt) *n.* a spear with three prongs.

tri·en·ni·al (trī-en'ē-əl) *adj.* **1** happening once every three years. **2** lasting three years.

tri·fle (trī'fəl) *n.* anything of very little value.

trig·ger (trig'ər) *n.* **1** a small lever that is squeezed to fire a gun. **2** anything that starts a train of actions or reactions.

tril·lion (tril'yən) *n.* **1** in the UNITED STATES and CANADA, a million millions. **2** in BRITAIN and EUROPE, a million million millions.

tri·lo·bite (trī'lə-bīt') *n.* any of various extinct sea animals, now found as fossils.

trim (trim) *vb.* **trim·ming, trimmed 1** to make neat and tidy, especially by clipping. **2** to make less by cutting: *to trim costs.* **3** to decorate with lace, ornaments, etc.

●**Trin·i·dad and To·ba·go** (trin'ə-dad', tə-bā'gō). See Supplement, **Countries.**

trin·i·ty (trin'ət-ē) *n.* **trin·i·ties** a group of three.

trin·ket (tring'kət) *n.* a cheap ornament.

tri·o (trē'ō) *n.* **trios 1** a group of three. **2** a piece of music for three performers.

trip (trip) *vb.* **trip·ping, tripped** to stumble or fall over. – *n.* **1** a journey or voyage. **2** a stumble.

trip·le (trip'əl) *adj.* **1** three times as great, as much, or as many. **2** made up of three parts or things.

trip·let (trip'lət) *n.* one of three offspring born to the same mother at the same time.

tri·pod (trī'päd') *n.* a stand with three legs for supporting a camera or telescope.

tri·reme (trī'rēm') *n.* an ancient Greek warship with three banks of oars on each side.

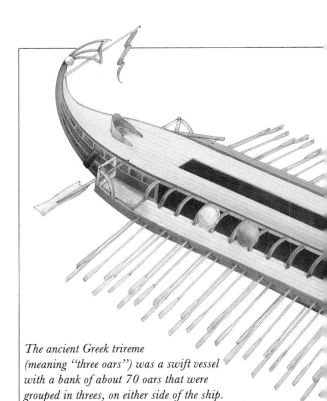

The ancient Greek trireme (meaning "three oars") was a swift vessel with a bank of about 70 oars that were grouped in threes, on either side of the ship.

tri·umph (trī′əmf) *n.* a great or notable victory, success, or achievement. − *vb.* **tri·umph·ing, tri·umphed** to win a victory.

tri·um·phal (trī-um′fəl) *adj.* of or celebrating a triumph.

tri·um·phant (trī-um′fənt) *adj.* feeling or showing great joy at a victory or success.

triv·i·a (triv′ē-ə) *n.* (*plural*) petty details.

triv·i·al (triv′ē-əl) *adj.* of very little importance.

trod, trodden. See **tread.**

Tro·jan (trō′jən) *n.* a citizen or inhabitant of ancient TROY in Asia Minor. − *adj.* of ancient Troy, its inhabitants, or citizens.

trom·bone (träm-bōn′) *n.* a brass wind instrument, with a U-shaped slide used to alter the pitch of the notes.

troop (trōōp) *n.* (in *plural*) soldiers.

troop·er (trōō′pər) *n.* **1** a soldier in a cavalry. **2** a state policeman.

tro·phy (trō′fē) *n.* **tro·phies** a cup, medal, or plate awarded as a prize for a contest.

trop·ic (träp′ik) *n.* **1** either of two imaginary circles running around the earth at 23°27′ north (the **Tropic of Cancer**) or 23°27′ south (the **Tropic of Capricorn**) of the equator. **2** (in *plural*) the part of the earth lying between these two circles, noted for its hot weather. − *adj.* **trop·i·cal** (träp′i-kəl).

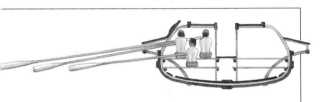

A cross section of a trireme showing the seating arrangement of a group of three oarsmen.

trot (trät) *vb.* **trot·ting, trot·ted 1** (of a horse) to move at a steady medium pace. **2** to move or proceed at a steady fairly brisk pace.

trou·ble (trub′əl) *n.* **1** something which causes distress, worry, concern, or annoyance. **2** a problem or difficulty. − *vb.* **trou·bling, trou·bled** to cause to feel distress, worry, etc.

trough (trôf, trôth) *n.* **1** a long narrow open container for holding water or feed for animals. **2** a long narrow hollow, as between two waves in the sea.

trou·sers (trou′zərz) *n.* (*plural*) a piece of clothing for the lower body, reaching from the waist and covering each leg separately.

trout (trout) *n.* **trout** or **trouts** any of several freshwater fish of the salmon family.

trow·el (trou′əl) *n.* **1** a small tool with a flat blade, used for spreading mortar, plaster, etc. **2** a garden tool like a small spade.

● **Troy** (troi) was an ancient city in Asia Minor which, according to Greek mythology, was besieged for ten years.

tru·ant (trōō′ənt) *n.* someone who stays away from school or work without good reason.

truce (trōōs) *n.* an agreement to stop fighting.

truck (truk) *n.* **1** a large motor vehicle for transporting goods. **2** a frame with wheels and handles for transporting heavy goods.

true (trōō) *adj.* **1** agreeing with fact or reality; not false or wrong: *This is a true story.* **2** accurate or exact. **3** faithful; loyal.

Triumphal arches date back to Roman times and usually were built to commemorate a great victory. The Arc de Triomphe in Paris (here clad in protective boards during the 1870 siege of the city) was ordered to be built by Napoleon in 1806 to commemorate his great victory over the Austrians and Russians at Austerlitz. It was completed in 1836.

Truant once had the meaning "idle rogue," but in the 1500s took on the meaning of a pupil absent from school. It is related to the Welsh word *truan*, meaning "wretched."

tru·ly (trōō′lē) *adv.* really; genuinely; honestly.

trum·pet (trum′pət) *n.* **1** a brass instrument with a powerful, high, clear tone. **2** anything like this in shape, such as the flower of a daffodil. **3** the loud cry of an elephant.

trunk (trungk) *n.* **1** the main stem of a tree without the branches and roots. **2** a person's or animal's body without the head, arms, and legs. **3** a large box or chest for storing or transporting clothes and other items. **4** the storage area of a car. **5** the long muscular nose of an elephant. **6** (in *plural*) men's short pants worn for swimming.

trust (trust) *n.* **1** belief or confidence in the goodness, character, and ability of someone or something. **2** charge or care: *The child was placed in my trust.* — *vb.* **trust·ing, trust·ed 1** to have confidence or faith in; to depend or rely on: *I trust her to be able to cope.* **2** to give credit to: *I'll trust you for the $5.* **3** to give to the care of: *We trust the child to him.* **4** to hope or suppose: *I trust you had a good journey.*

trust·wor·thy (trust′wur′thē) *adj.* able to be trusted or depended on.

trust·y (trus′tē) *adj.* **trust·i·er, trust·i·est** able to be trusted or depended on.

truth (trōōth) *n.* **truths** (trōōthz, trōōths) **1** the state of being true. **2** something that is established or generally accepted as true.

truth·ful (trōōth′fəl) *adj.* **1** (of a person) telling the truth. **2** true; realistic. — *n.* **truth·ful·ness**.

try (trī) *vb.* **tries, try·ing, tried 1** to attempt or make an effort to do something. **2** to test or to experiment with. **3** to judge or conduct the trial of someone in a law court. — *n.* **tries** an attempt or effort. — *n.* **tri·er** (trī′ər).

try·ing (trī′ing) *adj.* causing strain or anxiety.

tsar or **tzar** (zär, sär, tsär) *n.* Same as **czar**.

tsa·ri·na or **tza·ri·na** (zär-ē′nə, sär-ē′nə, tsär-ē′nə) *n.* Same as **czarina**.

T-shirt (tē′shurt′) *n.* a light casual shirt with no collar and usually short sleeves.

tub (tub) *n.* any of various round containers.

tu·ba (tōō′bə, tyōō′bə) *n.* a large brass musical instrument with a low tone.

tub·by (tub′ē) *adj.* **tub·bi·er, tub·bi·est** (*informal*) plump. — *n.* **tub·bi·ness**.

tube (tōōb, tyōōb) *n.* **1** a long hollow pipe used for carrying liquids or as a container. **2** a cylindrical container with a cap at one end, used for holding toothpaste, etc. **3** a tunnel.

tu·ber (tōō′bər, tyōō′bər) *n.* a short fleshy stem growing underground, such as the potato.

tu·ber·cu·lo·sis (tə-bur′kyə-lō′səs) *n.* a serious infectious disease that affects the lungs.

●**Tub·man** (tub′mən), **Harriet** (1820-1913) was one of the black Americans who organized the "underground railroad," which helped slaves escape captivity from the Southern states in the 1850s.

A slave family finds shelter on the journey north along the "Underground Railroad." It was not a real railroad, but the people who worked for it — notably Harriet Tubman — used railroad terms to describe the system. As many as 100,000 slaves may have been helped to freedom by the Railroad.

tuck (tuk) *vb.* **tuck·ing, tucked 1** to push or fold the outer edges of to make secure or neat: *You must tuck your shirt in.* **2** to put into a folded position: *she tucked her legs up.* **3** to fold the edges of sheets, blankets, etc. tightly around someone: *Father tucked us in.* — *n.* a flat pleat or fold sewn in a garment or piece of material.

Two of the leading monarchs of the House of Tudor: Henry VIII, who broke all ties with the pope and the Catholic Church, and Elizabeth I, under whom England became powerful and prosperous.

Tu·dor (tōōd′ər, tyōōd′ər) *adj.* **1** of the royal family which ruled ENGLAND from 1485 until the death of ELIZABETH I in 1603, or of this period in English history. **2** in or of the style of architecture characteristic of this period. – *n.* a member of the Tudor royal family.

Tues·day (tōōz′dē, tōōz′dā, tyōōz′dē, tyōōz′dā) *n.* the day of the week between Monday and Wednesday.

tuft (tuft) *n.* a small bunch or clump of grass, hair, feathers, wool, etc. attached or growing together at the base.

tug (tug) *vb.* **tug·ging, tugged 1** to pull sharply and strongly: *She tugged at the door until it opened.* **2** to tow with a tugboat. – *n.* **1** a strong sharp pull. **2** (in full **tug·boat** (tug′bōt′)) a boat with a very powerful engine for towing larger ships and barges.

tug-of-war (tug′əv-wôr′) *n.* **1** a contest in which two people or teams pull at opposite ends of a rope, trying to pull their opponents over a center line. **2** any struggle between two opposing sides.

tu·i·tion (tōō-ish′ən, tyōō-ish′ən) *n.* **1** money paid by a student for private school, college, etc. **2** teaching or instruction.

tu·lip (tōō′ləp, tyōō′ləp) *n.* a plant of the lily family grown from a bulb with a brightly colored flower.

tum·ble (tum′bəl) *vb.* **tum·bling, tum·bled 1** to fall helplessly or clumsily. **2** to perform as an acrobat, especially turning somersaults.

tum·bler (tum′blər) *n.* **1** a large drinking glass without a stem or handle. **2** an acrobat, especially one who performs somersaults.

tum·ble·weed (tum′bəl wēd) *n.* a plant that breaks away from its roots in the fall and is blown by the wind.

tu·mor (tōō′mər, tyōō′mər) *n.* a sometimes dangerous mass of tissue in the body formed by a new growth of cells.

tu·mult (tōō′məlt, tyōō′məlt) *n.* **1** a great or confused noise; an uproar. **2** the state of feeling confused emotions.

tu·na (tōō′nə, tyōō′nə) *n.* **tuna** or **tunas** a large saltwater fish of the mackerel family caught for food.

tun·dra (tun′drə) *n.* a vast flat ARCTIC plain with a layer of permanently frozen soil.

tune (tōōn, tyōōn) *n.* **1** a pleasing succession of musical notes; a melody. **2** the state of being set to the correct musical pitch: *The guitar's out of tune.* – *vb.* **tun·ing, tuned 1** to adjust to the correct musical pitch. **2** to adjust a radio to pick up signals clearly. **3** to adjust an engine, machine, etc. so as to run efficiently.

tu·nic (tōō′nik, tyōō′nik) *n.* **1** a loose sleeveless garment reaching to the hip or knee. **2** a jacket worn as part of a uniform.

● **Tu·ni·sia** (tōō-nē′zhə, tōō-nizh′ə). See Supplement, **Countries**.

tun·nel (tun′l) *n.* **1** an underground passage for pedestrians, vehicles, trains, etc. **2** an underground passage dug by an animal.

The word tulip comes from a Turkish word, *tulbend*, meaning turban, which the opened bloom was thought to resemble. Other Turkish words that have taken root in English are *divan* (a kind of couch), *kiosk* (a small shop), *kismet* (fate), and *yogurt*.

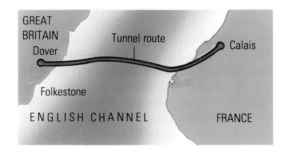

GREAT BRITAIN
Dover
Tunnel route
Calais
Folkestone
ENGLISH CHANNEL
FRANCE

The Eurotunnel linking Great Britain with France is nearly 30 mi. long. It is in fact three tunnels — two railroad and one service. The rail tunnels measure 25 ft. across. The service tunnel, which is about 16 ft. across, is used by workers to carry out repairs and it is also an emergency escape route. Trains carry cars and passengers across the Channel in about 35 minutes.

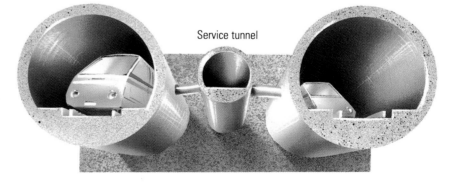

Service tunnel

Kemal Atatürk was elected the first president of the modern republic of Turkey in 1923. His name "Atatürk" means "Father of Turks."

tur·ban (tur′bən) *n.* a man's headdress consisting of a long piece of cloth wound around the head, worn especially by MUSLIMS and SIKHS.

tur·bine (tur′bən, tur′bīn′) *n.* a motor in which a wheel or drum with blades is driven by a flow of water, steam, gas, etc.

tur·bo *prefix* driven by a turbine attached to a propeller.

tu·reen (tə-rēn′, tyōō-rēn′) *n.* a deep dish with a cover, from which soup is served at the table.

turf (turf) *n.* **turfs** or **turves** (turvz) the surface of the soil consisting of grass and matted roots.

● **Tu·rin** (toor′ən, toor-in′) is a city on the Po River in northern ITALY.

Turk (turk) *n.* a person from TURKEY.

Turk·ish (tur′kish) *adj.* of TURKEY, its people, language, etc. − *n.* the official language of Turkey.

● **Tur·key** (tur′kē). See Supplement, **Countries**.

tur·key (tur′kē) *n.* **turkeys** a large domestic bird of the pheasant family, valued as food.

● **Turk·men·i·stan** (tərk-men′ə-stan′, tərk-men′ə-stan′). See Supplement, **Countries**.

tur·moil (tur′moil′) *n.* wild confusion or disorder; upheaval: *His mind was in turmoil.*

turn (turn) *vb.* **turn·ing, turned 1** to move or go around in a circle. **2** to move so that a different side or part comes to the top or front: *She turned the pages slowly.* **3** to change direction or take a new direction: *Turn left at the corner.* **4** to direct, aim, or point: *He turned his thoughts to supper.* **5** to become or change into: *They have turned the book into a movie.* **6** to move or swing around a point: *A gate turns on its hinge.* − *n.* **1** an act of turning; a rotation: *He gave the wheel a turn.* **2** a change of direction, course, or position: *At the light take a turn to the right.* **3** a change in nature, character, condition, etc.: *a turn for the worse.* **4** an opportunity that comes to each of several people in succession: *It's her turn to bat.* − *vb.* **turn out 1** to send away. **2** to make or produce. **3** to happen or prove to be: *She turned out to be right.* − *vb.* **turn up** to be found by accident.

turn·pike (turn′pīk′) *n.* a highway, especially one on which a toll is paid.

turn·stile (turn′stīl′) *n.* a revolving gate with arms which allows only one person to pass through at a time, often after paying a fee.

turn·ta·ble (turn′tā′bəl) *n.* the revolving platform on which a record turns on a record player.

tur·nip (tur′nup′) *n.* a plant of the cabbage family with a large edible root.

tur·quoise (tur′kwoiz′, tur′koiz′) *n.* **1** a light blue-green gemstone. **2** its color.

tur·ret (tur′ət) *n.* a small tower on a castle or other building. − *adj.* **tur·ret·ed**.

tur·tle (turt′l) *n.* any of several reptiles that live on land or in water, with a hard shell and flippers for swimming.

tur·tle·neck (turt′l-nek′) *n.* **1** a high turnover close-fitting collar. **2** a shirt or sweater with such a collar.

tusk (tusk) *n.* one of a pair of long curved pointed teeth which project from the mouth of certain animals including the elephant, walrus, and wild boar. − *adj.* **tusked**.

The gold mask that covered the face of the mummy of the Egyptian boy-king Tutankhamen. He was buried surrounded by treasure and beautiful furniture.

● **Tu·tankh·a·men** (tōō′tang-käm′əm, tōō′täng-käm′ən) was a pharaoh of ancient EGYPT whose tomb was discovered in 1922.

tu·tor (tōōt′ər, tyōōt′ər) *n.* a teacher or instructor, especially a private one.

TWINNED BUT TIRED

Clichés are words or phrases that have been used too often and so have become tired, and hackneyed. Here are some clichés using "twinned" words: by leaps and bounds, to pick and choose, tooth and nail, trials and tribulations, slow but sure, fast and furious.

●**Tu·va·lu** (tōō-vä-lōō) See Supplement, **Countries**.

●**Twain** (twān), **Mark** (1835-1910) was the pen-name of the American story-teller and humorist Samuel Clemens. His best known novels are *The Adventures of Tom Sawyer* and *The Adventures of Huckleberry Finn*.

twee·zers (twē′zərz) *n.* (*plural*) a small pair of pincers for pulling out individual hairs, etc.

twelfth (twelfth) *n.* **1** one of twelve equal parts. **2** the last of twelve; the next after the eleventh.

twelve (twelv) *n.* the number or figure 12. – *pron.* 12 people or things.

twen·ties (twent′ēz) *n.* (*plural*) **1** the period of time between someone's 20th and 30th birthdays. **2** the period of time between the 20th and 30th years of a century.

twen·ty (twent′ē) *n.* **twen·ties** the number or figure 20. – *pron.* 20 people or things. – *n., adj.,* & *adv.* **twen·ti·eth** (twent′ē-əth).

twice (twīs) *adv.* **1** two times; on two occasions. **2** double in amount.

twig (twig) *n.* a small branch of a tree, bush, etc.

twi·light (twī′līt′) *n.* **1** the faint light in the sky when the sun is below the horizon just after sunset. **2** the time of day when this occurs.

twin (twin) *n.* either of two people or animals born to the same mother at the same time – *vb.* **twin·ning, twinned** to bring together to form a pair.

twinge (twinj) *n.* a sudden sharp stabbing or shooting pain.

twin·kle (twing′kəl) *vb.* **twin·kling, twin·kled 1** (of a star, etc.) to shine with a bright flickering light. **2** (of the eyes) to shine or sparkle with amusement or mischief.

twirl (twûrl) *vb.* **twirl·ing, twirled** to spin.

twist (twist) *vb.* **twist·ing, twist·ed 1** to wind or turn: *He twisted around in his seat.* **2** to follow a winding course: *The road twisted through the mountains.* **3** to wrench out of the correct shape or position with a sharp turning movement: *He twisted his ankle.* – *n.* **1** the act of twisting. **2** turn or coil; a bend. **3** a sharp turning movement which pulls something out of shape; a wrench.

twitch (twich) *vb.* **twitch·ing, twitched 1** to move jerkily. **2** to pull sharply or jerkily.

twit·ter (twit′ər) *n.* a light repeated chirping sound made by small birds.

two (tōō) *n.* the number or figure 2. – *pron.* two people or things.

ty·coon (tī′kōōn′) *n.* a rich and powerful businessman or businesswoman.

type (tīp) *n.* **1** a class or group of people, animals, or things which share similar characteristics; a kind or variety. **2** (*informal*) a person, especially of a specified kind: *He is a quiet type.* – *vb.* **typ·ing, typed** to write words, text, etc. using a typewriter or word processor. – *n.* **typ·ing**.

type·writ·er (tīp′rīt′ər) *n.* a machine with a keyboard that prints letters.

typ·ist (tī′pəst) *n.* a person who types.

ty·phoid (tī′foid′) *n.* (in full **typhoid fever**) a dangerous infectious disease, caused by a bacterium in food or drinking water.

ty·phoon (tī-fōōn′) *n.* a violent hurricane occurring in the western PACIFIC area.

typ·i·cal (tip′i-kəl) *adj.* being a characteristic or representative example. – *adv.* **typ·i·cal·ly** (tip′i-klē).

ty·ran·no·saur (tə-ran′ə-sôr′) or **ty·ran·no·sau·rus** (tə-ran′ə-sôr′əs) *n.* a large flesh-eating dinosaur with two large hind legs for walking on and smaller front legs.

With its powerful legs and razorlike jaws, Tyrannosaurus must have been a terrifyingly efficient killer. It measured about 40 ft. — the length of three cars. It had tiny arms with only two claws — used perhaps for picking its teeth!

ty·rant (tī′rənt) *n.* **1** a cruel and unjust ruler. **2** a person who uses power unjustly.

tyre (tīr) *n.* British spelling of **tire**².

PRONUNCIATION SYMBOLS			
ə	away lemon		focus
a	fat	oi	boy
ā	fade	oo	foot
ä	hot	ōō	moon
âr	fair	ou	house
e	met	th	think
ē	mean	th	this
g	get	u	cut
hw	which	ur	hurt
i	fin	w	witch
ī	line	y	yes
îr	near	yōō	music
ô	often	yoor	pure
ō	note	zh	vision

U u

u·biq·ui·tous (yoo-bik′wət-əs) *adj.* found everywhere; everpresent.

U-boat (yoo′bōt′) *n.* a German submarine, especially of WORLD WARS I and II.

ud·der (ud′ər) *n.* the baglike organ of a cow, sheep, or goat, that produces milk.

●**UFO** an unidentified flying object.

●**U·gan·da** (yoo-gan′də, yoo-gän′də). See Supplement, **Countries**.

ug·ly (ug′lē) *adj.* **ug·li·er, ug·li·est** **1** unpleasant to look at. **2** threatening or involving danger or violence.

●**Uk·raine** (yoo-krān′). See Supplement, **Countries**.

ul·cer (ul′sər) *n.* a slow-healing internal or external wound. – *adj.* **ul·cer·ous** (ul′sə-rəs).

●**Ul·ster** (ul′stər) is the name of a former kingdom of IRELAND. Six of its nine counties have, since 1921, formed Northern Ireland, part of the UNITED KINGDOM.

ul·ti·mate (ul′tə-mət) *adj.* **1** last or final. **2** most important; greatest possible. **3** fundamental.

ultra- *prefix* **1** beyond in place, range, or limit: *ultramicroscopic.* **2** extremely: *ultraconservative.*

um·brel·la (um-brel′ə) *n.* a device carried to give shelter against rain, etc., consisting of a fabric canopy on a folding framework fitted around a central handle.

um·pire (um′pīr′) *n.* a person supervising play in various sports, as baseball and tennis.

un- *prefix* **1** not, or the opposite of: *unacceptable; unattractive.* **2** the reversal of a process: *unplug; unhook.* **3** a release from, or depriving of: *uncage; unthrone.* If the meaning of the main word is known then the sense of the word with the added prefix should usually be clear, for example *unable, unclear, unkind, untrue, unwell,* etc.

u·nan·i·mous (yoo-nan′ə-məs) *adj.* all in complete agreement.

un·be·com·ing (un′bi-kum′ing) *adj.* **1** not suited to the wearer. **2** not appropriate.

un·can·ny (un-kan′ē) *adj.* **un·can·ni·er, un·can·ni·est** strange or mysterious: *There was an uncanny sound in the cave.*

un·cer·tain (un-surt′n) *adj.* **1** not sure, certain, or confident. **2** not definitely known or decided. – *n.* **un·cer·tain·ty** (un-surt′n-tē), **un·cer·tain·ties**.

un·cle (ung′kəl) *n.* the brother or brother-in-law of a parent; the husband of an aunt.

Uncle Sam *n.* a representation or a nickname of the UNITED STATES.

un·com·for·ta·ble (un-kum′fərt-ə-bəl, un-kumf′tər-bəl) *adj.* **1** not comfortable. **2** feeling, involving, or causing discomfort or unease; awkward.

un·con·scious (un-kän′shəs) *adj.* **1** without consciousness; senseless. **2** not aware.

un·con·sti·tu·tion·al (un′kän′stə-too′shə-nəl, un′kän′stə-tyoo′shə-nəl) *adj.* not allowed by or consistent with a nation's constitution.

un·couth (un-kooth′) *adj.* coarse in behavior.

un·der (un′dər) *prep.* **1** below or beneath; on the downward-facing surface of. **2** at the foot of. **3** less than; short of: *It costs under $5.* **4** lower in rank than. **5** during the reign or administration of: *Under King George the American colonies rebelled.* – *adv.* in or to a lower place: *The swimmer went under again.*

un·der- *in compounds* **1** beneath or below: *underfoot.* **2** too little in quantity or degree; insufficient: *underpaid.* **3** lower in rank or importance: *undersecretary.* **4** less than: *underbid.* **5** less or lower than expectations or potential: *underdeveloped.* When the meaning of the main word is known the sense of the prefixed word should be clear, for example *underfed,* etc.

un·der·car·riage (un'dər-kar'ij) *n.* the landing gear of an aircraft.

un·der·go (un'dər-gō') *vb.* **un·der·goes, un·der·go·ing, un·der·went** (un'dər-went'), **un·der·gone** (un'dər-gôn') to endure, experience, or suffer.

un·der·grad·u·ate (un'dər-graj'ə-wət) *n.* a college or university student who has not yet earned a degree.

un·der·ground (un'dər-ground') *n.* **1** a place or area below ground level. **2** a secret organization fighting a government or

Electricity
Gas
Water
Telephones
Drains
Sewer

The underground world of city streets is a maze of drains, sewers, pipes, and cables. These are the city's lifelines — bringing gas, water, and electricity and taking away waste from kitchens and bathrooms.

occupying force. **3** (*British*) a subway. − (un'dər-ground') *adj.* existing or operating below the surface of the ground.

un·der·growth (un'dər-grōth') *n.* a thick growth of shrubs and bushes among trees.

un·der·mine (un'dər-mīn') *vb.* **un·der·min·ing, un·der·mined** **1** to dig or wear away the base or foundation of. **2** to weaken or destroy.

un·der·neath (un'dər-nēth') *prep.* & *adv.*

beneath or below; under.

un·der·pants (un'dər-pants') *n.* (*plural*) short pants worn beneath outer garments.

un·der·pass (un'dər-pas') *n.* a tunnel or road under a road or railroad.

un·der·priv·i·leged (un'dər-priv'ə-lijd) *adj.* not having the basic living standards and rights enjoyed by most people in society.

un·der·stand (un'dər-stand') *vb.* **un·der·stand·ing, un·der·stood** (un'dər-stood') **1** to grasp with the mind the meaning, nature, or explanation: *I understand Spanish.* **2** to know, believe, or infer, from information received. − *adj.* **un·der·stand·a·ble.**

un·der·stood (un'dər-stood'). See **understand.** − *adj.* implied but not stated.

un·der·take (un'dər-tāk') *vb.* **un·der·tak·ing, un·der·took** (un'dər-took'), **un·der·tak·en** (un'dər-tā'kən) **1** to begin or set about: *to undertake a new job.* **2** to promise or agree: *She undertook their care.*

un·der·wear (un'dər-wâr') *n.* clothes worn under shirts, pants, dresses, and skirts.

un·do (un-dōō') *vb.* **un·does** (un-duz'), **un·do·ing, un·did** (un-did'), **un·done** (un-dun') **1** to open, unfasten, or untie: *I can't undo my shoelaces.* **2** to cancel or reverse the result of.

un·doubt·ed (un-dout'əd) *adj.* clear; evident.

un·dress (un-dres') *vb.* **un·dress·ing, un·dressed** to take clothes off.

un·due (un-dōō', un-dyōō') *adj.* unjustifiably great; excessive. − *adv.* **un·du·ly.**

un·ea·sy (un-ē-zē) *adj.* **un·ea·si·er, un·ea·si·est** nervous, anxious, or ill at ease.

un·fold (un-fōld') *vb.* **un·fold·ing, un·fold·ed** to open or spread out.

un·for·tu·nate (un-fôr'chə-nət) *adj.* **1** having bad luck. **2** resulting from bad luck: *an unfortunate injury.* **3** regrettable.

un·hap·py (un-hap'ē) *adj.* **un·hap·pi·er, un·hap·pi·est** sad; in low spirits.

uni- *prefix* one; a single: *unicycle.*

un·i·corn (yōō'ni-kôrn') *n.* a mythical animal like a white horse with a long straight horn on its forehead.

u·ni·form (yōō'nə-fôrm') *n.* distinctive clothing worn by members of a particular organization or profession: *Mark wears his nurse's uniform at work.* − *adj.* not changing or varying in form or nature: *The books are of a uniform size.*

Perhaps of all uniforms military uniforms are the most colorful. At one time both dress and field uniforms were bright and colored — and conspicuous. In order to be less noticeable and less a target for firearms, armies adopted khaki-colored field and service uniforms, following the British army lead during the South African Boer War (1899-1902).

PRONUNCIATION SYMBOLS		
ə away	lemon	focus
a fat	oi	boy
ā fade	oo	foot
ä hot	ōō	moon
âr fair	ou	house
e met	th	think
ē mean	th	this
g get	u	cut
hw which	ur	hurt
i fin	w	witch
ī line	y	yes
îr near	yōō	music
ô often	yoor	pure
ō note	zh	vision

The countries of the United Kingdom of Great Britain and Northern Ireland. The rest of Ireland (now the Republic of Ireland) became independent of Great Britain after the Anglo-Irish Treaty of 1921.

u·ni·fy (yōō′nə-fī′) *vb.* **u·ni·fies, u·ni·fy·ing, u·ni·fied** to bring together to form a single unit or whole.

u·nion (yōōn′yən) *n.* **1** the act of uniting or the state of being united. **2** an association of people or groups united in a common, especially political, purpose. **3 the Union** The UNITED STATES or those states that formed the federal government during the CIVIL WAR. **4** a trade union.

Union Jack *n.* the national flag of the UNITED KINGDOM.

u·nique (yōō-nēk′) *adj.* **1** being the only one of its kind; having no equal. **2** found solely in or belonging solely to: *Kangaroos and koalas are unique to Australia.* – *n.* **u·nique·ness**.

u·nit (yōō′nət) *n.* **1** a single item or element regarded as the smallest subdivision of a whole. **2** a set of mechanical or electrical parts, or a group of workers, that is part of a larger construction or organization. **3** a standard measure in which a particular quantity, for example time or distance, is expressed. **4** any whole number less than 10.

u·nite (yoo-nīt′) *vb.* **u·nit·ing, u·nit·ed 1** to make or become a single unit. **2** to bring or come together in a common purpose or belief.

● **United Arab Em·i·rates** (em′ə-rəts). See Supplement, **Countries.**

● **United Kingdom**. The full title is the United Kingdom of Great Britain and Northern Ireland. (Great Britain consists of ENGLAND, SCOTLAND, and WALES.) The longest rivers are the Severn and the Thames on which London, the capital, stands. The south of the country is flat with rolling hills in parts. The north of the country, especially the Highlands of Scotland, is mountainous. The country has a moist temperate climate. Some 91 percent of the population lives in towns, though farming is highly efficient. Industry is varied and the country is rich in natural gas and oil. The country has only about one percent of the world's people, but the United Kingdom has a rich history. The British started the Industrial Revolution in the 1700s and they founded the largest empire in history. See separate entries: **England, Ireland, Scotland, Wales.** See Supplement, **Countries.**

The United Nations aims to maintain international peace and to solve problems through international cooperation.

● **United Nations** Most countries belong to the United Nations. Each member country sends delegates to regular meetings of the General Assembly in New York City. The UN works largely through 14 agencies. The Food and Agricultural Organization helps countries to grow more food. The World Health Organization fights disease. The International Monetary Fund lends countries money.

● **United States of America** 48 of the U.S. states are in the same part of NORTH AMERICA. The other two are Alaska in the north and the Pacific islands of Hawaii. The U.S. mainland stretches from the Atlantic Ocean to the Pacific. Long mountain ranges run down the Pacific coast. Inland are flat-topped mountains and basins. In this region is the GRAND CANYON. Farther east beyond the Rocky Mountains are the great plains where the Mississippi River flows.

The first Americans were the native "In-

Key Facts
Capital: Washington, D.C.
Area: 9,399,320 sq. km (3,615,123 sq. mi.)
Population: 256,600,000
Largest city: New York City
Highest point: Mount McKinley, Alaska, 6194m (20,320 feet).

dians." Europeans started colonies in the 1500s, bringing black slaves from Africa. In 1776, 13 colonies rebelled against British rule and set up a republic. George WASHINGTON became its first president. The United States is now the world's richest, most powerful nation and the largest producer of many industrial goods. It produces more farm goods than any other country and is almost self-supporting in gas, oil, and coal. See Supplement, **Countries.**

u·ni·ver·sal (yōō′nə-vur′səl) *adj.* **1** present or

existing everywhere. **2** of, relating to, or affecting the whole world or all people.

u·ni·verse (yoo′nə-vurs′) *n.* everything that exists everywhere, on earth and in space.

u·ni·ver·si·ty (yoo′nə-vur′sət-ē) *n.* **u·ni·ver·si·ties** a place of higher education that often is composed of colleges and schools for professional study, such as law or medicine.

un·lead·ed (un-led′əd) *adj.* (of gasoline) with a low lead content.

un·leav·ened (un-lev′ənd) *adj.* (of bread) made without yeast.

un·less (ən-les′) *conj.* if not; except if.

un·like (un-līk′) *prep.* **1** different from. **2** not typical or characteristic of: *It's unlike you to go for a walk.* – *adj.* different; dissimilar.

un·like·ly (un-līk′lē) *adj.* **1** probably untrue. **2** not expected or likely to. **3** not obviously suitable: *an unlikely choice of partner.*

un·load (un-lōd′) *vb.* **un·load·ing,**

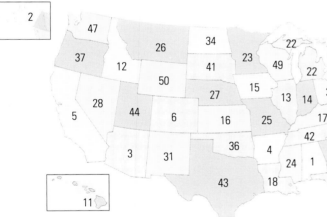

un·load·ed **1** to remove cargo from. **2** to remove ammunition from: *to unload a gun.*

un·mis·tak·a·ble (un′mə-stā′kə-bəl) *adj.* too easily recognizable to be mistaken for anything or anyone else: *Her voice is unmistakable.* – *adv.* **un·mis·tak·a·bly.**

un·na·tur·al (un-nach′ə-rəl) *adj.* **1** different from the way things usually happen in nature. **2** insincere; affected. – *adv.* **un·na·tur·al·ly.**

un·rul·y (un-roo′lē) *adj.* **un·rul·i·er,** **un·rul·i·est** disorderly: *an unruly mob.*

un·sa·vor·y (un-sā′və-rē) *adj.* unpleasant.

un·scathed (un-skāthd′) *adj.* not harmed.

un·so·phis·ti·cat·ed (un′sə-fis′ti-kāt′əd) *adj.* **1** simple. **2** not experienced in life.

un·tie (un-tī′) *vb.* **un·ty·ing, un·tied 1** to

undo from a tied state. **2** to set free.

un·til (ən-til′) *prep.* and *conj.* **1** up to the time of. **2** up to the time of reaching a place; as far as: *I slept until Chicago.* **3** (with a *negative*) before: *The dentist can't give you an appointment until next week.*

un·told (un-tōld′) *adj.* **1** not told. **2** too severe to be described: *The storm did untold damage.*

up (up) *prep.* at or to a higher position on, or a position farther along: *They climbed up the stairs.* – *adv.* **1** at or to a higher position or level: *Turn up the volume.* **2** in or to a more erect position: *Jake stood up.* **3** fully or completely: *All the food was eaten up.* **4** into the state of being gathered together: *I saved up for it.* **5** out of bed: *Anthony got up.* **6** to or toward: *The teacher walked up to him.* – *adj.* **1** placed in, or moving or directed to, a higher position: *Take the up escalator.* **2** out of bed. **3** (of the sun) above the horizon.

● **Up·dike** (up′dīk′), **John** (1932-) is an American writer whose novels include *Rabbit, Run.*

up·hea·val (up-hē′vəl) *n.* a violent change or disturbance.

up·keep (up′kēp′) *n.* the cost of keeping something in good order or condition.

up·on (ə-pän′, ə-pôn′) *prep.* on or onto.

up·per (up′ər) *adj.* **1** higher; situated above. **2** high or higher in rank or status.

up·right (up′rīt′) *adj.* **1** standing straight up; erect or vertical. **2** honest, good, moral.

up·ris·ing (up′rī′zing) *n.* a rebellion or revolt.

up·roar (up′rôr′, up′rōr′) *n.* a noisy protest.

up·set (up-set′) *vb.* **up·set·ting, up·set 1** to cause to be emotionally distressed: *We were upset to hear your sad news.* **2** to ruin or spoil: *to upset plans.* **3** to disturb the proper function of: *an upset stomach.* **4** to knock over: *The cat upset the milk.* – (up′set) *n.* **1** a disturbance, as of plans. **2** an unexpected defeat.

up·shot (up′shät′) *n.* the final outcome or ultimate effect.

up·side-down (up′sīd′doun′) *adj.* with the top part at the bottom. – *adv.* **upside down.**

up·stairs (up′stârz′) *adj.* & *adv.* on or to an upper floor. – (up-stârz′) *n.* an upper floor.

up·stream (up-strēm′) *adv.* toward the source of a river.

up·tight (up-tīt′) *adj.* (*informal*) **1** nervous; anxious; tense. **2** prudish or conventional.

up·ward (up′wərd) *adv.* (also **up·wards** (up′wərdz)) to or toward a higher place or a more important position. − *adj.* moving or directed upward. − *adv.* **up·ward·ly**.

●**U·ral Mountains** (yoor′əl) This range of mountains in RUSSIA forms a natural boundary between EUROPE and ASIA.

u·ra·ni·um (yə-rā′nē-əm) *n.* an element (symbol **U**), a silvery radioactive metal.

●**U·ra·nus** (yə-rā′nəs, yoor′ə-nəs) is one of our sun's planets. It is 19 times farther away from the sun than Earth is. One of its years lasts 84 of ours.

ur·ban (ur′bən) *adj.* of, or relating to, a town or city; not rural.

urge (urj) *vb.* **urg·ing, urged 1** to persuade forcefully; to beg or entreat. **2** to recommend earnestly: *I urge you to leave before it's too late.* **3** to drive onward. − *n.* a strong desire or impulse.

ur·gent (ur′jənt) *adj.* needing immediate attention or action. − *n.* **ur·gen·cy** (ur′jən-sē).

u·rine (yoor′ən) *n.* the yellow liquid mixture of waste protein and salts produced by the kidneys and discharged from the body via the bladder.

urn (urn) *n.* **1** a vase with a rounded body and a small narrow neck. **2** a large metal cylinder with a tap for serving of tea or coffee.

●**U·ru·guay** (yoor′ə-gwī′, oor′ə-gwī). See Supplement, **Countries**.

us (us) *pron.* the speaker or writer together with another person or other people; the object form of **we**: *He saw us at the game today.*

use[1] (yooz) *vb.* **us·ing, used 1** to put to a particular purpose: *We use scissors to cut cloth.* **2** to consume; to take as a fuel. − *adj.* **us·a·ble.** − *n.* **us·er.** − **used to** accustomed to: *She's not used to exercising.* − *vb.* **used** (*auxiliary*) was or were formerly: *They used to be friends. She never used to be so grumpy.*

use[2] (yoos) *n.* **1** the act of using. **2** the state of being used: *This room is not in use.* **3** a practical purpose a thing can be put to: *What use are these old shirts?* **4** the quality of serving a practical purpose: *It's no use complaining.* **5** the length of time for which a thing can be used.

used (yoozd) *adj.* not new; second-hand.

use·ful (yoos′fəl) *adj.* serving a helpful purpose or various purposes. − *n.* **use·ful·ness**.

●**U.S.S.R.** (**Union of Soviet Socialist Republics**). See **Commonwealth of Independent States** and **Russia**.

●**U·tah** (yoo′tô′, yoo′tä′). See Supplement, **U.S.A**.

u·ten·sil (yoo-ten′səl) *n.* an implement or container, especially for everyday use.

Utopia, *by the English scholar and politician, Sir Thomas More, was published in 1516. It describes an ideal land where everything is shared and everyone is educated.*

u·ter·us (yoot′ə-res) *n.* **u·ter·i** (yoot′ə-rī′) the womb.

u·til·i·ty (yoo-til′ət-ē) *n.* usefulness.

u·to·pi·a (yoo-tō′pē-ə) *n.* any imaginary place or situation of ideal perfection.

ut·ter (ut′ər) *vb.* **ut·ter·ing, ut·tered** to express as speech or a sound; to speak.

U-turn (yoo-turn′) *n.* a maneuver in which a vehicle is turned to face the other way.

●**Uz·bek·i·stan** (ooz-bek′i-stän′, ooz-bek′i-stan′). See Supplement, **Countries**.

A glass scent bottle in the shape of an urn made in Phoenicia sometime between 1000 and 775 B.C. The Phoenicians were skilled craft workers who traded their goods all around the Mediterranean coasts.

V v

va·cant (vā′kənt) *adj.* empty or unoccupied.

va·ca·tion (vā-kā′shən) *n.* a period of free time when work or study is suspended.

vac·cine (vak-sēn′) *n.* a substance containing usually dead bacteria or viruses, injected into the blood to give immunity to a specific disease. – *n.* **vac·ci·na·tion** (vak′sə-nā′shən).

vac·uum (vak′yoo-əm, vak′yoom′) *n.* **vacuums** a space from which all matter, air, or other gas has been removed. *adj.* using or

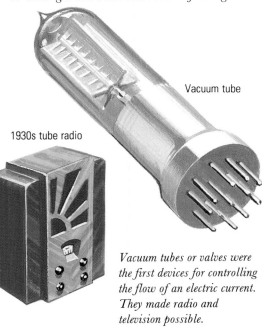

1930s tube radio

Vacuum tube

Vacuum tubes or valves were the first devices for controlling the flow of an electric current. They made radio and television possible.

producing a vacuum.

vacuum cleaner *n.* an electrically powered machine that lifts dust and dirt by suction.

va·gi·na (və-jī′nə) *n.* the passage connecting the external female sex organs to the womb.

vague (vāg) *adj.* indistinct, imprecise, unclear.

vain (vān) *adj.* **1** having too much pride in oneself; conceited. – **in vain** with no success; fruitlessly.

val·en·tine (val′ən-tīn′) *n.* a message of love sent on February 14, St. Valentine's Day.

Val·hal·la (val-hal′ə) *n.* in Scandinavian mythology, the place where the souls of slain heroes live in eternal bliss.

val·iant (val′yənt) *adj.* brave; heroic.

val·id (val′əd) *adj.* **1** based on truth or sound reasoning. **2** (of a ticket, passport, etc.) legally acceptable for use.

val·ley (val′ē) *n.* **valleys** an area of low flat land between hills or mountains, often with a river running through.

val·u·a·ble (val′yoo-ə-bəl, val′yə-bəl) *adj.* of considerable value or usefulness.

val·ue (val′yoo) *n.* **1** worth in money terms: *That painting has great value.* **2** the quality of being useful or desirable: *A knowledge of Russian is of great value today.* **3** (in *plural*) moral principles or standards. – *vb.* **val·u·ing, val·ued 1** to esteem. **2** to prize.

valve (valv) *n.* a device that controls the flow of a liquid or gas in a pipe by opening and closing an aperture.

van (van) *n.* a covered truck or other vehicle for transporting goods.

●**Van·cou·ver** (van-koo′vər) in British Columbia, is CANADA's third largest city and chief Pacific port.

van·dal (van′dəl) *n.* **1** a person who damages public property. **2 Vandal** a member of a Germanic people that attacked Rome in A.D. 455. – *n.* **van·dal·ism** (van′də-liz′əm).

van·dal·ize (van′də-līz′) *vb.* **van·dal·iz·ing,**

The letter *V*, like all the letters, has a long history. The earliest alphabets were taken and adapted by the Greeks. The Greek *beta*, when combined with the first letter, *aleph*, gives us the word alphabet.

The Greeks passed on their letters to the Romans, who developed the alphabet we use today, although they used only capital letters. Small letters developed in the A.D. 700s.

An early form of the letter V, used in the Middle East more than 3,000 years ago.

Ƴ

This letter was taken by the Greeks and became upsilon.

𝓋

Over the years different versions of the letter V have been developed.

van·dal·ized to inflict willful and senseless damage on: *to vandalize property*.

● **Van·der·bilt** (van′dər-bilt′) An important family in the history of American business. Their fortune was founded by Cornelius (1794-1877) in shipping and railroads.

vane (vān) *n.* any of the blades of a windmill.

● **Van Gogh** (van gō′, van gäkh), **Vincent** (1853-1890) was a Dutch painter of colorful landscapes and portraits with a simple form.

va·nil·la (və-nil′ə, və-nel′ə) *n.* a flavoring obtained from the pod of a Mexican orchid.

The Vatican, government headquarters of the Roman Catholic Church, is the world's smallest independent state, covering 108 acres. It is dominated by the basilica of St. Peter's, the largest Christian church in the world. The Vatican publishes its own daily newspaper and has its own postal and broadcasting services.

var·nish (vär′nish) *n.* a liquid containing resin, painted onto a surface, especially wood, to give a hard glossy finish.

var·y (vâr′ē) *vb.* **var·ies, var·y·ing, var·ied** **1** to change, especially according to different circumstances: *Veronica's moods vary*. **2** to make or become more diverse.

vase (vās, vāz) *n.* a container for flowers.

vast (vast) *adj.* great in size, extent, or amount. – *n.* **vast·ness**.

vat (vat) *n.* a large barrel or tank for storing or holding liquids, especially alcoholic drinks.

Vat·i·can (vat′i-kən) *n.* **1** the Pope's palace in Vatican City. **2** the government of the Pope.

van·ish (van′ish) *vb.* **van·ish·ing, van·ished** **1** to disappear. **2** to cease to exist; to die out.

● **Van·u·a·tu** (vän′yoo-ä′too, vän′ə-wä′too). See Supplement, **Countries**.

va·por (vā′pər) *n.* tiny droplets of moisture rising as a cloud or mist from a liquid or solid.

var·i·a·ble (vâr′ē-ə-bəl) *adj.* not steady or regular; changeable: *variable weather*.

var·i·a·tion (vâr′ē-ā′shən) *n.* **1** the act or process of varying or changing. **2** a thing that varies from a standard. **3** the extent to which a thing varies from a standard.

va·ri·e·ty (və-rī′ət-ē) *n.* **va·ri·e·ties** any of various types of the same thing; a kind or sort.

var·i·ous (vâr′ē-əs) *adj.* **1** several different: *She has worked for various companies*. **2** diverse.

● **Vat·i·can Cit·y** (vat′i-kən sit′ē) an independent state within Rome, is the POPE's official residence and the headquarters of the ROMAN CATHOLIC CHURCH.

vault¹ (vôlt) *n.* **1** an arched roof, as in a church. **2** a fortified room for storing valuables.

vault² (vôlt) *vb.* **vault·ing, vault·ed** to leap over.

VCR *n.* the abbreviation for videocassette recorder.

veal (vēl) *n.* the flesh of a calf, used as food.

veg·e·ta·ble (vej′tə-bəl, vej′ə-tə-bəl) *n.* any part of a plant used for food, for example the tuber, root, leaves, or fruit of numerous plants.

Parts of plants that are eaten as vegetables include tubers (potatoes), bulbs (onions), roots (carrots), leaves (spinach), and flower clusters (cauliflower). We also eat the seeds of plants (peas).

veg·e·tar·i·an (vej′ə-ter′ē-ən) *n.* a person who does not eat meat or fish.

veg·e·ta·tion (vej′ə-tā′shən) *n.* plants.

ve·hi·cle (vē′i-kəl, vē′hik′əl) *n.* anything, especially self-propelling, that is used for transporting people or things.

veil (vāl) *n.* **1** a fine netting covering for a woman's head: *a bride's veil.* **2** the hoodlike part of a nun's habit.

vein (vān) *n.* any of the vessels or tubes that carry blood back to the heart.

ve·loc·i·ty (və-läs′ət-ē) *n.* **ve·loc·i·ties 1** rate of motion in a particular direction. **2** speed.

vel·vet (vel′vət) *n.* a fabric with a short soft closely woven pile on one side.

vend·ing machine (ven′ding) *n.* a coin-operated machine dispensing candy, drinks, etc.

Ve·ne·tian (və-nē′shən) *adj.* of, or relating to, VENICE, Italy.

●**Ven·e·zu·e·la** (ven′ə-zoo-ā′lə). See Supplement, **Countries**.

●**Ven·ice** (ven′əs) is a beautiful city in northeastern ITALY built on islands in a lagoon of the Adriatic Sea.

ven·om (ven′əm) *n.* **1** a poisonous liquid that some creatures, as scorpions and certain snakes, inject in a bite or sting. **2** spitefulness.

vent (vent) *n.* an opening allowing air, gas, or liquid into or out of a confined space.

ven·ti·late (vent′l-āt′) *vb.* **ven·ti·lat·ing, ven·ti·lat·ed** to allow fresh air to circulate throughout. – *n.* **ven·ti·la·tion** (vent′l-ā′shən).

ven·tril·o·quism (ven-tril′ə-kwiz′əm) *n.* the art of speaking in a way that makes the sound appear to come from elsewhere. – *n.*

ven·tril·o·quist (ven-tril′ə-kwəst).

ven·ture (ven′chər) *vb.* **ven·tur·ing, ven·tured** to dare, or dare to go.

●**Ve·nus** (vē′nəs) is the the brightest planet in the solar system and is named after the Roman goddess of beauty and love. Venus takes only 225 days to orbit the sun but it spins so slowly that one day on Venus lasts 243 days on Earth.

ve·ran·da or **ve·ran·dah** (və-ran′də) *n.* a covered porch or portico.

verb (vurb) *n.* a class of words that represent an action, experience, occurrence, or state; *do, feel, happen,* and *remain* are all verbs.

ver·bal (vur′bəl) *adj.* **1** of, relating to, or consisting of words: *verbal abuse.* **2** spoken, not written: *verbal communication.*

●**Ver·di** (verd′ē), **Giuseppe** (1813-1901) was the Italian composer of such operas as *Aida.*

ver·dict (vur′dikt) *n.* **1** the decision arrived at by the jury in a court of law. **2** any decision.

verge (vurj) *n.* **1** a limit, boundary, or border. **2** a point or stage immediately beyond or after which something lies or occurs: *I was on the verge of striking him.*

●**Ver·mont** (vər-mänt′). See Supplement, **U.S.A.**

●**Ver·sailles** (vur-sī′, ver-sī′) is a town just outside Paris, famous for its luxurious palace, begun by LOUIS XIV in 1661.

ver·sa·tile (vur′sət-l) *adj.* **1** adapting easily to different tasks. **2** having numerous uses or abilities. – *n.* **ver·sa·til·i·ty** (vur′sə-til′ət-ē).

verse (vurs) *n.* **1** a division of a poem; a stanza. **2** poetry, as opposed to prose.

ver·sion (vər′zhən, vər′shən) *n.* any of

This figure of Aphrodite, the Greek goddess of love, is generally known as the Venus de Milo (Venus is the Roman name for Aphrodite). It was sculpted in 130 B.C. by Alexandros of Antioch.

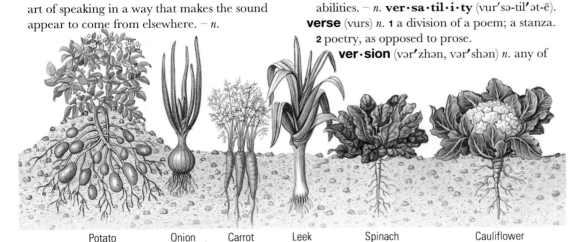

Potato   Onion   Carrot   Leek   Spinach   Cauliflower

several types or forms in which a thing exists or is available, for example a particular translation of a book, or one person's account of an incident: *the King James version of the Bible.*

ver·sus (vur′səs, vur′səz) *prep.* **1** in a contest against: *our team versus yours.* **2** in contrast to.

ver·te·bra (vurt′ə-brə) *n.* **ver·te·brae** (vurt′ə-brā′, vurt′ə-brē) any of the segments of bone that form the spine.

ver·te·brate (vurt′ə-brət) *adj.* having a spine. – *n.* any creature that has a spine, as fishes, birds, and mammals.

ver·ti·cal (vurt′i-kəl) *adj.* perpendicular to the horizon; upright.

ver·ti·go (vurt′ə-gō′) *n.* dizziness; giddiness.

ver·y (ver′ē) *adv.* **1** to a high degree or great extent: *very kind.* **2** (used with *own* and *same*, and with superlative adjectives) absolutely; truly: *the very same day; my very best effort.*

● **Ves·puc·ci** (ves-pōō′chē), **Amerigo** (1451-1512) was an Italian explorer after whom AMERICA is named.

ves·sel (ves′əl) *n.* **1** a container, especially for liquid. **2** a ship or large boat.

vest (vest) *n.* a sleeveless waist-length garment often worn under a jacket.

● **Ves·u·vi·us** (və-sōō′vē-əs) is a volcano that rises above the Bay of Naples, Italy. In A.D. 79 it erupted and buried the city of POMPEII.

vet[1] (vet) *n.* (*informal*) a veterinarian.
vet[2] (vet) *n.* (*informal*) a veteran.
vet·er·an (vet′ə-rən) *n.* **1** a person with long experience in a particular activity. **2** a former member of the armed forces.

vet·er·i·nar·i·an (vet′ə-rə-ner′ē-ən, vet′n-er′ē-ən) *n.* a person trained to treat animals.

vet·er·i·nar·y (vet′ə-rə-ner′ē, vet′n-er′ē) *adj.* concerned with diseases of animals.

ve·to (vē′tō′) *n.* **ve·toes** the right to reject a proposal or forbid an action, as in a law-making assembly; the act of using such a right.

vi·a (vē′ə, vī′ə) *prep.* by way of or by means of; through: *We went home via the park.*

vi·brate (vī-brāt′) *vb.* **vi·brat·ing, vi·brat·ed** to move back and forth very rapidly; to shake or tremble; to oscillate. – *n.* **vi·bra·tion** (vī-brā′shən).

vice (vīs) *n.* an immoral or evil habit or activity, as drinking too much alcohol.

vice- *prefix* next in rank to, and acting as deputy for: *vice-regent.*

vice president *n.* an official ranking below a president.

vi·ce ver·sa (vī′si vur′sə, vīs′vur′sə) *adv.* with elements reversed; the other way around.

vi·cin·i·ty (və-sin′ət-ē) *n.* **vi·cin·i·ties** a neighborhood.

vi·cious (vish′əs) *adj.* violent or ferocious.

vic·tim (vik′təm) *n.* a person or animal subjected to death, suffering, ill-treatment, or trickery.

vic·tor (vik′tər) *n.* the winner or winning side in a war or contest.

● **Vic·to·ri·a** (vik-tôr′ē-ə, vik-tōr′ē-ə) is an Australian state. Its capital is Melbourne.

● **Vic·to·ri·a** (vik-tôr′ē-ə, vik-tōr′ē-ə), **Queen** (1819-1901) became queen in 1837 and ruled BRITAIN for 64 years.

Vic·to·ri·an (vik-tôr′ē-ən, vik-tōr′ē-ən) *adj.* of, or relating to, QUEEN VICTORIA or the period of her reign (1837-1901).

vic·to·ri·ous (vik-tôr′ē-əs, vik-tō′ē-əs) *adj.* **1** winning a war or contest. **2** marking or representing a victory.

vic·to·ry (vik′tə-rē, vik′trē) *n.* **vic·to·ries** success against an opponent.

vid·e·o (vid′ē-ō′) *adj.* of, or relating to, the recording or broadcasting of visual, especially televised, images on magnetic tape. – *n.* **videos** **1** television or the visual part of television. **2** a program, movie, or the performance of a song recorded on videotape.

video camera *n.* a camera recording moving images and sound onto videotape.

A video camera (camcorder) converts an image into an electronic signal that can be recorded on videotape. It can also record the sound. The tape, contained in a cassette, can then be played back through an ordinary television using a VCR.

Viewfinder

Videotape

Video cassette

Lens   Zoom lens control

vid·e·o·cas·sette (vid′ē-ō-kə-set′) *n.* a cassette containing videotape.

vid·e·o·tape (vid′ē-ō-tāp′) *n.* magnetic tape on which visual images and sound can be recorded and played back.

vie (vī) *vb.* **vies, vy·ing, vied** to compete.

●**Vi·en·na** (vē-en′ə) is the capital of AUSTRIA.

●**Vi·et·nam** (vē-et′näm′, vē′ət-näm′). See Supplement, **Countries**.

view (vyōō) *n.* **1** an act or opportunity of seeing without obstruction: *We have a good view of the stage.* **2** something, especially a landscape, seen from a particular point: *There is a magnificent view from the summit.* – *vb.* **view·ing, viewed 1** to see or look at. **2** to inspect or examine: *They viewed the house before buying it.* – **in view of** taking account of; because of.

Vi·king (vī′king) *n.* any of the Danes, Norwegians, and Swedes who raided by sea, and settled in, much of northern Europe between the 700s and 1000s A.D.

vil·lage (vil′ij) *n.* a cluster of houses and stores smaller than a town. – *n.* **vil·lag·er**.

vil·lain (vil′ən) *n.* a violent or wicked person.

vine (vīn) *n.* a climbing plant, especially one that produces grapes.

vin·e·gar (vin′ə-gər) *n.* a sour liquid made by fermenting malt, wine, or cider, used for flavoring or pickling food.

vine·yard (vin′yərd) *n.* a plantation of vines.

vi·o·la (vē-ō′lə) *n.* a musical instrument similar to, but larger than, the violin.

vi·o·late (vī′ə-lāt′) *vb.* **vi·o·lat·ing, vi·o·lat·ed** to disregard or break: *to violate the law.* – *n.* **vi·o·la·tion** (vī′ə-lā′shən).

vi·o·lence (vī′ə-ləns) *n.* violent behavior.

vi·o·lent (vī′ə-lənt) *adj.* marked by or using great physical force: *a violent explosion.*

vi·o·let (vī′ə-lət) *n.* **1** a flowering plant with large purple or blue petals. **2** a bluish-purple color.

vi·o·lin (vī′ə-lin′) *n.* a four-stringed musical instrument played with a bow.

vi·per (vī′pər) *n.* **1** any of a family of poisonous snakes, including the adder. **2** a spiteful person.

vir·gin (vur′jən) *n.* a person who has never had sexual intercourse.

●**Vir·gin·ia** (vər-jin′yə). See Supplement, **U.S.A**.

From the late 700s until about 1100 **Vikings** ventured from their Scandinavian homelands in their lightweight, flat-bottomed ships in search of treasure and farmland. They plundered and in places they settled. They colonized Iceland and Greenland and even reached America.

Thor, the Viking god of thunder and war. Thursday is named after him.

Swords were highly valued by the Vikings and were often richly decorated with gold and silver.

Vir·go (vur′gō) *n.* See **zodiac**.

vir·tue (vur′chōō) *n.* a quality regarded as morally good: *Patience is a virtue.*

vi·rus (vī′rəs) *n.* any of numerous types of microorganism, smaller than bacteria, that grow on living cells and often cause disease.

vise (vīs) *n.* a tool with movable metal jaws, for gripping objects being worked on.

vis·i·ble (viz′ə-bəl) *adj.* able to be seen.

vis·i·bil·i·ty (viz′ə-bil′ət-ē) *n.* **1** the state or fact of being visible. **2** the extent to which things can be seen: *Visibility is down to 50 feet.*

vi·sion (vizh′ən) *n.* **1** the ability to see. **2** an image conjured up vividly in the imagination.

vis·it (viz′ət) *vb.* **vis·it·ing, vis·it·ed** to go to see a person or place.

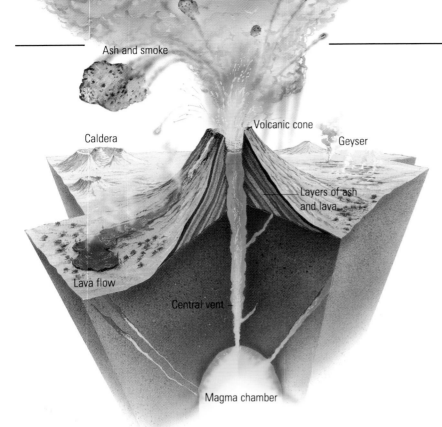

Ash and smoke

Caldera

Volcanic cone

Geyser

Layers of ash
and lava

Lava flow

Central vent

Magma chamber

*A typical "central" kind
of volcano has a crater
and cone of solidified
lava and ash. The
activity takes place in
the central vent through
which the material
erupts.*

VITAMINS	
Vitamin	Used for
A	Fighting disease
B	Healthy appetite; skin and nerves
C	Healthy blood; help against colds
D	Strong bones
E	We don't know!
K	Clotting blood

vi·sor (vī′zər) *n.* the movable part of a helmet.

vi·su·al (vizh′ōō-əl, vizh′wəl) *adj.* of, relating to, or received through sight or vision.

vi·tal (vīt′əl) *adj.* **1** of, relating to, or essential for life. **2** essential. – *adv.* **vi·tal·ly**.

vi·tal·i·ty (vī-tal′ət-ē) *n.* liveliness and energy.

vi·ta·min (vīt′ə-mən) *n.* any of a group of substances essential for healthy life, present in small quantities in various natural foods, and referred to by the letters A, B, C, D, E, etc.

●**Vi·val·di** (və-vôl′dē), **Antonio** (1678-1741) was the Italian composer who wrote *The Four Seasons*.

viv·id (viv′əd) *adj.* **1** (of color) very bright. **2** creating a clear mental picture.

vo·cab·u·lar·y (vō-kab′yə-ler′ē) *n.* **vo·cab·u·lar·ies** the words of a particular language.

vo·cal (vō′kəl) *adj.* **1** of, relating to, or produced by the voice. **2** expressing opinions freely.

vocal cords *n.* (*plural*) folds in the membrane lining the larynx, vibrated by the breath to produce sound.

voice (vois) *n.* **1** the ability to speak using the mouth and vocal chords; the power of speech: *Ali lost his voice.* **2** a way of speaking or singing

peculiar to each individual.

void (void) *adj.* **1** not valid or legally binding. **2** containing nothing; empty or unoccupied.

vol·can·o (väl-kā-nō, vôl-kā′nō) *n.* **vol·can·oes** an opening in the earth's crust, through which molten rock, ash, and gases erupt periodically.

vole (vōl) *n.* a small mouselike rodent.

●**Vol·ga** (väl′gə, vôl′gə, vōl′gə) the longest river in EUROPE flowing from near St. Petersburg, in RUSSIA, to the Caspian Sea.

volt (vōlt) *n.* the standard unit for measuring the force of an electric current.

volt·age (vōl′tij) *n.* electrical force measured in volts.

vol·ume (väl′yəm, väl′yōōm) *n.* **1** the amount of space occupied by an object, gas, or liquid. **2** loudness of sound; the control that adjusts it on a radio, stereo, etc. **3** a book.

vol·un·tar·y (väl′ən-ter′ē) *adj.* **1** done, given, taken, etc. by choice, not by accident or compulsion. **2** (of work) unpaid.

vol·un·teer (väl′ən-tir′) *vb.* **vol·un·teer·ing, vol·un·teered** to offer help or services willingly, without being persuaded or forced.

vom·it (väm′ət) *vb.* **vom·it·ing, vom·it·ed** to throw out the contents of the stomach through the mouth.

voo·doo (vōō′dōō) *n.* witchcraft of African origin.

vote (vōt) *n.* **1** a formal indication of choice or opinion, for example in an election or debate. – *vb.* **vot·ing, vot·ed** **1** to cast a vote for or against. **2** to decide, state, grant, or bring about by casting votes. – *n.* **vot·er**.

vow (vou) *n.* a solemn promise. – *vb.* **vow·ing, vowed** to promise or declare solemnly.

vow·el (vou′əl) *n.* **1** any speech-sound made with an open mouth and no blocking from lips, teeth, or tongue. **2** a letter representing such a sound – in English the letters *a, e, i, o, u,* and in some words *y*.

voy·age (voi′ij) *n.* a long journey to a distant place. – *vb.* **voy·ag·ing, voy·aged** to travel. – *n.* **voy·ag·er**.

vul·gar (vul′gər) *adj.* showing a lack of manners or taste; coarse.

vul·ner·a·ble (vul′nə-rə-bəl) *adj.* **1** easily hurt. **2** unprotected against attack.

vul·ture (vul′chər) *n.* a large bird of prey which feeds chiefly on dead animals.

Ww

wad (wäd) *n.* **1** a thick mass of soft material used for packing, etc. **2** a bundle of money, etc.

wad·dle (wäd'l) *vb.* **wad·dling, wad·dled** to sway from side to side when walking.

wade (wād) *vb.* **wad·ing, wad·ed 1** to walk through deep water. **2** to make one's way laboriously through.

wad·er (wād'ər) *n.* any long-legged bird that wades in shallow waters in search of food.

wa·fer (wā'fər) *n.* **1** a light finely layered kind of crisp cake. **2** a thin disk of flat bread.

waf·fle (wäf'əl, wô'fəl) *n.* a crisp cake made of batter, with a gridlike surface pattern.

wag (wag) *vb.* **wag·ging, wagged 1** to wave back and forth vigorously: *The dog wagged its tail.* **2** to move busily in chatter: *Their tongues wagged with the new gossip.*

wage (wāj) *vb.* **wag·ing, waged** to fight: *to wage war.* – *n.* payment from an employer to an employee.

wag·on (wag'ən) *n.* **1** a four-wheeled vehicle for carrying loads, often pulled by a horse or tractor. **2** a child's four-wheeled vehicle.

waist (wāst) *n.* the narrow part of the human body between the ribs and hips.

wait (wāt) *vb.* **wait·ing, wait·ed 1** to delay action, or remain in a certain place, in expectation of something: *We must wait for the bus.* **2** (of a task, etc.) to remain temporarily undealt with: *The ironing can wait.* **3** to serve people with food at a restaurant, etc.

wait·er (wāt'ər) or **wait·ress** (wā'trəs) *n.* a man or woman who serves food to people at a restaurant, etc.

wake¹ (wāk) *vb.* **wak·ing, woke** (wōk), **wok·en** (wō'kən) **1** to rouse or be roused from sleep. **2** to make aware of a fact, situation, etc.

wake² (wāk) *n.* a trail of disturbed water left by a ship, or of disturbed air left by an aircraft.

wak·en (wā'kən) *vb.* **wak·en·ing, wak·ened** to rouse or be roused from sleep.

●**Wales** (wālz) is one the countries that make up the UNITED KINGDOM. It consists largely of mountains, fertile valleys, and fertile coastal plains. The capital is Cardiff.

Settlers traveling westward across North America took all their possessions with them in huge wagons drawn by oxen or mules.

PRONUNCIATION SYMBOLS			
ə away	lemon		focus
a fat		oi	boy
ā fade		oo	foot
ä hot		ōō	moon
âr fair		ou	house
e met		th	think
ē mean		th	this
g get		u	cut
hw which		ur	hurt
i fin		w	witch
ī line		y	yes
îr near		yōō	music
ô often		yoor	pure
ō note		zh	vision

Walruses lie on beaches and ice floes, diving to great depths to catch clams from the seabed with their long curving tusks. Apart from humans their only enemies are polar bears and killer whales.

● **Wa·le·sa** (və-wen′sə, və-len′sə), **Lech** (1943-) a Polish trade-union leader and since 1990 president of POLAND.

walk (wôk) *vb.* **walk·ing, walked 1** to go in some direction on foot, by putting one foot in front of the other on the ground. **2** to take out for exercise: *to walk a dog.* – *n.* **1** the motion, or pace, of walking: *She slowed to a walk.* **2** an outing or trip on foot, especially for exercise: *They went for a walk in the hills.*

wall (wôl) *n.* **1** a solid vertical brick or stone structure that surrounds or divides an area of land. **2** the side of a building or room. – *vb.* **wall·ing, walled** to surround with a wall.

wall·pa·per (wôl′pā′pər) *n.* paper used to decorate the interior walls of houses, etc.

wal·let (wäl′ət) *n.* a flat folding case for holding money, credit cards, etc.

wal·low (wäl′ō) *vb.* **wal·low·ing, wal·lowed 1** to lie or roll around in water, mud, etc. **2** to indulge excessively in self-pity.

wal·nut (wôl′nut′) *n.* **1** an edible nut with a hard wrinkled shell. **2** the tree bearing it.

wal·rus (wôl′rəs) *n.* **wal·rus·es** or **walrus** a large sea mammal of the ARCTIC, with large tusks, related to the seal.

waltz (wôls, wôlts) *n.* **1** a ballroom dance in triple time. **2** a piece of music for this dance.

wand (wänd) *n.* a slender rod used by magicians.

wan·der (wän′dər) *vb.* **wan·der·ing, wan·dered 1** to walk about, heading for no particular destination. **2** to stray.

wane (wān) *vb.* **wan·ing, waned** (of the moon) to grow narrower as the sun illuminates less of its surface.

want (wônt, wänt, wunt) *vb.* **want·ing, want·ed 1** to feel a desire for; to wish: *She doesn't want you to leave.* **2** to need or lack: *May you never want friends.* – *n.* a need or requirement; a lack: *She shows a want of discretion.*

war (wôr) *n.* **1** an openly acknowledged state of armed conflict, especially between nations. **2** any long-continued struggle or campaign: *We are fighting a war against drug-dealing.*

ward (wôrd) *n.* **1** any of the rooms in a hospital with beds for patients. **2** any of the areas into which a town, etc. is divided for administration or elections. **3** a child under the legal protection of a guardian or court.

war·den (wôrd′n) *n.* **1** the officer in charge of a prison. **2** a person in charge of an area or who maintains certain laws: *a game warden.*

ward·er (wôrd′ər) *n.* a guard or watchman.

ward·robe (wôr′drōb′) *n.* **1** a room or piece of furniture in which to hang clothes. **2** a collection of garments.

ware (wâr) *n.* **1** manufactured goods of a specified material: *glassware, silverware,* or type of use: *kitchenware.* **2** (in *plural*) goods for sale.

ware·house (wâr′hous′) *n.* a building in which goods are stored.

war·head (wôr′hed′) *n.* the front part of a missile containing the explosives.

● **War·hol** (wôr′hôl′, wôr′hōl′), **Andy** (1926-1987) was an American artist, famous for his "pop art."

war·like (wôr′līk′) *adj.* fond of fighting.

warm (wôrm) *adj.* **1** comfortably or pleasantly hot. **2** (of clothes) providing and keeping in heat: *She put on a warm pair of socks.* **3** kind-hearted and affectionate. **4** enthusiastic or lively: *They gave him warm support.* – *vb.* **warm·ing, warmed** to heat gently.

warm-blood·ed (wôrm′blud′əd) *adj.* (of animals, etc.) having a relatively high blood temperature that remains constant.

warm-heart·ed (wôrm′härt′əd) *adj.* kind, affectionate, and generous.

warmth (wôrmth) *n.* the condition of being warm; moderate or comfortable heat.

warn (wôrn) *vb.* **warn·ing, warned 1** to make aware of possible or approaching danger. **2** to advise strongly. **3** to inform in advance.

warn·ing (wôr′ning) *n.* something that is said or happens that warns someone.

● **War of 1812** *n.* the war of 1812-1815 between the UNITED STATES and GREAT BRITAIN.

war·rant (wôr′ənt, wär′ənt) *n.* a written legal authorization for doing something, as arresting someone or searching property. – *vb.* **war·rant·ing, war·rant·ed 1** to justify. **2** to guarantee.

war·ren (wôr′ən, wär′ən) *n.* a place where rabbits live.

war·rior (wôr′yər, wôr′ē-ər) *n.* a person skilled

in fighting especially of earlier times.

●**War·saw** (wôr′sô′) is the capital of POLAND.

wart (wôrt) *n.* a small hard growth of horny skin, for example on the hands or face.

war·y (wâr′ē) *adj.* **war·i·er, war·i·est** cautious and distrustful.

was. See **be.**

wash (wôsh, wäsh) *vb.* **wash·ing, washed 1** to clean with water and soap or detergent. **2** (of flowing water) to sweep: *The river washed away the debris.* – *n.* **1** the process of washing or being washed. **2** a quantity of clothes, etc. for washing. – **wash one's hands of** to abandon responsibility for.

wash·er (wôsh′ər, wäsh′ər) *n.* **1** a machine for washing. **2** a flat ring of rubber or metal for keeping a joint tight.

wash·ing (wôsh′ing, wäsh′ing) *n.* clothes to be, or which have just been, washed.

●**Wash·ing·ton, D.C.** (wôsh′ing-tən dē′sē′, wäsh′ing-tən) is the capital of the UNITED STATES. It stands on a piece of land on the border between Maryland and Virginia called the District of Columbia (D.C.). Washington is the seat of the Congress and Supreme Court. It also contains the WHITE HOUSE, the official residence of the president.

●**Wash·ing·ton** (wôsh′ing-tən, wäsh′ing-tən), **George** (1732-1799) was the first president

In 1787 George Washington chaired a series of meetings held in Philadelphia to discuss a draft Constitution among delegates of the 13 new states that made up the newly formed United States of America.

(1789-1797) of the UNITED STATES. He led the victorious colonists during the AMERICAN REVOLUTION. He is buried at Mount Vernon.

●**Wash·ing·ton State** (wôsh′ing-tən, wäsh′ing-tən). See Supplement, **U.S.A.**

was·n't (wuz′ənt, wäz′ənt) was not.

wasp (wäsp, wôsp) *n.* a stinging insect with black and yellow stripes.

wast·age (wā′stij) *n.* something that is lost through wasting, use, etc.

waste (wāst) *vb.* **wast·ing, wast·ed 1** to use or spend extravagantly; to squander. **2** to fail to make the best of. **3** to throw away unused. – *adj.* **1** rejected as useless. **2** (of ground) lying unused, uninhabited, or uncultivated. – *n.* **1** failure to take advantage of something: *a waste of talent.* **2** refuse; rubbish. **3** a devastated or barren region. – **lay waste** to devastate.

waste·ful (wāst′fəl) *adj.* causing waste.

waste·land (wāst′land′) *n.* a desolate and barren region.

watch (wäch, wôsh) *vb.* **watch·ing, watched 1** to look at with close attention. **2** to guard, look after, or keep an eye on. **3** to keep track of, follow, or monitor: *We must watch developments in the Middle East.* **4** to take care: *Watch you don't slip.* – *n.* **1** a small instrument for telling the time, usually worn strapped to the wrist. **2** the activity or duty of watching or guarding: *You must keep watch.* – **keep a watch on** to keep under observation. – *vb.* **watch out 1** to be careful. **2** to be on guard against.

watch·dog (wäch′dôg′, wôch′dôg′) *n.* a dog kept to guard premises, etc.

watch·ful (wäch′fəl, wôch′fəl) *adj.* alert, vigilant, and wary.

Many kinds of wasp dig nest-tunnels in the ground. Potter wasps make beautiful nests out of clay. They lay an egg in each pot and fill it with food for the developing grub.

Water is the most common substance on our planet. Seven-tenths of the Earth's surface is covered with water. Without water, life as we know it would be impossible. Life, scientists say, started in water and the bodies of all living things are mainly water. Besides supporting life, water helps to shape the land by wearing away valleys and depositing material elsewhere. Water exists in three forms: it is normally a liquid; at 32°F (0°C) it freezes into solid ice; at 212°F (100°C) it turns into steam.

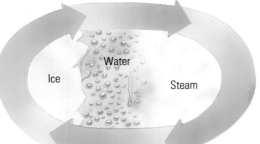

Water exists in three states. Ice takes a lot of energy to melt to water, just as water does to become vapor. This latent heat is given out again when vapor condenses to water.

Water is vital for all life. When water is added, the plant embryo inside a seed bursts out of the seed case and starts to grow.

Water power was used in medieval water wheels to drive hammers for iron working.

Most of the world's water (below left) is found in the oceans. Of the 3 per cent of the rest of the water some 77 per cent is frozen in the ice caps and glaciers of the Arctic and Antarctic.

Fresh water 3%

Sea water 97%

Animals around a waterhole in central Africa — again water is vital for all life.

Water has the amazing property of expanding when it freezes solid while all other liquids slowly contract as they cool. A frozen water pipe may split because of this; and when the ice melts you will have a leak.

Groundwater 22%

Ice sheets and glaciers 77%

Water vapor 0.05%
Moisture in soil 0.2%
Rivers and lakes 0.35%
Salt water lakes and inland seas 0.4%

WATERFALLS
The world's longest unbroken falls of water

Angel Falls, Venezuela 3,209 ft.
Yosemite Falls, CA 2,424 ft.
Mardalsfossen, Norway 2,150 ft.
Tugela, Africa 2,014 ft.

If soft rock over which a river flows is eroded enough for its face to be vertical, the river will cascade over as a waterfall.

watch·man (wäch′mən, wôch′mən) *n.* **watch·men** a person hired to guard a building or other premises.

wa·ter (wôt′ər, wät′ər) *n.* a colorless, transparent, tasteless, and odorless liquid that is a compound of hydrogen and oxygen, falls as rain, and forms oceans, lakes, and rivers. – *vb.* **wa·ter·ing, wa·tered 1** to wet, soak, or sprinkle with water. **2** to irrigate. **3** (of the mouth) to produce saliva in response to the expectation of food. **4** (of the eyes) to fill with tears, as when irritated. – **hold water** to prove sound; to be valid. – **in deep water** in trouble, danger, or difficulty. – **throw cold water on** to be discouraging or unenthusiastic about. – *vb.* **water down 1** to dilute or thin with water. **2** to reduce the impact of; to tone down. – **water under the bridge** experiences that are past and done with.

water buffalo *n.* **buffalo** or **buffaloes** the common domestic buffalo of ASIA, with backward-curving horns.

wa·ter·col·or (wôt′ər-kul′ər, wät′ər-kul′ər) *n.* **1** a paint thinned with water, not oil. **2** a painting done in such paint.

wa·ter·fall (wôt′ər-fôl′, wät′ər-fôl′) *n.* a place in a river or stream where the water drops a considerable height down steep rocks, over a precipice, etc.; a cascade.

wa·ter·fowl (wôt′ər-foul′, wät′ər-foul′) *n.* a bird living on or near water, especially a swimming bird such as a duck.

wa·ter hole (wôt′ər-hōl′, wät′ər-hōl′) *n.* a pond, pool, or spring in a desert area, where animals can drink.

water lily *n.* **lilies** a floating plant with large flat circular leaves and cup-shaped flowers.

wa·ter·logged (wôt′ər-lôgd′, wät′ər-lägd′) *adj.* completely full of water.

● **Wa·ter·loo** (wôt′ər-lōō′, wät′ər-lōō′), near Brussels, BELGIUM, was the scene of a battle in 1815 in which British and Prussian forces defeated the French under NAPOLEON.

water main *n.* a large underground pipe carrying a public water supply.

wa·ter·mel·on (wät′ər-mel′ən, wôt′ər-mel′ən) *n.* a large melon with dark green skin and juicy red flesh.

wa·ter·proof (wôt′ər-prōōf′, wät′ər-prōōf′) *adj.* treated or coated so as to resist water.

wa·ter·shed (wôt′ər-shed′, wät′ər-shed′) *n.*

1 the high land separating two river basins. **2** a crucial point that decides events.

wa·ter·tight (wôt′ər-tīt′, wät′ər-tīt′) *adj.* so well sealed as to be impenetrable by water.

wa·ter·way (wôt′ər-wā, wät′ər-wā′) *n.* a channel used by ships or boats.

wa·ter·wheel (wôt′ər-hwēl′, wät′ər-hwēl′) *n.* a wheel driven by water to work machinery, etc.

wa·ter·y (wôt′ər-ē, wät′ər-ē) *adj.* **1** of, or consisting of, water. **2** containing too much water; weak or thin: *She likes watery tea.*

watt (wät) *n.* a unit of power, equal to one joule per second.

● **Watt** (wät), **James** (1736-1819) was a Scottish engineer who improved the steam engine.

wave (wāv) *vb.* **wav·ing, waved 1** to move the hand back and forth in greeting, farewell, or as a signal: *She waved to her father.* **2** to direct with a gesture of the hand: *He waved at the waiter.* – *n.* **1** any of a series of ridges moving across the ocean or other expanse of water. **2** the form in which light, sound, etc. travel. **3** the circles of disturbance moving outward from the site of a shock such as an earthquake. **4** a loose soft curl in the hair.

wa·ver (wā′vər) *vb.* **wa·ver·ing, wa·vered** to falter, weaken, etc.; to hesitate.

wav·y (wā′vē) *adj.* **wav·i·er, wav·i·est 1** (of hair) falling in waves. **2** (of a line or outline) curving alternately upward and downward.

wax[1] (waks) *n.* any of various fatty substances, typically shiny and easily molded, used to make candles and polishes.

wax[2] (waks) *vb.* **wax·ing, waxed** (of the moon) to appear larger as more of its surface is illuminated by the sun.

way (wā) *n.* **1** a route providing access somewhere: *This is the way in.* **2** a direction: *This is a one-way street.* **3** position: *That picture is the wrong way up.* **4** a distance in space or time: *My birthday is a long way off.* **5** a distinctive manner or style: *She has a funny way of walking.* **6** a method: *I'll show you an easy way to cook fish.* **7** a mental approach, attitude, or opinion: *There are different ways of looking at it.* – **by the way** incidentally. – *adv.* by far; much: *This homework is way too hard for me.*

-ways *suffix* direction or manner: *sideways.*

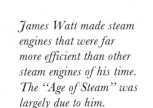

James Watt made steam engines that were far more efficient than other steam engines of his time. The "Age of Steam" was largely due to him.

anticyclone a region of high pressure usually associated with good weather.

convection the transfer of heat by flow of air from hotter to colder parts of the atmosphere.

cyclone a system of winds blowing spirally inward toward a center of low pressure.

front a boundary between air masses.

isobar a line drawn on a weather map to connect points of equal pressure.

precipitation any form of moisture that falls from a cloud.

sleet a mixture of snow and rain.

thunder the noise caused by a lightning flash when it heats air so that it expands explosively.

The weasel family includes the stoat, the common weasel, the American mink, the polecat (the ferret when domesticated), the pine marten, and the bearlike wolverine.

we (wē) *pron.* the speaker or the writer together with another person or other people: *We all left together.*

weak (wēk) *adj.* **1** lacking physical strength: *Her voice was weak.* **2** liable to give way or fail.

weak·en (wē'kən) *vb.* **weak·en·ing, weak·ened** to become weaker.

weak·ling (wēk'ling) *n.* a weak person.

weak·ness (wēk'nəs) *n.* **1** the condition of being weak. **2** a fault or failing. **3** a liking.

wealth (welth) *n.* **1** the possession of riches and property. **2** abundance of resources.

wealth·y (wel'thē) *adj.* **wealth·i·er, wealth·i·est** possessing riches; rich.

wean (wēn) *vb.* **wean·ing, weaned** to accustom to taking food other than mother's milk: *They weaned the baby onto solid foods.*

weap·on (wep'ən) *n.* **1** a device used to kill or injure people in a war or fight. **2** something that can be used to get the better of others.

wear (wâr) *vb.* **wear·ing, wore** (wôr), **worn** (wôrn) **1** to be dressed in: *She was wearing a red skirt.* **2** to have in a certain style: *He wears his hair long.* **3** to display: *to wear a smile.* **4** (of a carpet or garment) to become thin or threadbare through use. − *n.* **1** clothes suitable for a certain purpose, person, occasion, etc.: *menswear; children's wear.* **2** the amount or type of use that clothing, carpeting, etc. gets: *This carpet is subjected to heavy wear.* − *adj.*

wear·a·ble (wâr'ə-bəl). − *n.* **wear·er.** − *vb.*

wear off (of a feeling, pain, etc.) to become less intense; to disappear gradually.

wea·ry (wir'ē) *adj.* **wea·ri·er, wea·ri·est 1** tired out; exhausted. **2** tired; fed up.

wea·sel (wē'zəl) *n.* a small slender short-legged, reddish-brown animal that feeds on frogs, mice, etc.

weath·er (weth'ər) *n.* the atmospheric conditions in any area at any time, with regard to sun, cloud, temperature, wind, rain, etc. − *vb.* **weath·er·ing, weath·ered 1** to be exposed to the effects of wind, sun, rain, etc.; to alter in color or shape through such exposure. **2** to come safely through.

weath·er vane (weth'ər-vān') *n.* a revolving arrow on a fixed base that turns to point in the direction of the wind.

weave¹ (wēv) *vb.* **weav·ing, wove** (wōv),

wo·ven (wō'vən) to make on a loom, passing threads under and over each other.

weave² (wēv) *vb.* **weav·ing, weaved** to move to and fro or wind in and out.

web (web) *n.* **1** a network of slender threads constructed by a spider to trap insects. **2** a piece of skin connecting the toes of a swimming bird or animal.

● **Web·ster** (web'stər), **Noah** (1758-1843) compiled the first American dictionary in 1806. His *American Dictionary of the English Language*, published in 1828, had 70,000 entries. Webster simplified American spelling and eliminated many silent letters that remain in British English.

wed (wed) *vb.* **wed·ding, wed·ded** or **wed 1** to unite or combine. **2** to marry.

we'd (wēd) we had, we would, or we should.

wed·ding (wed'ing) *n.* a marriage ceremony.

wedge (wej) *n.* a piece of solid material, with a thick edge tapering to a thin edge, driven into wood to split it, or used to hold something in place, for example a door.

Wed·nes·day (wenz'dē, wenz'dā) *n.* the day between Tuesday and Thursday.

weed (wēd) *n.* a wild plant growing where unwanted. − *vb.* **weed·ing, weed·ed** to uproot weeds from.

week (wēk) *n.* a period of seven consecutive days, usually beginning on Sunday.

week·day (wēk'dā') *n.* any day except Saturday and Sunday.

week·end (wē'kend') *n.* the nonworking period from Friday evening to Sunday night.

weep (wēp) *vb.* **weep·ing, wept** (wept) to cry.

weigh (wā) *vb.* **weigh·ing, weighed 1** to measure the weight of. **2** to have a certain weight: *The books weigh eight pounds.*

weight (wāt) *n.* **1** the amount anything weighs. **2** a piece of metal of a standard weight, against which to

1 On Earth

Force of Gravity

2 On Moon

measure the weight of other objects. **3** a heavy load.

weight·less (wāt′ləs) *adj.* not subject to gravity, so able to float free.

weird (wîrd) *adj.* strange or bizarre.

wel·come (wel′kəm) *vb.* **wel·com·ing, wel·comed 1** to receive with a warm greeting and kind hospitality. **2** to invite and encourage: *The museum welcomes children.* − *interjection* an expression of pleasure on receiving someone: *Welcome home!* − *n.* the act of welcoming; a reception. − *adj.* used in the phrase "You're welcome" as a reply to an expression of thanks.

weld (weld) *vb.* **weld·ing, weld·ed** to join pieces of metal or plastic by first heating the edges to soften them then letting them harden together. − *n.* a joint made by welding.

wel·fare (wel′fâr′) *n.* **1** the health, comfort, happiness, and general well-being of a person, group, etc. **2** financial or other support given to those in need.

well¹ (wel) *adv.* **bet·ter** (bet′ər), **best** (best) *adv.* **1** skillfully: *She plays well.* **2** satisfactorily: *All went well.* **3** kindly: *I was well treated.* **4** thoroughly; properly: *Wash it well.* **5** intimately: *I don't know her well.* **6** by a long way: *It's well past midnight.* − *adj.* **better** (bet′ər), **best** (best) **1** healthy. **2** sensible; advisable: *It would be as well to check.* − **as well** too; in addition. − **as well as** in addition to.

well² (wel) *n.* a hole bored into the ground to give access to a supply of water, oil, or gas.

we'll (wēl) **1** we will. **2** we shall.

● **Wel·ling·ton** (wel′ing-tən) is the capital of NEW ZEALAND.

● **Wel·ling·ton** (wel′ing-tən), **Duke of** (1769-1852) was a British soldier and statesman.

Astronauts become weightless as they escape Earth's gravity. On the Moon, where gravity is weak, an astronaut would weigh less.

In Space

Welsh (welsh) *adj.* **1** of, or belonging to, WALES. **2** of, or in, the language of Wales. − *n.* **1** the Celtic language of Wales. **2** the people of Wales.

went. See **go**.

wept. See **weep**.

were. See **be**.

we're (wîr) we are.

Gas welding uses heat from a gas torch to join two metal parts which then melt and mix. As they cool, the parts fuse together.

weren't (wurnt) were not.

● **Wes·ley** (wes′lē, wez′lē) **Brothers** John (1703-1791) was an English religious leader who founded Methodism; Charles (1707-1788) wrote more than 6,000 hymns.

west (west) *n.* the direction in which the sun sets, or any part of the earth, a country, town, etc. lying in that direction. − *adj.* **1** in the west; on the side that is on or nearer the west. **2** (of a wind) blowing from the west. − *adv.* toward the west. − **the West** the countries of EUROPE and NORTH AMERICA, in contrast to those of ASIA.

west·er·ly (wes′tər-lē) *adj.* **1** (of a wind) coming from the west. **2** of, or in, the west. − *n.* **west·er·lies** a westerly wind.

west·ern (west′ərn) *adj.* of the west.

● **Western Aus·tra·lia** (ô-strāl′yə) is the largest state in AUSTRALIA. Its capital is Perth.

● **west·ern·er** (west′ər-nər) *n.* a person who lives in or comes from the west, or the WEST.

● **Western Sa·mo·a** (sə-mō′ə). See Supplement, **Countries**.

West In·di·an (west in′dē-ən) *n.* & *adj.* a native or inhabitant of the West Indies.

● **West Indies** an island chain separating the Caribbean Sea from the ATLANTIC. The largest islands are CUBA, the DOMINICAN REPUBLIC and HAITI, JAMAICA, and PUERTO RICO.

● **Wes·ting·house** (west′ing-hous′), **George** (1846-1914) was an American inventor.

Welsh is from the Old English word *waelisc* meaning "foreign." It is the second part of the name "Cornwall." The word "walnut" means literally "foreign nut."

PRONUNCIATION SYMBOLS		
ə **a**way	l**e**mon	f**o**cus
a	f**a**t	oi	b**oy**
ā	f**a**de	oo	f**oo**t
ä	h**o**t	ōō	m**oo**n
âr	f**air**	ou	h**ou**se
e	m**e**t	th	**th**ink
ē	m**ea**n	th	**th**is
g	**g**et	u	c**u**t
hw	**wh**ich	ur	h**ur**t
i	f**i**n	w	**w**itch
ī	l**i**ne	y	**y**es
îr	n**ear**	yōō	m**u**sic
ô	**o**ften	yoor	p**u**re
ō	n**o**te	zh	vi**s**ion

● **Westminster Ab·bey** is a church in London where British monarchs are crowned.

● **West Vir·gin·ia** (west′vər-jin′yə). See Supplement, **U.S.A.**

west·ward (west′wərd) (also **west·wards** (west′wərdz)) *adv.* & *adj.* toward the west.

wet (wet) *adj.* **wet·ter, wet·test 1** covered or soaked in water, rain, or other liquid. **2** (of weather) rainy. **3** (of paint, cement, etc.) not yet dried. – *n.* **1** moisture. **2** rainy weather; rain. – *vb.* **wet·ting, wet** or **wet·ted** to make wet; to splash or soak.

whale (wāl) *n.* any of several huge sea mammals that breathe air through an opening on the head. – *vb.* **whal·ing, whaled** to hunt whales.

The blue whale is by far the largest animal. The elephant is the largest land animal and the giraffe the tallest, while the ostrich is the largest bird.

● Because they are mammals, whales must swim to the surface to breathe. They take in air through a blowhole, or two slits, on top of the head. Baby whales are born in water. As soon as they are born they swim up to the surface to breathe.

wharf (hwôrf, wôrf) *n.* **wharves** (hwôrvz, wôrvz) or **wharfs** a structure built along a waterfront for loading and unloading vessels.

what (hwät, hwut, hwət, wät, wut, wət) *pron.* & *adj.* used in requesting information about a thing or person: *What month are we in?* – *adj.* used in exclamations: *What awful clothes!* – **what about ...? 1** what is your opinion of ...? **2** aren't you forgetting ...? – **what ... for?** why? – **what if ...?** what will happen if ...?

what·ev·er (hwät-ev′ər, hwut-ev′ər, wät-ev′ər, wut-ev′ər) *relative pron.* & *relative adj.* any things or quantity that: *Take whatever money you need.* – *pron.* & *adj.* no matter what: *I must finish, whatever else I do.* – *adj.* at all: *It has nothing whatever to do with you.*

wheat (hwēt, wēt) *n.* any of a variety of grasses, or their grain, providing flour for bread, etc.

wheel (hwēl, wēl) *n.* **1** a circular object rotating on an axle, on which a vehicle moves. **2** a device in the shape of a wheel: *a steering wheel.*

wheel·bar·row (hwēl′bar′ō, wēl′bar′ō) *n.* a cart with one wheel and two handles.

when (hwen, wen) *adv.* at what time?; during what period?; how soon?: *When does the plane arrive?* – *conj.* **1** at the time, or during the period, that: *She locks the door when she goes to bed.* **2** as soon as: *I'll come when I've finished.* **3** but just then: *I was about to leave when the telephone rang.* – *relative pron.* which time; at or during which: *an era when life was harder.*

when·ev·er (hwen-ev′ər, wen-ev′ər) *conj.* **1** at every time that: *He gets furious whenever he loses.* **2** if ever; no matter when: *Come whenever you like.*

where (hwâr, wâr) *adv.* in, at, or to which place?; in what direction?: *Where is she going?* – *pron.* what place?: *Where have you come from?* – *conj.* or *relative pron.* in, at, or to the place that: *We visited the town where I was born.*

where·a·bouts (hwâr′ə-bouts′, wâr′ə-bouts′) *n.* the position of a person or thing.

whereas (hwâr-az′) *conj.* while on the contrary: *Fish have gills whereas whales are mammals and breathe air.*

wher·ev·er (hwâr-ev′ər, wâr-ev′ər) *relative pron.* in, at, or to every place that: *She takes it wherever she goes.* – *conj.* in, at, or to whatever place: *They were welcomed wherever they went.* – *adv.* **1** no matter where: *I won't lose touch, wherever I go.* **2** an emphatic form of **where.**

From log wheel to pneumatic (air-filled) wheel — the wheel, some 5,000 years old, is one of the most important of all human inventions, making heavy loads much easier to move.

weth·er (hwe<u>th</u>′ər, we<u>th</u>′ər) *conj.* **1** used to introduce an indirect question: *I asked whether it was raining.* **2** used to introduce an indirect question involving alternative possibilities: *I was uncertain whether or not he liked her.* **3** used to state the certainty of something, whichever of two circumstances applies: *He promised to marry her, whether or not his parents agreed.*

which (hwich, wich) *adj.* or *pron.* used in requesting information about a thing or person from a known set or group: *Which twin did you mean? – relative pron.* **1** used to introduce a clause: *These are all animals which hibernate.* **2** used to add a commenting clause: *She moved her car, which was in the street, into the garage.*

which·ev·er (hwich-ev′ər, wich-ev′ər) *relative pron. & relative adj.* **1** the one or ones that; any that: *Take whichever coat fits better.* **2** according to which: *You can come at 10:00 or 10:30, whichever is more convenient. – adj. & pron.* no matter which: *We'll be late, whichever way we go.*

whiff (hwif, wif) *n.* **1** a slight smell. **2** a hint.

while (hwīl, wīl) *conj.* **1** at the same time as: *She worked while I gardened.* **2** for as long as; for the whole time that: *He guards us while we sleep.* **3** during the time that: *It happened while we were abroad. – n.* a space or lapse of time: *She came in after a while.*

whim·per (hwim′pər, wim′pər) *vb.* **whim·per·ing, whim·pered** to cry feebly.

whine (hwīn, wīn) *vb.* **whin·ing, whined** to complain. *– n.* a whimper.

whip (hwip, wip) *n.* a thin piece of leather or cord attached to a handle, for hitting animals or people. *– vb.* **whip·ping, whipped 1** to strike with, or with the force, of a whip.

whirl (hwurl, wurl) *vb.* **whirl·ing, whirled** to spin rapidly. *– n.* a circling or spiraling movement or pattern.

whirl·pool (hwurl′pōōl′, wurl′pōōl′) *n.* a fast-circling current.

whirl·wind (hwurl′wind, wurl′wind) *n.* a violently spiraling column of air. *– adj.* rapid.

whisk (hwisk, wisk) *vb.* **whisk·ing, whisked 1** to brush or sweep lightly: *She whisked the crumbs off the table.* **2** to transport rapidly. **3** to beat or whip: *to whisk eggs.*

whis·ker (hwis′kər, wis′kər) *n.* **1** any of the long coarse hairs growing around the mouth of a cat, mouse, etc. **2** (in *plural*) a man's beard.

whis·key or **whis·ky** (hwis′kē, wis′kē) *n.* **whis·keys** or **whis·kies** an alcoholic spirit distilled from fermented grain.

whis·per (hwis′pər, wis′pər) *vb.* **whis·per·ing, whis·pered** to speak quietly so that other people cannot hear.

whis·tle (hwis′əl, wis′əl) *n.* **1** a shrill sound produced through pursed lips or through the teeth. **2** any of several similar sounds, for example the call of a bird. **3** any of many devices producing a similar sound. *– vb.* **whis·tling, whis·tled 1** to produce a whistle. **2** to blow or play on a whistle.

● **Whis·tler** (hwis′lər, wis′lər), **James** (1834-1903) was an American painter.

white (hwīt, wīt) *adj.* **1** of the color of snow, milk, salt, etc. **2** (of people) belonging to one of the pale-skinned races; Caucasian. *– n.* **1** white color. **2** the clear fluid surrounding the yolk of an egg. **3** the white part of the eyeball, surrounding the iris.

white blood cell or **white corpuscle** *n.* one of the colorless cells in blood, that protect the body against disease and infection.

● **White House** the official residence and office of the president of the UNITED STATES since 1900. It is situated in Washington, D.C.

white lie *n.* a forgivable lie.

● **Whit·man** (hwit′mən, wit′mən), **Walt** (1819-1892) was an American poet, best known for his *Leaves of Grass.*

● **Whit·ney** (hwit′nē, wit′nē), **Eli** (1765-1825) was the American inventor of the cotton gin.

whit·tle (hwit′l, wit′l) *vb.* **whit·tling, whit·tled** to cut or carve a stick, piece of wood, etc.; to shape or fashion in this way.

who (hōō) *pron.* what person or people?: *Who gave it to you? – relative pron.* used to introduce a clause **1** that: *I saw the boy who gave you the frog.* **2** used to add a commenting clause: *Bellini, who was born in 1801, was a great composer.*

who·ev·er (hōō-ev′ər) *relative pron.* any person or people that: *Whoever is appointed must face this challenge. – pron.* **1** no matter who: *Whoever calls, I'm not available.* **2** an emphatic form of **who.**

who'd (hōōd) **1** who would. **2** who had.

whole (hōl) *n.* all of something. *– adj.* **1** all of; no less than: *I'd like to eat the whole cake.* **2** in one piece: *I swallowed it whole.* **3** unbroken.

Eli Whitney's cotton gin was used to remove seeds and impurities from cotton fibers. It was worked by hand.

Wife comes from an Old English word meaning "woman."

whole·sale (hōl′sāl′) *n.* the sale of goods in large quantities to a storekeeper.

whole·some (hōl′səm) *adj.* attractively healthy: *That bread has a wholesome appearance.*

whole wheat *adj.* made from the entire grain of wheat: *whole wheat flour.*

whol·ly (hōl′lē) altogether.

whom (hoōm) the object form of **who**: *To whom am I speaking?*

whoop (hoōp, hoop, hwoōp, hwoop) *n.* **1** a loud cry of delight, triumph, etc. **2** a noisy indrawn breath typical in whooping cough. – *vb.*
whoop·ing, whooped to make a loud cry.

whooping cough *n.* an infectious disease with bouts of violent coughing.

who's (hoōz) **1** who is. **2** who has.

whose (hoōz) *pron. & adj.* belonging to which person or people: *Whose is this jacket?* – *relative pron. & relative adj.* used to introduce a clause of whom or which: *I am talking about the children whose parents are divorced.*

why (hwī, wī) *adv.* for what reason: *Why do you ask?* – *relative pron.* for, or because of, which: *There is no reason why I should go.* – *n.* a reason.

wick (wik) *n.* the string running up through a candle, that burns when lit.

wick·ed (wik′əd) *adj.* **1** evil. **2** mischievous.

wick·er (wik′ər) *n.* flexible twigs, cane, or rush woven together. – *adj.* made of wicker.

wide (wīd) *adj.* **1** large in extent from side to side. **2** measuring a certain amount from side to side. **3** (of eyes) open to the fullest extent. **4** (of a range, selection, etc.) covering a great variety. **5** extensive; widespread: *He had wide support.* **6** general, as opposed to particular: *We must consider the wider issues.* – *adv.* **1** over an extensive area: *far and wide.* **2** to the fullest extent: *She stood with legs wide apart.*

wide·spread (wīd′spred′) *adj.* extending over a wide area: *There is widespread flooding.*

wid·ow (wid′ō) *n.* a woman whose husband is dead and who has not remarried.

wid·ow·er (wid′ō-ər) *n.* a man whose wife is dead and who has not remarried.

width (width, witth) *n.* extent from side to side.

wife (wīf) *n.* **wives** (wīvz) the woman to whom a man is married; a married woman.

wig (wig) *n.* an artificial covering of hair.

wig·wam (wig′wäm′) *n.* a domed tent made by NATIVE AMERICANS.

Wigs today are worn mainly by actors, legal officials in some countries, and some bald people. Wigs have been found on Egyptian mummies and were worn by the Persians, Greeks, and Romans. Wig wearing by men and women became fashionable in 17th-century France. Above are shown a French officer's campaign wig of 1670 and the wig of a wealthy Spanish lady of the 1650s.

wild (wīld) *adj.* **1** (of animals) untamed; not dependent on humans. **2** (of plants) growing in a natural, uncultivated state. **3** (of country) desolate and rugged. **4** unrestrained; uncontrolled; frantically excited: *The spectators went wild.* **5** (of weather) stormy: *It was a wild night.* – *n.* a wild animal's or plant's natural environment: *The zoo returned the cub to the wild.*

wild·cat (wīld′kat′) *n.* a fierce undomesticated variety of cat living in the wild.

wild·life (wīld′līf′) *n.* wild animals, birds, and plants in general.

●**Wilde** (wīld), **Oscar** (1854-1900) was an Irish poet, dramatist, and wit.

●**Wil·der** (wīl′dər), **Thornton** (1897-1975) was an American playwright and novelist.

wil·der·ness (wil′dər-nəs) *n.* an uncultivated or uninhabited region.

will¹ (wil, wəl, əl) *vb.* (*auxiliary*) used **1** to form a future tense: *He will arrive soon.* **2** to express intention or determination: *We will not give in.* **3** to make requests: *Please will you shut the door?* **4** to express commands: *You will apologize to her!* **5** to indicate readiness or willingness: *Any of our stores will exchange the goods.* **6** to make an invitation: *Will you have some coffee?*

will² (wil) *n.* **1** the determination to succeed; desire: *She has lost the will to live.* **2** a document containing instructions for the disposal of one's possessions and money after death. **3** feelings toward someone: *I felt no ill will toward her.*

●**Wil·liam** (wil′yəm) **I** was king of ENGLAND (1066-1087), and known as "the Conqueror" because he defeated King Harold.

●**Wil·liams** (wil′yəmz), **Tennessee** (1911-1983) was an American dramatist whose plays include *A Streetcar Named Desire.*

will·ing (wil′ing) *adj.* **1** ready to do something. **2** eager and cooperative.

wil·low (wil′ō) *n.* a tree with flexible branches.

wilt (wilt) *vb.* **wilt·ing, wilt·ed** (of flowers) to droop or wither, for example from heat.

wil·y (wī′lē) *adj.* **wil·i·er, wil·i·est** cunning.

win (win) *vb.* **win·ning, won** (wun) **1** to come first in a contest, war, election, etc. **2** to obtain by struggle or effort: *The team won support.* – *n.* a victory or success. – *n.* **win·ner.**

wind¹ (wind) *n.* **1** a current of air moving across the earth's surface. **2** breath or breath supply: *She was panting and short of wind.* – *vb.* **wind·ing, wind·ed** to deprive of breath temporarily: *She was winded by her fall.*

wind² (wīnd) *vb.* **wind·ing, wound** (wound) **1** to wrap or coil around something. **2** to move along a path with many twists and turns: *The road winds a lot.* **3** to tighten the spring of by turning a knob or key: *She winds the clock every day.* – *vb.* **wind up 1** to tighten the spring of. **2** to come or bring to a close.

wind instrument *n.* a musical instrument such as a clarinet, flute, or trumpet, played by blowing air through it.

wind·mill (wind'mil') *n.* a mill for grinding grain, or a machine for pumping water or generating electricity, operated by sails driven by the wind.

win·dow (win'dō) *n.* **1** an opening in a wall, roof, vehicle, etc. to look out through, or let in light and air, usually covered with glass. **2** an area into which a computer display may be divided.

Window means "wind's eye" for, besides letting in light, windows let in air. For centuries the windows of ordinary European houses had no glass in them.

wind·shield (wind'shēld') *n.* the front window or clear screen of a car, motorcycle, etc.

wind·surf·ing (wind'sur'fing) *n.* a sport that combines elements of sailing and surfing, using a board equipped with a sail.

wind·y (win'dē) *adj.* **wind·i·er, wind·i·est** exposed to, or affected by, strong wind.

wine (wīn) *n.* an alcoholic drink made from the fermented juice of grapes, or one made from other fruits, plants, etc.

wing (wing) *n.* **1** the part of the body on a bird, insect, or bat that is adapted for flying. **2** the structure projecting from either side of an aircraft body. **3** a part of a building projecting from the central or main section.

wing·span (wing'span') *n.* the distance from tip to tip of the wings of an aircraft or a bird.

wink (wingk) *vb.* **wink·ing, winked** to shut an eye briefly, often as a signal to someone.

●**Win·ni·peg** (win'ə-peg') is the capital of Manitoba province, CANADA.

An 18th-century fantail windmill. The small fantail attached to the main sail kept the main sail turned toward the wind.

win·ter (wint'ər) *n.* the coldest season of the year, coming between fall and spring. – *adj.* of, or belonging to, winter.

wipe (wīp) *vb.* **wip·ing, wiped 1** to clean or dry with a cloth, on a mat, etc. **2** to remove by rubbing. **3** to apply by rubbing: *Wipe the surface with wax.* – *vb.* **wipe out 1** to clean out the inside of. **2** to remove or get rid of.

wip·er (wī'pər) *n.* a person or thing that wipes, as the mechnical arm on a car's windshield.

wire (wīr) *n.* **1** metal drawn out into a narrow flexible thread. **2** a length of this, usually wrapped in insulating material, used for carrying an electric current.

wir·ing (wīr'ing) *n.* the arrangement of electrical wires used in a circuit or system.

wir·y (wīr'ē) *adj.* **wir·i·er, wir·i·est 1** of slight build, but strong and agile. **2** (of hair) coarse and wavy.

●**Wis·con·sin** (wis-kän'sən). See Supplement, **U.S.A**.

wis·dom (wiz'dəm) *n.* **1** the ability to make sensible judgments on the basis of experience and common sense. **2** knowledge.

wise (wīz) *adj.* **1** having or showing wisdom; prudent; sensible. **2** educated or informed.

-wise *suffix* denoting direction or manner: *lengthwise; clockwise; likewise; otherwise.*

PRONUNCIATION SYMBOLS		
ə **a**way	l**e**mon	f**o**cus
a f**a**t	oi	b**o**y
ā f**a**de	oo	f**oo**t
ä h**o**t	ōō	m**oo**n
âr f**ai**r	ou	h**ou**se
e m**e**t	th	**th**ink
ē m**ea**n	t͟h	**th**is
g **g**et	u	c**u**t
hw **wh**ich	ur	h**ur**t
i f**i**n	w	**w**itch
ī l**i**ne	y	**y**es
îr n**ea**r	yōō	m**u**sic
ô **o**ften	yoor	p**u**re
ō n**o**te	zh	vi**si**on

wish (wish) *vb.* **wish·ing, wished** **1** to want; to desire: *I wish I'd known.* **2** to long vainly for: *I've often wished for a quieter life.* − *n.* **1** a longing or desire. **2** (in *plural*) a hope expressed for someone's welfare: *Best wishes to your parents.*

wit (wit) *n.* **1** humor; the ability to express oneself amusingly. **2** a person with this ability. **3** (*in plural*) common sense; intelligence.

witch (wich) *n.* a person, especially a woman, supposed to have magical powers.

witch·craft (wich′kraft′) *n.* magic or sorcery of the kind practiced by witches.

with (wit͟h, with) *prep.* **1** in the company of: *I danced with him.* **2** by means of; using: *They raised it with a crowbar.* **3** used after verbs of covering, providing, etc.: *The pit was filled with garbage; They are equipped with firearms.* **4** as a result of: *She was shaking with fear.* **5** at the same time or rate as: *Discretion comes with age.* **6** used in describing: *They saw a man with a limp.*

with·draw (wit͟h-drô′, with-drô′) *vb.* **with·draw·ing, with·drew** (wit͟h-drōō′, with-drōō′), **with·drawn** (wit͟h-drôn′, with-drôn′) **1** to move somewhere else more secluded: *She withdrew into her bedroom.* **2** (of troops) to move back; to retreat. **3** to pull in or back: *She withdrew her hand from his.*

with·er (wit͟h′ər) *vb.* **with·er·ing, with·ered** **1** (of plants) to dry up and die. **2** to cause to dry up and die.

with·in (wit͟h-in′, with-in′) *prep.* **1** inside; enclosed by.

with·out (wit͟h-out′, with-out′) *prep.* **1** not having the company of: *She went home without him.* **2** deprived of: *I can't live without her.* **3** not having: *There was a blue sky without a cloud.* **4** not giving, showing, etc.: *He did as requested without a murmur.*

with·stand (with-stand′, wit͟h-stand′) *vb.* **with·stand·ing, with·stood** (with-stood′, wit͟h-stood′) to resist.

wit·ness (wit′nəs) *n.* **1** someone who sees and can give a direct account of an event, occurrence, etc. **2** a person who gives evidence in a court of law. − *vb.* **wit·ness·ing, wit·nessed** to be present as an observer at: *to witness an event.*

wit·ty (wit′ē) *adj.* **wit·ti·er, wit·ti·est** able to express yourself cleverly and amusingly.

wiz·ard (wiz′ərd) *n.* a person, especially a man, supposed to have magic powers.

woe (wō) *n.* **1** grief; misery. **2** (in *plural*) problems and afflictions.

wolf (woolf) *n.* **wolves** (woolvz) a wild animal of the dog family, that hunts in packs. − **cry wolf** to give a false alarm.

General James Wolfe's capture in 1759 of Quebec, the capital of New France (present-day Canada), ensured that Britain gained vast areas of France's lands in North America.

●**Wolfe** (woolf), **James** (1727-1759) was a British general who fought against the French in North America.

wom·an (woom′ən) *n.* **wom·en** (wim′ən) **1** an adult human female. **2** women generally: *The book is aimed at today's woman.*

wom·an·ly (woom′ən-lē) *adj.* feminine; considered natural or suitable to a woman.

women's liberation *n.* a movement, started by women, aimed at freeing them from the disadvantages they suffer in a male-dominated society.

In 1893 New Zealand became the world's first country to give women equal voting rights. In the U.S.A. and Britain the struggle for suffrage (the right to vote) continued for many more years. Women demonstrated in the streets and publicized injustices through poster campaigns.

● At the beginning of this century women did not have the right to vote, so they were powerless to get changes through Congress. In the UNITED STATES a women's rights convention was organized as early as 1848 by Lucretia Mott and Elizabeth Cady Stanton. Women received the right to vote in 1920.

womb (wōōm) *n.* the uterus, the organ in female mammals in which the baby develops until birth.

wom·bat (wäm′bat′) *n.* an Australian marsupial that eats plants and lives in burrows.

won. See **win**.

won·der (wun′dər) *n.* **1** the state of mind produced by something extraordinary, new, or unexpected; awe. **2** a marvel. – **work wonders** to achieve marvelous results. – *adj.* notable for accomplishing marvels: *It is a wonder drug.* – *vb.* **won·der·ing, won·dered 1** to be curious: *I often wondered about her background.* **2** to be surprised: *I shouldn't wonder if she won.* **3** to be uncertain: *I wonder whether to go.* **4** used politely to introduce requests: *I wonder if you could help me?*

won·der·ful (wun′dər-fəl) *adj.* **1** extraordinary. **2** excellent; splendid.

won't (wōnt) will not.

wood (wood) *n.* **1** the hard substance which forms the trunk and branches of trees. **2** this material used in building, for making furniture, etc., or as a fuel. **3** (in *singular* or *plural*) an expanse of growing trees.

● Wood is one of the most useful materials that we use. It can be sawn, carved, and worked into all kinds of shapes. There are two types of wood: softwood and hardwood. Softwood comes mostly from conifers. Much of it is turned into pulp for making paper and plastics. Hardwood comes from oaks, ash trees, etc. and is used for furniture and construction work.

wood·chuck (wood′chuk′) *n.* a gray or brown rodent of NORTH AMERICA with a stocky body and a short tail.

wood·cut (wood′kut′) *n.* a design cut into a wooden block, or a print taken from it.

wood·en (wood′n) *adj.* **1** made of or like wood. **2** stiff; lacking expression and liveliness.

wood·peck·er (wood′pek′ər) *n.* a bird with a strong, sharp beak with which it bores into tree bark searching for insects to eat.

wood·wind (wood′wind′) *n.* any of the orchestral wind instruments including the flute, oboe, clarinet, and bassoon.

wood·work (wood′wurk′) *n.* the art of making things out of wood; carpentry.

wood·y (wood′ē) *adj.* **wood·i·er, wood·i·est 1** (of countryside) wooded. **2** made of wood: *She studies plants with woody stems.* **3** like wood: *a woody appearance.*

wool (wool) *n.* **1** the soft wavy hair of sheep and certain other animals. **2** yarn made from wool. – *adj.* made of, or relating to, wool.

wool·en (wool′ən) *adj.* **1** made of wool. **2** producing, or dealing in, goods made of wool. – *n.* (often in *plural*) a woolen, especially knitted, piece of clothing.

wool·ly (wool′ē) *adj.* **wool·li·er, wool·li·est 1** made of wool or covered with wool. **2** vague: *woolly thinking.*

● **Woolf** (woolf), **Virginia** (1882-1941) was an English novelist, author of *To the Lighthouse.*

word (wurd) *n.* **1** a meaningful unit of spoken or written language that can stand alone. **2** a brief conversation on a particular matter: *I'd like a word with you.* **3** news or notice: *She sent word she'd arrive tomorrow.* **4** a solemn promise: *He gave his word of honor.* – *vb.* **word·ing, word·ed** to express in carefully chosen words: *She worded her refusal tactfully.* – **as good as your word** careful to keep your promise. – **have words** to quarrel.

word processor *n.* an electronic machine with a screen, into which text can be entered by a keyboard and organized, stored, updated, and printed out. – *n.* **word processing**.

● **Words·worth** (wurdz′wurth′), **William** (1770-1850) was an English poet.

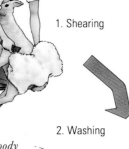

1. Shearing

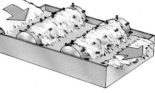

2. Washing

3. Squeezing

4. Dyeing

5. Carding

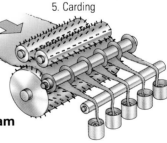

6. Roving

The fleece is clipped with electric shears and washed to remove grease and dirt (1&2). The wool is then squeezed to remove water and dyed (3&4). The wool is "carded" through wire-toothed rollers to produce loose ropes called "slivers" (5). A number of slivers are rolled (roving) into a thin rope which will be used to spin yarn (6).

work (wurk) *n.* **1** physical or mental effort made in order to achieve or make something; labor, study, research, etc. **2** employment: *He is out of work.* **3** a place of employment: *She leaves work at 4:30.* **4** the product of mental or physical labor: *This is a splendid piece of work.* **5** a literary, artistic, musical, or dramatic composition or creation. **6** (in *plural*) a factory or mill. **7** (in *plural*) the operating parts of a watch or machine. – *adj.* relating to, suitable for work: *I'm wearing my work clothes.* – *vb.* **work·ing, worked 1** to do work; to toil, labor, or study. **2** to be employed; to have a job; to perform the tasks and duties involved in a job: *He works a nine-hour day.* **3** to operate properly: *Does this radio work?* – *vb.* **work off** to get rid of by energetic activity: *to work off nervous tension.* – *vb.* **work out 1** to solve, sort out, or reason out. **2** to go successfully. **3** to perform a set of energetic physical exercises.

work·er (wur'kər) *n.* **1** a person who works. **2** among social insects such as bees or ants, a female that does the work of the colony.

work force (wurk'fôrs', wurk'fōrs') *n.* the number of workers engaged in a particular industry, factory, etc.

work·load (wurk'lōd') *n.* the amount of work expected of a person or machine.

work·shop (wurk'shäp') *n.* **1** a room or building where construction and repairs are carried out. **2** a course of study or work for a group of people on a particular project.

work station *n.* a person's seat at a computer terminal.

world (wurld) *n.* **1** the earth; the planet we inhabit. **2** the people inhabiting the earth; humankind: *We must tell the world.* **3** human affairs: *They discussed the present state of the world.* **4 World** the people of a particular region or period, and their culture: *the Third World.* – *adj.* of, relating to, or important throughout the whole world: *I took part in the world championships.*

world·ly (wurld'lē) *adj.* **world·li·er, world·li·est** relating to this world; material, not spiritual or eternal.

World Series (wurld sîr ēz) *n.* a series of baseball games, played in North America, that determines the champions of professional baseball.

●**World War I** (1914-1918) between the Allied Powers (Britain, France, Russia, and later the United States) and the Central Powers (Germany, Austria-Hungary, and Turkey) was caused by territorial rivalries. The Allied Powers eventually won this futile, costly war. In the Treaty of Versailles ending the war, the seeds were sown for the rise of Nazism in Germany and WORLD WAR II.

A gas mask. Gas was one of the new horrors of warfare.

For four years, fighting in World War I centered on two lines of trenches stretching across western Europe—the Western Front. There was no decisive battle. Conditions in the dirty, waterlogged trenches became increasingly intolerable.

● **World War II** (1939-1945) was between the Allies (led by Britain, France, Russia, and later the United States) and the Axis Powers (HITLER's Germany, Mussolini's Italy, and Japan). The immediate causes were Hitler's invasion of Poland (1939) and the Japanese attack on Pearl Harbor (December 1941). The Allied invasion of France in 1944 led to the defeat of Germany. The dropping of two atomic bombs on Japan in 1945 ended the war in the east.

worm (wurm) *n.* **1** a long slender animal without backbone or limbs, found in soil; an earthworm. **2** the larva of any of various insects; a grub.

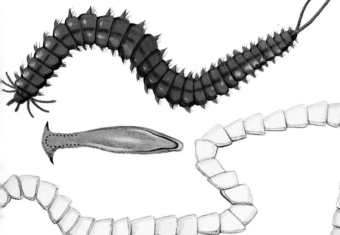

There are more than 20,000 species of worm. They include segmented worms such as earthworms, marine worms (lugworms) and leeches, parasites such as the tapeworm or flatworms.

worn (wôrn, wōrn). See **wear**. – *adj.* **1** looking old and weary. **2** thin and threadbare through long use or wear. – **worn out 1** exhausted. **2** too badly worn to be any further use.

wor·ry (wur′ē) *vb.* **wor·ries, wor·ry·ing, wor·ried 1** to be anxious. **2** to cause anxiety to. **3** to bother or harass. – *n.* **wor·ries 1** a state of anxiety. **2** a cause of anxiety. – *adj.* **wor·ried.** – *n.* **wor·ri·er**.

worse (wurs) *adj.* (*comparative* of **bad**) **1** more unfavorable: *To be blind or deaf — which is worse?* **2** more grave, serious, or acute. – *n.* something worse: *Worse was to follow.* – *adv.* less well.

wors·en (wur′sən) *vb.* **wors·en·ing, wors·ened** to grow worse.

People first worshiped life-giving mother goddesses. Early farmers worshiped and asked the help of nature gods, such as the sun and moon.

wor·ship (wur′shəp) *vb.* **wor·ship·ing** or **wor·ship·ping, wor·shiped** or **wor·shipped 1** to honor God or a god with praise, prayer, hymns, etc. **2** to love or admire, especially blindly; to idolize.

worst (wurst) *adj.* (*superlative* of **bad**) **1** most awful, unpleasant, etc. **2** most grave or severe. – *n.* the worst thing or possibility: *I fear the worst.* – *adv.* most severely; most badly.

worth (wurth) *n.* **1** value; importance; usefulness. **2** the quantity of anything that can be bought for a certain sum, accomplished in a certain time, etc.: *a dollar's worth of candy; three days' worth of work.* – *adj.* **1** having a value of: *This painting is worth a fortune.* **2** deserving.

worth·less (wurth′ləs) *adj.* of no value or merit.

worth·while (wurth-hwīl′, wurth-wīl′) *adj.* worth the time, money, or energy spent; useful.

wor·thy (wur′thē) *adj.* **wor·thi·er, wor·thi·est** admirable; excellent; deserving: *I support several worthy causes.*

would (wood) *vb.* used as past tense of **will 1** in reported speech: *She said she would leave at ten.* **2** to indicate willingness, readiness, or ability: *He was asked to help, but would not.* **3** to indicate habitual action: *He would always telephone at six.* **4** in making polite invitations, offers, or requests: *Would you like to go?*

would-be (wood′bē′) *adj.* hoping to be.

wound¹. See **wind²**.

wound² (woond) *n.* an injury to a living animal or plant tissue, caused by a cut, blow, etc. – *vb.* **wound·ing, wound·ed 1** to inflict an injury on. **2** to injure the feelings of.

wrap (rap) *vb.* **wrap·ping, wrapped** *vb.* **1** to fold or wind around something: *She wrapped the shawl around the baby.* **2** to cover in something.

wrath (rath) *n.* anger; fury.

wreath (rēth) *n.* a ring-shaped garland of flowers and leaves placed on a grave, or hung up as a decoration.

wreck (rek) *n.* **1** the destruction of a ship at sea. **2** a hopelessly damaged ship; a crashed aircraft; a ruined vehicle. – *vb.* **wreck·ing, wrecked** to break; to destroy.

Worm has not always meant "earthworm." It was originally used to describe dragons and serpents.

wrench (rench) *vb.* **wrench·ing, wrenched**
1 to pull or twist violently. **2** to sprain or injure.
– *n.* **1** a violent pull or twist. **2** a tool for
gripping and turning nuts and bolts, etc.

wres·tle (res′əl, ras′əl) *vb.*
wres·tling, wres·tled 1 to fight
by trying to grip and throw your
opponent; to do this as a
sport. **2** to struggle: *She
wrestled with her*

*Wrestling, the oldest sport
of all, goes back over 4,500
years. In Japan today,
Sumo wrestlers (left) are
national heroes.*

conscience before going to the police. – *n.* **wres·tler**
(res′lər, ras′lər). – *n.* **wres·tling**.

wrig·gle (rig′əl) *vb.* **wrig·gling, wrig·gled**
1 to twist and turn. **2** to manage cleverly to get
out of doing something you don't want to do.

wright (rīt) *n. suffix* a maker or repairer: *a
playwright, shipwright, wheelwright,* etc.

• **Wright** (rīt) **Brothers** Orville (1871-1948) and
Wilbur (1867-1912) were American inventors
who built and flew the first airplane near Kitty
Hawk, North Carolina, in 1903.

• **Wright** (rīt), **Frank Lloyd** (1867-1959)

was an American architect, famous for both his
public buildings and private homes.

wring (ring) *vb.* **wring·ing, wrung** (rung) **1** to
force liquid out of by twisting or squeezing.
2 to break by twisting: *to wring a chicken's neck.* –
wringing wet soaking wet.

wrin·kle (ring′kəl) *n.* **1** a crease or line in the
skin. **2** a slight crease or ridge in any surface.
– *vb.* **wrin·kling, wrin·kled** to develop
wrinkles.

wrist (rist) *n.* **1** the joint between the hand and
arm. **2** the part of a sleeve covering this.

wrist·watch (rist′wäch′) *n.* a watch worn
strapped around the wrist.

write (rīt) *vb.* **writ·ing, wrote** (rōt), **writ·ten**
(rit′n) **1** to produce letters, symbols, numbers,
words, sentences, etc. on a surface, usually
using a pen or pencil. **2** to compose or create a
book, music, newspaper articles, etc. **3** to fill in:
The doctor wrote a prescription. **4** to compose a
letter to. **5** to express in written form: *to write
your thoughts.* **6** to display clearly: *There was guilt
written all over his face.* – *vb.* **write down** to put
down in writing.

writ·er (rīt′ər) *n.* a person who writes, especially
as a living; an author.

writ·ing (rīt′ing) *n.* **1** written or printed words.
2 handwriting. **3** the art or activity of writing
books, poetry, etc.

writ·ten (rit′n). See **write**. – *adj.* taken down in
writing, and so undeniable: *written evidence.*

wrong (rông) *adj.* **1** not correct. **2** mistaken: *I
was quite wrong about her motives.* **3** not
appropriate or suitable: *I'm always saying the
wrong thing.* **4** not good; not sensible: *It's wrong
to waste the good weather.* **5** bad: *It's wrong to tell
lies.* **6** defective or faulty: *There is something
wrong with the radio.* **7** causing trouble, pain,
etc.: *She wouldn't cry unless something was wrong
with her.* – *adv.* incorrectly: *I spelled her name
wrong.* – *n.* **1** whatever is not right or just: *I
know right from wrong.* **2** any injury done to
someone else: *He did her wrong.* – *vb.*
wrong·ing, wronged to treat unjustly.

• **Wy·o·ming** (wī-ō′ming). See Supplement,
U.S.A.

*The Guggenheim Museum in New York City,
completed in 1960, is perhaps Frank Lloyd Wright's
best known building. Inside a spiral ramp runs from
the floor to the ceiling.*

X x

X (eks) *symbol* **1** (especially in mathematics; also **x**) an unknown quantity. **2** the Roman numeral for ten.

●**Xa·vi·er** (zā′vē-ər, ig-zā′vē-ər)**, Saint Francis** (1506-1552) was a Spanish missionary who helped to found the JESUITS.

xe·no·pho·bi·a (zen′ə-fō′bē-ə, zē′nə-fō′bē-ə) *n.* intense fear or dislike of foreigners or strangers.

Xe·rox (zir′äks′, zē′räks′) *n.* a trademark for a process for copying documents.

Xerxes, king of Persia, failed to conquer Greece. In 480 B.C. he watched from a hillside overlooking the Bay of Salamis as the swift Greek triremes crushed his fleet.

●**Xer·xes** (zurk′sēz′) **I** (**the Great**) (519-465 B.C.) was a king of PERSIA who won a decisive victory over GREECE but his fleet was later defeated.

Xmas (kris′məs, ek′sməs) *n.* (*informal*) short for **Christmas**.

●**Xmas** comes from the ancient practice of using the Greek letter *chi* (**X**) as an abbreviation for the Greek *Christos*, the Latin *Christus*, and the English *Christ*. The ending *-mas* is the same as in *Christmas* and comes from the word *mass*. **Xmas** has been used in English since the 1500s.

X-ray or **x-ray** (eks′rā′) *n.* **1** (usually in *plural*) an electromagnetic ray that can pass through most substances except metal and bone, producing an image on photographic film. The image shows the outline of the objects through which the X-ray does not pass, as the bones of a hand. **2** a photograph taken using X-rays. – *vb.* **X-ray·ing, X-rayed** to take a photograph using X-rays.

●X-rays were discovered in 1895 by Wilhelm ROENTGEN.

xy·lo·phone (zī′lə-fōn′) *n.* a musical instrument consisting of a series of wooden, or sometimes metal, bars of different lengths, played by being struck by wooden hammers.

The letter *X*, like all the letters, has a long history. The earliest alphabets were taken and adapted by the Greeks. The Greek *beta*, when combined with the first letter, *aleph*, gives us the word alphabet.

The Greeks passed on their letters to the Romans, who developed the alphabet we use today, although they used only capital letters. Small letters developed in the A.D. 700s.

An early form of the letter X, used in the Middle East more than 3,000 years ago.

X

This letter was taken by the Greeks and became xi.

Over the years different versions of the letter X have been developed.

Y y

yacht (yät) *n.* a boat or small ship, usually with sails, built and used for racing or cruising.

yak (yak) *n.* **yaks** or **yak** a type of long-haired ox of TIBET and central ASIA.

● **Yang·tze** (yang′sē′) (**Chang Jiang** (chäng′jē-äng′) the longest river in CHINA.

yard¹ (yärd) *n.* a unit of length equal to 3 feet (0.9144m).

yard² (yärd) *n.* **1** an area of ground around a home, school, farmhouse, etc. **2** an area of enclosed ground used for a special purpose.

yard·stick (yärd′stik′) *n.* a stick three feet in length, used in measuring.

yarn (yärn) *n.* thread spun from wool, cotton, etc.

yash·mak (yash′mak′) *n.* a veil worn by MUSLIM women, covering the face.

yawn (yôn) *vb.* **yawn·ing, yawned** to open the mouth wide and take a deep breath when tired or bored. − *n.* an act of yawning.

ye (yē) *pron.* a form of *you* or *your* used in the past.

A Muslim woman is expected to cover herself when she goes out. Some Muslims believe her face should also be covered with a yashmak.

year (yîr) *n.* **1** the period of time the earth takes to go once around the sun, about 365 days. **2** the period from January 1 to December 31, being 365, or in a leap year, 366 days.

year·ly (yîr′lē) *adj.* happening every year.

yearn (yurn) *vb.* **yearn·ing, yearned** to feel a great desire; to long. − *n.* **yearn·ing.**

yeast (yēst) *n.* a substance, consisting of fungi, which causes fermentation and is used to produce bread and alcoholic drinks.

yell (yel) *n.* a loud shout or cry. − *vb.* **yell·ing, yelled** to shout: *Yvonne yelled with anger.*

Old Faithful in Yellowstone National Park, a geyser that spouts a plume of hot water every hour.

yel·low (yel′ō) *adj.* of the color of gold, egg yolk, a lemon, etc.

● **Yellow River** (China). See **Huang Ho.**

● **Yel·low·stone National Park** (yel′ə-stōn′) was established in 1872 and is the oldest and largest park in the United States. It lies in Wyoming, Idaho, and Montana.

● **Yel·tsin** (yelt′sən), **Boris** (1931-) was elected president of RUSSIA in 1991.

● **Ye·men Republic** (yem′ən, yä′mən). See Supplement, **Countries.**

yen (yen) *n.* **yen** the standard unit of currency in JAPAN.

yeo·man (yō′mən) *n.* **yeomen** a petty officer in a navy who performs clerical duties.

yes (yes) *interjection* used to express agreement or consent.

yes·ter·day (yes′tər-dē, yes′tər-dā) *n.* **1** the day before today. **2** the recent past.

yet (yet) *adv.* **1** up till now or then; by now or by that time: *He had not yet arrived.* **2** at this time; now; as early as this: *You can't leave yet.* **3** at some time in the future; before the matter is finished; still: *She may yet make a success of it.*

yew (yōō) *n.* a type of evergreen tree with dark needlelike leaves and red berries.

Yid·dish (yid′ish) *n.* a language spoken by many Jews, based on medieval German.

yield (yēld) *vb.* **yield·ing, yield·ed**
1 to produce or supply as a crop or natural product: *Cows yield milk.* **2** to give or produce: *Shares yield dividends.* **3** to surrender.

yo·del (yōd′l) *vb.* **yo·del·ing, yo·deled** to sing, changing frequently from a normal to a falsetto voice and back again. – *n.* **yo·del·er**.

yo·ga (yō′gə) *n.* **1** a system of HINDU philosophy showing how to reunite the soul with God. **2** a physical and mental discipline based on this.

yo·gurt or **yo·ghurt** (yō′gərt) *n.* a food made from fermented milk, often flavored with fruit.

yoke (yōk) *n.* **1** a wooden frame placed over the necks of oxen to hold them together when they are pulling a plow, cart, etc. **2** something oppressive; a great burden: *the yoke of slavery.*

yolk (yōk) *n.* the yellow part of an egg.

Yom Kip·pur (yäm kip′ər, yōm kə-poor′) *n.* the Day of Atonement, an annual Jewish religious festival devoted to repentance for past sins.

yon·der (yän′dər) *adj.* in or at that place over there. – *adv.* in or at that place over there.

you (yōō) *pron.* **1** the person or persons, etc. spoken or written to. **2** any or every person: *You don't often see that nowadays.*

you'd (yōōd, yəd) **1** you would. **2** you had.

you'll (yōōl, yəl) **1** you will. **2** you shall.

young (yung) *adj.* **1** in the first part of life, growth, development, etc.; not old. **2** in the early stages. – *n.* (*plural*) young animals or birds: *Some birds feed their young on insects.*

young·ster (yung′stər) *n.* a young person.

● **Young** (yung), **Brigham** (1801-1877) was the American religious leader of the MORMONS, who led his followers to settle in Salt Lake City.

your (yoor, yôr, yōr, yər) *adj.* belonging to you.

you're (yoor, yôr, yōr, yər) you are.

yours (yoorz, yôrz, yōrz) *pron.* something belonging to you: *Is this scarf mine or is it yours?*

your·self (yər-self′) *pron.* **your·selves** (yər-selvz′) **1** the reflexive form of **you**. **2** used for emphasis: *Do what you yourself think best.* **3** your normal self: *You're not yourself today.*

Yoga is intended to remove all distractions that may prevent a person from reaching a physical and mental state to live a life of the spirit. The physical training gets more and more difficult and its aim is to bring the body under complete control.

youth (yōōth) *n.* **1** the early part of life, between childhood and adulthood. **2** a boy or young man. **3** (*plural*) young people in general.

youth·ful (yōōth′fəl) *adj.* young, especially in manner or appearance.– *n.* **youth·ful·ness**.

you've (yōōv, yəv) you have.

yo-yo (yō′yō) *n.* **yo-yos** a toy consisting of a reel that spins up and down on a string.

● **Yu·go·slav·i·a** (yōō′gə-släv′ē-ə) is a country in southeastern Europe (in the Balkans) and until 1992 consisted of six federal republics: Serbia, Croatia, Slovenia, Montenegro, Bosnia-Herzegovina, and Macedonia. Today it comprises Serbia and Montenegro. See also Supplement, **Countries**.

● **Yu·kon Territory** (yōō′kän′) is a region of northwestern CANADA, along the eastern border of Alaska.

Yule (yōōl′) *n.* Christmas.

yup·pie or **yup·py** (yup′ē) *n.* **yup·pies** (*informal*) an ambitious young professional person with a career in a city.

PRONUNCIATION SYMBOLS

ə	**a**way	lemon	focus
a	f**a**t	oi	b**oy**
ā	f**a**de	oo	f**oo**t
ä	h**o**t	ōō	m**oo**n
âr	f**air**	ou	h**ou**se
e	m**e**t	th	**th**ink
ē	m**ea**n	t͟h	**th**is
g	**g**et	u	c**u**t
hw	**wh**ich	ur	h**ur**t
i	f**i**n	w	**w**itch
ī	l**i**ne	y	**y**es
îr	n**ear**	yōō	m**u**sic
ô	**o**ften	yoor	p**u**re
ō	n**o**te	zh	vi**s**ion

YE OLDE TEA SHOPPE Strictly speaking it is quite incorrect to pronounce the Ye in "Ye Olde Tea Shoppe" as *yee*. The *y* represents a discarded Anglo-Saxon letter called *thorn*, which looked a bit like *Y*. (It survives in modern Icelandic.) The letter has been replaced by *th*. So we should really say "The Olde Tea Shoppe"!

Z z

●**Za·ire** (zä-îr′). See Supplement, **Countries**.

●**Za·ire River** (zä-îr′) in central AFRICA, is Africa's second longest river, after the NILE.

●**Zam·bi·a** (zam′bē-ə). See Supplement, **Countries**.

za·ny (zā′nē) *adj.* **za·ni·er, za·ni·est** amusingly crazy.

Modern Zimbabwe is named after the African walled city of Great Zimbabwe which was built between the 11th and 14th centuries. Nobody knows who built it or why it was built, but the city seems to have been a center of religion and the gold trade.

●**Zan·zi·bar** (zan′zə-bär′) is an island in the Indian Ocean off AFRICA. It forms part of TANZANIA.

zeal (zēl) *n.* great enthusiasm or keenness.

zeal·ous (zel′əs) *adj.* enthusiastic; keen.

ze·bra (zē′brə, *in Canada* zeb′rə) *n.* **zebras** or **zebra** a black-and-white striped animal of the horse family, living in AFRICA.

ze·nith (zē′nith) *n.* the highest point in the sky.

ze·ro (zîr′ō, zē′rō) *n.* **zeros** the number or figure 0.

zest (zest) *n.* **1** keen enjoyment; enthusiasm: *a zest for life.* **2** in cooking, the peel of an orange or lemon, used for flavoring.

Zeus (zo͞os). See **Myths and Legends**.

zig·gu·rat (zig′ə-rat′) *n.* a pyramid-like temple in ancient Mesopotamia.

zig·zag (zig′zag′) *n.* one of two or more sharp bends to right and left in a path, etc. – *adj.* having sharp bends to right and left. – *vb.* **zig·zag·ging, zig·zagged** to move in a zigzag path or manner: *John zigzagged down the road on his bike.*

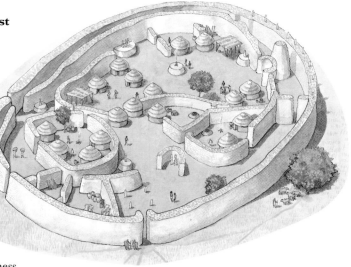

●**Zim·bab·we** (zim-bäb′wā). See Supplement, **Countries**.

zinc (zingk) *n.* a bluish-white metallic element (symbol **Zn**) used in brass.

zin·ni·a (zin′ē-ə, zin′yə) *n.* an originally tropical American plant cultivated for its showy flowers.

Zi·on (zī′ən) *n.* **1** the hill on which part of Jerusalem stands, often taken as representing Jerusalem itself. **2** the Jewish people.

zip (zip) *n.* **1** a whizzing sound. **2** (*informal*) energy; vitality. **3** (*informal*) a zip code. – *vb.* **zip·ping, zipped 1** to fasten with a zipper. **2** to make, or move with, a whizzing sound.

zip code or **ZIP code** (zip'kōd') *n.* a number that identifies each postal delivery area in the UNITED STATES.

zip·per (zip'ər) *n.* a device for fastening clothes, bags, etc. in which two rows of metal or nylon teeth are opened or closed by a sliding tab.

zith·er (zith'ər, zith'ər) *n.* a stringed musical instrument which is played by plucking while resting on a table or on the player's knees.

zlo·ty (zlôt'ē) *n.* **zloty** or **zlotys** the principal money currency of POLAND.

zo·di·ac (zō'dē-ak') *n.* an imaginary belt across the sky through which the sun, moon, and planets appear to move, divided into twelve equal parts, or signs. Each sign is named for a constellation which used to lie in it (although the signs and constellations now no longer match up).

● **Zo·la** (zō-lä', zō'lə), **Emile** (1840-1902) was a French novelist.

zom·bie or **zom·bi** (zäm'bē) *n.* **1** in VOODOO belief, a corpse brought to life again by magic. **2** (*informal*) a person who is sluggish in behavior.

zone (zōn) *n.* an area or region of a country, town, etc., especially one marked out for a special purpose or by a particular feature. – *vb.* **zon·ing, zoned** to divide into zones; to mark as a zone. – *adj.* **zon·al** (zōn'l).

zoo (zōō) *n.* a place where animals are kept for the public to see, and for study, breeding, etc.

zo·ol·o·gy (zō-äl'ə-jē, zōō-äl'ə-jē) *n.* the scientific study of animals. – *n.* **zo·ol·o·gist** (zō-äl'ə-jəst, zōō-äl'ə-jəst).

zoom (zōōm) *vb.* **zoom·ing, zoomed 1** to move very quickly, making a loud low buzzing noise. **2** to move very quickly: *The aircraft zoomed past us.* – *n.* the act or sound of zooming.

zuc·chi·ni (zōō-kē'nē) *n.* a green squash shaped like a cucumber and eaten as a vegetable.

● **Zu·lu** (zōō'lōō) a member of a people of southeast AFRICA.

● **Zü·rich** (zoor'ik) is the largest city in SWITZERLAND and famous for its banking.

The first people to study the **zodiac**, over 4,000 years ago, were the astronomers of ancient Babylon. They divided it into 12 sections with a group of stars in each section.

Thousands of years ago people divided the stars into groups or constellations. Few of these patterns resemble what they are supposed to be, although with a bit of imagination Leo can look quite lionlike!

The Egyptian mummy case (above) shows Nut, sky goddess, surrounded by signs of the zodiac, many of which are still in use.

1 Capricorn (Goat) Dec. 22 – Jan. 19
2 Aquarius (Water carrier) Jan. 20 – Feb. 18
3 Pisces (Fish) Feb. 19 – March 20
4 Aries (Ram) March 21 – April 19
5 Taurus (Bull) April 20 – May 20
6 Gemini (Twins) May 21 – June 21

7 Cancer (Crab) June 22 – July 22
8 Leo (Lion) July 23 – Aug. 22
9 Virgo (Virgin) Aug. 23 – Sept. 22
10 Libra (Scales) Sept. 23 – Oct. 23
11 Scorpio (Scorpion) Oct. 24 – Nov. 21
12 Sagittarius (Archer) Nov. 22 – Dec. 21

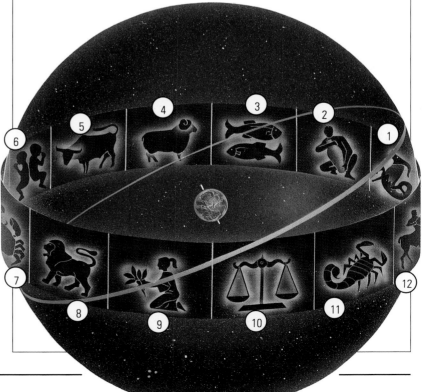

SUPPLEMENT

COUNTRIES OF THE WORLD

Country	Adjective	Capital	Currency	Language
Afghanistan	Afghan	Kabul	Afghani	Pushtu
Albania	Albanian	Tirane	Lek	Albanian
Algeria	Algerian	Algiers	Dinar	Arabic
Andorra	Andorran	Andorra la Vella	Franc/Peseta	Catalan
Angola	Angolan	Luanda	Kwanza	Portuguese
Antigua & Barbuda	Antiguan/Barbudan	St. John's	Dollar	English
Argentina	Argentinian or Argentine	Buenos Aires	Peso	Spanish
Armenia	Armenian	Yerevan	Ruble	Armenian
Australia	Australian	Canberra	Dollar	English
Austria	Austrian	Vienna	Schilling	German
Azerbaijan	Azerbaijani	Baku	Manat ·	Azerbaijani
Bahamas	Bahamian	Nassau	Dollar	English
Bahrain	Bahraini	Al Manamah	Dinar	Arabic/English
Bangladesh	Bangladeshi	Dhaka	Taka	Bengali
Barbados	Barbadian	Bridgetown	Dollar	English
Belarus	Belarussian	Minsk	Ruble	Belorussian
Belgium	Belgian	Brussels	Franc	Dutch/French
Belize	Belizian	Belmopan	Dollar	English
Benin	Beninese	Porto Novo	Franc	French
Bhutan	Bhutanese	Thimphu	Ngultrum	Dzongkha
Bolivia	Bolivian	La Paz	Boliviano	Spanish
Bosnia & Herzegovina	Bosnian	Sarajevo	Dinar	Serbo-Croatian
Botswana	Botswanan	Gaborone	Pula	English/Setswana
Brazil	Brazilian	Brasilia	Cruzeiro	Portuguese
Brunei	Bruneian	Bandar Seri Begawan	Brunei Dollar	Malay
Bulgaria	Bulgarian	Sofia	Lev	Bulgarian
Burkina Faso	Burkinese	Ouagadougou	Franc	French
Burundi	Burundian	Bujumbura	Franc	French/Rundi
Cambodia	Cambodian	Phnom Penh	Riel	Khmer
Cameroon	Cameroonian	Yaoundé	Franc	English/French
Canada	Canadian	Ottawa	Dollar	English/French
Cape Verde	Cape Verdean	Praia	Escudo	Portuguese
Central African Republic		Bangui	Franc	French
Chad	Chadian	N'Djamena	Franc	French
Chile	Chilean	Santiago	Peso	Spanish
China	Chinese	Beijing	Yuan	Mandarin Chinese
Colombia	Colombian	Bogotá	Peso	Spanish
Comoros	Comoran	Moroni	Franc	French/Arabic
Congo	Congolese	Brazzaville	Franc	French

Country	Adjective	Capital	Currency	Language
Costa Rica	Costa Rican	San José	Colón	Spanish
Côte d'Ivoire		Abidjan	Franc	French
Croatia	Croatian	Zagreb	Dinar	Serbo-Croatian
Cuba	Cuban	Havana	Peso	Spanish
Cyprus	Cypriot	Nicosia	Pound	Greek/Turkish
Czech Republic	Czech	Prague	Koruna	Czech
Denmark	Danish	Copenhagen	Krone	Danish
Djibouti	Djiboutian	Djibouti	Franc	French/Arabic
Dominica	Dominican	Roseau	Dollar	English
Dominican Republic	Dominican	Santo Domingo	Peso	Spanish
Ecuador	Ecuadorean	Quito	Sucre	Spanish
Egypt	Egyptian	Cairo	Pound	Arabic
El Salvador	Salvadorean	San Salvador	Colón	Spanish
Equatorial Guinea	Guinean	Malabo	Franc	Spanish
Eritrea	Eritrean	Asmara	Birr	Tigrinya
Estonia	Estonian	Tallinn	Kroon	Estonian
Ethiopia	Ethiopian	Addis Ababa	Birr	Amharic
Fiji	Fijian	Suva	Dollar	English
Finland	Finnish	Helsinki	Markka	Finnish/Swedish
France	French	Paris	Franc	French
Gabon	Gabonese	Libreville	Franc	French
Gambia, The	Gambian	Banjul	Dalasi	English
Georgia	Georgian	Tbilisi	Ruble	Georgian
Germany	German	Berlin	Mark	German
Ghana	Ghanaian	Accra	Cedi	English
Greece	Greek	Athens	Drachma	Greek
Grenada	Grenadian	St. George's	Dollar	English
Guatemala	Guatemalan	Guatemala City	Quetzal	Spanish
Guinea	Guinean	Conakry	Franc	French
Guinea-Bissau	Guinean	Bissau	Peso	Portuguese
Guyana	Guyanese	Georgetown	Dollar	English
Haiti	Haitian	Port-au-Prince	Gourde	French
Honduras	Honduran	Tegucigalpa	Lempira	Spanish
Hungary	Hungarian	Budapest	Forint	Hungarian
Iceland	Icelandic	Reykjavik	Krona	Icelandic
India	Indian	New Delhi	Rupee	Hindi/English
Indonesia	Indonesian	Jakarta	Rupiah	Bahasa Indonesian
Iran	Iranian	Tehran	Rial	Farsi (Persian)
Iraq	Iraqi	Baghdad	Dinar	Arabic
Ireland, Republic of	Irish	Dublin	Punt	English/Gaelic
Israel	Israeli	Jerusalem	Shekel	Hebrew/Arabic
Italy	Italian	Rome	Lira	Italian
Ivory Coast *see* Côte d'Ivoire				
Jamaica	Jamaican	Kingston	Dollar	English
Japan	Japanese	Tokyo	Yen	Japanese
Jordan	Jordanian	Amman	Dinar	Arabic
Kazakhstan	Kazakh	Alma Ata	Ruble	Kazakh
Kenya	Kenyan	Nairobi	Shilling	English/Swahili
Kiribati	Kiribati	Tarawa	Dollar	English/Gilbertese
Korea, North	Korean	Pyongyang	Won	Korean
Korea, South	Korean	Seoul	Won	Korean

Country	Adjective	Capital	Currency	Language
Kuwait	Kuwaiti	Kuwait	Dinar	Arabic
Kyrgyzstan	Kyrgyz	Bishkek	Som	Kyrgyz
Laos	Laotian	Vientiane	Kip	Lao
Latvia	Latvian	Riga	Lat	Latvian
Lebanon	Lebanese	Beirut	Pound	Arabic
Lesotho	Lesuthan	Maseru	Loti	English/Sesotho
Liberia	Liberian	Monrovia	Dollar	English
Libya	Libyan	Tripoli	Dinar	Arabic
Liechtenstein	Liechtenstein	Vaduz	Franc	German
Lithuania	Lithuanian	Vilnius	Litas	Lithuanian
Luxembourg	Luxembourger	Luxembourg	Franc	French/German
Macedonia	Macedonian	Skopje	Denar	Macedonian
Madagascar	Madagascan	Antananarivo	Franc	French/Malagasy
Malawi	Malawian	Lilongwe	Kwacha	English/Chichewa
Malaysia	Malaysian	Kuala Lumpur	Ringgit	Malay
Maldives	Maldivian	Male	Rufiyaa	Divehi
Mali	Malian	Bamako	Franc	French
Malta	Maltese	Valletta	Lira	English
Marshall Islands	Marshallese	Majuro	U.S. Dollar	English
Mauritania	Mauritanian	Nouakchott	Ouguiya	Arabic/French
Mauritius	Mauritian	Port Louis	Rupee	English
Mexico	Mexican	Mexico City	Peso	Spanish
Micronesia	Micronesian	Kolonia	U.S. Dollar	English
Moldova	Moldavian	Kishinev	Ruble	Romanian
Monaco	Monegasque	Monaco	Franc	French
Mongolia	Mongolian	Ulan Bator	Tugrik	Mongolian
Morocco	Moroccan	Rabat	Dirham	Arabic
Mozambique	Mozambican	Maputo	Metical	Portuguese
Myanmar	Burmese	Yangon	Kyat	Burmese
Namibia	Namibian	Windhoek	Rand	English/Afrikaans
Nauru	Nauruan	Yaren	Dollar	English/Nauruan
Nepal	Nepalese	Kathmandu	Rupee	Nepali
Netherlands	Dutch	Amsterdam	Guilder	Dutch
New Zealand	New Zealand	Wellington	Dollar	English
Nicaragua	Nicaraguan	Managua	Cordoba	Spanish
Niger	Nigerien	Niamey	Franc	French
Nigeria	Nigerian	Abuja	Naira	English
Norway	Norwegian	Oslo	Krone	Norwegian
Oman	Omani	Muscat	Rial	Arabic
Pakistan	Pakistani	Islamabad	Rupee	Urdu
Panama	Panamanian	Panama City	Balboa	Spanish
Papua New Guinea	Papua New Guinean	Port Moresby	Kina	English
Paraguay	Paraguayan	Asunción	Guarani	Spanish
Peru	Peruvian	Lima	Sol	Spanish
Philippines	Filipino	Manila	Peso	English/Filipino
Poland	Polish	Warsaw	Zloty	Polish
Portugal	Portuguese	Lisbon	Escudo	Portuguese
Qatar	Qatari	Doha	Riyal	Arabic
Romania	Romanian	Bucharest	Leu	Romanian
Russia	Russian	Moscow	Ruble	Russian
Rwanda	Rwandan	Kigali	Franc	French/Kinyarwanda

Country	Adjective	Capital	Currency	Language
St. Kitts & Nevis	Kittsian/Nevisian	Basseterre	Dollar	English
St. Lucia	St. Lucian	Castries	Dollar	English
St. Vincent & the Grenadines	St. Vincentian	Kingstown	Dollar	English
San Marino	Sanmarinese	San Marino	Lira	Italian
São Tomé and Príncipe	São Toméan	São Tomé	Dobra	Portuguese
Saudi Arabia	Saudi Arabian	Riyadh	Riyal	Arabic
Senegal	Senegalese	Dakar	Franc	French
Seychelles	Seychellois	Victoria	Rupee	English/French
Sierra Leone	Sierra Leonean	Freetown	Leone	English
Singapore	Singaporean	Singapore	Dollar	Malay/Tamil/Chinese
Slovakia	Slovak	Bratislava	Koruna	Slovak
Slovenia	Slovenian	Ljubljana	Tolar	Slovenian
Solomon Islands	Solomon Islander	Honiara	Dollar	English
Somalia	Somali	Mogadishu	Shilling	Somali
South Africa	South African	Pretoria & Capetown	Rand	Afrikaans/English
Spain	Spanish	Madrid	Peseta	Spanish
Sri Lanka	Sri Lankan	Colombo	Rupee	Sinhalese/Tamil
Sudan	Sudanese	Khartoum	Pound	Arabic
Suriname	Surinamese	Paramaribo	Guilder	Dutch
Swaziland	Swazi	Mbabane	Lilangeni	English/Swazi
Sweden	Swedish	Stockholm	Krona	Swedish
Switzerland	Swiss	Berne	Franc	French/German/Italian
Syria	Syrian	Damascus	Pound	Arabic
Taiwan	Taiwanese	Taipei	Dollar	Chinese
Tajikistan	Tajikistan	Dushanbe	Ruble	Tajik
Tanzania	Tanzanian	Dar es Salaam	Shilling	Swahili/English
Thailand	Thai	Bangkok	Baht	Thai
Togo	Togolese	Lomé	Franc	French
Tonga	Tongan	Nuku'alofa	Pa'anga	Tongan/English
Trinidad & Tobago	Trinidadian/Tobagian	Port of Spain	Dollar	English
Tunisia	Tunisian	Tunis	Dinar	Arabic
Turkey	Turkish	Ankara	Lira	Turkish
Turkmenistan	Turkmen	Ashkhabad	Ruble	Turkmen
Tuvalu	Tuvaluan	Fongafale	Dollar	Tuvaluan/English
Uganda	Ugandan	Kampala	Shilling	English
Ukraine	Ukrainian	Kiev	Grivna	Ukrainian
United Arab Emirates	Emirian	Abu Dhabi	Dirham	Arabic
United Kingdom	British	London	Pound	English/Welsh
United States	American	Washington, D.C.	Dollar	English
Uruguay	Uruguyan	Montevideo	Peso	Spanish
Uzbekistan	Uzbek	Tashkent	Ruble	Uzbek
Vanuatu	Vanuatuan	Port Vila	Vatu	Bislama/English/French
Vatican City			Lira	Latin/Italian
Venezuela	Venezuelan	Caracas	Bolívar	Spanish
Vietnam	Vietnamese	Hanoi	Dong	Vietnamese
Western Samoa	Samoan	Apia	Tala	Samoan/English
Yemen	Yemeni	Sana'a	Rial	Arabic
Yugoslavia (Serbia & Montenegro)	Yugoslavian	Belgrade	Dinar	Serbo-Croatian
Zaire	Zairean	Kinshasa	Zaire	French
Zambia	Zambian	Lusaka	Kwacha	English
Zimbabwe	Zimbabwean	Harare	Dollar	English

THE UNITED STATES OF AMERICA

State	Abbreviation	Capital	Bird	Flower
Alabama	AL	Montgomery	Yellowhammer	Camellia
Alaska	AK	Juneau	Willow ptarmigan	Forget-me-not
Arizona	AZ	Phoenix	Cactus wren	Saguaro
Arkansas	AR	Little Rock	Mockingbird	Apple blossom
California	CA	Sacramento	Valley quail	Golden poppy
Colorado	CO	Denver	Lark bunting	Rocky Mountain columbine
Connecticut +	CT	Hartford	Robin	Mountain laurel
Delaware +	DE	Dover	Blue hen chicken	Peach blossom
Florida	FL	Tallahassee	Mockingbird	Orange blossom
Georgia +	GA	Atlanta	Brown thrasher	Cherokee rose
Hawaii	HI	Honolulu	Hawaiian goose	Hibiscus
Idaho	ID	Boise	Mountain bluebird	Mock orange
Illinois	IL	Springfield	Cardinal	Native violet
Indiana	IN	Indianapolis	Cardinal	Peony
Iowa	IA	Des Moines	Eastern goldfinch	Wild rose
Kansas	KS	Topeka	Western meadowlark	Sunflower
Kentucky	KY	Frankfort	Kentucky cardinal	Goldenrod
Louisiana	LA	Baton Rouge	Brown pelican	Magnolia
Maine	ME	Augusta	Chickadee	White pine cone and tassel
Maryland +	MD	Annapolis	Baltimore oriole	Black-eyed Susan
Massachusetts +	MA	Boston	Chickadee	Mayflower
Michigan	MI	Lansing	Robin	Apple blossom
Minnesota	MN	St. Paul	Common loon	Pink and white lady's-slipper
Mississippi	MS	Jackson	Mockingbird	Magnolia
Missouri	MO	Jefferson City	Bluebird	Hawthorn
Montana	MT	Helena	Western meadowlark	Bitterroot
Nebraska	NE	Lincoln	Western meadowlark	Goldenrod
Nevada	NV	Carson City	Mountain bluebird*	Sagebrush*
New Hampshire +	NH	Concord	Purple finch	Purple lilac
New Jersey +	NJ	Trenton	Eastern goldfinch	Purple violet
New Mexico	NM	Santa Fe	Roadrunner	Yucca flower
New York +	NY	Albany	Bluebird	Rose
North Carolina +	NC	Raleigh	Cardinal	Flowering dogwood
North Dakota	ND	Bismarck	Western meadowlark	Wild prairie rose
Ohio	OH	Columbus	Cardinal	Scarlet carnation
Oklahoma	OK	Oklahoma City	Scissor-tailed flycatcher	Mistletoe
Oregon	OR	Salem	Western meadowlark	Oregon grape
Pennsylvania +	PA	Harrisburg	Ruffed grouse	Mountain laurel
Rhode Island +	RI	Providence	Rhode Island Red	Violet
South Carolina +	SC	Columbia	Carolina wren	Carolina jessamine
South Dakota	SD	Pierre	Ring-necked pheasant	American pasqueflower
Tennessee	TN	Nashville	Mockingbird	Iris
Texas	TX	Austin	Mockingbird	Bluebonnet
Utah	UT	Salt Lake City	Sea gull	Sego lily
Vermont	VT	Montpelier	Hermit thrush	Red clover
Virginia +	VA	Richmond	Cardinal	Flowering dogwood
Washington	WA	Olympia	Willow goldfinch	Coast rhododendron
West Virginia	WV	Charleston	Cardinal	Rhododendron
Wisconsin	WI	Madison	Robin	Wood violet
Wyoming	WY	Cheyenne	Meadowlark	Indian paintbrush

+ One of the 13 original states   * Unofficial

PRESIDENTS OF THE UNITED STATES

	In office	Party
1. George Washington (1732-1799)	1789-97	Federalist
2. John Adams (1735-1826)	1797-1801	Federalist
3. Thomas Jefferson (1743-1826)	1801-09	Democratic-Republican
4. James Madison (1751-1836)	1809-17	Democratic-Republican
5. James Monroe (1758-1831)	1817-25	Democratic-Republican
6. John Quincy Adams (1767-1848)	1825-29	Democratic-Republican
7. Andrew Jackson (1767-1845)	1829-37	Democratic
8. Martin Van Buren (1782-1862)	1837-41	Democratic
9. William Henry Harrison (1773-1841)	1841	Whig
10. John Tyler (1790-1862)	1841-45	Whig
11. James Knox Polk (1795-1849)	1845-49	Democratic
12. Zachary Taylor (1784-1850)	1849-50	Whig
13. Millard Fillmore (1800-74)	1850-53	Whig
14. Franklin Pierce (1804-69)	1853-57	Democratic
15. James Buchanan (1791-1868)	1857-61	Democratic
16. Abraham Lincoln+ (1809-65)	1861-65	Republican
17. Andrew Johnson (1808-75)	1865-69	National Union*
18. Ulysses Simpson Grant (1822-85)	1869-77	Republican
19. Rutherford B. Hayes (1822-93)	1877-81	Republican
20. James Abram Garfield+ (1831-81)	1881	Republican
21. Chester Alan Arthur (1829-86)	1881-85	Republican
22. Grover Cleveland (1837-1908)	1885-89	Democratic
23. Benjamin Harrison (1833-1901)	1889-93	Republican
24. Grover Cleveland (1837-1908)	1893-97	Democratic
25. William McKinley+ (1843-1901)	1897-1901	Republican
26. Theodore Roosevelt (1858-1919)	1901-09	Republican
27. William Howard Taft (1857-1930)	1909-13	Republican
28. Woodrow Wilson (1856-1924)	1913-21	Democratic
29. Warren Gamaliel Harding (1865-1923)	1921-23	Republican
30. Calvin Coolidge (1872-1933)	1923-29	Republican
31. Herbert Clark Hoover (1874-1964)	1929-33	Republican
32. Franklin Delano Roosevelt (1882-1945)	1933-45	Democratic
33. Harry S. Truman (1884-1972)	1945-53	Democratic
34. Dwight David Eisenhower (1890-1969)	1953-61	Republican
35. John Fitzgerald Kennedy+ (1917-63)	1961-63	Democratic
36. Lyndon Baines Johnson (1908-73)	1963-69	Democratic
37. Richard Milhous Nixon (1913-94)	1969-74	Republican
38. Gerald Rudolph Ford (1913-)	1974-77	Republican
39. James Earl Carter (1924-)	1977-81	Democratic
40. Ronald Wilson Reagan (1911-)	1981-89	Republican
41. George H.W. Bush (1924-)	1989-93	Republican
42. William Jefferson Clinton (1946-)	1993 -	Democratic

+ Assassinated in office

* The National Union Party consisted of Republicans and Democrats; Johnson was a Democrat.

IMPORTANT DATES IN UNITED STATES HISTORY

1492 Christopher Columbus sighted the Bahamas.

1565 St. Augustine, Florida founded by Pedro Menendes.

1607 Capt. John Smith founded a settlement at Jamestown.

1620 Pilgrims founded Plymouth Colony.

1624 Dutch established the settlement of New Netherland.

1672 The Boston Post Road was completed, linking Boston and New York City.

1704 *The Boston News-Letter,* first regular newspaper, began publication.

1732 Benjamin Franklin published first *Poor Richard's Almanac.*

1744 King George's War pitted British and Colonials against the French.

1752 Benjamin Franklin proved that lightning is electricity by flying a kite in a thunderstorm.

1754 French and Indian War began.

1763 Britain defeated France in the French and Indian War and gained control of eastern North America.

1765 British Parliament passed the Stamp Act to help defray cost of troops.

1767 British imposed taxes on paper, tea, and glass.

1770 British troops killed American civilians in the Boston Massacre.

1773 Colonists dumped tea into harbor in the Boston Tea Party.

1774 First Continental Congress held in Philadelphia.

1775 Revolutionary War began.

1776 Colonists adopted the Declaration of Independence and formed the United States of America.

1777 Washington defeated Cornwallis at Princeton. Continental Congress adopted the "Stars and Stripes" flag.

1781 British defeated at Yorktown in last major battle of Revolutionary War.

1783 Britain and U.S.A. signed peace treaty. Washington disbanded army.

1787 Founding Fathers wrote the Constitution.

1789 George Washington chosen as first president.

1793 Eli Whitney developed the cotton gin.

1796 Washington's farewell address as president.

1800 Washington, D.C. became the national capital.

1803 Louisiana Purchase almost doubled the size of the United States.

1804 Lewis and Clark expedition ordered by President Jefferson to explore northwest.

1807 Robert Fulton made first steamboat trip from New York City to Albany.

1812 War of 1812 began between the U.S.A. and Britain.

1815 Treaty of Ghent ended War of 1812.

1819 Spain ceded Florida to U.S.A.

1823 Monroe Doctrine warned Europeans against interference in the Americas.

1825 Erie Canal opened.

1828 Noah Webster published his *American Dictionary of the English Language.*

1834 Cyrus McCormick patented the reaper.

1837 Samuel Morse demonstrated the first successful telegraph.

1846 Mexican War began.

1848 Victory in Mexican War gave the U.S.A. vast new territory in the West.
Gold discovered in California started gold rush.

1852 Harriet Beecher Stowe's *Uncle Tom's Cabin* published.

1854 Republican Party formed.

1858 First Atlantic cable completed.

1859 Abolitionist John Brown seized U.S. armory at Harpers Ferry. Brown captured and hanged.

1860 Abraham Lincoln elected president.
Pony Express began carrying mail between Sacramento, California, and St. Joseph, Missouri.

1861 Seven southern states set up Confederate States of America and Civil War began.

1862 Union forces victorious in western campaigns. Battles in east inconclusive.

1863 Union forces victorious at Gettysburg. Lincoln gave his Gettysburg Address.

1864 General Sherman marched through Georgia to take Atlanta.

1865 Robert E. Lee surrendered at Appomattox.
President Lincoln shot by John Booth.
The 13th Amendment outlawed slavery in U.S.A.

1867 Alaska sold to U.S.A. by Russia.

1869 Transcontinental railroad completed.
Woman suffrage law passed in Wyoming.

1871 Great fire destroyed Chicago.

1876 Col. George A. Custer and 264 soldiers killed in "last stand" Battle of the Little Big Horn.
Alexander Graham Bell invented telephone.
Mark Twain published *Tom Sawyer.*

1877 Thomas Edison invented the phonograph.

1881 President Garfield shot in Washington, D.C.

1884 World's first skyscraper begun in Chicago.

1886 Statue of Liberty dedicated.
American Federation of Labor founded.

1898 The U.S.A. defeated Spain in Spanish-American War.

1903 Wright Brothers made first successful airplane flight at Kitty Hawk, North Carolina.

1909 Robert Peary with five companions reached North Pole.

1914 World War I began in Europe.
1917 U.S.A. entered World War I.
1918 World War I ended.
1920 The U.S. Senate rejected American participation in League of Nations.
The 19th Amendment ratified, giving women the right to vote.
1921 Limitation of Armaments Conference in Washington, D.C.
1925 John T. Scopes found guilty of teaching evolution in Dayton, Tennessee, high school.
1927 Charles A. Lindbergh made first solo flight across the Atlantic.
1927 *The Jazz Singer*, the first "talkie" movie appeared.
1928 Amelia Earhart became the first woman to fly the Atlantic.
1929 American depression began with stock market crash.
1933 President Roosevelt began the New Deal program.
1939 U.S.A. declared its neutrality in World War II.
1941 The Atlantic Charter signed by Roosevelt and Churchill. Japan attacked Pearl Harbor and U.S.A. declared war on Japan, Germany, and Italy.
1942 Battle of Midway, Japan's first major defeat.
1944 Allied and U.S. forces invaded Europe.

1945 Harry S. Truman became president on death of Roosevelt.
Atomic bombs dropped on Hiroshima and Nagasaki. Japan surrendered.
The U.S.A. became a charter member of the U.N.
1947 President Truman announced the Truman Doctrine.
1950 U.S.A. entered Korean War.
1953 Korean War ended.
1961 Alan B. Shepard became first American in space.
1962 Soviet Union removed missiles from Cuba, ending a threat of war with U.S.
1963 President John F. Kennedy assassinated.
Lyndon B. Johnson inaugurated president.
1965 American troops entered Vietnam War.
1969 Neil Armstrong became first person to set foot on the Moon.
1974 Watergate scandal led to President Nixon's resignation.
1975 End of Vietnam War.
1986 U.S.A. officially celebrated Martin Luther King Day.
1991 U.S. forces aid defeat of Iraq in Persian Gulf War.
1993 William (Bill) Clinton became the 42nd president of the United States.

WEIGHTS AND MEASURES

LENGTH

Customary Units
1 foot (ft.) = 12 inches (in.)
1 yard (yd.) = 3 feet
1 mile (mi.) = 1,760 yards = 5,280 feet

Metric Units
1 centimeter (cm) = 10 millimeters (mm)
1 meter (m) = 100 centimeters
1 kilometer (km) = 1,000 meters

Conversion Table

Unit	Conversion Number
1 inch	= 2.54 centimeters
1 foot	= 0.3048 meter
1 yard	= 0.914 meter
1 mile	= 1.609 kilometers

CAPACITY

Customary Units
1 cup (c.) = 8 fluid ounces (oz.)
1 pint (pt.) = 2 cups
1 quart (qt.) = 2 pints
1 gallon (gal.) = 4 quarts

Metric Units
1 liter (L) = 1,000 milliliters (mL)
1 kiloliter (kL) = 1,000 liters

Conversion Table

Unit	Conversion Number
1 fluid ounce	= 29.57 milliliters
1 quart	= 0.946 liter
1 gallon	= 3.785 liters

WEIGHT

Customary Units
1 pound (lb.) = 16 ounces (oz.)
1 ton (tn.) = 2,000 pounds

Metric Units
1 gram (g) = 1,000 milligrams
1 kilogram (kg) = 1,000 grams
1 metric ton = 1,000 kilograms

Conversion Table

Unit	Conversion Number
1 ounce	= 28.35 grams
1 pound	=0.4536 kilogram
1 ton	= 907.2 kilograms

supplement

RULERS OF ENGLAND, SCOTLAND, AND GREAT BRITAIN

House of Normandy

William I the Conqueror	1066-87
William II	1087-1100
Henry I	1100-35
Stephen I	1135-54

House of Plantagenet

Henry II	1154-89
Richard I	1189-99
John	1199-1216
Henry III	1216-72
Edward I	1272-1307
Edward II	1307-27
Edward III	1327-77
Richard II	1377-99

House of Lancaster

Henry IV	1399-1413
Henry V	1413-22
Henry VI	1422-61

House of York

Edward IV	1461-83
Edward V	1483
Richard III	1483-85

House of Tudor

Henry VII	1485-1509
Henry VIII	1509-47
Edward VI	1547-53
Mary I	1553-58
Elizabeth I	1558-1603

House of Stuart

Rulers of Scotland

Robert II	1371-90
Robert III	1390-1406
James I	1406-37
James II	1437-60
James III	1460-88
James IV	1488-1513
James V	1513-42
Mary	1542-67
James VI	1567-1625

Rulers of Great Britain

James I (VI of Scotland)	1603-25
Charles I	1625-49
(Commonwealth	1649-60)
Charles II	1660-85
James II (VII)	1685-88
William III 1689-1702 jointly with Mary II	1689-94
Anne	1702-14

House of Hanover

George I	1714-27
George II	1727-60
George III	1760-1820
George IV	1820-30
William IV	1830-37
Victoria	1837-1901
Edward VII	1901-10

House of Windsor

George V	1910-36
Edward VIII	1936
George VI	1936-52
Elizabeth II	1952-

CANADIAN PRIME MINISTERS

Sir John A. Macdonald	1867-1873
Alexander Mackenzie	1873-1878
Sir John A. Macdonald	1878-1891
Sir John J. C. Abbott	1891-1892
Sir John S. D. Thompson	1892-2894
Sir Mackenzie Bowell	1894-1896
Sir Charles Tupper	1896
Sir Wilfrid Laurier	1896-1911
Sir Robert L. Borden	1911-1917
Sir Robert L. Borden	1917-1920
Arthur Meighen	1920-1921
W. L. Mackenzie King	1921-1926
Arthur Meighen	1926
W. L. Mackenzie King	1926-1930
Richard B. Bennett	1930-1935
W. L. Mackenzie King	1935-1948
Louis S. St. Laurent	1948-1957
John G. Diefenbaker	1957-1963
Lester B. Pearson	1963-1968
Pierre Elliott Trudeau	1968-1979
Charles Joseph Clark	1979-1980
Pierre Elliott Trudeau	1980-1984
John N. Turner	1984
Brian Mulroney	1984-1993
Kim Campbell	1993
Jean Chrétien	1993-

IMPORTANT DATES IN WORLD HISTORY

B.C.

2780	First pyramid built in Egypt.
565	Birth of Buddha.
509	Founding of Roman republic.
331	Alexander the Great led Greeks to victory over the Persian Empire.
221	Building of the Great Wall of China begun.

A.D.

4?	Birth of Christ.
330	Roman emperor Constantine founded Constantinople.
476	Roman Empire collapsed.
570	Birth of Muhammad.
800	Charlemagne crowned first Holy Roman Emperor.
1066	William of Normandy conquered England.
1096	First of six crusades by Christian armies against Islam in Holy Land.
1100	Maoris sailed to New Zealand from Pacific islands.
1190	Genghis Khan began to conquer an empire for the Mongols.
1215	English barons drew up Magna Carta.
1300s	The Renaissance in arts and sciences.
1348	The Black Death killed millions.
1400s	The Inca empire ruled in Peru.
1492	Columbus said to "discover" America.
1498	Vasco de Gama sailed from Portugal to India.
1517	Martin Luther's protest began the Reformation.
1518	Cortes began conquest of Mexico, defeating Aztecs.
1533	Pizarro conquered Inca empire for Spain.
1584	Raleigh founded English colony in Virginia.
1588	English defeated Spanish Armada.
1620	Voyage of the Pilgrim ship *Mayflower*.
1642	Civil war in England. Abel Tasman discovered Tasmania; French found Montreal.
1700s	Revolutions in agriculture and industry; beginning of the Age of Machines.
1763	Britain gained control of Canada after defeating France.
1770	Cook explored coast of Australia and New Zealand.
1776	Declaration of Independence written.
1783	End of Revolutionary War in U.S.A.
1789	French Revolution George Washington first U.S. president.
1857	Indian Mutiny
1861	Civil War began in U.S.A.
1865	Civil War ended; Northern states defeated South.
1867	Canada became self-governing dominion.
1869	Opening of Suez Canal created shorter sea route from Europe to Asia.
1871	Prussia defeated France in Franco-Prussian War.
1914	World War I began.
1917	Communist revolution in Russia.
1918	World War I ended; Germany and allies defeated by Britain, France, Russia, U.S.A, and others. More than 10 million soldiers killed.
1930s	Depression and unemployment in U.S.A.
1933	Rise of Japan as military power. Hitler became ruler in Germany.
1936	Civil war broke out in Spain.
1939	Civil war in Spain ended; Franco became dictator. World War II began.
1941	Japanese attack on Pearl Harbor brought U.S.A. into World War II.
1945	World War II ended; Allies defeated Germany and Italy in Europe. First atomic bombs dropped on Japan.
1947	India gained independence from Britain.
1948	Creation of state of Israel.
1949	Mao Zedong's Communists won civil war in China.
1954	French pulled out of Indochina: beginnings of Vietnam War.
1956	President Nasser of Egypt nationalized Suez Canal, led to brief war with Britain and France.
1957	Treaty of Rome established European Community (EC).
1959	Fidel Castro led Communist revolution in Cuba.
1960s	Many former European-ruled states in Africa became self-governing.
1963	President John F. Kennedy assassinated.
1965	U.S. troops sent to Vietnam.
1969	U.S. astronauts land on Moon.
1975	Last U.S. forces left Vietnam.
1976	Vietnam War ended.
1979	Shah of Iran overthrown; Iran became an Islamic republic.
1980s	U.S. is strongest world power; EC moved toward free market; Gorbachev government brought new ideas in U.S.S.R.; Eastern bloc countries moved toward democracy; war between Iran and Iraq (ended 1988); apartheid eased in South Africa.
1990	Iraq invaded Kuwait.
1991	War in Persian Gulf; Allies defeated Iraq. Serbs and Croats fight in Yugoslavia. Soviet Union broken up into independent states.
1992	Soviet Union ceased to exist.
1993	Czechoslovakia was divided into 2 independent states — the Czech Republic and Slovakia; Eritrea became an independent nation.